NTC's GULF ARABIC-

NTC's GULF ARABIC-ENGLISH DICTIONARY

Hamdi A. Qafisheh, Ph.D.

in consultation with

Tim Buckwalter and Ernest N. McCarus

NTC Publishi

Library of Congress Cataloging-in-Publication Data

Qafisheh, Hamdi A.
NTC's Gulf Arabic–English dictionary / Hamdi A. Qafisheh ; in consultation with Tim Buckwalter and Ernest N. McCarus.
p. cm.
Includes index.
ISBN 0-8442-4606-9 (cloth)
ISBN 0-8442-0299-1 (paper)
1. Arabic language—Dialects—Persian Gulf States—Dictionaries—English.
I. NTC Publishing Group. II. Title.
PJ6856.Q24 1997
492'.7'09536—dc21 97-26231
CIP

Published by NTC Publishing Group
A division of NTC/Contemporary Publishing Group, Inc.
4255 West Touhy Avenue, Lincolnwood (Chicago), Illinois 60646-1975 U.S.A.

Printed in the United States of America
International Standard Book Number: 0-8442-4606-9 (cloth)
0-8442-0299-1 (paper)

99 00 01 02 03 04 QP 19 18 17 16 15 14 13 12 11 10 9 8 7 6 5 4 3 2 1

Dedicated to my wife

Kalida

in affection and gratitude

The research reported herein was performed pursuant to a grant from the U.S. Department of Education under the International Research and Studies Program, authorized by Title VI of the Higher Education Act of 1965, as amended.

ACKNOWLEDGMENTS

I would like to express my thanks and appreciation to all those who helped in the preparation of this study. First, to the administrators of the International Research and Studies Program of the U.S. Department of Education, Title VI of the Higher Education Act of 1965, as amended, for the grant which made the present study possible. To Professor Ernest N. McCarus, Emeritus Professor of Arabic and Kurdish Linguistics, University of Michigan, for having made a number of corrections and instructive suggestions, and for having edited the English translations of the GA phrases and illustrative sentences; to Tim Buckwalter, Arabic Software Developer, Orem, Utah, for having served in a number of ways, including creating the custom font for Arabic phonetic transcription, text formatting and page layout, printing, and preparing a camera-ready copy of the manuscript; to Dr. Benjamin T. Hoffiz for having served as a research assistant; to my Gulf Arab consultants and language informants, Abdalla S. Kaddas, Muhamma Mijrin Al-Rumaithi, Hamad Bin Tamim, and Salim Khamis for their intelligence, patience, humor, and hospitality.

H.A.Q.

Tucson, Arizona

CONTENTS

INTRODUCTION

NTC's Gulf Arabic-English Dictionary is a bilingual dictionary which includes most of the colloquial Arabic spoken by semi-educated native speakers of Gulf Arabic (GA) in Abu Dhabi, U.A.E. Gulf Arabic is here defined as the conversational language of the U.A.E., Qatar, and Bahrain. Forms which are characteristically Qatari or Bahraini are understood and most often used by Abu Dhabians, e.g., for "motorcycle" Abu Dhabians usually use دباب *dabbaab*; Bahrainis use بطبطة *buṭbuṭa*, but both words, *dabbaab* and *buṭbuṭa*, are used and/or understood by all speakers. Another example, ماميش *maamiiš* "there isn't; there aren't" is typically Qatari, which Abu Dhabians understand, but do not use. Variants, i.e., forms that exhibit phonetic variation or different forms are given in order of frequency of occurrence, starting with the most frequent form, e.g., الجمعة *l-yimᶜa, l-jimᶜa, l-jumaᶜ*, سمكة *smiča, simča,* هني *hni, hini,* etc. All the utterances in this dictionary have been compiled from the oral data collected.

In order to be as clear as possible and to give a wider range of information about the entries, both grammatical and lexical, numerous illustrative phrases and sentences, except for a few items that have a relatively low frequency of occurences in GA, are given. For example, in the meaning section of تفاح *tiffaaḥ* "apples" the illustrative sentences show that *tiffaaḥ* is a masculine singular collective noun, the unit of which is تفاحة *-a* and the plural is تفاحات *-aat* "individual apples"; if *tiffaaḥ* is used in a generic sense, it takes the article prefix *l-* التفاح *t-tiffaaḥ*; otherwise, *tiffaaḥ* without the article prefix implies "some apples." Many frequently used proverbs, sayings, and proverbial phrases are given in addition to the illustrative sentences or phrases. In those cases where no equivalent English proverb has been found, only a literal translation of the proverb is given.

The entries are arranged according to the traditional Arabic root system, with the roots arranged in accordance with the Arabic alphabet, including the GA phonemes چ *č*, گ *g*, and پ *p*. Foreign words and Arabic words no longer identified with their roots, e.g., جولة *čuula* "kerosene stove," are listed alphabetically. Under the root (which might have the long vowel ا *aa*) the first ten forms of the verb are listed. Many historically form IV verbs in GA have acquired perfect forms corresponding to those of form II verbs, e.g., خبر *xabbar* instead of form IV أخبر *'axbar* "to inform." Form I verbs are entered in the third person masculine singular form of the perfect, followed by the imperfect form. For forms II-X only the perfect form is given. After the verbs come the nominal forms, arranged generally by length and complexity. After the nominal forms come the elative and the active and passive participles. Plurals of nouns, adjectives, etc., are given and only the sound plural suffixes *-iin* and *-aat* are used to indicate masculine and feminine plurals, respectively. Roots including radicals associated with a literary phoneme are given in their GA forms, with cross-references from the literary form of the root. In cases where two or more Gulf forms of a literary Arabic root exist, these are sometimes brought together and sometimes kept separate, always with cross-references, according to the semantic criteria.

In order to preserve the root, the assimilation of root consonants to adjacent consonants is not shown. In the illustrative examples, however, assimilated consonants will be shown, e.g., under the root س ل ف *slf* form V is shown as تسلف *tsallaf* "to borrow (money)," but in the examples it is shown as تسلف *ssallaf.* Verbs with prepositions, conjunctional and adverbial forms are not treated as separate entries, e.g., ثبت على *θibat ᶜala* "to hold to s.th., be firm in s.th." is under ثبت *θibat* "to be firm, steady," عقبما *ᶜugub-ma* is after the preposition عقب *ᶜugub* "after," and أبداً *'abdan* "never" is under the root ء ب د *'bd.*

There are a few headwords that are of roughly equal frequency of occurrence. these forms are shown with an equal sign =, e.g., تحكى *tḥačča* V = حكى *ḥiča.* A few words occur in the illustrative examples, but are not included with the headwords because they have a low frequency of occurrence, e.g. محاكمة *muḥaakama* in رحنا المحكمة يوم المحاكمة *riḥna l-maḥkama yoom l-muḥaakama* "We went to court on the trial day," تصبح *tiṣbiḥ* in the proverb قطرة على قطرة وتصبح غدير *gaṭra ᶜala gaṭra w-tiṣbiḥ ġadiir* "If you take care of the pennies, the dollars will take care of themselves."

The Arabic script, as opposed to the romanized script, does not provide a one-to-one correspondence between sound and letter, e.g., ماحد stands for *maḥḥad* "no one," وايا stands for *wiyya* "with," والا stands for *walla* "or," انشاالله stands for *nšaaḷḷa* "God willing," etc. The reason for doing this is to make the Arabic script unambiguous and not cumbersome (see also Arabic and English Scripts).

ARABIC AND ENGLISH SCRIPTS

1. Consonants

Arabic	English	Arabic	English
ء	'	ص	*ṣ*
ب	*b*	ط	*ṭ*
پ	*p*	ظ	*ð̣*
ت	*t*	ع	ᶜ
ث	*θ*	غ	*ġ*
ج	*j*	ف	*f*
چ	*č*	ق	*q*
ح	*ḥ*	ك	*k*
خ	*x*	گ	*g*
د	*d*	ل	*l*
ذ	*ð*	م	*m*
ر	*r*	ن	*n*
ز	*z*	ه	*h*
س	*s*	و	*w*
ش	*š*	ي	*y*

2. Vowels

Short vowels are not represented by the Arabic script. The long vowels are:

ي *ii/ee* ا *aa*

و *uu/oo*

3. Diphthongs

او *iw/aw/aaw* اي *iy/ay/aay*

ABBREVIATIONS AND SYMBOLS

act. part.	active participle
adj.	adjective
adv.	adverb
anat.	anatomy
approx.	approximately
astron.	astronomy
bot.	botany
coll.	collective
com.	commerce
conj.	conjunction
def.	definite
derog.	derogatory
dipl.	diplomatic
e.g.	for example
elat.	elative
ele.	electricity
esp.	especially
f.	feminine
fig.	figuratively
foll.	following
geom.	geometry
i.e.	that is
imp.	imperative
imperf.	imperfect
intens.	intensive
intran.	intransitive
invar.	invariable
jur.	jurisprudence
lit.	literally
m.	masculine
math.	mathematics
med.	medicine
mil.	military
naut.	nautical
neg.	negative
n. of inst.	noun of instance
opp.	opposite/opposed to
pass.	passive
p.p.	passive participle
perf.	perfect
phot.	photography
p.	plural
pol.	politics
prep.	preposition
pron.	pronoun
rel. pron.	relative pronoun
s.	singular
s.o.	someone
s.th.	something
suff. pron.	suffixed pronoun
tran.	transitive
var.	variant
v.	verb
v.n.	verbal noun
zool.	zoology

NOTES ON PRONUNCIATION

1. The Article Prefix

Before nouns and adjectives beginning with one consonant, the article prefix is ال *l-*; before nouns and adjectives with clusters of two consonants it is ال *li-*, e.g., الكويت *li-kweet* "Kuwait," الصخلة *li-ṣxaḷa* "the young goat," المحسن *li-mḥassin* "the barber," etc. In a post consonantal position, it is ال *l-*, e.g., مـن القوطي *min l-guuṭi* "from the can," دريول اللوري *dreewil l-loori* "the truck driver," etc. Before a noun or an adjective beginning with *t*, *θ*, *č*, *d*, *ð*, *r*, *z*, *s*, *š*, *ṣ*, *ṭ*, *ḍ*, *n*, the *l-* is assimilated, e.g., التانكي *t-taanki* "the reservoir," الثلوث *θ-θuluuθ* "Tuesday," الشاي *č-čaay* "the tea," etc.

2. The Helping Vowel *i*

The helping vowel *i* is not used, e.g., من عمان *min ᶜmaan* "from Oman," صك حلجك *ṣikk ḥaljak* "Shut up!," رحت هناك *riḥt hnaak* "I went there," من دبي *min dbayy* "from Dubai."

3. Vowel Elision

A word that ends with *-vc*, where *-v-* is an unstessed vowel, drops its *-v-* when a vowel-initial suffix is added.

'asim	"name"	+	*-a*	→	*'asma*	"his name"
		+	*-i*	→	*'asmi*	"my name"
		+	*-ič*	→	*'asmič*	"your (f.s.) name"
'uxut	"sister"	+	*-een*	→	*'uxteen*	"two sisters"
ftiham	"to understand"	+	*-aw*	→	*ftihmaw*	"they understood"

However, words of the *fiᶜal* pattern usually change into *fᶜal-* when a vowel-initial suffix is added, except for the suffix *-een*:

faḥam	"coal"	+	*-a*	→	*fḥama*	"piece of coal"
ᶜiraf	"to know"	+	*-ak*	→	*ᶜrafak*	"he knew you"
					ᶜirafk	(is possible)
gaḷam	"pen; pencil"	+	*-a*	→	*gḷumi*	"my pen"

Note the change of *-a-* into *-u-* in the latter example because of the velarized *ḷ*.

4. Assimilation

In GA the feature of assimilation covers the sound *h* when preceded by the consonant *t* and both sounds occur medially, as well as the sounds *d*, *s*, *z*, *j*, *θ*, *ṭ*, and *ḍ* when preceded by initial or medial *t*. In the latter case the *t* is almost always an inflectional prefix of the imperfect form of the verb or the first sound in a form V verb. Examples:

beet	+	*-hum*	→	*beettum*	"their house"
beet	+	*-ha*	→	*beetta*	"her house"
beet	+	*-hin*	→	*beettin*	"their (f.p.) house"
t-	+	*sallaf*	→	*ssallaf*	"to borrow (money)"
t-	+	*θallaj*	→	*θθallaj*	"to be refrigerated"
t-	+	*ḍ̄aḥḥač*	→	*ḍ̄ḍ̄aḥḥač*	"to borrow (money)"

Some examples involve both anaptyxis and assimilation:

čift	+	*-hum*	→	**čifithum*	→	*čifittum*	"I saw them"
ḍ̄irabt	+	*-ha*	→	**ḍ̄irabitha*	→	*ḍ̄irabitta*	"I hit her"

Forms with *-Vt* where *V* is a short vowel change *t* into *č* before a *-č* suffix, e.g.:

ᶜrafat "she knew" + *-č* → *ᶜrafačč* "she knew you (f.s.)"

5. Word Stress

Word stress in GA is governend by the following two rules: (1) All words are stressed on the penultimate syllabe, i.e., on the next to last syllable unless (2) the ultimate or final syllable is long, in which case it is stessed:

šáaffin	"he saw them (f.)"	*béettum*	"their house"
ṭṭárraš	"it was sent"	*fannášt*	"I resigned"
máḥḥad	"no one"	*drísan*	"they (f.) studied"

The syllable *CVV* is treated as a long syllable:

daráahim	"money"	*ᶜalée*	"on him"
xaašúuga	"spoon"	*ᶜaṭóoha*	"they gave her"

Three consecutive short syllables of the pattern *CV CV CV* do not normally occur; instead, they change into *CCVCV*:

šyara	"tree"	*nᶜaya*	"ewe"
wruga	"piece of paper"	*gḷumi*	"my pen, pencil"

Note the following shift in stress:

gáablaw	"they met"	→	*gaablóo*	"they met him"
símač	"fish"	→	*simáčč*	"your fish"
'úxut	"sister"	→	*'uxútta*	"her sister"

For a detailed study of the phonology of GA, see Qafisheh, Hamdi A., *A Short Reference Grammar of Gulf Arabic*, University of Arizona Press, Tucson, AZ, 1977.

ء

ءاب *'aab*

آب *'aab* August (month). syn. أغسطس *'ağusṭuṣ.*

ءاخ *'aax*

آخ *'aax* 1. (exclamation) ouch! 2. cry of pain. آخ رجلـي تعـورني *'aax riili tᶜawwirni.* Oh, my foot hurts! 3. cry of regret. آخ على ذيك الأيام *'aax ᶜala ðiič l-'ayyaam*! Oh, the good old days!

ءادم *'aadm*

آدم *'aadam* Adam. بني آدم *bani 'aadam* human beings, people.

آدمي *aadmi p.* أوادم *'awaadim* person, human beings. إبن أوادم *'ibin 'awaadim* man of good family, well-bred man. f. آدمية *'aadmiyya* p. *-aat.*

ءاذار *'aaðaar*

آذار *'aaðaar* the month of March. syn. مارس *maaris.*

ءازم *'aazm*

آزم *'aazam* (يـازم *yaazam)* 1. to become. آزم القاضي هو الخصـم *'aazam l-gaaḍi huwa l-xaṣim.* The judge became the enemy.

ءاسيا *'aasyaa*

آسيا *'aasya* Asia.

آسيوي *'aasyawi* p. *-yya, -yyiin.* 1. an Asian. 2. Asiatic, characteristic of Asia.

ءاشر *'aašr*

آشار *'aašaar* old boat, old house. var. عشار *ᶜšaar,* عشاري *ᶜšaari.* no known plural.

ءال *'aal*

آل *'aal* the family of. آل نهيان *'aal nhayyaan* the ruling family in the U.A.E. آل ثاني *'aal θaani* the ruling family in Qatar. آل خليفة *'aal xaliifa* the ruling family in Bahrain.

ءالة *'aala*

آلـة *'aala* p. آلات *'aalaat* instrument. آلة موسـيقية *'aala muusiqiyya* musical instrument. آلـة كاتبـة *'aala kaatba* typewriter.

آلي *'aali* mechanical, mechanized.

ءالو *'aalw*

آلو *'aalo* coll. potatoes. syn. علي وللم *ᶜali willam,* بطاط *buṭaaṭ.* s. *-a.*

ءانا *'aanaa*

آنـا *'aana* I. var آني *'aani,* أنا *'ana,* أني *'ani.* p. نحـن *nihin,* حنا *ḥinna.* آنا تحت أمـرك *'aana taḥt 'amrak.* I am at your service. أنا وأنـت *'aana w-inta* you (m.s.) and I. آنـا مسـتانس *'aana mistaanis.* I am having a good time; I am comfortable.

ءايل *'aayl*

آيـل *'aayil.* 1. motor oil. السيارة تحتاج قوطـي آيـل *s-sayyaara tiḥtaaj guuṭi 'aayil.* The car needs a can of motor oil. 2. petroleum.

ءبد *'bd*

أبد *'abbad* (يبد *yabbid)* to last forever,

be eternal. ماحد يبد mahhad yabbid. No one lives forever. أبد 'abad (with neg.) never, not ever أبد ما دشيت الحفيز 'abad ma daššeet l-hafiiz. I have never entered the office. أبد ما رحت أمريكا 'abad ma riht 'amriika. I have never been to America. var. أبدا 'abdan. ما أشرب بيرة أبدا ma 'ašrab biira 'abdan. I never drink beer. أبدا موب هني 'abdan muub hini. certainly not here, never here.

أبدي 'abadi adj. eternal, everlasting. حكم أبدي hukum 'abadi life imprisonment.

ء ب ر 'br

إبرة 'ibra p. إبر 'ibar. 1. needle. إبرة وخيط 'ibra w-xeet needle and thread. 2. injection, inoculation. خذيت إبرة xaðeet 'ibra. I had an injection.

ء ب ر گ 'brg

إبريق 'ibriig p. أباريق 'abaariig pitcher (for water, of water). var. إبريج 'ibriij.

ء ب ل س 'bls

إبليس 'ibliis the Devil. هو مثل إبليس ما تقدرله huwa miθil 'ibliis ma tigdarla. He is like the Devil; you cannot overcome him. p. أبالسة 'abaalsa devil. ذاك الإبليس لعوزني ðaak l-'ibliis la^{c}wazni. That devil bothered me.

ء ب ن ١ 'bn

أبن 'abban (يبن yabbin) to eulogize a deceased person.

تأبين v.n. ta'biin eulogizing. كان فيه ناس وايدين في حفلة التأبين čaan fii naas waaydiin fi haflat t-ta'biin. There were a lot of people in the commemorative ceremony (in honor of a deceased person).

ء ب ن ٢ 'bn

ابن 'ibin p. أبناء 'abnaa' 1. son. 2. one of, descendent of, member of. ابن آدم 'ibin 'aadam son of Adam; human being, man. كلنا أبناء آدم وحوا killana 'bnaa' 'aadam w-hawwa. We are all the descendents of Adam and Eve. ابن إبن 'ibin 'ibin (with foll. n. or suff. pron.) grandson of. ابن كلب 'ibin čalb scoundrel, knave. ابن حلال 'ibin halaal decent, respectable man. تزوجت ابن حلال tazawwajat 'ibin halaal. She married a good man. f. بنت حلال bint halaal. ابن أخو 'ibin 'uxu (with foll. n. or suff. pron.) nephew, son of one's brother. ابن أخت 'ibin 'uxut nephew, son of one's sister. ابن بنت 'ibin bint grandson, son of one's daughter. ابن حرام 'ibin haraam p. ولاد حرام wlaad haraam illegitimate son, bastard; knave. (prov.) ابن الحرام لا ينام ولا يخلي الناس تنام 'ibn l-haraam la ynaam wala yxalli n-naas tnaam. A dog in the manger. ابن خال 'ibin xaal cousin (m.), son of one's maternal uncle. f. بنت خال bint xaal. ابن عرب 'ibin ^{c}arab an Arab. ابن عم 'ibin ^{c}amm cousin (m.) son of one's paternal uncle.

ء ب و 'bw

أبو 'ubu p. آباء 'aabaa', أبهات 'abbahaat father. أبوه 'ubuu his father. أبوك 'ubuuk your (m.s.) father. أبوك 'ubuuč your (f.s.) father. أبوي 'ubuuya my father. (with foll. n. usually بو bu) بو علي bu ^{c}ali Ali's father (a form of address for a married or a single man whose father's name is Ali). أبو بريجع

أثاث *'aθaaθ* furniture. تأثيث *ta'θiiθ* (v.n. from II أثث *'aθθaθ*) furnishing.

ء ث ر *'θr*

أثر *'aθθar (يثر yaθθir)* II 1. to influence, have an effect (on s.o. or s.th). أثر علي *'aθθar ᶜalayya.* He influenced me. 2. to harm, be hazardous. الجقاير تؤثر على صحة بني آدم *j-jigaayir taθθir ᶜala taθθir ṣīḥḥāṭ bani 'aadam.* Cigarettes are hazardous to people's health.

تأثر ب *t'aθθar b-* V to be influenced, affected by.

أثر *'aθar* p. آثار *'aaθaar* 1. trace. ماتوا كلهم وما تركوا أثر وراهم *maataw killahum w-ma trikaw 'aθar waraahum.* They all died and did not leave any trace. 2. (esp. p.) ruins, historical monuments, antiquities. فيه آثار واجد في أم النار *fii 'aaθaar waayid fi 'umm n-naar.* There are many historical ruins in Umm al-Nar. دايرة الآثار *daayrat l-'aaθaar* the department of antiquities.

أثري *'aθari* adj. historical, ancient.

تأثير *ta'θiir* (v.n. from أثر *'aθθar*) influence, effect. ما له أي تأثير *ma la 'ayya ta'θiir.* It does not have any effect.

مأثور *ma'θuur* handed down, traditional. قول مأثور *gool ma'θuur* traditional saying.

مؤثر *mu'θθir* (act. part. of *'aθθar*) moving, touching. كلام مؤثر *kalaam mu'aθθir* moving words.

'ubu breejiᶜ partial paralysis that afflicts the top half of the body. أبو جاسم *'ubu jaasim* (cognomen for s.o. named Muhammad). أبو جني *'ubu jinni* (cognomen for a water snake). أبو جنيب *'ubu jneeb* kidney pain. أبو حمير *'ubu ḥmayyir* whooping cough. أبو خليل *'ubu xaliil* (cognomen for s.o. named Ibrahim). أبو خميس *'ubu xamiis* (cognomen for a lion). أبو زيزي *'ubu ziizi* hippopotamus. أبو سرحان *'ubu sarḥaan* (cognomen for a fox). أبو سنيدة *'ubu sneeda* (cognomen for s.o. named Rashid). أبو سيف *'ubu seef* (cognomen for a kind of shark). أبو شلاخ *'ubu šlax* (epithet for s.o. who lies a lot). أبو شهاب *'ubu šhaab* (cognomen for s.o. named Ahmad or Hamadi). أبو طبيلة *'ubu ṭbeela* (s.o. who beats the drum during the month of Ramadan to wake up people to eat the *suḥuur*, a light meal before daybreak). أبو ظبي *'ubu ḍabi* or *bu ḍabi* capital city of the U.A.E. or the Emirate of Abu Dhabi. أبو عريك *'ubu ᶜreek* (s.o. named Mubarak). أبو عسيكر *'ubu ᶜseekir* (s.o. named Said). أبو الأبيض *'ubu l-'abyaḍ* island in Abu Dhabi whose old name is *mġeetis*. أبو الحصين *'ubu li-ḥṣeen* (cognomen for a fox). أبو العرس *'ubu l-ᶜirs* or إبن عرس *'ibin ᶜirs* (name of a rat). (with the vocative particle يا *ya*) يا يبا *ya yuba*! Father!

ء ث ث *'θθ*

أثث *'aθθaθ (يثث yaθθiθ)* II to furnish (a house, etc.) أثثت بيتي الجديد *'aθθaθt beeti l-yidiid.* I furnished my new house.

تأثث *t'aθθaθ* V to be furnished.

ء ث ي ر *'θyr*

أثير *'aθiir* ether.

ء ث ي ن ا *'θynaa*

أثينا *'aθiina* Athens.

ء ث ي و ب ي ا *'θywbyaa*

إثيوبيا *'iθyoobya* Ethiopia.

إثيوبي *'iθyoobi* p. *-yyiin* 1. an Ethiopian. 2. characteristic of Ethiopia.

ء ج ر *'jr*

أجر *'ajjar* (يجر *yajjir*) II 1. to rent, hire, lease a house, an apartment, etc. أجرله شقة *'ajjarla šigga*. He rented an apartment. أجرله شقة ودفع دبوزيت *'ajjarla šigga w-difa^c dippozeet*. He rented an apartment and paid a deposit. 2. to rent. أجر البيت اللي على السيف حق السفير الأمريكي *'ajjar l-beet illi ^cala s-siif ḥagg s-safiir l-'amriiki*. He rented the house on the beach to the American Ambassador.

تأجر *t'ajjar* V to be rented. البناية تأجرت *li-bnaaya t'ajjarat*. The building was rented.

أجر *'ajir* 1. reward, recompense. الأجر على الله *l-'ajir ^cala lla*. God rewards people. الأجر والثواب *l-'ajir w-θ-θawaab* reward for good deeds. 2. p. أجور *'ujuur* expenses, wages. أجور السفر *'ujuur s-safar* travel expenses; the coolie's wages. أجور الكولي *'ujuur l-kuuli*.

إيجار *'iijaar* rent money, rental. How much is the rent? عندنا بيت حق الإيجار *^cindana beet ḥagg l-'iijaar*. We have a house for rent.

مأجور *ma'juur* bribed, bought. خله يولي هذا واحد مأجور *xalla ywalli haaða waaḥid ma'juur*. Don't pay attention to him; he is in the pay of someone.

مؤجر *m'ajjir* p. *-iin* landlord, lessor. هو اللي مؤجرني البيت *huwa lli m'ajjirni l-beet*. He is the one who leased the house to me.

مستأجر *mista'jir* p. *-iin*. tenant, lessee. ذالحين المستأجر ما يقدر يحصل شقة. لازم يدفع عمولة *ðalḥiin l-mista'jir ma yigdar yḥaṣṣil šigga. laazim yidfa^c ^cmuula*. Now, a tenant cannot find an apartment. He has to pay a broker's fee.

ء ج ل *'jl*

أجل *'ajjal* (يجل *yajjil*) II to postpone. أجلنا السفر إلى السنة الجاية *'ajjalna s-safar 'ila s-sana l-yaaya*. We postponed our travel till next year. لا تؤجل عملك حق باكر *la t'ajjil ^camalak ḥagg baačir*. Do not postpone your work until tomorrow. مدير البنك أجل الدفعة إلى الشهر الجاي *mudiir l-bank 'ajjal d-daf^ca 'ila š-šahar l-yaay*. The bank manager deferred the payment till next month.

تأجل *t'ajjal* V to be postponed. الامتحان تأجل حق يوم الربوع *li-mtiḥaan t'ajjal ḥagg yoom r-rubuu^c*. The examination was postponed till Wednesday.

لأجل *li-'ajil* usually. لاجل *lajil*. 1. for the sake of. يعمل لاجل بلاده *y^camil lajil blaada*. He works for the sake of his country. 2. in order to, so that. رحت لاجل آكل *riḥt lajil 'aakil*. I went in order to eat. 3. because of. لاجل

هذا ما نقدر نفنش الكولية *lajil haaða ma nigdar nfanniš l-kuuliyya.* Because of this, we cannot lay off the coolies.

أجل *'ajal.* 1. instant of death. كل واحد أجله بيد الله *kill waaḥid 'ajala b-yadd aḷḷa.* Everyone's life is in God's hands.

تأجيل *ta'jiil* (v.n. of II أجل *'ajjal*) to postpone. التأجيل حق باكر زين *t-ta'jiil hagg baačir zeen.* Postponement until tomorrow is good.

مؤجل *mu'ajjal* (p.p. of II أجل *'ajjal*) 1. postponed. الاجتماع مؤجل *li-jtimaa*ᶜ *mu'ajjal.* The meeting has been postponed. 2. sum of money paid to a woman in the event of divorce. المؤجل مليون درهم *l-mu'ajjal malyoon dirhim.* The *mu'ajjal* is one million dirhams.

ء ح د *'ḥd*

أحد *'aḥad.* See under **و ح د** *wḥd.*

ء خ *'x*

أخ *'ax* p. إخوان *'ixwaan.* usually أخو *'uxu* p. إخوان *'ixwaan* brother. أخوك *'uxuuk* your (m.s.) brother. أخوك *'uxuuč* your (f.s.) brother. أخوي *'uxuuy, 'uxuuya* (for construct state, see **ء خ و** *'xw.*

ء خ ت *'xt*

أخت *'uxut* p. خوات *xawaat* 1. sister. أختي تدرس ممرضة *'uxti tidris mumarriḍa.* My sister is studying to be a nurse. 2. (polite form of addressing a woman of approximately the same age). شو أسم الأخت؟ *šu 'asim l-luxut?* What is your name, sister? 3. (with inanimate n.) the same as. هذه السيارة أخت ذيك *haaði s-sayyaara 'uxut ðiič.* This car is the same as that one.

ء خ ذ *'xð*

أخذ *'axað* (ياخذ *yaaxið, yaaxuð)* usually خذ *xað*, conjugated like Form I doubled verb. خذيت *xaðeet* I took. 1. to take s.o. or s.th. خذيته السوق *xaðeeta s-suug.* I took him to the market. خلنا ناخذ الموتر *xalna naaxið l-mootar.* Let's take the car. 2. to take s.o. or s.th. along. رايح آخذك واياي *raayiḥ 'aaxðak wiyyaay.* I am going to take you with me. 3. to get, obtain خذيت حقوقي وفنشت *xaðeet ḥguugi w-fannašt.* I took my due and resigned. خذيت الشهادة ودشيت الجيش *xaðeet š-šahaada w-daššeet l-jeeš.* I took my diploma and enlisted in the military. 4. to accept, take. خذ على خاطره *xað* ᶜ*ala xaaṭra.* He took it personally. لا ياخذ ولا يعطي *laa yaaxið wala y*ᶜ*aṭi.* He doesn't give and take. 5. to take, require. خذوا علي دبوزيت *xaðu* ᶜ*alayya deppoozeet.* They required a deposit from me. الامتحان خذ ساعتين *l-mtiḥaan xað saa*ᶜ*teen.* The examination took two hours. 6. to rank. خذت الأولى على بنات صفها *xaðat l-'uula* ᶜ*ala banaat ṣafha.* She ranked first among her classmates. 7. to occupy. دش هالحين وخذ الصف الأول *dišš halḥiin w-xið ṣ-ṣaff l-'awwal.* Enter now and take the front row. 8. to engage in, take. لين ينش يتسبح *leen yništ yitsabbaḥ.* When he gets up, he takes a bath. 9. to take up (a position, pose, etc.) خذيت حذري منه لأنه بطال *xaðeet ḥaðari minna linna baṭṭaal.* I was on my guard against him because he was a bad person. 10. to surprise, get the better of. خذني *xaðni* He took me by surprise. 11. (with راس *raas*) to behead s.o. قال الشيخ «إخذوا راس المطوع» *gaal š-šeex 'ixðu raas li-mṭawwa*c. The ruler said, "Cut off the holy man's head."

تؤاخذ *waaxað* III to blame. لا تواخذه بعده جاهل *laa twaaxða ba*c*da yaahil.* Don't blame him; he is still a young boy.

انوخذ *nwaxað* VII 1. to be taken. كله انوخذ *killa nwaxað*. It was all taken. 2. to be stolen. الموتر انوخذ *l-mootar nwaxað*. The car was stolen. ما ينوخذ *ma yinwixið* cannot be taken, is not fit to be taken. الجاهل ما ينوخذ السينما *l-yaahil ma yinwixið s-siinama*. A child should not be taken to the cinema. هذا طماط ما ينوخذ *haaða ṭamaaṭ ma yinwixið*. These are tomatoes that cannot be taken (i.e. bought).

اتخذ *ttaxað* VIII 1. to take as, use as. اتخذ غيابه عذر *ttaxað ġyaaba* c*uður*. He used his absence as an excuse. 2. (with ب *b-*) to adopt, take. اتخذت الحكومة قرار بتسفير الأجانب *ttaxaðat l-ḥukuuma garaar b-tasfiir l-'ayaanib*. The government took a decision to deport the foreigners.

أخذ *'axð* (v.n. from أخذ *'axað*) taking, receiving. أخذ ورد *'axð w-radd*, or أخذ وعطا *'axð w-*c*aṭa* give and take.

مؤاخذة *mu'aaxaða* censure, blame. بدون مؤاخذة. رايح أقطه *b-duun mu'aaxða. raayiḥ 'aguṭṭa*. No offense, I am going to throw it away.

ءخر *'xr*

أخر *'axxar* II 1. to delay, hold up. أخرني واجد *'axxarni waayid.* He delayed me for a long time. أخر الفلوس إلى آخر الشهر *'axxar li-fluus 'ila 'aaxir š-šahar*. He held up the money until the end of the month. 2. to postpone. أخر الامتحان *'axxar li-mtiḥaan.* He postponed the exam. لا تؤخر الخط إلى باكر. طرشه اليوم *la t'axxir l-xaṭṭ 'ila baačir. ṭarrša l-yoom*. Do not put off the letter until tomorrow. Send it today.

تأخر *t'axxar* V 1. to be late. تأخرت الطايرة *t'axxarat ṭ-ṭaayra.* The plane was late. 2. to get late. الدنيا تأخرت *d-dinya t'axxarat.* It has gotten late. 3. (with على c*ala*) to come late to s.o. متأسف. تأخرت عليك *mit'assif. t'axxart* c*aleek*. I am sorry. I came late to (see) you. 4. (with عن c*an*) to fall behind. تأخر عن ربعه *t'axxar* c*an rab*c*a.* He fell behind his group.

آخر *'aaxir* p. أواخر *'awaaxir*. 1. the last part, portion of. آخر ريال شفته *'aaxir rayyaal šifta*. the last man I saw. آخر الشهر *'aaxir š-šahar* the last part of the month. أواخر الصفري *'awaaxir li-ṣfiri.* the last part of Autumn. 2. last, final. آخر كلام: الطماط خمسة درهم الربعة *'aaxir kalaam: ṭ-ṭamaaṭ xamsa dirhim r-rub*c*a*. The last word (i.e., the final price): tomatoes are five dirhams per *rub*c*a*. 3. latest, most recent. آخر موديل *'aaxir modeel* the latest model. آخر شي قال لي ما يبغى يعرس *'aaxir šayy gal-li ma yibġa y*c*arris*. Finally, he told me he did not want to get married. 4. (with ما *ma*)

آخر مـا *'aaxir-ma* the last that. ذوله آخر مـا عنـدي مـن كنـادر *ðoola 'aaxir-ma ᶜindi min kanaadir.* These are the last men's dresses (dishdashes) I have. الآخـرة *l-'aaxra* the hereafter, as opposed to الدنيا *'id-dunya* this world.

تأخير *ta'xiir* (v.n. from أخر *'axxar*) delay, postponement.

مؤخر *m(u)'axxar* (p.p. from أخر *'axxar*) 1. delayed, postponed. الاجتماع مؤخر *l-'ijtimaaᶜ m'axxar.* The meeting has been postponed. 2. (as n.) sum of money paid to a divorced wife.

متأخر *mit'axxir* (act. part. from تأخر *t'axxar*) p. *-iin.* 1. having come late. جيـت متـأخر *yiit mit'axxir.* I came late. 2. late, delayed. الطيـارة متـأخرة *ṭ-ṭayyaara mit'axxra.* The plane is delayed. البلـدان المتـأخرة *l-bildaan l-mit'axxra* the underdeveloped countries.

ء خ ط ب ط *'xṭbṭ*

أخطبوط *'axṭabuuṭ* p. *-aat.* octopus.

ء خ و *'xw*

أخو *'uxu,* خـو *xu* p. إخوان *'ixwaan.* 1. brother. أخـوك *'xuuk* your (m.s.) brother. أخـوك *'uxuuč* your (f.s.) brother. أخـوي *'uxuuy, 'uxxuuya* my brother. 2. fellow, friend. يا أخي *ya 'axi,* يا خـوي *ya xuuya* my dear friend. الإخـوان المسلمين *l-'ixwaan l-muslimiin* (society of) the Muslim Brotherhood. 3. like, the same as. (prov.) عنبر خو بـلال *ᶜambar xu blaal.* Anbar is Bilal's brother = Two peas in a pod. f. أخت *'uxut* p. خـوات *xawaat.* see under **ء خ ت** *'xt.*

ء د ب *'db*

أدب *'addab* II 1. to teach manners, teach a lesson. الأب والأم يؤدبون عيالهم *l-'ubu w-l-'umm y'addbuun ᶜyaalhum.* The parents teach their kids manners. 2. to punish. الشـرطة أدبتهـم *š-širṭa 'addabattum.* The police punished them.

تأدب *t'addab* V to be, become polite. عقـب مـا زخـوه الشـرطة تـأدب *ᶜugub-ma zaxxoo š-širṭa t'addab.* He became polite after the police arrested him.

أدب *'adab* p. آداب *'aadaab* 1. literature تدرس أدب؟ *tidris 'adab?* Are you studying literature. كليـة الآداب والعلـوم *kulliyyat l-'aadaab w-l-ᶜuluum.* the College of Arts and Sciences. 2. manners. شك حلجك! ما عندك أدب *šikk ḥaljak! ma ᶜindak 'adab!* Shut up! You have no manners.

أديب *'adiib* p. أدبـاء *'udaba* man of letters. جمعيـة أدبـاء الخليـج *jamᶜiyyat 'udaba l-xaliij* The Society of the Gulf Authors.

تأديب *ta'diib* (v.n. from أدب *'addab*) disciplinary punishment. دايرة التـأديب *daayrat t-ta'diib.* The Department of Discipline. مجلـس التـأديب *majlis t-ta'diib* disciplinary board.

مؤدب *m'addab* p. *-iin.* (p.p. of أدب *'addab*) well behaved, well brought up.

ء د ر *'dr*

أدار *'adaar* p. *-aat* radar. يزخـون المخـالف بـالأدار *yzixxuun li-mxaalif b-l-'adaar.* They catch the violator by radar.

ءدم *'dm*

آدمي *'aadmi* see under **ءادم** *'adm.*

ءدو *'dw*

أداة *'adaa* p. أدوات *'adawaat* tool, instrument. أدوات الحرب *'adawaat l-ḥarb* war tools, war materiel.

ءذا١ *'ðaa*

إذا *'iða* syn. إن كان كان لو *nčaan čaan loo* 1. if إذا رحت سلم عليه *'iða riht sallim ᶜalee.* If you go, give him my regards. (prov.) إذا برق البرق طالع عين ثورك *'iða barag l-barg ṭaaliᶜ ᶜeen θoorak.* lit., "If lightning strikes, look your bull in the eye." = Look before you leap. (prov.) إذا كفت رفيجك حلو لا تاكله كله *'iða čift rifiijak ḥilu la taakla killa.* lit. "If you think your friend is sweet, do not eat him up all at once." = Do not use up all of your credit at once. 2. whether, if. إذا تسير لو ما تسير كله واحد *'iða tsiir loo ma tsiir killa waaḥid.* Whether you go or not it's the same.

ءذا٢ *'ðaa*

إذا *'iðan* (informal عيل *ᶜayal*) therefore. See عيل *ᶜayal* under **عيل** *ᶜyl.*

ءذر *'ðr*

إذرى *'iðra* see under **ذري** *ðry.*

ءذن *'ðn*

أذن *'aðan* (يـذن *yiiðan)* to give permission (to do s.th.) هو اللي أذن لي أدش *huwa lli 'aðan-li 'adišš.* He is the one who gave me permission to enter.

أذن *'aððan* II (يـذن *yaððin)* var. وذن *waððan* to call to prayer. أذن الظهر *'aððan ḍ-ḍuhur* The muezzin called to the noon-time prayer.

استأذن *sta'ðan* X to ask permission (to do s.th.) استأذنت أروح الدختر *sta'ðant 'aruuḥ d-daxtar.* I asked permission to go to the doctor. لازم تستأذن قبل لا تدش *laazim tista'ðin gabil-la d-dišš.* You must ask permission before you enter.

إذن *'iðin* permission. بإذن الله *b-'iðn l-laah* with God's permission, God willing.

إذن *'iðin* p. إذون *'iðuun* (f.) ear. راح الدختر لأن إذونه توجعه *raaḥ d-daxtar li'an 'iðuuna twayyᶜa.* He went to the doctor because his ears hurt him.

أذان *'aðaan* call to prayer. جا وقت الأذان *ya wagt l-'aðaan.* The time for the call to prayer has come.

ءذي *'ðy*

أذى *'aðða* II (يأذي *y'aðði)* 1. to hurt, harm. كانوا يابون يأذونا *čaanaw yabuun y'aððuuna.* They wanted to hurt us. لا تأذي ربعك *la t'aðði rabᶜak* Do not hurt your people. 2. to annoy. طلباته الكثيرة أذتني *ṭalabaata l-kaθiira 'aððatni.* His many requests annoyed me. 3. to molest. لا تأذي عيالك *la t'aðði ᶜyaalak.* Do not molest your kids.

تأذى *t'aðða* V 1. to be hurt, suffer. تأذيت واجد من الدعمة *t'aððeet waayid min d-daᶜma.* I was hurt a lot because of the car accident. 2. to feel hurt. تأذيت واجد من هذا الخبر *t'aððeet waayid min haaða l-xabar.* I felt hurt because of this news item.

أذى *'aða* 1. harm. (prov.) الأذى ما يحيط إلا بأهله *l-'aða ma yḥiiṭ 'illa* *b-'ahla*. Harm destroys only its doers. 2. annoyance, irritation. ما يجي منه أذى *ma yaji minna 'aða.* He does not annoy anyone.

ء ر ت و ز *'rtwz*

إرتــوازي *'irtiwaazi* (adj.) artesian. artesian well.

ء ر ث *'rθ*

إرث *'irθ* see under **و ر ث** *wrθ.*

ء ر د ن *'rdn*

الأردن *l-'ardun* Jordan. نهر الأردن *nahr l-'ardun* the River Jordan. شرق الأردن *šarg l-'ardun* Transjordan.

أردنـي *'arduni* p. أردنـيـن *'arduniin* p. *-yyiin* 1. A Jordanian. هو أردنـي مـن عمـان *huwa 'arduni min ᶜammaan.* He is a Jordanian from Amman. 2. characteristic of Jordan. طمـاط أردنـي *ṭamaaṭ 'arduni* Jordanian tomatoes. الإذاعة الأردنية *l-'iðaaᶜa l-'arduniyya* the Jordanian Broadcasting Station.

ء ر ظ *'rð̣*

أرض *'arð̣* (f.) p. أراضـي *'araað̣i.* 1. land, ground. الأرض استوت غالية هالحين *l-'arð̣ stawat ġaalya halḥiin.* Land has become expensive now. حصـل دعمـة ورفيقـي طـاح علـى الأرض *ḥiṣal daᶜma w-rifiiji ṭaaḥ ᶜala l-'arð̣* There was a car accident and my buddy fell down to the ground. 2. soil, land أرض راس الخيمة خصيبـة *'arð̣ raas l-xeema xaṣiiba.* The land in Ras Al-Khayma is fertile.

أرضـي *'arð̣i* situated on the ground. يسكن في الطابق الأرضي *yiskin fi ṭ-ṭaabig l-'arð̣i.* He lives on the ground floor.

أرضيـة *'arð̣iyya* p. *-aat* area of a building, ground on which a building stands, foundation. الأرضيـة رمـل مـوب زينـة *l-'arð̣iyya ramil muub zeena.* The foundation (of the building) is sand; it is not good.

ء ر م ن *'rmn*

أرمن *'arman* (coll.) Armenians. s. أرمني *'armani.* الأرمـن مـا لهـم وطـن حقهـم *l-'arman ma lahum waṭan ḥaghum.* The Armenians do not have a homeland of their own.

أرمـني *'armani* 1. Armenian 2. an Armenian.

ء ر ن ب *'rnb*

أرنـب *'arnab* p. أرانب *'araanib* rabbit. عمـرك كليـت لحـم أرنـب؟ *ᶜumrak kaleet laḥam 'arnab?* Have you ever eaten rabbit?

ء ر ي ل *'ryl*

أريـل *'aryal* pl. أريلات *'aryalaat* aerial, antenna.

ء ز م *'zm*

تـأزم *t'azzam* V to become critical. تأزم الوضع عقب الحرب *t'azzam l-wað̣iᶜ ᶜugb l-ḥarb.* The situation became critical after the war.

أزمة *'azma* p. *-aat* crisis.

ء س ب ا ن *'sbaan*

الإسـبان *l-'isbaan* or الإسـبانيين *l-'isbaaniyyiin.* The Spaniards.

إسباني *'isbaani* 1. A Spaniard. هو إسباني من مدريد بعـد *huwa 'isbaani min madriid baᶜad.* He is a Spaniard from Madrid too. 2. Spanish, characteristic of Spain.

إسـبانيا *'isbaanya* or سـبانيا *sbaanya* Spain. العـرب تركـوا آثـار في إسـبانيا *l-ᶜarab trakaw 'aaθaar fi sbaanya* The Arabs have left traces in Spain.

ء س ت ا ذ *'staað*

أسـتاذ *'ustaað* var. ستاذ *staað* p. أساتذة *'asaatiða* 1. professor. يشتغل أستاذ في الجامعـة *yištagil 'ustaað fi l-yaamᶜa.* He works as a teacher at the university. 2. craftsman, master. ستاذ في البنا *staað fi l-bina* a master at construction. 3. (a polite form of addressing an educated man). !يا ستاذ *ya staað!* Sir!

ء س ت ر ل *'strl*

أسـتراليا *'ustraalya* Australia. أسـترالي *'ustraali* p. *-yyiin.* 1. an Australian. 2. characteristic of Australia.

ء س ت ر ل ن *'strln*

إسـترليني *'istarliini* sterling. جنيه إسترليني *jineeh istarliini* pound sterling.

ء س د *'sd*

أسـد *'asad* p. أسود *'usuud* 1. lion syn. سـبع *sabiᶜ* p. سـباع *sbaaᶜ.* الأسد ملك الحيوانات *l-'asad malilk l-ḥayawaanaat.* The lion is the king of animals. سرنا القنـص وقنصنـا أسـد *sirna l-ganaṣ w-ginaṣna 'asad.* We went hunting and hunted a lion. فيـه أسـد في حديقـة الحيـوان في الدوحـة *fii 'asad fi ḥadiigat l-ḥayawaan fi d-dooḥa.* There is a lion in the zoo in Doha. 2. brave man.

ء س ر *'sr*

إسـر *'isar (يئسـر yi'sir)* 1. to capture, take prisoner. واجد مـن جنودنـا إسـرهم العـدو *waayid min jinuudna 'isarhum l-ᶜadu.* The enemy captured many of our soldiers. 2. to captivate, fascinate. أم كلثوم كانت تئسـر النـاس بصوتهـا *'umm kalθuum kaanat ti'sar n-naas b-ṣootha.* Umm Kalthum held people spellbound by her voice.

مأسـور *ma'suur* p. *-iin* p.p. of إسر *'isar* 1. captivated. 2. fascinated.

أسر *'asir* v.n. from إسر *'isar*, captivity. وقـع في الأسـر *wigaᶜ fi l-'asir* to be captured.

أسـير *'asiir* p. أسـرى *'asra* captive, prisoner of war. في حرب الخليج كان فيه أسـرى واجـد مـن الجيـش العراقـي *fi ḥarb l-xaliij čaan fii 'asra waayid min l-jeeš li-ᶜraagi.* During the Gulf war there were many captives from the Iraqi army.

ء س س *'ss*

أسـس *'assas* II 1. to lay a foundation. أسـس وبنـى عمـارتين علـى السـيف *'assas w-bina ᶜamarteen ᶜala s-siif.* He laid a foundation and built two buildings on the beach. 2. to establish, set up. أسسوا مجلـس سمـوه مجلس التعـاون الخليجـي *'assasaw majlis sammoo majlis t-taᶜaawan l-xaliiji.* They established a council which they called the Gulf Cooperation Council.

تأسـس *t'assas* V to be founded, established. الجمعيـة تأسسـت مـن زمـان *l-jamᶜiyya t'assasat min zamaan.* The society was founded a long time ago.

أسـاس *'asaas* (common var. ساس *saas*) 1. foundation. أسـاس العمـارة *'asaas li-ᶜmara* the foundation of the building. 2. basis على ها الأساس *ᶜala hal-'asaas* based on this. ما له أساس *ma* *la 'asaas* unfounded, baseless. على ها الأساس *ᶜala hal-'asaas* on the basis of this, on account of this.

أساسي *'asaasi* basic, fundamental. السبب الأساسي *s-sabab l-'asaasi* The basic reason.

تأسيس *ta'siis* (v.n. from II أسس *'assas*) founding, establishing.

مؤسس *mu'assis* (act. part. from II أسس *'assas*), founder. من هو مؤسس الجمعية؟ *man huwa mu'assis l-jamᶜiyya?* Who is the founder of the association?

مؤسسة *mu'assasa* p. *-aat* establishment. مؤسسة النقد الدولي *mu'assasat n-nagd d-dawli* The International Monetary Fund.

ء س ط ل *'sṭl*

أسطول *'usṭuul* p. أساطيل *'asaaṭiil.* fleet. الأسطول الأمريكي *l-'usṭuul l-'amriiki* the American fleet. الأسطول البحري *l-'usṭuul l-baḥri* the naval fleet.

ء س ط و ن *'sṭwn*

أسطوانة *'usṭuwaana* p. *-aat* 1. music record. var. سطوانة *sṭuwaana,* سنطوانة *sinṭuwaana.* عندي سطوانات حق مغنيين عرب واجدين *'indi sṭuwaanaat ḥagg mġanyiin ᶜarab waajdiin.* I have music records by many Arab singers. 2. cylinder. نحتاج سطوانتين غاز كل شهر *niḥtaaj sṭuwaanteen ġaaz kill šahar.* We need two cylinders of gas every month.

ء س ف *'sf*

تأسف *t'assaf* V to feel sorry, regret. ما بنيت! ما عملت شي! تأسفت على حالتك يا بو علي *ma baneet! ma ᶜimalt šayy! t'assaft ᶜala ḥaltak ya bu ᶜali.* You haven't built! You haven't done anything! I feel sorry for your situation, Abu Ali. تأسف على *t'assaf ᶜala* to feel sorry for, regret having done s.th. تأسفت على اللي عملته *t'assaft ᶜala lli ᶜimalta.* I regretted what I had done.

أسف *'asaf* v.n. regret. للأسف *l-l-'asaf* unfortunately.

متأسف *mit'assif* (act. part. from V تأسف *t'assaf*) sorry. متأسف على اللي سويته *mit'assif ᶜala lli sawweeta.* I am sorry for what I have done متأسف ما أقدر أساعدك *mit'assif ma 'agdar 'asaaᶜdak.* I am sorry, I cannot help you.

ء س ف ن ج *'sfnj*

إسفنج *'isfanj* or سفنج *sfanj* sponge.

ء س م ر *'smr*

أسمرة *'asmara* Asmara (capital of Eritrea).

ء س ي *'sy*

مأساة *ma'saa* calamity, tragedy (see also **و س ي** *wsy*).

ء ش ر *'šr*

أشر *'aššar* II 1. to indicate, point out. أشرت له على التنديل اللي فنش العمال *'aššart-la ᶜala t-tindeel illi fannaš l-ᶜummaal.* I pointed out to him the supervisor who had laid off the workmen. 2. to give a signal, gesture. العرب يؤشرون واجد لين يحكون *lᶜarab y'aššruun waayid leen yiḥčuun.* The Arabs make gestures when they talk.

3. to check (as a sign of approval). المدير أشر لي على الطلب *l-mudiir 'aššar-li ᶜala ṭ-ṭalab.* The manager checked my application.

إشارة *'išaara* p. *-aat.* signal, sign. قبل لا تلف يمين اعطي إشارة *gabil la tliff yimiin ᶜaṭi 'išaara.* Before you turn right, give a signal. هذي الإشارة معناتها لا تدق الهرن *haaδi l-'išaara maᶜnaatta la t-digg l-haran.* This sign means: Don't sound your horn.

تأشيرة *ta'šiira* p. *-aat* visa. قدمت طلب تأشيرة حق لندن *gaddamt ṭalab ta'šiira ḥagg landan.* I applied for a visa to London. تأشيرة مرور *ta'šiirat muruur* transit visa.

مؤشر *m'aššir* (act. part. from II أشر *'aššar*) indicator, pointer. مؤشر الحرارة ما يشتغل *m'aššir l-ḥaraara ma yištaġil.* The temperature indicator doesn't work.

ءصفهن *'ṣfhn*

إصفهان *'iṣfahaan* Isfahan (city in Iran).

ءصل *'ṣl*

أصل *'aṣl* p. أصول *'uṣuul* 1. origin, source. أنا ما أعرفه. أصله منين؟ *'aana ma ᶜarfa. 'aṣla mneen?* I do not know him. Where is he from originally? 2. foundation, basis. هذي القصة ما لها أصل *haaδi l-ġiṣṣa ma laha 'aṣil* This story does not have any foundation. 3. (with ال *'al-* the important one, the main one. خله يولي! أنت الأصل يا بو علي *xal̩la ywalli! 'inta l-'aṣil, ya bu ᶜali* The hell with them! You are the important one, Abu Ali. 4. descent, lineage. هو ريال زين. شعلينا من أصله وفصله *huwa rayyaal zeen. š-ᶜaleena min 'aṣla w-faṣla.* He is a good man. What have we got to do with his origin and ancestry! 5. (p. only) properly, in accordance with regulations. قدم طلب حسب الأصول *gaddam ṭalab ḥasb l-'uṣuul.* He applied properly.

أصلا *'aṣlan* actually. أصلا آنا قلت نفس الشي *'aṣlan 'aana gilt nafs š-šayy* Actually, I said the same thing.

أصلي *'asli* p. *-yyiin* 1. original. السبب الأصلي *s-sabab l-'aṣli.* The original cause. البتري الأصلي *l-batri l-laṣli* the original battery. 2. genuine, authentic. قطع غيار أصليين *giṭaᶜ ġayaar 'aṣliyyiin* genuine spare parts. 3. chief, main. الثمن الأصلي *θ-θaman l-'aṣli* the cost price.

متأصل *mit'aṣṣil* 1. deep-rooted, deep-seated. عادات متأصلة *ᶜaadaat mit'aṣṣla* deep-rooted customs. 2. chronic (illness) مرض متأصل *maraḍ mit'aṣṣil* chronic illness.

ءطر *'ṭr*

إطار *'iṭaar* p. إطارات *'iṭaaraat* frame (of a picture).

ءطلس *'ṭls*

أطلس *'aṭlas* p. أطالس *'aṭaalis* atlas, collection of maps. أطلس *'aṭlas* (adj.) p. طلس *ṭils*, طلسان *ṭilsaan* dark (color).

أطلسي *'aṭlasi* Atlantic. المحيط الأطلسي *l-muḥiiṭ l-'aṭlasi* The Atlantic Ocean.

ءفرگ *'frg*

أفريقيا *'afriigya* Africa. أفريقي *'afriigi* p. *-yyiin,* أفارقة *'afaarga* 1. an African.

2. characteristic of Africa.

ء ف غ ن *'fġn*

الأفغان *l-'afġaan* 1. the Afghans (coll.) 2. Afghanistan

أفغـــاني *'afġaani* 1. an Afghan, an Afghanistani. 2. characteristic of Afghanistan.

أفغانستان *'afġaanistaan* Afghanistan.

ء ف ف *'ff*

أف *'uff* (exclamation of displeasure or despair) oh! أف يا الله! *'uff ya 'aḷḷaah!* Oh, God. أف راسي يعـــورني *'uff raasi yᶜawwirni.* Oh! I have a headache.

أفـــة *'affa* (foll. by على *ᶜala*) shame أفة عليك! *'affa ᶜaleek!* Shame on you!

ء ف ي ن *'fyn*

أفيون *'afyuun* opium.

ء ك ت ب ر *'ktbr*

أكتوبر *'aktoobar*. October. نحن ما نعرف أكتوبر. نعرف الأشهر الهجريـــة *niḥin ma nᶜarf 'aktoobar. nᶜarf l-'ašhir l-hijriyya.* We do not know October. We know the hegira months.

ء ك د *'kd*

أكـــد *'akkad* II 1. to confirm s.th. (usually with على *ᶜala*). أكد على الموعد *'akkad ᶜala l-mawᶜid.* He confirmed the appointment. أكد علي أشوف الدختر *'akkad ᶜalayya 'ačuuf d-daxtar.* He made sure that I see the doctor. أكدت الخـــبر *'akkatt l-xabar.* I confirmed the news. 2. to assure, give assurance to s.o. أكد لنا إنه حب يد الشيخ *'akkad lana 'inna ḥabb yad š-šeex.* He assured us that he kissed the Shaikh's hand. أكدت له الحجز *'akkadt-la l-ḥajiz.* I confirmed the reservation for him.

تأكد *t'akkad* V 1. to be sure. تأكدت إنه باق الفلوس *t'akkatt 'inna baag li-fluus.* I was sure that he stole the money. تأكد من نفســـه *t'akkad min nafsa.* He was sure of himself. 2. to be convinced. تأكدت إنه ما يبغاهـــا *t'akkadat 'inna ma yibġaaha.* She was sure that he did not want her.

تـــأكيد *ta'kiid* (v.n. of V تأكد *t'akkad*) 1. assurance. بكل تـــأكيد *b-kill ta'kiid* certainly, of course. 2. confirmation تـــأكيد الحجـــز ضـــروري *ta'kiid l-ḥajiz ḍaruuri.* The confirmation of the reservation is necessary.

أكيد *'akiid* (adj.) certain. شي أكيد *šayy 'akiid* sure thing. (adv.) certainly, surely. أكيد هو ياي بـــاكر *'akiid huwa yaay baačir.* Certainly he is coming tomorrow. موب أكيد *muub 'akiid* not for sure, not certain.

مؤكـــد *m'akkad* (p.p. of II أكد *'akkad*) certain, confirmed. sure thing. الحجز مؤكد *l-ḥajiz m'akkad.* The reservation is confirmed.

متأكد *mit'akkid* (act. part. from V تأكد *t'akkad*) p. *-iin* positive, certain, sure. آنا متأكد إنه ريال زيـــن *'aana mit'akkid 'inna rayyaal zeen.* I am certain that he is a good man. أنت متأكد؟ *'inta mit'akkid?* Are you sure? أي نعم أنا متأكد. ليش موب متأكد؟ *'ii naᶜam 'aana mit'akkid. leeš muub mit'akkid?* Yes, I am sure. Why am I not sure?

ء ك ل see **ك ل** *kl.*

ء ك و *'kw*

أكو *'aku* (Kuwaiti and Bahraini) 1. there is, there are. أكو لحم بقر في السوق *'aku laḥam bagar fi s-suug.* There is beef in the market. أكو عيالة في الساحة *'aku ᶜayyaala fi s-saaḥa.* There are male dancers in the courtyard. أكو يحّ في السوق؟ *'aku yiḥḥ fi s-suug?* Are there watermelons in the market? 2. (with عند *ᶜind*) to have أكو شغل عندكم؟ *'aku šuġul ᶜindakum?* Do you have work? أكو فلوس في مخباي *'aku fluus fi maxbaaya.* There is money in my pocket.

ماكو *maaku* (neg.) there isn't, there aren't. ماكو فلوس *maaku fluus.* There is no money. ماكو قزازين في البلدية أبد؟ *maaku gazzaaziin fi l-baladiyya 'abad?* Aren't there any surveyors at all in the municipality? *maaku* = Qatari ما ميش *ma miiš* (corruption of literary ما من شيء *ma min šay'*).

ء ل ف *'lf*

ألف *'alf* p. ألوف *'uluuf* thousand (syn. لك *lakk*, an old form not commonly used). ألف ريال *'alf rayyaal* 1,000 men. خمسة أف *xamsa 'alf* or خمسة آلاف *xamsat 'aalaaf* 5,000.

ء ل ل *'ll*

إلا *'illa* 1. except. ماحد جا إلا حمد *maḥḥad ya 'illa ḥamad.* No one came except Hamad. لا إله إلا الله *la 'ilaaha 'illa ḷḷaah.* There is no god but He. 2. just, only ما أبغى إلا قشاري *ma abġa 'illa gšaari.* I just want my personal effects. 3. yes, indeed. جا محمد؟ إلا جا *ya mḥammad? 'illa ya.* Has Muhammad come? Yes, he certainly has. 4. (in telling time) minus, to. الساعة خمس إلا عشر *s-saaᶜa xams 'illa ᶜšir.* It's ten minutes to five. 5. (with preceding neg. v.) except that, it wasn't long until, no sooner ... than. ما شفته إلا نط جدامي ودعمته *ma čifta 'illa naṭṭ jiddaami w-daᶜamta.* No sooner had I seen him than he jumped in front of me, and I hit him.

وإلا *w-'illa,* ولا *willa* 1. or تابي هذا ولا ذاك؟ *tabi haaða willa ðaak?* Do you want this one or that one? محمد ولا خميس كله واحد *mḥammad willa xmayyis killa waaḥid.* Muhammad or Khmayis, it's all the same. 2. otherwise. ما دريت ولا كان رحت *ma dareet willa čaan riḥt.* I did not know; otherwise I would have gone.

ء ل ه *'llh*

الله *'aḷḷa* God (var. *'aḷḷaah*) الله رحيم *'aḷḷa raḥiim.* God is merciful. لا إله إلا الله *la 'ilaaha 'illa ḷḷaah.* There is no god but God. محمد رسول الله *muḥammad rasuula ḷḷaah.* Muhammad is God's messenger. صبحك الله بالخير! *ṣabbaḥk aḷḷa b-l-xeer.* Good morning! مساك الله بالخير *massaak aḷḷa b-l-xeer.* Good evening (or afternoon). الله وياك *'aḷḷa wiyyaak.* God be with you. Good luck. Goodbye! الله بالخير! *'aḷḷa b-l-xeer!* (polite expression used after someone arrives and sits down. It is said at any time of the day; it is characteristic of Kuwaiti and Iraqi. The response is the same). الله راد لي ولد *'aḷḷa raad-li walad.* God willed that I have a baby boy. بيت الله *beet 'aḷḷa* the Kaaba; Mecca. الله الله *'aḷḷaah*

aḷḷaah. (used by Bedouins) (an expression of amazement, admiration). How nice is...! الله بالستر *'aḷḷah b-s-sitir:* (expression used to forestall a calamity). God protect, shield us!

الله على *'aḷḷaah ᶜala ...* What a splendid thing is...! الله على أيام زمان! *'aḷḷaah ᶜala 'ayyaam zamaan!* The good old days. (expression said by someone offering condolences). God reward you with His blessing! = literary: عظم الله أجركم *ᶜaḏḏama ḷḷaahu 'ajrakum.* God make your reward greater (in the hereafter).

الله يسلمك *'aḷḷa ysallimk* or سلمك الله *sallamk aḷḷa* 1. (response to goodbye: مع السلامة *maᶜ s-salaama*) Goodbye. 2. (parenthetical phrase said when speaking to a man of higher rank or status) الله يسلمك باكر عطلة *'aḷḷa ysallimk baačir ᶜuṭla.* Tomorrow, God protect you, is a holiday. f. الله يسلمك *'aḷḷa ysallimč.*

الله يغربلك *'aḷḷa yǧarbilk* 1. (used to invoke God against s.o.) Damn you! God's curse fall on you. 2. darn you. الله يغربلك على هذه النكت *'aḷḷa yǧarbilk ᶜala haaḏi n-nikat.* Darn you for these jokes. الله يهداك *'aḷḷa yhadaak* or الله يهديك *'aḷḷa yhadiik* (used when giving advice and guidance; lit., "May God guide you to the correct path.")

ماشاالله *maašaaḷḷa* = literary ما شاء الله *maa šaa'a ḷḷaah!* (an exclamation of surprise or amazement) ماشاالله توظفت وعرست وبنيت *maašaaḷḷa twaḏḏaft w-ᶜarrast w-baneet* Amazing! You were employed, got married, and built (a house).

انشاالله *nšaḷḷa* = literary. إن شاء الله *'in šaa'a ḷḷaah* if God wills. 1. God willing, if possible (generally used for I hope so; I hope that, it is to be hoped that). انشاالله المدير في الحفيز *'inšaaḷḷa l-mudiir fi l-ḥafiiz.* I hope the manager is in the office. 2. (as a response to a request) yes; gladly, willingly. تشايك التاير *čaayik t-taayir.* Check the tire. انشاالله *'inšaaḷḷa.* Yes, certainly.

والله *waḷḷa* 1. honestly, really. والله ما أدري *waḷḷa ma dri.* Honestly, I do not know. والله هذي واجد زين *waḷḷa haaḏi waajid zeen.* Really! This is very good. 2. (expression of surprise) really? والله عدل طرش لكم فلوس؟ *waḷḷa' ᶜadil ṭarraš lakum fluus?* Really? Did he really send you money? 3. (more emphatic than *waḷḷa*) والله *waḷḷaahi* most certainly.

ياالله *yaḷḷa* 1. till, until. تريته ياالله جا *trayyeeta yaḷḷa ya.* I waited for him until he came. 2. hurry up. ياالله يا أم سارة زهبي لنا العشا *yaḷḷa ya 'umm saara zahhbii-lna l-ᶜaša.* Hurry up Umm Sara! Prepare dinner for us. 3. let's go. ياالله ما محمد! *yaḷḷa ma mḥammad!* Let's go, Muhammad! 4. just, just barely. المعاش على قد الحال ياالله يكفي *l-maᶜaaš ᶜala gadd l-ḥaal yaḷḷa yakfi.* The salary is not much. It's barely enough.

حياالله *ḥayyaḷḷa* (to s.o. who has just arrived) welcome! حياالله عبدالله *ḥayyaḷḷa ᶜabdaḷḷa.* Abdalla, you are welcome.

ء ل ل ي *'lly*

اللي *'illi* (rel. pron.) 1. who, that,

which. الريـال اللـي سـار *r-rayyaal illi saar* the man who has left. 2. whatever, whoever. (prov.) اللي فات مـات *'illi faat maat.* Let bygones be bygones. (prov.) اللي ما يعـرف الصغيـر يشـوي *'illi ma y^c^arf ṣ-ṣagir yišwii.* Do not kill the goose that lays the golden egg. (prov.) اللي ما يطلع على أبوه نغـل *'illi ma yiṭla^c^ ^c^ala 'ubuu naġaḷ.* Like father like son. (prov.) إللي صار صار *'illi ṣaar ṣaar.* Don't cry over spilled milk. 3. that which, what اللي تبغـاه عنـدي *'illi tibġaa ^c^indi.* I have what you want.

الذي *'illiði* var. of اللي *'illi* (corruption of literary الذي *'allaði*).

ء ل م ن *'lmn*

الألمان *l-'aḷmaan* (coll.) the German people.

ألماني *'aḷmaani* 1. a German p. ألمان *'aḷmaan* 2. characteristic of Germany.

ألمانيا *'aḷmaanya* Germany.

ء ل م ن ي م *'lmnym*

ألمنيم *'alaminyam* aluminum.

ء ل ه *'lh*

إلـه *'ilaah* p. آلهة *'aaliha* god, deity. يا إلهي *ya 'ilaahi* my God!

ء ل و ي ش *'lwyš*

إلويـش *'ilweeš* = ليـش *leeš* why. See **ل ي ش** *lyš.*

ء م ب ر ط و ر *'mbrṭwr*

إمـبراطور *'imbaraaṭoor* emperor (no recorded p.).

إمبراطوري *'imbaraaṭoori* imperial.

إمبراطوريـة *'imbaraaṭooriyya* p. *-aat* empire.

ء م د ي *'mdy*

أمـدى *'amda* (يمـدي *yimdi)* (with suff. pron.) to be able to do s.th. أمداه يوصل *'amdaa yooṣal.* He was able to arrive. ما أمداني أشـتغل *ma 'amdaani 'aštaġil.* I wasn't able to work.

ء م ر *'mr*

أمـر *'amar* (يـامر *yaamir)* to order, command s.o. تامر شي؟ *taamir šayy?* Can I help you? شو تـامر؟ *šu taamir?* What can I do for you? آمر وأنا أخوك *'aamir w-aana 'uxuuk.* Ask (for anything) and I am your brother, i.e., I am at your service. I will stand up for you.

تـأمر *t'ammar* V to be domineering, behave arrogantly. رجع من أمريكا وجـا يتـأمر علينـا *rija^c^ min 'amriika w-ya yit'ammar ^c^aleena.* He returned from America and came to push us around.

تـآمر *t'aamar* VI (with علـى *^c^ala*) to conspire, plot against. الجيش تآمر علـى حيـاة الرئيـس *l-jeeš t'aamar ^c^ala ḥayaat r-ra'iis.* The army plotted against the (life of) the president.

أمـر *'amir* p. أمور *'umuur* 1. command, order. الأمـر أمـرك *l-'amir 'amrak.* You are in command. باكر عطلة. أمر الحـاكم *baačir ^c^uṭla. 'amr l-ḥaakim.* Tomorrow is a holiday. It's the ruler's order. 2. will, will power. دعمته سيارة ومـات. هـذا أمـر الله *di^c^mata sayyaara w-maat. haaða 'amr aḷḷa.* A car hit him and he died. This is God's will. آنا تحت أمرك *'aana taḥt 'amrak.* I am at your service. 3. affair, matter. هذي أمور تخص الحريم *haaði 'umuur txiṣṣ l-ḥariim.* These are matters that concern women.

إمارة *'imaara* p. *-aat* emirate, principality. إمارة دبي *'imaarat dbayy* the Emirate of Dubai. الإمارات العربية المتحدة *l-'imaaraat l-ᶜarabiyya l-mittaḥada.* the United Arab Emirates.

أمير *'amiir* p. أمرا *'umara* 1. prince, emir (title of a member of the ruling family). 2. ruler of a region, esp. in Saudi Arabia. أمير المنطقة الشرقية *'amiir l-mantaga š-šargiyya* the ruler of the Eastern Province in Saudi Arabia. 3. commander. أمير البحر *'amiir l-baḥar* admiral. أمير لوا *'amiir liwa* brigadier. أمير المؤمنين *'amiir l-mu'miniin* Prince of the Faithful, Caliph.

أميرة *'amiira* p. *-aat* princess.

أميري *'amiiri* 1. governmental, Emiri. الديوان الأميري *l-diwaan l-'amiiri.* the Emiri Court or Bureau. 2. state-owned. state land.

مؤامرة *mu'aamara* p. *-aat* plot, conspiracy.

مأمور *ma'muur* p. مأمورين *ma'muuriin* (p.p. from أمر *'amar*) 1. one who takes order, subordinate. كل شي بيد التنديل. آنا كولي مأمور *kill šayy b-yadd t-tindeel. 'aana kuuli ma'muur.* Everything is in the supervisor's power. I am a coolie; I take orders. 2. official, civil official. مأمور البريد *ma'muur l-bariid* the postmaster. مأمور الشرطة *ma'muur š-širṭa* the commissioner of police.

مؤتمر *mu'tamar* p. *-aat.* conference, convention. مؤتمر صلح *mu'tamar ṣulḥ* peace conference.

ء م ر ك *'mrk*

تأمرك *t'amrak* to become Americanized. كل عاداته تغيرت. تأمرك *kill ᶜaadaata tġayyarat. ta'amrak.* All his habits have changed. He has become Americanized.

أمريكا *'amriika* (var. أميركا *'ameerka* or ميركا *mriika*) America. حصل الدكتوراه من أمريكا *ḥaṣṣal d-daktooraa min 'amriika.* He got the Ph.D. degree from America.

أمريكي *'amriiki* (var. أمريكاني *'amrikaani*) p. أمريكان *'amrikaan* 1. an American. 2. American, characteristic of America. السفير الأمريكي *s-safiir l-'amriiki* the American Ambassador. سيارة أمريكية *sayyaara 'amriikiyya* American car.

ء م س *'ms*

أمس *'ams* (syn. البارحة *l-baarḥa*) yesterday. أمس الخميس *'ams l-xamiis.* Yesterday was Thursday. هذا باقي من أمس *haaða baagi min 'ams.* This is left (over) from yesterday. أمس المسا *'ams l-masa* last night. أمس الصباح *'ams ṣ-ṣabaaḥ* yesterday morning. قبل أمس *gabl 'ams* the day before yesterday.

ء م ل *'ml*

تأمل *t'ammal* V to hope ما درس زين بس تأمل ينجح في الامتحان *ma diras zeen bass t'ammal yinjaḥ fi l-'imtiḥaan.* He did not study well, but he hoped to pass the examination.

أمل *'amal* p. آمال *'aamaal* hope. أملي يا يبا أكمل دراستي قبـــل الـــزواج *'amali ya yuba 'akammil diraasti gabl z-zawaaj.* My hope, father, is to complete my studies before marriage.

ء م م [1] *'mm*

أم *'amm* (يئم *y'imm*) (with في *fi*) to lead people in prayer. المطوع هو اللي يئم في النـــاس *li-mṭawwa^c huwa lli y'imm fi n-naas.* The *muṭawwa^c* is the one who leads the people in prayer.

أمـــم *'ammam* II to nationalize. الحكومة أممـــت المصـــانع *li-ḥkuuma 'ammamat l-maṣaani^c* The government nationalized the factories.

تـــأمم *t'ammam* V (p.p. from أمـــم *'ammam*). to be nationalized. كـــل شركـــات البـــترول تـــأممت *kill šarikaat l-batrool t'ammamat.* All the petroleum companies were nationalized.

تـــأميم *ta'miim* (v.n. from أمم *'ammam*) nationalization.

أم *'umm* p. أمهات *'ummahaat.* 1. أمي وأبوي *'ummi w-'ubuuya* my mother and my father (my parents). أم عيالي *'umm ^cyaali* my wife. يامـــا! *yumma!* (addressing one's mother) Mother! 2. the one with, the woman with. أم الشعر الطويـــل *'umm š-ša^car ṭ-ṭawiil.* the woman (or girl) with long hair. سيارة أم أربـــع بيبـــان *sayyaara 'umm 'arba^c biibaan.* car with four doors, four-door car. أم القيويـــن *'umm l-giiween.* Umm al-Qaiwain (one of the emirates of the U.A.E). أم النـــار *'umm n-naar* Umm al-Nar, small town in Abu Dhabi, known as an archaeological site. أم حمير *'umm ḥmayyir* whooping cough. أم خمـــس *'umm xams* five-bullet rifle. أم سبع وسبعين قايمة *'umm sab^ca w-sab^ciin gaayma* centipede. أم شيف *'umm šeef* (oil field in Abu Dhabi). أم الصبيان *'umm ṣ-ṣibyaan* epilepsy. أم عامر *'umm ^caamir* hyena. أم عشـــر *'umm ^cašir* ten-bullet rifle.

أمام *'amaam* see جدام *jiddaam.*

إمـــام *'imaam* p. أئمـــة *'a'imma* 1. religious official, imam. 2. prayer leader.

ء م م [2] *'mm*

أما *'amma* (conj.) 1. as for (introduces a topic--comment sentence) أما هذي يرجـــع لشيمتـــك *'amma haaδi yirja^c la-šiimatk.* As for this (thing), it's up to you. أما المدير ما عليك منـــه *'amma l-mudiir ma ^caleek minna.* As for the director, don't worry about him. 2. but أما هذي السيارة بس حق للاستعمال الرسمي *'amma haaδi s-sayyaara bass hagg li-sti^cmaal r-rasmi.* But this car is just for official use.

ء م ن *'mn*

أمـــن *'amman* (يـــمن *yammin*) II 1. to ensure, guarantee. أمن على حياته وحياة عايلتـــه *'amman ^cala ḥayaata w-ḥayaat ^caayilta.* He got life insurance for himself and his family. 2. to leave in trust. أمن الحيـــول عنـــد أبـــوه *'amman li-ḥyuul ^cind ubuu.* He placed the bracelets in his father's keeping. 3. to trust, have faith in. هالحين الواحد ما يمن بـــأحد *halḥiin l-waaḥid ma yammin b-'aḥad.* Nowadays people do not trust anyone.

آمن *'aaman* (يـامن *yaamin)* to believe (in s.th. or s.o.) يـامن بـالله *yaamin b-'aḷḷa.* He believes in God. هو كافر مـا يـامن بـأي شـي *huwa kaafir ma yaamin b-'ayya šayy.* He is an atheist, he doesn't believe in anything.

تـأمن *t'amman* V 1. to be placed in safekeeping. تأمنت السيارة في الجراج إلين أرجـع *t'ammanat s-sayyaara fi l-garaaj 'ileen 'arja*ᶜ The car was placed in safekeeping at the garage until I return. 2. to be trusted. لا تبوح له بأي سر ما يتـأمن *la tbuuḥ-la b-'ayya sirr ma yit'amman.* Do not tell him any secret. He cannot be trusted. 3. to be ensured. الحيـول والصوغـة وبـاقي الذهـب تـأمنوا *li-ḥyuul w-ṣ-ṣooġa w-baagi ð-ðahab ta'ammanaw.* The bracelets, the jewelry, and the rest of the gold have been ensured.

أمـن *'amin* security, safety. ما فيه أمـن هالايـام *ma fii 'amin ha liyyaam.* There is no security (or protection) these days. دايـرة الأمـن *daayrat l-'amin* the police department. رجـال الأمـن *rijaal l-'amin* the police. الأمـن العـام *l-amin l-*ᶜ*aamm* public safety.

أمـان *'amaan* safety, security. ما لك أمان *ma lak 'amaan.* You cannot be trusted. في أمـان الله *fi 'amaan illaah* (usually في مـان الله *fiimaanillaa*)! Goodbye! (lit., in God's protection). (The response is the same, or مـع السلامة *ma*ᶜ *s-salaama.*)

أمـين *'amiin* p. أمنا *'umana,* or أمينين *'amiiniin* honest, faithful. الأمـين العـام *l-'amiin l-*ᶜ*aamm* the secretary general. أمين الصندوق *'amiin ṣ-ṣanduug* the treasurer. أمين السر *'amiin s-sirr* the permanent secretary of state. مجلس الأمنا *majlis l-'umana* the board of regents, board of trustees.

آمين *'aamiin* Amen.

أمانـة *'amaana* 1. trustworthiness, reliability. الأمانة خصلة زينـة *l-'amaana xiṣla zeena.* Trustworthiness is a good quality. 2. safekeeping. تركت الفلوس أمانـة عنـد أخـوي *tirakt li-fluus 'amaana* ᶜ*ind 'uxuuy.* I left the money in my brother's keeping. 3. office or position of trust. أمانـة الصنـــدوق *'amaanat ṣ-ṣanduug* position of treasurer or cashier.

تـأمين *ta'miin* (v.n. from II أمن *'amman*) insurance; insurance company. تـأمين علـى الحيـاة *ta'miin* ᶜ*ala l-ḥayaa* life insurance. تأمين ضد الحريق *ta'miin ḍiḍḍ l-ḥariig* fire insurance.

إيمـان *'iimaan* faith, belief. الإيمان بـالله *l-iimaan bi-llaah.* belief in God.

مـأمون *ma'muun* safe, secure. هاذ مكان مـأمون *haað mukaan ma'muun.* This is a safe place.

ء م ي *'my*

إمية *'imya* hundred. See مية *miya.*

ء م ر ل *'mrl*

أمـيـرال *'amiiraal* (no recorded p.) admiral.

ء ن ¹ *'n*

إن *'in* (conj.) if. (syn. إذا *'iða,* أكان *ačan,* إنكـان *'inčaan,* لـو *lo, law*) إن خـلاك الله تعيـش تشـوف *'in xallaak aḷḷa t*ᶜ*iiš tšuuf.* If you live long, you will see (what the future holds for you). (prov.) إن شفت رفيقك حلو لا تكلـه كلـه

'in čift rifiijak ḥilu la taakla killa. Don't use up all your credit at once. إن طاح البعير كثرت سكاكينه *'in ṭaaḥ l-biciir kiθrat sičaačiina.* When it rains it pours. Misfortunes come in groups.

ء ن ٢ *'n*

إن *'inn-* (conj.) that اتفقوا إنهم يروحوا يتونسون *ttafgaw 'inhum yruuḥuun yitwannsuun.* They agreed to go to have a good time. قال إنه يابي زيادة. معاشه على قد الحال *gaal 'inna yabi ziyaada. macaša cala gadd l-ḥaal.* He said that he wanted a raise. His salary was not up to much. قال لي إنه مستانس *gaal-li 'inna mistaanis.* He told me that he was happy (or comfortable). على أن *cala 'an* if, provided that. وافق يقبل الوظيفة على أن يعطوه ستة ألف درهم في الشهر *waafag yigbal l-waḍiifa cala an yacṭuu sitta 'alf dirhim fi š-šahar.* He agreed to accept the job provided that they paid him six thousand dirhams a month. ولو إن *walaw inn* even though. قال إنه يدش الشغل ولو إنه مريض *gaal 'inna ydišš š-šuġul walaw inna mariiḍ.* He said that he would go to work even though he was ill.

ء ن ب ب *'nbb*

أنبوب *'unbuub* or أنبوبة *'unbuuba* p. أنابيب *'anaabiib* tube, pipe. أنبوب غاز *'unbuub ġaaz* gas pipe. خط أنابيب بترول *xaṭṭ 'anaabiib batrool* oil pipeline.

ء ن ت *'nt*

أنت *'inta, 'int, 'init* p. أنتم *'intum,* إنتو *'intu* you (m.s.). أنت شتابي *'inta š-tabi?* What do you want? أنت ظبياني من هني؟ *'inta ḍibyaani min hini?* Are you Abu Dhabian, from here? أنت شعليك؟ *'inta š-caleek?* What's it to you? (f.) أنت *'inti* p. أنتن *'intin.* أنتن وين سرتن *'intin ween sirtin?* Where did you (f.p.) go? أنتن قطريات؟ *'intin gṭariyyaat?* Are you (f.p.) Qataris?

ء ن ت ي ن *'ntyn*

أنتين *'antiin* p. *-aat* antenna.

ء ن ث *'nθ*

أنثى *'unθa,* إنثى *'inθa* p. نثا *niθa* female. النعجة أنثى الكبش *li-ncaya 'unθa č-čabš.* A ewe is the female of a ram. الأنثى تاخذ نص حصة الذكر في الإسلام *l-'unθa taaxiḏ nuṣṣ ḥissat ḏ-ḏakar fi l-'islaam.* The female gets half the portion of a male in Islam.

ء ن ج ر *'njr*

أنجر *'anjar,* أنقر *'angar* p. أناجر *'anaajir,* أناقر *'anaagir* (var. أنير *'anyar* p. أناير *'anaayir*) anchor. أنجر الجلبوت *'anjar l-jalbuut* the anchor of the jolly boat. (syn. باورة *paawra*).

ء ن چ *'nč*

إنج *'inč, 'inj* p. *-aat* inch. طولها خمسة إنج *ṭuulha xamsa 'inč.* It's five inches long.

ء ن س *'ns*

استانس *staanas* X 1. to have a good time, enjoy oneself. لعبنا ورق وتغدينا واستانسنا في النادي *licabna warag w-tġaddeena w-staanasna fi n-naadi.* We played cards, had lunch, and had a good time at the clubhouse. أنت ما تستانس هني *'inta ma tistaanis hini.* You will not enjoy yourself here. 2. to be happy (with s.th.) or comfortable (in a place). أنت استانست في الشقة؟ *'inta* *staanaast fi š-šigga?* Were you comfortable in the apartment?

إنس *'ins* man, mankind. الإنس والجن *l-'ins w-l-jinn* man and jinn, man and beast.

إنسي *'insi* human (being).

ناس *naas* people. الناس في عيد رمضان يلبسون أحسن شي عندهم *'in-naas fi ᶜiid rumđaan yilbisuun 'aḥsan šayy ᶜindahum.* People during the Ramadhan Feast wear the best clothes they have. فيه ناس وايدين *fii naas waaydiin.* There are a lot of people. (prov.) ناس بنعيم وناس بجحيم *naas b-naᶜiim w-naas b-jaḥiim.* People are not the same.

إنسان *'insaan* 1. human being, man. هو إنسان طيب *huwa 'insaan ṭayyib.* He is a good man. 2. (with ال *l-*) man, mankind. الإنسان فاني *l-'insaan faani.* Man is mortal.

إنساني *'insaani* pertaining to or characteristic of human beings, humane, humanitarian. عمل إنساني *ᶜamal 'insaani* good, charitable deed.

إنسانية *'insaaniyya* humaneness, kindness

آنسة *'aanisa* p. *-aat* (polite form of address) Miss. الآنسة موزة *l-'aanisa mooza.* Miss Moza.

ء ن ف *'nf*

استأنف *sta'naf* X to appeal, make an appeal. استأنف الحكم *sta'naf l-ḥukum.* He appealed the sentence.

استئناف *sti'naaf* (v.n. from X استأنف *sta'naf*) appeal. محكمة الاستئناف *maḥkamat li-sti'naaf* appeals court.

ء ن گ ل ت ر *'ngltr*

إنكلترا *'ingiltra* England. رحت إنكلترا؟ *riḥt 'ingiltara?* Have you been to England?

ء ن گ ل ي ز *'nglyz*

الإنكليز *l-'ingiliiz* the English people, the British.

إنكليزي *'ingiliizi* 1. an Englishman. هو إنكليزي من لندن *huwa 'ingiliizi min landan.* He is an Englishman from London. 2. the English language. يدرس إنكليزي *yidris 'ingiliizi.* He is studying English. 3. characteristic of England. كتاب إنكليزي *ktaab 'ingiliizi* English book.

ء ن ن س *'nns*

أنناس *'ananaas* pineapple.

ء ه ل *'hl*

أهل *'ahhal* II to qualify, make suitable. معلوماته ما تؤهله يصير تنديل *maᶜluumaata ma t'ahhla yiṣiir tindeel.* His knowledge does not qualify him to become a supervisor. شهادتك تؤهلك تصير قزاز *šahaadtak t'ahhilk tṣiir gazzaaz.* Your certificate qualifies you to be a surveyor.

تأهل *t'ahhal* V to be or become qualified. لين خذيت الشهادة تأهلت حق الوظيفة *leen xađeet š-šahaada t'ahhalt ḥagg l-wađiifa.* When I obtained the certificate, I became qualified for the job.

استاهل *staahal* X 1. to deserve, be worthy of. ما يستاهل أي شي *ma yistaahal 'ayya šayy.* He doesn't deserve anything. يستاهل كل خير *yistaahal kill xeer.* He deserves the best. بنية لطيفة ما يستاهلها. ما علينا من أصله وفصله *bnayya laṭiifa ma yistaahalha. ma ᶜaleena min 'aṣla w-faṣla.* She is a good girl whom he doesn't deserve. Never mind his origin and ancestry. 2. to be entitled to صارلك تشتغل دريول من زمان. تستاهل زيادة *ṣaar-lak tištaġil dreewil min zamaan. tistaahal ziyaada.* You have been working as a driver for a long time. You deserve a raise.

أهل *'ahil* p. أهالي *'ahaali* (var. هل *hal*) 1. family, relatives. أهلك وياك؟ *'ahlak wiyyaak?* Is your family with you? أهل سالم *'ahil saalim* Salim's relatives. 2. people, inhabitants. أهل بو ظبي *'ahil bu ḍabi* the people of Abu Dhabi, the Abu Dhabians. 3. wife. هل المدير جاوا ويتريونه برة *hal l-mudiir yaw w-yitrayyuuna barra.* The manager's wife came and she is waiting for him outside. أهل شرف *'ahil šaraf* honorable, magnanimous people. 4. followers, adherents. أهل الكتاب *'ahl l-kitaab* the followers of the heavenly books, usually Christians and Jews.

أهلا *'ahlan* (usually أهلا وسهلا! *'ahlan wa-sahlan!*) welcome!

أهلي *'ahli* 1. national. البنك الأهلي *l-bank l-'ahli* the national bank. 2. private, non-governmental. مدرسة أهلية *madrasa 'ahliyya* private school. 3. civil حرب أهلية *harb 'ahliyya* civil war.

مؤهلات *mu'ahhilaat* qualifications, credentials. بس أعرف القراية والكتابة. ما عندي مؤهلات ثانية *bass 'aᶜrif li-graaya w-li-ktaaba. ma ᶜindi mu'ahhilaat θaanya.* I know only reading and writing. I do not have any other qualifications.

ء و *'w*

أو *'aw* or. تابي هذا أو ذاك؟ *tabi haaða 'aw ðaak?* Do you want this one or that one? (ولا *walla* is more commonly used than أو *'aw*. See **و ل ل** *wll*).

ء و ت ي ل *'wtyl*

أوتيل *'uteel* pl. *-aat* hotel. أوتيل الهلتون *'uteel l-hilton* the Hilton Hotel. الأوتيلات استوت غالية *l-'uteelaat stawat ġaalya.* Hotels have become expensive.

ء و ر ب ب ا *'wrbbaa*

أوروبا *'uroobba* Europe.

أوروبي *'uroobbi* p. *-yyiin* 1. a European. 2. characteristic of Europe. باخرة أوروبية *baaxra 'uroobbiyya* European steamship.

ء و س ت ر ا ل ي *'wstraaly*

أستراليا *'ustraalya* Australia.

أوسترالي *'ustraali* 1. an Australian. 2. characteristic of Australia, Australian.

ء و ك ز ي و ن *'wkzywn*

أكازيون *'ukazyoon* clearance sale, special sale.

ء و ك س ج ن *'wksjn*

أكسجين *'uksijiin* oxygen.

ء و ل *'wl*

أول *'awwal* f. أولى *'uula, 'awwala* p. أوايل *'awaayil* 1. first. أول مرة *'awwal marra* the first time. أول شي *'awwal* *šayy* the first thing. البنت الأولى *l-bint l-'awwala, l-bint l-'uula* the first girl. 2. beginning, first part of. أول القيظ *'awwal l-geeḍ* the beginning of the summer. أول الصفري *'awwal li-ṣfiri* the beginning of autumn. مـن الأول *min l-'awwal* from the beginning. قتله كل شي من الأول *git-la kill šayy min l-'awal* I told him everything from the beginning. (prov.) اللي ما له أول ما له تـالي *'illi ma lah 'awwal ma lah taali* (describes s.o. who pretends to be, e.g., loyal and faithful after he has proved to be otherwise). 3. before, previous. The day before yesterday. كنت واياهم أول أمـس *čint wiyyaahum 'awwal ams.* I was with them the day before yesterday. أول أمـس الجمعـة *'awwal ams l-yimᶜa.* The day before yesterday was Friday. أولا *'awwalan* first of all, firstly. أولا المعرس لازم يزهب سـامانه *'awwalan l-miᶜris laazim yzahhib saamaana.* First of all, the bridegroom has to get his things (i.e., personal effects) ready.

أولي *'awwali* 1. first, initial اجتماع أولي *jtimaaᶜ 'awwali* preliminary meeting. 2. old, bygone. في الزمـان الأولي *fi z-zamaan l-'awwali* in olden times, a long time ago.

ء و ل م ب ي *'wlmby*

أولمـبي *'olimbi* Olympic. the Olympic games.

ء ي ي ١ *'yy*

إي *'ii* 1. yes. إي نعم *'ii naᶜam,* إي والله *'ii waḷḷa* yes, indeed, certainly. 2. look, alright! إي ليش ما تنكب عاد! *'ii leeš ma tinčabb ᶜaad!* Look, why don't you go away!

ء ي ي ٢ *'yy*

أي *'ay* (var. *'ayya*) 1. what, which. أي واحد تبغاه؟ *'ay waaḥid tibġaa?* Which one do you want? أي حزة *'ay ḥazza?* which hour? what time? when? من أي بلد أنـت؟ *min 'ay balad 'inta?* Which country are you from? 2. any whichever, whatever. عطني أي واحـد *ᶜaṭni 'ay waaḥid.* Give me anyone.

ء ي ر *'yr*

أيار *'ayyaar* May (month).

ء ي د ١ *'yd*

أيـد *'ayyad* II to support, back. الناس يؤيدون الشيخ زايد طويل العمـر *n-naas y'ayyduun š-šeex zaayid ṭawiil l-ᶜumur.* People support Shaikh Zayid, may he live long. 2. to confirm, endorse. الحكومة أيدت خبر استقالة الوزارة *li-ḥkuuma 'ayyadat xabar stigaalat l-wizaara.* The government confirmed the news of the resignation of the ministry.

تـأييد *ta'yiid* 1. support, backing. 2. confirmation, endorsement.

ء ي د ٢ *'yd*

إيـد *'iid* (f.) p. إيدين *'iideen* (var. more common يـد *yadd*) 1. hand. لف على إيدك اليمين *liff ᶜala 'iidak l-yimiin!* Turn right! عاشت إيـدك! *ᶜaašat iidič!* God protect your (f.) hand (for having brought or handed s.th. to s.o.). ساعة يد *saaᶜat yadd* wrist watch. شنطة يـد *šanṭat yad* handbag. (prov.) يدٍ ما تقدر عليها حبـها *yaddin ma tigdar ᶜaleeha ḥibbha* Kiss the hand that you cannot overpower. (prov.) أصابع يدك مـوب

واحدة *'aṣaabi^c yaddak muub waḥda.* Different strokes for different folks. (prov.) يد واحدة ما تصفق *yadd waḥda ma tṣaffig.* One hand washes the other. Cooperate with others. 2. power, control. ما له يد فيها *ma la yad fiiha.* He has nothing to do with it. بين إيديه *been 'iidee* in his power. تحت إيده *taḥat 'iida* in his control. ...حط يده على *ḥaṭṭ yadda ^{c}ala ...* he took possession or control of s.th.

ء ي ر ن *'yrn*

إيران *'iiraan* Iran.

إيراني *'iiraani* p. *-yyiin.* 1. an Iranian. فيه إيرانيين واجدين في الخليج *fii 'iiraaniyyiin waaydiin fi l-xaliij.* There are many Iranians in the Gulf. 2. characteristic of Iran, Iranian, Persian. ترى نقول الخليج الفارسي موب الخليج الإيراني *tara nguul l-xaliij l-faarsi muub l-xaliij l-'iiraani.* Look, we say the Persian Gulf, not the Iranian Gulf. زل إيراني *zall 'iiraani.* Persian rugs.

ء ي س *'ys*

أيس *'ayyas* II to lose hope, to despair. أيس من النجاح في امتحان الرياضيات *'ayyas min n-najaaḥ fi mtiḥaan r-riyaaḍiyyat.* He gave up hope of passing the mathematics examination.

ء ي ش *'yš*

أيش *'eeš* what? (syn. ويش *weeš,* شو *šu*). أيش اسمك *'eeš asmak?* What's your name? أش سويت *'eeš sawweet?* What did you do? أيشتغى *'eeštiġa?* What do you want? على ويش *^{c}ala weeš?* why? على ويش ها العفسة؟ *^{c}ala weeš ha l-^{c}afsa?* What is this commotion for?

ء ي ش ر ب *'yšrb*

إشارب *'iišaarb* p. *-aat* (woman's) scarf.

ء ي ل و ل *'ylwl*

أيلول *'ayluul* September.

ب

ب *b*

ب *b-* (prefixed to n.) 1. with, by means of. بالسكين *b-s-siččiin* with a knife. بالسيارة *b-s-sayyaara* by car. بالبر *b-l-barr* by land. بـالبحر *b-l-baḥar* by sea. بالباخرة *b-l-baaxra* by steamship. لعوزنا بروحته وييته *la^cwazna b-rooḥta w-yayta.* He bothered us with his goings and comings.

بدون *b-duun* without. يشرب قهوة بدون شكر *yišrab gahwa b-duun šakar.* He drinks coffee without sugar. بدون فلوس *b-duun fluus* (without money) free of charge, gratis. بدون قياس *b-duun gyaas* extremely, disproportionately. كان حمقان بدون قياس *čaan ḥamgaan b-duun gyaas.* He was very mad. بـالغصب *b-l-ġaṣb* by force, by hook or crook. عرست بـالغصب *^carrasat b-l-ġaṣb.* She got married by force. بـالحيل *b-l-ḥeel* hard. يشتغل بالحيل *yištaġil b-l-ḥeel.* He works hard. بـالطيب *b-ṭ-ṭiib* willingly. بتاخذينه بـالطيب والا بـالغصب. فهمت؟ *btaaxðiina b-ṭ-ṭiib walla b-l-ġaṣb. fahamti?* You must take him (as husband) by hook or crook. Do you understand? بقهر *b-gahar* unwillingly. بروحــ *b-ruuḥ-* (with suff. pron.) by oneself, alone. أسافر بروحي. كذي أحسن *'asaafir b-ruuḥi. čiði 'aḥsan.* I travel alone. It's better this way. بالزين *b-z-zeen* well, nicely. عاملهم بالزين *^caamilhum b-z-zeen.* Treat them well. بساع *b-saa^c* quickly. روح وتعال بساع *ruuḥ w-ta^caal b-šaa^c.* Go and come back quickly. بشكل *b-šakil* in a certain manner. بشكل ما يتصور *b-šakil ma yitṣawwar* to an inconceivable degree. بـالضبط *b-ḍ-ḍabt* exactly, acurately. أطلبك مية دينار بـالضبط *'aṭlubk miyat dinaar b-ḍ-ḍabt.* You owe me a hundred dinars exactly. بعجل *b-^cajal* quickly, fast. روح بعجل *ruuḥ b-^cajal.* Go quickly. لا تسوق بعجل *la tsuug b-^cajal.* Don't drive fast. 2. for. بكم الموز؟ *b-kam l-mooz?* How much are the bananas? الدرزن بعشرة درهم *d-darzan b-^cašara dirhim.* Ten dirhams for a dozen. بكم هذي الكندورة؟ *b-kam haaði l-kandoora?* How much is this dishdash? بخمسين درهم *b-xamsiin dirhim.* (It's) for 50 dirhams. 3. in, at. أبوي بالحفيز *'ubuuy b-l-ḥafiiz.* My father is at the office. هو بمكان وآنا بمكان ثاني *huwa b-mukaan w-aana b-mukaan θaani.* He is at one place and I am at another. حط سكر بالشاي *ḥaṭṭ šakar b-č-čaay.* He put sugar in the tea. 4. شبيك ما ترمس؟ *š-biik ma tirmis?* What's wrong with you? You are not talking. 4. by. فريقنا غلبهم بأربعة قوال *fariigna ġalabhum b-'arba^c gwaal.* Our team beat them by four goals. فزت عليه بخمس نقط *fuzt ^calee b-xams nigaṭ.* I beat him by five points. خمسة بستة بثلاثين *xamsa b-sitta b-θalaaθiin.* Five times six is thirty. 5. by (introducing an oath) بشرفي عمري ما شربت وسكي *b-šarafi ^cumri ma šribt wiski.* On my honor, I've never had any whiskey.

ب ا *baa*

با *baa* the name of the letter *b*.

ب ا ب *baab*

باب *baab* see ب و ب *bwb*.

ب ا ب ا *baabaa*

بابا *baaba* pope. *l-baaba* the Pope.

ب ا ب ل *baabl*

بابل *baabil* Babylon.

بـابلي *baabili* 1. a Babylonian. 2. characteristic of Babylon, Babylonian.

ب ا ب ط ي ن *baabṭyn*

بـابطين *baabaṭiin* (prominent Kuwaiti family).

آل بـابطين *'aal baabaṭiin* the Babateen family

ب ا ب ك و *baabkw*

بـابكو *baabko* BAPCo (Bahrain Petroleum Company).

ب ا ت ر ي *baatry*

باتري *baatri* p. *bataari* battery.

ب ا ج ل ل *baajll*

باجلة *baajilla* or *baagilla* (coll.) fava beans.

حبة باجلة *ḥabbat baajilla* a fava bean.

ب ا ر¹ *baar*

بـار *baar* strength, power. ما عطيت كل بـارك *ma ᶜaṭeet kill baark.* You did not exert all of your strength.

ب ا ر² *baar*

بـار *baar* p. *-aat* bar, tavern. ذالحين ما فيه بارات في الإمـارات، لكـن تقـدر تشـرب بـيرة ولا وسـكي في الفنـدق *ðalḥiin ma fii baaraat fi l-'imaaraat, laakin tigdar tišrab biira walla wiski fi l-fundug.* Now there are no bars in the U.A.E., but you can drink beer or whiskey at a hotel.

ب ا ر³ *baar*

بار *baar* fulcrum, center of weight.

ب ا ر ح *baarḥ*

بارح *baariḥ* (strong wind that blows in the summer and lasts for forty days, usually accompanied by a lot of dust).

ب ا ر د *baard*

بـارد *baarid* (n.) soft drink. أشرب بارد عقب الأكل *'ašrab baarid ᶜugb l-'akil.* I have a soft drink after food.

ب ا ز *baaz*

بـاز *baaz* falcon (also known as بازي *baazi*) p. بوازي *bawaazi.* (prov.) اللي مـا يعـرف البـازي يشـوي *'illi ma yᶜarf l-baazi yišwee.* Don't kill the goose that lays the golden egg.

ب ا ش ه *baašh*

باشـه *baaša* p. *-waat* 1. Pasha (title). (prov.) الاعور بـين العميـان باشـه *l-ᶜawar been l-ᶜimyaan baaša.* In the country of the blind the one-eyed man is king. 2. good guy, well-liked person.

ب ا ص ر *baaṣr*

بـاصور *baaṣuur* p. بواصـير *buwaaṣiir* piles, hemorrhoids. الباصور يلعوز الإنسان *l-baaṣuur ylaᶜwiz l-'insaan.* Hemorrhoids bother people.

ب ا ع *baaᶜ*

بـاع *baaᶜ* p. بواع *bwaaᶜ* span of the outstretched arms, fathom (six feet approx.). طولها خمس بواع *ṭuulha xams bwaa*ᶜ. It's about thirty feet long.

ب ا ك *baak*

باك *baak* p. *-aat* back player (in soccer). يلعب باك *yil*ᶜ*ab baak.* He is a back player.

ب ا ك س ت ن *baakstn*

الباكستان *l-baakistaan* Pakistan.

باكستاني *baakistaani* p. *-yyiin, -yya* 1. a Pakistani. 2. characteristic of Pakistan. فيه باكستانية واجدين في الخليج. *fii baakistaaniyya waaydiin fi l-xaliij.* There are many Pakistanis in the Gulf.

ب ا ل س *baals*

بالس *baalis* shoe polish.

ب ا ل و ل *baalwl*

بالول *baaluul* (coll.) salmon. s. بالولة *baaluula.* البالول طيب *l-baaluul ṭayyib.* Salmon is delicious.

ب ا م ي *baamy*

باميا *baamya* (coll.) okra. s. حبة باميا *ḥabbat baamya.* الباميا ويا طماط ولحم كلش زين *l-baamya wiyya ṭamaaṭ w-laḥam killiš zeen.* Okra with tomatoes and meat is very delicious.

ب ا ن ز ي ن *baanzyn*

بانزين *baanziin* gasoline. بانزين ممتاز *baanziin mumtaaz* premium gasoline. بانزين عادي *baanziin* ᶜ*aadi* regular gasoline. البانزين، شيشت البترول *l-baanziin, šiišt l-batrool* the gas station.

ب ا ن و ش *baanwš*

بانوش *baanuuš* p. بوانيش *buwaaniiš* canoe. خذينا البانوش ودشينا البحر. *xaðeena l-baanuuš w-daššeena l-baḥar.* We took the canoe and we went down to the sea.

ب ا و ر *baawr*

باور *baawar* power, force. باورهوز *baawar-hooz* p. *-aat* powerhouse.

ب ا و ر ة *baawra*

باورة *baawra* (var. *paawra*) p. بواير *buuwaayir, -aat* fisherman's anchor. syn. أنقر *'angar,* أنجر *'anjar.* غاطينا الباورة وقعدنا نحدق *gaaṭṭeena l-baawra w-ga*ᶜ*adna nḥadig.* We let down the anchor and started to fish.

ب ت ت *btt*

بت *batt* (يبت *ybitt*) (usu. with في *fi*) to decide on s.th. هو مترد. ما يقدر يبت في الأمر *huwa mitraddid. ma yigdar ybitt fi l-'amir.* He is hesitant. He cannot decide on the matter.

ب ت ت ة *btta*

بتة *batta* p. *-aat* (var. *patta*) 1. deck of playing cards. شتريت بتتين *štareet battateen.* I bought two decks of cards. رحنا النادي. تعشينا ولعبنا بتة واستانسنا *riḥna n-naadi. t*ᶜ*aššeena w-li*ᶜ*abna batta w-staanasna.* We went to the clubhouse. We had dinner, played cards and had a good time.

ب ت ر ل *btrl*

بترول *batrool* 1. petroleum. وزارة البترول *wizaarat l-batrool* the ministry of petroleum. أبو ظبي تنتج واجد بترول *'abu ḍabi tintij waajid batrool.* Abu Dhabi produces a lot of petroleum. طلع بترول *ṭila*ᶜ *batrool.* Petroleum gushed out. 2. gasoline. شيشة البترول *šiišt l-batrool* the gas station. بترول ممتاز *batrool mumtaaz* super gasoline. بترول عادي *batrool ᶜaadi* regular gasoline. عندنا هني بترول ممتاز بس. البترول العادي قليل *ᶜindana hini batrool mumtaaz bass. l-batrool l-ᶜaadi galiil.* We have here super gasoline only. Regular gas is rare.

ب ث ث *bθθ*

بث *baθθ (يبث ybiθθ)* to broadcast, transmit. راديو بو ظبي يبث الأخبار خمس مرات في اليوم *raadyo bu đabi ybiθθ l-'axbaar xams marraat fi l-yoom.* The Abu Dhabi Radio Station broadcasts the news five times a day.

بث *baθθ* (v.n.) بث الأخبار *baθθ l-'axbaar* broadcasting the news.

بثيث *baθiiθ* dessert made up of flour, dates, cardamom and butter.

ب ج ا م *bjaam*

بجامة *bijaama* p. *-aat* pajamas. نحن طال عمرك ما نلبس البجامة *niḥin ṭaal ᶜumrak ma nilbis l-bijaama.* We, God prolong your life, do not wear pajamas. لبس البجامة عادة أجنبية *libs l-bijaama ᶜaada 'aynabiyya.* Wearing pajamas is a foreign custom.

ب چ ر *bčr*

بچر *baččar* (less common var. بكر *bakkar*) 1. to come early. مبارك هني. اليوم بچر *mbaarak hini. l-yoom baččar.* Mubarak is here. He came early today. 2. to go out early, set out early. اليح بچر هذا العام *l-yiḥḥ baččar haađa l-ᶜaam.* Watermelons ripened early this year. بچر جمعة ودش الشغل *baččar yimᶜa w-dašš š-šuġul.* Jum‘a went out early and went to work.

بچر *bičir* (var. بكر *bikir*) p. بكارة *bakaara* 1. first-born (m. or f.). هي البچر *hiya l-bičir.* She is the first-born. هو بچر أمه *huwa bičir 'umma.* He is his mother's first-born baby. 2. virgin. هذي البنت بچر *haađi l-bint bičir.* This girl is a virgin.

مبچر *mbaččir* (act. part.) p. *-iin.* having come early. أتشوفك مبچر اليوم. زين.. *'ačuufak mbaččir l-yoom. zeen..* I see that you came early today. That's good.

باچر *baačir* (syn. غدوة *ġudwa,* بكرة *bukra*) 1. tomorrow. باچر السبت *baačir s-sabt.* Tomorrow is Saturday. عقب باچر *ᶜugub baačir.* the day after tomorrow. يجي باچر *yiji baačir.* He is coming (or he will come) tomorrow. أدش الشغل من باچر ورايح *'adišš -š-šuġul min baačir w-raayih.* I will report for work as of tomorrow. 2. soon, in the near future. إستح على روحك! باچر تستوي رجالن عود *'istaḥ ᶜala ruuḥak! baačir tistawi rayyaalin ᶜood.* Shame on you! Soon you will become an old man.

ب چ ي *bčy*

بچى *biča (يبچي yibči)* 1. to cry, weep. لين سمع الخبر قام يبچي *leen simaᶜ l-xabar gaam yibči.* When he heard the news, he started to weep. الناس بچوا وايد لين ماتت أم كلثوم *n-naas bičaw waayid leen maatat 'umm kalθuum.* The people cried very much when Umm Kalthum (an Egyptian singer) died. 2. (with على *ᶜala*) to mourn, lament. بچى

على الأموات *biča ᶜala l-'amwaat.* He mourned the dead. بجى على الزمان الأولي *biča ᶜala z-zamaan l-'awwali.* He cried over the olden times.

بجى *bačča* II to make s.o. cry. جاب خبر موب زين وبجانا *yaab xabar muub zeen w-baččaana.* He brought bad news and made us cry. هذا خبر يبجي *haaða xabar ybačči.* This is a news item that makes people cry.

انبجى *nbiča* VII (with على *ᶜala*) to be cried over. هذا الشي ما ينبجي عليه *haaða š-šayy ma yinbiči ᶜalee.* This thing is not worth crying over.

ب ح *bḥ*

بح *baḥ*, as in بح بح *baḥ baḥ* (said by a mother to her child as an encouragement to eat).

ب ح ت *bḥt*

بحت *baḥt* (invar.) pure, unmixed. هذا شلاخ بحت *haaða člaax baḥt.* That's pure lies.

ب ح ث *bḥθ*

بحث *biḥaθ (يبحث yibḥaθ)* 1. to look, search. بحث وما لقي شي *biḥaθ w-ma ligi šayy.* He looked and found nothing. (with عن *ᶜan*) to look for s.o. or s.th. بحثوا عنه وما لقيوه *bihaθu ᶜanna wa ma ligyuuh.* They looked for him but did not find him. 2. to investigate, examine. الوزارة تبحث المشكلة *l-wizaara tibḥaθ l-muškila.* The ministry is investigating the problem. 3. to discuss. يبحثون الوضع السياسي *yibhaθuun l-waðᶜ s-siyaasi.* They are discussing the political situation.

تباحث *tbaaḥaθ* VI to confer, discuss together. تباحثوا واتفقوا على الطلبة *tbaahaθaw w-ttafgaw ᶜala ṭ-ṭalba.* They conferred and agreed on the dowry.

انبحث *nbiḥaθ* VII to be discussed. هذا موضوع ما ينبحث *haaða mawðuuᶜ ma yinbaḥaθ.* This is a topic that cannot be discussed.

بحث *baḥθ* (v.n.) 1. discussion. بحث هذا الموضوع يحتاج وقت طويل *baḥθ haaða l-mawðuuᶜ yiḥtaaj wagt ṭawiil.* Discussing this topic needs a lot of time. 2. (research) paper. قدم بحث في الاجتماع *gaddam baḥθ fi l-'ijtimaaᶜ.* He submitted a paper at the meeting.

باحث *baaḥiθ* p. *-iin.* باحث اجتماع *baaḥiθ 'ijtimaaᶜ.* social worker.

ب ح ح *bḥḥ*

بح *baḥḥ (ybiḥḥ)* to make hoarse. الزعاق بح صوتي *li-zᶜaag baḥḥ ṣooti.* Shouting has made my voice hoarse. لا تبح صوتك! *la tbiḥḥ ṣootak!* Don't make yourself hoarse!

بحة *baḥḥa* hoarseness.

مبحوح *mabḥuuḥ* hoarse, husky. صوتي مبحوح *ṣooti mabḥuuḥ* my voice is hoarse.

ب ح ر *bḥr*

بحر *baḥḥar* II 1. to travel by sea. كان الهوا زين وبحرنا *čaan l-hawa zeen w-baḥḥarna.* The weather was good and we travelled by sea. عمرك بحرت؟ *ᶜumrak baḥḥart?* Have you ever travelled by sea? 2. to set sail, put to sea. الباخرة تبحر باكر انشالله *l-baaxra tbaḥḥir baačir nšaaḷḷa.* The steamship sails tomorrow, hopefully.

بحر *baḥar* p. بحور *bḥuur,* بحار *bḥaar* sea, ocean. بحر بو إمية *baḥar bu 'imya* sea, about 100 meters deep, very deep sea. بحر بو عشر *baḥar bu ᶜašir* sea, about 10 meters deep. البحر الأحمر *l-baḥar l-'aḥmar* the Red Sea. البحر الأسود *l-baḥar l-'aswad* the Black Sea. البحر الميت *l-baḥar l-mayyit* the Dead Sea. نقطة من بحر *nigṭa min baḥar* a drop in the ocean. 2. person (m. or f.) of extensive knowledge, learned person. يقولون فلان بحر من العلوم *yguuluun flaan baḥar min l-ᶜuluum.* They say so-and-so is a learned man.

البحر *l-baḥar* Al-Bahar (prominent family in the Gulf states).

البحرين *l-baḥreen* Bahrain. البحرين، الله يسلمك، جزيرة ولا عدة جزر *l-baḥreen, 'aḷḷa ysallimk, jiziira walla ᶜiddit juzur.* Bahrain, God protect you, is an island or many islands. البحرين ونسة *l-baḥreen winsa.* Bahrain is fun.

بحراني *baḥraani* p. بحارنة *baḥaarna* one belonging to the Shia sect in Bahrain. فيه بحارنة وايد في البحرين *fii baḥaarna waayid fi l-baḥreen.* There are many Shiites (i.e., followers of Ali) in Bahrain.

بحريني *baḥreeni* p. *-yyiin* 1. a Bahraini. البحرينيين خوش أوادم *l-baḥreeniyyiin xooš 'awaadim.* Bahrainis are good people. 2. characteristic of Bahrain, Bahraini. قماش بحريني *gmaaš bahreeni* pearls from Bahrain.

بحري *baḥri* 1. sea, marine. اليريور حيوان بحري *l-yaryuur ḥayawaan baḥri.* The shark is a sea animal. طير بحري *ṭeer baḥri* sea bird. سمك بحري *simač baḥri* sea fish, ocean fish. 2. naval. أسطول بحري *'usṭuul baḥri* naval fleet. قاعدة بحرية *gaaᶜda baḥriyya* naval base.

بحرية *baḥriyya* (usually with the article prefix ال *l-*) البحرية الأمريكية *l-baḥriyya l-'amriikiyya* the American Navy.

بحار *baḥḥaar* p. بحاير *bḥaaḥiir,* بحارة *baḥḥaara* sailor.

ب ح ل گ *bḥlg*

بحلق *baḥlag* (يبحلق *ybaḥlig)* to stare. فيه ناس لين يشوفون حرمة أجنبية يبحلقون *fii naas leen yšuufuun ḥurma 'ajnabiyya ybaḥilguun.* There are people who stare when they see a foreign woman.

ب خ ت *bxt*

بخت *baxt* p. بخوت *bxuut* (syn. حظ *ḥaḏḏ* p. حظوظ *ḥḏuuḏ*) luck. البخت يلعب دور كبير في حياته *l-baxt yilᶜab door kbiir fi ḥayaata.* Luck plays an important role in his life. ما ألعب. ما لي بخت *ma 'alᶜab. ma-li baxt.* I won't play. I have no luck.

ب خ ت ر *bxtr*

تبختر *tbaxtar* (يتبختر *yitbaxtar)* to strut, swagger. لا تتبختر في المشي! *la titbaxtar fi l-maši!* Do not strut when you walk.

بخترة *baxtara* (v.n.) strutting.

ب خ خ *bxx*

بخ *baxx* (يبخ *ybuxx)* to sprinkle, spray. لا تبخ واجد ماي على العيش *la tbuxx waajid maay ᶜala l-ᶜeeš.* Don't spray much water on the rice.

بخاخة *baxxaaxa* p. *-aat* sprinkler.

ب خ ر *bxr*

بخر *baxxar* II 1. to evaporate, vaporize. بخر الماي *baxxar l-maay.* He evaporated the water. 2. to perfume s.o. or s.th. with incense. بخروا القصر لأن خطار جايين من راس الخيمة *baxxaraw l-gaṣir li'an xuṭṭaar yayiin min raas l-xeema.* They burned incense in the palace because some guests are coming from Ras Al-Khaima. 3. to disinfect, fumigate. يبخرون المجمع مرة كل شهر *ybaxxruun li-mjamma^c^ marra kill šahar.* They fumigate the complex once every month.

تبخر *tbaxxar* V 1. to evaporate, be evaporated. تبخر الماي *tbaxxar l-maay.* The water evaporated 2. to perfume oneself with incense in a مبخرة *mabxara.* تبخر قبل لا طلع *tbaxxar gabil la ṭila^c^.* He perfumed himself (with incense) before he went out. 3. to vanish, disappear. كل كلامي تبخر في الهوا *kill kalaami tbaxxar fi l-hawa.* All my words (of advice, guidance, warning) vanished into the air.

بخار *buxaar* steam, vapor.

بخاري *buxaari* steam, steam-driven. سفينة بخارية *safiina buxaariyya* steamship.

بخار *baxxaar* p. *-aat* private garage.

بخور *baxxuur* (coll.) incense (s. عود بخور *^c^uud baxxuur* incense stick). يستعملون البخور في الأفراح *yista^c^imluun l-baxxuur fi l-'afraaḥ.* They use incense in weddings.

مبخرة *mabxara* p. مباخر *mabaaxir* censer, incense holder. جا الشيخ وقامت المباخر تشتغل *ya š-šeex w-gaamat l-mabaaxir tištaġil.* The Shaikh came and censers were put to use.

باخرة *baaxra* p. بواخر *buwaaxir* steamship عمرك سافرت بالباخرة؟ *^c^umrak saafart b-l-baaxra?* Have you ever travelled by steamship?

تبخير *tabxiir* II (v.n. from بخر *baxxar*) evaporation, vaporization.

ب خ ش ش *bxšš*

بخشش *baxšaš* (يبخشش *ybaxšiš*) 1. to tip s.o., give a tip to s.o. بخششته عشرة درهم *baxšašta ^c^ašara dirhim.* I tipped him ten dirhams. 2. to bribe. بخششه بمليون درهم *baxšaša b-malyoon dirhim.* He bribed him with a million dirhams. اللي ما يبخشش ما يتبخشش *'illi ma ybaxšiš ma yitbaxšaš.* He who doesn't bribe cannot be bribed.

تبخشش *tbaxšaš* (يتبخشش *yitbaxšaš*) 1. to be tipped. 2. to be bribed. أنت تقول فيه واحد ما يتبخشش *'inta tguul fii waaḥid ma yitbaxašaš?* Are you saying that there is someone who cannot be bribed?

بخشيش *baxšiiš* 1. tip, gratuity. الباقي لك بخشيش *l-baagi lak baxšiiš.* The change is a tip for you. 2. bribery. البخشيش منتشر في البلاد *l-baxšiiš mintišir fi li-blaad.* Bribery is widespread in the country.

ب خ ل *bxl*

بخل *bixal* (يبخل *yibxal*) to be stingy, miserly. بخل على *bixal ^c^ala* to be miserly toward s.o. or s.th. لا تبخل على روحك! *la tibxal ^c^ala ruuḥak!*

Don't live scantily! Don't be miserly! في امان الله! لا تبخلوا علينا بزيارتكم! *fi maan-i-llaah! la tibxalu ᶜaleena b-ziyaaratkum!* Goodbye! Don't be stingy with your visits to us.

بخل *bixil* stinginess. البخل صفة موب زينة *l-bixil ṣifa muub zeena.* Stinginess is not a good quality.

بخيل *baxiil* p. *-iin,* بخلا *buxala* 1. stingy, miserly. 2. a stingy person.

ب د ء *bd'*

ابتدا *btida* VIII (v.) to begin, start. الهوا حار وايد. القيظ ابتدا *l-hawa ḥaarr waayid. l-geeḍ btida.* The weather is very hot. Summer has started. ابتدا الزرع يطلع *btida z-zariᶜ yiṭlaᶜ.* Plants have started to sprout. (v.t.) to begin, start s.th. بخيت ابتدا زامه *bxiit btida zaama.* Bakhit started his work schedule. (with foll. imperf.) to start to do s.th. ابتدا يشتغل *btida yištaġil.* He started to work.

ابتدا *btida* (v.n.) beginning, start. دايما الابتدا صعب *daayman li-btida ṣaᶜb.* The beginning is always difficult.

مبدا *mabda* p. مبادى *mabaadi* 1. principle. رجال بدون مبدا *rayyaal biduun mabda* man of no principles. 2. starting point, beginning. المبدا هني *l-mabda hni.* The starting point is here. مبادى *mabaadi* 1. fundamentals, essentials. مبادى الهندسة *mabaadi l-handasa* fundamentals of engineering. 2. ideology. مبادى الحزب *mabaadi l-ḥizib* the ideology of the (political) party. مبادى هدامة *mabaadi haddaama* subversive ideology, i.e., communism.

مبدئي *mabda'i* original, initial.

مبدئيا *mabda'iyyan* initially, originally.

بدائي *bidaa'i* primitive. في الزمان الأولي حياة الناس كانت بدائية *fi z-zamaan l-'awwali ḥayaat n-naas čaanat bidaa'iyya.* In the olden times people's life was primitive.

ابتداء من *btidaa'an min* beginning from, as of. ابتداء من باكر عندي عطلة *btidaa'an min baačir ᶜindi ᶜuṭla.* As of tomorrow I will be on vacation.

ابتدائي *btidaa'i* elementary, primary. مدرسة ابتدائية *madrasa btidaa'iyya* elementary school.

ب د د *bdd*

بدد *baddad* II to waste, squander. بدد كل جهده على ولا شي *baddad kill jihda ᶜala wala šayy.* He wasted all his efforts for nothing. لا تبدد فلوسك! *la tbaddid fluusak!* Do not squander your money.

استبد *stabadd* X 1. to rule arbitrarily, tyrannically. الحاكم استبد بحكمه *l-ḥaakim stabadd b-ḥukma.* The ruler acted tyrannically in his rule. 2. to be independent (e.g., in one's opinion) استبد برايه *stabadd b-raaya.* He was obstinate. 3. to act arbitrarily. التنديل الزين ما يستبد بالعمال *t-tindeel z-zeen ma yistabidd b-l-ᶜummaal.* A good supervisor doesn't act arbitrarily with the workmen.

استبداد *stibdaad* (v.n. from استبد *stabadd*) despotism, arbitrariness.

استبدادي *stibdaadi* arbitrary, despotic. حكم استبدادي *ḥukum stibdaadi* despotic rule.

مستبد *mistibidd* p. *-iin* 1. a tyrant. 2. tyrannical.

بـد *bidd* (only in the set phrase لا بد من *la bidd min* it is inevitable that). (prov.) إذا هبت هبوبـك أذر عنها فـلا بـد لهبوب من السـكون *'iða habbat hbuubak 'aðir ᶜanha fa-la bidd la li-hbuub min s-sikuun.* If you are in luck's way move away from it; it is inevitable that there will be quiet after a storm.

ب د ر bdr

بـدر *badir* full moon. البدر يطلع ليلة خمسـة عشـر *l-badir yiṭlaᶜ leelat xamistaᶜšar.* There will be a full moon on the evening of the fifteenth (of the hegira month).

ب د ع bdᶜ

بدعـة *bidᶜa* p. بـدع *bidaᶜ* heresy, heretical doctrine. كل بدعـة ضلالـة *kill bidᶜa ḍalaala.* Every heresy is a departure from the right path (i.e., it is an error). هـل البـدع *hal l-bidaᶜ* the heretics.

ب د ل bdl

بـدل *baddal* II 1. to exchange for or replace s.o. or s.th. with s.o. or s.th. else. بـدل التـايرا *baddil t-taayir!* Change the tire! راح الدكـان وبـدل القميـص *raaḥ d-dikkaan w-baddal l-gamiiṣ.* He went to the store and exchanged the shirt. وصلت اليوم وبدلت فلوسي *wiṣalt l-yoom w-baddalt fluusi.* I arrived today and exchanged my money. لو تبدل فلوسك اليـوم أحسـن مـن بـاكر لأن سعر الـدلار يتخفض *lo tbaddil fluusak l-yoom 'aḥsan min baačir li'an siᶜr id-doolaar yitxaffaḍ.* If you exchange your money today, it's better than tomorrow because tomorrow the exchange rate for the dollar will be low. 2. to change, alter. بدلوا ساعات الـدوام *baddalaw saaᶜaat d-dawaam.* They changed the working hours. 3. to change clothes. قـوم بـدل هدومـك وتعـال نـاكل *guum baddil hduumak w-taᶜaal naakil.* Go change your clothes and come so that we might eat. ترجيتـه لـين بـدل هدومـه *trayyeeta leen baddal hduuma.* I waited for him until he got dressed.

تبـدل *tbaddal* V to be changed. The work schedule was changed. هذا الزام ما يتبـدل *haaða z-zaam ma yitbaddal.* This work schedule cannot be changed.

بـدل *bidal* (no p.) 1. substitute, alternate. عطاني بدل الكتاب اللـي ضيعتـه *ᶜaṭaani bidal li-ktaab illi ḍayyaᶜta.* He gave me a replacement for the book I lost. 2. compensation, reimbursement. بـدل مياومـة *bidal myaawama* per diem. 3. rate, fee. بدل اشـتراك *bidal ištiraak.* subscription rate. بدل ما *bidal-ma* (conj.) instead of. بدل ما يـدرس قـام يلعب *bidal-ma yidris gaam yilᶜab.* Instead of studying, he went to play.

بدل مـن *bidal min* (prep.) instead of, in place of. شـربت تشـاي بـدل مـن القهـوة *šribt čaay bidal min l-gahwa.* I had tea instead of coffee.

بدال *bidaal-* (with suff. pron.) in place of. بـدالي *bidaali* in place of me. بدالهم *bidaalhum* in place of them.

ب د ن *bdn*

بدن *badan* p. أبدان *'abdaan* body, trunk, torso. بدن بني آدم *badan bani 'aadam* human body.

بدني *badani* physical. رياضة بدنية *riyaaḍa badaniyya* physical exercise.

ب د و *bdw*

بدو *badu* (coll.) Bedouins. s. بدوي *bidwi*. البدو يسكنون البر *l-badu yaskunuun l-barr.* Bedouins live in the desert. البدوي عنده شيمة أخلاق *li-bdiwi ^cinda šiimat 'axlaag.* A Bedouin is of good moral character.

بدوي *bdiwi* (adj.) nomadic. حياة بدوية *ḥayaa bdiwiyya* nomadic life.

بدوية *bdiwiyya, badawiyya* p. *-aat* Bedouin woman or girl.

بادية *baadya* p. بوادي *bawaadi* semidesert, steppe (usually with *l-*) هو من هل البادية *huwa min hal l-baadya.* He is one of the desert dwellers.

بدون *biduun* (prep.) = *bi-duun*, see under **د و ن** *dwn.*

ب د ي ١ ابتدا *btida* VIII see under **ب د ء** *bd'.*

ب د ي ٢ بادية *baadya*, see under **ب د و** *bdw.*

ب د ي ٣ *bdy*

بدي *badi* p. *-yaat* body of a car. أبغاك ترنق بدي سيارتي *'abġaak trannig badi sayyaarti.* I want you to paint the body of my car.

ب ذ ء *bð'*

بذي *baði* p. بذيئين *baðii'iin* foul, obscene. كلام بذي *kalaam baði* foul talk. بذي اللسان *baði l-lisaan* foul-mouthed.

ب ذ خ *bðx*

بذخ *biðax* (يبذخ *yibðax)* to spend (money) lavishly. يبذخ وايد على يهاله *yibðax waayid ^cala yihhaala.* He spends a lot on his children.

بذاخ *baððaax* p. *-iin* spendthrift.

ب ذ ر *bðr*

بذر *baððar* II 1. to waste, squander. بذر كل فلوسه على السكر *baððar kill fluusa ^cala s-sikir.* He wasted all his money on drinking. 2. to go to seed. الزرع بذر *z-zari^c baððar.* The plants have gone to seed.

تبذر *tbaððar* V to be wasted. كل جهود التنديل حق تفنيش الكولية تبذرت *kill jhuud t-tindeel ḥagg tafniiš l-kuuliyya tbaððarat.* All the efforts of the supervisor for laying off the coolies were wasted.

بذر *biðir* (coll.) s. بذرة *biðra* seeds.

مبذر *mbaððir* p. *-iin* spendthrift.

ب ذ ل *bðl*

بذل *biðal* (يبذل *yibðil)* 1. to expend, exert. بذل جهد كبير في الدراسة *biðal jihd kabiir fi d-diraasa.* He exerted great efforts in studying. 2. to sacrifice. بذلت كل شي لاجل شرف عايلتي *biðalt kill šayy lajil šaraf ^caayilti.* I sacrificed everything for the sake of my family's honor.

ب ر ي *bry*

الباري *l-baari* God, the Creator.

برا *barra* II to acquit, clear. أخوي برته المحكمة من التهمة *'uxuuy barrata l-maḥkama min t-tuhma.* The court cleared my brother of the accusation.

تبرا *tbarra* V 1. to be acquitted, be cleared. 2. to disassociate oneself from. تبرا من ابنه *tbarra min ibna.* He disowned his son.

بري *bari,* بريء *barii'* p. *-iin* 1. innocent. حاكموه وطلع بري *ḥaakamoo w-ṭila^c bari.* They tried him (in court) and he turned out to be innocent. 2. free, having nothing to do with. عياله بطالين؛ هو بري منهم *^cyaala baṭṭaaliin; huwa bari minhum.* His kids are bad; he has nothing to do with them. 2. harmless. ياهل بري *yaahil bari* innocent child.

براءة *baraa'a* guiltlessness. طلع براءة *ṭila^c baraa'a.* He was found not guilty.

ب راغ *braaġ*

براغ *braaġ* bragh (Kuwaiti dish made up of rolled grape leaves with rice and meat).

ب رب ر ١ *brbr*

بربر *barbar* (يبربر *ybarbir*) to chatter, talk aimlessly. ما قال شي؛ بس راد يبربر *ma gaal šayy; bass raad ybarbir.* He did not say anything; he just wanted to chatter.

البربر *l-barbar* (coll.) the Berbers.

بربري *barbari* p. برابرة *baraabra* 1. a Berber. 2. characteristic of the Berbers. 3. barbaric, uncivilized.

بربرية *barbariyya* p. *-aat* (kind of Somali nanny goat, known for its good milk).

تبربر *tiburbur* (v.n.) chattering, talking aimlessly.

ب رب ر ٢ *brbr*

بربرة 1. Barbara (region along the coast of Somalia). 2. Barbara (city in the region of Barbara).

بربراوي *barbaraawi* p. *-yya* 1. person from Barbara. 2. characteristic of Barbara.

ب رب ي ر *brbyr*

بربير *barbiir* (coll.) 1. greens, herbaceous plants. s. عرج بربير *^cirj barbiir.* 2. parsley.

ب رت گ ل *brtgl*

برتقال *burtagaal* (coll.) oranges. s. برتقالة *burtagaala.* البرتقال غالي اليوم *l-burtagaal ġaali l-yoom.* Oranges are expensive today. كليت خمس برتقالات *kaleet xams burtagaalaat.* I ate five oranges. اشتريت برتقال *štareet burtagaal.* I bought oranges.

ب رث ن *brθn*

برثن *birθin* p. براثن *baraaθin* claw (of a bird of prey or of an animal).

ب رج *brj*

برج *birj* p. براج *braaj* (more common var. بري *biri* p. برايا *braaya*) 1. tower. كل إمارة لها بري كبير *kill 'imaara laha biri čibiir.* Every Emirate has a big tower. برج المطار *burj l-maṭaar* the airport tower. برج المراقبة *burj l-muraaġaba* the watch tower.

برج *burj* p. بروج *buruuj* sign of the zodiac.

بارجة *baarja* p. بوارج *buwaarij* battleship

ب ر چ brč

بـرك *birač (يـبرك yabrič)* 1. to kneel down. بـرك علـى ركبتينـه *birač ᶜla rkubteena.* He kneeled on his knees. 2. to sit down (usually said of an animal, e.g., a camel) برك البعير *birač l-biᶜiir.* The camel sat down.

بـارك *baarač* III 1. to bless, invoke a blessing on s.o. !الله يبـارك فيـك *'aḷḷa ybaarič fiik!* God bless you! 2. to offer congratulations. جانا ولـد. هلنا جـاوا وبـاركوا لنـا *yaana walad. halna yaw w-baarčaw lana.* We had a baby boy. Our relatives came and congratulated us.

بركـة *birča* p. برك *birak* pool, pond, swimming pool.

ب ر ح brḥ

البارحة *l-baarḥa* yesterday. أمس *'ams* is more common. See أمس *'ams.*

براحـة *baraaḥa* open space or alley between homes used as a playground.

ب ر د[1] brd

بـرد *birad (يـبرد yabrid)* to cool. فاح الشاي وذالحين برد. تقـدر تشـرب منه *faaḥ č-čaay w-ðalḥiin birad. tigdar tišrab minna.* The tea boiled. It has cooled off. You can drink some of it.

بـرد *barrad* II to cool, chill. الثلاجة تبرد المـاي *θ-θallaaja tbarrid l-maay.* A refrigerator cools the water. الكنديشن يبيرد الحجرة *l-kandeešin ybarrid l-ḥijra.* Air conditioning cools the room.

تـبرد *tbarrad* V 1. to be cooled. الماي تـبرد في الثلاجـة *l-maay tbarrad fi θ-θallaaja.* The water has been cooled in the refrigerator. 2. to cool oneself. فتحنـا الدريشـة وتبردنـا شـويـة *fitaḥna d-diriiša w-tbarradna šwayya.* We opened the window and cooled off a little bit.

استبرد *stabrad* X to catch a cold. رقد والدريشـة مفتوحـة. اسـتبرد *rigad w-d-diriiša maftuuḥa. stabrad.* He went to bed and the window was open; he caught a cold.

بـراد *baraad* cool weather, cool air. اليـوم بـراد *l-yoom baraad.* It's cool today.

براد *barraad* p. *-aat* (more common in Qatar) supermarket.

برودة *bruuda* coldness, coolness.

بـردان *bardaan* p. *-iin* cold. *'inta bardaan?* Are you cold?

أبـرد *'abrad* 1. colder, cooler الجو أبرد اليـوم *l-jaww 'abrad l-yoom.* The weather is colder today. 2. coldest, the coldest. هـذا أبـرد يـوم *haaða 'abrad yoom.* This is the coldest day. أبرد من *'abrad min* colder than.

بـارد *baarid* 1. cold, cool, chilly. الهوا بـارد اليـوم *l-hawa baarid l-yoom.* The weather is cold today. بارد الدم *baarid d-damm* cool headed.

بردي *bridi* (coll.) hail. s. بردية *bridiyya* hailstone.

ب ر د[2] brd

بـرد *birad (يبرد yabrid)* to file. الحداد برد البيـب *l-ḥaddaad birad l-peep.* The blacksmith filed the pipe. برادة *braada* 1. trade or profession of filing (iron, gold, etc.). 2. iron filings.

ب ر د ٣ brd

بريد *bariid* mail, letters, post. مكتب البريد *maktab l-bariid* the post office. بريد جوي *bariid jawwi* airmail. بريد عادي *bariid ᶜaadi* ordinary mail. بريد مسجل *bariid m(u)sajjal* registered, certified mail. طرشته بالبريد الجوي *ṭarrašta b-l-bariid l-jawwi.* I sent it airmail.

بريدي *bariidi* postal. طابع بريدي *ṭaabiᶜ bariidi* postal stamp (as opposed to طابع مالي *ṭaabiᶜ maali* revenue stamp).

ب ر د ٤ brd

برد *burd* side of a ship (no known p.).

ب ر د ٥ brd

بردة *burda* p. برد *burad* outer garment, esp. one worn by a dervish or a mystic.

ب ر ر ١ brr

بر *barr (يبر ybirr)* to keep (a promise), fulfill. إذا وعدت واحد لازم تبر بوعدك *'iða waᶜadt waaḥid laazim tbirr b-waᶜdak.* If you promise someone something, you have to keep your promise.

برر *barrar* II to justify. تقدر تبرر اللي سويته ذالحين؟ *tigdar tbarrir illi sawweeta ðalḥiin?* Can you justify what you have just done now?

مبرر *mbarrir* (act. part.) p. *-iin* having justified. هو المبرر موقفه *huwa li-mbarrir mawgifa.* He is the one who has justified his position.

ب ر ر ٢ brr

بر *barr* p. براري *baraari* (usually with ال *l-*) 1. desert. قيظوا في البر *gayyaḍaw fi l-barr.* They spent the summer in the desert. 2. open land. هذا هني كله بر *haaða hini killa barr.* Here, it's all open land. بالبر ولا بالبحر *b-l-barr walla b-l-baḥar* by land or by sea. (naut.) البر العالي *l-barr l-ᶜaali* the coast of the Arabian Gulf, stretching from Basra in Iraq to Muscat in Oman. (naut.) بر السواحلي *barr s-sawaaḥli* the coast of East Africa, stretching from Eritrea to Tanzania.

بري *barri* (adj.) 1. land. قوات برية وبحرية *guwwaat barriyya w-baḥriyya* land and sea forces. 2. wild (plants and animals). حيوان بري *ḥayawwan barri* wild animal. وحوش برية *wḥuuš barriyya* wild beasts.

برة *barra* outside, out. الشيخ طلع برة *š-šeex ṭalaᶜ barra.* The Shaikh went outside. موب هني برة *muub hini barra* not here, outside. (prov.) من برة الله الله ومن الداخل يعلم الله *min barra 'aḷḷa 'aḷḷa w-min d-daaxil yiᶜlam aḷḷa.* Fair without and foul within. برة برة *barra barra* Get out of here! (said with a loud harsh voice) phrase used to ask s.o. to leave, e.g., the office, room, house, etc.).

براني *barraani* 1. (adj.) outer, exterior. الحجرة البرانية *l-ḥijra l-barraaniyya* the outside room. 2. (p. برانية *barraaniyya)* foreigner. أكو برانية واجد في الكويت *'aku barraaniyya waayid fi li-kweet.* There are many foreigners in Kuwait. برانية يعني ناس من برة *barraaniyya yaᶜni naas min barra.* "barraaniyya" means people from outside (the country).

ب ر ر ٣ brr

بر *birr* good faith, piety. أعمال البر والتقوة *'acmaal l-birr w-t-tagwa* good deeds and fear of God.

ب ر ز brz

بر *baraz* (يبرز *yabriz*) 1. to be ready. برز العشا وكليناه *baraz l-caša w-kaleenaa.* The dinner was ready and we ate all of it. 2. to be finished. قال الميكانيكي السيارة تبرز باكر *gaal l-miikaaniiki s-sayyaara tabriz baačir.* The mechanic said that the car would be finished the following day.

برز *barraz* II to make s.o. or s.th. ready. برزت حرمتي العشا *barrazat ḥurumti l-caša.* My wife got dinner ready.

برزة *barza* p. *-aat* 1. social gathering. ما تقدر تشوف الشيخ لأن الشيوخ عندهم برزة ذالحين *ma tigdar ččuuf š-šeex li'an š-šyuux cindahum barza ðalḥiin.* You cannot see the Shaikh because the Shaikhs are having a social gathering now. برزة الشيوخ تكون عادة في الليل *barzat -š-šyuux tkuun caadatan fi l-leel.* The Shaikh's celebration is usually at night. 2. place where people meet, session room = مجلس *maylis.* See مجلس *maylis* under **ي ل س** *yls.*

بارز *baariz* (act. part.) p. *-iin.* ready, prepared. العشا بارز *l-caša baariz.* Dinner is ready. آنا بارز *'aana baariz.* I am ready.

ب ر س ت ي brsty

برستي *barasti* p. *-yya* shack, hut built with palm date leaves and branches. أهل البرستي *'ahl l-barasti* shack dwellers, slum dwellers. أهل البرستي اغتنوا *'ahl l-barasti ġtinaw.* Shack dwellers became rich.

ب ر ش م bršm

برشوم *baršuum* p. براشيم *baraašiim* little bell hung around the neck of an animal, such as a goat, a camel, a cow, etc.

ب ر ص ١ brṣ

برص *baraṣ* leprosy.

أبرص *'abraṣ* p. برص *birṣ* f. برصة *barṣa* p. *-aat* leper.

ب ر ص ٢ brṣ

بورصة *boorṣa* p. *-aat* stock exchange.

ب ر ص ص brṣṣ

برصيص *barṣiiṣ* p. براصيص *biraaṣiiṣ* very stingy person. «برصيص» يعني أكثر من بخيل *"barṣiiṣ" yacni 'akθar min baxiil.* "*barṣiiṣ*" means more than stingy.

ب ر ط ل brṭl

برطل *barṭal* (يبرطل *ybarṭil*) to bribe. برطله بألف درهم بس *barṭala b-'alf dirhim bass.* He bribed him with only a thousand dirhams.

تبرطل *tbarṭal* to be bribed. اللي ما يبرطل ما يتبرطل *'illi ma ybarṭil ma yitbarṭal.* He who doesn't bribe cannot be bribed.

برطيل *barṭiil* p. براطيل *baraaṭiil* bribe.

برطلة *barṭala* bribing, bribery. البرطلة منتشرة في البلاد *l-barṭala mintašra fi li-blaad.* Bribery is widespread in the country.

ب ر ط م *brṭm*

برطم *barṭam* (يبرطم *ybarṭim*) to pout. برطم لانه كان حمقان *barṭam linna čaan ḥamgaan.* He pouted because he was angry.

تبرطم *tbarṭam* (يتبرطم *yitbarṭam*) = برطم *barṭam.* See برطم *barṭam.*

برطمة *barṭama* (v.n.) pout, pouting.

مبرطم *mbarṭim* (act. part.) p. *-iin* having pouted. خله! مبرطم *xalla! mbarṭim.* Leave him be! He has just been pouting.

برطم *burṭum* p. براطم *baraaṭim* lip. أبو براطم *'ubu baraaṭim* s.o. with large thick lips. عض على برطمه *ᶜaðð ᶜala burṭuma.* He regretted s.th.

ب ر ع *brᶜ*

تبرع *tbarraᶜ* V (with بـ *b-*) to contribute, donate. تبرع بمليون درهم حق المؤسسة الخيرية *tbarraᶜ b-malyoon dirhim ḥagg l-mu'assasa l-xayriyya.* He donated one million dirhams to the charitable establishment. 2. to volunteer. تبرع يشتغل حق المشردين *tbarraᶜ yištaġil ḥagg li-mšarradiin.* He volunteered to work for the homeless people.

ب ر ع م *brᶜm*

برعم *burᶜum* p. براعم *baraaᶜim* bud (bot.).

ب ر غ م *brġm*

برغام *birġaam* p. براغيم *biraaġiim* (هارن *haaran*) car horn. هني يدقون البرغام حق كل شي *hini ydigguun l-birġaam ḥagg kill šayy.* Here they sound the car horn for everything.

ب ر غ ي *brġy*

برغي *burġi* p. براغي *baraaġi* (more common سكرو *sikruu*) screw. تيت البرغي بالمفك *tayyat l-burġi b-li-mfačč.* He tightened the screw with the screwdriver.

ب ر گ *brg*

برق *birag* (يبرق *yabrig*) to flash, glitter. برق البرق *birag l-barg.* There was lightning. (prov.) إذا برق البرق طالع عين ثورك *iða birag l-barg ṭaaliᶜ ᶜeen θoorak.* lit. "If lightning flashes, look your bull in the eye." It applies to s.o. who is in trouble and then finds a way out.

برق *barg* 1. lightning. 2. telegraph. دايرة البرق *daayrat l-barg* the telegraph department.

برقي *bargi* telegraphic. خطوط برقية *xuṭuuṭ bargiyya* telegraph lines.

برقية *bargiyya* p. *-aat* telegram, cable. طرش لي برقية *ṭarraš-li bargiyya.* He sent me a telegram.

أبرق *'abrag* p. برقان *birgaan* black or blue, yellow and white; black and white. حصان أبرق *ḥṣaan 'abrag* black horse. بقرة برقا *bgara barga* black cow. بعارين برقان *baᶜaariin birgaan* black camels.

ب ر گ ن *brgn*

برقان *burgaan* Burgan (oil field in Kuwait).

ب ر گ ع *brgᶜ*

برقع *birgiᶜ* p. براقع *baraagiᶜ* veil (long black drape that covers the whole face of a woman or a young girl).

ب ر ي گ *bryg*

بريق *briig* p. أباريق *'abaariig* (var., more common, بريج *briij*) 1. water pitcher. بريق لماي *briig li-maay* the water pitcher. 2. kettle. بريق الشاي *briig č-čaay* the tea kettle.

ب ر ك *brk*

برك *birak* = *birač*. See under **ب ر چ** *brč*.

بارك *baarak* III = *baarač*. See under **ب ر چ** *brč*.

تبارك *tabaarak* VI to be blessed, exalted, praised. تبارك الله! *tabaarak aḷḷa!* God is praised! (usually said in admiration of s.o. or s.th.).

بركة *birka* = *birča*. See under **ب ر چ** *brč*.

بركة *baraka* blessing, benediction. هذي بركة من الله *haaδi baraka min aḷḷa.* This is God's blessing. الله حط له البركة في معاشه *'aḷḷa ḥaṭṭ-la l-baraka fi maᶜaaša.* With God's blessing, his salary increased. هذي الساعة المباركة *haaδi s-saaᶜa li-mbaarka.* This is the blessed hour (said to s.o. who has just called on s.o. else) عيدك مبارك! *ᶜiidak mbaarak!* Happy holiday!

مبرك *mbaarik* p. *-iin* having congratulated, one who has offered congratulations for a newborn baby, passing an examination, etc.

ب ر ك ن *brkn*

بركان *burkaan* p. براكين *baraakiin* volcano.

بركاني *burkaani* volcanic. حجر بركاني *ḥiyar burkaani* volcanic rock.

ب ر ل م ن *brlmn*

برلمان *barlamaan* p. *-aat* parliament.

برلماني *barlamaani* parliamentary.

ب ر م ت *brmt*

برميت *barmeet* kind of sweets or candy, probably English peppermint.

ب ر م ل *brml*

برميل *barmiil* p. براميل *baraamiil* barrel, drum. كم سعر برميل البترول ذالحين؟ *čam siᶜr barmiil l-batrool δalḥiin?* What is the price of a barrel of oil nowadays? قطه في البرميل *gaṭṭa fi l-barmiil.* He threw it in the drum.

ب ر ن م ج *brnmj*

برنامج *barnaamij* p. *-aat*, برامج *baraamij* program, schedule.

ب ر ن و ص *brnwṣ*

برنوص *barnuuṣ* p. برانيص *baraaniiṣ* blanket. برنوص صوف *barnuuṣ ṣuuf* wool blanket.

ب ر ن ي و ش *brnywš*

برنيوش *barnyuuš* (popular dish made up of rice cooked with sugar, molasses or dates and eaten with fish).

ب ر ه ن *brhn*

برهن *barhan (ybarhin)* to prove, demonstrate. برهن إنه لحيتن غانمه *barhan 'inna liḥyatin ġaanma.* He proved that he was a religious, magnanimous person.

برهان *burhaan* p. براهين *baraahiin* proof.

ب ر و ز *brwz*

بروز *barwaz (يبروز ybarwiz)* to frame a

picture. رحنا حق العكاس. خذ لنا عكس وبروزناه *riḥna ḥagg l-ᶜakkaas. xað lana ᶜaks w-barwaznaa.* We went to the photographer. He took a picture of us and we framed it.

بـرواز *birwaaz* p. براويز *biraawiiz* picture frame.

ب ر و ش *brwš*

بروش *bruuš* p. *-aat* brush.

ب ر و ن *brwn*

بروانة *barwaana* (var. *parwaana*) p. *-aat.* 1. fan. في الزمان الأولي كانوا يستعملون بروانات من خوص *fi z-zamaan l-'awwali čaanaw yistaᶜimluun barwaanaat min xooṣ.* In the olden times, they used to use palm-leaf fans. 2. propeller. بروانة الطايرة *barwaanat ṭ-ṭaayra* the airplane propeller.

ب ر ي *bry*

بـرى *bira* (يبري *yabri*) to sharpen a pencil. بريت قلمي *bareet gḷumi.* I sharpened my pencil.

تبارى *tbaara* VI to meet in a contest. تبارينا واياه فريق العين وغلبناهم *tbaareena wiyya fariiġ l-ᶜeen wa ġallabnaahum.* We had a match with the Al-Ain team and we beat them.

مباراة *mbaaraa* p. مباريات *-yaat* match, tournament. مباراة كرة القدم *mbaaraat kurat l-ġadam* the soccer game.

براية *barraaya* p. *-aat* pencil sharpener.

ب ر ي ن *bryn*

بريـاني *biryaani* dish made of rice, meat, and spices, originally an Indian dish.

ب ر ي س م *brysm*

بريسم *breesim* silk.

ب ر ي ك *bryk*

بريك *breek* p. *-aat* car brake. تشيك البريكات! *čayyik li-breekaat!* Check the brakes! أبو البريك *'ubu li-breek* the one who fixes brakes.

ب ر ي م ي *brymy*

البريمي *li-breemi* 1. Buraymi (oasis and city by the same name in the U.A.E. 2. Al-Ain (city in Abu Dhabi) and the surrounding areas. دايماً نصيف في البريمي *daayman nṣayyif fi li-breemi.* We always spend the summer in Buraymi. البريمي، طال عمرك، واحة *li-breemi, ṭaal ᶜumrak, waaḥa.* Buraymi, may you live long, is an oasis.

ب ز ب ز *bzbz*

بزبوز *bazbuuz* p. بزابيز *bizaabiiz* spout of a pitcher.

ب ز ر ١ *bzr*

بزر *bizar* (يبزر *yabzir*) to sow seeds.

بـزر *bazzar* II to go to seed. الطماط بزر *ṭ-ṭmaaṭ bazzar.* The tomatoes have gone to seed.

بـزر *bazir* p. بـزور *bzuur* child, kid (only in Bahraini and Saudi Arabic). هـذا بـزر مـا عليك منه *haaða bazir ma ᶜaleek minna.* This is (only) a child. Ignore him; do not pay attention to him.

ب ز ر ٢ *bzr*

بزار *bzaar* spices.

ب ز ز *bzz*

بز *bazz* (coll.) cloth, material. أبو البز هو البزاز *'abu l-bazz huwa l-bazzaaz.* The one who sells cloth is the cloth merchant.

بزة *bazza* p. *-aat* piece of cloth or material.

بزاز *bazzaaz* p. *-iin* cloth merchant or dealer.

بزازة *bzaaza* cloth trade.

ب ز گ *bzg*

بزق *bizag* (يبزق *yubzug)* to spit. فيه ناس الله يسلمك يبزقون في كل مكان *fii naas, 'aḷḷa ysallimk, yubzuguun fi kill mukaan.* There are people, God protect you, who spit in every place. لا تبزق هني! *la tubzug hini!* Don't spit here!

بزق *bazg* (v.n. of بزق *bizag*) spitting. البزق ممنوع *l-bazg mamnuu^c* Spitting is forbidden. No spitting.

بزاق *bzaag* (coll.) spit, saliva. s. بزاقة *bzaaga.*

ب س ت ن *bstn*

بستان *bistaan* p. بساتين *bisaatiin* orchard, grove. بساتين نخيل *bisaatiin naxiil* date palm orchards.

بستنة *bastana* horticulture.

ب س ر *bsr*

بسر *bisir* (coll.) unripe dates. s. بسرة *bisra.*

ب س س¹ *bss*

بس *bass* (يبس *ybiss)* to mix. بس الشعير مع الذرا *bass š-ša^{c}iir ma^c ð-ðira.* He mixed the barley with the corn.

ب س س² *bss*

بس *bass* 1. only, just. آنا وأنت بس *'aana w-inta bass.* Only you and I. بس اشتريت سمك *bass štareet simač.* I only bought fish. 2. enough. بس عاد ترمس! *bass ^{c}aad trammis!* Enough; don't talk anymore! بسك عاد! *bassak ^{c}aad!* Enough (out of you)! Stop it! بسك شكاوى! *bassak šakaawi!* Enough of your complaints! بسك غشمرة *bassak ġašmara!* Enough of your kidding me! Enough of your bluffing! 3. (conj.) but, on the other hand. هو عاقل بس مرات مخبل *huwa ^{c}aagil bass marraat mxabbal.* He is rational but sometimes he is crazy. لا تنس إنك كولي وبس *la tansa 'innak kuuli wa bass.* Don't forget that you are a coolie (hired hand) and nothing more.

ب س س³ *bss*

بس *bass* (coll.) halyard, tackle (ship). s. بسة *bassa.*

ب س ط *bsṭ*

بسط *bisaṭ* (يبسط *yabsuṭ)* to spread, spread out. بسط ذراعينه *bisaṭ ðra^{c}eena.* He spread his arms.

بسط *bassaṭ* II 1. to open up, open for business. راعي الدكان بسط *raa^{c}i d-dikkaan bassaṭ.* The store owner opened up for business. 2. to simplify. ماحد يقدر يبسط هالمشكلة *maḥḥad yigdar ybassiṭ hal-muškila.* No one can simplify this problem.

بسط *basṭ* (v.n. of بسط *bisaṭ*) (characteristically Kuwaiti and Iraqi) flogging, beating. بسطوه خوش بسطة *bisaṭoo xooš basṭa.* They gave him a hard beating.

بسطة *basṭa* p. *-aat* 1. display of wares or merchandise. 2. (n. of inst.) a beating, flogging. بسطوه بسطة عراقية *bisaṭoo basṭa ᶜraagiyya.* They beat him an Iraqi (a hard) beating.

بسيط *basiiṭ* 1. simple, not complicated. عندي لك طلب بسيط *ᶜindi lak ṭalab basiiṭ.* I have a simple request of you. قضية بسيطة *gaðiyya basiiṭa* uncomplicated thing or problem. 2. little, modest. شي بسيط *šayy basiiṭ* little, trivial thing. طلب بسيط *ṭalab basiiṭ* modest request. 3. (p. *-iin*) naive, simple. رجال بسيط *rayyaal basiiṭ* simple man.

بساطة *basaaṭa* 1. simplicity, plainness. البساطة مطلوبة *l-basaaṭa maṭluuba.* Simplicity is desired, or called for. 2. naivete.

أبسط *'absaṭ* (elat.) 1. simpler or simplest. 2. more or most insignificant. 3. more or most naive.

ب س ك ت *bskt*

بسكوت *biskoot* (coll.) cookies, biscuits. s. بسكوتة *biskoota.*

ب س ل ١ *bsl*

بسال *bsaal* (coll.) dry dates. s. *bsaala.*

ب س ل ٢ *bsl*

بسيلة *bisiila* p. بسايل *bisaayil* braid, plait. أم البسايل *'umm l-bisaayil* girl or woman with long hair.

ب س م *bsm*

تبسم *tbassam* V to smile. لين يتحكى يتبسم *leen yitḥačča yitbassam.* When he talks, he smiles.

ابتسم *btisam* VIII = V. لما قلت له ابتسم وقال ما عليك منه *lamma gilit-la btisam w-gaal ma ᶜaleek minna.* When I told him, he smiled and said, "Don't pay attention to him."

بسمة *basma* p. *-aat* a smile.

ابتسام *btisaam* (v.n. from ابتسم *btisam*) smiling. الابتسام ما يفارق وجهه *li-btisaam ma yfaarig weeha.* lit., "Smiling doesn't leave his face." He is always smiling.

ابتسامة *btisaama* p. *-aat* a smile.

ب س م ت *bsmt*

بسمتي *basmati* (coll.) basmati (kind of Pakistani rice). s. حبة بسمتي *ḥabbat basmati.*

ب س ي س *bsys*

بسيس *basiis* = بثيث *baθiiθ.* See under **ب ث ث** *bθθ.*

ب ش ت *bšt*

بشت *bišt* p. بشوت *bšuut* (man's cloak or outer garment, usually white in the summer and dark in the winter). (prov.) عشت ولبست بشت *ᶜišt w-libast bišt* (said to a child or a young boy as a good wish.) May you live long and wear a cloak!

ب ش ت خ *bštx*

بشتاخة *bištaaxa* p. بشاتخ *bišaatix* wooden box or trunk used for keeping clothes and jewelry.

ب ش ر ١ *bšr*

بشر *baššar* II 1. to bring, announce

good news to s.o. !بشرك الله بالخير *baššark aḷḷa b-l-xeer!* (said as a response to s.o. who has brought good news) God bless you with good news. بشرته بنجاحه في الامتحان *baššarta b-najaaḥa fi li-mtiḥaan.* I broke the good news to him of (his) passing the examination. 2. (with ب *b-*) to spread, propagate (a religion, or doctrine) فيه ناس يبشرون بالإسلام *fii naas ybaššruun b-l-'islaam.* There are people who propagate Islam.

استبشر *stabšar* X to rejoice in hearing good news. استبشر بالخير لين سمع إنه حا ولد *stabšar b-l-xeer leen simaᶜ 'inna yaa walad.* He rejoiced when he heard that he had a baby boy.

بشارة *bšaara* p. بشاير *bišaayir* good news.

تبشير *tabšiir* (v.n. from بشر *baššar*) missionary activity. الحكومة هني ما تسمح بالتبشير *li-ḥkuuma hini ma tismaḥ b-t-tabšiir.* The government here does not allow missionary activity.

تبشيري *tabšiiri* (adj) missionary. مدرسة تبشيرية *madrasa tabšiiriyya* missionary school.

مبشر *mbaššir* (act. part.) p. *-iin* 1. bearer of good news. 2. a missionary.

ب ش ر[٢] *bšr*

باشر *baašar* III to begin, commence. باشرت شغلي قبل أمس *baašart šuġli gabl ams.* I began my work the day before yesterday.

بشر *bašar* 1. human being, man. هو بشر، مثلي ومثلك *huwa bašar, miθli w-miθlak.* He is a human being, like me and you. 2. mankind, the human race.

بشري *bašari* human (as opp. to animal) الجنس البشري *l-jins l-bašari* the human race. دختر بشري *daxtar bašari* medical doctor (as opposed to دختر بيطري *daxtar bayṭari* veterinarian).

بشرة *bašara* outer skin, complexion. معظم العرب بشرتهم سمرة *muᶜđam l-ᶜarab bašarittum samra.* Most Arabs have a dark complexion.

مباشرة *mubaašaratan* immediately. رحت الحفيز مباشرة *riḥt l-ḥafiiz mubaašaratan.* I went to the office immediately.

ب ش ر[٣] *bšr*

أبشر *'abšir* (imp.) = yes sir! with pleasure. نظف الجام! أبشر! *nađđif l-jaam! 'abšir!* Clean the glass! Yes sir!

ب ش ك ر *bškr*

بشكار *biškaar* p. بشاكر *bišaakir* servant, house servant. معظم البشاكر من الهند *muᶜđam l-bišaakir min l-hind.* Most house servants are from India.

ب ش م ك *bšmk*

بشمك *bašmak* (coll.) sweets made from sugar and sesame seed paste.

ب ص ب ص *bṣbṣ*

بصبص *baṣbaṣ (يبصبص ybaṣbis)* to ogle, cast amorous glances. يحب يبصبص على الحريم *yḥibb ybaṣbiṣ ᶜala l-ḥariim.* He likes to ogle women.

بصبصة *baṣbaṣa* (v.n. from بصبص *baṣbaṣ*) ogling, act of casting amorous glances. البصبصة هني توديك السجن *l-baṣbaṣa hni twaddiik is-siyin.* Amorous or coquettish glancing sends you to jail here.

ب ص ر ١ *bṣr*

تبصر *tbaṣṣar* V (with في *fi*) to reflect on s.th., ponder s.th. هذا أمر لازم تتبصر فيه *haaða 'amir laazim titbaṣṣar fii.* This is a matter you should reflect on.

بصر *baṣar* eyesight, vision. عمى بصرهم *ᶜima baṣarhum.* He blinded them. لمح البصر *lamḥ l-baṣar* glance of the eye. على مدى البصر *ᶜala mada l-baṣar* within sight, as far as the eye can see.

بصير *baṣiir* p. *-iin* 1. (with بـ *b-*) having insight into s.th. هو بصير بالأمور *huwa baṣiir b-l-'umuur.* He has insight into things. الله بصير بكل شي *'aḷḷaah baṣiir b-kill šayy.* God has profound knowledge of everything. 2. blind person. مسكين بصير بعيونه الثنتين *maskiin baṣiir b-ᶜyuuna θ-θinteen.* Poor man. He is blind in both eyes.

بصار *baṣṣaar* p. *-iin,* بصارة *baṣṣaara* fortune teller.

ب ص ر ٢ *bṣr*

البصرة *l-baṣra* Basra, city in southern Iraq.

بصراوي *baṣraawi* p. *-yya* 1. person from Basra. 2. characteristic of Basra. تمر بصراوي *tamir baṣraawi* dates from Basra.

ب ص ل *bṣl*

بصل *baṣal* (coll.) onions. s. بصلة *bṣala.* البصل يطلع هني *l-baṣal yiṭlaᶜ hini.* Onions grow here. اشتريت بصل *štareet baṣal.* I bought onions.

ب ص م *bṣm*

بصم *baṣam* (يبصم *yabṣum*) to stamp, print (a fingerprint). لا يقرا ولا يكتب بس يبصم *la yiġra wala yiktib bass yabṣum.* He neither reads nor writes; he just makes a fingerprint. بصمة *baṣma* imprint, impression. بصمة باليد *baṣma b-l-yadd* fingerprint.

ب ط ا ط *bṭaaṭ*

بطاط *buṭaaṭ* (coll.) potatoes. Also, less common علي وللم *ᶜali willam,* آلو *'aalo.* s. حبة بطاط *ḥabbat buṭaaṭ.*

ب ط ب ط ١ *bṭbṭ*

بطبط *baṭbaṭ* (يبطبط *ybaṭbiṭ*) to fall down (to the ground) gradually. الرطب بطبط *li-rṭabb baṭbaṭ.* The fresh dates (yellowish in color, not very ripe) fell down to the ground.

ب ط ب ط ٢ *bṭbṭ*

بطبطة *buṭbuṭa* p. بطابط *biṭaabiṭ* motorcycle. دعمت واحد راكب بطبطة في السوق *diᶜamt waaḥid raakib buṭbuṭa fi s-suug.* I hit a person riding a motorcycle in the marketplace.

ب ط خ *bṭx*

بطيخ *baṭṭiix* (coll.) cantaloupes. s. بطيخة *baṭṭiixa.* البطيخ غالي اليوم *l-baṭṭiix ġaali l-yoom.* Cantaloupes are expensive today. فيه بطيخ في السوق؟ *fii baṭṭiix fi s-suug?* Are there cantaloupes in the marketplace? اشتريت بطيختين *štareet baṭṭiixteen.* I bought two cantaloupes.

ب ط ري *bṭry*

بطاريـــة *baṭṭaariyya* p. *-aat* battery (mil.).

ب ط ط ١ *bṭṭ*

بـــط *baṭṭ* (يبط *ybiṭṭ*) 1. to knock out, gouge out. بـــط عيـــني *baṭṭ ᶜeeni.* He poked me in the eye. 2. to pop (a balloon). بط البالون *baṭṭ l-baaloon.* He popped the balloon.

انبـــط *nbaṭṭ* VII 1. to get poked. انبطت عينه *nbaṭṭat ᶜeena.* He got poked in the eye. 2. to be, get popped. انبط البالون *nbaṭṭ l-baaloon.* The balloon got popped.

ب ط ط ٢ *bṭṭ*

بـــط *baṭṭ* (coll.) ducks. s. بطة *baṭṭa* p. *-aat*.

ب ط غ *bṭġ*

بطاغـــة *biṭaaġa* (var. بطاقـــة *biṭaaqa, biṭaaga*) p. بطـــايق *biṭaayig, -aat* 1. (identity) card. وربي بطـــاغتك! *warrni biṭaaġatk!* Show me your identity card. بطاقة شخصيـــة *biṭaaġa šaxṣiyya* identity card. بطاقـــة دخـــول *biṭaaġat duxuul* entry card (e.g., for entering a lecture hall, a country, etc.) بطاقـــة معـــايدة *biṭaaġat muᶜaayada* greeting card. بطاقة خروج *biṭaaġat xuruug* exit card. بطاقـــة زيـــارة *biṭaaġat ziyaara* calling, visiting card. 2. ticket. بطاغة الطـــايرة *biṭaaġat ṭ-ṭaayra* the plane ticket.

ب ط گ *bṭg*

بطاقة *biṭaaga* (see بطاغة *biṭaaġa*).

ب ط ل ١ *bṭl*

بطل *biṭal* (يبطل *yabṭul*) to be nullified, void. إذا دخت جيقارة وأنت صايم بطـــل صومـــك *'iða duxt jiigaara w-inta ṣaayim biṭal ṣoomak.* If you smoke a cigarette while you are fasting, your fast becomes nullified. (prov.) لا حصل الماي بطل العـــافور *la ḥaṣal l-maay biṭal l-ᶜaafuur* lit., "If water can be gotten (or within reach) ablution is nullified."

بطالـــة *baṭaala* 1. idleness. 2. unemployment.

بطال *baṭṭaal* p. *-iin* 1. s.o. or s.th. bad (derog.) ما عليك منه. هذا رجال بطال *ma ᶜleek minna. haaða rayyaal baṭṭaal.* You have nothing to do with him. He is a bad man. 2. unemployed. ما فيه بطالين في الإمـــارات *ma fii baṭṭaaliin fi l-'imaaraat.* There are no unemployed people in the Emirates.

بـــاطل *baaṭil* unfounded, false. حجتك هذي باطلـــة *ḥijjatk haaði baaṭla.* This excuse of yours is groundless.

ب ط ل ٢ *bṭl*

بطـــل *baṭṭal* II to open (e.g., a door, a bottle, a can, etc.). بطل الدريشة. الهوا حـــار *baṭṭil d-diriiša. l-hawa ḥaarr.* Open the window! The weather is hot.

تبطـــل *tbaṭṭal* V to be opened, can be opened. هذا القوطي مـــا يتبطـــل *haaða l-guuṭi ma yitbaṭṭal.* This can cannot be opened.

ب ط ل ٣ *bṭl*

بطـــل *baṭṭal* II to stop, leave off. هذي عادة شينة. بطلـــها! *haaði ᶜaada šeena. baṭṭilha!* This is a bad habit. Stop it!

ب ط ل ٤ *bṭl*

بطـــل *baṭal* p. ابطال *bṭaal* 1. hero. من

هو البطل في هذا الفلم؟ *man huwa l-baṭal fi haaða l-filim?* Who is the hero in this film? 2. champion. بطل الكرة *baṭal l-kuura* the soccer champ. بطل السباحة *baṭal s-sibaaḥa* the swimming champ.

بطولة *buṭuula* 1. heroism, bravery, 2. championship

ب ط ل ٥ *bṭl*

بطل *boṭil* p. بطالة *bṭaala* bottle. كنت ظميان وشربت بطل ماي *čint ðamyaan w-šribt boṭil maay.* I was thirsty and I drank a bottle of water.

ب ط ن ١ *bṭn*

بطن *baṭṭan* II (with بـ *b-*) to line (a garment) with s.th. البزاز بطن الكوت بحرير *l-bazzaaz baṭṭan l-kuut b-ḥariir.* The tailor lined the jacket with silk. الحرمة بطنت برقعها بخلق أسود *l-ḥurma baṭṭanat birgiᶜha b-xalag 'aswad.* The woman covered the inside of her veil with black cloth.

بطن *baṭin* p. بطون *bṭuun* (كرش *karš* is more common. See under **ك ر ش** *krš*) 1. belly, stomach. 2. pregnancy, delivery. ثاني بطن الحرمة جابت ولد *θaani baṭin l-ḥurma yaabat walad.* On her second pregnancy the woman had a baby boy. القطوة جابت بطنين *l-gaṭwa yaabat baṭneen.* The cat had two pregnancies.

بطانة *bṭaana* lining (of a garment).

ب ط ن ٢ *bṭn*

بطن *baṭin* p. بطون *bṭuun* clan, kinsfolk. بطني منصوري *baṭni manṣuuri.* Mansouri is my clan.

ب ط ن ٣ *bṭn*

بطين *baṭiin* Bateen (name given to communities, sections or quarters in the U.A.E., e.g., there is ضاحية البطين *ðaaḥiyat l-baṭiin* in Abu Dhabi, حي البطين *ḥayy l-baṭiin* in Dubai, etc.).

ب ط ي ١ *bṭy*

أبطى *'abṭa* (يبطي *yibṭi*) 1. to be slow, take a long time. عادته يبطي في شرب القهوة *ᶜaadta yibṭi fi šurb l-gahwa.* He is accustomed to drinking coffee slowly. راح وأبطى *raaḥ w-'abṭa.* He went and took a long time 2. to be late, come late. ليش أبطيت هالقد؟ *leeš 'abṭeet ha-l-gadd?* Why did you come this late? 3. to slow down s.o., delay. بغيت أجي مبكر بس هو اللي أبطاني *baġeet 'ayi mbaččir bass huw alli 'abṭaani.* I wanted to come early, but it was he who slowed me down.

بطي *baṭi* p. *-yiin* slow. بطي في شغله *baṭi fi šuġla.* He is slow in his work. فيتر بطي *feetir baṭi* slow pipe fitter.

ب ط ي ٢ *bṭy*

بطي *buṭi* Buti (male's first name, common in the U.A.E.).

ب ظ ع *bðᶜ*

بضاعة *biðaaᶜa* p. بضايع *biðaayiᶜ* goods, merchandise, commodities.

ب ع ب ص *bᶜbṣ*

بعبوص *buᶜbuuṣ* p. بعابيص *biᶜaabiiṣ* 1. the middle finger. 2. coward. هو قاعد هناك مثل البعبوص *huwa gaaᶜid hnaak miθl l-buᶜbuuṣ.* He is sitting there like a coward.

بعبصة *baᶜbaṣa* (v.n.) 1. act of moving

the middle finger. 2. cowardice.

ب ع ث *bcθ*

بعث *bacaθ (يبعث yibcaθ)* to resurrect s.o. (from death). الله يبعث الناس من القبور يوم القيامة *'aḷḷaah yibcaθ n-naas min li-gbuur yoom li-gyaama.* God resurrects people from their graves on the Day of Resurrection.

بعث *bacθ* (v.n. from بعث *bacaθ*) resurrection. حزب البعث *ḥizb l-bacθ* the Ba'ath Party, Renaissance Party.

بعثي *bacθi* p. *-yyiin* 1. of or pertaining to the Ba'ath Party. 2. member of the Ba'ath Party.

بعثة *bicθa* p. *-aat* 1. mission, delegation. بعثة دبلوماسية *bicθa diblomaasiyya* diplomatic mission. 2. (student) scholarship. خلص المدرسة الثانوية وودوه بعثة *xallaṣ l-madrasa θ-θaanawiyya w-waddoo bicθa.* He finished secondary school and they sent him on a scholarship.

البعثات *l-bicθaat* the (student) scholarship section.

مبعوث *mabcuuθ* (p.p. from بعث *bacaθ*) p. *-iin* 1. dispatched, delegated. 2. emissary, delegate. مبعوث الحاكم *mabcuuθ l-ḥaakim* the ruler's emissary.

ب ع د *bcd*

بعد *baccad* II (with عن *can*) 1. to go far away from. ضلينا الطريق وبعدنا عن المدينة *ḍalleena ṭ-ṭariig w-baccadna can l-madiina.* We lost our way and went far away from the city. 2. to send s.o. or s.th. away. بعد الشر عنك! *baccid š-šarr cannak!* Move away from evil! (lit., "Send evil away from you!")

أبعد *'abcad* IV to deport s.o. الحكومة أبعدت الأجانب *li-ḥkuuma 'abcadat l-'ayaanib.* The government deported the foreigners.

ابتعد *bticad* VIII (with عن *can*) 1. to move, go away from. ابتعد عن الشر! *btacid can š-šarr!* Move away from evil (or harm's way)! 2. to avoid. ذوله بطالين. ابتعد عنهم! *ðoola baṭṭaaliin. btacid canhum!* Those people are bad. Avoid them!

استبعد *stabcad* X to find or consider s.th. remote, unlikely; to doubt. سمعت هذا الخبر لكن استبعدته *samact haaða l-xabar laakin stabcadta.* I had heard this news item, but I found it unlikely. أستبعد هذا الشي من الوجود *'astabcid haaða š-šayy min l-wijuud.* I doubt that this thing ever existed.

بعد *bacd* (prep.) 1. after (عقب *cugub* is more common. See under **ع ق ب** *cgb*). شفته بعد الظهر *čifta bacd ḍ-ḍuhur.* I saw him in the afternoon. بعد الصلاة *bacd ṣ-ṣalaa* after prayer. تعال بعد شوية! *tacaal bacd šwayya!* Come in a little while! 2. next to. الدايرة بعد شيشة البانزين *d-daayra bacd šiišt l-baanziin.* The department is next to the gas station.

بعد *bacad* 1. too, also. خذ هذا وذاك بعد! *xið haaða w-ðaak bacad!* Take this and that one too. آنا جيت بعد *'aana yiit bacad.* I came also. 2. still, yet. وصلنا البيت لو بعد؟ *wiṣalna l-beet lo bacad?* Have we reached the house or not yet? هم هناك بعد *humma hnaak bacad.* They are still there. بعد ما

سرت؟ *ba^c^ad ma sirt?* Haven't you left yet? 3. more. أريد بعد *'ariid ba^c^ad.* I want more. شتبي بعد؟ *š-tabi ba^c^ad?* What else do you want?

بعدما *ba^c^ad-ma* (conj.) after. بعدما وصلنا تريقنا *ba^c^ad-ma waṣalna trayyagna.* After we arrived, we had breakfast.

بعد *bi^c^id, bi^c^de* (v.n.) 1. farness. البعد عن الأهل صعب *l-bi-^c^d ^c^an l-'ahal ṣa^c^b.* Being far away from one's family is difficult. 2. (only بعد *bi^c^d*) distance. البعد من هني إلى دبي مية كيلو *l-bi^c^d min hini 'ila dbayy miyat keelo.* The distance from here to Dubai is a hundred kilometers.

بعيد *ba^c^iid* p. *-iin* far, distant. المدرسة بعيدة *l-madrasa ba^c^iida.* The school is far away. بعيد النظر *ba^c^iid n-naðar* farsighted, farseeing. موب بعيد يوصل اليوم *muub ba^c^iid yooṣal l-yoom.* It's not unlikely that he will arrive today. من بعيد *min ba^c^iid* from a distance. (prov.) جارك القريب ولا أخوك البعيد *yaarak l-gariib wa la 'axuuk l-ba^c^iid.* Out of sight out of mind. (lit., "Your close neighbor and not your distant brother.") بعدين *ba^c^deen* later on, afterwards. وصلت المطار وبعدين خذيت تكسي *wiṣilt l-maṭaar w-ba^c^deen xaðeet taksi.* I arrived at the airport and, later on, I took a taxi. رحنا السينما بعدين *riḥna s-siinama ba^c^deen.* We went to the cinema afterwards. أشوفك بعدين *'ačuufak ba^c^deen.* I will see you later on. وبعدين وياك؟ صك حلجك! *w-ba^c^deen wiyyaak? ṣikk ḥaljak!* What's next from you? Shut up!

إبعاد *ib^c^aad* (v.n. from أبعد *'ab^c^d*) deportation. إبعاد المجرمين *'ib^c^aad l-mujrimiin* the deportation of criminals.

مبعد *mub^c^ad* p. *-iin* deportee.

مستبعد *mistab^c^ad* (p.p. from استبعد *stab^c^ad*) improbable, unlikely. خبر مستبعد *xabar mistab^c^ad* unlikely news item.

ب ع ر *b^c^r*

بعر *ba^c^ar* (coll.) droppings, dung (of animals). s. بعرة *b^c^ara.*

بعير *bi^c^iir* p. بعارين *ba^c^aariin* camel. (prov.) البعير لو يطالع حدبته انكسرت رقبته *l-bi^c^iir lo yṭaali^c^ ḥidibta nkisrat rgubta.* (lit., "If a camel looks at its hump, his neck will be broken.") describes s.o. who does not see his own faults but sees the faults of others.

بعرور *ba^c^ruur* (coll.) dung, droppings of animals, less common than بعر *ba^c^ar.*

ب ع ظ *b^c^ð*

بعض *ba^c^ð* 1. some of, a few of. بعض الناس *ba^c^ð n-naas* some (of the) people. بعض الدهن *ba^c^ð d-dihin* some (of the) shortening. بعض الشي *ba^c^ð š-šayy* a little bit, something. يقرا ويكتب بعض الشي *yigra w-yiktib ba^c^ð š-šayy.* He reads and writes a little bit. 2. (as n. with preceding v.) one another; each other. ساعدوا بعض *saa^c^daw ba^c^ð.* They helped each other. (also) بعضهم بعض *ba^c^ðahum ba^c^að.* with/amongst each other. هاوشوا بعضهم بعض *haawšaw ba^c^ðahum ba^c^að.* They quarreled with each other. وياه بعض *wiyya ba^c^að.*

together, all together. درسنا وياه بعض *dirasna wiyya baᶜaḏ̣.* We studied together. بعض الأوقات *baᶜḏ̣ l-'awgaat* sometimes.

ب ع و ظ *bᶜwḏ̣*

بعوض *baᶜuuḏ̣* (coll.) mosquitoes, gnats. s. *-a.*

ب غ د د *bġdd*

بغداد *baġdaad* Baghdad (capital of Iraq).

بغدادي *baġdaadi* p. *-yya, -yyiin* 1. native of Baghdad 2. characteristic of Baghdad.

ب غ ظ *bġḏ̣*

بغض *baġaḏ̣ (يبغض yibġaḏ̣)* to hate, detest s.o. ليش تبغض ابن عمك؟ *leeš tibġaḏ̣ 'ibin ᶜammak?* Why do you hate your cousin?

انبغض *nbiġaḏ̣* VII to be hated. انبغض من ابن عمه *nbaġaḏ̣ min 'ibin ᶜamma.* He was hated by his cousin.

بغض *buġḏ̣* (v.n.) hatred.

مبغوض *mabġuuḏ̣* (p.p.) p. *-iin* hated, detested.

ب غ ل ١ *bġl*

بغل *baġal* p. بغال *bġaal* mule. f. بغلة *bġala.*

ب غ ل ٢ *bġl*

بغلة *bġala* p. *-aat* kind of big sailboat used for long trips.

ب غ م *bġm*

بغم *biġam* (coll.) gold necklaces. s. بغمة *bġuma*

بغام *baġġaam* p. *-iin* ingenuous person.

ب غ ي *bġy*

بغى *baġa (يبي yabi,* يبغي *yabġi,* يبغى *yibġa)* 1. to want, desire, wish, like to do s.th. بغى يروح ويانا *baġa yruuḥ wiyyaana.* He wanted to go with us. بغى يجي يدرس *baġa yaji yadris.* He wanted to come to study. هو يبغيك *huwa yabġiik.* He wants you. (prov.) بغى يكحلها عماها *baġa ykaḥḥilha ᶜmaaha.* He wanted to improve things, but he made them worse. (lit. "He wanted to put kohl in her eyes, (but) he blinded her.") بغيناها طرب صارت نشب *baġeenaaha ṭarab ṣaarat nišab.* prov. with a similar meaning. (prov.) اللي يبغى الصلاة ما تفوتها *illi yibġa ṣ-ṣalaa ma tifuuta.* Where there is a will there is a way. (lit., "He who wants prayer, won't be late for it.") 2. to need, require. المجلس يبغاله كنبات وزولية *l-maylis yibġaala kanabaat w-zuuliyya.* The living room needs sofas and a carpet.

مبغاي *mabġaay* (v.n. from بغى *baġa*) aim, purpose.

ب ف ت *bft*

بفت *baft* (coll.) calico, cotton cloth. s. *-a.*

ب گ ر *bgr*

بقر *bagar* (coll.) cows. s. بقرة *bgara.* لحم بقر *laḥam bagar* beef. بقرات المناخ *bgarat l-manaax* dolphin. (prov.) لو حجت البقر على قرونها *lo ḥajjat l-bagar ᶜala gruunha.* (lit., "If cows go on pilgrimage on their horns.") It is an impossible, absurd thing.

ب گ ش bgš

بقش *baggaš* II to wrap s.th. in a cloth bundle. بقش كل قشاره وسار *baggaš kill gšaara w-saar.* He wrapped all his personal effects and left.

بقشة *bugša* p. بقش *bugaš* 1. cloth bundle. حطوا المهر في بقشة وعطوها حق أبو العروس *ḥaṭṭaw l-mahar fi bugša w-ᶜaṭooha ḥagg 'ubu l-ᶜaruus.* They put the dowry in a bundle and gave it to the bride's father. 2. envelope حط الخط في بقشة وطرشه *ḥuṭṭ l-xaṭṭ fi bugša w-ṭarrša.* Put the letter in an envelope and send it.

ب گ گ bgg

بق *bagg* (coll.) bugs, gnats. s. *-a.* فيه بق واجد في الصيف *fii bagg waayid fi ṣ-ṣeef.* There are many bugs in the summer. شجرة البق *šyarat l-bagg* the elm tree.

ب گ گ ر bggr

بقارة *baggaara* p. *-aat* sailing ship with oars (tonnage: 10-30).

ب گ ل bgl

بقل *bagil* (coll.) greens, herbaceous plants. s. بقلة *bgala.*

بقال *baggaal* p. *-iin* greengrocer.

بقالة *baggaala* p. *-aat* grocery store.

ب گ ي bgy

بقي *bigi,* بقى *baga* (يبقى *yibga*) 1. to stay, remain. بقي هني يومين *bigi hni yoomeen.* He stayed here two days. بقي عندنا شهر *bigi ᶜindana šahar.* He stayed with us for a month. بقي على *bigi ᶜala* to have, e.g., time left. بقي علي سنتين *bigi ᶜalayy santeen* I have two more years left. بقي عليك امية درهم *bigi ᶜaleek 'imyat dirhim.* You still owe one hundred dirhams. 2. (with foll. imperf.) to continue, go on doing s.th. بقيت أشتغل وياهم *bigiit 'aštaġil wiyyaahum.* I continued to work with them.

بقى *bagga* II to make or cause s.o. or s.th. to stay, remain. بقاني عنده *baggaani ᶜinda.* He made me stay at his place. زخوه على الحدود وبقوه هناك *zaxxoo ᶜala l-ḥuduud w-baggoo hnaak.* They arrested him at the border and detained him there. لا تبقي شي! *la tbaggi šayy!* Don't leave anything behind! بقيته يترجى أخوه *baggeeta yitrayya 'uxuu.* I kept him waiting for his brother.

تبقى *tbagga* V to be left. كم يتبقى من الوقت؟ *čam yitbagga min-il-wagt?* How much time is left? تبقى علي ألف دينار *tbagga ᶜalayy 'alf diinaar.* I still owe 1,000 dinars.

استبقى *stabga* X to keep for oneself. استبقى الزين *stabga z-zeen.* He left the good ones for himself.

بقاء *bagaa', baqaa'* (v.n. from بقي *bigi*) (var. بغا *baġaa*) immortality, eternity. البقاء لله وحده *l-bagaa' li-ḷḷaah waḥdah.* Only God is eternal.

بقية *bagiyya* p. بقايا *bagaaya* remainder, rest. وين بقية الفلوس؟ *ween bagiyyat li-fluus?* Where is the rest of the money? تحصل بقايا خمام جدام البناية *thaṣṣil bagaaya xmaam jiddaam li-bnaaya.* You will find remains of garbage in front of the building.

باقي *baagi* (act. part.) (var. باجي *baaji*)

p. *-yiin.* 1. left over, remaining. عندنا حليب باقي من أمس *ᶜindana ḥaliib baagi min 'ams.* We have milk left over from yesterday. الباقي لك بخشيش *l-baagi l-ak baxšiiš.* The remainder (i.e., the change) is a tip for you. باقي عليك امية درهم *baagi ᶜaleek 'imyat dirhim.* You still owe one hundred dirhams. 2. staying, remaining. آنا باقي هني الليلة *'aana baagi hni l-leela.* I am staying overnight here. 3. immortal, eternal. الحي الباقي هو الله *l-ḥayy l-baagi huwa ḷḷaah.* The Eternal Being is God.

ب ك ت ي ر ي ا *bktyryaa*

بكتيريا *baktiirya* bacteria.

ب ك ر *bkr*

بكر *bakkar* II (var., more common *baččar*). See under **ب چ ر** *bčr.*

ابتكر *btikar* VIII to invent. ابتكر شي جديد *btikar šayy yidiiid.* He invented something new.

بكر *bikir* (var., more common *bičir*). See under **ب چ ر** *bčr.*

بكرة *bakra* p. *-aat* 1. spool, reel. 2. pulley. 3. (p. بكار *bkaar*) virgin nanny goat. 4. (only in عن بكرة أبيهم *ᶜan bakrat 'abiihim*) all of them (without exception).

بكرة *bukra* (var., more common باكر *baačir*). See under **ب چ ر** *bčr.*

ب ك ل *bkl*

بكلة *bukla* p. بكل *bukal* (more common قضلة *gaḍla.* See under **ق ض ل** *gḍl*).

ب ك م *bkm*

بكم *bakum* (var. *bakam*) p. بكمين *bukmiin* dumb, unable to talk. عبد بكم *ᶜabd bakum* (an African who speaks broken, incomprehensible Arabic). f. بكمة *bakma.*

ب ل ا *blaa*

بلا *bala* = بدون *b-duun* without. See **ب د ن** *bdn.*

ب ل ا ت ي ن *blaatyn*

بلاتين *blaatiin* (coll.) platinum.

ب ل ب ل *blbl*

بلبول *balbuul* p. بلابيل *bilaabiil* tap, faucet.

ب ل ح *blḥ*

بلح *bilḥ* (coll.) caviar.

ب ل د *bld*

بلد *balad* (m. or f.) p. بلدان *bildaan,* بلادين *balaadiin* country, town, city. من أي بلد أنت؟ *min 'ayy balad inta?* Which country are you from?

بلدي *baladi* 1. local, regional. يح بلدي *yiḥḥ baladi* local watermelons. لباس بلدي *libaas baladi* native dress. 2. municipal. مجلس بلدي *meelis baladi* municipal, town council. المجلس البلدي يوزع تو الأراضي *l-meelis l-baladi yuwazziᶜ to l-'araaḍi.* The town council distributes (pieces of) land.

بلدية *baladiyya* p. *-aat* municipality, municipal council or district, city government. أشتغل قزاز حق البلدية *'aštaġil gazzaaz ḥagg l-baladiyya.* I work as a surveyor for the municipality.

بليد *baliid* p. *-iin* stupid, dull-witted.

بلادة *balaada* (v.n.) stupidity.

أبلد *'ablad* (elat.) more or most stupid.

ب ل س م *blsm*

بلسم *balsam* balsam, balm.

ب ل ش *blš*

بلش *bilaš* (يبلش *yiblaš*) 1. to be or become involved, get mixed up. بلشت ويا جماعة بطالين *bilašt wiyya jamaaᶜa baṭṭaaliin.* I got mixed up with a bad group of people. 2. to get stuck, get a bad deal. بلشت بهالقضية العسيرة *bilašt b-hal-gaðiyya l-ᶜasiira.* I got stuck with this difficult problem. 3. to accuse s.o. falsely. بلشني *bilašni.* He made a false accusation of me.

تبالش *tbaalaš* VI to disagree with each other. تبالشوا على المهر *tbaalšaw ᶜala l-mahar.* They disagreed on the dower.

بلش *balaš* (only Bedouin) syphilis.

بلشة *bilša* (v.n.) entanglement, mess, critical situation. !والله هذي بلشة *walla haaði bilša!* What a mess this is!

بلاش *blaaš* (prob. a corruption of literary بلا شيء *bila šay'* without anything) free of charge. اليح بلاش بلاش اليوم *l-yiḥḥ blašš blaaš l-yoom.* Watermelons are very inexpensive today. (lit., "Watermelons are free of charge today.") كم السمك اليوم؟ الكيلو بخمسة درهم. والله بلاش *čam s-simač l-yoom? l-kiilo b-xamsa dirhim. walla blaaš.* How much is fish today? Five dirhams per kilogram. That's very cheap indeed. ببلاش *b-blaaš* for nothing, gratis.

ب ل ط ١ *blṭ*

بلط *ballaṭ* II to pave s.th. (with tiles). ذالحين يبلطون الحمام *ðalḥiin yballiṭuun l-ḥammaam* Now they are tiling the bathroom.

بلاط *bilaaṭ* (coll.) tiles. s. *-a*.

تبليط *tabliiṭ* (v.n. from بلط *ballaṭ*) paving with tiles.

مبلط *mballiṭ* (act. part.) 1. having paved. آنا مبلط الحمام *'aana mballiṭ l-ḥammaam.* I have tiled the bathroom. 2. one whose profession is to tile s.th., tiler.

مبلط *mballaṭ* (p.p. from بلط *ballaṭ*) tiled, having been tiled.

ب ل ط ٢ *blṭ*

بلطة *balṭa* p. *-aat* axe, hatchet.

ب ل ل ط *bllṭ*

بلاليط *bilaaliiṭ* (coll.) spaghetti or macaroni.

ب ل ع *blᶜ*

بلع *bilaᶜ* (يبلع *yiblaᶜ*) to swallow, gulp down s.th. بلع الأكل *bilaᶜ l-'akil.* He swallowed down the food. بلع ريقه *bilaᶜ riija.* He restrained himself; he had a respite (lit. "He swallowed his saliva.")

بلع *ballaᶜ* II 1. to make s.o. swallow s.th. المرضة بلعتني الحبة *l-mumarriða ballaᶜatni l-ḥabba.* The nurse forced me to swallow the pill.

بالوعة *baaluuᶜa* p. بواليع *buwaaliiᶜ* sewer, drain. ما تحصل بواليع هني لأن ما فيه مطر واجد *ma tḥaṣṣil buwaaliiᶜ hini li'an ma fii muṭar waayid.* You will not find sewers here because it doesn't rain much. انسدت البالوعة *nsaddat l-baaluuᶜa.* The sewer got clogged up.

مسلك البواليع *msallik l-buwaaliiᶜ* the one whose profession is to unclog sewers.

ب ل ع م *blᶜm*

بلعوم *balᶜuum* p. بلاعيم *bilaᶜiim* throat, pharynx.

ب ل ع س *blᶜs*

بلعيس *balᶜiis* (corruption of أبا العيس *'aba l-ᶜiis*) fox.

ب ل غ *blġ*

بلغ *bilaġ* (يبلغ *yiblaġ*) 1. to reach, get to. الشلاخ بلغ حده. ما أقدر أتحمل أكثر *š-šlaax bilaġ ḥadda. ma 'agdar 'atḥammal 'akθar.* Telling lies has reached its limit. I cannot take any more. 2. to reach puberty. بلغ سن الرشد *bilaġ sinn r-rušd.* He attained puberty, he came of age. يزوجونه لين يبلغ *yzawwjuuna leen yiblaġ.* They will get him married when he reaches puberty.

بلغ *ballaġ* II 1. to convey, transmit, report. بلغنا السلام *ballaġna s-salaam.* He conveyed the greeting to us. بلغه تحياتي *ballġa taḥiyyaati.* Send him my regards! 2. notify. بلغوه إنهم رايحين يفنشونه *ballaġoo 'inhum raayḥiin yfannšuuna.* They notified him that they were going to lay him off.

بالغ *baalaġ* III to exaggerate. يبالغ لين يتحكى *ybaaliġ leen yithačča.* He exaggerates when he talks.

تبلغ *tballaġ* V to be notified. تبلغ بقرار المحكمة *tballaġ b-ġaraar l-maḥkama.* He was notified of the decision of the court.

بلاغ *balaaġ* p. *-aat* communiqué, bulletin. بلاغ عسكري *balaaġ ᶜaskari* military communiqué.

بلوغ *buluuġ* (v.n. from بلغ *bilaġ*) puberty, sexual activity.

مبلغ *mablaġ* p. مبالغ *mabaaliġ* amount, sum of money. دفع مبلغ خمسين درهم *difaᶜ mablaġ xamsiin dirhim.* He paid the sum of fifty dirhams. البيت يكلف مبلغ كبير *l-beet ykallif mablaġ čibiir.* A house costs lots of money.

بالغ *baaliġ* p. *-iin* 1. having reached puberty. 2. adult, mature.

مبلغ *mballiġ* p. *-iin* 1. (court) messenger. 2. informer.

ب ل ك و ن *blkwn*

بلكون *balkoon* p. *-aat* balcony. أبغى شقة ويا بلكون *'abġa šigga wiyya balkoon.* I want an apartment with a balcony.

ب ل ل ١ *bll*

بلل *ballal* II to wet, moisten. المطر بلل الشنطة *l-muṭar ballal -š-šanṭa.* The rain got the suitcase wet.

تبلل *tballal* V to get wet, be moistened. هدومي تبللت *hduumi tballalat.* My clothes got wet. الشنطة تبللت من المطر *š-šanṭa tballalat min l-muṭar.* The suitcase got wet from the rain.

بل *ball* (v.n.) moistening, wetting.

بلة *balla* (n. of instance) moisture, humidity. زاد الطين بلة *zaad ṭ-ṭiin balla.* He made things worse. (lit. "He made mud wetter.")

ب ل ل٢ *bll*

بـــل *bill* (var., less common إبل *'ibil*) camels. s. بعير *bi^{c}iir*. See ب ع ر *b^{c}r*.

ب ل م١ *blm*

بلم *balam* p. بلام *blaam* sailing boat.

ب ل م٢ *blm*

بلـــم *ballam* II to be silent, hold one's tongue. لين سمع الخـــبر بلـــم *leen sima^c l-xabar ballam.* When he heard the news, he held his tongue.

مبلـــم *mballim* (act. part. from بلـــم *ballam*) p. *-iin.* silent, having kept silent.

ب ل ن ت ي *blnty*

بلنتي *balanti* penalty quick in soccer.

ب ل ه *blh*

بلـــه *balah* = بلاهة *balaaha* stupidity, foolishness.

أبلـــه *'ablah* p. بلهين *balhiin* stupid, dull-witted. f. بلهى *balha.*

ب ل و See under ب ل ي *bly.*

ب ل و ز *blwz*

بلـــوز *bluuz* = بلوســـة *bluusa* p. *-aat* blouse.

ب ل و ش *blwš*

بلـــوش *bluuš* (coll.) Baluchis (people originally from southwest Pakistan). s. *-i.* البلوش يشتغلون حمالين والا خمـــامين *li-bluuš yištaġluun ḥammaaliin walla xammaamiin.* Baluchis work as porters or garbage collectors.

ب ل ي١ *bly*

بلـــى *bala (*يبلى *yibla)* (with بـــ *b-*) to afflict, torment s.o. with s.th. الله بلاه بهالمرض *'aḷḷa balaa b-hal-marađ̣.* God afflicted him with this disease. الله يبلاك! *'aḷḷa yiblaak!* God's affliction be upon you! العيال بلوني بطلباقم *li-^{c}yaal balooni b-ṭalabaattum.* The kids bothered me a lot with their demands.

انبلى *nbila* VII = VIII ابتلى *btila* (*btila* is more common) 1. (with بـــ *b-*) to be afflicted by s.o. or s.th. انبليت بهالمرض *nbileet b-ha l-marađ̣* I was afflicted by this disease. 2. to get stuck by s.th. شريت هالسيارة وانبليـــت بهـــا *šareet ha s-sayyaara w-nbileet biiha.* I bought this car and got stuck with it. ابتليت بالفقر *btileet b-l-fagir.* I suffered from poverty. 3. to get into trouble. جاوا الشرطـــة. زخونـــا وابتلينـــا *yaw š-širṭa. zaxxoona w-btileena.* The police came. They arrested us and we got into trouble.

بـــلا *bala* (v.n. from بلـــى *bala*) 1. affliction, misfortune. عمري ما شفت مثـــل هـــا البـــلا *^{c}umri ma čift miθil ha l-bala.* I have never seen an affliction like this one. 2. trial, test (of courage, patience, etc.). هذا بلا مـــن الله *haađa bala min aḷḷa.* This is a trial ordained by God.

بلوى *balwa* p. بلاوى *bilaawi* (var. بلية *baliyya* p. بلاوى *bilaawi*) calamity, catastrophe. (prov.) بلاوى تـــابي صـــبر *bilaawi tabi ṣabir.* (lit. "Calamities need patience.") بليتن بلوى *baliyyatin balwa* very smart and cunning person.

مبالاة *mubaalaa* regard, attention. بدون مبـــالاة *b-duun mubaalaa* without a regard, carelessly.

ب ل ي[٢] *bly*

بلي *bali* yes, right (Bahraini and Kuwaiti), rarely used in the Emirates (var. بلى *bala* or إن بلى *mbala*).

ب ل ي ر د *blyrd*

بلياردو *bilyaardo* billiards.

ب ل ي ن *blyn*

بليون *bilyoon* p. بلايين *bilaayiin* billion. بليون درهم *balyoon dirhim* a billion dirhams.

ب ل ي ي *blyy*

بلاي *blayya* (prep.) without. قهوة بلاي حليب *gahwa blayya ḥaliib* coffee without milk.

ب م ب ي *bmby*

بمبي *bambi* Bombay.

ب ن ب س *bnbs*

بنباسي *banbaasi* p. بنابيس *banaabiis* black servant.

ب ن ت *bnt*

بنت *bint* p. بنات *banaat* 1. girl. عرس على بنت حلال *ᶜarras ᶜala bint ḥalaal.* He got married to a decent girl. البنت الكبيرة *l-bint li-čbiira* the oldest girl. بنت جميلة *bint yamiila* beautiful girl. 2. daughter. عنده بنتين *ᶜinda binteen.* He has two daughters. بنتي *binti* my daughter. بنت عمي *bint ᶜammi* my cousin (paternal uncle's daughter). بنت خالي *bint xaali* my cousin (maternal uncle's daughter). بنت أخوي *bint 'uxuuy* my niece (brother's daughter). بنت أختي *bint uxti* my niece (sister's daughter). بنت حرام *bint ḥaraam* illegitimate daughter. 3. member of. بنت عرب *bint ᶜarab* Arab woman or girl. بنت عشرين سنة *bint ᶜišriin sana* girl of twenty years.

ب ن ج *bnj*

بنج *bannaj* II to anesthetize. بنجني الدختر قبل العملية *bannajni d-daxtar gabl l-ᶜamaliyya.* The doctor anesthetized me before the operation.

بنج *binj* anesthetic. فيه عمليات بسيطة ما تحتاج بنج *fii ᶜamaliyyaat basiiṭa ma tiḥtaay banj.* There are simple operations that do not need anesthetic.

ب ن ج ر *bnjr*

بنجري *banjari* p. بناجر *banaajir* gold bracelet.

ب ن د *bnd*

بند *bannad* II 1. to shut, close. بند الباب *bannad l-baab.* He shut the door. باكر الجمعة. البنك يبند *baačir l-yimᶜa. l-bank ybannid.* Tomorrow is Friday. The bank will be closed. 2. to come to an end. الشغل بند *š-šuġul bannad.* Work finished. 3. to stop working, be idle. متى تبند اليوم؟ *mita tbannid l-yoom?* When do you stop working today? 3. to turn off. بند الماكينة! *bannid l-maakiina!* Turn off the engine. بند الليتات *bannad l-leetaat.* He turned the lights off.

بند *band* end, cessation of work. البند الساعة خمس *l-band s-saaᶜa xams.* Work finishes at five o'clock.

مبند *mbannid* (act. part.) p. *-iin* 1. closed. البنك مبند *l-bank mbannid.* The bank is closed. 2. not at work. الكولية مبندين اليوم *l-kuuliyya mbanndiin l-yoom.* The coolies are not at work today.

مبند *mbannad* (p.p.) p. *-iin* closed, shut. البيبان مبندين *l-biibaan mbannadiin.* The doors are closed.

ب ن د ر *bndr*

بندر *bandar* p. بنادر *banaadir* seaport. بندر دبي *bandar dbayy* The Dubai seaport. بندر عباس *bandar ᶜabbaas* Bandar Abbas (seaport in S. Iran).

ب ن د م *bndm*

بنادم *bnaadam* p. بناديم *bnaadmiin* (corruption of بني آدم *bani 'aadam*) human being, man. See **ء د م** *'dm.*

ب ن د ي ر *bndyr*

بنديرة *bindeera* p. *-aat,* بنادر *binaadir* banner, flag.

ب ن د گ *bndg*

بندق *bundug* (coll.) hazelnut. s. *-a.*

بندقية *bindigiyya* p. بندق *bindig* rifle, gun, shotgun.

ب ن د ل *bndl*

بندلة *bandala* p. بنادل *binaadil, -aat* bundle, parcel. بندلة قواطي جقاير *bandalat guwaaṭi jigaayir* bundle of cigarette packs.

ب ن س ل *bnsl*

بنسل *bensil* p. بناسل *binaasil* pencil.

ب ن ط ل *bnṭl*

بنطلون *banṭaloon* p. بناطلين *binaaṭliin* (pair of) pants or trousers. اشتريت أربعة بناطلين *štireet 'arbaᶜ binaaṭliin.* I bought four pairs of pants. هذا البنطلون غالي *haaða l-banṭaloon ġaali.* This pair of pants is expensive.

ب ن ك *bnk*

بنك *bank* p. بنوك *bnuuk* bank. هذا البنك يعطي فايدة خمسة في المية *haaða l-bank yᶜaṭi faayda xamsa fi l-miya.* This bank gives a five percent interest. بنك أبو ظبي الوطني *bank 'abu ḍabi l-waṭani* the National Bank of Abu Dhabi. البنك العربي *l-bank l-ᶜarabi* the Arab Bank. بنك عمان *bank ᶜumaan* the Bank of Oman. بنك قطر الوطني *bank giṭar l-waṭani* the National Bank of Qatar. البنك الأمريكي *l-bank l-'amriiki* the American bank. بنك الدم *bank d-damm* the blood bank. البنك الدولي *l-bank d-dawli* the World Bank.

ب ن ك ة *bnka*

بنكة *banka* p. *-aat* fan (orig. a canvas covered frame suspended from the ceiling). الهوا حار ورطب في القيظ والبنكة ما تفيد *l-hawa ḥaarr w-raṭib fi l-geeḍ w-l-banka ma tfiid.* The weather is hot and humid in the summer. A fan is not useful.

ب ن ن *bnn*

بن *bunn* (coll.) coffee beans, ground coffee beans.

بني *bunni* p. *-yyiin* brown, coffee colored. بنطلين بني *banṭaliin bunni* brown pants.

ب ن و ر *bnwr*

بنور *bannuur* (coll.) (pieces of) crystal. s. *-a* p. *-aat* piece of crystal (cf. literary بلور *balluur).*

ب ن ي ١ *bny*

بنى *bina* (يبني *yibni)* to build, construct. بنى له بيت على السيف *binaa-la beet*

^{c}ala s-siif. He built himself a house on the beach. رايح أبـني عمـارة وأجرهـا *raayiḥ 'abni ^{c}maara w-'ajjirha.* I am going to build a building and rent it out. بنيـت عمـارة في شـارع الشيـخ حمـدان *bineet ^{c}maara fi šaari^{c} š-šeex ḥamdaan.* I built a building on Shaikh Hamdan Street.

بنـا *bina* (v.n.) act of building, construction. تحـصل بنـا في كـل مكـان *tḥaṣṣil bina fi kill mukaan.* You will find construction everywhere. عامل بنا *^{c}aamil bina* construction worker.

انبنـى *nbina* VII to be built. العمارة انبنت *li-^{c}maara nbinat.* The building was built.

بناي *bannaay* p. *-a* mason, builder.

مبـني *mabni* (p.p.) p. *-yyiin* built, constructed. فيه هني بيوت مبنية من حجـر *fii hini byuut mabniyya min ḥiyar.* There are houses built of stone.

ب ن ي ٢ *bny*

تبنـى *tbanna* V 1. to adopt. في الغرب يتبنون العيال. نحن هني عادة ما نتبنـى أحـد *fi l-ġarb yitbannuun li-^{c}yaal. niḥin hini ^{c}aadatan ma nitbanna 'aḥad.* In the West people adopt children; here we do not usually adopt anyone. 2. to adopt, take up the cause of. الشيخ زايد طويل العمر تبنـى مشـروع الزراعـة في العـين *š-šeex zaayid ṭawiil l-^{c}umur tbanna mašruu^{c} z-ziraa^{c}a fi l-^{c}een.* Shaikh Zaayid, may he live long, embraced the agricultural project in the city of Al-Ain.

بنيـة *bnayya* p. *-aat* 1. girl. 2. daughter. 3. unmarried girl. (See also بنت *bint* under ب ن ت *bnt*.).

ب ه ت *bht*

بهـت *bihat* (يبهـت *yibhat*) to astonish, surprise, amaze s.o. هـا الخـبر يبهــت الإنســان *ha l-xabar yibhat l-'insaan.* This news item astonishes people. بهتـني خـبر تسـفير مديـر التلفزيـون *bihatni xabar tasfiir mudiir t-talavizyoon.* I was surprised by the news of the deportation of the T.V. station director.

انبهـت *nbihat* VII to be astonished, amazed. انبهتنا لين سمعنا إن الشرطة زخـوه *nbihatna leen sima^{c}na 'inna š-šurṭa zaxxoo.* We were amazed when we heard that the police had arrested him.

بهتان *buhtaan* untruth, slander.

مبهوت *mabhuut* (p.p. from بهت *bihat*) astonished, surprised. شفيك؟ مبهـوت؟ مـا ترمـس *š-fiik? mabhuut? ma trammis.* What's wrong with you? Are you flabbergasted? You are not talking.

ب ه ج *bhj*

ابتهـج *btihaj* VIII to be delighted, glad. ابتهج لين سمع إنه حصل المقاولـة *btihaj leen sima^{c} 'inna ḥaṣṣal l-muġaawala.* He was delighted when he heard that he was awarded the contract.

بهجـة *bahja* (n. of instance) p. *-aat* joy, delight.

ب ه د ل *bhdl*

بهـدل *bahdal* (يبهـدل *ybahdil*) 1. to ridicule, embarrass s.o. المديـر بهـدل الموظـف لانـه كـان يقـرا جرايد في المكتـب *l-mudiir bahdal l-muwaḏḏaf linna* *čaan yigra jaraayid fi l-maktab.* The director ridiculed the employee because he was reading newspapers in the office. 2. to make a mess of. الهبــوب بهدلــت النــاس *li-hbuub bahdalat n-naas.* The wind made a mess of people.

تبهـدل *tbahdal (*يتبهدل *yitbahdal)* 1. to be ridiculed, embarrassed. 2. to be or become mixed up, get in bad shape. تبهدل لين ابتدا يسكر ويلعب قمـار *tbahdal leen btida yiskar w-yilᶜab gmaar.* He got in bad shape when he began to drink and gamble.

بهدلـة *bahdala* (v.n. of بهدل *bahdal*) 1. insult, abuse. البهدلـة مـا تفيـد ويـاه *l-bahdala ma tfiid wiyyaa.* Insult will not do him any good. 2. mess, disorder. وايش ها العفسة والبهدلـة؟ *weeš ha l-ᶜafsa w-l-bahdala?* What's this mess?

مبهـدل *mbahdil* (act. part.) p. *-iin* having ridiculed, embarrassed s.o. المديـر مبهدلـه *l-mudiir mbahdila.* The director has ridiculed him.

مبهدل *mbahdal* (p.p.) p. *-iin* 1. having been ridiculed. 2. sloppy, miserable.

ب ه ر ١ *bhr*

بهر *bahhar* II to put spices in the food. دايما يبهر الأكل *daayman ybahhir l-'akil.* He always puts spices in the food.

بهار *bhaar* spices الأكل الهندي فيه بهار واجـد *l-'akil l-hindi fii bhaar waayid.* Indian food has a lot of spices.

ب ه ر ٢ *bhr*

بـاهر *baahir* (adj.) splendid, superb. عمل بـاهر *ᶜamal baahir* splendid piece of work. نجـاح بـاهر *najaaḥ baahir* brilliant success.

ب ه ظ *bhđ*

بـاهظ *baahiđ* (adj.) excessive, enormous. تكـاليف باهظـة *tikaaliif baahđa* excessive expenses.

ب ه ل *bhl*

ابتهـل *btihal* VIII to pray humbly to God. ابتهـل إلى الله *btihal 'ila ḷḷaah.* He beseeched God.

ابتهـال *btihaal* (v.n. from ابتهل *btihal*) supplication, prayer to God.

ب ه ل ل *bhll*

بهلـول *bahluul* p. بهـاليل *bihaaliil* buffoon, clown.

ب ه ل و ن *bhlwn*

بهلـوان *bahlawaan* p. *-yya, -aat* acrobat, tightrope walker. رحنا السيرك وحصلنـا بهلوانيـة واجـد *riḥna s-seerk w-ḥaṣṣalna bahlawaaniyya waayid.* We went to the circus and found many acrobats.

بهلوانـي *bahlawaani* (adj.) acrobatic. ألعاب بهلوانيـة *'alᶜaab bahlawaaniyya* acrobatics.

ب ه م *bhm*

بهيمـة *bhiima* p. بهايم *bahaayim* beast, animal.

بهام *bhaam* p. *-aat* thumb. عور بهامه في الشـركة وفنـش *ᶜawwar bhaama fi š-šarika w-fannaš.* He injured his thumb in the company and resigned.

ب ه ن س *bhns*

تبهنس *tbahnas (*يتبهنـس *yitbahnas)* to

buy luxury items. خلنا نسير السوق نتبهنس شوية *xalḷna nsiir s-suug nitbahnas šwayya.* Let's go to the market and buy luxury items.

ب ه ي *bhy*

تباهى *tbaaha* VI (with بـ *b-*) to boast of s.th., be proud of s.th., pride oneself on s.th. دايما يتباهى بأصله وفصله *daayman yitbaaha b-'aṣla w-faṣla.* He always boasts of his origin and lineage.

ب و *bw*

بو *buu* = أبو *'ubu.* See ء ب و *'bw*

ب و ب *bwb*

باب *baab* p. بيبان *biibaan* 1. door. صك الباب! *ṣikk l-baab!* Shut the door! فتح الباب *fitaḥ l-baab.* He opened the door. 2. gate, gateway. باب البحرين *baab l-baḥreen* the Bahrain Gateway. باب المندب *baab l-mandab* the Straits of Bab Al Mandeb (straights between SW Arabia and Africa). 3. class, group, category. عيش أول باب *ᶜeeš 'awwal baab* top quality rice. فتح باب جديد *fitaḥ baab yidiid.* He opened up a new way or possibility. من كل باب *min kill baab* from everywhere. (prov.) الباب اللي يجيك منه ريح سده واستريح *l-baab alli yajiik minna riiḥ sidda w-stariiḥ.* Rid yourself of what is harmful to you. (prov.) باب الفقر ما ينصك *baab l-fagir ma yinṣakk.* What have I or you got to lose? (lit. "The door of a poor man cannot be closed.")

بواب *bawwaab* p. *-iin* doorman, doorkeeper. يشتغل بواب ولا خمام *yištaġil bawwaab walla xammaam.* He works as a doorkeeper or a sweeper.

بوابة *bawwaaba* p. *-aat* gate, doorway. بوابة البيت *bawwaabat l-beet* the house gate.

ب و ب ز *bwbz*

بوبز *boobaz* (يبوبز *yboobiz*) to squat on the ground (with thighs against the stomach and arms enfolding the legs).

مبوبز *mboobiz* (act. part.) p. *-iin* squatting.

ب و ب ل ي ن *bwblyn*

بوبلين *boobliin* poplin.

ب و ب و *bwbw*

بوبو *booboo* water or food (only in baby talk).

ب و ت س *bwts*

بوتاس *buutaas* potash.

ب و ح *bwḥ*

باح *baaḥ* (يبوح *ybuuḥ*) 1. to be revealed, leaked out. السر باح *s-sirr baaḥ.* The secret leaked out. 2. (with بـ *b-*) to reveal. باح لي بسره *baaḥli b-sirra.* He revealed his secret to me.

بوح *booḥ* (v.n.) revealing, disclosure (of a secret) البوح بالسر *l-booḥ b-s-sirr* revealing a secret.

بيحة *beeḥa* p. *-aat* forgiveness. فلان توفى. يطلبك البيحة *flaan tawaffa. yaṭlubk l-beeḥa.* So-and-so passed away; he asks forgiveness (for his debt).

ب و د ر *bwdr*

بودرة *boodra* powder.

ب و ر *bwr*

بـار *baar* (يـبـور *ybuur*) 1. to be unsaleable, be dead stock. البضاعة بارت *l-biðaa*ᶜ*a baarat.* The goods did not sell. 2. to be unable to get a husband. البنت كبرت وبارت *l-bint kburat w-baarat.* The girl became older and didn't get married.

باير *baayir* (act. part.) 1. uncultivated, waste. أراضي بـايرة *'araaði baayra* wasteland. 2. unsold. بضاعة بايرة *biðaa*ᶜ*a baayra* unsold goods.

ب و ر ي *bwry*

بـوري *buuri* p. بـواري *buwaari* 1. trumpet. 2. pipe.

ب و ز *bwz*

بـوز *bawwaz* II to look glum, pout. لين قلت حق بنتي: «مـا تروحـين ويـاي» بـوزت *leen gilt ḥagg binti: "ma truuḥiin wiyyaay," bawwazat.* When I said to my daughter, "You're not going with me," she pouted. كان حمقان، قعد وبـوز *čaan ḥamgaan, ga*ᶜ*ad w-bawwaz.* He was mad; he sat down and was pouted.

بـوز *buuz* p. بـواز *bwaaz* mouth (ثم *θamm* p. ثمـام *θmaam* is more common).

مبوز *mbawwiz* (act. part.) p. *-iin* angry, mad.

ب و س ي ر *bwsyr*

بواسـير *bwaasiir* (or باسـور *baasuur*) piles, hemorrhoids.

ب و ش *bwš*

بـوش *booš* 1. empty tea glasses or coffee cups. شـيل البـوش! *šiil l-booš!* (said to a waiter) Take away the empty cups and glasses! 2. useless, vain. كل جهـدي راح بـوش *kill jihdi raaḥ booš.* All my efforts were useless. 3. loose (automotive). البريكات مال السيارة بـوش. *li-breekaat maal s-sayyaara booš.* The car brakes are loose.

ب و ص ل *bwṣl*

بوصلة *buuṣla* p. *-aat* compass. (ديرة *diira* is more common. See د ي ر *dyr*.).

ب و ع *bw*ᶜ

بـوع *buu*ᶜ p. بواع *bwaa*ᶜ metatarsal bone. (prov.) ما يعرف كوعه مـن بوعـه *ma y*ᶜ*arf kuu*ᶜ*a min buu*ᶜ*a.* He doesn't know his knee from his elbow (i.e., he is a stupid person).

بـاع *baa*ᶜ p. بـواع *bwaa*ᶜ span of the outstretched arms, fathom (six feet approx.) طولهـا خمـس بـواع *ṭuulha xams bwaa*ᶜ*.* It's about thirty feet long.

ب و ف ي ه *bwfy*

بوفيـه *bufee* p. بوفيهـات *bufeehaat* buffet.

ب و ك *bwk*

بـوك *buuk* p. بواك *bwaak* wallet. طلعت فلوس مـن بوكـي *ṭalla*ᶜ*t fluus min buuki.* I took money out of my wallet.

ب و گ *bwg*

بـاق *baag* (يـبـوق *ybuug*) 1. to steal. لا تبـوق! *la tbuug!* Don't steal! بـاقوا الفلوس منـه *baagu li-fluus minna.* They stole the money from him. (prov.) لا تبـوق ولا تخـاف *la tbuug w-la txaaf.* If you don't steal, you won't have to fear anything. 2. to rob. باقوا البنك *baagu l-bank.* They robbed the bank.

انبـاق *nbaag* VII 1. to be stolen. انباقت

الفلوس *nbaagat li-fluus.* The money was stolen. 2. to be robbed. انباق البنك *nbaag l-bank.* The bank was robbed.

بوق *boog* (v.n. from باق *baag*) 1. stealing. البوق يوديك السجن *l-boog ywaddiik s-siyin.* Stealing sends you to jail. 2. robbery.

بوقة *booga* (n. of instance) p. *-aat* a theft, a robbery.

بواق *bawwaag* p. *-iin, bawwaaga* thief, robber. زخوا البواق متلبس بالجريمة *zaxxu l-bawwaag mitlabbis b-l-jariima.* They arrested the thief redhanded.

ب و ل ١ *bwl*

بال *baal (يبول ybuul)* to urinate. لا تبول في الشارع! *la tbuul fi š-šaari*ᶜ*!* Don't urinate in the street! (prov.) ما يبول على جرح *ma ybuul* ᶜ*ala jarḥ.* He is very stingy. (lit., "He doesn't urinate on a wound.")

بول *bool* (v.n.) 1. urinating, urination. يلاقي صعوبة في البول *ylaagi ṣu*ᶜ*uuba fi l-bool.* He finds it difficult to urinate. 2. urine. عنده سكري في البول ᶜ*inda sukkari fi l-bool.* He has sugar diabetes. تسمم في البول *tasammum fi l-bool* uremia.

ب و ل ٢ *bwl*

بال *baal* 1. state of mind. باله مشغول *baala mašġuul.* He is worried. هذي الكلمة راحت من بالي *haaði -č-čalma raaḥat min baali.* I have forgotten this word. هذي القضية على بالي *haaði l-gaðiyya* ᶜ*ala baali.* I am thinking about this problem. خلنا على البال! *xallna* ᶜ*ala l-baal!* Don't forget us. هذي مشكلة موب على البال وموب على الخاطر *haaði muškila muub* ᶜ*ala l-baal wa-muub* ᶜ*ala l-xaaṭir.* This is a problem that is totally unexpected. 2. attention. لا تدير بال! *la ddiir baal!* Don't worry! Never mind. دير بالك من هذا الرجال المحتال! *diir baalak min haaða r-rayyaal l-muḥtaal!* Beware of this deceitful man. حط بالك! *ḥuṭṭ baalak!* Pay attention! بالك بالك! *baalak baalak!* (phrase repeated by porters and donkey drivers in a crowded marketplace to avoid accidents). دير بالك على ساماني! *diir baalak* ᶜ*ala saamaani!* Watch my things!

ب و ل ي س *bwlys*

بوليس *boliis* p. رجال البوليس *rijaal l-boliis* policeman (شرطي *širṭi* is more common. See ش ر ط ي *šrṭy*).

ب و م ١ *bwm*

بوم *buum,* بومة *buuma* p. *-aat* owl.

ب و م ٢ *bwm*

بوم *buum* (no recorded p.) large double-ended ship, usually fully decked, with the rudderhead high above it, used mainly for transporting passengers.

ب ي ب ت ت و *bybttw*

بيبتو *biibatto* p. *-waat* parrot.

ب ي ت *byt*

بات *baat (يبات ybaat)* 1. to stay overnight, spend the night. الخطار باتوا عندنا *l-xuṭṭaar baataw* ᶜ*indana.* The guests spent the night with us. بات عندنا الليلة! *baat* ᶜ*indana l-leela!* Spend the night with us! 2. to sit overnight. إذا بات الأكل ما عليه *'iða baat l-'akil ma ᶜalee.* If the food sits overnight, it is all right.

بيـــت *bayyat* II 1. to put up s.o. for the night. كان الوقت متأخر وبيتناهم عندنـــا *čaan l-wagt mit'axxir w-bayyat-naahum ᶜindana.* It had gotten late and we kept them overnight with us. 2. to keep s.th. overnight. الأكل اللي بيتوه خـــاس *l-'akil illi bayyatuu xaas.* The food which they left overnight went bad.

بيـــت *beet* p. بيوت *byuut* 1. house, home. في البيـــت *fi l-beet* at home. آنا رايح البيـــت *'aana raayiḥ l-beet.* I am going home. (prov.) بيت البايق باقوه *beet l-baayig baagoo* Tit for tat. There will come a day when the oppressor will be oppressed. (lit., "They robbed the house of the burglar.") بيت حجر *beet ḥiyar* stone house. بيت خلا *beet xaḷa* outhouse. 2. family. أهل البيت *'ahl l-beet* the family of Prophet Muhammad (cf. هل البيت *hal l-beet* the house occupants or owners). 3. place. بيـــت أمـــان *beet 'amaan* safe, secure place. بيت المال *beet l-maal* the treasury, the exchequer (Islamic law). بيت الحـــرام *beet l-ḥaraam* the Kaaba (in Mecca, Saudi Arabia). بيت شعـــر *beet šaᶜar* Bedouin tent (made of camel hair). 3. (p. ابيات *byaat*) line of poetry. ابيات من الشعر النبطي *byaat min -š-šiᶜir n-nabaṭi* lines of colloquial, vernacular poetry.

مبيـــت *mabiit* place for staying overnight.

بـــايت *baayit* (act. part. from بات *baat*) 1. staying or having stayed overnight. آنا بايت الليلة هنـــاك *'aana baayit l-leela hnaak.* I am staying overnight there, or I stayed overnight there. 2. stale, old. خبز بايت *xubiz baayit* stale bread.

ب ي ج م *byjm*

بيجامـــا *biijaama* = بجاما *bajaama.* See under ب ج ا م *bjaam.*

ب ي ح *byḥ*

باح *baaḥ.* See under ب و ح *bwḥ.*

ب ي د *byd*

بـــاد *baad* (يبيد *ybiid*) to exterminate, annihilate. يرشون البيت لاجل يبيـــدون الحشـــرات *yruššuun li-byuut lajil ybiiduun l-ḥašaraat.* They sprinkle the houses so as to exterminate insects.

بـــايد *baayid* (act. part.) past, bygone. العهد البايد *l-ᶜahd l-baayid* the former regime.

ب ي د ر *bydr*

بيدر *beedar* p. بيادر *biyaadir* 1. place for threshing corn or wheat. 2. heap, pile. بيـــدر تـــبن *beedar tibin* heap of straw.

بيدار *beedaar* p. *-iyya* farmer, peasant (whose job is to thresh corn or wheat).

ب ي د م *bydm*

بيـــدم *beedam* (coll.) almonds. s. *-a.* شجرة بيدم *šyarat beedam* almond tree.

ب ي ذ ن ج ن *byðnjn*

بيذنجان *beeðinjaan* (coll.) eggplant. s. *-a.* البيذنجان نحن ما نعرفـــه *l-beeðinjaan niḥin ma nᶜarfa.* We do not know what "*beeðinjaan*" is. طال عمرك فيـــه

بيذنجان أسود وبيذنجان حمر *ṭaal ᶜumrak fii beeðinjaan 'aswad w-beeðinjaan ḥamar.* May you live long, there is black eggplant and red eggplant.

ب ي ر ١ *byr*

بير *biir* p. ابيار *byaar,* آبار *'aabar* well. بير ماي *biir maay* water well. آبار بترول *'aabaar batrool* oil wells.

ب ي ر ٢ *byr*

بيرة *biira* beer. ما أشرب بيرة حرام *ma 'ašrab biira ḥaraam.* I do not drink beer. It's unlawful. بوطل بيرة *booṭil biira* beer bottle. bottle, glass of beer. عطني بيرة *ᶜaṭni biira!* Give me a beer!

ب ي ر گ *byrg*

بيرق *beerag* p. بيارق *bayaarig* flag, banner.

ب ي ر و ت *byrwt*

بيروت *beruut* Beirut.

بيروتي *beruuti* p. *-iyya* 1. a Beiruti 2. characteristic of Beirut.

ب ي ز *byz*

بيزة *beeza* p. *-aat* paise (Indian coin = 1/64 of a rupee, was in use until 1957).

بيزات *beezaat* money (فلوس *fluus* is more common). ورني بيزاتك! *warrni beezaatak!* Show me your money! ما عنده بيزات *ma ᶜinda beezaat.* He doesn't have any money.

ب ي ش *byš*

بيش *beeš* = بأيش *b-eeš.* See under **ء ي ش** *'yš.*

ب ي ظ *byḍ*

باض *baaḍ* (يبيض *ybiiḍ)* to lay eggs. دجاجنا كله يبيض *diyaayna killa ybiiḍ.* All of our hens lay eggs. الدجاجة باضت اليوم *d-diyaaya baaḍat l-yoom.* The hen laid today.

بيض *bayyaḍ* II 1. to make white, whitewash. بيضوا الطوفة حول البيت اليوم *bayyaḍu ṭ-ṭoofa ḥool l-beet l-yoom.* They whitewashed the wall around the house today. الكبر يبيض الشعر *l-kibar ybayyiḍ š-šaᶜr.* Old age turns hair white. بيض الله وجهك! *bayyaḍ aḷḷa weehak!* May God make you happy. (lit., "May God whiten your face!") 2. to tinplate. بيضنا الجدورة وكل المواعين *bayyaḍna li-juduura w-kill l-muwaaᶜiin.* We tinplated the cooking pots and all the pots and pans.

ابيض *byaḍḍ* IX to turn white, get white. شعره ابيض *šaᶜra byaḍḍ.* His hair turned white.

بيض *beeḍ* (coll.) eggs. s. *-a.* pl. *-aat* البيض غالي اليوم *l-beeḍ ġaali l-yoom.* Eggs are expensive today. شريت خمس بيضات *šareet xams beeḍaat.* I bought five eggs. كل يوم يتريق بيضتين *kill yoom yitrayyag beeḍteen.* Every day he has two eggs for breakfast. بيضة ديك *beeḍdat diič* (lit., "a rooster's egg.") It happens only once in a lifetime. صفار البيضة *ṣafaar l-beeḍa* the yolk of the egg. عندنا بيض؟ *ᶜindana beeḍ?* Do we have eggs? البيض يبيعونه بالدرزن لو بالكرتونة *l-beeḍ ybiiᶜuuna b-d-darzan lo b-l-kartoona.* They sell eggs by the dozen or by the carton. (carton of eggs = 24 eggs.)

بياض *bayaaḍ* whiteness. بياض البيضة *bayaaḍ l-beeḍa* the white of the eggs. بياض الوجه *bayaaḍ l-weeh* good name, reputation.

بياضة *bayyaaða* p. *-aat* 1. good layer (hen). عندنا خمس بياضات *ᶜindana xams bayyaaðaat.* We have five good laying hens. (2. kind of fish that lays many eggs).

أبيض *'abyað* f. بيضا *beeða* p. بيض *biið* white. أبيض أكثر *'abyað 'akθar* whiter. صحيفته بيضا *ṣaḥiifta beeða.* He has a clean slate. His record is clean. سلاح أبيض *silaaḥ 'abyað* (lit., "white weapon") cold steel (sword, knife, bayonet).

مبيض *mabiið* p. مبايض *mabaayið* ovary.

ب ي ط ر *byṭr*

بيطري *beeṭari* (n.) p. *-iyya, -yyiin* veterinarian. (also more common طبيب بيطري *ṭabiib beeṭari.*).

بيطري *beeṭari* (adj.) veterinary. الطب البيطري *t-ṭibb l-beeṭari* veterinary medicine.

ب ي ع *byᶜ*

باع *baaᶜ*(يبيع *ybiiᶜ*) to sell. باعني سيارته *baaᶜni sayyaarta.* He sold me his car. !لا تبيعني تشلاخ *la tbiiᶜni člaax!* Don't lie to me. (lit., "Don't sell me lies!") فلان داهية. يبيعك ويشتريك *flaan daahya. ybiiᶜk w-yištiriik.* So-and-so is smart. He is capable of manipulating you. (lit. "He can sell you and buy you.") (prov.) باع الكحيلة حق عشا ليلة *baaᶜ li-kḥeela ḥagg ᶜaša leela.* (He is) penny wise and pound foolish. (lit., "He sold the house for one [evening] dinner.")

بيع *bayyaᶜ* II to make s.o. sell s.th. المحكمة بيعتني بيتي *l-maḥkama bayyaᶜtni beeti.* The court forced me to sell my house. راح اشتكى علي وبيعني كل حلالي *raaḥ štika ᶜalayy w-bayyaᶜni kill ḥalaali.* He went and filed suit against me and forced me to sell all my possessions.

بيع *beeᶜ* sale. للبيع *la l-beeᶜ* for sale. بيع بالجملة *beeᶜ bi-l-jumla* wholesale. بيع بالمفرق *beeᶜ b-li-mfarrag* retail. البيع والشرا *l-beeᶜ wa š-šira* buying and selling.

بياع *bayyaaᶜ* p. *-iin* salesman, sales clerk.

ب ي ل *byl*

بيل *beel* p. ابيال *byaal* pickax, pick or shovel (also more common, شيول *šeewil*).

ب ي ل ر *bylr*

بيلر *beelar* p. *-aat* boiler. ماي بيلر *maay beelar* desalinated sea water. ماي الشرب بيلر *maay š-šurb beelar.* Drinking water is boiled (by the boiler) water.

ب ي م *bym*

بيمة *biima* p. إبيم *'ibyam* insurance. شركة البيمة *šarikat l-biima.* The insurance company. !روني بيمة السيارة *rawwni biimat s-sayyaara!* Show me the car insurance! أنت تسوق سيارة لازم يكون عندك بيمة *'inta tsuug sayyaara laazim ykuun ᶜindak biima.* If you drive a car, you have to have insurance. بعض الجماعة يسوقون بدون بيمة *baᶜð l-jamaaᶜa ysuuguun b-duun biima.* Some people drive cars without insurance.

ب ي ن *byn*

بـين *bayyan* II 1. to make s.th. clear, plain. بين لنـا كـل شـي *bayyan lana kill šayy.* He made everything clear to us. 2. to appear, become evident. كان فيه سـحاب بس بعدين بـين القمـر *čaan fii saḥaab bass baᶜdeen bayyan l-gumar.* There were clouds, but later on the moon appeared. ما تبين. مـاحد يشـوفك *ma tbayyin. maḥḥd yčuufak.* You don't show up. No one sees you. 3. to seem, appear to be. يبـين عليـك بـالك مشغول *ybayyin ᶜaleek baalak mašġuul.* It seems that you are preoccupied.

تبـين *tbayyan* V to appear, turn out. تبين لي إنه تشلاخ *tbayyan-li 'inna čallaax.* It became evident to me that he was a liar.

بـين *been* 1. between. هذا بيني وبينـك *haaða beeni w-beenak.* This is between you and me. بين يوم ويوم *been yoom w-yoom* from day to day. (prov.) بين حانه ومانـه ضيعنـا لحانـه *been ḥaana w-maana ḍayyaᶜna lḥaana.* Caught in the middle. Between the devil and the deep blue sea. 2. among. بـين العيـال *been li-ᶜyaal* among the children.

بيـان *bayaan* p. *-aat* announcement, proclamation.

باين على *baayin ᶜala* (with suff. pron.) it seems that, it appears that. باين عليك ظميـان *baayin ᶜaleek ḍamyaan.* It seems that you are thirsty.

پ

پ ا ت ش *paatš*

باتشـة *paača* Persian stew made of meat from the head, feet, and stomach of a sheep.

پ ا ص *paaṣ*

بـاص *paaṣ* p. *-aat* 1. bus. خذيت الباص إلى الدايرة *xaðeet l-paaṣ 'ila d-daayra.* I took the bus to the department. 2. passport. عطني البـاص والتذكـرة *ᶜaṭni l-paaṣ w-t-taðkara.* Give me the passport and the ticket.

پ ا ك ي ت *paakyt*

بـاكيت *paakeet* p. *-aat* 1. box (of cigarettes, candy, etc.). اشتريت باكيت تشـكليت *štareet paakeet čakleet.* I bought a box of chocolates. 2. paper bag. !حـط الطمـاط في بـاكيت *ḥuṭṭ ṭ-ṭamaaṭ fi paakeet!* Put the tomatoes in a paper bag!

پ ا ل *paal*

بالـة *paala* p. *-aat* 1. bale of cotton. 2. ream.

پ ا و ر *paawr*

بـاورة *paawra* p. *-aat,* بواير *puwaayir* (also أنقـر *'angar,* أنجـر *'anjar, 'anyar*) fisherman's anchor. قطينا البورة وقعدنـا نحـدق *gaṭṭeena l-pawra w-giᶜadna nḥadig.* We let down the anchor and started to fish.

پ ت ت *ptt*

بتـة *patta* (var., less common *batta*) p. *-aat* deck of playing cards. رحنا النادي تعشينا ولعبنا بتـة واستانسـنا *riḥna n-naadi tᶜaššeena w-liᶜabna patta w-staanasna.* We went to the clubhouse. We had dinner, played cards and enjoyed ourselves.

پ ت ي ت *ptyt*

بتيتـة *puteeta* (coll.) potatoes. s. بتيتـا *puteetaa,* حبـة بتيتـة *ḥabbat puteeta.* البتيتـة مـا تطلع هـني *l-puteeta ma tiṭlaᶜ hini.* Potatoes do not grow here.

پ ر د *prd*

بـردة *parda* p. *-aat* curtain, drape. هالحين الناس قـاموا يشـترون بـردات جـاهزة *halḥiin n-naas gaamaw yištiruun pardaat jaahza.* Nowadays people have started to buy ready-made curtains.

پ ر ك و ت *prkwt*

بركـوت *parkoot* (var. فركوت *farkoot*) p. *-aat* overcoat.

پ ر و ا ن *prwaan*

بروانـة *parwaana* p. *-aat* 1. fan. 2. (airplane) propeller.

پ ر ي م ز *prymz*

بريمز *preemez* p. *-aat* primus stove. بس في الزمان الأولي الناس كـانوا يسـتعملون الـبريمزات *bass fi z-zamaan l-'awwali n-naas čaanaw yistaᶜimluun li-preemzaat.* Only in olden times did people use primus stoves.

پ ل ا س ت ي ك *plaastyk*

بلاستيك *plaastiik* (coll.) plastic. شنطة بلاستيك *šanṭa plaastiik* plastic bag.

پ م پ *pmp*

بمب *pamp* p. *-aat* air pump, tire pump. نفخنا التيوبات بالبمب ونزلنا البحر *nifaxna t-tyuubaat b-l-pamp w-nizalna l-baḥar.* We inflated the tubes and went down to the sea.

پ ن ش ر *pnšr*

بنشر *panšar (ينبشر ypanšir)* to go flat. تاير من التايرات بنشر في نص الطريق *taayir min t-taayraat panšar fi nuṣṣ ṭ-ṭariig.* One of the tires went flat in the middle of the road.

بنشر *panšar* puncture, leak, hole. أبو البنشر *'ubu l-panšar* the tire repairman.

پ ن ك *pnk*

بنكة *panka* (var. *banka*). See under ب ن ك *bnk.*

پ و د ر *pwdr*

بودرة *puudra* (coll.) powder. حليب بودرة *haliib puudra* powdered milk.

پ ي ا ل *pyaal*

بيالة *pyaala* p. *-aat* (also more common ستكان *stikaan* p. *-aat*) small glass tea cup.

پ ي پ *pyp*

بيب *peep* p. *-aat* pipe. تيت بيب الماي *tayyat peep l-maay.* He tightened the water pipe.

ت

ت ا *taa*

تا *taa* name of the letter ت *t*.

ت ا ب و ت *taabwt*

تـابوت *taabuut* p. توابيـت *tiwaabiit* coffin, casket.

ت ا ر ي خ *taaryx*

تاريخ *taariix.* See under **ء ر خ** *'rx*.

ت ا ز *taaz*

تـازة *taaza* (invar.) fresh. ما نشتري إلا لحـم تـازة *ma ništiri 'illa laḥam taaza.* We buy only fresh meat. فواكـه تـازة *fawaakeh taaza* fresh fruit.

ت ا ن ك ي *taanky*

تـانكي *taanki* p. توانكي *tawaanki* tank (water, gasoline), reservoir. اتـرس التانكي! *'itris t-taanki!* Fill up the tank! تـانكي المـاي مـتروس *taanki l-maay matruus.* The water tank is full. (prov.) بـن مغامس عـرف ربعـه وزق في التانكي *bin mġaamis ^{c}iraf rab^{c}a w-zagg fi t-taanki.* Do not do favors for those who do not appreciate or deserve them. (lit., "Bin Mghamis was sure of his group and defecated in the tank.")

ت ا ي ر *taayr*

تـاير *taayir* p. تواير *tuwaayir, -aat* car tire. بدل التاير من فضلك! *baddil t-taayir min faðlak!* Change the tire, please! كنـت مسـرع وبنشـر التـاير *čint misri^c w-pančar t-taayir.* I was speeding and the tire went flat.

ت ب ب *tbb*

تـب *tabb* (يتـب *ytibb)* to pearl dive. الغـوص هـو اللـي يتـب *l-ġooṣ huwa lli ytibb.* A pearl diver is the one who (pearl) dives.

تبة *tabba* (n. of inst.) p. *-aat* one act of pearl diving.

ت ب ب ا ن *tbbaan*

تبـان *tabbaan* (coll.) fish of the king mackerel family. s. تبانة *-a*.

ت ب ع *tb^c*

تبـع *tiba^c* (يتبع *yitba^c)* 1. to belong to, be under the authority of. كلبة وخور فكـان ودبـا تتبـع الشـارجة *čalba w-xoor fakkaan w-diba titba^c š-šaarja.* Kalba, Khor Fakkan, and Diba belong to Sharja. 2. to follow, pursue. 3. to come after, follow. هالشمال يتبعـه هـوا زيـن *ha š-šamaal yitba^{c}a hawa zeen.* This northerly wind will be followed by good weather. 4. to adhere to. اتبع تعليمـــات المديـــر! *'itba^c ta^{c}liimaat l-mudiir!* Adhere to the director's structions!

تـابع *taaba^c* III to continue, go on with, follow. تـابعت دروسـها عقـب الصـلاة *taaba^{c}at druussa ^{c}ugb ṣ-ṣalaa.* She continued studying after the prayer.

اتبـع *ttaba^c* VIII = تبع *tiba^c* to adhere to, follow. اتبـع تعليمـات المديـر! *'ittabi^c ta^{c}liimaat l-mudiir!* Adhere to the director's instructions! مجلـس التعـاون الخليجـي يتبـع سياسـة دول الخليـج *majlis t-ta^{c}aawun l-xaliiji yittabi^c siyaasat* *duwal l-xaliij.* The Gulf Cooperation Council follows the policy of the Gulf states.

تبعية *tabaᶜiyya* (var. تابعية *taabᶜiyya*) p. *-aat* nationality, citizenship. وين التابعية؟ *ween t-taabᶜiyya?* Where is the citizenship (certificate)? تابعيتي قطري *taabᶜiiti gṭari.* My nationality is Qatari. I am a Qatari national.

متابعة *mtaabaᶜa* (v.n. from III تابع *taabaᶜ*) continuation, pursuing. متابعة القضية *mtaabaᶜt l-gaðiyya* the continuation of the problem. متابعة الدراسة *mtaabaᶜt d-diraasa* the continuation of studies.

اتباع *ttibaaᶜ* (v.n. from VIII اتبع *ttabaᶜ*) adherence, compliance with. اتباع التعليمات *ttibaaᶜ t-taᶜliimaat* adherence to instructions.

تابع *taabiᶜ* (act. part. from تبع *tibaᶜ*) p. *-iin,* أتباع *'atbaaᶜ* 1. follower, disciple. واحد من أتباع الحاكم *waaḥid min 'atbaaᶜ l-ḥaakim* one of the ruler's followers. 2. belonging to, under the rule of. خور فكان تابعة دبي *xoor fakkaan taabᶜa dbayy.* Khor Fakkan belongs to Dubai.

تابعة *taabᶜa* p. توابع *tawaabiᶜ* dependency, dependent territory.

تابعية *taabᶜiyya* (var. تبعية *tabaᶜiyya*). See *tabaᶜiyya* under **ت ب ع** *tbᶜ*.

متبع *mittabaᶜ* (p.p. from VIII اتبع *ttabaᶜ*) observed, adhered to. العادات المتبعة *l-ᶜadaat l-mittabᶜa* the observed customs.

ت ب ن *tbn*

تبن *tibin* (coll.) straw, threshed stalks of grain.

ت ت ن *ttn*

تتن *titin* (coll.) tobacco. s. حبة تتن *ḥabbat titin.* نشتري التتن من التتان *ništiri t-titin min t-tattaan.* We buy tobacco from the tobacconist.

تتان *tattaan* p. *-iin, -a* tobacconist. اشتريت سبيل من التتان *štireet sbiil min t-tattaan.* I bought a pipe from the tobacconist.

ت ج ر *tjr*

تاجر *taajar* III to do business, deal. يتاجر بالقماش *ytaajir b-li-gmaaš.* He deals in pearls.

تاجر *taajir* p. تجار *tijjaar* merchant, trader. شغله تاجر *šuġla taajir.* He works as a merchant. تاجر بالجملة *taajir b-l-jimla* wholesale dealer.

تجارة *tijaara* 1. trade, business. يشتغل في التجارة *yištaġil fi-t-tijaara.* He deals in trade. 2. commerce. درست تجارة *dirast tijaara.* I studied commerce. وزارة التجارة *wizaarat t-tijaara* the ministry of commerce.

تجاري *tijaari* commercial. الدكان في موقع تجاري *d-diččaan fi mawgiᶜ tijaari.* The store is in a commercial location.

ت ج ه *tjh*

اتجه *ttajah* VIII. See under **و ج ه** *wjh.*

ت ح ت *tḥt*

تحت *taḥat* 1. (prep.) under. الدكان تحت البناية *d-diččaan taḥat li-bnaaya.* The store is under the building. من تحت راس *min taḥat raas* due to, attributed to. هذي المشاكل من تحت راس الحريم *haaði l-mašaakil min taḥat raas l-ḥariim.*

These problems are caused by women. الموظف تحت التجربة *li-mwaððaf taḥt t-tajriba.* The employee is on probation. تحت إشراف *taḥat 'išraaf* under the supervision of. تحت تصرف *taḥat taṣarruf* at the disposal of. 2. (adv.) راح تحت *raaḥ taḥat.* He went downstairs. من تحت *min taḥat* from below, underneath.

تحتي *taḥti* located lower or beneath. هدوم تحتية *hduum taḥtiyya* underwear.

ت ح د *tḥd*

اتحد *ttiḥad* VIII. See under **و ح د** *wḥd.*

ت ر ا *traa*

ترى *tara* (invar.) 1. well, well then, well now. ترى اليوم عطلة *tara l-yoom* *ᶜuṭla.* Well, today is a holiday. 2. for your information, I tell you. المدير الجديد يا ترى *l-mudiir l-yidiid ya tara.* For your information, the new director has come. 3. because. لا تسير وياه، ترى يغثك! *la tsiir wiyyaa, tara ygiθθak!* Don't go with him because he will upset you.

ت ر ا ي *traay*

تراي *traay* p. *-aat* test, examination. خذ عليهم تراي *xað ᶜaleehum traay.* He gave them an examination. خذيت تراي على السيارة؟ *xaðeet traay ᶜala s-sayyaara?* Did you try the car?

ت ر ا ب *traab*

تراب *traab* (coll.) earth, soil, dirt. s. حفنة تراب *ḥafnat traab* a handful of earth. لا تخلي أخوك يلعب في التراب! *la txalli 'uxuuk yilᶜab fi t-traab!* Don't let your brother play in the dirt! التراب هني موب زين. ما يطلع فيه النبات *t-traab hini muub zeen. ma yiṭlaᶜ fii n-nabaat.* The soil here is not good. Plants will not grow in it.

ت ر ج م *trjm*

ترجم *tarjam* (يترجم *ytarjim)* to translate, interpret. ترجم من العربي إلى الإنكليزي *tarjam min l-ᶜarabi 'ila l-'ingiliizi.* He translated from Arabic into English. ما يعرفون عربي. يبون واحد يترجم لهم *ma yᶜarfuun ᶜarabi. yibuun waaḥid ytarjim-ilhum.* They do not know Arabic. They need someone to interpret for them.

ترجمة *tarjama* (v.n. from ترجم *tarjam)* translation, interpretation. ترجمة من العربي إلى الإنكليزي *tarjama min l-ᶜarabi 'ila l-'ingiliizi* translation from Arabic into English.

ترجمان *tirjimaan* p. *-iyya* translator, interpreter.

ت ر س ^1^ *trs*

ترس *tiras* (يترس *yitris)* to fill, fill up s.th. with. ترس التانكي ماي *tiras t-taanki maay.* He filled the tank with water. اترس التانكي! *'itris t-taanki!* Fill up the tank!

ترّس *tarras* II = *tiras.* See **ت ر س** *trs.*

انترس *ntiras* VII to be filled with s.th. التانكي انترس ماي *t-taanki ntiras maay.* The tank was filled with water. ياكل وايد. كرشه ما ينترس *yaakil waayid. karša ma yintiris.* He eats a lot. His belly is bottomless.

تارس *taaris* (act. part. from ترس *tiras)* p. *-iin* having filled with. توني تارسه ماي *tawwni taarsa maay.* I have just filled it with water.

مـتروس *matruus* (p.p. from ترس *tiras*) filled with, full of. الدرام مـتروس خمـام *d-draam matruus xmaam.* The can is full of garbage. السوق متروس رجـاجيل وحريـم *s-suug matruus rayaayiil w-ḥariim.* The marketplace is full of men and women.

ترس² *trs*

تـارس *taaris* strong wind. ونحن في البر طلع تارس والرمـل عمانـا *w-niḥin fi l-barr ṭilaᶜ taaris w-r-ramil ᶜamaana.* While we were in the desert, a strong wind blew and the sand blinded us.

ترفك *trfk*

ترفـك *trafik* traffic department, highway patrol. دايـرة الـترفك *daayrat t-trafik* the highway department. ضو الترفك *ðaww t-trafik* the traffic light.

ترك *trk*

تـرك *tirak* (يترك *yitrik)* 1. to leave s.th. كان ما شـفته اتـرك لـه خـبر *čaan ma čifta 'itrik-la xabar.* If you do not see him, leave him a message. ترك المطـار *tirak l-maṭaar.* He left the airport. 2. to give up (e.g., a habit). لازم تترك هذي العـادة الشـينة *laazim titrik haaði l-ᶜaada š-šeena.* You have to give up this bad habit.

تـرك *tarrak* II to cause s.o. to give up, abandon s.th. لازم أتركـه العـادة الشـينة *laazim 'atarrka l-ᶜaada š-šeena.* I have to make him give up the bad habit.

تارك *taarik* (act. part. from ترك *tirak*) p. *-iin* 1. leaving. آنـا تـارك بـاكر *'aana taarik baačir.* I am leaving tomorrow. 2. having left. آنـا تـاركهم هنـاك أمـس *'aana taarikhum hnaak 'ams.* I left them there yesterday.

مـتروك *matruuk* (p.p. from ترك *tirak*) left, having been left. السيارة متروكة في نص الطريق *s-sayyaara matruuka fi nuṣṣ ṭ-ṭariig.* The car is left in the middle of the road.

تركي *trky*

تركيـة *tirkiyya* Turkey. عمـرك رحـت تركيـة؟ *ᶜimrak riḥt tirkiyya?* Have you ever been to Turkey? تركيـة بلـد زيـن *tirkiyya balad zeen.* Turkey is a beautiful country.

تركـي *tirki* p. أتراك *'atraak* 1. a Turk. هــو تركــي مــن أنقـرة *huwa tirki min 'angara.* He is a Turk from Ankara. 2. Turkish. قهوة تركيـة *gahwa tirkiyya* Turkish coffee.

ترنج *trnj*

ترنـج *trinj* (coll.) citron. s. ترجة *-a.* يبيعـون الـترنج بالحبـة *ybiiᶜuun t-trinj b-l-ḥabba.* They sell citron by the piece. الترنج ما يطلع هني *t-trinj ma yiṭlaᶜ hini.* Citron doesn't grow here.

تسال *tsaal*

تسـالة *tissaala* special kind of ship (also known as the صندل *ṣandal*), used for transporting goods from steamships to the harbor.

تسع *tsᶜ*

تسـعة *tisᶜa* (var. تسـع *tisiᶜ*) nine. كم واحـد تـابي؟ تسـعة *čam waaḥid tabi? tisᶜa.* How many do you want? Nine. تسـعتهم *tisᶜattum* the nine of them. جـاوا تسـعتهم كلهـم *yaw tisᶜattum killhum.* They came, all nine of them.

تسعتعش *tisi^c^ta^c^aš,* تسعتعشر *tisi^c^ta^c^šar* nineteen.

تسع *tisi^c^* p. اتساع *tsaa^c^* one-ninth.

تسعين *tis^c^iin* ninety. تسعين درهم *tis^c^iin dirhim* ninety dirhams.

تسعمية *tisi^c^imya* 900.

تسعة ألف *tis^c^a 'alf* 9,000. تسعة مليون *tis^c^a malyoon* nine million.

تاسع *taasi^c^* (with foll. n.) the ninth. تاسع يوم *taasi^c^ yoom* the ninth day. تاسعهم *taasi^c^hum* the ninth (one) of them.

ت ش ر ي ن *tšryn*

تشرين أول *tišriin 'awwal* October. تشرين ثاني *tišriin θaani* November.

ت ص ل *tṣl*

اتصل *ttiṣal* VIII. See under **و ص ل** *wṣl.*

ت ع ب *t^c^b*

تعب *ti^c^ab* (يتعب *yit^c^ab*) 1. to be or become tired. تعبت من الشغل *ti^c^abt min š-šuġul.* I got tired of work. تعب من المشي. يبي يستريح *ti^c^ab min l-maši. yabi yistariiḥ.* He became tired of walking. He wants to rest. 2. to work hard. إذا بغيت تتوفق في حياتك لازم تتعب *'iða bağeet titwaffag fi ḥayaatak laazim tit^c^ab.* If you want to be successful in your life, you have to work hard.

تعب *ta^cc^ab* II 1. to make s.o. tired. هو رجال عود. المشي يتعبه *huwa rayyaal ^c^ood. l-maši yta^cc^iba.* He is an old man. Walking makes him tired. ذاك الشغل يتعب *ðaak š-šuġul yta^cc^ib.* That work makes one tired. 2. to bother, trouble s.o. التنديل موب زين. تعبني واجد *t-tindeel muub zeen. ta^cc^abni waayid.* The supervisor is not good. He caused me a lot of trouble. !لا تتعب روحك *la tta^cc^ib ruuḥak!* Don't bother yourself!

تعب *ta^c^ab* 1. tiredness, weariness. الشغل في جزيرة داس تعب واجد *š-šuġul fi yiziirat daas ta^c^ab waayid.* Work on Das Island is very tiring. 2. trouble, exertion.

تعبان *ta^c^baan* p. *-iin* tired, exhausted. تعبان. ما أقدر أشتغل *ta^c^baan. ma 'agdar 'aštaġil.* I am tired. I cannot work. كنت تعبان ورقدت *čint ta^c^baan w-ragatt.* I was tired and fell asleep.

أتعب *'at^c^ab* (elat.) more or most tired. هو أتعب مني *huwa 'at^c^ab minni.* He is more tired than I am. هو أتعب واحد *huwa 'at^c^ab waaḥid.* He is the most tired one.

متعب *mut^c^ib* 1. tiring, difficult. 2. dull, boring.

ت ع ت ع *t^c^t^c^*

تعتع *ta^c^ta^c^* (يتعتع *yta^c^ti^c^*) to stammer. ما يتكلم زين. يتعتع *ma yitkallam zeen. yta^c^ti^c^.* He doesn't talk well. He stammers.

تعتعة *ta^c^ta^c^a* (v.n. from تعتع *ta^c^ta^c^*) stammering, a stammer.

ت ع ظ *t^c^ð̣*

اتعظ *tti^c^að̣* VIII. See under **و ع ظ** *w^c^ð̣.*

ت ع ل *t^c^l*

تعال *ta^c^aal* (imp.) 1. Come, come here. (f. تعالي *ta^c^aali*). !تعال هني *ta^c^aal hini!* Come here! !روح وتعال بعجل *ruuḥ w-ta^c^aal b-^c^ajal!* Go and come back quickly! !تعالي ويانا *ta^c^aali wiyyaana!* Come (f.s.) with us! 2. (with foll.

imp.) come..! !تعال احكي واياي *taᶜaal 'iḥči wiyyaay!* Come talk to me! !تعال علمني *taᶜaal ᶜallimni!* Come tell me!

ت ف ح *tfḥ*

تفاح *tiffaaḥ* (coll.) apples. s. تفاحة *tiffaaḥa.* p. *-aat.* التفاح غالي اليوم *t-tiffaaḥ ġaali l-yoom.* Apples are expensive today. على كم التفاح؟ *ᶜala čam t-tiffaaḥ?* How much are apples? رحت السوق واشتريت تفاح *riḥt s-suug w-štireet tiffaaḥ.* I went to the market and bought apples. كل ثلاث تفاحات *kal θalaaθ tiffaaḥaat.* He ate three apples.

ت ف خ *tfx*

تفخ *tifax* (يتفخ *yitfix)* = more common نفخ *nifax* (ينفخ *yanfix).* See under **ن ف خ** *nfx.*

ت ف گ *tfg*

اتفق *ttifag* VIII. See under **و ف گ** *wfg.*

ت ك س ي *tksy*

تكسي *taksi* p. تكاسي *tikaasi* taxi. خذيت تكسي من المطار إلى الفندق *xaðeet taksi min l-maṭaar 'ila l-fundug.* I took a taxi from the airport to the hotel.

ت ف ل *tfl*

تفل *tifal* (يتفل *yatfil)* to spit. شلع ضروسه وقام يتفل على الأرض *čilaᶜ ḍruusa w-gaam yatfil ᶜala l-'arḍ.* He had his teeth pulled out and started to spit on the ground. تفل علي من غيظه *tifal ᶜalayy min ġeeḍa.* He spat on me because of his anger. لا تتفل *la titfil!* Don't spit!

تفل *taffal* II = *tifal.* See **ت ف ل** *tfl.*

تفال *tfaal* 1. spit, saliva. 2. spitting. التفال على الأرض ممنوع *t-tifaal ᶜala l-'arḍ mamnuuᶜ.* Spitting on the floor is forbidden.

تفلة *tafla* (n. of inst.) p. تفلات *-aat* an instance of spitting.

ت ف ه *tfh*

تفاهة *tfaaha* triviality, insignificance.

أتفه *'atfah* 1. (with foll. من *min*) more trivial than. 2. (with foll. n.) the most trivial.

تافه *taafih* p. *-iin* trivial, insignificant.

ت گ ي *tgy*

اتقى *ttiga* VIII. See **و گ ي** *wgy.*

ت ك ل *tkl*

اتكل *ttikal* VIII. See **و ك ل** *wkl.*

ت ك ك ي *tkky*

تكي *tikki* (coll.) mulberries, berries. s. تكية *-yya* or حبة تكي *ḥabbat tikki.* التكي ما يطلع هني *t-tikki ma yiṭlaᶜ hini.* Mulberries do not grow here.

ت ك ي *tky*

اتكى *ttika* VIII. See under **و ك ي** *wky.*

ت ل غ ر ف *tlġrf*

تلغراف *taliġraaf* 1. telegraph. دايرة التلغراف *daayrat t-taliġraaf* the telegraph department. 2. telegram, cable. طرشت له تلغراف *ṭarrašt-la taliġraaf.* I sent him a telegram.

تلغرافي *taliġraafi* telegraphic. اتصالات تلغرافية *ttiṣaalaat taliġraafiyya* graphic communications.

ت ل ف *tlf*

تلف *tilif (يتلف yitlaf)* 1. to be or become abandoned or deserted. المكان تلف يعني صار تلفان *l-mukaan tilif yaᶜni ṣaar talfaan.* The place was abandoned means that the place became or was deserted.

تلف *talaf* (v.n. from تلف *tilif*) abandonment, desertion.

تالف *taalif* (act. part.) p. *-iin* having become deserted. قرية تالفة *ġarya taalfa* deserted village.

تلفان *talfaan* p. *-iin* abandoned, deserted. عماير تلفانين *ᶜamaayir talfaaniin* abandoned, deserted buildings. المكان تلفان. ماحد فيه *l-mukaan talfaan. maḥḥad fii.* The place is deserted. There isn't anyone in it.

ت ل ف ز ي ن *tlfzyn*

تلفزيون *talafizyoon* p. *-aat* television. شفت فلم زين على التلفزيون *šift filim zeen ᶜala t-talafizyoon.* I saw a good movie on television.

ت ل ف ن *tlfn*

تلفن *talfan (يتلفن ytalfin)* to make a telephone call. تلفنت له أمس بس ما حصلته *talfant-la 'ams bass ma ḥaṣṣalta.* I telephoned him yesterday but did not find him.

تلفون *talafoon* p. *-aat* telephone. خط التلفون *xaṭṭ t-talafoon* the telephone line. التلفون مشغول *t-talafoon mašġuul.* The telephone is busy. شو رقم تلفونك؟ *šu ragam talafoonak?* What is your telephone number? بالتلفون *b-t-talafoon* by telephone, on the telephone. اتصلت فيك بالتلفون *ttaṣalt fiik b-t-talafoon.* I contacted you by telephone. حاكيته بالتلفون *ḥaačeeta b-t-talafoon.* I talked to him on the telephone.

ت ل ل *tll*

تل *tall (يتل ytill)* to pull. تل الحبل من يدي *tall l-ḥabil min yaddi.* He pulled the rope from my hand. تل السيب الغيص *tall s-seeb l-ġeeṣ.* The rope-man (in pearl diving) pulled the pearl diver.

تل *tall* (v.n. from *tall*) pulling. مباراة تل الحبل *mubaaraat tall l-ḥabil* the tug of war game.

تال *taall* (act. part.) p. *-iin* having pulled. آنا تاله قبل شوي *'aana taalla gabl šwayy.* I pulled it a short while ago.

متلول *matluul* (p.p.) p. *-iin* having been pulled.

ت ل و *tlw*

تلاوة *tilaawa* (v.n.) oral reading (esp. from the Quran). تلاوة من القرآن *tilaawa min l-ġur'aan* oral reading, recitation from the Quran.

تالي *taali* (adv.) 1. afterwards, then. وتالي؟ *w-taali?* And then what? 2. in the end, at long last. تاليها رحنا شربنا قهوة *taaliiha riḥna šribna gawha.* In the end we went and had coffee. أنت روح ذالحين. آنا أجي تالي *'inta ruuḥ ðalḥiin. 'aana 'ayi taali.* You go now, I will come later. 3. (only with suff. ـها *-ha*) هذي تاليها. ما تحاكيني؟ *haaði taaliiha. ma tḥaačiini?* Is this the end result? Aren't you talking to me?

ت م ب *tmb*

تمبة *tamba* p. *-aat* small ball (such as a tennis ball). العيال لعبوا التمبة *li-ᶜyaal liᶜbaw t-tamba.* The children played ball. الدنيا تمبة مدورة *d-dinya tamba mdawwara.* The world is a round ball.

ت م ب ك *tmbk*

تمباك *timbaak* (coll.) = (more common تتن *titin*) tobacco. التمباك نستورده من تركية *t-timbaak nistawirda min tirkiyya.* We import tobacco from Turkey. نشتري التمباك من التتان *ništiri t-timbaak min t-tattaan.* We buy tobacco from the tobacconist.

ت م ب ل *tmbl*

تمبل *tambal* (var. تنبل *tanbal*) p. تنابل *tanaabil* bum, loafer. بس تمبل قاعد ما يعمل شي *bass tambal gaaᶜid ma yᶜamil šayy.* He is only a bum. He is inactive and indolent.

ت م ت م *tmtm*

تمتم *tamtam* (يتمتم *ytamtim*) to stumble in speech, mutter, stammer. كان يتمتم. ما عرفنا اللي قاله *čaan ytamtim. ma ᶜirafna lli gaala.* He was stammering. We did not know what he had said.

تمتمة *tamtama* (v.n. from تمتم *tamtam*) stammering, muttering. كل كلامه كان تمتمة *kill kalaama čaan tamtama.* All his words were unintelligible.

ت م ر *tmr*

تمر *tamir* (coll.) dry dates, palm dates (usually of black or dark color). s. *-a,* حبة تمر *ḥabbat tamir* a fruit date. في رمضان الناس يفطرون على التمر *fi rumḍaan n-naas yifiṭruun ᶜala t-tamir.* During Ramadan people break their fast by eating dates. تمر هندي *tamir hindi* tamarind.

تمار *tammaar* p. *-iin,* تمامرة *tamaamra* one who sells dates.

ت م س ح *tmsḥ*

تمساح *timsaaḥ* p. تماسيح *timaasiiḥ* 1. crocodile. 2. alligator.

ت م م *tmm*

تم *tamm* (يتم *ytimm*) 1. to be completed, consummated. عقبما تم العرس المعرس خذ عرسته حق هلها *ᶜugubma tamm l-ᶜirs l-miᶜris xað ᶜaruusta ḥagg halha.* After the wedding was completed, the bridegroom took his bride to her folks' home. 2. (with foll. imperf.) to continue, go on doing s.th. تميت أشتغل إلين تعبت *tammeet 'aštaġil 'ileen tiᶜabt.* I continued to work until I got tired.

تمم *tammam* II to complete, finish. تمم شغلك! *tammim šuġlak!* Finish your work!

تمام *tamaam* 1. exactly. إي نعم تمام. أبي خمسين درهم *'ii naᶜam tamaam. 'abi xamsiin dirhim.* Yes, exactly. I want fifty dirhams. 2. well, perfectly. هذا الكولي يشتغل تمام *haaða l-kuuli yištaġil tamaam.* This coolie works well. 3. true, right. والله تمام! هذا شيبتن غانمه *waḷḷa tamaam! haaða šeebtin ġaanma.* This is really true! This is a magnanimous old man.

ت م م و ز *tmmwz*

تموز *tammuuz* July (month).

ت ن ب ل *tnbl*

تنبل *tanbal* (more common, تمبل *tambal*). See under ت م ب ل *tmbl*.

ت ن د ي ل *tndyl*

تنديل *tindeel* p. تناديل *tinaadil,* تنديلية *-iyya* foreman, supervisor. يشتغل تنديل حق الكولية *yištaġil tindeel ḥagg l-kuuliyya.* He works as a foreman for the coolies. التنديل هو اللي يوظف ويفنش *t-tindeel huwa 'illi ywaððif w-yfanniš.* The foreman is the one who hires and fires.

ت ن ك *tnk*

تنك *tanak* (coll.) tin sheets, aluminum. s. قطعة تنك *giṭᶜat tank* or تنكة *tnaka.* تنكة *tnaka* p. *-aat* tin container (= 4 gallons approx.) تنكة بانزين *tnakat baanziin* gas container. بيوت من تنك *byuut min tanak* aluminum houses.

تناك *tannaak* p. *-iin,* تناكة *tannaaka* tinsmith.

ت ن ك ر *tnkr*

تنكر *tankar* p. تناكر *tanaakir* tanker car, truck (usually used for carrying water). الماي حق الشرب موب زين. نشتري تنكرين ماي كل يوم *l-maay ḥagg š-širb muub zeen. ništiri tankareen maay kill yoom.* Water for drinking purposes is not good. We buy two trucks of water every day.

ت ن و ر *tnwr*

تنور *tannuur* p. تنانير *tanaaniir* mud oven (for baking bread). خبز تنور *xubiz tannuur* bread baked in a *tannuur*.

ت ه م *thm*

تهم *tiham* (يتهم *yitham)* 1. (with ب *b-*) to accuse, charge s.o. with s.th. تهموه بالبوق *tihmoo b-l-boog.* They accused him of stealing.

انتهم *ntiham* VII (with ب *b-*) to be accused, charged with s.th. انتهم بالبوق *ntiham b-l-boog.* He was accused of stealing.

اتهم *ttaham* VIII = more common تهم *tiham.* See ت ه م *thm.*

تهمة *tihma* (var. تهيمة *tahiima*) p. تهم *tiham* accusation, charge.

متهم *mittaham* (p.p. from اتهم *ttaham*) p. *-iin.* accused.

ت و ا ل ي ت *twaalyt*

تواليت *twaaleet* 1. coiffure, hairdo. راح المحسن وسوى تواليت مثل الخنفس *raaḥ li-mḥassin w-sawwa twaaleet miθl l-xunfus.* He went to the barber and had his hair styled like a Beatle. 2. toilet. راح التواليت وبال *raaḥ t-twaaleet w-baal.* He went to the toilet room and urinated.

ت و ب *twb*

تاب *taab (*يتوب *ytuub)* 1. to repent, do penance. كان يسكر وبعدين تاب *čaan yiskar w-baᶜdeen taab.* He used to get drunk and he repented later on. 2. (with عن *ᶜan*) to renounce, turn away from. تاب عن السكر *taab ᶜan s-sikir.* He turned away from drinking. تاب علي *taab ᶜala* to forgive s.o. (a sin). بطل السكر وتاب عليه الله *baṭṭal s-sikir w-taab ᶜalee 'aḷḷa.* He stopped drinking and God forgave him.

توب *tawwab* II to make s.o. repent. توبته وبطل السكر *tawwabta w-baṭṭal s-sikir.* I made him repent and he stopped drinking.

توبـة *tooba* (v.n. from تـاب *taab*) repentance, doing penance. التوبـة يـا رب! *t-tooba ya rabb!* I will never ...! I've learned my lesson, God! التوبـة خـلاص! *t-tooba xalaaṣ!* I repent all that I've done.

تـواب *tawwaab* (epithet of God, lit, "the forgiving one") forgiving, merciful. الله هـو التـواب الرحيـم *'aḷḷaah huwa t-tawwaab r-raḥiim.* God is the forgiving and merciful one.

ت و ج *twj*

تـوج *tawwaj* II to crown s.o. توجوه ملك علـى الأردن *tawwajoo malik ᶜala l-'ardun.* They crowned him king of Jordan.

تـاج *taaj* p. تيجان *tiijaan* crown. تاج الملك *taaj l-malik* the king's crown. لبس التـاج *libis t-taaj.* He wore the crown.

ت و ل *twl*

تولـة *tuula* p. *-aat* 1/40 lb. (originally used in weighing gold and other precious metals).

ت و م *twm*

تـوم *toom* p. توام *twaam* twins. حرمته جـابت تـوم *ḥurumta yaabat toom.* His wife had twins. خمس توام *xams twaam.* quintuplets.

ت و ن س *twns*

تونـس *tuunis* 1. Tunisia (the state of Tunisia). 2. Tunis (the capital city).

تونسـي *tuunsi* p. توانسة *tawaansa* 1. a Tunisian. هو مـوب تونسـي *huwa muub tuunsi.* He is not Tunisian. 2. Tunisian, characteristic of Tunisia. الحكومـة التونسـية *li-ḥkuuma t-tuunisiyya* the Tunisian government.

ت و و *tww*

تـو *taww-* (with foll. suff. pron.) have just ... توه وصـل *tawwa wiṣal.* He has just arrived. العيـال توهـم جـاوا *li-ᶜyaal tawwhum yaw.* The children have just come. توني مرمسه *tawwni mrammsa.* I have just talked to him.

ت ي ب ل *tybl*

تيبـل *teebil* p. تيابل *tayaabil* 1. table. فيه خمس تيابل في الحفيـز *fii xams tayaabil fi l-ḥafiiz.* There are five tables in the office. 2. desk. التيبل حق التنديل *t-teebil ḥagg t-tindeel* the foreman's desk.

ت ي ح *tyḥ*

تـاح *taaḥ (يتيـح ytiiḥ)* to throw, throw away. تاح الحجر في المـاي *taaḥ l-ḥiyar fi l-maay.* He threw the rock in the water.

تـايح *taayiḥ* (act. part.) p. *-iin* having thrown, having thrown away s.th. آنا تايحـه في الـدرام *'aana taayḥa fi d-draam.* I have thrown it away in the garbage can.

تايحـة *taayḥa* p. *-aat* misfortune, calamity. تايحات الدهر *taayḥaat d-dahir* misfortunes of fate.

ت ي ر *tyr*

تيـار *tayyaar* p. *-aat* current, flow, draft (of air). تيـار كرهـب *tayyaar karhab* electric current.

ت ي س *tys*

تيـس *tees* p. تيـوس *tyuus* billy goat. التيـس هـو ذكـر العنـز *t-tees huwa ðakar* *l-ᶜanz.* A billy goat is the male of a goat.

ت ي ل *tyl*

تيل *teel* p. تيول *tyuul* 1. wire. 2. power line.

ت ي م *tym*

تيم *teem* 1. time. 2. work shift. خلص تيمي *xilaṣ teemi.* My work shift has finished. التيم خلاص *t-teem xalaaṣ.* The time has expired.

ت ي ن *tyn*

تين *tiin* (coll.) figs. s. تينة -*a.* حبة تين *ḥabbat tiin.* تينة، شجرة تين *tiina, šyarat tiin* fig tree. التين هني موب واجد *t-tiin hini muub waayid.* Figs are not abundant here. اشتريت تين *štireet tiin.* I bought figs. التين غالي *t-tiin ġaali.* Figs are expensive. كليت خمس تينات *kaleet xams tiinaat.* I ate five figs.

ت ي ه *tyh*

تاه *taah (*يتيه *ytiih)* to get lost, lose one's way. طلعوا القنص وتاهوا في البر *ṭlaᶜaw l-ganaṣ w-taahaw fi l-barr.* They went out hunting and got lost in the desert. تاه عن الطريق *taah ᶜan ṭ-ṭariig.* He lost his way.

تيه *tayyah* II to lose, confuse s.o. البايق تيه الشرطي اللي كان لاحقه *l-baayig tayyah š-širṭi lli čaan laaḥga.* The thief lost the policeman who was following him.

تايه *taayih* (act. part.) p. -*iin* 1. having lost one's way. أنا تايه. لا تسألني *'aana taayih. la tis'alni.* I have lost my way. Don't ask me. 2. confused.

ت ي و ب *tywb*

تيوب *tyuub* p. -*aat* tire tube. نفخنا التيوبات ونزلنا البحر *nifaxna t-tyuubaat w-nizalna l-baḥr.* We inflated the (tire) tubes and went down to the sea. عندك تيوب جديد؟ *ᶜindak tyuub yidiid?* Do you have a new (tire) tube?

ت ي ي ت *tyyt*

تيت *tayyat* II to tighten s.th. تيت السكرو *tayyat s-sikruu.* He tightened the screw.

ث

ث ا θaa

ثا θaa name of the letter ث θ.

ث ا ر θaar

ثار θaar revenge, vengeance. خذ ثاره xað θaara. He avenged himself.

ث ا ل و ل θaalwl

ثالول θaaluul p. ثواليل θawaaliil wart. رحت الدختر لاجل الثواليل اللي في يدي *riḥt d-daxtar lajil θ-θawaaliil illi fi yaddi.* I went to the doctor for the warts in my hand.

ث ب ت θbt

ثبت θibat (يثبت yiθbit) 1. to be firm, steady. يشتغل زين وذالحين ثبت في شغله *yištaġil zeen w-ðalḥiin θibat fi šuġla.* He works well, and now he cannot be replaced in his work. 2. (with على ᶜala) to hold to s.th., be firm in s.th. ثبت على اللي قاله *θibat ᶜala lli gaala.* He held to what he had said. يثبت على كلامه *yiθbit ᶜala kalaama.* He sticks to his word. 3. to become established, proven. ثبت إن هو التشلاخ *θibat 'inna huwa č-čallaax.* It was established that he was the liar. ثبت لي إنه موب صديق مخلص *θibat-li 'inna muub ṣidiij muxliṣ.* It was proved to me that he wasn't a sincere friend.

ثبت θabbat II 1. to confirm. لازم تثبت الحجز والا يكنسلونه *laazim tθabbit l-ḥajiz walla ykansiluuna.* You have to confirm reservation; otherwise they will cancel it. 2. to appoint permanently. التنديل ثبت الكولي بشغله *t-tindeel θabbat l-kuuli b-šuġla.* The foreman appointed the coolie to his work permanently.

أثبت 'aθbat IV to prove. أثبتوا في المحكمة إنه مذنب *'aθbatu fi l-maḥkama 'inna miðnib.* They proved in court that he was guilty.

تثبت tθabbat V to verify, become certain of. تثبت من صحة كلامه *tθabbatt min ṣiḥḥat kalaama.* I established the truth of his words.

ثبات θbaat (v.n. from ثبت θibat) proof.

ثابت θaabit (act. part.) p. *-iin* permanent, stable. هو ثابت في وظيفته *huwa θaabit fi waḏiifta.* He is permanent in his position. 2. proven, established. هذا شي ثابت؛ ما يحتاج إلى برهان *haaða šayy θaabit; ma yiḥtaaj 'ila burhaan.* This is an established thing; it doesn't need proof.

ث ر ث ر θrθr

ثرثر θarθar (يثرثر yθarθir) to chatter. دايما يثرثر؛ ما يقدر يسكت *daayman yθarθir; ma yigdar yaskit.* He is always chattering; he cannot shut up.

ثرثرة θarθara (v.n.) chatter, iddle talk.

ثرثار θarθaar p. *-iin* chatterbox, prattler.

ث ر د θrd

ثريد θariid (coll.) bread crumbs with meat or meat broth. s. *-a* dish consisting of bread crumbs with meat.

ث ر م *θrm*

ثرم *θarram* II to chop up, cut up (e.g., onions, meat, etc.). اشتريت لحم وسألت القصاب يثرمه *štireet laḥam w-si'alt l-gaṣṣaab yθarrma.* I bought meat and asked the butcher to cut it up. ثرم البصل *θarram l-baṣal.* He chopped up the onions.

انثرم *nθiram* VII to be chopped up, cut up. البصل انثرم قبل اللحم *l-baṣal nθiram gabl l-laḥam.* The onions were chopped up before the meat.

ث ر ي *θry*

ثري *θari* p. *-yyiin,* أثريا *'aθriya.* rich, rich person. فيه ناس واجد ثريين في الخليج *fii naas waajid θariyyiin fi l-xaliij.* There are many rich people in the Gulf.

ثروة *θarwa* p. *-aat* wealth, fortune. ثروته تتقدر بمليون درهم *θariwta titgaddar b-malyoon dirhim.* His wealth is estimated to be one million dirhams.

ث ر ي ي ا *θryyaa*

ثريا *θurayya* p. *-aat* chandelier. (with the article prefix ال *'al-*) الثريا *'aθ-θurayya* Pleiades. (prov.) وين الثرا من الثريا *ween θ-θara min θ-θurayya* (used for things or persons of disproportional value or importance).

ث ع ل *θᶜm*

ثعل *θaᶜal* p. ثعالي *θaᶜaali* (also less common ثعلب *θaᶜlab*) fox, jackal.

ث ع ل ب *θᶜlb*

ثعلب *θaᶜlab* p. ثعالب *θaᶜaalib* fox.

ث غ ر *θrg*

ثغرة *θagra* p. *-aat* opening, rift.

ث گ ب *θgb*

ثقب *θagb* p. ثقوب *θguub* little hole, puncture. التاير بنشر. فيه ثقب *t-taayir banšar. fii θagb.* The tire went flat. There is a little hole in it.

ث گ ف *θgf*

ثقف *θaggaf* II to educate, impart culture or education. المدارس تثقف الناس *l-madaaris θθaggif n-naas.* Schools educate people.

تثقف *tθaggaf* V to become educated. إذا ردت تثقف دش المدرسة *'iδa ridt tiθθaggaf dišš l-madrasa.* If you want to get educated, go to school.

ثقافي *θagaafi* educational, cultural. المستوى الثقافي *l-mustawa θ-θagaafi* the educational level. الركز الثقافي *l-markaz θ-θagaafi* the cultural center. الملحق الثقافي *l-mulḥag θagaafi* the cultural attaché.

مثقف *mθaggaf* p. *-iin* educated, cultured.

ث گ ل *θgl*

ثقل *θigal* (يثقل *yiθgal*) to become heavy. من الكبر لسانه ثقل *min l-kubur lsaana θigal.* His tongue became heavy because of old age. الحمل ثقل *l-ḥimil θigal.* The load became heavy. الشنطة ثقلت. ما أقدر أشيلها *š-šanṭa θiglat. ma 'agdar 'ašiilha.* The bag became heavy. I cannot lift it.

ثقل *θaggal* II 1. to make s.th. heavy. ثقل الحمل واجد؛ البعير طاح على الأرض *θaggal l-ḥimil waayid; l-biᶜiir ṭaaḥ* *ᶜala l-'arđ̣.* He made the load too heavy; the camel fell down to the ground. 2. (with على *ᶜala*) to burden, inconvenience s.o. لا تثقل علي بطلباتك! *la θθaggil ᶜalayy b-ṭalabaatak!* Do not inconvenience me with your demands! في أمان الله! ثقلنا عليكم. *fii 'amaan-i-llaah! θaggalna ᶜaleekum.* Goodbye! We've bothered you.

ثقل *θigal* (v.n. from ثقل *θigal*) 1. heaviness, heavy weight. طاح على الأرض من ثقل الحمل *ṭaaḥ ᶜala l-'arđ̣ min θigal l-ḥimil.* He fell down to the ground because of the heavy load. 2. inconvenience, bothering.

ثقيل *θagiil* p. *-iin* 1. heavy, weighty. آنا شايل حمل ثقيل *'aana šaayil ḥimil θagiil.* I am carrying a heavy load. 2. insufferable, dull bore. ثقيل الدم *θagiil d-damm* insufferable, disagreeable.

ث ك ن *θkn*

ثكنة *θakana* p. *-aat* military barracks.

ث ل ث *θlθ*

ثلث *θallaθ* II to triple s.th., make s.th. threefold. دير بالك لا يثلث القيمة عليك! *diir balak la yθalliθ l-giima ᶜleek!* Be on the lookout so that he doesn't triple the cost to you!

ثلاثة *θalaaθa* p. *-aat* three. (with foll. n.) ثلاث، ثلاثة *θalaaθat,* ثلاث *θalaaθ.* ثلاث، ثلاثة رجاجيل *θalaaθ, θalaaθat rayaayiil* three men. ثلاثة وخمسين *θlaaθa w-xamsiin* fifty-three. ثلاثتهم *θalaaθattum* the three of them.

الثلاثة *θ-θalaaθa,* الثلوث *θ-θuluuθ* Tuesday. اليوم الثلوث *l-yoom θ-θuluuθ.* Today is Tuesday. يوم الثلوث *yoom θ-θuluuθ* 1. Tuesday. 2. on Tuesday. كل يوم ثلوث *kill yoom θuluuθ* every Tuesday.

ثلتعش *θalattaᶜaš* (var. ثلتعشر *θalattaᶜšar*) thirteen. (with foll. n. *θalattaᶜšar*). ثلتعشر مدرسة *θalattaᶜšar madrasa* thirteen schools. كم تبي؟ *čam tabi?* How many do you want? ثلتعش *θalattaᶜaš* (var. ثلتعشر *θalattaᶜšar*) thirteen.

ثلاثين *θalaaθiin* thirty. ثلاثين دولار *θalaaθiin duulaar* $30.00. في الثلاثينات *fi θθalaaθiinaat* during the thirties, in the thirties.

ثالث *θaaliθ* 1. third. يوم ثالث *yoom θaaliθ* a third day. 2. (w. foll. gen.) the third. ثالث يوم *θaaliθ yoom* the third day. ثالث يوم في الأسبوع هو الاثنين *θaaliθ yoom fi li-sbuuᶜ huwa l-'aθneen.* The third day of the week is Monday. ثالث شي *θaliθ šayy* the third thing, thirdly.

مثلث *mθallaθ* (p.p. from II ثلث *θallaθ*) 1. tripled. 2. (p. *-aat*) triangle.

ثلاثمية *θalaaθimya* three hundred. ثلاثمية *θalaaθimya* (var. *θalaaθimyat*) درهم *dirhim.* 300.00 dirhams. ثلاثة مليون *θlaaθa malyoon* three million.

ث ل ج *θlj*

ثلج *θallaj* II 1. to refrigerate, freeze s.th. ذالحين اللحم إما تثلجه والا تطبخه *đalḥiin l-laham 'imma θθallja walla tiṭbaxa.* Nowadays you either freeze meat or cook it . 2. to get cold, freeze. هني في بلادنا الدنيا ما تثلج *hini fi blaadna d-dinya ma θθallij.* Here, in our country, it doesn't get very cold (or

ث م م θmm

ثم θamm p. ثمام θmaam (also less common حلج ḥalj) mouth. !صك ثمك ṣikk θammak! Shut up!

ث م ن ١ θmn

ثمن θamman II to price, set a value on s.th. بكم تثمن هذا؟ b-kam θθammin haaδa? For much do you value this? قبل لا تبيع البيت لازم تثمنه gabil la tbiic l-beet laazim θθammna. Before you sell the house, you have to have it appraised. اللي ما يعرفك ما يثمنك 'illi ma ycarfak ma yθammink. He who doesn't know you doesn't respect you.

تثمن tθamman V to be appraised, assessed. جات البلدية وقالت، «بيتك لازم يتثمن قبل لا نهدمه yat l-baladiyya w-gaalat, "beetak laazim yiθθamman gabil-la nhadma." The municipal officials came and said, "Your house must be assessed before we demolish it." هذا شي ما يتثمن haaδa šayy ma yiθθamman. This is a priceless thing.

ثمن θaman p. أثمان 'aθmaan 1. price. كم ثمن هذي السيارة؟ kam θaman haaδi s-sayyaara? What is the price of this car? 2. value.

ثمين θamiin precious, costly. الذهب من المعادن الثمينة δ-δahab min l-macaadin θ-θamiina. Gold is one of the precious metals.

ث م ن ٢ θmn

ثمانية θamaanya (var. θamaaniya) eight. عندي ثمانية cindi θamaanya. I have eight. (with foll. n.) θamaanyat. ثمانية أنفار θamaaniyat 'anfaar 800 people, 800 individuals.

freeze). 3. to become frozen. اللحم ثلج l-laḥam θallaj. The meat became frozen.

ثلاجة θallaaja p. -aat 1. refrigerator. فيه ثلاجة وغسالة في الشقة fii θallaaja w-ġassaala fi š-šigga. There are a refrigerator and a washing machine in the apartment. 2. (only p. -aat) refrigerated (grocery) stores. الدكاكين القديمة هالحين ماكو. كلهم ثلاجات d-dikaakiin l-gadiima halḥiin maaku. killahum θallaajaat. There are no old shops now. They are all refrigerated (grocery) stores.

مثلج mθallaj (p.p. from II ثلج θallaj) refrigerated, frozen, iced, icy. لحم مثلج laḥam mθallaj frozen meat. شاي مثلج čaay mθallaj iced tea.

ث ل ت ت ع ش θlttcš

ثلتعش θalattacaš. See under ث ل ث θlθ.

ث م ر θmr

استثمر staθmar X to invest (e.g., money) profitably. استثمر فلوسه في التجارة staθmar fluusa fi t-tijaara. He invested his money in trade.

ثمرة θamara p. -aat benefit, gain. بدون ثمرة b-duun θamara without benefit.

مستثمر mistaθmir (act. part. from X استثمر staθmar) 1. an investor. 2. having invested. آنا مستثمر فلوس واجد في شركة البترول 'aana mistaθmir fluus waayid fi šarikat l-batrool. I have invested a lot of money in the petroleum company.

ثمانتعش *θamaantaᶜaš* (var. ثمانتعشر *θamaantaᶜšar*) eighteen. امية وثمانتعش *'imya w-θamaantaᶜaš.* 118. (with foll. n.) *θmaantaᶜšar.* ثمانتعشر نفر *θamaantaᶜšar nafar* 118 people.

ثمانين *θamaaniin* eighty. ثمانين درهم *θamaaniin dirhim* eighty dirhams. في الثمانينات *fi θ-θamaaniinaat* in the eighties, during the eighties.

ثمن *θumn* p. أثمان *θmaan* one eighth. ثمن الأربعين خمسة *θumn l-'arbaᶜin xamsa.* One eighth of forty is five.

ثامن *θaamin* 1. eighth. شرطي ثامن *širṭi θaamin* an eighth policeman. بنتي طلعت الثامنة في صفها *binti ṭlaᶜat θ-θaamna fi ṣaffha.* My daughter ranked eighth in her class. (with foll. n.) the eighth. ثامن بنية *θaamin bnayya* the eighth girl.

ث ن ع ش *θnᶜš*

اثنعش *θnaᶜaš* (var. اثنعشر *θnaᶜšar*) twelve. عندي اثنعش *ᶜindi θnaᶜaš.* I have twelve. إمية واثنعش *'imya w-θnaᶜaš* 112. (with foll. n.) اثنعشر *θnaᶜšar.* اثنعشر درهم *θnaᶜšar dirhim.* twelve dirhams.

ث ن ي ١ *θny*

ثنى *θanna* II 1. to do twice, repeat. كل وثنى *kal w-θanna.* He ate and went for seconds. إذا تثني تطيح مريض *'iδa θθanni ṭṭiiḥ miriiḍ.* If you do it again, you will fall ill. 2. (with على *ᶜala*) to second, support s.th. ثنى على اللي قلته *θanna ᶜala lli gilta.* He seconded what you had said.

استثنى *staθna* X to exclude, except. التنديل خذهم كلهم وما استثنى أحد *t-tindeel xaδhum killahum w-ma staθna 'aḥad.* The foreman took all of them and did not exclude anyone. القانون يستثني الأجانب من البعثات *l-ġaanuun yistaθni l-'ayaanib min l-biᶜθaat.* The law excludes foreigners from scholarships.

ثنين *θneen* (less common var. اثنين *'aθneen*) f. ثنتين *θinteen* 1. two. ثنين وعشرين *θneen w-ᶜišriin* twenty-two. تزوج ثنتين *zzawwaj θinteen.* He married two. 2. (with suff. pron.) the two of, both of. ثنينهم جاوا *θneenhum yaw.* Both of them came. ثنتينهن عرسن *θinteenhin ᶜarrasan.* Both of them (f.) got married.

الاثنين *l-'aθneen* (less common var. اللثنين *l-laθneen*) Monday. يوم الاثنين *yoom l-'aθneen* on Monday. اليوم الاثنين *l-yoom l-'aθneen.* Today is Monday. كل اثنين *kill 'aθneen* every Monday. كل الاثنين *kill l-'aθneen* Monday, all day long.

ثنينات *θneenaat-* (only with suff. pron.) = ثنين *θneen* + suff. pron. ثنيناتهم *θneenaattum* both of them. ثنيناتهن *θneenaattin* both of them (f.).

ثاني *θaani* p. *-yiin* (f. ثانية *θaanya*) 1. another. ولد ثاني *walad θaani* another boy. بنت ثانية *bint θaanya* another girl. أشيا ثانية *'ašya θanya* other things. 2. (with preced. def. n.) the second. الولد الثاني *l-walad θ-θaani* the second boy. البنت الثانية *l-bint θ-θaanya* the second girl. ثاني مرة *θaani marra* the second time, again.

ثانية *θaanya* p. ثواني *θawaani* one second. ثانية واحدة! *θaanya waḥda!*

just a minute! جرى المية متر في عشرين ثانية *yira l-miyat mitir fi ᶜišriin θaanya.* He ran the hundred meters dash in twenty seconds. خمس ثواني *xams θawaani* five seconds.

ثانوي *θaanawi* p. *-yyiin* 1. secondary. مدرسة ثانوية *madrasa θaanawiyya* secondary school. 2. minor, of less importance. شي ثانوي *šayy θaanawi* minor thing. قضية ثانوية *gaḍiyya θaanawiyya* minor problem.

ث ن ي ٢ *θny*

ثنى *θina* (يثني *yiθni)* to bend s.th. لا تثني هذا الواير! *la tiθni haaða l-waayar!* Don't bend this wire!

ثني *θani* (v.n.) bending.

مثني *maθni* (p.p.) p. *-yyiin* bent.

ث ن ي ٣ *θny*

ثني *θini* p. ثنيان *θinyaan* six-year-old camel.

ث ن ي ن *θnyn*

ثنين *θneen.* See under **ث ن ي** ١ *θny.*

ث و ب *θwb*

تثاوب *tθaawab* VI to yawn. يتثاوب واجد. يمكن نعسان *yiθθaawab waayid. yamkin naᶜsaan.* He is yawning a lot. He might be sleepy.

ثوب *θoob* p. اثواب *θwaab* (also less common كندورة *kandoora* and دشداشة *dišdaaša*) man's dress. (prov.) لو يدري عمير كان شق ثوبه *lo yidri ᶜmeer čaan šagg θooba.* Ignorance is bliss. (lit., "If Omeer had known, he would have ripped his clothes.") ثوب العافية *θoob l-ᶜaafya* good health. (prov.) ثوب العارية ما يدفي *θoob l-ᶜaariyya ma ydaffi.* Fair without and foul within. (lit., "The naked lady's clothes don't keep [her] warm.")

ثياب *θyaab* (also more common هدوم *hduum.* See under **ه د م** *hdm*) clothes. ضرب ثيابه أوتي *ðirab θyaaba 'uuti.* He ironed his clothes.

ثواب *θawaab* reward from God for good deeds. الثواب من الله *θ-θawaab min aḷḷaah.* Reward for good deeds is given by God. عطني درهم ثواب لك ولوالدينك *ᶜaṭni dirhim θawaab-lak w-li-waaldeenak* (said by a beggar). Give me a dirham as a reward from God for you and your parents.

ث و ر *θwr*

ثار *θaar* (يثور *yθuur)* 1. to revolt, rebel. الحاكم موب زين. رعيته ثاروا عليه *l-ḥaakim muub zeen. raᶜiita θaaraw ᶜalee.* The ruler is not good. His followers revolted against him. 2. to erupt, explode. البركان ثار *l-burkaan θaar.* The volcano erupted.

ثور *θoor* p. ثيران *θiiraan* bull, steer (prov.) الثور الحمر ما يموت إلا حمر *θ-θoor l-ḥamar ma ymuut 'illa ḥamar.* A leopard cannot change his spots. (prov.) نقول ثور يقول حلبه *nguul θoor yguul ḥilba.* (describes someone who is so dense that he cannot see an impossible thing, or who argues for an impossible thing. lit., "We say, 'Bull,' and he says, 'Milk it!'"). (prov.) إذا برق البرق طالع عين ثورك *'iða birag l-barg ṭaaliᶜ ᶜeen θoorak.* Look before you leap! (lit., "If lightning strikes, look your bull in the eye"!)

ثورة *θawra* p. *-aat* revolt, revolution

الثـورة العربيـة *θ-θawra l-ᶜarabiyya* the Arab Revolution. حصل ثورة على الفساد *ḥaṣal θawra ᶜala l-fasaad.* There was a revolt against corruption. ثورة أهلية *θawra 'ahliyya* civil strife.

ثـوري *θawri* p. *-yyiin* revolutionary, reactionary. عمـل ثـوري *ᶜamal θawri* revolutionary act.

ثـاير *θaayir* (act. part. from *θaar*) 1. rebellious 2. (p. ثوار *θuwwaar*) rebel, revolutionary person. الثوار المسـلمين في أفغانسـتان حـاربوا الـروس *θ-θuwwaar l-muslimiin fi 'afġaanistaan ḥarbaw r-ruus.* The Muslim rebels in Afghanistan fought against the Russians.

ثوم *θwm*

ثوم *θuum* (coll.) garlic. s. راس ثوم *raas θuum.* الثوم يطلع هني *θ-θuum yiṭlaᶜ hini.* Garlic grows here. حصلت ثوم في قوطي *ḥaṣṣalt θuum fi guuṭi.* I got garlic in a can.

ثير *θyr*

ثاير *θaayir.* See under **ثور** *θwr.*

ج

ج ا *jaa*

جا *jaa.* See under **ي ي** *yy.*

ج ا ث و م *jaaθwm*

جاثوم *jaaθuum.* See under **ي ا ث و م** *yaaθwm.*

ج ا خ و ر *jaaxwr*

جاخور *jaaxuur* p. جواخير *jiwaaxiir* (less common var. ياخور *yaaxuur*) stable. الخيل في الجاخور *l-xeel fi l-jaaxuur.* The horses are in the stable.

ج ا م *jaam*

جام *jaam* (coll.) glass, sheets of glass. s. *-a.* نظف الجام من فضلك *naððif l-jaam min faðlak!* Clean the glass, please!

ج ا م و س *jaamws*

جاموس *jaamuus* p. جواميس *jiwaamiis* buffalo, water buffalo. جاموسة *jaamuusa* buffalo cow.

ج ا ه *jaah*

جاه *jaah* dignity, honor. جاه الله عليك تساعدني! *jaah aḷḷa ᶜaleek tsaaᶜidni!* Please! I plead with you to help me!

ج ب ر *jbr*

جبر *jibar.* See under **ي ب ر** *ybr.*

ج ب س *jbs*

جبس *jibs* (coll.) jibs 1. gypsum 2. plaster of Paris.

ج ب ل ١ *jbl*

جابل *jaabal* III (more common var. قابل *gaabal*). 1. to meet, run across s.o. كنت ماشي في السوق وقابلته *čint maaši fi s-suug w-jaabalta.* I was walking in the marketplace and met him. 2. to have an interview with s.o. قابلت التنديل *jaabalt t-tindeel.* I had an interview with the foreman. 3. to face, encounter s.o. قابلته وجه لوجه *jaabalta weeh l-weeh.* I met him face to face.

ج ب ل ٢ *jbl*

جبل *jibal.* See under **ي ب ل** *ybl.*

ج ب ل ٣ *jbl*

الجابلة *l-jaabla.* See under **ق ب ل** *gbl.*

ج ب ن *jbn*

جبن *jibin* (coll.) cheese. الجبن الزين غالي *l-jibin z-zeen ġaali.* Good cheese is expensive. كليت جبن وخبز *kaleet jibin w-xubiz.* I ate cheese and bread. عندك جبن؟ *ᶜindak jibin?* Do you have cheese?

ج ب ه *jbh*

جابه *jaabah* III. See under **ي ب ه** *ybh.*

ج ت ت *jtt*

جت *jatt* (coll.; less common *gatt*) clover. s. عرق جت *ᶜirj jatt.* clover bunch. الجت تاكله البهايم *l-jatt taakla l-bihaayim.* Grazing animals eat clover.

ج ت ت ي *jtty*

جتي *jatti* p. جتاتي *jitaati* jetty, landing wharf.

ج ث ث *jθθ*

جثة *jiθθa* p. جثث *jiθaθ* corpse,

cadaver.

ج ث م ن *jθmn*

جثمان *jiθmaan* p. *-aat* corpse, remains.

ج ح ح *jḥḥ*

جح *jiḥḥ* (coll.). See **ي ح ح** *yḥḥ*.

ج ح ش *jḥš*

جحش *jahš* (less commmon var. *yaḥš*) p. جحوش *jḥuuš,* جحاش *jḥaaš* young donkey, ass. بغينا نبيع الجحش في سوق حرج *baġeena nbiiᶜ l-jaḥš fi suug ḥaraj.* We wanted to sell the young donkey at the auction. جحش ما يفتهم *jaḥš ma yiftihim.* He is an ass; he doesn't understand.

ج ح ي م *jḥym*

جحيم *jaḥiim* (less common var. *yaḥiim*) hell, hellfire. هو عايش في جحيم *huwa ᶜaayiš fi jaḥiim.* He is living in hell.

ج د ح *jdḥ*

جدح *jidaḥ* (يجدح *yijdaḥ*) (less common var. *yidaḥ*) 1. to drill (with a drill). 2. to spark, strike fire. فيه نوع من الحجر يجدح زين *fii nooᶜ min l-ḥiyar yijdaḥ zeen.* There is a kind of flint that sparks well.

جدح *jadḥ* (v.n.) 1. drilling. 2. sparking.

جداحة *jaddaaḥa* p. *-aat* cigarette lighter.

مجدح *majdaḥ* p. مجادح *mijaadiḥ* drill. المجدح نستعمله حق الجدح *l-majdaḥ nistaᶜimla ḥagg l-jadḥ.* We use a drill for drilling.

ج د د[١] *jdd*

جد *jadd.* See under **ي د د** *ydd.*

ج د د[٢] *jdd*

جد *jadd* (يجد *yjidd*) 1. to work hard. جديت في دراستي *jaddeet fi diraasti.* I worked hard at my studies. 2. to be serious, be in earnest. ما يجد في كلامه *ma yjidd fi kalaama.* He is not serious about what he says.

جدد *jaddad* II. See under **ي د د** *ydd.*

تجدد *tajaddad* V. See under **ي د د** *ydd.*

جد *jidd* (v.n.) seriousness, earnestness. بالجد والاجتهاد تحصل اللي تبغاه *b-l-jidd w-li-jtihaad tḥaṣṣil illi tibġaa.* Through seriousness and diligence you get what you want.

جدة *jadda* Jaddah (city in Saudi Arabia).

جديد *jadiid.* See under **ي د د** *ydd.*

أجد *'ajadd.* See under **ي د د** *ydd.*

جدر *jidir* p. جدور *jduur* pot, cooking pot. (prov.) اللي بالجدر يطلعه الملاس *'illi b-l-jidir yṭallᶜa l-millaas.* Time will tell one's good and bad qualities. (lit., "What's in the pot will be shown by the ladle.") (prov.) جدر ولقى غطاه *jidir w-liga ġaṭaa.* A man is known by the company he keeps. Birds of a feather flock together. (lit., "A cooking pot and it has found its lid.")

ج د ف *jdf*

جدف *jaddaf* II. See under **ي د ف** *ydf.*

مجداف *mijdaaf.* See under **ي د ف** *ydf.*

ج د ل[1] *jdl*

جادل *jaadal* III to argue, argue with s.o. بس يجادل. ما فيه فـايدة *bass yjaadil. ma fii faayda.* He only argues. It's fruitless. جـادلني بشـي مـا منـه فـايدة *jaadalni b-šayy ma minna faayda.* He argued with me about something that is of no use.

تجادل *tjaadal* VI to argue with each other. تجادلنـا مـدة طويلـة بـدون نتيجـة *tjaadalna mudda ṭawiila b-duun natiija.* We argued for a long time without any result.

جدل *jadal* argument, dispute. بدون جـدل *b-duun jadal* without any argument.

جدال *jidaal* = جـدل *jadal.* See جدل *jadal.*

ج د ل[2] *jdl*

جدل *jadal (يجدل yijdil)* to braid, plait (the hair, a rope, etc.) هـني بعـض الرجـاجيل يجدلـون شـعرهم *hini baᶜḍ r-rayaayiil yijidluun šaᶜarhum.* Here, some men braid their hair.

جديلة *jidiila* p. جدايل *jidaayil* (less common بسـيلة *bisiila*) braid, plait. جدايله مـا تقـول عنهـا إلا جدايـل عروسـة *jidaayla ma tguul ᶜanha 'illa jidaayil ᶜaruusa.* His braids are nothing but those of a bride. أبـو الجدايـل *'ubu l-jidaayil* the one (m.) with the braids.

ج د م *jdm*

جدم *jadam* p. جـدام *jdaam* (less common var. قدم *gadam, ġadam*) foot (part of a body).

جدام *jiddaam* 1. (prep.) in front of. وقـف قـدام البنايـة *wigaf jiddaam li-bnaaya.* He stood in front of the building. القضية اللي قدامنـا *l-gaḍiyya lli jiddaamna.* the problem we are facing, the problem under discussion. ليـش مـا تقـرا الخـط قدامنـا؟ *leeš ma tigra l-xaṭṭ jiddaamna?* Why don't you read the letter in our presence? 2. (adv.) in front. جلس قدام *yilas jiddaam.* He sat in front. روح قدام *ruuḥ jiddam.* Go in front.

ج د و ل *jdwl*

جدول *jadwal* p. جـداول *jidaawil* 1. schedule, chart, table. جـدول الدراسـة *jadwal d-diraasa* study schedule; schedule of studies. جـدول الضـرب *jadwal ḍ-ḍarb* multiplication table.

ج د و م *jdwm*

جدوم *jadduum* p. جدادم *jidaadiim* 1. hatchet. 2. adz.

ج ذ ر *jðr*

جذر *jaðir* p. جذور *juðuur* root of a plant. تشلعه من جـذره *člaᶜa min jaðra.* He uprooted it.

ج ر ء *jr'*

جرأ *jira' (يجرأ yijra')* to dare, venture, have the courage. ما تجرأ تطلع بدون برقع *ma tijra' tiṭlaᶜ b-duun birgiᶜ.* She doesn't dare go out without a veil. جرأ على *jira' ᶜala* to have the courage to do s.th. جرأ علينا بشـلاخه *jira' ᶜaleena b-člaaxa.* He had the gall to lie to us.

تجارأ *tjaara'* VI = جرأ *jira'.* See under ج ر ء *jr'.*

جريء *jarii'* p. جريئين *-iin* courageous, bold.

جرأة *jir'a* (v.n. from جرأ *jira'*) courage, daring. عنده الجرأة يتحكى هالشكل *ᶜinda l-jir'a yitḥačča haš-šikil.* He has the nerve to talk in this manner.

أجرأ *'ajra'* (elat.) 1. more courageous. 2. the most courageous.

ج ر ب ١ *jrb*

جرب *jarrab* II (less common var. *yarrab*) to try out, test. اخذ المفتاح وجرب هذي السيارة *'ixiđ l-miftaaḥ w-jarrib haađi s-sayyaara.* Take the key and try this car.

جرب *jarab.* See under **ي ر ب** *yrb.*

أجرب *'ajrab.* See under **ي ر ب** *yrb.*

جربان *jarbaan.* See under **ي ر ب** *yrb.*

تجربة *tajriba* p. تجارب *tajaarib* 1. experiment, test. حصلنا نتايج زينة من التجربة *ḥaṣṣalna nataayij zeena min t-tajriba.* We got good results from the experiment. 2. trial, test. هالموظف تحت التجربة *hal-muwađđaf taḥt t-tajriba.* This employee is on probation. السيارة تحت التجربة *s-sayyaara taḥt t-tajriba.* The car is being tested. 3. experience, practice. كل واحد يتعلم بالتجربة *kill waaḥid yitᶜallam b-t-tajriba.* Everyone learns by experience. هو شيبة. شاف تجارب واجدة *huwa šeeba. šaaf tajaarib waayda.* (He is) an old man. He has a lot of experiences.

مجرب *mjarrib* (act. part. from II جرب *jarrab*) p. *-iin* 1. having tested, tried out s.o. or s.th. آنا مجرب ذيك السيارة *'aana mjarrib điič s-sayyaara.* I have tried that car. 2. experienced. تنديل مجرب *tindeel mjarrib* experienced foreman.

ج ر ب ٢ *jrb*

جرب *jirba* = قرب *girba.* See under **گ ر ب** *grb.*

جريب *jiriib* = قريب *giiriib.* See under **گ ر ب** *grb.*

ج ر ب و ع *jrbwᶜ*

جربوع *jarbuuᶜ.* See under **ي ر ب و ع** *yrbwᶜ.*

ج ر ث م *jrθm*

جرثومة *jarθuuma* p. جراثيم *jiraaθiim* germ, microbe. تحصل جراثيم في الوسخ *tḥaṣṣil jiraaθiim fi l-waṣax.* You will find germs in dirt.

ج ر ج ر *jrjr*

جرجر *jarjar* (يجرجر *yjarjir*) to pull, drag. السيارة وقفت وجرجرناها حق الكراج *s-sayyaara wgufat w-jarjarnaaha ḥagg l-garaaj.* The car stalled and we pulled it to the garage.

ج ر ح *jrḥ*

جرح *jiraḥ* (يجرح *yijraḥ*) to wound, cut. جرحه في وجهه وودوه المستشفى *jraḥa fi weeha w-waddoo l-mustašfi.* He wounded him in his face and they took him to the hospital. جرح يده *jiraḥ yadda.* He cut his hand. كفى! لا تجرح شعوره! *kafa! la tijraḥ šuᶜuura!* Enough! Don't hurt his feelings!

جرح *jarraḥ* II to cut, wound many times. المحسن جرحني *li-mḥassin jarraḥni.* The barber nicked me.

تجرح *tjarraḥ* V (pass. of II جرح *jarraḥ*) to be cut, wounded many times.

انجرح *njiraḥ* VII to be wounded (pass. of جرح *jiraḥ*).

جرح *jarḥ* p. جروح *jruuḥ* wound, cut.

جراحة *jiraaḥa* surgery.

جـراح *jarraaḥ* p. *-iin* surgeon. نقول «دخـتر جـراح» والا «جـراح» بـس *ngull "daxtar jarraaḥ" walla "jarraaḥ" bass.* We say, "*daxtar jarraaḥ*" or "*jarraaḥ*" only.

ج ر د *jrd*

جـرد *jirad* (يجـرد *yujrud*) to make an inventory. كل راعي دكـان يجـرد بضاعتـه *kill raa*ᶜ*i dikkaan yujrud bđaa*ᶜ*ta.* Every store owner makes an inventory of his goods on hand.

انجـرد *njirad* VII to be inventoried, be taken stock of. كل دكان لازم ينجرد مرة في السـنة *kill dikkaan laazim yinjirid marra fi s-sana.* Every store has to be inventoried once a year.

جـراد *jaraad* = يراد *yaraad.* See under يرد *yrd.*

جريـدة *jariida* p. جرايد *jiraayid* (less common var. *yaraayid*) newspaper. قريت الجريدة *gareet l-jariida.* I read the newspaper. الجرايد مـا تكتـب أخبـار زينـة *l-jiraayid ma tiktib 'axbaar zeena.* Newspapers do not write good news.

جريـد *jiriid* (coll.) palm branches stripped of their leaves.

مجـرد *mujarrad* mere, nothing more than. هذا مجرد كلام لا أكثر ولا أقل *haađa mujarrad kalaam la 'akθar wala 'agall.* This is mere talk, nothing more or less.

ج ر ر *jrr*

جـر *jarr* (يجر *yjurr*) = (more common var. *yarr*) *yarr*. See under يرر *yrr*.

انجر *njarr* VII. See under يرر *yrr*.

جر *jarr* (v.n.). See under يرر *yrr*.

جرارة *jarraara.* See under يرر *yrr*.

ج ر س *jrs*

جرس *jiras* p. جراس *jraas* bell.

ج ر ش *jrš*

جرش *jiraš* (يجرش *yujruš*) to grind (e.g., corn). حرمتي جرشت ذرا *ḥurumti jrašat đira.* My wife ground corn.

جـرش *jarš* (v.n.) grinding (of corn, wheat, etc.)

جريش *jiriiš* (coll.) 1. dish in which the main ingredient is coarsely ground wheat. s. *-a* 2. coarsely ground wheat or corn.

جاروشـة *jaaruuša* p. جواريش *jiwaariiš* hand mill, grinder. ذالحين جواريش ماكو *đalḥiin jiwaariiš maaku.* There are no hand mills (for grinding grain) nowadays.

ج ر ع *jr*ᶜ

جـرع *jira*ᶜ (يجـرع *yijra*ᶜ) = (less common var.) جـرأ *jira'.* See under جرء *jr'.*

تجـارع *tjaara*ᶜ VI = (less common var.) تجارأ *tjaara'.* See under جرء *jr'.*

جريع *jarii*ᶜ = (less common var.) جريء *jarii'.* See under جرء *jr'.*

جرعـة *jur*ᶜ*a* = (less common var.) جرأة *jur'a.* See under جرء *jr'.*

أجـرع *'ajra*ᶜ (elat.) = (less common var.) أجرأ *'ajra'.* See under جرء *jr'.*

ج ر ف ١ *jrf*

جـرف *jiraf* (يجـرف *yujruf*) to wash

away, carry downstream. الماي جرف الجلبوت *l-maay jiraf l-jalbuut.* The water carried the jolly-boat downstream. الماي جرف الساماني اللي خليناه على السيف *l-maay jiraf s-saamaan illi xaḷḷeenaa ᶜala s-siif.* The water washed away the things we left on the seashore.

انجرف *njiraf* VII to be swept away.

ج ر ف ٢ *jrf*

جرفة *jirfa* (coll.; less common var. قرفة *girfa*) cinnamon.

ج ر م *jrm*

أجرم *'ajram* (يجرم *yijrim*) IV to commit a crime. أجرم مرة ثانية. عدموه *'ajram marra θaanya. ᶜadamoo.* He committed another crime. They executed him.

جرم *jurm* p. جرام *jraam* crime, offense.

إجرام *'ijraam* (v.n. from أجرم *'ajram*) act of committing a crime. مكافحة الإجرام *mkaafaḥat l-'ijraam* crime prevention.

جريمة *jariima* p. جرايم *jiraayim* crime, felony. البوق جريمة *l-boog jariima.* Stealing is a crime.

مجرم *mijrim* (act. part. from أجرم *'ajram*) p. *-iin* criminal.

ج ر ي *jry*

جرى *jira* (يجري *yijri*) 1. to run, flow. مطرت أمس والماي جرى في الوديان *muṭrat 'ams w-l-maay jira fi l-widyaan.* It rained yesterday and the water ran in the valleys. 2. to happen, occur. ويش اللي جرى لك؟ *weeš illi jaraa-lak?* What happened to you? كل شي جرى بساع *kill šayy jira b-saaᶜ.* Everything happened fast. شو اللي جرى منه؟ *šu lli jira minna?* What has he done?

جارى *jaara* III to go along with, adjust to. جاريته إلين حول *jaareeta 'ileen ḥawwal.* I went along with him until he moved.

جاري *jaari* (act. part. from جرى *jira*) 1. running, flowing. الماي الجاري *l-maay l-jaari* the running water. 2. current, present. الشهر الجاري *š-šahar l-jaari* the current month.

مجرى *majra* p. مجاري *majaari* 1. flow, stream. مجرى الماي *majra l-maay* the flow of water. 2. course, passage (of events). مجرى الحوادث *majra l-ḥwaadiθ* the course of events.

ج ز ر *jzr*

جزر *jizar* (coll.) carrots. s. جزرة *jzara* p. *-aat.* الجزر زين *l-jizar zeen.* Carrots are good. عندك جزر؟ *ᶜindak jizar?* Do you have carrots? كم الجزر؟ *čam l-jizar?* How much are carrots? كليت جزرتين *kaleet jazrateen.* I ate two carrots.

جزيرة *jaziira* (less common var. *yaziira*) p. جزاير *jazaayir* island, peninsula. الجزيرة العربية *l-jaziira l-ᶜarabiyya* the Arabian Peninsula. جزيرة داس *jaziirat daas.* Das Island (in Abu Dhabi). جزيرة السعديات *jaziirat s-saᶜdiyyaat* Sadiyat Island (in Abu Dhabi). جزيرة طوم الصغرى *jaziirat ṭuum ṣ-ṣiġra* Lesser Tumb Island. جزيرة طوم الكبرى *jaziirat ṭuum l-kubra* Greater Tumb Island (close to Bandar Abbas in Iran).

الجزاير *l-jazaayir* Algeria.

جزايـري *jazaayri* p. *-yyiin* 1. an Algerian. 2. from Algeria, characteristic of Algeria.

ج ز ز *jzz*

جـز *jazz* (يجـز *yjizz)* to shear hair or wool of an animal. يجـزون صـوف الخروف لـين يكـبر *yjizzuun ṣuuf l-xaruuf leen yikbar.* They shear the wool of a lamb when it gets older.

جـز *jazz* (v.n.) act of shearing the hair or wool of an animal.

جزة *jazza* (less common var. *jizza*) (n. of inst.) one act of shearing. (prov.) اللي ما يرضى بجزة يرضى بجزة وخروف *'illi ma yirđa b-jazza yirđa b-jazza w-xaruuf.* Cut your losses and run. Half a loaf is better than none.

ج ز ف[1] *jzf*

جـازف *jaazaf* III (with بـ *b-*) to risk, stake. لا تجـازف بحيـاتك! *la jjaazif b-ḥayaatak!* Don't risk your life!

مجازفة *mjaazafa* (v.n.) risk, hazard.

مجازف *mjaazif* (act. part. from III جازف *jaazaf*) p. *-iin* 1. having risked s.th. تـوه مجـازف بحياتـه *tawwa mjaazif b-ḥayaata.* He has just risked his life. 2. reckless. 3. adventurous.

ج ز ف[2] *jzf*

جزف *jizaf* (يجزف *yijzif*) to be abundant or plentiful. (more frequent var. يزف *yizaf* (يـزف *yizzif*). الخضار والفاكهة تزف في القيـظ *li-xđaar w-l-faakha tizzif fi l-geeđ.* Vegetables and fruit are plentiful in the summer.

مجزوف *majzuuf* (p.p.) (more frequent var. مـيزوف *mayzuuf*) plentiful, abundant.

جزاف *jazzaaf* p. جزازيف *jizaaziif* (less common يزاف *yazzaaf*) fish wholesale dealer; wholesale dealer.

ج ز ي *jzy*

جـزى *jiza* (يجزي *yijzi*) to reward, give. زجزاك الله خـير! *jazaak aḷḷa xeer!* May God reward or bless you (for it)!

جـازى *jaaza* III = 1. جـزى *jaza* to reward, repay. 2. to punish. الله يجـازيك يـا زمـان! *'aḷḷa yjaaziik ya zamaan!* May God punish you, time! أبوه جازاه لانـه كـان يسـكر *'ubuu jaazaa linna čaan yiskar.* His father punished him because he used to drink.

تجـازى *tjaaza* VI 1. to be rewarded. 2. to be punished.

جــزا *jaza* 1. reward. جـزاك على الله *jazaak ᶜala ḷḷa.* Your reward is in heaven. 2. punishment, penalty. فيـه جزا في الآخـرة *fii jaza fi l-'aaxra.* There is punishment in the hereafter. ضربة جـزا *đarbat jaza* penalty kick (in soccer).

ج س د *jsd*

جسد *jasad.* See under **ي س د** *ysd.*

ج س ر *jsr*

جسـر *jisir* p. جسـور *jsuur,* جسـورة *jsuura* bridge, beam (more common كبري *kubri* p. كباري *kabaari*).

جسـارة *jasaara* 1. strength. 2. boldness, impudence.

ج س س *jss*

جـس *jass* (يجـس *yjiss)* 1. to feel,

examine by touching. الدختر جس نبض المريض *d-daxtar jass nabð̣ l-miriið̣.* The doctor felt the patient's pulse. 2. to try to find out, try to get information. سار السوق لاجل يجس لنا الأخبار *saar s-suug lajil yjiss lana l-'axbaar.* He went to the marketplace in order to find out for us what was happening.

تجسس *tjassas* V to spy. طرشوه يتجسس لهم *ṭarrašoo yijjassas lahum.* They sent him to spy for them.

جاسوس *jaasuus* p. جواسيس *juwaasiis* spy.

جاسوسية *jaasuusiyya* spying, espionage.

ج ش ش *jšš*

جش *jišš* (coll.) kind of dates (the most important of which are جش الورد *jišš l-ward.*) s. جشة *jišša.*

جش *jašš* kind of fish.

ج ص ص *jṣṣ*

جص *jaṣṣ* (coll.) gypsum, plaster of Paris. s. *-a.*

جصاص *jaṣṣaaṣ* p. *-a* gypsum wholesale dealer.

ج ع د١ *jᶜd*

جعد *jiᶜad* (يجعد *yijᶜid*) to sit down. (more common var. قعد *giᶜad.*) See under **ق ع د** *gᶜd.*

جاعدة *jaaᶜda.* See under **ي ع د** *yᶜd.*

ج ع د٢ *jᶜd*

جعد *jaᶜad* (coll.) (kind of herbs used for medicinal purposes, e.g., a stomach ache). s. عرق جعد *ᶜirj jaᶜad.*

ج غ ر ف ي *jġrfy*

جغرافيا *juġraafya* geography. درست جغرافيا *dirast juġraafya.* I studied geography. درس في الجغرافيا *dars fi l-juġraafya* lesson in geography.

ج غ م *jġm*

جغم *jiġam* (يجغم *yijġam*). See under **ي غ م** *yġm.*

جغمة *jiġma* (n. of inst.). See under **ي غ م** *yġm.*

ج ف ر *jfr*

جفير *jifiir* p. جفران *jifraan* basket made from palm tree branches. يحطون التمر في جفير ويودونه السوق *yḥuṭṭuun t-tamir fi jifiir w-ywadduuna s-suug.* They put dates in a basket and take it to the marketplace.

ج ف ف *jff*

جف *jaff.* See under **ح ف ف** *ḥff.*

جفف *jaffaf* II. See under **ح ف ف** *ḥff.*

جاف *jaaff.* See under **ح ف ف** *ḥff.*

ج ف ل *jfl*

جفل *jifal* (يجفل *yijfil*) 1. to start, jump with fright. جفل البعير لين شاف الذيب *jifal l-biᶜiir leen čaaf ð-ðiib.* The camel got a start when it saw the wolf. 2. to shy. جفل الجاهل لين سمع الانفجار *jifal l-yaahil leen simaᶜ l-'infijaar.* The child shied when he heard the explosion.

جفل *jaffal* II to startle, frighten. صوت البارود جفلني *ṣoot l-baaruud jaffalni.* The sound of gunpowder startled me.

ج ف ن *jfn*

جفن *jifin.* See under **ي ف ن** *yfn.*

ج ل ب *jlb*

جلب *jilab (يجلب yijlib)* 1. to attract, draw s.th. هالمنظر جلب نظري *ha l-manđar jilab nađari.* This view attracted my attention. 2. to bring, cause. هذي القضايا تجلب مشاكل *haađi l-gađaaya tijlib mašaakil.* These matters cause problems.

جلاب *jallaab* p. جلاليب *jlaaliib* slave trader. هالحين ما تحصل جلاليب لأن الناس تمدنوا *halḥiin ma tḥaṣṣil jlaaliib li'an n-naas tmaddanaw.* Nowadays you will not find slave traders because people have become civilized.

ج ل د *jld*

جلد *jilad (يجلد yajlid)* to flog or beat s.o. with a whip. (less common var. *yalad.*) جلدوه إمية جلدة *jladoo 'imyat jalda.* They whipped him a hundred times.

جلد *jallad* II to bind (a book). جلدت الكتاب لانه تمزق *jallatt li-ktaab linna tmazzag.* I had the book bound because it got torn.

جلد *jild.* See under **ي ل د** *yld.*

جلدة *jalda* p. *-aat* stroke with a whip.

جلاد *jallaad* p. *-iin* executioner, hangman.

مجلد *mjallid* (act. part. from II جلد *jallad*) p. *-iin* book-binder.

مجلد *mjallad* (p.p. from جلد *jallad*) p. *-iin* 1. bound, having been bound (book) 2. (p. *-aat*) volume (of a book).

ج ل س *jls*

جلس *jilas.* See under **ي ل س** *yls.*

جلس *jallas* II. See under **ي ل س** *yls.*

جلسة *jalsa* p. *-aat* session (of a committee, a court, of ministers, etc.) meeting.

مجلس *majlis.* See under **ي ل س** *yls.*

جالس *jaalis.* See under **ي ل س** *yls.*

جلاس *jallaas* p. *-iin* ship cook.

ج ل ع *jl[c]*

انجلع *njila[c]* VII to be sent or driven away. انجلع وراح مرة *njila[c] w-raaḥ marra.* He was sent away for good. انجلع من وجهي! *njili[c] min weehi!* Go away! Beat it!

ج ل ل *jll*

جل *jall (يجل yjill)* 1. to be exalted, great. الله عز وجل *'aḷḷaah [c]azza wa jall.* God is powerful and exalted.

أجل *'ajall (يجل yjill)* IV to esteem highly, honor. كل الناس في الإمارات يجلون الشيخ زايد *kill n-naas fi l-'imaaraat yjilluun š-šeex zaayid.* All the people in the Emirates highly esteem Shaikh Zayid. أجلك الله *'ajallak aḷḷa* (an expression used as an apology for mentioning a distasteful thing) Excuse me for saying this, but... Pardon the expression, but... أجلك الله تطلع ريحة خايسة من البواليع *'ajallak aḷḷa tiṭla[c] riiḥa xaaysa min l-buwaalii[c].* Excuse me for saying that a rotten smell comes out of the sewers.

جلالة *jalaala* majesty. جلالة الملك *jalaalat l-malik* his majesty the king. جلالة الملوك *jalaalat l-muluuk* their majesties the kings. جلالـة السـلطان *jalaalat s-sulṭaan* his majesty the Sultan.

جليل *jiliil* p. *-iin* (more common var. *giliil*). See under گ ل ل *gll*.

ج م ب *jmb*

جمـب *jamb* = *yamm*. See under ي م م *ymm* and ج ن ب *jnb*.

ج م ب ا ز *jmbaaz*

جمباز *jimbaaz* gymnastics.

جمبازي *jimbaazi* p. *-yya* gymnast.

جمبيزي *jimbeezi* p. *-yyaat* gymnasium. رحنـا الجمبـيزي ولعبنـا كـورة *riḥna l-jimbeezi w-li^c^abna kuura.* We went to the gymnasium and played soccer.

ج م ج م *jmjm*

جمجمـة *jimijma* p. جماجم *jamaajim* skull.

ج م د *jmd*

جمـد *jimad* (يجمد *yijmad*) 1. to freeze, harden. الماي جمـد في الثلاجـة *l-maay jimad fi θ-θallaaja.* The water froze in the refrigerator. 2. to stand still, freeze (usually out of fear). جمدت لين شفته يفـهق *jimatt leen čifta yifhag.* I froze when I saw him breathe his last. 3. to harden, solidify. الصالونة جمدت في الثلاجة *ṣ-ṣaaloona jmidat fi θ-θallaaja.* The soup hardened in the refrigerator.

جمّد *jammad* II to freeze s.th. الهوا البارد يجمـد المـاي *l-hawa l-baarid yjammid l-maay.* Cold weather freezes water. 2. to freeze (assets). جمد أمواله وترك البلد *jammad 'amwaala w-tirak l-balad.* He froze his assets and left the country.

تجمـد *tjammad* V to be or become frozen. تجمـد المـاي *jjammad l-maay.* The water became frozen. تجمدت أموال الشركـة *jjammadat 'amwaal š-šarika.* The assets of the company were frozen.

جـامد *jaamid* p. *-iin* 1. frozen. 2. solid, hard.

جماد أول *jamaad 'awwal* Jumada I (the fifth month of the Islamic (Hegira) year). جماد ثاني *jamaad θaani* Jumada II (the sixth month of the Islamic (Hegira) year).

ج م ر *jmr*

جمر *jamir*. See under ي م ر *ymr*.

جمرة *jamra*. See under ي م ر *ymr*.

مجمـار *mijmaar* p. مجامـير *mjaamiir* censer, incense holder.

ج م ر ك *jmrk*

جمـرك *jamrak* (يجمرك *yjamrik*) to pay customs duty. قبل لا يسمحون لك تدخل البلد لازم تدفع جمرك على التلفزيـون *gabil la yismaḥuun lak tudxul l-balad laazim tidfa^c^ jumruk ^c^ala t-talavizyoon.* Before they let you enter the country, you have to pay duty for the television set.

جمـرك *jumruk* p. جمارك *jamaarik* 1. customs, customs duty. 2. (p. جمارك *jamaarik*) customhouse. رحت الجمارك ودفعت الرسوم *riḥt l-jamaarik w-difa^c^t r-rusuum.* I went to the customs and paid the customs duty.

ج م ع[1] *jm^c^*

جمـع *jima^c^* (يجمع *yijma^c^*). See under ي م ع *ym^c^*.

ج م ع ٢ jm^c

جمّع *jamma^c* II. See under ي م ع *ym^c*.

تجمّع *tajamma^c, tjamma^c* V to assemble, congregate together. الناس تجمعت قدام الجامع يوم الجمعة *n-naas jjamma^cat jiddaam l-yaami^c yoom l-yim^ca.* The people assembled in front of the mosque on Friday.

انجمع *njima^c* VII to be collected, gathered together.

اجتمع *jtima^c* VIII to meet, have a meeting. مجلس التعاون رايح يجتمع باكر *majlis t-ta^caawun raayiḥ yijtami^c baačir.* The (Gulf) Cooperation Council will meet tomorrow. اجتمعنا وياهم *jtima^cna wiyyaahum.* We met with them.

جمع *jam^c* 1. collecting together. جمع الجهال في مكان واحد صعب *jam^c l-yihhaal fi mukaan waaḥid ṣa^cb.* Gathering the kids in one place is difficult. 2. gathering (of people). كان فيه جمع كبير من الناس *čaan fii jam^c čibiir min n-naas.* There was a large crowd of people. 3. addition. توه صغير ما يعرف الجمع بعد *tawwa ṣġayyir ma y^carf l-jam^c ba^cad.* He is still a young boy; he doesn't know addition yet.

جمعة *jim^ca.* See under ي م ع *ym^c*.

جمعية *jam^ciyya* p. *-aat* association, organization, society. جمعية تعاونية *jam^ciyya ta^caawuniyya* cooperative society. الجمعية العامة *l-jam^ciyya l-^caamma* the General Assembly. جمعية ملكية *jam^ciyya malakiyya* royal academy. جمعية خيرية *jam^ciyya xayriyya* charitable organization. جمعية الأمم *jam^ciyyat l-'umam* the League of Nations.

جميع الناس *jimii^c n-naas* all of the people. الجميع *l-jimii^c* everyone, everybody.

أجمعين *'ajma^ciin* (reply to a wish for a good thing, e.g., good health, fortune, etc.) approx.: May it be the same for everyone.

جماعة *jamaa^ca* p. *-aat* 1. group of people. شفته يتحكى ويا جماعة *čifta yitḥačča wiyya jamaa^ca.* I saw him talking with a group of people. 2. (with foll. n. or suff. pron.) relations. جماعتي *jamaa^cti* my people, my relations.

تجميع *tajmii^c* (v.n. from II جمع *jamma^c*) assembly (of machinery parts). مصنع تجميع *maṣna^c tajmii^c* assembly plant.

إجماع *'ijmaa^c* unanimity, agreement, consensus. وافقوا بالإجماع *waafgaw b-l-'ijmaa^c.* They agreed unanimously.

اجتماع *jtimaa^c* p. *-aat* 1. meeting. اليوم عندنا اجتماع الساعة خمس *l-yoom ^cindana jtimaa^c s-saa^ca xams.* Today we have a meeting at five o'clock. 2. gathering, assembly.

اجتماعي *jtimaa^ci* 1. social. الحالة الاجتماعية *l-ḥaala li-jtimaa^ciyya* social conditions. وزارة الشؤون الاجتماعية *wizaarat š-ši'uun li-jtimaa^ciyya* the ministry of social affairs. 2. sociable, friendly. موب اجتماعي؛ ما يرمس أحد *muub jtimaa^ci; ma yrammis 'aḥad.* He is not sociable; he doesn't talk to anyone.

جامع *jaamiᶜ*. See under **ي م ع** *ymᶜ*.

جامعة *jaamᶜa*. See under **ي م ع** *ymᶜ*.

مجموع *majmuuᶜ* (p.p. from جمع *jimaᶜ*) 1. collected, gathered. الناس مجموعين في قصر الشيخ *n-naas majmuuᶜiin fi gaṣr š-šeex.* The people are gathered at the Shaikh's palace. 2. sum, total. كم مجموع المصاريف؟ *čam majmuuᶜ l-maṣaariif?* What is the total of the expenses?

مجتمع *mijtamaᶜ* p. *-aat* society, community.

ج م ل ١ *jml*

جمل *jammal* II. See under **ي م ل** *yml*.

جملة *jumla* total, sum. جملة أشيا *jumlat 'ašya* some things. بالجملة *b-l-jumla* in whole groups. ناس تركوا بالجملة *naas trikaw b-l-jumla.* People left in whole groups. 2. by wholesale. تاجر بالجملة *taajir b-l-jumla* wholesale dealer.

جمال *jamaal* beauty.

جميل *jamiil*. See under **ي م ل** *yml*.

جميل *jamiil* p. جمايل *jimaayil* favor. ناكر الجميل *naakir l-jamiil* ungrateful.

أجمل *'ajmal*. See under **ي م ل** *yml*.

ج م ل ٢ *jml*

جمل *jamal*. See بعير *biᶜiir* under **ب ع ر** *bᶜr*.

جمال *jammaal* p. جماميل *jmaamiil* 1. camel driver. 2. camel owner.

ج م ه ر *jmhr*

تجمهر *tjamhar* (يتجمهر *yitjamhar*) to gather together. تجمهروا الناس لين سمعوا ضرب النار *jjamharaw n-naas leen simᶜaw ḍarb n-naar.* The people gathered when they heard the sound of gunshots.

جمهور *jamhuur* p. جماهير *jamaahiir* 1. crowd, group of people. كان فيه جمهور كبير في المطار *čaan fii jamhuur čibiir fi l-maṭaar.* There was a big crowd in the airport. 2. الجماهير *l-jamaahiir* the masses, the people. الجماهير تؤيد الشيخ زايد *l-jamaahiir t'ayyid š-šeex zaayid.* The public support Shaikh Zayid.

جمهوري *jamhuuri* 1. republican. الحزب الجمهوري *l-ḥizb l-jamhuuri* the Republican Party. نظام جمهوري *niḍaam jamhuuri* republican system (of government) 2. (p. جمهوريين *jamhuuriyyiin*) Republican, member of the Republican Party.

جمهورية *jamhuuriyya* p. *-aat* republic. الجمهورية اللبنانية *l-jamhuuriyya l-libnaaniyya* the Lebanese Republic. جمهورية مصر العربية *jamhuuriyyat maṣir l-ᶜarabiyya.* the Arab Republic of Egypt.

ج ن ب *jnb*

جنب *jannab* II 1. to keep away. فلان جنب يعني ابتعد عن المشاكل *flaan jannab yaᶜni btiᶜd ᶜan l-mašaakil.* If (you say that) somebody *"jannab"*, that means he kept away from problems. 2. to keep s.o. out of the way of (e.g., problems, danger, etc.) هذا العمل يجنبك مشاكل واجدة *haaða l-ᶜamal yjannibk mašaakil waayda.* This practice will keep you away from many problems.

تجنب *tjannab* V to avoid, keep away from. لازم تتجنب الخطر *laazim tijjannab* *l-xaṭar.* You have to avoid danger.

جنب *janb* 1. side. 2. = يم *yamm.* See under **ي م م** *ymm.*

جنوب *jinuub* (prep.) 1. south of. جنوب المدينة *jinuub l-madiina* south of the city, the southern part of the city. 2. south. من الجنوب *min l-jinuub* from the south.

جنوبي *jinuubi* southern, south. أمريكا الجنوبية *'amriika l-jinuubiyya* South America (as opposed to جنوب أمريكا *jinuub 'amriika* the southern part of America).

جانب *jaanib* p. جوانب *juwaanib* side, direction. من هالجانب *min ha l-jaanib* from this side or angle. من كل جانب *min kill jaanib* or من كل الجوانب *min kill l-jawaanib* from everywhere, on all sides.

أجنبي *'ajnabi* 1. foreign, alien. البلاد الأجنبية *li-blaad l-'ajnabiyya* the foreign countries. بضاعة أجنبية *bḏaa*ᶜ*a 'ajnabiyya* foreign merchandise. 2. (p. أجانب *'ajaanib*) foreigner.

ج م ب ن *jmbn*

جمبن *jambin* (cf. English "jumping") speed bumps. (no known singular)

ج ن ج ف *jnjf*

جنجفة *jinjifa* p. *-aat* (more common ورق *warag* or بتة *patta*) deck of playing cards. لعبنا جنجفة *li*ᶜ*abna jinjifa.* We played cards.

ج ن ح *jnḥ*

جناح *janaaḥ* p. جنحان *jinḥaan,* أجنحة *'ajniḥa* wing (of a bird, airplane, building, etc.). جناح يسار *janaaḥ yisaar* left wing (in soccer). جناح يمين *janaaḥ yimiin* right wing (in soccer).

ج ن د *jnd*

جند *jannad* II to recruit, draft, enlist. جندت الحكومة ناس واجدين *jannadat li-ḥkuuma naas waaydiin.* The government drafted many people.

تجند *tjannad* V to be drafted, recruited. كل الشباب تجندوا *kill š-šabaab jjannadaw.* All the young men were drafted.

جندي *jindi* p. جنود *jnuud* soldier. جيشنا فيه خمسين ألف جندي *jeešna fii xamsiin 'alf jindi.* Our army has 50,000 soldiers. الجندي المجهول *l-jindi l-majhuul* the unknown soldier.

جندية *jindiyya* (usually with ال *l-*) 1. the army, the military. 2. military service.

ج ن ز *jnz*

جنازة *janaaza* p. *-aat* funeral, funeral procession.

ج ن س *jns*

تجنس *tjannas* V to become a naturalized citizen. تجنست بالجنسية الأمريكانية *jjannast b-l-jinsiyya l-'amrikaaniyya.* I became a naturalized American citizen.

جنس *jins* p. اجناس *jnaas* 1. kind, sort, species. عنده كراسي من كل جنس ᶜ*inda karaasi min kill jins.* He has all kinds of chairs. هذا رجال بطال موب من جنسك *haaða rayyaal baṭṭaal muub min jinsak.* This is a bad man; he is not your sort of person. 2. race. تحصل هني ناس من كل الأجناس *tḥaṣṣil hini* *naas min kill li-jnaas.* You find people of all races here. الجنس البشري *l-jins l-bašari* the human race.

جنسية *jinsiyya* nationality, citizenship. شو جنسيتك الأصلية؟ *šu jinsiitak l-'aṣliyya?* What is your original nationality?

ج ن ط *jnṭ*

جنطة *janṭa* p. جنط *jinaṭ* (more common var. شنطة *šanṭa*) suitcase, bag. حط الجنط على الميزان! *ḥuṭṭ l-jinaṭ ᶜala l-miizaan!* Put the suitcases on the scales! حطيت هدومي في جنطة وسرت *ḥaṭṭeet hduumi fi janṭa w-sirt.* I put my clothes in a bag and left.

ج ن گ ل ي *jngly*

جنقلي *jangali* p. *-yya* rogue, rascal. عمري ما شفت جنقلي مثل هذا *ᶜumri ma šift jangali miθil haaða.* I have never seen a rascal like this one. الجنقلي دوني *l-jangali duuni.* A rascal is a base person.

ج ن ن *jnn*

جن *jann.* See under **ي ن ن** *ynn.*

جنن *jannan* II. See under **ي ن ن** *ynn.*

انجن *njann* VII. See under **ي ن ن** *ynn.*

جن *jinn* (coll.). See under **ي ن ن** *ynn.*

جني *jinni.* See under **ي ن ن** *ynn.*

جن *janna.* See under **ي ن ن** *ynn.*

جنون *jnuun.* See under **ي ن ن** *ynn.*

مجنون *majnuun.* See under **ي ن ن** *ynn.*

ج ن ي *jny*

جنى *jina (يجني yijni)* to wrong or cause harm to s.o. جنى على عياله. تركهم جهال *jina ᶜala ᶜyaaḷa. tirakhum yihhaal.* He caused harm to his kids. He left them when they were very young. إذا فنشته تجني عليه *'iða fannašta tijni ᶜalee.* If you fire him, you will wrong him.

جناية *jnaaya* p. *-aat* crime, felony.

جاني *jaani* (act. part. from جنى *jina*) p. *-yiin* criminal, culprit.

ج ن ي ر *jnyr*

جنير *jiniir* (less common var. *jneer*) p. *-iyya* 1. engineer. يشتغل جنير حق شركة فلبس *yištaġil jiniir ḥagg šarikat fillips.* He works as an engineer for the Philips company. 2. skillful mechanic.

ج ه د *jhd*

جاهد *jaahad* III to fight, wage a holy war. جاهد في سبيل الله *jaahad fi sabiil llaah.* He fought for the cause of God. الأفغان يجاهدون في سبيل وطنهم *l-'afġaan yjaahduun fi sabiil waṭanhum.* The Afghans fight in their country's behalf.

أجهد *'ajhad (yijhid)* IV to exert, strain. أجهد نفسه في الشغل *'ajhad nafsa fi š-šuġul.* He strained himself with work.

اجتهد *jtihad* VIII to work hard, exert one's effort. اجتهد في دراسته *jtihad fi draasta.* He worked hard at his studies. اجتهد في شغله *jtihad fi šuġla.* He exerted his best effort at work.

جهد *jahd* p. جهود *jhuud* effort, endeavor. بذل كل جهده في شغله *biðal kill jahda fi šuġla.* He exerted every possible effort at work.

جهاد *jihaad* jihad, holy war.

اجتهاد *jtihaad* (v.n. from VIII اجتهد *jtihad*) pains, trouble, exertion, endeavor.

مجاهد *mjaahid* p. *-iin* religious warrior.

مجتهد *mijtahid* p. *-iin* hardworking, diligent, industrious. طالب مجتهد *ṭaalib mijtahid* hard working student. هو مجتهد *huwa mijtahid.* He is diligent.

ج ه ز *jhz*

جهز *jahhaz* II (with ب *b-*) to supply, furnish, equip with. جهزنا البيت الجديد بالزل *jahhazna l-beet l-yidiid b-z-zall.* We furnished the new house with carpets. المعرس جهز العروسة بالهدوم والذهب *l-miᶜris jahhaz l-ᶜaruusa b-li-hduum w-ð-ðahab.* The bridegroom provided the bride with clothes and gold.

تجهز *tjahhaz* V (with ب *b-*) to be provided with s.th. العيال تجهزوا بالكتب والقلامة *li-ᶜyaal jjahhazaw b-l-kutub w-l-gḷaama.* The kids were provided with books and pencils.

جهاز *jhaaz* 1. apparatus, set. جهاز التلفزيون *jhaaz t-talavizyoon* the TV set. جهاز لاسلكي *jhaaz laasilki* wireless set. 2. things bought for a bride.

جاهز *jaahiz* = بارز *baariz.* See under ب ر ز *brz.*

ج ه ل *jhl*

تجاهل *tjaahal* 1. to ignore s.o. or s.th. جاوا وقعدوا ولكن تجاهلناهم *jaw w-gaᶜdaw walaakin jjaahalnaahum.* They came and sat down, but we ignored them. 2. to feign ignorance, pretend to know nothing. لا تتجاهل الموضوع. أنت تعرفه *la tijjaahal l-mawḍuuᶜ. 'inta tᶜarfa.* Don't feign ignorance of the subject. You know it.

جهل *jahil* (v.n.) 1. ignorance. من جهله ضيع فلوسه *min jahla ḍayyaᶜ fluusa.* Because of his ignorance he lost his money. 2. illiteracy.

مجهول *majhuul* (p.p.) unknown. الجندي المجهول *l-jindi l-majhuul* the unknown soldier.

ج ه م *jhm*

جهام *jhaam* (coll.) dark clouds. s. *-a.*

ج ه ن م *jhnm*

جهنم *jhannam* hell, hellfire.

ج و ب *jwb*

جاوب *jaawab* III 1. to answer, reply to s.o. طرشت له خط وجاوبني *ṭarrašt-la xaṭṭ w-jaawabni.* I sent him a letter and he answered me. 2. (with على *ᶜala*) to answer (e.g., a letter, a request, etc.) جاوب على السؤال *jaawab ᶜala s-su'aal.* He answered the question.

استجاب *stajaab* X 1. to comply with a request. رمسته بالموضوع وهو استجاب لي *rammasta b-l-mawḍuuᶜ w-huwa stajaab-li.* I talked to him about the subject, and he complied with my request. الله استجاب لدعاي *'aḷḷa stajaab la duᶜaaya.* God answered my prayers.

استجوب *stajwab* X to interrogate, question s.o. الشرطة زخوه واستجوبوه

ساعتين *š-širṭa zaxxoo w-stajwaboo saaᶜteen.* The police arrested him and interrogated him for two hours.

جواب *jawaab* p. *-aat* answer, reply. ما فيه جواب *ma fii jawaab.* There is no answer.

ج و ت *jwt*

جوت *juut* (coll.) jute.

ج و ت ي *jwty*

جوتي *juuti* p. جواتي *juwaati* pair of shoes. اشتريت خمس جواتي حق العيال. *štireet xams juwaati ḥagg li-ᶜyaal.* I bought five pairs of shoes for the children.

ج و خ *jwx*

جوخ *juux* broadcloth. هالحين الناس قاموا يلبسون جوخ *halḥiin n-naas gaamaw yilbisuun juux.* Nowadays people have started to wear broadcloth.

ج و د *jwd*

جاد *jaad (يجود yjuud)* 1. to grant, give lavishly. الله جاد *'aḷḷa jaad.* God has given (us things) bountifully. 2. (with *b-*) to give s.th. to s.o. lavishly. الله جاد علينا بالمطر *'aḷḷa jaad ᶜaleena b-l-muṭar.* God has sent us a lot of rain. جاد عليهم بمليون درهم. *jaad ᶜaleehum b-malyoon dirhim.* He generously granted them one million dirhams. 3. to master s.th., be proficient in s.th. سجل في المدرسة الليلية وذالحين يجيد القراية والكتابة *sajjal fi l-madrasa l-layliyya w-ðalḥiin yjiid li-graaya w-li-ktaaba.* He enrolled in an evening school, and now he has mastered reading and writing. يجيد الإنكليزي *yjiid l-'ingiliizi.* He knows English well.

جود *jawwad* II 1. to get hold of s.o. or s.th., grab s.o. or s.th. جود فلوس وايدة *jawwad fluus waayda.* He got a lot of money. He saved a lot of money. (prov.) جود مجنونك لا يجيك أجن منه *jawwid maynuunak la yiik 'ayann minna.* A bird in the hand is worth two in the bush. (lit., "Hold on to your crazy person lest a crazier one come along.") 2. to arrest. الشرطة جودوه واستجوبوه *š-širṭa jawwadoo w-stajwaboo.* The police arrested him and interrogated him.

جود *juud* generosity, liberality.

ج و د ر ي *jwdry*

جودري *joodri* p. جوادر *juwaadir* rug made from flax fibers.

ج و ر *jwr*

جار *jaar (يجور yjuur)* to wrong, oppress (على *ᶜala* s.o.). جار علينا الزمان *jaar ᶜaleena z-zamaan.* Time has wronged us. Time has been unfair to us. أنت تجور على عيالك إذا ما تخليهم يشوفون التلفزيون *'inta jjuur ᶜala ᶜyaaḷak 'iða ma txaḷḷiihum yšuufuun t-talavizyoon.* You will be unfair to your children if you do not let them watch television.

جاور *jaawar* III 1. to live next door to s.o., be the neighbor of s.o. جاورناهم خمس سنين *jaawarnaahum xams sniin.* We lived next door to them for five years. 2. to be close to. دبي تجاور بو ظبي *dbayy jjaawir bu ḍabi.* Dubai is close to Abu Dhabi.

جور *joor* injustice, oppression.

جار *jaar* p. جيران *jiiraan*. See under ي و ر *ywr*.

ج و ز *jwz*

جاز *jaaz* (يجوز *yjuuz*) 1. to be allowed or permitted. الإفطار في شهر رمضان ما يجوز *l-'iftaar fi šahar rumđaan ma yjuuz.* Not to fast during the month of Ramadan is not allowed. الصلاة بدون وضو ما تجوز *ṣ-ṣalaa bduun wađu ma jjuuz.* Prayer without ablution is not permitted. (with ال *l-* + s.o. = s.o. is permitted, allowed to do s.th.) جازت له الصلاة *jaazat-la ṣ-ṣalaa.* He is permitted to pray. ما يجوز لك تفطر في شهر رمضان *ma yjuuz-lak tifṭir fi šahar rumđaan.* You are not allowed not to fast during the month of Ramadan. 2. (with من *min*) to stop, quit. ليش ما تجوز من التدخين؟ *leeš ma jjuuz min t-tadxiin?* Why don't you stop smoking?

جاوز *jaawaz* III to go beyond, exceed, surpass. جاوز أصول الأدب *jaawaz 'uṣuul l-'adab.* He went beyond the fundamentals of good manners. المصاريف جاوزت مليون درهم *l-maṣaariif jaawazat malyoon dirhim.* The expenses exceeded a million dirhams.

تجاوز *tjaawaz* VI to go beyond, overstep, exceed. تجاوز الحدود بتصرفاته *jjaawaz l-ḥuduud b-taṣarrufaata.* He stepped out of bounds in his dealings.

جواز *jawaaz* p. *-aat* passport. عطني التذكرة والجواز من فضلك *ᶜaṭni t-tađkara w-l-jawaaz min fađlak.* Give me the ticket and the passport please.

إجازة *'ijaaza* p. *-aat* leave, vacation. الإجازة الصيفية *l-'ijaaza ṣ-ṣayfiyya* the summer vacation.

جايز *jaayiz* (act. part. from جاز *jaaz*) possible, permissible. موب جايز *muub jaayiz* not possible.

جايزة *jaayza* p. جوايز *jawaayiz* prize, award.

جوز *jooz* (coll.) walnuts. s. *-a* جوز هند *jooz hind* coconuts.

ج و ع *jwᶜ*

جاع *jaaᶜ* (يجوع *yjuuᶜ*) to be or become hungry. يجوع بساع ولو إنه توه كل *yjuuᶜ b-saaᶜ walaw inna tawwa kal.* He gets hungry fast, although he has just eaten.

جوع *jawwaᶜ* II to starve s.o., make s.o. go hungry. الأم ما تجوع عيالها *l-'umm ma jjawiᶜ ᶜyaalha.* A mother won't let her children go hungry. (prov.) جوع كلبك يتبعك *jawwiᶜ čalbak yitbaᶜk.* (lit., "If you starve your dog, he will follow you.") approx. If you humiliate a lowly, base person, he will be on your side.

جوع *juuᶜ*. See under ي و ع *ywᶜ*.

جوعان *juuᶜaan.* See under ي و ع *ywᶜ*.

مجاعة *majaaᶜa* p. *-aat* famine, starvation.

ج و ل *jwl*

تجول *tjawwal* V to wander around, move around. بس تجولنا في شوارع المدينة *bass jjawwalna fi šawaariᶜ l-madiina.* We only wandered around in the streets of the city.

جوال *jawwaal.* See under ي و ل *ywl*.

مجال *majaal.* p. *-aat* 1. (with ل *l-*) room, space. ما فيه مجال للسيارة توقفها هني *ma fii majaal la s-sayyaara twaggiffa hini.* There is no room for the car to be parked here. 2. field, domain, sphere. عنده خبرة طويلة في مجال التعليم *cinda xibra ṭawiila fi majaal t-tacliim.* He has long experience in the field of teaching. 3. opportunity, free scope, free action. عنده مجال واسع يتوظف ويترقى *cinda majaal waasic yitwaḍḍaf w-yitragga.* He has great opportunity to be employed and promoted. إذا صار عنده مجال، هو يتصل فيك *'iða ṣaar cinda majaal, huwa yittaṣil fiik.* If he gets a chance, he will contact you.

تجول *tajawwul* (v.n. from V تجول *tjawwal*) wandering, moving around. منع التجول *manc t-tajawwul* curfew.

متجول *mitjawwil* (act. part. of V تجول *tjawwal*) p. *-iin* 1. wandering, moving. بياع متجول *bayyaac mijjawil* traveling salesman, peddler. 2. having wandered, moved around. آنا متجول في ذيك الشوارع *'aana mijjawwil fi ðiič š-šawaaric.* I have wandered around in those streets.

ج و هـ ر *jwhr*

جوهر *jawhar* essence, essential nature. جوهر الموضوع *jawhar l-mawḍuuc* the essence of the subject. جوهر كلامه *jawhar kalaama* the substance of his talk.

جوهرة *joohara* p. جواهر *jawaahir* jewel, gem.

مجوهرات *mjawharaat* jewelry, jewels, gems.

ج و و *jww*

جو *jaww* 1. atmosphere. آنا موب مستانس من الجو في الحفيز *'aana muub mistaanis min l-jaww fi l-ḥafiiz.* I am not happy with the atmosphere in the office. 2. weather, climate. الجوب هني حار ورطب في القيظ *l-jaww hini ḥaarr w-raṭib fi l-geeḍ.* The weather here is hot and humid in the summer. في الشتا الجو موب حار وموب بارد *fi š-šita l-jaww muub ḥaarr w-muub baarid.* In the winter the weather is neither hot nor cold. بالجو *b-l-jaww* by air.

جوي *jawwi* atmospheric, aerial. طرشته بالبريد الجوي *ṭarrašta b-l-bariid l-jawwi.* I sent it airmail. أسطول جوي *'usṭuul jawwi* air fleet. الضغط الجوي *ḍ-ḍagṭ l-jawwi* atmospheric pressure.

ج ي *jy*

جا *ja* (يجي *yaji*). See under ي ي *yy.*

ج ي ب[١] *jyb*

جاب *jaab* (يجيب *yjiib*). See under ي ي ب *yyb.*

ج ي ب[٢] *jyb*

جيب *jeeb* p. جيوب *jyuub* pocket. (مخبا *maxba* is more common.) See under خ ب ي *xby.*

ج ي ر *jyr*

جير *jiir* asphalt (coll.).

ج ي ر ن *jyrn*

جيرن *jiiran.* See under ي و ر *ywr.*

ج ي س *jys*

جاس *jaas* (يجيس *yjiis*) to feel, touch s.o. or s.th. الدختر جاس قلبي *d-daxtar jaas galbi.* The doctor felt my heart.

ج ي ش *jyš*

جيش *jeeš* p. جيوش *jyuuš* army, armed forces. الجيوش العربية *li-jyuuš l-ᶜrabiyya* the Arab armies. جيشنا فيه تقريب نـص مليـون جنـدي *jeešna fii tagriib nuṣṣ malyoon jindi.* Our army has approximately half a million soldiers.

ج ي ف *jyf*

جيفة *jiifa* p. إجيف *'ijyaf* 1. carrion. 2. bad odor, stinking smell.

ج ي گ ا ر *jygaar*

جيقارة *jiigaara* (common var. جقـارة *jigaara*) p. جقـاير *jigaayir* cigarette. أنت تـدوخ جقـاير؟ *'inta dduux jigaayir?* Do you smoke cigarettes? جقارة لـف *jigaarat laff* hand-rolled cigarettes.

ج ي ك *jyk*

جيك *jeek* p. *-aat* car jack. إذا ما عندك جيك ما تقـدر تبـدل التـاير *'iða ma ᶜindak jeek ma tigdar tbaddil t-taayir.* If you do not have a jack, you cannot change the tire.

ج ي ل *jyl*

جيل *jiil* p. اجيال *jyaal* generation.

ج ي م ١ *jym*

جيم *jiim* name of the letter ج *j*.

ج ي م ٢ *jym*

جيمة *jiima* (more common var. قيمة *giima*). See under **گ ي م** *gym*.

ج ي ي *jyy*

جي *jayya*. See under **ي ي** *yy*.

چ

چ ا د ر *čaadr*

شـادر *čaadir* p. شـوادر *čuwaadir* bedspread.

چ ا ك و چ *čaakwč*

شاكوش *čaakuuč* p. شواكيش *čuwaakiič* hatchet, hammer.

چ ا ي *čaay*

شـاي *čaay* (less common var. *šaay*) 1. tea. تشـرب شـاي والا بـارد؟ *tišrab čaay walla baarid?* Would you like to drink tea or a soft drink? كتلي الشاي *kitli č-čaay* the tea kettle. 2. cup of tea. شـربت شـايين *šribt čaayeen.* I had two cups of tea. عطنا خمس شايات *ᶜaṭna xams čaayaat.* Give us five teas.

چ ب ب ١ *čbb*

كـب *čabb (يكـب yčibb)* to pour out, spill. كب الشاي على هدومه *čabb č-čaay ᶜala hduuma.* He spilled the tea on his clothes.

انكـب *nčabb* VII to be poured out, be spilled. انكب الشاي *nčabb č-čaay.* The tea was spilled.

چ ب ب ٢ *čbb*

كـب *čabb!* (only imper.; expresses rebuke or reprimand) Shut up! Silence!

چ ب د *čbd*

كبـد *čabd* p. كبود *kbuud,* اكباد *kbaad* 1. liver. الكبد كلش مغـذي *č-čabd killiš mġaðði.* Liver is very nutritious. 2. stomach. كبــدي يعورنـــي *čabdi yᶜawwirni.* My stomach hurts.

چ ب ر ١ *čbr*

جـبرة *čabra* p. *-aat* kiosk, vender's stand. صدنـا سمـك ووديناه الجـبرة *ṣidna simač w-waddeenaa č-čabra.* We caught fish and took it to the market.

چ ب ر ٢ *čbr*

كبير *čibiir.* See under **ك ب ر** *kbr.*

چ ب ر ي ت *čbryt*

كـبريت *čabriit* (coll.) 1. matches. s. صلـب كـبريت *ṣilb čabriit* match stick. قوطـي كـبريت *guuṭi čabriit* box of matches. 2. sulfur. يستعملون الكبريت لاجـل يقتلــون دود الشــجر *yistaᶜimluun č-čabriit lajil yugutluun duud š-šiyar.* They use sulfur to kill tree maggots.

كبريتـة *čibriita* p. كباريت *čibaariit* box of matches.

چ ب ش *čbš*

كبش *čabš* (less common var. *kabš*) p. كبـاش *kbaaš* ram. الكبش ذكـر النعجـة *č-čabš ðakar li-nᶜaya.* The ram is the male of the ewe. ذبحنا كبـش في عيـد الضحيـة *ðibaḥna čabš fi ᶜiid ð̣-ð̣iḥiyya.* We slaughtered a ram for the Sacrifice Feast.

چ ت ف *čtf*

كتـف *čattaf* II (less common var. *kattaf*) to tie up, tie up the hands (and feet of s.o.) كتفوه الشرطة وودوه السجن *čattafoo š-širṭa w-waddoo s-sijin.* The police tied him up (and handcuffed him) and took him to jail.

تكتف *tčattaf* V 1. to be bound up, tied up. 2. to fold one's arms. ليش تتكتف وتوقف قدامي؟ *leeš tiččattaf w-toogaf jiddaami?* Why do you fold your arms and stand in front of me?

كتف *čatf* (less common var. *katf*) p. اكتاف *ktaaf,* كتوف *ktuuf* shoulder. دعم اللي قدامه وعور كتفه *diᶜam illi jiddaama w-ᶜawwar čatfa.* He hit (in a car accident) the one in front of him and hurt his shoulder.

چ ت ي *čty*

جتي *čatti* p. جتاتي *čitaati* written note, signed voucher, chit. إذا ما عندك جتي ما تقدر تدش *'iđa ma ᶜindak čatti ma tigdar ddišš.* If you don't have a chit, you cannot enter.

چ ح ت *čḥt*

جحت *čiḥat* (يجحت *yičḥat*) to dismiss s.o. (from a meeting, a house, an office, etc.), chase away, shove away. جحتوه من الحفيز لانه كان بواق *čiḥatoo min l-ḥafiiz linna čaan bawwaag.* They chased him away from the office because he was a thief.

جحت *čaḥt* (v.n.) dismissing, act of chasing away, shoving away s.o.

چ د *čd*

كد *čid* (with foll. perf. v.) 1. certainly, really. كد علمتك *čid ᶜallamtak.* Certainly I have told you. 2. already كد وصل *čid wiṣal.* He has already arrived. 3. (question particle) did, has. كد قال لك؟ *čid gal-lak?* Did he tell you? Has he told you? كد شفته؟ *čid šifta?* Have you (ever) seen him?

چ ذ ب *čđb*

كذب *čiđab* (يكذب *yačđib*) to lie, tell lies. لين قال لك جا الساعة ثمان كذب *leen gal-lak ya s-saaᶜa θamaan čiđab.* When he told you he came at eight, he lied. لا تصدقه. يكذب *la ṣṣaddga. yičđib.* Don't believe him. He tells lies. (with على *ᶜala* on) to tell lies to s.o. كذب علي *čiđab ᶜalayya.* He lied to me. قول الصدق لا تكذب علينا *guul ṣ-ṣidj la tačđib ᶜaleena.* Tell the truth. Don't lie to us. لانه كذب حكموا عليه بالسجن *linna čiđab ḥkamaw ᶜalee b-s-sijin.* Because he lied, they sentenced him to jail.

كذب *čađđab* II = 1. *čiđab.* 2. to call s.o. a liar, accuse s.o. of lying. كذبوه لين قال الصلاة ما تفوته *čađđaboo leen gaal ṣ-ṣalaa ma tfuuta.* They called him a liar when he said that he hadn't missed any prayer. 3. to deny, refute. الحكومة كذبت الخبر *li-ḥkuuma čađđabat l-xabar.* The government denied the news.

تكذب *tčađđab* V to be accused of lying, be proved as having lied. القاضي ما يتكذب *l-gaaḍi ma yiččađđab.* A judge cannot be accused of lying. تكذب قدام كل الناس *ččađđab jiddaam kill n-naas.* He was proved to be a liar in front of all the people.

كذب *čađb* (v.n.) lying, telling lies. الكذب حرام *č-čađb ḥaraam.* Lying is forbidden.

كذبة *čiđba* p. *-aat* lie, untruth.

كذاب *čađđaab* p. *-iin* liar.

أكذب *'ačđab* (elat.) 1. (with من *min*)

more untruthful. هـو أكـذب مـن أخـوه *huwa 'ačðab min 'uxuu.* His is more untruthful than his brother. 2. (with foll. n.) the most untruthful. هو أكذب واحـد *huwa 'ačðab waaḥid.* He is the biggest liar.

چ ذ ي *čðy*

كـذي *čiði* (adv.) like this, in this manner. العيالة يرقصـون بالسـيف والبنـدق ويروحـون يمـين ويسار كـذي *l-ᶜayyaala yurugṣuun b-s-seef w-l-bindig w-yruuḥuun yimiin w-yisaar čiði.* Male dancers dance with swords and rifles, swaying right and left in this manner. كـذي أحسـن *čiði 'aḥsan.* It's better this way. مـا يسـتوي كـذي *ma yistawi čiði* It's not possible in this manner. كذي وكذي *čiði w-čiði* so and so, such and such. قال كذي وكذي *gaal čiði w-čiði.* He said such and such.

چ ر چ ف *črčf*

شرشـف *čarčaf* p. شراشف *čaraačif.* 1. table cloth. 2. bedsheet.

چ ر خ *črx*

جـرخ *čarrax* II to whet, sharpen (knives, razors, etc.) on a whetstone.

جراخ *čarraax* p. *-a, -iin* one whose job is to whet, sharpen edge tools on a whetstone.

چ ر غ *črġ*

جراغي *čarraaġi* (coll.) fire crackers. s. *-yya.*

چ س ي *čsy*

كسـى *čisa* (يكسـي *yičsi)* to clothe, attire. كسى عيالـه هـدوم جديـدة في العيـد *čisa ᶜyaaḷa hduum yidiida fi l-ᶜiid.* He clothed his children in new clothes during the feast.

كسـوة *čiswa* p. *-aat* clothing, attire (usually given to a bride with the dower). المعرس لازم يوفر الكسوة *l-miᶜris laazim ywaffir č-čiswa.* The bride-groom has to provide the clothing.

چ ش م *čšm*

كشـمة *čašma* (less common var. *kašma*) p. *-aat* goggles, pair of eyeglasses. الكشمة هني ضرورية في القيـظ *č-čašma hini ḍaruuriyya fi l-geeḍ.* Goggles are necessary here in the summer.

چ ع ب *čᶜb*

كعب *čaᶜb* p. كعوب *kᶜuub* 1. heel of the foot. 2. bottom, lower part. كعب الكـوب *čaᶜb l-kuub* the bottom of the cup. 3. heel (of a shoe). كعب الجوتي *čaᶜb l-juuti* heel of the shoe.

چ ف ف *čff*

كف *čaff* p. كفوف *kfuuf* (less common var. *kaff*) palm of the hand. قاري الكـف *gaari č-čaff* palmist, chiromancer. قراية الكف *graayat č-čaff* palmistry, chiromancy. ضـرب كـف *ḍirab čaff* to slap (s.o.) on the face.

چ ف ن *čfn*

كفـن *čaffan* II (less common var. *kaffan*) to wrap s.o. in a shroud. كفنوه وودوه المقـبرة *čaffanoo w-waddoo l-maġbara.* They wrapped him (i.e. the dead person) and sent him to the cemetery.

كفـن *čafan* p. اكفـان *kfaan* shroud, winding sheet.

چ ف ي *čfy*

كفى *čifa* (يكفي *yakfi*) See under **ك ف ي** *kfy*.

كفية *čaffiyya* p. *-aat* (more common var. غترة *ġitra*) Arab headdress.

چ ك ل ي ت *čklyt*

تشكليت *čakleet* 1. chocolate. 2. candy.

چ ل ب *člb*

كلب *čallab* II (with ب *b-*) 1. to hold on to, cling to, stick to. كان في السوق ناس واجدين وولدي المسكين كلب بي *čaan fi s-suug naas waaydiin w-wildi l-maskiin čallab biyya.* There were a lot of people in the marketplace and my poor son held on to me. قميصه طار في الهوا وكلب بالشجرة *ġamiiṣa ṭaar fi l-hawa w-čallab b-li-šyara.* His shirt flew in the air and hung up in the tree. كلب بيك. شفيه؟ *čallab biik. š-fee?* He held onto you. What's the matter with him? 2. to insist. كلب بي أسير وياه *čallab biyya 'asiir wiyyaa.* He insisted that I go with him.

كلب *čalb* (less common var. *kalb*) p. كلاب *člaab* dog. ابن كلب *'ibin čalb* knave, rascal. كلب البحر *čalb l-baḥar* (more common var. يريور *yaryuur*) shark. (prov.) ولد الكلب كلبن مثله *wild č-čalb čalbin miθla.* (derog.) Like father like son. (lit., "The son of a dog is a dog like his father.") (prov.) ويش على السحاب من نبح الكلاب؟ *weeš ᶜala s-saḥaab min nabḥ li-člaab?* (lit., "What can the barking of dogs do to clouds?") (prov.) إذا أطريت الكلب ولم العصا *'iða 'aṭreet č-čalb wallim l-ᶜaṣa.* (lit., "If you think you are going to encounter a dog, get your stick ready.")

كلبة *čalba* p. *-aat* 1. female dog, bitch. 2. Kalba (dependency of Sharja, situated on the Gulf of Oman).

كلاب *čillaab* p. كلاليب *člaaliib* 1. hook. 2. clip. 3. safety pin.

كلابتين *čillabteen* p. كلابات *čillaabaat* pair of pliers.

كليب *čleeb* p. *-aat* (dim. of كلب *čalb*) small dog, puppy.

مكلوب *mačluub* p. *-iin* 1. rabid dog. 2. madman, lunatic.

چ ل م *člm*

كلمة *čalma* p. *-aat* 1. word. 2. brief speech. جمع الناس وقال كلمة زينة *yimaᶜ n-naas w-gaal čalmatin zeena.* He gathered the people and gave a good brief speech. 3. influence, authority. إله كلمة في الحكومة *'ila čalma fi li-ḥkuuma.* He has influence in the government. (See also **ك ل م** *klm.*).

چ ل و *člw*

كلوة *čilwa* p. كلاوي *čalaawi* kidney.

چ م *čm*

كم *čam* (less common var. *kam*) 1. (with foll. def. n.) how much? كم الطماط؟ *čam ṭ-ṭamaaṭ?* How much are the tomatoes? كم الهمبة؟ *čam l-hamba?* How much are the mangoes? 2. (with foll. indef. n.) how many? كم واحد تابي؟ *čam waaḥid tabi?* How many (ones) do you want? كم درهم دفعت؟ *čam dirhim difaᶜt?* How many dirhams did you pay? 3. (with foll. v.)

how much? how many? كم دفعت؟ *čam difaᶜt?* How much did you pay? كم تابي؟ *čam tabi?* How much do you want? How many (e.g., kilograms, ones, etc.) do you want? 4. (in a statement with foll. indef. s.n.) some, a few. بعد كم شهر أكمل دراستي *baᶜd čam šahar 'akammil diraasti.* I will complete my studies in a few months. بعد كم يوم تنقضي القضية على خير انشاالله *baᶜd čam yoom tingaðˌi l-gaðˌiyya ᶜala xeer nšaaḷḷa.* In a few days the problem will be solved, hopefully.

چ م م *čmm*

كم *čim* p. كموم *kmuum,* اكمام *kmaam* sleeve.

چ ن ع د *čnᶜd*

جنعد *čanᶜad* (coll.) king mackerel, king fish. s. *-a.* الجنعد سمك زين ولكن الهامور أطيب *č-čanᶜad simač zeen walaakin l-haamuur 'aṭyab.* King mackerel is good fish, but red snapper is more delicious. عمرك كليت جنعد؟ *ᶜumrak kaleet čanᶜad?* Have you ever eaten king fish?

چ ن ن *čnn*

كانـ *činn-* (with foll. suff. pron.) 1. as though, as if. كانه الشيخ زايد *činna š-šeex zaayid* as if he were Shaikh Zayid. تمشي كانها طاووس *tamši činnha ṭaawuus.* She walks as if she were a peacock. قاعدين كانهم حكام *gaaᶜdiin činnhum ḥikkaam.* They are sitting as though they were rulers. 2. like, similar to. أختها كانها حصة *'uxutta činnha ḥiṣṣa.* Her sister is like Hissa. هذي السيارة كانها سيارتنا *haaði s-sayyaara činnha sayyaaratna.* This car is similar to our car. 3. it looks as if, it appears that. كانه ما يبي يشتري أي شي *činna ma yabi yištiri 'ayya šayy.* It looks as if he doesn't want to buy anything. كانهم ما بندوا من الشغل *činnhum ma bannadaw min š-šuġul.* It looks as though they did not finish work.

چ ن گ ل *čngl*

جنقال *čingaaḷ* p. جناقيل *činaagiiḷ* fork (utensil). آنا ما آكل بالجنقال. آكل بيدي *'aana ma 'aakil b-č-čingaaḷ. 'aakil b-yaddi.* I do not eat with a fork. I eat with my hand.

چ و چ ب *čwčb*

جوجب *čoočab* p. جواجب *čiwaačib* spring (of water). تحصل جواجب واجد في الوديان في السعودية *tḥaṣṣil čiwaačib waayid fi l-widyaan fi s-suᶜuudiyya.* You find many springs in ravines in Saudi Arabia.

چ و د *čwd*

كود *čood* (less common var. *kood*) perhaps, possibly, maybe. كود جا *čood ya.* Perhaps he came. He might have come. كود يجي اليوم *čood yaji l-yoom.* He might come today.

چ و ف *čwf*

شاف *čaaf (*يشوف *yčuuf)* (less common var. *šaaf*) 1. to see. شفته أمس *čifta 'ams.* I saw him yesterday. لازم أشوف المدير حق الزيادة *laazim 'ačuuf l-mudiir ḥagg z-ziyaada.* I have to see the manager concerning the increment. شفتهم رايحين السوق *čifittum raayḥiin s-suug.* I saw them going to the marketplace. شوف، إذا بغيت تسكر

اسكر في بيتك *čuuf, 'iða bağeet tiskar 'iskar fi beetak.* Look, if you want to drink (liquor), drink at home. 2. find out, find. رحت لاجل أشوف ش صاير بيناتهم *riḥt lajil 'ačuuf š-ṣaayir beenaattum.* I went in order to find out what had happened between them. رحت وشفت ماكو شي بيناتهم *riḥt w-čift maaku šayy beenaattum.* I went and found there was nothing between them. 3. to encounter, experience. شاف مشاكل واجدة في حياته *čaaf mašaakil waayda fi ḥayaata.* He has encountered many problems in his life. ش بيك؟ كانك شايف الذل *š-biik? činnak čaayif ð-ðill.* What's wrong with you? It looks as if you have experienced humiliation. شاف نجوم الظهر *čaaf nyuum ḍ-ḍuhur.* He went through a lot of trouble. 4. to consider, think, be of the opinion. جربت السيارة وأشوف إنها موب زينة *jarrabt s-sayyaara w-'ačuuf 'innha muub zeena.* I have tried the car and think that it's not good. آنا أشوف إنه رايك في مكانه *'aana 'ačuuf 'inna raayak fi mukaana.* It seems to me that your opinion is sound. شو تشوف؟ أقول لها لو لا؟ *šu ččuuf? 'aguul laha loo la?* What do you think? Shall I tell her or not? آنا أشوف إنك تقول لها أحسن *'aana 'ačuuf 'innak tguul laha 'aḥsan.* It seems to me that it would be better if you tell her.

شوف *čawwaf* II 1. to cause to experience. شوفته نجوم الظهر *čawwafta nyuum ḍ-ḍuhur.* I made him go through a lot of trouble. (lit., "I showed him midday stars.") 2. to show, cause to see. شوفني اياها *čawwafni-yyaaha.* He showed it to me. شوفتهم المكان *čawwafittum l-mukaan.* I showed them the place.

انشاف *nčaaf* VII 1. to be seen. شفيه؟ ما تنشاف *š-fii? ma tinčaaf.* What's going on? You haven't been seen around. 2. وجه الحرمة ما ينشاف *weeh l-ḥurma ma yinčaaf.* A woman's face cannot be seen.

شوف *čoof* (v.n. from شاف *čaaf*) seeing. شوف الفلم عقب الظهر *čoof l-filim ^c^ugb ḍ-ḍuhur.* Seeing the film is in the afternoon.

شوفة *čoofa* (n. of inst.) p. *-aat* look, glance.

چ و ل *čwl*

جولة *čuula* p. *-aat* stove, kerosene stove. في الزمان الأولي الناس كانوا يطبخون على الجولة *fi-z-zamaan l-'awwali n-naas čaanaw yiṭbaxuun ^c^ala č-čuula.* In olden times people used to cook on kerosene stoves.

چ و ن ^١^ *čwn*

كان *čaan (يكون ykuun)* (less common var. *kaan*) 1. to be. كان هني قبل يومين *čaan hini gabil yoomeen.* He was here two days ago. كنت مريض في المستشفى *čint mariiḍ fi l-mustašfa.* I was sick in the hospital. الشيخ زايد رايح يكون هني باكر *š-šeex zaayid raayiḥ ykuun hini baačir.* Shaikh Zayid is going to be here tomorrow. السوق كان مترّوس رجاجيل وحريم *s-suug čaan matruus rayaayiil w-ḥariim.* The marketplace was filled with men and women. كان فيه *čaan fii* There was, there were. كان فيه مطوع في المسجد *čaan fii* *mṭawwaᶜ fi li-msiid.* There was a holy man in the mosque. كان عند *čaan ᶜind* to have. كان عندي إمية دولار. *čaan ᶜindi 'imiyat duulaar.* I had a hundred dollars. كان عندنا خطار أمس *čaan ᶜindana xuṭṭaar 'ams.* We had guests yesterday. 2. (with foll. imperf.) to be doing s.th. or used to do s.th. لين شفته كان يدرس *leen čifta čaan yidris.* When I saw him, he was studying. طاح على الأرض لين كان يحول يركب السيكل *ṭaaḥ ᶜala l-'arḍ leen čaan yḥaawil yirkab s-seekal.* He fell down to the ground when he was trying to ride the bicycle. كان يرقد عقب الغدا *čaan yargid ᶜugb l-ġada.* He used to take a nap after lunch. كنت أمشي كل يوم ساعتين. *čint 'amši kill yoom saaᶜteen.* I used to walk two hours every day. 3. (with foll. act. part.) to be doing s.th. or having done s.th. لما حصلته كان راكب بعيره *lamma ḥaṣṣalta čaan raakib biᶜiira.* When I caught up with him, he was riding his camel. كان حاط ميداره وقاعد يحدق *čaan ḥaaṭṭ miidaara w-gaaᶜid yḥadig.* He had already thrown his fishing line and was fishing. كانوا مغشمريني مدة طويلة. *čaanaw mġašmiriinni mudda ṭawiila.* They had played pranks on me for a long time. لين وصلنا الفندق كان شارب بوطلين بيرة *leen wiṣalna l-fundug čaan šaarib boṭleen biira.* When we arrived at the hotel, he had already had two bottles of beer. 4. (invar. كان *čaan* with foll. perfect in conditional sentences) would have, could have, should have. لو رحت هناك كان شفته *lo riḥt hnaak čaan čifta.* If you had gone there, you would have seen him. لو سمعت الخبر كان طرت من الفرح *lo simaᶜti l-xabar čaan ṭirti min l-faraḥ.* If you had heard the news, you would have been overjoyed. (prov.) لو يدري عمير كان شق ثوبه *lo yadri ᶜmeer čaan šagg θooba.* Ignorance is bliss. (lit., "If Omayr had known, he would have ripped his clothes.") لين حصلته كان حبيت يده *leen ḥaṣṣalta čaan ḥabbeet yadda.* When you found him, you should have kissed his hand. (prov.) لو بغيت الصلاة كان حصلتها *loo baġeet ṣ-ṣalaa čaan ḥaṣṣalitta.* Make hay while the sun shines. (lit., "If you had wanted the prayer, you could have gotten it.")

كون *kawwan* II. See under **ك و ن** *kwn.*

تكون *tkawwan* V. See under **ك و ن** *kwn.*

الكون *l-koon.* See under **ك و ن** *kwn.*

چ و ن[٢] *čwn*

كان *čaan* (conj.; more common var. ان كان *nčaan*) if. (prov.) ان كان شفت رفيقك حلو لا تاكله كله *nčaan čift rifiijak ḥilu la taakla killa.* Do not use up all of your credit at once. (lit., "If you find out that your friend is sweet, don't eat him up all at once.") ان كان عليك فلوس سدها *nčaan ᶜaleek fluus siddha.* If you owe money, pay it back. ان كان عازمني زين. *nčaan ᶜaazminni zeen.* If he has invited me, (it's) fine.

چ و ي *čwy*

كوى *čuwa (يكوي yičwi)* 1. to cauterize. في الزمان الأولي كانوا الناس يكوون الجرح بالصوفان *fi z-zamaan* *l-'awwali čaanaw n-naas yičwuun l-jarḥ b-ṣ-ṣuufaan.* In olden times people used to cauterize wounds with touchwood. 2. to burn. الماي الحار كوى وجهه *l-maay l-ḥaarr čuwa weeha.* The hot water burned his face.

كوى *čawwa* II = *čuwa.*

انكــوى *nčuwa* VII 1. to be cauterized. انكوى الجرح *nčuwa l-jarḥ.* The wound was cauterized. 2. to be burned.

كــوي *čayy* (v.n.; less common var. *kayy*) cauterization. داوي جرحك بالكي *daawi jarḥak b-č-čayy.* Treat your wound with cauterization.

١ چ ي س *čys*

كيــس *čayyas* II (less common var. *kayyas*) to put s.th. in a bag. كيسنا سامانا في اكياس كبيرة *čayyasna saamaanna fi čyaas čibiira.* We put our things in large bags.

كيـــس *čiis* p. اكياس *čyaas* bag, sack. كيس شكر *čiis šakar* bag of sugar, sugar bag. كيس عيش *čiis ᶜeeš* sack of rice, rice sack.

كيــاس *čyaas* p. *-aat* (approx.) half a kilogram. اشتريت عشر كياسات عيش *štireet ᶜašir čyaasaat ᶜeeš.* I bought five kilograms of rice.

٢ چ ي س *čys*

كيس *čiis* expense. على كيسي *ᶜala čiisi* at my expense. يدرس على كيس الحكومة *yidris ᶜala čiis li-ḥkuuma.* He is studying at the government's expense.

چ ي ف *čyf*

كيــف *čeef?* 1. how? كيف حالك؟ *čeef ḥaalak?* How are you? كيف الهوا اليوم؟ *čeef l-hawa l-yoom?* How is the weather today? كيفهم؟ *čeeffum?* How are they? 2. mood, state of mind. لا ترمسه! كيفه موب زين اليوم *la trammsa! čeefa muub zeen l-yoom.* Don't talk to him! He is not in a good mood today. 2. well-being, good humor. ما له كيف اليــوم *ma-la čeef l-yoom.* He is not feeling well today. 3. discretion, will. كل شي على كيفك *kill šayy ᶜala čeefak.* Everything is the way you want it. إذا ما بغيت تجي وايانا بكيفك *'iða ma baġeet tiyi wiyyaana b-čeefak.* If you do not want to come with us, that's up to you.

چ ي ك *čyk*

جيــك *čayyak* II 1. to check, control. تشيك الرديتر من فضلك! *čayyik r-radeetar min faðlak.* Check the radiator, please! هذا يجيك الضغط *haaða yčayyik ð-ðaġt.* This controls the pressure. 2. to examine s.th. for accuracy and safety. رحت الكراج لاجل أجيك البتري *riḥt l-garaaj lajil 'ačayyik l-batri.* I went to the garage in order to have the battery checked. رحت وجيكت عليه *riḥt w-čayyakt ᶜalee.* I went and examined it. 3. to correct, adjust s.th. ما كان يشتغل زين. جيكته *ma čaan yištaġil zeen. čayyakta.* It wasn't working well. I adjusted it. 4. to mark with a check mark. التنديل جيك لي بطاقة الدوام *t-tindeel čayyak-li biṭaaġat d-dawaam.* The supervisor checked the time card for me.

تجيــك *tčayyak* V to be checked الباتري تجيكت *l-baatri ččayyakat.* The battery was checked.

تجييــك *tačyiik* (v.n. from جيك *čayyak*) checking, act of checking.

مجيك *mčayyik* (act. part. from II جيك *čayyak*) 1. having checked s.th. تونى مجيك الماكينة *tawwni mčayyik l-maakiina.* I have just checked the engine. 2. (p. *-iin*) مجيك *mčayyak* having been checked. الماي والآيل والبتري مجيكين *l-maay w-l-'aayil w-l-batri mčayyakiin.* The water, the oil, and the battery have been checked.

چ ي ل *čyl*

كيل *čayyal* II (less common var. *kayyal*) 1. to store up, stockpile. كنا من زمان نكيل بر والا شعير والا اذرا *činna min zamaan nčayyil burr walla šaᶜiir walla 'iðra.* We used, some time ago, to store up wheat, barley, or corn. 2. to provide with grain, cereals, corn, etc.

كيل *čeel* dry measure (of no standard size) for grain.

كيل *čayyaal* p. *-iin* one who measures out grain, cereals, etc.

چ ي م *čym*

جمة *čima* (coll.; less common var. فقع *fagiᶜ*) mushrooms. s. جما *čimaa* a mushroom.

چ ي ن گ و *čyngw*

جينقو *čiingo* (coll.) aluminum sheets. s. لوح جينقو *looḥ čiingo* an aluminum sheet. فيه ناس يعيشون في برستي من جينقو *fii naas yᶜiišuun fi barasti min čiingo.* There are people who live in shacks of aluminum.

ح

ح ا *ḥaa*

حا *ḥaa* name of the letter ح *ḥ*.

ح ا ن ا *ḥaanaa*

حانـا *ḥaana* Hana (woman's name, made famous in the prov. بين حانا ومانا ضيعنـا لحانـا *been ḥaana w-maana ðayyaᶜna lḥaana.* Caught in the middle between the devil and the deep blue sea.). (lit., "Between Hana and Mana we lost our beards.").

ح ا م *ḥaam*

حـام *ḥaam* famous ravine in the Emirate of Fujaira.

ح ب ا ر *ḥbaar*

حبارة *ḥabaara* p. حبر *ḥubir* bustard, sand grouse. الحبـارة طـير صحـراوي *l-ḥabaara ṭeer ṣaḥraawi.* The bustard is a desert bird.

ح ب ب[1] *ḥbb*

حـب *ḥabb* (يحـب *yḥibb*) 1. to kiss. سـاعدني! أحـب علـى يـدك *saaᶜidni! 'aḥibb ᶜala yaddak.* Help me! I will kiss your hand. 2. to like, love s.o. or s.th. يحب القهـوة الحـارة *yḥibb l-gahwa l-ḥarra.* He likes hot coffee. تحب تجي وايانـا؟ *tḥibb tiyi wiyyaana?* Would you like to come with us? حبينا بعض وعرسنا *ḥabbeena baᶜaḍ w-ᶜarrasna.* We loved each other and got married.

حـبب *ḥabbab* II to cause to be liked or loved. يحبـب روحـه حـق النـاس *yḥabbib ruuḥa ḥagg n-naas.* He endears himself to people.

تحـابب *tḥaabab* VI to love each other. تحـابيوا وعرسـوا *tḥaababaw w-ᶜarrasaw.* They loved each other and got married.

حـب *ḥubb* love, affection. الحب عمي *l-ḥubb ᶜamay.* Love is blind. وقع في حبهـا *wugaᶜ fi ḥubbha.* He fell in love with her. حـب النفـس مـوب زيـن *ḥubb n-nafs muub zeen.* Self-love is not good. حـب الاسـتطلاع *ḥubb l-'istiṭlaaᶜ* curiosity. حـب الوطـن *ḥubb l-waṭan* patriotism. واقع في حب بنية جميلة *waagiᶜ fi ḥubb bnayya yimiila.* He is in love with a beautiful girl.

حبـة *ḥabba* p. *-aat* kiss. عطاها حبة *ᶜaṭaaha ḥabba.* He kissed her. He gave her a kiss.

حبيب *ḥabiib* p. حبايب *ḥabaayib,* احباب *ḥbaab* 1. loved one, sweetheart, lover. 2. dear friend. هذيـل أصحابنـا وحبايبنـا *haðeel 'aṣḥaabna w-ḥabaayibna.* These are our friends and loved ones. بنك حبيب *bank ḥabiib* Habib Bank.

محبة *mḥabba* affection, attachment.

محبـوب *maḥbuub* (p.p. from حب *ḥabb*) p. *-iin* 1. lovable, desireable. التواضع خصلـة محبوبـة *t-tawaaðuᶜ xiṣla maḥbuuba.* Modesty is a desirable trait. 2. popular. مغني محبـوب *mġanni maḥbuub* popular singer. محبـوب الجماهـير *maḥbuub l-jamaahiir* very popular (singer, ruler, poet, etc.) among the masses. 3. sweetheart, dear one. ما أقدر على فراق المحبوب *ma 'agdar ᶜala fraag l-maḥbuub.* I cannot put up with being separated from my dear one.

ح ب ب ٢ *ḥbb*

حب *ḥabb* (coll.) p. حبوب *ḥbuub* 1. grains, seeds. حب هيل *ḥabb heel* cardamom seeds. حب شمسي *ḥabb šamsi* sunflower seeds. 2. acne, pestules. حب شباب *ḥabb šabaab* adolescent pimples. 3. tablets, pills. حبوب أسبرين *ḥbuub 'asbiriin.* aspirin tablets. حبوب الحمل *ḥbuub l-ḥamil* contraceptive pills.

حبة *ḥabba* p. *-aat* 1. grain, granule. حبة بر *ḥabbat burr* wheat grain. حبة شعير *ḥabbat šaᶜiir* barley grain. 2. tablet, pill. شرب حبتين أسبرين *širib ḥabbateen 'asbiriin.* He took two aspirin tablets. 3. piece of s.th. (e.g., an orange, an apple, a banana, etc.) عطيته خمس حبات تفاح *ᶜaṭeeta xams ḥabbaat tiffaaḥ.* I gave him five apples. هذا برتقال زين. كم حبة تبي؟ *haaða burtagaal zeen. čam ḥabba tabi?* These are good oranges. How many (ones) do you want?

ح ب ب ٣ *ḥbb*

حب *ḥibb* p. حباب *ḥbaab* large pottery jar for storing drinking water.

ح ب چ *ḥbč*

حبك *ḥibač* (يحبك *yḥabič*) to bind a book. يحبكون الكتب في المطبعة *yḥabčuun l-kutub fi l-maṭbaᶜa.* They bind books at the printing press.

حباك *ḥbaač* (v.n.) bookbinding. الحباك شغلة ما هي بهالقد *li-ḥbaač šaġla ma hi b-hal-gadd.* Bookbinding is not that much of a good job.

حباك *ḥabbaač* p. حبابيك *ḥbaabiič, -a* bookbinder.

ح ب ح ب *ḥbḥb*

حبحب *ḥabḥab* valley in the Emirate of Fujaira.

ح ب ح ر *ḥbḥr*

حبحر *ḥabḥar* (coll.) hot (red) peppers. s. حبة حبحر *ḥabbat ḥabḥar,* حبحرة *-a.* الحبحر يسوي حارق *l-ḥabḥar ysawwi ḥaarig.* Hot (red) pepper causes heartburn.

ح ب س *ḥbs*

حبس *ḥibas* (يحبس *yḥabis*) 1. to jail, imprison. حبسوه خمس سنين *ḥabsoo xams siniin.* They locked him up for five years. 2. to block, confine. حبس علي الطريق. ما أقدر أطلع *ḥibas ᶜalayya ṭ-ṭariig. ma 'agdar 'aṭlaᶜ.* He blocked my way. I cannot go out. 3. to send (e.g. school kids) to detention, keep s.o. (after school) as punishment. المدرس حبس العيال المشاغبين *li-mdarris ḥibas li-ᶜyaaḷ li-mšaaġbiin.* The teacher sent the mischievous kids to detention.

انحبس *nḥibas* VII to be imprisoned, detained. انحبس عشر سنين وطلع *nḥibas ᶜašar siniin w-ṭilaᶜ.* He was imprisoned for ten years and was turned loose thereafter. انحبس مؤبد *nḥibas m'abbad.* He received life imprisonment.

حبس *ḥabs* (v.n. from حبس *ḥibas*) 1. imprisonment, confinement. الحبس حق المجرمين *l-ḥabs ḥagg l-mijirmiin.* Imprisonment is for criminals. حكموا عليه خمس سنين حبس *ḥakamu ᶜalee* *xams siniin ḥabs.* They sentenced him to five years in jail. 2. (p. حبوس *ḥbuus*) jail, prison.

محبوس *maḥbuus* (p.p. from حبس *ḥibas*) 1. locked up, confined. 2. (p. محابيس *maḥaabiis,* محبوسين *-iin*) inmate, convict. صار له محبوس عشرين سنة *ṣaar-la maḥbuus ᶜišriin sana.* He has been in jail for twenty years.

ح ب ش *ḥbš*

الحبشة *l-ḥabaša* Ethiopia, Abyssinia.

حبشي *ḥbaši* 1. Ethiopian, characteristic of Ethiopia. 2. (p. حبش *ḥabaš*) an Ethiopian, an Abyssinian.

ح ب ش ا ن *ḥbšaan*

حبشان *ḥibšaan* Hibshan (oil field in Abu Dhabi).

ح ب ل١ *ḥbl*

حبل *ḥabil* p. حبال *ḥbaal.* rope, cable, line (such as a clothes line). حبل الغسيل *ḥabl l-ġasiil* the clothes line.

ح ب ل٢ *ḥbl*

حبل *ḥibil* (coll.) p. حبول *ḥbuul* (more common syn. بلح *bilḥ* p. بلوح *bluuḥ*) caviar.

ح ب ي *ḥby*

حبى *ḥiba* (يحبي *yḥabi)* to crawl, creep. جا يحبي مثل الجاهل *ya yḥabi miθl l-yaahil.* He came crawling like a child. الطفل يقوم يحبي لين يكون عمره تسعة أشهر *ṭ-ṭifil yguum yḥabi leen ykuun ᶜumra tisᶜat 'ašhir.* A baby starts to crawl when it's nine months old.

ح ت ت١ *ḥtt*

حت *ḥatt (يحت yḥitt)* 1. (v.t.) to rub off, scrape off s.th. (e.g., dirt, hair, etc.). حت شعر شواربه *ḥatt šaᶜar šawaarba.* He rubbed off the hairs of his moustache. حت الوسخ *ḥatt l-wasax.* He rubbed off the dirt. 2. (v.i.) to fall out (hair), fall down. هو شيبة. شعره قام يحت *huwa šeeba. šᶜara gaam yḥitt.* He is an old man. His hair has started to fall out.

ح ت ت٢ *ḥtt*

حت *ḥatta.* See under **ح ت ي** *ḥty.*

ح ت م **حتم** *ḥattam* II (with على *ᶜala*) to impose on s.o., insist. حتم علي أسير وياهم *ḥattam ᶜlayya 'asiir wiyyaahum.* He insisted that I go with them. حتمنا عليهم يجون يتعشون عندنا *ḥattamna ᶜaleehum yiyuun yitᶜaššuun ᶜindana.* We insisted that they come to have dinner at our place.

ح ت ي١ *ḥty*

حاتى *ḥaata* III to attach importance (to), feel concern (for). لا تحاتي! *la tḥaati!* Don't be concerned! هذا شي ما يستاهل. لا تحاتيه! *haaδa šayy ma yistaahal. la tḥaatii!* This is a worthless thing. Don't attach importance to it!

ح ت ي٢ *ḥty*

حتى *ḥatta* (conj.) 1. in order that, so that. رحت المطعم حتى آكل *riḥt l-maṭᶜam ḥatta 'aakil.* I went to the restaurant in order to eat. سار الديوان الأميري حتى يشوف الشيخ *saar d-diiwaan l-'amiiri ḥatta yčuuf š-šeex.* He went to the Emiri Court so that he might see the Shaikh. 2. even. من ترك الفريج حتى مر مـــا يمـــر *min tirak l-firiij ḥatta marr ma ymurr.* Since he left the neighborhood, he hasn't even passed through. حتى ســـالم جـــا *ḥatta saalim ya.* Even Salim came. حتى لو *ḥatta law* even though, even if. ما أبغى أشوفه حتى لو جا *ma 'abġa 'ačuufa ḥatta law ya.* I do not want to see him even if he comes. حتى ولا *ḥatta wala* not even, never even. حتى ولا يقول «في امان الله» *ḥatta wala yguul, "fi maan illaa."* He doesn't even say, "Goodbye." 3. (prep.) until, till. تريتهم حتى نص الليل *trayyeettum ḥatta nuṣṣ l-leel.* I waited for them until midnight. بقي في الشغل حتى آخـــر دقيقـــة *bigi fi š-šuġul ḥatta 'aaxir digiiga.* He stayed at work until the last minute.

ح ث ث ١ *ḥθθ*

حث *ḥaθθ (يحث yḥiθθ)* (with على *ᶜala*) to encourage, urge. حثني على الشغـــل *ḥaθθani ᶜala š-šuġul.* He encouraged me to work. حثيته على الشغل والا يموت جـــوع *ḥaθθeeta ᶜala š-šuġul walla ymuut juuᶜ.* I urged him to work or he will starve.

ح ث ث ٢ *ḥθθ*

حـــث *ḥiθθ* (coll.) dry dates. (no recorded s.)

ح ج ب *ḥjb*

حجـــب *ḥijab (يحجب yḥajib)* to hide, obscure, block off. الغيم يحجب الشمس *l-ġeem yḥajib š-šams.* Clouds hide the sun. الطوفة حجبت المنظـــر *ṭ-ṭoofa ḥjibat l-manḍar.* The wall obscured the view.

تحجـــب *tḥajjab* V to wear a veil. الحرمة هني في بلادنا لازم تتحجب *l-ḥurma hini fi blaadna laazim titḥajjab.* A woman here in our country has to wear a veil.

حجاب *ḥjaab* p. *-aat* (woman's) veil.

حـــاجب *ḥaajib* p. حواجب *ḥawaajib* eyebrow.

محجـــب *mḥajjab* veiled, obscured, blocked off. حرمـــة محجبـــة *ḥurma mḥajjaba* veiled woman.

ح ج ج *ḥjj*

حـــج *ḥajj (يحـــج yḥijj)* to make the pilgrimage (to Mecca). الحجاج يحجون إلى مكـــة *l-ḥijjaaj yḥijjuun 'ila makka.* Pilgrims go on pilgrimage to Mecca. حجيـــت العـــام المـــاضي *ḥajjeet l-ᶜaam l-maaḍi.* I made the pilgrimage last year.

حاجج *ḥaajaj* III to argue with, reason with s.o. لا تحاججني. سويها ها الشكل *la tḥaajijni. sawwiiha ha š-šikil.* Don't argue with me. Do it in this manner.

تحجـــج *tḥajjaj* V to make excuses. لين قلت له تأخرت قـــام يتحجـــج *leen git-la ta'axxart gaam yitḥajjaj.* When I told him he was late, he started to make excuses. دايما يتحجج بمرضـــه *daayman yitḥajjaj b-maraḍa.* He always uses his illness as an excuse.

تحاجج *tḥaajaj* VI to carry on a dispute, debate. لا تتحاجج وايا اللي أكبر منك *la titḥaajaj wiyya lli 'akbar minnak.* Don't argue with those who are older than you.

احتـــج *ḥtajj* VIII to protest, object. دايما يحتـــج *daayman yiḥtajj.* He always objects. راحوا الوزارة واحتجـــوا *raaḥaw l-wizaara w-ḥtajjaw.* They went to the ministry and protested. احتج عند *ḥtajj ᶜind* protest to. احتجوا عند الوزير *ḥtajjaw ᶜind l-waziir.* They protested to the minister. 2. (with على *ᶜala*) to protest (about) s.th. احتجوا على الأوضاع الاجتماعية *ḥtajjaw ᶜala l-'awđaaᶜ l-'ijtimaaᶜiyya.* They protested about social conditions.

حج *ḥajj* pilgrimage, making the pilgrimage. الحج من أركان الإسلام *l-ḥajj min 'arkaan l-'islaam.* Pilgrimage is one of the pillars of Islam.

حجة *ḥijja* p. حجج *ḥijaj* excuse, pretext. حجته انه مريض *ḥijjta 'inna mariiđ.* His excuse is that he is sick. جاب حجة لاجل ما يدش الشغل *yaab ḥijja lajil ma ydišš š-šuġul.* He made up an excuse not to go to work. ذو الحجة *ðu l-ḥijja* Zu'lhijja (the last month of the Islamic calendar).

حجي *ḥajji,* حج *ḥajj* p. حجاج *ḥijjaaj* pilgrim, person who has made the pilgrimage. الحج سالم *l-ḥajj saalim* Hadj Salim, Salim, the pilgrim.

احتجاج *ḥtijaaj* (v.n. from VIII احتج *ḥtajj*) protest, objection

١ ح ج ر *ḥjr*

حجر *ḥajir* (v.n.) confinement, c tainment, as in حجر صحي *ḥajir ṣiḥḥi* quarantine.

حجرة *ḥijra* p. حجر *ḥijar,* احجر *'iḥjar* room in a house. أسكن في بيت فيه خمس حجر *'askin fi beet fii xams ḥijar.* I live in a house that has five rooms. حجرة النوم *ḥijrat n-noom* the bedroom. حجرة الأكل *ḥijrat l-'akil* the dining room.

٢ ح ج ر *ḥjr*

حجر *ḥijir* p. حجران *ḥijraan* (more common var. شليل *šiliil*) lap. (prov.) إذا عطاك الشيخ مرق حطه بشليلك *'iða ᶜaṭaak š-šeex marag ḥuṭṭa b-šiliilak.* Make hay while the sun shines. (lit., "If the Shaikh gives you meat broth, put it in your lap.")

٣ ح ج ر *ḥjr*

تحجر *tḥajjar* V to turn to stone, become petrified. فيه متحف هني يرويك بعض النباتات والحيوانات اللي تحجرت *fii matḥaf hini yrawwiik baᶜđ n-nabaataat w-l-ḥayawaanaat illi tḥajjarat.* There is a museum here that shows you some plants and animals that have become petrified. إذا أنت قلبك تحجر يعني قلبك موب رحيم *'iða 'inta galbak tḥajjar yaᶜni galbak muub raḥiim.* If you become hard-hearted, that means you are not kind-hearted.

حجر *ḥijar* (more common var. *ḥiyar*). See under ح ي ر *ḥyr.*

حجري *ḥajari* stony, stone. العصر الحجري *l-ᶜaṣr l-ḥajari* the Stone Age.

متحجر *mitḥajjir* p. *-iin* having turned to stone, petrified. حيوانات متحجرين *ḥayawaanaat mitḥajjriin* petrified animals. قلبه متحجر *galba mitḥajjir.* He is hard-hearted. هذا دماغه متحجر *haaða dmaaġa mitḥajjir.* This one is thick-headed.

ح ج ز *ḥjz*

حجز *ḥijaz (يحجز yḥajiz)* 1. to reserve, make a reservation. حجزنا محلين *ḥijazna maḥalleen.* We reserved two places. حجز وسافر *ḥijaz w-saafar.* He made a reservation and traveled. حجزت له غرفة في الفندق *ḥijazt-la ġurfa fi l-fundug.* I reserved him a room in the hotel. 2. (with على *ᶜala*) to seize, confiscate. فلس والحكومة حجزت على كل أملاكه *fallas w-li-ḥkuuma ḥijzat ᶜala kill 'amlaaka.* He went bankrupt and the government seized all his possessions. حجزوا على بيته *ḥijzaw ᶜala beeta.* They seized his house. 3. (with عن *ᶜan*) to keep away, block off s.th. الشجر يحجز ضو الشمس عن بيتنا *š-šiyar yḥajiz ðaww š-šams ᶜan beetna.* The trees keep away sunlight from our house.

حجز *ḥajz* (v.n.) 1. reservation. عملت حجز؟ *ᶜimalt ḥajz?* Have you made a reservation? ما فيه لك حجز *ma fii lak ḥajz.* You don't have a reservation. 2. seizure, confiscation. 3. separation.

الحجاز *li-ḥjazz* Hijaz (region in W. Arabia, or, by extension, Saudi Arabia).

حجازي *ḥjaazi* p. *-yyiin* 1. of, characteristic of Hijaz. 2. person from Hijaz or from Saudi Arabia.

حاجز *ḥaajiz* p. حواجز *ḥawaajiz* 1. divider. 2. partition. 3. (p. حاجزين *ḥaajziin*) having made a reservation, having reserved. آنا حاجز غرفتين *'aana ḥaajiz ġurufteen.* I have reserved two rooms.

ح ج ل *ḥjl*

حجل *ḥijil* (more common var. *ḥeel*). See under ح ي ل *ḥyl.*

ح ج م *ḥjm*

حجم *ḥajim* bulk, size, volume. حجم الحجرة كبير *ḥajim l-ḥijra čibiir.* The room is of a large size. حجم تانكي الماي *ḥajm taanki l-maay* the volume of the water tank.

ح چ چ *ḥčč*

حك *ḥačč* (يحك *yḥičč*) 1. to scratch. حك ظهره *ḥačč ðhara.* He scratched his back. 2. (with على *ᶜala*) to scratch s.th. against s.th. else. حك جلده على الشجرة *ḥačč yilda ᶜala li-šyara.* He scratched his skin against the tree. 2. to itch. ظهري يحكني *ðahri yḥični.* My back itches.

انحك *nḥačč* VII to become worn. الثوب انحك *θ-θoob nḥačč.* The (man's) dress got worn.

حكة *ḥačča* (n. of inst.) p. *-aat* 1. scratching. 2. itching.

ح چ ي *ḥčy*

حكى *ḥiča* (يحكي *yḥači*) 1. to tell, relate. حكى لي حكاية طويلة *ḥičaa-li ḥčaaya ṭawiila.* He told me a long story. احكي لي الصدق! *'iḥčii-li ṣ-ṣidj!* Tell me the truth! 2. to say, utter. كان قاعد ساكت وبعدين حكى *čaan gaaᶜid saakit w-baᶜdeen ḥiča.* He was silent and then he said (something). حكى واجد عن نفسه *ḥiča waayid ᶜan nafsa.* He said a lot about himself. 3. to talk, speak. حكى وايانا *ḥiča wiyyaana.* He talked to us. حكى عن الحالة السياسية *ḥiča ᶜan l-ḥaala s-siyaasiyya.* He talked about the political situation. صار له مدة ما يحكي وايانا *ṣaar-la mudda ma yḥači wiyyaana.* He hasn't been speaking to us for some time. دايما يحكي عليك *daayman yḥači ᶜaleek.* He always runs you down. أبغاك تحكي لي

وايـا الوزيـر *'abġaak tiḥčii-li wiyya l-waziir.* I want you to put in a good word for me with the minister.

حكّى *ḥačča* II to make s.o. talk, force s.o. to speak. رايح أحكّيه بالغصب *raayiḥ 'aḥaččii b-l-ġaṣb.* I am going to make him talk by force.

حـاكى *ḥaača* III to engage s.o. in conversation, talk to s.o. حاكيتـه عـن ذاك الشـي ومـا وافـق *ḥaačeeta ᶜan ðaak š-šayy w-ma waafag.* I talked to him about that thing and he did not agree. صار لي مدة ما أحاكيـه *ṣaar-li mudda ma 'aḥaačii.* I haven't been speaking to him for some time. حـاكي لي ايـاه *ḥaačii-li-yyaa.* Speak to him for me. شـفته لكـن مـا حاكيتـه *čifta laakin ma ḥaačeeta.* I saw him but I didn't speak to him.

تحكّى *tḥačča* V = حكى *hiča.*

تحاكى *tḥaača* VI to talk to each other. تقابلنـا وتحاكينـا واتفقنـا *tgaabalna w-tḥaačeena w-ttafagna.* We met, talked to each other and came to an agreement. صـار لهـم مـدة طويلـة مـا يتحاكون *ṣaar-lahum mudda ṭawiila ma yitḥaačuun.* They haven't been talking to each other for a long time. هـذا رجـال مـا يتحـاكى. متكـبر *haaða rayyaal ma yitḥaača. mitkabbir.* This is a man who cannot be talked to. He is arrogant.

انحكى *nḥiča* VII to be said, told. هذي السـالفة انحكـت مـن زمـان *haaði s-saalfa nḥičat min zamaan.* This story was told a long time ago. هـذا الكـلام مـا ينحكـي *haaða l-kalaam ma yinḥiči.* These words cannot be said.

حكي *ḥači* 1. talk, speech. هذا الحكي ما لـه أسـاس *haaða l-ḥači maa la 'asaas.* This talk is unfounded. هـذا حكـي *haaða ḥači.* This is mere talk. 2. talking, speaking. الحكي مـا ينفـع وايـاه *l-ḥači ma yinfaᶜ wiyyaa.* Talking doesn't do him any good.

حكاية *ḥčaaya* p. *-aat* tale, anecdote, story.

ح د ب *ḥdb*

حدبة *ḥidba* p. حدب *ḥidab* (less common var. حدبة *ḥdiba*) 1. hump, hunchback. (prov.) البعير لو يطالع حدبته انكسرت رقبتـه *l-biᶜiir lo yṭaaliᶜ ḥidbita nkisrat rgubta.* (lit., "If a camel looks at its hump, its neck will be broken.") Do not overlook your own faults and be concerned with the faults of others. 2. hill, sand hilltop.

حدب *ḥadab* (adj.) p. *-iin,* حدب *ḥudub* humped, hunchbacked, hunchback. f. حدبا *ḥadba.* ما يقدر يمشي عدل لانه حدب *ma yigdar yamši ᶜadil linna ḥadab.* He cannot walk well because he is a hunchback.

ح د ث *ḥdθ*

حدث *ḥidaθ (يحدث yḥadiθ)* to take place, occur. دعمات تحدث على الطريـق كل يوم *daᶜmaat tḥadiθ ᶜala ṭ-ṭariig kill yoom.* Car accidents take place on the road every day. شـحدث؟ *š-ḥidaθ?* What happened? الدعمـة حدثـت يـم الديـوان الأمـيري *d-daᶜma ḥdiθat yamm d-diiwaan l-'amiiri.* The accident occurred near the Emiri Court.

حدث *ḥaddaθ* II to tell, relate to s.o. حدثنا يا خوي عـن كشـتتكم *ḥaddiθna ya* *xooy ᶜan kaštatkum.* Talk to us, my dear friend, about your picnic. حدثنا عن الوضع السياسي *ḥaddaθna ᶜan l-waðᶜ s-siyaasi.* He talked to us about the political situation.

تحدث *tḥaddaθ* V to speak, talk. تحدث عن الحرب في البوسنة *tḥaddaθ ᶜan l-ḥarb fi l-boosna.* He talked about the war in Bosnia. تحدث عن الأمم المتحدة *tḥaddaθ ᶜan l-'umam l-mittaḥda.* He talked about the U.N.

حديث *ḥadiiθ* p. أحاديث *'aḥaadiiθ* 1. talk, speech. 2. Prophetic tradition, the sayings of the Prophet, Hadith.

محادثة *mḥaadaθa* p. *-aat* conversation, talk, discussion. محادثات السلام *mḥaadaθaat s-salaam* peace discussions, peace talks.

حادث *ḥaadiθ* p. حوادث *ḥawaadiθ* 1. event, incident. حادث بوق *ḥaadiθ boog* a theft. حادث وفاة *ḥaadiθ wafaa* a death. حادث تزوير *ḥaadiθ tazwiir* a case of forgery. حادث قتل *ḥaadiθ gatil* a killing. حادث اغتيال *ḥaadiθ ġtiyaal* an assassination.

ح د د *ḥdd*

حد *ḥadd* (يحد *yḥidd*) 1. (with من *min*) to reduce, impede, hinder, curb. الشمالي يحد من شدة القيظ *š-šamaali yḥidd min šiddat l-geeð.* The northerly wind reduces the intensity of the heat. كثرت الأحزاب تحد من تقدم البلد *kaθrat l-'aḥzaab tḥidd min tagaddum l-balad.* Too many (political) parties hinder the progress of the country. 2. to border, be adjoining. عجمان تحد الشارجة من الشمال *ᶜajmaan tḥidd š-šaarja min š-šamaal.* Ajman borders Sharja on the north. Ajman lies to the north of Sharja.

حدد *ḥaddad* II 1. to limit, restrict. الوزارة حددت المياومة *l-wizaara ḥaddadat li-myaawama.* The ministry limited per diem. تقدر تسوي شما تريد. ماحد يحددك *tigdar tsawwi š-ma triid. maḥḥad yḥaddidk.* You can do whatever you like. No one will restrict you. 2. to fix. ديوان الموظفين حدد أجور العمال *diiwaan li-mwaððafiin ḥaddad 'ujuur l-ᶜummaal.* The civil servant commission fixed the wages of workmen. 3. to schedule, set down, determine. وزارة التربية حددت المناهج *wazaarat t-tarbiya ḥaddadat l-manaahij.* The ministry of education determined the syllabi. حدد ساعات الزيارة *ḥaddad saaᶜaat z-ziyaara.* He set the visiting hours. 4. to delimit, demarcate. لازم يكون فيه لجنة تحدد الحدود بين العراق والكويت عقب حرب الخليج *laazim ykuun fii lajna tḥaddid li-ḥduud been li-ᶜraag w-li-kweet ᶜugub ḥarb l-xaliij.* There must be a committee that demarcates the border between Iraq and Kuwait after the Gulf War.

حادد *ḥaadad* III to border, adjoin. بو ظبي تحادد دبي من الجنوب *bu ðabi tḥaadid dbayy min l-januub.* Abu Dhabi borders Dubai on the south.

احتد *ḥtadd* VIII to be or become angry. ماأدري ليش يحتد بعجل *madri leeš yiḥtadd b-ᶜajal.* I do not know why he gets mad so fast. ما عنده شفقة. يحتد على عياله على ما ميش *ma ᶜinda šafaga. yiḥtadd ᶜala ᶜyaaḷa ᶜala ma miiš.* He is not affectionate. He gets mad at his kids for nothing.

حد *ḥadd* p. حدود *ḥduud* 1. border, boundary. هذي حدود الإمارات من الشرق *haaði ḥduud l-'imaaraat min š-šarg.* These are the borders of the Emirates from the east. حدود البلد طولها ميتين كيلومتر *ḥduud l-balad ṭuulha miiteen keelumitir.* The borders of the country are two hundred kilometers long. 2. limit, end. طمعه ما له حدود *ṭamaᶜa ma la ḥduud.* His greed is limitless. إلى هذا الحد *'ila haaða l-ḥadd* to this extent. كفى! هذا حدك *kafa! haaða ḥaddak.* Enough! That's enough from you. وقفته عند حده لانه طاش *waggafta ᶜind ḥadda linna ṭaaš.* I stopped him right there, because he flared up in anger. 3. extent, degree. إلى حد بعيد *'ila ḥadd baᶜiid* to a considerable degree. إلى حد *'ila ḥadd* until, till, up to. مشى إلى حد الكبري *miša 'ila ḥadd l-kubri.* He walked as far as the bridge. المسألة وصلت إلى حد ما يطاق *l-mas'ala wṣalat 'ila ḥadd ma yṭaag.* The problem reached an unbearable point. إلى حد الحين، لحد الحين *'ila ḥadd l-ḥiin, la ḥadd l-ḥiin* up to now, until now. ما شفته لحد الحين *ma čifta la ḥadd l-ḥiin.* I haven't seen him yet. 4. sharp edge. حد السكين *ḥadd s-siččiin* the edge of the knife. سيف بو حدين *seef bu ḥaddeen* two-edged sword.

حدة *ḥidda* intensity, severity. حدة القيظ *ḥiddat l-geeð* the intensity of the heat.

حداد *ḥdaad* mourning. مات الملك وأعلنوا الحداد عليه *maat l-malik w-'aᶜlanaw li-ḥdaad ᶜalee.* The king died and they declared (a period of) mourning for him. في حداد في القصر لمدة سبوع *fii ḥdaad fi l-gaṣir li-muddat subuuᶜ.* There is (a period of) mourning in the palace for a week.

حديد *ḥadiid* (coll.) iron, steel. s. حديدة *ḥadiida* piece of iron. فيه معادن في عجمان مثل الكروم والحديد وماأدري شبعد *fii maᶜaadin fi ᶜajman miθil li-kroom w-l-ḥadiid w-ma dri š-baᶜad.* There are metals in Ajman, such as chrome, iron, and I do not know what else.

حديدة *ḥadiida* p. حدايد *ḥadaayid* piece of iron.

حداد *ḥaddaad* p. *-iin* blacksmith. شغل الحدادين هالحين موب شي *šuġul l-ḥaddaadiin halḥiin muub šayy.* The work of a blacksmith (or blacksmithing) nowadays is not much (i.e., it is not profitable).

حدادة *ḥdaada* blacksmithing.

تحديد *taḥdiid* (v.n. from II حدد *ḥaddad*) 1. restriction. تحديد الأسعار *taḥdiid l-'asᶜaar* price restriction. بالتحديد *b-t-taḥdiid* specifically. 2. demarcation. تحديد الحدود *taḥdiid li-ḥduud* demarcation of the border.

أحد *'aḥadd* (elat.) 1. (with من *min*) sharper than. هذي السكين أحد من ذيك *haaði s-siččiin 'aḥadd min ðiič.* This knife is sharper than that one. 2. (with foll. n.) sharpest. هذا أحد خنجر *haaða 'aḥadd xanyar.* This is the sharpest dagger. 3. more or most intense, severe.

حاد *ḥaadd* 1. sharp, keen. خنجر حاد *xanyar ḥaadd* sharp dagger. بصر حاد *baṣar ḥaadd* keen eyesight. حاد في

الصـــدر *haadd fi ṣ-ṣadir* acute bronchitis. 3. fiery, vehement. طبعـه حـاد *ṭabᶜa ḥaadd.* He is hot-tempered. 4. sour. طرشـي حـاد *ṭurši ḥaadd* sour pickles.

محـدود *maḥduud* (p.p. from حد *ḥadd*) limited, restricted, fixed. شركة محدودة *šarika maḥduuda* limited company. مبلـغ محـدود *mablaġ maḥduud* limited sum of money. كمية محدودة *kammiyya maḥduuda* limited amount.

ح د ر *ḥdr*

حـدر *ḥadir* 1. below. قطيتـه حـدر *gaṭṭeeta ḥadir.* I threw it below. 2. downstairs. راح حـدر *raaḥ ḥadir.* He went downstairs. المجلس حـدر *l-maylis ḥadir.* The living room is downstairs. (prov.) شـفتك فـوق شـفتك حـدر *čiftak foog čiftak ḥadir.* (lit., "I saw you upstairs; I saw you downstairs") applies to s.o. who does not change.

حـدري *ḥadri* (adj.; more common var. تحـتي *taḥti*) located lower or below. الحفيز التحـتي *l-ḥafiiz t-taḥti* the office below.

ح د گ *ḥdg*

حـدق *ḥidag (يحـدق yḥadig)* to catch fish, fish. كنا نحدق بالميادير يعني بـالخيوط والدجيـج *činna nḥadig b-l-miyaadiir yaᶜni b-li-xyuuṭ w-d-dijiij.* We were fishing with lines, rods, and nets.

حـداق *ḥdaag* fishing, catching fish. من رحنا لجينا كلـه حـداق *min riḥna la yiina killa ḥdaag.* From the time we went until we came back we were fishing the whole time.

حـداق *ḥaddaag* p. *-iin* fisherman. معظم الناس في الزمان الأولي كـانوا يشـتغلون حداقـين *muᶜđam n-naas fi z-zamaan l-'awwali čaanaw yištaġluun ḥaddaagiin.* Most people in olden times used to work as fishermen. الحداق هو اللي يحدق والسماك هو اللي يبيـع السـمك *l-ḥaddaag huwa lli yḥadig w-s-sammaač huwa lli ybiiᶜ s-simač.* A fisherman is the one who catches fish and a fishmonger is the one who sells fish.

حديقـة *ḥadiiga* p. حدايـق *hadaayig* garden. حديقـــة الحيوانـــات *ḥadiigat l-ḥayawaanaat* zoological garden, zoo.

ح د ي *ḥdy*

تحـدى *tḥadda* V 1. to challenge. تحداني ألعـب بنـق بونـق وايـاه *taḥddaani 'alᶜab bing-bong wiyyaa.* He challenged me to play table tennis with him. 2. to defy, oppose, resist. لا تتحـدى سـلطة الأمـــير! *la titḥadda sulṭat l-'amiir!* Don't defy the Emir's authority.

ح ذ ر *ḥđr*

حـذر *ḥiđr (يحذر yḥađir)* to be cautious, be on the guard. احذر من ذاك الشخص! *'iḥđar min đaak š-šuxṣ!* Watch out for that guy. احـذر مـن الكلب! *'iḥđar min č-čalb!* Beware of the dog.

حـذر *ḥađđar* II to warn, caution. حذرتـك مـن ذاك الدجـال *ḥađđartak min đaak d-dajjaal.* I warned you against that swindler.

تحذر *tḥađđar* V to be careful, take care. تحذر من السياير *ṭḥađđar min s-siyaayiir.* Watch out for cars.

حـذر *ḥađar* caution, watchfulness.

خذيت حذري مــن ذاك الرجـال *xaðeet ḥaðari min ðaak r-rayyaal.* I was on my guard against that man. بحـذر *b-ḥaðar* cautiously.

تحذير *taḥðiir* (v.n. from II حذر *ḥaððar*) warning, cautioning.

ح ذ ف ١ *ḥðf*

حذف *ḥiðaf (يحذف yḥaðif)* 1. to throw, throw away, cast, hurl. حذف الحجر *ḥiðaf l-ḥiyar.* He threw the rock.

حـذف *ḥaðf* (v.n.) throwing, casting, hurling.

محـاذف *mḥaaðif* p. محاذيف *mḥaaðiif* rock or javelin thrower.

ح ذ ف ٢ *ḥðf*

حـذف *ḥiðaf (يحذف yḥaðif)* to delete, omit, drop, take away. احذف هذا السطر مــن الاتفاقيـة *'iḥðif haaða s-saṭir min l-'ittifaagiyya.* Delete this line from the agreement. ليش حذفوا اسمـك مـن الليستة؟ *leeš ḥðafaw 'ismak min l-liista?* Why did they remove your name from the list? وزارة المالية حذفت مليونين درهم من الميزانيـة *wizaarat l-maaliyya ḥðifat malyooneen dirhim min l-miizaaniyya.* The ministry of finance cut out two million dirhams from the budget.

حذف *ḥaðf* (v.n.) removal, dropping.

ح ذ ي *ḥðy*

حاذى *ḥaaða* III to parallel, run parallel to s.th. في شارع الشيخ حمدان السـيايير تحاذي بعـض *fi šaari*[c] *š-šeex ḥamdaan s-siyaayiir tḥaaði ba*[c]*aḍ.* On Shaikh Hamdan Street cars parallel each other. الطريق يحاذي المينا إلى مسافة مية متر *ṭ-ṭariig yḥaaði l-miina 'ila masaafat miyat mitir.* The road parallels the port for a distance of a hundred meters.

حـذا *ḥða* (prep.) near, close to, by. الفندق حذا بيتنـا *l-fundug ḥða beetna.* The hotel is near our house. اقعد حذاي *'ig*[c]*id ḥðaay.* Sit by me! بيتها حذانـا *beetta ḥðaana.* Her house is close to our house.

محاذي *mḥaaði* (act. part. from III حاذى *ḥaaða*) parallel to, along. الطريق محاذي السيف *ṭ-ṭariig mḥaaði s-siif.* The road is parallel to the seashore.

ح ر ب *ḥrb*

حـارب *ḥaarab* III to fight, combat, battle against. واجد دول حاربت العراق في حرب الخليج *waayid duwal ḥaarabat li-*[c]*raag fi ḥarb l-xaliij.* Many nations fought against Iraq in the Gulf War. حاربوا ولكن انهزمــوا *ḥaarbaw walaakin nhizmaw.* They fought but they were defeated. الحكومة تحارب الفقر والجـهل *li-ḥkuuma tḥaarib l-fagir w-l-jahil.* The government is fighting against poverty and ignorance (illiteracy). المواطنين يحاربوني لاني أجنبي *li-mwaaṭniin yḥaarbuunni linni 'aynabi.* The citizens are giving me a hard time because I am a foreigner.

تحـارب *tḥaarab* VI to be engaged in war, fight each other. تحاربوا وايا بعض مدة سنة *tḥaarbaw wiyya ba*[c]*aḍ muddat sana.* They fought with each other for a year.

حرب *ḥarb* (f.) p. حروب *ḥruub,* حرايب *ḥaraayib* 1. war, warfare. وقعت الحرب بينـهم *wig*[c]*at l-ḥarb beenhum.* War broke out between them. الحرب العالمية

الأولــــة *l-ḥarb l-ᶜaalamiyya l-'awwala* World War I. 2. fight, feud, combat. فيه حـــــرب بـــين القبـــايل *fii ḥarb been l-gabaayil.* There is a feud among the tribes.

حربي *ḥarbi* p. *-yyiin* military, martial, warlike. البوليس الحربي *l-buuliis l-ḥarbi* the military police. وزارة الحربيـــــة *wazaarat l-ḥarbiyya* the war ministry. الكلية الحربيـــة *l-kulliyya l-ḥarbiyya* the military academy.

حربة *ḥarba* p. *-aat* bayonet.

محـــراب *miḥraab* p. محاريب *maḥaariib* prayer niche (recess in a mosque indicating the direction of prayer).

ح ر ث *ḥrθ*

حــــرث *ḥiraθ (يحرث yḥariθ)* to plow. يحرثون الأرض ويزرعونهـــا بـــر *yḥarθuun l-'arḍ̄ w-yizraᶜuunha burr.* They plow up the land and plant it with wheat.

حرث *ḥarθ* (v.n.) plowing, tilling.

محــــراث *miḥraaθ* p. محاريث *maḥaariiθ* plow.

ح ر ج ١ *ḥrj*

حرج *ḥiraj (يحرج yḥarij)* to embarrass s.o., put s.o. in a tight spot. ليش حرجتني قدام الموظفـــــين؟ *leeš ḥirajtani jiddaam l-muwaḍḍafiin?* Why did you embarrass me in front of the employees?

حـــــرج *ḥarraj* II 1. (with على *ᶜala*) to persist in s.th. حرج علينا المدير ما ندوخ جقاير في الحفيز *ḥarraj ᶜaleena l-mudiir ma nduux jigaayir fi l-ḥafiiz.* The manager insisted that we not smoke in the office.

أحـــــرج *'aḥraj* IV = حرج *ḥiraj.* أحرجتني بـــاللي قلتــه *'aḥrajtani b-lli gilta.* You embarrassed me with what you said.

انحــــــرج *nḥiraj* VII to be embarrassed. انحرج قدام رفيقــه *nḥiraj jiddaam rifiija.* He was embarrassed in front of his friend. انحرج بســــؤالي *nḥiraj b-su'aali.* He was embarrassed by my question.

حــــرج *ḥaraj* (v.n. from *ḥiraj*) embarrassment.

ح ر ج ٢ *ḥrj*

حــــرج *ḥarraj* II (with على *ᶜala*) to auction off. في سوق حراج يحرجون على أشيا قديمة وأشيـــا مســـتعملة بعــد *fi suug ḥaraaj yḥarrjuun ᶜala 'ašya gadiima w-'ašya mistaᶜmala baᶜad.* At the auction they auction off old things and used things too. قلت حق المحرج، «حرج على الكرفاية هذي» *gilt ḥagg li-mḥarrij, "ḥarrij ᶜala l-kirfaaya haaði."* I said to the auctioneer, "Auction off this bed."

تحرج *tḥarraj* V to be auctioned off. الميز والكنبة والكريولة كلهم تحرجـــوا في نـــص ساعة *l-meez w-l-kanaba w-l-karyoola killahum tḥarrajaw fi nuṣṣ saaᶜa.* The table, the sofa, and the bed were all auctioned off in half an hour.

حــــراج *ḥaraaj* auctioning. سوق حراج *suug ḥaraaj* the market or place where auctioning takes place.

محرج *mḥarrij* p. *-iin* 1. auctioneer. 2. agent, broker.

ح ر ر *ḥrr*

حــــرر *ḥarrar* II 1. to liberate, set free. الأفغان جاهدوا لاجـــل يحـــررون وطنـــهم *l-'afġaan jaahdaw lajil yḥarriruun*

حرية *ḥurriyya* freedom, liberty.

حرير *ḥariir* (coll.) silk. s. قطعة حرير *ġiṭᶜat ḥariir.* هالحين الناس قاموا يلبسون حرير *halḥiin n-naas gaamaw yilbisuun ḥariir.* Now people have started to wear silk. (prov.) إن لبست البس حرير وإن عاشرت عاشر أمير *'in libist 'ilbis ḥariir w-in ᶜaašart ᶜaašir 'amiir.* Elegant appearance and good friends are both important. Aim high. (lit., "When you dress, dress in silk, and when you crave company, accompany a prince.")

حرارة *ḥaraara* 1. temperature. 2. fever.

حران *ḥarraan* p. *-iin* hot, perspiring, sweating. آنا حران؛ ما أقدر أشتغل *'aana ḥarraan; ma 'agdar 'aštaġil.* I am hot; I cannot work.

أحر *'aḥarr* (elat.) 1. (with من *min*) hotter than. اليوم أحر من أمس *l-yoom 'aḥarr min 'ams.* Today is hotter than yesterday. 2. (with foll. n.) the hottest. أحر أيام القيظ *'aḥarr 'ayyaam l-geeḍ* the hottest days of the summer.

تحرير *taḥriir* (v.n. from II حرر *ḥarrar*) 1. liberation, emancipation. تحرير العبيد *taḥriir l-ᶜabiid* the emancipation of slaves. 2. editing. مدير التحرير *mudiir t-taḥriir* editor-in-chief.

حار *ḥaarr* 1. hot. الهوا حار في القيظ *l-hawa ḥaarr fi l-geeḍ.* The weather is hot in the summer. راسه حار *raasa ḥaarr.* He is hot-tempered. 2. strong, hot, biting. طرشي حار *ṭurši ḥaarr* hot pickles. تتن حار *titin ḥaarr* strong tobacco.

waṭanhum. The Afghans fought a holy war to liberate their country. 2. to set free. 2. to edit, redact. من يحرر هذي الجريدة؟ *man yḥarrir haaḏi l-jariida?* Who edits this newspaper?

تحرر *tḥarrar* V to be freed, be liberated. العبيد في أمريكا تحرروا من زمان *l-ᶜabiid fi 'amriika tḥarraraw min zamaan.* The slaves in America were freed a long time ago.

احتر *ḥtarr* VIII to be or become hot. احتريت. بطل الدريشة من فضلك *ḥtarreet. baṭṭil d-diriiša min faḏlak.* I am hot. Open the window, please. إذا احتريت شغل الكنديشن *'iḏa ḥtarreet šaġġil l-kandeešin.* If you are hot, turn the air conditioning on.

حر *ḥarr* heat, hot weather. الحر واجد اليوم *l-ḥarr waajid l-yoom.* It's very hot today. الحر يكون في القيظ *l-ḥarr ykuun fi l-geeḍ.* Hot weather is in the summer. الدنيا حر *d-dinya ḥarr.* It's hot.

حر *ḥurr* p. أحرار *'aḥraar* 1. freeman, not a slave. 2. free, living in freedom. آنا حر. أسوي اللي أبغاه *'aana ḥurr. 'asawwi lli 'abġaa.* I am free. I do whatever I want. فيه صحافة حرة هني *fii ṣaḥaafa ḥurra hini.* There is free press here. 3. genuine, pure. ذهب حر *ḏahab ḥurr* pure gold. دهن حر *dihin ḥurr* clarified butter. 4. (no recorded p.) peregrine, hawk, falcon.

حرة *ḥarra* jealousy. الحرة مرات تقتل الواحد *l-ḥarra marraat tugtul l-waaḥid.* Jealousy kills people sometimes.

حرورة *ḥruura* = حر *ḥarr.* اليوم حرورة *l-yoom ḥruura.* It's hot today.

محرر *mḥarrir* (act. part. from II حرر *ḥarrar*) 1. liberator, emancipator. 2. editor.

متحـرر *mitḥarrir* p. *-iin* 1. emancipated. 2. liberal-minded. الحاكم الحالي متحـرر *l-ḥaakim l-ḥaali mitḥarrir.* The present ruler is liberal-minded. هـو متحـرر بتفكيره *huwa mitḥarrir b-tafkiira.* He is emancipated (or liberal-minded) in his thinking.

ح ر ص ١ *ḥrṣ*

حـرص *ḥiraṣ (يحرص yḥariṣ)* 1. to guard, watch. فيه جنـود يحرصـون بيـت الوزيـر *fii jnuud yḥarṣuun beet l-waziir.* There are soldiers guarding the minister's house. 2. to protect, keep, preserve. ورا وقـدام سيارة الشـيخ كـان فيـه سـيارات تحرصـه *wara w-jiddaam sayyaarat š-šeex čaan fii saayaaraat tḥarṣa.* In front of and behind the Shaikh's car there were cars protecting him. الله يحرصك! *'aḷḷa yḥarṣak!* God keep you!

تحرص *tḥarraṣ* V (with من *min*) to be on one's guard (against), be wary (of). تحرص من هذا الرجال *tḥarraṣ min haaða r-rayyaal.* Be wary of this man.

احترص *ḥtiras* VIII = V تحرص *tḥarraṣ.*

حـرص *ḥaras* 1. guard, watch. واقف حرص *waagif ḥaraṣ* standing guard. 2. escort, guard, detachment guard. الحـرص الأمـيري *l-ḥaraṣ l-'amiri* the Emiri guard. الحـرص الوطـني *l-ḥaraṣ l-waṭani* the national guard.

حراصة *ḥraasa* 1. guarding, watching. 2. guard duty. أخوي عنده حراصة الليلـة *'uxuuy ᶜinda ḥraaṣa l-leela.* My brother has guard duty tonight.

حـارص *ḥaariṣ* p. حرص *ḥaraṣ,* حراص *ḥirraaṣ* guard, watchman. حارص البناية *ḥaariṣ li-bnaaya* the watchman of the building. حارص المرمـى *ḥaaris l-marma* the goalkeeper, goalie.

محـروص *maḥruuṣ* (p.p. of حرص *ḥiraṣ*) guarded, safeguarded القصر محروص زين *l-gaṣir maḥruuṣ zeen.* The palace is well-guarded.

ح ر ص ٢ *ḥrṣ*

حـرص *ḥiraṣ (يحـرص yḥariṣ)* (with على *ᶜala*) to be concerned (with), be intent (upon). الحكومة تحرص على نظافة الشوارع *li-ḥkuuma tiḥriṣ ᶜala naðaafat š-šawaariᶜ.* The government is concerned with the cleanliness of the streets. أحرص على تربية عيالي *'aḥriṣ ᶜala tarbiyat ᶜyaaḷi.* I am concerned with the upbringing of my children.

حـرص *ḥirṣ* (v.n.) dedication, concern. حرص على تربية الأولاد *ḥirṣ ᶜala tarbiyat l-'awlaad* dedication to the upbringing of children. حرص على الشـغل *ḥirṣ ᶜala š-šuġul* dedication to work.

حريـص *ḥariiṣ* p. *-iin* concerned, dedicated. حريص علـى شـرف عايلتـه *ḥariiṣ ᶜala šaraf ᶜaayilta* concerned about the honor of his family. حريص علـى دراسـته *ḥariiṣ ᶜala draasta* dedicated to his studies.

أحـرص *'aḥraṣ* (elat.) 1. (with من *min*) more concerned than. 2. (with foll. n.) most concerned.

ح ر ص ٣ *ḥrṣ*

حـرص *ḥiraṣ (يحـرص yḥariṣ)* to be stingy, niggardly, miserly. حرص على الطراد. ما عطانا اياه *ḥiraṣ ᶜala ṭ-ṭarraad.*

ma ᶜaṭaana-yyaa. He was stingy about the motorboat. He did not give it to us. لا تحرص على روحك بهاالأشيا الضرورية *la tḥariṣ ᶜala ruuḥak b-ha l-'ašya ḏ̣-ḏ̣aruuriyya.* Don't stint yourself on these necessities. لا تحرص علينا بزيارتك *la tḥariṣ ᶜaleena b-ziyaartak.* Don't be stingy with your visits to us.

حرص *ḥirṣ* (v.n.) stinginess.

حريص *ḥariiṣ* p. *-iin* 1. stingy, miserly. 2. stingy person.

ح ر ط م *ḥrṭm*

حرطم *ḥarṭam* (يحرطم *yḥarṭim*) 1. to mutter, grumble, growl. ما يتكلم عدل. يحرطم بالكلام *ma yitkallam ᶜadil. yḥarṭim b-l-kalaam.* He doesn't talk well. He mutters. 2. to chatter, prattle. صار له ساعة يحرطم *ṣaar-la saaᶜa yḥarṭim.* He has been chattering for an hour.

حرطمة *ḥarṭama* (v.n.) chatter, idle talk.

محرطم *mḥarṭim* p. *-iin* chatterbox, prattler.

ح ر ظ *ḥrḏ̣*

حرض *ḥarraḏ̣* II to incite, provoke, stir up. حرض الكولية على الإضراب *ḥarraḏ̣ l-kuuliyya ᶜala l-'iḏ̣raab.* He incited the coolies to strike.

محرض *mḥarriḏ̣* (act. part.) p. *-iin* instigator, inciter.

ح ر ف *ḥrf*

حرف *ḥarraf* II to distort, twist, misconstrue. ليش حرفت كلامي؟ آنا ما قلت هذا. *leeš ḥarraft kalaami? 'aana ma gilt haaða.* Why did you distort my words? I did not say that.

انحرف *nḥiraf* VII to deviate, digress, turn away. انحرف عن الطريق الصحيح *nḥiraf ᶜan ṭ-ṭariig ṣ-ṣaḥiiḥ.* He deviated from the right path.

احترف *ḥtiraf* VIII to practice s.th. as a profession, do s.th. professionally. احترف التدريس *ḥtiraf t-tadriis.* He made teaching his profession.

حرف *ḥarf* p. حروف *ḥruuf* letter (of the alphabet). حكى الحكاية حرف بحرف *ḥiča li-ḥčaaya ḥarf b-ḥarf.* He told the story word for word.

احتراف *ḥtiraaf* (v.n. from VIII احترف *ḥtiraf*) professionalism.

محترف *miḥtarif* (act. part. from VIII احترف *ḥtiraf*) p. *-iin* professional. لاعب كرة محترف *laaᶜib kuura miḥtarif* professional soccer player. ملاكم محترف *mulaakim miḥtarif* professional boxer.

ح ر گ *ḥrg*

حرق *ḥirag* (يحرق *yḥarig*) 1. to burn s.th. يحرقون الخمام بعيد عن المدينة *yḥarguun li-xmaam baᶜiid ᶜan l-madiina.* They burn the garbage far away from the city. الجقارة حرقت يدي *l-jigaara ḥrigat yaddi.* The cigarette burned my hand. الهندوس يحرقون الميت *l-hindoos yḥarguun l-mayyit.* The Hindus cremate the dead. حرق قلبي *ḥirag galbi.* He exasperated me. He burned me up. (lit. "He burned my heart.") 2. to sting, smart. عور يده وهالحين يده تحرقه *ᶜawwar yadda w-halḥiin yadda tḥarga.* His hand was

ح ر ك *ḥrk*

حرك *ḥarrak* II 1. to move s.th., set s.th. in motion, operate. حرك نفسك شوية. خلني أشوف التلفزيون *ḥarrik nafsak šwayya. xaḷni 'ačuuf t-talafizyoon.* Move yourself a little. Let me watch TV. تعرف تحرك البورهوز؟ *t*c*arf tḥarrik l-bawarhooz?* Do you know how to operate the powerhouse? لا تحرك ساكن! *la tḥarrik saakin!* Let sleeping dogs lie! قعد وما حرك ولا ساكن *gi*c*ad w-ma ḥarrak wala saakin.* He sat down and never lifted a finger. 2. to start s.th., get s.th. started. ما أقدر أحرك الداو *ma 'agdar 'aḥarrik d-daaw.* I cannot start the dhow. 3. to incite, stir up, provoke. ظل يحرك الكولية لين أضربوا *ẟall yḥarrik l-kuuliyya leen 'aẟrabu.* He continued to stir up the coolies until they went on strike.

تحرك *taḥarrak* V 1. to move, stir, budge. لا تتحرك! *la titḥarrak!* Don't move! Stand still! الأولاد يخافون من مدرسهم. لين يقعدون ما يتحركون أبد *l-'awlaad yxaafuun min mdarrissum. leen yigi*c*duun ma yitḥarrakuun 'abad.* The children fear their teacher. When they sit down, they never move (out of their places). 2. to get moving, start moving. تحرك ياالله! *tḥarrak yaḷḷa!* Get moving! 3. to leave, depart. الباص يتحرك من المحطة الساعة ست *l-paaṣ yitḥarrak min l-mahaṭṭa s-saa*c*a sitt.* The bus leaves the station at six o'clock. 4. to be agitated, be excited. تحركت مشاعره لين شاف المنظر وقام يبكي *tḥarrakat mašaa*c*ra leen čaaf l-manẟar w-gaam yibči.* He was excited when he saw the scene and injured, and now his hand stings. عين الجاهل قامت تحرقه من الصابون c*een l-yaahil gaamat tḥarga min ṣ-ṣaabuun.* The child's eye started to sting from the soap.

تحرق *tḥarrag* V to be consumed (by emotion), eat one's heart out. فنشوه وبعده يتحرق على الوظيفة *fannašoo w-ba*c*da yitḥrrag* c*ala l-waẟiifa.* They laid him off and he is still eating his heart out over the job.

احترق *ḥtirag* VIII 1. to catch fire, burn, burn up. هدومهم احترقت كلها *ḥduumhum ḥtirgat killaha.* All of their clothes caught fire. احترق البيت كله *ḥtirag l-beet killa.* The whole house burned. قلبي يحترق على المصابين في البوسنة *gaḷbi yiḥtarig* c*ala li-mṣaabiin fi l-boosna.* My heart bleeds for the casualties in Bosnia. 2. to burn out. الليت احترق *l-leet ḥtirag.* The light bulb burned out.

حريق *ḥariig* p. حرايق *ḥiraayig* (more common var. *ḥariij*) fire, conflagration. شب حريق في سوق السمك وحرقه كله *šabb ḥariij fi suug s-simač w-ḥriga killa.* Fire broke out in the fish market and burned it up, all of it.

محرق *mḥarrag* (usually المحرق *li-maḥrrag*) Muharraq (city in Bahrain).

محروق *maḥruug* (p.p. from حرق *ḥirag*) 1. burned, charred, burned up. 2. irritated, burned up. شدعوة قلبك محروق؟ *š-da*c*wa gaḷbak maḥruug?* What are you burned up about? 3. burned out. ليت محروق *leet maḥruug* burned out light bulb.

started to cry.

حركة *ḥaraka* 1. movement, motion. كل شي ساكن. ما فيه حركة *kill šayy saakin. ma fii ḥaraka.* Everything is quiet. There is no movement. 2. activity. كل شي غالي. ما فيه حركة في السوق *kill šayy ġaali. ma fii ḥaraka fi s-suug.* Everything is expensive. There is no activity in the marketplace. 3. traffic. حركة المرور *ḥarakat l-muruur* traffic. 4. social movement. حركة أدبية *ḥaraka 'adabiyya* literary movement.

محرك *mḥarrik* (act. part. from II حرك *ḥarrak*) 1. instigator, trouble-maker, stirrer. 2. (p. *-aat*) motor, engine.

متحرك *mitḥarrik* (act. part. from V تحرك *tḥarrak*) 1. moving. صور متحركة *ṣuwar mitḥarrka* motion pictures. 2. having left or departed. الجلبوت تحرك قبل ساعة *l-jalbuut tḥarrak gabil saa*ʿ*a.* The jolly-boat left an hour ago.

ح ر م *ḥrm*

حرم *ḥiram (يحرم yḥarim)* 1. to deprive, dispossess, take away s.th. في امان الله! لا تحرمنا من شوفتك! *fi maan illaa! la tiḥrimna min šooftak.* Goodbye! Don't deprive us of seeing you. مسكينة، حرمها من كل شي *maskiina, ḥiramha min kill šayy.* Poor thing, he has deprived her of everything. حرمهم من شوف الفلم *ḥaramhum min šoof l-filim.* He prevented them from seeing the film. 2. to exclude, cut off. ضد الإسلام انك تحرم ابنك من الميراث *ðidd l-'islaam 'innak tḥarim 'ibnak min l-miiraaθ.* It's against (the teaching of) Islam to exclude your son from the inheritance. 3. to enter into the state of ritual consecration during pilgrimage. (See إحرام *'iḥraam* below).

حرم *ḥarram* II 1. to forbid s.th., declare s.th. unlawful. الإسلام حرم شرب الخمر *l-'islaam ḥarram šurb l-xamir.* Islam has forbidden the drinking of wine. 2. (with على ʿ*ala*) to forbid s.o. أبوها حرم عليها تكشف وجهها *'ubuuha ḥarram* ʿ*aleeha tikšif weehha.* Her father ordered her not to uncover her face. 3. (with على ʿ*ala* + نفس *nafs*) to deny oneself s.th., abstain from s.th. حرم على نفسه الونسة *ḥarram* ʿ*ala nafsa l-winsa.* He denied himself having a good time. He abstained from pleasure.

انحرم *nḥiram* VII to be deprived. جهالي انحرموا من أشيا واجدة *yihhaali nḥirmaw min 'ašya waayda.* My kids were deprived of many things. ليش انحرموا من شوف الفلم؟ *leeš nḥirmaw min šoof l-filim?* Why were they prevented from watching the film?

احترم *ḥtiram* VIII to respect, esteem. الإنسان لازم يحترم اللي أكبر منه *l-'insaan laazim yiḥtirim illi 'akbar minna.* People ought to respect those who are older than they. لازم تحترم نفسك! *laazim tiḥtirim nafsak!* Be self-respecting!

حرم *ḥaram* (no recorded p.) 1. sacred, holy thing (e.g., place, possessions, etc.) الحرم *l-ḥaram* the holy mosque in Mecca. الحرم الشريف *l-ḥaram š-šariif* the Holy Sanctuary in Jerusalem (known as the Dome of the Rock and the Al-Aqsa Mosque).

الحرمين *l-ḥarameen* the two holy

mosques in Mecca and Medina. ثالث الحرمـــين *θaaliθ l-ḥarameen* the third holy mosque (i.e., the one in Jerusalem).

حرمة *ḥurma* p. حريم *ḥariim* 1. woman, lady. سوق السمك مترس رجاجيل وحريم *suug s-simač matruus riyaayiil w-ḥariim.* The fish market is full of men and women. 2. wife. حرمتي جابت ست جهال *ḥurumti yaabat sitt yihhaal.* My wife gave birth to six children.

حــرام *ḥaraam* forbidden, prohibited (opp. حــلال *ḥalaal*). شرب الخمر حرام *šurb l-xamir ḥaraam.* Drinking alcoholic drinks is forbidden. ابن حرام *'ibin ḥaraam* p. اولاد حرام *wlaad ḥaraam* illegitimate son, bastard. f. بنت حرام *bint ḥaraam*, p. بنــات حــرام *banaat ḥaraam*. حرام عليــك! *ḥaraam ᶜaleek!* Shame on you! You must not do that. ياكل مال حرام *yaakil maal ḥaraam.* He is dishonest. He cheats. (lit. "He eats forbidden property."). البيت الحـــرام *l-beet l-ḥaraam* the Kaaba. الشهر الحرام *š-šahar l-ḥaraam* the Holy Month, Muharram.

حريـــمي *ḥariimi* characteristic of women, for women. جــواتي حريـــمي *juwaati ḥariimi* women's shoes.

حرمـــان *ḥirmaan* 1. deprivation, bereavement. يتصرف ها الشكـــل مـــن الحرمـــان *yitṣarraf ha š-šikil min l-ḥirmaan.* He behaves in this manner because of deprivation. 2. exclusion. الحرمان مـــن الإرث *l-ḥirmaan min l-'irθ* exclusion from inheritance. 3. excommunication (in Christianity).

إحــرام *'iḥraam* state of ritual consecration, during which a Mecca pilgrim wears two seamless linen sheets and abstains from sexual intercourse.

احــترام *ḥtiraam* (v.n. from VIII احترم *ḥtiram*) respect, regard, esteem. عامل الناس باحترام! *ᶜaamil n-naas b-ḥtiraam!* Treat people with respect! الاحـــترام مطلوب *li-ḥtiraam maṭluub.* Respect is required. بكـــل احـــترام *b-kill ḥtiraam* with all due respect.

احتراما *ḥtiraaman* out of respect. وقفوا احترامـــا للحـــــاكم *wigfaw ḥtiraaman l-l-ḥaakim.* They stood up out of respect for the ruler.

محروم *maḥruum* (p.p. from حرم *ḥiram*) deprived, bereaved.

محــرم *mḥarram* (p.p. from II حـــرم *ḥarram*) 1. forbidden, interdicted. لعب القمـــار محـــرم *liᶜb li-gmaar mḥarram.* Gambling is forbidden. أكل لحم الخنزير محـــرم في الإســـلام *'akil laḥam l-xanziir mḥarram fi l-'islaam.* Eating pork is forbidden in Islam. 2. Muharram (first month of the Islamic calendar).

محرم *miḥrim* p. *-iin* Mecca pilgrim in a state of إحرام *'iḥraam.*

محــترم *muḥtaram* p. *-iin* respected, esteemed. الدختر محترم بين الناس *d-daxtar muḥtaram been n-naas.* A medical doctor is respected among the people.

ح ر ي *ḥry*

تحـــرى *tḥarra* V (with عـــن *ᶜan*) to investigate. قبل لا تحصل وظيفة في الشرطة لازم يتحـــرون عنـــك *gabil la tḥaṣṣil waðiifa fi š-širṭa laazim yitḥarruun* ᶜannak. Before you get a job in the police department, they will have to investigate you. يتحرون عنه لانه مشبوه *yitḥarruun ᶜanna linna mašbuuh.* They are investigating him because he is a suspect.

تحـــري *taḥarri* (v.n.) p. *-yaat* 1. investigation. 2. inquiry, check.

ح ز ب *ḥzb*

حـــزب *ḥizib* p. أحـــزاب *'aḥzaab* 1. political party. أحزاب ما ميش في الخليج *'aḥzaab ma miiš fi l-xaliij.* There are no political parties in the Gulf area. 2. faction, group, clique. أنت من حـــزب الأمير؟ *'inta min ḥizb l-'amiir?* Do you belong to the Emir's clique? Are you one of the followers of the Emir?

حـــزبي *ḥizbi* p. *-yyiin* factional, party (adj.) أفكـــار حزبيـــة *'afkaar ḥizbiyya* party ideas. جريـــدة حزبيـــة *jariida ḥizbiyya* party newspaper.

ح ز ي ر ن *ḥzyrn*

حزيران *ḥaziiraan* June (month).

ح ز ز *ḥzz*

حـــزة *ḥazza* p. *-aat* time, appointed time. ها الحزة *hal-ḥazza* now. أي حزة؟ *'ayya ḥazza?* When? What time? في ذيك الحـــزة *fi ðiič l-ḥazza* at that time. حزة الزرع *ḥazzat z-zariᶜ* the time when seeds are planted. هذي حزتـــه *haaði hazzata.* This is the appointed time of his arrival.

حـــزازة *ḥzaaza* enmity, hatred. القبايل يتهاوشون. فيه حـــزازة بينـــهم *l-gabaayil yithaawšuun. fii ḥzaaza beenhum.* The tribes are quarreling with one another. There is enmity among them.

ح ز م *ḥzm*

حـــزام *ḥzaam* p. حزم *ḥizim* 1. belt, girdle, waistband. 2. supporter. هو حزامي؛ أعتمد عليه وقت الشدايـــد *huwa ḥzaami; 'aᶜtimid ᶜalee wagt š-šadaayid.* He is my supporter; I depend on him in distress.

ح ز ن *ḥzn*

حـــزن *ḥizin* (يحزن *yḥazin*) to be sad, grieved. حزن لين عرف انـــه ســـقط في الامتحـــان *ḥizin leen ᶜiraf 'inna saġaṭ fi l-'imtiḥaan.* He was sad when he knew that he failed the examination. 2. to mourn, be in mourning. حزنت علـــى رجلها خمـــس ســـنين *ḥiznat ᶜala rajilha xams siniin.* She mourned her husband for five years. ولده مات وحزن عليه واجـــد *wilda maat w-ḥizan ᶜalee waayid.* His son died and he mourned him for a long time.

حزن *ḥazzan* II to make s.o. sad, grieve s.o. منظر الطرار حزني *manðar ṭ-ṭarraar ḥazzanni.* The sight of the beggar made me sad. موت الرئيس حزن الناس واجـــد *moot r-ra'iis ḥazzan n-naas waayid.* The death of the president grieved the people a lot.

حـــزن *ḥizin* (v.n. from حـــزن *ḥizin*) sorrow, sadness, grief.

حـــزين *ḥaziin* p. *-iin,* حزانة *hazaana* mournful, grieved.

حزنـــان *ḥaznaan* p. *-iin* in mourning. أبوهم توفى من زمان. بعدهم حزانين عليـــه *'ubuuhum tawaffa min zamaan. baᶜadhum ḥaznaaniin ᶜalee.* Their father died a long time ago. They are still in mourning.

ح ز و *ḥzw*

حازى *ḥaaza* III 1. to tell a fairy tale, tell stories. دايما تحازي الجهال قبل لا يرقدون *daayman tḥaazi l-yihhaal gabil la yarigduun.* She always tells stories to the children before they fall asleep. 2. to ask s.o. a riddle, quiz s.o. حازاني بشي ما يخطر على البال *ḥaazaani b-šayy ma yxaṭir ᶜala l-baal.* He asked me a riddle about something you'd never think of.

حزا *ḥzaa* p. حزاوي *ḥazaawi* 1. story, anecdote. 2. fairy tale. 3. nursery rhyme.

حزوة *ḥazwa* p. حزايات *ḥzaayaat* (more common var. فزورة *fazzuura* p. فوازير *fawaaziir*) riddle, puzzle. سمعت فوازير من الراديو في شهر رمضان *simaᶜt fawaaziir min r-raadyo fi šahar rumðaan.* I heard riddles on the radio during the month of Ramadan.

ح س ب *ḥsb*

حسب *ḥisab (yḥasib)* 1. to compute, calculate, count. حسبت كم نفر جاوا؟ *ḥisabt čam nafar yaw?* Did you count how many people came? حسب مصروفه الشهري *ḥisab maṣruufa š-šahri.* He calculated his monthly expenses. حسب الفلوس وقال ناقصين مية درهم *ḥisab li-fluus w-gaal naagṣiin miyat dirhim.* He counted the money and said it was one hundred dirhams short. 2. to consider, deem, think. يحسب نفسه رجال *yḥasib nafsa rayyaal.* He considers himself a man. آنا أحسبك واحد من إخواني *'aana 'aḥsibk waaḥid min 'ixwaani.* I consider you one of my brothers. احسبه من اللي دشوا الشغل الساعة ثمان *'iḥsiba min illi daššu š-šuġul s-saaᶜa θamaan.* Count him as one of those who came to work at eight. حسب حساب *ḥisab ḥsaab* to take s.o. or s.th. into account or into consideration, attach importance to s.o. or s.th. هذا شين ما حسبت له حساب *haaða šayyin ma ḥisabt-la ḥsaab.* This is something I haven't taken into consideration. لازم تحسب حسابك قبل لا تشتري السيارة *laazim tḥasib ḥsaabak gabil la tištiri s-sayyaara.* You have to take everything into account before you buy the car. دايما يحسب حساب المستقبل *daayman yḥasib ḥsaab l-mustagbal.* He always considers the future. حسبت له ألف حساب *ḥisabt-la 'alf ḥsaab.* I took into consideration every little thing about him. 3. to price. زين. إذا تشتري الحيول، أحسب لك الخاتم بألفين درهم *zeen. 'iða tištiri li-ḥyuul, 'aḥsib-lak l-xaatim b-'alfeen dirhim.* Fine. If you buy the bracelets, I will sell you the ring for two thousand dirhams.

حسب *ḥassab* II 1. to think, consider. ما حسبت ينجح في الامتحان *ma ḥassabt yinjaḥ fi l-'imtiḥaan.* I did not think he would pass the examination. تشوفه تحسبه خنفس *ččuufa tḥassba xunfus.* If you look at him, you will think he is a Beatle. 2. to be or become apprehensive, anxious. لا تحسب! الفلوس في أمان *la tḥassib! li-fluus fi 'amaan.* Don't be apprehensive! The money is safe.

حاسب *ḥaasab* III 1. to call to account, ask for an accounting. الله يحاسب كل واحد *'aḷḷa yḥaasib kill waaḥid.* God calls everyone to account. يسوي اللي

العرض والطلب *ḥasab l-ᶜarđ w-ṭ-ṭalab.* according to supply and demand.

حسبما *ḥasb-ma* (conj.) according to what..., depending on how.... حسبما تريد *ḥasb-ma triid* according to what you want. حسبما أعرف *ḥasb-ma ᶜarf* as far as I know. العيد باكر حسبما يقولون *l-ᶜiid baačir ḥasab-ma yguuluun.* The feast day is tomorrow, according to what they say.

حساب *ḥsaab* 1. arithmetic. لازم تدرس أكثر. أنت ضعيف في الحساب *laazim tidris 'akθar. 'inta đaᶜiif fi li-ḥsaab.* You have to study harder. You are weak in arithmetic. 2. count, score. أنت بس امسك الحساب *'inta bass 'imsik li-ḥsaab.* You just keep score. ما اله حساب *ma 'ila ḥsaab* countless, innumerable. الاولاد في هذا الصف ما الهم حساب *li-wlaad fi haađa ṣ-ṣaff ma 'ilhum ḥsaab.* The kids in this class are innumerable. يقزرون الفلوس بدون حساب *ygazzruun li-fluus b-duun ḥsaab.* They spend money foolishly and blindly. 3. account, bank account. عندك حساب في البنك؟ *ᶜindak ḥsaab fi l-bank?* Do you have a bank account? عطيه حسابه وخله يولي *ᶜaṭii ḥsaaba w-xaḷḷa ywalli.* Give him what he is entitled to and make him go away. على حساب *ᶜala ḥsaab* s.o. at someone's expense. التذاكر على حسابي *t-tađaakir ᶜala ḥsaabi.* The tickets are at my expense. لا والله. العشا على حسابي *la waḷḷa. ḷ-ᶜaša ᶜala ḥsaabi.* No, the dinner is on me. 4. by oneself, on the account of. كنت مستعجل وخذيت سيارة على حسابي *čint mistaᶜjil w-xađeet sayyaara ᶜala ḥsaabi.* I was

يبغاه؛ ما ميش أحد يحاسبه *ysawwi lli yibġaa; ma miiš 'aḥad yḥaasba.* He does whatever he wants; there isn't anyone to call him to account. 2. (with على *ᶜala*) to hold s.o. responsible for s.th. حاسبني على كل صغيرة وكبيرة *ḥaasabni ᶜala kill ṣaġiira w-čibiira.* He held me responsible for every detail. 3. pay the bill. عقب الأكل حاسبت راعي المطعم وسرت *ᶜugb l-'akil ḥaasabt raaᶜi l-maṭᶜam w-sirt.* After eating I paid the restaurant owner the bill and left.

تحاسب *tḥaasab* VI to settle a mutual account. خلنا نقعد نتحاسب *xaḷḷna nagᶜid nitḥaasab.* Let's sit down and settle accounts. روح تحاسب واياه لانه حكى عليك! *ruuḥ tḥaasab wiyyaa linna ḥiča ᶜaleek!* Go settle with him because he talked about you. تحاسبنا وتم كل شي على خير *tḥaasabna w-tamm kill šayy ᶜala xeer.* We settled accounts and everything ended well.

حسب *ḥasab* noble descent. ما علينا من حسبه ونسبه *ma ᶜaleena min ḥasaba w-nasaba.* We have nothing to do with his esteemed, noble family.

حسب *ḥasb* (prep.; less common var. *ḥasab*) according to, depending on, in accordance with. المصروف حسب المعاش *l-maṣruuf ḥasab l-maᶜaaš.* Expenditure is according to salary. قدمت طلب شغل حسب الأصول *gaddamt ṭalab šuġul ḥasb l-'uṣuul.* I submitted a job application according to regulations. أسويه على ها الخشم، حسب طلبك *'asawwii ᶜala ha l-xašim, ḥasab ṭalabič.* I will do it with great pleasure, according to your request. حسب

in a hurry and took a taxi all to myself. 5. reckoning. يوم الحساب *yoom li-ḥsaab* Day of Reckoning. الله يحاسب الناس على أعمالهم يوم الحساب *'aḷḷa yḥaasib n-naas ᶜala 'aᶜmaalhum yoom li-ḥsaab.* God will call people to account for their deeds on the Day of Reckoning.

محاسبة *mḥaasaba* (v.n. from III حاسب *ḥaasab*) 1. accounting. درست محاسبة *dirast mḥaasaba.* I studied accounting. 2. bookkeeping.

محسوب *maḥsuub* (p.p. from حسب *ḥisab*) 1. calculated, counted, reckoned. الخدمة محسوبة وايا السعر *l-xidma maḥsuuba wiyya s-siᶜir.* Service is included in the price. 2. considered, deemed, looked upon. هي محسوبة واحدة من الشاعرات *hiya maḥsuuba waaḥida min š-šaaᶜiraat.* She is considered one of the poets.

محاسب *mḥaasib* (act. part. from III حاسب *ḥaasab*) p. *-iin* 1. accountant, bookkeeper. يشتغل محاسب *yištaġil mḥaasib.* He works as an accountant. 2. paymaster. جا المحاسب وعطانا رواتبنا. *ya li-mḥaasib w-ᶜaṭaana rawaatibna.* The paymaster came and paid us our salaries.

ح س ب ل *ḥsbl*

حسبال *ḥasbaal* (with suff. pron.) in the opinion of. حسبالي *ḥasbaali* I think, in my opinion. حسبالهم *ḥasbaalhum* they think, in their opinion. حسبالي جات واياهم *ḥasbaali yat wiyyaahum.* I think she came with them. سلفته فلوس. حسبالي خوش رجال *sallafta fluus. ḥasbaali xooš rayyaal.* I lent him some money. I thought he was a good man.

ح س د *ḥsd*

حسد *ḥisad* (يحسد *yḥasid*) to envy, be envious. حسده على ماله *ḥsida ᶜala maala.* He envied him his possessions.

انحسد *nḥisad* VII to be envied. انحسدت على وظيفتي الجديدة *nḥisatt ᶜala waðiifati l-yidiida.* I was envied my new job. انحسدت من يوم اشتريت بيت *nḥisatt min yoom štireet beet.* I have been envied since I bought a house.

حسد *ḥasad* (v.n. for حسد *ḥisad*) envy. الحسد شيمة بطالة *l-ḥasad šiima baṭṭaala.* Envy is a bad quality.

حسود *ḥasuud* p. *-iin* envious.

ح س س *ḥss*

حس *ḥass* (يحس *yḥiss*) 1. to feel, sense. حست انهم بيخطبونها *ḥassat 'inhum b-yxaṭbuunha.* She sensed that they were going to ask her hand in marriage. ما تبغي تتحكى واياه. ما يحس *ma tabġi titḥačča wiyyaa. ma yḥiss.* She doesn't want to talk to him. He can't sense it. 2. to notice. صارت عفسة كبيرة لكنه ما حس *ṣaarat ᶜafsa čibiira laakinna ma ḥass.* There was a big commotion, but he did not notice.

حس *ḥiss* 1. feeling, sensation. 2. voice. 3. sound, noise.

حساس *ḥassaas* p. *-iin* 1. sensitive, readily affected. شخص حساس واجد *šuxṣ ḥassaas waayid* very sensitive person. 2. delicate, touchy. مسألة حساسة *mas'ala ḥassaasa* delicate matter.

بو ظبي ذالحين تحسنت واجد *bu ḍabi ḍalḥiin tḥassanat waayid.* Abu Dhabi has improved a lot now. صحته تحسنت انشاالله *ṣiḥḥta tḥassanat nšaaḷḷa.* I hope his health has improved.

استحسن *staḥsan* X to regard s.th. as right or appropriate. أستحسن يروح هو قبل *'astaḥsin yruuḥ huwa gabil.* I think it's appropriate that he go first. أستحسن السفر بالسيارة هذي الأيام *'astaḥsin s-safar b-s-sayyaara haaḍi l-'ayyaam.* I think it's appropriate to travel by car during these days.

حسن *ḥisin* beauty, prettiness, liveliness.

حسن *ḥusun* excellence, goodness. شهادة حسن سلوك *šahaadat ḥusun suluuk* certificate of good behavior. لحسن الحظ *li-ḥusn l-ḥaḍḍ* fortunately. حسن التصرف *ḥusn t-taṣarruf* good judgement. حسن النية *ḥusn n-niyya* good intent, good faith. لا تلومه. سواه بحسن نية *la tluuma. sawwaa b-ḥusun niyya.* Don't blame him. He did it in good faith. لحسن الحظ *li-ḥusn l-ḥaḍḍ* fortunately. لحسن الحظ، حصلته في المكتب *li-ḥusn l-ḥaḍḍ, ḥaṣṣalta fi l-maktab.* Fortunately, I found him in the office.

أحسن *'aḥsan* (elat.) 1. (with من *min*) better than. الهوا اليوم أحسن من أمس *l-hawa l-yoom 'aḥsan min 'ams.* The weather today is better than yesterday. آنا أسافر بروحي. كذي أحسن *'aana 'asaafir b-ruuḥi. čiḍi 'aḥsan.* I travel alone. It's better this way. أحسن لك تروح تشوفه قبل *'aḥsan-lak truuḥ ččuufa gabil.* It's better for you to go see him first. 2. (with foll. n.) the best. هذا أحسن مقنطر *haaḍa 'aḥsan mġanṭir.*

حساسية *ḥasaasiyya* 1. sensitivity. 2. allergy.

إحساس *'iḥsaas* sensitivity, sense, perception. قليل الإحساس *galiil l-'iḥsaas* insensitive.

حاسة *ḥaassa* p. حواس *ḥawaass* sense. الحواس الخمسة *l-ḥawaass l-xamsa* the five senses. حاسة الشم *ḥaassat š-šamm* the sense of smell.

محسوس *maḥsuus* tangible, noticeable. تقدم محسوس *tagaddum maḥsuus* noticeable progress.

ح س ن *ḥsn*

حسّن *ḥassan* II 1. to have a haircut. رحت المحسن يوم الخميس وحسنت شعري *riḥt li-mḥassin yoom l-xamiis w-ḥassant šᶜari.* I went to the barber on Thursday and had a haircut. يحسن شعره مرتين في الشهر *yḥassin šᶜara marrateen fi š-šahar.* He has a haircut twice a month. 2. to shave. يحسن لحيته كل يوم *yḥassin liḥyita kill yoom.* He shaves (his beard) every day.

أحسن *'aḥsan* (يحسن *yiḥsin*) IV 1. to do s.th. well, be proficient at s.th. يحسن القراية والكتابة *yiḥsin li-graaya w-li-ktaaba.* He reads and writes well. يحسن اللغة الإنكليزية *yiḥsin l-luġa l-'ingliiziyya.* He is proficient in English. 2. to give alms, give charity. يحسن إلى الفقرا والمساكين *yiḥsin 'ila l-fugara w-l-masaakiin.* He gives alms to the poor. أحسنت! *'aḥsant!* 1. Thank you, you did well! 2. Bravo!

تحسن *tḥassan* V to be or become improved, get better. الشغل تحسن *š-šuġul tḥassan.* Work has improved.

This is the best contractor. أحسن واحد فيهم *'aḥsan waaḥid fiihum* the best one among them. هو أحسنهم في الكورة *huwa 'aḥsanhum fi l-kuura.* He is the best one among them in soccer.

أحسن ما *'aḥsan-ma* 1. the best (that)... أحسن ما يكون *'aḥsan ma ykuun* the best there is. هذا اليح أحسن ما عندي *haaða l-yiḥḥ 'aḥsan-ma ᶜindi.* These watermelons are the best I have. 2. rather than, in preference to. أحسن ما نقرا عنه، خلنا نروح نشوفه *'aḥsan-ma nigra ᶜanna, xaḷḷna nruuḥ nčuufa.* Better than reading about it, let's go see it. يمشي على رجوله أحسن ما ياخذ تكسي *yamši ᶜala ryuula 'aḥsan-ma yaaxið taksi.* He walks rather than take a taxi.

الحسنى *l-ḥusna* fair means, fair way. عامل الناس بالحسنى! *ᶜaamil n-naas b-l-ḥusna!* Treat people in a friendly manner. الأسماء الحسنى *l-'asmaa' l-ḥusna* the 99 attributes of God.

حسنة *ḥasana* p. *-aat* 1. good deed, charitable deed. سواها حسنة لله *sawwaaha ḥasana li-llaah.* He did it as a charitable deed for the sake of God. 2. (only in the p.) advantages, merits. هذي الطريقة الها حسناتها *haaði ṭ-ṭariiga 'ilha ḥasannaatta.* This way has its own advantages.

حسانة *ḥsaana* barbering, barber's trade. (prov.) يتعلم الحسانة في روس القرعان *yitᶜallam li-ḥsaana fi ruus l-gurᶜaan.* The blind leading the blind. (lit., "He learns barbering on bald people's heads.")

تحسين *taḥsiin* (v.n. from II حسن *ḥassan*) improving, improvement.

تحسونة *taḥsuuna* shave, shaving, act of having a haircut.

محسن *miḥsin* p. *-iin* (act. part. from IV أحسن *'ahsan*) philanthropist, charitable person.

محسن *mḥassin* (act. part. from II حسن *ḥassan*) barber. رحت المحسن وحسنت شعري *riḥt li-mḥassin w-hassant šᶜari.* I went to the barber and had a haircut.

ح ش ا *ḥšaa*

حشا *ḥiša* not at all, certainly not, on the contrary.

ح ش د *ḥšd*

حشد *ḥišad (يحشد yḥašid)* to gather, mass, mobilize. العراق حشد جيشه على الحدود الكويتية *li-ᶜraag ḥišad jeeša ᶜala li-ḥduud li-kweetiyya.* Iraq massed its army on the Kuwaiti border.

تحشد *tḥaššad* V to be massed, be concentrated. الجيش تحشد في هذي المنطقة *l-jeeš tḥaššad fi haaði l-manṭaġa.* The army is concentrated in this region.

ح ش ر *ḥšr*

حشر *ḥišar (يحشر yḥašir)* to stick, pack, squeeze, force. حشر الكتب بين القمصان في الشنطة *ḥišar l-kutub been l-gumṣaan fi š-šanṭa.* He stuck the books in between the shirts in the suitcase. هذا مكان صغير واجد. ما أقدر أحشر الولد فيه *haaða mukaan ṣaġiir waayid. ma 'agdar 'aḥšir l-walad fii.* This is a very small place. I cannot squeeze the boy into it. هني الدريولية يحشرون ناس واجد في السيارات *hini d-dreewliyya yḥašruun naas waayid fi s-sayyaaraat.*

Here, drivers jam a whole crowd of people into cars.

الحشر *l-ḥašir* or يوم الحشر *yoom l-ḥašir* Day of Resurrection.

حشرة *ḥšira* p. *-aat* insect, bug. علم الحشرات *ᶜilm l-ḥašaraat* entomology.

ح ش ش *ḥšš*

حش *ḥašš (يحش yḥišš)* to mow, cut grass. في الزمان الأولي كانوا بعض الناس يحشون الحشيش ويودونه السوق *fi z-zamaan l-'awwali čaanaw baᶜđ n-naas yḥiššuun l-ḥašiiš w-ywadduuna s-suug.* In olden times some people used to cut grass and take it to the marketplace.

حشش *ḥaššaš* II to smoke hashish. اللي يحشش يزخونه الشرطة ويودونه السجن *'illi yḥaššis yzixxuuna š-širṭa w-ywadduuna s-sijin.* He who smokes hashish will be arrested by the police and taken to jail.

حشيش *ḥašiiš* (coll.) 1. wild grass, hay, herbs. 2. hashish (or loosely, any narcotic). s. *-a* hashish, hemp (or loosely, any narcotic).

حشاش *ḥaššaaš* 1. (p. حواشيش *ḥiwaašiiš*) one who cuts grass and sells it as animal feed (in the old times). 2. (p. *-iin*) 1. one who smokes hashish. 2. narcotics addict.

محشش *mḥaššiš* (act. part. from II حشش *ḥaššaš*) 1. having smoked hashish or other narcotic. لقيوه محشش. زخوه ووده السجن *ligyoo mḥaššiš. zaxxoo w-waddoo s-sijin.* They found him doped. They arrested him and took him to jail. 2. s.o. under the influence of hashish or other narcotic.

ح ش ف *ḥšf*

حشف *ḥašaf* (coll.) s. حشفة *ḥšifa* dried up, poor quality dates, used as cattle feed. الحشف أخس أنواع التمر *l-ḥašaf 'axass 'anwaaᶜ t-tamir.* *ḥašaf* is the worst kind of dates.

ح ش م *ḥšm*

حشم *ḥaššam* II to treat s.o. politely or hospitably, treat with deference. حشمته لاجل خاطرك لانه ما يستحق الحشيمة *ḥaššamta lajil xaaṭrak linna ma yistaḥigg l-ḥašiima.* I treated him politely and reverentially for your sake because he doesn't deserve to be treated with respect or politeness.

تحشم *tḥaššam* V to be treated politely or hospitably.

احتشم *ḥtišam* VIII to be modest, conservative. يحتشم. ما يمدح نفسه *yiḥtišim. ma yimdaḥ nafsa.* He is modest. He doesn't praise himself. الحرمة هني لازم تحتشم في لبسها *l-ḥurma hini laazim tiḥtišm fi libissa.* Women here have to be conservative in their dress.

حشمة *ḥišma* modesty, decency, conservativeness. الحشمة مطلوبة *l-ḥišma maṭluuba.* Modesty is required. الحشمة من شيمة الحرمة الزينة *l-ḥišma min šiimat l-ḥurma z-zeena.* Conservativeness is one of the qualities of a good woman.

ح ش و *ḥšw*

حشى *ḥiša (يحشي yḥaši)* to stuff, fill. حشى المخدة بالقطن *ḥiša li-mxadda b-l-guṭun.* He stuffed the pillow with cotton. حشى الدجاجة بالعيش والزبيب

ḥiša d-diyaaya b-l-ᶜeeš w-z-zibiib. He stuffed the chicken with rice and raisins. 2. to stick, stuff. ليش حشيت هالقد قطن في المخدة؟ *leeš ḥašeet hal-gadd guṭun fi li-mxadda?* Why have you stuffed so much cotton in the pillow? 3. to fill (teeth). كم ضرس حشى لك طبيب الأسنان؟ *čam ðirs ḥašaa-lak ṭabiib l-'asnaan?* How many teeth has the dentist filled for you?

حشى *ḥašša* II = حشى *ḥiša* (يحشي *yḥaši).*

تحشى *tḥašša* V to be stuffed, be filled. المخدة تحشت قطن *li-mxadda tḥaššat guṭun.* The pillow was stuffed with cotton. ها الضرس ما يتحشى؛ لازم ينشلع *ha ð-ðirs ma yithašša; laazim yinšiliᶜ* This tooth cannot be filled; it will have to be pulled out.

تحاشى *tḥaaša* VI 1. to avoid, keep away or abstain from s.o. or s.th. تحاشى الرجال البطال *tḥaaša r-rayyaal l-baṭṭaal.* Keep away from bad men. تحاشيت أقول له أي شي عن الموضوع *tḥaašeet 'agul-la 'ayya šayy ᶜan l-mawðuuᶜ.* I avoided telling him anything about the subject. 2. to ignore. تحاشاه! ما عليك من اللي يقوله *tḥaašaa! ma ᶜaleek min illi yguula.* Avoid him. Don't pay attention to anything he says.

انحشى *nḥiša* VII = تحشى V *tḥašša.*

حشو *ḥašu* (v.n. from حشى *ḥiša*) 1. stuffing, filling, s.th. that is filled. حشو حق مخدة *ḥašu ḥagg mxadda* stuffing for a pillow. الحشو في الديك الرومي *l-ḥašu fi d-diič r-ruumi* the turkey stuffing. 2. filling (teeth). حشو مال ضرس *ḥašu maal ðirs* tooth filling.

حاشية *ḥaašiya* p. حواشي *ḥawaaši* followers, entourage. مطارزية الأمير وحاشيته جاوا *maṭaarziyyat l-'amiir w-ḥaašiita jaw.* The prince, his bodyguards, and his entourage came.

محشي *maḥši* (p.p. from حشى *ḥiša*) stuffed, filled. كوسا محشي *kuusa maḥši* stuffed squash. بقلاوة محشية جوز والا لوز *baglaawa maḥšiyya jooz walla looz* baklava filled with walnuts or almonds.

ح ص د *ḥṣd*

حصد *ḥiṣad* (يحصد *yḥaṣid)* to reap, harvest. في راس الخيمة يحصدون بر وإذرا *fi raas l-xeema yḥaṣduun burr w-'iðra.* In Ras Al-Khaima they harvest wheat and corn.

انحصد *nḥiṣad* VII to be harvested. ما أدري متى يحصدون الشعير *ma dri mita yḥaṣduun š-šaᶜiir.* I don't know when they harvest barley.

ح ص ر ١ *ḥṣr*

حصر *ḥiṣar* (يحصر *yḥaṣir)* to narrow down, confine. الشرطة حصروا الشبهة بالبوق بالبلوشي *š-širṭa ḥṣaraw š-šubha b-l-boog b-l-bluuši.* The police narrowed down the suspicion of theft to the Baluchi. حصر تفكيره وحاول يذكر، بس ما قدر *ḥiṣar tafkiira w-ḥaawal yiððakkar, bass ma gidar.* He put his mind to it and tried to remember, but he couldn't.

حاصر *ḥaaṣar* III 1. to surround, encircle. الشرطة حاصروا الطلاب المتظاهرين في الجامعة *š-širṭa ḥaaṣraw* *ṯ-ṯullaab l-miðǒaahriin fi l-yaamᶜa.* The police surrounded the demonstrating students in the university. 2. to besiege. الجيش حاصر المدينة شهر قبلما سقطت *l-jeeš ḥaaṣar l-madiina šahar gabil-ma sagṭat.* The army besieged the city for a month before it fell.

انحصر *nḥiṣar* VII 1. to be caught, be trapped. انحصروا في الدكان إلين وقف إطلاق النار *nḥiṣraw fi d-dikkaan 'ileen wugaf 'iṭlaag n-naar.* They got caught in the shop until shooting (lit. "the opening of fire") stopped. 2. to be crowded, be jammed. انحصرنا بالتكسي وما قدرنا نتحرك *nḥiṣarna b-t-taksi w-ma gidarna nitḥarrak.* We were crowded in the taxi and couldn't move. 3. to have a full bladder, to have to go. الشيبة انحصر بوله. فيه حمام هني؟ *š-šeeba nḥiṣar boola. fii ḥammaam hini?* The old man has to go to the bathroom. Is there a toilet here?

حصير *ḥaṣiir* (coll.) woven mats, mats made from bamboo. s. *-a.* في الزمان الأولي الناس كانوا يناموں على الحصير *fi z-zamaan l-'awwali n-naas čaanaw ynaamuun ᶜala l-ḥaṣiir.* In the olden times, people used to sleep on bamboo mats.

حصار *ḥiṣaar* 1. siege, blockade. حصار اقتصادي *ḥiṣaar 'igtiṣaadi* economic blockade.

انحصار *nḥiṣaar* (v.n. from VII انحصر *nḥiṣar*) confinement, limitation, restrictedness.

محصور *maḥṣuur* (act. part. from حصر *ḥiṣar*) 1. limited, restricted, confined. شركات السيارات محصورة في ثلاثة أنفار *šarikaat s-sayyaaraat maḥṣuura fi θalaaθat 'anfaar.* Car companies are restricted to three people. 2. bored, depressed. كان محصور في ذيك القرية الصغيرة *čaan maḥṣuur fi ðiič l-ġarya ṣ-ṣaġiira.* He was bored in that little village. 3. feeling the need to urinate. إذا محصور الحمام تحت *'iða maḥṣuur l-ḥammaam taḥat.* If you've got to go, the bathroom is downstairs.

ح ص ر٢ *ḥṣr*

تحصر *tḥaṣṣar* V 1. (with على *ᶜala)* to sigh over s.th. تحصر على ذيك الأيام الحلوة *tḥaṣṣar ᶜala ðiič l-'ayyaam l-ḥilwa.* He sighed over the good old days. 2. to grieve, be grieved (for s.th.). قزر فلوسه كلها وقام يتحصر على درهم *gazzar fluusa killaha w-gaam yitḥaṣṣar ᶜala dirhim.* He spent all his money foolishly and began to grieve for one dirham.

حصرة *ḥaṣra* p. *-aat* 1. sigh. 2. longing, nostalgia. يا حصرتي على الأيام اللي فاتت *ya ḥaṣrati ᶜala l-'ayyaam illi faatat.* Ah, what good days those were!

ح ص ل *ḥṣl*

حصل *ḥiṣal (يحصل yḥaṣil)* 1. to happen, take place, occur. حصل دعمة في سوق السمك *ḥiṣal daᶜma fi suug s-simač.* A car accident took place in the fish market. عسى ما حصل شي! *ᶜasa ma ḥiṣal šayy!* I hope nothing bad happened. هذا شي يحصل مرة في العمر *haaða šayy yḥaṣil marra fi l-ᶜumur.* This is a thing that happens once in a lifetime. حصلت الموافقة على الترفيع

ḥṣalat li-mwaafga ᶜala t-tarfiiᶜ. The approval for the promotion went through. ليش تلومني؟ ما حصل مني شي *leeš tluumni? ma ḥiṣal minni šayy.* Why do you blame me? I haven't done anything. 2. (with *ᶜala*) to obtain, get, receive. حصل على بعثة من وزارة التربية *ḥiṣal ᶜala biᶜθa min wazaarat t-tarbiya.* He got a scholarship from the Ministry of Education. حصل على الشهادة عقب خمس سنين *ḥaṣal ᶜala š-šahaada ᶜugub xams siniin.* He obtained his certificate in five years. 3. to be found, be available, obtainable. دورت على نارجيلة في السوق لكن ما حصل *dawwart ᶜala naariila fi s-suug laakin ma ḥiṣal.* I looked for a water pipe in the market but it wasn't available. (prov.) لا حصل الماي بطل العافور *la ḥiṣal l-maay biṭal l-ᶜaafuur.* (lit., "If water is available, ablution with clean earth becomes invalid.")

حصل *ḥaṣṣal* II 1. to find. حصلت سمك في السوق؟ *ḥaṣṣalt simač fi s-suug?* Did you find fish in the market? ما حصلت شي *ma ḥaṣṣalt šayy.* I did not find anything. حصلته عند المدير *ḥaṣṣalta ᶜind l-mudiir.* I found him at the director's (office). 2. to obtain, get, receive. حصل السيارة اللي يبغيها *ḥaṣṣal s-sayyaara lli yabġiiha.* He got the car he wanted. تقدر تحصل لي حقوقي من الشركة؟ *tigdar tḥaṣṣil-li ḥguugi min š-šarika?* Can you get for me my due from the company? كم تحصل في الشهر؟ *čam tḥaṣṣil fi š-šahar?* How much do you make a month? أحصل خمسة ألف درهم في الشهر *'aḥaṣṣil xamsa 'alf dirhim fi š-šahar.* I make five thousand dirhams a month. 3. to profit, make a profit. بعت العمارة بخمسة مليون درهم وحصلت منها مليون درهم *biᶜt li-ᶜmaara b-xamsa malyoon dirhim w-ḥaṣṣalt minha malyoon dirhim.* I sold the building for five million dirhams and made a million dirham profit on it.

تحصل *tḥaṣṣal* V 1. to be obtained. ها الشي ما يتحصل إلا في مركز حمدان *ha š-šayy ma yitḥaṣṣal 'illa fi markaz ḥamdaan.* This thing cannot be obtained except at Hamdan Center. 2. to be collected. هذا الدين ما يتحصل بسهولة *haaða d-deen ma yitḥaṣṣal b-suhuula.* This debt cannot be easily collected.

حصول *ḥuṣuul* (v.n. from حصل *ḥiṣal*) obtaining, attaining. الحصول على ويزة *l-ḥuṣuul ᶜala wiiza* obtaining a visa.

حاصل *ḥaaṣil* p. *-aat* 1. product. أهم حاصلات الإمارات البترول *'ahamm ḥaaṣilaat l-'imaaraat l-batrool.* The most important of the products of the Emirates is petroleum. 2. crop, harvest. الحر يدمر بعض الحاصلات *l-ḥarr ydammir baᶜð̣ l-ḥaaṣilaat.* Heat destroys some crops. 3. (with the article prefix ال *l-*) briefly, in brief. الحاصل راح تونس وقزر فلوسه *l-ḥaaṣil raaḥ twannas w-gazzar fluusa.* To make a long story short, he had a good time and spent his money foolishly. الحاصل ما حصلت شقة تعجبني *l-ḥaaṣil ma ḥaṣṣalt šigga tiᶜjibni.* In the end, I did not find an apartment I liked.

محصول *maḥṣuul* (p.p. from حصل *ḥiṣal*) p. محاصيل *maḥaaṣiil* 1. product. 2. crop, harvest. 3. yield, gain.

ح ص ن ḥṣn

حصـــن ḥaṣṣan II to fortify, entrench. الجيش الأمريكي حصن مواقعـــه في هـــذي المنطقة في حرب الخليــج *l-jeeš l-'amriiki ḥaṣṣan mawaagᶜa fi haaði l-manṭiga fi ḥarb l-xaliij.* The American army fortified its positions in this area during the Gulf War.

تحصن *tḥaṣṣan* V pass. of II *ḥaṣṣan.*

حصـــن *ḥiṣin* p. حصون *ḥṣuun* fortress, fort (usually for an Emir and his followers).

حصـــني *ḥiṣni* p. حصنية *hiṣniyya* (واوي *waawi* is more common) jackal.

حصان *ḥṣaan* p. حصن *ḥuṣun* 1. horse (f. فـــرس *faras*). 2. horsepower. قوة الماكينة مية حصـــان *guwaat l-maakiina miyat ḥṣaan.* The motor is one hundred horsepower.

ح ص و ḥṣw

حصـــي *ḥiṣa* (يحصـــي *yḥaṣi*) to count, enumerate. عنده فلوس ماحد يقدر يحصيها *ᶜinda fluus maḥḥad yigdar yiḥṣiiha.* He has more money than anyone could count. ها الناس اللي في السوق شيحصيهم؟ *han-naas illi fi s-suug š-yiḥṣiihum?* How could anyone count the people in the marketplace?

حصى *ḥaṣa* (coll.) pebbles, little stones. s. حصاة *ḥaṣaa.*

إحصـــا *'iḥṣa* 1. count, counting. إحصا الســـكان *'iḥṣa s-sukkaan* census. 2. statistics درست إحصـــا؟ *dirast 'iḥṣa?* Have you studied statistics?

ح ط ب ḥṭb

حطـــب *ḥaṭṭab* II to gather firewood. حرمة البدوي هي اللـــــي تحطـــب *ḥurmat li-bdiwi hiya lli tḥaṭṭiib.* A Bedouin's wife is the one who gathers firewood.

حطـــب *ḥaṭab* (coll.) 1. firewood. 2. wood. s. احطبة *ḥṭuba.*

حطـــاب *ḥaṭṭaab* p. حطاطيب *ḥaṭaaṭiib, -iin* one who cuts firewood or one who sells firewood.

ح ط ط ḥṭṭ

حـــط *ḥaṭṭ* (يحط *yḥuṭṭ*) 1. put, place, set down. حط الشنط على الميزان *ḥuṭṭ š-šinaṭ ᶜala l-miizaan.* Put the suitcases on the scale(s). لا تحط نفسك بمشاكل مثل هذي *la tḥuṭṭ nafsak b-mašaakil miθil haaði.* Don't get yourself into problems similar to these. حطيت عيني على ذيك البنية، لكن عرست *ḥaṭṭeet ᶜeeni ᶜala ðiič li-bnayya, laakin ᶜarrasat.* I had my eye on that girl, but she got married. 2. to land, settle. الطايرة حطت الساعة خمـــس *ṭ-ṭaayra ḥaṭṭat s-saaᶜa xams.* The plane landed at five o'clock. 3. (with من *min*) to lower, detract from, diminish. السكر يحط من قيمة الإنســـان *s-sikir yḥuṭṭ min giimt l-'insaan.* Drinking lowers one's prestige.

انحـــط *nḥaṭṭ* VII 1. to be put, placed. الشنط انحطوا على الميزان *š-šinaṭ nḥaṭṭaw ᶜala l-miizaan.* The suitcases were put on the scale(s). الشنط انحطوا فوق بعض *š-šinaṭ nḥaṭṭaw foog baᶜaḍ.* The suitcases were placed on top of each other. 2. to deteriorate, decay, decline. انحطت صحته لين بدا يسكر *nḥaṭṭat ṣiḥḥta leen bida yiskar.* His health deteriorated when he started to drink. أخلاقه انحطـــت *'axlaaga nḥaṭṭat.* His moral behavior has declined.

محطة *maḥaṭṭa* p. *-aat* 1. stop, stopping place. محطة الباص *maḥaṭṭat l-paaṣ* the bus stop. 2. station. محطة القطار *maḥaṭṭ l-giṭaar* the railroad station. محطة الإذاعة *maṭṭat l-'iðaaᶜa* the broadcasting station.

أحط *'aḥaṭṭ* (elat.) 1. (with من *min*) more deteriorated, more debased. 2. (with foll. n.) the most deteriorated, the most debased.

منحط *minḥaṭṭ* p. *-iin* degraded, low, base. أجلك الله، هذا رجال منحط *'ajallak aḷḷa, haaða rayyaal minḥaṭṭ.* Pardon the expression, this is a low-based, degraded man. حرمة منحطة *ḥurma minḥaṭṭa* fallen woman.

ح ظ ر *ḥðr*

حضر *ḥiðar* (يحضر *yḥaðir*) 1. to attend, be present. حضرت اجتماع في البلدية *ḥiðart 'ijtimaaᶜ fi l-baladiyya.* I attended a meeting in the municipality. حضرت حفلة التخرج أمس؟ *ḥiðart ḥaflat t-taxarruj 'ams?* Did you attend the graduation ceremony yesterday? سالم حضر؟ *saalim ḥiðar?* Was Salim present? اي نعم، حضر. ليش ما يحضر؟ *'ii naᶜam, ḥiðar. leeš ma yḥaðir?* Yes, indeed. He was present. I cannot see why he cannot be present. 2. to arrive, get to s.o., or to some place. هل المعرس حضروا. نبغى نتحكى واياهم *hal l-miᶜris ḥiðraw. nibġa nitḥačča wiyyaahum.* The bridegroom's folks arrived. We would like to talk to them. حضرنا إلى الديوان الأميري والشيخ، طويل العمر، رمسنا *ḥiðarna 'ila d-diiwaan l-'amiiri w-š-šeex, ṭawiil l-ᶜumur, rammasna.* We arrived at the Emiri Court, and the Shaikh, may he live long, addressed us.

حضر *ḥaððar* II (و لم *wallam,* برز *barraz* are more common) 1. to prepare, make ready. حضروا ساماهم وتركوا *ḥaððaraw saamaanhum w-trikaw.* They got their things ready and left. أنت صيدلي؟ الصيدلي هو اللي يحضر الدوا *'inta ṣaydali? ṣ-ṣaydali huwa lli yḥaððir d-duwa.* Are you a pharmacist? A pharmacist is the one who prepares medicine. 2. to produce, make. الطلاب حضروا غاز الهيدروجين في المختبر *ṭ-ṭullaab ḥaððaraw ġaaz l-heedrojiin fi l-muxtabar.* The students produced hydrogen gas in the laboratory.

حاضر *ḥaaðar* III to lecture, give a course of lectures. حاضر عن الوضع الاقتصادي في الإمارات *ḥaaðar ᶜan l-waðᶜ l-'igtiṣaadi fi l-'imaaraat.* He lectured on the economic situation in the Emirates. حاضر في الكلية سنتين *ḥaaðar fi l-kulliyya santeen.* He lectured at the college for two years.

تحضر *tḥaððar* V 1. to prepare oneself, get ready. تحضرنا للسفر قبل سبوع *tḥaððarna la s-safar gabil subuuᶜ.* We got ready for travelling a week ago. 2. to become urbanized, become a town dweller. البدو صعب عليهم يتحضرون *l-badu ṣaᶜb ᶜaleehum yitḥaððaruun.* It's difficult for Bedouins to become urbanized. 3. to become civilized. شفتك فوق شفتك حدر. طول عمرك موب رايح تتحضر *šiftak foog šiftak ḥadir. ṭuul ᶜumrak muub raayiḥ titḥaððar.* You never change (lit., "I saw you upstairs, I saw you downstairs.") You'll never in your life become civilized.

حضر *ḥaðar* (coll.) settled population, town dwellers (as opposed to بدو *badu* Bedouins or nomads). s. حضري *ḥðari.*

حضرة *ḥaðra* presence. في حضرة كل الناس *fi ḥaðrat kill n-naas* in the presence of all the people. 2. respectful form of address, esp. in letters, e.g. حضرة الرئيس! *ḥaðrat r-ra'iss!* Mr. President! حضرة السيد سالم *ḥaðrat s-sayyid saalim* Dear Mr. Salim.

حضور *ḥuðuur* (v.n. from حضر *ḥiðar*) 1. presence. حضور الاجتماع *ḥuðuur li-jtimaa*ᶜ attending the meeting. حضور هذا الشاهد في المحكمة موب لازم *ḥuðuur haaða š-šaahid fi l-maḥkama muub laazim.* The attendance of this witness in the law court is not required. عد الفلوس بحضوره ᶜ*idd li-fluus b-ḥuðuura.* Count the money in his presence. 2. attendance. الحضور في الاجتماع ضروري *l-ḥuðuur fi li-jtimaa*ᶜ *ðaruuri.* Attendance at the meeting is necessary. 3. (with the article prefix ال *l-*) those present, the people attending. كل الحضور وافقوا على المشروع *kill l-ḥuðuur waafgaw* ᶜ*ala l-mašruu*ᶜ. All of those present approved the project.

حضارة *ḥaðaara* p. *-aat* civilization, 2. culture.

حضيرة *ḥaðiira* p. حضاير *ḥaðaayir* squad (small number of soldiers, about 6-12).

محضر *maḥðar* p. محاضر *maḥaaðir* minutes (of a meeting, etc.), record of factual findings (of a case, etc.)

محاضرة *muḥaaðara* p. *-aat* lecture.

حاضر *ḥaaðir* (act. part. from حضر *ḥiðar*) 1. having attended (e.g., a lecture, a meeting, etc.) آنا حاضر الاجتماع *'aana ḥaaðir li-jtimaa*ᶜ. I have attended the meeting. 2. present. الوقت الحاضر *l-wagt l-ḥaaðir* the present time. 3. ready (بارز *baariz* is more common. See under ب ر ز *brz*). العشا حاضر *l-*ᶜ*aša ḥaaðir.* Dinner is ready. 4. (with the article prefix ال *l-*) the one present, those present, the people attending) الحاضر يعلم الغايب *l-ḥaaðir yi*ᶜ*lim l-ġaayib.* Those present will tell those who are absent.

متحضر *mitḥaððir* p. *-iin* civilized. بلد متحضر *balad mitḥaððir* civilized country.

ح ظ ر م و ت *ḥðrmwt*

حضرموت *ḥaðramuut* Hadhramaut.

حضرمي *ḥaðrami* p. حضارمة *ḥaðaarma, -yyiin* (حضرموتي *ḥaðramuuti* is less common) 1. of, characteristic of Hadhramaut. 1. man from Hadhramaut, Hadhramauti.

ح ظ ظ *ḥðð*

حظ *ḥaðð* p. حظوظ *ḥðuuð* 1. lot, fate, destiny. 2. luck, fortune. الحظ يلعب دور كبير في الحياة *l-ḥaðð yil*ᶜ*ab door čbiir fi l-ḥayaa.* Luck plays an important role in life. سوء الحظ *suu' l-ḥaðð* bad luck, misfortune. من سوء الحظ *min suu' l-ḥaðð* or لسوء الحظ *li-suu' l-ḥaðð* unfortunately. حسن الحظ *ḥusn l-ḥaðð* good luck. لحسن الحظ *li-ḥusn l-ḥaðð* fortunately, luckily. من حسن حظك عفوا عنك *min ḥusn ḥaððak* ᶜ*afaw* ᶜ*annak.* Fortunately for you, they have forgiven you.

محظـوظ *maḥðuuð* p. *-iin* lucky, fortunate. محظوظ. موب لازم يدرس ويشتغل *maḥðuuð. muub laazim yidris w-yištaġil.* He is fortunate. He doesn't have to study and work. محظوظ. لعب ورق وربح *maḥðuuð. licab warag w-ribaḥ.* He's lucky. He played cards and won.

ح ظ ن *ḥðn*

حضـن *ḥiðan* (يحضـن *yḥaðin*) 1. to embrace, hug s.o. حضن صديقه وعطاه حبة *ḥiðan ṣadiiga w-caṭaa ḥabba.* He embraced his friend and kissed him. 2. to put in one's lap. الأم حضنت طفلها *l-'umm ḥðanat ṭiflaha.* The mother put her baby on her lap.

حضـن *ḥaðin* (v.n. from حضن *ḥiðan*) embracing, hugging. الحضن هني تحصله بين الرجاجيل لو بين حريم لوحدهم *l-ḥaðin hini tḥaṣṣla been r-rayaayiil lo been ḥariim la-waḥdahum.* Here you find embracing among men or among women by themselves.

حضن *ḥuðun* p. أحضان *'aḥðaan* (شليل *šiliil* is more common) 1. lap. 2. bosom.

ح ف ر *ḥfr*

حفـر *ḥifar* (يحفر *yḥafir*) 1. to dig. حفر حفرة في الأرض *ḥifar ḥifra fi l-'arð.* He dug a hole in the ground. يحفرون خنادق حـول القصـر *yḥafruun xanaadig ḥool l-gaṣir.* They are digging trenches around the palace. حفروا قـبر *ḥifraw gabir.* They dug a grave. 2. to drill. الشركة حفرت بير بترول جديـد *š-šarika ḥfarat biir batrool yidiid.* The company drilled a new oil well.

حفر *ḥaffar* II to dig up, tear up. الكولية حفروا الشارع وما لقيـوا بيـب المـاي المكسـور *l-kuuliyya ḥaffaraw š-šaaric w-ma ligyu peep l-maay l-maksuur.* The coolies dug up the street and did not find the broken water pipe.

تحفر *tḥaffar* V to be or become dug up. الشارع تحفـر مـن الشاحنـات *š-šaaric tḥaffar min š-šaaḥinaat.* The street got dug up by the trucks.

انحفـر *nḥifar* VII 1. to be dug up. 2. to be drilled.

حفـر *ḥafir* (v.n. from حفر *ḥifar*) 1. digging, digging up. 2. drilling.

حفرة *ḥifra* p. حفر *ḥifar* hole, pothole. ما نحصل إلا حفـر في هـذا الشـارع *ma nḥaṣṣil 'illa ḥifar fi haaða š-šaaric.* We find only potholes in this street.

حفريات *ḥafriyyaat* excavations. أجهزة الحفريـات *'ajhizat l-ḥafriyyaat* the excavations equipment.

حفار *ḥaffaar* p. حفافير *ḥafaafiir, -iin* 1. digger. حفـارين القبـور *ḥaffaariin li-gbuur* gravediggers. 2. driller. يشتغل حفـار *yištaġil ḥaffaar.* He works as a driller.

حافر *ḥaafir* p. حوافر *ḥawaafir* hoof.

محفور *maḥfuur* (p.p. from حفر *ḥifar*) 1. dug up. 2. inscribed, engraved. اسمه محفور علـى القـبر *'isma maḥfuur cala l-gabir.* His name is engraved on the tombstone.

ح ف ظ *ḥfð*

حفـظ *ḥifað* (يحفـظ *yḥafið*) 1. to preserve. الثلاجة تحفظ الأشيا مدة طويلـة *θ-θallaaja tḥafið l-'ašya mudda*

الشـرطة يحـافظون علـى الأمـن *š-širṭa yḥaafðuun ᶜala l-'amin.* The police maintain security. حافظ على وعدك؛ لا تخلـف *ḥaafið ᶜala waᶜdak; la tixlif.* Keep your promise; don't break it.

تحفظ *tḥaffað* V 1. to learn by heart, learn. تحفـظ القـرآن *tḥaffað l-qur'aan.* He learned the Quran by heart. تحفظت دروسها *tḥaffaðat druussa.* She learned her lessons. 2. to protect oneself. تحفـظ مـن الحـر *tḥaffað min l-ḥarr.* Protect yourself from the heat. 2. to be cautious, careful, be on guard. ما قال كل شي. تحفـظ في حكيـه *ma gaal kill šayy. tḥaffað fi ḥačya.* He didn't say everything. He was careful with what he said. تحفـظ منـه. هـو مجـرم *tḥaffað minna. huwa mijrim.* Be careful of him. He is a criminal.

انحفظ *nḥifað* VII to be preserved. 2. to be protected or guarded. 3. to be kept away. 4. to be memorized.

احتفظ *ḥtifað* VIII (with ب *b-*) 1. to keep, save. احتفظ بصورتهـا كـل الوقـت *ḥtifað b-ṣuuratta kill l-wagt.* He kept her picture the whole time. 2. to reserve, maintain, uphold. احتفظت بحقـي أقـول اللـي أبغيـه *ḥtifaðt b-ḥaggi 'aguul illi 'abġii.* I reserved the right to say all that I wanted. 3. to keep up, maintain. كان يحتفظ بصحتـه قبلمـا مـات *čaan yiḥtafið b-ṣiḥḥta gabil-ma maat.* He used to keep his health up before he died. 4. to retain, keep. احتفـظ بمسـتواه العلمـي طـول حياتـه *ḥtifað b-mustawaa l-ᶜilmi ṭuul ḥayaata.* He retained his scholarly standard throughout his lifetime. الحاكم احتفـظ بوزارة الدفـاع حق نفسـه *l-ḥaakim ḥtifað*

ṭiwiila. A refrigerator preserves things for a long time. 2. to protect, guard, watch over. الله يحفظـك *'aḷḷa yiḥfaðk* God protect you. 3. to keep, put away, save, store. احفـظ هـذا في مخبـاك *'iḥfað haaða fi maxbaak.* Keep this in your pocket. خلصنا من هذيل الملفات. احفظهـم كلهـم *xaḷḷaṣna min haðeel l-malaffaat. 'iḥfaðhum killahum.* We have finished with these files. Put them away. لازم تحفـظ كـل الطلبـات *laazim tḥafið kill ṭ-ṭalabaat.* You have to file all the applications. حفـظ لي أوراقـي وايـاه في المكتـب *ḥifað-li 'awraagi wiyyaa fi l-maktab.* He held my papers for me in the office. 4. to memorize, commit to memory, know by heart. حفـظ الـدرس كلـه *ḥifað d-dars killa.* He memorized the whole lesson. فيه ناس يحفظـون القـرآن *fii naas yḥafðuun l-qur'aan.* There are some people who know the Quran by heart.

حفظ *ḥaffað* II 1. to cause to memorize. أمـي حفظتـني القصيـدة *'ummi ḥaffaðatni l-gaṣiida.* My mother helped me memorize the poem. المـدرس حفظنـا سـورتين مـن القـرآن *l-mudarris ḥaffaðna suurteen min l-qur'aan.* The teacher helped us learn two chapters from the Quran by heart.

حـافظ *ḥaafað* III (with على *ᶜala*) 1. to maintain, preserve, sustain, keep up, uphold. الضغط حافظ على مستواه *ð-ðaġṭ ḥaafað ᶜala mustawaa.* Pressure maintained its level. عقبمـا طلع مـن المستشـفى، حـافظ علـى صحتـه *ᶜugub-ma ṭilaᶜ min l-mustašfa, ḥaafað ᶜala ṣiḥḥta.* After he was discharged from the hospital, he kept up his health.

b-wazaarat d-difaaᶜ ḥagg nafsa. The ruler retained the ministry of defense for himself.

محفظة *maḥfaða* p. محافظ *maḥaafið, -aat* briefcase, attaché case.

محافظة *mḥaafaða* (v.n. from III حافظ *ḥaafað*) 1. safeguarding. 2. protection, defense. 3. preservation, maintenance. المحافظة على الأمن *li-mḥaafaða ᶜala l-'amin* preservation of the peace. المحافظة على مناطق الآثار *li-mḥaafaða ᶜala manaaṭig l-'aaθaar* maintenance of archaeological sites.

حافظ *ḥaafið* (act. part. from حفظ *ḥifað*) p. *-iin,* حفاظ *ḥuffaað* 1. having learned s.th. حافظ دروسه *ḥaafið druusa.* He has learned his lessons. حافظ جدول الضرب *ḥaafið jadwal ð-ðarb.* He has learned the multiplication table. 2. (p. حفاظ *ḥuffaað*) one who has learned the Quran by heart.

محافظ *mḥaafið* (act. part. from III حافظ *ḥaafað*) 1. (p. *-iin*) a conservative. حزب المحافظين *ḥizb li-mḥaafðiin* the conservative party. 2. (with على *ᶜala*) complying with, preserving, keeping. محافظ على التعليمات *mḥaafið ᶜala t-taᶜliimaat* complying with instructions. محافظ على وعده *mḥaafið ᶜala waᶜda* keeping his promise.

ح ف ف *ḥff*

حف *ḥaff (يحف yḥiff)* 1. to be or become dry. يحطون السمك في الشمس لين يحف *yḥuṭṭuun s-simač fi š-šams leen yḥiff.* They put fish in the sun until it gets dry. الهوا حف *l-hawa ḥaff.* The weather became dry. 2. to pluck, remove, scratch off. الحرمة إما تحف لو تزين شعر رجولها *l-ḥurma 'imma tḥiff lo tzayyin šaᶜar ryuulha.* A woman either plucks or shaves the hair on her legs. حف الشعر الأبيض من شواربه *ḥaff š-šaᶜar l-'abyað min šawaarba.* He removed the grey hairs from his moustache. حف العود *ḥaff l-ᶜuud.* He stripped off the stick. 3. to be or become weak. بدن الشيبة يحف *badan š-šeeba yḥiff.* An old man's body becomes weak.

حاف *ḥaaff* dry, not humid. الهوا في القيظ هني موب حاف *l-hawa fi l-geeð hini muub ḥaaff.* The weather in the summer here is not dry. في العين حاف *fi l-ᶜeen ḥaaff.* In the city of Al-Ain it's dry.

ح ف ل *ḥfl*

احتفل *ḥtifal* VIII (with ب *b-*) to celebrate, have a celebration. احتفلنا بالعيد *htifalna b-l-ᶜiid.* We celebrate the feast day.

حفلة *ḥafla* p. *-aat* 1. party. سويت حفلة *sawwet ḥafla.* I gave a party. 2. ceremony. كان فيه حفلة في قصر الشيخ *čaan fii ḥafla fi gaṣr š-šeex.* There was a ceremony at the Shaikh's palace. حفلة عرس *ḥaflat ᶜirs* wedding ceremony. حفلة غدا *ḥaflat ġada* luncheon. 3. concert. حفلة غنا *ḥaflat ġina* concert of vocal music.

احتفال *htifaal* p. *-aat* celebration, festival. احتفلنا احتفال كلش زين *ḥtifalna ḥtifaal killiš zeen.* We had a great celebration.

ح ف ي ت *ḥfyt*

حفيت *ḥafiit* 1. (better known as جبل

حفيت *yibal ḥafiit*) Mount Hafit (near the city of Al-Ain). 2. Hafit (small town near Al-Ain).

ح ف ي ز *ḥfyz*

حفيز *hafiiz* p. *-aat* office. وين حفيز الشركة؟ *ween ḥafiiz š-šarika?* Where is the company office?

ح گ ب *ḥgb*

حقب *ḥugub* p. احقاب *ḥgaab* belt (usually worn by women). حقب ذهب *ḥugub ðahab* gold belt.

ح گ ر *ḥgr*

حقر *ḥigar* (يحقر *yḥagir*) to despise, scorn. ماحد يحكي وياه. كلهم يحقرونه *maḥḥad yḥači wiyyaa. killhum yḥagruuna.* Nobody talks to him. All of them despise him.

حقر *ḥaggar* II to humiliate, degrade. ما عطوه زيادة في الراتب. حقروه *ma ᶜaṭoo ziyaada fi r-raatib. ḥaggaroo.* They didn't give him a salary increment. They humiliated him. حقر نفسه وراح الحفلة بدون دعوة *ḥaggar nafsa w-raaḥ l-ḥafla b-duun daᶜwa.* He degraded himself and went to the party without invitation.

حقير *ḥagiir* p. *-iin,* حقارى *ḥagaara.* 1. low, base, vulgar. من عايلة حقيرة *min ᶜaayla ḥagiira* from a low family. 2. mean, cheap. تصرف حقير *taṣarruf ḥagiir* contemptible behavior. 3. contemptible, despicable. شخص حقير *šuxṣ ḥagiir* contemptible person.

حقران *ḥigraan* (v.n. from حقر *ḥigar*) contempt, disdain, scorn. الحقران يقطع المصران *l-ḥigraan ygaṭṭiᶜ l-muṣraan.* (lit., "Contempt cuts up one's intestines.")

ح گ گ[1] *ḥgg*

حقق *ḥaggag* II 1. to realize, fulfill. حقق كل آماله *ḥaggag kill 'aamala.* He has realized all his hopes. 2. (with ب *b-*) to investigate. المباحث حققت بحادث القتل *l-mabaaḥiθ ḥaggagat b-ḥaadiθ l-gatil.* The government agency of investigation investigated the killing. 3. (with وايا *wiyya*) to interrogate. زخوه وخذوه مكتب التحقيق وحققوا واياه *zaxxoo w-xaðoo maktab t-taḥgiig w-ḥaggagu wiyyaa.* They arrested him, took him to the office of investigations and interrogated him.

تحقق *tḥaggag* V 1. to be realized, be effected. تحققت كل آماله *tḥaggagat kill 'aamaala.* All his hopes were realized. 2. to make sure, reassure oneself, be sure. تحقق انه فيه أمان في بيروت قبل لا تروح هناك *tḥaggag 'inna fii 'amaan fi bayruut gabil la truuḥ hnaak.* Make sure that there is peace in Beirut before you go there. 3. to turn out to be true, be confirmed. تحقق خبر استقالة الوزارة *tḥaggag xabar stigaalat l-wazaara.* The news of the resignation of the ministry has turned out to be true. إشاعة زيادة الرواتب تحققت *'išaaᶜat ziyaadat r-rawaatib tḥaggagat.* The rumor of an increase in salary has been confirmed.

استحق *staḥagg* X 1. to deserve, merit s.th., be worthy of s.th. يحقرونه، ما يستحق معاملة مثل هذي *yḥaggruuna, ma yistaḥigg muᶜaamala miθil haaði.* They humiliate him. He doesn't deserve such treatment. حصلت قرض؟ اي حصلت بس ما يستحق الذكر *ḥaṣṣalt* *garḏ? 'ii ḥaṣṣalt bass ma yistaḥigg ð-ðikr.* Did you get a loan? Yes, I did, but it is not worth mentioning. 2. to be entitled, have a claim to s.th. كل موظف يستحق شهر إجازة *kill muwaḏḏaf yistaḥigg šahar 'ijaaza.* Every employee is entitled to one month's leave. يستحق زيادة سنوية *yistaḥigg ziyaada sanawiyya.* He is entitled to an annual increment. أنت كسرت السيكل حقه؛ يستحقك بميتين درهم *'inta kisart s-seekal ḥagga; yistaḥiggak b-miiteen dirhim.* You broke his bicycle; he has a claim on you for two hundred dirhams. 3. to become due or payable, mature. الكمبيالة تستحق عقب شهر *l-kumbyaala tistaḥigg ᶜugub šahar.* The note becomes due in one month. المقنطر ما خلص العمارة في وقتها؛ لذلك يستحق غرامة *li-mganṭir ma xaḷḷaṣ li-ᶜmaara fi wagitta; liðaalik yistaḥigg ġaraama.* The contractor did not finish the building on time; for that reason there is a penalty due against him.

حق *ḥagg* p. حقوق *ḥguug* 1. right, title, legal claim. الحرمة هني بعد ما لها حق تصوت *l-ḥurma hini baᶜd ma laha ḥagg tṣawwit.* Women here do not yet have the right to vote. الها حق فيها *'ilha ḥagg fiiha.* She has a claim to it. من حقك تطالب بفلوسك *min ḥaggak ṭṭaalib b-fluusak.* You have the right to ask for your money. ما لك حق عليه *ma lak ḥagg ᶜalee.* You have no claim against him. 2. one's due عطوني فلوسي وفنشوني *ᶜaṭooni fluusi w-fannašuuni.* They gave me what was due me and laid me off. موب حقي؟ كان موب لازم يعيب علي *muub ḥaggi? čaan muub laazim yᶜayyib ᶜalayya.* Isn't it my right? He shouldn't have called me bad names. صدق هو اللي حكى علي؟ لين أشوفه آخذ حقي منه *ṣidj huwa lli hiča ᶜalayya? leen 'ačuufa 'aaxið ḥaggi minna.* Is it true that he said bad things about me? When I see him, I will get my revenge on him. 3. truth. الحق وياك *l-ḥagg wiyyaak.* You are right. وحق الله ما سمعت أي شي *w-ḥagg aḷḷa ma simaᶜt 'ayya šayy.* I swear (lit., "It's God's truth."), I haven't heard anything. هسة طلع الحق. المحكمة برتني *hassa ṭilaᶜ l-ḥagg. l-maḥkama barratni.* Now the truth has come out. The court found me innocent. 4. (p. only) l prudence. كلية الحقوق *kulliyyat l-ḥuguug* the college of law, the law school. 5. (as prep.) to, towards (e.g., a place). رحت حق التنديل ورمسته *riḥt ḥagg t-tindeel w-rammasta.* I went to the supervisor and talked to him. المفتاح حق الدار *l-miftaaḥ ḥagg d-daar* the house key. 6. (with من *man*) whose, belonging to whom. هذي السيارة حق من؟ *haaði s-sayyaara ḥagg man?* Whose is this car? 7. for, for the purpose of. ها البز حق بناطلين *ha l-bazz ḥagg binaaṭliin.* This material is for pants.

أحق *'aḥagg* (elat.) 1. (with من *min*) more worthy, entitled, deserving. 2. (with foll. n.) the most worthy, entitled, deserving.

أحقية *'aḥaggiyya* p. *-yyaat* legal claim, title, right.

حقيقة *ḥagiiga* p. حقايق *ḥagaayig* 1. fact. هذي حقيقة ما أقدر أنكرها *haaði* *ḥagiiga ma 'agdar 'ankirha.* This is a fact I cannot deny. 2. truth, reality. في الحقيقة *fi l-ḥagiiga* in fact, actually. في الحقيقة أختها أجمل منها *fi l-ḥagiiga 'uxutta 'aymal minha.* Actually, her sister is more beautiful than she is. 3. true nature, essence. ذالحين عرفتها على حقيقتها *ðalḥiin ᶜarafitta ᶜala ḥagiigatta.* Now I know her true nature.

حقاني *ḥaggaani* p. حقانية *ḥaggaaniyya, -yyiin* 1. just, honest, fair. 2. an honest person.

تحقيق *taḥgiig* (v.n. from II حقق *ḥaggag*) 1. realization, fulfillment. تحقيق أهداف الشركة *taḥgiig 'ahdaaf š-šarika* the realization of the goals of the company. 2. investigation, check. تحقيق الهوية *taḥgiig l-hawiyya* identity check.

محقق *mḥaggig* (act. part. from II حقق *ḥaggag*) 1. investigator. 2. interrogator.

محقق *mḥaggag* (p.p. from II حقق *ḥaggag*) 1. confirmed, established. جيته صارت محققة *yayyta ṣaarat mḥaggaga.* His arrival has been confirmed. 2. sure, certain, unquestionable. محقق رايح يترقى *mḥaggag raayiḥ yitragga.* It's certain he will be promoted.

مستحق *mistaḥigg* (act. part. from X استحق *staḥagg*) p. *-iin* 1. entitled to. مستحق خمسمية ريال *mistaḥigg xamsmiyat ryaal.* He is entitled to five hundred riyals. صار له سنة مستحق ترفيع *ṣaar-la sana mistaḥigg tarfiiᶜ.* He's been entitled to promotion for a year. 2. deserving, worth. مستحق كل خير *mistaḥigg kill xeer* deserving good things. 3. due, payable. الكمبيالة مستحقة *l-kumbyaala mistaḥigga.* The note is due.

ح گ گ ٢ *ḥgg*

حقة *ḥagga* p. *-aat* net used for trapping birds.

حقة *ḥigga* (less common var. *ḥijja*) p. إحقق *'iḥgag* young female camel, about two years old.

ح گ ن ١ *ḥgn*

حقن *ḥigan* (يحقن *yḥagin*) to give an enema. حقن المريض ماي لاجل يمشي بطنه *ḥigan l-mariiḍ maay lajil yamši baṭna.* He gave the patient a water enema so that he'd have a bowel movement.

احتقن *ḥtigan* VIII 1. to be given an enema. 2. to be congested.

حقنة *ḥugna* p. *-aat,* حقن *ḥugan* 1. enema. 2. syringe.

احتقان *ḥtigaan* (v.n. from VIII احتقن *ḥtigan*) congestion. احتقان الرئة *ḥtigaan r-ri'a* lung congestion.

ح گ ن ٢ *ḥgn*

محقان *miḥgaan* p. محاقن *maḥaagin* funnel.

ح ك ك *ḥkk*

حك *ḥakk* (less common var. of *ḥačč*). See under ح چ چ *ḥčč.*

ح ك م *ḥkm*

حكم *ḥikam* (يحكم *yḥakim*) 1. to govern, rule. الشيخ حكم عشر سنين *š-šeex ḥikam ᶜašar siniin.* The Shaikh ruled for ten years. 2. (with على *ᶜala*)

a. to sentence s.o. القاضي حكم عليه بخمس سنين سجن *l-ġaaḏi ḥikam ᶜalee b-xams siniin sijin.* The judge sentenced him to five years in jail. b. to insist, demand, order. حكم علي أروح وياه *ḥikam ᶜalayya 'aruuḥ wiyyaa.* He forced me to go with him. ولدي حكم علي أشتري له سيكل *wildi ḥikam ᶜalayya 'aštirii-la seekal.* My son insisted that I should buy him a bicycle. 3. to pass judgment, express an opinion, judge. الحاكم لازم يحكم بالعدل *l-ḥaakim laazim yḥakim b-l-ᶜadil.* A judge must judge fairly. 4. to deliver a judgment, rule. حكم الكورة ما يعرف القوانين؛ ما يحكم زين *ḥakam l-kuura ma yᶜarf l-gawaaniin; ma yḥakim zeen.* The soccer game referee doesn't know the rules; he isn't doing a good job. الحكم حكم انها ضربة جزا *l-ḥakam ḥikam 'innaha ḏarbat jaza.* The referee ruled that it was a penalty kick. 4. to be due, come due, arrive (prayer time). هالحين حكمت صلاة المغرب. أذن المؤذن *halḥiin ḥkamat ṣalaat li-mġarb. 'aððan l-mu'aððin.* Now the sunset prayer is due. The muezzin has made the call to prayer.

حكم *ḥakkam* II to appoint s.o. as ruler, choose an arbitrator. الشيخ طال عمره قال، «حكم عقلك وشوف الحق على من» *š-šeex ṭaal ᶜumra gaal, "ḥakkim ᶜaglak w-čuuf l-ḥagg ᶜala man."* The Shaikh, may he live long, said, "Let your reason be the judge, and see who is at fault."

حاكم *ḥaakam* III to try s.o. in a law court, arraign, try. حاكموه ووجدوه مذنب *ḥaakmoo w-wajadoo miðnib.* They tried him and found him guilty.

تحكم *tḥakkam* V to have one's own way, handle s.th. arbitrarily. التنديل يتحكم في الكولية مثلما يريد *t-tindeel yitḥakkam fi l-kuuliyya miθil-ma yriid.* The supervisor can do anything he wants with the coolies. بعض الأساتذة يتحكمون في الطلاب *baᶜḏ l-'asaatða yitḥakkamuun fi ṭ-ṭullaab.* Some teachers handle students arbitrarily.

انحكم *nḥikam* VII to be sentenced. انحكم مؤبد *nḥikam m'abbad.* He was sentenced to life imprisonment. انحكم بالإعدام *nḥikam b-l-'iᶜdaam.* He was sentenced to death.

احتكم *ḥtikam* VIII to seek judgment, appeal for a legal decision. تهاوشوا واحتكموا عند الشيخ *thaawšaw w-ḥtikmaw ᶜind š-šeex.* They quarreled with each other and sought judgment from the ruler.

حكم *ḥukum* p. أحكام *'aḥkaam* 1. rule, government, regime. حكم جمهوري *ḥukum jumhuuri* republican form of government. الحكم التركي *l-ḥukum t-tirki* the Turkish rule. حكم ذاتي *ḥukum ðaati* self-rule, autonomy. 2. judgment, verdict, sentence. حكم مؤبد *ḥukum m'abbad* life sentence. حكم بالإعدام *ḥukum b-l-'iᶜdaam* death sentence. حكم غيابي *ḥukum ġiyaabi* sentence in absentia. حكم خفيف *ḥukum xafiif* light sentence. 3. rule, regulation, provision, decree. أحكام القانون *'aḥkaam l-ġaanuun* provisions of the law. أحكام عرفية *'aḥkaam ᶜurfiyya* martial law. الضرورة الها أحكام *ḏ-ḏaruura 'ilha 'aḥkaam.* Necessity knows no law. (lit., "Necessity has its own rules".) بحكم *b-ḥukum* a. by virtue of, by force of. بحكم القانون *b-ḥukum l-ġaanuun* by force of the law. بحكم العادة *b-ḥukum l-ᶜaada* by the force of habit. b. almost, virtually, as good as. بحكم المستحيل *b-ḥukum l-mustaḥiil* virtually impossible.

حكم *ḥakam* p. حكام *ḥikkaam* referee, umpire.

حكمة *ḥikma* p. حكم *ḥikam* 1. wisdom. 2. maxim. 3. rationale.

حكيم *ḥakiim* p. حكما *ḥukama* 1. wise, judicious. 2. wise man, sage. 3. doctor, physician.

حكومة *ḥukuuma* p. *-aat* government. دواير الحكومة *dawaayir l-ḥukuuma* the government departments, the government offices.

حكومي *ḥukuumi* 1. government, governmental, official. مكاتب حكومية *makaatib ḥukuumiyya* government offices. وفد حكومي *wafd ḥukuumi* official delegation. 2. public, state, state owned. مدرسة حكومية *madrasa ḥukuumiyya* public school. أرض حكومية *'arḏ ḥukuumiyya* public land 3. administration, government. السياسة الحكومية *s-siyaasa l-ḥukuumiyya* the administration's policy. المنهج الحكومي *l-manhaj l-ḥukuumi* the administration program.

محكمة *maḥkama* p. محاكم *maḥaakim* court, tribunal. المحكمة الشرعية *l-maḥkama š-šarᶜiyya* the Islamic court (with jurisdiction in marital and family matters). رحنا المحكمة يوم المحاكمة *riḥna l-maḥkama yoom l-muḥaakama.* We went to court on the trial day. محكمة الاستئناف *maḥkamat li-sti'naaf* court of appeal. محكمة عسكرية *maḥkama ᶜaskariyya* military court.

حاكم *ḥaakim* (act. part. from حكم *ḥikam*) p. حكام *ḥikkaam* 1. ruler. حاكم البحرين الشيخ عيسى *ḥaakim l-baḥreen š-šeex ᶜiisa.* The ruler of Bahrain is Shaikh Isa. حكام الإمارات *ḥikkaam l-'imaaraat* the rulers of the Emirates. 2. governor. حاكم عسكري *ḥaakim ᶜaskari* military governor. 3. judge. حكم عليه الحاكم بالسجن *ḥikam ᶜalee l-ḥaakim b-s-sijin.* The judge sentenced him to jail. حاكم الصلح *ḥaakim ṣ-ṣulḥ* justice of the peace.

محكوم عليه *maḥkuum ᶜalee* 1. having been sentenced. محكوم عليهم بالإعدام *maḥkuum ᶜaleehum b-l-'iᶜdaam* (those) sentenced to death. 2. person who has been sentenced. المحامي تحكى وايا المحكوم عليه بالسجن *li-mḥaami tḥačča wiyya l-maḥkuum ᶜalee b-s-sijin.* The lawyer talked with the man sentenced to prison.

ح ل ب *ḥlb*

حلب *ḥilab (يحلب yḥalib)* to milk. حلب النعجة *ḥilab li-nᶜaya.* He milked the ewe. (prov.) نقول ثور يقول حلبه *nguul θoor yguul ḥilba.* (lit., "We say, 'Bull,' and he says, 'Milk it.'")—(describes s.o. who argues for an impossible thing).

انحلب *nḥilab* VII to be milked. البقرة انحلبت مرتين اليوم *li-bgara nḥilbat marrateen l-yoom.* The cow was milked twice today.

حلبة *ḥalba* (n. of inst.) p. *-aat* one act of milking.

حلبة *ḥilba* (coll.) 1. fenugreek. 2. tonic (prepared of yellowish or reddish grain for women in childbed and during menstruation).

حليب *ḥaliib* 1. milk. الحليب هني عادة العيال يشربونه، ويشربونه حار، موب بارد *l-ḥaliib hini ᶜaadatan li-ᶜyaaḷ yišrabuuna, w-yišrabuuna ḥaarr, muub baarid.* Here, children drink milk usually, and they drink it hot, not cold. 2. one's nature or breeding. حليبه ما يخليه يسوي هذي الأشيا *ḥaliiba ma yxaḷḷii ysawwi haaði l-'ašya.* His breeding won't let him do these things. (prov.) اللي ما يجيبه حليبه ما يجيبه الزور *'illi ma yjiiba ḥaliiba ma yjiiba z-zoor.* You can lead a horse to water, but you can't make him drink. (lit., "He who cannot be brought by one's milk won't be brought by force").

حالوب *ḥaaluub* heavy rain, often followed by hail. يجي حالوب في الشتا *yiji ḥaaluub fi š-šta.* There is (a period of) heavy rain and hail in the winter.

ح ل ج *ḥlj*

حلق *ḥalj* (less common var. *ḥalg*) p. حلوق *ḥluuj.* 1. throat. 2. mouth. صك حلقك! *ṣikk ḥaljak!* Shut up!

ح ل ح ل *ḥlḥl*

حلحل *ḥalḥal* (يحلحل *yḥalḥil*) 1. to tilt a heavy object, move, budge. ما قدر يحلحل الحجر لانه ثقيل واجد *ma gidar yḥalḥil l-ḥiyar linna θagiil waayid.* He couldn't move the rock because it was very heavy. 2. to work s.th. back and forth, wiggle, jiggle. دختور الاسنان حلحل ضرسي قبلما تشلعه *daxtoor s-snaan ḥalḥal ðirsi gabil-ma člaᶜa.* The dentist worked my tooth back and forth before he pulled it out.

تحلحل *tḥalḥal* (يتحلحل *yitḥalḥal)* 1. to be tilted, moved. هذا الحجر ما يتحلحل. ثقيل واجد *haaða l-ḥiyar ma yitḥalḥal. θagiil waayid.* This rock cannot be moved. It's very heavy. 2. to wiggle, shake. ضرسي يتحلحل؛ يبغى له تشلع *ðirsi yitḥalḥal; yibġaa-la čaliᶜ.* My tooth is loose; it needs to be pulled out.

ح ل ز و ن *ḥlzwn*

حلزون *ḥalazoon* (coll.) snail. s. *-a.*

ح ل ف *ḥlf*

حلف *ḥilaf* (يحلف *yḥalif)* to take an oath, swear, vow. حلف يمين بالله *ḥilaf yamiin b-llaah.* He swore (by God). حلف يمين *ḥilaf yamiin.* He took an oath. حلف انه ما يسكر بعد *ḥilaf 'inna ma yiskar baᶜad.* He swore that he would never drink again. حلف انه ما باق شي *ḥilaf 'inna ma baag šayy.* He took an oath that he hadn't stolen anything. جا الشاهد وحلف يمين بالله انه يقول الصدق *ya š-šaahid w-ḥilaf yimiin b-'aḷḷa 'inna yguul ṣ-ṣidj.* The witness came and swore by God that he would tell the truth. حلف على القرآن *ḥilaf ᶜala l-qur'aan.* He swore by the Quran.

حلف *ḥallaf* II 1. to put s.o. under oath, swear in. حلفوا الشاهد قبلما يعطي شهادته في المحكمة *ḥallafaw š-šaahid gabil-ma yᶜaṭi šahaatta fi l-maḥkama.* They swore the witness in before he gave his testimony in court.

حالف *ḥaalaf* III to enter into an alliance with, become an ally of. بلدان واجدة حالفت أمريكا في حرب الخليج

bildaan waayda ḥaalafat 'amriika fi ḥarb l-xaliij. Many countries formed an alliance with America during the Gulf War.

تحالف *tḥaalaf* VI to join together in an alliance, make an alliance with. دول واجدة تحالفت في الحـــرب *duwal waayda tḥaalafat fi l-ḥarb.* Many nations allied themselves during the war. تحالفنا وايـــاهم *tḥaalafna wiyyaahum.* We allied ourselves with them.

حلـف *ḥilf* p. أحلاف *'aḥlaaf* pact, alliance. حلـف عسـكري *ḥilf ᶜaskari* military alliance. الحلف الأطلنطي *l-ḥilf l-'aṭlanṭi* the Atlantic Pact (NATO).

حلفـــان *ḥilfaan* (v.n. from حلف *ḥilaf*) swearing, oath taking. حلفان اليمـــين *ḥilfaan l-yimiin* taking the oath. حلفان اليمين قبل الشهادة *ḥilfaan l-yimiin gabil š-šahaada.* Taking the oath is before testifying.

حليـف *ḥaliif* 1. allied. الدول الحليفة *d-duwal l-ḥaliifa* the allied nations. 2. (p. حلفا *ḥulafa*) ally.

ح ل گ *ḥlg*

حلقة *ḥalga* 1. (p. حلق *ḥilag*) earring. الحريم بس اللي يلبسون الحلق *l-ḥariim bass illi yilibsuun l-ḥilag.* Only women wear earrings. 2. wedding band. 3. ring, door knocker.

ح ل ل *ḥll*

حـل *ḥall* (يحل *yḥill*) 1. to solve, figure out. حـل المسألة *ḥall l-mas'ala.* He solved the problem. حل دروسه *ḥall druusa.* He did his homework. هذي مسألة ما أقدر أحلـها *haaδi mas'ala ma 'agdar 'aḥillha.* This is a problem I cannot solve. تقدر تحل هذي الفـــزورة؟ *tigdar tḥill haaδi l-fazzuura?* Can you figure out this riddle? 2. to untie, unfasten, unravel. ما أقدر أحل هـــذي العقدة *ma 'agdar 'aḥill haaδi l-ᶜugda.* I cannot untie this knot. فلان ما يقدر يحل ولا يربـط *flaan ma yigdar yḥill wala yarbuṭ.* So-and-so has no power or influence. (lit., "so-and-so can neither untie nor tie a knot".) 3. to dissolve, disband. الحكومة حلت المجلس *li-ḥkuuma ḥallat l-majlis.* The government dissolved the parliament. 4. to be allowed, permitted, lawful. ما يحل لك تفطر في شهر رمضان *ma yḥill-lak tifṭir fi šahar rumδaan.* You are not allowed not to fast during Ramadan. ما يحل للمسلمة تتجوز غـير المسلم *ma yḥill la l-muslima tijjawwaz ġeer l-muslim.* A Muslim girl is not permitted to marry anyone but a Muslim. أختك ما تحل لك *'uxtak ma tḥill-lak.* It is not lawful for you to marry your sister. 5. to occur, take place. حلـت البركـة! *ḥallat l-baraka!* (said to s.o. who comes to visit you, e.g., at home, in the office, etc.) 6. to set down, land, alight. حل الطير *ḥall ṭ-ṭeer.* The bird came down. حلت الطايرة *ḥallat ṭ-ṭaayra.* The plane landed. 7. to take the place of, replace. باكر ما أدش الشغل. أبغاك تحل محلي *baačir ma 'adišš š-šuġul. 'abġaak tḥill maḥalli.* Tomorrow I won't go to work. I want you to substitute for me.

حلل *ḥallal* II 1. to make permissible or lawful, sanction. الله حلل الزواج بـأربع حـريم *'aḷḷa ḥallal z-zawaaj b-'arbaᶜ ḥariim.* God sanctioned marriage to four women. 2. to declare permissible, allow. الدين حلل أكل لحم الميتـة، يعـني

الســمكة *d-diin ḥallal 'akil laḥam l-mayta, yaᶜni li-smiča.* The (Islamic) religion has permitted the eating of the meat of one animal not slaughtered in accordance with Islam, i.e., the fish. 3. to make a chemical analysis. حللنا المحلول في المختبر *ḥallalna l-maḥluul fi l-muxtabar.* We analyzed the solution in the laboratory.

انحل *nḥall* VII 1. to be solved. المشكلة انحلت *l-muškila nḥallat.* The problem has been solved. 2. to be untied. العقدة انحلت *l-ᶜugda nḥallat.* The knot was untied.

احتل *ḥtall* VIII to occupy, take over. بدت حرب الخليج لين الجيش العراقي احتل الكويت *bidat ḥarb l-xaliij leen l-jeeš li-ᶜraagi ḥtall li-kweet.* The Gulf War broke out when the Iraqi army occupied Kuwait.

حل *ḥall* (v.n. from حل *ḥall*) 1. solving, figuring out. حل المسألة *ḥall l-mas'ala* solving the problem. حل الفزورة *ḥall l-fazzuura* figuring out the riddle. 2. untying, unfastening.

حلال *ḥalaal* 1. allowed, permitted, permissible, lawful. حلال في الإسلام *ḥalaal fi l-'islaam* permissible, lawful in Islam. ابن حلال *'ibin ḥalaal* respectable man, nice guy. 2. s.th. meritorious and deserving reward in the hereafter, such as voluntary contribution of alms, e.g., صدقة عيد الفطر *ṣadagat ᶜiid l-fiṭir* alms at the Ramadan Feast. 3. one's possessions, lawful possessions, such as cattle, real estate, money, etc. يريد ياخذ مني حلالي اللي حصلته بعرق جبيني *yriid yaaxið minni ḥalaali 'illi ḥaṣṣalta b-ᶜirag yibiini.* He wants to take away my possessions which I earned with the sweat of my brow. كل حلالي *kal ḥalaali.* He stole my legal property. 4. owed, due. السيارة حلال عليك. خذها! *s-sayyaara ḥalaal ᶜaleek. xiðha!* The car is rightfully yours. Take it!

محل *maḥall* p. *-aat* (مكان *mukaan* is more common). 1. place, location, site, spot. ما فيه محل هني *ma fii maḥall hini.* There is no place here. فنش وما فيه أحد يحل محله *fannaš w-ma fii 'aḥad yḥill maḥalla.* He resigned and there isn't anyone to replace him. هذا الكلام موب في محله *haaða l-kalaam muub fi maḥalla.* These words are not a priate. 2. room, space. ما لك محل هني *ma lak maḥall hini.* You have no room here. 3. shop, store, place. عندنا محلات في قطر *ᶜindana maḥallaat fi giṭar.* We have stores in Qatar.

محلي *maḥalli* 1. local. أخبار محلية *'axbaar maḥalliyya* local news. 2. native, indigenous, local. إنتاج محلي *'intaaj maḥalli* local production.

تحليل *taḥliil* (v.n. from II حلل *ḥallal*) analysis. تحليل دم *taḥliil damm* blood test. تحليل نفساني *taḥliil nafsaani* psychoanalysis. مختبر التحليل الطبي *muxtabar t-taḥliil ṭ-ṭibbi* medical analysis laboratory.

انحلال *nḥilaal* (v.n. from VII انحل *nḥall*) dissolution, degeneration. فيه انحلال في الأخلاق في كل مكان *fii nḥilaal fi l-'axlaag fi kill mukaan.* There is moral degeneration everywhere.

احتلال *ḥtilaal* (v.n. from VIII احتل *ḥtall*) occupation (mil.).

محلول *maḥluul* 1. loose, loosened. سكرو محلول *sikruu maḥluul* loose screw. 2. untied, unfastened. العقدة محلولة *l-ᶜugda maḥluula.* The knot has been untied. 3. (p. محاليل *maḥaaliil*) solution. محلول مالح *maḥluul maaliḥ* saline solution.

محلل *mḥallil* (act. part. from II حلل *ḥallal*) p. *-iin* analyzer, analyst.

منحل *minḥall* 1. solved. مسائل منحلة *masaa'il minḥalla* solved problems. 2. loosened, relaxed. أخلاق منحلة *'axlaag minḥalla* loose morals.

ح ل م *ḥlm*

حلم *ḥilim* (يحلم *yḥalim*) 1. to dream. حلمت حلم مزعج ليلة أمس *ḥlimt ḥilim muzᶜij leelat 'ams.* I had a bad dream last night. حلمت فيك البارحة *ḥlimt fiič l-baarḥa.* I dreamed about you yesterday. حلمت اني كنت أميرة *ḥlimt 'inni čint 'amiira.* I dreamed I was a princess. 2. to daydream. بس قاعد في الصف يحلم *bass gaaᶜid fi ṣ-ṣaff yḥalim.* He is sitting in class daydreaming.

حلم *ḥilim* p. أحلام *'aḥlaam* dream. ما درينا هذا حلم والا علم *ma dareena haaða ḥilim walla ᶜilim.* We don't know whether this is a dream or reality. عايش في دنيا الأحلام *ᶜaayiš fi dinya l-'aḥlaam* living in a dream world.

حلمة *ḥlima* p. *-aat*, حلم *ḥilam* 1. nipple, teat, mammilla (of the female breast). 2. (baby) pacifier.

حلمان *ḥalmaan* p. *-iin* dreaming, in a state of dreaming.

ح ل و *ḥlw*

حلى *ḥala* (يحلي *yḥali*) 1. to be or become sweet. إذا تحط شكر في الشاي، يحلي *'iða tḥuṭṭ šakar fi č-čaay, yḥali.* If you put sugar in tea, it becomes sweet. 2. to become pleasant, nice, enjoyable. تحلى لي القعدة على السيف في الليل *tiḥlaa-li l-gaᶜda ᶜala s-siif fi l-leel.* I enjoy sitting on the seashore at night.

حلى *ḥalla* II 1. to make sweet, sweeten. حليت الشاي *ḥalleet č-čaay.* I sweetened the tea. 2. to make pleasant, enjoyable. الصحة الزينة تحلي الحياة *ṣ-ṣiḥḥa z-zeena tḥalli l-ḥayaa.* Good health makes life enjoyable. 3. to make pretty, beautify. النفنوف الحمر يحليها أكثر من الخضر *n-nafnuuf l-ḥamar yḥalliiha 'akθar min l-xaðar.* The red dress becomes her more than the green one.

حلو *ḥilu* 1. sweet, sweetened. شاي حلو *čaay ḥilu* sweetened tea. البدو ما يشربون قهوة حلوة *l-badu ma yišrabuun ghawa ḥilwa.* Bedouins do not drink sweetened coffee. 2. pleasant, nice, enjoyable. حكي حلو *hači ḥilu* pleasant talk.

حلويات *ḥalawiyyaat* sweet pastries.

حلاوة *ḥalaawa* (v.n. from حلى *ḥala*) 1. sweetness. 2. candies, confectionary. 3. dessert. كلينا حلاوة عقب الأكل *kaleena ḥalaawa ᶜugb l-'akil.* We had dessert after the food. 4. reward, gratuity, recompense. (حلوان *ḥalawaan* is more common. See حلوان *ḥalawaan* below.)

حلوان *ḥalawaan* reward, present of money, gratuity. علي حلوانك مية درهم.

آنـا *ḥalawaanak miyat dirhim. ᶜalayya 'aana.* Your reward is one hundred dirhams. It's on me. عطتني خمسة درهم حلـوان *ᶜaṭatni xamsa dirhim ḥalawaan.* She gave me five dirhams as a gratuity.

حلوانـي *ḥalawaani* p. *-yya, -yyiin* candy dealer, confectioner.

تحلية *taḥliya* (v.n. from II حلى *ḥalla*) 1. desalination. محطة تحلية *maḥaṭṭat taḥliya* desalination plant. 2. decoration, embellishment.

ح م د *ḥmd*

حمد *ḥimad* (يحمد *yḥamid*) 1. to praise, commend, laud. حمدنا الله على ها الولـد *ḥimadna ḷḷa ᶜala hal-walad.* We praised God for this (baby) boy. احمد الله واشكره! شو تريد بعد؟ *'iḥmid aḷḷa w-uškura! šu triid baᶜad?* Praise God and thank Him! What else do you want? التنديـل يحمـدك واجـد *t-tindeel yḥamdak waayid.* The supervisor praises you a lot.

حمد *ḥamd* (v.n.) praise, commendation. الحمـد لله! *l-ḥamdu lil-laah!* Praise be to God! Thank God! (usually as a response to شلونك؟ *šloonak?* How are you?). الحمـد لله، جـابت ولـد *l-ḥamdu lil-laah, yaabat wald.* Thank God, she gave birth to a (baby) boy.

حميـد *ḥamiid* praiseworthy, commendable. أخـلاق حميـدة *'axlaag ḥamiida* commendable character (of a person). ربك حميـد، الدعمـة كـانت بسـيطة *rabbak ḥamiid, d-daᶜma čaanat basiiṭa.* Thank goodness, the (car) accident was minor.

ح م ر *ḥmr*

حمـر *ḥammar* II 1. to roast. حمر الدجاجة علـى النـار *ḥammar d-diyaaya ᶜala n-naar.* He roasted the chicken on the fire. 2. to brown. الدجاجة بارزة، بـس رجعهـا وحمرهـا علـى النـار *d-diyaaya baarza, bass rajjiᶜha w-ḥammirha ᶜala n-naar.* The chicken is done; just put it back on the fire and brown it.

تحمـر *tḥammar* V 1. to be roasted. 2. to be browned.

احمـر *ḥmarr* IX to turn red, become red, redden. لين رمستها، خجلت وامر وجهها *leen rammasitta, xijlat w-ḥmarr weehha.* When I talked to her, she was embarrassed and (her face) turned red. احمر وجهه من الخجـل *ḥmarr weeha min l-xajal.* He blushed from embarrassment. فرك عيونه مـن الحساسـية واحمـروا *firak ᶜyuuna min l-ḥasaasiyya w-ḥmarraw.* He rubbed his eyes because of the allergy, and they turned red.

حمرة *humra* redness, red color.

حمـر *ḥamar* f. حمرا *ḥamra* p. حمر *ḥumur* red. أريد تفاح حمـر *'ariid tiffaaḥ ḥamar.* I want red apples. اليح الحمر زين *l-yiḥḥ l-ḥamar zeen.* Red watermelons are good. مـوت حمـر *moot ḥamar* violent death. (prov.) الثور الحمر ما يموت إلا حمر *θ-θoor l-ḥamar ma ymuut 'illa ḥamar.* A leopard cannot change his spots. (lit., "A red bull dies only as a red bull.")

الحمـر *l-ḥamar* Al-Hamar (prominent Bahraini family).

أحمر *'aḥmar* red (used only with proper

names). البحر الأحمر *l-baḥar l-'aḥmar* the Red Sea.

حمار *ḥmaar* p. حمير *ḥamiir* 1. donkey, ass. 2. (used as derog. term for a human being) jackass, stupid person. حمار! ما يفتهم *ḥmaar! ma yiftihim.* He is stupid; he doesn't understand. شعليك منه، ها الحمار *š-ᶜaleek minna, ha li-ḥmaar.* You have nothing to do with him, that jackass.

حمار *ḥammaar* p. حمارة *ḥammaara* donkey driver.

محمر *mḥammar* (p.p. from II حمر *ḥammar*) roasted, baked, grilled. دجاج محمر *diyaay mḥammar* roasted chicken. بتيتة محمرة *puteeta mḥammara* baked potatoes.

ح م س ١ *ḥms*

حمس *ḥammas* II to make enthusiastic, stir up, excite. حمسني على السفر حق أمريكا *ḥammasni ᶜala s-safar ḥagg 'amriika.* He made me enthusiastic about traveling to America. خطاب الرئيس حمس الجماهير *xiṭaab r-ra'iis ḥammas l-jamaahiir.* The president's speech stirred up the crowd.

تحمس *tḥammas* V 1. to be excited, stirred. تحمست لين سمعت الخطاب *tḥammast leen simaᶜt l-xiṭaab.* I was stirred when I heard the speech. 2. to become enthusiastic, eager, zealous. تحمست أروح وياه *tḥammast 'aruuḥ wiyyaa.* I was enthusiastic about going with him. تحمس حق المشروع واستعد يموله *tḥammas ḥagg l-mašruuᶜ w-staᶜadd ymawwla.* He became enthusiastic about the project and was ready to finance it.

حماس *ḥamaas* enthusiasm, zeal, ardor. بحماس *b-ḥamaas* with enthusiasm, enthusiastically.

حماسي *ḥamaasi* stirring, rousing. أغاني حماسية *'aqaani ḥamaasiyya* stirring songs.

متحمس *mitḥammis* (act. part. from V تحمس *tḥammas*) enthusiastic, ardent, zealous. وطني متحمس *waṭani mitḥammis* zealous nationalist.

ح م س ٢ *ḥms*

حمسة *ḥmisa* p. حمس *ḥamas* turtle. فيه حمس كبير في الخليج *fii ḥamas čibiir fi l-xaliij.* There are big turtles in the Gulf.

ح م ص *ḥmṣ*

حمص *ḥammaṣ* II to roast (coffee beans, peanuts, and other seeds). حمص القهوة زين وبعدين طحنها *ḥammaṣ li-ghawa zeen w-baᶜdeen ṭaḥanha.* He roasted the coffee beans well and then ground them.

تحمص *tḥammaṣ* V to be roasted. اللبوب تحمص *li-lbuub tḥammaṣ.* The seeds were roasted.

حمص *ḥummoṣ* (coll.) 1. chick peas. s. حبة حمص *ḥabbat ḥummoṣ* 2. dish made of ground chick peas and sesame seed paste, usually known as حمص بطحينة *ḥummoṣ b-ṭḥiina.*

ح م ظ *ḥmð̣*

حمض *ḥimað̣ (يحمض yḥamið̣)* to sour, become sour, unpleasant. حمض يعني استوى حامض *ḥimað̣ yaᶜni stiwa ḥaamið̣. ḥimað̣* means it became sour.

حمض *ḥammað̣ II* to sour, become sour

or unpleasant. حط الحليب في الثلاجة قبل لا يحمض *ḥuṭṭ l-ḥaliib fi θ-θallaaja gabil la yḥammiḍ.* Put the milk in the refrigerator before it sours.

حموضة *ḥmuuḍa* 1. sourness. 2. acidity. اخذ مالوكس حق الحموضة *'ixiđ maaluks ḥagg li-ḥmuuḍa.* Take Maalox for an acid stomach.

حامض *ḥaamiḍ* (act. part. from حمض *ḥimaḍ*) sour, acid. الحصرم حامض كلش *l-ḥiṣrim ḥaamiḍ killiš.* Green grapes are very sour. ما أحب التفاح الحامض *ma 'aḥibb t-tiffaaḥ l-ḥaamiḍ.* I don't like sour apples. (prov.) اللي ما يطول العنقود يقول حامض *'illi ma yṭuul l-ᶜanguud yguul ḥaamiḍ.* Sour grapes. (lit., "He who cannot get the cluster of grapes will say it is sour.") شاي حامض *čaay ḥaamiḍ* hot drink made by boiling crushed dried Omani lemons or limes.

ح م گ *ḥmg*

حمق *ḥimig* (يحمق *yḥamig*) to be or become angry, mad, furious. حمق بساع وطلع برة *ḥimig b-saaᶜ w-ṭilaᶜ barra.* He got mad right away and went outside. أبوي حمق لين قلت له، «اشتري لي جوتي» *'ubuuya ḥimig leen git-la, "štirii-li juuti."* My father became furious when I said to him, "Buy me shoes."

حمقي *ḥamagi* p. *-iyya* 1. hot-tempered, easily angered. 2. hot-tempered person.

حماقة *ḥamaaga* 1. stupidity, foolishness. 2. stupid or foolish act.

حمقان *ḥamgaan* p. *-iin* angry, mad, upset. كان حمقان علينا وبعدين راضيناه *čaan ḥamgaan ᶜaleena w-baᶜdeen raaḍeena.* He was angry with us and later we tried to please him.

ح م ل *ḥml*

حمل *ḥimal* (يحمل *yḥamil*) 1. to carry, bear, hold, support. حملناه ووديناه تشبرة السمك *ḥimalnaa w-waddeenaa čabrat s-simač.* We carried it and took it to the fish market. هذا الكرسي ما يحملك *haađa l-kirsi ma yḥamlak.* This chair won't bear your weight. 2. (with على *ᶜala*) to attack, launch or make an attack against s.o. or s.th. لين سمع اني ترقيت قبله، حمل علي قدام الناس *leen simaᶜ 'inni traggeet gabla, ḥimal ᶜalayya jiddaam n-naas.* When he heard that I was promoted before he was, he attacked me in front of the people. 3. to accept, entertain, harbor. العقل السليم ما يحمل هذي الأفكار *l-ᶜagil s-saliim ma yḥamil haađi l-'afkaar.* A sane mind won't accept these ideas. يحمل أفكار شيوعية *yḥamil 'afkaar šuyuuᶜiyya.* He harbors communist ideas. 4. to become pregnant. حملت وجابت ولد *ḥmilat w-yaabat walad.* She got pregnant and gave birth to a (baby) boy. حملت منه *ḥmilat minna.* She got pregnant by him. 5. to bear fruit. شجرة التين حملت هذي السنة *šyarat t-tiin ḥmilat haađi s-sana.* The fig tree bore fruit this year.

حمل *ḥammal* II 1. to load. حملنا اللوري طماط *ḥammalna l-loori ṭamaaṭ.* We loaded the truck with tomatoes. 2. to charge s.o. with s.th., burden, impose on. حملني مسؤولية كبيرة *ḥammalni mas'uuliyya čibiira.* He charged me with a big responsibility. لا تحمله أكثر من طاقته *la tḥammla 'akθar min ṭaagta.* Don't burden him with more than he can put up with.

تحمل *tḥammal* V 1. to be loaded. اللوري تحمل يح *l-loori tḥammal yiḥḥ.* The truck was loaded with watermelons. 2. to hold, support, bear. هذا الكبري قديم؛ ما يتحمل لوريات *haaδa l-kubri gadiim; ma yitḥammal looriyyaat.* This bridge is old; it cannot take trucks. 3. to bear, stand, put up with. ما أقدر أتحمل بعد *ma 'agdar 'atḥammal baᶜad.* I cannot take any more. لا تغشمره ترى ما يتحمل *la tġašimra tara ma yitḥammal.* Don't tease him because he can't take it. ما أقدر أتحمل هذي اللغوة *ma 'agdar 'atḥammal haaδi l-laġwa.* I cannot stand this gibberish. ما يتحمل ألم *ma yitḥammal 'alam.* He can't stand pain. 4. to undergo, suffer. تحمل واجد بسلوك ولده *tḥammal waayid b-suluuk wilda.* He suffered a lot because of his son's behavior.

تحامل *tḥaamal* VI (with على *ᶜala*) to attack, criticize unjustly. لا تتحامل على الغير في غيابهم *la titḥaamal ᶜala l-ġeer fi ġyaabhum.* Don't attack others in their absence. التنديل دايما يتحامل علي *t-tindeel daayman yitḥaamal ᶜalayya.* The supervisor always picks on me.

انحمل *nḥimal* VII to be borne, endured, tolerated. ذاك ثقيل الدم ما ينحمل *δaak θagiil d-damm ma yinḥimil.* That disagreeable person is unbearable. الوجع ما ينحمل أكثر *l-wujaᶜ ma yinḥimil 'akθar.* The pain cannot be endured any more.

احتمل *ḥtimal* VIII to feel that something is possible, conceivable or likely. أحتمل يجي اليوم *'aḥtamil yiyi l-yoom.* I suppose he will come today. يحتمل *yiḥtamal* it's possible, it's conceivable. يحتمل يجي باكر *yuḥtamal yiyi baačir.* It's possible he will come tomorrow.

حمل *ḥamil* (v.n. from حمل *ḥimal*) 1. carrying, bearing. 2. pregnancy.

حمل *ḥimil* p. احمال *ḥmaal* load, cargo, burden. حمل ثقيل *ḥimil θagiil* heavy load.

حملة *ḥamla* p. حملات *ḥamlaat* 1. attack, criticism. 2. campaign. حملة صحافية *ḥamla ṣaḥaafiyya* press campaign. حملة انتخابية *ḥamla 'intixaabiyya* election campaign. حملة ضد الجهل *ḥamla ḍidd l-jahil* illiteracy campaign.

حمال *ḥammaal* p. حماميل *ḥamaamiil, -iin* porter, carrier. قلت حق الحمال، «شيل الجنط» *gilt ḥagg l-ḥammaal, "šiil l-jinaṭ."* I said to the porter, "Carry the suitcases."

حمولة *ḥmuula* p. *-aat* 1. load capacity, load limit. 2. tonnage (of a vessel).

حمولة *ḥamuula* p. حمايل *ḥamaayil* stock, extended family. ابن حمولة *'ibin ḥamuula* man from good stock.

تحامل *taḥaamul* (v.n. from VI تحامل *tḥaamal*) 1. prejudice, bias. 2. intolerance.

احتمال *ḥtimaal* (v.n. from VIII احتمل *ḥtimal*) 1. probability, likelihood. فيه احتمال أشوف الحاكم اليوم *fii ḥtimaal 'ačuuf l-ḥaakim l-yoom.* There's a good chance I will see the ruler today. 2. tolerance, endurance, resistance. احتمال للحر *ḥtimaal lil-ḥarr* tolerance for heat.

حامل *ḥaamil* (act. part. from حمل *ḥimal*) p. *-iin* 1. carrying, bearing. هو حامل الصندوق *huwa ḥamil ṣ-ṣanduug.* He is carrying the box. 2. holder (of a document, of a diploma, etc.) أنت حامل جواز سفرك؟ *'inta ḥaamil jawaaz safarak?* Are you carrying your passport? Do you have your passport on you? وين الهوية؟ أنت حاملها؟ *ween l-hawiyya? 'inta ḥaamilha?* Where is your identity card? Is it on you? هي حاملة شهادة دكتوراه *hiya ḥaamla šahaadat daktooraa.* She is a holder of a Ph.D. degree. 3. (p. حوامل *ḥawaamil*) pregnant. حرمة حامل *ḥurma ḥaamil* pregnant woman.

حاملة *ḥaamila* p. *-aat* carrier, device for carrying or holding s.th. حاملة طائرات *ḥaamilat ṭaa'iraat* aircraft carrier.

محمول *maḥmuul* (p.p. from حمل *ḥimal*) p. *-iin* carried, borne. جنود محمولين بالجو *jnuud maḥmuuliin b-l-jaww* airborne troops. (prov.) محمول ويترفس *maḥmuul w-yitraffas.* Don't bite the hand that feeds you. Don't do favors to those who do not appreciate or deserve them. (lit., "He is carried and he kicks.")

محمل *mḥammal* (p.p. from II حمل *ḥammal*) loaded, having been loaded. اللوري محمل أكثر من اللازم *l-loori mḥammal 'akθar min l-laazim.* The truck is overloaded. اللوري توه محمل *l-loori tawwa mḥammal.* The truck has just been loaded.

ح م م *ḥmm*

حمة *ḥumma* fever. عنده حمة يعني هو مسخن *ᶜinda ḥumma yaᶜni huwa mṣaxxan.* He has a fever means "he is feverish."

حمام *ḥamaam* (coll.) pigeons, doves. s. *-a.* فيه ناس ياكلون الحمام *fii naas yaakluun l-ḥamaam.* There are people who eat pigeons. كم حمامة عندك؟ *čam ḥamaama ᶜindak?* How many pigeons do you have? خمس حمامات *xams ḥamaamaat* five pigeons.

حمام *ḥammaam* p. *-aat* 1. bathroom, lavatory. 2. bathroom, room for bathing. رحت الحمام وسبحت *riḥt l-ḥammaam w-sibaḥt.* I went to the bathroom and took a bath.

ح م ن ي *ḥmny*

حمني *ḥamanni* (dim. of عبد الرحمن *ᶜabd r-raḥmaan*) Abd Al-Rahman (used for endearment).

١ ح م ي *ḥmy*

حمي *ḥima* (coll.) stinky dark brown mud.

٢ ح م ي *ḥmy*

حمى *ḥamma* to heat, make warm. حميت شوية ماي *ḥammeet šwayyat maay.* I heated some water.

تحمى *tḥamma* V to warm oneself. تحميت يم النار *tḥammeet yamm n-naar.* I got warm by the fire.

حمية *ḥamiyya* 1. zeal, fervor, ardor. حمية وطنية *ḥamiyya waṭaniyya* nationalistic zeal. 2. enthusiasm. صاحب حمية *ṣaaḥib ḥamiyya* man with enthusiasm. 3. passion, rage, fury.

٣ ح م ي ḥmy

حمى ḥima (يحمي yḥami) (with من min) to defend, protect, shelter, shield. الجيش يحمي المدينة من العدو *l-jeeš yḥami l-madiina min l-ᶜadu.* The army defends the city against the enemy. المظلة تحميك من الشمس *li-mðalla tḥamiik min š-šams.* The umbrella protects you from the sun. لا تخاف! آنا أحميك *la txaaf! 'aana 'aḥmiik.* Don't worry! I will protect you.

احتمى ḥtima VIII to protect oneself, defend oneself. الجاهل احتمى من الكلب *l-jaahil ḥtima min č-čalb.* The child protected himself from the dog.

حماية ḥimaaya (v.n. from حمى ḥima) protection, protecting.

حامي ḥaami (act. part. from حمى ḥima) protector, defender, guardian. حامي الديار المقدسة *ḥaami d-diyaar l-muġaddasa* guardian of the holy shrines. (prov.) حاميها حراميها *ḥaamiiha ḥaraamiiha.* The protector turned out to be a thief.

محمي maḥmi (p.p. from حمى ḥima) protected. السيارة محمية من الشمس *s-sayyaara maḥmiyya min š-šams.* The car is protected from the sun. البيت محمي من الشمس بالشجر *l-beet maḥmi min š-šams b-š-šiyar.* The house is protected against the sun by the trees.

محمية maḥmiyya p. -aat protectorate (pol.). بورتوريكو محمية أمريكانية *poortoriiko maḥmiyya 'amriikaaniyya.* Puerto Rico is an American protectorate.

محاماة mḥaamaa profession, practice of law.

محامي mḥaami p. -iin lawyer, attorney.

محامية mḥaamya p. -aat woman lawyer.

٤ ح م ي ḥmy

حمى ḥama (p. حميان ḥimyaan) father-in-law. حماي ḥamaaya my father-in-law. حماها ḥamaaha her father-in-law.

حماة ḥamaa (p. حموات ḥamawaat) mother-in-law. حماتي ḥamaati my mother-in-law. حماتك ḥamaatič your (f.) mother-in-law.

ح م ي ن ḥmyn

حمين ḥmayyin (dim. of عبد الرحمن ᶜabd r-raḥmaan) Abd Al-Rahman (used for endearment).

ح ن چ ḥnč

حنج ḥinič p. حنوج ḥnuuč chin.

ح ن ش ḥnš

حنش ḥanaš p. حنشان ḥinšaan long poisonous snake.

ح ن ط ḥnṭ

حنط ḥannaṭ II to embalm, mummify (a corpse). المصريين في الزمان الأولي كانوا يحنطون الميت *l-maṣriyyiin fi z-zamaan l-'awwali čaanaw yḥanniṭuun l-mayyit.* In old times the Egyptians used to mummify the dead.

حنطة ḥinṭa (coll.) (بر burr is more common) wheat. s. حبة حنطة ḥabbat ḥinṭa grain of wheat.

ح ن ظ ل *ḥnðl*

حنظل *ḥanðal* (علقم *ᶜalgam* is more common) colocynth (kind of very bitter gourd). أمر من الحنظل *'amarr min l-ḥanðal* more bitter than colocynth.

ح ن ف *ḥnf*

حنفي *ḥanafi* 1. Hanafitic (pertaining to an orthodox school of theology, founded by Abu Hanifa). 2. (p. *-iyyiin, -iyya*) Hanafi (member of the Hanafite school).

ح ن ن ١ *ḥnn*

حن *ḥann* (يحن *yḥinn*) 1. to long, yearn, be anxious. يحن إلى ذيك الأيام *yḥinn 'ila ðiič l-'ayyaam.* He longs for those days. كل واحد يحن حق بلاده *kill waaḥid yḥinn ḥagg blaada.* Everyone yearns for their country. يحن إلى شوفتها مرة ثانية *yḥinn 'ila šoofatta marra θaanya.* He is looking forward to seeing her again. 2. (with على *ᶜala*) to feel affection, compassion, sympathy for. المعلم حن عليه ونجحه *li-mᶜallim ḥann ᶜalee w-najjaḥa.* The teacher took pity on him and passed him. قلبها حن على الفقير وعطته عشرة درهم *galbaha ḥann ᶜala l-fagiir w-ᶜaṭata ᶜašara dirhim.* Her heart went out for the poor man and she gave him ten dirhams.

حنان *ḥanaan* (v.n. from حن *ḥann*) 1. sympathy, affection, tenderness. 2. compassion, pity. ما عنده ذرة من الحنان *ma ᶜinda ðarra min l-ḥanaan.* He doesn't have the least bit of affection.

حنين *ḥaniin* (v.n. from حن *ḥann*) longing, yearning, nostalgia. الحنين إلى الوطن *l-ḥaniin 'ila l-waṭan* homesickness.

حنون *ḥanuun* 1. compassionate, affectionate. شوف شقد أخوه حنون. يعطيه كل اللي يطلبه *čuuf š-gadd 'uxuu ḥanuun. yᶜaṭii kill illi yuṭulba.* Look how compassionate his brother is! He gives him all that he asks for. 2. kind, gentle. صوت حنون *ṣoot ḥanuun* gentle, moving voice.

أحن *'aḥann* (elat.) 1. (with من *min*) more compassionate, affectionate. 2. (with foll. n.) the most compassionate, affectionate.

ح ن ن ٢ *ḥnn*

حنا *ḥinna* (نحن *niḥin* is more common) we. حنا ربع الشيخ *ḥinna rabiᶜ š-šeex.* We are the Shaikh's followers.

ح ن ي ١ *ḥny*

حنى *ḥanna* II to dye red (with henna). البنات والحريم هن اللي يحنون إيدينهن ورجولهن *l-banaat w-l-ḥariim hin illi yḥannuun 'iideenhin w-ryuulhin.* Girls and women are the ones who dye their hands and feet red.

حنة *ḥinna* (coll.) henna (redish-orange cosmetic made from the henna plant).

ح ن ي ٢ *ḥny*

حنى *ḥina* (يحني *yḥani*) to bend, bow, bend forward. حنى العود *ḥina l-ᶜuud.* He bent the stick. احني راسك حتى تقدر تدش *'iḥni raasak ḥatta tigdar d-dišš.* Bend your head forward so that you can enter. الكبر يحني الظهر *l-kibar yḥani ð-ðahir.* Old age bends one's back.

انحنى *nḥina* VII 1. to curve, twist, turn. الرستة تنحني إلى اليمين هناك *r-rasta* *tinḥani 'ila l-yimiin hunaak.* The paved road curves to the right over there. 2. to bow. ينحنون للشيخ لين يسلمون عليه *yinḥinuun liš-šeex leen ysallmuun ᶜalee.* They bow to the Shaikh when they greet him. 3. to bend forward. انحنى وشال الصندوق *nḥina w-šaal ṣ-ṣanduug.* He bent forward and picked up the box. انحنى ظهره من الكبر *nḥina ḍahra min l-kibar.* His back bent forward from old age.

حنو *ḥunu* = حنان *ḥanaan* affection, compassion, sympathy.

منحني *minḥini* 1. bent, bowed. ظهره منحني من الكبر *ḍahra minḥini min l-kibar.* His back is bent with age. 2. leaning, inclined. الشجرة منحنية ورايحة توقع *li-šyara minḥanya w-raayḥa toogaᶜ.* The tree is leaning over and it's about to fall.

ح و ت *ḥwt*

حوت *ḥuut* p. حيتان *ḥiitaan* whale. ما في حيتان في الخليج هني بس فيه جراجير واجد *ma fii ḥiitaan fi l-xaliij hini bass fii yaraayiir waayid.* There are no whales in the Gulf here, but there are many sharks.

ح و ج *ḥwj*

احتاج *ḥtaaj* VIII to need, want, require. تحتاج شي؟ *tiḥtaaj šayy?* Do you need anything? العيال يحتاجون كتب وقلامة وجواتي بعد *li-ᶜyaaḷ yiḥtajuun kutub w-gḷaama w-juwaati baᶜad.* The children want books, pencils, and shoes too. يحتاج لك سيارة *yiḥtaaj-lak sayyaara.* You are in need of a car. الترفيع حقك يحتاج له موافقة التنديل *t-tarfiiᶜ ḥaggak yiḥtaaj-la mwaafagat t-tindeel.* Your promotion requires the supervisor's approval.

حاجة *ḥaaja* p. *-aat* 1. need, necessity. ما لي حاجة فيها *ma-li ḥaaja fiiha.* I don't need it. فيه حاجة تنش الصباح الساعة خمس؟ *fii ḥaaja tnišš ṣ-ṣabaaḥ s-saaᶜaa xams?* Is there any need to wake up at five in the morning? عند الحاجة *ᶜind l-ḥaaja* at the time of need, when necessary. ما عندي مانع تستعمل سيارتي عند الحاجة *ma ᶜindi maaniᶜ tistaᶜmil sayyaarati ᶜind l-ḥaaja.* I have no objection to your using my car if necessary. في حاجة إلى *fi ḥaaja 'ila* in need of. السيارة في حاجة إلى قوطي آيل *s-sayyaara fi ḥaaja 'ila guuṭi 'aayil.* The car is in need of a can of motor oil. 2. pressing need, poverty, destitution. لوما الحاجة كان ما رحت له *looma l-ḥaaja čaan ma riḥt-la.* Had it not been for the pressing need, I would not have gone to him. 3. need, s.th. needed, necessary article. حاجتي عندك *ḥaajti ᶜindak.* You have what I need. إذا كانت حاجتي عند صديق، ما يقصر *ᶜiða kaanat ḥaajti ᶜind ṣadiig, ma ygaṣṣir.* If a friend has what I need, he won't let me down. اخذ حاجتك وفي امان الله *'ixið ḥaajtak w-fi maan illaah.* Take what you need and good-bye. 4. matter, concern, business. قضيت حاجتي عنده *gaðeet ḥaajti ᶜinda.* I took care of my business at his place. ما لك حاجة في غيرك *ma-lak ḥaaja fi ġeerak.* You've got no concern with others. مر من هني الشرطي ما له حاجة فيك *murr min ihni š-širṭi ma-la ḥaaja fiik.* Walk from here; the policeman has no concern with you. 5. (p. *-aat*) goods, wares, merchandise. روح له؛ يبيع

حاجات أجنبية ruuḥ-la; ybiiᶜ ḥaajaat 'aynabiyya. Go to him; he sells foreign goods.

محتاج *miḥtaaj* p. *-iin* 1. in need, needy, poor. 2. person in need of s.th., poor person.

ح و چ *ḥwč*

حاچ *ḥaač* = حاك *ḥaak.* See under **ح و ك** *ḥwk.*

ح و د *ḥwd*

حاد *ḥaad* (يحود *yḥuud)* to turn aside, turn away, drive away. حود البهايم من البستان *ḥuud l-bahaayim min l-bistaan.* Drive away the animals from the orchard.

ح و ز *ḥwz*

حاز *ḥaaz* (يحوز *hḥuuz)* see under **ح ي ز** *ḥyz.*

ح و ش *ḥwš*

حاش *ḥaaš* (يحوش *yḥuuš)* to gather, collect. راح وحاش حشيش حق الغنم *raaḥ w-ḥaaš ḥašiiš ḥagg l-ġanam.* He went and gathered some grass for the sheep.

حوش *ḥawwaš* II 1. to amass, accumulate, gather. حوش فلوس *ḥawwaš fluus.* He got some money. 2. to save, put by (money). حوش مليون درهم *ḥawwaš malyoon dirhim.* He saved one million dirhams.

حوش *ḥooš* p. احواش *ḥwaaš* court, courtyard.

ح و ط *ḥwṭ*

حوط *ḥaaṭ* (يحوط *yḥuuṭ)* 1. to surround, encircle. جا الشيخ وحاطوه الناس. ما قدرت أشوفه *yaa š-šeex w-ḥaaṭoo n-naas. ma gidart 'ačuufa.* The Shaikh came and the people clustered around him. I couldn't see him. 2. (with ب *b-*) to overcome, overtake. نيتك البطالة حاطت بيك *niitič l-baṭṭaala ḥaaṭat biič.* Malice has overcome you.

حوط *ḥawwaṭ* II to build a wall around, wall in, encircle, surround. حوطوا البيت بحوطة عالية *ḥawwaṭu l-beet b-ḥooṭa ᶜaalya.* They built a high wall around the house.

احتاط *ḥtaaṭ* VIII to be careful, be cautious, to prepare onself, make provision. لازم تحتاط للمشاكل *laazim tiḥtaaṭ lil-mašaakil.* You should be prepared for problems. إذا ما تحتاط للمشكلة حيف عليك *'iða ma tiḥtaaṭ lil-muškila ḥeef ᶜaleek.* If you aren't prepared for the problem, you will be sorry.

حوطة *ḥooṭa* p. احواط *ḥwaaṭ* 1. fence, wall. بنينا حوطة حول البيت *baneena ḥooṭa ḥool l-beet.* We built a wall around the house. 2. sheep pen. الغنم ينامون في الحوطة *l-ġanam ynaamuun fi l-ḥooṭa.* Sheep (and goats) sleep in a sheep pen.

احتياط *ḥtiyaaṭ* (v.n. from VIII احتاط *ḥtaaṭ*) 1. caution, carefulness. 2. provision, precaution, care. للاحتياط *la li-ḥtiyaaṭ* as a precaution, just in case. اخذ واياك برنوص للاحتياط *'ixið wiyyaak barnuuṣ la li-ḥtiyaaṭ.* Take a blanket with you, just in case. 3. (p. *-aat*) precautionary measures, precautions. خذوا كل الاحتياطات اللازمة حق سلامة المسافرين *xaðaw kill li-ḥtiyaaṭaat l-laazma ḥagg salaamat li-msaafriin.* They took all the precautions necessary for the safety of travelers. 4. substitute (sports). عندنا أربعة احتياط في هذي المباراة *ᶜindana 'arbaᶜa ḥtiyaaṭ fi haaði l-mubaaraa.* We have four substitute players in this match.

احتياطي *ḥtiyaaṭi* 1. replacement, spare. فيه أدوات احتياطية في المختبر والمكتبة *fii 'adawaat ḥtiyaaṭiyya fi l-muxtabar w-l-maktaba.* There are spare instruments in the laboratory and the library. 2. reserve. قوات احتياطية *guwwaat ḥtiyaaṭiyya* reserve forces, reserves. احتياطي زيت *ḥtiyaaṭi zeet* oil reserves.

محيط *muḥiiṭ* p. *-aat* 1. ocean. المحيط الهندي *l-muḥiiṭ l-hindi* the Indian Ocean. 2. environment, surroundings.

ح و ظ *ḥwð̣*

حوض *ḥooð̣* p. احواض *ḥwaað̣* basin, trough. خذيت البعير حق الحوض لاجل يشرب *xaðeet l-biᶜiir ḥagg l-ḥooð̣ lajil yišrab.* I took the camel to the trough so that it might drink.

ح و گ *ḥwg*

احواق *ḥwaag* left-overs. حرمتي ما طبخت اليوم. كلينا احواق *ḥurumti ma ṭbaxat l-yoom. kaleena ḥwaag.* My wife did not cook today. We ate left-overs.

ح و ك *ḥwk*

حاك *ḥaak* (يحيك *yḥiik*) 1. to weave. حاكت برنوص صوف *ḥaakat barnuuṣ ṣuuf.* She wove a woolen blanket. 2. to knit. بنت عمي حاكت لي سويتر *bint ᶜammi ḥaakat-li sweetar.* My uncle's daughter knitted me a sweater.

حياكة *ḥyaaka* (v.n. from حاك *ḥaak*) 1. weaving. 2. knitting.

حايك *ḥaayik* p. حياك *ḥiyyaak, -iin* weaver.

ح و ل *ḥwl*

حال *ḥaal* (يحول *yḥuul*) 1. to intervene, interfere, interpose. ما فيه شي يحول بيننا وبين غرضنا *ma fii šayy yḥuul beenna w-been ġarað̣na.* Nothing is going to come between us and our goal.

حال *ḥaal* (يحيل *yḥiil*) (with *ᶜala*) to transfer, refer to s.o. حال المشكلة على المدير *ḥaal l-muškila ᶜala l-mudiir.* He handed the problem to the manager. الإدارة حالت الموظف على التقاعد *l-'idaara ḥaalat l-muwað̣ð̣af ᶜala t-tagaaᶜud.* The administration retired the employee. المدير حالني على دايرة ثانية *l-mudiir ḥaalni ᶜala daayra θaanya.* The manager referred me to another office.

حول *ḥawwal* II 1. to change, convert, exchange. حولت ألف درهم إلى دولارات *ḥawwalt 'alf dirhim 'ila duulaaraat.* I changed a thousand dirhams into dollars. 2. transfer, move. التنديل حولني إلى وظيفة ثانية *t-tindeel ḥawwalni 'ila wað̣iifa θaanya.* The supervisor transferred me to another job. 3. to remit, send, transmit (e.g., money by mail). حولت ألف دولار بالبريد اليوم حق هلي *ḥawwalt 'alf duulaar b-l-bariid l-yoom ḥagg hali.* I sent a thousand dollars through the post office to my folks today. 4. (with عن *ᶜan*) to turn s.th. aside, move s.th. away from. ما حول عيونه عن وجهها *ma ḥawwal ᶜyuuna ᶜan weehha.* He did not move his eyes away from her. 5. to descend, dismount, get off. قوم! حول! *guum! ḥawwil!* Stand up! Go downstairs! حول عند الليت الثاني *ḥawwil ᶜind l-leet θ-θaani.* Get off at the second (traffic) light.

حاول *ḥaawal* III to try, attempt to do s.th., make an attempt. حاول ينتشل الغريق، لكن ما قدر *ḥaawal yintašil l-ġariig, laakin ma gidar.* He tried to pick up the drowned person, but he couldn't. حاول ينهزم *ḥaawal yinhazim.* He tried to escape.

تحول *tḥawwal* V 1. to be changed, be converted. كل الخلال تحول إلى رطب *kill l-xaḷaaḷ tḥawwal 'ila rṭabb.* All the green unripe dates turned to ripe dates. (prov.) زمان أول تحول والغزل انقلب صوف *zamaan 'awwal tḥawwal w-l-ġazal ngaḷab ṣuuf.* Time changes. Things are no longer the same. (lit., "The olden times have changed and spun thread, yarn, has changed to wool.") 2. to be transferred, reassigned. إذا ما أتحول من ها المكان، أفنش *'iða ma 'atḥawwal min hal-mukaan, 'afanniš.* If I don't get transferred from this place, I will quit. 3. to be remitted, be changed. المبلغ تحول *l-mablaġ tḥawwal.* The sum of money was remitted. 4. to move.تحولنا من بيتنا القديم إلى بيت جديد *tḥawwalna min beetna l-gadiim 'ila beet yidiid.* We moved from our old house to a new house.

احتال *ḥtaal* VIII (with على *ᶜala*) to cheat, deceive, dupe. احتال علينا وخذ منا ألف دينار *ḥtaal ᶜaleena w-xað minna 'alf diinaar.* He cheated us and took a thousand dinars from us.

حال *ḥaal* p. أحوال *'aḥwaal* 1. condition, state. كيف حالك؟ *čeef ḥaalak?* How are you? 2. situation. 3. circumstance. أحواله زينة *'aḥwaala zeena.* He is doing very well. على كل حال *ᶜala kull ḥall* at any rate, in any case. على كل حال، ما عليك منه *ᶜala kull ḥaal, ma ᶜaleek minna.* At any rate, don't pay attention to him. 4. (p. أحوال *'aḥwaal*) matters, affairs, concerns. كيف أحوالك؟ *čeef 'aḥwaalak?* How are things? دايرة الأحوال الشخصية *daayrat l-'aḥwaal š-šaxṣiyya* vital statistics department.

حالما *ḥaal-ma* (conj.) as soon as, the moment that. قل لي حالما يوصل *gul-li ḥaal-ma yooṣal.* Tell me as soon as he arrives.

حالا *ḥaalan* (adv.) immediately. اتصل فيه حالا *ttaṣil fii ḥaalan.* Contact him immediately.

حالة *ḥaala* p. *-aat* 1. condition, state. حالة طوارئ *ḥaalat ṭawaari'* state of emergency. 2. situation. آنا عارف حالتك يا بو علي *'aana ᶜaarif ḥaaltak ya bu ᶜali.* I know your situation, Abu Ali. 3. case. هذي حالة من الحالات الصعبة *haaði ḥaala min l-ḥaalaat ṣ-ṣaᶜba.* This is one of the difficult cases. في هذي الحالة أدش الشغل وياك *fi haaði l-ḥaala 'adišš š-šuġul wiyyaak.* In this case, I will go to work with you.

حول *ḥool* (*ḥawl* is a var. in literary utterances) 1. might, power. لا حول ولا قوة إلا بالله *la ḥawla wa-la guwwata 'illa bil-laah.* (expression of resignation) There's nothing I can do about it. (lit., "There's no power and no strength except in God.") 2. (prep.) around, about, in the area of. فيه طوفة حـــول البنايـــة *fii ṭoofa ḥool li-bnaaya.* There is a wall around the building. 3. approximately, about. يا حول خمسمية نفـــر *ya ḥool xamsimyat nafar.* About five hundred people came. 4. about, concerning. حكيت وياه حـــول ذيـــك القضية لـــو لا؟ *ḥačeet wiyyaa ḥool ðiič l-gaðiyya lo la?* Did you speak with him about that problem or not?

حيل *ḥeel* strength, power, vigor, force. ما له قوة ولا حيـــل *ma la guwwa wala ḥeel.* He is completely helpless.

حيلة *ḥiila* p. حيل *ḥiyal* trick, wile. ما في اليد ولا حيلة *ma fi l-yadd wala ḥiila.* There is no recourse; there's nothing I can do. صاحب حيل *ṣaaḥib ḥiyal* tricky person; man of excuses.

حوالة *ḥwaala* p. *-aat* money order. طرشت حوالة حق القنصلية *ṭarrašt ḥwaala ḥagg l-ġunṣuliyya.* I sent a money order to the consulate.

حوالي *ḥawaali* (prep.; less common var. حول *ḥool*) about, approximately. حوالي مليـــون درهـــم *ḥawaali malyoon dirhim* about one million dirhams. حوالي الســـاعة خمـــس *ḥawaali s-saaᶜa xams* about five o'clock. عنده حوالي عشرة مليون درهم *ᶜinda ḥawaali ᶜašara malyoon dirhim.* He has about ten million dirhams.

حول *ḥawal* crossing of the eyes. فيه حول في عيونها *fii ḥawal fi ᶜyuunha.* She is cross-eyed.

حول *ḥawal* f. حولا *ḥoola* p. حول *ḥuul* 1. cross-eyed. 2. cross-eyed person.

محول *mḥawwil* (act. part. from II حول *ḥawwal*) p. *-aat* transformer (el.). إذا انقطعت الكهربا، عندنا محول *'iða ngiṭaᶜat l-kahraba, ᶜindana mḥawwil.* If the electricity is cut off, we have a transformer.

تحويلة *taḥwiila* p. *-aat,* تحاويل *taḥaawiil* 1. detour. تحصل تحويلة قدامك لأن الكولية يشتغلـــون في الطريـــق *tḥaṣṣil taḥwiila jiddaamak li'an l-kuuliyya yištaġluun fi ṭ-ṭariig.* You will find a detour in front of you because the coolies are working in the road.

محاولة *mḥaawala* p. *-aat* attempt, endeavor, try.

محتال *muḥtaal* (act. part. from VIII احتـــال *ḥtaal*) p. *-iin* swindler, cheat, imposter. 2. crook, scoundrel.

مستحيل *mustaḥiil* (less common var. *mistaḥiil*) 1. impossible, absurd, preposterous. هذا شـــين مســـتحيل *haaða šayyin mustaḥiil.* This is an impossible thing. 2. (with foll. imperf.) it is impossible that ... مستحيل تروح صوبهـــم *mustaḥiil truuḥ ṣoobhum.* It is impossible that you go to their place.

ح و م *ḥwm*

حام *ḥaam* (يحـــوم *yḥuum*) 1. to go around, circle. ظل يحوم في السوق لين لقى اللي يريده *ðall yḥuum fi s-suug leen liga lli yriida.* He kept going around in the marketplace until he found what he wanted. صار له مدة يحوم على ها الشغـــل *ṣaar-la mudda yḥuum ᶜala ha š-šuġul.* He's been after this job for a while. 2.

to hover, fly around. الطير حام وحام وبعدين حط *ṭ-ṭeer ḥaam w-ḥaam w-bacdeen ḥaṭṭ.* The bird kept circling and then it came down.

ح وو ا *ḥwwaa*

حوا *ḥawwa* Eve. آدم وحوا *'aadam w-ḥawwa* Adam and Eve.

ح ي چ *ḥyč*

حايچ *ḥaayič* = حايك *ḥaayik.* See under **ح ي ك** *ḥyk.*

ح ي د [1] *ḥyd*

حاد *ḥaad* (يحيد *yḥiid*) to remember, recall, recollect. ما تحيد يوم كنت مريض *ma tḥiid yoom čint mariiḍ?* Don't you remember when you were ill?

ح ي د [2] *ḥyd*

حاد *ḥaad* (يحيد *yḥiid*) (with عن *can*) to deviate, stray, move away from. ما يحيد عن الصدق ولو ضد مصلحته *ma yḥiid can ṣ-ṣidj walaw ḍidd maṣlaḥta.* He doesn't deviate from truth even though it's against his own welfare.

حياد *ḥiyaad* neutrality. على الحياد *cala l-ḥiyaad* neutral. هو على الحياد؛ ما يتدخل في مشاكل الآدمين *huwa cala l-ḥiyaad; ma yiddaxxal fi mašaakil l-'aadmiin.* He is neutral; he doesn't interfere in people's problems.

محايد *mḥaayid* (act. part. from حاد *ḥaad*) neutral الدول المحايدة *d-duwal li-mḥaayda* the neutral states.

ح ي ر [1] *ḥyr*

حير *ḥayyar* II to confuse, puzzle, bewilder. أنت حيرتني. قل لي شو تريد: هذا والا ذاك *'inta ḥayyartani. gul-li šu triid: haaða walla ðaak.* You've confused me. Tell me what you want: this one or that one. لا تحيرني. عندي موعد، أريد أروح *la tḥayyirni. cindi mawcid, 'ariid 'aruuḥ.* Don't waste my time. I have an appointment. I want to go. ولدي حيرني. مرة يريد سيكل ومرة يريد بطبطة *wildi ḥayyarni. marra yriid seekal w-marra yriid buṭbuṭa.* My son's given me a hard time. One moment he wants a bicycle and the next he wants a motorcycle.

تحير *tḥayyar* V to be or become confused, perplexed, puzzled, bewildered. تحيرت وما دريت شأسوي *tḥayyart w-ma dareet š-asawwi.* I was confused and didn't know what to do. تحيرت أشتري هذا البيت لو ذاك *tḥayyart 'aštiri haaða l-beet lo ðaak.* I was undecided whether to buy this house or that one.

احتار *ḥtaar* VIII = V تحير *tḥayyar.*

حيرة *ḥiira* confusion, perplexity, puzzlement. تركتهم أمهم وخلتهم في حيرة *trakattum 'ummhum w-xaḷḷattum fi ḥiira.* Their mother abandoned them and left them helpless.

ح ي ر [2] *ḥyr*

حير *ḥayyar* II to hold up, impede, hinder. لا تحيرني! إذا حيرتني أتأخر عن الباص *la tḥayyirni! 'iða ḥayyartani 'at'axxar can l-paaṣ.* Don't hold me up! If you hold me up, I will miss the bus.

تحير *tḥayyar* V to be late, come late. تحيرت عن الموعد يا دختر *tḥayyart can l-mawcid, ya daxtar.* I am late for the appointment, Doctor.

حيرة *ḥiira* (v.n.) delay, postponement, deferment.

ح ي ر ٣ *ḥyr*

حجر *ḥiyar* (coll.) 1. stone, pebble. s. -*a*. رمى حجرة عليّ *rima ḥiyara ᶜalayya.* He threw a stone at me. بيوت من حجر *byuut min ḥiyar* stone houses. 2. rock. ما أقدر أحلحل هالحجرة *ma 'agdar 'aḥalḥil hali-ḥyara.* I can't move this rock.

ح ي ز *ḥyz*

حاز *ḥaaz* (يحوز *yḥuuz*) (with على *ᶜala*) to obtain, achieve, get. حاز على شهادة المدرسة *ḥaaz ᶜala šahaadat l-madrasa.* He obtained the school certificate. فريقنا حاز على كاس العالم في الكورة *fariiġna ḥaaz ᶜala kaas l-ᶜaalam fi l-kuura.* Our team got the World Cup in soccer.

تحيز *tḥayyaz* V to take sides, to be partial, be biased. المعلم يتحيز حق ولد الشيخ *l-muᶜallim yitḥayyaz ḥagg wild š-šeex.* The teacher is partial to the Shaikh's son.

انحاز *nḥaaz* VII = V تحيز *tḥayyaz.*

حيازة *ḥyaaza* (v.n. from حاز *ḥaaz*) 1. obtainment, attainment. 2. possession. لقيوا في حيازة البايق فلوس وذهب وما ادري شبعد *ligyu fi ḥyaazat l-baayig fluus w-ðahab w-ma dri š-baᶜad.* They found money, gold, and I don't know what else, in the thief's possession.

تحيز *taḥayyuz* (v.n. from V تحيز *tḥayyaz*) bias, prejudice. هذا الكاتب عنده تحيز ضد العرب *haaða l-kaatib ᶜinda taḥayyuz ḍidd l-ᶜarab.* This writer is prejudiced against the Arabs.

ح ي ط *ḥyṭ*

حاط *ḥaaṭ* (يحيط *yḥiiṭ*), احتاط *htaaṭ,* محيط *muḥiit,* etc., see under ح و ط *ḥwṭ.*

ح ي ظ *ḥyð̣*

حاض *ḥaað̣* (يحيض *yḥiið̣*) to menstruate. ما ادري بأي سن تحيض البنية هني *ma dri b-'ayy sinn tḥiið̣ li-bnayya hini.* I don't know at what age a girl begins to menstruate here.

ح ي ف *ḥyf*

حيف *ḥeef* (v.n.) 1. injustice, wrong. 2. pity, shame. حيف على...! *ḥeef ᶜala...!* What a pity! Too bad! حيف عليه، فنشوه! *ḥeef ᶜalee, fannašoo!* It's a pity they laid him off!

ح ي ك *ḥyk*

حايك *ḥaayik,* حياكة *ḥyaaka,* etc., see under ح و ك *ḥwk.*

ح ي ل ١ *ḥyl*

حال *ḥaal,* حيل *ḥeel,* حيلة *ḥiila*, etc., see under ح و ل *ḥwl.*

ح ي ل ٢ *ḥyl*

حيل *ḥeel* p. حيول *ḥyuul* bracelet. حيل ذهب *ḥeel ðahab* gold bracelet. المعرس هو اللي يشتري الحيول *l-miᶜris huwa lli yištiri li-ḥyuul.* The bridegroom is the one who buys the bracelets.

ح ي ل ي ن *ḥylyn*

حيليانة *ḥiilyaana* (قبقوبة *gabguuba* is more common) lobster. الناس هني ما ياكلون حيليان واجد *n-naas hini ma yaakluun ḥiilyaan waayid.* People here do not eat a lot of lobster.

ح ي ن *ḥyn*

حين *ḥiin* p. أحيان *'aḥyaan* time, period of time. الحـــين *'alḥiin,* ذالحين *ðalḥiin* now. بعـض الأحيــان *ba*^{c}*ð l-'aḥyaan* sometimes, occasionally, once in a while. كل حين وحين *kill ḥiin w-ḥiin* every now and then. أدوخ جقاير بعض الأحيان *'aduux jigaayir ba*^{c}*ð l-'aḥyaan.* I occasionally smoke cigarettes.

أحيانـــا *'aḥyaanan* (rare) = بعض الأحيان *ba*^{c}*ð l-'aḥyaan.*

ح ي و ن *ḥywn*

حيوان *ḥayawaan.* See under **ح ي ي** *ḥyy.*

ح ي ي *ḥyy*

حـيّى *ḥayya* II 1. to greet, hail. الناس يحيون الشيــخ *n-naas yḥayyuun š-šeex.* The people are cheering the Shaikh. حياهم وقعـــد *ḥayyaahum w-gi*^{c}*ad.* He greeted them and sat down. حياك الله! *ḥayyaak aḷḷa!* or يا حــي الله! *ya ḥayy aḷḷa!* = أهلا وسهلا! *'ahlan wa sahlan!* (used for greeting s.o.) Welcome! (lit., "May God preserve your life.") 2. to salute. الجنود يحيون العلم *li-jnuud yḥayyuun l-*^{c}*alam.* The soldiers are saluting the flag.

اســتحى *stiḥa* X 1. to feel ashamed, be ashamed. استحي على وجهك! *stiḥi* ^{c}*ala weeyhak!* Shame on you! ما تستحي! قوم وحب على يد أبوك *ma tistiḥi! guum w-ḥibb* ^{c}*ala yadd 'ubuuk.* Aren't you ashamed? Get up and kiss your father's hand! هو واحد ما يستحي. يسكر قــدام النـــاس *huwa waaḥid ma yistiḥi. yiskar jiddaam n-naas.* He is someone who doesn't know shame. He drinks (liquor) in front of the people. 2. to be or become embarrassed, feel embarrassed. استحى يطلب سيارتي ثـــاني مـــرة *stiḥa yuṭlub sayyarti θaani marra.* He was embarrassed to ask for my car again. ما أقدر أطلب فلوس أكثر، أستحي *ma 'agdar 'aṭlub fluus 'akθar, 'astiḥi.* I can't ask for more money. I'd be embarrassed. 3. to be bashful, shy. يستحي واجد، ما يتحكى وايا الحريم *yistiḥi wayyid, ma yitḥačča wiyya l-ḥariim.* He is very bashful. He wouldn't talk to women.

حــي *ḥayy* 1. alive, living, not dead. أبوك حي؟ *'ubuuk ḥayy?* Is your father alive? حــي مــوب ميــت *ḥayy muub mayyit.* He's alive, not dead. 2. (p. أحيـــاء *'aḥyaa'*) living being, living thing. علــم الأحيـــاء ^{c}*ilm l-'aḥyaa'* biology. الأحيـــاء والأمــوات *l-'aḥyaa' w-l-'amwaat* the living and the dead.

حي *ḥayya* (inv.) come! حي على الصلاة! *ḥayya* ^{c}*ala ṣ-ṣalaa!* Come to prayer!

حيــة *ḥayya* p. *-aat,* حيايا *ḥayyaaya* (حنـــش *ḥanaš* or داب *daab* are more common) snake.

حيا *ḥaya* shame, bashfulness.

حياة *ḥayaa* 1. life. ما يفكر في الحياة اللي هو فيها الحــين *ma yfakkir fi l-ḥayaa 'illi huwa fiiha l-ḥiin.* He doesn't think of the life he is leading now. حياة البدوي *ḥayaat li-bdiwi* Bedouin life. 2. living, cost of living. الحياة غاليـــة في الخليـــج *l-ḥayaa ġaalya fi l-xaliij.* The cost of living is expensive in the Gulf. الحياة في البر *l-ḥayaa fi l-barr* life in the desert.

حيــوي *ḥayawi* vital, essential to life. مسألة حيويـــة *mas'ala ḥayawiyya* vital matter.

حيـوان *ḥayawaan* p. *-aat* animal, beast. حديقـة حيوانـات *ḥadiigat ḥayawaanaat* zoo. حيـوان! مـا يفكـر *ḥayawaan! ma yfakkir.* He is (as stupid as) an animal. He doesn't think.

خ

خ ا *xaa*

خا *xaa* name of the letter خ *x*.

خ ا ز و گ *xaazwg*

خازوك *xaazuug*. See **خ و ز گ** *xwzg*.

خ ا ش و گ *xaašwg*

خاشوكة *xaašuuga*. See **خ و ش گ** *xwšg*.

خ ا م *xaam*

خـــام *xaam* (invar.) 1. raw, unprocessed. بترول خام *batrool xaam* crude oil. مواد خام *mawaad xaam* raw materials. حديـــد خـــام *ḥadiid xaam* iron ore. 2. inexperienced, naive, wet behind the ears. هذا الكـــولي خـــام *haaða l-kuuli xaam*. This coolie is inexperienced.

خ ا ن *xaan*

خان *xaan* pl. *-aat* 1. stable (for beasts of burden). 2. old fashioned inn. 3. warehouse, storehouse.

خ ب ب *xbb*

خب *xabba* II. See under **خ ب ي** *xby*.

خ ب ث *xbθ*

خبـــث *xubθ* (v.n.) viciousness, troublemaking, vicious behavior.

خبيـــث *xabiiθ* p. *-iin* 1. troublesome, vicious, malicious. 2. dangerous, serious. مـــرض خبيـــث *marað xabiiθ*. serious disease. المرض الخبيث *l-marað l-xabiiθ*. tuberculosis.

أخبـــث *'axbaθ* 1. (with من *min*) more troublesome, vicious, etc. 2. (with foll. n.) most troublesome, vicious, etc.

خ ب ر *xbr*

خبر *xibar* (يخبر *yxabir*) to perceive, have insight into, know. الله يخبر كل شي *'aḷḷa yxabir kill šayy*. God knows everything (i.e., God is the Omniscient). تخبر متى راح؟ *txabir mita raaḥ?* Do you know when he left?

خـــبر *xabbar* II to tell, inform, let s.o. know. خبرنا باللي صـــار *xabbirna b-lli ṣaar*. Tell us what happened. خبرته باكر بـــآمر عليـــه *xabbarta baačir b-aamurr ᶜalee*. I told him I would stop by tomorrow.

خـــابر *xaabar* III to telephone, phone. خابرته أمس بس ما حصلته *xaabarta 'ams bass ma ḥaṣṣalta*. I telephoned him yesterday but I didn't find him.

تخـــابر *txaabar* VI to telephone, get in touch with each other. تخابرنا واتفقنـــا نتقـــابل بـــاكر *txaabarna w-ttafagna nitgaabal baačir*. We telephoned each other and agreed to meet the following day. تخابرت واياهم *txaabart wiyyaahum*. I got in touch with them.

اختـــبر *xtibar* VIII to test, examine, experience. اختبرناهم وطلعوا نـــاس أوادم *xtibarnaahum w-ṭliᶜaw naas 'awaadim*. We tested them, and they turned out to be good people.

اســـتخبر *staxbar* X 1. to inquire, ask (about s.o. or s.th.). استخبرت عنه وعن أصله وفصله *staxbart ᶜanna w-ᶜan 'aṣla w-faṣla*. I inquired about him and about his origin and family. 2. to learn, find out. استخبرت انه جا أمس *staxbart 'inna ya 'ams.* I learned that he came yesterday.

خبر *xabar* p. أخبار *'axbaar* news, news item. سمعت الأخبار؟ *sim^c^at l-'axbaar?* Have you heard the news? ما سمعت أي خبر *ma sim^c^at 'ayya xabar.* I haven't heard any news item. عندي خبر يطيرك من الفرح *^c^indi xabar yṭayyirk min l-faraḥ.* I have a piece of news that will overcome you with joy.

خبرة *xibra* p. *-aat* experience. خبرة في التعليم *xibra fi t-ta^c^liim* experience in teaching. خبرة في الحسانة *xibra fi li-ḥsaana.* experience in barbering.

خبير *xabiir* p. خبرا *xubara* expert, experienced. خبير في التربية *xabiir fi t-tarbiya* expert in education.

مخابرة *muxaabara* p. *-aat* 1. telephone call. مخابرة دولية *muxaabara dawliyya.* international call. مشكور على المخابرة *maškuur ^c^ala l-muxaabara.* Thank you for the telephone call. 2. (p. only) المخابرات *l-muxaabaraat* the investigation department.

خ ب ز *xbz*

خبز *xibaz (يخبز yxabiz)* to bake bread. حرمتي دايما تخبز خبز في البيت *ḥurumti daayman txabiz xubiz fi l-beet.* My wife always bakes bread at home. خبزت عشرين قرص خبز *xibzat ^c^išriin garṣ xubiz.* She baked twenty loaves of bread. تعرفه؟ عجنته وخبزته *t^c^arfa? ^c^ijanta w-xibazta.* Do you know him? I know him very well. (lit., "I kneaded and baked him.").

خبز *xubiz* (coll.) bread. s. قرص خبز *garṣ xubiz.* loaf of bread. الخبز هني رخيص *l-xubiz hini raxiiṣ.* Bread is inexpensive here. عندك خبز؟ *^c^indak xubiz?* Do you have bread? كليت خبز ولحم *kaleet xubiz w-laḥam.* I ate bread and meat. خبز رقاق *xubiz rgaag* thin sheets of bread. خبز عربي *xubiz ^c^arabi* Arabic bread.

خبزة *xabza* (n. of inst.) p. *-aat* batch, mixture (of bread dough).

خباز *xabbaaz* p. خبابيز *xabaabiiz, -iin* baker, bread maker. الخباز هو اللي يخبز الخبز *l-xabbaaz huwa lli yxabiz l-xubiz.* A baker is the one who bakes bread.

مخبز *maxbaz* p. مخابز *maxaabiz* bakery, bread shop.

خ ب ص *xbṣ*

خبص *xubaṣ (يخبص yxabuṣ)* to mix up, distract, confuse. لا تخبص روحك! على كيفك *la txabuṣ ruuḥak! ^c^ala keefak.* Don't mix yourself up! Take it easy. سالم خبص الدنيا *saalim xubaṣ d-dinya.* Salim caused a lot of confusion.

انخبص *nxubaṣ* VII to be or become confused, preoccupied, rushed. انخبص وما درى شو يسوي *nxubaṣ w-ma dira šu ysawwi.* He was confused and didn't know what to do. كان عندنا خطار أمس وانخبصنا بهم *čaan ^c^indana xuṭṭaar 'ams w-nxubaṣna biihum.* We had guests yesterday and we were completely occupied with them.

خبصة *xabṣa* commotion, confusion, hustle and bustle.

خ ب ط *xbṭ*

خبط *xubaṭ (يخبط yxabuṭ)* 1. to mix.

خبط شعير وتبن وعطاه حق الحصان *xubaṭ šaᶜiir w-tibin w-ᶜaṭaa ḥagg li-ḥṣaan.* He mixed barley and straw and gave it to the horse. 2. to slam, strike, beat. صار حمقان. خرج وخبط الباب *ṣaar ḥamgaan. xiraj w-xubaṭ l-baab.* He became furious. He walked out and slammed the door.

خبطة *xabṭa* (n. of inst.) p. *-aat* 1. instance of mixing, mixing. 2. mixture, batch.

خباطة *xabbaaṭa* (خلاطة *xaḷḷaaṭa* is more common) p. *-aat* mixer, cement mixer.

خ ب ل *xbl*

خبل *xabbaḷ* II to drive s.o. insane, make s.o. crazy. اخذه عني! خبلني *'ixða ᶜanni! xabbaḷni.* Take him away! He's driven me out of my mind. ها المنظر يخبل *hal-manðar yxabbiḷ.* This scenery stuns you.

تخبل *txabbaḷ* V to go crazy, go wild. تخبل لين خسر فلوسه *txabbaḷ leen xisar fluusa.* He went crazy when he lost his money. لين شاف البنية الحلوة تخبل *leen čaaf li-bnayya l-ḥilwa txabbaḷ.* When he saw the beautiful girl, he went crazy.

خبال *xbaaḷ* madness, insanity.

مخبل *mxabbaḷ* (p.p. from II خبل *xabbaḷ*) insane person, madman.

خ ت م *xtm*

ختم *xitam (يختم yxatim)* 1. to seal. ختم الخط *xitam l-xaṭṭ*. He sealed the letter. ختم المظروف *xitam l-maðruuf.* He sealed the envelope. 2. to stamp, impress with a stamp. ختم الطلب ووداه الوزير *xitam ṭ-ṭalab w-waddaa l-waziir.* He stamped the application and took it to the minister. ختم الطوابع *xitam ṭ-ṭawaabiᶜ.* He canceled the stamps. 3. to conclude, terminate. ختم كلامه بساع وقال «في أمان الله» *xitam kalaama b-saaᶜ w-gaal fi 'amaan illaah.* He concluded his speech in a hurry and said, "Good-bye!" 4. to read (the Quran) from cover to cover, read through. ختم القرآن لين كان عمره عشر سنين *xitam l-qur'aan leen čaan ᶜumra ᶜašir siniin.* He read the Quran from cover to cover when he was ten years old.

ختم *xattam* II to have s.o. read through (the Quran). ختموه القرآن *xattamoo l-qur'aan.* They made him read the Quran.

ختم *xatim* p. اختام *xtaam* seal, stamp.

ختمة *xatma* (n. of inst.) p. *-aat* a reading of the whole Quran. ختمة القرآن على روح الميت *xatmat l-qur'aan ᶜala ruuḥ l-mayyit* the reading of the Quran to bless the soul of the dead person.

خاتم *xaatim* (act. part. from ختم *xitam*) p. ختام *xittaam* graduate of a Quranic school. خاتم القرآن *xaatim l-qur'aan* one who has learned the Quran by heart. كان فيه مسابقة حق ختام القرآن *čaan fii musaabaġa ḥagg xittaam l-qur'aan.* There was a contest for learners of the Quran (by heart).

خ ت ن *xtn*

ختن *xattan* II to perform circumcision, circumcise. اللي يختن هو الختان *'illi yxattin huwa l-xattaan.* The one who circumcises is the *xattaan*. نحن ما نختن النسا *niḥin ma nxattin n-nisa*. We don't circumcise women.

تختن *txattan* V to be circumcised. الصبي يتختن وهو صغير *li-ṣbayy yitxattan w-huwa ṣaġiir*. A boy is circumcised when he is young. البنت، الله يسلمك، ما تتختن *l-bint, 'aḷḷa ysallimk, ma titxattan*. A girl, God keep you safe, is not circumcised.

ختان *xitaan* circumcision. كان اللي يسوي الختان المحسن، لكن ذالحين الناس قاموا يروحون الدختر *čaan illi ysawwi li-xtaan li-mḥassin, laakin ðalḥiin n-naas gaamaw yruuḥuun d-daxtar*. The one who used to perform circumcision was the barber, but now people have started to go to the doctor. الختان واجب على كل مسلم *li-xtaan waajib ᶜala kill muslim*. Circumcision is required of every Muslim. الختان عبارة عن الطهور *li-xtaan ᶜbaara ᶜan ṭ-ṭahuur*. Circumcision is, in other words, cleansing.

ختان *xattaan* p. ختاتنة *xataatna*, *-iin* one who performs circumcision. في الزمان الأولي الختان كان المحسن، بس الحين الناس قاموا يروحون الدختر *fi z-zamaan l-'awwali l-xattaan čaan li-mḥassin, bass alḥiin n-naas gaamaw yruuḥuun d-daxtar*. A long time ago, the one who performed circumcision was the barber, but now people have started to go to the doctor.

خ ج ل *xjl*

خجل *xijil (يخجل yxajil)* 1. to be or become embarrassed. والله خجلت من مصارحتك *waḷḷa xjilt min muṣaaraḥtak*. Honestly, I was too embarrassed to be frank with you. يخجل من أبوه *yxajil min 'ubuu*. He is embarrassed in front of his father. 2. to be ashamed, feel shame. هو شخص ما يخجل *huwa šaxṣ ma yxajil*. He is a person who feels no shame. 3. to be or become shy. خجل وما قال شي *xijil w-ma gaal šaay*. He became shy and said nothing.

خجل *xajjal* II to embarrass, put s.o. to shame. خجلني بكلامه الفارغ *xajjalni b-kallama l-faariġ*. He embarrassed me with his useless talk.

خجل *xajal* (v.n. from خجل *xijil*) embarrassment.

خجول *xajuul* p. *-iin* shy, bashful, timid. ولد خجول وايد *walad xajuul waayid* very shy boy.

خجلان *xajlaan* p. *-iin* embarrassed. ترك الحجرة وهو خجلان *tirak l-ḥijrah w-huwa xajlaan*. He left the room in embarrassment.

أخجل *'axjal* (elat.) 1. (with من *min*) more shy, etc. 2. (with foll. n.) the most shy, etc.

مخجل *mixjil* (act. part.) embarrassing, shocking. عمل مخجل *ᶜamal mixjil* shameful act.

خ د د *xdd*

خد *xadd* p. خدود *xduud* cheek. خدودها حمر مثل التفاح الحمر *xduudha ḥumur miθil t-tiffaaḥ l-ḥamar*. Her cheeks are as red as red apples.

مخدة *mxadda* p. *-aat* pillow, cushion.

خ د ر *xdr*

خدر *xaddar* II 1. to numb, deaden.

الدختر ضربني إبرة حتى يخدر المكان قبل العملية *d-daxtar ḍirabni 'ibra ḥatta yxaddir l-mukaan gabl l-^{c}amaliyya.* The doctor gave me a shot in order to deaden the area before the operation. 2. to anesthetize. خدروا الضفدع قبل ما شرحوه *xaddaraw ḍ-ḍifda^{c} gabil-ma šarraḥoo.* They had anesthetized the frog before they dissected it.

خدران *xadraan* numb, asleep. رجلي خدرانة *riili xadraana.* My leg is asleep.

مخدر *muxaddir* (act. part. from II خدر *xaddar*) 1. anesthetic, painkilling, tranquilizing. مادة مخدرة *maadda mxaddra* painkilling material. 2. (p. *-aat*) narcotics, drugs, dope.

خ د ع *xd^{c}*

خدع *xida^{c} (يخدع yxadi^{c})* to deceive, mislead, dupe. المظاهر مرات تخدع الإنسان مثلما يقول المثل «بالنهار عمايم وبالليل خمايم *l-maḍaahir marraat txadi^{c} l-'insaan miθil-ma yguul l-maθal b-n-nahaar ^{c}amaayim w-b-l-leel xamaayim.* Appearances sometimes fool people, as the proverb says, "Fair without and foul within." (lit. "In daylight they are turbans, i.e., holy men with turbans, and at night they are garbage, i.e., rascals, knaves, etc.").

انخدع *nxida^{c}* VII to be deceived, misled, duped. انخدعت باللي قال لي اياه *nxida^{c}t b-lli gal-li-yyaa.* I was taken in by what he told me. ينخدع بساع *yinxidi^{c} b-saa^{c}.* He is easily taken in.

خداع *xaddaa^{c}* 1. deceptive, deceiving. المظاهر خداعة بعض الأحيان *l-maḍaahir xaddaa^{c}a ba^{c}ḍ l-'aḥyaan.* Appearances are deceptive sometimes.

2. (p. *-iin*) swindler, cheat, crook.

خ د م *xdm*

خدم *xidam (يخدم yxadim)* 1. to serve, be of service, work for. الحاكم خدم بلاده والمواطنين *l-ḥaakim xidam blaada w-l-muwaaṭniin.* The ruler served his country and the citizens. سيارتي قديمة بس تخدمني زين *sayyaarti gadiima bass txadimni zeen.* My car is old, but it is of good service to me. 2. to be a servant, serve. الهندي خدمنا خمس سنين *l-hindi xidamna xams siniin.* The Indian boy served us (or served in our household) for five years.

استخدم *staxdam* X 1. to employ, hire. الحكومة تستخدم ناس واجد *li-ḥkuuma tistaxdim naas waayid.* The government employs a lot of people. 2. to use, make use of. في الخليج هني نستخدم أحسن موديلات السيارات *fi l-xaliij hini nistaxdim 'aḥsan modeelaat s-sayyaaraat.* Here, in the Gulf, we use the best car models.

خدمة *xidma* (v.n.) p. *-aat* 1. service. خدمني خدمة عظيمة *xidamni xidma ^{c}aḍiima.* He rendered me great service. 2. service, attendance. خدمة عسكرية *xidma ^{c}askariyya* military service.

خدوم *xaduum* p. *-iin* obliging. حمد إنسان خدوم؛ ما يقصر *ḥamad 'insaan xaduum; ma ygaṣṣir.* Hamad is an obliging person; he doesn't let you down.

خادم *xaadim* p. خدم *xadam,* خدام *xiddaam* 1. servant, manservant. عندنا خادمة هندية في البيت *^{c}indana xaadma hindiyya fi l-beet.* We have an Indian maid at home. الخادمة، طال عمرك، تطبخ

وتغسل المواعين وتنظف البيت *l-xaadma, ṭaal ᶜumrak, tiṭbax w-tġasil l-muwaaᶜiin w-tnaððif l-beet.* A female domestic servant, may you live long, cooks, does the dishes, and cleans the house. 2. servant, custodian. هو خادم من خدام الحرم في مكة *huwa xaadim min xiddaam l-ḥaram fi makka.* He is one of the custodians of the Holy Mosque in Mecca.

خدامة *xaddaama* (خادمة *xaadma* is more common) p. *-aat* woman servant, maid.

خ د و ي *xdwy*

خديوي *xdeewi* (no recorded p.) kind of an old rifle.

خ ر ب *xrb*

خرب *xirib (يخرب yxarib)* 1. to break down, get out of order, broken. السيارة خربت *s-sayyaara xribat.* The car broke down. فيه ساعات تخرب بساع *fii saaᶜaat tixrab b-saaᶜ.* There are watches that get out of order easily. 2. to be ruined, destroyed, spoiled. البلد خربت بعد غلا المعيشة *l-balad xribat baᶜd ġala l-maᶜiiša.* The country was ruined after the rise in the cost of living. خربت العمارة *xribat li-ᶜmaara.* The building was destroyed. 3. to go bad, spoil (of food). خرب الأكل *xirib l-'akil.* The food got spoiled.

خرب *xarrab* II 1. to destroy, ruin, break down. مطرت الدنيا والمطر خرب كل شي *muṭrat d-dinya w-l-muṭar xarrab kill šayy.* It rained and the rain destroyed everything. خرب السيارة لانه يسوق مثل المجنون *xarrab s-sayyaara linna ysuug miθil l-maynuun.* He ruined the car because he drives like a crazy person. 2. to put out of order, damage. خرب الساعة *xarraab s-saaᶜa.* He messed up the watch.

خراب *xaraab* ruin, state of being destroyed or ruined. السيارة خراب *s-sayyaara xaraab.* The car is ruined.

خرابة *xaraaba* p. *-aat*, خرايب *xaraayib,* disintegrating structure.

خربان *xarbaan* broken, out of order. السيارة خربانة *s-sayyaara xarbaana.* The car is broken down. إذا ساعتك خربانة، خذها حق المصلح *'iða saaᶜtak xarbaana, xiðha ḥagg li-mṣalliḥ.* If your watch is out of order, take it to the repairman.

خ ر ب ط *xrbṭ*

خربط *xarbaṭ (يخربط yxarbiṭ)* 1. to mix up, confuse, throw into disorder. خربطني بكلامه *xarbaṭni b-kalaama.* He mixed me up with his words. خربط القراطيس ولازم أسويهم عدل *xarbaṭ l-garaaṭiis w-laazim 'asawwiihum ᶜadil.* He mixed up the pieces of paper and I have to put them in order. 2. to get mixed up, malfunction. سكر وقام يخربط واجد *sikir w-gaam yxarbiṭ waayid.* He got drunk and went wild. لين يتحكى يخربط *leen yitḥačča yxarabiṭ.* When he talks, he gets mixed up. صار مريض مرة ثانية لانه خربط في الأكل *ṣaar mariið marra θaanya linna xarbaṭ fi l-'akil.* He became ill for the second time because he didn't eat right.

تخربط *txarbaṭ* to get mixed up, be confused. تخربطوا القراطيس *txarbaṭu l-garaaṭiis.* The sheets of paper got mixed up. أتخربط إذا واحد يتحكى وآنا

أقـــرا *'atxarbaṭ 'iða waaḥid yitḥačča w-aana 'agra.* I get mixed up if someone is talking while I am reading. تخربط وما درى شو يسوي *txarbaṭ w-ma dira šu ysawwi.* He got mixed up and did not know what to do. استعمل الدوا حسبما قال له الدختر، بس تخربط *sta^c^mal d-duwwa ḥasab-ma gal-la d-daxtar, bass txarbaṭ.* He used the medicine according to what the doctor told him, but he got worse.

خربطة *xarbaṭa* (v.n. from خربط *xarbaṭ*) mess, disorder confusion.

مخربط *mxarbaṭ* (p.p. from خربط *xarbaṭ*) p. *-iin* 1. mixed up, confused. القراطيس مخربطـــين *l-garaaṭiis mxarbaṭiin.* The pieces of paper are mixed up. البتـــة مخربطة *l-patta mxarbaṭa.* The (playing) cards are shuffled. 2. disorderly, messed up. شعـــرك مخربـــــط *ša^c^rak mxarbaṭ.* Your hair is messed up.

مخربـــــط *mxarbiṭ* (act. part. from خربط *xarbaṭ*) having confused, mixed up s.o. or s.th. هـــو المخربطــــــني *huwa li-mxarbiṭni.* He is the one who mixed me up. توني مخربط البتة *tawwni mxarbiṭ l-patta.* I have just shuffled the deck of cards.

خ ر ج *xrj*

خــــرج *xiraj (يخرج yxarij)* 1. to go out, walk out. خرج برة *xiraj barra.* He went outside. 2. to come out, emerge from. خرج من البيت الســـاعة ســـت *xiraj min l-beet s-saa^c^a sitt.* He left the house at six o'clock. 3. to drive or ride out, go out (in a vehicle). خرج بالسيارة *xiraj b-s-sayyaara.* He drove out in the car. 4. (with عــن *^c^an*) to disagree with, disobey. خرج عن طاعـــــة الله *xiraj ^c^an ṭaa^c^at-llaah.* He disobeyed God. الباص خرج عن سيده ودعم سيارتين *l-baaṣ xiraj ^c^an seeda w-di^c^am sayyaarteen.* The bus ran off its line and hit two cars.

خــــرج *xarraj* II 1. to graduate s.o. كم طالب تخرج الجامعـــة هـــذي الســـنة؟ *kam ṭaalib txarrij l-yaam^c^a haaði s-sana?* How many students will the university graduate this year?

أخرج *'axraj* IV 1. to throw out, eject, expel. المعلم أخرج ثلاث مشــــاغبين مـــن الصــــف *l-mu^c^allim 'axraj θalaaθ mšaaġbiin min ṣ-ṣaff.* The teacher threw out three troublemakers from class. الحكومة قامت تخرج الأجانب مـــن البلد *li-ḥkuuma gaamat tixrij l-'ayaanib min l-balad.* The government started to expatriate foreigners from the country. أخرجوه من السينما لانـــه كـــان يزعـــق *'axrajoo min s-siinama linna čaan yza^cc^ig.* They ejected him from the cinema because he was shouting. 2. to direct the production of a film. منو أخرج هذا الفلم؟ *minu 'axraj haaða l-filim?* Who directed this movie?

تخــرج *txarraj* V (less common var. *taxarraj*) to graduate. متى تخرجت؟ *mita txarrajt?* When did you graduate? تخرجت قبل سنتين *txarrajt gabil santeen.* I graduated two years ago.

اســـتخرج *staxraj* X to extract, mine, recover. يستخرجون البانزين من البـــترول *yistaxirjuun l-baanziin min l-batrool.* They extract gasoline from petroleum. صدق يستخرجون العطور من الـــورد؟ *ṣidj yistaxirjuun l-^c^uṭuur min l-ward?* Is it true that they extract perfume from flowers? الفحم ما يستخرج بسهولة مـــن

الأرض *l-faḥam ma yistaxraj b-suhuula min l-'arð̣.* Coal is not easily extracted from the ground.

خـروج *xuruuj* (v.n. from خرج *xiraj*) 1. exit. الخروج مـن هـني والدخـول منـاك *l-xuruuj min hini w-d-duxuul minnaak.* Exit is from here and entrance is from there. 2. departure. باب الخروج *baab l-xuruuj* the departure gate. 3. (with عـن *ᶜan*) disobeying, disobedience, disagreement with. الخروج عن طاعة الله *l-xuruuj ᶜan ṭaaᶜat illaah* disobeying God.

خريـج *xirriij* p. *-iin* graduate (of a school, college, etc.) هو خريـج جامعـة الإمــارات *huwa xirriij jaamiᶜat l-'imaaraat.* He is a graduate of the U.A.E. University. مؤتمر الخريجين العرب *mu'tamar l-xirriijiin l-ᶜarab* Congress of Arab Graduates.

مخـرج *maxraj* p. مخارج *maxaarij* (place of) exit, way out. ما فيـه أي مخـرج مـن هـذي الحالة الصعبة *ma fii 'ayya maxraj min haaði l-ḥaala ṣ-ṣaᶜba.* There is no way out of this difficult situation. المطار اله عشـر مخارج *l-muṭaar 'ila ᶜašar maxaarij.* The airport has ten exits.

تخـرج *taxarruj* (v.n. from V تخرج *txarraj*) graduation (from a school, college, etc.).

استخراج *stixraaj* (v.n. from X استخرج *staxraj*) extracting, mining, recovering.

خـارج *xaarij* 1. (as n.) exterior, outside. مـن الخـارج *min l-xaarij* from (the) outside. 2. foreign country or countries, the outside. من الخـارج *min l-xaarij* from abroad, foreign. *fi l-xaarij* abroad, in foreign countries. سـافر للخـارج *saafar la l-xaarij.* He traveled abroad. 3. (as prep.) out of, outside. خـارج البلـد *xaarij l-balad* outside the country.

خـارجي *xaariji* external, exterior. اسـتعمال خـارجي *stiᶜmaal xaariji* external use. عيـادة خارجيـة *ᶜiyaada xaarijiyya* outpatient clinic. وزارة الخارجيـة *wazaarat l-xaarijiyya* The Ministry of Foreign Affairs.

مخـرج *muxrij* p. *-iin* (stage or screen) director.

متخرج *mitxarrij* (act. part. from V تخرج *txarraj*) having graduated (from a school, college, etc.) هـو متخـرج مـن جامعـة الكويـت *huwa mitxarrij min jaamiᶜat li-kweet.* He has graduated from Kuwait University. من وين أنـت متخـرج؟ *min ween 'inta mitxarrij?* Where did you graduate from?

خ ر خ ر *xrxr*

خرخـر *xarxar* (يخرخـر *yxarxir)* to drip, leak. السـقف يخرخـر مـن المطـر *s-sagf yxarxir min l-muṭar.* The ceiling is dripping from the rain. السقف يخرخر *s-sagf yxarxir.* The ceiling leaks.

خ ر د *xrd*

خـردة *xarda* change, small change. ما عنـدي خـردة *ma ᶜindi xarda.* I don't have change. خردوات *xardawaat* small goods, miscellaneous small articles.

خ ر د ل *xrdl*

خـردل *xardal* (coll.) 1. mustard seeds. 2. mustard.

خ ر ر *xrr*

خر *xarr (يخر yxurr)* to drip, leak. الماي بقى يخر من السقف *l-maay biga yxuur min s-sagf.* The water continued to drip from the ceiling. الماي يخر من التانكي *l-maay yxuur min t-taanki.* The water leaks out of the (water) tank. نجمة من نجوم السما خرت *neema min nyuum s-sama xarrat.* One of the stars of the sky fell.

خ ر ز *xrz*

خرز *xiraz* (coll.) beads. s. خرزة *xraza.* p. *-aat.*

خراز *xarraaz* p. خراريز *xaraariiz* 1. cobbler, maker of old shoes and other leather goods. 2. one who works with an awl.

خ ر س¹ *xrs*

خرس *xarras* II to silence, make s.o. dumb. المدير صاح فيهم وخرسهم *l-mudiir ṣaaḥ fiihum w-xarrassum.* The manager yelled at them and shut them up.

خرس *xaras* p. خرسان *xirsaan* f. خرسا *xarsa* (غتم *ġaxam* is more common) 1. mute, dumb. 2. dumb, mute person.

خ ر س² *xrs*

خرس *xirs* p. خراس *xraas* (less common var. حب *ḥibb*) large jar made of clay, for storing water.

خ ر ش *xrš*

خرش *xaraš* p. خرش *xirš* f. خرشا *xarša* 1. inflicted with smallpox. 2. person inflicted with smallpox.

خ ر ط *xrṭ*

خرط *xiraṭ (يخرط yxariṭ)* to talk nonsense. ظليت أسمع له وهو يخرط وعقبه سكته *ðalleet 'asmaᶜ-la w-huw yxariṭ w-ᶜugba sakkatta.* I kept listening to him while he was talking nonsense, and then I silenced him.

خراط *xarraaṭ* p. خراطة *-a, -iin* braggart, bluffer.

خراطة *xraaṭa* 1. rubbish, nonsense, baloney. فلان يرمس خراطة *flaan yarmis xraaṭa.* So-and-so talks nonsense. 2. worthless thing, junk. هذي القضية أحسبها خراطة *haaði l-gaðiyya 'aḥsibha xraaṭa.* I think this problem is worthless. لا تشتري هذي السيارة، ترى خراطة *la tištiri haaði s-sayyaara, tara xraaṭa.* Don't buy this car because it's a piece of junk. الدنيا خراطة *d-dinya xraaṭa.* The world (as opposed to the hereafter) is a trifle.

خرطي *xriṭi* lies, nonsense. خرطي في خرطي *xriṭi fi xriṭi* lies, lies, and more lies.

خريطة *xariiṭa* p. خرايط *xaraayiṭ* (less common var. خارطة *xaarṭa*) 1. map, chart. خريطة العالم *xariiṭat l-ᶜaalam* world map. 2. ground, building plan, map of a small area. القزاز رسم خريطة حق أرضي *l-gazzaaz risam xariiṭa ḥagg 'arði.* The surveyor drew up a plan for my land.

خ ر ط و م *xrṭwm*

خرطوم *xarṭuum* p. خراطيم *xaraaṭiim* 1. water hose. روى الشجر بالخرطوم *riwa š-šiyar b-l-xarṭuum.* He watered the trees with a hose. 2. trunk (of an elephant). خرطوم الفيـــل *xarṭuum l-fiil* elephant trunk. (prov.) يسوي الإبـــرة خرطـــوم *ysawwi l-'ibra xarṭuum.* He makes mountains out of molehills.

الخرطـــوم *l-xarṭuum* Khartoum (capital city of the Sudan).

خ رع و ب *xr^c^wb*

خرعـــوب *xar^c^uub* p. خراعيب *xaraa^c^iib* 1. beautiful girl. 2. well-bred she-camel.

خ ر ف *xrf*

خرف *xarraf* II to be or become senile and feeble-minded. ما عليك منه. يخرف يوم عن يـــوم *ma ^c^aleek minna. yxarrif yoom ^c^an yoom.* Don't pay attention to him. He's getting more senile every day.

خريـــف *xariif* (usually الخريف *l-xariif*) autumn, fall. فصل الخريف *faṣl l-xariif* the fall season. (الصفري *li-ṣifri* is more common).

خـــروف *xaruuf* p. خرفان *xirfaan* young lamb, sheep. لحم خروف *laḥam xaruuf* lamb (meat). ذبحنا خروف علـــى عيـــد رمضـــــان *ðibaḥna xaruuf ^c^ala ^c^iid rumðaan.* We slaughtered a lamb for the Ramadan Feast.

خرافـــة *xuraafa* p. *-aat* 1. superstition. 2. fairy tale.

خرافي *xuraafi* p. *-yiin* legendary. شخص خرافي *šuxṣ xuraafi* legendary character.

مخـــرف *mxarrif* (act. part. from II خرف *xarraf*) p. *-iin* senile, feeble-minded.

خ ر گ *xrg*

خـــرق *xirag (يخرق yxarig)* to violate, break (e.g., the law). خرق القانون *xirag l-gaanuun.* He broke the law.

اخـــترق *xtirag* VIII 1. to go through, pierce. الإبرة اخترق صبعه *l-'ibra xtirgat ṣub^c^a.* The needle pierced his finger. 2. to penetrate, pass through. السيارة ما وقفت؛ اخترقت الحـــدود *s-sayyaara ma waggafat; xtirgat li-ḥduud.* The car didn't stop; it passed through the border. الجيش اخترق خطوط العدو *l-jeeš xtirag xṭuuṭ l-^c^adu.* The army penetrated the enemy lines.

خـــرق *xarg* (v.n. from خرق *xirag*) 1. piercing, boring. 2. violating, breaking (e.g., the law). خرق القانون *xarg l-gaanuun* breaking the law.

خ ر ي *xry*

خري *xiri* p. خروي *xruny* (less common var. خـــــرج *xirj* p. خروج *xruuj*) horse saddlebag. خري الخيـــل *xiri l-xeel* the horse saddlebag.

خ ز ف *xzf*

خـــزف *xizaf* (coll.) glazed pottery, earthenware.

خزفي *xzafi* (adj.) pottery, earthenware. مواعـــين خزفيـــة *muwaa^c^iin xzafiyya* earthenware dishes.

خ ز ن *xzn*

خـــزن *xizan (يخزن yxazin)* to store s.th. يخزنون الماي في توانكي كبـــيرة *yxaznuun l-maay fi tuwaanki čibiira.* They store water in big reservoirs.

خزن *xazzan* II to accumulate, store up. ما يتونســـون؛ بـــس يخزنـــون فلـــوس *ma yitwannsuun; bass yxazznuun fluus.* They don't have fun; they just accumulate money.

خزنة *xazna* p. *-aat* treasure.

خزينة *xaziina* treasury, public treasury.

مخزن *maxzan* p. مخازن *maxaazin*. 1. storeroom, warehouse. 2. supply room, stockroom. 3. store, shop (دكان *dikkaan* is more common).

تخزين *taxziin* (v.n. from II خزن *xazzan*) 1. storing, warehousing. 2. accumulation, storing up.

مخزون *maxzuun* (p.p. from خزن *xizan*) stored up, warehoused.

خ س ء *xs'*

خسى *xisa (يخسي yxasi)* to lie, not to tell the truth. فلان يخسي في كلامه *flaan yxasi fi kalaama.* So-and-so lies (in his speech).

اخس *'ixis!* (imp.) 1. Shut up! 2. Beat it! Scram!

خسة *xissa* (v.n. from خسى *xisa*) baseness, meanness.

خسيس *xasiis* p. *-iin* 1. low, mean. 2. low, mean person. هو خسيس ما له صديق *huwa xasiis ma-la ṣadiig.* He is a mean person who has no friends.

خ س س *xss*

خس *xass* (coll.) lettuce s. *-a* head of lettuce. الخس غالي اليوم *l-xass ġaali l-yoom.* Lettuce is expensive today. نبغى خس *nibġa xass.* We want (some) lettuce. اشتريت خستين *štireet xassateen.* I bought two heads of lettuce.

خ س ر *xsr*

خسر *xisir (يخسر yxasir)* to lose. خسر كل فلوسه في القمار *xisir kill fluusa fi li-gmaar.* He lost all his money in gambling. خسر الدعوة في المحكمة أمس *xisir d-daᶜwa fi l-maḥkama 'ams.* He lost the case in court yesterday. خسرناه؛ موب لاقيين أحسن منه *xisirnaa; muub laagyiin 'aḥsan minna.* We lost him; we cannot find a better person than he. فريقنا خسر أمس *fariigna xisir 'ams.* Our team lost yesterday.

خسر *xassar* II to cause loss or damage. صرت شريك واياه وخسرني كل فلوسي *ṣirt širiič wiyyaa w-xassarni kill fluusi.* I became a partner with him; he made me lose all my money. هو اللي خسرنا المباراة *huwa lli xassarna l-mubaaraa.* He is the one who caused us to lose the game.

خسارة *xasaara* (v.n. from خسر *xisir*) 1. loss. 2. waste, loss. كان دايما سكران؛ راح عمره خسارة *čaan daayman sakraan; raaḥ ᶜumra xasaara.* He was always intoxicated; his life went to waste. !خسارة *xasaara!* Pity! What a loss!

خ س ف *xsf*

خسوف *xusuuf* lunar eclipse. خسوف القمر عبارة عن غضب من الله *xusuuf l-gumar ᶜibaara ᶜan ġaḏab min 'aḷḷa.* Lunar eclipse means God's anger.

خ ش ب *xšb*

خشب *xišab* p. خشبان *xišbaan* 1. kind of a passenger ship. 2. (coll.) wood (حطب *ḥiṭab* is more common). s. خشبة *xšiba* piece or board of wood. صندوق خشب *ṣanduug xišab* wooden box.

خ ش ر xšr

خاشر *xaašar* III to be or become a partner with s.o., enter into partnership. خاشرتهم وخسرت فلوسي *xaašartahum w-xsirt fluusi.* I went into partnership with them and lost my money.

تخاشر *txaašar* VI to enter into partnership (together), form a partnership together. آنا وصاحبي تخاشرنا في التجارة *'aana w-ṣaaḥbi txaašarna fi t-tijaara.* My friend and I formed a partnership in trade.

خشير *xašiir* p. خشرا *xašra* partner (in trade).

خ ش ش xšš

خش *xašš (يخش yxišš)* to hide, conceal s.th. قل لي. لا تخش عني شي *gul-li. la txišš ᶜanni šayy.* Tell me. Don't hide anything from me.

خش *xašš* (v.n.) hiding, concealing. خش السر *xašš s-sirr* hiding the secret.

خاش *xaašš* (act. part.) p. *-iin* 1. hiding, concealing. أحس انك خاش عني شي *'aḥiss 'innak xaašš ᶜanni šayy.* I feel that you are hiding something from me. 2. having hidden or concealed s.th. ما ادري شأسوي؛ هو خاش عني شي *ma dri š-asawwi; huwa xaašš ᶜanni šayy.* I don't know what to do; he has hidden something from me.

مخشوش *maxšuuš* (p.p.) hidden, concealed. سر مخشوش *sirr maxšuuš* hidden secret.

خ ش ع xšᶜ

خشع *xišaᶜ (يخشع yxašiᶜ)* to humble oneself, be submissive. يصوم ويصلي ويخشع لله *yṣuum w-yṣaḷḷi w-yxašiᶜ li-llaah.* He fasts, prays, and humbles himself to God.

خشوع *xušuuᶜ* (v.n.) submissiveness, humbleness. الخشوع لله بس *l-xušuuᶜ li-llaah bass.* Submissiveness is to God only.

خاشع *xaašiᶜ* (act. part) p. *-iin* submissive, humble.

خ ش گ xšg

خاشوقة *xaašuuga* p. خواشيق *xuwaašiig* spoon. خاشوقة شاي *xaašuugat čaay* teaspoon.

خ ش م xšm

خشم *xašim* p. خشوم *xšuum* nose. على هاالخشم *ᶜala hal-xašim.* Consider it done. I will do it willingly. Yes, sir. (prov.) خشمك منك لو كان عوج *xašmak minnak lo čaan ᶜaway.* Do not be ashamed of your folks. (lit., "Your nose is a part of you even if it were crooked."). فلان نفسه بطرف خشمه *flaan nafsa b-ṭaraf xašma.* So-and-so is arrogant and supercilious. هذي على خشمك *haaði ᶜala xašmak.* You will do this against your will. صار قص خشوم بيناتهم *ṣaar gaṣṣ xšuum beenaattum.* They were at the brink of war. (lit., "There was a cutting off of noses between them."). يتكلم من راس خشمه *yitkallam min raas xašma.* He is haughty.

خ ش ن xšn

خشن *xašin* p. *-iin* 1. coarse, rough. بز خشن *bazz xašin* coarse cloth. جلد خشن *yild xašin* rough skin. 2. crude, uncouth. أخلاق خشنة *'axlaag xašna* crude manners. 3. hoarse, low-pitched. صوت خشن *ṣoot xašin* low pitched voice.

خشونة *xašuuna* 1. coarseness, crudeness. 2. rudeness.

أخشن *'axšan* (elat.) 1. (with من *min*) coarser, rougher than. 2. (with foll. n.) the coarsest, the roughest.

خ ش ي *xšy*

خشي *xiša* (يخشي *yxaši)* to fear, dread. ما يخشي إلا الله *ma yxaši 'illa llaah.* He does not fear anyone except God. إذا تخشى ربك تصلي وتصوم *'iða txaši rabbak tṣalli w-tṣuum.* If you fear your God, you (will have to) pray and fast.

اختشى *xtiša* VIII to feel shame, be ashamed. ما يختشي وما يستحي *ma yixtiši w-ma yistiḥi.* He doesn't feel any shame at all.

خ ص ب *xṣb*

خصيب *xaṣiib* fertile. راس الخيمة فيها أرض خصيبة *raas l-xeema fiiha 'arḍ xaṣiiba.* There is fertile land in Ras Al-Khaima. الهلال الخصيب *l-hilaal l-xaṣiib.* The Fertile Crescent.

خ ص ر *xṣr*

خصر *xaṣir* p. خصور *xuṣuur* waist

اختصار *xtiṣaar* summarization. باختصار *b-xtiṣaar* briefly, in a few words.

مختصر *mixtaṣar* brief, short. 1. عنوان مختصر *ᶜinwaan mixtaṣar* brief title. مختصر مفيد *mixtaṣar mufiid* in brief, in short, to make a long story short. 2. (p. *-aat*) summary, synopsis, abstract.

خاصرة *xaaṣra* p. خواصر *xuwaaṣir* hip, side (between the hip bone and false rib).

خ ص ص *xṣṣ*

خص *xaṣṣ* (يخص *yxuṣṣ)* to concern, pertain to s.o., be of importance to s.o. هذا شي ما يخصك *haaða šayy ma yxuṣṣak.* This is something that doesn't concern you. ما ادري؛ ما يخصني *madri; ma yxuṣṣni.* I don't know; it's not my business. عندي لك كلام يخصك *ᶜindi li-č kalaam yxuṣṣič.* I have for you some words that are of importance to you.

خصص *xaṣṣaṣ* II 1. to reserve, assign. الوزير خصص حجرة حق الاجتماعات *l-waziir xaṣṣas ḥijra ḥagg l-'ijtimaaᶜaat.* The minister reserved a room for meetings. خصصنا مكان حق الحريم *xaṣṣaṣna mukaan ḥagg l-ḥariim.* We have reserved a place for women. 2. to set aside, designate. لازم تخصص ساعتين كل يوم حق الراحة *laazim txaṣṣiṣ saaᶜteen kill yoom ḥagg r-raaḥa.* You have to set aside two hours a day for resting. 3. to appropriate, allot, allocate. الحكومة خصصت خمسة مليون درهم حق الزراعة *li-ḥkuuma xaṣṣaṣat xamsa malyoon dirhim ḥagg z-ziraaᶜa.* The government has appropriated five million dirhams for agriculture.

تخصص *txaṣṣaṣ* V to specialize, become a specialist. تخصص في الزراعة *txaṣṣaṣ fi z-ziraaᶜa.* He specialized in agriculture.

اختص *xtaṣṣ* VIII = V تخصص *txaṣṣaṣ.* هذا المحامي اختص في القانون الدولي *haaða li-mḥaami xtaṣṣ fi l-gaanuun d-dawli.* This attorney specialized in international law.

خصوصاً *xuṣuuṣan* especially. يحب اللحم، خصوصاً لحم الخروف *yḥibb l-laḥam, xuṣuuṣan laḥam l-xaruuf.* He likes meat, especially lamb.

خصوصي *xuṣuuṣi* 1. special. جواز سفر خصوصي *jawaaz safar xuṣuuṣi* special passport. 2. private, personal. سيارة خصوصية *sayyaara xuṣuuṣiyya* private car.

خاص *xaaṣṣ* 1. special. سعر خاص *si^c^ir xaaṣṣ* special price. خصم خاص *xaṣim xaṣṣ* special discount. ظروف خاصة *ðuruuf xaaṣṣa* special circumstances. بصورة خاصة *b-ṣuura xaaṣṣa* particularly, especially. 2. private. مدرسة خاصة *madrasa xaaṣṣa* private school. 3. reserved, limited. هذا الكراج خاص للموظفين *haaða l-garaaj xaaṣṣ lil-muwaððafiin.* This car park is reserved for the employees.

مخصصات *mxaṣṣaṣaat* allowances. هذي المخصصات فوق المعاش *haaði li-mxaṣṣaṣaat foog l-ma^c^aaš.* These allowances are in addition to the salary.

خ ص ل *xṣl*

خصلة *xiṣla* p. خصل *xiṣal, -aat* trait, good characteristic. الصدق خصلة زينة *ṣ-ṣidj xiṣla zeena.* Telling the truth is a good quality.

خ ص م *xṣm*

خصم *xiṣam (يخصم yxaṣim)* to deduct, discount (a bill, a note, etc.) كم تخصم لي من السعر إذا اشتريت خمسين درزن بيض؟ *čam txaṣim-li min s-si^c^ir 'iða štireet xamsiin darzan beeð?* How much would you deduct from the price if I buy fifty dozen eggs?

انخصم *nxiṣam* VII to be deducted, be discounted. انخصم ستة درهم من السعر *nxiṣam sitta dirhim min s-si^c^ir.* Six dirhams were deducted from the price.

خصم *xaṣim* (v.n. from خصم *xiṣam)* 1. discount. ما فيه خصم *ma fii xaṣim.* There is no discount. خصم خمسين في الميّة *xaṣim xamsiin fi l-miya* 50% discount. 2. (p. خصوم *xuṣuum)* opponent. خصمنا في الكورة اليوم الفريق السعودي *xaṣimna fi l-kuura l-yoom l-fariig s-su^c^uudi.* Our opposing soccer team today is the Saudi team. هذا خصم خاص لك *haaða xaṣim xaaṣṣ lak.* This is a special discount for you.

خصومة *xṣuuma* p. *-aat* dispute, quarrel, feud. فيه خصومة بيناتهم *fii xṣuuma beenattum.* There is a dispute among them.

مخاصم *mxaaṣim* (act. part. from III خاصم *xaaṣam)* having quarreled with s.o., having opposed s.o. هو اللي مخاصمني *huwa lli mxaaṣimni.* He is the one who has quarreled with me.

خ ص ي *xṣy*

خصى *xiṣa (يخصي yxaṣi)* to castrate, emasculate s.o. خصينا الخروف لاجل يمتن *xaṣeena l-xaruuf lajil yimtan.* We castrated the lamb so that it might become fat.

خصي *xaṣi* p. خصيان *xiṣyaan,* خصية *xiṣya* 1. castrate, eunuch. 2. one who cannot have sexual intercourse (with a woman).

مخصي *maxṣi* (p.p. from خصى *xiṣa*) p. *-yyiin* 1. castrated, emasculated. 2. (p. مخاصي *maxaaṣi*) castrated male, eunuch.

خ ط ء *xṭ'*

خطى *xiṭa* (يخطي *yixṭi*) to make a mistake, commit an error. آنا خطيت في حقك وأطلب منك السماح *'aana xiṭeet fi ḥaggak w-'aṭlub minnak s-samaaḥ.* I did wrong to you and I ask your forgiveness.

خطى *xaṭṭa* II to cause to make a mistake, incriminate. ما عليك منه. يخطي كل واحد *ma ᶜaleek minna. yxaṭṭi kill waaḥid.* Never mind him. He causes everyone to make mistakes.

خطا *xaṭa* p. أخطاء *'axṭaa'* mistake, wrongdoing. آنا سويت خطا وأطلب منك السماح *'aana sawweet xaṭa w-'aṭlub minnak s-samaaḥ.* I made a mistake and I ask your forgiveness. عن خطا *ᶜan xaṭa* by mistake. آنا شايلنه عن خطا *'aana šaaylinna ᶜan xaṭa.* I am carrying it by mistake. زين، كيف تصلح خطاك؟ *zeen, čeef tṣalliḥ xaṭaak?* Fine, how are you going to correct your mistake?

مخطي *mixṭi* p. *-yiin* mistaken, at fault. حصل دعمة في سوق السمك وآنا المخطي *ḥiṣal daᶜma fi suug s-simač w-aana l-mixṭi.* A car accident took place in the fish market, and I was at fault.

خ ط ب *xṭb*

خطب *xiṭab* (يخطب *yxaṭib*) 1. to make a speech, give a public address. يوم الجمعة قبل الصلاة الشيخ يخطب في الناس *yoom l-yimᶜa gabl ṣ-ṣalaa š-šeex yxaṭib fi n-naas.* On Friday, before prayer, the Shaikh gives a speech to the people. 2. to propose to, ask for a girl's hand in marriage. خطبنا البنت من أبوها *xiṭabna l-bint min 'ubuuha.* We asked the father for the girl's hand in marriage. طرش أمه لاجل تخطب له بنية جميلة *ṭarraš 'umma lajil txaṭib-la bnayya yimiila.* He sent his mother to propose to a beautiful girl for him.

خاطب *xaaṭab* III to address s.o., talk or speak to s.o. آنا أخاطبك أنت، موب واحد ثاني *'aana 'axaaṭibk 'inta, muub waaḥid θaani.* I am talking to you, not to someone else.

انخطب *nxiṭab* VII to be betrothed, become engaged. انخطبت البنت يوم الجمعة وقرينا الفاتحة *nxaṭbat l-bint yoom l-yimᶜa w-gareena l-faatḥa.* The girl got engaged on Friday and we read the first sura (from the Quran).

خطبة *xiṭba* p. خطب *xiṭab* 1. address, speech. 2. sermon. خطبة الجمعة كانت عن أعمال الخير *xiṭbat l-yimᶜa čaanat ᶜan 'aᶜmaal l-xeer.* The Friday sermon was about charitable deeds. 3. (p. *-aat*) betrothal, engagement ceremony.

خطاب *xiṭaab* p. *-aat* 1. speech, address. 2. formal letter. الوزير طرش لي خطاب تهنية بالترفيع *l-waziir ṭarraš-li xiṭaab tahniya b-t-tarfiiᶜ.* The minister sent me a letter of congratulations for promotion.

خاطب *xaaṭib* (act. part. from خطب *xiṭab*) p. خطاب *xiṭṭaab* 1. fiancé, betrothed.

خطيبة *xaṭiiba* p. *-aat* fiancée, betrothed.

خطابة *xaṭṭaaba* p. *-aat* matchmaker (f.).

خ ط ر *xṭr*

خطر *xiṭar (يخطر yxaṭir)* to occur. ما خطر على بالي شي *ma xiṭar ^cala baali šayy.* Nothing came to (my) mind. ترفع وصار تنديل. افتهمنا. والله هذا شي ما يخطر على البال *traffa^c w-ṣaar tindeel. ma ftihamna. waḷḷa haaðа šayy ma yxaṭir ^cala l-baal.* He was promoted and became supervisor. We didn't know (what was going on). This is something I can't imagine.

خطر *xaṭṭar* II to notify, inform s.o., serve s.o. notice. البلدية خطرته يطلع من البيت *l-baladiyya xaṭṭarata yiṭla^c min l-beet.* The municipal council notified him to vacate the house.

خطر *xaṭar* p. أخطار *'axṭaar* 1. danger, risk. 2. menace, danger, peril. واحد ها الشكل خطر على المجتمع *waaḥid haš-šikil xaṭar ^cala l-mijtama^c.* Someone like this is a menace to society.

خطير *xaṭiir* 1. serious, grave. ارتكب ذنب خطير *rtikab ðanb xaṭiir.* He committed a serious crime. 2. important, significant, weighty. إعلان خطير *'i^claan xaṭiir.* important announcement.

أخطر *'axṭar* (elat.) 1. (with من *min*) more dangerous, riskier. 2. (with foll. n.) the most dangerous.

خاطر *xaaṭir* p. خواطر *xawaaṭir* 1. idea, thought, notion. خطر لي خاطر *xiṭar-li xaaṭir.* I had an idea. It occurred to me. 2. sake, desire, inclination. لاجل خاطرك *lajil xaaṭrak.* for your sake. من كل خاطر *min kill xaaṭir* gladly. لخاطر الله اسكت! *la xaaṭir aḷḷa 'iskit!* For God's sake, be quiet! لخاطر الله بس عاد! *la xaaṭir 'aḷḷa bass ^caad!* For the sake of Allah, quit it! على خاطرك *^cala xaaṭrak.* as you like. خذ بخاطر *xað b-xaaṭir.* to offer condolences. خلنا نروح ناخذ بخاطره. أبوه مات أمس *xaḷḷna nruuḥ naaxið b-xaaṭra. 'ubuu maat 'ams.* Let's go offer our condolences. His father died yesterday. خاطري في هذي البنت *xaaṭri fi haaði l-bint.* I like this girl. This girl appeals to me. 2. (p. خطار *xuṭṭaar*) guest. عندنا خطار على العشا *^cindana xuṭṭaar ^cala l-^caša.* We have guests for dinner.

خطارة *xṭaara* visit, visiting (friends or relatives). جينا خطارة بس *yiina xṭaara bass.* We came only for a visit.

خ ط ط *xṭṭ*

خطط *xaṭṭaṭ* II 1. to mark off, line. خططوا ملعب الكورة *xaṭṭaṭaw mal^cab l-kuura.* They marked off the soccer field. 2. to plan, project. مجلس التخطيط يخطط حق البلد *majlis t-taxṭiiṭ yxaṭṭiṭ ḥagg l-balad.* The planning commission plans for the country.

خط *xaṭṭ* p. خطوط *xṭuuṭ* 1. line. لازم ترسم خط هني *laazim tirsim xaṭṭ hini.* You have to draw a line here. 2. line, line of communication, route. خط الباص *xaṭṭ l-paaṣ* the bus line. خط سكة الحديد *xaṭṭ sikkat l-ḥadiid* the railroad line. الخطوط الجوية الكويتية *li-xṭuuṭ l-jawwiyya l-kweetiyya* Kuwait Airlines. الخطوط الجوية العالمية *li-xṭuuṭ l-jawwiyya l-^caalamiyya* Trans World Airlines. 3. telephone line. الخط مشغول

l-xaṭṭ mašguul. The line is busy. عنده خط ثاني *ᶜinda xaṭṭ θaani.* He has another (extension) line. 4. letter. طرشت خط حق هالي *ṭarrašt xaṭṭ ḥagg hali.* I sent a letter to my family. 5. (milit.) line. الخطوط الأمامية *li-xṭuuṭ l-'amaamiyya* the front lines. 6. penmanship, handwriting. خط يد *xaṭṭ yadd* penmanship, handwriting. 7. calligraphy. الخط العربي *l-xaṭṭ l-ᶜarabi* Arabic calligraphy.

خطي *xaṭṭi* written, handwritten. جواب خطي *jawaab xaṭṭi* written answer.

خطة *xiṭṭa* p. خطط *xiṭaṭ* 1. plan, project, design. 2. policy, line of action.

خطاط *xaṭṭaaṭ* p. *-iin* calligrapher. 2. sign painter.

مخطوط *maxṭuuṭ,* مخطوطة *maxṭuuṭa* p. *-aat* (old) manuscript.

خ ط ف *xṭf*

خطف *xiṭaf* (يخطف *yxaṭif*) 1. to snatch, seize, grab. خطفوا منه فلوسه في السوق *xṭafaw minna fluusa fi s-suug.* They snatched his money from him in the marketplace. 2. to abduct, kidnap s.o. خطفوا البنت وقتلوها *xṭafaw l-bint w-gataluuha.* They kidnapped the girl and killed her. 3. to hijack. خطفوا الطيارة *xṭafaw ṭ-ṭayyaara.* They hijacked the plane.

انخطف *nxiṭaf* VII 1. to be kidnapped, abducted. ابن الوزير انخطف *'ibn l-waziir nxiṭaf.* The minister's son was kidnapped.

مخطوف *maxṭuuf* (p.p. from خطف *xiṭaf*) p. *-iin* 1. victim of kidnapping. 2. having been kidnapped, abducted. ابن الوزير مخطوف *'ibn l-waziir maxṭuuf.* The minister's son has been kidnapped. 3. having been hijacked. الطيارة مخطوفة *ṭ-ṭayyaara maxṭuufa* The plane has been hijacked.

خ ط و *xṭw*

تخطى *txaṭṭa* V to overstep, transgress. لا تتخطى حدود الله *la titxaṭṭa ḥduud 'alla.* Don't overstep the bounds (or the restrictions) that God has placed on man's freedom of action. تخطى أصول التعارف *txaṭṭa 'uṣuul t-taᶜaaruf.* He violated the customs of getting acquainted.

خطوة *xaṭwa* p. *-aat* step, pace, stride. سويه خطوة خطوة *sawwii xaṭwa xaṭwa.* Do it one step at a time.

خ ظ خ ظ *xḍxḍ*

خضخض *xaḍxaḍ* (يخضخض *yxaḍxiḍ*) to shake, rock. لا تخضخض بطل البيرة *la txaḍxiḍ boṭil l-biira.* Don't shake the beer bottle.

خ ظ ر *xḍr*

خضر *xaḍḍar* II 1. to dye or color green, to make green. خضرنا باب الدار *xaḍḍarna baab d-daar.* We colored the house door green. خضر الكفية *xaḍḍar č-čaffiyya.* He dyed the head dress green. الرنق الخضر يخضر الأشيا *r-rang l-xaḍar yxaḍḍir l-'ašya.* Green paint makes things green. 2. to turn green. الزرع كله خضر عقب المطر *z-zariᶜ killa xaḍḍir ᶜugb l-muṭar.* All the young crops turned green after the rain.

اخضر *xḍarr* IX to turn green. اخضرت

الأرض من المطر *xḍarrat l-'arḍ min l-muṭar.* The land turned green from the rain. الشجر يخضر في الربيع *š-šiyar yixḍarr fi r-rabiiᶜ*. Trees turn green in the spring.

خضر *xaḍar* p. خضر *xuḍur* f. خضرا *xaḍra* green. سيارتي خضرا *sayyaarti xaḍra.* My car is green. عيون خضر *ᶜyuun xuḍur* green eyes.

خضرة *xuḍra* 1. greens, salad greens. 2. (p. خضروات *xuḍrawaat*) vegetables.

خضار *xaḍaar* 1. green, green color. 2. vegetation, greenery.

خضيري *xḍeeri* p. *-yya* bird whose feathers are green and yellow.

خ ظ ظ *xḍḍ*

خض *xaḍḍ (يخض yxuḍḍ)* to shake. لا تخض بطل البيرة *la txuḍḍ boṭil l-biira.* Don't shake the beer bottle. خض البطل قبل ما تشرب الدوا *xuḍḍ l-boṭil gabil-ma tišrab d-duwa.* Shake the bottle before you take the medicine.

خض *xaḍḍ* (v.n.) shaking

خضة *xaḍḍa* (n. of inst.) p. *-aat* an instance of shaking. خضيت البطل خضتين *xaḍḍeet l-boṭil xaḍḍateen.* I shook the bottle twice.

خ ظ ع *xḍᶜ*

خضع *xiḍaᶜ (يخضع yxaḍiᶜ)* to submit, yield, be under one's control. البدو يخضعون حق الحاكم؟ *l-badu yxaḍᶜuun ḥagg l-ḥaakim?* Do Bedouins yield to the ruler? هذي الحرمة ما تخضع حق رجلها *haaḍi l-ḥurma ma txaḍiᶜ ḥagg riilha.* This woman doesn't obey her husband.

خضع *xaḍḍaᶜ* II to subdue, humble, subjugate. الحكومة تخضع القبايل بالطيب والا بالغصب *li-ḥkuuma txaḍḍiᶜ l-gabaayil b-ṭ-ṭiib walla b-l-ġaṣb.* The government subdues the tribes by hook or by crook.

تخضع *txaḍḍaᶜ* V to base oneself, grovel. عقبما فنشوه راح يتخضع حق الديوان الأميري *ᶜugub-ma fannašoo raaḥ yitxaḍḍaᶜ ḥagg d-diiwaan l-'amiiri.* After they fired him, he went to grovel at the Emiri Court.

تخضع *xuḍuuᶜ* (v.n. from خضع *xiḍaᶜ*) submission, obedience. الخضوع لله بس *l-xuḍuuᶜ li-llaah bass.* Submission is only to God.

خاضع *xaaḍiᶜ* (act. part. from خضع *xiḍaᶜ*) p. *-iin* having been submissive or obedient.

خ ف ر *xfr*

خفر *xaffar* II prevent a young girl from going out without a veil, as in خفروا البنت *xaffaraw l-bint.* They prevented the girl from going unveiled.

خفرة *xafra* p. *-aat* young girl, lass.

تخفير *taxfiir* (v.n. from II خفر *xaffar*) the practice of preventing a young girl from going out without a veil.

مخفر *maxfar* p. مخافر *maxaafir* guardroom, control post. مخفر شرطة *maxfar širṭa* police substation, precinct station. مخفر الحدود *maxfar li-ḥduud* the border post.

خ ف ظ *xfḍ*

خفض *xaffaḍ* II to lower, decrease,

reduce (e.g., price). إذا تخفض السعر أشتري أكثر *'iða txaffið s-si^c^ir 'aštiri 'akθar.* If you lower the price, I will buy more. لا ترفع صوتك! خفضه! *la tirfa^c^ ṣootak! xaffḍa!* Don't raise your voice! Lower it!

انخفض *nxifað* VII to drop, go down, decrease. مستوى الماي في التانكي انخفض *mustawa l-maay fi t-taanki nxifaḍ.* The water level in the reservoir went down. سعر برميل زيت انخفض هالأيام *si^c^ir barmiil zeet nxifað hal-iyyam.* The price of a barrel of oil has dropped these days.

منخفض *minxafið* (act. part.) low. أسعار منخفضة *'as^c^aar minxafða* low prices. صوت منخفض *ṣoot minxafið* low voice.

خ ف ف *xff*

خف *xaff (يخف yxiff)* 1. to become lighter, decrease in weight, lose weight. وزني خف *wazni xaff.* My weight decreased. لين تعوم وزنك يخف *leen t^c^uum waznak yxiff.* When you swim, your weight decreases. الحمل خف عليه لانه قط شنطة *l-ḥimil xaff ^c^alee linna gaṭṭ šanṭa.* The load was lighter for him because he threw away a bag. 2. to decrease. الوجع بعد ما خف *l-wuja^c^ ba^c^ad ma xaff.* The pain hasn't let up yet. 3. to get easier, lighter. الشغل حقي خف لين جا واحد يساعدني *š-šuġul ḥaggi xaff leen ya waaḥid ysaa^c^idni.* My work got lighter when someone came to assist me. 4. to be thin or sparse, to thin. السوق ذالحين زحمة. تربي شوي لين يخف الازدحام *s-suug ðalḥiin zaḥma. trayya šwayy leen yxiff li-zdiḥaam.* The market-place is now crowded. Wait a little until the crowd thins out. هو شيبة؛ شعره بدا يخف *huwa šeeba; š^c^ara bada yxiff.* He is an old man; his hair has started to thin. 5. to hurry, speed up, hasten. خف رجلك لاجل ما يفوتك الباص *xuff riilak lajil ma yfuutak l-paaṣ.* Hurry up if you don't want to miss the bus.

خفف *xaffaf* II 1. to make lighter, lighten. هذا الحمل ثقيل؛ لازم تخففه *haaða l-ḥimil θagiil; laazim txaffifa.* This load is heavy; you have to lighten it. 2. to decrease, lessen. لين توصل الجسر خفف السرعة *leen tooṣal l-jisir xaffif s-sur^c^a.* When you get to the bridge, slow down. 3. to lighten, ease, relieve. القاضي خفف عنه الحكم *l-gaaḍi xaffaf ^c^anna l-ḥukm.* The judge gave him a lighter sentence. راح الدختر لاجل يضربه إبرة تخفف الوجع *raaḥ d-daxtar lajil yuðurba 'ibra txaffif l-wuja^c^.* He went to the doctor so that he might give him a shot to ease the pain. خففوا عني الشغل أمس *xaffafaw ^c^anni š-šuġul 'ams.* They made the work lighter on me yesterday. هذي المرة المدرس رايح يخفف الأسئلة عنا *haaði l-marra l-mudarris raayiḥ yxaffif l-'as'ila ^c^anna.* This time the teacher is going to give us easier questions. 4. to lighten, thin. هذا الشاي ثقيل. خفف لي اياه *haaða č-čaay θagiil. xaffif-li-yyaa.* This tea is strong. Lighten it for me. المحسن خفف لي شعري بالمقص *li-mḥassin xaffaf-li š^c^ari b-li-mgaṣṣ.* The barber thinned out my hair with the scissors.

خف *xuff* p. اخفاف *xfaaf* hoof. خف البعير *xuff l-bi^c^iir* the camel hoof.

خفة *xiffa* (v.n. from خف *xaff*) agility, nimbleness. خفة الحركة *xiffat l-ḥaraka* nimbleness, agility. خفة الدم *xiffat d-damm* amiability, charm.

أخف *'axaff* (elat.; with من *min*) 1. lighter than, more lightweight. 2. slighter, less. 3. weaker, more diluted. 4. more agile. (with foll. n.). 1. the lightest, the most lightweight. 2. the slightest, the least. 3. the weakest, the most diluted. 4. the most agile. (See examples under خفيف *xafiif* below).

خفيف *xafiif* p. *-iin*, خفاف *xfaaf.* 1. light, not heavy, lightweight. هذا الكيس خفيف؛ تقدر تشيله *haaða č-čiis xafiif; tigdar tšiila.* This bag is light; you can carry it. شنطة خفيفة *šanṭa xafiifa* light suitcase. أكل حفيف *'akil xafiif* light, easily digestible food. حكم خفيف *ḥukum xafiif* light sentence. 2. slight, little, insignificant. وجع خفيف *wuja*ᶜ *xafiif* slight pain. شغل خفيف *šuġul xafiif* easy work. 3. thin, sparse. شعر خفيف *ša*ᶜ*ar xafiif* thin hair. 4. thin, diluted. رنق خفيف *rang xafiif* thin paint. 5. agile, nimble, quick. يده خفيفة *yadda xafiifa.* He is a fast worker. خفيف الدم *xafiif d-damm* amiable, charming. خفيف الظل *xafiif ð-ðill* likable, nice (person). شاي خفيف *čaay xafiif* weak tea. خفيف العقل *xafiif l-*ᶜ*agil* feeble-minded, simple-minded.

تخفيف *taxfiif* (v.n. from II خفف *xaffaf*) 1. lightening, easing. 2. decreasing, lessening. 3. thinning, lightening.

خ ف گ *xfg*

خفق *xifag* (يخفق *yxafig*) 1. to palpitate, throb, beat. قلبه يخفق من الخوف *galba yxafig min l-xoof.* His heart is palpitating out of fear. 2. to beat, whip (eggs, cream, etc.) خفق له بيضتين *xifag-la beeðteen.* He beat two eggs for himself.

خ ف ي *xfy*

تخفى *txaffa* V 1. to hide, keep oneself out of view. تخفى وماحد عرف وين راح *txaffa w-maḥḥad* ᶜ*iraf ween raaḥ.* He was in hiding and nobody knew where he went. 2. to disguise oneself. تخفى بعباية وبرقع *txaffa b-*ᶜ*ibaaya w-birgi*ᶜ. He disguised himself in an aba and a veil.

اختفى *xtifa* VIII 1. to hide, keep oneself out of sight. البايق اختفى حتى ما يعرفه الشرطي *l-baayig xtifa ḥatta ma y*ᶜ*arfa š-širṭi.* The thief concealed himself so the policeman wouldn't recognize him. 2. to disappear, vanish. اختفى عن الأنظار *xtifa* ᶜ*an l-'anðaar.* He disappeared from sight. تحصل هني كل شي. ولا شي يختفي من السوق *tḥaṣṣil hini kill šayy. wala šayy yixtifi min s-suug.* You can find everything here. Nothing vanishes from the market.

خفية *xifya* secretly, covertly. يروح الفندق ويشرب بيرة خفية *yruuḥ l-fundug w-yišrab biira xifya.* He goes to the hotel and drinks beer secretly.

مخفي *maxfi* p. *-yyiin* hidden, concealed. هذا طال عمرك سر مخفي *haaða ṭaal* ᶜ*umrak sirr maxfi.* This, may you live long, is a hidden secret.

متخفي *mitxaffi* p. *-yiin* disguised, in disguise. لين زخوه كان متخفي *leen zaxxoo čaan mitxaffi.* When they caught him, he was in disguise.

خ ل ب *xlb*

مخلب *mixlab* p. مخالب *maxaalib* claw, talon.

خ ل ج *xlj*

خليج *xaliij* p. خلجان *xiljaan* gulf, bay. خليج عمان *xaliij ᶜmaan* the Gulf of Oman. الخليج العربي *l-xaliij l-ᶜarabi* the Arabian Gulf. الخليج الفارسي *l-xaliij l-faarsi* the Persian Gulf.

خليجي *xaliiji* 1. characteristic of the Arabian Gulf. سمعنا أغاني خليجية *simaᶜna 'aġaani xaliijiyya.* We listened to Gulf songs. علي عبدالله خليفة شاعر خليجي *ᶜali ᶜabdaḷḷa xaliifa šaaᶜir xaliiji.* Ali Abdalla Khalifa is a Gulf poet. مجلس التعاون الخليجي *majlis t-taᶜaawun l-xaliiji.* The Gulf Cooperation Council. 2. (p. *-yyiin*) Gulf Arab. هو خليجي وهي خليجية *huwa xaliiji w-hiya xaliijiyya.* He is a Gulf Arab and she is a Gulf Arab too.

خ ل خ ل *xlxl*

خلخل *xalxal (يخلخل yxalxil)* 1. to shake. خلخل الميز لين قعد *xalxal l-meez leen giᶜad.* He shook the table when he sat down. 2. to tilt. تقدر تخلخل هذي الصخرة؟ *tigdar txalxil haaði li-ṣxara?* Can you tilt this big rock?

خ ل د *xld*

خلد *xallad* II to perpetuate, immortalize. خلدوا ذكره *xalladaw ðikra.* They perpetuated his memory.

تخلد *txallad* V to be perpetuated, immortalized. رايح يتخلد ذكره عقبما يتوفى *raayiḥ yitxallad ðikra ᶜugub-ma yitwaffa.* His memory will be immortalized after he passes away.

خالد *xaalid* p. *-iin* 1. eternal, immortal, undying. المؤمنين خالدين في الجنة *l-mu'umniin xaaldiin fi l-janna.* The faithful will be immortal inhabitants of paradise. 2. Khalid (popular male's first name); f. خالدة *xaalida* Khalida.

خ ل س *xls*

اختلس *xtilas* VIII to embezzle. اختلس مليون درهم من فلوس الشركة *xtilas malyoon dirhim min fluus š-šarika.* He embezzled one million dirhams from the company's funds.

اختلاس *xtilaas* (v.n.) embezzlement.

مختلس *mixtalis* (act. part.) p. *-iin* embezzler.

خ ل ص *xlṣ*

خلص *xilaṣ (يخلص yxaliṣ)* 1. to be freed, get rid of. انتقل وخلص من ها الشغل *ntigal w-xilaṣ min haš-šuġul.* He transferred and was relieved of this work. رايح أشتري سيارة وأخلص *raayiḥ 'aštiri sayyaara w-'axlaṣ.* I am going to buy a car and be done with it. 2. (with من *min*) to escape from, avoid. خلص من الموت بمشيئة الله *xilaṣ min l-moot b-mašii'at illaah.* He escaped from death by God's will. صيفنا في لندن وخلصنا من حر بو ظبي *ṣayyafna fi landan w-xilaṣna min ḥarr bu ḍabi.* We spent the summer in London and escaped the heat of Abu Dhabi.

خلص *xallaṣ* II 1. to finish, complete. خلصت المدرسة الثانوية *xallaṣt l-madrasa θ-θaanawiyya.* I finished high school. خلص شغله *xallaṣ šuġla.* He finished his work. خلصت سنتين وباقي عليها سنة

l-batrool l-xaamm. They extract several things (i.e., products) from crude oil.

خلاص *xalaaṣ* 1. way out, deliverance. هذي مشكلة؛ ما منها خلاص *haaδi muškila; ma minha xalaaṣ.* This is a problem. There is no way out of it. 2. it's done, there's nothing else to be said. خلاص! العشا عندنا باكر *xalaaṣ! l-ᶜaša ᶜindana baačir.* That's it! Dinner is at our place tomorrow. خلاص! الدعوة عندي *xalaaṣ! d-daᶜwa ᶜindi.* It's done! I am responsible for the case. 3. kind of dates. s. خلاصة *-a.*

خلاصة *xulaaṣa* gist, summary. خلاصة الموضوع *xulaaṣat l-mawḍuuᶜ* the gist, summary of the subject. الخلاصة *l-xulaaṣa* in short, briefly. الخلاصة، هذا موب رجال *l-xulaaṣa, haaδa muub rayyaal.* In short, that's not a man.

خلصان *xalṣaan* p. *-iin* (with من *min*) 1. rid of, free of. الحمد لله نحن خلصانين من شلاخه *l-ḥamdu lillaah niḥin xalṣaaniin min člaaxa.* Thank God, we're rid of his lying. آنا خلصان من مشاكلهم *'aana xalṣaan min mašaakilhum.* I am free of their problems. 2. finished, done, over. سيارتك خلصانة. تعال خذها *sayyaartak xalṣaana. taᶜaal xiδha.* Your car is finished. Come get it. كل شي خلصان. بس تعال *kill šayy xalṣaan. bass taᶜaal.* Everything is done. Just come over. الحفلة خلصانة *l-ḥafla xalṣaana.* The party's over. 3. gone, finished, used up. الخبز الحار كله خلصان *l-xubiz l-ḥaarr killa xalṣaan.* All the hot bread is gone. الوقت خلصان. بس خلاص *l-wagt xalṣaan. bass xalaaṣ.* The time's up.

واحدة *xallaṣat santeen w-baagi ᶜaleeha sana waḥda.* She completed two years and has one more year to go. متى تخلص من شغلك؟ *mita txalliṣ min šuġlak?* When do you get off your work? أقدر أخلص لك السيارة من الجمرك بألف درهم *'agdar 'axalliṣ-lak s-sayyaara min l-jimrig b-'alf dirhim.* I can get you the car from customs for a thousand dirhams. 2. to be or become finished, used up. متأسف ما فيه خبز حار؛ كله خلص *mit'assif ma fii xubiz ḥaarr; killa xallaṣ.* I am sorry. There is no hot bread; it's all gone. السيارة خلصت. تعال خذها *s-sayyaara xallaṣat. taᶜaal xiδha.* The car is finished. Come and take it. الكندورة حقك خلصت *l-kandoora ḥaggak xallaṣat.* Your dishdash is finished. 3. to use up, finish. لا تخلصين كل الأكل؛ أختك بعد ما كلت *la txallṣiin kill l-'akil; 'uxtič baᶜad ma kalat.* Don't eat up all the food; your sister hasn't eaten yet.

أخلص *'axlaṣ* IV to be faithful, devoted. أخلص الها إلى آخر يوم من حياته *'axlaṣ-'ilha 'ila 'aaxir yoom min ḥayaata.* He was faithful to her till the last day of his life.

تخلص *txallaṣ* V (with من *min*) to rid oneself of s.o. or s.th. لازم تتخلصين منه بالطيب والا بالغصب *laazim titxallaṣiin minna b-ṭ-ṭiib walla b-l-ġaṣb.* You will have to get rid of him by hook or crook. تخلصنا من ها القضية *txallaṣna min hal-gaḍiyya.* We got rid of this problem.

استخلص *staxlaṣ* X to extract. يستخلصون أشيا واجدة من البترول الخام *yistaxilṣuun 'ašya waayda min*

That's it. It's done.

مخلص *maxlaṣ* final offer, firm, final price. كم المخلص علـى الراديـو؟ *čam l-maxlaṣ ᶜala r-radyo?* How much is the final offer on the radio? المخلص بخمسماية درهـم *l-maxlaṣ b-xamsimyat dirham.* The final price is 500 dirhams.

أخلص *'axlaṣ* 1. (with من *min*) more faithful, loyal than. 2. (with foll. n.) the most faithful.

تخليص *taxliiṣ* (v.n. from II خلص *xallaṣ*) customs clearance, payment of duty. تخليـص البضـايع *taxliiṣ l-biðaayiᶜ* the payment of duty on merchandise.

إخلاص *'ixlaaṣ* faithfulness, loyalty, sincerity.

خالص *xaaliṣ* pure, unmixed, unadulterated. ذهـب خـالص *ðahab xaaliṣ* pure gold.

مخلص *muxliṣ* p. *-iin* loyal, faithful. صديق مخلـص *ṣadiig muxliṣ* loyal friend. رجلها مخلـص الها *riilha muxliṣ-ilha.* Her husband is faithful to her.

خ ل ط *xlṭ*

خلط *xilaṭ (يخلط yuxluṭ)* 1. to mix, blend, mingle. خلط التفاح وايـا البرتقـال *xilaṭ t-tifaaḥ wiyya l-burtagaal.* He mixed the apples with the oranges. خلـط السـميت بالمـاي *xilaṭ s-smiit b-l-maay.* He mixed the cement with water. 2. to be or become confused, mixed up. هذيل توم؛ أخلط بيناتهم *haðeel toom; 'axluṭ beenaattum.* These are twins; I confuse them with each other.

خالط *xaalaṭ* III to mix, associate with s.o. يخالط ناس مـوب زينـين *yxaaluṭ naas muub zeeniin.* He is mixing with bad people.

اختلط *xtilaṭ* VIII 1. to be mixed, blended. اختلـط الحـابل بالنـابل *xtilaṭ l-ḥaabil b-n-naabil.* Everything became confused, got into a state of confusion. اختلط السـميت بالمـاي *xtilaṭ s-smiit b-l-maay.* The cement was mixed with water. 2. to associate or mix. يختلـط وايـا الحريـم *yixtaluṭ wiyya l-ḥarim.* He associates with women.

خلط *xalṭ* (v.n. from خلط *xilaṭ*) 1. mixing, blending. 2. confusing, mistaking.

خلاطة *xallaaṭa* p. *-aat* mixer, mixing machine. خلاطة سميـت *xallaaṭat smiit* cement mixer.

اختلاط *xtilaaṭ* (v.n. from VIII اختلط *xtilaṭ*) associating, dealings (وايا *wiyya* with). يحب الاختلاط وايا الحريم *yḥibb li-xtilaaṭ wiyya l-ḥarim.* He likes to associate with women.

مختلط *mixtalaṭ* mixed. تعليم مختلط *taᶜliim mixtalaṭ* coeducation.

خ ل ع *xlᶜ*

خلع *xilaᶜ* *(يخلع yxaliᶜ)* see under چ ل ع *člᶜ.*

خ ل ف *xlf*

خلف *xilaf (يخلف yxalif)* 1. to succeed, be the successor. مات الملك وخلفه ولي العهـد *maat l-malik w-xlifa wali l-ᶜahd.* The king died and the crown prince succeeded him.

خلف *xallaf* II 1. to have descendants, have offspring. خلف درزن جهال *xallaf darzan yihhaal.* He had a dozen children. !الله يلعن اللي خلفك *'aḷḷaah yilᶜan illi xallafk!* Damn your father! 2. to leave, leave behind. لين مات خلف الهم ثروة كبيرة *leen maat xallaf-ilhum θarwa čibiira.* When he died, he left them a fortune.

خالف *xaalaf* III 1. to issue a traffic violation to s.o. كنت مسرع والشرطي خالفني *čint misriᶜ w-š-širṭi xaalafni.* I was speeding and the police officer gave me a ticket. 2. to break, violate, disobey. الدريول خالف قوانين السير *d-dreewil xaalaf ġawaaniin s-seer.* The driver violated the traffic regulations. خالف القانون *xaalaf l-ġaanuun.* He broke the law. لا تخالف رغبة أبوك *la txaalif raġbat 'ubuuk.* Don't go against your father's wishes. 3. to contradict. يخالف نفسه بساع *yxaalif nafsa b-saaᶜ.* He contradicts himself fast. 4. to be different, differ from, be inconsistent, incompatible with. اللي قلته يخالف اللي قاله *'illi gilta yxaalif illi gaala.* What I said is different from what he said. خالفته بذاك الموضوع *xaalafta b-ðaak l-mawðuuᶜ.* I differed with him on that subject. خالف تعرف *xaalif tuᶜraf.* Be different and you will be known. شرب الخمر يخالف الدين والقانون *šurb l-xamir yxaalif d-diin w-l-ġaanuun.* Drinking wine is not in keeping with religion and the law. 5. to matter, make a difference. ما يخالف *ma yxaalif* It doesn't matter. It's all right.

تخلف *txallaf* V 1. to lag behind, fall behind. كلهم جاوا. بس هو تخلف عن جماعته *killahum yaw. bass huwa txallaf ᶜan jammaᶜta.* They all came. Only he fell behind his group. 2. to fail to appear, fail to show up. تخلف عن حضور المحكمة *txallaf ᶜan ḥuðuur l-maḥkama.* He failed to appear in court. تخلف عن الخدمة العسكرية *txallaf ᶜan l-xidma l-ᶜaskariyya.* He failed to appear for his military service.

اختلف *xtilaf* VIII 1. to differ, be different. ما أبغى هذي السيارة؛ تختلف *ma 'abġa haaði s-sayyaara; tixtilif.* I don't want this car; it's different. اختلف عن *xtilaf ᶜan* to be different from. هذي السيارة تختلف عن ذيك *haaði s-sayyaara tixtilif ᶜan ðiič.* This car is different from that one. 2. to disagree, differ in opinion, argue. أختلف وياك في رايي *'axtilif wiyyaak fi raayi.* I differ with you in my opinion. اختلفوا على بداية شهر رمضان *xtilfaw ᶜala bidaayat šahar rumðaan.* They disagreed on the beginning of the month of Ramadan. اختلفوا على ملكية الأرض *xtilfaw ᶜala milkiyyat l-'arḍ.* They quarreled over the ownership of the land.

خليفة *xaliifa* p. خلفا *xulafa* 1. caliph. عقبما مات نبينا محمد الخلفا جاوا بعده *ᶜugub-ma maat nabiina muḥammad l-xulafa yaw baᶜda.* After our Prophet Muhammad had died, the caliphs came after him. 2. Khalifa (popular male's name).

خلافة *xilaafa* caliphate.

خلاف *xilaaf* p. *-aat* 1. difference. خلاف في الراي *xilaaf fi r-raay* difference of opinion. 2. disagreement. 3. dispute, controversy. 4. (with suff. pron. or foll. n.) others (than those mentioned). عطني خلافهم *ᶜaṭni xlaaffum.* Give me other than these. شفت خلاف ذوليــــك؟ *čift xlaaf ðooliik?* Have you seen other than these?

مخالفـة *mxaalafa* (v.n. from III خالف *xaalaf*) p. *-aat* 1. violation, disobeying. مخالفة القانون *mxaalafat l-ġaanuun* breaking the law. 2. traffic violation. كنت مسرع والشرطي عطاني مخالفـــة *čint misri^c w-š-širṭi ^caṭaani mxaalafa.* I was speeding and the policeman gave me a ticket.

اختــلاف *xtilaaf* (v.n. from VIII اختلف *xtilaf*) p. *-aat* 1. difference, disparity. 2. disagreement, difference of opinion. اختــلاف في الـــراي *xtilaaf fi r-raay* difference of opinion.

متخلــف *mitxallif* p. *-iin* 1. underdeveloped, backward. البلاد المتخلفـــة *li-blaad l-mitxallfa* the underdeveloped countries. 2. retarded. متخلف في عقله *mitxallif fi ^cagla.* He is mentally retarded. 3. one left behind. كلهم جاوا، بس هـــو المتخلـــف *killahum yaw, bass huwa l-mitxallif.* All of them came, but he is the one who hasn't shown up.

مختلــف *mixtilif* (act. part. from VIII اختلــف *xtilaf*) 1. different. 2. (p. *-iin*) having a different opinion, disagreeing. هو مختلف وايانا *huwa mixtilif wiyyaana.* He is in disagreement with us.

خ ل گ *xlg*

خلــق *xilag* (يخلق *yuxlug*) to create. الله خلق الدنيـــا في ســبعة أيـــام *'aḷḷa xilag d-dinya fi sab^cat 'ayyaam.* God created the world in seven days. الله خلق الناس ســوا *'aḷḷa xilag n-naas siwa.* God created people equal. (prov.) الله يخلق ومحمد يبتلي *'aḷḷa yuxlug w-muḥammad yibtili.* God proposes and man disposes (lit., "God creates and Muhammad suffers.").

اختلــق *xtilag* VIII to fabricate, make up, think up. اختلق عذر وقال إنه كـــان مريــض *xtilag ^cuður w-gaal 'inna čaan mariiḏ.* He made up an excuse and said he was sick. هذي قصة خيالية. من اختلقـــها؟ *haaði ġiṣṣa xayaaliyya. man xtilagha.* This is a fanciful story. Who made it up?

خلق *xulg* 1. temper, nature, temperament. لا تتحكى وياه ذالحين؛ ما له خلق *la tithačča wiyyaa ðalḥiin; ma-la xulg.* Don't talk to him now, he is not in the mood; he is upset. ظاج خلقـــي *ḏaaj xulgi.* I am bored. 2. (p. أخــلاق *'axlaag*) character, behavior. أخلاقه زينة *'axlaaga zeena.* He is of good character.

خلقــة *xilga* p. خلقان *xilgaan*, خلاقين *xilaagiin* 1. piece of cloth. اشتريت لك خلقة جميلـــة *štareet-lič xilga yimiila.* I bought you a beautiful piece of cloth. 2. (pl. *-aat*) natural disposition, nature. خلقـــة الله *xilgat aḷḷa* God's creation.

خلــق *xalag* p. خلقان *xilgaan* shabby, worn piece of cloth. يمش بالخلق *ymišš b-l-xalag.* He dusts with an old piece of cloth.

خلــوق *xaluug* p. *-iin* polite, of good character, well-mannered. ذاك الرجال خلوق *ðaak r-rayyaal xaluug.* That man is polite.

الخلاق *l-xallaag* God, The Creator. بنية

جميلة وخلوقة. سبحان الخلاق! *bnayya yimiila w-xaluuga. subḥaan l-xallaag!* She is a beautiful and well-mannered girl. Praise the Lord!

أخلاقي *'axlaagi* moral, ethical. فنشوه لأسباب أخلاقية *fannašoo li-'asbaab 'axlaagiyya.* They fired him for moral reasons.

مخلوق *maxluug* p. مخاليق *maxaaliig* creature, created being.

خ ل ل *xḷḷ*

خل *xaḷḷ* (coll.) vinegar.

خل *xiḷḷ* p. خلان *xiḷḷaan* friend, acquaintance.

خلل *xaḷaḷ* defect, deficiency. خلل ميكانيكي *xaḷaḷ miikaaniiki* mechanical defect.

خلال *xaḷaaḷ* (coll.) unripe dates. s. خلالة *xḷaaḷa.* الخلال، طال عمرك، هو التمر قبل ما يستوي. يكون شي خضر *l-xaḷaaḷ, ṭaal ᶜumrak, huwa t-tamir gabil-ma yistawi. ykuun šayy xaðar. xaḷaaḷ,* may you live long, are hard, firm dates before they ripen. They are somewhat green. خلالة العين *xḷaaḷat l-ᶜeen* 1. the eye ball. 2. the pupil of the eye.

خ ل و *xlw*

خلى *xaḷḷa* II 1. to leave, allow or cause s.o. or s.th. to remain. خلى السيارة في الكراج *xaḷḷa s-sayyaara fi l-garaaj.* He left the car in the garage. خليتهم في السوق. يبغون يشترون أغراض واجدة *xaḷḷeettum fi s-suug. yibġuun yištiruun 'aġraað waayda.* I left them in the marketplace. They want to buy many things. صك الباب؛ لا تخليه مفتوح *ṣikk l-baab; la txaḷḷii maftuuḥ.* Shut the door; don't leave it open. قبل ما مات خلى لهم فلوس في البنك *gabil-ma maat xaḷḷaa-lhum fluus fi l-bank.* Before he died, he left them money in the bank. ما خلت واحدة ما تحكت واياها *ma xaḷḷat waḥda ma tḥaččat wiyyaaha.* She didn't leave anyone without talking to her. 2. to keep, retain. خلها عندي الين تحتاج الها *xaḷḷha ᶜindi 'ileen tiḥtaaj-ilha.* Keep it with me until you need it. خلي عينك على الشنط *xaḷḷi ᶜeenak ᶜala š-šinaṭ.* Keep your eye on the suitcases. خلي بالك من ها القضية *xaḷḷi baalak min hal-gaðiyya.* Keep this matter in mind. خلوا له مكان جمبكم *xaḷḷuu-la mukaan yammkum.* Save him a place near you. 3. to put, place. خليت خمسة قلن بانزين في السيارة *xaḷḷeet xamsa galan baanziin fi s-sayyaara.* I put five gallons of gas in the car. خلي قشارك على الأرض *xaḷḷi gšaarak ᶜala l-'arḍ.* Put your things on the floor. 4. (with foll. imp.) a. to let, allow. خله يروح يرقد *xaḷḷa yruuḥ yargid.* Let him go to sleep. خله يلبس هدومه *xaḷḷa yilbas hduuma.* Let him get dressed. خلني أساعدك *xaḷḷni 'asaaᶜidk.* Let me help you. b. to cause, make. خله يولي! *xaḷḷa ywalli!* The hell with him! (lit. "Make him go away or get lost!") خله يروح الدريشة الثانية *xaḷḷa yruuḥ d-diriiša θ-θaanya.* Have him go to the second window. ها الأريل يخلي التلفزيون يشتغل زين *hal-'aryil yxaḷḷi t-talafizyoon yištaġil zeen.* This antenna makes the television operate well.

أخلى *'axla* IV 1. to vacate. الحكومة قالت لازم يخلون البيت حقهم *li-ḥkuuma* gaalat laazim yixluun l-beet ḥagghum. The government said that they had to vacate their house. 2. to evacuate. أخلوا المدينة 'axlaw l-madiina. They evacuated the city.

تخلى *txaḷḷa* V (with عن *ᶜan*) 1. to give up, abandon, relinquish. خلوه يتخلى عن كل أملاكه *xaḷḷoo yitxaḷḷa ᶜan kill 'amlaaka.* They made him give up all his property. ما يتخلى عن أصدقاءه عند الحاجة *ma yitxaḷḷa ᶜan 'aṣdigaa'a ᶜind l-ḥaaja.* He doesn't abandon his friends at the time of need. 2. to give up, lay down, surrender. خلوه يتخلى عن مركزه *xaḷḷoo yitxaḷḷa ᶜan markiza.* They made him give up his position. الجيش تخلى عن سلاحه *l-jeeš txaḷḷa ᶜan silaaḥa.* The army laid down its weapons.

خلا *xaḷa* open air, country.

خلة *xilla* p. *-aat* lazy, sluggish woman. بس قاعدة تتقهوى طول اليوم؛ خلة *bass gaaᶜda titgahwa ṭuul l-yoom; xilla.* She is doing nothing except drink coffee all day long; she is a lazy, sluggish woman.

خلوة *xalwa* p. *-aat* secluded room or place in a mosque for prayer and invocation of God.

خالي *xaaḷi* 1. empty, void. مكان خالي *mukaan xaaḷi* empty place. بطل خالي *boṭil xaaḷi* empty bottle. 2. vacant. بيت خالي *beet xaaḷi* vacant house. 3. free, clear, devoid (of من *min*). حليب خالي الدهن *ḥaliib xaaḷi d-dihin* fat-free milk. خالي البال *xaaḷi l-baal* clear of mind.

خ م ر *xmr*

خمر *xammar* II 1. to rise. خمر العجين زين *xammar l-ᶜajiin zeen.* The dough has risen well. 2. to let rise, leaven, raise. لازم تخمر العجين قبل ما تخبزه *laazim txammir l-ᶜajiin gabil-ma txabza.* You have to let the dough rise before you bake it. هذي الخميرة ما تخمر العجين زين *haaði l-xamiira ma txammir l-ᶜajiin zeen.* This yeast doesn't raise dough well. 3. to ferment. إذا خمر عصير العنب ما ينشرب *'iða xammar ᶜaṣiir l-ᶜinab ma yinširib.* If grape juice ferments, it won't be drinkable. 4. to cause to ferment. فيه ناس يخمرون عصير العنب ويسوون منه خمر *fii naas yxammruun ᶜaṣiir l-ᶜinab w-ysawwuun minna xamir.* There are people who ferment grape juice and make wine from it.

تخمر *txammar* V 1. to rise. خلي العجين يتخمر قبل ما تخبزه *xaḷḷi l-ᶜajiin yitxammar gabil-ma txabza.* Let the dough rise before you bake it. 2. to ferment, be in a state of fermentation. عصير العنب تخمر *ᶜaṣiir l-ᶜinab txammar.* The grape juice has fermented.

خمر *xamir* (coll.) wine. الإسلام حرم الخمر *l-'islaam ḥarram l-xamir.* Islam declared wine unlawful.

خمري *xamri* 1. rosy, reddish brown. لون خمري *loon xaxmri* wine color. 2. (p. خمارة *xmaara*) one who belongs to the Khmara tribe.

خمير *xamiir* kind of bread, the dough of which is mixed with eggs and then baked.

خميرة *xamiira* yeast.

خمّار *xammaar* p. *-a* (less common than خباز *xabbaaz*) baker.

خ م س *xms*

خمّس *xammas* II 1. to make fivefold, quintuple. عطيتني خمسة. بس ليش ما خمستهم؟ *ᶜaṭeetni xamsa. bass leeš ma xammasittum?* You gave me five. Why didn't you make them fivefold? إذا تخمس العشرة تحصل خمسين *'iða txammis l-ᶜašara tḥaṣṣil xamsiin.* If you multiply ten by five, you get fifty. 2. to divide into five parts. خمستنا اشتغلنا وحصلنا ألف درهم. خمسناهم *xamsatna štaġalna w-ḥaṣṣalna 'alf dirhim. xammasnaahum.* The five of us worked and earned one thousand dirhams. We divided them (الدراهم *d-daraahim* the dirhams) into five parts.

خمس *xums* p. اخماس *xmaas* one fifth. خمس الفلوس *xums li-fluus* one fifth of the money. خمسين *xumseen* two fifths. ثلاث اخماس *θalaθ xmaas* three fifths.

خمسة *xamsa* p. *-aat* five. كنا خمسة *činna xamsa.* We were five. كنا خمسة أنفار *činna xamsat 'anfaar.* We were five people. خمستهم *xamsattum* the five of them. خمسة دولار *xamsa duulaar* five dollars. خمسة كيلو *xamsa keelu* five kilograms. عندك دراهم خمسات؟ *ᶜindak daraahim xamsaat?* Do you have five-dirham bills?

خمستعش *xamistaᶜaš* (var. خمستعشر *xamistaᶜšar*) fifteen. ميتين وخمستعش *miiteen w-xamistaᶜaš* 215. خمستعشر دينار *xamistaᶜšar diinaar.* fifteen dinars.

خمسين *xamsiin* p. *-aat* fifty. خمسين درهم *xamsiin dirhim* fifty dirhams. خمسين كيلو *xamsiin keelu* fifty kilograms. عندك دراهم خمسينات؟ *ᶜindak daraahim xamsiinaat?* Do you have fifty-dirham bills?

الخميس *l-xamiis,* يوم الخميس *yoom l-xamiis* 1. Thursday. اليوم الخميس *l-yoom l-xamiis.* Today is Thursday. كل خميس *kill xamiis* every Thursday. كل الخميس *kill l-xamiis* Thursday, all day long. 2. on Thursday. تعال (يوم) الخميس *taᶜaal (yoom) l-xamiis.* Come on Thursday.

خميّس *xmayyis* (dim of خميس *xamiis*) Khamis (male's name).

خامس *xaamis* (the) fifth. خامس يوم *xaamis yoom* (on) the fifth day. خامس مرة *xaamis marra* the fifth time. هو الخامس *huwa l-xaamis.* He is the fifth one. خامسهم *xaamissum* The fifth (one) of them.

مخمّس *mxammas* (p.p. from II خمس *xammas*) pentagonal, having five sides or corners.

خ م ش *xmš*

خمّش *xammaš* II 1. to scratch, e.g., the face, the skin, etc., with nails or claws. القطو خمش وجهي *l-gaṭu xammaš weehi.* The cat scratched my face. 2. to pierce, go through. المسمار خمش صبع يدي *l-mismaar xammaš ṣubiᶜ yaddi.* The nail went through my finger.

خمش *xamš* (v.n.) 1. scratching. 2. piercing, going through s.th.

خ م ل *xml*

خامل *xaamil* p. *-iin* lazy, sluggish.

خ م م xmm

خم *xamm* (يخم *yximm*) 1. to sweep. الخادم كل يوم يخم الأرض *l-xaadim kill yoom yximm l-'arḍ.* The servant sweeps the floor every day. 2. to clean. خمت البيت كله *xammat l-beet killa.* She cleaned the whole house.

خمام *xmaam* p. خمايم *xamaayim* (less common var. خمة *ximma*) garbage, rubbish, sweepings. (prov.) بالنهار عمايم وبالليل خمايم *b-n-nahaar ᶜamaayim w-b-l-leel xamaayim.* Fair without and foul within. (lit., "In daylight they are turbans, i.e., holy men with turbans, and at night they are garbage, i.e., rascals, knaves, etc."). تل من الخمام في وسط المدينة؟! *tall min li-xmaam fi wisṭ l-madiina?!* (Isn't it embarrassing to find) a heap of garbage downtown?!

مخمة *mxamma* p. *-aat* broom.

خمام *xammaam* p. *-iin, -a* 1. garbage collector. 2. street sweeper.

خ ن ث xnθ

خنث *xannaθ* II to have sexual intercourse with s.o.

تخنث *txannaθ* V to be or become effeminate. فيه ناس يتخنثون في لبسهم وكلامهم بعد *fii naas yitxannaθuun fi libishum w-kalaamhum baᶜad.* There are people who are effeminate in their dress and in their speech too.

مخنث *mxannaθ* p. مخانيث *maxaaniiθ, -iin* 1. effeminate (person). 2. powerless, weak (person).

خ ن ج ر xnjr

خنجر *xanjar* p. خناجر *xanaajir* (more common var. خنير *xanyar* p. خناير *xanaayir*) dagger (usually with a curved blade). العيالة يرقصون بالسيف والخنير *l-ᶜayyaala yurguṣuun b-s-seef w-l-xanyar.* Male dancers dance with swords and daggers.

خ ن خ ن xnxn

خنخن *xanxan* (يخنخن *yxanxin*) to speak nasally, speak through the nose. لين يتحكى يخنخن *leen yitḥačča yxanxin.* When he speaks, he speaks through his nose.

خنخنة *xanxana* (v.n.) nasal twang, nasalization.

خ ن د ر xndr

خندر *xandar* (يخندر *yxandir*) to be absent-minded, distracted. لا تخندر! اسمع! *la txandir! 'ismaᶜ!* Don't be distracted! Listen!

مخندر *mxandir* (act. part.) p. *-iin* absent-minded, distracted. بس مخندر دايما *bass mxandir daayman.* He is always absent-minded.

خ ن د ر س xndrs

خندريس *xandariis* (coll.) dry, old dates, usually used as animal feed. s. *-a.*

خ ن د گ xndg

خندق *xandag* p. خنادق *xanaadig* 1. ditch. 2. trench. في الزمان الأولي كانوا الناس يحفرون خنادق حول المدينة *fi z-zamaan l-'awwali čaanaw n-naas yḥafruun xanaadig ḥool l-madiina.* In olden times, people used to dig ditches around the city.

خ ن ز ر *xnzr*

خنزير *xanziir* p. خنازير *xanaaziir* pig, hog, swine. لحم خنزير *laḥam xanziir* pork or ham. ياكل مثل الخنزير *yaakil miθl l-xanziir.* He eats like a pig.

خنزيرة *xanziira* p. *-aat,* female pig, sow. (prov.) خنزيرة ومخنوقة *xanziira w-maxnuuga.* Another black mark against him. (lit., "A sow and it has been suffocated.")

خ ن س *xns*

خنس *xinas (يخنس yxanis)* to shrink back, cower, withdraw. لين صاح عليه أبوه خنس *leen ṣaaḥ ᶜalee 'ubuu xinas.* When his father yelled at him, he shrank back. القطو خنس تحت الميز *l-gaṭu xinas taḥt l-meez.* The cat cowered under the table.

خنس *xannas* II to make cower, cow. خنس عياله بصراخه وزعاقه *xannas ᶜyaaḷa b-ṣraaxa w-zᶜaaga.* He made his children cower with yelling and shouting.

الخناس *l-xannaas* name for the Devil. أعوذ بالله من الوسواس الخناس *'aᶜuuðu b-llaah min l-wiswaas l-xannaas.* God save me from the Devil. (lit., "I seek refuge in God from the Tempter, the Devil.").

خ ن ص ر *xnṣr*

خنصر *xunṣur* p. خناصر *xanaaṣir* 1. little finger. الخنصر والبنصر *l-xunṣur w-l-bunṣur* the little finger and the ring finger. 2. gold ring women wear on the little finger.

خ ن ف س *xnfs*

خنفس *xunfus* p. خنافس *xanaafis* 1. dung beetle, scarab. 2. a Beatle.

خ ن ف ر *xnfr*

خنفر *xunfur* p. خنافر *xanaafir* (less common var. خنفرة *xanfara*) big nose. أبو خنفر *'ubu xunfur* nickname for a black slave.

خ ن گ *xng*

خنق *xinag (يخنق yxanig)* 1. to choke to death, suffocate, strangle. الجاهل خنق القطو *l-yaahil xinag l-gaṭu.* The kid strangled the cat. كان ميت في الحجرة. القاز خنقه *čaan mayyit fi l-ḥijra. l-qaaz xnaga.* He was dead in the room. The gas had suffocated him. 2. to choke. عظمة من عظم السمك خنقتني *ᶜaðma min ᶜaðim s-simač xnagatni.* One of the fishbones choked me. دخان السياير في بعض شوارع القاهرة يخنق *dixxaan s-siyaayiir fi baᶜð šawaariᶜ l-ġaahira yxanig.* The smoke from cars in some streets in Cairo chokes people.

خنق *xannag* II intens. of خنق *xinag.* شفتهم يخنقون الدجاج *šifittum yxannguun d-diyaay.* I saw them choking the chickens.

تخانق *txaanag* VI to quarrel, dispute, pick a fight (with each other). شفت عيال يتخانقون في الشارع *čift ᶜyaaḷ yitxaanguun fi š-šaariᶜ.* I saw kids quarreling in the street. ما فيه حاجة تتخانق وايا الناس *ma fii ḥaaja titxaanag wiyya n-naas.* There is no reason for you to jump down people's throats.

اختنق *xtinag* VIII 1. to choke to death, suffocate. وقف الأكل في حلقه واختنق

wugaf l-'akil fi ḥalja w-xting. The food caught in his throat and he choked to death. ما يعوم. وقع في الماي واختنق *ma yᶜuum. wugaᶜ fi l-maay w-xtinag.* He doesn't swim. He fell into the water and drowned. صار حريق في الحجرة حقه واختنق *ṣaar ḥariij fi l-ḥijra ḥagga w-xtinag.* There was a fire in his room and he suffocated.

خنق *xang* (v.n. from خنق *xinag*) strangulation, suffocation. مات خنق *maat xang.* He died by strangulation.

خنقة *xanga* (n. of inst.) p. *-aat* 1. congestion, crowding, jam. 2. madhouse, mess, crowded place. اليوم الخميس؛ السوق خنقة *l-yoom l-xamiis; s-suug xanga.* Today is Thursday; the market is a madhouse.

خ ن ن *xnn*

خنن *xannan* II to perfume, scent s.o. جاوا الخطار وخنناهم *yaw l-xuṭṭaar w-xannannaahum.* The guests came and we perfumed them.

تخنن *txannan* V to perfume oneself. تخنن قبل ما طلع *txannan gabil-ma ṭilaᶜ.* He perfumed himself before he went out.

خنين *xaniin* (less common var. خنة *xinna*) fragrance, sweet smell. (prov.) لا خنينة ولا بنت رجال *la xniina wala bint rjaal.* It's utterly useless. (lit., "She is neither sweet-smelling nor of a good family.")

خ و خ *xwx*

خوخ *xoox* (coll.) peaches. s. *-a* p. *-aat.* طال عمرك، الخوخ ما يطلع هني *ṭaal ᶜumrak, l-xoox ma yiṭlaᶜ hini.* May you live long, peaches do not grow here. اشتريت خوخ *štireet xoox.* I bought (some peaches). كم الخوخ؟ *čam l-xoox?* How much are peaches? كليت ثلاث خوخات *kaleet θalaθ xooxaat.* I ate three peaches.

خ و ر ١ *xwr*

خور *xawwar* II to embroider s.th. الخياطة خورت نفنوف العروسة *l-xayyaaṭa xawwarat nafnuuf l-ᶜaruusa.* The seamstress embroidered the bride's dress.

تخور *txawwar* V to be embroidered. النفنوف تخور *n-nafnuuf txawwar.* The dress was embroidered.

مخور *mxawwar* (p.p. from II خور *xawwar*) embroidered.

خ و ر ٢ *xwr*

خور *xoor* p. خيران *xiiraan* gulf, bay. الخور عبارة عن قسم من البحر *l-xoor ᶜibaara ᶜan gisim min l-baḥar.* A *xoor* is, in other words, a part of the sea. خور فكان *xoor fakkaan* Khor Fakkan (dependency of Sharja). خور دبي *xoor dbayy* The Gulf of Dubai (which divides Dubai into two parts).

خ و ز *xwz*

خاز *xaaz (يخوز yxuuz)* (with عن *ᶜan*) to keep away from, avoid s.o. or s.th. لازم تخوز عن الشر *laazim txuuz ᶜan š-šarr.* You should keep away from evil. إذا كنت بلنش وضربك الطوفان تقدر في طرف تخوز عنه *'iða čint b-lanč w-ðarabk ṭ-ṭuufaan tigdar fi ṭaraf txuuz ᶜanna.* If you were in a boat and were hit by the waves, you can avoid them by moving aside. خوز عني! *xuuz* goodness!

خ و ش گ *xwšg*

خاشوقة *xaašuuga* p. خواشيق *xawaašiig* spoon. خاشوقة مال أكل *xaašuuga maal 'akil* table spoon. خاشوقة مال شاي *xaašuuga maal čaay,* خاشوقة مال كوب *xaašuuga maal kuub* teaspoon.

خ و ص *xwṣ*

خوص *xooṣ* (coll.) palm leaves. s. *-a* p. خوص *xuwaṣ* 1. palm leaf. 2. gold bracelet in the form of a coil.

خ و ظ *xwð̣*

خوض *xaað̣ (يخوض yxuuð̣)* to wade in the water. رفع الكندورة حقه وطب يخوض في الماي *rifa*c *l-kandoora ḥagga w-ṭabb yxuuð̣ fi l-maay.* He lifted his dishdash and went wading in the water.

خ و ف *xwf*

خاف *xaaf (يخاف yxaaf)* to be scared, afraid, worried, concerned. (prov.) لا تبوق ولا تخاف *la tbuug w-la txaaf.* If you don't steal, you don't have to be scared (of anyone or anything). لا تخاف؛ روح! ما فيه شرطي *la txaaf; ruuḥ! ma fii širti.* Don't be afraid; go! There isn't a policeman. أخاف ما أقدر أشوفه *'axaaf ma 'agdar 'ašuufa.* I am afraid I won't be able to see him. يخاف من الكلاب *yxaaf min li-člaab.* He is afraid of dogs. لا تخاف عليه؛ يعرف كيف يتصرف *la txaaf* c*alee; y*c*arf čeef yitṣarraf.* Don't worry about him; he knows how to conduct himself. خاف الله! ما تصوم رمضان؟ *xaaf 'aḷḷa! ma tṣuum rumð̣aan?* Fear God! Why don't you fast the month of Ramadan? ما جا

c*anni!* Go away! Beat it! الحريم ما يخوزن من الدار *l-ḥariim ma yxuuzin min d-daar.* Women do not leave the house.

خوز *xawwaz* II to take away, move away (usually s.th. bad or evil). الله يخوز عنك الشر إذا صليت وصمت *'aḷḷa yxawwwiz* c*annak š-šarr 'iða ṣalleet w-ṣumt.* God will keep away evil from you if you pray and fast.

خ و ز گ *xwzg*

خوزق *xoozag (يخوزق yxoozig)* to cheat, get s.o. into a bad fix, take in s.o. ما اشتري منه؛ يخوزق الناس *ma 'aštiri minna; yxoozig n-naas.* I won't buy from him; he cheats people.

تخوزق *txooxag (يتخوزق yitxoozag)* to get stuck, to be taken in. اشتريتها منه وتخوزقت *štireetha minna w-txoozagt.* I bought it from him and I was taken in.

خازوق *xaazuug* p. خوازيق *xawaaziig* post, stake, pole. كل خازوق *kal xaazuug.* He got the shaft, he was taken in.

خ و ش *xwš*

خوش *xooš* 1. good, fine, excellent. خوش بيت *xooš beet* good house. خوش سيارة *xooš sayyaara* good car. هذا حقي وهذا حقك. خوش *haaða ḥaggi w-haaða ḥaggak. xooš.* This is mine and this is yours. Fine. خوش حكي *xooš ḥači.* Good idea, now you're talking. 2. (expresses surprise or scorn) my-oh-my! my goodness! سرق أموال الشركة. خوش والله! *sirag 'amwaal š-šarika. xooš waḷḷa!* He stole the company funds. My-oh-my! My

وايانا يتونس. أخاف ما عنده فلوس *ma ya wiyyaana yitwannas. 'axaaf ma* ᶜ*inda fluus.* He didn't come with us to have a good time. I'm afraid he didn't have money.

خوف *xawwaf* II to scare, frighten, alarm. خوفني لين طمر ووقف قدامي *xawwafni leen ṭumar w-wugaf jiddaami.* He scared me when he jumped and stood in front of me. القطو طمر من الدرام وخوفني *l-gaṭu ṭumar min d-draam w-xawwafni.* The cat jumped out of the (garbage) can and scared me. خوفني كلش لين شفته ينزف دم *xawwafni killiš leen čifta yinzif damm.* He scared me to death when I saw him bleeding. ها الزلازل والبراكين تخوف *ha z-zalaazil w-l-baraakiin txawwif.* These earthquakes and volcanoes are alarming.

خوف *xoof* (v.n. from خاف *xaaf*) fear, fright. شرد من الخوف *širad min l-xoof.* He ran away out of fear. خوفي عليك *xoofi* ᶜ*aleeč.* I am concerned about you; I care for you.

خايف *xaayif* (act. part. from *xaaf*) p. *-iin* afraid, scared. هو خايف من الكلب *huwa xaayif min č-čalb.* He is afraid of the dog. خايف يعوم *xaayif y*ᶜ*uum.* He is afraid to swim.

خ و ل *xwl*

خول *xawwal* II to authorize. من خولك توقع على ذيل الأوراق؟ *man xawwalk twaggi*ᶜ ᶜ*ala ðeel l-'awraag?* Who authorized you to sign these papers?

خال *xaaḷ* p. أخوال *'axwaaḷ* maternal uncle. خالي بغى يزوج أختي حق ولده *xaaḷi baġa yzawwij 'ixti ḥagg wilda.* My maternal uncle wanted to marry my sister to his son.

خالة *xaaḷa* p. *-aat* 1. maternal aunt. 2. (form of addressing an old lady) madam (approx.)! يا خالة، وين تبين تروحين *ya xaaḷa, ween tabiin truuḥiin?* Ma'am, where do you want to go?

تخويل *taxwiil* (v.n. from II خول *xawwal*) authorization.

خ و ن ١ *xwn*

خان *xaan* (يخون *yxuun*) 1. to betray. زخوه وقطوه السجن لانه خان وطنه *zaxoo w-gaṭṭoo s-sijin linna xaan waṭana.* They arrested him and put him in jail because he betrayed his country. لا تعلمه بشي ترى يخونك *la t*ᶜ*allma b-šayy tara yxuunak.* Don't tell him anything or he will give you away. 2. to cheat, deceive. حرمته تخونه دايما *ḥurumta txuuna daayman.* His wife is cheating on him all the time.

خون *xawwan* II 1. to consider or call s.o. treacherous, unfaithful, disloyal. خوني بشي طول عمري ما سويته *xawwanni b-šayy ṭuul* ᶜ*umri ma sawweeta.* He made me out to be dishonest in something I have never done. 2. to mistrust, be suspicious of. دايما يخون الناس اللي يشتغلون وياه *daayman yxawwin n-naas illi yištaġluun wiyyaa.* He always mistrusts the people who work with him.

خاين *xaayin* p. خونة *xawana* traitor.

خ و ن ٢ *xwn*

خان *xaan.* See under خ ا ن *xaan.*

خ و ي *xwy*

خـوي *xawi* p. خويـان *xwayyaan* 1. travelling companion. الحرمة مـا تسـافر بروحها؛ لازم يكـون وياهـا خـوي *l-ḥurma ma tsaafir b-ruuḥḥa; laazim ykuun wiyyaaha xawy.* A woman doesn't travel by herself; there has to be a travelling companion with her.

خ ي ب *xyb*

خـاب *xaab (يخيب yxiib)* to be lowered, let down, dashed. خاب ظني فيك *xaab ḍanni fiik.* My opinion of you has been lowered. خاب أملي في القزاز الجديد *xaab 'amali fi l-gazzaaz l-yidiid.* My hope in the new surveyor was dashed.

خيـب *xayyab* II to disappoint, let down, dash. خيـب أملي فيـه *xayyab 'amali fii.* He disappointed my hope for him.

خـايب *xaayib* (act. part. from خـاب *xaab*) p. *-iin* unsuccessful, failing. خـايب في حياتـه *xaayib fi ḥayaata.* He is unsuccessful in his life.

خ ي ا ر *xyaar*

خيـار *xyaar* (coll.) cucumbers. s. *-a* p. *-aat.* الخيـار غـالي اليـوم *li-xyaar ġaali l-yoom.* Cucumbers are expensive today. ما فيه خيـار زيـن في السـوق *ma fii xyaar zeen fi s-suug.* There aren't good cucumbers in the market. كليت خيارتين *kaleet xyaarteen.* I ate two cucumbers. أبي خمـس خيـارات *'abi xams xyaaraat.* I want five cucumbers.

خ ي ر *xyr*

خير *xayyar* II to let s.o. choose, to give a choice to s.o. الشركة خيرتني بين الشـغل في دبـي والا بوظـبي *š-šarika xayyaratni been š-šuġul fi dbayy walla bu ḍabi.* The company gave me the choice between work in Dubai or Abu Dhabi.

تخير *txayyar* V to choose, take one's choice. تخير: لو تروح الشارجة والا عجمان *txayyar: lo truuḥ š-šaarja walla ᶜayman.* Take your choice: either you go to Sharja or Ajman.

اختـار *xtaar* VIII to choose, select, pick. اخـترت الأزيـن *xtart l-azyan.* I chose the best. منـو اختـار هـا القميص *minu xtaar hal-gamiiṣ?* Who picked this shirt?

خـير *xeer* 1. good thing, blessing. حصل خـير انشـاالله *ḥiṣal xeer nšaaḷḷa.* I hope something good happened. I hope there was a good thing. ما حصل إلا خـير *ma ḥiṣal 'illa xeer.* Nothing bad happened. هـذا كلـه خـير مـن الله *haaḍa killa xeer min aḷḷa.* All of this is a blessing from God. 2. wealth. فيه خير واجد في الخليج *fii xeer waayid fi l-xaliij.* There is great wealth in the Gulf. هذيل أهـل خـير *haḍeel 'ahil xeer.* These are wealthy people. 3. good, benefit, advantage. هـذا رجـال مـا فيـه خـير. مـا يسـاعد أحـد *haaḍa rayyaal ma fii xeer ma ysaaᶜid 'aḥad.* This is a man from whom no benefit can be expected. He doesn't help anyone. إذا فيه خير، يقـدر يجـي يسـاعدنا *'iḍa fii xeer, yigdar yiji ysaaᶜidna.* If he is the man he thinks he is, he can come to help us. 4. good, excellent, outstanding, prosperous. اليوم خير. حدقنا وصدنا سمك واجد ودينـاه الجـبرة *l-yoom xeer. ḥidagna w-ṣidna simač waayid w-waddeenaa č-čabra.* Today was prosperous. We went fishing, caught a lot of fish, and took them to the (fish) market. 5. charity. أعمـــال الخـــير *'acmal l-xeer* charitable deeds. صبحك الله بالخـــير *ṣabbaḥk aḷḷa b-l-xeer.* Good morning. مساك الله بالخير *massaak aḷḷa b-l-xeer.* Good afternoon. Good evening. خير انشاالله *xeer nšaaḷḷa.* I hope everything's all right. مشكور. آنا بخير *maškuur. 'aana bxeer.* Thanks. I am fine. 6. (p. خـــيرات *xeeraat*) resources, treasures. خيرات بلادنا ما لها عد *xeeraat blaadna ma laha cadd.* The resources of our country are innumerable.

خـــيري *xayri* charitable. جمعية خيريـــة *jamciyya xayriyya* charitable organization. أعمـــال خيريـــة *'acmaal xayriyya* charitable deeds.

اختيـــار *xtiyaar* (v.n. from VIII اختار *xtaar*) choice, selection. عرســـت باختيارها *carrasat b-xtiyaarha.* She got married of her own accord.

اختيـــاري *xtiyaari* 1. voluntary. خدمة اختياريـــة *xidma xtiyaariyya* voluntary service. تبرع اختياري *tabarruc xtiyaari* voluntary contribution. 2. optional. الحضـــور اختيـــاري *l-ḥuðuur xtiyaari.* Attendance is optional. 3. elective. مـــواد اختياريـــة *mawaadd xtiyaariyya* elective courses (of study).

خ ي ز ن *xyzn*

خـــيزران *xeezaraan* (coll.) 1. cane, rattan. 2. cane plant. خيزرانـــة *xeezaraana* p. *-aat* cane, stick.

خ ي س *xys*

خاس *xaas (يخيس yxiis)* to spoil, go bad. خاس الحليب لانه ما كان في الثلاجـــة *xaas l-ḥaliib linna ma čaan fi θ-θallaaja.* The milk spoiled because it wasn't in the refrigerator. الماي في الحوض يخيس إذا تركته مدة طويلـــة *l-maay fi l-ḥooð yxiis 'iða tirakta mudda ṭawiila.* The water in the trough will get stagnant if you leave it for a long time.

خيـــس *xayyas* II to cause to spoil, rot. الحر يخيس الحليب *l-ḥarr yxayyis l-ḥaliib.* Heat spoils milk. (prov.) الســـمكة الخايسة تخيـــس الســـمك كلـــه *li-smiča l-xaaysa txayyis s-simač killa.* A rotten apple spoils the whole barrel.

خيـــاس *xyaas* (v.n. from خاس *xaas*) rotten smell. إذا رحت جبرة السمك مـــا تشم إلا خيـــاس *'iða riḥt čabrat s-simač ma tšimm 'illa xyaas.* If you go to the fish market, you will smell nothing except rottenness.

خيســـة *xeesa* (فطيســـة *ftiisa* is more common) 1. carcass, carrion. 2. rotten smell.

خـــايس *xaayis* (act. part. from خاس *xaas*) 1. rotten, spoiled. سمك خايس *simač xaayis* rotten fish. 2. (p. *-iin*) dishonest, mannerless person.

خايسة *xaaysa* p. *-aat* whore, prostitute.

خ ي ش *xyš*

خيش *xeeš* (coll.) canvas, sackcloth. s. خيشة *-a* p. *-aat* 1. piece of sackcloth. 2. bag, sack of canvas, sackcloth (for keeping grains, flour, sugar or onions). نحن نشتري العيش بالخيشـــة *niḥin ništiri l-cееš b-l-xeeša.* We buy rice in big canvas bags. خـــم الأرض بخيشـــة! *xim l-'arð b-xeeša!* Mop the floor with a piece of coarse canvas!

خ ي ط xyṭ

خـــاط *xaaṭ (يخيط yxiiṭ)* 1. to sew. أمي تخيط كلش زيــــن *'ummi txiiṭ killiš zeen.* My mother sews very well. 2. to tailor. من خاط لك ها الثوب؟ *man xaaṭ-lak ha θ-θoob?* Who made this dishdash for you?

خيط *xayyaṭ* II = خاط *xaaṭ.*

خيــــط *xeeṭ* p. خيوط *xuyuṭ* 1. thread, string. 2. (fishing) line. كنا نحــــدق بالميادير، يعني بـــــالخيوط والدجيــــج *činna nḥadig b-l-mayaadiir, yaᶜni b-li-xyuuṭ w-d-dijiij.* We were fishing with lines, rods, and nets. 3. necktie. فلان شاد خيـــــط *flaan šaadd xeeṭ.* So-and-so is wearing a necktie.

خياطـــة *xyaaṭa* (v.n. from خاط *xaaṭ*) sewing. ماكينة خياطة *maakiinat xyaaṭa* sewing machine.

خياط *xayyaaṭ* p. *-iin* tailor.

خياطة *xayyaaṭa* p. *-aat* seamstress.

خ ي ل ١ xyl

تخيـــــل *txayyal* V to imagine. تخيل نفسه حـــــاكم *txayyal nafsa ḥaakim.* He imagined being a ruler.

خيال *xayaal* 1. imagination. خيال واسع *xayaal waasiᶜ* vivid imagination. 2. shadow. يخاف مـــــن خيالــــه *yxaaf min xayaala.* He is afraid of his own shadow.

خ ي ل ٢ xyl

خيــــل *xiyil (يخيـــــل yxayil)* = خجل *xijil (يخجل yxajil).* See under **خ ج ل** *xjl.*

تخيــــل *txayyal* V 1. to cover, veil oneself. الحرمة تخيلت قبل ما طلعت بـــــرة *l-ḥurma txayyalat gabil-ma ṭlaᶜat barra.* The woman veiled herself before she went out. 2. to be or feel embarrassed. سالم يطلبني بألف درهـــــم. أتخيل أسير حقــــه *saalim yuṭlubni b-'alf dirhim. 'atxayyal 'asiir ḥagga.* I owe Salim one thousand dirhams. I am embarrassed to go to him.

خيل *xayal* (v.n. from خيل *xiyil*) = خجل *xijil.* See under **خ ج ل** *xjl.*

خ ي ل ٣ xyl

خيل *xeel* horses. s. حصان *ḥsaan* horse.

خيال *xayyaal* p. *-a* horseman, rider.

خيالة *xayyaala* cavalry. شرطة خيالة *širṭa xayyaala* mounted police.

خ ي م xym

خيم *xayyam* II 1. to pitch a tent, set up camp. كشتنـــا وخيمنـــا في راس الخيمـــة *kišatna w-xayyamna fi raas l-xeema.* We had a picnic and set up camp in Ras Al-Khaima. 2. to settle (said of the night). خيـــم الليـــل *xayyam l-leel.* Night settled. It was night.

خيمـــــة *xeema* p. خيام *xyaam* tent. البدو يســـكنون في الخيـــام *l-badu yiskinuun fi li-xyaam.* Bedouins live in tents. راس الخيمـــة *raas l-xeema* Ras Al-Khaima (one of the U.A.E. emirates).

مخيــــــم *mxayyam* p. *-aat* campground, camp. مخيم لاجئـــــين *mxayyam laaj'iin* refugee camp.

د

داب daabb

داب *daabb* p. ديبان *diibaan* snake. (prov.) من عضه الداب ينقز من الحبل *man* *ᶜaḏḏa d-daab yangiz min l-ḥabil.* Once bitten twice shy. (lit., "He who has been bitten by a snake fears a rope.")

داحوس daaḥws

داحوس *daaḥuus* p. دواحيس *dawaaḥiis* small reddish snake.

دارسين daarsyn

دارسين *daarsiin* (coll.) cinnamon. شاي دارسين *čaay daarsiin.* tea flavored with cinnamon.

داس daas

داس *daas* or جزيرة داس *yiziirat daas.* Das Island (in Abu Dhabi).

دال daas

دال *daal* 1. name of the letter *d* د. 2. (coll.) lentils. s. *-a* p. *-aat* شوربة دال *šuurbat daal.* lentil soup.

دان daan

دان *daan* (coll.) 1. cannonballs. 2. bombs. s. *-a* pl. *-aat* 1. cannonball. 2. large pearl.

داي daay

داية *daaya* pl. *-aat* 1. midwife. 2. female servant. 3. wet nurse.

دبا dbaa

دبا *diba* 1. Deba (dependency of Sharja). 2. (coll.) locusts. s. دبا *dibaa.*

دبب dbb

دب *dabb* (يدب *ydibb)* to fall down and hit the ground with a thud. سنهو اللي دب؟ *šinhu lli dabb?* What is the thing that fell down with a thud?

دب *dubb* p. ادباب *dbaab* bear. الدب الأصغر *d-dubb l-'aṣġar* Little Bear, Ursa Minor. الدب الأكبر *d-dubb l-'akbar* Great Bear, Ursa Major.

دبة *dabba* p. *-aat* (*šanṭa* is less common) car trunk.

دباب *dabbaab* p. *-aat* (بطبطة *buṭbuṭa* is less common) motorcycle.

دبابة *dabbaaba* p. دواب *dawaabb* 1. animal, beast. 2. riding animal (donkey, mule, horse).

دبدب dbdb

دبدب *dabdab* (يدبدب *ydabdib)* 1. to make noise like a motorcycle. 2. to tap, tread heavily.

دبدبة *dabdaba* (v.n.) 1. motorcycle noise. 2. sound of heavy footsteps.

دبر dbr

دبر *dabbar* II 1. to manage, handle, arrange. أقدر أدبر لك سيارة *'agdar 'adabbir-lak sayyaara.* I can manage to get a car for you. هو دبر لي شغل في الشركة *huwa dabbar-li šuġul fi š-šarika.* He arranged a job for me with the company. ما يقدر يدبرها *ma yigdar ydabbir-ha.* He cannot handle it. 2. to contrive, devise, work at

دبروا خطة يتخلصون فيها من الحاكم *dabbaraw xiṭṭa yitxallaṣuun fiiha min l-ḥaakim.* They worked out a plan for getting rid of the ruler.

تدبر *ddabbar* V to be arranged, managed. الكشتة تدبرت *l-kašta ddabbarat.* The picnic was arranged. الفلوس رايحة تتدبر *li-fluus raayḥa tiddabbar.* The money will come through.

تدبير *tadbiir* (v.n.) 1. organization, planning, preparation. تدبير منزلي *tadbiir manzili.* home economics. 2. (p. تدابير *tadaabiir*) measure, step, move. سوي لي تدبير. ما عندي تأشيرة *sawwii-li tadbiir. ma ᶜindi ta'šiira.* Show me a way out. I don't have a visa.

مدبر *mdabbar* (p.p.) well-organized. كل شي مدبر، الحمد لله *kill šayy mdabbar, l-ḥamdu li-llaah.* Everything is well-organized, thank God.

د ب س *dbs*

دبس *dibs* (coll.) date molasses. (prov.) ما تقدر تطول الدبس من طيز النمس *ma tigdar ṭṭuul d-dibs min ṭiiz n-nims.* You cannot gather grapes from thorns. (lit., "You cannot get molasses from the anus of a weasel.")

د ب ش *dbš*

دبش *dabaš* (coll.) animals, such as sheep, goats, cows and donkeys. s. دبشة *dabša.* (used figuratively) stupid, dull-witted person. (prov.) كان ما عندك سند اقبض فلوسك من دبش *čaan ma ᶜindak sanad 'igbaḍ fluusak min dabaš.* You have no proof. Where's your proof? (lit., "If you don't have legal papers, collect your money from animals."). عنده أراضي وحريم ودبش وما ادري شبعد *ᶜinda 'araaḍi w-ḥariim w-dabaš w-ma dri š-baᶜad.* He has land, women, cattle, and I don't know what else.

د ب غ *dbġ*

دبغ *dibaġ* (يدبغ *yidbaġ*) to tan s.th. يشترون جلود ويدبغونها *yištiruun jluud w-yidbaġuunha.* They buy hides and tan them.

دباغة *dbaaġa* (v.n.) tanning, tanner's trade.

دباغ *dabbaaġ* p. *-a, -iin* tanner.

مدبغة *madbaġa* p. مدابغ *madaabiġ* tannery.

مدبوغ *madbuuġ* (p.p. from دبغ *dibaġ*) tanned. جلود مدبوغين *jluud madbuugiin* tanned hides.

د ب ل *dbl*

دبل *dabbal* II to double s.th. دبلت له المبلغ *dabbalt-la l-mablaġ.* I doubled the amount of money for him.

دبل *dabal* double. عطيته المبلغ دبل *ᶜaṭeeta l-mablaġ dabal.* I gave him double the amount of money.

د ب ل و م *dblwm*

دبلوم *dibloom* p. *-aat* diploma or certificate (awarded after the completion of two years at a training or a commercial college).

د ب ل و م س *dblwms*

دبلوماسي *diblomaasi* 1. diplomatic. 2. (p. *-yiin*) diplomat.

دبلوماسية *diblomaasiyya* diplomacy.

د ب ي ي *dbyy*

دبي *dbayy* (less common var. *dubayy*) 1. the Emirate of Dubai. 2. Dubai (the capital city).

د ج ج *djj*

دجاج *dijaaj*. See under **د ي ي** *dyy*.

د ج ل ۱ *djl*

دجل *dajjal* II (with على *ᶜala*) to swindle, cheat. خله يولي، هذا يدجل على كل واحد *xalla ywalli, haaða ydajjil ᶜala kill waaḥid.* Don't listen to him; he cheats everyone.

دجل *dajal* (v.n.) trickery, deceit.

دجال *dajjaal* p. *-iin* impostor, swindler.

د ج ل ۲ *djl*

دجلة *dijla* or نهر دجلة *nahar dijla* the Tigris River.

د ج ي ج *djyj*

دجيج *dijiij* 1. net used for trapping fish, fishing net. بعض السماميك يصيدون سمك بالدجيج *baᶜð̣ s-simaamiič yṣiiduun simač b-d-dijiij.* Some fishermen catch fish with nets. 2. (adj.) thin, skinny. See under **د گ گ** *dgg.*

د چ چ ۱ *dčč*

دك *dačč* (يدك *ydičč*) to fill, stuff, pack. دك بطنه دجاج *dačč baṭna diyaay.* He filled his stomach with chicken. دك أربع بناطلين في الشنطة *dačč 'arbaᶜ banaaṭliin fi š-šanṭa.* He stuffed four pairs of pants into the suitcase.

دك *dačč* (v.n.) stuffing, filling, packing.

د چ چ ۲ *dčč*

دج *dačč* (يدج *ydičč*) to lose one's way, to get lost. دج في البر *dačč fi l-barr.* He got lost in the desert.

دج *dačč* (v.n.) losing one's way, getting lost.

د خ ت ر *dxtr*

دختر *daxtar* p. دخاتر *daxaatir,* دخاترة *daxaatra* (less common var. دختور *daxtoor*) doctor (medical doctor and Ph.D.). f. دختورة *daxtoora* p. *-aat.* كشف علي الدختر وقال لازم أنام في المستشفى *kišaf ᶜalayya d-daxtaar w-gaal laazim 'anaam fi l-mustašfa.* The doctor examined me and said that I had to be hospitalized.

د خ ل *dxl*

دخل *dixal* (يدخل *yadxul)* 1. to enter, go in. (دش *dašš* is more common). ما قدرت أدخل لأن الباب كان مصكوك *ma gidart 'adxul li'an l-baab čaan maṣkuuk.* I couldn't enter because the door was locked. ادخل، الباب مفتوح *'udxul, l-baab maftuuḥ.* Come in, the door is open. ماحد يقدر يدخل على المدير ذالحين *maḥḥad yidgar yudxul ᶜala l-mudiir ðalḥiin.* No one can go in to (see) the director now. البايق يدخل السجن *l-baayig yadxul s-sijin.* A thief will be imprisoned. اللي يچلخ يدخل جهنم *'illi yčallix yadxul jahannam.* He who lies will go to hell. دخل كلية الزراعة *dixal kulliyyat z-ziraaᶜa.* He entered the college of agriculture. دخل الكلية الحربية *dixal l-kulliyya* *l-ḥarbiyya.* He enlisted in the military college. 2. (with علـى *ᶜala*) to consummate a marriage, cohabit, sleep with one's wife (for the first time). دخل المعرس على عروسته عقب الزفة *dixal l-miᶜris ᶜala ᶜaruusta ᶜugb z-zaffa.* The bridegroom slept with his bride after the wedding ceremony. 3. to be included. الضريبـة مـا تدخـل في السـعر *ð̣-ð̣ariiba ma tadxul fi s-siᶜir.* Tax is not included in the price. العمولة حقي تدخل في السعر *l-ᶜumuula ḥaggi tadxul fi s-siᶜir.* My commission is included in the price.

دخـل *daxxal* II 1. to make or let enter, bring in, let in s.o. or s.th. فتح الباب ودخلني *fitaḥ l-baab w-daxxalni.* He opened the door and let me in. دخلني المستشـفى *daxxalni l-mustašfa.* He placed me in the hospital. قـال لي التنديـل، «لا تدخـل أحـد علـيّ» *gal-li t-tindeel, "la ddaxxil 'aḥad ᶜalayya."* The supervisor said to me, "Don't let anyone go in to see me." لا دخل نفسك في هـا المشـاكل *la daxxil nafsak fi hal-mašaakil!* Don't drag yourself into these problems! قـال لي، «لا تدخـل نفسـك بكـل شـي!» *gal-li, "la ddaxil nafsak b-kill šayy!"* He said to me, "Don't meddle in everything!" 2. to insert, include, enter. دخل الواير في البيب *daxxal l-waayir fi l-peep.* He inserted the wire in the pipe. ما دخلوا الخدمة في الحسـاب *ma daxxalaw l-xidma fi li-ḥsaab.* They did not include service in the bill. دخلوا اسمه في ليستة المشبوهين *daxxalaw 'isma fi liistat l-mašbuuhiin.* They entered his name on the list of the suspects.

تدخـل *tadaxxal* V (common var. *ddaxxal*) 1. to interfere, meddle, involve oneself. آنا ما أتدخل في السياسة *'aana ma 'addaxxal fi s-siyaasa.* I don't involve myself in politics. لا تتدخـل بشـؤوني! *la tiddaxxal b-šu'uuni!* Don't interfere in my affairs! الشرطة تدخلت في الانتخابات *š-širṭa ddaxxalat fi l-'intixaabaat.* The police rigged the elections. 2. to be inserted, put in, entered. الوايـر تدخـل في البيـب *l-waayir ddaxxal fi l-peep.* The wire was inserted in the pipe.

دخـل *daxil* 1. income. ضريبـة الدخـل *ð̣ariibat d-daxil* income tax. مـا فيـه ضريبـة دخـل هـني *ma fii ð̣ariibat daxil hini.* There is no income tax here. 2. interference, intervention. ما لي دخل في هـا القضيـة *ma lii daxil fi hal-gað̣iyya.* I have nothing to do with this matter. أنت شو دخلك؟ هذي حـق الرجـاجيل *'inti šu daxlič? haaði ḥagg r-rayaayiil.* What's this got to do with you? (It's none of your business). This is men's business.

دخلـة *daxla* (n. of inst.) p. *-aat* consummation. ليلـة الدخلـة *leelat d-daxla* the wedding night.

دخيـل *daxiil* (in certain expressions) دخيلـك، لا توجـع راسـي *daxiilak, la twajjiᶜ raasi.* Please don't give me a headache. دخيلك، لا تطقـني *daxiilak, la ṭṭigni.* Please don't hit me. دخيل الله ليش الأسعار غالية ها القد؟ *daxiil aḷḷa leeš l-'asᶜaar ġaalya hal-gadd?* For the love of God, why are prices so high?

دخـول *duxuul* (v.n. from *dixal*) entry, entrance, admittance, admission. الدخول مني والخروج مناك *d-duxuul minni* *w-l-xuruuj minnaak.* Entrance is from here and exit is from there. ممنوع الدخول! *mamnuu*ᶜ *d-duxuul!* Don't enter! (lit., "Entry is forbidden.") تذكرة دخول *taðkarat duxuul* admission ticket. بطاقة دخول الطايرة *biṭaaġat duxuul ṭ-ṭaayra* airplane boarding pass. ما أسمح لك بالدخول إلا بعد يومين *ma 'asmaḥ-lak b-d-duxuul 'illa ba*ᶜ*d yoomeen.* I will not permit you to enter except after two days. سعر الدخول عشرين درهم *si*ᶜ*r d-duxuul* ᶜ*išriin dirhim.* The admission fee is twenty dirhams.

مدخل *madxal* p. مداخل *madaaxil* entrance.

داخل *daaxil* 1. (prep.) inside. داخل الحجرة *daaxil l-ḥijra* inside the room. 2. (adv.) inside. راح داخل *raaḥ daaxil.* He went inside.

داخلي *daaxili* internal, interior, inside. أمور داخلية *'umuur daaxiliyya* internal affairs. اضطرابات داخلية *ðṭiraabaat daaxiliyya* internal disturbances. هدوم داخلية *hduum daaxiliyya* underwear, underclothes. وزارة الداخلية *wazaarat d-daaxiliyya* the ministry of internal affairs, ministry of the interior. مدرسة داخلية *madrasa daaxiliyya* boarding school. قسم داخلي *gisim daaxili* (of a school) boarding section, dormitory. طب الأمراض الداخلية *ṭibb l-'amraað d-daaxiliyya* internal (diseases) medicine.

دخن *dxn*

دخن *daxxan* II 1. to fumigate, fume s.th. دخنوا العمارة لاجل يموت البق *daxxanaw li-*ᶜ*maara lajil ymuut l-bagg.* They fumigated the building so that the mosquitoes would die. 2. to smoke, emit smoke. فيه سيارات تدخن واجد في الشوارع *fii sayyaaraat ddaxxin waayid fi š-šawaari*ᶜ*.* There are cars that give off a lot of smoke in the streets.

دخان *dxaan* 1. smoke, fumes. (prov.) ماكو دخان بلا ضو *maaku dxaan bala ðaww.* Where there is smoke there is fire. (lit., "There is no smoke without fire."). (prov.) كل عود براسه دخان *kill* ᶜ*uud b-raasa dxaan.* No one is perfect. (lit., "Every stick has smoke in its upper part."). 2. (more common var. دخان *duxaan*) Dukhan, city in Qatar, famous for its port on the Gulf of Bahrain.

تدخين *tadxiin* (v.n. from II دخن *daxxan*) smoking (tobacco). التدخين ممنوع *t-tadxiin mamnuu*ᶜ*.* Smoking is forbidden.

مدخن *mdaxxin* (act. part. from II دخن *daxxan*) p. *-iin* smoker. مركز المدخنين *markaz li-mdaxxniin* the smokers' corner or shop.

درام *draam*

درام *draam* p. *-aat* 1. barrel. درام زيت *draam zeet* oil barrel. 2. (garbage) can. قطه في الدرام *giṭṭa fi d-draam.* Throw it away in the garbage can.

درب *drb*

درب *darrab* II to train, coach, drill. دربهم على الملاكمة *darrabhum* ᶜ*ala l-mulaakama.* He trained them in boxing. درب فريق كرة السلة قبل المباراة *darrab fariiġ kurat s-salla gabl* *l-mubaaraa.* He coached the basketball team before the game. الضابط درب الجنود على استعمال السلاح *ð-ðaabiṭ darrab li-jnuud ᶜala stiᶜmaal s-silaaḥ.* The officer drilled the soldiers in the use of weapons.

تدرب *tadarrab* V to be trained, drilled. رحت أمريكا وتدربت على التعليب *riḥt 'amriika w-tadarrabt ᶜala t-tᶜaliib.* I went to America and was trained in canning. هذا المدرس ما تدرب على التدريس *haaða l-mudarris ma tadarrab ᶜala t-tadriis.* The teacher was not trained to teach. هذيل ما تدربوا وايا باقي الجنود *haðeel ma tadarrabaw wiyya baagi li-jnuud.* Those did not drill with the rest of the soldiers.

درب *darb* p. دروب *druub* 1. street, road. رحت من ذاك الدرب ودشيت *riḥt min ðaak d-darb w-daššeet.* I took that road and got lost. (prov.) كل من سار على الدرب وصل *kill man saar ᶜala d-darb wuṣal.* Where there is a will there is a way. (lit., "He who treads the (proper) path will arrive (at his destination."). (prov.) يا ماشي درب الزلق لا تيمن طيحتك *ya maaši darb z-zalag la teeman ṭeeḥtak.* Don't stand in harm's way. (lit., "If you are on a slippery road, don't guarantee you won't fall down."). 2. way, route. ممكن تشتري لي تفاح بدربك؟ *mumkin tištirii-li tiffaaḥ b-darbak?* Will you buy me apples on your way? خلني أشوف دربي *xaḷḷni 'ačuuf darbi.* Let me concentrate on what I am doing.

تدريب *tadriib* (v.n. from II درب *darrab*) practice, drill, training. مركز تدريب المعلمين *markaz tadriib l-muᶜallimiin* the teacher training center. تدريب عسكري *tadriib ᶜaskari* military training. دورة تدريبية *dawra tadriibiyya* training course. رحت في دورة تدريبية شهرين *riḥt fi dawra tadriibiyya šahreen.* I went for a two-month training course.

مدرب *mudarrib* p. *-iin* trainer, coach.

د ر ب ي ل *drbyl*

دربيل *darbiil* p. درابيل *diraabiil* binoculars.

د ر ج *drj*

تدرج *tadarraj* II to advance gradually. تدرج في الوظيفة إلين صار تنديل على الكولية *tadarraj fi l-waðiifa 'ileen ṣaar tindeel ᶜala l-kuuliya.* He advanced gradually in his job until he became a supervisor over the coolies.

استدرج *stadraj* X to coax, tempt, lure. استدرجته إلين اعترف بالبوق *stadrajta 'ileen ᶜtiraf b-l-boog.* I coaxed him until he confessed the theft.

درج *daraj* (more common var. *daray*) steps, stairs, staircase. فيه درج طويل يوديك الديوان الأميري *fii daray ṭawiil ywaddiik d-diiwaan l-'amiiri.* There is a long flight of stairs that leads you to the Emiri palace.

درجة *draja* (more common var. درية *draya*) 1. step, stair. 2. (p. *-aat*) degree. درجة الحرارة *drajat l-ḥaraara* the temperature. 3. degree, extent. كريم إلى درجة بعيدة *kariim 'ila daraja baᶜiida* generous to an extreme degree. 4. class. درجة أولى *daraja 'uula* first class. درجة سياحية *daraja siyaaḥiyya* tourist class. شلاخ من الدرجة الأولى

čallaax min d-daraja l-'uula first-class liar. 5. grade, mark (in school). حصل بس درجة نجاح *ḥaṣṣal bass darajat najaaḥ.* He obtained only a passing grade.

دراج *darraaj* (coll.) game birds resembling the sand grouse.

مدرج *madraj* p. مدارج *madaarij* (airfield) runway. مدرج الطايرة *madraj ṭ-ṭaayra* the (airplane) runway.

بالتدريج *b-t-tadriij* gradually, step-by-step. by degrees. الحالة الاقتصادية تتحسن بالتدريج *l-ḥaala l-'igtiṣaadiyya titḥassan b-t-tadriij.* The economic situation is getting better gradually.

دارج *daarij* prevalent, common, popular. الأمثال الدارجة *l-'amθaal d-daarja* the common, widespread proverbs. اللغة الدارجة *l-luġa d-daarja* the colloquial language.

مدرج *mudarraj* (p.p.) amphitheater. المدرج الروماني *l-mudarraj r-ruumaani* the Roman amphitheater.

د ر د ر *drdr*

دردور *darduur* (p. unknown) whirlpool, eddy.

د ر ر *drr*

در *darr (يدر ydirr)* 1. to give milk abundantly, be productive. درت الناقة *darrat n-naaga.* The female camel gave a lot of milk. 2. to be abundant, plentiful. ما ادري من وين درت عليهم الفلوس *ma dri min ween darrat ᶜaleehum li-fluus.* I don't know from where the money showered on them.

در *durr* (coll.) 1. pearls. 2. gems. s. *-a* p. *-aat.*

د ر ز *drz*

درز *darraz* (خيط *xayyaṭ* II is less common) to sew. أمه تدرز كلش زين *'umma ddarriz killiš zeen.* His mother sews very well. اللي يدرزون هني معظمهم هنود وباكستانيين *'illi ydarrzuun hini muᶜđamhum hnuud w-baakistaaniy-yiin.* Most of those who sew here are Indians and Pakistanis. أمي درزت لي دراعة *'ummi darrazat-li darraaᶜa.* My mother made a (woman's) dress for me.

درزي *darzi* p. *-iyya* tailor.

د ر ز ن *drzn*

درزن *darzan* p. درازن *daraazin* dozen. اشتريت درزن تفاح *štireet darzan tiffaaḥ.* I bought a dozen apples. يبيعون البرتقال بالدرزن *ybiiᶜuun l-burtagaal b-d-darzan.* They sell oranges by the dozen.

د ر س *drs*

درس *diras (يدرس yidris)* to study. درست إنكليزي وتاريخ *dirast 'ingiliizi w-taariix.* I studied English and history. درسنا وايا بعض خمس سنين *dirasna wiyya baᶜađ xams sniin.* We studied together for five years. درست القضية وقدمت تقرير حق الوزير *dirast l-gađiyya w-gaddamt tagriir ḥagg l-waziir.* I studied the case and submitted a report to the minister.

درس *darras* II to teach, instruct. درست في دار المعلمين سنتين *darrast fi daar l-muᶜallimiin santeen.* I taught at the men's teacher training college for two years. درسني إنكليزي *darrasni* *'ingiliizi.* He taught me English.

درس *dars* p. دروس *duruus.* 1. lesson, chapter (of a textbook). درس عشرين طويل *dars ᶜišriin ṭawiil.* Lesson Twenty is long. 2. class, class period. عندنا خمسة دروس في اليوم *ᶜindana xamsat duruus fi l-yoom.* We have five class periods a day. 3. lesson (from experience). تعلمت درس ما أنساه أبد *taᶜallamt dars ma 'ansaa 'abad.* I learned a lesson I will never forget.

دراسة *diraasa* 1. (v.n. from درس *diras*) study, studying. كملت دراستي الثانوية في المدرسة الليلية *kammalt diraasti θ-θaanawiyya fi l-madrasa l-layliyya.* I completed my secondary education at the night school. 2. (p. *aat*) study, investigation. عقب دراسة الموضوع قررت أسافر *ᶜugub diraasat l-mawḏuuᶜ garrart 'asaafir.* After investigating the problem, I decided to travel.

دراسي *diraasi* academic, scholastic. سنة دراسية *sana diraasiyya* academic year.

مدرسة *madrasa* p. مدارس *madaaris* school. هو في المدرسة *huwa fi l-madrasa.* He is at school. مدرسة حكومية *madrasa ḥukuumiyya* public school.

تدريس *tadriis* (v.n. from II درس *darras*) teaching.

مدرس *mudarris* p. *-iin* teacher, instructor.

د ر ع *drᶜ*

درع *diriᶜ* p. دروع *druuᶜ* 1. shield. 2. armor, suit of armor.

دراعة *darraaᶜa* p. *-aat* woman's dress (worn at home).

مدرع *mudarraᶜ* armored. سيارة مدرعة *sayyaara mudarraᶜa* armored car. قوات مدرعة *guwwaat mudarraᶜa* armed forces.

د ر ك *drk*

أدرك *'adrak* IV to realize, understand, become aware of s.th. أدرك إنه كان المخطي *'adrak 'inna čaan l-mixṭi.* He realized that he was at fault.

تدارك *tadaarak* VI to take care of, takes steps to prevent (s.th. from happening), make amends. تدارك الموقف *tadaarak l-mawgif.* He took charge of the situation. تدارك السألة قبل ما كبرت *tadaarak l-mas'ala gabil-ma kbarat.* He took charge of the matter before it got worse.

إدراك *'idraak* (v.n. from IV أدرك *'adrak*) realization, understanding.

د ر ن ف ي س *drnfys*

درنفيس *darnafiis* p. *-aat* screwdriver.

د ر ه م *drhm*

درهم *dirhim* p. دراهم *daraahim.* 1. dirham (unit of money in the U.A.E. = 100 fils). دفعت له خمسين درهم *difaᶜt-la xamsiin dirhim.* I paid him fifty dirhams. 2. (p. دراهم *daraahim*) money. وين دراهمك؟ *ween daraahmak?* Where is your money?

د ر و ا ز *drwaaz*

دروازة *dirwaaza* p. *-aat,* دراويز *diraawiiz* doorway, gate. دروازة القصر *dirwaazat l-gaṣir* the castle gate. دروازة البحرين *dirwaazat l-baḥreen* = بوابة البحرين *bawwaabat l-baḥreen* the

Bahrain Doorway.

د ر و ي ش *drwyš*

درويش *darwiiš* p. دراويش *diraawiiš* 1. dervish (member of a Muslim sect that professes poverty and self-denial), Sufi. 2. poor person. درويش سندي *darwiiš sindi* poor person from the province of Sind (of West Pakistan).

دروشة *darwaša* act of behaving like a dervish.

د ر ي *dry*

درى *dira (يدري yidri)* 1. to know. ما ادري ليش ما جا وايانا *ma dri leeš ma ya wiyyaana.* I don't know why he hasn't come with us. تدري؟ ها الرجال ما يعجبني *tidri? ha-r-rayyaal ma yi^c^jibni.* You know what? I don't like this man. ما ادري وين هو *ma 'adri ween huwa.* I don't know where he is. ما ادري كيف أبدل التاير *ma dri čeef 'abaddil t-taayir.* I don't know how to change the tire. دريت انه جاي عقب باكر *direet 'inna yaay ^c^ugub baačir.* I knew that he was coming the day after tomorrow. 2. to find out. (prov.) لو يدري عمير كان شق ثوبه *lo yidri ^c^meer čaan šagg θooba.* Ignorance is bliss. (lit., "If Omayr had found out, he would have ripped his clothes.") دريت بترفيعك لو بعد *direet b-tarfii^c^ak lo ba^c^ad?* Have you heard of your promotion yet?

درى *darra* II to inform, let s.o. know, acquaint s.o. of s.th. دريته بكل شي *darreeta b-kill šayy.* I have told him everything. شدراني؟ *š-darraani?* Who would have told me? I don't know.

دارى *daara* III to treat with flattery or gentle courtesy, to flatter. كنت في دارهم وداريته. شأساوي بعد *čint fi daarhum w-daareeta. š-asawwi ba^c^ad.* I was at their home and I was courteous to him. What else could I have done? ما ادري ليش فنش. كل الموظفين يحبونه ويدارونه *ma dri leeš fannaš. kill l-muwaððafiin yḥibbuuna w-ydaaruuna.* I don't know why he has resigned. All the employees like him and are courteous to him.

اندرى *ndira* VII to be known. ما يندرى شو اللي صار *ma yindara šu lli ṣaar.* What has happened cannot be known. ما يندرى يجي اليوم والا باكر *ma yindara yiyi l-yoom walla baačir.* It is not known if he's coming today or tomorrow.

مدارة *m(u)daaraa* (v.n. from III دارى *daara*) care, attention.

أدرى *'adra* (elat.) 1. (with من *min*) more knowledgeable, more informed than. هو أدرى منك *huwa 'adra mink.* He is more knowledgeable than you are. 2. (with foll. n.) the most knowledgeable, the most informed. هو أدرى واحد *huwa 'adra waaḥid.* He is the most knowledgeable one.

د ر ي س *drys*

دريس *drees* p. *-aat* military uniform.

تدرس *tadarras* V to wear a military uniform.

د ر ي ش *dryš*

دريشة *diriiša* p. درايش *diraayiš* window. افتح الدريشة! الهوا موب حار *'iftaḥ d-diriiša! l-hawa muub ḥaarr.* Open the window! The weather is not hot.

د ر ي ل *dryl*

دريـل *dreel* p. *-aat* 1. (oil) drill. 2. oil rig.

د ر ي و ل *drywl*

دريول *dreewil* p. *-iyya* driver (of a taxi or a car), chauffeur. (سايق *saayig,* سواق *sawwaag* are less common). آنا أشتغل دريـول حـق شـركة «أدمـا» *'aana 'aštaġil dreewil ḥagg šarikat 'adma.* I am now working as a driver for the ADMA (Abu Dhabi Marine Areas Ltd.) company.

د ز ز *dzz*

دز *dazz* (يـدز *ydizz)* to send. (طـرش *ṭarraš* is more common). See under **ط ر ش** *ṭrš.*

دزة *dazza* clothes and jewelry sent to a bride before the wedding night.

د س ت و ر *dstwr*

دستور *dastuur* p. دساتير *dasaatiir* constitution (pol.).

د س س *dss*

دس *dass* (يدس *ydiss)* 1. to slip, shove, insert s.th. (into). دس الفلـوس في مخبـاه *dass li-filuus fi maxbaa.* He slipped the money into his pocket. 2. to hide, conceal s.th. دست الفلوس في الصرة حقها *dassat li-fluus fi ṣ-ṣurra ḥaggaha.* She hid the money in her bundle of clothes. 3. to administer surreptitiously. دست له السـم في الشـاي لاجـل تموتـه *dassat-la s-samm fi č-čaay lajil tmawwta.* She slipped him the poison in the tea to kill him.

دساس *dassaas* p. *-iin* intriguer, schemer, plotter.

دسيسة *dasiisa* p. دسايس *dasaayis* scheme, intrigue, plot.

د س ع *ds*ᶜ

دسع *disa*ᶜ (يدسع *yidsa*ᶜ) to ruminate. البعـارين والغنـم مـن الحيوانـات اللـي تدسـع *l-ba*ᶜ*aariin w-l-ġanam min l-ḥayawaanaat illi tidsa*ᶜ*.* Camels, sheep, and goats are among the animals that ruminate.

داسع *daasa*ᶜ III to belch, burp.

دسعة *das*ᶜ*a* (v.n. from دسـع *disa*ᶜ or داسع *daasa*ᶜ) (animal) rumination.

د ش د ش *dšdš*

دشداشة *dišdaaša* p. دشادش *dašaadiiš* (كنـدورة *kandoora* or ثـوب *θoob* are more common) men's outer garment, dress (usually white in the summer and dark in the winter), the standard dress for children and adults.

د ش ش *dšš*

دش *dašš* (يدش *ydišš)* 1. to enter, go in. ما قدرت أدش لأن الباب كان مصكـوك *ma gidart 'adišš li'an l-baab čaan maṣkuuk.* I couldn't enter because the door was locked. دش! البـاب مفكـوك *dišš! l-baab mafkuuk.* Enter! The door is unlocked. ماحد يقدر يدش على المدير ذالحـين *maḥḥad yigdar ydišš* ᶜ*ala l-mudiir ðalḥiin.* No one can go in to (see) the director now. البـايق يـدش السـجن *l-baayig ydišš s-sijin.* A thief will be imprisoned. اللي يجلخ يدش جهنم *'illi yčallix ydišš jahannam.* He who lies will go to hell. دش الكليـة الحربيـة *dašš l-kulliyya l-ḥarbiyya.* He enlisted in the military college. 2. to report for duty, go to work. أدش الزام الساعة ست الصباح *'adišš z-zaam s-saa^{c}a sitt ṣ-ṣabaaḥ.* I report for duty at six in the morning. 3. (with على *^{c}ala*) to drop in on s.o. توه دش علينا *tawwa dašš ^{c}aleena.* He has just dropped in on us.

دش *dašš* (v.n.) entry, entering. الدش مني والخروج مناك *d-dašš minni w-l-xuruuj minnaak.* Entrance is from here and exit is from there.

دشة *dašša* p. *-aat* (n. of inst.) (preceded by يوم *yoom* as in يوم الدشة *yoom d-dašša*) the first day of pearl diving.

د ع ث ر *d^{c}θr*

دعثر *da^{c}θar* (يدعثر *yda^{c}θir*) 1. to cause s.o. to fall down. دفعني ودعثرني على الأرض *difa^{c}ni w-da^{c}θarni ^{c}ala l-'arḏ.* He pushed me and knocked me down on the ground. 2. to get s.o. into a bad fix, involve, entangle s.o. دعثروه بمشكلة *da^{c}θaroo b-muškila.* They got him involved with a problem. دعثرتني وايا التنديل. ليش قلت له ما دشيت الزام اليوم؟ *da^{c}θartani wiyya t-tindeel. leeš git-la ma daššeet z-zaam l-yoom?* You got me into a bad fix with the supervisor. Why did you tell him I did not go to work today?

تدعثر *tda^{c}θar* (يتدعثر *yitda^{c}θar*) 1. to fall down. ما شفته إلا نط قدامي وتدعثر *ma čifta 'illa naṭṭ jiddaami w-dda^{c}θar.* No sooner had I seen him, than he fell down. 2. to get oneself into a mess, get into trouble, become entangled. تدعثر بالمشكلة *dda^{c}θar b-l-muškila.* He got himself entangled with the problem.

دعثور *da^{c}θuur* 1. (عرقوب *^{c}arguub* is more common) 2. (p. دعاثير *di^{c}aaθiir*) sand hill, dune.

د ع س *d^{c}s*

دعس *di^{c}as* (يدعس *yid^{c}as*) 1. to knock down, run over. السيارة دعسته ومات *s-sayyaara di^{c}sata w-maat.* The car ran over him and he died. 2. to tread underfoot, trample down. لا تدعس على الخبز. حرام *la tid^{c}as ^{c}ala l-xubiz. ḥaraam.* Don't tread on the bread. It's unlawful. You mustn't do that.

اندعس *ndi^{c}as* VII to be run over. راعي السيكل اندعس ورجله تعورت *raa^{c}i s-seekal ndi^{c}as w-riila t^{c}awwarat.* The cyclist was run over and his leg was injured.

دعس *da^{c}s* (v.n. from دعس *di^{c}as*) 1. running over (pedestrians). حوادث الدعس *ḥawaadiθ d-da^{c}s* pedestrian accidents. 2. treading s.th. underfoot, trampling down.

د ع ل ي *d^{c}ly*

دعلي *d^{c}alay* p. دعلية *d^{c}aliyya* hedgehog.

د ع م *d^{c}m*

دعم *di^{c}am* (يدعم *yid^{c}am*) 1. to run into, collide with. العمي كان ماشي ودعم الطوفة *l-^{c}amay čaan maaši w-di^{c}am ṭ-ṭoofa.* The blind man was walking and ran into the wall. اللوري دعمني لانه كان مسرع *l-loori di^{c}amni linna čaan misri^c.* The truck ran into me (i.e., into my car) because it was speeding. سيارته دعمت سيارتي *sayyaarta di^{c}mat sayyaarti.* His car collided with my car. 2. to hit s.o. (in a car accident). دعمـت راعـي السـيكل وطاح علـى الأرض *di^c^amt raa^c^i s-seekal w-ṭaaḥ ^c^ala l-'arḍ̱.* I hit the cyclist and he fell down (to the ground).

تداعـم *tdaa^c^am* VI 1. to collide, run into each other. سـياراتنا تداعمــوا *sayyaaraartna ddaa^c^maw.* Our cars collided.

اندعـم *ndi^c^am* VII to be run into, be hit. اندعم في وسط السوق *ndi^c^am fi wiṣṭ s-suug.* He was hit (in a car accident) in the middle of the marketplace. اندعمـت سـيارته ثـلاث مـرات *ndi^c^mat sayyaarta θalaaθ marraat.* His car has been in three collisions.

دعمـة *da^c^ma* p. *-aat* car accident, collision.

داعـم *daa^c^im* (act. part. from دعـم *di^c^am*) p. *-iin* having run into s.o. or s.th. هو اللي داعمـني *huwa lli daa^c^imni.* He is the one who ran into me.

مدعمية *mad^c^amiyya* (less common var. دعاميـة *da^c^^c^aamiyya*) p. *-aat* bumper (auto).

د ع ي *d^c^y*

دعـى *di^c^a* (يدعـي *yid^c^i*) 1. to invite. دعيتهم على العشـا *da^c^eettum ^c^ala l-^c^aša.* I invited them to dinner. 2. to summon, call for s.o., send for s.o. المحكمة دعتني لاجـل أشـهد في ذيـك القضيـة *l-maḥkama da^c^atni lajil 'ašhad fi ðiič l-gaḍ̱iyya.* The court summoned me to testify in that case. 3. to pray. أدعـي لـك بطـول العمــور *'ad^c^ii-lak b-ṭuul l-^c^umur.* I wish you a long life. أدعي لك بالنجاح *'ad^c^ii-lak b-n-najaaḥ.* I pray for your success. دعت عليه بالموت *di^c^at ^c^alee b-l-moot.* She prayed for his death.

ادعـى *ddi^c^a* VIII 1. to claim, allege, maintain. ليش تدعـي انـك تعـرف أصلـه وفصلـه؟ *leeš tidda^c^i 'innak t^c^arf 'aṣla w-faṣla?* Why do you claim that you know his origin and lineage? 2. (with علـى *^c^ala*) to start, initiate (legal action). راح وادعى علـي في المحكمـة *raaḥ w-ddi^c^a ^c^alayya fi l-maḥkama.* He went and filed suit against me in court.

اسـتدعى *stad^c^a* X 1. to apply, submit an application. راح واستدعى حق البلدية وحصـل فلـوس *raaḥ w-stad^c^a ḥagg l-baladiyya w-ḥaṣṣal fluus.* He went and applied to the municipality, and got some money. 2. to recall. استدعت الحكومة سفيرنا في لندن *stad^c^at li-ḥkuuma safiirna fi landan.* The government summoned our ambassador in London. 3. to summon, call in, send for s.o. الحـاكم اسـتدعى وزيـر الماليـة إلى القصـر *l-ḥaakim stad^c^a waziir l-maaliyya 'ila l-gaṣir.* The ruler summoned the minister of finance to the palace. 4. to call for, request, necessitate. ها الوضع يسـتدعي إجــراءات شــديدة *hal-waḍ̱i^c^ yistad^c^i 'ijraa'aat šadiida.* This situation calls for strict measures.

دعـوة *da^c^wa* p. *-aat* 1. matter, case, affair. هذي بس دعوة درهمين *haaði bass da^c^wat dirhimeen.* This is only a matter of two dirhams. لـك دعـوة بهاالقضيـة؟ *lak da^c^wa b-hal-gaḍ̱iyya?* Do you have anything to do with this matter? Is this matter any concern of yours? ما لي دعوة فيـه. خلـه يسـوي اللـي يبغـاه *ma-li da^c^wa fii. xaḷḷa ysawwi lli yibġaa.* He's no concern of mine. Let him do whatever he wants. شدعوة ليش غالية هـا الكـثر؟ *š-dacwa leeš ġaalya hal-kiθir?* How come it's so expensive? شـدعوة هـا التـبربر في الحفيز؟ *š-dacwa ha-t-tiburbur fi l-ḥafiiz?* Why all this gibberish in the office? شدعوة شايل خشمك علينا كانك التنديل؟ *š-dacwa šaayil xašmak caleena činnak t-tindeel?* Why are you looking down on us as if you were the supervisor? شدعوة مـاحد يشـوفك؟ *š-dacwa maḥḥad yšuufak?* What's up? We don't see you anymore. 2. invitation. جات لنا دعوة من السفير الأمريكـي *jat lana dacwa min s-safiir l-'amriiki.* We had an invitation from the American ambassador. 3. دعوى *dacwa* (p. دعاوي *dacaawi*) lawsuit, case, legal proceedings. رفع دعـوى علـي في المحكمـة *rifac dacwa calayya fi l-maḥkama.* He filed a lawsuit against me in court.

دعـا *duca* (no recorded p.) prayer, invocation (of God), supplication.

دعاية *dicaaya* p. *-aat* 1. propaganda. 2. promotion, advertising.

داعي *daaci* (act. part. from دعى *dica*) 1. (p. *-iin*) having invited s.o. هـو الداعينا على العشـا *huwa d-daaciina cala l-caša.* He is the one who invited us to dinner. 2. (p. دعاة *ducaa*) proponent, propagandist. 3. (p. دعاوي *dacaawi*) reason, cause, motive. مـن كلامـك عرفـت طلبـك ولا داعـي لذكـره *min kalaamak ciraft ṭalabak wala daaci li-ðikra.* From what you said, I knew your request and there is no need for mentioning it.

د غ ش *dġš*

دغش *diġaš* (يدغش *yidġaš*) 1. to cheat. لا تشـتري منـه. يدغشـك *la tištiri minna. yidġašk.* Don't buy from him. He will cheat you. دغشـني بالسـعر *diġašni b-s-sicr.* He cheated me on the price. 2. to insinuate, imply. ترى يدغش بحكيه *tara yidġaš b-ḥačya.* Well, he makes insinuations in his speech.

دغـش *daġaš* (v.n.) 1. deception, cheating, swindle. كلامه دغش *kalaama daġaš.* His words are deceptive.

د غ ص *dġṣ*

دغص *duġṣ* (less common var. دغس *duġs*) p. دغصان *duġṣaan* dolphin.

د ف ت ر *dftr*

دفتر *daftar* p. دفاتر *dafaatir* notebook, copybook. بـاكر تفتح المدرسـة والعيـال يبغون دفاتر وقلامة ومـا ادري شـبعد *baačir tiftaḥ l-madrasa w-li-cyaaḷ yibġuun dafaatir w-gḷaama w-ma dri š-bacad.* Tomorrow the school will open and the children need notebooks, pencils, and I don't know what else.

د ف ع *dfc*

دفع *difac* (يدفع *yidfac*) 1. to pay. إذا بغيت تشتري بيت لازم تدفع أقل شي مليـون والا مليونين درهـم *'iða baġeet tištiri beet laazim tidfac 'agall šayy malyoon walla malyooneen dirhim.* If you want to buy a house, you have to pay at least one or two million dirhams. كم تدفـع حـق هـذا الراديـو؟ *čam tidfac ḥagg haaða r-raadu?* How much would you pay for this radio? لازم تدفع ضريبة المطار *laazim tidfac ḍariibat l-maṭaar.* You have to pay the airport tax. 2. to offer ndifa^c waayid leen takallam ^can l-muslimiin fi l-boosna. He got worked up when he talked about the Muslims in Bosnia.

دفع dafi^c (v.n. from دفع difa^c) 1. paying, act of paying. إخذه هالحين والدفع باكر 'ixða halḥiin w-d-dafi^c baačir. Take it now and pay for it tomorrow. 2. pushing, shoving.

دفعة daf^ca (n. of inst.) p. -aat 1. payment. علي دفعتين حق البنك ^calayya daf^citeen ḥagg l-bank. I have to make two payments to the bank. دفعة واحدة daf^ca waḥda one payment, full payment. 2. push, shove, thrust. 3. group, bunch. دفعة جنود daf^cat jnuud group of soldiers, shipment of troops.

مدفع madfa^c p. مدافع madaafi^c cannon, gun. مدفع رشاش madfa^c raššaaš machine gun.

مدفعية madfa^ciyya artillery.

دفاع difaa^c 1. defense. وزارة الدفاع wazaarat d-difaa^c the ministry of defense. mḥaami d-difaa^c the defense attorney. 2. back (soccer).

مدافع mdaafi^c p. -iin defender (of s.o. or s.th).

د ف ف dff

دف daff p. دفوف dfuuf tambourine.

دفة daffa p. -aat women's cloak-like wrap (usually black), women's aba.

د ف ن dfn

دفن difan (يدفن yadfin) 1. to bury. من الأفضل في الإسلام انك تغسل الميت وتدفنه على طول min l-'afðal fi l-'islaam 'innak tġasil l-mayyit w-tadfina ^cala ṭuul. In

(to pay). دفعت له ألفين درهم لكن ما باعني اياها difa^ct-la 'alfeen dirhim laakin ma baa^cani-yyaaha. I offered him two thousand dirhams but he didn't sell it to me. 3. to push. لا تدفع الباب. سحبه! la tidfa^c l-baab. siḥba! Don't push the door. Pull it! بغيت واحد يدفع سيارتي baġeet waaḥid yidfa^c sayyaarti. I wanted someone to push my car. السوق متروس رجاجيل وحريم والناس يدفعون بعض s-suug matruus rayaayiil w-ḥariim w-n-naas yidfa^cuun ba^cað. The marketplace is full of men and women, and people push each other aside.

دفع daffa^c II to shove, push. لا تدفع. كلنا ندش la ddaffi^c. killana ndišš. Don't shove! We'll all get in.

دافع daafa^c III 1. to offer resistance, oppose. الجيش دافع l-jeeš daafa^c. The army offered resistance. 2. (with عن ^can) to defend. الجيش دافع عن المدينة l-jeeš daafa^c ^can l-madiina. The army defended the city. المحامي دافع عني li-mḥaami daafa^c ^canni. The attorney defended me.

تدافع tdaafa^c VI to push each other. الناس تدافعوا لين فتح الدكان n-naas ddaaf^caw leen fitaḥ d-dikkaan. The people pushed each other when the store opened.

اندفع ndifa^c VII 1. to be paid. المبلغ اندفع كله l-mablaġ ndifa^c killa. The sum of money was paid in full. 2. to be pushed. ما يندفع ها الصندوق. ثقيل ma yindafa^c ha-ṣ-ṣanduug. θagiil. The box cannot be pushed. It's heavy. 3. to be carried away, to get worked up. اندفع واجد لين تكلم عن المسلمين في البوسنة

Islam, it's better to wash a dead person and bury him right away. الكلب دفن العظمة تحت الشجرة *č-čalb difan l-ᶜaðma taḥat li-šyara.* The dog buried the bone under the tree. 2. to hide, conceal, keep s.th. secret. دفن الملف بين الملفات الثانيين *difan l-malaff been l-malaffaat θ-θaanyiin.* He concealed the folder among the other folders. دفنوا القضية وما خلوها تطلع *difnaw l-gaðiyya w-ma xaḷḷooha tiṭlaᶜ.* They kept the problem secret and did not let it leak out.

اندفن *ndifan* VII to be buried. الميت اندفن أمس *l-mayyit ndifan 'ams.* The dead person was buried yesterday.

دفن *dafin* (v.n. from دفن *difan*) burial, burying. غسل الميت قبل دفنه فرض *ġasl l-mayyit gabil dafna farð.* Washing a dead person before burying him is required (in Islam).

مدفن *madfan* p. مدافن *madaafin* burial ground, burying place, cemetery (مقبرة *maqbara* is more common).

مدفون *madfuun* (p.p. from دفن *difan*) buried. فيه كنز مدفون هني *fii kanz madfuun hini.* There is a buried treasure here.

د ف ي *dfy*

دافي *daafi* warm. ماي دافي *maay daafi* warm water.

د گ د گ *dgdg*

دقدق *dagdag* (يدقدق *ydagdig)* to knock, rap, bang (with على *ᶜala* on, e.g., the door). دقدق على الباب في نص الليل *dagdag ᶜala l-baab fi nuṣṣ l-leel.* He knocked on the door at midnight.

دقداقة *digdaaga* Digdaga (city in Ras Al-Khaima, U.A.E, known for its fertile land).

د گ گ *dgg*

دق *dagg* (يدق *ydugg)* 1. to ring. دق التلفون *dagg t-talafoon.* The telephone rang. دقيت له تلفون *daggeet-la talafoon.* I telephoned him. الناس هني يدقون الهرن *n-naas hini ydugguun l-haran.* People here sound the horns of their cars. 2. to beat (e.g., the drums). الناس يدقون الطبول في الأعياد وحفلات الزواج *n-naas ydugguun li-ṭbuul fi l-'aᶜyaad w-ḥaflaat z-zawaaj.* People beat the drums at festivals and wedding ceremonies. دق سلف! *dugg self!* Start the car!

دقق *daggag* II to examine closely, examine exactly. المحاسب رايح يجي يدقق الحسابات *li-mḥaasib raayiḥ yiyi ydaggig li-ḥsaabaat.* The accountant is coming to check the accounts. قبل ما تشتريه لازم تدقق النظر فيه *gabil-ma tištirii laazim ddaggig n-naðir fii.* Before you buy it, you have to examine it closely.

اندق *ndagg* VII 1. to be rung. اندق جرس الباب *ndagg jiras l-baab.* The door bell was rung. 2. to be beaten. اندقت الطبول في العيد *ndaggat li-ṭbuul fi l-ᶜiid.* The drums were beaten during the feast. 3. to be struck or hit. اندق دق قوي *ndagg dagg gawi.* He was beaten hard.

دق *dagg* (v.n. from دق *dagg*) 1. ringing. 2. beating (the drums). 3. banging, rapping. 4. striking, beating. 5. (adv.) fast, quickly, right away.

طلعوا وراحوا عليه دق *ṭlaᶜaw w-raaḥaw ᶜalee dagg.* They left and went right away to him. 6. (in certain expressions with وقع *wugaᶜ*). قبضه ووقع فيه دق *gbaḏa w-wugaᶜ fii dagg.* He grabbed him and beat the hell out of him. وقع بالدراسة دق *wugaᶜ b-d-diraasa dagg.* He really studied hard. يوقع في الأكل دق *yoogaᶜ fi l-'akil dagg.* He really digs into food.

دقيق *digiig* 1. (coll.) flour. 2. (adj. p. *-iin*) thin, skinny (more common var. *dijiij*) هو طويل ودقيق *huwa ṭawiil w-dijiij.* He is tall and skinny. دقيق عكس متين *dijiij ᶜaks mitiin.* Skinny is the opposite of fat.

دقيقة *digiiga* p. دقايق *digaayig* 1. minute. الساعة ثنتين إلا خمس دقايق *s-saaᶜa θinteen 'illa xams digaayig.* It's five minutes to two. 2. a very short while. صبر، دقيقة! *ṣabir, digiiga!* Just a minute! Wait a minute!

مدقة *mdagga* p. *-aat* 1. pounder, pestle. مدقة الهيل *mdaggat l-heel* the cardamom pounder. 2.(door) knocker. مدقة الباب *mdaggat l-baab* the door knocker.

تدقيق *tadgiig* (v.n. from II دقق *daggag*) act of examining closely or exactly. تدقيق الحسابات *tadgiig li-ḥsaabaat* the checking of accounts.

مدقق *mdaggig* (act. part. from II دقق *daggag*) 1. having checked or examined (e.g., accounts). توه مدقق الحساب *tawwa mdaggig li-ḥsaab.* He has just checked the account. 2. (p. *-iin*) account examiner or checker.

مدقق *mdaggag* (p.p. from II دقق *daggag*) having been checked or examined. الحساب مدقق *li-ḥsaab mdaggag.* The account has been checked.

د گ ل ١ *dgḷ*

دقل *digiḷ* p. ادقال *dgaal* mast of a ship. الدقل العود *d-digiḷ l-ᶜood* the mainmast of a ship.

د گ ل ٢ *dgḷ*

دكلة *dugḷa* p. دكل *dugaḷ* jubba (long outer garment of a holy man).

د گ م *dgm*

دقم *daggam* II to button. دقم السويتر مالك؛ الهوا بارد اليوم *daggim s-sweetar maalak; l-hawa baarid l-yoom.* Button up your sweater. It's cold today.

تدقم *tdaggam* V to button up oneself. تدقم قبل لا تخرج برة *ddaggam gabil-la tuxruj barra.* Button up before you go outside.

دقمة *digma* p. دقم *digam.* 1. button. تقدر تشتري دقم من سوق البزازين *tigdar tištiri digam min suug l-bazzaaziin.* You can buy buttons at the cloth market. 2. button, pushbutton. دقمة الليت *digmat l-leet* the light switch.

د ك ت و ر *dktwr*

دكتور *daktoor* (دختر *daxtar,* دختور *daxtoor* are more common) p. دكاتر *dakaatir,* دكاترة *dakaatra* (دخاتر *daxaatir* is more common) doctor, physician and Ph.D. أنت مريض ومسخن. روح الدختر *'inta mariiḏ w-mṣaxxan. ruuḥ d-daxtar.* You are sick and running a temperature. Go see the doctor.

دكتوراه *daktooraa* Ph.D. شهادة دكتوراه *šahaadat daktooraa* Ph.D. degree.

د ك ك ن *dkkn*

دكان *dikkaan* (*diččaan* is more common) p. دكاكين *dikaakiin* shop, store. راعي الدكان *raa*ᶜ*i d-diččaan* the shopkeeper. دكان حلوى *diččaan ḥalwa* sweets, pastry shop.

د ل ا غ *dlaaġ*

دلاغ *dlaaġ* p. *-aat* 1. pair of socks. 2. pair of stockings. 3. pair of gloves or mittens.

د ل خ *dlx*

أدلخ *'adlax* (يدلخ *yidlix*) to be or become turbid, muddy. البحر يدلخ مرات في الشتا *l-baḥar yidlix marraat fi š-šita.* The sea sometimes becomes turbid in the winter.

دلخ *dalix* turbid, muddy.

د ل گ م *dlgm*

دلقم *dalgam* (يدلقم *ydalgim*) to make s.th. round or ball-shaped. يدلقمون التمر ويحطونه في تنك قبل لا يودونه السوق *ydalgimuun t-tamir w-yḥuṭṭuuna fi tanak gabil-la ywadduuna s-suug.* They stack dates and put them in tin cans before they take them to the market. يدلقمون العيش *ydalgimuun l-*ᶜ*eeš.* They heap rice.

دلقمة *dalgama* (v.n.) 1. act of making things round or ball-shaped. 2. (p. *dalaagim*) bite, morsel, mouthful.

مدلقم *mdalgam* heaped, ball-shaped. (prov.) موب كل مدلقم جوز *muub kill mdalgam jooz.* Don't judge people or things by their appearance. You cannot judge a book by its cover. (lit. "Not every ball-shaped thing is a walnut.").

د ل ك *dlk*

دلك *dilak* (يدلك *yudluk*) to rub. دلكت وجهها وخلت عليه بودرة *dlakat weehha w-xaḷḷat* ᶜ*alee puudra.* She rubbed her face and put powder on it.

دلك *dallak* II to massage. حرمته دلكت له ظهره *ḥurumta dallakat-la ðhara.* His wife massaged his back for him.

دلاك *dallaak,* مدلك *mdallik* p. *-iin* masseur.

د ل ل *dll*

دل *dall* (يدل *ydill*) 1. (with على ᶜ*ala*) to show, demonstrate, point out s.th. ممكن تدلني على الطريق؟ *mumkin tadillani* ᶜ*ala ṭ-ṭariig?* Will you please show me the way? اللي قلته ما يدل على أي شي *'illi gilta ma ydill* ᶜ*ala 'ayya šayy.* What you have just said doesn't show anything. كلامه يدل على رحابة صدره *kalaama ydill* ᶜ*ala raḥaabat ṣadra.* His words demonstrate his open-mindedness. 2. to prove. هذا يدل على انه جلاخ *haaða ydill* ᶜ*ala 'inna čallaax.* This proves that he is a liar.

دلل *dallal* II 1. (with على ᶜ*ala*) to auction off s.th. كان الدلال يدلل على الكرفاية *čaan d-dallaal ydallil* ᶜ*ala l-kirfaaya.* The auctioneer was auctioning off the bed. في سوق هرج يدللون على كل شي *fi suug haraj ydalliluun* ᶜ*ala kill šayy.* At the auction (place) they auction off everything. 2. (with على ᶜ*ala*) = دل

dall. ضعنا وحصلنا واحد شيبة دللنا على الطريق *ðiᶜna w-ḥaṣṣalna waaḥid šeeba dallalna ᶜala ṭ-ṭariig.* We lost our way. We found an old man who showed us the way. 3. to pamper, spoil. يدلل بناته واجد *ydallil banaata waayid.* He pampers his daughters a lot.

تدلل *tdallal* V 1. to be coy, behave affectedly. هو موافق بس يتدلل عليهم لانه يبغى فلوس أكثر *huwa mwaafig bass yiddallal ᶜaleehum linna yibġa fluus 'akθar.* He is in agreement but he is playing hard to get with them because he wants more money. هي تتدلل على رجلها *hiya tiddallal ᶜala riilha.* She is acting coy with her husband. 2. to make demands, take advantage. تتدلل على أبوها لانه يحبها واجد *tiddallal ᶜala 'ubuuha linna yiḥbbha waayid.* She makes demands of her father because he loves her a lot.

اندل *ndall* VII 1. to find. اندليت الطريق *ndalleet ṭ-ṭariig.* I found my way. اختفى وراح مكان ما نندله *xtifa w-raaḥ mukaan ma nindalla.* He disappeared and went to a place we cannot find. 2. to know, know where. تندل ذاك المكان؟ *tindall ðaak l-mukaan?* Do you know where that place is? ماحد يندل بيت التنديل *maḥḥad yindall beet t-tindeel.* No one knows where the supervisor's house is.

دلة *dalla* p. ادلال *dlaal* large coffee pot (with long curved spout, usually made of brass).

دلال *dalaal* 1. coyness, coquettishness. 2. pampering, spoiling.

دليل *daliil* p. دلايل *dalaayil* 1. proof, evidence. عندك دليل على اللي تقولينه؟ *ᶜindič daliil ᶜala lli tguuliina?* Do you have proof of what you are saying? 2. directory, guidebook. دليل التلفون *daliil t-talafoon* the telephone directory.

دلال *dallaal* p. *-iin,* دلالوة *dlaalwa* 1. auctioneer. تحصل دلالين واجد في سوق هرج *tḥaṣṣil dallaaliin waayid fi suug haraj.* You will find many auctioneers at the auction (place). 2. dealer, agent, broker. إذا بغيت تشتري سيارة لازم تتفق وايا دلال *'iða baġeet tištiri sayyaara laazim tittafig wiyya dallaal.* If you want to buy a car, you have to come to an agreement with a dealer. 3. street crier, hawker.

دلالة *dlaala* brokerage commission (commission taken by a دلال *dallaal*).

د ل و *dlw*

دلو *dalu* p. دلاوة *dlaawa* bucket, pail. دندل الدلو في البير *dandal d-dalu fi l-biir.* He lowered the bucket into the well.

د م ب س *dmbs*

دمبس *dambas* (يدمبس *ydambis)* 1. to pin s.th. الدرزي يدمبس بطانة الهدوم *d-darzi ydambis bṭaanat li-hduum.* A tailor pins in the lining of clothes. 2. to dip. دمبس الأوراق بالكلبس *dambas l-'awrag b-li-klips.* He clipped the papers with a paper clip.

دمبوس *dambuus* p. دنابيس *danaabiis* (safety) pin.

د م ب ك *dmbk*

دمبك *dumbuk* p. دنابك *danaabik* clay or brass drum with skin head.

د م ج *dmj*

دمج *dimaj* (يدمج *yidmij*) to merge, join, combine. الحلفا دمجوا قواتهم وحاربوا سوى *l-ḥulafa dmajaw guwwaattum w-ḥaarbaw siwa.* The Allies merged their forces and fought together. دمجت الصفين ودرستهم *dimajt ṣ-ṣaffeen w-darrasittum.* I combined the two classes and taught them.

د م ر *dmr*

دمر *dammar* II to annihilate, destroy, ruin, demolish. الزلزال دمر المدينة *z-zilzaal dammar l-madiina.* The earthquake destroyed the city. العدو دمر جيشنا *l-ᶜadu dammar jeešna.* The enemy wiped out our army. دمر السيارة لانه سواق طايش *dammar s-sayyaara linna sawwaag ṭaayiš.* He ruined the car because he is a reckless driver. فريقنا لعب ضد فريقهم ودمرونا *fariigna liᶜab ḍidd fariiġhum w-dammaruuna.* Our team played their team and they slaughtered us. المدرب دمر الجنود بالتدريبات العسكرية *li-mdarrib dammar li-jnuud b-t-tadriibaat l-ᶜaskariyya.* The trainer annihilated the soldiers with military exercises. دمر روحه *dammar ruuḥa.* He ruined himself.

تدمر *tdammar* V to be annihilated, destroyed, ruined, demolished. المدينة تدمرت بالزلزال *l-madiina ddammarat b-z-zilzaal.* The city was destroyed in the earthquake. ما صار فيه شي في الدعمة لكن سيارته تدمرت *ma ṣaar fii šayy fi d-daᶜma laakin sayyaarta ddammarat.* Nothing happened to him in the car accident, but his car was wrecked. كل شي تدمر في الحرب *kill šayy ddammar fi l-ḥarb.* Everything was destroyed in the war.

دمار *damaar* destruction, ruin, annihilation. الحرب ما تجلب إلا الدمار *l-ḥarb ma tijlib 'illa d-damaar.* War brings about nothing except destruction.

مدمور *madmuur* ruined, messed up, in a bad shape.

مدمرة *mdammra* p. *-aat* destroyer (naut.).

د م ع *dmᶜ*

دمع *dammaᶜ* II to tear, shed tears. دمعت عيونه لين سمع انهم خسروا الحرب *dammaᶜat ᶜyuuna leen simaᶜ 'inhum xsaraw l-ḥarb.* His eyes shed tears when he heard that they had lost the war. عيونك تدمع لين تقشر بصل؟ *ᶜyuunak ddammiᶜ leen tgaššir baṣal?* Do your eyes water when you peel onions?

دمع *damiᶜ* (coll.) tears. s. دمعة *damᶜa.* لين كانوا يدللون على بيته كان الدمع ينزل من عيونه *leen čaanaw ydalliluun ᶜala beeta čaan d-damiᶜ yinzil min ᶜyuuna.* When they were auctioning off his house, tears were coming down from his eyes.

د م غ *dmġ*

دماغ *damaaġ* p. *-aat* 1. brain. 2. mind, brains.

د م غ ر ط *dmġrṭ*

ديموغراطي *dimoġraaṭi* 1. (adj.) democratic. الحزب الديموغراطي *l-ḥizb d-dimoġraaṭi* the democratic party (p. *-yyiin*) a democrat. هو ديموغراطي *huwa dimoġraaṭi.* He is a democrat. ذالحين

الديموغراطيين يسـيطرون علـى الكونغـرس الأمريكـي *ðalḥiin d-dimoġraaṭiyyiin yṣayṭruun ᶜala l-konġres l-'amriiki.* Now the Democrats are in control of the U.S. Congress.

ديموغراطية *dimoġraaṭiyya* democracy.

د م م *dmm*

دم *damm* 1. blood. وجه حمر مثل الـدم *weeha ḥamar miθil d-damm.* His face is red as blood. His face is blood red. مـن دمي ولحمـي *min dammi w-laḥmi* (said of a person) my own, my own flesh and blood. بنك الدم *bank d-damm* the blood bank. 2. a killing, a death, a life. فيـه دم بـين القبيلتـين *fii damm been l-gabiilteen.* Blood has been shed between the two tribes. There has been a killing between the two tribes. دمه ما يـروح بـلاش *damma ma yruuḥ balaaš.* His death won't go for nothing. 3. (in certain constructions). خفيف الدم *xafiif d-damm* amiable, charming. ثقيل الـدم *θagiil d-damm* insufferable, disagreeable, unpleasant.

دموي *damawi* bloody. حرب دموية *ḥarb damawiyya* bloody war.

الدمـام *d-dammaam* Dammam (city in eastern Saudi Arabia, known as a seaport).

د م ن¹ *dmn*

أدمـن *'adman* IV (يدمـن *yidmin)* (with على *ᶜala*) to be addicted to s.th. أدمن على شرب الخمـر وصحتـه تدمـرت *'adman ᶜala šurb l-xamir w-ṣiḥḥta ddammarat.* He addicted himself to drinking liquor and his health was ruined.

مدمـن *midmin* (act. part. from IV أدمن *'adman*) p. *-iin* 1. addict. هو مدمن من جملـة المدمنـين الثـانيين *huwa midmin min jimlit l-midimniin θ-θaanyiin.* He is an addict among the other addicts. 2. being an addict. هو المدمن علـى الخمـر، مـوب آنـا *huwa l-midmin ᶜala l-xamir, muub 'aana.* He is the one addicted to liquor, not I.

د م ن² *dmn*

دمـن *dimin* (coll.) (بعـرور *baᶜruur* is more common) droppings, dung of animals. s. دمنة *dimna.*

د ن ب س *dnbs*

دنبـس *danbas,* دنبوس *danbuus* = دمبس *dambas,* دمبـوس *dambuus.* See under **د م ب س** *dmbs.*

د ن ب ك *dnbk*

دنبك *dunbuk* p. دنابك *danaabik* = دمبك *dumbuk* p. دنابك *danaabik.* See under **د م ب ك** *dmbk.*

د ن د ل *dndl*

دنـدل *dandal (*يدندل *ydandil)* to lower, let down, dangle. دنـدل الدلـو في البـير *dandal d-dalu fi l-biir.* He lowered the bucket in the well. دندل الحبل من فوق *dandil l-ḥabil min foog.* Let down the rope from upstairs.

تدنـدل *tdandal* to hang down, hang, dangle. خلي الحبل يدندل مني *xalli l-ḥabil yiddandal minni.* Let the rope hang from here. تدندل من الدريشة وطاح على الأرض *ddandal min d-diriiša w-ṭaaḥ ᶜala l-'arḍ.* He hung down from the window and fell to the ground.

د ن گ *dng*

دنق *dannag* II to bend, bow. لين ذكرته بماضيه دنق راسه من الحيا *leen ðakkarta b-maaðii dannag raasa min l-ḥaya.* When I reminded him of his past, he bowed his head out of shame. الطفل دنق واجد من الدريشة ووقع *ṭ-ṭifil dannag waayid min d-diriiša w-wugaᶜ.* The child leaned too far out of the window and fell.

د ن ي *dny*

دنى *danna* II 1. to be low, mean, base, contemptible. يدني حق أي شي *ydanni ḥagg 'ayya šayy.* He lowers himself for anything. دنى نفسه وراح يتوسل بالتنديل *danna nafsa w-raaḥ yitwassal b-t-tindeel.* He lowered himself and went to beg the supervisor. 2. to bring s.th. close, move s.th. near. دنيه؛ ما أقدر أشوفه *dannii; ma 'agdar 'ačuufa.* Bring it closer; I can't see it.

تدنى *tdanna* V 1. to move close, go near. تدنى من الطوفة *ddanna min ṭ-ṭoofa.* He moved closer to the wall. تدنى جمبي! *ddanna yamni!* Come nearer to me! 2. to move over, scoot over. تدنى شوية. ما فيه مكان الي *ddanna šwayya. ma fii mukaan 'ili.* Move over a little. There's no room for me.

دني *dini* (in نفسه دنية *nafsa diniyya*) greedy, self-indulgent. نفسه دنية. كل شي يشوفه يبغاه *nafsa diniyya. kill šayy yčuufa yibġaa.* He is greedy. He wants everything he sees.

أدنى *'adna* (elat.) 1. (with من *min*) more contemptible, vile. هو أدنى من أي واحد *huwa 'adna min 'ayya waaḥid.* He is more contemptible than any other one. 2. (with foll. n.) the most contemptible, vile. هو أدنى شخص *huwa 'adna šuxṣ.* He is the most contemptible person. 3. (in certain expressions) أدنى حد *'adna ḥadd* the minimum, the lowest limit. الشرق الأدنى *š-šarg l-'adna* the Near East.

دنيا *dinya* (less common var. *dunya*) 1. world. الدنيا غير *d-dinya ġeer.* The world (nowadays) is different. The world has changed. 2. this world (as opposed to الآخرة *l-'aaxra* the hereafter), this life. 3. life, existence. بس! هذي الدنيا *bass! haaði d-dinya.* That's enough! That's life.

د ه د ه *dhdh*

دهده *dahdah (يدهده ydahdih)* 1. to roll down, cause to roll, let roll. دهده الحجر *dahdah l-ḥiyar.* He rolled down the rock. لا تدهده الدرام في الشارع *la ddahdih d-draam fi š-šaariᶜ.* Don't roll the barrel down the street.

تدهده *tdahdah (يتدهده yitdahdah)* to roll, be rolled down. الصخرة تدهدهت *li-ṣxara ddahdahat.* The rock rolled down. التانكي انكسر والماي تدهده كله *t-taanki nkisar w-l-maay ddahdah killa.* The water reservoir broke and the water ran down.

دهدهية *dihdihiyya* (adv.) quickly, fast. روح وتعال دهدهية *ruuḥ w-taᶜaal dihdihiyya.* Go out and come back quickly.

د ه ر *dhr*

دهر *dahir* p. دهور *dhuur* 1. long time, age. 2. fate, destiny. مصايب الدهر

maṣaayib d-dahir afflictions, trials of fate.

دهريز *dhryz*

دهريز *dihriiz* (less common var. دهليز *dihliiz*) p. دهاريز *dahaariiz* narrow passage, corridor.

دهم *dhm*

دهم *diham* (يدهم *yidham*) to be or become insane. دهم قبل ما ودوه مستشفى المجانين *diham gabil-ma waddoo mustašfa l-mayaaniin.* He went insane before they took him to the lunatic asylum.

دهم *dahham* II to make insane, to madden. مرات الجهال يدهمون الإنسان *marraat l-yihhaal ydahhimuun l-'insaan.* Sometimes children drive people nuts. جمال هذي البنت يدهم *jamaal haaði l-bint ydahhim.* This girl's beauty is maddening.

دهمان *dahmaan* p. *-iin* insane, mad.

دهن *dhn*

دهن *dihan* (يدهن *yidhan*) 1. to oil, grease. الماكينة فيها صوت عالي؛ لازم تدهنها *l-maakiina fiiha ṣoot ᶜaali; laazim tidhanha.* The machine is noisy; you have to oil it. 2. (with ب *b-*) to rub, massage. دهنت رجولها بزيت زيتون *dhanat ryuulha b-zeet zaytuun.* She massaged her legs with olive oil.

دهن *dihin* (coll.) 1. fat, butter fat, shortening. اشتريت قوطي دهن *štireet guuṭi dihin.* I bought a can of shortening. هذا اللحم فيه دهن واجد *haaða l-laḥam fii dihin waayid.* This meat has a lot of fat in it. حليب خالي الدهن *ḥaliib xaali d-dihin* non-fat milk. 2. oil (for lubricating, or for the skin).

دهني *dihni* fatty, oily. مواد دهنية *mawadd dihniyya* fatty substances.

دهور *dhwr*

دهور *dahwar* (يدهور *ydahwir*) to destroy, ruin, damage. الخمر دهور صحته *l-xamir dahwar ṣiḥḥta.* Liquor has destroyed his health.

تدهور *tadahwar* (يتدهور *yitdahwar*) to deteriorate. صحته تدهورت من المرض *ṣiḥḥta ddahwarat min l-maraḏ.* His health deteriorated because of the disease. تدهور الوضع السياسي *ddahwar l-waḏᶜ s-siyaasi.* The political situation deteriorated.

دهي *dhy*

داهية *daahiya* p. دواهي *dawaahi* disaster, calamity, catastrophe. وقع في داهية *wugaᶜ fi daahiya.* A disaster befell him. هذي داهية. ما لنا إلا الصبر *haaði daahiya. ma lana 'illa ṣ-ṣabir.* This is a calamity. We have no recourse except patience.

دوب ١ *dwb*

دوب *doob* (no known p.) nature, natural disposition, temperament. هذا دوبه. عرفناه من زمان *haaða dooba. ᶜirafnaa min zamaan.* This is his nature. We have known him for a long time.

دوب ٢ *dwb*

دوب *doob* (coll.) kind of light wood used in shipbuilding, esp. in making oars. s. *-a* p. دوب *duwab.*

د و ب ٣ dwb

دوبة *duuba* p. دوب *duwab* barge, cargo ship (that transports merchandise from anchored ships to the wharf).

د و ب ل ج dwblj

دوبلاج *dublaaj* dubbing (in motion pictures).

مدبلج *mdablaj* p. *-iin* dubbed.

د و ح dwḥ

دوح *dooḥ* (coll.) tall trees with many branches. s. *-a* p. *-aat*.

دوحة *dooḥa* p. *-aat* place with trees. دوحة السيلة، دوحة قميس، دوحة القويفرية *dooḥat s-seela, dooḥat ġamiis, dooḥat l-gaweefriyya* are names of doḥas in the U.A.E.

الدوحة *d-dooḥa* Doha, capital city of Qatar.

د و خ ١ dwx

داخ *daax (يدوخ yduux)* 1. to be or become dizzy, feel dizzy. يدوخ إذا يشتغل مدة طويلة *yduux 'iða yištaġil mudda ṭawiila.* He gets dizzy if he works for a long time. راسه يدوخ عقب أول بطل بيرة *raasa yduux ᶜugub 'awwal boṭil biira.* His head starts spinning after the first bottle of beer. 2. to get a headache. دخت من الزعاق والصراخ *duxt min li-zᶜaag w-ṣ-ṣraax.* Shouting and screaming gave me a headache. داخ راسي من القراية *daax raasi min l-graaya.* I got a headache from reading. 3. to have a lot of trouble, be put to a lot of bother. اشتريت سيارة قديمة ودخت بها *štireet sayyaara gadiima w-duxt biiha.* I bought an old car and it gave me a lot of trouble. 4. to feel nausea, get sick. ما يسافر بالباخرة لانه يدوخ *ma ysaafir b-l-baaxra linna yduux.* He doesn't travel by ship because he gets sick.

دوخ *dawwax* II 1. to make s.o. dizzy. السفر بالطيارة يدوخني *s-safar b-ṭ-ṭayyaara ydawwixni.* Travel by plane makes me dizzy. 2. to give s.o. a headache, bother s.o. a lot. دوخني من كثرة لغوته *dawwaxni min kaθrat laġiwta.* He gave me a headache because of his gibberish.

دوخة *dooxa* 1. dizziness. 2. headache, trouble, nuisance. 3. nausea, motion sickness.

د و خ ٢ dwx

داخ *daax (يدوخ yduux)* to smoke (a cigarette, a cigar, a pipe). أدوخ جقاير ما أدوخ مدواخ *'aduux jigaayir ma 'aduux midwaax.* I smoke cigarettes. I don't smoke a pipe. أنت تدوخ؟ *'inta dduux?* Do you smoke? لا، ما أدوخ *la, ma 'aduux.* No, I don't smoke.

دوخة *dooxa* (v.n.) 1. smoking. 2. (p. *-aat*) puff of smoke. خذيت دوخة من ها السيكار وداخ راسي *xaðeet dooxa min has-siigaar w-daax raasi.* I took a puff of smoke from that cigar and I felt dizzy. 3. confusion, disorder, hustle and bustle. رحت السوق وكان متروس رجاجيل وحريم وسياير. دوخة! *riḥt s-suug w-čaan matruus rayaayiil w-ḥariim w-siyaayiir. dooxa!* I went to the marketplace and it was full of men, women, and cars. It was a nuisance.

دايخ *daayix* (act. part. from داخ *daax*) 1. having smoked (a cigarette, a pipe,

تبغي جقارة؟ لا، مشكور. توني دايخ سبيل *tibġa jigaara? la, maškuur. tawwni daayix sbiil.* Do you want a cigarette? No, thanks. I have just smoked a pipe. 2. dizzy. دايخ من الجوع *daayix min l-yuu*ᶜ. He is dizzy from hunger.

مدواخ *midwaax* p. مداويخ *midaawiix* smoking pipe. يدوخ مدواخ *yduux midwaax.* He smokes a pipe.

د و د *dwd*

دود *dawwad* II to be or become worm-eaten. لين الثمر يدود ما ينوكل *leen θ-θamar ydawwid ma yinwikil.* When fruits get wormy, they cannot be eaten.

دود *duud* (coll.) 1. worms. s. -*a*. p. -*aat*. 2. worm-like larva, e.g., maggots, woodworms, etc. مثل الدود، ما ينعدون *miθil d-duud, ma yin*ᶜ*adduun.* There are so many of them; they are innumerable. دودة الأرض *duudat l-'arđ* earthworm. الدودة الوحيدة *d-duuda l-waḥiida* tapeworm.

د و ر *dwr*

دار *daar* (يدور *yduur*) 1. to go round, rotate, circulate, spread. دار حول البيت *daar ḥool l-beet.* He went round the house. إشاعة استقالة الحكومة دارت في البلد *'išaa*ᶜ*at stigaalat l-ḥukuuma daarat fi l-balad.* The rumor of the government resignation has gone around the country. ارتفاع سعر البانزين دار في السوق *rtifaa*ᶜ *si*ᶜ*r l-baanziin daar fi s-suug.* The increase in the price of gasoline spread in the market. 2. to turn, circle, revolve. لا تدور مني *la dduur minni.* Don't turn here. درت لين سمعت الصوت *durt leen sima*ᶜ*t ṣ-ṣoot.* I turned when I heard the noise. روح إلى آخر الشارع ودور على اليمين *ruuḥ 'ila 'aaxir š-šaari*ᶜ *w-duur* ᶜ*ala l-yimiin.* Go to the end of the street and turn right. الأرض تدور حول الشمس *l-'arđ dduur ḥool š-šams.* The earth revolves around the sun. راسي دار وما دريت شي *raasi daar w-ma dareet šayy.* I was confused and didn't know anything. 3. to tour, travel, wander around. هذي السنة درنا في أوروبا كلها *haaði s-sana durna fi 'urooppa killaha.* This year we travelled all over Europe. تقدر تدور الإمارات كلها في يومين *tigdar dduur l-'imaaraat killaha fi yoomeen.* You can tour the whole of the U.A.E. in two days. 4. (with في *fi*) to stun, bewilder. القصة اللي سمعتها دارت فيني *l-ġissa lli sima*ᶜ*taha daarat fiini.* The story I have heard stunned me.

دور *dawwar* II 1. (with على ᶜ*ala*) to look for s.o. or s.th. دورت عليه وما لقيته *dawwart* ᶜ*alee w-ma ligeeta.* I looked for him and did not find him. ضيعت الشنطة. دورت عليها وما حصلتها *đayya*ᶜ*t š-šanṭa. dawwart* ᶜ*aleeha w-ma ḥaṣṣaltaha.* I lost the suitcase. I looked for it and did not find it. 2. to look, search. دورت في كل مكان وما لقيته *dawwart fi kill mukaan w-ma ligeeta.* I looked everywhere and didn't find it. إذا تدور زين تلقاه *'iða ddawwir zeen tilgaa.* If you search carefully, you will find it. ما عليك منه؛ بس يدور مشاكل *ma* ᶜ*aleek minna; bas yidawwir mašaakil.* Never mind him. He is only looking for trouble.

اندار *ndaar* VII 1. to turn. لين سمع الصوت اندار *leen sima*ᶜ *ṣ-ṣoot ndaar.*

When he heard the sound, he turned. 2. (with على *ᶜala*) to turn against. الكولية انداروا على التنديل *l-kuuliyya ndaaraw ᶜala t-tindeel.* The coolies turned against the supervisor. واحد منهم اندار علي وشتمني *waaḥid minhum ndaar ᶜalayya w-šitamni.* One of them turned on me and cursed me.

دار *daar* (f.) p. دور *duur* 1. house, home. هذي الدار انباعت *haaði d-daar nbaaᶜat.* This house was sold. دارنا، الله يسلمك، بعيدة مني *daarna, 'aḷḷa ysallimk, baᶜiida minni.* Our home, God protect you, is far from here. دار الأيتام *daar l-'aytaam* the orphanage. دار المعلمين *daar l-muᶜallimiin* the men's teacher training college. دار المعلمات *daar l-muᶜallimaat* the women's teacher training college. 2. household, family. دار عمي جاوا عندنا أمس *daar ᶜammi yaw ᶜindana 'ams.* My (paternal) uncle's family came to our place yesterday.

دور *door* p. ادوار *dwaar* 1. turn. الدور عليك *d-door ᶜaleek.* It's your turn. اخذ رقم دورك *'ixið ragam doorak.* Take a number for your turn. صبر! الدور رايح يوصلك *ṣabir! d-door raayiḥ yooṣalk.* Be patient! Your turn will come. كل واحد يدش بالدور *kill waaḥid ydišš b-d-door.* Everyone enters in turn. 2. role, part. شو دورك في ها الرواية؟ *šu doorak fi har-riwaaya?* What is your role in this play? لعبوا دور مهم في المحادثات *liᶜbaw door muhimm fi l-muḥaadaθaat.* They played an important role in the discussions. 3. once, one time. دور يصوم ودور يفطر *door yṣuum w-door yifṭir.* Sometimes he fasts, sometimes he doesn't fast.

دورة *doora* p. *-aat* one rotation, revolution, circulation. خمس دورات في الثانية *xams dooraat fi θ-θaanya* five revolutions per second.

دورة *dawra* p. *-aat* 1. course, training course. 2. session (of parliament).

دوري *dawri* periodic, recurring, intermittent. ألعاب دورية *'alᶜaab dawriyya* periodic sports. سباق دوري *sibaag dawri* round robin tournament.

دورية *dawriyya* p. *-aat* patrol.

دوارة *dwaara* (v.n. from II دور *dawwar*) looking for s.o. or s.th. دورت عليه دوارة وما حصلته *dawwart ᶜalee dwaara w-ma ḥaṣṣalta.* I really looked hard for him, but I didn't find him.

دوار *dawwaar* p. دواوير *dawaawiir* circle, roundabout, square. دعمتني سيارة عند الدوار الأول *diᶜmatni sayyaara ᶜind d-dawwaar l-'awwal.* A car hit me at the first circle.

دوار *dawaraan* 1. act of revolving, going round. دوران الأرض حول الشمس *dawaraan l-'arḍ ḥool š-šams* the revolution of the earth around the sun. 2. evasion, dodging. بدون لف ودوران *b-duun laff w-dawaraan* without ceremony, without detours and evasion.

دايرة *daayra* p. دواير *dawaayir* circle. رسم دايرة *risam daayra.* He drew a circle.

مدور *mdawwar* (p.p. from II دور *dawwar*) round, circular. الدنيا تمبة مدورة *d-dinya tamba mdawwara.* The world is a round ball. وجه مدور *weeh mdawwar* round face.

دوربين *dwrbyn*

دوربين *doorbiin* p. *-aat* telescope.

دوس *dws*

داس *daas (يدوس yduus)* 1. (with على *ᶜala*) to step, tread on s.th. لا تدوس على هذي الأرض *la dduus ᶜala haaði l-'arḍ̣.* Don't step on this floor. لا تدوس على الزولية بالجوتي حقك *la dduus ᶜala z-zuuliyya b-l-juuti ḥaggak*. Don't step on the carpet with your shoes. دوس على البانزين، دوس بانزين! *duus ᶜala l-baanziin, duus baanziin!* Step on the gas, step on the gas! أدوس على راس كل خاين *'aduus ᶜala raas kill xaayin*. I will humiliate every traitor. I will hurt every traitor.

انداس *ndaas* to be stepped on. أرض الحرم ما يندلاس عليها *'arḍ̣ l-ḥaram ma yindaas ᶜaleeha.* The floor of the mosque shouldn't be stepped on. السميت موب يابس بعد. ما يندلاس عليه *s-smiit muub yaabis baᶜad ma yindaas ᶜalee.* The cement isn't dry yet. It cannot be walked on. انداس على راس أبوه *ndaas ᶜala raas 'ubuu.* He was hurt (or humiliated) a lot.

دوسر *dwsr*

دوسري *doosari* p. دواسر *duwaasir* 1. belonging to the Dosari tribe, who originally came from وادي الدواسر *waadi d-duwaasir* in the Arabian Peninsula. 2. very large camel.

دوش *dwš*

دوش *duuš* shower, shower bath.

دوشگ *dwšg*

دوشك *doošag* (شبرية *šibriyya* is more common) p. دواشك *duwaašig* 1. mattress. 2. bench. تحصل دواشك في المنتزهات *tḥaṣṣil duwaašig fi l-muntazahaat.* You find benches in parks.

دوكر *dwkr*

دوكر *dookar (يدوكر ydookir)* to confuse s.o. لا تدوكرني. خلني أفكر *la ddookirni. xaḷḷni 'afakkir.* Don't confuse me. Let me think.

تدوكر *tdookar (يتدوكر yitdookar)* to become confused. تدوكرت لين سألني ذاك السؤال وما قدرت أجاوبه زين *ddookart leen si'alni ðaak s-su'aal w-ma gidart 'ajaawba zeen.* I was confused when he asked me that question and couldn't answer him properly.

دول *dwl*

دولة *dawla* (p. دول *duwal*) state, power, country. دولة قطر *dawlat giṭar* the State of Qatar. دولة البحرين *dawlat l-baḥreen* the State of Bahrain. الدول العربية *d-duwal l-ᶜarabiyya* the Arab States. الدول النامية *d-duwal n-naamya* the developing countries.

دولي *dawli* international. مطار أبو ظبي الدولي *maṭaar 'abu ḍ̣abi d-dawli* Abu Dhabi International Airport. القانون الدولي *l-ġaanuun d-dawli* international law.

دولاب *dwlaab*

دولاب *duulaab* p. دواليب *duwaaliib* 1. steering wheel. 2. wardrobe. علق هدومه في الدولاب *ᶜallag hduuma fi* *d-duulaab.* He hung his clothes in the wardrobe.

دولار *dwlaar*

دولار *duulaar* p. *-aat* dollar. عطيته خمسة دولار *ᶜaṭeeta xamsa duulaar.* I gave him five dollars. دفع لي خمسين دولار *difaᶜ-li xamsiin duulaar.* He paid me fifty dollars. كم سعر الدولار اليوم؟ *čam siᶜr d-duulaar l-yoom?* How much is the dollar exchange rate (lit., "the price of the dollar") today?

دولم *dwlm*

دولمة *doolma* Turkish dish made up of stuffed vegetables, such as grape leaves, squash, peppers, etc.

دوم *dwm*

دام *daam* (يدوم *yduum)* to last, continue, go on. حرب الخليج دامت شهرين *ḥarb l-xaliij daamat šahreen.* The Gulf War lasted two months. أيام العز دامت لهم *'ayyaam l-ᶜizz daamat lahum.* The good old days lasted long for them. الدنيا ما تدوم حق أحد *d-dinya ma dduum ḥagg 'aḥad.* The world doesn't stand still for anyone.

دام *daam* (يديم *ydiim)* to make permanent, perpetuate, cause to last or continue. الله دام النعمة عليهم *'aḷḷa daam n-niᶜma ᶜaleehum.* God perpetuated prosperity for them. الله يديم الشيخ لنا *'aḷḷa ydiim š-šeex lana.* God keep the Shaikh for us. مشكور. الله يديمك *maškuur. 'aḷḷa ydiimak.* Thank you. God keep you.

داوم *daawam* III 1. to go to work, report for duty. فيه ناس بتداوم الصباح وفيه ناس يتداوم العصر *fii naas b-ddaawim ṣ-ṣabaaḥ w-fii naas b-ddaawim l-ᶜaṣir.* There are people who go to work in the morning, and there are people who go to work in the afternoon. لازم تداوم باكر الساعة تسع *laazim ddaawim baačir s-saaᶜa tisiᶜ.* You have to report for duty tomorrow at nine. 2. to continue, carry on. أحسن لك تداوم على شغلك *'aḥsan-lak ddaawim ᶜala šuġlak.* It's better for you to continue to do your work. داوم على الدراسة *daawam ᶜala d-diraasa.* He continued to study.

مادام *ma-daam* 1. as long as, while. تونس مادمت حي *twannas ma-dumt ḥayy.* Enjoy life as long as you are alive. مادام (هو) هني *ma-daam (huwa) hni* while, as long as he is here. 2. since, because, inasmuch as. مادام ما عندك فلوس، ما تقدر تتونس *ma-daam ma ᶜindak fluus, ma tigdar titwannas.* Since you don't have any money, you cannot have a good time.

دوام *dawaam* work schedule, working day. ساعات الدوام *saaᶜaat d-dawaam* working hours, office hours. الدوام في الشركة *d-dawaam fi š-šarika* company hours. دوامي صعب *dawaami ṣaᶜb* My work schedule is difficult. عندنا نص دوام باكر *ᶜindana nuṣṣ dawaam baačir.* We have a half day (work schedule) tomorrow. على الدوام *ᶜala d-dawaam* at all times, always.

دايم *daayim* (act. part. from دام *daam*) 1. continuous, continual, constant. عمل خير دايم *ᶜamal xeer daayim* constant charitable deed. 2. eternal, everlasting. الله هو الدايم *'aḷḷaah huwa d-daayim.* God is the (only) eternal one. بصورة دايمة *b-ṣuura daayma* permanently.

دايماً *daayman* (less common var. دوم *doom*) always. دايما سكران *daayman sakraan.* He is always drunk. يجي دايما هني *yaji daayman hini.* He always comes here. موب دايما *muub daayman* not always.

دومن *dwmn*

دومنة *doomna* p. *-aat* dominoes.

دون *dwn*

بدون *b-duun* (prep.) without. يشرب قهوة بدون شكر *yišrab gahwa b-duun šakar.* He drinks coffee without sugar. بدون فلوس *b-duun fluus* free of charge, gratis. بدون قياس *b-duun gyaas* extremely, disproportionately, very. كان حمقان بدون قياس *čaan ḥamgaan b-duun gyaas.* He was very mad. الماي بدون قياس *l-maay b-duun gyaas.* The water is very plentiful. There is a lot of water. بدونهم ما نقدر نسوي شي *b-duunhum ma nigdar nsawwi šayy.* Without them we cannot do anything.

بدون ما *b-duun-ma* (conj.) without. لا تروح بدون ما تسترخص *la truuḥ b-duun-ma tistarxiṣ.* Don't go without taking permission.

دوني *duuni* 1. (p. *-iin,* دونية *duuniyya*) rascal, knave. لا تعاشره؛ هو دوني *la tᶜaašra; huwa duuni.* Don't associate with him; he is a rascal. 2. (adj.) close, nearby. رحت الدكان الدوني واشتريت حليب *riḥt d-dikkaan d-duuni w-štireet ḥaliib.* I went to the close store and bought milk.

ديوان *diiwaan* p. دواوين *dawaawiin* reception room. الديوان الأميري *d-diiwaan l-'amiri* the Emiri court. 2. central office, bureau, central building (of a ministry). ديوان الموظفين *diiwaan l-muwaððafiin* service commission. 3. collected works of a poet.

دونم *dwnm*

دونم *dunum* p. *-aat* land measure of about 2,500 square meters.

دووام *dwwaam*

دوامة *dawwaama* p. *-aat* 1. top (child's toy). 2. whirlpool, eddy.

دوي *dwy*

دوى *dawa* (يدوي *yadwi)* 1. to boom, resound, ring out. سمعت صوت يدوي؟ يمكن صوت الماكينة *simaᶜt ṣoot yadwi? yamkin ṣoot l-maakiina.* You heard a booming sound? It might be the sound of the machine. 2. to drone. الطيارة تدوي فوق روسنا *ṭ-ṭayyaara tadwi foog ruusna.* The plane is droning over our heads.

داوى *daawa* III to treat (a wound, an ailment, etc.). خذوه الدختر لاجل يداوي الجرح حقه *xaðoo d-daxtar lajil ydaawi l-jarḥ ḥagga.* They took him to the doctor to treat his wound. داويت السل اللي فيك؟ *daaweet s-sill illi fiik?* Have you had your tuberculosis treated?

تداوى *tdaawa* VI to be treated, get treated. يروح أمريكا ويتداوي هناك *yruuḥ 'amriika w-yiddaawa hnaak.* He goes to America and gets treated there.

دوا *duwa* p. أدوية *'adwiya* medicine, medication, remedy. رحت الدختر وكتب لي دوا *riḥt d-daxtar w-kitab-li duwa.* I went to the doctor and he prescribed some medicine for me. دواك عندي *duwaak ᶜindi.* I have your best medicine (i.e., I know you and know how to deal with you). دوا الجرح الكي *duwa l-jarḥ l-kayy.* The best medicine for a wound is cauterization.

دوي *dawi* (v.n. from دوا *dawa*) boom, rumbling, resounding sound. سمعت دوي المدفع؟ *simaᶜt dawi l-midfaᶜ?* Have you heard the roar of the cannon?

د ي ث *dyθ*

ديوث *dayyuuθ* (less frequent var. ديوس *dayyuus*) p. *-iin* pimp, procurer. ديوث ابن ديوث *dayyuuθ 'ibin dayyuuθ* son of a bitch.

د ي چ *dyč*

ديك *dayyač* II (with على *ᶜala*) to be proud or haughty, to swagger. لا تديك على ربعك *la ddayyič ᶜala rabᶜak.* Don't look down upon your people.

ديك *diič* p. ديوك *dyuuč* rooster. (prov.) يوم صخنا الماي شرد الديك *yoom ṣaxxanna l-maay širad d-diič.* Forewarned is forearmed. (lit., "When we heated the water, the rooster ran away."). (prov.) بيضة ديك *beeđat diič.* It happens only once in a lifetime. (lit., "A rooster's egg."). ديك رومي *diič ruumi* turkey cock.

مديك *mdayyič* p. *-iin* (with على *ᶜala*) proud, haughty. سالم مديك على الناس *saalim mdayyič ᶜala n-naas.* Salim looks down upon people.

د ي د *dyd*

ديد *deed* p. ديود *dyuud* 1. female breast. الديد اللي رضعك *d-deed illi rađđaᶜk* the breast which nursed you. 2. udder.

د ي ر *dyr*

دار *daar* (يدير *ydiir*) 1. to pour. دير لي شوية ماي في هذا القلاس *diir-li šwayyat maay fi haađa li-glaaṣ.* Pour me some water in this glass. 2. to turn, turn (one's face), direct. دير راسك! *diir raasak!* Turn your head! دير وجهك على الناس! *diir weeyhak ᶜala n-naas!* Turn your face to the people. دار باله *daar baala* to pay attention, be careful. دير بالك! فيه شرطي مرور قدامنا *diir baalak! fii širṭi muruur jiddaamna.* Be careful! There's a traffic policeman in front of us. لا تدير بال *la ddiir baal.* Don't worry. لا تدير له بال *la ddiir-la baal.* Don't worry about him. Don't pay attention to him. دار باله على السيارة الجديدة *daar baala ᶜala s-sayyaara l-yidiida.* He took care of the new car. دير بالك على صحتك *diir baalak ᶜala ṣiḥḥatk.* Look after your health. 3. (with على *ᶜala*) to turn s.o. against s.o. else. هذا يدير الكولية على التنديل *haađa ydiir l-kuuliyya ᶜala t-tindeel.* This one turns the coolies against the supervisor. دار علي وشتمني *daar ᶜalayya w-šitamni.* He turned on me and cursed me. 4. to direct, manage, run, be in charge of s.th. من اللي يدير ها الدايرة؟ *man illi ydiir had-daayra?* Who is the one who manages this department? هو اللي يدير كل شي هني *huwa lli ydiir kill šayy hini.* He is the one who runs everything here. يقدرون يديرون بلدهم بروحهم *yigdaruun ydiiruun baladhum b-ruuḥḥum.* They can run their country by themselves.

دير *deer* (v.n.) 1. pouring. دير الماي علـى الأرض *deer l-maay ^c^ala l-'arḍ* pouring the water on the ground. 2. managing, directing.

ديـرة *diira* p. *-aat* 1. town, hometown. حدرنـا للديـرة *ḥaddarna li-d-diira.* We went to town. رحت الديرة وشفت حالي *riḥt d-diira w-čift hali.* I went to my hometown and saw my folks. 2. compass. الديـرة ترويـك ويـن أنـت رايـح *d-diira trawwiik ween 'inta raayiḥ.* A compass shows you where you are heading. 3. district, region, area. ديرة دبـي *diirat dbayy* the commercial district of Dubai.

إدارة *'idaara* management, administration. إدارة الأعمـال *'idaarat l-'a^c^maal* business management. إدارة الجامعـة *'idaarat l-yaam^c^a* the university administration. مجلـس الإدارة *majlis l-'idaara* board of directors.

إداري *'idaari* 1. administrative. إجـراءات إداريـة *'ijraa'aat 'idaariyya* administrative measures. 2. (p. *-yyiin*) administrator. كم إداري في هذي الدايرة؟ *čam 'idaari fi haaði d-daayra?* How many administrators are there in this department?

دايـرة *daayra* p. دواير *dawaayir* 1. department, department of a ministry. دايـرة الجمـرك *daayrat l-jimrig* the customs department. دايـرة التربيـة *daayrat t-tarbiya* the department of education. كم دايرة في هذي الوزارة؟ *čam daayra fi haaði l-wazaara?* How many departments are there in this ministry?

مدير *mudiir* p. *-iin,* مدرا *mudara.* 1. director, manager. مديـر الماليـة *mudiir l-maaliyya* the director of finance. مديـر البنـك *mudiir l-bank* the bank manager. مديـر أعمـال *mudiir 'a^c^maal* business manager. 2. principal (of a school). مدير المدرسة *mudiir l-madrasa* the school principal. 3. president (of a university). مديـر الجامعـة *mudiir l-yaam^c^a* the university president.

د ي ر م *dyrm*

ديرم *deerum* lipstick

د ي س *dys*

ديـوس *dayyuus* (more frequent var. ديوث *dayyuuθ*) p. *-iin* pimp, procurer.

د ي ك *dyk*

ديـك *diik* (more common var. *diič*). See under **د ي چ** *dyč.*

د ي ن ١ *dyn*

ديـن *deen* p. ديـون *dyuun* 1. debt. عليه ديـن *^c^alee deen.* He is in debt. عطني امية درهـم ديـن *^c^aṭni 'imyat dirhim deen.* Give me one hundred dirhams as debt. 2. money owed one. الي دين عليه ألـف دينـار *'ili deen ^c^alee ^c^alf diinaar.* He owes me one thousand dinars. عليه دين لازم يسده *^c^alee deen laazim ysidda.* He owes money he should pay back.

مديـون *madyuun* p. *-iin* in debt, indebted. نشـتري بـالدين. مديونـين بـألف درهـم *ništiri b-d-deen. madyuuniin b-'alf dirhim.* We buy (things) on credit. We owe one thousand dirhams. آنا مديون لك بحيـاتي *'aana madyuun-lak b-ḥayaati.* I owe you my life.

د ي ن ٢ *dyn*

ديـن *diin* p. أديان *'adyaan* religion. الدين

الإسلامي *d-diin l-'islaami* the Islamic religion. الأديان السماوية *l-'adyaan s-samaawiyya* the heavenly religions. ما يامن بأي دين *ma yaamin b-'ayya diin.* He doesn't believe in any religion. يوم الدين *yoom d-diin* the Day of Judgement.

ديني *diini* religious, spiritual. أمور دينية *'umuur diiniyya* religious matters, religious affairs.

د ي ن ا ر *dynaar*

دينار *diinaar* p. دنانير *dinaaniir* dinar. كم يسوى الدينار البحريني؟ *čam yiswa d-diinaar l-baḥreeni?* How much is a Bahraini dinar worth?

د ي ن م ي ت *dynmyt*

ديناميت *diinamiit* dynamite. صبع ديناميت *ṣubi*[c] *diinamiit* stick of dynamite.

د ي ن م و *dynmw*

دينامو *diinamo* p. ديناموات *-waat* generator, dynamo.

د ي ي ١ *dyy*

دجاج *diyaay* (coll.) 1. chicken. كلينا دجاج ولحم مشوي *kaleena diyaay w-laḥam mašwi.* He ate chicken and grilled meat. 2. (s. دجاجة *diyaaya*. p. *-aat*) chicken, hen. عندنا خمس دجاجات بياضات [c]*indana xams diyaayaat bayyaađ̣aat.* We have five egg-laying chickens. (prov.) تموت الدجاجة وعينها بالسبوس *tmuut d-diyaaya w-*[c]*eenha b-s-sibuus.* (derogatory expression for a very greedy person) (lit., "A chicken dies looking at chicken feed.").

د ي ي ٢ *dyy*

دية *diyya.* See under **و د ي** *wdy.*

ذ

ذ ا *ðaa*

ذا *daa* (dem. pron.; more common var. هذا *haaða*) f. ذي *ðii* p. ذيل *ðeel,* ذيلا *deela* this, this one. See under هذا *haaða*.

ذ ا ك *ðaak*

ذاك *ðaak* (dem. pron.; more common var. هذاك *haðaak*) f. ذيك *ðiič* p. ذول *ðool,* ذولا *ðoola* that, that one. See under هذاك *haðaak.*

ذ ا ل *ðaal*

ذال *ðaal* name of the letter ذ *ð.*

ذ ب ب *ðbb*

ذب *ðabb (يذب yðibb)* 1. to throw, toss. لا تذب خمام على الأرض *la ððib xmaam ᶜala l-'arḍ.* Don't throw garbage on the floor. ذب له الكورة من بعيد *ðabb-la l-kuura min baᶜiid.* He threw the ball to him from a far distance. ذب نفسه منيك *ðabb nafsa minniik.* He jumped from there. ذبوه بقرية صغيرة لان ما له أحد يتوسط له *ðabboo b-ġarya ṣaġiira linn ma-la 'aḥad yitwassaṭ-la.* They sent him to a small village because he didn't have anyone to intercede for him. ذب كل شغله علي *ðabb kill šuġla ᶜalayya.* He pushed all of his work off on me. 2. to throw away, discard. ما يسوى شي. ذبه في الدرام *ma yiswwa šayy. ðibba fi d-draam.* It's not worth anything. Throw it away in the (garbage) can. أخيرا ذب القميص عقب ما لبسه عشرين مرة *'axiiran ðabb l-ġamiiṣ ᶜugub-ma libsa ᶜišriin marra.* At long last he threw away the shirt after he had worn it forty times. ذبت البرقع لين دشت بيتها *ðabbat l-birgiᶜ leen daššat betta.* She discarded the veil when she entered her house. ذب كبده *ðabb čabda.* He threw up.

ذ ب ح *ðbḥ*

ذبح *ðibaḥ (يذبح yiðbaḥ)* 1. to slaughter, butcher. القصاب ذبح خروفين *l-gaṣṣaab ðibaḥ xaruufeen.* The butcher slaughtered two lambs. قبل لا تذبح خروف والا بقرة والا بعير لازم تقول، «بسم الله والله أكبر» *gabil-la tiðbaḥ xaruuf walla bgara walla biᶜiir laazim tguul, "bismi-llah w-'aḷḷaahu 'akbar."* Before you slaughter a lamb, or a cow, or a camel, you have to say, "In the name of God, and God is the greatest." ذبحوا خروف على العيد *ðbaḥaw xaruuf ᶜala l-ᶜiid.* They slaughtered a lamb for the feast. 2. to cut someone's throat, kill s.o. ذبحوا بعضهم بعض *ðbaḥaw baᶜḍahum baᶜaḍ.* They beat each other. باقوه وذبحوه *baagoo w-ðbaḥoo.* They robbed him and cut his throat. هذا الشغل يذبح *haaða š-šuġul yiðbaḥ.* This work is murder. ذبحوه من الضرب وانحاشوا *ðbahoo min ḍ-ḍarb w-nhaašaw.* They almost beat him to death and ran away. ذبح روحه الين خلص الشغل *ðibaḥ ruuḥa 'ileen xaḷḷaṣ š-šuġul.* He almost killed himself until he finished his work. 3. to massacre. الجيش ذبح أهل القرية *l-jeeš ðibaḥ 'ahl l-ġarya.* The army massacred the people of the village.

ذبح *ðabbaḥ* II 1. to slaughter (large numbers). صار له مدة طويلة قاعد يذبح دجاج *ṣaar-la mudda ṭawiila gaacid yðabbiḥ diyaay.* He's been slaughtering chickens for a long time.

انذبح *nðibaḥ* VII 1. to be slaughtered. الخرفان انذبحوا كلهم *l-xirfaan nðibḥaw killahum.* All the lambs have been slaughtered. 2. to be killed. انذبحت من الشغل *nðibaḥt min š-šuġul.* I am dead tired from the work.

ذبح *ðabḥ* (v.n. from ذبح *ðibaḥ*) 1. slaughtering, killing. ذبح الخروف واجب على كل حاج *ðabḥ l-xaruuf waajib cala kill ḥaajj.* Slaughtering (or sacrificing) a lamb is required of every pilgrim. 2. cutting someone's throat. زخوا القاتل وذبحوه ذبح *zaxxaw l-gaatil w-ðbaḥoo ðabḥ.* They caught the killer and brutally cut his throat.

ذبيحة *ðibiiḥa* p. ذبايح *ðibaayiḥ* 1. slaughtered animal. المعرس لازم يدفع ثمن الذبايح حق الضيوف *l-micris laazim yidfac θaman ð-ðibaayiḥ ḥagg ḍ-ḍuyuuf.* The bridegroom has to pay for the cost of the slaughtered animals for the guests. 2. sacrificial animal. في عيد الأضحى لازم كل حاج يذبح ذبيحة *fi ciid l-'aḍḥa laazim kill ḥaajj yiðbaḥ ðibiiḥa.* On the day of the Feast of Immolation every pilgrim has to have a sacrificial animal. لحم الذبيحة يعطونه حق الفقارا *laḥam ð-ðibaayiḥ yacṭuuna ḥagg l-fagaara.* They give the meat of sacrificial animals to the poor.

مذبح *maðbaḥ* p. مذابح *maðaabiḥ* slaughterhouse.

مذبحة *maðbaḥa* p. مذابح *maðaabiḥ* massacre, slaughter.

مذبوح *maðbuuḥ* (p.p. from ذبح *ðibaḥ*) p. *-iin* 1. slaughtered, having been slaughtered. الكبش مذبوح *č-čabš maðbuuḥ.* The ram is slaughtered. 2. killed, having been killed.

ذ ب ل ðbl

ذبل *ðibal* (يذبل *yiðbal*) 1. to wilt, wither. الخس ذبل من الحر *l-xass ðibal min l-ḥarr.* The lettuce wilted in the heat. كل شي يذبل هني في الصيف *kill šaay yiðbal hini fi ṣ-ṣeef.* Everything wilts here in the summer. 2. to waste away, get run down. ذبل من المرض اللي فيه *ðibal min l-maraḍ illi fii.* He wasted away with his illness.

ذبلان *ðablaan* p. *-iin* 1. wilted, withered. الرويد ذبلان *r-rweed ðablaan.* The radishes are wilted. 2. wasted away, run down. ما ادري شفيه. باين عليه ذبلان *ma dri š-fee. baayin calee ðablaan.* I don't know what's wrong with him. He seems to be run down.

ذ ب ن ðbn

ذبان *ðibbaan* (coll.; less common var. ذباب *ðbaab*) flies. s. *-a.* الذبان يكثر في القيظ *ð-ðibbaan yikθar fi l-geeḍ.* Flies increase in the summer.

ذبابي *ðabbaabi* p. *-yya* flycatcher.

ذ ر ر ðrr

ذر *ðarr* (coll.) ants, small ants. s. *-a.* p. *-aat.* لازم نتعلم التعاون والجد من الذر *laazim nitcallam t-tacaawun w-l-jidd min ð-ðarr.* We ought to learn cooperation and hard work from ants.

ذرة *ðarra* p. *-aat* 1. atom. 2. speck, mote. ما عنده ولا ذرة من الحنان *ma ᶜinda wala ðarra min l-ḥanaan.* He doesn't have a bit of affection. 3. small ant.

ذري *ðarri* atomic. قنبلة ذرية *gunbula ðarriyya* atomic bomb.

ذرية *ðurriyya* p. *-aat* descendants, offspring.

ذ ر ع *ðrᶜ*

ذراع *ðraaᶜ* p. ذرعان *ðirᶜaan,* ذراعات *-aat* 1. arm (of a person), forearm. حصل الترقية بذراعه *ḥaṣṣal t-targiya b-ðraaᶜa.* He got the promotion by his own effort. 2. (p. ذراعات *-aat,* أذرع *'aðriᶜ*) unit of measure (= approx. 1½ feet).

ذ ر ي *ðry*

ذرى *ðarra* II to winnow (grain). يذرون البر في الهوا *yðarruun l-burr fi l-hawa.* They are winnowing wheat in the air.

إذرة *'iðra* (coll.) corn. حبة إذرة *ḥabbat 'iðra* grain of corn. الإذرة ما تطلع هني *l-'iðra ma tiṭlaᶜ hini.* Corn does not grow here. إذرة صفرا *'iðra ṣafra* maize. إذرة بيضا *'iðra beeḍa* sorghum.

ذروة *ðarwa* peak, apex, top (of power, happiness, success, etc.) هو في ذروة السعادة *huwa fi ðarwat s-saᶜaada.* He is at the peak of happiness.

ذ ع ن *ðᶜn*

أذعن *'aðᶜan* (يذعن *yiðᶜin*) to yield, submit, give in, obey. يذعن حق اللي يهدده *yiðᶜin ḥagg illi yhaddida.* He gives in to those who threaten him. الشرطة تستعمل القوة حق اللي ما يذعن *š-širṭa tistaᶜmil l-guwwa ḥagg illi ma yiðᶜin.* The police use force on those who do not obey.

ذ گ ن *ðgn*

ذقن *ðagin* p. ذقون *ðguun* chin.

ذ ك ر *ðkr*

ذكر *ðikar* (يذكر *yaðkur*) 1. to mention. ذكر انه رايح يجي باكر *ðikar 'inna raayiḥ yiyi baačir.* He mentioned that he was going to come tomorrow. ما ذكر في الخط أي شي عن دراسته *ma ðikar fi l-xaṭṭ 'ayya šayy ᶜan diraasta.* He didn't mention anything about his studies in the letter. 2. to recall, remember. تذكر يوم جيت الإمارات؟ *taðkur yoom yiit l-'imaaraat?* Do you recall the day you came to the Emirates? ما أذكر اني قلت ها الكلام *ma 'aðkur 'inni gilt hal-kalaam.* I don't recall I have said these words. 3. to speak of, talk about. رجال زين. دايماً نذكره بالخير *rayyaalin zeen. daayman naðkura b-l-xeer.* He is a good man. We always speak well of him.

ذكر *ðakkar* II to remind, call to mind. ذكرني بذيك الأيام *ðakkarni b-ðiič l-'ayyaam.* He reminded me of those days. حرمتي ذكرتني أشتري عيش وسمك *ḥurumti ðakkaratni 'aštiri ᶜeeš w-simač.* My wife reminded me to buy rice and fish. ذكرته بالزيادة اللي وعدني فيها *ðakkarta b-z-ziyaada lli waᶜadni fiiha.* I reminded him of the raise he had promised me. إذا نسيت ذكرني *'iða niseet ðakkirni.* If I forget, remind me. ها الوجه ما يذكرك بالمدير علي؟ *hal-weeh ma yðakkirk b-l-mudiir ᶜali?* Doesn't this face remind you of Director Ali?

ذاكر *ðaakar* III to learn, study one's lessons. ما شاالله عليها يا بو علي. كل يوم تقعد تذاكر دروسها *ma šaa-ḷḷa ᶜaleeha ya bu ᶜali. kill yoom tagᶜid ððaakir druussa.* She is amazing, Abu Ali. Every day she sits down to study her lessons.

تذكر *tðakkar* to remember, recollect. تذكر انه لازم يروح البريد *ððakkar 'inna laazim yruuḥ l-bariid.* He remembered that he had to go to the post office. ما أتذكر *ma 'aððakkar.* I don't remember.

ذكر *ðikir* (v.n. from ذكر *ðikar*) 1. mentioning, mention. نتبدا بذكر الله *nitbadda b-ðikr aḷḷa.* We begin by mentioning the Lord's name. ذالحين كنا بذكر أخوك *ðalḥiin činna b-ðikir 'uxuuk.* We were just talking about your brother. ها الشي اله ذكر في القرآن؟ *haš-šayy 'ila ðikir fi l-ġur'aan?* Is this thing mentioned in the Quran? على ذكر بنتك لطيفة، شو تسوي ذالحين؟ *ᶜala ðikir bintak laṭiifa, šu tsawwi ðalḥiin?* Speaking of your daughter Latifa, what is she doing now? واسع الذكر *waasiᶜ ð-ðikir* widely known. 2. religious ceremony in which the attributes of God are recited.

ذكر *ðakar* p. ذكور *ðukuur* male. الكبش ذكر النعجة *č-čabš ðakar li-nᶜaya č-čabš ðakar li-nᶜaya.* A ram is the male of an ewe.

ذكرى *ðikra* p. ذكريات *-yaat* 1. remembrance, recollection. اليوم ذكرى مولد النبي *l-yoom ðikra mawlid n-nabi.* Today is the anniversary of the birth of the Prophet. 2. (p. *-aat*) memoirs, reminiscences.

تذكار *tiðkaar* p. *-aat* souvenir, memento. خذ هذا تذكار *xið haaða tiðkaar.* Take this as a souvenir.

تذكرة *taðkara* p. تذاكر *taðaakir* 1. ticket, admission ticket. شغلي قطع تذاكر حق المتحف *šuġli ġaṭiᶜ taðaakir ḥagg l-matḥaf.* My job is to sell tickets for the museum. قبل لا تدش المتحف لازم تقطع تذكرة *gabil-la ddišš l-matḥaf laazim tiġṭaᶜ taðkara.* Before you enter the museum, you have to buy a ticket. شباك التذاكر *šubbaak t-taðaakir* the ticket window. 2. (bus, train, airplane) ticket. قطعت تذكرة رايح جاي *ġiṭaᶜt taðkara raayiḥ yaay.* I bought a round-trip ticket.

مذاكرة *muðaakara* (v.n. from III ذاكر *ðaakar*) studying one's lessons, learning.

ذاكرة *ðaakira* memory. عنده ذاكرة قوية *ᶜinda ðaakira gawiyya.* He has a strong power of recollection.

مذكور *maðkuur* p. *-iin* (p.p. from ذكر *ðikar*) 1. mentioned. 2. said, above-mentioned.

مذكرة *muðakkara* p. *-aat* memorandum. دايرة الآثار طرشت مذكرة حق وزارة السياحة *daayrat l-'aaθaar ṭarrašat muðakkara ḥagg wazaarat s-siyaaḥa.* The department of antiquities sent a memorandum to the ministry of tourism.

ذ ك ي *ðky*

ذكا *ðaka* intelligence, brightness. ذكاه عجيب *ðakaa ᶜajiib.* He is very intelligent.

ذكي *ðaki* p. *-yyiin,* أذكيا *'aðkiya*

intelligent, bright, clever. ذكية كلش. تطلع الأولى على بنات صفها *ðakiyya killiš. tiṭlac l-'uula cala banaat ṣaffha.* She is very intelligent. She ranks the first among her classmates.

ذ ل ل *ðll*

ذل *ðall (يذل yðill)* to be or become despised, contemptible, lowly. نفسه تذل على درهم *nafsa ððill cala dirhim.* He humiliates himself for a dirham. ذل يعني أصبح ذليل *ðall yacni 'aṣbaḥ ðaliil. ðall* means he became servile.

ذلل *ðallal* II 1. to humble, humiliate. لا تذلل نفسك على درهم *la ððallil nafsak cala dirhim.* Don't humiliate yourself for a dirham. 2. to overcome, surmount. مشكور. مساعدتك ذللت كل الصعوبات *maškuur. musaacadatak ðallalat kill ṣ-ṣucuubaat.* Thank you. Your help has overcome all the difficulties.

تذلل *tðallal* V 1. to lower, humble oneself, be humble. لين يحتاج أحد يتذلل له *leen yiḥtaaj 'aḥad yiððall-la.* Whenever he needs someone, he will humiliate himself for him. 2. to be overcome, be surmounted. كل الصعوبات اللي قدامي تذللت *kill ṣ-ṣucuubaat illi jiddami ððallalat.* All the difficulties facing me have been overcome.

ذل *ðull* (v.n. from ذل *ðall*) humiliation, submission, subjugation. عاشوا عيشة ذل *caašaw ciišat ðull.* They lived a life of humiliation. الذل، طال عمرك، ما ينقبل *ð-ðull, ṭaal cumrak, ma yingabal.* Subjugation, may you live long, is unacceptable.

ذليل *ðaliil* p. *-iin,* ذلة *ðilla* humble, submissive, servile.

ذلول *ðaluul* p. ذلل *ðulal* young female riding camel.

مذلة *maðalla* = ذل *ðull*

ذ م ا ر *ðmaar*

ذمار *ðamaar* Dhamar (city in Yemen).

ذ م ر *ðmr*

تذمر *tðammar* V to complain, grumble. لاتدير بال! يتذمر من كل شي *la ddiir baal! yiððammar min kill šayy.* He grumbles about everything.

تذمر *taðammur* (v.n. from V تذمر *tðammar*) complaining, grumbling.

ذ م م *ðmm*

ذم *ðamm (يذم yðimm)* to find fault with s.o., criticize s.o. يذم غيره على ماميش *yðimm ġeera cala maamiiš.* He finds fault with others for nothing. يذم التنديل بس يمدح المدير *yðimm t-tindeel bass yimdaḥ l-mudiir.* He criticizes the supervisor but praises the manager.

ذمة *ðimma* p. ذمم *ðimam* 1. conscience, moral sense. بالذمة؟ *b-ð-ðimma?* Honestly! Really! بذمتي ما عندي علم بهذا الشي *b-ðimmati ma cindi cilim b-haaða š-šayy.* I swear I have no knowledge of this matter. بذمتك، شو سويت؟ *b-ðimmatk, šu sawweet?* Honestly, what have you done? 2. financial obligation. لا تزال على ذمته *la tazaal cala ðimmta.* She is still financially dependent on him.

ذ ن ب *ðnb*

أذنب *'aðnab* IV *(يذنب yiðnib)* to commit a sin, a crime, an offense. إن

حلفت تقول الصدق وما قلت الصدق أذنبت *'in ḥilaft tguul ṣ-ṣidj w-ma gilt ṣ-ṣidj 'aðnabt.* If you swear to tell the truth and you don't tell the truth, you have sinned.

ذنب *ðanb* p. ذنوب *ðnuub* 1. sin, offense, misdeed. ذنبه خطير *ðanba xaṭiir.* His sin is serious. 2. mistake, fault, error. موب ذنبي؛ ذنبك *muub ðanbi; ðanbak.* It's not my fault; it's your fault. ذنبه على جنبه *ðanba ᶜala jamba.* He is at fault. It's his mistake.

ذنب *ðanab* p. اذناب *ðnaab* (ذيل *ðeel* is more common) tail. See under **ذ ي ل** *ðyl.*

مذنب *miðnib* (act. part. from IV أذنب *'aðnab*) p. *-iin* 1. guilty. 2. sinner.

ذ ه ب *ðhb*

ذهب *ðahab* (coll.) gold. الذهب غالي *ð-ðahab ġaali.* Gold is expensive. رحت السوق واشتريت حلقة ذهب *riḥt s-suug w-štireet ḥilga ðahab.* I went to the market and bought a gold ring. شدعوة غالي ها القد؟ باين عليه ذهب *š-daᶜwa ġaali hal-gadd? baayin ᶜalee ðahab.* Why is it that expensive? It seems it's gold. ساعة ذهب *saaᶜa ðahab* gold watch.

ذهبي *ðahabi* golden, gold (color). لون السيارة ذهبي *loon s-sayyaara ðahabi.* The color of the car is gold. لون ذهبي *loon ðahabi* gold color.

مذهب *maðhab* p. مذاهب *maðaahib* 1. denomination, faith, religious denomination. فيه أربع مذاهب في الإسلام *fii 'arbaᶜ maðaahib fi l-'islaam.* There are four denominations in Islam. المذهب الكاثوليكي *l-maðhab l-kaaθooliiki* the Catholic faith, Catholicism.

مذهب *mðahhab* gilded. صينية مذهبة *ṣiiniyya mðahhaba* gilded tray. بردة مذهبة *parda mðahhaba* gilded curtain.

ذ ه ن *ðhn*

ذهن *ðihin* p. أذهان *'aðhaan* mind.

ذهني *ðihni* intellectual, mental. سؤال ذهني *su'aal ðihni* question requiring thought.

ذهين *ðihiin* clever, intelligent, bright.

أذهن *'aðhan* (elat.) 1. (with من *min*) more intelligent, brighter. ما فيه أذهن منه *ma fii 'aðhan minna.* There isn't any other more intelligent person. 2. (with foll. n.) the most intelligent, the brightest. هو أذهن واحد *huwa 'aðhan waaḥid.* He is the most intelligent one.

ذ و ب *ðwb*

ذاب *ðaab (يذوب yðuub)* 1. to dissolve. الشكر ذاب في القهوة *š-šakar ðaab fi li-gahwa.* The sugar dissolved in the coffee. 2. to melt. الثلج اللي في القلاص ذاب *θ-θalj illi fi li-glaaṣ ðaab.* The ice in the glass has melted.

ذوب *ðawwab* II 1. to dissolve s.th. ذوب الشكر في الشاي *ðawwab š-šakar fi č-čaay.* He dissolved the sugar in the tea. 2. to melt s.th. الصايغ يذوب الذهب *ṣ-ṣaayiġ yðawwib ð-ðahab.* The jeweler is melting the gold.

ذ و ت *ðwt*

ذات *ðaat* 1. self, ego. حب الذات *ḥubb ð-ðaat* egoism, self-love, selfishness. 2. self. جاوا بذاتهم *yaw b-ðaattum.*

They came themselves. هو بذاته رمسني *huwa b-ðaata rammasni.* He himself talked to me. بحد ذاته *b-ḥadd ðaata* in itself, by itself. الوظيفة بحد ذاتها زينة، بس العمل الحر أحسن *l-waðiifa b-ḥadd ðaatta zeena, bass l-ᶜamal l-ḥurr 'aḥsan.* Employment in itself is good, but business is better.

ذوات *ðawaat*, as in ابن ذوات *'ibin ðawaat* person from a prominent family.

ذاتي *ðaati* self-produced, self-acting. حكم ذاتي *ḥukum ðaati* autonomy, self-rule.

ذ و گ *ðwg*

ذاق *ðaag (يذوق yðuug)* 1. to taste, sample. ذاق الأكل وقال إنه زين *ðaag l-'akil w-gaal 'inna zeen.* He tasted the food and said it was good. عمرك ذقت ها الأكل؟ *ᶜumrak ðugt hal-'akil?* Have you ever tasted this food? 2. to experience, undergo, suffer. ذاق العذاب في السجن *ðaag l-ᶜaðaab fi s-sijin.* He experienced torture in jail. ذاق الأمرين *ðaag l-'amarreen.* He went through hell. He suffered the greatest hardships.

استذوق *staðwag* X to like, appreciate, relish. الريوق اليوم بيض وجبن وزبد. رايح تستذوقه *r-riyuug l-yoom beeḍ w-jibin w-zibid. raayiḥ tistaðwiga.* Breakfast today is eggs, cheese, and butter. You are going to like it. أستذوق طبخ أمي *'astaðwig ṭabx 'ummi.* I appreciate my mother's cooking.

ذوق *ðoog* 1. taste (of food, clothing, etc.). 2. manners, sense of propriety, tact. ذوقه سليم *ðooga saliim.* He has good taste.

ذ و ل *ðwl*

ذول *ðool,* ذولا *ðoola.* See under هذا *haaða.*

ذ ي *ðy*

ذي *ðii,* هذي *haaði.* See under هذا *haaða.*

ذ ي ب *ðyb*

ذيب *ðiib* p. ذياب *ðyaab* wolf. (prov.) ويش على الذيب من ضراط النعجة؟ *weeš ᶜala ð-ðiib min ðraaṭ li-nᶜaya?* (lit., "What harm can the fart of a ewe do to the wolf?"). ذيب ظلما *ðiib ḍalma* very courageous person.

ذ ي چ *ðyč*

ذيك *ðiič,* هذيك *haðiič* that (f.), that one (f.). See under هذاك *haðaak.*

ذ ي د *ðyd*

ذيد *ðeed* beautiful oasis in Sharja.

ذ ي ر *ðyr*

ذار *ðaar (يذير yðiir)* 1. to avoid, keep away from. لازم تذير عن هذا الرجال *laazim ððiir ᶜan haaða r-rayyaal.* You've got to avoid this man. أذر عن الخطر *'aðir ᶜan l-xaṭar.* Keep away from danger. 2. to go far away, become distant. البعير ذار عن المرعى *l-biᶜiir ðaar ᶜan l-marᶜa.* The camel went far away from the grazing land. ليش ذرت عن المجلس؟ *leeš ðirt ᶜan l-majlis?* Why didn't you attend the council meeting?

ذ ي ع *ðyᶜ*

ذاع *ðaaᶜ (يذيع yðiiᶜ)* 1. to broadcast, transmit. ذاعوا الخبر الساعة خمس *ðaaᶜaw* *l-xabar s-saaᶜa xams.* They broadcast the news at five o'clock. ذاعوا انهم رايحين يفتشون البيوت *ðaaᶜaw 'inhum raayḥiin yfattšuun li-byuut.* They broadcast that they were going to search the houses. 2. to spread, circulate. الخبر ذاع بين الناس *l-xabar ðaaᶜ been n-naas.* The news became widespread among the people.

انذاع VII *nðaaᶜ* = ذاع *ðaaᶜ*.

إذاعة *'iðaaᶜa* 1. broadcasting. إذاعة الأخبار *'iðaaᶜat l-'axbaar* broadcasting of the news. محطة الإذاعة *maḥaṭṭat l-'iðaaᶜa* the broadcasting station. 2. announcement, disclosure. 3. (p. إذاعات *'iðaaᶜaat*) broadcasting station.

مذيع *muðiiᶜ* p. *-iin* radio or television announcer.

ذ ي ل *ðyl*

ذيل *ðeel* p. ذيول *ðyuul* 1. tail (of an animal, a bird, an airplane). 2. hem, border. ذيل الثوب *ðeel θ-θoob* the hem of the dress. ذيل العباية *ðeel l-ᶜabaaya* the hem of the aba.

ر

را *raa*

را *raa* name of the letter ر *r*.

رادو *raadw*

رادو *raadu* p. رادوات *-waat* radio. سمعنا الأخبار من الـرادو *sima*ᶜ*na l-'axbaar min r-raadu.* We heard the news on the radio.

رازجي *raazjy*

رازجـي *raazji* (coll.) white flowers. (unit noun unknown).

رءس *r's*

رأس *ri'as (يرأس yir'as)* to lead, be at the head, be in charge. مـن اللـي رأس الاجتمـاع؟ *man illi ri'as l-'ijtimaa*ᶜ*?* Who chaired the meeting? رأس اللجنة *ri'as l-lajna.* He chaired the committee.

رأس *ra''as* II (less common var. ريس *rayyas*) to appoint as leader or head, place in charge. منـو اللـي رأسـك هـني؟ *minu lli ra''ask hini?* Who made you the boss here?

تـرأس *tra''as* V to lead, head, be in charge. ترأس وفدنا إلى هيئـة الأمـم *tra''as wafdana 'ila hay'at l-'umam.* He headed our delegation to the United Nations.

راس *raas* p. روس *ruus* 1. head. راسي يعورنـي *raasi y*ᶜ*awwirni.* I have a headache. عورت راسـي ᶜ*awwart raasi.* You gave me a headache. راسـي دار *raasi daar.* I was confused. راسه حار *raasa ḥaarr.* He is bad-tempered. خـذوا راس القـاتل *xaðu raas l-gaatil.* They beheaded the killer. (prov.) راس بالسـما وطـيز بالمـاي *raasin b-s-sima w-ṭiizin b-l-maay.* Fair without and foul within. (lit., "A head in the sky and a rear end in the water."). 2. head of ... راس غنـم *raas ġanam* head of sheep. راس خـس *raas xass* head of lettuce. راس بصـل *raas baṣal* an onion. 3. top, summit, peak. راس الجبـل *raas l-yibal* the top of the mountain. راس الخيمـة *raas l-xeema* Ras Al-Khaima. راس النخلة *raas li-nxaḷa* the top of the palm tree. 4. beginning. راس الشـهر *raas š-šahar* the first of the month. راس السـنة *raas s-sana* the beginning of the year. عيد راس السنة ᶜ*iid raas s-sana* New Year's Day. روس الأصـابع *ruus l-'aṣaabi*ᶜ tiptoes.

راسمـال *raasmaal* capital, financial assets.

راسمـالي *raasmaali* 1. capitalistic, capitalist. نظام راسمالي *niðaam raasmali* capitalist system. (p. *-yyiin*) capitalist.

راسمالية *raasmaaliyya* capitalism.

رئيس *ra'iis* p. رؤسا *ru'asa* 1. president. رئيـس دولـة الإمـارات *ra'iis dawlat l-'imaaraat* the president of the U.A.E. رئيـس الجامعـة *ra'iis l-yaam*ᶜ*a* the university president. رئيس الوزرا *ra'iis l-wuzara* the prime minister. رئيـس البلديـة *ra'iis l-baladiyya* the mayor. رئيـس الأركـان *ra'iis l-'arkaan* the chief of staff (mil.). 2. head, leader, boss, chief. رئيس الدايـرة *ra'iis d-daayra* the head of the department. رئيس العصابة *ra'iis l-ᶜiṣaaba* the leader of the gang. رئيس التحرير *ra'iis t-taḥriir* the e in-chief.

رئيسي *ra'iisi* main, chief, principal. السبب الرئيسي *s-sabab r-ra'iisi* the main reason. شارع رئيسي *šaariᶜ ra'iisi* main street. دور رئيسي *door ra'iisi* leading role.

رئاسة *ri'aasa* (informal var. رياسة *riyaasa*) 1. presidency, presidentship. رئاسة الوزرا *ri'aasat l-wuzara* the prime ministry, the premiership. 2. chairmanship. رياسة اللجنة *riyaasat l-lajna* the committee chairmanship. رياسة الجمعية *riyaasat l-jamᶜiyya* the chairmanship of the association.

مرؤوس *mar'uus* (p.p. from رأس *ri'as*) p. *-iin* subordinate, underling.

ر ء ف *r'f*

رأف *ri'af (يرأف yir'af)* to show mercy, be kind, merciful. رأف على الفقير *ri'af ᶜala l-fagiir.* He was kind to the poor person.

رؤوف *ra'uuf* p. *-iin* merciful, compassionate.

ر ء ي *r'y*

رأي *ra'i* no p. (more common var. راي *raay*) opinion, view. شو رايك؟ *šu raayak?* What do you think? ما لك راي؟ *ma lak raay?* Don't you have your own opinion? رايك نسير *raayak nsiir?* Do you think we should go? رايي ان هذا الموضوع خطير *raayi 'inna haaða l-mawḍuuᶜ xaṭiir.* I am of the opinion that this case is serious. في رايي *fi raayi* in my opinion. الراي العام *r-raay l-ᶜaamm* (the) public opinion.

راية *raaya* p. *-aat* banner, flag.

مرية *mrayya* p. *-aat* mirror, looking glass.

ر ب ب *rbb*

رب *rabb* 1. lord, master. رب البيت *rabb l-beet* the provider, the head of the family. ربة البيت *rabbat l-beet* the homemaker, the housewife. يا رب، يا ربي! *ya rabb, ya rabbi!* my Lord! my God! الرب *r-rabb* God. يا ربي، شو هذا *ya rabbi šu haaða?* My God, what's this? رب العالمين *rabb l-ᶜaalamiin.* God, the Lord of the Universe. (prov.) ربي كما خلقتني *rabbi kama xalagtani.* (used to describe someone who never changes). (lit., "I am, my God, the same as you created me."). 2. (only in p. أرباب *'arbaab*) a. proprietors, owners, as in أرباب أموال *'arbaab 'amwaal* capitalists. أرباب الحكم *'arbaab l-ḥukum* the rulers. b. (adj.) well-liked, respected, refined. ريس أرباب *rayyis 'arbaab* well-liked boss. رجال أرباب *rayyaal 'arbaab* refined gentleman.

ربابة *rbaaba* p. *-aat* stringed musical instrument resembling the fiddle.

ر ب ح *rbḥ*

ربح *ribaḥ (يربح yirbaḥ)* 1. to gain, profit. ربح خمسة مليون درهم من المشروع *ribaḥ xamsa malyoon dirhim min l-mašruuᶜ.* He gained five million dirhams from the project. من ذيك الصفقة ربح مليون دينار *min ðiič ṣ-ṣafġa ribaḥ malyoon diinaar.* On that deal he made a million dinars. 2. to win.

لـو تربـح لـو تخسـر *lo tirbaḥ lo txasir.* Either you win, or lose. البطاقة ربحت ألـف درهـم *l-biṭaaġa rbiḥat 'alf dirhim.* The ticket won a thousand dirhams. يخسـر في القمـار أكـثر مما يربـح *yxasir fi l-gimaar 'akθar mim-ma yirbaḥ.* He loses more than he gains in gambling.

ربح *rabbaḥ* II to make s.o. gain, grant s.o. a profit, allow s.o. to profit. ذيك الصفقـــة ربحتـــني واجـــد *ðiič ṣ-ṣafġa rabbaḥatni waayid.* That transaction made me a large profit.

ربح *ribḥ* p. أربـاح *'arbaaḥ* 1. profit, gain. أربـاح الشـركة خمسـة مليـون درهـم *'arbaaḥ š-šarika xamsa malyoon dirhim.* The company made a five million dirham profit. 2. interest (on money). الربح من البنوك حرام في الإسـلام. *r-ribḥ min li-bnuuk ḥaraam fi l-'islaam.* Interest from banks is not allowed in Islam.

ربحان *rabḥaan* p. *-iin* gainer, winner, profiter. هو الربحان وأنـت الخسـران *huwa r-rabḥaan w-inta l-xasraan.* He is the winner and you are the loser.

رابح *raabiḥ* (act. part. from ربح *ribaḥ*) 1. having gained, won. هو رابـح ألـف دينـار *huwa raabiḥ 'alf diinaar.* He has gained one thousand dinars. 2. (adj.) winning. الرقم الرابـح *r-ragam r-raabiḥ* the winning number.

ر ب ر ب *rbrb*

ربرب *rabrab (*يربـرب *yrabrib)* to chatter, talk aimlessly. ما عليـك منهـا؛ بـس تربـرب *ma ᶜaleek minha; bass trabrib.* Don't pay attention to her. She just chatters.

ربربة *rabraba* chattering, gibberish. لويش هـا الربربـة؟ مـا فهمـت شـي *li-weeš har-rabraba? ma fihamt šayy.* What's this gibberish for? I don't know what's going on.

ربربي *rabrabi* p. *-yya, -iin* talkative, chatterbox. ما عنده إلا الكلام. ربربـي *ma ᶜinda 'illa l-kalaam. rabrabi.* He has nothing but words. He's a chatterbox.

ربربية *rabrabiyya* p. *-aat* female chatterbox.

ر ب ش *rbš*

ربش *ribaš (*يربش *yirbiš)* 1. to confuse s.o. ربشني بحكيه *ribašni b-ḥačya.* He confused me with what he said. 2. to mess up s.th. لا تربش النظام في ها الدايرة. *la tirbiš n-niðaam fi had-daayra.* Don't mess up the system in this department.

أربش *'arbaš* IV = ربش *ribaš*

ارتبش *rtibaš* VIII 1. to be confused, mixed up. يرتبش مـن أقـل شـي *yirtabiš min 'agall šayy.* He gets confused for the slightest thing. لا تحكي وانـا أقـرا؛ تـرى أرتبـش *la tḥači w-aana 'agra; tara 'artibiš.* Don't talk while I am reading; otherwise I will get mixed up.

ربشة *rabša* confusion, disorder, mess. صارت ربشة حينمـا وزعـوا الفلـوس *ṣaarat rabša ḥiin-ma wazzaᶜaw li-fluus.* There was confusion when they distributed the money. كان فيه ربشة في السـوق *čaan fii rabša fi s-suug.* There was disorder in the marketplace.

مرتبش *mirtibiš* p. *-iin* confused, mixed up. مـا يحكـي عـدل؛ مرتبـش *ma yḥači*

^{c}*adil; mirtibiš.* He doesn't talk properly; he's confused.

ر ب ط *rbṭ*

ربـــط *ribaṭ (*يربط *yarbuṭ)* 1. to tie up, bind. زخوه وربطوه بحبل وخذوه الشرطـــة *zaxxoo w-ribṭoo b-ḥabil w-xaðoo š-širṭa.* They caught him, tied him up with a rope, and took him to the police. 2. to fasten, tie, attach. اربط الحزام! *'urbuṭ li-ḥzaam!* Fasten the seat belt! ربط الخروف بالشجرة *ribaṭ l-xaruuf b-š-šyara.* He tied the lamb to the tree. 3. to connect. ما فيه جسر يربط بو ظبي بالســـعديات *ma fii jisir yarbuṭ bu ḍabi b-s-sa^{c}diyyaat.* There is no bridge that connects Abu Dhabi with Sadiyaat (Island). 4. attach, annex. ربطوا ديوان الموظفين بوزارة التخطيط *ribṭaw diiwaan l-muwaḍḍafiin b-wazaarat t-taxṭiiṭ.* They attached the civil service commission to the ministry of planning.

ربط *rabbaṭ* II = ربط *ribaṭ*

تربط *trabbat* V to be tied up, bound.

ارتبـــط *rtibaṭ* VIII 1. to bind oneself, commit oneself. ارتبطنا بالموعد *rtibaṭna b-l-maw^{c}id.* We got tied up with the appointment. 2. to be connected. ارتبطت السيارة بالحبل *rtibṭat s-sayyaara b-l-ḥabil.* The car was connected to the rope.

ربـــط *rabṭ* (v.n. from ربـــط *ribaṭ*) connecting, attaching. حكيه ما فيه ربط *ḥačya ma fii rabṭ.* His words don't make sense. ربط السيارتين بحبل ما يفيد *rabṭ s-sayyaarteen b-ḥabil ma yfiid.* Connecting the two cars with a rope doesn't help.

ربطـــة *rabṭa* (n. of inst.) p. *-aat* bunch, bundle.

رابطـــة *raabiṭa* p. روابط *rawaabiṭ* 1. bond, tie. فيه رابطـــة صداقـــة بيننـــا *fii raabiṭat ṣadaaga beenna.* There is a bond of friendship between us. 2. league, union, association. الرابطـــة الإســـلامية *r-raabiṭa l-'islaamiyya* the Muslim League. رابطة الطلاب العـــرب *raabiṭat ṭ-ṭullaab l-^{c}arab* the Arab Student League.

مربـــوط *marbuuṭ* (p.p. from ربط *ribaṭ*) 1. tied up, bound. 2. fastened, attached. 3. connected. 4. attached, annexed.

مرتبـــط *mirtibiṭ* p. *-iin* committed, tied up, tied down. مرتبط بكلامـــه *mirtibiṭ b-kalaama* committed to his words. مرتبط بموعـــد *mirtibiṭ b-maw^{c}id* tied up with an appointment.

ر ب ع *rb^{c}*

ربـــع *rabba^{c}* II to quadruple, increase fourfold. نقلـــوه وربعـــوا راتبـــه *nigloo w-rabba^{c}aw raatba.* They transferred him and quadrupled his salary.

رابـــع *raaba^{c}* III to befriend s.o., associate closely with s.o. رابعناه لانه خـــوش رجـــال *raaba^{c}naa linna xooš rayyaal.* We made friends with him because he is a good man. (prov.) رابع واوي ولا ترابع حســـاوي *raabi^{c} waawi wa-la traabi^{c} ḥasaawi.* (lit., "Befriend a jackal and don't befriend one from Al-Hasa."). (prov.) من رابـــع المصلـــين صلى، ومن رابع المغنين غـــنى *man raaba^{c} li-mṣalliin ṣalla, w-man raaba^{c} li-mġanniin ġanna.* A man is known

أربعة *'arbaᶜa* p. *-aat* 1. four. أبي أربعة *'abi 'arbaᶜa.* I want four. أربعة وخمسين *'arbaᶜa w-xamsiin* fifty-four. امية وأربعة *'imya w-'arbaᶜa* one hundred and four. 2. (with foll. money and weights) أربعة دولار *'arbaᶜa duulaar* four dollars. أربعة كيلو *'arbaᶜa keelu* four kilograms. 3. (with foll. n.) أربع *'arbaᶜ*, أربعة *'arbaᶜat.* أربع بعارين *'arbaᶜ baᶜaariin* four camels. 4. (with foll. suff. pron.) أربعة *'arbaᶜat.* جاوا أربعتهم *yaw 'arbaᶜattum.* The four of them came.

أربعتعش *'arbaᶜtaᶜaš* (common var. أربعتعشر *'arbaᶜtaᶜšar*) fourteen. أبي أربعتعش *'abi 'arbaᶜtaᶜaš.* I want fourteen. (with foll. n.) أربعتعشر *'arbaᶜtaᶜšar.* أربعتعشر دجاجة *'arbaᶜtaᶜašar diyaaya* fourteen chickens.

أربعين *'arbaᶜiin* forty. أربعين نفر *'arbaᶜiin nafar* forty people. علي بابا والأربعين حرامي *ᶜali baaba w-l-'arbaᶜiin ḥaraami* Ali Baba and the forty thieves.

الربوع *r-rubuuᶜ*, يوم الربوع *yoom r-rubuuᶜ* Wednesday, on Wednesday. الربوع عقب الثلوث *r-rubuuᶜ ᶜugb θ-θuluuθ.* Wednesday is after Tuesday. اليوم الربوع *l-yoom r-rubuuᶜ.* Today is Wednesday.

يربوع *yarbuuᶜ* p. يرابيع *yaraabiiᶜ* jerboa, desert rat.

رابع *raabiᶜ* fourth (ordinal). رابع يوم *raabiᶜ yoom* the fourth day, on the fourth day. في اليوم الرابع *fi l-yoom r-raabiᶜ* on the fourth day. رابعهم أخوي *raabiᶜᶜum 'uxuuy.* The fourth one of them is my brother.

by the company he keeps. Birds of a feather flock together.

ربع *rabiᶜ* 1. friends, associates (s. ربيع *ribiiᶜ* but rarely used). ربعي *rabᶜi* my friends, my associates. هو من ربعك؟ *huwa min rabᶜak?* Is he one of your friends? 2. relatives. ربعي راحوا وخلوني *rabᶜi raaḥaw w-xaḷḷooni.* My relatives went and left me.

ربع *rubᶜ* p. ارباع *rbaaᶜ* quarter, one-fourth, fourth part. ربع دينار *rubᶜ diinaar* quarter of a dinar. ثلاثة ارباع *θalatt rbaaᶜ* three-fourths. ربع الفلوس *rubᶜ li-fluus* one-fourth of the money. الساعة خمسة وربع *s-saaᶜa xamsa w-rubᶜ.* It's a quarter past five.

رباع *rbaaᶜ* (less common var. رباعية *rbaaᶜiyya*) p. *-yyaat* six-year old female camel.

ربعة *rubᶜa* p. *-aat* robbah (weight) = 4 lbs. كم ربعة الطماط *čam rubᶜat ṭ-ṭamaaṭ?* How much is a robbah of tomatoes? عشرة درهم الربعة *ᶜašara dirhim r-rubᶜa.* Ten dirhams per robbah.

ربيع *rabiiᶜ* 1. spring, springtime. فصل الربيع *faṣil r-rabiiᶜ* the spring season. عطلة الربيع *ᶜuṭlat r-rabiiᶜ* the spring vacation, the spring break. الربيع ما يطول هني *r-rabiiᶜ ma yṭawwil hini.* Spring doesn't last long here. ربيع أول *rabiiᶜ 'awwal* Rabia I (the third Islamic month). ربيع ثاني *rabiiᶜ θaani* Rabia II (the fourth Islamic month). 2. grass, herbage. في الشتا الربيع يطلع وترعاه الغنم *fi š-šita r-rabiiᶜ yiṭlaᶜ w-tirᶜaa l-ġanam.* In the winter grass grows and sheep and goats feed on it.

مربع *mrabba*[c] (p.p. from II ربع *rabba*[c]) 1. squared, square. خمسين متر مربع *xamsiin mitir mrabba*[c] fifty square meters. 2. (p. *-aat*) square (geom.). 3. square, raised to the power of two (math.).

ر ب ل *rbl*

ربل *rabal* (coll.) rubber. يستخرجون الربل من الشجر *yistaxirjuun r-rabal min š-šiyar.* Rubber is obtained (or extracted) from trees.

ر ب ي ١ *rby*

ربى *rabba* II 1. to raise, bring up. ربى عياله تربية زينة *rabba* *[c]yaala tarbiya zeena.* He raised his kids well. 2. to raise, breed. في ناس واجدين يربون دجاج في المزارع *fii naas waaydiin yrabbuun diyaay fi l-mazaari*[c]. There are many people who raise chickens on farms. 3. to cause to grow, grow. ربى له لحية طويلة *rabbaa-la liḥya ṭawiila.* He grew himself a long beard.

تربى *trabba* V 1. to be raised, brought up, reared. تربت تربية زينة في بيت أبوها *trabbat tarbiya zeena fi beet 'ubuuha.* She was well brought up in her father's home. 2. to be punished, to learn a lesson. ضربوه وتربى وما عاد يسويها مرة ثانية *ḍarboo w-trabba w-ma* *[c]aad ysawwiiha marra θaanya.* They hit him; he learned a lesson, and he has never done it again.

تربية *tarbiya* (v.n. from II ربى *rabba*) 1. bringing up, upbringing, raising. تربية العيال ماهي بسهلة *tabiyat li-*[c]*yaaḷ ma-hi b-sahla.* Raising children is not easy. تربوا تربية زينة *trabbaw tarbiya zeena.* They were well brought up. 2. education, instruction. وزارة التربية *wazaarat t-tarbiya* the ministry of education. 3. breeding, raising (of animals).

ربيان *ribyaan* (coll.) shrimp. s. *-a.* الربيان كلش طيب بس غالي *r-ribyaan killiš ṭayyib bass ġaali.* Shrimp is very delicious but it's expensive. كليت ربيان *kaleet ribyaan.* I ate shrimp. ما حصلت ربيان في السوق *ma ḥaṣṣalt ribyaan fi s-suug.* I didn't find shrimp in the marketplace.

ربيبة *rabiiba* p. *-aat* female peregrine.

ربية *rubbiyya* p. *-yyaat* rupee (Indian coin = U.A.E. dirham = Qatari riyal). dual ربيتين *rubbiiteen.*

ر ب ي ٢ *rby*

ربى *rabba* II to give birth, bear a child. حرمتي ربت أمس وجابت ولد *ḥurumti rabbat 'ams w-yaabat walad.* My wife gave birth to a baby boy yesterday.

ر ت ب *rtb*

رتب *rattab* II 1. to arrange, put into proper order, organize. رتب الطلبات وخذهم حق الوزير *rattab ṭ-ṭalabaat w-xaðhum ḥagg l-waziir.* He arranged the applications and took them to the minister. رتبت حجر النوم *rattabat ḥijar n-noom.* She straightened up the bedrooms. 2. to prepare, arrange (هزب *hazzab* is more common). See under ه ز ب *hzb.*

ترتب *trattab* V 1. to be arranged, put into proper order. ها الطلبات بعد ما ترتبت *haṭ-ṭalabaat ba*[c]*ad ma trattabat.* These papers haven't been arranged yet. 2. (with على *ᶜala*) to be the result or consequence of s.th. تدري شو يترتب على عملك هذا؟ *tidri šu yitrattab ᶜala ᶜamalak haaða?* Do you know what's going to result from this action of yours?

رتبة *rutba* p. رتب *rutab* rank. ترفع إلى رتبة ضابط *traffaᶜ 'ila rutbat ḍaabiṭ.* He was promoted to the rank of officer.

ترتيب *tartiib* (v.n. from II رتب *rattab*) 1. order, arrangement. بالترتيب *b-t-tartiib* in order, one by one. اوقفوا طابور بالترتيب *'oogafu ṭaabuur b-t-tartiib.* Stand in line, one by one. من غير ترتيب *min ġeer tartiib* disorderly, in confusion. رتبت الحرمة بيتها ترتيب زين *rattabat l-ḥurma betta tartiib zeen.* The wife straightened up her home very well. 2. (p. *-aat*) measures, steps. عمل الترتيبات اللازمة *ᶜimil t-tartiibaat l-laazma.* He took the necessary measures.

راتب *raatib* p. رواتب *rawaatib* (common var. معاش *maᶜaaš*) salary, pay, stipend. راتبه ألفين دينار في الشهر *raatba 'alfeen diinaar fi š-šahar.* His salary is two thousand dinars a month. صرفوا له راتب شهرين *ṣarafuu-la raatib šahreen.* They paid him a two-month salary. راتبي على قد الحال *raatbi ᶜala gadd l-ḥaal.* My salary is not up to much. My salary doesn't go far.

مرتب *murattab* (p.p. from II رتب *rattab*) 1. arranged, organized. 2. neat, orderly. مرتبين. يلبسون هدوم زينة ونظيفة *murattabiin. yilibsuun hduum zeena w-naðiifa.* They are neat. They wear good and clean clothes.

رتوش *rtwš*

رتوش *rituuš* retouching (phot.).

رجب *rjb*

رجب *rajab* Rajab (name of the seventh month of the Islamic calendar).

رجج *rjj*

رج *rajj* (يرج *yrujj*) to shake, rock. رج الغرشة قبل لا تشرب الدوا *rujj l-ġarša gabil-la tišrab d-duwa.* Shake the bottle before you take the medicine. رج الدار بصوته العالي *rajj d-daar b-ṣoota l-ᶜaali.* He shook the house with his loud voice.

ارتج *rtajj* VIII to be shaken, to shake. ارتجت البلد من صوت الطايرات الحربية *rtajjat l-balad min ṣoot ṭ-ṭaayraat l-ḥarbiyya.* The city shook from the noise of the fighter planes.

رج *rajj* (v.n. from رج *rajj*) shaking, rocking.

رجة *rajja* (n. of inst.) one act of shaking, shock, concussion.

رجح *rjḥ*

رجح *rajjaḥ* II to prefer, give preference to, favor. آنا أرجح الراي الثاني *'aana 'arajjiḥ r-raay θ-θaani.* I prefer the other opinion.

أرجح *'arjaḥ* (only in certain expressions) على الأرجح *ᶜala l-'arjaḥ* most probably, most likely. على الأرجح أشوفه باكر *ᶜala l-'arjaḥj 'ačuufa baačir.* Most probably, I will see him tomorrow. من الأرجح ان *min l-'arjaḥ 'inn* it's most likely that. من الأرجح انه رايح يوفق *min l-'arjaḥ 'inna raayiḥ* *ywaafig.* It's most likely that he's going to agree.

راجح *raajiḥ* 1. preferable, more acceptable. هذا راي راجح *haaða raay raajiḥ.* This is a preferable opinion. 2. having more weight, superior in weight (i.e., a merchant's weight). عطاك ثنين كيلو راجحين *ᶜaṭaak θneen keelu raajḥiin.* He gave you more than two kilograms. هذا وزن راجح *haaða wazin raajiḥ.* This is more than a fair weight.

رجع *rjᶜ*

رجع *rijaᶜ (يرجع yirjaᶜ)* 1. to return, come back, come again. رجعت من السعودية أمس *rijaᶜt min s-suᶜuudiyya 'ams.* I returned from Saudi Arabia yesterday. روح ولا ترجع *ruuḥ w-la tirjaᶜ.* Go and don't come back. لا تروح وياهم. ارجع! *la truuḥ wiyyaahum. 'irjaᶜ!* Don't go with them. Go back! ارجع لورا *'irjaᶜ la-wara!* Back up! Move back! رجع إلى عقله وبطل السكر *rijaᶜ 'ila ᶜagḷa w-baṭṭal s-sikir.* He came to his senses and quit drinking. رجع في كلامه *rijaᶜ fi kalaama.* He went back on his word. 2. to recur, come back, return. الأسعار العالية رجعت *l-'asᶜaar l-ᶜaalya rijᶜat.* High prices recurred. رجع حر القيظ *rijaᶜ ḥarr l-geeḍ.* The summer heat came back. المرض رجع عليه *l-maraḍ rijaᶜ ᶜalee.* His sickness returned. 3. to resume, begin again. رجع إلى الشلاخ *rijaᶜ 'ila č-člaax.* He resumed telling lies. 4. to go back, revert to, become again. رجع مريض *rijaᶜ mariiḍ.* He became ill again. صلحته بس رجع عوج *ṣallaḥta bass rijaᶜ ᶜaway.* I straightened it but it turned crooked again. 5. (with إلى *'ila*) to depend on, rely on. هذا يرجع إلى شيمتك *haaða yirjaᶜ 'ila šiimatk.* This depends on your character. آنا ما لي دخل. كل شي يرجع له *'aana maa-li daxil. kill šayy yirjaᶜ-la.* It's none of my business. Everything is up to him. 6. to go back, be traceable. يقولون أصلهم يرجع إلى الفراعنة *yguuluun 'aṣlahum yirjaᶜ 'ila l-faraaᶜna.* They say that their ancestry goes back to the Pharaohs. 7. (with عن *ᶜan*) to withdraw from, revoke, go back on. رجع عن رايه *rijaᶜ ᶜan raaya.* He changed his mind. رجع عن وعده *rijaᶜ ᶜan waᶜda.* He broke his promise. رجع عن كلامه *rijaᶜ ᶜan kalaama.* He went back on his word.

رجع *rajjaᶜ* II 1. to return, give back s.th. or s.o. اشتريت جوتي ورجعته *štireet juuti w-rajjaᶜta.* I bought a pair of shoes and returned them. رجعت له السيارة *rajjaᶜt-la s-sayyaara.* I returned the car to him. I gave him back his car. الشركة رجعت لنا الضو عقب ما دفعنا الفلوس *š-šarika rajjaᶜat la-na ḍ-ḍaww ᶜugub-ma difaᶜna li-fluus.* The company turned on the electricity for us after we paid the money. 2. to put back, return. رجعوه للسجن *rajjaᶜoo lis-sijin.* They returned him to jail. رجعوه إلى وظيفته القديمة *rajjaᶜoo 'ila waḍiifta l-gadiima.* They returned him to his old job. 3. to take back. ما أبغيكم ترجعون القميص؛ بس أريد أبدله *ma 'abġiikum trajjᶜuun l-gamiiṣ; bass 'ariid 'abaddla.* I don't want you to take the shirt back; I just want to exchange it. 4. to set back, move back. ساعتك مقدمة. رجعها خمس دقايق

saa^c^atk mjaddma. rajji^c^ha xams digaayig. Your watch is too fast. Set it back five minutes. رجـع السـيارة لـورا شوية *rajji^c^ s-sayyaara la-wara šwayya.* Move the car back a little.

راجـع *raaja^c^* III 1. to ask for information, consult, look up (in the book), check with. راجعـت المدرسـة وقـالوا ابـني مقبـول السـنة الجايـة *raaja^c^t l-madrasa w-gaalaw 'ibni magbuul s-sana l-yaaya.* I went to the school for information, and they said that my son was accepted for next year. راجعنا باكر *raaji^c^na baačir.* Check with us tomorrow. راجعتهـم بخصـوص قـز الأرض *raaja^c^ittum b-xuṣuuṣ gazz l-'arđ.* I checked with them concerning the land survey. راحـت حـق المطـوع وقـال، «بـاراجع الكتـاب» *raaḥat ḥagg li-mṭawwa^c^ w-gaal, "b-araaji^c^ li-ktaab."* She went to the holy man and he said, "I will look things up in the book." راجعت دختر ثاني وقال أحتاج كشـف مـن جديـد *raaja^c^t daxtar θaani w-gaal 'aḥtaaj kašf min yidiid.* I consulted another doctor, and he said that I needed a new medical examination. 2. to check, review (a book), examine critically. راجع أغلاطك *raaji^c^ 'aġlaaṭak.* Check your errors. المدير راجع الحساب وقال فيه غلط *l-mudiir raaja^c^ li-ḥsaab w-gaal fii ġalaṭ.* The manager checked the accounts and said that there was something wrong. سـألوه يراجـع الكتـاب قبـل طبعـه *si'loo yraaji^c^ li-ktaab gabil ṭab^c^a.* They asked him to review the book before printing it.

ترجـع *trajja^c^* V 1. to be returned, given back. 2. to be put back, returned. هذا شي مـا يـترجع *haađa šayy ma yitrajja^c^.* This is something that can't be returned.

تراجـع *traaja^c^* VI 1. to withdraw, retreat, fall back. الجيـش تراجـع *l-jeeš traaja^c^.* The army retreated. 2. (with عـن *^c^an*) to go back on, rescind. ما قبل يتراجع عن موقفـه *ma gibal yitraaja^c^ ^c^an mawgifa.* He didn't agree to go back on his position.

اسـترجع *starja^c^* X to get back, recover, regain. اسـترجعوا كـل الفلـوس اللـي باقهـا *starja^c^aw kill li-fluus illi baagha.* They recovered all the money he had stolen.

رجعـي *raj^c^i* 1. reactionary. حكم رجعي *ḥukum raj^c^i* reactionary rule. 2. (p. -*yyiin*) reactionary person.

رجعية *raj^c^iyya* reactionism.

رجعة *raj^c^a* p. -*aat* return, returning.

رجـوع *rujuu^c^* (v.n. from رجع *rija^c^*) 1. return, coming back. 2. recurring, coming back. 3. resumption, beginning again. 4. (with عـن *^c^an*) withdrawing from, going back on, revocation.

مرجـع *marji^c^* p. مراجـع *maraaji^c^* 1. authority to which one turns or appeals. مـا لـك مرجـع إلا الله *maa-lak marji^c^ 'illa aḷḷaah.* You have no one to turn to (for help) except God. 2. authoritative reference work. القـرآن مرجع حق كل شـي *l-qur'an marji^c^ ḥagg kill šayy.* The Quran is an authoritative reference for everything.

مراجعة *muraaja^c^a* (v.n. from III راجع

raajaᶜ) 1. asking for information, consultation. 2. checking, review (of a book).

استرجاع *stirjaaᶜ* X 1. reclamation. استرجاع الأراضي *stirjaaᶜ l-'araađi* land reclamation. 2. recovery, getting back s.th.

راجع *raajiᶜ* (act. part. from رجع *rijaᶜ*) p. *-iin* 1. will return. نحن راجعين عقب باكر *niḥin raajᶜin ᶜugub baačir.* We are returning the day after tomorrow. 2. returning. هو في الطريق؛ راجع *huwa fi ṭ-ṭariig; raajiᶜ.* He is on the way; he's returning. 3. having returned. صار له راجع يومين *ṣaar-la raajiᶜ yoomeen.* It's been two days since he returned.

مراجع *muraajiᶜ* p. *-iin* (act. part. from III راجع *raajaᶜ*) one who asks for information, checker, verifier. المراجعين يجون هني كل يوم *l-muraajᶜiin yiyuun hini kill yoom.* People asking for information come here every day. مراجع الحسابات *muraajiᶜ l-ḥisaabaat* the auditor, the comptroller.

رج ف *rjf*

رجف *rijaf* (يرجف *yirjif*) to tremble, shiver, shake. يرجف من البرد *yirjif min l-bard.* He is shivering from the cold. يرجف من المرض *yirjif min l-marađ.* He is trembling from the illness.

ارتجف *rtijaf* VIII = رجف *rijaf.*

رج ل *rjl*

رجل *rijil*, see under ري ل *ryl.*

رجال *rajjaal*, see under ري ل *ryl.*

رج م *rjm*

رجم *rijam* (يرجم *yirjim*) to stone, throw a rock at s.o. في الحج الحجاج يرجمون ابليس *fi l-ḥajj l-ḥijjaaj yirijmuun bliis.* During the pilgrimage, pilgrims stone the devil.

رجم *rajim* (v.n.) stoning. رجم ابليس من ضروريات الحج *rajim bliis min đaruuriyyat l-ḥajj.* Stoning the devil is one of the requirements of the pilgrimage.

رجيم *rajiim* (said of the devil) cursed, damned. أعوذ بالله من الشيطان الرجيم *'aᶜuuđu bil-laah min aš-šayṭaan ir-rajiim.* God save me from the cursed devil.

رج و *rjw*

رجى *rija* (يرجي *yarji*) 1. to request, ask. رجاني أسلفه ألف درهم *rajaani 'asallfa 'alf dirhim.* He asked me to lend him one thousand dirhams. رجيته يطرش لي الخط *rajeeta yṭarriš-li l-xaṭṭ.* I asked him to mail the letter for me. أرجوك لا تلعوزني *'arjuuk la tlaᶜwizni.* Please don't bother me. أرجوك! آنا شدراني؟ *'arjuuk! 'aana š-darraani?* Now, I ask you! How would I have known? أرجو لك كل خير *'arjuu-lak kill xeer.* I wish you the best.

ترجى *trajja* V to beg s.o., appeal to s.o. راح ودش مكتب المدير ترجاه يعطيه زيادة *raaḥ w-dašš maktab l-mudiir w-trajjaa yᶜaṭii ziyaada.* He went and entered the director's office, and begged him to give him a raise. أترجاك تسوي لي هالمعروف *'atrajjaak tsawwii-li hal-maᶜruuf.* I beg you to do me this favor. ترجيته يساعدني *trajjeeta ysaaᶜidni.* I asked him to help me.

him.

ركب *raččab* II 1. to give a ride to, cause to ride. ركبني بسيارته إلى بيتي *raččabni b-sayyaarta 'ila beeti.* He gave me a ride in his car to my house. 2. to put aboard, put on. خذيت أمي وركبتها بالباص *xaðeet 'ummi w-raččabitta b-l-paaṣ.* I took my mother and put her on the bus. 3. to install, set, place, mount. ركب الليتات *raččab l-leetaat.* He installed the lights. ركب الكنديشن في الدريشة *raččab l-kandeešin fi d-diriiša.* He placed the air conditioner in the window. 4. to assemble, put together, fit together. تقدر تركب قطع الغيار ذولا؟ *tigdar traččib ġiṭa^c l-ġayaar ðoola?* Can you assemble those spare parts? 5. to prepare and put together a meal. قومي ركبي الأكل وحطيه على الجولة *guumi raččbi l-'akil w-ḥuṭṭii ^cala č-čuula.* Get up, prepare the ingredients of the food, and put it on the stove.

تركب *traččab* V to be fitted, mounted, set in. ها الجامة ما تتركب لانها كبيرة واجد *hal-jaama ma titraččab linha čibiira waayid.* This piece of glass won't fit because it's very big.

ركاب *rčaab* (less common var. *rkaab*) p. *-aat* stirrup.

رح ب *rḥb*

رحب *raḥḥab* II (with ب *b-* or في *fi*) to welcome s.o., make s.o. welcome. رحبوا فينا لين وصلنا بيتهم *raḥḥabu fiina leen wiṣalna beettum.* They welcomed us when we reached their home. أنت بس روحي. يرحبون بك *'inti bass ruuḥi. yraḥḥbuun biič.* You just go. They will

رجا *raja* hope, request, plea. رجاي انك تخلصين المدرسة *rajaay 'innič txallṣiin l-madrasa.* I hope that you will finish school. رجاني رجا حار *rajaani raja ḥaarr.* He pleaded heartily with me.

رجاءً *rajaa'an* please. رجاء لا ترفع صوتك *rajaa'an la tirfa^c ṣootak.* Please don't shout.

رج ي م *rjym*

رجيم *rijiim* diet. سوى رجيم *sawwa rijiim.* He went on a diet.

رچ ب *rčb*

ركب *ričab* (يركب *yirčab*) 1. to ride (an animal). ركب البعير *ričab l-bi^ciir.* He rode the camel. أقدر أركب الحصان. ليش ما أقدر *'agdar 'arčab li-ḥṣaan. leeš ma 'agdar?* I can ride a horse. Why can't I? 2. to ride in, ride on, travel in, on or on board. عمرك ركبت قطار؟ *^cumrak ričabt ġiṭaar?* Have you ever ridden on a train? ركب الطيارة وراح البحرين *ričab ṭ-ṭayyaara w-raaḥ l-baḥreen.* He boarded the plane and went to Bahrain. الجاهل ما قدر يمشي. ركب على ظهري *l-yaahil ma gidar yamši. ričab ^cala ḍahri.* The child couldn't walk. He rode on my back. 3. to mate with, breed with, mount. الديك ركب الدجاجة *d-diič ričab d-diyaaya.* The rooster mounted the chicken. 4. to get in, get on, climb aboard. ركب سيارته وانهزم *ričab sayyaarta w-nhizam.* He got in his car and took off. 5. to dominate, bully, intimidate. مسكين ضعيف. الناس يركبوه *miskiin ḍa^ciif. n-naas yirčabuu.* Poor man. He's weak. People would bully welcome you.

مرحباً *marḥaba* (common var. مرحب *marḥab*) hi! hello! أهلاً وسهلاً *'ahlan wa sahlan!* (answer to مرحبا *marḥaba*).

ترحيب *tarḥiib* (v.n. from II رحب *raḥḥab*) welcoming, greeting. الترحيب بالزاير من عادات العرب *t-tarḥiib b-z-zaayir min ᶜaadaat l-ᶜarab.* Welcoming a visitor is an Arab custom. حفلة ترحيب *ḥaflat tarḥiib* welcoming party, reception party.

ر ح ل *rḥl*

رحل *riḥal* (يرحل *yirḥal)* to move about, migrate, move away. البدو يرحلون في الخلا *l-badu yirḥaluun fi l-xaḷa.* Bedouins move about in the desert. رحلوا عن ذاك المكان لأن ما فيه ماي *rḥalaw ᶜan ðaak l-mukaan li'an ma fii maay.* They moved away from that place because there was no water in it.

رحل *raḥḥal* II to cause to leave, relocate, resettle. الحكومة رحلت كثير من الأجانب *li-ḥkuuma raḥḥalat kaθir min l-'ayaanib.* The government deported many of the foreigners. رحلوا كل القبايل في هذي المنطقة *raḥḥalaw kill l-gabaayil fi haaði l-manṭiga* They relocated all the tribes in this area.

رحال *raḥḥaal* p. *-a, -iin* moving, roaming, migrating, nomadic. قبايل رحالة *gabaayil raḥḥaala* nomadic tribes. طيور رحالة *ṭyuur raḥḥaala* migratory birds.

مرحلة *marḥala* p. مراحل *maraaḥil* phase, stage.

ر ح م *rḥm*

رحم *riḥam* (يرحم *yirḥam)* to have mercy upon s.o., have compassion for s.o. الله يرحم أمواتنا! *'aḷḷaah yirḥam 'amwaatna!* God have mercy upon our dead! الله يرحم روحه! *'aḷḷaah yirḥam ruuḥa!* God bless his soul! القاضي رحمك بهالحكم *l-gaaði rḥamak b-hal-ḥukum.* The judge was merciful toward you in this verdict.

ترحم *traḥḥam* V (with على *ᶜala*) to be merciful, be kind, show mercy to s.o. ترحم على الفقير بعشرة درهم *traḥḥam ᶜala l-fagiir b-ᶜašara dirhim.* He was merciful to the poor man by giving him ten dirhams.

استرحم *starḥam* X to plead for mercy, to ask s.o. to have mercy. قدم طلب يسترحم فيه تخفيف الحكم *gaddam ṭalab yistarḥim fii taxfiif l-ḥukum.* He submitted an application in which he pleaded for a shortening of the sentence.

رحمة *raḥma* (v.n. from رحم *riḥam*) 1. mercy. أطلب الرحمة من الله سبحانه وتعالى *'aṭlub r-raḥma min aḷḷa subḥaanahu wa taᶜaalaa.* I seek mercy from God, be he praised and sublime. المطر رحمة من الله *l-muṭar raḥma min aḷḷa.* Rain is a blessing from God. توفت. رحمة الله عليها! *tawaffat. raḥmat aḷḷa ᶜaleeha!* She passed away. God have mercy upon her!

رحيم *raḥiim* merciful, compassionate. الله رحيم *'aḷḷaah raḥiim.* God is merciful. قلبه رحيم *galba raḥiim.* He's kind-hearted.

الرحمن *r-raḥmaan* the Merciful (i.e., God). بسم الله الرحمن الرحيم *b-ismi-llaah ir-raḥmaan r-raḥiim* in the name of God, the Merciful, the Compassionate.

أرحم *'arḥam* (elat.) 1. (with من *min*) more merciful, compassionate. 2. (with foll. n.) the most merciful, compassionate.

استرحام *stirḥaam* (v.n. from X استرحم *starḥam*) plea for mercy. قدم طلب استرحام حق الحاكم *gaddam ṭalab stirḥaam ḥagg l-ḥaakim.* He submitted a plea for clemency to the ruler.

مرحوم *marḥuum* (p.p. from رحم *riḥam*) (usually with the article prefix ال *l-*) the deceased, the late.

رخص *rxṣ*

رخص *rixaṣ (يرخص yirxaṣ)* to become inexpensive, cheap. الطماط رخص واجد *ṭ-ṭamaaṭ rixaṣ waayid.* Tomatoes got very cheap. السعر يرخص في القيظ *s-si^c^ir yirxaṣ fi l-geeḍ.* The price decreases in the summer.

رخص *raxxaṣ* II 1. to give permission to s.o. to leave. كنت مريض والتنديل رخصني *čint mariiḍ w-t-tindeel raxxaṣni.* I was ill and the supervisor gave me permission to leave. 2. to authorize, license. رخصوا له يبيع ذهب *raxxaṣuu-la ybii^c^ ḍahab.* They authorized him to sell gold. رخصوا لي أفتح دكان *raxxaṣuu-li 'aftaḥ dikkaan.* They gave me license to open a store. 3. to make cheap, inexpensive. الحكومة رخصت سعر الشكر والشاي *li-ḥkuuma raxxaṣat si^c^r š-šakar w-č-čaay.* The government decreased the price of sugar and tea. 4. to license, have s.th. licensed. رخصت السيارة عقب ما اشتريتها *raxxaṣt s-sayyaara ^c^ugub-ma štireetta.* I had the car licensed after I (had) bought it.

استرخص *starxaṣ* X 1. to excuse oneself. استرخص ومشى لانه كان تعبان *starxaṣ w-miša linna čaan ta^c^baan.* He excused himself and left because he was tired. 2. to find s.th. cheap. استرخص الطماط واشترى صندوقين *starxaṣ ṭ-ṭamaaṭ w-štira ṣanduugeen.* He found the tomatoes cheap and bought two boxes.

رخصة *ruxṣa* 1. permission, authorization. من رخصتك *min ruxṣatk* with your permission, if you please. خذيت رخصة من التنديل وسافرت *xaḍeet ruxṣa min t-tindeel w-saafart.* I took permission from the supervisor and travelled. 2. vacation. قدمت طلب حق رخصة *gaddamt ṭalab ḥagg ruxṣa.* I submitted an application for a vacation. أشوفك هني. شو تسوي؟ عندك رخصة *'ačuufak hini. šu tsawwi? ^c^indak ruxṣa?* I see you're here. What are you doing? Are you on vacation? 3. (p. رخص *ruxaṣ*) license. رخصة استيراد *ruxṣat stiiraad* import license. رخصة تصدير *ruxṣat taṣdiir* export license. رخصة سواقة *ruxṣat swaaga* driving permit, operator's license.

رخيص *raxiiṣ* cheap, inexpensive. الطماط رخيص اليوم *ṭ-ṭamaaṭ raxiiṣ l-yoom.* Tomatoes are cheap today. لا، موب رخيص؛ غالي *la, muub raxiiṣ; ġaali.* No, it's not cheap; it's expensive. ما فيه شي رخيص هني *ma fii šayy raxiiṣ hini.* There isn't anything inexpensive here.

أرخص *'arxaṣ* (elat.) 1. (with من *min*) cheaper than, more inexpensive than. هذا أرخص من ذاك *haaða 'arxaṣ min ðaak.* This is cheaper than that one. هذا أرخص *haaða 'arxaṣ.* This is cheaper. 2. (with foll. n.) the cheapest. هذا أرخص سعر *haaða 'arxaṣ si^c^ir.* This is the cheapest price. أرخص ما *'arxaṣ-ma* the cheapest thing that... أرخص ما عندي *'arxaṣ-ma ^c^indi* the cheapest thing that I have. أرخص ما اشتريت *'arxaṣ-ma štireet* the cheapest thing that I bought.

رخ ي *rxy*

رخى *raxxa* II 1. to lower, let down, drop. رخى الحبل *raxxa l-ḥabil.* He lowered the rope. 2. to loosen, slacken. الحبل مشدود. رخيه *l-ḥabil mašduud. raxxii.* The rope is tight. Loosen it.

ترخى *traxxa* V 1. to be lowered, let down, dropped. 2. to be loosened, slackened. ها السكرو ما يترخى. فيه حالى *has-sikruu ma yitraxxa. fii ḥala.* This screw can't be loosened. It's rusty.

ارتخى *rtixa* VIII 1. = V ترخى *traxaa.* 2. to relax. أنت تعبان. لازم ترتخي شوية *'inta ta^c^baan. laazim tirtixi šwayya.* You are tired. You have to relax a little. 3. to lose force or vigor. ارتخى عقب الشغل *rtixa ^c^ugb š-šuġul.* He lost vigor after work.

رخا *raxa* 1. abundance, opulence, prosperity. الناس هني عايشين في رخا *n-naas hini ^c^aayšiin fi raxa.* People here are living comfortably. 2. decrease, lowness (of prices). فيه رخا في الأسعار ذالحين *fii raxa fi l-'as^c^aar ðalḥiin.* Prices are low now.

ر د ء *rd'*

تردا *tradda* V to become bad. الحالة السياسية تردت في البلاد العربية *l-ḥaala s-siyaasiyya traddat fi li-blaad l-^c^arabiyya.* The political situation became bad in the Arab countries.

ر د د *rdd*

رد *radd* (يرد *yrudd*) 1. to return. قلت له: «السلام عليكم» وما رد السلام *gitla: "s-salaam ^c^aleekum," w-ma radd s-salaam.* I said to him: "Peace be upon you," and he didn't return the greeting. 2. (with على *^c^ala*) to reply, answer. خابرتك أمس بس ما رد علي أحد *xaabartak 'ams bass ma radd ^c^alayya 'aḥad.* I telephoned you yesterday but no one answered me. ما تقدر ترد عليه؟ *ma tigdar trudd ^c^alee?* Can't you answer him? 3. to bring back, take back. تقدر ترد بعض الأشيا اللي تشتريها *tigdar trudd ba^c^ḍ l-'ašya lli tištiriiha.* You can return some of the things you buy. 4. to put back, return. رديت الكتاب بمكانه على الميز *raddeet li-ktaab b-mukaana ^c^ala l-meez.* I put the book back in its place on the table. رد الباب وراك من فضلك *rudd l-baab waraak min faḍlak.* Close the door behind you, place. 5. to refuse, reject, turn down. خوش رجال؛ ما يفشل ولا يرد أحد *xooš rayyaal; ma yfaššil wala yrudd 'aḥad.* He is a good man; he doesn't disappoint or turn anyone down. عمري ما رديت له أي طلب *^c^umri ma raddeet-la 'ayya ṭalab.* I have never refused him any request. 6. to give back, hand back, return. ثمن التذكرة

أربعة دينار. عطيته خمسة دينار ومـــا رد لي الباقي *θaman t-taðkara 'arba^ca diinaar.* *^caṭeeta xamsa diinaar w-ma radd-li l-baagi.* The price of the ticket is four dinars. I gave him five dinars and he didn't give me back the change. 7. to return, come back, go back. روح ذالحين ورد بساع *ruuḥ ðalḥiin w-rudd b-saa^c.* Go now and come back fast. ردت صحته لين وقف السكر *raddat ṣiḥḥta leen waggaf s-sikir.* His health has returned since he stopped drinking. رد على عادته القديمة *radd ^cala ^caatta l-gadiima.* He's back to his old habit.

ردد *raddad* II to repeat constantly. ما له راي؛ يردد اللي تقولـــه الجرايـــد *ma la raay; yraddid illi tguuḷa l-jaraayid.* He has no opinion. He repeats what the newspapers say. الجاهل يردد اللي يسمعه *l-yaahil yraddid illi ysam^ca.* A child repeats what he hears.

تردد *traddad* V 1. (with على *^cala*) to frequent, visit frequently. ليش تتردد على هذي المنطقة بالذات؟ *leeš titraddad ^cala haaði l-manṭiga b-ð-ðaat?* Why do you frequently visit this area of all places? شعندك؟ دايم تتردد علـــى الحفـــيز *š-^cindak? daayim titraddad ^cala l-ḥafiiz.* What are you up to? You're always coming into the office. 2. to hesitate, be reluctant, uncertain. ترددت أسافر ذالحين لو بعديـــن *traddatt 'asaafir ðalḥiin lo ba^cdeen.* I was uncertain whether to travel now or later. لا تتردد. روح. الله واياك *la titraddad. ruuḥ. 'aḷḷa wiyyaak.* Don't hesitate. Go. God be with you. ترددت آخذه واياي *traddatt 'aaxða wiyyaay.* I was reluctant to take him with me.

اســترد *staradd* X to get back, regain. استردت الشركة منه كل المبلـــغ *staraddat š-šarika minna kill l-mablaġ.* The company got the whole amount back from him. استرد صحته عقب مـــا تـــرك الجقـــاير *staradd ṣiḥḥta ^cugub-ma tirak j-jigaayir.* He regained his health after he quit smoking.

رد *radd* (v.n. from رد *radd*) 1. (p. ردود *rduud*) answer, reply. طرشت له خط وما حصلـــت رد بعـــد *ṭarrašt-la xaṭṭ w-ma ḥaṣṣalt radd ba^cad.* I sent him a letter and I haven't received an answer yet. 2. taking back, bringing back, returning s.th. رد البضاعـــة *radd li-bḍaa^ca* taking back the merchandise. 3. returning. رد الســـلام *radd s-salaam* returning the greeting. 4. refusal, rejection, denial. رد الطلبـــات *radd ṭ-ṭalabaat* the refusal of applications. 5. reaction, reversal, change of heart. رد فعـــل *radd fi^cil* reaction. صار عنده رد فعل ورخص حرمته *ṣaar ^cinda radd fi^cil w-raxxaṣ ḥurumta.* He had a change of heart and divorced his wife. أخذ ورد *'axð w-radd* give and take. المسألة فيـــها أخـــذ ورد *l-mas'ala fiiha 'axð w-radd.* The problem is still in dispute.

ترديد *tardiid* (v.n. from II ردد *raddad*) repetition.

مرتـــد *mirtadd* p. *-iin* 1. (with عن *^can*) having renounced a faith. هو مرتد عن الإسلام *huwa mirtadd ^can l-'islaam.* He has renounced Islam. 2. apostate.

ر د م *rdm*

ردم *ridam* (يردم *yardim)* to fill in with

dirt, fill up with earth. ردموا الحفر اللي في الرستة *radmaw l-ḥifar illi fi r-rasta.* They filled in the potholes in the road.

ر د ن *rdn*

ردن *ridin* p. اردان *rdaan* (less common var. اردانات *rdaanat*) sleeve (of a shirt, or a jacket, etc.). ردن القميص *ridin l-gamiiṣ* the shirt sleeve. ردن الكندورة *ridin l-kandoora* the dishdash sleeve.

ر ذ ل *rðl*

رذيل *raðiil* 1. base, mean, contemptible. 2. (p. *-iin*) despicable person.

رذالة *raðaala* (v.n.) profanity, meanness.

ر ز ب *rzb*

مرزاب *mirzaab* p. مرازيب *maraaziib* roof gutter. ماي المطر ينزل في المرزاب ويروح البير *maay l-muṭar yanzil fi l-mirzaab w-yruuḥ l-biir.* Rain water flows down the roof gutter and goes to the well.

ر ز ز *rzz*

رزة *razza* p. *-aat* 1. door latch. 2. stopper.

ر ز ف *rzf*

رزف *rizaf* (يرزف *yarzif*) 1. to celebrate, engage in merry-making. في العيد الوطني الناس يرزفون في الشوارع *fi l-ᶜiid l-waṭani n-naas yarzifuun fi š-šawaariᶜ.* On National Day people celebrate in the streets. 2. to dance. العيالة هم اللي يرزفون *l-ᶜayyaala hum illi yarzifuun.* Male dancers are the ones who dance.

رزيف *raziif* 1. celebration, merry-making. ليلة العرس هل المعرس ياخذونه حق بيت العروسة ويتقهوون ويعملون رزيف *leelt l-ᶜirs hal l-miᶜris yaaxðuuna ḥagg beet l-ᶜaruusa w-yitgahuwuun w-yᶜamluun raziif.* On the wedding night, the bridegroom's relatives take the bridegroom to the bride's home, have coffee, and celebrate. 2. dance, dancing. رقص العيالة نسميه «رزيف» ورقص النعاشات نسميه «نعيش» *rags l-ᶜayyaala nsammii "raziif" w-rags n-naᶜᶜaašaat nsamii "niᶜiiš."* We call male dancing "*raziif*" and female dancing "*niᶜiiš.*"

ر ز گ *rzg*

رزق *rizag* (يرزق *yarzig*) 1. (said of God) to provide s.o. with wealth and sustenance. الله يرزق عباده *'aḷḷa yarzig ᶜibaada.* God provides his servants with a livelihood. 2. to bless s.o. with (a child). الله رزقنا ولد *'aḷḷa rizagna walad.* God blessed us with a baby boy.

رزق *rizg* livelihood, subsistence, means of living. هذا رزقي ورزق العيال *haaða rizgi w-rizg li-ᶜyaaḷ.* This is my and my children's livelihood. الرزق على الله *r-rizg ᶜala-ḷḷa.* One's livelihood is from God. (prov.) رزق اليوم خذيناه ورزق باكر على الله *rizg l-yoom xaðeenaa w-rizg baačir ᶜala-ḷḷa.* Whatever will be will be. (lit., "We have taken today's sustenance, and tomorrow's sustenance will be from God.").

ر ز م *rzm*

رزمة *rizma* p. رزم *rizam* parcel, package.

رزن *rzn*

رزين *riziin* p. *-iin* rational, prudent, wise, of sound judgement. هو رجال رزين *huwa rayyaalin riziin.* He is a wise man. (Go and ask him his opinion).

رزانة *razaana* prudence, wisdom, sound judgement.

رس ب *rsb*

رسب *risab (يرسب yarsib)* to fail, flunk. رسب في الامتحان *risab fi li-mtiḥaan.* He flunked the examination. رسب بموضوعين في الامتحان *risab b-mawḏuuᶜeen fi li-mtiḥaan.* He failed two subjects on the examination.

رسب *rassab* II to cause to fail, give a failing grade. غش في الامتحان؛ عيل رسبه المعلم *ġašš fi li-mtiḥaan; ᶜayal rassaba l-muᶜallim.* He cheated on the examination; consequently the teacher flunked him.

رسوب *rusuub* (v.n. from رسب *risab*) failure (in an examination).

راسب *raasib* p. *-iin* 1. one who has failed an examination. 2. repeater. العام الماضي كان في الصف الرابع وبعده في الصف الرابع. راسب *l-ᶜaam l-maaḏi čaan fi ṣ-ṣaff r-raabiᶜ w-baᶜda fi ṣ-ṣaff r-raabiᶜ. raasib.* Last year he was in fourth grade and he is still in fourth grade. He is a repeater.

رس ت *rst*

رستة *rasta* p. *-aat* paved road. هذي الطريق ذالحين استوت رستة زينة *haaði t-ṭariig ðalḥiin stawat rasta zeena.* The road has now turned into a good paved road.

رس خ *rsx*

رسخ *risax (يرسخ yirsax)* to be or become firmly established, to sink in, stick (in the mind). الدرس رسخ في عقله عقب ما درسته اياه ثلاث مرات *d-dars risax fi ᶜagla ᶜugub-ma darrasta-yyaa θalaaθ marraat.* The lesson stuck in his mind after I had taught it to him three times.

رسخ *rassax* II to make take root, establish, impress s.th. on s.o.'s mind. المعلم رسخ الدرس في عقول تلاميذه *l-muᶜallim rassax d-dars fi ᶜguul talaamiiða.* The teacher made the lesson stick to his pupils' minds. The teacher impressed the lesson on his pupils' minds.

رس غ *rsġ*

رسغ *rusuġ* p. رسوغ *rusuuġ* wrist.

رس ل *rsl*

راسل *raasal* III to correspond with, exchange letters. ولدي يراسلني من أمريكا *wildi yraasilni min 'amriika.* My son sends letters to me from America. راسلته وراسلني *raasalta w-raasalni.* We exchanged letters.

أرسل *'arsal* IV (طرش *ṭarraš* is more common). See under **طرش** *ṭrš*.

تراسل *traasal* VI to correspond with each other, exchange correspondence. ظلينا نتراسل سنتين وبعدين انقطعت الرسايل *ðalleena nitraasal santeen w-baᶜdeen ngiṭᶜat r-rasaayil.* We continued to exchange letters for two years and then the letters stopped.

رسـول *rasuul* p. رسل *rusul.* 1. messenger, emissary. 2. prophet. الرسول، رسـول الله *r-rasuul, rasuul aḷḷaaḥ* the Messenger, the Messenger of God (i.e., Mohammad). محمـد رسـول الله *muḥammad rasuul aḷḷaah.* Mohammad is God's messenger.

رسـالة *risaala* (خـط *xaṭṭ* is more common). See under **خ ط ط** *xṭṭ.*

مراسلة *muraasala* (v.n. from VI تراسل *traasal*) correspondence, exchange of letters. تقدر تدرس بالمراسلة *tigdar tidris b-l-muraasala.* You can study by correspondence.

مراسل *muraasil* p. *-iin* (act. part. from III راسـل *raasal*) correspondent, reporter. مراسـل الجريـدة *muraasil l-jariida* the newspaper reporter.

مرسل *mursil* p. *-iin* (act. part. from IV أرسل *'arsal*) sender (of letters).

ر س م *rsm*

رسـم *risam* (يرسم *yarsim*) 1. to draw, sketch. ولدي رسم صورة سوق السـمك *wildi risam ṣuurat suug s-simač.* My son drew a picture of the fish market. تقدر ترسـم بعـير؟ *tigdar tirsim bicciir?* Can you draw a camel? القزاز رسم لي خارطـة حـق الأرض *l-gazzaaz risam-li xaarṭa ḥagg l-'arḍ.* The surveyor drew for me a map of the land. رسم لوحة جميلة *risam looḥa yimiila.* He painted a beautiful picture.

انرسـم *nrisam* VII 1. to be drawn. 2. to be painted.

رسـم *rasim* (v.n. from رسم *risam*) 1. drawing, sketching. يدرس رسم *yidris rasim.* He is studying drawing. يرسم رسم كلش زين *yarsim rasim killiš zeen.* He draws very well. 2. (p. رسـوم *rusuum*) picture, sketch, drawing. هذا رسم بستان *haaða rasim bistaan.* This is a drawing of an orchard. 3. duty, fee, tariff. رسم الدخول *rasm d-duxuul* the admission fee. رسوم الجامعـة *rusuum l-yaamᶜa* the university fees. رسـوم جمركيـة *rusuum jimrigiyya* customs duty.

رسمي *raṣmi* official, formal. هدوم رسمية *hduum rasmiyya* formal clothes, formal dress. زيـارة رسميـة *zyaara rasmiyya* official visit. بصورة رسميـة *b-ṣuura rasmiyya* officially.

رسميـات *rasmiyyaat* formalities, conventions.

رسميـاً *rasmiyyan* officially, formally. رسميا، ما أقدر أقول لـك *rasmiyyan, ma 'agdar 'agul-lak.* Officially, I can't tell you.

رسام *rassaam* p. *-iin* 1. draftsman. 2. painter, artist.

مرسوم *marsuum* (p.p. from رسم *risam*) 1. drawn, sketched. 2. painted. 3. (p. مراسيم *maraasiim*) edict, decree. مرسوم ملكي *marsuum malaki* royal decree. 4. regulation, ordinance. مراسيم الاحتفال *maraasiim li-ḥtifaal* the rules of the ceremony, the protocol.

ر س ن *rsn*

رسـن *risan* p. ارسان *rsaan* reins (of a horse, a mule, etc.). ربط رسن الحصان في الشجرة *ribaṭ risan li-ḥṣaan fi li-šyara.* He tied the reins of the horse to the tree.

رش ح *ršḥ*

رشح *raššaḥ* II to nominate, put up as a candidate. رشحناه حق رياسة المجلس البلدي *raššaḥnaa ḥagg riyaasat l-majlis l-baladi.* We nominated him for the chairmanship of the municipal council. رشح نفسه لاجل يصير تنديل على الكولية *raššaḥ nafsa lajil yiṣiir tindeel ᶜala l-kuuliyya.* He nominated himself to be a supervisor over the coolies.

ترشح *traššaḥ* V to be nominated as a candidate, be a nominee. ترشح للوظيفة *traššaḥ lal-waðiifa.* He was nominated for the job.

مرشح *mraššaḥ* (p.p. from II رشح *raššaḥ*) 1. having been nominated. هو مرشح عن منطقتنا *huwa mraššaḥ ᶜan manṭigatna.* He has been nominated from our district. 2. (p. *-iin*) candidate, nominee. مرشحين ما ميش *mraššaḥiin ma miiš.* There are no candidates.

رش د *ršd*

رشد *rišad* (يرشد *yiršid*) to lead, guide, show the right way. العيال يحتاجون واحد يرشدهم على الطريق الصحيح *li-ᶜyaaḷ yiḥtaajuun waaḥid yiršidhum ᶜala ṭ-ṭariig ṣ-ṣaḥiiḥ.* The children need someone to show them the right way.

رشد *rušd*, as in بلغ سن الرشد *bilaġ sinn r-rušd.* He came of age.

إرشاد *'iršaad* 1. guidance, direction, showing the right way. طايشين؛ هم بحاجة إلى إرشاد *ṭaayšiin; hum b-ḥaaja 'ila 'iršaad.* They are reckless; they are in need of guidance.

مرشد *miršid* p. مرشدين *mirišdiin* (act. part. from رشد *rišad*) 1. having guided, shown s.o. the right way. توني مرشده على الطريق الصحيح *tawwni mirišda ᶜala ṭ-ṭariig ṣ-ṣaḥiiḥ.* I have just shown him the right way. 2. advisor. فيه مرشدين في وزارة الأوقاف *fii mirišdiin fi wazaarat l-'awgaaf.* There are advisors in the wakf ministry. 3. Mirshid (popular male's name).

رش رش *ršrš*

رشرش *rašraš* (يرشرش *yrašriš*) to sprinkle, spray. رشرش الشجر بالماي *rašraš š-šiyar b-l-maay.* He sprinkled the trees with water.

رش ش *ršš*

رش *rašš* (يرش *yrišš*) 1. to spray. رش دوا على الشجر *rašš duwa ᶜala š-šiyar.* He sprayed the trees with an insecticide. 2. to sprinkle. البلدية رشت الأرض بالماي *l-baladiyya raššat l-'arð b-l-maay.* The municipality sprinkled the ground with water. 3. to water. نرش البستان مرتين في السبوع *nrišš l-bistaan marrateen fi s-subuuᶜ.* We water the lawn twice a week.

رش *rašš* (v.n. from رش *rašš*) 1. spraying. 2. sprinkling. رش السيارة بالماي ما يفيد *rašš s-sayyaara b-l-maay ma yfiid.* Sprinkling the car with water doesn't help.

رشة *rašša* p. *-aat* (n. of inst.) light drizzle. رشهم رشتين *raššum raššateen.* He sprayed them twice.

راش *raašš* drizzle, light misty rain. (prov.) من بغى العالي يصبر على الراش *man baġa l-ᶜaali yaṣbir ᶜala r-raašš.*

Where there is a will, there is way. (lit., "He who desires excellence will have to put up with the drizzle.").

رشاش *raššaaš* p. *-aat* 1. sprinkling can, watering can. 2. machine gun, usually مدفع رشاش *midfa*ᶜ *raššaaš* machine gun.

رش گ *ršg*

رشق *rišag (يرشق yaršig)* to drop excrement (bird). رشقت الدجاجة *ršigat d-diyaaya.* The chicken dropped excrement.

رشق *rišag* (coll.) excrement (of birds).

رش م *ršm*

رشم *rašim* p. رشوم *ršuum* seal, signet. رشم البريد *rašim l-bariid* the postal cancellation stamp.

رش و *ršw*

رشا *riša (يرشي yirši)* to bribe. (برطل *barṭal* is more common). رشا التنديل بمية دينار. *riša t-tindeel b-miyat diinaar.* He bribed the supervisor with one hundred dinars. اللي ما يرشي ما يرتشي *'illi ma yirši ma yirtiši.* He who doesn't bribe can't be bribed.

ارتشى *rtiša* VIII to be bribed, accept bribery. (تبرطل *tabarṭal* is more common). ارتشى وسوى اللي نبغاه *rtiša w-sawwa lli nibġaa.* He was bribed and did what we wanted. ما يرتشي *ma yirtiši.* He cannot be bribed. He won't ever take a bribe.

رشوة *rašwa* p. رشاوي *rašaawi* (برطيل *barṭiil* and بخشيش *baxšiiš* are more common) bribe. يخش رشوة *yxišš rašwa.* He takes bribes. بدون رشوة ما تحصل شي *b-duun rašwa ma tḥaṣṣil šayy.* Without bribery you cannot get anything done.

رص د *rṣd*

رصد *riṣad (يرصد yarṣid)* 1. to observe, watch (stars). يرصدون النجوم من المرصد *yarṣiduun li-nyuum min l-marṣad.* They observe stars from the observatory. 2. to appropriate, earmark. الجامعة رصدت عشرة مليون درهم حق رواتب الأساتذة *l-yaam*ᶜ*a rṣidat* ᶜ*ašara malyoon dirhim ḥagg rawaatib l-'asaatða.* The university appropriated ten million dirhams for the salaries of the professors.

ترصد *traṣṣad* V to keep an eye on, watch, observe, lie in wait. في ناس يترصدون للي يفطر في شهر رمضان *fii naas yitraṣṣaduun la-lli yifṭir fi šahar rumðaan.* There are people who keep an eye on those who do not fast during the month of Ramadan. الحنش يترصد للطير *l-ḥanaš yitraṣṣad laṭ-ṭeer.* The snake is lying in wait for the bird.

رصيد *raṣiid* 1. balance. 2. available funds. شيك بدون رصيد *šeek b-duun raṣiid* bad check, check without sufficient funds to cover it.

رص ص *rṣṣ*

رص *raṣṣ (يرص yriṣṣ)* to press together, pack well. رص التمر في الكونية *raṣṣ t-tamir fi l-guuniyya.* He packed the dates very well in the container.

ارتص *rtaṣṣ* VIII to be pressed or packed together. ارتص التمر في الكونية *rtaṣṣ t-tamir fi l-guuniyya.* The dates were very well packed in the container.

رص *raṣṣ* (v.n. from رص *raṣṣ*) pressing together, packing well. رص هذي الأشيا بعضها على بعض ما يفيد *raṣṣ haaði l-'ašya ba^c^ðaha ^c^ala ba^c^að ma yfiid.* Pressing these things together on top of each other doesn't help.

رصة *raṣṣa* p. *-aat* 1. bundle, parcel, package. رصة كتب *raṣṣat kutub* bundle of books. 2. ream (of paper) رصة ورق *raṣṣat warag* ream of paper.

رصاص *raṣaaṣ* (coll.) 1. lead. حصلوا أشيا من رصاص من قرية هيلي الأثرية *ḥaṣṣalaw 'ašiya min raṣaaṣ min ġaryat hiili l-'aθariyya.* They found things made of lead in the archeological village of Hili. قلم رصاص *gaḷam raṣaaṣ* pencil. 2. (s. رصاصة *raṣaaṣa* p. *-aat*) bullet. ضرب ست رصاصات *ðirab sitt raṣaaṣaat.* He fired six bullets.

رصاصة *raṣṣaaṣa* p. *-aat* clothespin.

رصف *rṣf*

رصف *riṣaf* (يرصف *yarṣif*) to pave, lay with stone. البلدية ترصف شوارع كل يوم *l-baladiyya tarṣif šawaari^c^ kill yoom.* The municipality paves streets every day.

رصيف *raṣiif* p. أرصفة *'arsifa* 1. pavement. 2. sidewalk. 3. dock, wharf.

رظرظ *rðrð*

رضرض *raðrað* (يرضرض *yraðrið*) 1. to tenderize. القصاب يرضرض لك اللحم *l-gaṣṣaab yraðrið-lič l-laḥam.* The butcher will tenderize the meat for you (f.s.). 2. to crack, smash, break. فيه طيور ترضرض العظم *fii ṭyuur traðrið l-^c^aðim.* There are birds that crack bones.

رظظ *rðð*

رض *raðð* (يرض *yriðð*) to bruise s.th. طاح على الأرض ورض راسه *ṭaaḥ ^c^ala l-'arð w-raðð raasa.* He fell to the ground and bruised his head.

انرض *nraðð* VII to be or become bruised. انرض صبعه من الشاكوش *nraðð ṣub^c^a min č-čaakuuč.* His finger got bruised by the hammer.

رض *raðð* (v.n. from رض *raðð*) bruising, bruise.

رضة *raðða* p. *-aat* (n. of inst.) one bruise, one act of bruising. طاح على الأرض ورض راسه رضة قوية *ṭaaḥ ^c^ala l-'arð w-raðð raasa raðða gawiyya.* He fell to the ground and bruised his head badly.

رظع *rð^c^*

رضع *riða^c^* (يرضع *yirða^c^*) to nurse, suck milk at a mother's breast. ظل يرضع الين صار عمره سنتين *ðall yirða^c^ 'ileen ṣaar ^c^umra sanateen.* He continued to nurse until he was two years old.

رضع *raðða^c^* II to breast-feed a baby. أمه ظلت ترضعه الين صار عمره سنتين *'umma ðallat traðð^c^a 'ileen ṣaar ^c^umra sanateen.* His mother continued to breast-feed him until he became two years old. يالله قومي رضعيه! *yaḷḷa guumay raðð^c^ii!* Come on, go nurse him!

رضيع *raðii^c^* p. رضعان *rið^c^aan,* رضع *riðða^c^* suckling, infant, baby. شفت حرمة شايلة رضيع في السوق *čift ḥurma šaayla raðii^c^ fi s-suug.* I saw a woman carrying a baby in the marketplace.

رضاعة *raǒǒaa^c^a* p. *-aat* 1. nursing bottle. نحن ما نستعمل الرضاعة وايا أطفالنا أبداً *nihin ma nista^c^mil r-raǒǒaa^c^a wiyya 'atfaalna 'abdan.* We never use nursing bottles with our babies. 2. wet nurse. الرضاعة تجي كل يوم وترضع أطفالنا *r-raǒǒaa^c^a tiyi kill yoom w-traǒǒi^c^ 'atfaalna.* The wet nurse comes every day and suckles our young.

رظف *rǒf*

رظيف *riǒiif* p. رظفان *riǒfaan* young boy whose job is to help the rope-man on a ship (See سيب *seeb* rope-man under **سيب** *syb*).

رظي *rǒy*

رضى *riǒa* (يرضى *yirǒa*) 1. to be satisfied, be content. ما رضى بالفلوس اللي عطيته اياها *ma riǒa b-li-fluus illi ^c^ateeta-yyaaha.* He wasn't satisfied with the money I gave him. ما يرضى بأي شي *ma yirǒa b-'ayya šayy.* He isn't satisfied with anything. 2. to agree, accept. رضى يجي وايانا *riǒa yiyi wiyyaana.* He agreed to come with us. 3. to be pleased. ماحد يرضى على هالأوضاع *mahhad yirǒa ^c^ala hal-'awǒaa^c^.* No one is pleased with these circumstances. الله يرضى عليك *'alla yirǒa ^c^aleek.* May God be pleased with you. (prov.) اللي ما يرضى بجزة يرضى بجزة وخروف *'illi ma yirǒa b-yizza yirǒa b-yizza w-xaruuf.* Cut your losses and run. Half a loaf is better than none. (lit., "He who doesn't like to give the shorn wool of a lamb may [one day] have to give the shorn wool and the lamb.")

رضى *raǒǒa* II 1. to satisfy, please, gratify. مو بالسهل ترضيه *muu b-s-sahil traǒǒii.* He's not easy to please. ما ادري شو يرضيه *ma-dri šu yraǒǒii.* I don't know what can satisfy him. 2. to appease, pacify, mollify. رضيت أبوي لانه كان حمقان من طرفي *raǒǒeet 'ubuuy linna čaan hamgaan min tarafi.* I made up with my father because he was mad at me. رضت الجاهل بالرضاعة *raǒǒat l-yaahil b-r-raǒǒaa^c^a.* She placated the child with the nursing bottle.

راضى *raaǒa* III 1. = II رضى *raǒǒa.* حمقان من طرفك. روح راضيه *hamgaan min tarafak. ruuh raaǒii.* He is mad at you. Go make up with him. 2. to reconcile, conciliate. صار لهم مدة طويلة ما يتحاكون. رحنا نراضيهم *saar-lahum mudda tawiila ma yithaačuun. rihna nraaǒiihum.* They haven't spoken to each other for a long time. We went to reconcile them.

تراضى *traaǒa* VI to come to terms, settle differences with each other. بس خلهم. هم يتراضون بروحهم *bass xallhum. hum yitraaǒuun b-ruuhhum.* You just leave them alone. They will settle their differences by themselves.

رضى *riǒa* (v.n. from رضى *riǒa*) satisfaction, agreement, approval. هذا من رضى الوالدين *haaǒa min riǒa l-waaldeen.* This (e.g., success, wealth, etc.) is due to my parent's satisfaction. أبغى رضاك علي *'abġa riǒaač ^c^alayya.* I seek your satisfaction.

بالمراضاة *b-li-mraaǒaa* amicably, with mutual satisfaction.

راضي *raađi* p. *-yiin* (act. part. from رضى *riđa*) 1. (with عن *ᶜan*) satisfied with s.o. الوالدين راضيين عني *l-waalden raađyiin ᶜanni.* My parents are satisfied with me. 2. (with ب *b-*) content with. مسكينة. راضية بحالتها *miskiina. raađya b-ḥaalatta.* Poor thing. She is content with her situation. 3. willing, ready. أنت راضي تجي وايانا؟ *'inta raađi tiyi wiyyaana?* Are you willing to come with us?

رطب *rṭb*

رطب *raṭib* p. *-iin* humid, wet. الهوا هني حار ورطب في القيظ *l-hawa hni ḥaarr w-raṭib fi l-geeđ.* The weather here is hot and humid in the summer. الهدوم رطبين *li-hduum raṭbiin.* The clothes are wet.

رطوبة *ruṭuuba* humidity, dampness, moisture. فيه رطوبة هني واجد في القيظ *fii ruṭuuba hini waayid fi l-geeđ.* There is high humidity here in the summer.

رعد *rᶜd*

رعد *riᶜad* (يرعد *yirᶜid*) to thunder. الدنيا ما ترعد واجد هني *d-dinya ma tirᶜid waayid hni.* It doesn't often thunder here.

ارتعد *rtiᶜad* VIII to shiver, tremble, shake. ارتعد من البرد *rtiᶜad min l-bard.* He shivered from the cold. ارتعد لين سمع صوت الأسد *rtiᶜad leen simaᶜ ṣoot l-'asad.* He trembled when he heard the lion's sound.

رعد *raᶜad* thunder.

رعدة *raᶜda* p. *-aat* (رعشة *raᶜša* is more common) (n. of inst.) shiver, trembling. انصاب برعدة من البرد *nṣaab b-raᶜda min l-bard.* He shivered from the cold.

رعش *rᶜš*

رعش *riᶜaš* (يرعش *yraᶜiš*) to shake, tremble (from the cold or illness). هو رجال كبير. يرعش *huwa rayyaal čibiir. yraᶜiš.* He's an old man. He is trembling.

ارتعش *rtiᶜaš* VIII to tremble, shake. يرتعش من المرض اللي فيه *yirtiᶜiš min l-marađ illi fii.* His body is trembling from the illness he's afflicted with.

رعشة *raᶜša* p. *-aat* (n. of inst.) shiver, trembling, shaking.

رعف *rᶜf*

رعف *riᶜaf* (يرعف *yirᶜif*) to have a nosebleed. خشمه يرعف لين يكون حران *xašma yirᶜif leen ykuun ḥarraan.* He has a nosebleed when he is hot.

رعاف *rᶜaaf* (v.n.) nosebleed, nosebleeding.

مرعف *mirᶜif* (act. part.) nosebleeding. خشمه مرعف *xašma mirᶜif.* He is nosebleeding. (lit., "His nose is bleeding.").

رعي *rᶜy*

رعى *riᶜa* (يرعى *yirᶜa*) 1. to graze, eat herbs and grass. الغنم يرعون والراعي وياهم *l-ġanam yirᶜuun w-r-raaᶜi wiiyyaahum.* The sheep are grazing and the shepherd is with them. 2. to take care of, tend, guard. الراعي يرعى الغنم *r-raaᶜi yirᶜa l-ġanam.* A shepherd tends a flock of sheep. 3. to protect, guard, take care of. رعاك الله! *raᶜaak aḷḷaah!* God protect you!

راعى *raa^c^a* III 1. to observe, heed, respect. لازم تراعي قوانين السواقة *laazim traa^c^i ġawaaniim s-swaaga.* You must observe driving regulations. لازم تراعي عادات البلادين الثانية *laazim traa^c^i ^c^aadaat l-balaadiin θ-θaanya.* You have to respect the customs of other countries. راعى خاطري *raa^c^a xaaṭri.* He respected my feelings. 2. to be lenient with s.o. المعلم راعاه في الامتحان ونجحه. موب عدل *l-mu^c^allim raa^c^aa fi li-mtiḥaan w-najjaḥa. muub ^c^adil.* The teacher was lenient with him on the examination and passed him. This is not justice. 3. to make provision, see to it that. لا تشتري منه. ما يراعي أحد بالسعر *la tištiri minna. ma yraa^c^i 'aḥad b-s-si^c^ir.* Don't buy from him. He doesn't do well to anyone on the price. إذا تراعيني أشتري منك *'iđa traa^c^iini 'aštiri minnak.* If you treat me well, I will buy from you.

رعية *ra^c^iyya* p. رعايا *ra^c^aayaa* subjects, citizens.

مرعى *mar^c^a* p. مراعي *maraa^c^i* grazing land, pasture. كل يوم الصباح الراعي ياخذ الغنم حق المرعى *kill yoom ṣ-ṣabaaḥ r-raa^c^i yaaxiđ l-ġanam ḥagg l-mar^c^a.* Every day in the morning the shepherd takes the sheep to the grazing land.

المراعي *l-maraa^c^i* well-known dairy company in the Emirates and in Saudi Arabia.

رعاية *ri^c^aaya* 1. care, attention, consideration. مركز رعاية الطفل *markaz ri^c^aayat ṭ-ṭifil* center for child care, health center for children. 2. sponsorship, patronage. مباراة الكورة اليوم تحت رعاية الحاكم *mubaaraat l-kuura l-yoom taḥat ri^c^aayat l-ḥaakim.* The soccer game today is sponsored by the ruler.

راعي *raa^c^i* (act. part. from رعى *ri^c^a*) 1. (p. رعيان *ri^c^yaan*) shepherd, herdsman. 2. (p. *-yiin*) owner, proprietor. راعي التكسي *raa^c^i t-taksi* the taxicab owner. راعي الدكان *raa^c^i d-dikkaan* the shopkeeper. (prov.) راعي النصيفة سالم *raa^c^i n-niṣiifa saalim.* Half a loaf is better than none. Cut your losses and run. 3. (p. رعاة *ru^c^aa*) only in رعاة البقر *ru^c^aat l-bagar* the cowboys.

رغ ب *rġb*

رغب *raġġab* II (with في *fi*) to interest s.o. in s.th., excite s.o.'s interest in s.th. ما بغيت أدرس. هو اللي رغبني في الدراسة *ma baġeet 'adris. huwa lli raġġabni fi d-diraasa.* I didn't want to study. He is the one who got me interested in studying. الدلال رغبني في السيارة واشتريتها *d-dallaal raġġabni fi s-sayyaara w-štareetta.* The dealer got me enthusiastic about the car and I bought it.

رغبة *raġba* p. *-aat* wish, desire. عندي رغبة يا يبا أكمل دراستي *^c^indi raġba ya yuba 'akammil diraasti.* I intend, Dad, to complete my studies. البنت ما عندها رغبة تعرس هالحين *l-bint ma ^c^indaha raġba t^c^arris halḥiin.* The girl doesn't have a desire to get married now.

مرغوب *marġuub* in demand, coveted, sought after, desirable. السيارات الجابانية مرغوبة أكثر شي في الخليج *s-sayyaaraat l-jaabaaniyya marġuuba 'akθar šayy fi l-xaliij.* Japanese cars are the most in demand in the Gulf.

شخص مرغـوب فيـه *šuxṣ marġuub fii.* persona grata. شخص غير مرغوب فيـه *šuxṣ ġeer marġuub fii.* persona non grata. الحكومة سفرت كل الغير مرغـوب فيـهم *li-ḥkuuma saffarat kill l-ġeer marġuub fiihum.* The government deported all the undesirable people.

رغم *rġm*

أرغـم *'arġam* IV to force, compel. أرغموه يستقيل *'arġamoo yistagiil.* They forced him to resign. أرغمته الوزارة على تفنيش التنديـل *'arġamta l-wazaara ᶜala tafniiš t-tindeel.* The ministry forced him to fire the supervisor.

رفج *rfj*

رافـق *raafaj* III (less common var. *raafag*) 1. to accompany s.o. رافقناه لين دش الطـائرة *raafajnaa leen dašš ṭ-ṭaayra.* We accompanied him until he entered the plane. 2. to become friends with s.o. associate closely with s.o. لا ترافق مثل هذيل النـاس *la traafij miθil haðeel n-naas.* Don't associate with people like these. 3. to be on intimate terms with, go with. مـا تزوجها؛ بس رافقها مدة خمس سـنين *ma tazawwajha; bass raafaja muddat xams siniin.* He didn't marry her; he was just her intimate friend for five years.

ترافق *traafaj* VI to become friends, be intimate with each other. ترافقت وايا أخوها لاجل أزوج اختـه *traafajt wiyya 'uxuuha lajil 'azzawwaj 'ixta.* I became friends with her brother so that I could marry his sister. ترافقنا في الطريق لـين وصلنـا دبي *traafajna fi ṭ-ṭariig leen wiṣalna dbayy.* We were companions on the way until we arrived in Dubai.

رفيـق *rifiij* p. رفـايق *rifaayij,* رفقان *rifjaan.* 1. friend, buddy, pal. رفيقي سالم يسلم عليـك *rifiiji saalim ysallim ᶜaleek.* My friend Salim sends you his regards. 2. companion. موب صديق؛ بس رفيق سـفر *muub ṣidiij; bass rifiij safar.* He's not a friend; he's only a travel companion.

رفيقـة *rifiija* p. *-aat* 1. girl friend. 2. mistress.

رفرف *rfrf*

رفرف *rafraf* (يرفرف *yrafrif*) 1. to flap the wings. الطير ظل يرفرف لين حط على الشجرة *t-ṭeer ðall yrafrif leen ḥaṭṭ ᶜala li-šyara.* The bird continued to flap its wings until it lit on the tree. 2. to flutter. العلم يرفـرف *l-ᶜalam yrafrif.* The flag is fluttering.

رفس *rfs*

رفـس *rifas* (يرفس *yarfis*) to kick. هذا البغل يرفـس *haaða l-baġal yarfis.* This mule kicks. رفسه الحصان *rfasa li-ḥṣaan.* The horse kicked him.

رفسـة *rafsa* p. *-aat* (n. of inst.) one kick, a kick.

رفظ *rfð*

رفـض *rifað* (يرفض *yarfuð*) to refuse to accept, reject, turn down. رفض يوافق على طلب الزيادة في الراتب *rifað ywaafig ᶜala ṭalab z-ziyaada fi r-raatib.* He refused to approve the request for the salary increase. رفض المدير المعاملة *rifað l-mudiir l-muᶜaamala.* The director rejected the (business) transaction. القـاضي رفـض القضيـة *l-gaaði rifað l-gaðiyya.* The judge dismissed the case. رفض شوري *rifaḍ šoori.* He turned down my suggestion.

رفض *rafḍ* refusal, rejection. أبد ما كنت أتصور الجواب يكون بالرفض *'abad ma čint 'atṣawwar l-jawaab ykuun b-r-rafḍ.* It never occurred to me that the answer would be a refusal.

ر ف ع *rf^c*

رفع *rifa^c* (يرفع *yirfa^c*) 1. to lift, raise, lift up. تقدر ترفع امية كيلو؟ *tigdar tirfa^c 'imyat keelu?* Can you lift one hundred kilograms? 2. to raise. رفعته وحطيته على الميزان *rifa^cta w-ḥaṭṭeta ^cala l-miizaan.* I raised it and put it on the scale لا ترفع صوتك من فضلك! *la tirfa^c ṣootak min faḍlak!* Don't raise your voice, please! يرفعون العلم كل يوم خميس *yirfa^cuun l-^calam kill yoom xamiis.* They raise the flag every Thursday. 3. to increase, mark higher. رفعوا سعر الشكر والقهوة *rfa^caw si^cr š-šakar w-li-ghawa.* They raised the prices of sugar and coffee. 4. to take away, remove. ارفع يدك! لا تلمسني! *'irfa^c yaddak! la tilmasni!* Take your hand off! Don't touch me! رفعوا اسمه من ليستة المشبوهين *rfa^caw 'isma min liistat l-mašbuuhiin.* They removed his name from the list of suspects. 5. to submit, present, forward. وزارة التجارة رفعت تقرير عن الصادرات والواردات *wazaarat t-tijaara rfa^cat tagriir ^can ṣ-ṣaadiraat w-l-waaridaat.* The ministry of commerce submitted a report about exports and imports. رئيس الديوان الأميري رفع الطلب حق الأمير *ra'iis d-diiwaan l-'amiiri rifa^c ṭ-ṭalab ḥagg l-'amiir.* The director of the Emiri court forwarded the request to the Emir. 6. (with دعوى *da^cwa*) to sue, bring legal action against s.o. رفع دعوى على الشركة *rifa^c da^cwa ^cala š-šarika.* He sued the company.

رفّع *raffa^c* II to promote, raise s.o. in salary or rank. رفعوه وصار تنديل على الكولية *raffa^coo w-ṣaar tindeel ^cala l-kuuliyya.* They promoted him and he became a supervisor over the coolies. بس رفعوه اشتري سيارة جديدة *bass raffa^coo štira sayyaara yidiida.* As soon as they promoted him, he bought a new car.

ترفّع *traffa^c* V 1. to be promoted. ترفع إلى رتبة ضابط *traffa^c 'ila rutbat ḍaabiṭ.* He was promoted to the rank of officer. 2. to be too proud, look down. ترفع يروح يزور هله في بيتهم القديم *traffa^c yruuḥ yzuur hala fi beettum l-gadiim.* He was too proud to go visit his folks in their old home. يترفع عن أشغال مثل هذي *yitraffa^c ^can 'ašġaal miθil haaði.* He looks down upon jobs similar to these.

ارتفع *rtifa^c* VIII 1. to become higher, go up, rise. سعر الطماط رايح يرتفع في القيظ *si^cr ṭ-ṭamaaṭ raayiḥ yirtifi^c fi l-geeḍ.* The price of tomatoes is going to go up in the summer. الرطوبة ما ترتفع في الشتا *r-ruṭuuba ma tirtifi^c fi š-šita.* Humidity doesn't increase in the winter. صوته ارتفع لين صار حمقان *ṣoota rtifa^c leen ṣaar ḥamgaan.* His voice rose when he got mad.

رفع *rafi^c* (v.n. from رفع *rifa^c*) lifting, raising, hoisting. رفع الأثقال *raf^c l-'aθgaal* weight lifting. رفع العلم *raf^c l-^calam* raising the flag.

رفيــــع *rifiiᶜ* thin, slender (دقيق *dijiij* is more common. See under **د گ گ** *dgg*).

ترفيــــع *tarfiiᶜ* p. *-aat* (v.n. from II رفّع *raffaᶜ*) promotion. صار له يشتغل عشر سنين وما حصل ترفيع بعد *ṣaar-la yištaġil ᶜašar siniin w-ma ḥaṣṣal tarfiiᶜ baᶜad.* He's been working for ten years and hasn't been promoted yet.

ارتفـــاع *rtifaaᶜ* p. *-aat* (v.n. from VIII ارتفـــع *rtifaᶜ*) 1. rise. ارتفاع الأسعار *rtifaaᶜ l-'asᶜaar* rise of prices. 2. increase. ارتفاع المعيشة *rtifaaᶜ l-maᶜiiša* high cost of living. 3. height, elevation, altitude. ارتفاع الجبل *rtifaaᶜ l-yibal* the altitude of the mountain.

مــترفع *mitraffiᶜ* p. *-iin* 1. having been promoted. مترفع قبـــل ســـنتين *mitraffiᶜ gabil santeen.* He was promoted two years ago. 2. arrogant, snobbish, haughty.

ر ف ف *rff*

رف *raff (*يرف *yriff)* to twitch, quiver. عينــه تـــرف *ᶜeena triff.* His eye is twitching.

رف *raff* p. رفـــوف *rfuuf* 1. shelf. 2. ledge. 3. flight (of birds).

ر ف گ *rfg*

رافــق *raafag* III (more common var. *raafaj*) to accompany, escort. See under **ر ف ج** *rfj*.

ترافــق *traafag* VI (more common var. *traafaj*) to become friends, intimate with each other. See under **ر ف ج** *rfj*.

رفيــق *rifiig* p. رفـــايق *rifaayig,* رفقان *rifgaan* (more common var. *rifiij*) friend, buddy, etc. See under **ر ف ج** *rfj*.

مرافق *mraafig* p. *-iin* (act. part. from III رافـــق *raafag*) 1. escort. 2. aide, aide-de-camp.

ر گ ب *rgb*

راقـــب *raagab* III to watch, observe, keep an eye on. العريف يراقب الصف اليوم *l-ᶜariif yraagib ṣ-ṣaff l-yoom.* The prefect is watching over the class today. ماحد يراقبك. روحـــي! *maḥḥad yraagibč. ruuḥi!* Nobody is watching you. Go! هو من المشبوهين. الشرطة يراقبونه *huwa min l-mašbuuhiin. š-širṭa yraagbuuna.* He's one of the suspects. The police have him under surveillance.

رقبـــة *rguba* p. رقاب *rgaab* neck. قطعوا رقبته *gṭaᶜaw rgubta.* They cut through his neck. خطيتـــه في رقبتـــك *xaṭiita fi rgubtak.* His mistake is your responsibility. برقبته عايلة كبيرة *b-rgubta ᶜaayla čibiira.* He's got the responsibility of a large family.

رقيـــب *ragiib* p. رقبـــا *rugaba* (less common var. رقيب *raqiib, raġiib*) 1. sergeant. رقيـــب أول *ragiib 'awwal* sergeant-major. 2. censor. يشتغل رقيب حق وزارة الإعـــلام *yištaġil ragiib ḥagg wazaarat l-'iᶜlaam.* He works as a censor for the ministry of information.

رقابة *ragaaba* censorship.

مراقبـــة *mraagaba* (v.n. from III راقب *raagab*) 1. observation, surveillance. 2. monitoring, overseeing.

مراقب *mraagib* p. *-iin* (act. part. from III راقب *raagab*) prefect, monitor.

ر گ د *rgd*

رقد *rigad (*يرقد *yargid)* 1. to sleep. هني

الناس يرقدون ساعة الظهر *hini n-naas yarigduun saa^c^t ð̣-ð̣uhur.* Here people take a nap at noontime. قال لي الدختر لازم أرقد سبع ساعات كل يوم *gal-li d-daxtar laazim 'argid sabi^c^ saa^c^aat kill yoom.* The doctor told me I had to sleep seven hours a night. لا ترقد ذالحين *la targid ðalḥiin.* Don't sleep now. 2. to go to bed, retire. خلنا نروح نرقد *xaḷḷna nruuḥ nargid.* Let's go to bed. الدجاجة رقدت على البيض *d-diyaaya rgadat ^c^ala l-beeð̣.* The chicken sat on the eggs.

رقد *raggad* II to put s.o. to bed, to put s.o. to sleep. الأم رقدت عيالها *l-'umm raggadat ^c^yaaḷha.* The mother put her children to sleep. جا عندنا خطار أمس. رقدناهم عندنا ذيك الليلة *yaa ^c^indana xuṭṭaar 'ams. raggadnaahum ^c^indana ðiič l-leela.* We had guests yesterday. We put them up at our place that night.

رقدة *ragda* p. *-aat* (n. of inst.) manner of lying, lying position. رقد رقدة هنية *rigad ragda haniyya.* He slept soundly.

رقاد *rgaad* (v.n. from رقد *rigad*) sleep, sleeping. من جينا لنشينا ساعة الصبح كله رقاد *min yiina la-naššeena saa^c^at ṣ-ṣubḥ killa rgaad.* From the time we came until we woke up in the morning, we were sleeping the whole time. الرقاد عقب الأكل موب زين *r-rgaad ^c^ugb l-'akil muub zeen.* Going to bed after eating is not healthy.

راقد *raagid* p. *-iin* (act. part. from رقد *rigad*) sleeping, asleep. الدجاجة راقدة على البيض *d-diyaaya raagda ^c^ala l-beeð̣.* The chicken is sitting on the eggs.

ر گ ص *rgṣ*

رقص *rigaṣ* (يرقص *yargiṣ*) to dance. النعاشات قامن يرقصن ويغنن *n-na^cc^aašaat gaaman yarigṣin w-yġannin.* The female dancers started to dance and sing. في أمريكا هني ما اعرف أرقص *fi 'amriika hni ma ^c^arf 'argiṣ.* In America here I don't know how to dance. رقصت من الفرح *rigaṣt min l-faraḥ.* I danced for joy.

رقص *raggaṣ* II to make dance. جاب سباله ورقصه وحصل فلوس من وراه *yaab sbaala w-raggaṣa w-ḥaṣṣal fluus min waraa.* He brought his monkey, made him dance, and got money because of him.

ترقص *traggaṣ* V to prance, swagger. يترقص بمشيته. *yitraggaṣ b-mašyita.* He prances in his gait. He prances when he walks.

رقص *ragṣ* (v.n. from رقص *rigaṣ*) dancing, dance. الرقص والغنا *r-ragṣ w-l-ġina* dancing and singing. رقصت رقص عربي *rigṣat ragṣ ^c^arabi.* She belly-danced.

رقصة *ragṣa* p. *-aat* (n. of inst.) a dance, one dance.

رقاص *raggaaṣ* p. *-aat* as in رقاص الساعة *raggaaṣ s-saa^c^a* the pendulum.

ر گ ط *rgṭ*

رقط *raggaṭ* II to speckle, spot s.th. رحت المورس وقلت له: «رقط لي الخلقة حمرا وخضرا» *riḥt li-mwarris w-git-la: "raggiṭ-li l-xalga ḥamra w-xað̣ra."* I went to the dyer and said to him: "Speckle this piece of cloth red and green for me."

أرقـط *'argaṭ* p. رقـط *rugṭ* speckled, spotted. f. رقطا *ragṭa.* ديك أرقط *diič 'argaṭ* speckled rooster. دجاجـة رقطا *diyaaya ragṭa* speckled chicken.

ر گ ع *rg^c*

رقـع *riga^c* (يرقع *yirga^c*) to patch. كان في ثوبـه ثقـب. رقعـه *čaan fi θooba θagb. rga^ca.* There was a whole in his dishdash. He patched it.

رقـع *ragga^c* II to patch, mend. طال عمرك هـني نـاس مـا يرقعـون الثـواب ولا الجواتـي. بـس يقطونهـم *ṭaal ^cumrak hini naas ma yrgg^cuun li-θwaab walla l-juwaati. bass yigiṭṭuunhum.* People here, may you live long, don't patch dishdashes or mend shoes. They just throw them away.

رقعـة *rug^ca* p. رقع *ruga^c* 1. patch. هذي الرقعـة مـن غـير لـون *haaδi r-rug^ca min ġeer loon.* This patch is of a different color. 2. lot, piece of land. عندي رقعة في راس الخيمـة *^cindi rug^ca fi raas l-xeema.* I have a piece of land in Ras Al-Khaima. 3. gold piece of jewelry worn on the forehead by women. 4. stern of a ship.

ر گ گ *rgg*

رك *rigg* p. ركـوك *rguug* oil rig. تحصل ركـوك واجـد هـني *tḥaṣṣil rguug waajid hini.* You will find many oil rigs here.

ركي *raggi* (coll.) watermelons (only in Ras Al-Khaima, Saudi and Iraqi Arabic). s. ركيـة *raggiyya* p. *-aat.* الركـي نسـميه هـني «اليـح» ولا «الجـح» *r-raggi nsammii hni "l-yiḥḥ" walla "l-jiḥḥ."* We call *r-raggi "l-yiḥḥ"* or *"l-jiḥḥ"* here. الركي مال السعودية كلش طيـب *r-raggi maal s-su^cuudiyya killiš ṭayyib.* The watermelons of Saudi Arabia are very delicious.

رقـاق *rgaag* (coll.) thin, flat bread. s. رقاقة *rgaaga* p. *-aat.*

ر گ م *rgm*

رقـم *raggam* II to number, give a number to s.th. رقم هذيل الطلبات حسب الأصـول *raggim haδeel ṭ-ṭalabaat ḥasb l-'uṣuul.* Number these applications according to regulations.

رقم *ragam* p. أرقام *'argaam* 1. numeral. الأرقام من واحد إلى عشـرة *l-'argaam min waaḥid 'ila ^cašara* the numerals from one to ten. 2. number, No. نمرة واحد *numra waaḥid* No. 1, the best. سجل رقم قياسـي *sajjal ragam giyaasi.* He set a record (in athletics).

ترقيم *targiim* (v.n. from II رقم *raggam*) numbering, numeration.

مرقـم *mraggam* (p.p.) numbered, having been given a number.

ر ك ب *rkb*

ركـب *rikab* (*ričab* is more common). See under **رچ ب** *rčb.*

ركـب *rakkab* II (*raččab* is more common). See under **رچ ب** *rčb.*

تركـب *trakkab* V (*traččab* is more common). See under **رچ ب** *rčb.*

ارتكـب *rtikab* VIII to commit, perpetrate (a sin, a crime). ارتكب أكثر مـن جريمـة في حق بنتـه *rtikab 'akθar min jarrima fi ḥagg binta.* He committed more than one crime with respect to his daughter.

ركبـة *rukba* (common var. *ričba*) p.

ركب *rikab* knee. ركبتي تعورني *rkubti tᶜawwirni.* My knee hurts. My knee is hurting me. يوم الركبة *yoom r-rukba* (also known as يوم الدشة *yoom d-dašša*) the first day of pearling season.

ركاب *rkaab* (*rčaab* is more common). See under **رچب** *rčb*.

مركب *markab* p. مراكب *maraakib* ship, boat, vessel.

راكب *raakib* (عبري *ᶜibri* is more common). See under **ع ب ر** *ᶜbr*.

ر ك د *rkd*

ركد *rikad (*يركد *yarkid)* to be motionless, still, stagnant. ركد الماي ونزل الطين تحت *rikad l-maay w-nizal ṭ-ṭiin tahat.* The water became still and the mud settled to the bottom. اركد لاجل آخذ ضغط دمك! *'irkid lajil 'aaxið ðagṭ dammak!* Be still so that I can take your blood pressure.

ركد *rakkad* II 1. to make quiet, motionless. إذا ما تركده ما أقدر أشتغل *'iða ma trakkda ma 'agdar 'aštaġil.* If you don't calm him down, I cannot work. 2. to make less painful, alleviate. الدختر عطاني دوا يركد الوجع *d-daxtar ᶜaṭaani duwa yrakkid l-wujaᶜ.* The doctor gave me medicine to ease the pain.

ركادة *rkaada* (v.n. from ركد *rikad*) 1. quietness, tranquility. 2. prudence, wisdom, discernment.

بركادة *b-rkaada* (adv.) intelligently, judiciously.

راكد *raakid* (act. part. from ركد *rikad*) 1. stagnant, still, motionless. ماي راكد *maay raakid* stagnant water. 2. sluggish. سوق السمك راكد اليوم *suug s-simač raakid l-yoom.* The fish market is sluggish today. البيع والشرا راكد *l-beeᶜ w-š-šira raakid.* Buying and selling is very slow. 3. (p.*-iin*) peaceful, tranquil, quiet.

ر ك ز *rkz*

ركز *rakkaz* II 1. to plant or ram in the ground, set up. ركز العمود في الأرض *rakkaz l-ᶜamuud fi l-'arḍ.* He set up the pole in the ground. 2. to concentrate. ركز كل تفكيره بهالشي *rakkaz kill tafkiira b-haš-šayy.* He concentrated all his thinking on this matter. 3. to fix, implant. ركز كل التعليمات بذهنه *rakkaz kill t-taᶜliimaat b-ðihna.* He fixed all the instructions in his mind.

تركز *trakkaz* V 1. to be set up, planted or rammed in the ground. 2. to be concentrated (on s.th.). 3. to be fixed, implanted.

ارتكز *rtikaz* VIII (with على *ᶜala*) 1. to lean, support one's weight on s.th. هو رجال عود لحيته بيضا يرتكز على العصا *huwa rayyaal ᶜood liḥyita beeḍa yirtakiz ᶜala l-ᶜaṣa.* He is an old man whose beard is grey. He supports his weight on the cane. 2. to rest, be based on. الباب يرتكز على الطوفة *l-baab yirtakiz ᶜala ṭ-ṭoofa.* The wall is supporting the door.

مركز *markaz* p. مراكز *maraakiz.* 1. center. مركز التدريب حق أدما *markaz t-tadriib ḥagg 'adma* the ADMA Training Center. 2. station. مركز البوليس *markaz l-pooliis* the police station.

مركزي *markazi* central. السوق المركزي *s-suug l-markazi* the central marketplace. حكومة مركزية *ḥkuuma markaziyya* central government.

مركز *murakkaz* (p.p. from II ركز *rakkaz*) 1. centralized, concentrated. 2. condensed. حليب مركز *ḥaliib murakkaz* condensed milk.

ر ك ظ *rkḍ*

ركض *rikaḍ* (يركض *yarkuḍ*) to run, race, rush. ركض ميلين *rikaḍ miileen.* He ran two miles. اركض لايفوتنا الباص *'urkuḍ la yfuutna l-paaṣ.* Run so that we don't miss the bus. كلما صار عنده مشكلة يركض على المدير *kill-ma ṣaar cinda muškila yarkuḍ cala l-mudiir.* Whenever he faces a problem, he runs to the director.

ركض *rakkaḍ* II to make run, race, rush. ركضني ميلين *rakkaḍni miileen.* He made me run two miles.

ركض *rakḍ* (v.n. from ركض *rikaḍ*) running. ركض ركض سريع *rikaḍ rakḍ sariic.* He ran fast.

راكض *raakiḍ* p. *-iin* (act. part. from ركض *rikaḍ*) 1. having run. توه راكض ميلين *tawwa raakiḍ miileen.* He has just run two miles. 2. runner, racer.

ر ك ع *rkc*

ركع *rikac* (يركع *yirkac*) to kneel down, drop to one's knees (in prayer). في صلاة الظهر المصلين يركعون أربع مرات *fi ṣalaat ḍ-ḍuhur li-mṣalliin yirkacuun 'arbac marraat.* During the midday prayer worshippers kneel down four times.

ركعة *rukca* p. ركع *rukac* bowing and kneeling down in prayer.

ر ك ك *rkk*

رك *rakk* (يرك *yrikk*) to be or become weak or feeble. (less common var. *račč*) ركت الدجاجة، خلاص *rakkat d-diyaaya, xalaaṣ.* The chicken no longer had eggs. الرجال العود يرك *r-rayyaal l-cood yrikk.* An old man becomes weak.

راك *raakk* (act. part.) جاسم مثل الدجاجة الراكة *jaasim miθl d-diyaaya r-raakka.* Jasim is like a weakened chicken.

ركة *rakka* beginning of the pearling season. الركة عادةً تكون في أول القيظ *r-rakka caadatan tkuun fi 'awwal l-geeḍ.* The pearling season is usually at the beginning of the summer.

ر ك ن *rkn*

ركن *rukun* p. أركان *'arkaan* 1. corner. ها الحجرة فيها أربع أركان *hal-ḥijra fiiha 'arbac 'arkaan.* This room has four corners. 2. principle, basic element. أركان الإسلام خمسة *'arkaan l-'islaam xamsa.* The principles or pillars of Islam are five. 3. (mil.) staff. رئيس أركان الجيش *ra'iis 'arkaan l-jeeš* the military chief of staff.

ر ك ي *rky*

ركية *rikya* (بير *biir* is more common). See under **ب ي ر** *byr*.

ر م ح *rmḥ*

رمح *rumḥ* p. رماح *rmaaḥ* spear, javelin.

ر م د *rmd*

رمـــاد *rmaad* (less common var. *rumaad*) ashes. انحرق البيت وصار رمـاد *nḥirag l-beet w-ṣaar rmaad.* The house burned up and turned into ashes.

رمـادي *rmaadi* p. *-yyiin* gray, grayish, ash-colored. لـون رمـادي *loon rmaadi* gray color.

ر م ز *rmz*

رمـز *ramz* p. رمـوز *rmuuz* 1. symbol, emblem. 2. secret sign, code sign.

رمـزي *ramzi* symbolic. هذي موب شي. بـس هدية رمزيـة *haaði muub šayy. bass hadiyya ramziyya.* This is not much. It's only a symbolic gift.

ر م س *rms*

رمـس *rimas* (يرمـس *yarmis)* to speak, talk. بس قاعد يرمس *bass gaa^c^id yarmis.* He's just talking. (prov.) المن أقـول والمـن أرمـس *'il-man 'aguul w-'il-man 'armis.* Nobody is listening. There's no use. (lit., "Whom will I tell and whom will I speak to?")

رمـس *rammas* II to speak to s.o. الشيخ رمس المطـارزي وقـال لـه: «نبغـي نـروح القنـص» *š-šeex rammas l-maṭaarzi w-gal-la: "nabġi nruuḥ l-ganaṣ."* The Shaikh talked to the bodyguard and said to him: "We would like to go hunting."

رمس *rams* (v.n.) talk, talking, speech.

رمسة *ramsa* (n. of inst.) one act of speech or talk. شـها الرمسة!؟ *š-har-ramsa!?* = شها الكلام!؟ *š-hal-kalaam!?* What kind of talk is this!?

ر م ش *rmš*

رمش *rimš* p. رموش *rmuuš* eyelash.

ر م ظ *rmð̣*

رمضـان *rumð̣aan* Ramadan (name of the ninth month of the Islamic calendar, the month of fasting). المسلم لازم يصوم شـهر رمضـان *l-muslim laazim yṣuum šahar rumð̣aan.* A Muslim must fast the month of Ramadan. عيد رمضـان *^c^iid rumð̣aan* the Ramadan Feast, Lesser Bairam. كلب رمضان *čalb rumð̣aan* the dog of Ramadan (fig. s.o. who doesn't fast the month of Ramadan). (prov.) شو فاكر من رمضان غـير الجـوع والعطـش *šu faakir min rumð̣aan ġeer l-yuu^c^ w-l-^c^aṭaš.* Don't bite the hand that feeds you. Be good to those who have done you a favor. Don't dirty your own nest. (lit. "He remembers only the hunger and thirst of Ramadan.").

ر م ل *rml*

ترمـل *trammal* V to become a widow. مسـكينة. ترملـت وهـي صغـيرة *maskiina. trammalat w-hiya ṣaġiira.* Poor thing. She became a widow when she was young.

رمـل *ramil* (coll.) sand. السيارة قرزت في الرمـل *s-sayyaara ġarrazat fi r-ramil.* The car got stuck in the sand. يضرب بـالرمل *yað̣rib b-r-ramil.* He tells one's fortune in the sand.

رملـي *ramli* sandy. صخـر رملـي *ṣaxar ramli* sandy rocks. لون رملي *loon ramli* sandy color.

ر م ن *rmn*

رمان *rummaan* (coll.) pomegranates. s.

-a p. -aat. ما فيه رمان في السوق *ma fii rummaan fi s-suug.* There are no pomegranates in the market. الرمان يطلع هني *r-rummaan yiṭlaᶜ hni.* Pomegranates grow here. كليت رمانتين *kaleet rummaanteen.* I ate two pomegranates.

رمانة *rummaana* p. *-aat* 1. pomegranate. 2. wooden piece on the poop deck used for securing sheets on a ship or a boat.

ر ن د *rnd*

رندة *randa* p. *-aat* (carpenter's) plane. النجاجير يشتغلون بالرندة والشاكوش *n-nijaajiir yištağluun b-r-randa w-č-čaakuuč.* Carpenters work with planes and hammers. يضربون الليحان بالرندة *yaðribuun l-liiḥaan b-r-randa.* They use a plane on boards.

ر ن گ *rng*

رنق *rannag* II to paint, dye, stain, color, tint. رنق باب البيت خضر *rannag baab l-beet xaðar.* He painted the house door green. فيه ناس يرنقون شعرهم *fii naas yrannguun šaᶜarhum.* There are people who dye their hair. هذا الرجال يرنق الهدوم *haaða r-rayyaal yrannig li-hduum.* This man dyes clothes.

رنق *rang* p. رناق *rnaag* 1. paint. رنقنا الصندوق برنق خضر *rannagna ṣ-ṣanduug b-rang xaðar.* We painted the box green. 2. dye. 3. color.

مرنق *mrannig* p. *-iin* (act. part. from II رنق *rannag*) 1. painter. 2 dyer.

ر ن ن *rnn*

رن *rann (يرن yrinn)* to ring, resound. التلفون يرن *t-talafoon yrinn.* The telephone is ringing. صوته عالي ويرن في كل البيت *ṣoota ᶜaali w-yrinn fi kill l-beet.* His voice is loud, and it resounds in the whole house.

ران *raann* (act. part. from رن *rann*) having rung. التلفون توه ران *t-talafoon tawwa raann.* The telephone has just rung.

رنان *rannaan* ringing, resounding. صوت رنان *ṣoot rannaan* resounding voice.

ر ه ب *rhb*

إرهاب *'irhaab* (v.n.) terror, terrorism.

إرهابي *'irhaabi* 1. terroristic. عمل إرهابي *ᶜamal 'irhaabi* terroristic act. 2. (p. *-yyiin*) terrorist.

راهب *raahib* p. رهبان *ruhbaan* priest, monk.

راهبة *raahiba* p. *-aat* nun.

ر ه ش *rhš*

رهش *rihaš (يرهش yirhaš)* 1. to glitter, shine, sparkle. فستان النعاشة كان يرهش *fustaan n-naᶜᶜaaša čaan yirhas.* The female dancer's dress was glittering. 2. to twinkle. بعض النجوم ترهش في الليل *baᶜð li-nyuum tirhaš fi l-leel.* Some stars twinkle at night.

رهش *rahaš* 1. kind of dessert made of sesame seeds and date molasses. 2. thick sauce made of sesame oil and sesame seed paste.

ر ه م *rhm*

رهم *riham (يرهم yirham)* 1. to fit, be suitable for. الجوتي يرهم *l-juuti yirham.* The shoes fit. ها السكروب ما يرهم

has-sakruub ma yirham. This screw doesn't fit. ها الكـوت يرهـم عليـك زيـن *hal-kuut yirham ᶜaleek zeen.* This coat fits you well. الرنق ما يرهم وايـا الزوليـة *r-rang ma yirham wiyya z-zuuliyya.* The paint doesn't go with the carpet.

ر ه ن *rhn*

رهـم *rihan* (يرهـن *yirhan*) 1. to pawn, deposit as security. رهنت صوغتها لاجل تشـتري بيـت *rhinat ṣooġatta lajil tištiri beet.* She pawned her jewelry in order to buy a house. ما تقدر تتسلف فلوس إلا إذا رهنـت سـاعتك الذهبيـة *ma tigdar titsallaf fluus 'illa 'iða rihant saaᶜtak ð-ðahabiyya.* You cannot borrow any money unless you leave your gold watch as security. 2. to mortgage. رهـن بيتـه بمليـون درهـم *rihan beeta b-malyoon dirhim.* He mortgaged his house for a million dirhams.

راهـن *raahan* III to make a bid with s.o., to bet, wager. راهنتـه وخسـر *raahanta w-xisar.* I made a bet with him and he lost. أراهنك انه رايح يخسـر *'araahink 'inna raayiḥ yxasir.* I bet you he is going to lose. راهن بخمسامية درهـم علـى ذاك البعـير *raahan b-xamsimyat dirhim ᶜala ðaak l-biᶜiir.* He wagered five hundred dirhams on that camel.

تراهـن *traahan* VI to bet with each other. تراهنـا علـى امية دينـار *traahanna ᶜala 'imyat diinaar.* We bet each other a hundred dinars.

رهـان *rhaan* 1. bet, wager. 2. money deposited on a bet. 3. pawn, pledge, security.

رهينـة *rahiina* p. رهـاين *rahaayin* hostage.

ر و ب *rwb*

راب *raab* (يـروب *yiruub*) to curdle. الحليـب راب *l-ḥaliib raab.* The milk curdled. (prov.) لا ماي يروب ولا قحبة تتـوب *la maay yruub wala gaḥba tituub.* A leopard cannot change his spots. (lit., "Water doesn't curdle and a prostitute doesn't repent.").

روب *rawwab* II to curdle, make curdle. حرمتي روبت الحليـب وسـوت لـبن *ḥurumti rawwabat l-ḥaliib w-sawwat laban.* My wife curdled the milk and made yoghurt.

ر و ث *rwθ*

روث *rooθ* dung, manure (of a horse, a camel, a donkey, etc.)

ر و ج *rwj*

راج *raaj* (يـروج *yruuj*) 1. to increase, become greater, become more. المـاي راج في التـانكي *l-maay raaj fi t-taanki.* The water increased in the reservoir. 2. to sell well, find a good market, be in demand. البضاعـة راجـت في الأسـواق *l-biðaaᶜa raajat fi l-'aswaag.* The merchandise sold well in the marketplace.

روج *rawwaj* II 1. to spread (rumors, news), circulate. فيـه نـاس يروجـون الإشـاعات *fii naas yrawwjuun l-'išaaᶜaat.* There are people who spread rumors. 2. to push the sale of, open a market for. يروجـون بيـع التلفزيونـات في مركـز الحـامد *yrawwjuun beeᶜ t-talafizyoonaat fi markaz il-ḥaamid.* They are pushing the sale of television sets at the Hamid

Shopping Center.

رواج *rawaaj* (v.n. from راج *raaj*) increase, circulation.

ترويـج *tarwiij* (v.n. from II روج *rawwaj*) spreading, sale, distribution.

روح *rwḥ*

راح *raaḥ (يـروح yiruuḥ)* 1. to go, go away, leave, depart. راح وايـاي *raaḥ wiyyaay.* He went with me. لا تـروح وايـاهم *la truuḥ wiyyaahum.* Don't go with them. (prov.) راحت روحه وورمت جروحه *raaḥat ruuḥa w-wurmat jruuḥa.* Good riddance! Good riddance to bad rubbish! (lit., "His soul has gone and his wounds have become swollen."). (prov.) راحـوا اليقـرون وظلـوا اليخـرون *raaḥaw l-yigruun w-ḍallaw l-yixruun.* The good old days. Things are no longer the same. (lit., "Those who feed the poor are gone, and those who (eat and) defecate have stayed."). تعبي عليهـم راح سدى *ta*ᶜ*abi* ᶜ*aleehum raaḥ suda.* My efforts to raise them went for nothing. راح السـاعة خمـس *raaḥ s-saa*ᶜ*a xams.* He left at five o'clock. 2. to go to s.o. or to some place. راح الدوحـة *raaḥ d-dooḥa.* He went to Doha. راح سـوق السـمك *raaḥ suug s-simač.* He went to the fish market. 3. (with foll. imperf.) to go to do s.th., go in order to do s.th. راح يشتغل *raaḥ yištaġil.* He went in order to work. رحت أرمس الشـيخ *riḥt 'arammis š-šeex.* I went to speak with the Shaikh. يروح يلعـب كـورة *yruuḥ yil*ᶜ*ab kuura.* He goes to play soccer. 4. imperf. يروح *yruuḥ* with foll. imperf. expresses likelihood, future, or alternate action. لا تقول قدامـه هـا الشـكل. يـروح يحمـق *la tguul jiddaama haš-šikil. yruuḥ yḥamig.* Don't say such things in his presence; he might get mad. لا تبوق لا تـروح السـجن *la tbuug la truuḥ s-sijn.* Don't steal so you might not go to jail. إذا الله هداه، يروح يـترك السـكر *'iða 'aḷḷa hadaa, yruuḥ yitrik s-sikir.* If God leads him to the true faith, he will quit drinking. بدل التاير لا يروح يبنشر *baddil t-taayir la yruuḥ ybanšir.* Change the tire or it will go flat.

روح *rawwaḥ* II 1. to go home (usually in the evening). يـدش الشـغل الصبـاح ويـروح العصـر *ydišš š-šuġul ṣ-ṣabaaḥ w-yrawwiḥ l-*ᶜ*aṣir.* He goes to work in the morning, and goes home in the afternoon. 2. to cause or allow s.th. to go away. الصابون يروح الوسـخ *ṣ-ṣaabuun yrawwiḥ l-waṣax.* Soap removes dirt. لا تروح ها الصفقـة مـن يـدك *la trawwiḥ haṣ-ṣafga min yaddak.* Don't let this deal slip through your hands. كـانت شـقة زينـة. روحهـا مـن يـده *čaanat šigga zeena. rawwaḥḥa min yadda.* It was a good apartment. He let it get through his hands.

روح *ruuḥ* p. ارواح *rwaaḥ* 1. soul, breath of life. قرا الفاتحة على روح الموات *gira l-faatḥa* ᶜ*ala ruuḥ li-mwaat.* He read the first sura of the Quran for blessing the soul of the dead. الروح بيد الله سبحانه وتعـالى *r-ruuḥ b-yadd 'aḷḷa subḥaanahu wa-ta*ᶜ*aalaa.* A person's life is in the hands of God, be He praised and exalted. طلعت روحه ساعة الصبـح *ṭla*ᶜ*at ruuḥa saa*ᶜ*t ṣ-ṣubḥ.* He died early in the morning. خفيف الروح *xafiif r-ruuḥ* amiable. طويل الروح *ṭawiil* *r-ruuḥ* patient. (prov.) روح قطو *ruuḥ gaṭu.* (lit., "The life of a cat.") (describes s.o. who has the capability to put up with a lot of suffering). يا روحي *ya ruuḥi* (endearing term of address) dear, my dear. ويش فيك يا روحي؟ *weeš fiik ya ruuḥi?* What's wrong with you, dear? 2. (with prefix ب *b-* and suff. pron.) by oneself, alone. سافرت بروحي *saafart b-ruuḥi.* I traveled by myself. إذا تجي، تعال بروحك *'iđa tiyi, ta^c^aal b-ruuḥak.* If you come, come alone.

روحة *rooḥa* (n. of inst.) p. *-aat* an act of leaving, going away, departing.

روز *rwz*

راز *raaz (يريز yriiz)* to estimate the weight of s.th. راز قلة السح وقال «هذي خمسة كيلو بمية درهم» *raaz gallat s-siḥḥ w-gaal haađi xamsa keelu b-miyat dirhim.* He estimated the weight of the basket of ripe dates and said, "This is five kilograms for one hundred dirhams." تقدر تريز لي صندوق الطماط هذا؟ *tigdar triiz-li ṣanduug ṭ-ṭamaaṭ haađa?* Can you estimate the weight of this box of tomatoes for me?

روس¹ *rws*

ريوس *reewas (يريوس yreewis)* to back up, go in reverse. ريوس هني وبعدين لف على اليمين *reewas hni w-ba^c^deen laff ^c^ala l-yimiin.* He backed up here and then turned right. ريوس هني ولف على شمالك وبرك سيارتك هني *reewis hni w-liff ^c^ala šmaalak w-barrik sayyaaratk hni.* Back up here, turn left, and park your car here.

روس² *rws*

روسي *ruusi* p. روس *ruus* 1. a Russian. 2. characteristic of Russia.

روسيا *ruusya* Russia.

راس *raas* p. روس *ruus.* See under **رءس** *r's.*

روظ *rwđ*

روضة *roođa* p. *-aat,* رياض *riyaađ* 1. low-lying area of grass and shrubs. هذي روضة جنة *haađi roođat yanna.* This is a garden of paradise. 2. kindergarten, nursery school. توه جاهل. يدرس في الروضة *tawwa yaahil. yidris fi r-roođa.* He's still a child. He goes to kindergarten.

روع *rw^c^*

روع *rawwa^c^* II to frighten, scare s.o. روع عياله وحرمته بصوته العالي *rawwa^c^ ^c^yaala w-ḥurumta b-ṣoota l-^c^aali.* He frightened his kids and his wife with his loud voice.

تروع *trawwa^c^* V = VIII ارتاع *rtaa^c^* to be frightened, scared, alarmed. الجاهل تروع من سمع صوت الأسد *l-yaahil trawwa^c^ min sima^c^ ṣoot l-'asad.* The child was terrified when he heard the roar of the lion.

روعة *raw^c^a* beauty, splendor, magnificence. منظر روعة *manđar raw^c^a* beautiful view. مناظر روعة *manaađir raw^c^a* beautiful views. كانت ضربة روعة في الكول *čaanat đarba raw^c^a fi l-gool.* It was a splendid kick in the goal.

أروع *'arwa^c^* 1. (with من *min*) more splendid or marvellous than. عمري ما

شفت أروع مـن هـا الضربـة *ᶜumri ma čift 'arwaᶜ min haδ̣-δ̣arba.* I have never seen a more splendid kick (in sports) than this one. 2. (with foll. n.) the most splendid or marvellous.

روغ *rwġ*

راغ *raaġ* (يـروغ *yruuġ*) to dismiss, drive out, expel, evict. راغوه من المكتب لانـه لغـوي واجـد *raaġoo min l-maktab linna laġwi waayid.* They dismissed him from the office because he was very talkative. المعلـم راغ الطـالب لانـه كان يغش *l-muᶜallim raaġ ṭ-ṭaalib linna čaan yġišš.* The teacher dismissed the student because he was cheating. ترى المؤجـر يروغـك إذا مـا تدفـع الإيجـار *tara l-mu'ajjir yruuġak 'iδa ma tidfaᶜ l-'iijaar.* The landlord, I tell you, will evict you if you don't pay the rent.

رول *rwl*

رولة *roola* p. *-aat* 1. roller, road roller. 2. hair roller, hair curler.

روم *rwm*

مرام *maraam* wish, desire. على مرام *ᶜala maraam* according to one's desire or wish. كل يغني على مرامه *killin yġanni ᶜala maraama.* Everyone sings according to one's desire.

روي *rwy*

روى *rawa* (يـروي *yarwi*) 1. to water, irrigate. روى البستان *rawa l-bistaan.* He watered the garden. لازم تـروي الشـجر هني كل يوم *laazim tarwi š-šiyar hni kill yoom.* You have to water the trees every day. 2. to quench one's thirst. المـاي تـروي العطشـان *l-maay tarwi l-ᶜaṭšaan.* Water quenches one's thirst.

روى *rawwa* II to show, demonstrate. تحصل ناس هناك يروونك البلد *tḥaṣṣil naas hnaak yrawwuunak l-balad.* You will find people there who will show you the city. رواني الشقة *rawwaani š-šigga.* He showed me the apartment. روح! لا ترونا وجهك مـرة ثانيـة *ruuḥ! la trawwna weehak marra θaanya.* Beat it! Don't show us your face again. إذا تحكي علي ذالحـين، أرويـك بعديـن *'iδa tḥači ᶜalayya δalḥiin, 'arawwiik baᶜdeen.* If you talk (bad things) about me now, I will show you later.

ارتوى *rtiwa* VIII 1. to be watered, irrigated. الشجر ارتوي زين *š-šiyar rtiwa zeen.* The trees got plenty of water. 2. to quench one's thirst. شرب ماي الين ارتوى *širib maay 'ileen rtiwa.* He drank water until he quenched his thirst.

ري *rayy* (v.n. from روى *rawa*) irrigation, watering. دايرة الري العامة *daayrat r-rayy l-ᶜaamma* the general directorate of irrigation.

رويـان *rawyaan* well-watered, well-irrigated. النخل رويان وما نحتاج ماي بعـد *n-naxal rawyaan w-ma niḥtaaj maay baᶜad.* The palm trees are well-watered, and we don't need any more water.

روايـة *riwaaya* p. *-aat* 1. tale, story. 2. play, drama. 3. novel. روايـة هزليـة *riwaaya hazaliyya* comedy. كـاتب روايـات *kaatib riwaayaat* 1. novelist. 2. playwright, dramatist.

ريل[١] *ryl*

ريـال *ryaal* p. *-aat,* أريل *'aryil* Qatari or Saudi riyal (= U.A.E. dirham = approx. $.28).

ريل٢ ryl

رجال *rayyaal* p. رجاجيل *rayaayiil* man, person. رجال زين. يحب يساعد كل واحد. *rayyaalin zeen. yḥibb ysaacid kill waaḥid.* He is a good man. He likes to help everyone. كنا خمسة رجاجيل *činna xamsat rayaayiil.* We were five men. هـذا رجـال شكـبره؟! *haaða rayyaal š-kubra?!* What an old man this is! He's a very old man.

رجيم rjym

رجيـم *rijiim* diet, regimen. ما أقدر آكل هذا. مسـوي رجيـم *ma 'agdar 'aakil haaða. msawwi rijiim.* I can't eat this. I am on a diet. الحريم يسون رجيم أكثر من الرجـاجيل *l-ḥariim ysawwin rijiim 'akθar min r-rayaayiil.* Women go on a diet more than men.

ريح ryḥ

ارتـاح *rtaaḥ* VIII 1. to be satisfied, content, happy. أريد أدرس وأشتغل لاجل أرتاح من صوبين *'ariid 'adris w-'aštaġil lajil 'artaaḥ min ṣoobeen.* I would like to study and work in order to be satisfied in both ways. نحن مرتاحين في شغلنـا *niḥin mirtaaḥiin fi šuġulna.* We are satisfied with our work. 2. to rest, relax. تفضل ارتاح في حجرة النوم *tfaððal rtaaḥ fi ḥijrat n-noom.* Please go rest in the bedroom. كنت تعبان؛ خلاني أرتاح شويـة *čint tacbaan; xal̦l̦aani 'artaaḥ šwayya.* I was tired; he let me rest a while. تفضل ارتاح *tfaððal rtaaḥ.* Please take a seat. 3. (with من *min*) to be relieved of s.o. or s.th. هديت المدرسة وارتاحيت من الدراسة *haddeet l-madrasa w-rtaaḥeet min d-diraasa.* I dropped out of school and was relieved of studying. فنشوه وارتـاحوا مـن شـره *fannašoo w-rtaaḥaw min šarra.* They fired him and were done with him. 4. to be at ease, be relieved. قلت الهم الصدق وارتاح ضمـيري *gilt-ilhum ṣ-ṣidj w-rtaaḥ ðamiiri.* I told them the truth and my mind was at ease.

اسـتراح *staraaḥ* X 1. to take a rest, have a break. تفضل اسـتريح! *tfaððal stariiḥ!* Please sit down! Please take a seat! كل ساعتين في الشغل نستريح ربـع سـاعة *kill saacteen fi š-šuġul nistariiḥ rubc saaca.* Every two hours at work we take a break for a quarter of an hour. 2. to make oneself comfortable, feel comfortable. هذا بلد زين. تجي هني وتستريح انشـالله *haaða balad zeen. tiyi hni w-tistariiḥ nšaal̦l̦a.* This is a good country. You will come here and feel comfortable, God willing.

راحـة *raaḥa* 1. rest, repose. كله شغل دق؛ ما فيه راحة *killa šuġul dagg; ma fii raaḥa.* It's all hard work. There is no rest. مريض ومسخن. يحتاج راحة *mariið w-mṣaxxan. yiḥtaay raaḥa.* He's sick and running a temperature. He needs a rest. على راحتك؛ آنا قـاعد هـني *cala raaḥtak; 'aana gaacid hni.* You take it easy; I'm sitting here. 2. comfort. والله الشغـل راحـة *w-al̦l̦a š-šuġul raaḥa.* Believe me, work is comfortable. وسائل الراحة متوفرة في الإمارات *wasaa'il r-raaḥa mitwaffra fi l-'imaaraat.* Conveniences are abundant in the Emirates.

أريـح *'aryah* (more common أروح *'arwaḥ*) 1. (with مـن *min*) easier or more comfortable than. الشغل هني أروح منـاك *š-šuġul hni 'arwaḥ minnaak.*

هـا الأرض يـنـراد الهـا قـز *hal-'arḍ yinraad-ilha gazz.* This land needs to be surveyed. يـنراد لـك حيـول ذهـب *yinraad-lič ḥyuul ðahab.* You need gold bracelets.

إرادة *'iraada* 1. wish, desire. سويت كل شـي بحسـب إرادتـه *sawweet kill šayy b-ḥasb 'iraatta.* I did everything according to his wish. 2. (p. *-aat*) decree. إرادة ملكيـة *'iraada malakiyya* royal decree. 3. will, will power. إرادته ضعيفـة *'iraatta ḍacifa.* His will is weak.

مـراد *muraad* design, intention, purpose. حصلت مرادي منها وتركتها *ḥaṣṣalt muraadi minha w-trakitta.* I got what I wanted from her and left her. هذا مرادي *haaða muraadi.* This is my intention.

ريس *rys*

ريـس *rayyis* p. *-iin.* 1. boss, man in charge. مـن هـو ريسـك؟ *man huw rayysak?* Who is your boss? الريس قال كـذي *r-rayyis gaal čiði.* The boss said this. 2. captain of a ship. في المركب الريس هو اللي يـامر *fi l-markab r-rayyis huwa lli yaamir.* On a passenger ship, the captain is the one who gives orders. الريس رخصني *r-rayyis raxxaṣni.* The ship captain gave me permission to leave.

ريش *ryš*

ريـش *riiš* (coll.) feathers. s. *-a.* أخف من الريشـة *'axaff min r-riiša* lighter than a feather. هذي المخدة فيها ريش بط *haaði li-mxadda fiiha riiš baṭṭ.* There are duck feathers in this pillow.

ريشـة *riiša* p. *-aat,* ريـش *riyaš* 1.

Work here is easier than there. 2. (with foll. n.) the easiest, the most comfortable. هـذا أروح شـغل *haaða 'arwaḥ šuġul.* This is the easiest work.

ريحان *riiḥaan* (coll.) sweet basil. s. *-a.*

صلاة الـتراويح *ṣalaat t-taraawiiḥ* prayer performed during the nights of Ramadan.

ريد *ryd*

راد *raad (يريـد yriid)* to want, wish, desire. ما يقنع باللي حصله. يريد كل شـي *ma yignac b-illi ḥaṣṣala. yriid kill šayy.* He's not satisfied with what he has gotten. He wants everything. بعد شـو يريـد مـني؟ *bacad šu yriid minni?* What else does he want from me? الله راد لي ولـد *'aḷḷa raad-li walad.* God ordained that I have a baby boy. جينا نطلب القرب منكم. ابننـا يريـد بنتكـم *yiina nuṭlub l-gurb minkum. 'ibnana yriid bintakum.* We came to ask to be related to you by marriage. Our son would like the hand of your daughter in marriage. أريـدك تعلمـني *'ariidak tcallimni.* I want you to let me know. مـا أريـد لـك إلا الخير *ma 'ariid-lak 'illa l-xeer.* I wish you nothing but the best. 2. (with foll. imperf.) to like to do s.th. يريد يطـرش الخـط *yriid yṭarriš l-xaṭṭ.* He wants to send the letter. شو تريد تاكل؟ *šu triid taakil?* What do you want to eat? أريـد أشـرب بـارد *'ariid 'ašrab baarid.* I would like to have a soft drink.

انـراد *nraad* VII 1. to be wanted, desired, needed. ها الشـقة صـوب البحـر تـنراد *haš-šigga ṣoob l-baḥar tinraad.* This apartment by the sea is desired.

feather. 2. nib of a fountain pen.

ريظ *ryð̣*

الريــاض *r-riyaað̣* Riyadh (capital of Saudi Arabia). رحــت الريــاض؟ *riḥt r-riyaað̣?* Did you go to Riyadh?

رياضة *riyaað̣a* 1. physical exercise. 2. sports, athletics.

ريــاضي *riyaað̣i* 1. athletic, sporting. ألعاب رياضية *'al^c^aab riyaað̣iyya* sports, sporting events. 2. (p. *-yyiin*) sportsman, athlete. 3. mathematical. مسألة رياضية *mas'ala riyaað̣iyya* mathematical problem.

رياضيات *riyaað̣iyyaat* mathematics.

ريف *ryf*

ريــف *riif* p. ارياف *ryaaf* countryside, rural area. ما عندنا رياف هني مثل، مثلا، الريف المصــري *ma ^c^indana riyaaf hini miθil, maθalan, r-riif l-maṣri.* We don't have rural areas here, such as, e.g., the Egyptian countryside.

ريگ *ryg*

ريق *rayyag* II to give breakfast to s.o., provide s.o. with breakfast. حرمــتي ريقت العيال قبل ما راحوا المدرسة *ḥurumti rayyagat li-^c^yaal gabil-ma raaḥaw l-madrasa.* My wife fed breakfast to the kids before they went to school. ريقتهم بيض ولحــم وخــبز *rayyagattum beeð̣ w-laḥam w-xubiz.* She gave them, eggs, meat, and bread for breakfast.

تريق *trayyag* V to have breakfast. كنا دايمــا نــتريق في المطعــم *činna daayman nitrayyag fi l-maṭ^c^am.* We always used to have breakfast at the restaurant. تريقت جبن وبيــض اليــوم *trayyagt jibin w-beeð̣ l-yoom.* I had cheese and eggs for breakfast today.

ريق *riij* (less common var. *riig*) p. ريوق *ryuuj* saliva, spittle. ما قدرت أبلع ريقي لاني كنت مريــض ومســخن *ma gidart 'abla^c^ riiji linni čint mariið̣ w-mṣaxxan.* I couldn't swallow my saliva because I was sick and running a temperature. ريقي ناشف *riiji naašif.* My mouth is dry. نشف ريقــه *naššaf riija.* He gave him a hard time. آنا إلى ذالحين على الريق *'aana 'ila ðalḥiin ^c^ala r-riij.* Up to now I haven't had breakfast. لا تدوخ جقارة على الريــق *la dduux jigaara ^c^ala r-riij.* Don't smoke a cigarette before having breakfast.

ريوق *ryuug* breakfast.

رين *ryn*

ريان *rayyaan* see under **روي** *rwy.*

ريي *ryy*

ري *rayy* see under **روي** *rwy.*

ز

زار zaar

زار *zaar* (no known p.) jinni, demon. فيه زار *fii zaar.* He has been possessed by jinnis.

زاروگ zaaruug

زاروق *zaaruug* p. زواريق *zuwaariig* 1. kind of a rowboat. 2. skiff. خذينا زاروق وعبرنا النهر *xaðeena zaaruug w-ᶜibarna n-nahar.* We took a skiff and crossed the river.

زام zaam

زام *zaam* p. *-aat.* 1. work schedule, work shift. الزام يتغير: مرات في الليل ومرات في النهار *z-zaam yitġayyar: marraat fi l-leel w-marraat fi n-nahaar.* The work schedule is changeable: sometimes it is at night and sometimes it's during the day. زامي في الليل *zaami fi l-leel.* I work a night shift. I have a night shift. الزام هني من الساعة تسع الين الساعة ثنتين *z-zaam hini min s-saaᶜa tisiᶜ 'ileen s-saaᶜa θinteen.* The working hours here are from nine o'clock till two o'clock. 2. turn, one's turn. الزم زامك! *'ilzam zaamak!* Take your turn! عد من الزام؟ *ᶜid man z-zaam?* Whose turn is it? الزام زامي *z-zaam zaami.* It's my turn.

زان zaan

زانة *zaana* p. *-aat* fishing tackle, fish hook.

زبب zbb

زب *zibb* p. أزباب *'azbaab,* زباب *zbaab,* زبابة *zibaba* penis.

زبيب *zibiib* (coll.) raisins. s. *-a.* إذا حطيت العنب في الشمس ويبسته يستوي زبيب *'iða ḥaṭṭeet l-ᶜinab fi š-šams w-yabbasta yistawi zibiib.* If you put grapes in the sun and dry them, they will become raisins.

زبد zbd

زبدة *zibda* butter.

زبدة *zubda* gist, main point. زبدة الموضوع *zubdat l-mawḍuuᶜ* the gist of the matter.

زبن zbn

زبن *ziban* (يزبن *yazbin*) to seek protection, seek refuge (with s.o. from s.th.), appeal to s.o. for aid. فيه قبايل صغيرة تزبن إلى قبايل أكبر وأقوى *fii gabaayil ṣaġiira tazbin 'ila gabaayil 'akbar w-'agwa.* There are small tribes who seek protection with bigger and stronger tribes.

زابن *zaabin* (act. part.) p. *-iin* (less common var. زبين *zabiin*) refugee, one who seeks protection with s.o.

مزبن *mizbin* p. *-iin* protector, one who provides protection to s.o.

زبون zbwn

زبون *zibuun* p. زباين *zibaayin* customer, client.

ز ب ي د ي *zbydy*

زبيدي *zbeedi* (coll.) bass (fish) s. *-yya.* الحامور أطيب من الزبيدي *l-haamuur 'aṭyab min z-zbeedi.* Red snapper is more delicious than bass.

ز چ م *zčm*

زكمة *začma* (less common var. زكام *zukaam*) common cold, head cold.

ز ح ز ح *zḥzḥ*

زحزح *zaḥzaḥ (يزحزح yzaḥziḥ)* to move (s.th. from its place), shift. هذا الكبت ثقيل واجد؛ ما أقدر أزحزحه *haaða l-kabat θagiil waayid; ma 'agdar 'azaḥizḥa.* The cupboard is very heavy; I can't move it. هو من جماعة الشيخ؛ ماحد يقدر يزحزحه *huwa min yamaa^cat š-šeex; maḥḥad yigdar yzaḥizḥa.* He's one of the followers of the ruler; no one can move him out.

تزحزح *tazaḥzaḥ* 1. to be moved, shifted. ها الكبت ثقيل واجد وما يتزحزح *hal-kabat θagiil waayid w-ma yitzaḥzaḥ.* This cupboard is very heavy and can't be moved. 2. to move, move over. تزحزح شوية لاجل أقعد *tzaḥzaḥ šwayya lajil 'ag^cid.* Move over so that I may sit down.

ز ح ف *zḥf*

زحف *ziḥaf (يزحف yizḥaf)* 1. to crawl, creep on the ground. ها الفقير يزحف؛ رجوله مقطعة *hal-fagiir yizḥaf; ryuula mgaṭṭa^ca.* This poor man is crawling; his legs are amputated. ما يقدر يمشي؛ بعده يزحف *ma yigdar yamši; ba^cda yizḥaf.* He can't walk; he is still crawling. 2. to march. زحف على *ziḥaf ^cala* to march toward or against. الجيش زحف على المدينة ساعة الصبح *l-jeeš ziḥaf ^cala l-madiina saa^ct ṣ-ṣubḥ.* The army marched toward the city at dawn.

زحف *zaḥf* 1. crawling, creeping. 2. marching.

زاحف *zaaḥif* (act. part.) 1. having crawled, having crept. 2. having marched. الجيش زاحف مية كيلو *l-jeeš zaaḥif miyat keelu.* The army has marched one hundred kilometers. 3. (p. زواحف *zawaaḥif*) reptiles (no known s.).

ز ح ل گ *zḥlg*

زحلق *zaḥlag (يزحلق yzaḥlig)* 1. to slide, roll. كان ماشي وزحلق في الطين *čaan maaši w-zaḥlag fi ṭ-ṭiin.* He was walking and slid into the mud. 2. to cause to slide, slip. دفعني وزحلقني في الطين *difa^cni w-zaḥlagni fi ṭ-ṭiin.* He pushed me and made me slide into the mud.

تزحلق *tzaḥlag (يتزحلق yitzaḥlag)* 1. to slip, slide, skid. الأرض مبلولة؛ دير بالك لا تتزحلق *l-'arð mabluula; diir baalak la tizzaḥlag.* The floor is wet; be careful so you won't slip. 2. to ski. تحصل محلات هني يروحون العيال لها لاجل يتزحلقون على الثلج *tḥaṣṣil maḥallaat hini yruuḥuun li-^cyaal laha lajil yizzaḥlaguum ^cala θ-θalj.* You will find places here to which kids go to skate on snow.

زحلقة *zaḥlaga* (v.n. from زحلق *zaḥlag*) 1. sliding, rolling. 2. skiing. 3. skating.

ز ح م *zḥm*

زاحم *zaaḥam* III to compete, vie

with. ذكية واجد. تطلع الأولى على بنات صفها وماحد يقدر يزاحمها *ðakiyya waayid. tiṭlaᶜ l-'uula ᶜala banaat ṣaffha w-maḥḥad yigdar yzaaḥimha.* She is very clever. She ranks first among her classmates, and no one can compete with her. يزاحمون على كاس الشيخ زايد *yizzaaḥmuun ᶜala kaas š-šeex zaayid.* They are competing for the Shaikh Zayid Cup (in sports).

ازدحم *zdiḥam* VIII to be crowded, to teem, swarm (with people). سوق السمك ازدحم بالرجاجيل والحريم *suug s-simač zdiḥam b-r-rayaayiil w-l-ḥariim.* The fish market was crowded with men and women.

زحمة *zaḥma* 1. crowd, throng. السوق زحمة. متروس رجاجيل وحريم *s-suug zaḥma. matruus rayaayil w-ḥariim.* The marketplace is crowded. It's full of men and women. 2. jam, crush. كان فيه زحمة سيارات *kaan fii zaḥmat sayyaaraat.* There was a traffic jam.

ازدحام *zdiḥaam* (v.n. from VIII ازدحم *zdiḥam*) 1. crowd, crush, jam, congestion.

مزاحمة *mzaaḥama* (v.n. from III زاحم *zaaḥam*) 1. competition. 2. rivalry.

زخخ *zxx*

زخ *zaxx (يزخ yzixx)* 1. to arrest. زخوا البايق وودوه الشرطة *zaxxu l-baayig w-waddoo š-širṭa.* They arrested the thief and took him to the police station. 2. to hold, get hold of s.o. or s.th. زخيته من يده *zaxxeeta min yadda.* I held his arm.

زخرف *zxrf*

زخرف *zaxraf (يزخرف yzaxrif)* to decorate, ornament. زخرفوا البيبان والطواف قبل العرس *zaxrafaw l-biibaan w-ṭ-ṭwaaf gabl l-ᶜirs.* They decorated the doors and the walls before the wedding.

تزخرف *tzaxraf (يتزخرف yitzaxraf)* to be decorated, ornamented.

زخرفة *zaxrafa* (v.n. from زخرف *zaxraf*) decoration, ornamentation.

زرب *zrb*

زريبة *ziriiba* p. زرايب *ziraayib* cattle pen, corral, fold.

زربول *zrbwl*

زربول *zarbuul* p. زرابيل *zaraabiil* 1. kind of shoe worn by people traveling in the desert. 2. woolen sock.

زرد *zrd*

زرد *zarad* p. زرود *zruud* chain mail, coat of mail.

زرر *zrr*

زر *zirr* p. ازرار *zraar* push button, button.

زرط *zrṭ*

زرط *ziraṭ (يزرط yazruṭ)* to swallow, gulp down without chewing. زرط العنب *ziraṭ l-ᶜinab.* He swallowed the grapes. زرط اللقمة *ziraṭ l-lugma.* He swallowed the morsel.

انزرط *nziraṭ* VII to be swallowed, gulped down. الخبز ما ينزرط مثل الموز *l-xubiz ma yinzariṭ miθil l-mooz.* Bread doesn't go down as easily as bananas.

زرط *zarṭ* (v.n. from زرط *ziraṭ*) swallowing, gulping down.

زرع *zr^c^*

زرع *zira^c^ (* يزرع *yizra^c^)* to plant, grow. البلدية زرعت شجر على طول الطريق *l-baladiyya zra^c^at šiyar ^c^ala ṭuul ṭ-ṭariig.* The municipality planted trees alongside the street. السنة الجاية رايحين نزرع خضار *s-sana l-yaaya raayḥiin nizra^c^ xiðaar.* Next year we are going to grow vegetables. زرع الله يرعاه الله *zar^c^ aḷḷa yir^c^aah aḷḷa.* (lit., "God's growing crop is protected by God."). God is the lone protector. (prov.) زرعنا لو طلعت لا شي *zira^c^na law ṭla^c^at la šayy.* If me no if's. (lit., "We planted 'if'; nothing broke forth.").

زرع *zari^c^* (v.n.) 1. planting, growing, cultivation (of crops). زرع الطماط ذالحين *zar^c^ ṭ-ṭamaaṭ ðalḥiin.* The right time for the planting of tomatoes is now. 2. green crop. لا تخلي الغنم تاكل الزرع *la txaḷḷi l-ganam taakil z-zari^c^.* Don't let the sheep eat the green crop.

زراعة *ziraa^c^a* agriculture, farming. وزارة الزراعة *wazaarat z-ziraa^c^a* the ministry of agriculture.

زراعي *ziraa^c^i* agricultural, agrarian. ما تحصل أراضي زراعية واجد هني *ma tḥaṣṣil 'araaði ziraa^c^iyya waayid hini.* You will not find many arable lands here. دايرة الاستصلاح الزراعي *daayrat l-'istiṣlaaḥ z-ziraa^c^i* the department of agrarian reform.

مزرع *mazra^c^a* p. مزارع *mazaari^c^* farm, plantation. في مزارع دجاج واجد هني *fii mazaari^c^ diyaay waayid hini.* There are many chicken farms here.

مزروع *mazruu^c^* (p.p. from زرع *zira^c^*) planted, cultivated.

مزارع *muzaari^c^* p. *-iin* farmer, farm-owner.

زرف *zrf*

زرافة *zaraafa* p. *-aat* giraffe.

زرفل *zrfl*

زرفل *zarfal (*يزرفل *yzarfil)* 1. to walk fast, hasten. الناقة زرفلت *n-naaga zarfalat.* The camel (f.) walked fast. 2. to jog. أزرفل كل يوم *'azarfil kill yoom.* I jog every day.

زرگ *zrg*

زرق *zirag (*يزرق *yazrug)* 1. to go quickly, dash, hurry. زرق للسوق واشترى سمك *zirag lis-suug w-štira simač.* He dashed to the market and bought fish. 2. to slip away, escape. الشرطة شافوه لكنه زرق *š-širṭa šaafoo lakinna zirag.* The policemen saw him but he slipped away.

ازرق *zragg* IX to turn blue, become blue. وجهه ازرق من البرد *weeha zragg min l-bard.* His face turned blue from the cold.

زرقة *zarga* (v.n.) 1. dashing, going quickly, hurrying. زرق زرقة رمح *zirag zargat rumḥ.* He dashed speedily. (lit., "He dashed like a javelin.").

زراقة *zirraaga* p. *-aat* light speedy ship.

زراق *zaraag* (v.n. from IX ازرق *zragg*) blueness, blue color.

أزرق *'azrag* p. زرق *zurg* f. زرقا *zarga* p. زرق *zurg* blue. السما أزرق *s-sama 'azrag.* The sky is blue. عيونها زرق

^{c}*yuunha zurg.* Her eyes are blue.

زركش *zrkš*

زركش *zarkaš (يزركش yzarkiš)* to embroider, decorate. زركشت البردة *zarkašat l-parda.* She embroidered the curtain.

زرنيخ *zrnyx*

زرنيخ *zarniix* (coll.) arsenic. يستعملون الزرنيخ دوا حق الإبل الجربانة *yista^{c}imluun z-zarniix duwa ḥagg l-'ibil l-yarbaana.* They use arsenic as medicine for scabby camels.

زطط *zṭṭ*

زطي *ziṭṭi* p. زطوط *zṭuuṭ* vagabond, tramp.

زعتر *z^{c}tr*

زعتر *za^{c}tar* (coll.) thyme. زعتر عن تسعة وتسعين علة *za^{c}tar ^{c}an tis^{c}a w-tis^{c}iin ^{c}illa.* Thyme cures ninety-nine maladies.

زعط *z^{c}ṭ*

زعطوط *za^{c}ṭuuṭ* p. زعاطيط *za^{c}aaṭiiṭ* (derog. term) young person, young punk.

زعفران *z^{c}fraan*

زعفران *za^{c}faraan* (coll.) saffron.

زعل *z^{c}l*

زعل *zi^{c}al (يزعل yiz^{c}al)* to be a little angry or mad. زعل لين ذكرته باللي سواه *zi^{c}al leen ðakkarta b-lli sawwaa.* He got mad when I reminded him of what he had done. زعل على *zi^{c}al ^{c}ala* to be or get mad at s.o. زعل علينا وبعدين راضيناه *zi^{c}al ^{c}aleena w-ba^{c}deen raaðeenaa.* He got mad at us, and later on we conciliated him.

زعل *za^{cc}al* II to annoy, anger, make s.o. mad. زعلته وعقبه راضيته *za^{cc}alta w-^{c}ugba raaðeeta.* I made him mad and then I conciliated him.

تزاعل *tzaa^{c}al* VI to be a little angry at each other. هذيل عيال يتزاعلون وبعدين يتصالحون *haðeel ^{c}yaal yizzaa^{c}luun w-ba^{c}deen yiṣṣaalḥuun.* These are kids; they become angry at each other and then they make up. تزاعلوا على شي بسيط *zzaa^{c}law ^{c}ala šayy basiiṭ.* They stopped speaking to each other over a simple matter.

زعل *za^{c}al* (v.n. from زعل *zi^{c}al*) displeasure, annoyance. من زعله علينا حتى مر ما يمر *min z^{c}ala ^{c}aleena ḥatta marr ma ymurr.* Because he was a little angry with us, he doesn't even stop by. تری لا تزعل علي! *tara la tiz^{c}al ^{c}alayya!* Now don't get mad at me! بزعل *b-za^{c}al* in anger, angrily. رمسنا بزعل *rammasna b-za^{c}al.* He talked to us angrily.

زعلان *za^{c}laan* p. *-iin* (حمقان *ḥamgaan* is more common) angry, annoyed. التنديل كان زعلان على الكولي وفنشه *t-tindeel čaan za^{c}laan ^{c}ala l-kuuli w-fannaša.* The supervisor was mad at the coolie and laid him off.

زعم *z^{c}m*

تزعم *tza^{cc}am* V (with على *^{c}ala*) to be the leader of. تزعم علينا *zza^{cc}am ^{c}aleena.* He put himself in charge of us.

زعيم *za^{c}iim* p. زعما *zu^{c}ama* 1. leader. 2. brigadier general. 3. colonel.

زعامة *za^caama* leadership, controlling position.

زغب *zġb*

زغب *ziġab* (يزغب *yizġab*) 1. to drink in large gulps, gulp. زغب كلاصين بيرة *ziġab glaaṣeen biira.* He gulped two glasses of beer. 2. to have sexual intercourse with s.o. زغبها بالغصب وزخوه الشرطة *ziġabha b-l-ġaṣb w-zaxxoo š-širṭa.* He raped her and the police arrested him.

زغر *zġr*

زغر *ziġar, zuġur* = صغر *ṣiġar, ṣuġur.* See under **صغر** *ṣġr.*

زغط *zġṭ*

زغط *ziġaṭ* (يزغط *yizġaṭ*) to choke to death, suffocate. وقف الأكل في حلقه وزغط *wugaf l-'akil fi ḥalja w-ziġaṭ.* The food caught in his throat and he choked to death. زغط من دخان الحريق *ziġaṭ min dixxaan l-ḥariij.* He suffocated from the smoke of the fire.

زغطة *zaġṭa* (v.n.) strangulation, suffocation.

مزغوط *mazġuuṭ* strangled, suffocated.

زغل *zġl*

زغل *zaġal* p. زغاغيل *zaġaaġiil* person whose parents are unknown.

زفف *zff*

زف *zaff* (يزف *yziff*) 1. to escort the bride or bridegroom in a solemn procession to the new home. هني نزف المعرس على عروسته عقب صلاة العشا *hini nziff l-mi^cris ^cala ^caruusta ^cugub ṣalaat l-^ciša.* Here we escort the bridegroom to his bride after the evening prayer. 2. to carry water and sell it. لين نقول «يزف الماي» يعني ينقله ويبيعه إلى البيوت *leen nguul, "yziff l-mayy," ya^cni yungula w-ybii^ca 'ila l-byuut.* When we say, "*yziff l-mayy,*" we mean he transports the water and sells it to homes.

زفة *zaffa* (n. of inst.) p. *-aat* wedding procession. كان في الزفة مطبلين ومغنين وعيالة *čaan fi z-zaffa mṭabbliin w-mġanniin w-^cayyaala.* There were drummers, singers, and male dancers in the wedding procession.

زفاف *zafaaf* (v.n.) wedding ceremony. كان فيه ناس واجدين ليلة زفافه *čaan fii naas waaydiin leelat zafaafa.* There were a lot of people on his wedding night.

زگر *zgr*

زقر *zigar* (يزقر *yizgur*) to call s.o. زقرني ورحت له *zigarni w-riḥt-la.* He called me and I went to him.

زقر *zagir* (v.n.) calling s.o.

زاقر *zaagir* (act. part.) p. *-iin* caller.

زگرتي *zgrty*

زقرتي *zgirti* p. *-yya* 1. bachelor, unmarried. نحن ما نسكن زقرتية هني *niḥin ma nsakkin zgirtiyya hini.* We don't put up bachelors here. 2. elegantly dressed young man. اليوم صاير زقرتي *l-yoom ṣaayir zgirti.* He has become an elegantly dressed man nowadays. 3. young man who chases girls. 4. noble, decent young man.

زگزگ *zgzg*

زقزق *zagzag* (يزقزق *yzagzig*) to chirp,

cheep. العصفور يزقزق *l-ᶜaṣfuur yzagzig.* The sparrow is chirping.

زقزقة *zagzaga* (v.n.) chirping, cheeping.

زگگ *zgg*

زق *zagg (يزق yzigg)* to defecate. (prov.) لا تزق في ماعون أكلت فيه *la zzigg fi maaᶜuun 'akalt fii.* Don't bite the hand that feeds you. Don't dirty your own nest. (prov.) بن مغامس عرف ربعه وزق في التانكي *bin mġaamis ᶜiraf rabᶜa w-zagg fi t-taanki.* Do not do favors for those who do not appreciate or deserve them. (lit., "Bin Mgaamis got acquainted with his fellows and defecated in the water tank.").

زق *zagg* (v.n.) defecating.

زق *zigg* (coll.) excrement, feces. يا ابن الزق! *ya 'ibn z-zigg!* Son of a bitch!

زگلب *zglb*

زقلب *zaglab (يزقلب yzaglib)* 1. to turn upside down (esp. heavy items, such as rocks, barrels, etc). كان حمقان وزقلب الأشيا اللي في وجهه *čaan ḥamgaan w-zaglab l-'ašya lli fi weeha.* He was mad and turned upside down the things he saw. 2. to hurl or push s.o. or s.th. downhill. زقلب الصخرة *zaglab li-ṣxara.* He hurled down the rock.

زكم *zkm*

زكام *zukaam* (*zučaam,* زكمة *začma* are more common variants). See under **زچم** *zčm.*

زكي *zky*

زكى *zakka* 1. to give alms to the poor. المسلم لازم يزكي كل سنة *l-muslim laazim yzakki kill sana.* A Muslim should give alms to the poor every year. 2. to vouch for, support, testify in favor of. طلب ترقية والمدير زكاه عند الوزير *ṭalab targiya w-l-mudiir zakkaa ᶜind l-waziir.* He requested promotion and the manager vouched for his credentials to the minister. إذا تبي تدش الجيش آنا أزكيك *'iða tabi ddišš l-jeeš 'aana 'azakkiik.* If you want to join the army, I will vouch for you. 3. to recommend. كلهم زكوه حق رياسة المجلس *killhum zakkoo ḥagg riyaasat l-majlis.* They all recommended him for presiding over the council.

زكاة *zakaa* 1. alms-giving, alms, charity. 2. alms tax (2.5% in Islamic law).

تزكية *tazkiya* (v.n. from II زكى *zakka*) pronouncement of one's support of favorable testimony. بالتزكية *b-t-tazkiya* by acclamation.

زلزل *zlzl*

زلزال *zilzaal* p. زلازل *zalaazil* earthquake.

زلط *zlṭ*

زلط *zalaṭ* (common var. زلاطة *zalaaṭa*) salad. طلبت لحم وعيش وزلاطة *ṭilabt laḥam w-ᶜeeš w-zalaaṭa.* I ordered meat, rice, and salad.

زلگ *zlg*

زلق *zilag (يزلق yazlig)* 1. to slip, slide. زلق لانه داس على قشر موز *zilag linna daas ᶜala gišir mooz.* He slipped because he stepped on a banana peel. 2. to make a mistake, make a slip. زلق

لسانه *zilag lsaana.* He made a slip of the tongue. احكي شوي شوي. لا تزلق *'iḥči šwayy šwayy. la tazlig.* Talk slowly. Don't make a slip.

زلق *zallag* II to cause to slip, slide. دفعني وزلقني *difaᶜni w-zallagni.* He pushed me and made me slip.

زلق *zalag* (v.n.) slipperiness. (prov.) يا ماشي درب الزلق لا تيمن طيحتك *ya maaši darb z-zalag la teeman ṭeeḥtak.* Keep away from harm's way. (lit., "If you walk on a slippery road, you will not be safe from falling down.").

ز ل ل *zll*

زل *zall* (يزل *yzill)* 1. to slip, make a mistake. اسمح لي يا خوي! زل لساني *'ismaḥ-li ya xuuy! zall lsaani.* Pardon me, brother! My tongue slipped. 2. to pour s.th. زل الماي *zall l-mayy.* He poured the water. 3. to come to an end, be over. زل النهار *zall n-nahaar.* The daytime came to an end.

ز م ر *zmr*

زمر *zammar* II to blow, play a wind instrument. في العرس يطبلون ويزمرون ويغنون وما ادري شبعد *fi l-ᶜirs yṭabbluun w-yzammruun w-yġannuun w-ma dri š-baᶜad.* In a wedding ceremony, they beat the drums, play wind instruments, sing, and I don't know what else.

زمارة *zummaara* p. *-aat* wood-wind instrument.

ز م ر د *zmrd*

زمرد *zumurrud* (coll.) emerald. s. *-a* p. *-aat.*

ز م ز م *zmzm*

زمزم *zamzam* Zamzam (name of a well in Mecca).

زمزمية *zamzamiyya* p. *-aat* thermos (flask in which pilgrims carry water from Zamzam).

ز م ل *zml*

زامل *zaamal* III to be a friend or colleague of s.o., maintain a friendship with s.o. زاملته مدة عشر سنين *zaamalta muddat ᶜašar siniin.* I maintained a friendship with him for ten years.

زمالة *zamaala* 1. colleagueship. 2. fellowship, friendship. 3. comradeship.

زمال *zmaal* p. زمايل *zmaayil* donkey, jackass.

ز م ل و ط *zmlwṭ*

زملوط *zamluuṭ* p. زماليط *zamaaliiṭ* sheet of paper folded up in the shape of a conc by a shopkccpcr in which things like tea, coffee, spices, etc, are put.

ز م ن *zmn*

زمان *zamaan* p. *-aat* time, period, era. في الزمان الأولي كنا نسكن في البرستية *fi z-zamaan l-'awwali činna niskin fi l-barastiyya.* In olden times we used to live in shacks. في زمان أجدادنا ها الأشيا ما كانت تصير *fi zamaan 'aydaadna hal-'ašya ma čaanat tṣiir.* In the days of our forefathers these things wouldn't have happened. زمان أول *zamaan 'awwal* the past time. (prov.) زمان أول تحول والغزل انقلب صوف *zamaan 'awwal taḥawwal w-l-ġazal* *ngaḷab ṣoof.* Times have changed. Things are no longer the same. (lit., "Old times have changed and [spun] yarn has changed into wool."). في ها الزمان ماميش صديق مخلص *fi haz-zamaan ma-miiš ṣadiij muxliṣ.* These days there aren't any sincere friends. من زمان *min zamaan* for a long time, for quite a long while. آنا صار لي هني من زمان *'aana ṣaar-li hini min zamaan.* I have been here for a long time. صار لي من زمان ما شفتك *ṣaar-li min zamaan ma šiftič.* I haven't seen you in quite a while. في زمان الأتراك *fi zamaan l-'atraak* during the Turkish period.

زنبر *znbr*

زنبور *zanbuur* p. زنابير *zanaabiir* wasp, hornet.

زنبل *znbl*

زنبيل *zanbiil* p. زنابيل *zanaabiil* basket woven from straw or branches of palm trees.

زنجر *znjr*

زنجر *zanjar (يزنجر yzanjir)* to rust, be or become rusted. كل شي يزنجر هني من الرطوبة *kill šayy yzanjir hini min r-ruṭuuba.* Everything becomes rusted here from humidity.

زنجار *zinjaar* (common var. زنقار *zingaar*) rust.

مزنجر *mzanjir* (act. part. from زنجر *zanjar*) rusty, rust-covered. القفل مزنجر؛ ما ينفتح *l-guful mzanjir; ma yinfitiḥ.* The lock is rusty; it cannot be opened.

زنجبل *znjbl*

زنجبيل *zanjabiil* (coll.) (less common var. زنزبيل *zanzabiil*) ginger. هذا زنجبيل خالص *haaða zanjabiil xaaliṣ.* This is pure ginger.

زند *znd*

زند *zand* p. زنود *znuud* forearm. زنده يمشي عليه التيس *zanda yamši ᶜalee t-tees.* (lit., "A billy goat can walk on his forearm.") He has a huge body.

زندگ *zndg*

زنديق *zandiig* p. زناديق *zanaadiig* atheist, unbeliever.

زنزبل *znzbl*

زنزبيل *zanzabiil* (coll.) (more common var. زنجبيل *zanjabiil*) ginger.

زنگن *zngn*

زنقين *zangiin* p. زناقين *zanaagiin* 1. wealthy, rich. 2. rich man.

زني *zny*

زنى *zina (يزني yazni)* 1. to commit adultery. إذا تزني مصيرك جهنم *'iða tizni maṣiirak jahannam.* If you commit adultery, your fate is hell.

زنى *zina* (v.n.) adultery. ابن زنى *'ibin zina* bastard.

زاني *zaani* (act. part.) p. *-iin* adulterer.

زهب *zhb*

زهب *zahhab* II to prepare, get things ready. زهبنا الغدا *zahhabna l-ġada.* We prepared lunch. (prov.) زهبنا الماي وطار الديك *zahhabna l-maay w-ṭaar d-diič.* Forewarned is forearmed. (lit., "We got the water ready and the rooster flew away."). (prov.) زهبنا الدوا قبل الفلعة *zahhabna d-duwa gabl l-fal^c^a.* Be prepared for what comes next. Forewarned is forearmed. (lit., "We got the medicine before the head wound.").

زاهب *zaahib* (act. part.) p. *-iin* ready, prepared. آنا زاهب للسفر *'aana zaahib las-safar.* I am ready to travel.

ز ه ر *zhr*

زهر *zahir* (coll.) s. *-a* 1. flowers. 2. blossoms.

زهرة *zahra* 1. morning star. 2. (p. *-aat*) flower. 3. blossom.

مزهرية *mazhariyya* p. *-aat* flower vase.

زاهر *zaahir* shining, luminous. نجمة زاهرة *niyma zaahira* shining star.

ز و ج *zwj*

زوج *zawwaj* II to marry off, give in marriage. زوجها ابن عمها *zawwajha 'ibn ^c^ammha.* He married her off to her cousin. رايح أزوجه عقب ما يتخرج من الجامعة *raayiḥ azawwja ^c^ugub-ma yitxarraj min l-yaam^c^a.* I am going to get him married after he graduates from the university.

تزوج *tazawwaj* V (عرس *^c^arras* is more common) 1. to get married. تزوج لين تخرج من الجامعة *tazawwaj leen taxarraj min l-yaam^c^a.* He got married when he graduated from the university. 2. to marry s.o. تزوجت بنت خالتي *tazawwajt bint xaaḷati.* I married my maternal aunt's daughter.

زوج *zawj, zooj* p. ازواج *zwaaj* 1. husband. 2. couple of, pair of. زوج دجاج *zooj diyaay* two chickens. زوجها قزاز في البلدية *zawijha gazzaaz fi l-baladiyya.* Her husband is a surveyor in the municipality.

زوجة *zawja* p. *-aat wife.*

زواج *zawaaj* 1. marriage. الزواج يكلف واجد *z-zawaaj ykallif waayid.* Getting married costs a lot. الزواج بدون مهر ما يتم *z-zawaaj b-duun mahar ma ytimm.* Marriage without a dowry cannot be contracted. 2. wedding. حفلة زواج *ḥaflat zawaaj* wedding ceremony. 3. matrimony.

مزوج *mitzawwij* (act. part. from V تزوج *tazawwaj*) p. *-iin* married.

ز و د *zwd*

زود *zawwad* II to provide, furnish, supply. قبل لا تسافر روح مكتب السفر وهم يزودونك بكل المعلومات *gabil-la tsaafir ruuḥ maktab s-safar w-hum yzawwduunak b-kill l-ma^c^luumaat.* Before you travel, go to the travel office and they will furnish you with all the information. زودني معلومية عنه *zawwadni ma^c^luumiyya ^c^anna.* He provided me with information about him.

زاد *zaad* food.

ز و ر *zwr*

زار *zaar (يزور yzuur)* to visit s.o. or s.th., call on or pay a visit to s.o. زرت صديقي في السبيتار *zirt ṣadiiji fi s-sbeetaar.* I visited my friend in the hospital. زرنا قبر النبي في المدينة *zirna ġabir n-nabi fi l-madiina.* We visited the Prophet's tomb in Madina. زارني في بيتي *zaarani fi beeti.* He called on me at my home.

زور *zawwar* II 1. to guide, show around. رحت القدس وشفت واحد زورني الحرم الشريف *riḥt l-guds w-šift waaḥid zawwarni l-ḥaram š-šariif.* I went to Jerusalem and saw someone who guided me around the Holy Sanctuary. تزوج بنتي وكان يزورنا اياها مرة كل شـهر *tazawwaj binti w-čaan yzawwirna-yyaaha marra kill šahar.* He married my daughter and he used to let her visit us once a year. 2. to forge, falsify, counterfeit. زور إمضا الوزيـر *zawwar 'imḍ̄a l-waziir.* He forged the minister's signature. فيه ناس يزورون المية درهـم *fii naas yzawwruun il-miyat dirhim.* There are people who counterfeit the one hundred dirham bill. زوروا الانتخابـات *zawwaru l-'intixaabaat.* They rigged the elections.

تزاور *tzaawar* VI to visit each other, exchange visits. كنا جيران وكنا نتزاور علـى طـول *činna yiiraan w-činna nizzaawar ᶜala ṭuul.* We were neighbors and we used to visit each other for a long time.

زور *zuur* 1. force, compulsion. بالزور *b-z-zuur* by force. (prov.) اللي ما يجيبه حليبه، مـا يجيبه الـزور *'illi ma yjiiba ḥaliiba, ma yjiiba z-zuur.* You can lead a horse to water, but you cannot make him drink. (lit., "He who cannot be brought along by one's milk, cannot be brought along by force."). لازم تتزوجينه بـالطيب والا بـالزور *laazim tizzawwajiina b-ṭ-ṭiib walla b-z-zuur.* You have to get married to him by hook or by crook. 2. untruth. شهادة زور *šahaadat zuur* false testimony.

زيـارة *ziyaara* (v.n. from زار *zaar*) 1. visiting. سـاعات الزيـارة *saaᶜaat z-ziyaara* visiting hours. زيارة المتحف *ziyaarat l-matḥaf* visiting the museum. 2. (p. *-aat*) visit.

تزوير *tazwiir* (v.n. from II زور *zawwar*) forgery, falsification. تزوير الشـهادات *tazwiir š-šahaadaat* falsification of certification.

زايـر *zaayir* (as act. part.) 1. going to visit. زايرنا باكر *zaayirna baačir.* He's going to visit us tomorrow. 2. having visited. نحن زايرين القدس *niḥin zaayriin l-guds.* We have visited Jerusalem. 3. (p. زوار *zuwwaar*) visitor, caller, guest. زوار من إنكلترا *zuwwaar min 'ingiltara* visitors from England. أنت زاير هـني ولازم تراعي تقاليد المواطنـين *'inta zaayir hini w-laazim traaᶜi tağaaliid li-mwaṭniin.* You are a guest here and you have to respect the citizen's traditions.

مـزور *mzawwar* (p.p. from II زور *zawwar*) forged, counterfeit.

زوع *zwᶜ*

زاع *zaaᶜ* (يزوع *yzuuᶜ*) to vomit, throw up. يزوع لين يركب الطيـارة *yzuuᶜ leen yirkab ṭ-ṭayyaara.* He throws up when he rides a plane.

زوع *zawwaᶜ* II to cause to vomit. الدختر عطاه دوا لاجـل يزوعـه *d-daxtar ᶜaṭaa duwa lajil yzawwᶜa.* The doctor gave him medicine to make him throw up.

زواع *zwaaᶜ* (v.n. from زاع *zaaᶜ*) vomiting, throwing up.

زول zwl

زال *zaal* (يزول *yzuul)* 1. to go away, leave. زال الهم عنا *zaal l-hamm* *ᶜanna.* We are no longer burdened by worry. (lit., "Worry has gone away from us."). زال الخطر عنه عقب العملية *zaal l-xaṭar* *ᶜanna ᶜugub l-ᶜamaliyya.* He's out of danger after the operation. زول عن وجهي! *zuul ᶜan weehi!* Go away! Beat it! 2. (with neg. particle لا *la* or ما *ma*) still, yet. لا يزال يدش الشغل الصبح *la yazaal ydišš š-šuġul ṣ-ṣubḥ.* He still goes to work in the morning. لا نزال موجودين هني *la nazaal mawjuudiin hini.* We are still here.

زول *zawwal* II to cause to go away, leave. زول عن وجهي! زولك الله! *zuul ᶜan weeyhi! zawwalk aḷḷa!* Go away! May God take you away!

زولية *zuuliyya* p. زل *zall,* زوالي *zawaali* carpet, rug.

زوي zwy

انزوى *nzuwa* VII to hide oneself, go into seclusion. انزوى وماحد يعرف وين راح *nzuwa w-maḥḥad yᶜarf ween raaḥ.* He hid himself and no one knows where he went. لين سقط في الامتحان انزوى *leen ṣigaṭ fi li-mtiḥaan nzuwa.* When he didn't pass the examination, he went into seclusion.

زاوية *zaawiya* p. زوايا *zawaaya* 1. angle. هذي الزاوية خمسين درجة *haaði z-zaawiya xamsiin daraja.* The angle is fifty degrees. 2. corner. بكى وقعد في زاوية من زوايا الحجرة *biča w-giᶜad fi zaawiya min zawaaya l-ḥijra.* He cried and sat in one of the corners of the room.

زيبگ zybg

زيبق *zeebag* (less common var. زوبق *zoobag*) mercury.

زيت zyt

زيت *zeet* p. زيوت *zyuut* oil (edible, fuel, etc.) زيت زيتون *zeet zaytuun* olive oil. شركة زيت *šarikat zeet* petroleum company. زيت سمك *zeet simač* cod-liver oil.

زيتي *zeeti* oily, oil. لون زيتي *loon zeeti* green, oily color. رنق زيتي *rang zeeti* oil paint. لوحة زيتية *lawḥa zeetiyya* oil painting.

زيتون zytwn

زيتون *zaytuun* (coll.) 1. olives. 2. olive trees. s. *-a* p. *-aat* 1. olive. 2. olive tree.

زيح zyḥ

زاح *zaaḥ* (يزيح *yziiḥ)* to take away, remove, drive away. زيح الكرسي من قدامي حتى أقدر أشوف التلفزيون *ziiḥ l-kirsi min jiddaami ḥatta 'agdar 'ačuuf t-talafizyoon.* Move the chair away from me so that I can watch television. المدير الجديد زاح التنديل من وظيفته *l-mudiir l-yidiid zaaḥ t-tindeel min waðiifta.* The new director ousted the supervisor from his position. ما أقدر أزيح الميز لانه ثقيل واجد *ma 'agdar 'aziiḥ l-meez linna θaagii waayid.* I cannot move the table because it's very heavy.

زيد zyd

زاد *zaad* (يزيد *yziid)* 1. to increase, become greater, become more. ربحنا من التجارة زاد *ribiḥna min t-tijaara* zaad. Our profit from trade increased. عـدد الموظفـين بزيـد ^c^adad li-mwaððafiin b-ziid. The number of employees is increasing. وجـع ضروسـي بزيـد wuja^c^ ðruusi b-ziid. My toothache is getting more severe. 2. to augment, add to, increase. أبغى أزيـدك معلوميـة عـني 'abġa 'aziidak ma^c^luumiyya ^c^anni. I want to give you more information about me. المدير زاد معاشـي l-mudiir zaad ma^c^aaši. The manager increased my salary. زيد القهـوة شـكر ziid l-gahwa šakar. Add some sugar to the coffee. (an answer to تفضـل tfaððal) الله يزيـد فضلـك aḷḷa yziid faðlak. Thank you. (lit., "May God increase your graciousness."). زاد الطـين بلـة zaad ṭ-ṭiin balla. He made things worse. 3. to be left over. إذا زاد أكل عطني اياه 'iða zaad 'akil ^c^aṭni-yyaa. If any food is left over, give it to me. 4. (with على ^c^ala or عن ^c^an) to be more than, exceed. الـواردات زادت علـى الصـادرات l-waaridaat zaadat ^c^ala ṣ-ṣaadiraat. Imports exceeded exports.

زيـادة ziyaada 1. increase, rise. صار فيه زيـادة في الأسـعار ṣaar fii ziyaada fi l-'as^c^aar. There has been an increase in prices. 2. excess, surplus. عنـدك زيادة خمسة كيلو في العفش ^c^indak ziyaada xamsa keelu fi l-^c^afš. You have five kilograms of excess baggage. طلع زيـادة في الميزانيـة ṭila^c^ ziyaada fi l-miizaaniyya. There was a surplus in the budget. غلـط وعطـاني خمسـة درهـم زيـادة ġilaṭ w-^c^aṭaani xamsa dirhim ziyaada. He made a mistake and gave me five dirhams too much. 3. increment, increase. ها الكولي صـار لـه خمـس سـنين ومـا حصـل زيـادة hal-kuuli ṣaar-la xams siniin w-ma ḥaṣṣal ziyaada. This coolie hasn't had an increment for five years. زيـادة عـن ziyaada ^c^an over and above, in excess of. عطـوه ألـف درهـم زيـادة عـن العـلاوة السـنوية ^c^aṭoo 'alf dirhim ziyaada ^c^an l-^c^alaawa s-sanawiyya. They gave him a thousand dirhams over and above the annual allowance. وزيـادة علـى ذلـك wa-ziyaada ^c^ala ðaalik and moreover, and in addition to that. فنشوه وزيـادة علـى ذلـك غرمـوه fannašoo w-ziyaada ^c^ala ðaalik ġarramoo. They terminated his services, and in addition to that they fined him.

أزيـد 'azyad 1. (with مـن min) more excessive, high, etc. 2. (with foll. n.) the most excessive, high, etc.

مـزاد mazaad p. -aat auction, public sale.

زايد zaayid (act. part. from زاد zaad) 1. excessive. بغيت الفـايدة وجـاتني المصـايب زايـدة bağeet l-faayda w-jatni l-maṣaayib zaayda. I was after profit, but I was beset by excessive problems. 2. increasing, becoming more or greater. العكاسات تزخ المسرع اللـي زايـد عـن قـانون السـواقة l-^c^akkaasaat zzixx l-misri^c^ illi zaayid ^c^an ġaanuun s-swaaga. Cameras catch the speeding motorist. 3. having increased. المعيشة زايدة هذي السنة l-ma^c^iiša zaayda haaði s-sana. The cost of living has increased this year. 4. additional, extra. عنـدك درهـم زايـد ^c^indak dirhim zaayid. You have an extra dirhim. 5. more than necessary, excess. سعر كيلو اللحـم زايـد هـا الايام si^c^ir keelu l-laḥam zaayid hal-iyyaam. The price of a kilogram of meat is more than necessary these days.

زي ر *zyr*

زيارة *ziyaara,* زاير *zaayir.* See under **زور** *zwr.*

زي غ *zyġ*

زاغ *zaaġ (يزيغ yziiġ)* to swerve, deviate. يزيغ في السواقة لانه سكران *yziiġ fi s-swaaga linna sakraan.* He swerves in driving because he is drunk.

زاغى *zaaġa* III 1. to cause to swerve, deviate. الجلبوت يزاغيه الريح *l-jalbuut yzaaġiii r-riiḥ.* The wind rocks the jolly-boat. 2. to deceive, mislead. يزاغيك في حكيه المعسول *yzaġiik fi ḥačya l-maᶜsuul.* He misleads you with his sweet words.

زوغ *zooġ* (v.n. from زاغ *zaaġ*) 1. swerving, deviation. 2. deceit.

زغيوي *zġeewi* p. *-iyya* swindler, cheat, crook.

زي ل *zyl*

زال *zaal* see under **زول** *zwl.*

زي ن ١ *zyn*

زين *zeen* name of the letter ز *z.*

زي ن ٢ *zyn*

زين *zayyan* II 1. to decorate, adorn, ornament. في العيد الوطني الناس يزينون الشوارع *fi l-ᶜiid l-waṭani n-naas yzayynuun š-šawaariᶜ.* On National Day (Independence Day in the U.A.E.) people display decorations in the streets. زينوا الحفيز بالورد *zayyanaw l-ḥafiiz b-l-ward.* They decorated the office with flowers. الحرمة زينت نفسها *l-ḥurma zayyanat nafissa.* The woman made herself up. 2. to shave, give a shave to. زين لحيته *zayyan liḥyita.* He shaved his beard. منو اللي زين لك شواربك؟ *minu lli zayyan-lak šawaarbak?* Who shaved your moustache for you? 3. to shave, get a shave. بزين. لحيته طويلة *b-zayyin; liḥyita ṭawiila.* He is shaving; his beard is long. ليش ما تزين؟ *leeš ma zzayyin?* Why don't you shave?

تزين *tzayyan* V 1. to be decorated, be adorned, be beautified. الشوارع تزينت بأقواس النصر *š-šawwariᶜ zzayyanat b-'agwaas n-naṣir.* The streets have been decorated with triumphal arches. شارع المطار تزين بالشجر *šaariᶜ l-maṭaar zzayyan b-š-šiyar.* The airport road has been improved by trees. 2. to shave, get a shave. يتزين كل يوم الصبح *yizzayyan kill yoom ṣ-ṣubḥ.* He shaves every day in the morning.

زين *zeen* 1. fine, good, nice. الحمد لله، كلنا زين *l-ḥamdu li-llaah, killana zeeniin.* Thanks to God. We're all fine. عنده سيارة زينة *ᶜinda sayyaara zeena.* He has a good car. آنا موب زين اليوم *'aana muub zeen l-yoom.* I'm not feeling well today. موب زين منه عطاكم الجلبوت حقه؟ *muub zeen minna ᶜaṭaakum l-jalbuut ḥagga?* Wasn't that nice of him to give you his jolly-boat? هم زين *hamm zeen* it's a good thing that. هم زين ما رحت وياه *hamm zeen ma riḥt wiyyaa.* It's a good thing you didn't go with him. 2. beautiful, pretty. عنده بنية زينة *ᶜinda bnayya zeena.* He has a beautiful daughter. زينة والا شينة، ما عليه. بنته *zeena walla šeena, ma ᶜalee. binta.* Beautiful or ugly, it doesn't matter. She's his daughter. 3. (n.) beautiful person. (prov.) الزين زين لو قعد من منامه والشـين شين لـو غسـل بصـابون *z-zeen zeenin law gicad min manaama w-š-šeen šeenin law ġassal b-ṣaabuun.* A leopard cannot change his spots. (comp. or derog.) (lit., "A beautiful person is always beautiful even if he wakes up and an ugly person is always ugly even if he washes with soap."). 4. (adv.) well, excellently. هـا الحـين التلفزيون يشتغل زين *halḥiin t-talafizyoon yištaġil zeen.* Now the T.V. works well. زين سويت *zeen sawweet.* You did well. Well done! Bravo! 5. (interjection of approval) O.K., all right, fine, good. زين، أشوفك باكر *zeen, 'ašuufak baačir.* All right, I'll see you tomorrow. زين، بند البـاب *zeen, bannid l-baab!* O.K., shut the door! (ان زين *nzeen* is a more common var.).

زينة *ziina* p. *-aat* decoration, ornament.

مزيـون *mazyuun* p. *-iin* handsome. f. *-a* p. *-aat* beautiful, pretty.

س

س ا ب *saab*

ساب *saab* p. سياب *syaab*. 1. small river, tributary. لين ينزل المطر السياب تسيب في كل مكان *leen yanzil l-muṭar li-syaab tsiib fi kill mukaan.* When it rains, small rivers flow everywhere. فيه سياب تسيب في البحر الأحمر *fii syaab tsiib fi l-baḥar l-'aḥmar.* There are tributaries that pour into the Red Sea. 2. (roof) gutter.

س ا ج *saaj*

ساج *saaj* (coll.) kind of hardwood used in making ships, gates, water tanks, etc. s. *-a.* (var. ساي *saay*).

س ا د *saad*

ساد *saad* Sad (region, close to Al-Ain, famous for its fresh water).

سادة *saada* (invar.) 1. plain, uncolored. حمر سادة *ḥamar saada* solid red. لون سادة *loon saada* solid color. 2. plain, straight. قهوة سادة *gahwa saada* unsweetened coffee.

س ا ر و ج *saarwj*

ساروج *saaruuj* p. *sawaariij* valley.

س ا م ا ن *saamaan*

سامان *saamaan* 1. things, objects, odds and ends. المخزن متروس سامان *l-maxzan matruus saamaan.* The storeroom is full of things. 2. personal effects. شل سامانه ومشى *šall saamaana w-miša.* He picked up his belongings and left.

س ا ن *saan*

سان *saan* (invar.) (adj. or adv.) going southward. المركب سان *l-markab saan.* The boat is going southward. سان! سان! *saan! saan!* Steer (the boat) toward the south!

س ا ع *saa^c^*

ساع *saa^c^* (with ب *b-*) quickly, fast, right away. روح وتعال بساع *ruuḥ w-ta^c^aal b-saa^c^.* Go and come back fast. وديته وجيت بساع *waddeeta w-yiit b-saa^c^.* I took it and hurried back. (common var. سع *sa^c^*).

ساعة *saa^c^a* p. *-aat* 1. hour. ترييته ساعتين *trayyeeta saa^c^teen.* I waited for him for two hours. يرجع عقب ساعة *yirja^c^ ^c^ugub saa^c^a.* He will be back in an hour. 2. time, moment. كم الساعة؟ *čam s-saa^c^a?* What time is it? الساعة المباركة *s-saa^c^a li-mbaarka* blessed, happy time. (prov.) ساعة لقلبك وساعة لربك *saa^c^a l-galbak w-saa^c^a l-rabbak.* Stop and smell the roses. All work and no play makes Jack a dull boy. (lit., "One hour for your heart and one hour for your God."). 2. (with foll. n.) 1. at the time of. نش ساعة الصبح *našš saa^c^t ṣ-ṣubḥ.* He woke up early in the morning. 2. short time, only one hour. كلها ساعة زمان *killha saa^c^at zamaan.* It's only for a short time. 3. watch, clock. ساعة يد *saa^c^at yadd* wrist watch. ساعتك مقدمة *saa^c^atk mjaddma.* Your watch is (too) fast. ساعتي مؤخرة

saa^c^ti m'axxra. My watch is (too) slow.

ساعاتي *saa^c^aati* p. *-yya* watch or clock repairman, watch dealer.

س ا م *saam*

سامي *saami* 1. Semitic. 2. Semite.

س ا م ر ي *saamry*

سامري *saamri* folk songs, sung to the accompaniment of a rebab (ربابة *rbaaba*).

س ا ن ي *saany*

سانية *saanya* p. سواني *sawaani* 1. animal (horse, mule, donkey) used for carrying heavy loads. 2. riding animal.

س ء ل *s'l*

سأل *si'al* (يسأل *yis'al)* to ask, inquire. سألته سؤال *si'alta su'aal.* I asked him a question. تفضل اسأل *tfaððal 'is'al!* Go ahead, ask! ما شفته من زمان. سألت عنه *ma čifta min zamaan. si'alt ^c^anna.* I haven't seen him for a long time. I inquired about him. سألته يساعدني *si'alta ysaa^c^idni.* I requested him to help me.

سؤال *su'aal* p. أسئلة *'as'ila,* سؤالات *su'aalaat* question, inquiry. ممكن أسألك سؤال؟ *mumkin 'as'alak su'aal?* May I ask you a question? سألوه واجد سؤالات في المطار *si'loo waayid su'aalaat fi l-maṭaar.* They asked him many questions at the airport.

مسألة *mas'ala* p. مسائل *masaa'il* 1. problem, question. هذي مسألة ما يحلها إلا الشيخ *haaði mas'ala ma yḥillha 'illa š-šeex.* This is a problem only the Shaikh can solve. 2. matter, affair, case. مسألة بسيطة *mas'ala basiiṭa* simple matter. شو المسألة؟ *šu l-mas'ala?* What's going on?

مسؤول *mas'uul* p. *-iin* 1. person in charge, such as a director, a manager, a foreman, etc. من المسؤول هني؟ *man l-mas'uul hini?* Who's the one in charge here? 2. responsible, accountable. من المسؤول عن اللي صار؟ *man l-mas'uul ^c^an illi ṣaar?* Who is responsible for what has happened?

مسؤولية *mas'uuliyya* responsibility.

س ب ب *sbb*

سب *sabb* (يسب *ysibb)* to insult, abuse, call s.o. bad names. هو اللي سبني في السوق قدام الناس *huwa lli sabbani fi s-suug jiddaam n-naas.* He is the one who insulted me in the marketplace in front of the people. التنديل سب الكولي والكولي ضربه *t-tindeel sabb l-kuuli w-l-kuuli ðraba.* The foreman called the coolie bad names and the coolie hit him.

سبب *sabbab* II to cause, bring about, provoke. ها السيارة العتيقة تسبب لك مشاكل *has-sayyaara l-^c^atiija tsabbib-lak mašaakil.* This old car will cause you problems. ما نعرف شو اللي سبب الربشة في السوق *ma n^c^arf šu lli sabbab r-rabša fi s-suug.* We don't know who caused the commotion in the market place.

تسابب *tsaabab* VI to insult each other, call each other bad names. تساببوا وتصالحوا عقبه *tsaabbaw w-ṣṣaalḥaw ^c^ugba.* They exchanged insults and made up later on.

سبب *sabab* p. أسباب *'asbaab* (var. سباب *sbaab)* reason, cause. شنهو السبب؟ *šinhu s-sabab?* What's the reason? سبب الهجرة الفقر *sabab l-hijra l-fagir.* The reason for emigration is poverty. هي سبب كل المشاكل *hiya sabab kill l-mašaakil.* She's the cause of all the problems. بسبب *b-sabab* because of, due to. ما داومت بسبب المرض *ma daawamt b-sabab l-marað̣.* I didn't go to work because of illness.

مسبة *masabba* p. *-aat* insult, abuse. كل مسبات كثيرة من الشرطي *kal masabbaat kaθiira min š-širṭi.* He took many insults from the policeman.

س ب ت *sbt*

السبت *s-sabt* Saturday. اليوم السبت *l-yoom s-sabt.* Today is Saturday. يوم السبت *yoom s-sabt* on Saturday. السبت الماضي *s-sabt l-maað̣i* last Saturday. كل يوم سبت *kill yoom sabt* every Saturday.

س ب چ *sbč*

سبك *sibač (يسبك yisbič)* to mold, form, shape a metal. السباك هو اللي يسبك السبايك *s-sabbaač huwa lli yisbič s-sibaayič.* A smelter is the one who molds pieces of gold.

سبيكة *sbiiča* p. سبايك *sibaayič* piece of gold, ingot. سبايك ذهب *sibaayič ðahab* gold ingots.

سباك *sabbaač* p. سبابيك *sibaabiič* smelter, founder.

س ب ح *sbḥ*

سبح *sibaḥ (يسبح yisbaḥ)* 1. to take a bath, bathe. آنا مجنب؛ لازم أسبح قبل الصلاة *'aana mujnib; laazim 'asbaḥ gabil ṣ-ṣalaa.* I am ritually unclean; I must take a bath before prayer. يسبح قبل لا يروح الشغل *yisbaḥ gabil-la yruuḥ š-šuġul.* He bathes before he goes to work. قوم تفصخ واسبح وتعال لاجل ناكل *guum tfaṣṣax w-isbaḥ w-taᶜaal lajil naakil.* Get up, undress, take a bath, and come so that we might eat. 2. to swim (عام *ᶜaam* is more common; look up under ع و م *ᶜwm*). تعرف تسبح؟ *tᶜarf tisbaḥ?* Do you know how to swim? رحنا نسبح *riḥna nisbaḥ.* We went swimming.

سبح *sabbaḥ* II 1. to give a bath to s.o. الأم سبحت عيالها *l-'umm sabbaḥat ᶜyaaḷha.* The mother gave a bath to her children. 2. to praise, glorify God (by saying سبحان الله *subḥaan aḷḷaah* praise the Lord!) المؤذن يسبح قبل صلاة الصبح *l-mu'aððin ysabbiḥ gabil ṣalaat ṣ-ṣubḥ.* The muezzin calls to prayer before the morning prayer. 3. to toy with a string of prayer (worry) beads. في ناس يسبحون طول اليوم *fii naas ysabbḥuun ṭuul l-yoom.* There are people who play with their prayer (worry) beads all day long.

تسبح *tsabbaḥ* V = سبح *sibaḥ.*

انسبح *nsibaḥ* VII (with في *fi*) to be swum in. هذا الماي موب صافي؛ ما ينسبح فيه *haaða l-maay muub ṣaafi; ma yinsibiḥ fii.* This water is not clear; it cannot be swum in.

سبحة *sibḥa* p. سبح *sibaḥ,* مسابح *masaabiḥ* prayer beads, rosary.

تسبيح *tasbiiḥ* (v.n. from II سبح *sabbaḥ*) glorification of God (by saying سبحان الله *subḥaan aḷḷaah* praise the Lord!).

سباح *sabbaaḥ* p. *-iin* swimmer.

مسبح *masbaḥ* p. مسابح *masaabiḥ* swimming pool, swimming place.

س ب س *sbs*

سبوس *sibuus* (coll.) rice husks, rice hulls (used as chicken feed). (prov.) تموت الدجاجة وعينها بالسبوس *tmuut d-diyaaya w-ᶜeenha b-s-sibuus.* The good old days. (lit., "The chicken is dying with its eye on the chicken food.").

س ب ع *sbᶜ*

سبع *sabiᶜ* p. سباع *sbaaᶜ* 1. lion. سرنا القنص وقنصنا سبع *sirna l-ganaṣ w-ginaṣna sabiᶜ*. We went hunting and caught a lion. 2. (adj.) brave, courageous.

سبعة *sabᶜa* p. *-aat* seven, the numeral seven. سبعة وسبعين *sabᶜa w-sabᶜiin* seventy-seven. سبعة دولار *sabᶜa duulaar* seven dollars. سبعتهم *sabᶜatum* the seven of them. سبع جهال *sabiᶜ yihhaal* seven children.

سبعتعش *sabiᶜtaᶜaš*, سبعتعشر *sabiᶜtaᶜašar* seventeen. امية وسبعتعش *'imya w-sabiᶜtaᶜaš* 117. كنا سبعتعشر نفر *činna sabiᶜataᶜašar nafar.* We were seventeen people.

سبع *subuᶜ* p. اسباع *sbaaᶜ* one-seventh, seventh part.

سبعين *sabᶜiin* p. *-aat* seventy, the numeral seventy. سبعين نفر *sabᶜiin nafar* seventy people. سبعة وسبعين *sabᶜa w-sabᶜiin* seventy-seven.

أسبوع *'usbuuᶜ* (more common var. سبوع *subuuᶜ*) p. أسابيع *'asaabiiᶜ* week. السبوع الماضي *s-subuuᶜ l-maaḏi* last week. السبوع الجاي *s-subuuᶜ l-yaay* next week. آخر سبوع *'aaxir subuuᶜ* the last week.

أسبوعي *'usbuuᶜi* (more common var. سبوعي *subuuᶜi*) weekly. جريدة سبوعية *yariida subuuᶜiyya* weekly newspaper.

أسبوعياً *'usbuuᶜiyyan* (more common var. سبوعياً *subuuᶜiyyan*) weekly, by the week.

سابع *saabiᶜ* seventh. سابع يوم *saabiᶜ yoom* the seventh day. في اليوم السابع *fi l-yoom s-saabiᶜ* on the seventh day. سابعهم *saabiᶜhum* the seventh one of them.

س ب گ *sbg*

سبق *sibag* (يسبق *yisbig*) 1. to be, come, go, or happen before or ahead of, precede, arrive before s.o. صلاة السنة تسبق صلاة الفرض *ṣalaat s-sunna tisbig ṣalaat l-farḏ.* The sunna prayer precedes the obligatory prayer. البرق يسبق الرعد *l-barg yisbig r-raᶜd.* Lightening comes before thunder. يسبقني في الخدمة *yisbigni fi l-xidma.* He is ahead of me in service. أختها تسبقها بصف واحد *'uxutta tisbigha b-ṣaff waaḥid.* Her sister is one class (grade) ahead of her. 2. to surpass, beat, do better than (in sports). سبقني في سباق الامية متر *sibagni fi sibaag l-'imyat mitir.* He beat me in the one hundred meter dash.

سبق *sabbag* II to cause to precede or come ahead of. سبقني عليهم *sabbagni ᶜaleehum.* He made me come ahead of them.

تسابق *tsaabag* VI to try to get ahead of each other, seek to outdo each other, racc, compete. تسابقنا: هو بسيارته وانا بسيارتي *tsaabagna: huwa b-sayyaarta w-aana b-sayyaarti.* We had a race: he in his car and I in my car. تسابقنا وهو سبقني *tsaabagna w-huwa sibagni.* We had a race and he beat me.

سباق *sibaag* p. *-aat* race, contest. سباق الامية متر *sibaag l-'imyat mitir* the one hundred meter dash.

أسبق *'asbag* earlier, or earliest, antecedent. ماحد أسبق مني في الترفيع *maḥḥad 'asbag minni fi t-tarfiiᶜ*. I, and nobody else, am the first in line for promotion.

أسبقية *'asbagiyya* 1. precedence, priority. 2. seniority. الأسبقية في الخدمة *l-'asbagiyya fi l-xidma* seniority in service. الأسبقية في الترفيع *l-'asbagiyya fi t-tarfiiᶜ* seniority for promotion.

مسابقة *musaabaga* p. *-aat* contest. مسابقة معلومات *musaabagat maᶜluumaat* a contest of knowledge.

سابق *saabig* 1. previous, prior, preceding. المرة السابقة *l-marra s-saabga* the previous time. 2. former, ex-. المدير السابق *l-mudiir s-saabig* the former director. السابق واللاحق *s-saabig w-l-laaḥig* the former and the latter. في السابق *fi s-saabig* formerly, in the past. في السابق ناس واجدين كانوا يسكنون في برستية *fi s-saabig naas waaydiin čaanaw yiskinuun fi barastiyya.* In the past many people used to live in shacks. سابق لأوانه *saabig li-'awaana* premature, untimely. الترفيع سابق لأوانه *t-tarfiiᶜ saabig li-'awaana.* The promotion is premature. حر سابق لأوانه *ḥarr saabig li-'awaana* unseasonably hot weather.

سابقة *saabga* p. سوابق *sawaabig* previous (criminal) case, precedent. هو من أصحاب السوابق *huwa min 'aṣḥaab s-sawaabig.* He's one of those who have a criminal record.

س ب ك *sbk*

سبك *sibak* (يسبك *yisbik*), see under **س ب چ** *sbč*.

س ب ل *sbl*

سبل *sibil* (coll.) ear, stalk of wheat or barley, s. *-a.*

سبال *sbaal* 1. (coll.) peanuts. s. *-a.* 2. (p. سيابيل *siyaabiil*) monkey. f. *-a* p. *-aat.*

سبيل *sabiil* s.th., esp. water, donated for charitable use. ها الماي سبيل، بدون فلوس *hal-maay sabiil, b-duun fluus.* This water has been donated; it's free. في سبيل الله *fi sabiil il-laah* for the sake of God, in behalf of God and His religion. ابن السبيل *'ibn s-sabiil* wayfarer, traveler. على سبيل المثال *ᶜala sabiil l-miθaal* as an example.

سبيل *sbiil* p. سبلان *siblaan* smoking pipe. أنت تدوخ سبيل؟ *'inta dduux sbiil?* Do you smoke a pipe? السبيل يدوخني *li-sbiil ydawwixni.* A pipe makes me dizzy.

س ب ن *sbn*

سبن *sibin* (coll.) moonfish. s. *-a.*

س ب ي ت *sbyt*

سبيت *sbeet* spades (in card games).

س ب ي ت ر *sbytr*

سبيتار *sbeetaar* (more common var. مستشفى *mustašfa*) p. *-aat* hospital. See *mustašfa* under **ش ف ي** *šfy*.

س ب ي ط ي *sbyṭy*

سبيطي *sbeeṭi* (coll.) kind of fish s. *-yya*.

س ب ي ن غ *sbynġ*

سبيناغ *sbeenaaġ* (coll.) spinach.

س پ ر ن گ *sprng*

سبرنك *sipring* p. *-aat* spiral spring, coil spring.

س ت ت *stt*

ستة *sitta* p. *-aat* six, the numeral six. ستة وخمسين *sitta w-xamsiin* fifty-six. ستة درهم *sitta dirhim* six dirhams. كنا ستة *činna sitta.* We were six (people). (with foll. n. ستة *sittat*). كنا ستة أنفار *činna sittat 'anfaar.* We were six people.

ستعش *sittaᶜaš,* ستعشر *sittaᶜšar* sixteen. امية وستعش *'imya w-sittaᶜaš* 116. (with foll. n. ستعشر *sittaᶜšar*). ستعشر مدرسة *sittaᶜšar madrasa* sixteen schools.

ستين *sittiin* p. *-aat* sixty. ستين درهم *sittiin dirhim* sixty dirhams. امية وستين *'imya w-sittiin* 160. كم عمره؟ *čam ᶜumra?* How old is he? في الستينات *fi s-sittiinaat* in his sixties. في الستينات *fi s-sittiinat* during the 1960's.

سات *saatt* (common var. سادس *saadis*) sixth. See under **س د س** *sds*.

س ت د *std*

ستاد *staad* p. *-iyya* mason, builder. شفت لي ستاد أمين وبنيت البيت *šifit-li staad 'amiin w-baneet l-beet.* I found for myself an honest builder and built the house.

س ت ر *str*

ستر *sitar* (يستر *yustur*) 1. to hide, conceal, cover up. هذي بنية كبيرة؛ لازم تستر على نفسها *haaδi bnayya čibiira; laazim tustur ᶜala nafissa.* This is an old girl; she will have to cover up. 2. to shield, protect, watch over, guard. الله يستر من ها الدعمة. يمكن يموت *'aḷḷa yustur min had-daᶜma. yamkin ymuut.* God protect us from this car accident. He may die. الله يستر عليك. أنت خوش حرمة *'aḷḷa yustur ᶜaleeč. 'inti xooš ḥurma.* God watch over you. You are a fine woman. كان الجاهل رايح يوقع من الدريشة. الله ستر *čaan l-yaahil raayiḥ yuugaᶜ min d-diriiša. 'aḷḷa sitar.* The child was about to fall down from the window. God prevented it. لا ما تسقط في الامتحان. الله يستر *la ma tuṣġuṭ fi li-mtiḥaan. 'aḷḷa yustur!* No, you won't fail in the examination. God forbid!

تستر *tsattar* V to cover up, hide, conceal oneself. خوش حرمة. دايماً تتستر *xooš ḥurma. dayman titsattar.* She's a fine woman. She always covers up.

ستر *sitir* (v.n.) 1. covering up. ستر العورة *sitr l-ᶜoora* covering up parts of a woman's body, such as the face, hair, the legs, etc. 2. protection, guard, shield. يا الله سترك! نحن ما ندور إلا الستر *ya 'aḷḷaah sitrak! niḥin ma ndawwir 'illa s-sitir.* God protect us! We look only for (God's) protection. (prov.) ستر عنز وصلاح قطوة *sitir ᶜanz w-ṣalaaḥ gaṭwa.* The behind of a nanny goat is always uncovered, and a cat is always cunning.

مستور *mastuur* (p.p. from ستر *sitar*) 1. hidden, covered up, concealed. 2. chaste, proper, honorable. بنية مستورة *bnayya mastuura* nice girl. مستور الحال *mastuur l-ḥaal* of meager means.

س ت ك ن *stkn*

ستكان *stikaan* p. *-aat* small glass used for drinking tea.

س ج د *sjd*

سجد *sijad (يسجد yasjid)* to bow down, prostrate oneself in prayer. ما يقدر يسجد لانه مريض *ma yigdar yasjid linna mariiḍ.* He cannot prostrate himself (in prayer) because he is ill. المسلم ما يسجد إلا لله *l-muslim ma yasjid 'illa li-llaah.* A Muslim doesn't bow down to anyone but God.

سجدة *sajda* (n. of inst.) p. *-aat* one prostration in prayer.

سجود *sujuud* (v.n. from سجد *sijad*) prostration in prayer.

مسجد *masjid* (more common var. *msiid*) p. مساجد *masaayid* mosque. الناس يصلون في المسجد والا في البيت *n-naas yṣalluun fi li-msiid walla fi l-beet.* People pray in a mosque or at home. المسجد العود *li-msiid l-ᶜood* the large mosque (where the Friday prayer is conducted).

س ج ل *sjl*

سجل *sajjal* II 1. to register, record, enter in a register. سجلت اسمي وعنواني في الدفتر *sajjalt 'ismi w-ᶜinwaani fi d-daftar.* I entered my name and address in the notebook. سجلني؛ أريد أتبرع بألف درهم *sajjilni; 'ariid atbarraᶜ b-'alf dirhim.* Put me down; I want to donate a thousand dirhams. 2. to enter, enroll (in a school, etc.) سجلت في المدرسة الليلية *sajjalt fi l-madrasa l-layliyya.* I enrolled in the evening school. 3. to record, make a recording of. سجلت كل أغاني محمد عبده *sajjalt kill 'aġaani mḥammad ᶜabdo.* I recorded all of Muhammad Abdo's songs.

سجل *sijill* p. *-aat* register, record, list. السجل التجاري *s-sijill t-tijaari* the commercial register. سجل الزيارات *sijill z-ziyaaraat* the visitor's book, guest book. سجلات المحكمة *sijillaat l-maḥkama* the court records.

مسجل *msajjil* (act. part. from II سجل *sajjal*) p. *-iin* 1. having registered, enrolled. آنا تونى مسجل ابني في المدرسة *'aana tawwni msajjill 'ibni fi l-madrasa.* I have just enrolled my son in the school. 2. (as occupational n. p. *-iin*) registrar, recorder. مسجل الكلية *msajjil l-kulliyya* the college registrar. 3. (p. *-aat*) tape recording, recording device.

مسجل *msajjal* (p.p. from II سجل *sajjal*) registered, recorded, entered, listed. بريد مسجل *bariid msajjal* registered mail. بريد جوي مسجل *bariid jawwi msajjal* registered air mail. طرشت خط مسجل *ṭarrašt xaṭṭ msajjal.* I sent a registered letter. اسمي مسجل هناك *'ismi msajjal hnaak.* My name is entered there.

س ج ن *sjn*

سجن *sijan* (يسجن *yasjin)* to jail, imprison s.o. سجنوه لانه باق فلوس من البنك *sijnoo linna baag fluus min l-bank.* They put him in jail because he stole money from the bank. أبوها قال الها «لازم أسجنك هني في البيت» *'ubuuha gaal il-ha laazim 'asjinč hni fi l-beet.* Her father said to her: "I have to confine you to the house."

انسجن *nsijan* VII to be jailed, imprisoned. انسجن خمس سنين *nsijan xams siniin.* He was imprisoned for five years.

سجن *sijin* p. سجون *sujuun* 1. prison, jail. حطوه في السجن لانه باق فلوس من الشيخ *ḥaṭṭoo fi s-sijin linna baag fluus min š-šeex.* They put him in jail because he stole money from the Shaikh. 2. imprisonment, prison sentence. حكم عليه القاضي خمس سنين سجن *ḥikam ᶜalee l-gaaḍi xams siniin sijin.* The judge sentenced him to five years imprisonment.

مسجون *masjuun* (p.p. from سجن *sijan*) 1. imprisoned, jailed, confined. كام صار لك مسجون؟ *čam ṣaar-lak masjuun?* How long have you been imprisoned? 2. (p. مساجين *masaajiin*) prison inmate, convict. مسجون محكوم عليه خمس سنين سجن *masjuun maḥkuum ᶜalee xams siniin sijin* inmate sentenced to five years in jail.

س ج ي *sjy*

سجي *saji* rising tide, flow of the sea. السجي هني يكون ساعات الصبح *s-saji hini ykuun saaᶜat ṣ-ṣubḥ.* The rising tide here takes place in the early morning.

س چ ن *sčn*

سكين *siččiin* p. سكاكين *sičaačiin* knife. ها الحين الناس قاموا ياكلون بالسكين والجنقال *halḥiin n-naas gaamaw yaakluun b-s-siččiin w-č-čingaaḷ.* Now people have started to eat with fork and knife. (prov.) إذا طاح البعير كثرت سكاكينه *'iða ṭaaḥ l-biᶜiir kiθrat sičaačiina.* When it rains, it pours. Misfortune comes in groups. (lit., "If the camel falls down, its knives will be plenty.").

س ح ب *sḥb*

سحب *siḥab* (يسحب *yisḥab)* 1. to take out, withdraw (e.g., money). سحبت فلوس من البنك *siḥabt fluus min l-bank.* I withdrew money from the bank. سحبوا أرقام الفايزين *sḥibaw 'argaam l-faayziin.* They drew the names of the winners. 2. to pull down, drag. سحبت الباب *siḥabt l-baab.* I pulled the door. اللوري سحب سيارتي الخربانة *l-loori siḥab sayyaarti l-xarbaana.* The truck towed my broken car. البنكة في المطبخ تسحب الهوا *l-panka fi l-maṭbax tisḥab l-hawa.* The fan in the kitchen draws the air out. 3. to recall, call back, withdraw. أمريكا سحبت سفيرها من العراق *'amriika sḥabat safiira min li-ᶜraag.* America recalled its ambassador from Iraq. سحبوا الجيش من الحدود *sḥabaw l-jeeš min li-ḥduud.* They pulled their army back from the borders. 4. to take back, withdraw. سحب كلامه لانه خاف *siḥab kalaama linna xaaf.* He took back what he said because he was afraid.

المسرع يسحبون الليسن حقه *l-misri^c yisḥabuun l-leesan ḥagga.* They will take away the license of the speeding motorist. 5. to pull, draw (a weapon). سحب المسدس وقتله *siḥab l-musaddas w-gtala.* He drew the gun and killed him.

انسحب *nsiḥab* VII to withdraw, retreat, pull back. الجيش انسحب من الحدود *l-jeeš nsiḥab min li-ḥduud.* The army withdrew from the borders. إذا ما تقدر تدفع المهر انسحب *'iða ma tigdar tidfa^c l-mahar nsiḥib.* If you cannot pay the dowry, back off. انسحب من الانتخابات *nsiḥab min li-ntixaabaat.* He withdrew from the elections.

سحب *saḥb* (v.n. from سحب *siḥab*) 1. pulling. 2. drawing (in a lottery). 3. withdrawal (of money, troops, etc.).

انسحب *nsiḥaab* (v.n. from VII انسحب *nsiḥab*) retreat, pulling out.

مسحوب *masḥuub* (p.p. from سحب *siḥab*) withdrawn. المبلغ المسحوب *l-mablaġ l-masḥuub* the amount withdrawn. هذا الشيك مسحوب على بنك في انكلترا *haaða š-šeek masḥuub ^cala bank fi ngiltara.* The check is drawn on a bank in England.

س ح ت *sḥt*

سحت *saḥḥat* II to sharpen a knife, a pencil, etc. سحت السكين *saḥḥat s-siččiin.* He sharpened the knife.

س ح ر *sḥr*

سحر *siḥar (يسحر yisḥar)* to bewitch, enchant, charm. ها البنية جمالها سحرني *ha li-bnayya jamaalha siḥarni.* The girl's beauty bewitched me.

سحر *saḥḥar* II to serve the Suhuur, a light meal (shortly before daybreak taken during Ramadan). سحروني جبن وزبد وخبز *saḥḥarooni jibin w-zibid w-xubiz.* They served me cheese, butter, and bread for the Suhuur.

تسحر *tsaḥḥar* V to eat the Suhuur. شو تسحرت أمس؟ *šu tsaḥḥart 'ams?* What did you have for the Suhuur yesterday?

سحر *siḥir* 1. bewitchment, enchantment. 2. sorcery, witchcraft.

سحري *siḥri* magic, magical. فانوس سحري *faanuus siḥri* magic lantern, slide projector. ألعاب سحرية *'al^caab siḥriyya* magic tricks.

سحور *suḥuur* suhuur (meal taken before dawn during Ramadan).

ساحر *saaḥir* 1. (act. part. from سحر *siḥar*) having bewitched, enchanted s.o. ساحرته بجمالها *saaḥirta b-jamaalha.* She cast a spell on him with her beauty. 2. (p. *-iin,* سحرا *suḥara*) magician, wizard, sorcerer, charmer.

ساحرة *saaḥira* p. *-aat* sorceress, witch.

سحارة *saḥḥaara* p. *-aat* box, crate, case. سحارة طماط *saḥḥaarat ṭamaaṭ* 1. box of tomatoes. 2. tomato box.

س ح ح *sḥḥ*

سح *siḥḥ* (coll.) ripe dates, usually of a dark brown color. s. *-a* قلة السح كانت بخمسين ربية *gaḷḷat s-siḥḥ čaanat b-xamsiin rubbiyya.* A basket of dates was for fifty rupees.

س ح گ *sḥg*

سحق *siḥag (يسحق yisḥag)* 1. to crush, mash. سحق الجقارة لاجل تنطفي *siḥag* *j-jigaara lajil tinṭifi.* He crushed the cigarette so it would go out. ها اللوري يسحق الرستة *ha l-loori yisḥag r-rasta.* This truck packs down the (paved) road. 2. to run over, trample, run down. سحقته السيارة في نص الشارع. *siḥgata sayyaara fi nuṣṣ š-šaari*[c]. The car ran over him in the middle of the street. الجاهل سحقه حمار في سوق الخضار *l-yaahil siḥga ḥmaar fi suug li-xđaar.* A donkey trampled a child in the vegetable marketplace. 3. to annihilate, destroy, wipe out. الجيش سحق جيش العدو *l-jeeš siḥag jeeš l-*[c]*adu.* The army crushed the enemy army.

مسحوق *masḥuug* p. مساحيق *masaaḥiig* powder.

س ح ل *sḥl*

ساحل *saaḥil* p. سواحل *sawaaḥil* seashore, coastline. ساحل عمان *saaḥil* [c]*maan* the coast of Oman.

١ س ح ي *sḥy*

سحية *siḥiyya* p. *-aat,* سحايا *saḥaaya* (usually سحية الليل *siḥiyyat l-leel*) bat (zool.).

٢ س ح ي *sḥy*

استحى *stiḥa* X. See under ح ي ي *ḥyy.*

س خ ت ي ن *sxtyn*

سختيان *sixtyaan* (coll.) fine, thin leather.

س خ ر *sxr*

سخر *sixar (*يسخر *yisxar)* (with من *min*) to laugh at, mock, make fun of. سخر مني قدام الناس *sixar minni jiddaam n-naas.* He made fun of me in front of the people.

سخر *saxxar* II to employ, utilize, make use of. سخرنا كل إمكانيات الدولة ضد المخدرات *saxxarna kill 'imkaaniyyaat d-dawla đidd l-muxaddaraat.* We have employed all the available means of the state against drugs.

مسخرة *masxara* frivolousness, state of lacking in seriousness. هذا الحكم موب عادل؛ مسخرة *haađa l-ḥukum muub* [c]*aadil; masxara.* This verdict is not just; it's a joke.

س خ ف *sxf*

See under ص خ ف *ṣxf.*

س خ ل *sxl*

See under ص خ ل *ṣxl.*

س خ ن *sxn*

See under ص خ ن *ṣxn.*

س خ ي *sxy*

See under ص خ ي *ṣxy.*

س د د *sdd*

سد *sadd (*يسد *ysidd)* 1. to close up, plug. الوسخ سد المغسلة *l-waṣax sadd l-maġsala.* The dirt stopped up the sink. مطرت الدنيا وسدوا مجرى الماي *muṭrat d-dinya w-saddaw majra l-maay.* It rained and they dammed the water course. 2. to pay back. سد الفلوس اللي عليه *sadd li-fluus illi* [c]*alee.* He paid back the money he owed. 3. to close, shut. سد الباب من فضلك *sidd l-baab min fađlak.* Close the door, please. هذا البنك موب زين. روح سد حسابك! *haađa l-bank muub zeen. ruuḥ sidd ḥsaabak!* This bank is not good. Go close your account! (prov.)

البالوعة *sadd l-baaluu^c^a* the clogging of the sewer. 2. paying back. سد المبلغ *sadd l-mablaġ* paying back the amount. 3. closing, shutting. سد الباب *sadd l-baab* closing, shutting the door. سد الحساب *sadd li-ḥsaab* closing of the account. 4. obstructing, blocking. *sadd ṭ-ṭariig* the blocking of the way. 5. meeting, covering (e.g., a deficit). 6. filling, closing. سد الفراغ *sadd l-faraaġ* filling the gap.

سد *sadd* p. سدود *sduud* 1. dam. 2. dike. 3. barrier.

س د ر *sdr*

سدر *sidir* (coll.) 1. lotus trees. s. *-a*. فيه سدر واجد هني *fii sidir waayid hini.* There are many lotus trees here. 2. leaves of lotus trees. في قديم الزمان بعض الناس كانوا يستعملون السدر بدل الصابون *fi gadiim z-zamaan ba^c^ḍ n-naas čaanaw yista^c^imluun s-sidir bidal ṣ-ṣaabuun.* A long time ago some people used the leaves of lotus trees instead of soap.

س د س *sds*

سدس *suds* p. اسداس *sdaas* one-sixth.

سادس *saadis* (common var. سات *saatt*) sixth, the sixth. See also under **س ت ت** *stt*.

س ر ب *srb*

تسرب *tsarrab* V 1. to leak, seep out. الماي يتسرب من البيب *l-maay yitsarrab min l-peep.* The water is leaking from the pipe. 2. to leak out, spread, get out. بعض الأخبار تسربت من مكتب الوزير *ba^c^ḍ l-'axbaar tsarrabat min maktab l-waziir.* Some news leaked out from the minister's office. 3. to infiltrate.

الدريشة اللي يجيك منها دخان سدها *d-diriiša lli yjiik minha daxxaan sidda.* Prevent a bad thing from happening at the start. Nip bad things in the bud. (lit., "Close the window that lets in smoke on you."). 4. to obstruct, block. حصل دعمة وسدوا الطريق *ḥiṣal da^c^ma w-saddaw ṭ-ṭariig.* There was a car accident and they blocked the way. ها الدريول سد الطريق علي *had-drwweil sadd ṭ-ṭariig ^c^alayya.* This driver blocked my way. ها الطوفة عالية واجد، ورايحة تسد علينا منظر المنتزه *haṭ-ṭoofa ^c^aalya waayid, w-raayḥa tsidd ^c^aleena manðar l-muntazah.* This wall is very high and it's going to obstruct our view of the park. 5. to meet, cover, satisfy. بعض البلادين تتسلف فلوس لاجل تسد العجز في الميزانية *ba^c^ð l-balaadiin titsallaf fluus lajil tsidd l-^c^ajiz fi l-miizaaniyya.* Some countries borrow money in order to meet the deficit in the budget. 6. to fill, close. توفى. الله يرحمه. ترك فراغ ما يسده أحد *twaffa. 'aḷḷaah yirḥama. tarak faraaġ ma ysidda 'aḥad.* He passed away. May God bless his soul. He left a gap that no one can fill.

سدد *saddad* II to pay up, settle. سدد كل المبلغ اللي عليه *saddad kill l-mablaġ illi ^c^alee.* He paid up the whole amount he owed.

تسدد *tsaddad* V 1. to be paid back. 2. to meet, cover, satisfy.

انسد *nsadd* VII 1. to be blocked, obstructed, plugged up. 2. to be closed, shut.

سد *sadd* (v.n. from سد *sadd*) 1. closing, plugging, stopping up. سد

فيه عساسة يتسربون إلى خطوط العدو *fii ᶜassaasa yitsarrabuun 'ila xṭuuṭ l-ᶜadu.* There are spies who infiltrate enemy lines.

س ر ج srj

سرج *sarj* p. سروج *sruuj* saddle.

سراج *siraaj* p. سروج *sruuj* lamp, lantern.

سراج *sarraaj* p. *-iin* 1. saddler. 2. leather craftsman.

س ر ح srḥ

سرح *siraḥ* (يسرح *yisraḥ*) 1. to move away, go away, leave. الراعي سرح بالغنم *r-raaᶜi siraḥ b-l-ġanam.* The shepherd left with the sheep. 2. to graze freely. الغنم يسرحون في السهول والوديان *l-ġanam yisraḥuun fi s-suhuul w-l-widyaan.* Sheep graze freely in meadows and valleys. 3. to be distracted, let one's mind wander. يقدر ينتبه شوية بس وبعدين يسرح *yigdar yintabih šwayya bass w-baᶜdeen yisraḥ.* He can pay attention for only a while, and then his mind wanders.

سرح *sarraḥ* II 1. to discharge, dismiss, release s.o. from a job, lay off. الحكومة سرحت معظم الأجانب *li-ḥkuuma sarraḥat muᶜḍam l-'ayaanib.* The government has laid off most of the foreigners. 2. to comb, do up (the hair). بنتي دايماً توقف قدام المنظرة وتسرح شعرها *binti daayman toogaf jiddaam l-minḍara w-tsarriḥ šaᶜraha.* My daughter always stands in front of the mirror and combs her hair.

سراح *saraaḥ* release. أطلقوا سراحه *'aṭlagaw saraaḥa.* They released him.

سارح *saariḥ* (act. part. from سرح *siraḥ*) 1. having gone or moved away, having left. الراعي سارح بالغنم *r-raaᶜi saariḥ b-l-ġanam.* The shepherd has left with the sheep. 2. being distracted (mind), wandering. تفكيره سارح *tafkiira saariḥ.* He is distracted.

س ر ر srr

سر *sarr* (يسر *ysirr*) 1. to make happy, cheer, delight. سرني نجاح ولدي في الامتحان *sarrani najaaḥ wildi fi li-mtiḥaan.* My son's passing the examination pleased me. يسرني انك تجي تزورنا الليلة *ysirrani 'innak tiyi tzuurna l-leela.* It makes me very happy that you will come to visit us tonight. 2. to tell a secret, confide in s.o. سر علي بشي وما أقدر أقوله *sarr ᶜalayya b-šayy w-ma 'agdar 'aguula.* He let me in on s.th. and I can't tell it.

انسر *nsarr* VII to be or become happy, be delighted. انسر لين سمع بنجاح ولده في الامتحان *nsarr leen simaᶜ b-najaaḥ wilda fi li-mtiḥaan.* He became happy when he heard of his son's passing the examination.

سر *sirr* p. أسرار *'asraar* secret. كلمة السر *čalmat s-sirr* the password. باح بالسر *baaḥ b-s-sirr.* He revealed the secret.

سري *sirri* 1. secret. رسالة سرية *risaala sirriyya* secret letter. اجتماع سري *jtimaaᶜ sirri* secret meeting. 2. classified, confidential. معلومات سرية *maᶜluumaat sirriyya* classified information.

سرور *suruur* joy, happiness, pleasure. بكل سرور! *b-kull suruur!* With pleasure, gladly!

مسرور *masruur* p. *-iin* glad, happy, pleased. آنـا مسـرور بهالوظيفـة *'aana masruur b-hal-waðiifa.* I am pleased with this job. آنا مسرور بنجاحك *'aana masruur b-najaaḥak.* I am happy about your success.

س ر ع sr^c

أسـرع *'asra^c^* IV to speed up, hasten, hurry. أسـرع ومـا قـدروا يزخـوه *'asra^c^ w-ma gdaraw yizixxuu.* He speeded up and they couldn't catch him. لا تسرع! فيـه شـرطي مـرور هـني *la tisri^c^! fii širṭi muruur hini.* Don't speed up! There is a traffic policeman here. إذا تسرع تقدر تلحـق البـاص *'iða tisri^c^ tigdar tilḥag l-paaṣ.* If you hurry, you can catch the bus.

تسـرع *tsarra^c^* V to be hasty, rash, do s.th. in a hurry. راح تسـرع وفنـش مـن الشـركة *raaḥ tsarra^c^ w-fannaš min š-šarika.* He was rash and resigned from the company. لا تتسرع! فكـر! *la titsarra^c^! fakkir!* Don't do things in a hurry! Think!

سرعة *sur^c^a* 1. speed. معظم الدريولية هـني يسـوقون بسـرعة *mu^c^ðam d-dreewliyya hni ysuuguun b-sur^c^a.* Most drivers here drive fast. تعرف كم سرعة الصوت؟ *t^c^arf čam sur^c^at ṣ-ṣoot?* Do you know what the speed of sound is? 2. quickness, promptness. روح وتعال بسـرعة *ruuḥ w-ta^c^aal b-sur^c^a.* Go and come back right away.

سريع *sarii^c^* fast, quick, speedy. روح بالقطـار السريع *ruuḥ b-l-giṭaar s-sarii^c^.* Go by express train.

أسـرع *'asra^c^* (elat.) 1. (with من *min*) faster than. السـيارة أسـرع مـن البطبطـة *s-sayyaara 'asra^c^ min l-buṭbuṭa.* A car is faster than a motorcycle. 2. (with foll. n.) the fastest. هذي أسرع طريقـة *haaði 'asra^c^ ṭariiga.* This is the fastest way.

مسـرع *misri^c^* (act. part. from IV أسرع *'asra^c^*) going at a fast speed, speeding. النجدة بتخـالف المسـرع *n-najda b-txaalif l-misri^c^.* The police squad issues violations to speeding motorists. كان مسـرع *čaan misri^c^.* He was speeding. العكاسات تزخ المسرع *l-^c^akkaasaat zzixx l-misri^c^.* Cameras catch speeding motorists.

س ر ف *srf*

أسـرف *'asraf* IV to spend lavishly, be extravagant. مـا يفكـر في مستقبله. دايمـاً يسـرف *ma yfakkir fi mustaġbala. daayman yisrif.* He doesn't think of his future. He is always extravagant.

مسـرف *misrif* (act. part. from IV أسرف *'asraf*) 1. extravagant, wasteful. 2. spendthrift.

س ر ي *sry*

سـرى *sara* (يسري *yisri*) 1. to travel at night. سـرينا في الليـل لـين وصلنـا مكـة *sareena fi l-leel leen wiṣalna makka.* We travelled at night until we reached Mecca. 2. (with على *^c^ala*) to go very early in the morning to some place. سـرى على الشـغل *sara ^c^ala š-šuġul.* He went to work very early in the morning. 3. to spread. رباط الدم يسري في عروقنا ويشدنا حق بعض *rbaaṭ d-damm yisri fi ^c^ruugna w-yšiddna ḥagg ba^c^að.* Blood relationship flows through our veins and pulls us together. السرطان يسري في عظامه *s-saraṭaan yisri fi* *ᶜð̣aama.* Cancer is spreading throughout his bones. 4. to be effective, be in force, take effect. هذا القانون يسري مفعوله باكر *haaða l-ġaanuun yisri mafᶜuula baačir.* This law will be in force tomorrow. 5. (with على *ᶜala*) to apply to, be applicable to. القانون يسري على الجميع *l-ġaanuun yisri ᶜala l-jimiiᶜ.* The law applies to all people.

سرية *sariyya* p. سرايا *saraaya* detachment (mil.), squadron.

سريان *sarayaan* (v.n. from سرى *sara*) 1. flow, spread, diffusion. سريان الدم *sarayaan d-damm* the flow of blood. 2. validity, coming into force.

إسرا *'isra* (lit. إسراء *'israa'*) night journey, midnight journey. الإسرا *l-'isra* Muhammad's midnight journey to heaven. الإسرا والمعراج *l-'isra w-l-miᶜraaj* Muhammad's midnight journey and ascension to heaven.

س س ر *ssr*

ساسر *saasar* III to whisper in s.o.'s ear. تعال ساسرني في اذني *taᶜaal saasirni fi 'iðni.* Come and whisper in my ear

مساسرة *msaasara* (v.n. from III ساسر *saasar*) whispering, whisper.

س ط ل *sṭl*

See under **ص ط ل** *ṣṭl.*

س ع د *sᶜd*

سعد *siᶜad (يسعد yisᶜad)* 1. (with ب *b-*) to be happy, be pleased. سعدت بلقاءه *siᶜatt b-liġaa'a.* I am happy to meet him. 2. to please, make happy. الله يسعدك! *'aḷḷaah yisᶜidk!* God make you happy! حرمته تسعده *ḥurumta tisᶜida.* His wife makes him happy. يسعدني أشوفك متزوج ومتوفق في حياتك *yisᶜidni 'ačuufak mitzawwij w-mitwaffig fi ḥayaatak.* It pleases me to see you married and getting ahead in your life.

ساعد *saaᶜad* III to help, assist. ساعدني! *saaᶜidni!* Help me! لحيةٍ غانمة. يساعد كل واحد *liḥyatin ġaanma. ysaaᶜid kill waaḥid.* He's a good man. He helps everyone. المدارس تساعد على محو الأمية *l-madaaris tsaaᶜid ᶜala maḥw l-'ummiyya.* Schools help with the eradication of illiteracy.

تساعد *tsaaᶜad* VI to help each other. تساعدنا في الدراسة *tsaaᶜadna fi d-diraasa.* We helped each other in studying.

سعيد *saᶜiid* p. سعدا *suᶜada, -iin* 1. happy. أتمنى انك تكون سعيد في حياتك *'atmanna 'innak tkuun saᶜiid fi ḥayaatak.* I hope you will be happy in your life. سعيد الحظ *saᶜiid l-ḥað̣ð̣* lucky, fortunate.

سعيد *sᶜiid* Said (common name in the U.A.E.). (prov.) سعيد أخو مبارك *sᶜiid 'uxu mbaarak.* Two peas in a pod. (lit., "Said is Mubarak's brother."). عنبر خو بلال *ᶜambar xu bḷaaḷ* has the same meaning, and it's more common. (prov.) سعيد بعين أمه بدر *sᶜiid b-ᶜeen 'umma badir.* Beauty is only in the eye of the beholder. (lit., "Said is a full moon in his mother's eye.").

سعادة *saᶜaada* 1. happiness. السعادة في راحة البال *s-saᶜaada fi raaḥat l-baal.*

Happiness lies in the relaxed state of mind. 2. title, roughly equivalent to His Excellency, His Grace, etc. سعادة المدير! *sa^{c}aadat l-mudiir!* His Excellency, the Director! يا سعادة المدير! *ya sa^{c}aadat l-mudiir!* Your Excellency, the Director!

سعودي *su^{c}uudi* 1. Saudi, characteristic of Saudi Arabia. البترول السعودي *l-batrool s-su^{c}uudi* the Saudi petroleum. 2. a Saudi Arab. أنت سعودي والا خليجي؟ *'inta su^{c}uudi walla xaliiji?* Are you a Saudi or a Gulf Arab?

سعدان *sa^{c}daan* p. سعادين *sa^{c}aadiin* 1. monkey. فيه سعادين في حديقة الحيوان في الدوحة *fii sa^{c}aadiin fi ḥadiigat l-ḥayawaan fi d-dooḥa.* There are monkeys in the zoo in Doha. 2. ape.

أسعد *'as^{c}ad* (elat.) 1. (with من *min*) happier than. 2. (with foll. n.) the happiest.

مساعدة *musaa^{c}ada* p. *-aat* help, assistance. البنك قدم لي مساعدة مالية *l-bank gaddam-li musaa^{c}ada maaliyya.* The bank offered me financial assistance. مساعدات اقتصادية *musaa^{c}adaat 'igtiṣaadiyya* economic aid.

ساعد *saa^{c}id* p. سواعد *sawaa^{c}id* 1. forearm. 2. hilt (of a sword). ساعد السيف *saa^{c}id s-seef* the hilt of a sword.

مساعد *msaa^{c}id* III (act. part. from III ساعد *saa^{c}ad*) 1. having helped s.o. هو مساعدني أمس *huwa msaa^{c}idni 'ams.* He helped me yesterday. 2. helper, assistant. مساعد المدير *msaa^{c}id l-mudiir* the assistant to the director.

س ع ر *s^{c}r*

سعر *sa^{cc}ar* II to price, set a price on s.th. الحكومة سعرت الشكر والعيش والبيض *li-ḥkuuma sa^{cc}arat š-šakaar w-l-^{c}eeš w-l-beeḍ.* The government has fixed the price of sugar, rice and eggs.

سعر *si^{c}ir* p. أسعار *'as^{c}aar* price. كم سعر الطماط؟ *čam si^{c}ir ṭ-ṭamaaṭ?* What is the price of tomatoes? سعر الحكومة *si^{c}ir l-ḥukuuma* the price set by the government.

س ع ف *s^{c}f*

أسعف *'as^{c}af* IV 1. to help, aid, assist. جا بوقته وأسعفني *yaa b-wagta w-'as^{c}afni.* He came at the right moment and helped me. 2. to give medical assistance. طاح على الأرض. خذوه العيادة وأسعفوه *ṭaaḥ ^{c}ala l-'arḍ. xaðoo l-^{c}iyaada w-'as^{c}afoo.* He fell to the ground. They took him to the clinic and rendered medical service to him.

إسعاف *'is^{c}aaf* (v.n.) 1. aid, relief, help. 2. medical assistance. سيارة الإسعاف *sayyaarat l-'is^{c}aaf* the ambulance. إسعاف أولي *'is^{c}aaf 'awwali,* إسعافات أولية *'is^{c}aafaat 'awwaliyya* first aid.

سعف *sa^{c}af* (coll.) branches or stalks (esp. of palm trees). s. سعفة *s^{c}ifa.*

س ع و *s^{c}w*

سعوة *s^{c}awa* p. *-aat* yellow wagtail (bird).

س ع ي *s^{c}y*

سعى *sa^{c}a (يسعى yis^{c}a)* to work, endeavor, try. سعى لي في البلدية بس ما حصلت الوظيفة *sa^{c}aa-li fi l-baladiyya* *bass ma ḥaṣṣalt l-waðiifa.* He tried for me in the municipality but I didn't get the job. الإنسان لازم يسعى زين *l-'insaan laazim yisᶜa zeen.* People should strive hard. يسعى لك بالقتل *yisᶜaa-lak b-l-gatil.* He's trying to have you killed.

ساعي *saaᶜi* (act. part.) p. سعاة *suᶜaa* messenger, delivery boy. ساعي البريد *saaᶜi l-bariid* mail carrier.

س ف ر *sfr*

سفر *saffar* II 1. to send on a journey, send away. في الصيف هني الناس يسفرون عوايلهم *fi ṣ-ṣeef hni n-naas ysaffruun ᶜawaayilhum.* In the summer here people send their families away. 2. to deport, expel. الحكومة سفرت أجانب واجدين *li-ḥkuuma saffarat 'ayaanib waaydiin.* The government expelled many foreigners. سفروه لانه ما عنده إقامة *saffaroo linna ma ᶜinda 'igaama.* They deported him because he didn't have a residence permit.

سافر *saafar* III 1. to travel, take a trip. سافر بالسيارة *saafar b-s-sayyaara.* He traveled by car. سافرت بروحي *saafart b-ruuḥi.* I traveled alone. رايح أسافر لندن هذا الصيف *raayiḥ 'asaafir landan haaða ṣ-ṣeef.* I am going to travel to London this summer. 2. to leave, depart. الممثلين رايحين يسافرون باكر *l-mumaθθliin raayḥiin ysaafruun baačir.* The representatives are going to leave tomorrow. شفته قبل ما سافر *čifta gabil-ma saafar.* I saw him before he left.

سفر *safar* (v.n.) traveling, travel. شركة سفر *šarikat safar* travel company.

سفرة *safra* (n. of inst.) p. *-aat* 1. trip, journey, tour.

سفرة *sufra* p. سفر *sufar* mat on which food is put. حضري السفرة *ḥaððri s-sufra.* Set the table.

سفير *safiir* p. سفرا *sufara.* ambassador. السفير الأمريكي *s-safiir l-'amriiki* the American ambassador. السفرا جاوا وسلموا على الشيخ *s-sufara yaw w-sallamaw ᶜala š-šeex.* The ambassadors came and greeted the Shaikh.

سفور *sufuur* 1. unveiling, uncovering the face of a woman. 2. with the face uncovered, without a veil. البنت لين كبرت لازم ما تطلع سفور *l-bint leen kubrat laazim ma tiṭlaᶜ sufuur.* When a girl is older, she mustn't go around unveiled.

سفارة *safaara* p. *-aat* embassy. ممكن تقول لي وين السفارة الأمريكانية؟ *mumkin tgul-li ween s-safaara l-'amrikaan-iyya?* Will you please tell me where the American embassy is?

سافرة *saafra* (f.) p. *-aat* unveiled, wearing no veil. سافرة، ما تتحجب *saafra, ma titḥajjab.* She goes unveiled; she doesn't wear a veil.

مسافر *msaafir* (act. part. from III سافر *saafar*) 1. away, out of town. وين سالم؟ مسافر *ween saalim? msaafir.* Where is Salim? He's out of town. 2. traveling, going on a trip. متى مسافر حق أمريكا؟ *mita msaafir ḥagg 'amriika?* When are you traveling to America? 3. (as noun p. *-iin*) traveler.

4. passenger.

س ف ر ج ل *sfrjl*

سفرجل *safarjal* (coll.) quinces. s. *-a.*

س ف ل *sfl*

سافل *saafil* p. سفلا *sufala* 1. lowly, mean, despicable. 2. despicable person.

س ف ن *sfn*

سفينة *safiina* p. سفن *sufun* ship, boat. تقدر تسافر من هني إلى الهند بالسفينة *tigdar tsaafir min hni 'ila l-hind b-s-safiina.* You can travel from here to India by ship. النوخذه حق السفينة *n-nooxaða ḥagg s-safiina* the ship captain.

س ف ن ج *sfnj*

سفنج *sfanj* (coll.) sponges. s. *-a.*

س ف ه *sfh*

سفيه *safiih* p. سفها *sufaha* 1. foolish, silly. 2. impudent, shameless.

سفاهة *safaaha* (v.n.) 1. foolishness, stupidity. 2. impudence, shamelessness.

س گ ط *sgṭ* See under **ص گ ط** *ṣgṭ.*

س گ ف *sgf*

سقف *saggaf* II to provide with a roof or ceiling. باكر انشاالله نسقف البيت *baačir nṣaaḷḷa nsaggif l-beet.* Tomorrow, God willing, we will roof the house.

سقف *sagf* p. سقوف *sguuf* roof of a house or a building. سقف البيت طاح من المطر *safg l-beet ṭaaḥ min l-muṭar.* The roof of the house fell down because of the rain.

س گ م *sgm*

سقم *saggam* II to pay money to pearl divers in advance. اللي يسقم هو النوخذه *'illi ysaggim huwa n-nooxaða.* The one who pays money in advance to pearl divers is the ship captain.

تسقام *tisgaam* money paid in advance by a ship captain.

س گ ي *sgy*

سقى *siga* (يسقي *yisgi*) 1. to water, provide water for. هني في القيظ يسقون الشجر كل يوم *hini fi l-geeḍ yisguun š-šiyar kill yoom.* Here, in the summer, they water trees every day. كنت ظميان وحرمتي سقتني *čint ḍamyaan w-ḥurumti sigatni.* I was very thirsty and my wife gave me water to drink. رحنا الفندق ورفيقي سقاني بيرة *riḥna l-fundug w-rifiiji sigaani biira.* We went to the hotel and my friend treated me to a beer.

س ك ت *skt*

سكت *sikat* (يسكت *yaskit*) 1. to be or become silent. اسكت! ما تعرف *'iskit! ma t*ᶜ*arf.* Hush! Shut up! You don't know. اسكت، ترى يسمعك المدير *'iskit, tara yisma*ᶜ*ak l-mudiir.* Shut up! The director will probably hear you. عقبه سكت وما قال شي ᶜ*ugba sikat w-ma gaal šayy.* Later on, he became silent and said nothing. 2. to quiet down, calm down. لين دش التنديل كل الكولية سكتوا *leen dašš t-tindeel kill l-kuuliyya siktaw.* When the foreman entered, all the coolies quieted down. اهو اللي ضربك. ليش سكت له؟ *'uhu lli ḍarabk. leeš sikatt-la?* He is the one who hit you. Why did you take it from him?

سكت *sakkat* II to silence, quiet, calm. الأم سكتت الجاهل بالرضاعة *l-'umm sakkatat l-yaahil b-r-raḍḍaaᶜa.* The mother quieted the child with the nursing bottle. ويش ها الضجة؟ روحي سكتي العيال! *weeš haḍ-ḍajja? ruuḥi sakkti li-ᶜyaaḷ!* What's this noise? Go silence the kids.

سكتة *sakta* (n. of inst.) p. *-aat* silence, quiet. سكتة قلبية *sakta gaḷbiyya* heart failure.

سكوت *sukuut* (v.n. from سكت *sikat*) silence, quiet. (prov.) إن كان الكلام من فضة، السكوت من ذهب *'in čaan l-kalaam min fiḍḍa, s-sukuut min ðahab.* Speech is silver; silence is golden.

س ك ر *skr*

سكر *sikar* (يسكر *yiskar*) 1. to get drunk, become intoxicated. بعض الجماعة يسكرون وبيركبون سيايير *baᶜḍ l-jamaaᶜa b-yiskaruun w-byirkabuun siyaayiir.* Some people get drunk and drive cars. سكر وقام يخربط في حكيه *sikar w-gaam yxarbiṭ fi ḥačya.* He got drunk and his speech became muddled. 2. to drink liquor. صحته تدهورت لانه يسكر *ṣiḥḥata tadahwarat linna yiskar.* His health deteriorated because he drinks. يروحون الفندق ويسكرون كل يوم خميس في الليل *yruuḥuun l-fundug w-yiskaruun kill yoom xamiis fi l-leel.* They go to the hotel and drink every Thursday night.

سكر *sakkar* II to make drunk, intoxicate. خذوني، سكروني، وباقوا فلوسي *xaðooni, sakkarooni, w-baagaw fluusi.* They took me, got me drunk, and stole my money.

سكر *sikir* (v.n. from سكر *sikar*) drunkenness, drinking. السكر حرام في الإسلام *s-sikir ḥaraam fi l-'islaam.* Drinking is unlawful in Islam. معظم حوادث السيايير من السكر *muᶜḍam ḥawaadiθ s-siyaayiir min s-sikir.* Most car accidents are due to drunkenness.

سكرة *sakra* (n. of inst.) p. *-aat* instance of drunkenness, drinking spree. (prov.) راحت السكرة وجات الفكرة *raaḥat s-sakra w-yat l-fakra.* (lit., "Drunkenness has gone and careful thinking has come.").

سكران *sakraan* p. سكارى *skaara, -iin* 1. drunk, intoxicated. 2. intoxicated person.

مسكر *muskir* p. *-aat* 1. alcoholic beverage, intoxicating liquor. 2. (adj.) البيرة موب مسكرة مثل الوسكي *l-biira muub muskira miθil l-wiski.* Beer is not as intoxicating as whiskey.

س ك ر ت ي ر *skrtyr*

سكرتير *sikirteer* p. *-iyya, -iin* male secretary. عندي موعد وايا السكرتير باكر *ᶜindi mawᶜid wiyya s-sikirteer baačir.* I have an appointment with the secretary tomorrow. يشتغل سكرتير *yištaġil sikirteer.* He works as a secretary.

س ك ن [1] *skn*

سكن *sikan* (يسكن *yiskin*) 1. to dwell, live (in a place), reside. سكنت في هذا البيت خمس سنين *sikant fi haaða l-beet xams siniin.* I have lived in this house for five years. أخوه يسكن في دبي *'uxuu yiskin fi dbayy.* His brother lives in

Dubai. 2. to subside, calm, become still. شربت الدوا وعقب نص ساعة الوجـع سـكن *šribt d-duwa w-ᶜugub nuṣṣ saaᶜa l-wujaᶜ sikan.* I took the medicine, and the pain subsided after half an hour.

سـكن *sakkan* II 1. to lodge, provide living quarters for s.o. الحكومة سكنت العمـــال في بيـــوت شـــعبية *li-ḥkuuma sakkanat l-ᶜummaal fi byuut šaᶜbiyya.* The government settled the workers in low income housing. 2. to calm, alleviate, soothe. الدوا اللي شربته يسكن الوجـع *d-duwa lli šribta ysakkin l-wajaᶜ.* The medicine I took alleviates pain.

انسكن *nsikan* VII to be lived in, inhabited. هذا البيت ما ينسكن فيه *haaða l-beet ma yinsikin fii.* This house cannot be lived in.

مسـكن *maskan* p. مسـاكن *masaakin* home, residence.

إسكان *'iskaan* 1. settling. مشاريع إسكان *mašaariiᶜ 'iskaan* settling projects, housing projects. 2. housing. وزارة الإسـكان *wazaarat l-'iskaan* the ministry of housing.

سـاكن *saakin* (act. part. from سـكن *sikan*) 1. living, residing, dwelling. آنـا سـاكن هنـاك ذالحـين *'aana saakin hnaak ðalḥiin.* I am living there now. 2. (p. سـكان *sikkaan*) dweller, inhabitant, resident. سـكان هـا المنطقـة كلهـم بلـوش *sikkaan hal-manṭiga killhum bluuš.* The inhabitants of this region are all Baluchis. 3. (p. only) population. سكان الإمـارات أكـثر مـن مليونـين *sikkaan l-'imaaraat 'akθar min malyooneen.* The population of the U.A.E. is more than two million. 4. calm, still, motionless. الريـح سـاكن ذالحـين *r-riiḥ saakin ðalḥiin.* The wind is calm now.

مسـكون *maskuun* (p.p. from سـكن *sikan*) 1. inhabited, populated. 2. haunted. هـا المكـان مسـكون. فيـه جـن *hal-mukaan maskuun. fii jinn.* This place is haunted; there are *jinn*s in it.

مسـكن *musakkin* (act. part. from II سـكن *sakkan*) 1. (p. *-iin*) pacifier, calmer, soother. 2. (p. *-aat*) tranquilizer, sedative.

س ك ن ٢ *skn*

سـكين *sikkiin* = *siččiin.* See under **س چ ن** *sčn.*

س ل ب *slb*

سـلبي *salbi* 1. having a negative attitude. لا تدير له بال. هو سلبـي دايمـاً *la ddiir-la baal. huwa salbi daayman.* Don't listen to him. He always has a negative attitude. 2. passive. دفـاع سلبـي *difaaᶜ salbi* passive resistance.

أسـلوب *'usluub* p. أساليب *'asaaliib* 1. way, method, procedure. 2. manner, style, fashion.

س ل ح *slḥ*

سـلح *sallaḥ* II 1. to arm, provide with weapons. سـلحنا جيشـنا بأسـلحة حديثـة *sallaḥna jeešna b-'asliḥa ḥadiiθa.* We have equipped our army with modern weapons. 2. to reinforce, strengthen. سلحنا الساس بالسـميت والحديـد *sallaḥna s-saas b-s-smiit w-l-ḥadiid.* We reinforced the foundation with cement and iron.

تسلح *tsallaḥ* V 1. to arm oneself. تسلحنا ورحنا القنص *tsallaḥna w-riḥna l-ganaṣ.* We armed ourselves and went hunting. 2. to be armed, be provided with weapons. جيشنا تسلح بأسلحة حديثة *jeešna tsallaḥ b-'asliḥa ḥadiiθa.* Our army was provided with modern weapons.

سلاح *silaaḥ* p. أسلحة *'asliḥa* weapons, armor. سلاح الجو *silaaḥ l-jaww* the air force. العرب ما عندهم سلاح قوي *l-ᶜarab ma ᶜindahum silaaḥ gawi.* The Arabs don't have powerful weapons. سلم سلاحه *sallam silaaḥa.* He laid down his weapons. He surrendered.

تسليح *tasliiḥ* (v.n. from II سلح *sallaḥ*) arming, providing with weapons.

مسلح *musallaḥ* (p.p. from II سلح *sallaḥ*) 1. armored. سيارة مسلحة *sayyaara musallaḥa* armored car. 2. armed. جيشنا مسلح زين *jeešna musallaḥ zeen.* Our army has been well-armed. 3. reinforced, armored. القوات المسلحة *l-ġuwwaat l-musallaḥa* the armed forces. سميت مسلح *smiit musallaḥ* reinforced concrete.

س ل خ *slx*

سلخ *silax* (يسلخ *yislax*) 1. to skin (an animal). اشترينا جدي على العيد وسلخناه. *štireena yidi ᶜala l-ᶜiid w-silaxnaa.* We bought a young billy goat for the feast and skinned it.

انسلخ *nsilax* VII to be skinned. جديان وخرفان واجدين ينذبحون يوم العيد *yidyaan w-xirfaan waaydiin yinðibḥuun yoom l-ᶜiid.* Many billy goats and lambs are killed and skinned on the day of the feast.

سلخ *salx* (v.n. from سلخ *silax*) skinning (an animal).

مسلخ *maslax* p. مسالخ *masaalix* slaughterhouse.

س ل ط *slṭ* See under ص ل ط *ṣlṭ*.

س ل ع *slᶜ*

سلعة *silᶜa* p. سلع *silaᶜ* commodity, commercial article.

س ل ف *slf*

سلف *sallaf* II to lend (money to s.o.), loan, advance. أي نعم أسلفك فلوس. ليش ما أسلفك؟ *'ii naᶜam 'asallifk fluus. leeš ma 'asallifk?* Yes, indeed, I will lend you some money. Why wouldn't I lend it to you? سلفني فلوس! أبغى أروح أعرس *sallifni fluus! 'abġa 'aruuḥ 'aᶜarris.* Lend me some money. I want to go get married. البنك العقاري يسلف فلوس حق المواطنين بس *l-bank l-ᶜaġaari ysallif fluus ḥagg li-mwaaṭniin bass.* The real-estate bank loans money only to citizens. البنك اللي أشتغل فيه يسلف فلوس حق موظفينه *l-bank illi 'aštaġil fii ysallif fluus ḥagg mwaððafiina.* The bank where I work advances loans to its employees.

تسلف *tsallaf* V to borrow (money), to get a loan. تسلف نص مليون درهم من البنك العقاري وبنى دكاكين *ssallaf nuṣṣ malyoon dirhim min l-bank l-ᶜaġaari w-bina dikaakiin.* He borrowed half a million dirhams from the real-estate bank and built stores.

سلف *salaf* 1. advance payment (originally paid to a sailor), money borrowed. عطيته ميتين درهم سلف *ᶜaṭeeta miiteen dirhim salaf.* I gave him an advance of two hundred dirhams. I loaned him two hundred dirhams. 2. ancestors, forefathers. الخلف والسلف *l-xalaf w-s-salaf* our successors and forefathers.

س ل گ *slg*

سلق *silag* (يسلق *yuslug)* to boil, cook in boiling water. سلق بيضتين وتريقهم *silag beeđteen w-trayyaghum.* He boiled two eggs and had them for breakfast.

سلق *salg* (v.n.) boiling. سلق البيض *salg l-beeđ* the boiling of eggs.

سلوقي *saluugi* (common var. *suluugi*) p. سلق *salag* saluki (Asiatic or African breed of a hunting dog similar to the greyhound).

مسلوق *masluug* (p.p. from سلق *silag*) boiled, cooked in water. بيض مسلوق *beeđ masluug* boiled eggs. لحم مسلوق *laḥam masluug* boiled meat.

س ل ك *slk*

سلك *silak (*يسلك *yusluk)* 1. to behave oneself. ما يسلك سلوك زين *ma yusluk suluuk zeen.* He doesn't behave well. 2. be on good terms, get along with. ما يسلك وايا الموظفين في الدايرة *ma yusluk wiyya li-mwađđafiin fi d-daayra.* He is not on good terms with the employees in the department. ما يسلك زين وايا والدينه *ma yusluk zeen wiyya waaldeena.* He's not getting along well with his parents.

سلك *sallak* II 1. *sallak* = سلك *silak.* يسلك نفسه زين وايا الموظفين *ysallik nafsa zeen wiyya li-mwađđafiin.* He is on good terms with the employees. 2. to unclog sewers or drains. جبنا واحد فيتر يسلك البالوعة *yibna waaḥid feetir ysallik l-baaluu^c^a.* We brought a certain pipe fitter to unclog the sewer. فيه دختر هني يسلك مجاري البول *fii daxtar hini ysallik majaari l-bool.* There's a doctor here who opens clogged urethra.

سلك *silk* p. أسلاك *'aslaak* 1. wire (واير *waayir* p. *-aat* is more common. See also under و ي ر *wyr*). 2. (only s.) corps. السلك الدبلوماسي *s-silk d-diblomaasi* the diplomatic corps. سلك التعليم *silk t-ta^c^liim* the teaching profession.

لاسلكي *laa-silki* wireless.

سلوك *suluuk* behavior, manners. حسن السلوك *ḥasan s-suluuk* of good behavior. شهادة حسن السلوك *šahaadat ḥusun suluuk* certificate of good behavior.

مسلك *maslak* p. مسالك *masaalik* passage, course. مسالك البول *masaalik l-bool* the urinary passages (anat.).

تسليك *tasliik* (v.n. from II سلك *sallak*) unclogging, clearing. تسليك البواليع *tasliik l-buwaalii^c^* the unclogging of sewers.

مسلك *msallik* p. *-iin* one who unclogs. مسلك البواليع *msallik l-buwaali^c^* one who unclogs sewers. مسلك مجاري البول *msallik majaari l-bool* one (a doctor) whose specialization is to open clogged urinary passages or urethra.

س ل ل *sll*

تسلل *tsallal* V to infiltrate, enter. فيه ناس يتسللون إلى الإمارات من إيران *fii naas* *yitsallaluun 'ila l-'imaaraat min 'iiraan.* There are people who infiltrate to the U.A.E. from Iran.

انسل *nsall* VII to catch tuberculosis, become consumptive. انسل لين كان صغير *nsall leen čaan ṣaġiir.* He got tuberculosis when he was young.

استل *stall* VIII to draw, unsheathe. العيالة يستلون سيوفهم ويرقصون *l-ᶜayyaala yistalluun syuuffum w-yargiṣuun.* Male dancers draw their swords and dance.

سل *sill* tuberculosis, consumption.

سلة *salla* p. سلال *slaal, -aat* basket. كرة السلة *kurat s-salla* basketball. سلة المهملات *sallat l-muhmalaat* waste basket.

مسلة *masalla* p. *-aat* 1. obelisk. 2. large needle.

تسلل *tasallul* (v.n. from V تسلل *tasallal*) infiltration.

مسلول *masluul* 1. drawn, unsheathed (sword). 2. infected with tuberculosis. 3. person having tuberculosis.

س ل م *slm*

سلم *silim* (يسلم *yislam*) 1. to be safe, secure, unharmed. حصل دعمة لكن الحمد لله سلمنا *ḥaṣal daᶜma laakin l-ḥamdu li-llaah slimna.* There was a car accident, but we were all safe, thanks to God. 2. (with من *min*) to escape from, get away from. سلمنا من الموت *slimna min l-moot.* We escaped death. سلم من الخطر *silim min l-xaṭar.* He escaped from danger. 3. (with من *min*) to pass, get by. لو بس يسلم من الرياضيات، كان يترفع *loo bass yislam min r-riyaaḍiyyaat, čaan yitraffaᶜ.* If he only passes mathematics, he will be promoted. فكر انه رايح يسلم من سؤالات المدرس *fakkar 'inna raayiḥ yislam min su'aalaat l-mudarris.* He thought that he was going to get by without answering the teacher's questions.

سلم *sallam* II 1. (with على *ᶜala*) to greet, salute s.o. جا وسلم علينا *ya w-sallam ᶜaleena.* He came and greeted us. مر وما سلم علينا *marr w-ma sallam ᶜaleena.* He passed by and didn't say hello to us. سلم على أخوك في الخط *sallim ᶜala 'uxuuk fi l-xaṭṭ.* Send my regards to your brother in the letter. جيت أسلم عليكم. أسافر باكر انشاالله *yiit 'asallim ᶜaleekum. 'asaafir baačir nšaaḷḷa.* I came to say good-bye to you. I am leaving tomorrow, God willing. 2. to protect from harm, keep safe. الله يسلمك *'aḷḷa ysallimk* (reply to مع السلامة *maᶜ s-salaama* or كيف حالك؟ *čeef ḥaalak?*) God protect you. الله سلمني. كان طحت على الأرض وتعورت *aḷḷa sallamni. čaan ṭiḥt ᶜala l-'arḍ w-tᶜawwart.* God saved me. I would have fallen to the ground and got hurt. الله يسلمه؛ لحيةٍ غانمة. يحب يساعد كل واحد *'aḷḷa ysallma; liḥyatin ġaanma. yḥibb ysaaᶜid kill waaḥid.* God bless him; he's a real nice guy. He likes to help everyone. 3. to turn over, hand over, surrender. سلمت كل التقارير إلى المدير *sallamt kill t-tagaariir 'ila l-mudiir.* I turned all the reports over to the manager. المدرس سلمنا الكتب الجديدة *l-mudarris sallamna l-kutub l-yidiida.* The teacher handed the new books over to us. سلم أمرك لله! *sallim 'amrak li-llaah!* Surrender your fate to God! Resign yourself to the will of God. سلم نفسه للشرطة *sallam nafsa l-š-širṭa.* He gave himself up to the police. 4. to deliver, hand over, give s.th. to s.o. سلمني الخط اللي جا من ولدي *sallamni l-xaṭṭ illi ya min wlidi.* He delivered to me the letter that came from my son. أجرت شقة والمؤجر سلمني المفتـــــاح *'ajjart šigga w-l-mu'ajjir sallamni l-miftaaḥ.* I rented an apartment and the landlord gave me the key. ســـلمني المســـؤولية *sallamni l-mas'uuliyya.* He gave me the responsibility. 5. to surrender, lay down one's arms. خمسين جنـــدي ســـلموا في النهايـــــة *xamsiin jindi sallamaw fi n-nihaaya.* Fifty soldiers surrendered at the end.

أسلم *'aslam* IV to become a Muslim, embrace Islam. إذا تبـــي تسلم، مـــاحد يجبرك *'iða tabi tislim, maḥḥad yijbirk.* If you want to become a Muslim, no one forces you.

تسلم *tsallam* V 1. to receive, obtain, get. تسلمت خط من أبوي أمس *tsallamt xaṭṭ min 'ubuuy 'ams.* I received a letter from my father yesterday. 2. to take over, take possession of. تسلم إدارة الشغل *tsallam 'idaarat š-šuġul.* He took over the work management. شو تسلمت منـــه؟ *šu tsallamt minna?* What did you take over from him?

استلم *stilam* VIII = تسلم *tsallam* V.

استســـــلم *staslam* X to submit, yield, give in. أقنعني واستسلمت لـــــه *'agnaᶜni w-staslamt-la.* He convinced me and I gave in to him.

ســـلمي *silmi* peaceful. مظاهرة سلمية *muðaahara silmiyya* peaceful demonstration.

سلام *salaam* 1. peace, peacefulness. ما فيـــــه ســـــلام في العـــالم *ma fii salaam fi l-ᶜaalam.* There's no peace in the world. السلام العالمي *s-salaam l-ᶜaalami* world peace. سلام الله عليهم؛ رجـــاجيل زينين! *salaam aḷḷa ᶜaleehum; rayaayiil zeeniin!* God's peace on them; they are good men! 2. security, safety. السلام عليكــــــم! *'as-salaamu ᶜaleekum!* سلام عليكــــــم! *salaamu ᶜaleekum!* Peace be with you! (standard greeting). 3. (p. *-aat*) greeting, salutation. بعثت له ســـــــلامي *biᶜaθt-la salaami.* I sent him my regards. ليش ما ضربت ســـــلام حـــق الضابط لين مـــــر؟ *leeš ma ðirabt salaam ḥagg ð-ðaabiṭ leen marr?* Why didn't you give a salute to the officer when he passed by? 4. (national) anthem. السلام الجمــــــهوري *s-salaam l-jamhuuri* the national anthem of the republic. الســـــلام الأمــــيري *s-salaam l-'amiiri* the national anthem of an emirate. السلام الملكـــــي *s-salaam l-malaki* the royal national anthem.

ســـلامة *salaama* 1. safety, security. الحمدلله علـــــى الســـــلامة *l-ḥamdilla ᶜala s-salaama!* Welcome back! Thank goodness you are all right! مـــع الســـــــلامة *maᶜ s-salaama.* Good-bye (response: الله يسلمك! *aḷḷa ysallimk!* or ســــلمك الله! *sallamk aḷḷa!*) 2. well-being, welfare. ســـلامتك *salaamatk!* (said in response to a question, such as, Do you need anything?) Thanks for asking. I don't need anything. (also said to a person wishing him a speedy recovery). 3. soundness, flawlessness.

سلامة الصحة *salaamat ṣ-ṣiḥḥa* good, sound health. سلامة النية *salaamat n-niyya* good faith, sincerity. لا تواخذه. قالها بسلامة نية *la twaaxða. gaalha b-salaamat niyya.* Don't blame him. He said it in good faith. لازم نتأكد من سلامة البلد من المخدرات *laazim nit'akkad min salaamat l-balad min l-muxaddaraat.* He must make sure that the country is free of drugs.

سليم *saliim* 1. safe, secure. أماكن سليمة *'amaakin saliima* safe places. 2. sound, unhurt, undamaged. (prov.) العقل السليم في الجسم السليم *l-ᶜagl s-saliim fi l-jism s-saliim.* A sound mind in a sound body. بضاعة سليمة *biðaaᶜa saliima* undamaged goods. 3. faultless, flawless. ذوق سليم *ðoog saliim* good taste. سليم النية *saliim n-niyya* sincere, good-natured.

أسلم *'aslam* (elat.) 1. (with من *min*) safer than, more secure than, etc. 2. (with foll. n.) the safest, the most secure, etc.

سليمان *sulaymaan* Solomon. سليمان الحكيم *sulaymaan l-ḥakiim* Solomon the Wise.

إسلام *'islaam* (v.n. from IV أسلم *'aslam*) submission, resignation (to the will of God). الإسلام *l-'islaam* Islam, the religion of Islam.

إسلامي *'islaami* Islamic. الدين الإسلامي *d-diin l-'islaami* the Muslim religion. المركز الإسلامي *l-markaz l-'islaami* the Islamic center.

سالم *saalim* (act. part. from سلم *silim*) 1. safe, secure. (prov.) راعي النصيفة سالم *raaᶜi n-niṣiifa saalim.* Cut your losses and run. Half a loaf is better than none. 2. safe and sound. (prov.) روح بعيد وتعال سالم *ruuḥ bᶜiid w-taᶜaal saalim.* Don't meddle in people's affairs. Keep your nose clean. (lit., "Keep away (from meddling) and come back safe and sound.").

مسالم *musaalim* peaceful, peaceable, peace-loving. شعب مسالم *šaᶜb musaalim* peace-loving nation.

مسلم *muslim* p. *-iin* Muslim. المسلم هو اللي يامن بالإسلام *l-muslim huwa lli yaamin b-l-'islaam.* A Muslim is one who believes in Islam.

س ل ن د ر *slndr*

سلندر *silindar* p. *-aat* cylinder (of a motor).

س ل ي *sly*

تسلية *tasliya* p. تسالي *tasaali* p. *-aat* amusement, entertainment, pastime.

س م ب ل *smbl*

سمبلة = سنبلة *sunbula.* See under **س ن ب ل** *snbl.*

س م چ *smč*

سمك *simač* (coll.) fish. s. سمكة *smiča, simča.* سوق السمك دايما متروس رجاجيل وحريم *suug s-simač daayman matruus rayaayiil w-ḥariim.* The fish market is always full of men and women. (p. أسماك *'asmaak*). من أسماك الخليج الصافي والهامور والربيان *min 'asmaak l-xaliij ṣ-ṣaafi w-l-haamuur w-r-ribyaan.* Among the fishes of the Gulf are rabbitfish, groupers, and shrimp. الحداق هو اللي يصيد سمك *l-ḥaddaag* *huwa lli yṣiid simač.* A fisherman is one who catches fish.

سمكة *smiča* (less common var. *simča*) a fish. (prov.) السمكة الخايسة تخيس السمك كلها *li-simča l-xaaysa txayyis s-simač killa.* A rotten apple spoils the barrel. (lit., "A rotten fish spoils all the fish.").

سماك *sammaač* p. سماميك *simaamiič* fisherman. هالحين سماميك واجدين ماكو *halḥiin simaamiič waaydiin maaku.* Now there aren't many fishermen.

س م ح *smḥ*

سمح *simaḥ (يسمح yismaḥ)* to permit, allow, grant permission. اسمح لي أقول لك إنك رجال موب زين *'ismaḥ-li 'agul-lak 'innak rayyaal muub zeen.* Allow me to tell you that you are not a good man. ما سمح لنا بالدخول *ma simaḥ lana b-d-duxuul.* He didn't allow us to enter. لا سمح الله! *la simaḥ aḷḷaa!* God forbid! اسمح لي بس دقيقة *'ismaḥ-li bass digiiga.* Excuse me for just a minute. ممكن تسمح لي أقول لك شي؟ *mumkin tismaḥ-li 'agul-lak šayy?* Will you please permit me to say something to you? اسمح لي أبطيت *'ismaḥ-li 'abṭeet.* Pardon me. I came late. سمح لنا بالزيارة *simaḥ l-ana b-z-ziyaara.* He gave us permission to visit.

سامح *saamaḥ* III to forgive, pardon. سامحني! هذي آخر مرة *saamiḥni! haaði 'aaxir marra.* Forgive me! This is the last time. باق فلوسهم بس سامحوه *baag fluussum bass saamḥoo.* He stole their money, but they forgave him.

تسامح *tsaamaḥ* V to forgive or pardon each other, practice mutual tolerance. هذيل جهال: يتهاوشون وبعدين يتسامحون *haðeel yihhaal: yithaawšuun w-ba*ᶜ*deen yissaamḥuun.* These are children: they fight with each other and later on they forgive each other.

سماح *samaaḥ* (v.n. from سمح *simaḥ*) 1. forgiveness, pardon, tolerance. آنا أخطيت وأطلب منك السماح *'aana 'axṭeet w-'aṭlub minnak s-samaaḥ.* I have made a mistake, and I ask you for forgiveness. 2. permission. السماح بالزيارة *s-samaaḥ b-z-ziyaara* permission to visit.

سماحة *samaaḥa* as in, e.g., سماحة المفتي *samaaḥat l-mufti* His Eminence the Mufti.

مسموح *masmuuḥ* (p.p. from سمح *simaḥ*) permitted, permissible, allowed. المشي هني موب مسموح *l-maši hini muub masmuuḥ.* Walking here is not allowed. موب مسموح تاكلون في الشارع في رمضان *muub masmuuḥ taakluun fi š-šaari*ᶜ *fi rumðaan.* You are not allowed to eat in the street during Ramadan.

س م د *smd*

سمد *sammad* II to fertilize, manure. يحرثون الأرض وبعدين يسمدونها *yḥarθuun l-'arð w-ba*ᶜ*deen ysammduunha.* They till the land and then they fertilize it.

سماد *samaad* 1. manure, dung. 2. fertilizer. سماد كيماوي *samaad kiimaawi* chemical fertilizer.

س م ر *smr*

اسمر *smarr* IX to turn brown. اسمرت من الشمس *smarrat min š-šams.* She had a tan from the sun. يقعدون في الشمس لاجل يسمرون جلدهم *yigiᶜduun fi š-šams lajil yisammruun jilidhum.* They sit in the sun so their skin will tan.

سمار *samaar* brownness, brown color.

أسمر *'asmar* p. سمر *sumur,* سمرين *sumuriin* dark-skinned, brown-skinned. f. سمرا *samra.* معظم العرب سمر *muᶜđam l-ᶜarab sumur.* Most Arabs are brown-skinned. حرمته بيضا بس بنته سمرا *ḥurumta beeđa bass binta samra.* His wife is white but his daughter is brunette.

س م س م *smsm*

سمسم *simsim* (coll.) sesame.

س م ع *smᶜ*

سمع *simaᶜ* (يسمع *yismaᶜ*) 1. to hear. سمعتهم يتكلمون *simaᶜthum yitkallamuun.* I heard them talking. سمعت الأخبار؟ *simaᶜt l-'axbaar?* Have you heard the news? سمعت من ابنك في لندن؟ *simaᶜt min 'ibnak fi landan?* Have you heard from your son in London? 2. to listen, pay attention, take heed. أنت بس اسمعني *'inta bass ismaᶜni.* You just listen to me. اسمع! نحن دايرة موب بنك *'ismaᶜ! niḥin daayra muub bank.* Listen! We are a department, not a bank. يسمع كلام أبوه *yismaᶜ kalaam 'ubuu.* He heeds his father's words. He does what his father wants.

سمع *sammaᶜ* II 1. to make hear, cause to hear. سمعنا صوتك *sammiᶜna ṣootak.* Let's hear your voice. سمعنا أغاني عربية *sammaᶜna 'aġaani ᶜarabiyya.* He played Arabic songs to us. 2. to recite. سمعنا شي من القرآن *sammiᶜna šayy min l-ġur'aan.* Recite to us something from the Quran. 3. to say (one's lessons). تعالي سمعي دروسك *taᶜaali sammᶜi druusič.* Come say your lessons.

تسمع *tsammaᶜ* V to eavesdrop, listen in on s.th. يتسمع الحكي من ورا الباب *yitsammaᶜ l-ḥači min wara l-baab.* He's eavesdropping from behind the door.

انسمع *nsimaᶜ* VII to be heard. يحكي بشيش؛ صوته ما ينسمع *yihči b-šweeš; soota ma yinsimiᶜ.* He doesn't talk loud; his voice cannot be heard.

استمع *stimaᶜ* VIII (with ل *l-*) to listen closely to, lend one's ear to s.o. or s.th. استمعنا لخطاب الرئيس *stimaᶜna la-xiṭaab r-ra'iis.* We listened closely to the president's speech.

سمعة *sumᶜa* reputation, name, standing. سمعته زينة عند الشيوخ *sumᶜata zeena ᶜind š-šyuux.* He has a good reputation among the Shaikhs.

سماع *samaaᶜ* (v.n. from سمع *simaᶜ*) hearing, listening. سماع الأخبار *samaaᶜ l-'axbaar* hearing the news.

السميع *s-samiiᶜ* the All-hearing (one of the epithets of God). الله السميع العليم *'aḷḷaah s-samiiᶜ l-ᶜal* God, the All-hearing, the Omniscient.

سماعة *sammaaᶜa* p. *-aat* 1. earphone, headset. 2. (telephone) receiver. 3. hearing aid.

سامع *saamiᶜ* (act. part. from سمع *simaᶜ*) 1. having heard s.th. آنا سامع الأخبار *'aana saamiᶜ l-'axbaar.* I have heard the news. أنت سامع الأغنية الجديدة؟ *'inta saami^c l-'uġniyya l-yidiida?* Have you heard the new song? 2. having paid attention to s.o. or s.th., having heeded (someone's words or advice, etc.). أنت سـامع كلامـي والا لا؟ *'inta saami^c kalaami walla la?* Have you paid attention to what I have said or not?

مسموع *masmuu^c* (p.p. from سمع *sima^c*) 1. audible. الصوت موب مسموع *ṣ-ṣoot muub masmuu^c.* The voice is not audible. 2. paid attention to. كلمته مسـموعة *čilmita masmuu^ca.* His word carries weight. His word is law.

مستمع *mustami^c* (act. part. from VIII استمع *stima^c*) p. *-iin* 1. hearer, listener. المستمعين *l-mustami^ciin* the audience. 2. auditor (in a class).

س م م ١ *smm*

اسم *'asim,* etc., see under **س م ي** *smy.*

س م م ٢ *smm*

سم *samm (يسم ysimm)* 1. to poison s.o. or s.th. سموه ومات *sammoo w-maat.* They poisoned him and he died. 2. to poison s.th., put poison in s.th. سمموا الأكل *sammaw l-'akil.* They poisoned the food.

تسمم *tsammam* V to be poisoned. إذا تشرب هذا الحليب تتسمم *'iđa tišrab haađa l-ḥaliib titsammam.* If you drink this milk, you will be poisoned.

سم *samm* p. سموم *smuum* 1. poison. 2. venom.

سام *saamm* (act. part. from سم *samm*) 1. poisonous. 2. venomous. داب سام *daabb saamm,* حنش سام *ḥanaš saamm* venomous, poisonous snake.

مسموم *masmuum* (p.p. from سم *samm*) poisoned, containing poison.

س م ن *smn*

سمن *simman* (coll.) quail. s. *-a* لحم السمن طيب *laḥam s-simman ṭayyib.* Quail meat is delicious.

س م و *smw*

سما *sama* p. سماوات *-waat* heaven, sky. في السما السابع *fi s-sama s-saabi^c* in the seventh heaven. سبع سماوات *sabi^c samaawaat* seven heavens.

سماوي *samaawi* 1. heavenly, celestial. 2. bluish, sky-blue. اشتريت قميص سماوي *štareet gamiiṣ samaawi.* I bought a sky-blue skirt.

سمو *sumuww* (invar.) as in سمو الأمير *sumuww l-'amiir* His Highness the Prince. صاحب السمو الملكي *ṣaaḥib s-sumuww l-malaki* His Royal Highness.

س م ي *smy*

سمى *samma* II 1. to name, designate, call. ها الشي عمري ما شفته. شو تسميه؟ *haš-šayy ^cumri ma čifta. šu tsammii?* I have never seen this thing. What do you call it? 2. to give a name to, call, name. جانا ولد وسميناه محمد *yaana walad w-sammeenaa mḥammad.* We had a boy and we named him Muhammad. سموه باسم أبوه *sammoo b-'asim 'ubuu.* They named him after his father. They gave him his father's name. 3. to say, بسم الله الرحمن الرحيم *"b-ism illaahi r-raḥmaan r-raḥiim"* in the name of God, the Merciful, the Compassionate. قبل ما تاكل لازم تسمي *gabil-ma taakil laazim tsammi.* Before you eat, you have to say grace (by saying, بسم الله *"b-ism illaahi..."*).

تسمى *tsamma* V to be named, called. الولد تسمى باسم جده *l-walad tsamma b-'asim yadda.* The boy was name after his grandfather.

اسم *'asim* p. أسامي *'asaami* 1. name. اسمي سالم *'asmi saalim.* My name is Salim. شو اسمك؟ *šu smak?* What's your name? بالاسم بس *b-l-'asim bass* nominally, in name only. بسم الله *b-ism illaah* in the name of God. حجزت في الفندق باسمك *ḥijazt fi l-fundug b-ismak.* I made a reservation at the hotel in your name. لازم تقدم الطلب باسم الوزير، موب باسمي آنا *laazim tgaddim ṭ-ṭalab b-ism l-waziir, muub b-ismi 'aana.* You have to address the application to the minister, not to me. 2. reputation, standing, prestige. ما له اسم زين في الغرفة التجارية *ma-la 'asim zeen fi l-ġurfa t-tijaariyya.* He doesn't have a good reputation in the chamber of commerce.

س ن ا س ن *snaasn*

سناسين *sanaasiin* (coll.) okra. نحن ما عرفنا السناسين لين إخواننا العرب جاوا *niḥin ma ᶜirafna s-sinaasiin leen 'ixwaanna l-ᶜarab yaw.* We had not known okra before our Arab brothers came.

س ن ب ل *snbl*

سنبلة *sunbula* p. سنابل *sanaabil* ear (of grain).

س ن ت ر *sntrl*

سنترال *santraal* telephone exchange.

س ن ت م ت ر *sntmtr*

سنتيمتر *santimitir* (less common var. سانتي *saanti*) p. *-aat* centimeter.

س ن ج *snj*

سنجة *sinja* p. *-aat, sinaj* bayonet.

س ن ح *snḥ*

سنح *sinaḥ* (يسنح *yisnaḥ)* to present itself, offer itself (to s.o., esp. an opportunity). إذا تسنح لي الفرصة، أمر عليك الليلة *'iða tisnaḥ-li l-furṣa, 'amurr ᶜaleek l-leela.* If I have the opportunity, I will stop by at your place tonight.

س ن د¹ *snd*

سند *sinad* (يسند *yisnid)* to support, provide support for, prop up. إذا ما فيه واحد يسندك، ماحد يسمع لك *'iða ma fii waḥid yisnidak, maḥḥad yismaᶜ-lak.* If there is nobody to support you, no one is going to listen to you. تقدر تسند التاير بحجر *tigdar tisnid t-taayir b-ḥiyar.* You can prop up the tire with a rock.

استند *stinad* VIII 1. lean, recline. استند على المخدة *stinad ᶜala li-mxadda.* He leaned on the pillow. 2. to be based, founded, supported. هذا بس حكي ما يستند على برهان *haaða bass ḥači ma yistinid ᶜala burhaan.* This is mere talk that is not based on proof. 3. (with على *ᶜala*) to rest one's case, have as evidence, use as a basis. لازم تستند على شي ثاني، غير أقوال الشهود *laazim tistinid ᶜala šayy θaani, ġeer 'agwaal š-šuhuud.* You have to have something else as evidence, not only the testimony of the witnesses.

سـنـد *sanad* p. *-aat* 1. support, prop. 2. legal instrument, deed, document.

مسـنـد *masnad* p. مسـانـد *masaanid* cushion, pillow.

س ن د٢ *snd*

السـنـد *s-sind* Sind (province of West Pakistan).

سـنـدي *sindi* p. سـنـادوة *sanaadwa* 1. Sindhi. 2. the Indic language of Sind.

س ن د ر *sndr*

سـنـدر *sandar* (يسندر *ysandir)* to irritate or bother s.o. والله سندرني بكثرة طلباته *wallaahi sandarni b-kaθrat ṭalabaata.* By God, he irritated me with his many requests.

س ن د ن *sndn*

سـنـدان *sindaan* p. سـنـادين *sinaadiin* anvil.

س ن د و ش *sndwš*

سـنـدويش *sandawiiš* p. *-aat* sandwich. كليـت سـندويش بيـض *kaleet sandawiiš beeḍ.* I ate an egg sandwich.

س ن ط و ن *snṭwn*

سـنـطوانة *sinṭwaana* p. *-aat* pillar. المسجد قايم على أربع سـنطوانات *li-msiid gaayim ᶜala 'arbaᶜ sinṭwaanaat.* The mosque rests on four pillars.

س ن گ ي ن *sngyn*

سـنـكين *sangiin* strong, dark, concentrated. شاي سنكين *čaay sangiin* strong tea.

س ن م *snm*

سـنـام *sanaam* p. *-aat* hump (of a camel). فيه بعض البعارين بسنامين *fii baᶜḍ l-baᶜaariin b-sanaameen.* There are some camels with two humps.

س ن ن *snn*

سـن *sann* (يسـن *ysinn)* 1. to sharpen, whet. اخـذ السـكاكين وسـنهم *'ixiδ s-sičaačiin w-sinnhum.* Take the knives and have them sharpened. 2. to enact, introduce, pass. سنوا قانون جديد يمنـع شـرب الخمـر في الفنـادق *sannaw ġaanuun yidiid yimnaᶜ širb l-xamir fi l-fanaadig.* They passed a new law that prohibits drinking liquor in hotels.

سنن *sannan* II 1. to pray the prayer of سـنة *sunna,* which is optional before and/or after the prayer of فرض *farḍ*, which is obligatory. 2. to grow teeth, teethe. الجـاهل سـنن قبـل سـنة *l-yaahil sannan gabil sana.* The child teethed a year ago.

سن *sann* (v.n.) enactment, issuance (of laws) سن القوانين *sann l-ġawaaniin* the passing of laws.

سـن *sinn* p. سنون *snuun,* أسنان *'asnaan* 1. tooth. سـنوني تعورنـي *snuuni tᶜawwirni.* My teeth ache. طبيب أسنان *ṭabiib 'asnaan* dentist. طبيـب الأسـنان شـلع سـني *ṭabiib l-'asnaan čilaᶜ sinni.* The dentist pulled my tooth out. 2. tooth (of a comb, a saw blade, of a gear wheel, etc.) 3. age. كم سنك؟ *čam sinnak?* How old are you? بلغ سن الرشد *bilaġ sinn r-rušd.* He has attained puberty. He came of age. كبـير السـن *čibiir s-siin* old.

سـنة *sunna* 1. customary practice, usage sanctioned by tradition. سنة النبي *sunnat n-nabi* the Sunna of the Prophet (i.e., his sayings and doings, later established as legally binding). 2. optional (as opposed to فرض *farḍ* religious duty). صلاة التراويح سنة، موب فرض *ṣalaat t-taraawiiḥ sunna, muub farḍ.* Prayer during the nights of Ramadan (after the evening prayer) are optional, not obligatory. هذي سنة النبي؛ نمشي عليها *haaði sunnat n-nabi; namši ᶜaleeha.* This is Prophet Muhammad's tradition; we follow it.

سني *sunni* p. سنة *sunna, -yyiin* 1. Sunni (belonging to the orthodox sect of Islam). 2. a Sunni, a Sunnite.

مسن *musinn* old, advanced in years.

مسنن *msannan* (p.p. from II سنن *sannan*) toothed, indented, jagged. سكين مسنن *siččiin msannan* sharp, toothed knife.

سنة *sana* pl. *siniin* year. عمري خمسين سنة *ᶜumri xamsiin sana.* I am fifty years old. سنة هجرية *sana hijriyya* year of the Muslim era, A.H. سنة ميلادية *sana miilaadiyya* year of the Christian era, A.D. سنة القحط *sanat l-gaḥṭ* the year of the drought.

سنوي *sanawi* annual, yearly. زيادة سنوية *ziyaada sanawiyya* annual increment. دخل سنوي *daxil sanawi* annual income.

سنوياً *sanawiyyan* yearly, every year, annually.

س ه ر *shr*

سهر *sihir* (يسهر *yishar*) 1. to stay up at night, stay awake, go without sleep. يسهر ويدرس وما ينام إلا ساعة الصبح *yishar w-yidris w-ma ynaam 'illa saaᶜt ṣ-ṣubḥ.* He stays up at night, studies, and doesn't go to bed except early in the morning. أمس سهرنا سهرة زينة *'ams shirna sahra zeena.* Last night we had a pleasant evening. جاوا يسهرون عندنا *yaw yisharuun ᶜindana.* They came to our place to have a pleasant evening. 2. (with على *ᶜala*) to guard or look after s.o.'s interest. يسهر على مصلحة عياله *yishar ᶜala maṣlaḥat ᶜyaaḷa.* He attends to his kids' interest.

سهرة *sahra* p. *-aat* evening gathering, evening party. سهرة عيد الميلاد *sahrat ᶜiid l-miilaad* the Christmas evening party. سهرة زينة *sahra zeena* pleasant evening gathering.

سهران *sahraan* sleepless, awake.

س ه ل *shl*

سهل *sihil* (يسهل *yishal*) 1. to be or become easy, convenient. لين دفع الفلوس اللي عليه سهلت المسألة *leen difaᶜ li-fluus illi ᶜalee sihlat l-mas'ala.* When he paid the money he owed, the problem became easy. 2. (with على *ᶜala*) to be or become easy for s.o. عقب سنة سهل عليه الشغل *ᶜugub sana sihil ᶜalee š-šuġul.* In a year's time work became easier for him. 3. (imperf. يسهل *yishil*) to purge, relieve of constipation. الدختر عطاني دوا يسهل البطن *d-daxtar ᶜaṭaani duwa yishil l-baṭin.* The doctor gave me medicine that purges the bowels.

سهل *sahhal* II to make easier, to facilitate. ها الإشارة تسهل حركة المرور *hal-'išaara tsahhil ḥarakat l-muruur.* This (traffic) signal makes the flow of traffic easier. النظام الجديد يسهل الشغل واجد *n-niðaam l-yidiid ysahhil š-šuġul* *waayid.* The new system makes work a lot easier.

تساهل *tsaahal* VI to be lenient, tolerant, indulgent. هذا معلم شـديد. ما يتساهل وايا أحد *haaða mu^{c}allim šadiid. ma yitsaahal wiyya 'aḥad.* This teacher is strict. He is not lenient with anybody. هذا البقال ما يتساهل وايـا أي زبـون *haaða l-baggaal ma yitsaahal wiyya 'ayya zibuun.* This grocer is not obliging to any customer.

استسهل *stashal* X to find or consider s.th. easy, deem s.th. easy. الطلاب استسـهلوا الأسـئلة *ṭ-ṭullaab stashalaw l-'as'ila.* The students found the questions easy. لا تستهل القضيـة. ترى فيه مشاكل *la tistashil l-gaḍiyya. tara fii mašaakil.* Don't consider the matter easy. Mind you, there are problems.

سهل *sahil* easy, not difficult, convenient. هـذا الـدرس سـهل *haaða d-dars sahil.* This lesson is easy. سهل انـك تشـوف الشـيخ *sahil 'innak tšuuf š-šeex.* It's easy for you to see the Shaikh.

سهل *sahal* p. سهول *shuul* meadow, plain. فيه سـهول واجـد في راس الخيمـة *fii shuul waayid fi raas l-xeema.* There are many meadows in Ras Al-Khaima.

سهولة *suhuula* (v.n. from سهل *sihil*) ease, easiness, facility, convenience. ما تقدر تجـي بهاالسـهولة اللي تتصورهـا *ma tigdar tiyi b-has-suhuula lli titṣawwarha.* You cannot come as easily as you think. نجـح في الامتحـان بسـهولة *nijaḥ fi li-mtiḥaan b-suhuula.* He passed the examination easily.

سهيل *sheel* canopus (star).

أسهل *'ashal* (elat.) 1. (with من *min*) easier than. هـذا الشـغل أسـهل مـن ذاك *haaða š-šuġul 'ashal min ðaak.* This work is easier than that one. 2. (with foll. n.) the easiest, the most convenient. هذا أسهل درس *haaða 'ashal dars.* This is the easiest lesson.

إسهال *'ishaal* diarrhea.

مسهل *mushil* p. *-aat* laxative, purgative.

س ه م *shm*

ساهم *saaham* III to have a share, to participate, share, take part. ساهمت في بنـك أبـو ظبـي الوطـني *saahamt fi bank 'abu ḍabi l-waṭani.* I had shares in the National Bank of Abu Dhabi. ساهم وايانا في جمع الكتـب *saaham wiyyaana fi jam^c l-kutub.* He participated with us in collecting the books. هـني فيـه نـاس غنيـين واجـد يساهمون بمعظـم روس أمـوال الشركات *hini fii naas ġaniyyiin waayid ysaahmuun b-mu^{c}ḍam ruus 'amwaal š-šarikaat.* Here there are very rich people who contribute most of the capital to the companies.

سهم *sahim* p. أسـهم *'ashim* 1. share, share (of stocks), portion. كم سهم لك في الشـركة؟ *čam sahim lak fi š-šarika?* How many shares do you have in the company? 2. arrow. 3. dart.

مساهم *musaahim* (act. part. from III ساهم *saaham*) p. *-iin* shareholder, stockholder.

س ه و *shw*

سهى *siha* (يسهى *yisha*) 1. to be forgetful, inattentive. كنت قاعد وسهيت ومـا دريت شو اللي صـار *čint gaa^{c}id w-siheet*

ســيئة *sayyi'a* p. *-aat* sin, misdeed, offense.

س و چ *swč*

ســوچ *siwič* p. *-aat* switch. السوچ حق السيارة *s-siwič ḥagg s-sayyaara* the car switch.

س و ح *swḥ*

ساحة *saaḥa* p. *-aat* 1. courtyard, open square. ساحة الــدار *saaḥat d-daar* the house courtyard. 2. open space, field. ســاحة المعركــة *saaḥat l-macraka* the battlefield, battleground. ساحة المدرسة *saaḥat madrasa* school yard. ســاحة الألعــاب *saaḥat l-'alcaab* the sports field.

س و د *swd*

ســود *sawwad* II to blacken, make black, darken. الدخان ســود القرطــاس *d-daxxaan sawwad l-girṭaas.* The smoke made the paper black. سود وجه فــلان *sawwad weeh flaan* to discredit, dishonor, shame s.o. سود الله وجهك! *sawwad aḷḷa weehak!* God shame you! Damn you! سود وجهي قــدام النــاس *sawwad weeyhi jiddaam n-naas.* He made a fool of me in front of the people.

اسود *swadd* IX to be or become black or dark, to turn black or dark. فيه معادن تسود من الرطوبــة *fii macaadin tiswadd min r-rṭuuba.* There are metals that turn dark from humidity. اسود وجهه *swadd weeha.* He was disgraced.

ســواد *sawaad* blackness, darkness. ما يجــي إلا في ســواد الليــل *ma yiyi 'illa fi sawaad l-leel.* He comes only late at night.

w-ma direet šu lli ṣaar. I was sitting down and I was inattentive and I didn't know what was going on. سهيت ومــا خابرتــه *siheet w-ma xaabarta.* I forgot and didn't call him. 2. (with عن *can*) to neglect, forget about, overlook. سهيت عنه *siheet canna.* I forgot about it.

ســهى *sahha* II to cause to forget. قعد واياي يسولف وسهاني عن الدراســة *gicad wiyyaay ysoolif w-sahhaani can d-diraasa.* He sat down to talk with me and made me forget about my studies.

ســهو *sahu* (v.n. from ســهى *siha*) 1. inattentiveness, absent-mindedness. 2. negligence, forgetfulness. 3. oversight.

س و ء *sw'*

ساء *saa'* (يسيء *ysii'*) to act meanly, do harm (to s.o.) ما ادري ليش دايماً يسيء للنــاس *ma dri leeš daayman ysii' lan-naas.* I don't know why he always acts meanly toward people. هو اللي ساء التصرف *huwa lli saa' t-taṣarruf.* He is the one who misbehaved. ساء فهمي *saa' fahmi.* He misunderstood me. الشرطة تسيء معاملة المساجين *š-širṭa tsii' mucaamlat l-masaajiin.* The police mistreat inmates. يسيء الظن بكل واحد *ysii' ð̣-ð̣ann b-kill waaḥid.* He has a low opinion of everyone.

سوء *suu'* (v.n. from ساء *saa'*) evil, ill. سوء الحظ *suu' l-ḥað̣ð̣* bad luck. سوء النية *suu' n-niyya* evil intention. لسوء الحظ *l-suu' l-ḥað̣ð̣* unfortunately. سوء المعاملة *suu' l-mucaamala* mistreatment. سوء الفهم *suu' l-fahim* misunderstanding.

أسـود *'aswad* f. سودا *sooda* p. سود *suud* black, dark. أسـود كلش *'aswad killiš* jetblack. أسـود الوجـه *'aswad l-weeh* disgraced, dishonored.

سـويدة *sweeda* (dim. of سـودا *sooda*) black. (f.) (prov.) سويدة وبايقة *sweeda w-baayga.* Still waters run deep (derog.). (lit., "She is black and she has stolen.").

السودان *s-suudaan* the Sudan.

سـوداني *suudaani* 1. characteristic of the Sudan. فـول سـوداني *fuul suudaani* peanuts. 2. a Sudanese. هو سوداني من الخرطـوم *huwa suudaani min l-xarṭuum.* He is a Sudanese from Khartoum.

مسـودة *miswadda* p. *-aat* rough draft, rough sketch.

س و ر *swr*

سـوار *suwaar* (coll.) beams, deck beams. s. *-a.*

س و ر ي *swry*

سـوريا *suuriyya* Syria. سوريا قريبـة مـن الأردن *suuriyya gariiba min l-'ardun.* Syria is close to Jordan.

سـوري *suuri* 1. characteristic of Syria. جبن سـوري *jibin suuri* Syrian cheese. حلوى سـورية *ḥalwa suuriyya* Syrian sweets. 2. a Syrian. هي سورية من حلب *hiya suuriyya min ḥalab.* She is Syrian from Aleppo.

س و س *sws*

سـوس *sawwas* II 1. to decay, rot, cause to decay (esp. the teeth). الحلوى تسوس السنون *l-ḥalwa tsawwis li-snuun.* Sweets decay teeth. دختر السـنون شلع ضرسي لانـه سـوس *daxtar li-snuun čilaᶜ ḍirsi linna sawwas.* The dentist pulled my tooth out because it was decayed. 2. to be or become worm-eaten. الحطـب سـوس *l-ḥaṭab sawwas.* The wood was decayed.

سـوس *suus* (coll.) 1. woodworms, termites. 2. caterpillars. s. *-a.* السوس كل الحطب *s-suus kal l-ḥaṭab.* Termites have eaten the wood.

س و س ن *swsn*

سوسن *sawsan* lily of the valley.

س و گ *swg*

سـاق *saag (يسـوق ysuug)* 1. to drive, operate (a vehicle). يسوق السيارة بدون بيمـة *ysuug s-sayyaara b-duun biima.* He drives the car without insurance. مـا يعـرف يسـوق لـوري *ma yᶜarf ysuug loori.* He doesn't know how to drive a truck. 2. to force to go. الشرطي ساقه للمحكمـة *š-širṭi saaga lil-maḥkama.* The policeman brought him to court.

تسـوق *tsawwag* V to go shopping. أتسوق يوميـة *'atsawwag yawmiyya.* I go shopping every day.

انسـاق *nsaag* VII to be carried away. انسـاق بعواطفـه *nsaag b-ᶜawaatfa.* He was carried away by his emotions.

سـوق *suug* p. أسـواق *'aswaag* 1. marketplace, bazaar. رحت السـوق *riḥt s-suug.* I went to the marketplace. السـوق الحـرة *s-suug l-ḥurra* the free market. السـوق السـودا *s-suug s-sooda* the black market. سـوق السـمك *suug s-simač* the fish market.

سـواقة *swaaga* (v.n. from سـاق *saag*) (less common var. سـياقة *syaaga*) driving. النجدة يزخون اللي زايد عن قانون

السواقة *n-najda yzixxuun illi zaayid ᶜan ġaanuun s-swaaga.* The police squad catch the speeding motorist.

تسويق *taswiig* marketing, sale (of merchandise). البضاعة تحتاج تسويق *l-biđaaᶜa tiḥtaay taswiig.* The merchandise needs marketing.

سايق *saayig* (common var. سواق *sawwaag*) p. *-iin,* سواق *suwwaag* 1. driver. 2. chauffeur. 3. driver (of animals). سايق الغنم *saayig l-ġanam.* He's driving the sheep and goats.

س و ك *swk*

سوك *sawwak* II to brush the teeth with a chewed twig. فيه ناس يسوكون سنونهم قبل وعقب الصلاة *fii naas ysawwkuun snuunhum gabil w-ᶜugb ṣ-ṣalaa.* There are people who brush their teeth before and after prayer.

مسواك *miswaak* p. مساويك *masaawiik* small chewed stick or twig used for brushing and cleaning teeth, esp. before and after prayer.

س و ل ف *swlf*

سولف *soolaf (*يسولف *ysoolif)* to chat, chatter, carry on idle conversation. قعد جنبي وظل يسولف مدة ساعتين *giᶜad yammi w-đall ysoolif muddat saaᶜteen.* He sat by me and kept on chatting for two hours. ياالله سولف *yaḷḷa soolif.* Come on, talk.

سالفة *saalfa* p. سوالف *suwaalif* story, tale, anecdote. بس قاعدين يسولفون سوالف *bass gaaᶜdin ysoolfuun suwaalif.* They are just telling old stories. المسألة صارت سالفة *l-mas'ala ṣaarat saalfa.* It took a long time. سوالف مكسرة *suwaalif mkassara* bad deeds, such as drinking liquor, chasing women, etc. عليك السالفة *ᶜaleek s-saalfa.* You are at fault. You are wrong.

س و م *swm*

سام *saam (*يسوم *ysuum)* to ask for the price of s.th. سام أسعار الطماط في السوق *saam 'asᶜaar ṭ-ṭamaaṭ fi s-suug.* He asked for the price of tomatoes in the marketplace.

ساوم *saawam* III to haggle, bargain with s.o. السعر محدود. لا تساوم *s-siᶜir maḥduud. la tsaawim.* The price is fixed. Don't haggle. لا تساومني على سعر ها البضاعة *la tsaawimni ᶜala siᶜir hal-biđaaᶜa.* Don't bargain with me over the price of this merchandise.

مساومة *msaawama* (v.n. from III ساوم *saawam*) haggling, bargaining.

س و ي *swy*

يسوى *yiswa* (no perfect form) to be worth, equal to. كم تسوى هذي السيارة؟ *čam tiswa haađi s-sayyaara?* How much is this car worth? ما تسوى شي *ma tiswa šayy.* It's not worth anything.

سوى *sawwa* II 1. to do, perform, commit. شو سويت هناك؟ *šu sawweet hnaak?* What did you do there? تبي الخط. شو رايح تسوي فيه؟ *tabi l-xaṭṭ. šu raayiḥ tsawwi fii?* You want the letter. What are you going to do with it? خذوه المستشفى وسووا له عملية *xaðoo l-mustašfa w-sawwoo-la ᶜamaliyya.* They took him to the hospital and performed an operation on him. سحبوا منه الليسن لانه سوى مخالفة *sḥabaw minna* *l-leesan linna sawwa muxaalafa.* They withdrew his (driving) license because he committed a violation. (prov.) سواها واستوت *sawwaaha w-stawat.* It's too late. Don't cry over spilled milk. (lit., "He has done it and it's done."). 2. to make, produce, manufacture. سوينا عشا واستانسنا *sawweena ^caša w-staanasna.* We made dinner and had a good time. سوى غلطة *sawwa ġalṭa.* He made a mistake. فيه مصانع هني تسوي أشيا من بلاستيك *fii maṣaani^c hini tsawwi 'ašya min blaastiik.* There are factories here that manufacture things made of plastic. (prov.) يسوي من الحبة قبة *ysawwi min l-ḥabba gubba.* He makes a mountain out of a molehill. (lit., "He makes a dome out of a grain."). سوينا حفلة عشا *sawweena ḥaflat ^caša.* We had a dinner party.

ساوى *saawa* III 1. to equal, be equal to, be equivalent to. خمسة في خمسة يساوي خمسة وعشرين *xamsa fi xamsa yswaawi xamsa w-^cišriin.* Five times five equals twenty-five. 2. to settle, smooth over, put in order. ساوينا الخلاف بينهم وخلاص *saaweena l-xilaaf beenhum w-xalaaṣ.* We settled the disagreement between them and that was the end of it. 3. to treat alike, put on the same footing. ما تقدر تساوي بينهم؛ هذا تنديل وذاك حارس *ma tigdar tsaawi beenhum; haaða tindeel w-ðaak ḥaaris.* You can't treat them alike; this one is a foreman and that one is a guard.

تساوى *tsaawa* VI to be equal or similar, equivalent to each other. الناس يتساوون أمام القانون *n-naas yitsaawuun 'amaam l-ġaanuun.* People are equal before the law.

استوى *stawa* VIII 1. to occur, happen. القضا ما بغيناه واستوى *l-gaða ma baġeenaa w-stawa.* Fate is something we didn't want, but it took its course. 2. (with foll. n. or adj.) to become, change into s.th. الماي استوى ثلج *l-maay stawa θalj.* The water became ice. الرطب يستوي زين في آخر القيظ *r-rṭabb yistawi zeen fi 'aaxir l-geeð.* Dates become good at the end of the summer. 3. to ripen, mature. اليح ما استوى بعد *l-yiḥḥ ma stawa ba^cad.* Watermelons haven't ripened yet.

سوية *sawiyya* (p.) equal, alike. في نظري هم سوية *fi naðari hum sawiyya.* In my opinion they are equals. (prov.) ظلمٍ بالسوية عدلٍ بالرعية *ðulmin b-s-sawiyya ^cadlin b-r-ra^ciyya.* Treat people equally. Injustice done equally to all people is preferable to justice for some and injustice for others. (lit., "Injustice to all is justice to everyone.").

تسوية *taswiya* (v.n. from II سوى *sawwa*) 1. leveling, smoothing. لازم تسوي تسوية قبل لا تبني *laazim tsawwi taswiya gabil-la tibni.* You have to have a leveling of the ground before you build. 2. settlement, adjustment (of a dispute). دايرة تسوية الأراضي *daayrat taswiyat l-'araaḍi* the office of land dispute settlement.

مساواة *musaawaa* (v.n. from III ساوى *saawa*) equality, equal rights.

تساوي *tasaawi* (v.n. from VI تساوى *tsaawa*) equality, sameness. بالتساوي *b-t-tasaawi* equally.

استواء *stiwaa'* only in خط الاستواء *xaṭṭ l-'istiwaa'* the equator.

استوائي *stiwaa'i* tropical, equatorial. منطقة استوائية *manṭiga stiwaa'iyya* tropical region.

مستوي *mistawi* (act. part. from VIII استوى *stawa*) 1. having changed into. الماي مستوي ثلج *l-maay mistawi θalj.* The water has changed into ice. 2. having ripened. الرطب مستوي زين *r-rṭabb mistawi zeen.* The dates have ripened.

مستوى *mustawa* level, standard. مستوى الماي في التانكي *mustawa l-maay fi t-taanki* the water level in the reservoir. مستوى البحر *mustawa l-baḥar* sea level. مستوى المعيشة *mustawa l-maᶜiiša* standard of living.

س و ي د *swyd*

السويد *s-sweed* Sweden.

سويدي *sweedi* 1. characteristic of Sweden, Swedish. 2. a Swede.

س و ي س *swys*

السويس *'is-swees* Suez (seaport in Egypt). قناة السويس *ganaat s-swees* the Suez Canal.

س و ي س ر *swysr*

سويسرا *swiisra* Switzerland.

سويسري *swiisri* 1. characteristic of Switzerland. 2. a Swiss.

س ي ب *syb*

سيب *seeb* p. سيوب *syuub* rope-man (in pearling). السيب يمسك الحبل حق الغيص *s-seeb yamsik l-ḥabil ḥagg l-ġeeṣ.* The *seeb* is the one who holds the rope for the diver.

س ي ح *syḥ*

سياحة *siyaaḥa* 1. traveling, touring, tourism. دايرة السياحة *daayrat s-siyaaḥa* the department of tourism. 2. tour, trip.

س ي د *syd*

سيد *seed* p. سيود *syuud* 1. queue, line (esp. of people or vehicles). الزم سيدك! *'ilzam seedak!* Stay in your line! 2. turn. السيد على من ذالحين؟ *s-seed ᶜala man ðalḥiin?* Whose turn is it now?

سيدة *siida* (adv.) straight. روح سيدة لين توصل الدوار الأول *ruuḥ siida leen tooṣal d-dawwaar l-'awwal.* Go straight until you reach the first circle (or roundabout). عند الليت لا تروح سيدة. لف على اليمين *ᶜind l-leet la truuḥ siida. liff ᶜala l-yimiin.* At the (traffic) light don't go straight. Turn right.

سيد *sayyid* p. اسياد *syaad,* سادة *saada* 1. lord, master (as opp. to عبد *ᶜabd* slave, serf). 2. (with the article prefix) السيد *s-sayyid* Mr. السيد حمد *s-sayyid ḥamad.* Mr. Hamad. 3. one of the descendants of Prophet Muhammad. سيدنا *sayyidna* honorific title used before the name of a prophet or a saint in Islam.

سيدة *sayyida* p. *-aat* 1. lady. 2. (with the article prefix) Mrs.

سيادة *siyaada* 1. sovereignty, rule, dominion. 2. title and form of address of a president. سيادة الرئيس *siyaadat r-ra'iis* His Excellency the President.

س ي ر *syr*

سار *saar (يسير ysiir)* 1. to leave, go. خميس موب هني. سار *xamiis muub hini. saar.* Khamis is not here. He has left. سار حق لبنان *saar ḥagg libnaan.* He went to Lebanon. سار من ساعة الصبح *saar min saaᶜat ṣ-ṣubh.* He left early in the morning. 2. to walk. سار وايانا *saar wiyyaana.* He walked with us. 3. (with على *ᶜala*) to follow, pursue, maintain. يسير على ترتيب معين *ysiir ᶜala tartiib muᶜayyan.* He's following a specific arrangement. (prov.) من سار على الدرب وصل *man saar ᶜala d-darb wiṣal.* Where there is a will there is a way. (lit., "He who follows the right path will get there."). 4. to be or become loose, move, have diarrhea. بطني تسير *baṭni tsiir.* I have diarrhea. سارت بطنه مرتين اليوم *saarat baṭna marrateen l-yoom.* He had two bowel movements today.

سير *sayyar* II 1. (with على *ᶜala*) to drop in on, call on. سيرنا على ربعنا ليلة أمس *sayyarna ᶜala rabiᶜna leelat 'ams.* We dropped in on our relatives last night. 2. to order s.o. around, make s.o. do one's bidding. مثل الجاهل. تسيره مثل ما تريد *miθl l-yaahil. tsayyra miθil-ma triid.* He's like a child. She orders him around however she wants.

ساير *saayar* III to put up with s.o., get along with s.o. دايما يلعوزهم بس يسايرونه *daayman ylaᶜwizzum bass ysaayruuna.* He always bothers them, but they put up with him.

سير *seer* p. سيور *syuur* 1. leather string or strap. 2. leather belt. ما أشتري إلا سير جلد *ma 'aštiri 'illa seer yild.* I will buy only a leather belt.

سيرة *siira* 1. trip, travel. توي واصل من سيرتي *tawwi waaṣil min siirti.* I have just arrived from my trip. 2. behavior, conduct. السيرة النبوية *s-siira n-nabawiyya* the biography of Prophet Muhammad.

سيارة *sayyaara* (less common var. موتر *mootar*) p. *-aat,* سياير *siyaayiir.* 1. car, automobile. سافرت بالسيارة *saafart b-s-sayyaara.* I traveled by car. وديت السيارة شيشة البانزين *waddeet s-sayyaara šiišt l-baanziin.* I took the car to the gas station. 2. vehicle. سيارة إسعاف *sayyaarat 'isᶜaaf* ambulance. سيارة أجرة *sayyaarat 'ujra* taxi cab.

مسايرة *msaayara* (v.n. from III ساير *saayar*) showing patience or tolerance toward s.o., putting up with s.o.

س ي ر ك *syrk*

سيرك *seerk* p. *-aat* circus.

س ي س *sys*

سياسة *siyaasa* 1. policy. السياسة الخارجية *s-siyaasa l-xaarijiyya* foreign policy. سياسة أمريكا *siyaasat 'amriika* the policy of the United States. 2. politics, political science. يدرس سياسة *yidris siyaasa.* He is studying political science. 3. diplomacy.

سياسي *siyaasi* 1. political. الوضع السياسي *l-waðᶜ s-siyaasi* the political situation. 2. diplomatic. 3. diplomat, politician.

س ي ط ر *syṭr*

سيطر *sayṭar* see under ص ي ط ر *ṣyṭr.*

س ي ف *syf*

سيف *seef* p. سيوف *syuuf* sword, saber. العيالة يرقصون بالسيف والخنجر *l-ᶜayyaala yarguṣuun b-s-seef w-l-xanyar.* Male dancers dance with swords and daggers.

سيفوه *seefoo* (dim. of سيف *seef*) Seef (male's name). (prov.) هذا سيفوه وهذي ثيابه *haaða seefoo w-haaði θyaaba.* A leopard cannot change its spots (derog.) (lit., "This is Seef and these are his clothes.").

سيف *siif* p. سياف *syaaf,* أسياف *'asyaaf* seashore, seacoast. البناية اللي على السيف هو صاحبها *li-bnaaya lli ᶜala s-siif huwa ṣaaḥibha.* He is the owner of the building which is on the seashore.

س ي گ *syg*

سايق *saayig,* سواقة *swaaga,* etc., see under **س و گ** *swg.*

س ي ك ل *sykl*

سيكل *seekal* p. سياكل *siyaakil* bicycle. تركب سيكل؟ *tirkab seekal?* Do you ride a bicycle?

س ي ل *syl*

سال *saal* (يسيل *ysiil)* 1. to flow (out of s.th.), stream, run. الماي يسيل من التانكي *l-maay ysiil min t-taanki.* The water is flowing out of the reservoir. 2. to leak. القوطي يسيل صلصة طماط *l-guuṭi ysiil ṣalṣat ṭamaaṭ.* The can is leaking tomato sauce.

سيل *seel* p. سيول *syuul* 1. flood. نزل مطر وقامت السيول تسيل *nizal muṭar w-gaamat li-syuul tsiil.* It rained and floods started to flow. 2. torrent, torrential stream. سيل من الشكاوي *seel min š-šakaawi* innumerable complaints.

س ي ل ا ن *sylaan*

سيلان *siilaan* Ceylon.

س ي م *sym*

سيم *siim* p. سيام *syaam,* سيامة *syaama* 1. wire, thin metal wire. 2. barbed wire. لا تتعدى هذا السيم *la titᶜadda haaða s-siim.* Don't go beyond this barbed wire.

س ي ن *syn*

سين *siin* p. *-aat* name of the letter س *s.*

س ي ن م ا *synmaa*

سينما *siinama* p. *-aat* cinema, movie theater. رحنا السينما وشفنا فلم هندي *riḥna s-siinama w-čifna filim hindi.* We went to the cinema and saw an Indian film.

سينمائي *siinamaa'i* cinematic, movie (adj.) نجم سينمائي *najim siinamaa'i* movie star.

ش

ش š

ش *š-* (inter. part.) 1. what. شـدعوة *š-daᶜwa?* What's wrong? What's going on? شـفيك؟ *š-fiik?* What's wrong with you? شـــهالحاكي؟ *š-hal-ḥači?* You don't say! (lit., "What's this talk?") شاسمك؟ *š-asmak?* (less common var. *š-ismak?*) What's your name? شـصاير؟ *š-ṣaayir?* What has happened? What's going on? 2. how much, how many. شقد؟ *š-gadd?* How much? How many? 3. (with foll. حقه *ḥagga*) why. شحقه؟ *š-hagga?* Why? 4. (with foll. v.) what. شتبـي؟ *š-tabi?* What do you want? شسويت؟ *š-sawweet?* What have you done?

شما *š-ma* whatever. خذت شما تريد *xaðat š-ma triid.* She took whatever she wanted.

ش اح و ف šaaḥwf

شـاحوف *šaaḥuuf* p. شواحيف *šuwaaḥiif* small rowboat.

ش ا د ر šaadr

شـادر *šaadir* p. شوادر *šawaadir* (more common var. *čaadir*) bedspread, bedsheet.

ش ا ص šaaṣ

شاص *šaaṣ* p. *-aat* chassis.

ش ا ك و ش šaakwš

شـاكوش *šaakuuš* p. شواكيش *šuwaakiiš* (more common var. *čaakuuč*) hatchet, hammer.

ش ا ل šaal

شال *šaal* p. شيلان *šiilaan* 1. shawl. 2. (coll.) kind of wool cloth. غـترة شـال *ġitra šaal* wool headcloth.

ش ا م šaam

شـام *šaam* (with the article prefix الشام *š-šaam*) 1. Syria. 2. Damascus.

شـامي *šaami* 1. (p. شـوام *šwaam*) a Syrian. 2. characteristic of Syria, Syrian. 3. cool wind that blows from the northwest or from Syria.

ش ا م س šaams

شامسي *šaamsi* p. شوامس *šuwaamis* 1. Shamsi (person belonging to the Shamsi tribe in the U.A.E.). 2. characteristic of the Shamsi tribe.

ش ا ه šaah

شـاه *šaah* 1. (p. *-aat*) Shah, emperor. شاه إيران *šaah 'iiraan* the Shah of Iran. f. *-a* p. *-aat* queen, empress. الشاهة *š-šaaha* the queen of Iran. 2. (p. شياه *šyaah*) ewe. الشـاه نثيـة الكبـش *š-šaah niθyat č-čabš.* A ewe is the female of a ram.

ش ا ه ي ن šaahyn

شـاهين *šaahiin* p. شـواهين *šuwaahiin* peregrine. يربـون الشـواهين لاجـل الصيـد *yrabbuun š-šuwaahiin lajil ṣ-ṣeed.* They raise peregrines for hunting.

ش ا ي šaay

شـاي *šaay* (more common var. *čaay*) tea. See under **چ ا ي** *čaay*.

ش ء م š'm

تشاءم *tšaa'am* VI 1. to be pessimistic. لا تتشاءم، الله يدبرهـــا *la tiššaa'am, aḷḷa ydabbirha.* Don't be pessimistic. God will take care of it. لا تتشاءم من النتيجة *la tiššaa'am min n-natiija.* Don't be pessimistic about the result. 2. to be superstitious. فيه ناس يتشاءمون من صوت الرعـــد *fii naas yiššaa'muun min ṣoot r-ra^c^d.* There are people who see ill omens in the sound of thunder.

شـــوم *šuum* (less common var. شؤم *šu'um*) misfortune, bad luck.

مشـــؤوم *maš'uum.* unlucky, unfortunate. ثلّتعش عـــدد مشـــؤوم *θallatta^c^aš ^c^adad maš'uum.* Thirteen is an unlucky number.

متشـــائم *mitšaa'im* (act. part. from VI تشاءم *tšaa'am*) 1. a pessimist. 2. pessimistic.

ش ء ن š'n

شان *šaan* p. شؤون *š'uun* 1. matter, affair. وزارة الشؤون الاجتماعية *wazaarat š-šu'uun l-'ijtimaa^c^iyya* the ministry of social affairs. 2. esteem, respect. شانك عندنا كبير *šaanak ^c^indana čibiir.* You are highly esteemed by us. 3. (with على ^c^ala) sake. عملت كل هذا على شانك *^c^imalt kill haaδa ^c^ala šaanak.* I've done all of this for your sake. 4. (with ب b-) concerning, about. رمسته بشان ذيـــك القضيـــة *rammasta b-šaan δiič l-gaδiyya.* I talked to him concerning that matter.

ش ب ب šbb

شب *šabb* (يشب *yšibb*) 1. to become a young man, grow up. شب لين صار عمره ســـتّعشر ســـنة *šabb leen ṣaar ^c^umra sitta^c^šar sana.* He became a young man when he was sixteen years old. 2. to break out (fire, war, etc.) الحريق شب في الـــــداو *l-ḥariij šabb fi d-daaw.* Fire broke out on the dhow. 3. (v.t.) to turn on (the light). !شب الليت *šibb l-leet!* Turn on the light!

شـــب *šabb* (coll.) alum, aluminum sulphate. s. *-a* نستعمل الشب حـــق التنظيف *nista^c^mil š-šabb ḥagg t-tanδiif.* We use alum for cleansing.

شبـــة *šabba* p. *-aat* telephone pole. حطوا شبة قريب من بيتنا وجانـــا التلفـــون *ḥaṭṭaw šabba gariib min beetna w-yaana t-talafoon.* They put up a telephone pole near our house and we got a telephone.

شباب *šabaab* 1. youth, youthfulness. 2. young men, juveniles.

شـــاب *šaabb* p. شبان *šubbaan,* شباب *šabaab* youth, young man. شاب طايش *šaabb ṭaayiš* reckless young man. f. *-a* young woman, girl.

ش ب چ šbč

شبك *šibač* (يشبك *yišbič*) to tie, fasten, attach. شبـــك الســـيارة بحبـــل *šibač s-sayyaara b-ḥabil.* He tied the car to a rope.

شبـــك *šabač* (coll.) nets, netting. s. شبكة *šibča* p. *-aat.* نحدق بأشيا كثيرة مثل الشبـــك *nḥadig b-'ašya kaθiira miθil š-šibač.* We fish with many things, such as nets.

ش ب ح šbḥ

شبـــح *šabaḥ* p. أشباح *'ašbaaḥ* spirit, ghost.

ش ب ر *šbr*

شبر *šibir* p. شبور *šbuur* span of the hand (used as a unit of measurement). شبر بشبر *šibir b-šibir* inch by inch. شبر من الأرض *šibir min l-'arḍ* foot or inch of the land.

شبرية *šibriyya* p. شباري *šabaari* 1. mattress. 2. bedstead.

ش ب ش *šbš*

شباشة *šbaaša* p. شبابيش *šibaabiiš* 1. clothespin. 1. binder clip.

ش ب ط *šbṭ*

شباط *šbaaṭ* February. شباط من أشهر الشتا *šbaaṭ min 'ašhir š-šita.* February is one of the winter months.

ش ب ع *šb^c^*

شبع *šiba^c^ (يشبع yišba^c^)* 1. to eat one's fill, become satiated, full. كليت لين شبعت *kaleet leen šiba^c^t.* I ate until I got full. 2. to be or become fed up or sick and tired. نبغي فعل. شبعنا من الكلام *nabġi fi^c^il. šiba^c^na min l-kalaam.* We need action. We've become fed up with words. 3. (v.t.) to fill, sate, satisfy. ولا شي يشبعه. قطو مطابخ *wala šayy yišbi^c^a. gaṭu maṭaabix.* Nothing fills him up. He has a bottomless belly. (lit., "He's a cat of kitchens.")

شبع *šabba^c^* II 1. to satiate, fill. عيش بروحه ما يشبع *^c^eeš b-ruuḥa ma yšabbi^c^.* Rice by itself doesn't fill one up. 2. to satisfy, gratify. لو عطيته أموال الدنيا كلها ما تشبعه *lo ^c^aṭeeta 'amwaal d-dinya killaha ma tšabb^c^a.* If you give him the wealth of the whole world, you will not satisfy him. 3. to make s.o. fed up or sick and tired. شبعونا كلام؛ ما فيه فعل *šabba^c^oona kalaam; ma fii fi^c^il.* They made us fed up with words; there's no action.

شبعان *šab^c^aan* 1. full, sated, satisfied. آنا شبعان، موب جوعان *'aana šab^c^aan, muub juu^c^aan.* I am full, not hungry. 2. fed up, sick and tired. آنا شبعان من ها الحكي *'aana šab^c^aan min hal-hači.* I am fed up with these words.

ش ب ك *šbk*

شبك *šibak* (see also *sibač* under **ش ب چ** *šbč*).

اشتبك *štibak* VIII to get entangled, involved, engaged. الجيش اشتبك وايا العدو في معركة كبيرة *l-jeeš štibak wiyya l-^c^adu fi ma^c^raka čibiira.* The army got engaged in a big battle with the enemy.

شبكية *šabakiyya.* p. *-aat* retina (of the eye).

ش ب ه *šbh*

شبه *šibah (يشبه yišbah)* to resemble, look like, be similar to. ها الولد يشبه أبوه *hal-walad yišbah 'ubuu.* This boy looks like his father.

شبك *šabbah* II (with ب *b-*)1. to liken, compare to. ها المغني يشبه حبيبته بغزالة *hal-muġanni yšabbih ḥabiibta b-ġazaala.* This singer likens his sweetheart to a female gazelle. 2. to consider similar or identical, to find a resemblance in. هذي البنية شبهتها ببنتي *haaði li-bnayya šabbahitta b-binti.* I thought this girl was my daughter. ها البيت أشبها ببيتنا في الشارجة *hal-beet 'ašabbha b-beetna fi š-šaarja.* This house reminds me of our house in

Sharja.

شابه *šaabah* III, only as in وما شابه *w-ma šaabah* and the like, and others of the same type. فيه مغنيين ومغنيات وشعرا وما شابه *fii mġannyiin w-mġannyaat w-šuᶜara w-ma šaabah.* There are male and female singers, poets, and the like.

تشبه *tšabbah* V (with ب *b-*) to copy, imitate, try to be like. ها الولد يتشبه بالخنافس *hal-walad yitšabbah b-l-xanaafis.* This boy copies the Beatles.

تشابه *tšaabah* VI to look alike, resemble each other, be similar to each other. هي وأختها يتشابهون واجد *hiya w-'uxutta yiššaabhuun waayid.* She and her sister look a lot alike.

اشتبه *štibah* VIII 1. to be mistaken, make a mistake. اشتبهت. القزاز هو اللي يقز الأرض *štibaht. l-gazzaaz huwa lli ygizz l-'arḍ.* I am mistaken. A surveyor is the one who surveys land. 2. (with في *fi*) to suspect, be suspicious about. الشرطة اشتبهوا فيه وخذوه المركز *š-širṭa štabhaw fii w-xaðoo l-markaz.* The police suspected him and took him to the station.

شبه *šibih* p. اشباه *šbaah* semi-, half-, -like. شبه رسمي *šibih rasmi* semi-official. شبه دفاع *šibih difaaᶜ* half-back (soccer). شبه جزيرة *šibih yiziira* peninsula.

شبه *šabah* p. اشباه *šbaah* 1. resemblance, similarity, likeness. فيه شبه بينه وبين أخوه *fii šabah beena w-been 'uxuu.* There is resemblance between him and his brother. 2. image.

شبهة *šubha* p. *-aat* suspicion. فيه عليه شبهة *fii ᶜalee šubha.* He's under suspicion.

مشبوه *mašbuuh.* 1. under suspicion, suspect. بيت مشبوه *beet mašbuuh* house of ill repute. 2. (p. *-iin*) a suspect. ليستة المشبوهين *liistat l-mašbuuhiin* the list of suspects, the black list.

ش ت ت *štt*

شتت *šattat* II (usually used with شمل *šamil* gathering) to route, break up, disperse. العدو شتت شملهم *l-ᶜadu šattat šamilhum.* The enemy routed them.

تشتت *tšattat* V to be dispersed, scattered. تشتت شملهم *ššattat šamilhum.* They were dispersed. الجيش العراقي تشتت في الكويت *l-jeeš li-ᶜraagi ššattat fi li-kweet.* The Iraqi army fell apart in Kuwait.

تشتيت *taštiit* (v.n. from II شتت *šattat*) dispersion, scattering, dissolution.

ش ت ل *štl*

شتلة *šatla* p. شتايل *šataayil,* شتول *štuul* young plant, seedling.

مشتل *maštal* p. مشاتل *mašaatil* nursery, arboretum.

ش ت م *štm*

شتم *šitam* (يشتم *yaštim*) to call s.o. bad names, curse s.o. هو اللي شتمني قدام الناس *huwa lli šitamni jiddaam n-naas.* He's the one who called me bad names in front of the people.

شتم *šattam* II intensive of شتم *šitam.* شتم عليه في السوق *šattam ᶜalee fi s-suug.* He cursed him repeatedly in the marketplace.

شتيمة *šatiima* p. شتايم *šataayim* insult. عمري ما أنسى شتيمتك أبداً *ᶜumri ma 'ansa šatiimatk 'abdan.* I will never forget your insulting me.

ش ت و *štw*

شتى II *šatta* to spend the winter. دايماً نشتي هني *daayman nšatti hni.* We always spend the winter here.

شتا *šita* winter. فصل الشتا هني زين، موب بارد *faṣl š-šita hni zeen, muub baarid.* The winter season here is good; it's not cold. الهوا في الشتا كلش زين هني *l-hawa fi š-šita killiš zeen hni.* The weather in the winter is very good here.

شتوي *šitwi* winter, wintry. هدوم شتوية *hduum šitwiyya* winter clothes.

مشتى *mašta* p. مشاتي *mašaati* winter resort.

ش ج ر *šjr*

شجر *šijar* see under **ش ي ر** *šyr.*

ش ج ع *šjᶜ*

شجع *šajjaᶜ* II 1. to encourage. هو اللي شجعني على الدراسة والشغل *huwa lli šajjaᶜni ᶜala d-diraasa w-š-šuġul.* He's the one who encouraged me to study and work. رحنا لاجل نشجع فريقنا *riḥna lajil nšajjiᶜ fariigna.* We went to encourage our team. 2. to support, back, promote. لازم نشجع الإنتاج الوطني *laazim nšajjiᶜ l-'intaaj l-waṭani.* We should support national production.

تشجع *tšajjaᶜ* V to be encouraged. تشجع يدرس في المدرسة الليلية *tšajjaᶜ yidris fi l-madrasa l-layliyya.* He was encouraged to study at night school.

شجاع *šijaaᶜ* p. شجعان *šijᶜaan* 1. brave, courageous, bold. 2. courageous person.

شجاعة *šajaaᶜa* courage, bravery, boldness.

أشجع *'ašjaᶜ* (elat.) 1. (with من *min*) more courageous than, etc. 2. (with foll. n.) the most courageous, etc.

ش ح ح *šḥḥ*

شح *šaḥḥ* (يشح *yšiḥḥ)* to become scarce, run short, decrease. التمر يشح في الشتا *t-tamir yšiḥḥ fi š-šita.* Dates become scarce in the winter.

شحة *šiḥḥa* (v.n. from شح *šaḥḥ*) scarcity, shortage.

شحيح *šiḥiiḥ* scarce, short, meager. الطماط شحيح في القيظ *ṭ-ṭamaaṭ šiḥiiḥ fi l-geeḍ̌.* Tomatoes are scarce in the summer.

ش ح ش ط *šḥšṭ*

شحشط *šaḥšaṭ (يشحشط yšaḥšiṭ)* to drag, drag along. ما أقدر أشيل الصندوق؛ لازم أشحشطه *ma 'agdar 'ašiil ṣ-ṣanduug; laazim 'ašaḥišṭa.* I cannot carry the box; I have to drag it.

ش ح ط *šḥṭ*

شحط *šiḥaṭ (يشحط yišḥaṭ)* to scuff, drag along, scrape. لا تمشي وتشحط بالجوتي حقك *la tamši w-tišḥaṭ b-l-juuti ḥaggak.* Don't walk and scuff your shoes.

ش ح م *šḥm*

شحم *šaḥḥam* II to lubricate, grease. اخذ السيارة وشحمها في الكراج *'ixiđ* *s-sayyaara w-šaḥḥimha fi l-garaaj.* Take the car and have it lubricated in the garage.

تشحم *tšaḥḥam* V (pass. of II شحم *šaḥḥam*) to be lubricated.

شحم *šaḥam* (coll.) fat, grease, suet. s. شحمة *šḥama* piece of fat or suet. شحمة الاذن *šḥamat l-'iðin* the earlobe. (prov.) موب كل بيضة شحمة ولا كل سودة فحمة *muub kill beeḍa šḥama wala kill sooda fḥama.* Do not judge people or things by their appearance. You cannot judge a book by its cover. (Lit. "Not every white thing is a piece of fat and not every black thing is a piece of charcoal.")

ش ح م ط *šḥmṭ*

شحموط *šaḥmuuṭ* p. شحاميط *šiḥaamiiṭ* 1. young, not old. 2. young boy, youth, lad. الولد بعده شحموط *l-walad ba^c da šaḥmuuṭ.* The boy is still young.

ش ح ن *šḥn*

شحن *šiḥan (يشحن yišḥan)* 1. to ship, freight. فنش وشحن قشاره حق قطر *fannaš w-šiḥan gšaara ḥagg giṭar.* He resigned and shipped his belongings to Qatar. شحنوا اليح باللوري *šḥanaw l-yiḥḥ b-l-loori.* They shipped the watermelons by truck.

شحن *šaḥin* (v.n.) shipping, freighting. سيارة شحن *sayyaarat šaḥin* truck, lorry.

شحنة *šaḥna* (n. of inst.) p. *-aat* load, shipment, cargo.

شاحنة *šaaḥina* p. *-aat* truck, lorry.

مشحون *mašḥuun* (p.p.) loaded, freighted. اللوريات مشحونين عيش وشكر *l-looriyyaat mašḥuuniin ^c eeš w-šakar.* The trucks are loaded with rice and sugar.

ش ح ي *šḥy*

شحي *šiḥḥi* p. شحوح *šḥuuḥ* Bedouin belonging to the tribe known as the *šḥuuḥ* الشحوح.

ش خ ب ط *šxbṭ*

شخبط *šaxbaṭ (يشخبط yšaxbiṭ)* to scribble, scrawl. الجاهل قاعد يشخبط على الورقة *l-yaahil gaa^c id yšaxbiṭ ^c ala li-wruga.* The child is scribbling on the piece of paper.

ش خ ب و ط *šxbwṭ*

شخبوط *šaxbuuṭ* Shakhbout (common male's name in the Gulf).

ش خ ر *šxr*

شخر *šixar (يشخر yašxur)* to snore. لين يرقد دايماً يشخر *leen yargid daayman yašxur.* When he goes to bed, he always snores.

شخير *šaxiir* snoring.

ش خ ص *šxṣ*

شخص *šaxxaṣ* II to diagnose. الدخاتر هني ما قدروا يشخصون ها المرض العجيب *d-daxaatir hni ma gdaraw yšaxxṣuun hal-maraḍ l-^c ajiib.* The doctors here couldn't diagnose this strange disease.

شخص *šuxṣ* p. أشخاص *'ašxaaṣ,* شخاص *šxaaṣ* person, individual, someone. فيه هني خمسين شخص *fii hni xamsiin šuxṣ.* There are fifty persons here. نحن محتاجين حق أشخاص يقرون ويكتبون *niḥin miḥtaajiin ḥagg 'ašxaaṣ yigruun* *w-yikitbuun.* We are in need of people who (can) read and write.

شخصي *šaxṣi* personal, private. همه الوحيد مصلحته الشخصية *hamma l-waḥiid maṣlaḥta š-šaxṣiyya.* His only concern is his personal interest.

شخصياً *šaxṣiyyan* personally. آنا شخصياً كنت هناك *'aana šaxṣiyyan čint hnaak.* I personally was there.

شخصية *šaxṣiyya* p. *-aat* 1. personality. ضعيف الشخصية *ðaᶜiif š-šaxṣiyya* incompetent. 2. person of importance and prominence. 3. identity. ما قدروا يعرفون شخصية القتيل *ma gidraw yᶜarfuun šaxṣiyyat l-gatiil.* They couldn't know the murdered man's identity.

ش خ ط *šxṭ*

شخط *šixaṭ (يشخط yišxaṭ)* 1. to strike (a match). شخط صلب كبريت وولع الجقارة *šixaṭ ṣilb čabriit w-wallaᶜ j-jigaara.* He struck a match and lit the cigarette. 2. to cross out, strike out. شخط اسمي من الليستة *šixaṭ 'asmi min l-liista.* He crossed out my name from the list. 3. to make a mark, scratch. شخط بالقلم على الأرض *šixaṭ b-l-gaḷam ᶜala l-'arḍ.* He made a mark on the floor with the pen. شخط شخطين على الطوفة *šixaṭ šaxṭeen ᶜala ṭ-ṭoofa.* He scratched two marks on the wall.

شخط *šaxxaṭ* II intensive of شخط *šixaṭ.* قاعد يشخط كبريت *gaaᶜid yšaxxiṭ čabriit.* He's striking a lot of matches. شخط على الأرض *šaxxaṭ ᶜala l'arḍ.* He made many marks on the floor.

شخط *šaxṭ* (v.n. from شخط *šixaṭ*) 1. striking (a match). 2. crossing out, striking out. 3. scratching, making a mark. 4. (p. شخوط *šxuuṭ*) scratch, mark, line.

شخاط *šaxxaaṭ* (coll.) matches, lucifers. عود شخاط *ᶜuud šaxxaaṭ* match, stick of matches.

شخاطة *šaxxaaṭa* p. *-aat* box of matches.

مشخوط *mašxuuṭ* (p.p. from شخط *šixaṭ*) 1. scratched, marked. 2. (p. *-iin*) s.o. slightly crazy, foolish.

مشخط *mšaxxaṭ* (p.p. from II شخط *šaxxaṭ*) having been scratched. 2. having been crossed out or struck out.

ش د خ *šdx*

شداخة *šiddaaxa* p. *-aat* mouse trap.

ش د د *šdd*

شد *šadd (يشد yšidd)* 1. to load up (animals) to go. شدينا البل وسرنا *šaddeena l-bil w-sirna.* We loaded up the camels and left. 2. to pull or drag s.o. or s.th. شدني من ثوبي *šaddani min θoobi.* He dragged me by my dress. شد ذاك الحبل *šidd ðaak l-ḥabil.* Pull that rope. 3. to tie up, tie together. حط قشاره في بقشة وشدها *ḥaṭṭ gšaara fi bugša w-šaddha.* He put his things in a bag and tied it up. 4. to bring together, muster (e.g., up strength). شد حزامك واشتغل زين *šidd ḥzaamak w-štağil zeen.* Gather your strength and work hard.

شدد *šaddad* II 1. to make strong, intensify, strengthen. القاضي شدد الحكم عليه لانه جلخ *l-gaaḍi šaddad l-ḥukum* ᶜalee linna čallax. The judge made his sentence heavier because he lied. لا تشــدد علــى عيــالك la tšaddid ᶜala ᶜyaaḷak. Don't be hard on your kids. 2. to exert pressure, press. إذا تشـدد عليـه، يقـول الصـدق 'iða tšaddid ᶜalee, yguul ṣ-ṣidj. If you are firm with him, he will tell the truth.

تشدد tšaddad V to be strict, harsh, severe. جـابوا مدير جديـد يتشــدد علـى العمـال yaabaw mudiir yidiid yitšaddad ᶜala l-ᶜummaal. They brought a new manager who is strict with the workmen.

انشد nšadd VII pass. of شد šadd to be pulled or dragged. 2. to be tied up, tied together.

اشتد štadd VIII 1. to become hard, harsh, severe. في القيـظ يشـتد الحـر fi l-geeộ yištadd l-ḥarr. In the summer hot weather becomes intense. اشتدت العـداوة بينهـم štaddat l-ᶜadaawa beenhum. Enmity became more intense between them. اشـتد وجـع ضروسـي štadd wujaᶜ ộruusi. My toothache became more severe.

شد šadd (v.n. from شد šadd) 1. loading up. 2. pulling or dragging. شد الحبـل šadd l-ḥabil tug of war. 3. tying up, tying together. 4. bringing together, mustering, gathering (strength). شـد الحـزام šadd li-ḥzaam gathering of strength.

شدة šidda p. شدايد šadaayid distress, hardship, adversity.

شديد šadiid severe, strong, hard, harsh, intense. ها المعلم شديد وايا الطلاب hal-muᶜallim šadiid wiyya ṭ-ṭullaab. This teacher is severe with the students. رطوبة شـديدة ruṭuuba šadiida intense humidity.

شداد šdaad p. -aat riding saddle of a camel.

أشد 'ašadd (elat.) 1. (with من min) more forceful, intense, rigorous, stronger, harder, harsher. 2. (with foll. n.) the most forceful, rigorous, etc.

ش د ر šdr

شادر šaadir see under چ د ر čdr.

شدري šadri having a roof made of cloth. سـيارة شـدري sayyaara šadri convertible car.

ش د ه šdh

شده šidah (يشده yišdah) 1. to amaze, surprise, astonish. هـا المنظـر يشـده hal-manðar yišdah. This sight is amazing. 2. to distract, confuse. شدهت بـالي. مـا أقـدر أفكـر šidaht baali. ma 'adgar 'afakkir. You distracted me. I can't think.

انشده nšidah VII 1. to be surprised, astonished. انشده بالها لين شـافت الحيـول والصوغـة nšidah baalha leen čaafat li-ḥyuul w-ṣ-ṣooġa. She was amazed when she saw the bracelets and the jewelry. 2. to be distracted, preoccupied. انشده بالـه nšidah baala. He was distracted.

مشدوه mašduuh (p.p. from شده šidah) 1. surprised, astonished. 2. distracted, preoccupied. مشـدوه البـال mašduuh l-baal distracted.

ش د ي šdy

شدى šida (يشدي yišdi) to sing. (more

common var. غنى *ġanna*. See under **غ ن ي** *ġny*).

شادى *šaada* III to resemble, look like s.o. or s.th. ها السيارة تشادي السيارة اللي اشتريته *has-sayyaara tšaadi s-sayyaara lli štareetta.* This car looks like the car I bought.

شادي *šaadi* p. *-yiin* singer. شادي الخليج *šaadi l-xaliij* title, pseudonym of Abd Al-Aziz Khalid, a Kuwaiti singer.

ش ذ ر *šðr*

شذر *šaðir* (coll.) turquoise. s. *-a*, piece of turquoise.

شذري *šaðri* turquoise blue, turquoise. لون الصوغة شذري *loon ṣ-ṣooġa šaðri.* The color of the jewelry is turquoise.

ش ر ب *šrb*

شرب *širib (*يشرب *yišrab)* 1. to drink. شربت قهوة بدوية *šribt gahwa bdiwiyya.* I had Bedouin coffee. ما أبغى بيرة، ترى ما أشرب *ma 'abġa biira, tara ma 'ašrab.* I don't want beer because I don't drink.

شرب *šarrab* II 1. to make or let drink. الأم شربت عيالها الدوا *l-'umm šarrabat ᶜyaaḷha d-duwa.* The mother made her kids drink the medicine. تعال واياي أشربك بيرة *taᶜaal wiyyay 'ašarribk biira.* Come with me. I'll buy you a beer. شربهم ماي *šarrabhum maay.* He gave them water to drink. 2. to soak, saturate. شرب هدومه بالماي *šarrab hduuma b-l-maay.* He soaked his clothes in water.

تشرب *tšarrab* V to be soaked, saturated. تشربت الهدوم بالماي *tšarrabat li-hduum b-l-maay.* The clothes were soaked in water.

انشرب *nširab* VII to be drunk. ها القهوة باردة. ما تنشرب *hal-gahwa baarda. ma tinširib.* This coffee is cold. It can't be drunk.

شرب *šurb* (v.n. from شرب *širab*) drinking. شرب الخمر حرام في الإسلام *šurb l-xamir ḥaraam fi l-'islaam.* Drinking liquor is unlawful in Islam. ها الأيام الشرب بيلر *hal-iyyaam š-šurb beelar.* (lit., "During these days drinking is boiled water.") i.e., people no longer drink regular water; they drink boiled water.

شربة *šurba* (n. of inst.) p. *-aat* drink, sip, draught. خلني بس أشرب شربة واحدة *xaḷḷni bass 'ašrab šurba waḥda.* Let me have only one sip.

شراب *šaraab* sherbet, fruit drink, fruit juice.

شارب *šaarib* (act. part. from شرب *širib*) 1. having drunk s.th. توني شارب شاي *tawwni šarib čaay.* I have just had some tea. 2. (p. شاربين *šaarbiin*) drinker. 3. (p. شوارب *šawaarib*) mustache. (prov.) لحية ولحيّة وكل شارب اله مقص *liḥya w-lḥayya w-kill šaarib 'ila mgaṣṣ.* Your fingers are not the same. Different strokes for different folks. (Lit., "There is a beard and there is a small beard and each mustache has its scissors.")

مشروب *mašruub* (p.p. from شرب *širib*) 1. having been drunk. ما فيه شاي. كله مشروب *ma fii čaay. killa mašruub.* There isn't any tea. It has all been drunk. 2. drink, alcoholic drink. المشـــروبات مـــا تنبـــاع هـــني *l-mašruubaat ma tinbaa*[c] *hni.* Alcoholic drinks are not sold here.

ش ر ب ت *šrbt*

شـــربت *šarbat* fruit drink, non-carbonated soft drink. مـا حصلنا إلا شـربت عنـده *ma ḥaṣṣalna 'illa šarbat* [c]*inda.* We found only a fruit drink at his place.

ش ر ب چ *šrbč*

شـربك *šarbač* (يشـربك *yšarbič*) 1. to entangle, snarl. لا تشربكني بهالمشكلة *la tšarbični b-hal-muškila.* Don't get me into this problem. 2. to complicate. لا تشـربك الأمـور *la tšarbič l-'umuur.* Don't complicate things.

ش ر ج *šrj*

شرج *šarraj* II (less common var. شرق *šarrag*) to go east. شرق وغـرب ومـا حصـل شـي *šarraj w-ġarrab w-ma ḥaṣṣal šayy.* He went everywhere and got nothing.

شـرج *šarj* (less common var. شـرق *šarg*) east.

شـرجي *šarji* (less common var. شرقي *šargi*) eastern. هـوا شـرقي *hawa šarji* eastern wind. المنطقة الشـرقية *l-manṭiga š-šarjiyya* the eastern district.

الشـارجة *š-šaarja* Sharja (one of the U.A.E. emirates).

شـــارجي *šaarji* 1. (p. *-yiin*) Sharji (someone from Sharja). أنت شـارجي؟ *'inta šaarji?* Are you from Sharja? 2. characteristic of Sharja.

ش ر ح *šrḥ*

شـرح *širah* (يشرح *yišrah*) to explain, make clear or plain, illustrate. المدرس شـرح لنـا الـدرس *l-mudarris širaḥ lana d-dars.* The teacher explained the lesson to us.

شـرح *šarraḥ* II to dissect, perform an autopsy on a corpse. شـرحنا أرنـب في المختـبر *šarraḥna 'arnab fi l-muxtabar.* We dissected a rabbit in the laboratory. شـرحوا الجثـة لاجـل يعرفـون سـبب المـوت *šarraḥaw l-jiθθa lajil y*[c]*arfuun sabab l-moot.* They performed an autopsy on the corpse to find out the cause of death. 2. to slice, cut up into slices. القصاب شرح لي اللحم *l-gaṣṣaab šarraḥ-li l-laḥam.* The butcher sliced the meat for me.

شـــرح *šarḥ* (v.n. from شـرح *širaḥ*) explanation, illustration.

شـريحة *šriiḥa* p. شـرايح *širaayiḥ* thin slice (of meat).

تشـــريح *tašriiḥ* (v.n. from II شـرح *šarraḥ*) dissecting, dissection. علـم التشريح [c]*ilm t-tašriiḥ* anatomy.

ش ر د *šrd*

شـرد *širad* (يشرد *yašrid*) to run away, flee, escape. شرد من الشـرطة *širad min š-širṭa.* He ran away from the police. شـرد مـن السـجن *širad min s-sijin.* He escaped from jail. (prov.) يوم سخنا المای شرد الديـك *yoom ṣaxxanna l-maay širad d-diič.* Forewarned is fore-armed. (lit. "When we heated the water, the rooster ran away.") شرد ذهنه *širad ðihna.* He was distracted. His mind was far away.

شــــرد *šarrad* II to cause to run away, flee. شرد العيال بصوتــه *šarrad li-ᶜyaaḷ b-ṣoota.* He made the children run away with his voice. الحرب شردت ناس مــن بيوهّـم *l-ḥarb šarradat naas min byuuttum.* The war drove people away from their homes.

تشرد *tšarrad* V 1. = شرد *širad.* تشرد من الشرطة *tšarrad min š-širṭa.* He ran away from the police. 2. to be driven away. ناس واجدين تشردوا من بيوهّم *naas waaydiin tšarradaw min byuuttum.* Many people were driven away from their homes.

شــرود *šruud* (v.n. from شرد *širad*) running away, fleeing, escape.

شارد *šaarid* (act. part. from شرد *širad*) 1. having escaped. المســجون شــارد *l-masjuun šaarid.* The inmate has escaped. 2. fleeing, running away, at large.

ش ر ر ١ *šrr*

شــــر *šarr* (يشر *yšurr*) 1. to hang (on a line). حرمتي شرت الغسيل *ḥurumti šarrat l-ġasiil.* My wife hung the wash. 2. to scatter. شر الحبــوب *šarr li-ḥbuub.* He scattered the seeds.

ش ر ر ٢ *šrr*

شـــر *šarr* p. شرور *šruur* evil, wickedness. انشاالله ما حصل شـــر *nšaaḷḷa ma ḥiṣal šarr.* I hope nothing bad happened. عطيه اللي يبغاه. نبــي نفتك مــن شــره *ᶜaṭii lli yibġaa. nabi niftakk min šarra.* Give him what he wants. We would like to rid ourselves of his trouble.

شــرار *šaraar* (coll.) sparks. s. *-a* spark.

ش ر ط *šrṭ*

شرط *širaṭ* (يشرط *yašruṭ*) to stipulate, impose as a condition. شرط انه لازم نــروح وايــاه *širaṭ 'inna laazim nruuḥ wiyyaa.* He stipulated that we must go with him.

شرط *šarraṭ* II intens. of شرط *širaṭ.*

شارط *šaaraṭ* III to bet, wager. أشارطك انه بــاكر عطلــة *'ašaariṭk 'inna baačir ᶜuṭla.* I bet you tomorrow will be a holiday.

تشـــارط *tšaaraṭ* VI to make an agreement, to fix mutual conditions. تشارطنا إذا نجح في الامتحان أعطيه ميتــين درهــم *tšaaraṭna 'iða nijaḥ fi li-mtiḥaan 'aᶜṭii miiteen dirhim.* We made an agreement that if he passed the examination, I would give him two hundred dirhams. تشارطت واياهم آخذ ربح أول سنة *tšaaraṭṭ wiyyaahum 'aaxið ribḥ 'awwal sana.* I made an agreement with them to take the profit of the first year.

اشـــترط *štiraṭ* VIII (with على *ᶜala*) to stipulate, impose as a condition on s.o. الحكومة اشترطت عليه انه يــدرس هندســة بــترول *li-ḥkuuma štarṭat ᶜalee 'inna yidris handasat batrool.* The government imposed on him the cond i tion that he study petroleum engineering.

شـــرط *šarṭ* p. شروط *šruuṭ* condition, stipulation. عندنا واجد أشغال وكل شغلة تحتــاج شــروط معينــة *ᶜindana waayid 'ašġaal w-kill šaġla tiḥtaaj šruuṭ mᶜayyana.* We have many jobs and each job requires specified conditions.

بشـرط ان *b-šarṭ 'inn-*, على شرط ان *ᶜala šarṭ 'inn-* on condition that, provided that.

شـرطي *širṭi* p. شرطة *širṭa* policeman. شرطي مرور *širṭi muruur* traffic officer. شرطة المرور *širṭat l-muruur* the traffic, highway department.

شـريط *šariiṭ* p. أشـرطة *'ašriṭa* tape, recording tape.

مشـرط *mišraṭ* p. مشـارط *mašaariṭ* sharp knife used by a circumcisor.

ش ر ع *šrᶜ*

شـرع *šarraᶜ* II to open (a door, a window, etc.). صك الباب. لا تشرعه *ṣikk l-baab. la tšarrᶜa.* Close the door. Don't open it.

مشـرع *mšarraᶜ* (p.p. from II شـرع *šarraᶜ*) open. الباب مشـرع، مـوب مصكـوك *l-baab mšarraᶜ, muub maṣkuuk.* The door is open, not closed.

الشـرع *š-šarᶜ* the canonical law of Islam. في الشـرع الإسـلامي *fi š-šarᶜ l-'islaami* according to Islamic law. خلاف الشـرع *xilaaf š-šarᶜ* violation of religious law.

شـرعاً *šarᶜan* legally, lawfully, in a legal sense.

شـرعي *šarᶜi* 1. legal, lawful, legitimate. الربا شـي مـوب شـرعي في الإسـلام *r-riba šayy muub šarᶜi fi l-'islaam.* Usury is something unlawful in Islam. 2. dealing with Islamic law. قاضي شـرعي *gaaḍi šarᶜi* cadi, Islamic judge. محكمـة شـرعية *maḥkama šarᶜiyya* religious court.

شـراع *šraaᶜ* p. شرع *širᶜ*, شرايع *širaayiᶜ* sail. تفصيل الشـراع *tafṣiil š-šraaᶜ* sail-making.

شـراعي *šraaᶜi* sail-, sailing, rigged with sails. مركب شراعي *markab šraaᶜi* sailboat.

الشـريعة *š-šariiᶜa* the Sharia, the canonical law of Islam.

تشريع *tašriiᶜ* legislation.

تشـريعي *tašriiᶜi* legislative. السلطة التشـريعية *s-sulṭa t-tašriiᶜiyya* the legislative branch, the legislature.

شارع *šaariᶜ* p. شوارع *šawaariᶜ* street. تسـكن في أي شـارع؟ *tiskin fi 'ayya šaariᶜ?* Which street do you live on? في آخـر الشـارع *fi 'aaxir š-šaariᶜ* at the end of the street.

مشـروع *mašruuᶜ* 1. (p. مشـاريع *mašaariiᶜ*) project, undertaking, enterprise. مشـروع زراعـي *mašruuᶜ ziraaᶜi* agricultural project. مشـاريع الحكومـة تشـغل نـاس كثـيرين *mašaariiᶜ li-ḥkuuma tšaġġil naas kaθiiriin.* The government projects employ a lot of people. 2. legal, lawful. عمل مشروع *ᶜamal mašruuᶜ* legal action. 3. acceptable, allowable. هذي كلها أعذار مـوب مشـروعة *haaði killaha 'aᶜðaar muub mašruuᶜa.* These are all unacceptable excuses.

ش ر ف *šrf*

شـرف *šarraf* II 1. to honor. شرفتونا بزيـارتكم *šarraftuuna b-ziyaaratkum.* You honored us with your visit. 2. to be more noble, eminent, honorable than. أشرفك وأشرف أبـوك بعـد *'ašarrifk w-'ašarrif 'ubuuk baᶜad.* I am more honorable than you and your father too.

أشرف *'ašraf (يشرف yišrif)* (with على *ᶜala*) 1. to watch, supervise, oversee. مدير الديوان الأميري هو اللي يشرف على المطارزية *mudiir d-diiwaan l-'amiiri huwa lli yišrif ᶜala l-maṭaarziyya.* The director of the Emiri Court is the one who supervises the bodyguards. من يشرف على المشروع؟ *man yišrif ᶜala l-mašruuᶜ?* Who oversees the project? 2. to overlook, command a view of. ها البلكونة تشرف على البستان *hal-balkoona tišrif ᶜala l-bistaan.* This balcony overlooks the garden.

شرف *šaraf* 1. honor. سوينا حفلة على شرف الوزير *sawweena ḥafla ᶜala šaraf l-waziir.* We had a party in honor of the minister. 2. eminence, nobility, distinction.

شريف *šariif* p. شرفا *šurafa,* أشراف *'ašraaf* 1. eminent, noble, distinguished. 2. honorable, respectable, honest. بنت شريفة *bint šariifa* honorable girl. 3. sherif, descendant of Muhammad.

أشرف *'ašraf* (elat.) 1. (with من *min*) more honorable, respectable. 2. (with foll. n.) the most honorable, respectable.

إشراف *'išraaf* (v.n. from IV أشرف *'ašraf*) supervision, control. تحت إشراف *taḥt 'išraaf* under the auspices of.

ش ر گ *šrg*

شرق *šarrag* II (more common var. II *šarraj*) to go east. See also under **ش ر ج** *šrj.* البدو يشرقون وقت القيظ. *l-badu yšarrguun wagt l-geeḏ.* Bedouins go east at summer time. شرق وغرب *šarrag w-ġarrab.* He went everywhere.

أشرق *'ašrag (يشرق yišrig)* IV to rise (sun). الشمس أشرقت *š-šams 'ašragat.* The sun rose.

شرق *šarg* east. الشرق الأوسط *š-šarg l-'awsaṭ* the Middle East. شرق المدينة *šarg l-madiina* east of the city. شمال شرق *šamaal šarg* northeast. جنوب شرق *yinuub šarg* southeast.

شرقي *šargi* eastern. المنطقة الشرقية *l-manṭiga š-šargiyya* the Eastern Province in Saudi Arabia.

ش ر ك *šrk*

شرك *širak (يشرك yišrik)* to include, make a partner or participant. شركناه في المشروع *širaknaa fi l-mašruuᶜ.* We included him in the project.

شارك *šaarak* III to go into partnership with, participate with, be or become a partner with. شاركتهم في المشروع وخسرنا *šaarakittum fi l-mašruuᶜ w-xisarna.* I went into partnership with them and we lost money.

أشرك *'ašrak (يشرك yišrik)* IV 1. (أشرك بالله *'ašrak b-llaah)* to be a polytheist, hold others equal with God. إذا تشرك بالله تروح جهنم *'iða tišrik b-llaah truuḥ jahannam.* If you hold others equal to God, you will go to hell. 2. = شرك *širak.*

تشارك *tšaarak* VI to enter into partnership. تشاركت وايا النوخذة *tšaarakt wiyya n-nooxaða.* I went into partnership with the captain of the ship.

اشترك *štirak* VIII 1. to participate, take part, join in, collaborate. اشتركت في الجمعية *štirakt fi l-jamᶜiyya.* I became a member of the society. اشترك في الألعاب الأولمبية *štirak fi l-'alᶜaab l-'oolampiyya.* He took part in the Olympic Games. 2. to subscribe. قال المدير لازم نشترك في ذيك المجلة *gaal l-mudiir laazim ništarik fi ðiič l-majalla.* The manager said we had to subscribe to that magazine.

شركة *širka* partnership, association.

شركة *šarika* p. *-aat* company, firm, corporation. شركة «شل» *šarikat šal* the Shell Company. شركة تأمين *šarikat ta'miin* insurance company.

شريك *širiik* p. شركا *šuraka* 1. partner. شريكي في التجارة *širiiki fi t-tijaara* my business partner. جاسم وشركاه *jaasim w-šurakaa* Jasim & Co. 2. accessory, accomplice. شريك في الجريمة *širiik fi li-jariima* accessory to the crime.

شريكة *širiika* p. *-aat* (common var. *širiiča*) second wife. (prov.) شريكة ولو هي في القبر *širiika walaw hii fi l-gabir* (derog.). A leopard cannot change his spots. (lit. "She is a second wife although she is in the grave.")

اشتراك *štiraak* (v.n. from VIII اشترك *štirak*) 1. participation, joining, collaboration. 2. (p. *-aat*) subscription. اشتراك في المجلة *štiraak fi l-majalla* subscription to the magazine. اشتراك سنوي *štiraak sanawy* annual subscription. 3. subscription fee, rate. الاشتراك السنوي امية درهم *l-'ištiraak s-sanawy 'imyat dirhim.* The annual subscription is one hundred dirhams. 4. (بدل اشتراك *bidal štiraak*) dues, participation fee.

اشتراكي *štiraaki* 1. social, socialistic. 2. (p. *-yyiin*) a socialist.

اشتراكية *štiraakiyya* (usually with ال *l-*) socialism.

مشرك *mišrik* (act. part. from IV أشرك *'ašrak*) polytheist.

مشترك *mištarik* (act. part. from VIII اشترك *štirak*) p. *-iin* 1. subscriber. 2. participant.

مشترك *mištarak* (p.p. from VIII اشترك *štirak*) joint, combined, collective, common, communal. بلاغ مشترك *balaaġ mištarak* joint communique. جهود مشتركة *jihuud mištarka* combined efforts. السوق المشتركة *s-suug l-mištarka* the Common Market. حمام مشترك *ḥammaam mištarak* communal bathroom. شعور مشترك *šuᶜuur mištarak* solidarity.

ش ر ك س *šrks*

شركس *šarkas* (coll.) Circassian. s. *-i.* فيه شركس في الأردن *fii šarkas fi l-'ardun.* There are Circassians in Jordan.

ش ر م *šrm*

أشرم *'ašram* p. شرم *širm* s.o. whose upper lip is split.

ش ر و *šrw*

شروا *šarwaa-* (usually with suff. pron.) like, similar to. شرواك *šarwaak* like you. شرواهم *šarwaahum* like them. نبغى ناس شرواك *nibġa naas* *šarwaak.* We want people like you, of your caliber.

ش ر ي *šry*

اشترى *štira* VIII to buy, purchase. اشترى لحم وعيش *štira laḥam w-ᶜeeš.* He bought meat and rice. ما اشتريت أي شي لان كل شي غالي اليوم *ma štireet 'ayya šayy linn kill šayy ġaali l-yoom.* I didn't buy anything because everything is expensive today. يشتريك ويبيعك بساع *yištiriik w-ybiiᶜak b-saaᶜ.* He's a swindler; he'll take the shirt off your back.

شرا *šira* (v.n.) buying, purchasing. البيع والسرا *l-beeᶜ w-š-šira* buying and selling.

مشتري *mištari, mištiri* (act. part. from VIII اشترى *štira*) p. *-yiin* buyer, customer.

مشترى *mištara* (p.p. from VIII اشترى *štira*) 1. bought, having been bought. البيت مشترى *l-beet mištara.* The house has been bought. 2. (p. مشتريات *mištaryaat*) purchased goods or groceries. المشترى اليوم كلفني خمسين دينار *l-mištara l-yoom kallafni xamsiin diinaar.* The things I bought today cost me fifty dinars.

ش ش م *ššm*

ششمة *šašma* (more common var. جشمة *čašma*). See under **چ ش م** *čšm.*

ش ط ح *šṭḥ*

شاطوحة *šaaṭuuḥa* p. شواطيح *šawaaṭiiḥ* (baby) cradle.

ش ط ر *šṭr*

تشاطر *tšaaṭar* VI to show cleverness, smartness, skill. لا تتشاطر وياه. يبيعك ويشتريك *la tiššaaṭar wiyyaa. ybiiᶜak w-yištiriik.* Don't be smart with him. He's a swindler. He'll take the shirt off your back.

شطارة *šaṭaara* cleverness, smartness, skill.

أشطر *'ašṭar* (elat.) 1. (with من *min*) more clever, smarter than. 2. (with foll. n.) the most clever, the smartest.

شاطر *šaaṭir* (act. part.) p. *-iin,* شطار *šiṭṭaar* clever, smart, skillful. شاطرة. لا تخاف عليها *šaaṭra. la txaaf ᶜaleeha.* She's clever. Don't worry about her. هو شاطر في المدرسة *huwa šaaṭir fi l-madrasa.* He's good at school.

ش ط ر ن ج *šṭrnj*

شطرنج *šiṭranj* chess. تلعب شطرنج؟ *tilᶜab šiṭranj?* Do you play chess?

ش ط ط[1] *šṭṭ*

شط *šaṭṭ* (more common var. سيف *siif*). See under **س ي ف** *syf.*

ش ط ط[2] *šṭṭ*

شطة *šaṭṭa* (no p.) hardship, difficulty. جمع المال اليوم صار شطة *jamᶜ l-maal l-yoom ṣaar šaṭṭa.* Nowadays the accumulation of wealth has become difficult. المعيشة صارت شطة *l-maᶜiiša ṣaarat šaṭṭa.* The cost of living has become very expensive.

ش ع ب *šᶜb*

تشعب *tšaᶜᶜab* V to branch out, split. الرستة رايحة تتشعب قدام *r-rasta raayḥa titšaᶜᶜab giddaam.* The road will branch out later on.

شعب *šaᶜb* p. شعوب *šᶜuub* 1. people.

2. nation. الشعب العربي *š-šacb l-carabi* the Arab people. هذا كله حق مصلحة الشعب *haaða killa ḥagg maṣlaḥat š-šacb.* This is all for the welfare of the people.

شعبي *šacbi* 1. popular, folk-. أغاني شعبية *'aġaani šacbiyya* popular songs, folk songs. 2. having to do with poor, low income people. بيوت شعبية *byuut šacbiyya* low income housing.

شعبية *šacbiyya* popularity.

شعبان *šacbaan* Shaban, the eighth month of the Islamic year.

شعيب *šceeb* p. شعب *šicb,* شعبان *šicbaan* small valley. نزل مطر وانترست الشعبان ماي *nizal muṭar w-ntirsat š-šicbaan maay.* It rained and the small valleys filled up with water.

ش ع ر *šcr*

شعر *šicar (*يشعر *yašcir)* (with ب *b-*) 1. to sense, feel. البنت شعرت بانهم جاوا يخطبونها من أبوها *l-bint šcarat b-inhum yaw yxaṭbuunha min 'ubuuha.* The girl sensed that they came to ask her father for her hand in marriage. 2. to realize, notice. ما شعر بأنهم يغشمرونه *ma šicar b-'anhum ygašmiruuna.* He didn't realize that they were playing tricks on him.

شعر *šacar* (coll.) hair. s. شعرة *šcara.* البنت عيونها صاحية وجميلة وشعرها طويل *l-bint cyuunha ṣaaḥya w-yimiila w-šacarha ṭawiil.* The girl's eyes are sound and beautiful and she has long hair. شعر بنات *šacar banaat* cotton candy. بيوت من شعر *byuut min šacar* tents (lit., "homes of camel hair").

شعر *šicir* poetry. يكتب شعر *yiktib šicir.* He writes poetry. بيت من شعر *beet min š-šicir* line of poetry. شعر نبطي *šicir nabaṭi* colloquial poetry.

شعري *šicri* (coll.) kind of fish. s. *-yya.*

شعار *šicaar* p. *-aat* 1. motto, slogan. 2. emblem, distinguishing feature.

شعير *šiciir* (coll.) barley. s. حبة شعير *ḥabbat šiciir.*

شعور *šucuur* (v.n. from شعر *šicar*) 1. feeling, awareness. عندي شعور انها رايحة توافق *cindi šucuur 'inha raayḥa twaafig.* I have a feeling that she is going to agree. 2. capacity to respond emotionally. مشكور على هالشعور الطيب *maškuur cala haš-šucuur ṭ-ṭayyib.* Thank you for your noble feelings. 3. sensitivity, perceptiveness. ما عنده شعور *ma cinda šucuur.* He has no sensitivity.

شاعر *šaacir* p. شعرا *šucara,* شعاعير *šicaaciir* poet.

ش ع ع *šcc*

شعاع *šucaac* rays, beams (no known s.) شعاع الشمس *šucaac š-šams* the rays of the sun.

أشعة *'ašicca* (p. of شعاع *šucaac*) x-ray. لازم ناخذ أشعة حق صدرك *laazim naaxið 'ašicca ḥagg ṣadrak.* We have to take an x-ray of your chest. عيادة الأشعة *ciyaadat l-'ašicca* the x-ray clinic.

ش ع ل *šcl*

اشتعل *šticial* VIII to catch fire, flare

up, ignite, be on fire. صلب الكبريت هذا ما يشتعل *ṣilb č-čabriit haaða ma yištaᶜil.* This match stick doesn't light. الضو ظل يشتعل الين رجال المطافي جاوا *ḍ-ḍaww ḍall yištaᶜil ileen rijaal l-maṭaafi yaw.* The fire kept burning until the firemen came.

شعلة *šuᶜla* p. *-aat* flame, blaze. موزة شعلة من الذكا *mooza šuᶜla min ð-ðaka.* Moza is very brilliant.

مشعل *mašᶜal* p. مشاعل *mašaaᶜil* 1. lantern. من زمان الناس كانوا يستعملون مشاعل زيت *min zamaan n-naas čaanaw yistaᶜimluun mašaaᶜil zeet.* A long time ago people used oil lanterns. 2. torch.

ش غ ب *šġb*

شاغب *šaaġab* III to make trouble, disturb the peace. دايماً يشاغب في هذا الصف *daayman yšaaġib fi haaða ṣ-ṣaff.* He always makes trouble in this class. ترى يشاغب عليك *tara yšaaġib ᶜaleek.* Mind you, he'll make trouble for you.

شغب *šiġab* (v.n.) trouble, disturbance, unrest. الطرب صار شغب *ṭ-ṭarab ṣaar šiġab.* Merry-making became a disturbance.

مشاغب *mšaaġib* (act. part. from III شاغب *šaaġab*) p. *-iin* troublemaker, agitator.

ش غ ر *šġr*

شغر *šiġar (يشغر yišġar)* to be vacant, free, unoccupied. شغرت وظيفة في البنك. قدمت طلب عليها *šiġrat waðiifa fi l-bank. gaddamt ṭalab ᶜaleeha.* There was an open position at the bank. I applied for it.

شاغر *šaaġir* (act. part.) 1. vacant, free, unoccupied. فيه مكان شاغر ذالحين *fii mukaan šaaġir ðalḥiin.* There's an open position now. 2. (p. شواغر *šawaaġir*) vacancy, opening. البنك أعلن عن شواغر حق السنة المالية الجديدة *l-bank 'aᶜlan ᶜan šawaaġir ḥagg s-sana l-maaliyya l-yidiida.* The bank advertised vacancies for the new fiscal year.

ش غ ل *šġl*

شغل *šiġal (يشغل yišġal)* 1. (with ب *b-*) to occupy, busy s.o. with s.th. شغلني بحكيه عن تصرفاته *šiġalni b-ḥačya ᶜan taṣarrufaata.* He took up my time talking about his problems. 2. (with بال *baal*) to make uneasy, apprehensive, to disturb. ها الأشيا اللي تصير تشغل البال *hal-'ašya lli tṣiir tišġil l-baal.* These things that are happening make one uneasy. 3. to occupy, take up. يشغل وظيفتين *yišġal waðiifteen.* He's holding two jobs.

شغل *šaġġal* II (less common var. *šaqqal*) 1. to employ, provide employment. شغلني ويا أخوي في الزراعة *šaġġalni wiyya 'uxuuy fi z-ziraaᶜa.* He employed me and my brother in agriculture. 2. to make, let work. يشغلهم من الصبح إلى العصر *yšaġġilhum min ṣ-ṣubḥ 'ila l-ᶜaṣir.* He makes them work from the morning till late afternoon. 3. to put to work, put in operation. شغل السيارة *šaġġil s-sayyaara.* Start the car. ما أقدر أشغل هذي الماكينة *ma 'agdar 'ašaġġil haaði l-maakiina.* I cannot operate this engine. نبغى نسمع الأخبار. شغل الرادو

nibġa nisma^c l-'axbaar. *šaġġil r-raadu.* We would like to hear the news. Turn on the radio.

انشغل *nšiġal* VII (with ب *b-*) to be or become busy, occupied, distracted with. جانا خطار أمس وانشغلنا بيهم *yaana xuṭṭaar 'ams w-nšiġalna biihum.* We had company yesterday and we were all tied up with them.

اشتغل *štiġal* VIII 1. to work, to be busy, occupied, engaged. اشتغلت دريول حق الشركة سنتين *štiġalt dreewil ḥagg š-šarika sanateen.* I worked as a driver for the company for two years. أدرس وأشتغل لاجل أرتاح من صوبين *'adris w-'aštaġil lajil 'artaaḥ min ṣoobeen.* I study and work so that I might be satisfied in both ways. 2. to run, work, be in operation. روح جرب السيارة وشوف إذا تشتغل *ruuḥ jarrib s-sayyaara w-čuuf 'iða tištaġil.* Go try the car and see if it runs. ها الساعة تشتغل على البتري *has-saa^ca tištaġil ^cala l-batri.* This watch operates by battery. اشتغلت السيارة لين ضربت سوتش *štaġlat s-sayyaara leen ḍirabt siwič.* The car started when I turned the ignition on. 3. to do business, be in business. شيشة البترول هذي تشتغل زين *šiišt l-batrool haaði tištaġil zeen.* This gas station does a brisk business. فيه مطاعم هني تشتغل أربعة وعشرين ساعة في اليوم *fii maṭaa^cim hini tištaġil 'arba^ca w-^cišriin saa^ca fi l-yoom.* There are restaurants here that are open twenty-four hours a day. يشتغل على حسابه *yištaġil ^cala ḥsaaba.* He's self-employed.

شغل *šuġul* 1. work, job. شو شغلك؟ *šu šuġlak?* What's your work? What do you do? شغلي قزاز في البلدية *šuġli gazzaaz fi l-baladiiya.* I work as a surveyor for the municipality. 2. workmanship. شغل ها الساعة زين *šuġul has-saa^ca zeen.* The workmanship on this watch is good. ها الجوتي شغل يد *hal-juuti šuġul yadd.* These shoes are hand-made. 3. business, concern. هذا موب شغلك *haaða muub šuġlak.* That's none of your business.

شغلة *šaġla* p. *-aat* piece of work, task. كل شغلة محتاجة لشروط معينة *kill šaġla miḥtaaja la šruuṭ m^cayyana.* Each job requires certain conditions.

مشغول *mašġuul* (p.p. from شغل *šiġal*) busy, occupied. الوزير مشغول *l-waziir mašġuul.* The minister is busy. الخط مشغول *l-xaṭṭ mašġuul.* The line is busy.

ش ف ر *šfr*

شفرة *šafra* p. *-aat* 1. code, cipher. 2. vertical edge of a sail.

شفر *šafar* Chevrolet. سيارة شفر *sayyaara šafar* Chevrolet car.

ش ف ع *šf^c*

شفع *šifa^c (يشفع yišfa^c)* intercede, intervene, plead. إذا ماحد يشفع لك يفنشونك *'iða maḥḥad yišfa^c-lak yfannšuunak.* If nobody intercedes for you, they will fire you.

تشفع *tšaffa^c* V = شفع *šifa^c*.

شفيع *šafii^c* p. شفعا *šufa^ca, -iin* mediator, intercessor.

شفاعة *šafaa^ca* (v.n. from شفع *šifa^c*) mediation, intercession. ما لك شفاعة

عند أي إنسان *ma-lak šafaaᶜa ᶜind 'ayya 'insaan.* No one is going to plead in your behalf.

شافعي *šaafᶜi* 1. Shafiitic. المذهب الشافعي *l-maðhab š-šaafᶜi* the Shafiitic school (of Islamic thought). 2. (p. *-yyiin*) a Shafiite.

ش ف گ *šfg*

شفق *šifag (يشفق yišfag)* (with على *ᶜala*) to feel pity for, sympathize with. شفق عليه التنديل وما فنشه *šifag ᶜalee t-tindeel w-ma fannaša.* The foreman felt pity for him and didn't fire him

شفقة *šafaga* pity, sympathy, compassion. ما فيه عنده ولا ذرة من الشفقة *ma fii ᶜinda wala ðarra min š-šafaga.* He doesn't have a bit of pity in him.

ش ف ي *šfy*

شفى *šifa (يشفى yišfa)* to be cured, be healed, to get well. شربت الدوا وشفيت الحمد لله *šribt d-duwa w-šifiit l-ḥamdu li-llaah.* I drank the medicine and was cured, praise be to God.

مستشفى *mustašfa* (less common var. مستشفي *mustašfi*) p. *-yaat* hospital. مستشفى العيون *mustašfa l-ᶜuyuun* the eye hospital. مستشفى المخبلين *mustašfa li-mxabbliin* the lunatic asylum (also known as العصفورية *l-ᶜaṣfuuriyya*). المستشفى العسكري *l-mustašfa l-ᶜaskari* the military hospital.

ش گ ر *šgr*

أشقر *'ašgar* p. شقر *šugur* f. شقرا *šagra* blond.

شقرا *šagra* p. *-aat,* شقر *šugur* 1. blond (f.). 2. light brown mare.

ش گ گ *šgg*

شق *šagg (يشق yšigg)* 1. to rip, tear s.th. شق قميصة *šagg gamiiṣa.* He tore his shirt. (prov.) لو يدري عمير كان شق ثوبه *lo yadri ᶜmeer čaan šagg θooba.* Ignorance is bliss. (lit., "If Omeer had known, he would have ripped his dress.") قرا الخط وشقه وقطه في الدرام *gira l-xaṭṭ w-šagga w-gaṭṭa fi d-draam.* He read the letter, tore it up and threw it away in the garbage can. 2. to cut through, construct, build (a road or a street). البلدية تشق شوارع كل يوم *l-baladiyya tšigg šawaariᶜ kill yoom.* The municipality builds streets every day.

شقق *šaggag* II to tear up, tear to pieces. شقق الخط عقب ما قراه *šaggag l-xaṭṭ ᶜugub-ma garaa.* He tore up the letter after he had read it.

تشقق *tšaggag* V to be torn up or torn to pieces.

انشق *nšagg* VII = تشقق *tšaggag* V.

شق *šagg* p. شقوق *šguug* rip, tear, crack.

شقة *šigga* p. شقق *šigag* apartment, flat. الشقة فيها حجرتين نوم ومجلس *š-šigga fiiha ḥijrateen noom w-maylis.* There are two bedrooms and a living room in the apartment. رفيقي في الشقة *rifiiji fi š-šigga* my roommate.

ش گ ل ب *šglb*

شقلب *šaglab (يشقلب yšaglib)* 1. to turn things upside down, upset things. كان حمقان وشقلب كل شي في الشقة *čaan ḥamgaam w-šaglab kill šayy fi š-šigga.* He was furious and turned everything upside down in the apartment. 2. to send tumbling. دفعني وشقلبني على الدرج *difa^cni w-šaglabni ^cala d-daray.* He pushed me and sent me tumbling down the stairs.

تشقلب *tšaglab (يتشقلب yitšaglab)* 1. to be turned upside down. 2. to fall head over heels, tumble. دفعني وتشقلبت على الدرج *difa^cni w-ššaglabt ^cala d-daray.* He pushed me and I took a tumble down the stairs.

ش گ ي *šgy*

تشاقى *tšaaga* VI to kid around, joke with each other. هو بس يتشاقى وياك. لا تزعل عليه *huwa bass yiššaaga wiyyak. la tiz^cal ^calee.* He is just kidding around with you. Don't get mad at him.

شقى *šiga* misery, pain, suffering. الحياة شقى *l-ḥayaa šiga.* Life is difficult.

شقي *šagi* p. أشقيا *'ašgiya* 1. naughty, mischievous. 2. rogue, scoundrel.

شقاوة *šagaawa* naughtiness.

ش ك ر ١ *škr*

شكر *šikar (يشكر yaškur)* to thank, express gratitude to s.o. أشكرك على اللي سويته *'aškurak ^cala lli sawweeta.* I thank you for what you've done.

شكر *šukur* (v.n.) 1. thankfulness, gratefulness. 2. thanks, acknowledgement. كتاب شكر *kitaab šukur* letter of appreciation. الشكر والحمد لله وحده *š-šukur w-l-ḥamd li-llaah waḥda.* Thanks and praise be only to God.

شكراً *šukran* (more common var. مشكور *maškuur*). See below.

مشكور *maškuur* p. *-iin.* thanks, thank you (lit., "you are thanked.") مشكور، ما أدوخ جقاير *maškuur, ma 'aduux jigaayer.* Thanks, I don't smoke cigarettes.

ش ك ر ٢ *škr*

شكر *šakar* (coll.) sugar. قهوة بدون شكر *gahwa b-duun šakar* coffee without sugar. الشكر مدعوم من الحكومة *š-šakar mad^cuum min li-ḥkuuma.* Sugar is subsidized by the government.

ش ك ك *škk*

شك *šakk (يشك yšikk)* 1. to have doubt, doubt. أشك في حكيك *'ašikk fii hačyak.* I doubt your words. أشك انه باكر عطلة *'ašikk 'inna baačir ^cuṭla.* I doubt that tomorrow will be a holiday. 2. to suspect, distrust. يشك في كل واحد *yšikk fi kill waaḥid.* He suspects everyone.

شك *šakk* (v.n.) p. شكوك *škuuk* doubt, suspicion. بدون شك *b-duun šakk* without doubt, undoubtedly. ما فيه شك *ma fii šakk.* There's no doubt.

مشكوك *maškuuk* (p.p.) (usually with فيه *fii*) doubtful, uncertain. شي مشكوك فيه *šayy maškuuk fii* an unlikely thing.

ش ك ل *škl*

شكل *šakkal* II 1. to form, shape, fashion, create. شكلوا لجنة تراقب الأسعار *šakkalaw lajna traagib l-'as^caar.* They formed a committee to study prices. المخدرات تشكل مشاكل كثيرة *li-mxaddaraat tšakkil mašaakil* *kaθiira.* Drugs create many problems. 2. to diversify, vary, variegate. اشتريت سكريم وراعي الدكان شكل لي اياها *štireet sikriim w-raaᶜi d-dikkaan šakkal-li iyyaaha.* I bought ice cream and the store owner made it several flavors for me.

تشكل *tšakkal* V pass. of II شكل *šakkal.*

شكل *šakil* p. أشكال *'aškaal* 1. outward appearance, figure. شكله شكل السعدان *šakla šakil s-saᶜdaan.* He looks like a monkey. شو شكل الوزير الجديد؟ *šu šakil l-waziir l-yidiid?* What does the new minister look like? 2. shape, form, configuration. شكل هندسي *šakil handasi* geometrical figure. بشكل دائرة *b-šakil daa'ira* in the shape of a circle. بشكل ما يتصور *b-šakil ma yitṣawwar* to an inconceivable degree. 3. sort, kind, class, type. هني فيه أشكال من الشواهين *hini fii 'aškaal min š-šuwaahiin.* Here there are various kinds of peregrines. عندها أشكال واجدة من الحيول *ᶜindaha 'aškaal waayda min li-ḥyuul.* She has many kinds of bracelets. أبغى شكل ثاني *'abġa šakil θaani.* I want another kind. هاالشكل *haš-šakil* like this, in this manner.

شكلي *šakli* formal, conventional. هذي أشيا شكلية *haaði 'ašya šakliyya.* These are only formalities.

شكليات *šakliyyaat* (no singular) formalities.

تشكيلة *taškiila* p. *-aat* assortment, variety, selection.

مشكل *mšakkal* (p.p. from II شكل *šakkal*) different, variegated. عطني حلويات مشكلة *ᶜaṭni ḥalawiyyaat mšakkala.* Give me different kinds of sweets.

مشكلة *muškila* p. مشاكل *mašaakil* problem. هذي مشكلتك *haaði muškiltak.* This is your problem. عندي مشكلة *ᶜindi muškila.* I have a problem. مشكلة المشاكل *muškilat l-mašaakil* the most difficult, serious problem.

ش ك و *škw*

شكو؟ *šaku?* (Kuwaiti) What? What's there? شكو من أخبار اليوم؟ *šaku min 'axbaar l-yoom?* What's the news today?

ش ك ي *šky*

شكى *šika* (يشكي *yiški*) 1. complain about. شكى لي عنه *šikaa-li ᶜanna.* He complained to me about it (or him). 2. to suffer, make a complaint. يشكي من مرض قديم *yiški min maraḍ gadiim.* He is suffering from an old illness.

اشتكى *štika* VIII 1. (with على *ᶜala*) to file a complaint about. اشتكى عليه عند الشيخ *štika ᶜalee ᶜind š-šeex.* He complained about him to the Shaikh. 2. to sue, file complaint against. اشتكى عليّ في المحكمة *štika ᶜalayya fi l-maḥkama.* He sued me (in court).

شكوى *šakwa* p. شكاوي *šakaawi* complaint, grievance. رفع شكوى على الشركة *rifaᶜ šakwa ᶜala š-šarika.* He sued the company.

مشتكي *mištiki* (act. part. from VIII اشتكى *štika*) 1. having complained, filed a complaint, sued. هو المشتكي عليّ

huwa l-mištiki ᶜalayya. He's the one who filed a complaint against me. 2. (p. *-yiin*) complainant, plaintiff.

ش ل خ *šlx*

شلخ *šallax* II = كذب *čiðab.* See under **چ ذ ب** *čðb* and under **چ ل خ** *člx.*

ش ل ع *šlᶜ*

شلع *šilaᶜ (يشلع yišlaᶜ)* to extract, remove, pull out. رجال لحيته بيضا شلع ضروسه *rayyaal liḥyita beeḍa šilaᶜ ḍruusa.* An old man with a gray beard had his teeth extracted. شلع الدريشة *šilaᶜ d-diriiša.* He removed the window. شلع المسمار *šilaᶜ l-mismaar.* He pulled out the nail.

شلع *šallaᶜ* II intens. of شلع *šilaᶜ*.

تشلع *tšallaᶜ* V to be pulled out. تشلعت كل ضروسه *ššallaᶜat kill ḍruusa.* All of his teeth were pulled out.

شلع *šaliᶜ* (v.n. from شلع *šilaᶜ)* pulling out, extracting, removing.

ش ل غ م *šlġm*

شلغم *šalġam* (coll.) turnips. s. راس شلغم *raas šalġam* a turnip.

ش ل ل ١ *šll*

شل *šall (يشل yšill)* 1. to take, carry away. شل قشاره ومشى *šall gšaara w-miša.* He took his personal effects and left. شلوه الشرطة لانه باق *šalloo š-širṭa linna baag.* The police took him away because he had stolen. 2. to carry, lift (= شال *šaal*). See under **ش ي ل** *šyl*. 3. to steal, pilfer. شل أوراق وقلامة من الحفيز *šall 'awraag w-gḷaama min l-ḥafiiz.* He stole paper and pens from the office.

انشل *nšall* VII 1. to be taken, carried away. 2. to be carried, lifted. 3. to be stolen.

شل *šall* (v.n. from شل *šall*) 1. taking, carrying away. 2. carrying, lifting. 3. stealing.

شال *šaall* (act. part. from شل *šall*) p. *-iin* 1. having carried, lifted. آنا شال الصندوق قبل شوية *'aana šaall ṣ-ṣanduug gabil šwayya.* I have just carried the box. 2. having stolen, pilfered s.th. هو شال الساعة *huwa šaall s-saaᶜa.* He's the one who has stolen the watch.

مشلول *mašluul* (p.p. from شل *šall*) 1. having been taken, carried away. 2. having been carried, lifted. 3. having been stolen.

ش ل ل ٢ *šll*

شل *šall (يشل yšill)* to sew by hand. بنتي تشل واجد زين *binti tšill waajid zeen.* My daughter hand sews very well.

انشل *nšall* VII to be hand sewn.

شلالة *šlaala* (v.n. from شل *šall*) sewing by hand.

شليل *šiliil* p. شلايل *šilaayil* lap. (prov.) لو عطاك الشيخ مرق حطه بشليلك *lo ᶜaṭaak š-šeex marag ḥuṭṭa b-šiliilak.* Make hay while the sun shines. Seize the opportunity. (lit., "If the Shaikh gives you broth, put it in your lap.")

شلال *šallaal* p. *-aat* waterfall, cataract.

ش ل و ن *šlwn*

شلون *šloon* (contraction of *š-loon* or

شــو لــون *šu loon*) 1. how, in what condition. شــلونك؟ *šloonak?* How are you? شلون الأهل؟ *šloon l-'ahil?* How's the family? 2. how, in what manner. ما يعرف شلون يروح هناك *ma y^c^arf šloon yruuḥ hnaak.* He doesn't know how to go there 3. why, for what reason? شـلون تقـول هـذا؟ *šloon tguul haaða?* How could you say this? شلون ما بنيت بيـت بعـد؟ *šloon ma bineet beet ba^c^ad?* How come you haven't built a house yet? 4. what, what sort of, what kind of. شلون؟ أنـت اللي وافقـت علـى الـزواج *šloon? 'inti llii waafagti ^c^ala z-zawaaj.* What? You are the one who agreed to get married. شلون حكي هـذا؟ أنـت تغشـمـر *šloon ḥači haaða? 'inta tġašmir.* What kind of talk is this? You're kidding.

شـلون مـا *šloon-ma* however, howsoever. أسـوي لـك اياهـا شـلون مـا تريـد. *'asawii-lak-iyyaaha šloon-ma triid.* I will do it for you any way you want.

ش م ح ط *šmḥṭ*

شمحوط *šamḥuuṭ* p. شماحيط *šamaaḥiiṭ* very tall person. التنديل رجـال شـطوله! شمحـوط *t-tindeel rayyaal š-ṭuula! šamḥuuṭ.* What a tall man the supervisor is! He's a very tall man.

ش م ر *šmr*

شمري *šammari* p. شمر *šammar* or بني شمر *bani šammar* large Arab tribe in the north of the Arabian Peninsula. أنت شمري والا دوسـري؟ *'inta šammari walla doosari* Are you one of the *šammari* or *doosari* tribesmen?

ش م س *šms*

شمس *šammas* II to expose to the sun, lay out in the sun. نـاس واجديـن هـني يشمسـون هدومهـم *naas waaydiin hni yšammsuun hduumhum.* Many people here lay their clothes out in the sun.

تشمس *tšammas* V to bask in the sun, expose oneself to the sun. اللـي يتشمسـون هـني الأمريكـان والأوروبيـين *'illi yitšammasuun hini l-'amrikaan w-l-'urooppiyyiin.* Those who bask in the sun here are the Americans and the Europeans.

شمس *šams* p. شموس *šmuus* sun. ساعة شـروق الشـمس *saa^c^at šruug š-šams* at sunrise. غـروب الشـمس *ġruub š-šams* sunset. غـابت الشـمس *ġaabat š-šams.* The sun set. ضربـة شمس *ḍarbat šams* sunstroke.

شمسي *šamsi* (coll.) kind of pigeons. (s. unknown). (coll.) حب شمسي *ḥabb šamsi* sunflower seeds. s. حبة شمسي *ḥabbat šamsi.*

شمسي *šamsi* solar, sun-. ساعة شمسية *saa^c^a šamsiyya* sundial. حمـام شمسـي *ḥammaam šamsi* sunbath. طاقة شمسية *ṭaaga šamsiyya* solar energy.

ش م ش و ل *šmšwl*

شمشول *šamšuul* p. شماشيل *šamaašiil* loose trousers (usually worn by pearl divers or women under the *aba*).

ش م غ *šmġ*

شماغ *šmaaġ* p. *-aat* headdress (غترة *ġitra* is more common. See under غ ت ر *ġtr*).

ش م م šmm

(continued)

شم šamm (v.n. from شم šamm) smelling, sniffing.

ش ن گ šng

شنق šinag (يشنق yušnug) to hang s.o. (on a gibbet). شنقوه ساعة الصبح *šingoo saaᶜat ṣ-ṣubḥ.* They hanged him early in the morning.

شنق šang hanging. الشنق يكون نص الليل والا الفجر *š-šang ykuun nuṣṣ l-leel walla l-fajir.* Hanging takes place either at midnight or at dawn. حكموا عليه بالشنق *ḥikmaw ᶜalee b-š-šang.* They sentenced him to death by hanging.

مشنقة mašnaga p. مشانق *mašaanig* gallows, hanging place.

ش ن ن šnn

شن šann (يشن yšinn) to launch an attack, make an attack. شن حملة *šann ḥamla* to launch a campaign. شن غارة *šann ġaara* to make a raid.

ش ن و šnw

شنو šinu (inter. pron.) (short for شنهو *šinhu* or *šinhaw*) What? What is it? What do you mean? شنو تريد؟ *šinu triid?* What do you want?

ش ه د šhd

شهد šihad (يشهد *yišhad)* 1. to testify, bear witness, give testimony. شهد عليه في المحكمة *šihad ᶜalee fi l-maḥkama.* He testified against him in court. أشهد لك *'ašhad-lak.* I will testify for you. أشهد بالله انه لحيةٍ غانمة *'ašhad bil-laah 'inna liḥyatin ġaanma.* I swear by God he's a very nice man. 2. (with على *ᶜala* s.th.) to sign as a witness. شهد على

ش م ل ١ šml

شمل šimal (يشمل *yišmil)* to include, imply. السعر يشمل الضريبة *s-siᶜir yišmil ḍ-ḍariiba.* The price includes tax. الزيادة تشمل الأجانب *z-ziyaada tišmil l-'ayaanib.* The increase (in salary) includes the foreigners.

اشتمل štimal VIII (with على *ᶜala*) to contain, include, be made up of. الشقة تشتمل على حجرتين نوم وحمام ومطبخ *š-šigga tištamil ᶜala ḥijirteen noom w-ḥammaam w-maṭbax.* The apartment consists of two bedrooms, a bathroom, and a kitchen.

شمل šamil uniting, gathering. اجتمع شملنا *jtimaᶜ šamlana.* We had a reunion. We got together.

شامل šaamil (act. part. from شمل *šimal*) comprehensive, inclusive. امتحان شامل *mtiḥaan šaamil* comprehensive examination.

ش م ل ٢ šml

شمال šamaal (common var. *šmaal*) north. شمال شرق *šamaal šarg* northeast. شمال المدينة *šamaal l-madiina* north of the city.

شمالي šamaali 1. northerly wind. 2. northern, north. القسم الشمالي *l-gism š-šamaali* the northern section.

ش م م šmm

شم šamm (يشم *yšimm)* to smell, sniff. شميت شي خايس *šammeet šayy xaayis.* I smelled a rotten thing. يشم سعوط *yšimm sᶜuuṭ.* He sniffs snuff.

اشتم štamm VIII = شم *šamm.*

عقد الـــزواج *šihad ᶜala ᶜagd z-zawaaj.* He signed the marriage contract as a witness.

شـــهد *šahhad* II to make or cause to give testimony. شهدت باق من الدكان. *baag min d-dikkaan. šahhatt* جماعة عليه *jamaaᶜa ᶜalee.* He stole from the store. I had people testify against him.

تشـاهد *tšaahad* VI 1. to recite the creed to Islam. كل مسلم يعرف كيـف يتشـــاهد *kill muslim yᶜarif keef yitšaahad.* Every Muslim knows how to recite the creed of Islam. 2. to say one's last words, be near death. قبل ما وقعت الطيارة تشاهدنــا *gabil-ma wugᶜat ṭ-ṭayyaara tšaahadna.* Before the plane crashed, we said our last words.

اســتشهد *stašhad* X 1. to die as a martyr. اســتشهد في المعركــة *stašhad fi l-maᶜraka.* He gave his life in the battle. 2. (with ب *b-*) to cite as authority, quote as evidence. استشهدت بآية مـــن القـــرآن *stašhatt b-'aaya min l-ġur'aan.* I quoted a verse from the Quran as evidence.

شهيد *šahiid* p. شهدا *šuhada* martyr.

شهادة *šahaada* p. شهايد *šahaayid, -aat* 1. certificate, degree, diploma. 2. testimony, deposition.

شــاهد *šaahid* p. شهود *šhuud* 1. witness. الشاهد شهد واياي *š-šaahid šihad wiyyaay.* The witness testified in my favor. 2. (p. شـــهاد *šuhhaad*) headstone. 3. (p. شواهـــد *šawaahid*) the pointer (finger). 4. (p. شواهـــد *šawaahid*) the largest bead in a prayer rosary.

ش ه ر *šhr*

اشتــهر *štihar* VIII to be or become famous, well-known. اشتهر عقب ما تعين وزيـــر *štihar ᶜugub-ma tᶜayyan waziir.* He became famous after he was appointed minister. راس الخيمة تشتـــهر بالزراعـــــة *raas l-xeema tištahir b-z-ziraaᶜa.* Ras Al-Khaima is famous for agriculture.

شهر *šahar* p. أشهر *'ašhir,* شهور *šuhuur* month. الشهر الجاي *š-šahar l-yaay* next month. شهر العســـل *šahar l-ᶜasal* the honeymoon.

شـــهري *šahri* monthly. معاش شهري *maᶜaaš šahri* monthly salary. إيجار شهري *'iijaar šahri* monthly rent.

شهرية *šahriyya* p. *-aat* monthly rent.

شهرة *šuhra* fame, reputation.

أشـــهر *'ašhar* (elat.) 1. (with من *min*) more famous, well-known. 2. (with foll. n.) the most famous, well-known,

مشهور *mašhuur* famous, well-known. لاعـــب كـــورة مشـــهور *laaᶜib kuura mašhuur* famous soccer player. مشهور ب *mašhuur b-* famous, well-known for. هيلي مشهورة بآثارها *hiili mašhuura b-'aaθaarha.* Hili is famous for its ruins.

ش ه گ *šhg*

شـــهق *šihag (يشهق yišhag)* 1. to sigh deeply. شهق لين سمع الأخبار *šihag leen simaᶜ l-'axbaar.* He sighed deeply when he heard the news. 2. to burst into tears, weep loudly. شهق من الفرح *šihag min l-faraḥ.* He burst into tears of joy.

ش ه م *šhm*

شـهـم *šahim* p. *-iin* decent, noble, gentlemanly.

ش ه ي *šhy*

شهى *šahha* II to whet the appetite, be appetizing. ها الأكـل يشـهي *hal-'akil yšahhi.* This food whets the appetite.

اشتـهى *štiha* VIII to have an appetite or craving for s.th. ما أشتهي آكل *ma 'aštihi 'aakil.* I have no appetite for eating. اشتهت الرمـان الحـامض *štihat r-rummaan l-ḥaamiḍ.* She had a craving for sour pomegranates.

شهية *šahiyya* appetite, craving.

ش و ت¹ *šwt*

شات *šaat (يشوت yšuut)* to shoot, kick a ball. شات الكورة برجله اليسـار *šaat l-kuura b-riila l-yisaar.* He kicked the ball (into the goal) with his left foot.

ش و ت² *šwt*

شاوت *šaawat* III to argue a lot. يشاوت ويلاوت *yšaawit w-ylaawit.* He argues incessantly.

ش و چ *šwč*

See under **ش و ك** *šwk.*

ش و ر *šwr*

شار *šaar (يشور yšuur)* = شار *šaar* (يشير *yšiir)* (with على *ᶜala*) to offer advice to s.o. المطوع شار عليّ أروح أشوف الشيخ *li-mṭawwaᶜ šaar ᶜalayya 'aruuḥ 'ačuuf š-šeex.* The holy man advised me to go to see the Shaikh.

شاور *šaawar* III to consult with s.o., ask s.o.'s advice. شاوروا أبوها وصـار قسمة ونصيب وخطبوهـا منـه *šaawraw 'ubuuha w-ṣaar jisma w-naṣiib w-xaṭabuuha minna.* They consulted with her father and they were fortunate and asked him for her hand in marriage.

تشـاور *tšaawar* VI to consult with each other, deliberate. تقابلنا وتشاورنا وخطبنا البنـت *tgaabalna w-ššaawarna w-xiṭabna l-bint.* We met, consulted with each other, and asked for the girl's hand in marriage.

استشار *stašaar* X to consult s.o., ask for s.o.'s advice. عنيد؛ ما يستشير أحد *ᶜaniid; ma yistašiir 'aḥad.* He's stubborn; he doesn't consult anyone. الواحد لازم يستشير اللي أكبر منه *l-waaḥid laazim yistašiir illi 'akbar minna.* People should consult those who are older than they are.

شور *šoor* (v.n. from شار *šaar*) counsel, advice, suggestion. الشور شورك يا يبا وانا أطيع أمرك *š-šoor šoorak ya yuba w-aana 'aṭiiᶜ 'amrak.* The decision is yours, father, and I will obey you.

مشاورة *mšaawara* (v.n. from III شاور *šaawar*) consultation, deliberation.

إشـارة *'išaara* p. *-aat* 1. sign, signal. أوقف عند إشـارة الـترافيك *'oogaf ᶜind 'išaarat t-trafik.* Stop at the traffic sign.

اسـتشارة *stišaara* (v.n. from X استشار *stašaar*) seeking of advice, consultation.

اسـتشاري *stišaari* advisory. مجلـس اسـتشاري *majlis stišaari* advisory council.

مستشار *mustašaar* (p.p. from X استشار

stašaar) adviser, counselor. مستشار عسكري *mustašaar ᶜaskari* military adviser. مستشار تعليمي *mustašaar taᶜliimi* educational, cultural adviser. مستشار السفارة *mustašaar s-safaara* the embassy counselor.

ش و ش *šwš*

شاش *šaaš* (coll.) muslin. s. -*a* piece of muslin.

شاشة *šaaša* p. -*aat* (movie) screen.

ش و ط *šwṭ*

شوط *šooṭ* p. اشواط *šwaaṭ* round, half, course (in sports and games). الشوط الأول *š-šooṭ l-'awwal* the first round, the first half.

ش و ف *šwf* = *čwf.* See under **چ و ف** *čwf.*

ش و ك *šwk*

شوك *šook* (coll.) (common var. *šooč*) thorns. s. -*a* طحت حدر ونخزني شوك الصبر *ṭiht ḥadir w-nixazni šooč ṣ-ṣabir.* I fell down there and the cactus thorns pricked me.

ش و گ *šwg*

اشتاق *štaag* VIII to long, yearn, have a desire, nostalgia. سافر أمريكا واشتاق حق هله *saafar 'amriika w-štaag ḥagg hala.* He traveled to America and longed to see his family. اشتاقيت أسافر وإياه *štaageet 'asaafir wiyyaa.* I liked to travel with him. أشتاق إلى ذيك الأيام الحلوة *'aštaag 'ila ðiič l-'ayyaam l-ḥilwa.* I yearn for those pleasant times.

شوق *šoog* p. أشواق *'ašwaag* longing, yearning, desire.

مشتاق *mištaag* (act. part. from VIII اشتاق *štaag*) longing, yearning, desirous. مشتاق لك *mištaag-lič.* I have been longing for you (f.). I miss you (f.).

ش و ل *šwl*

شوال *šawwaal* Shawwal (the tenth month of the Islamic calendar).

ش و ه *šwh*

شوه *šawwah* II to disfigure, make ugly, distort, debase. الجدري يشوه الوجه *l-jidri yšawwih l-weeh.* Smallpox mars the face. يشوه الحقيقة *yšawwih l-ḥagiiga.* He distorts the truth. اللي يتعاطون المخدرات يشوهون سمعة البلد *'illi yitᶜaaṭuun l-muxaddaraat yšawwhuun sumᶜat l-bald.* Those who deal in drugs debase the reputation of the country.

تشوه *tšawwah* V pass. of II شوه *šawwah.* وجهها تشوه بالعملية *wehha tšawwah b-l-ᶜamaliyya.* Her face was marred by the operation.

ش و ي ١ *šwy*

شوى *šuwa* (يشوي *yišwi*) to broil, grill, roast. كشتنا وشوينا لحم واستانسنا *kišatna w-šuweena laḥam w-staanasna.* We went on a picnic, grilled meat, and enjoyed ourselves. الشمس شوتني *š-šams šuwatni.* I got a sunburn. (prov.) اللي ما يعرف الصقر يشويه *'illi ma yᶜarf ṣ-ṣagir yišwii.* Don't kill the goose that lays the golden egg.

انشوى *nšuwa* VII to be broiled, grilled, roasted. انشوى اللحم ونحن بارزين حق الأكل *nšuwa l-laḥam w-niḥin baarziin ḥagg l-'akil.* The meat was broiled and we are ready to eat.

ش ي ء šy'

شاء *šaa'* (reduced to شا *-šaa-* in a few phrases, of God) to want, wish, desire. انشاالله = إن شاء الله *('in)šaaḷḷa* 1. God willing, I hope, it is to be hoped (that). انشاالله مستانس هني *nšaaḷḷa mistaanis hini.* I hope you are comfortable here. انشاالله المدير هني *nšaaḷḷa l-mudiir hni.* I hope the director is here. 2. (as a response to a request or a command) yes, gladly, willingly. تشيك التاير! *čayyik t-taayir!* Check the tire! انشاالله! *nšaaḷḷa!* yes, certainly. ما شاء الله = ماشاالله *maašaaḷḷa* (lit., "whatever God intended.") 3. (expresses a great amount, quantity, or number) ماشاالله عندهم فلوس ودكاكين وشركات *maašaaḷḷa ᶜindhum fluus w-dikaakiin w-šarikaat.* They have a lot of wealth, stores, and companies. 4. (expresses surprise, astonishment, etc.) Great! Wonderful! Bravo! ماشاالله خذت الأولى على بنات صفها *maašaaḷḷa xaðat l-'uula ᶜala banaat ṣaffha.* Great! She ranked "first" among students of her class.

ش ي ب šyb

شاب *šaab (يشيب yšiib)* to grow old, become an old man, become gray-haired. (prov.) عقب ما شاب ودوه الكتاب *ᶜugub-ma šaab waddoo l-kuttaab.* You cannot teach an old dog new tricks. (lit., "After he had become an old man, they sent him to school.")

شيب *šayyab* II = شاب *šaab.* رجال عود كبير. شيب *rayyaal ᶜood čibiir. šayyab.* He's a very old man. He got old.

مشوي *mašwi* (p.p. from شوى *šuwa*) grilled, roasted, broiled. سمك مشوي *simač mašwi* grilled fish. لحم مشوي *laḥam mašwi* broiled meat.

ش و ي ٢ šwy

شاوي *šaawiy* p. شويان *šiwyaan* 1. shepherd. 2. sheep dealer.

ش و ي ٣ šwy

شوية *šwayya* (less common var. شوي *šwayy*) 1. small amount, a little, a few, some. عندي شوية فلوس *ᶜindi šwayyat fluus.* I have a small amount of money. عطني شوية قهوة *ᶜaṭni šwayyat gahwa.* Give me some coffee. شوية دولارات *šwayyat duulaaraat* a few dollars. 2. a short time. أنت تدش عقب شوية *'inta ddišš ᶜugb šwayya.* You enter in a little while. استنا شوية! *stanna šwayya!* Wait a minute! Just a minute! 3. a little bit, somewhat. ريوس شوية *reewis šwayya.* Back up a little. هو حمقان شوية *huwa ḥamgaan šwayya.* He's a little mad.

ش ي ي šyy

شي *šayy* p. أشيا *'ašya* 1. thing. شي زين *šayy zeen* good thing. تبغى شي؟ *tibġa šayy?* Do you want anything? ما عندي شي *ma ᶜindi šayy.* I don't have anything. نفس الشي *nafs š-šayy* the same thing. بعض الشي *baᶜð̣ š-šayy* to a certain degree, a little. تحسن بعض الشي *tḥassan baᶜð̣ š-šayy.* He improved a little. 2. something جبت له شي يبغاه *yibt-la šayy yibġaa.* I brought him something he wanted. شي عجيب *šayy ᶜajiib* something strange.

شيب *šeeb* grayness of the hair, gray or white hair.

شيبة *šeeba* p. شواب *šuwwaab* old man. آنا أخبر بو علي شيبة والعصا بيده *'aana axbar bu ᶜali šeeba w-l-ᶜaṣa b-yadda.* I know that Abu Ali is an old man and he carries a cane.

ش ي خ *šyx*

شيخ *šeex* p. شيوخ *šyuux* 1. Shaikh, leader, head (of a tribe). الشيخ زايد *š-šeex zaayid* Shaikh Zaid. هذا شيخ الدواسر *haaða šeex d-duwaasir.* This is the leader of the Dosaris (tribesmen of the Dosari tribe). 2. ruler (of a country) رحت القصر وسلمت على الشيخ *riḥt l-gaṣir w-sallamt ᶜala š-šeex.* I went to the palace and greeted the ruler. 3. religious scholar or teacher. 4. senator. مجلس الشيوخ *majlis š-šyuux* the senate. الشيوخ *š-šyuux* the Shaikhs (members of the ruling family).

شيخة *šeexa* p. *-aat* Shaikh's wife, sister or relative. الشيخة فاطمة *š-šeexa faaṭma* Shaikha Fatima (the ruler's wife).

شيخوخة *šeexuuxa* old age, senility.

ش ي ر *šyr*

شجر *šiyar* (coll.) trees. s. شجرة *šyara* p. *-aat.* شجرة موز *šyarat mooz* banana tree. عندهم خمس شجرات عنب في البستان *ᶜindahum xams šyaraat ᶜinab fi l-bistaan.* They have five grape vines in the orchard.

ش ي ش *šyš*

شاش *šaaš* (يشيش *yšiiš*) to be or become furious, angry. شاش وقام يكسر الأشيا *šaaš w-gaam ykassir l-'ašya.* He became furious and began to break things.

شيش *šiiš* p. شياش *šyaaš* 1. skewer. 2. metal rod or bar.

شيشة *šiiša* p. إشيش *'išyaš* bottle, flask. شيشة بترول *šiišat batrool* gas station.

شيشاوي *šiišaawi* 1. of glass, having to do with glass. 2. (p. *-yyiin*) one who makes or sells bottles. 2. (coll.) fish (also known as صافي *ṣaafi* rabbitfish). s. *-yya* p. *-aat.*

ش ي ط ن *šyṭn*

تشيطن *tšeeṭan* (يتشيطن *yitšeeṭan*) to behave like a little rascal. بس! لا تتشيطن. ماحد يقدر عليك *bass! la tiššeeṭan. maḥḥad yigdar ᶜaleek.* Enough! Don't behave like a little rascal. Nobody can control you.

شيطان *šiiṭaan* p. شياطين *šiyaaṭiin* 1. devil, demon. 2. little rascal, mischief-maker. 3. wise guy, smart alec.

ش ي ع *šyᶜ*

شاع *šaaᶜ* (يشيع *yšiiᶜ*) to spread, become known or widespread. شاع الخبر بين الناس *šaaᶜ l-xabar been n-naas.* The news item spread among the people. شاع استعمال الكمبيوتر في الإمارات *šaaᶜ stiᶜmaal l-kombyuutar fi l-'imaaraat.* The use of computers has spread in the Emirates.

شيع *šayyaᶜ* II (شيع الجنازة *šayyaᶜ l-janaaza*) to attend a funeral procession, attend a funeral. ناس واجدين شيعوا جنازته *naas waaydiin šayyaᶜaw janaazta.* Many people attended his funeral.

الشيعـــة *š-šiiᶜa* the Shiites (the branch of Muslims who recognize Ali as Prophet Muhammad's successor).

شيعـــي *šiiᶜi* 1. Shiitic. المذهب الشيعي *l-maðhab š-šiiᶜi* the Shiitic religious creed. 2. (p. شيعة *šiiᶜa*) a Shiite.

شيوعـــــي *šuyuuᶜi* 1. communist, communistic. المبدا الشيوعــــي *l-mabda š-šuyuuᶜi* the communist ideology. 2. (p. *-yyin*) a communist.

الشيوعية *š-šuyuuᶜiyya* communism.

إشاعــــة *'išaaᶜa* (v.n.) spreading, circulation of news. 2. (p. *-aat*) rumor, gossip.

ش ي ك[١] *šyk*

شيك *šayyak* II (more common var. II جيك *čayyak*). See چ ي ك *čyk*.

ش ي ك[٢] *šyk*

شيك *šeek* p. *-aat* check. صرفت الشيك في البنك *ṣiraft š-šeek fi l-bank.* I cashed the check at the bank. شيكات سياحية *šeekaat siyaaḥiyya* traveler's checks. شيك بـــدون رصيـــد *šeek b-duun raṣiid* uncovered check.

ش ي ل *šyl*

شـــال *šaal* (يشيل *yšiil*) 1. to lift, raise, pick up. شيل الشنط وحطهم على الميزان *šiil š-šinaṭ w-ḥuṭṭhum ᶜala l-miizaan.* Lift the suitcases and put them on the scale. 2. to carry, transport. شـــال صندوق الطماط إلى السيارة *šaal ṣanduug ṭ-ṭamaaṭ 'ila s-sayyaara.* He carried the box of tomatoes to the car. ها التكسي يشيل خمس عبريـــة *hat-taksi yšiil xamas ᶜibriyya.* This taxicab carries five passengers. 3. to carry on one's person, wear, bear. ما تقدر تشيل مسدس خفيـــة *ma tigdar tšiil musaddas xifya.* You cannot carry a concealed revolver. عنده درزن جهال. يشيل هم كبير *ᶜinda darzan yihhaal. yšiil hamm čibiir.* He has a dozen kids. He is burdened with worry. يشيل فلوس واجد وايـــاه *yšiil fluus waayid wiyyaa.* He (usually) has a lot of money on him. 4. to leave, change location, change residence. شالوا من زمـــان *šaalaw min zamaan.* They left a long time ago.

شيل *šeel* (v.n.) 1. lifting. 2. carrying.

شـــال *šaall* (act. part. from شال *šaal*) (common var. شايل *šaayil*) 1. carrying, transporting. التكسي شايل خمس أنفـــار *t-taksi šaayil xamas 'anfaar.* The taxicab is carrying five people. 2. carrying on one's person, wearing. bearing. شايل فلوس واياك؟ *šaayil fluus wiyyaak?* Do you have any money on you?

شيال *šayyaal* p. *-aat* 1. suspenders. 2. bra.

ش ي م *šym*

شيمـــة *šiima* good moral character, integrity, magnanimity, virtue.

ش ي ن[١] *šyn*

شـــين *šeen* 1. bad. أشتريه، زين والا شين *'aštirii, zeen walla šeen.* I'll buy it, good or bad. 2. ugly. (prov.) الزين زين لو قعد منّ منامه والشين شـــين لـــو غســـل بصـــابون *z-zeen zeenin lo giᶜad min manaama w-š-šeen šeenin lo ġassal b-ṣaabuun.* A leopard cannot change its spots.

ش ي و ل *šywl*

شيول *šeewil* p. *-aat* shovel.

ش ي ن[٢] *šyn*

شين *šiin* name of the letter ش *š*.

ص

ص ا ج *ṣaaj*

صاج *ṣaaj* (coll.) thin sheets of metal. s. *-a*.

صاجة *ṣaaja* p. *-aat* bread tin, baking tin.

ص ا د *ṣaad*

صاد *ṣaad* name of the letter ص *ṣ*.

ص ا ر و ج *ṣaarwj*

صاروج *ṣaaruuj* (coll.) roof sealer.

ص ا ع *ṣaa^c^*

صاع *ṣaa^c^* p. صيعان *ṣii^c^aan* grain measure (approx.) 2½ kilograms. صاع بصاع *ṣaa^c^ b-ṣaa^c^* tit for tat. كال الصاع بصاعين *kaal ṣ-ṣaa^c^ b-ṣaa^c^een* to pay s.o. back twofold.

ص ا ل و ن١ *ṣaalwn*

صالون *ṣaaloon* p. *-aat* six-passenger car, more commonly known as سيارة صالون *sayyaara ṣaaloon.*

ص ا ل و ن٢ *ṣaalwn*

صالونة *ṣaaloona* soup. كليت صالونة وسمك *kaleet ṣaaloona w-simač.* I ate soup and fish.

ص ب ب *ṣbb*

صب *ṣabb (يصب yṣibb)* to pour, pour out. صب الماي على ايديني *ṣabb l-maay ^c^ala 'iideeni.* He poured the water on my hands. صب الشاي في الاستكان *ṣibb č-čaay fi li-stikaan.* Pour the tea into the tea cup. صب لي فنجان قهوة *ṣibb-li finyaan ghawa.* Pour me a cup of coffee.

صبيب *ṣibiib* dish made from dough, onions, and shortening.

ص ب ب ا ن *ṣbbaan*

صبان *ṣabbaan* (coll.) snails. s. *-a.* نحن ما ناكل الصبان *niḥin ma naakil ṣ-ṣabbaan.* We don't eat snails.

ص ب ح *ṣbḥ*

صبح *ṣabbaḥ* II to bid s.o. good morning. صبحك الله بالخير! *ṣabbaḥk 'aḷḷa b-l-xeer!* Good morning! جا وصبح علينا *yaa w-ṣabbaḥ ^c^aleena.* He came and said, "Good morning," to us.

أصبح *'aṣbaḥ* IV to be or become in the morning. كيف أصبحت اليوم *čeef 'aṣbaḥt l-yoom?* How are you this morning?

صبح *ṣubḥ* daybreak. ساعة الصبح *saa^c^t ṣ-ṣubḥ* at dawn. صلاة الصبح *ṣalaat ṣ-ṣubḥ* the morning prayer (at dawn).

صباح *ṣabaaḥ* morning. اليوم الصباح *l-yoom ṣ-ṣabaaḥ* this morning. الصباح *ṣ-ṣabaaḥ* in the morning. يدش الشغل الصباح *yidišš š-šuġul ṣ-ṣabaaḥ.* He goes to work in the morning. باكر الصباح *baačir ṣ-ṣabaaḥ* tomorrow morning. صباح الجمعة *ṣabaaḥ l-yim^c^a* Friday morning. (prov.) الصباح رباح *ṣ-ṣabaaḥ rabaaḥ.* The early bird gets the worm.

صباحة *ṣbaaḥa* money or gift a bridegroom gives to his bride on the morning of the wedding day.

ص ب خ ṣbx

صبخة *ṣabxa* infertile, alkaline soil.

ص ب ر ١ ṣbr

صبر *ṣibar (يصبر yaṣbir)* to be patient, wait patiently. صبر وحصل اللي يبغيه *ṣibar w-ḥaṣṣal illi yabġii.* He was patient and got what he wanted. !اصبر !صبر *'iṣbir! ṣabir!* Be patient! Wait a minute! صبرت خمس سنين وجابت ولد *ṣbarat xamas siniin w-yaabat walad.* She waited for five years until she had a baby boy.

صبر *ṣabbar* II to make s.o. wait. شو !اللي يصبرني *šu lli yṣabbirni!* There's nothing that can make me wait!

صبر *ṣabir* (v.n. from صبر *ṣibar*) patience. (prov.) الصبر مفتاح الفرج *ṣ-ṣabir miftaaḥ l-faraj.* Patience is the key to a happy ending. صبر أيوب *ṣabir 'ayyuub* the patience of Job.

صابر *ṣaabir* (act. part.) p. *-iin* patient, enduring. صابر على الذل *ṣaabir* *ᶜala ð-ðull* enduring humiliation.

ص ب ر ٢ ṣbr

صبار *ṣbaar* drink made from tamarind.

ص ب ع ṣbᶜ

صبع *ṣubiᶜ* p. صبوع *ṣbuuᶜ*, صوابع *ṣuwaabiᶜ* finger. (prov.) صوابع يدك موب واحدة *ṣuwaabiᶜ yaddak muub waḥda.* Your fingers are not the same. Different strokes for different folks. صبع رجل *ṣubiᶜ reel* toe.

ص ب ن ṣbn

صابون *ṣaabuun* see under **ص و ب ن** *ṣwbn.*

ص ب ي ṣby

صبي *ṣbayy* p. صبيان *-aan* young boy, lad.

صبيانية *ṣbyaaniyya* childish actions.

ص ب ي ط ṣbyṭ

صبيطي *ṣbeeṭi* (coll.) kind of fish. s. *-yya.*

ص پ ا ن ṣpaan

صبانة *ṣpaana* (common var. *sbaana*) p. *-aat* wrench, spanner.

ص چ م ṣčm

صچمة *ṣačma* p. صچم *ṣičam* ball bearing.

ص ح ب ṣḥb

صاحب *ṣaaḥab* III 1. to be or become a friend with s.o. صاحب جماعة أكبر منه *ṣaaḥab yamaaᶜa 'akbar minna.* He became friends with a group older than he was. 2. to associate with s.o. يصاحب اللي يسكر *yṣaaḥib illi yiskar.* He associates with those who drink wine.

صاحب *ṣaaḥib* p. أصحاب *'aṣḥaab* 1. friend, associate. واحد من أصحابي جا واياي *waaḥid min 'aṣḥaabi ya wiyyaay.* One of my friends came with me. 2. owner, holder, possessor. صاحب الدكان *ṣaaḥib d-dikkaan* the shop owner. صاحب الجلالة *ṣaaḥib l-jalaala* p. أصحاب الجلالة *'aṣḥaab l-jalaala* His Majesty. صاحب الحق *ṣaaḥib l-ḥagg* the one who is in the right. صاحب السمو *ṣaaḥib s-sumuww* His Royal Highness.

ص ح ح ṣḥḥ

صح *ṣaḥḥ (يصح yṣiḥḥ)* 1. to be true,

correct. اللي تقوله ما يصح *'illi tguula ma yṣiḥḥ.* What you say cannot be true. إذا يصح الخبر ما فيه مشكلة *'iδa yṣiḥḥ l-xabar ma fii muškila.* If the news is correct, there will be no problem. 2. (with ل *l-*) to be found by s.o., come to s.o. صحت له وظيفة زينة *ṣaḥḥat-la waδiifa zeena.* He got a good position. 3. to give a chance, allow an opportunity. يصح لك تجي وايانا؟ *yṣiḥḥ-lak tiyi wiyyaana?* Will you have a chance to come with us? مشغول واجد. اسمح لي. ما يصح لي أروح *mašġuul waayid. smaḥ-li. ma yṣaḥḥ-li 'aruuḥ.* I'm very busy. Please excuse me. I don't have the time to come. ما يصح لك تفطر في شهر رمضان *ma yṣaḥḥ-lak tifṭir fi šahar rumδaan.* You are not allowed to break your fast during the month of Ramadan.

صحح *ṣaḥḥaḥ* II to correct, grade, mark. الأستاذ صحح الامتحان *l-'ustaaδ ṣaḥḥaḥ li-mtiḥaan.* The teacher has graded the exam.

صحة *ṣiḥḥa* 1. health. وزارة الصحة *wazarat ṣ-ṣiḥḥa* the ministry of health. صحته زينة *ṣiḥḥta zeena.* He's in good health. 2. truth, validity.

صحي *ṣiḥḥi* 1. wholesome, healthy. اكل هذا. صحي *'ikil haaδa. ṣiḥḥi.* Eat this. It's wholesome. 2. sanitary, hygienic. لا تشرب ها الماي. موب صحي *la tišrab hal-maay. muub ṣiḥḥi.* Don't drink this water. It's not sanitary.

صحيح *ṣaḥiiḥ* true, correct, right. صحيح راحت وياك؟ *ṣaḥiiḥ raaḥat wiyyaak?* Is it true that she went with you? لا، موب صحيح *la, muub ṣaḥiiḥ.* No, it's not true. حلف يمين وقال الصحيح *ḥilaf yamiin w-gaal ṣ-ṣaḥiiḥ.* He took an oath and told the truth.

أصح *'aṣaḥḥ* 1. (with من *min*) more correct, complete than. 2. (with foll. n.) the most authentic, reliable.

تصحيح *taṣḥiiḥ* (v.n. from II صحح *ṣaḥḥaḥ*) correction, correcting.

صحر *ṣḥr*

صحرا *ṣaḥra* p. صحاري *ṣaḥaari* desert.

صحراوي *ṣaḥraawi* desert, desolate. أراضي صحراوية *'araaδi ṣaḥraawiyya* desert lands.

صحارة *ṣaḥḥaara* see سحارة *saḥḥaara* under **سحر** *sḥr.*

صحف *ṣḥf*

صحيفة *ṣaḥiifa* p. صحايف *ṣaḥaayif* 1. page, leaf (of a book, etc.). صحيفته بيضا *ṣaḥiifta beeδa.* He has a clean slate. 2. (p. صحف *ṣuḥuf*) newspaper (جريدة *jariida* is more common).

صحافة *ṣaḥaafa* 1. journalism. يدرس صحافة *yidris ṣaḥaafa.* He's studying journalism. 2. the press. حرية الصحافة *ḥurriyyat ṣ-ṣaḥaafa* the freedom of the press.

صحافي *ṣaḥaafi* 1. journalistic, press (adj.). مؤتمر صحافي *mu'tamar ṣaḥaafi* press conference. 2. (p. *-yyiin, -yya*) journalist, reporter.

مصحف *muṣḥaf* p. مصاحف *maṣaaḥif* copy, edition of the Quran.

صحن *ṣḥn*

صحن *ṣaḥan* (less common var. *ṣaḥin*) p. صحون *ṣuḥuun* plate, dish. غسلت الصحون *ġisalt ṣ-ṣuḥuun.* I did the dishes. صحن عيش *ṣaḥan ᶜeeš* plate of rice.

صخخ١ *ṣxx*

صخ *ṣaxx* (يصخ *yṣixx*) to hold, hold s.th. forth. الغيص صخ الحمسة *l-ġeeṣ ṣaxx li-ḥmisa.* The pearl diver held the turtle.

صخخ٢ *ṣxx*

صخة *ṣaxxa* 1. stillness, quiet, calmness. 2. heavy rain.

صخر *ṣxr*

صخر *ṣaxar* (coll.) rocks, boulders. s. صخرة *ṣxara.* صخر مرجاني *ṣaxar marjaani* coral rocks. راسه يابس مثل الصخر *raasa yaabis miθl ṣ-ṣaxar.* His head is as hard as rocks. الصخرة *ṣ-ṣaxra,* قبة الصخرة *gubbat ṣ-ṣaxra* the Dome of the Rock.

صخف *ṣxf*

صخيف *ṣixiif* 1. narrow. هذا درب صخيف؛ ما تقدر تفوت منه السيارة *haaða darb ṣixiif; ma tigdar tfuut minna s-sayyaara.* This is a narrow alley; the car cannot go through it. 2. skinny, thin. صخيف الساق *ṣixiif s-saag* thin-legged.

صخل *ṣxl*

صخل *ṣaxal* p. صخول *ṣxuul* young goat, kid. f. صخلة *ṣxala* (prov.) الطول طول نخلة والعقل عقل صخلة *ṭ-ṭuul ṭuul nxaḷa w-l-ᶜagil ᶜagil ṣxala.* The body of a man and the mind of a child.

صخم *ṣxm*

صخم *ṣaxxam* II to blacken, besmudge. الجولة صخمت يده *č-čuula ṣaxxamat yadda.* The stove made his hand black.

تصخم *tṣaxxam* V to be blackened. تصخمت يده من الجولة *tṣaxxamat yadda min č-čuula.* His hand got dirty from the stove.

صخام *ṣxaam* soot.

صخن *ṣxn*

صخن *ṣaxxan* II (less common var. صخم *saxxam*) to heat, warm s.th. الشمس تصخن الماي *š-šams tṣaxxin l-maay.* The sun heats the water. (prov.) يوم صخنا الماي شرد الديك *yoom ṣaxxanna l-maay širad d-diič.* Forewarned is forearmed. (lit., "When we heated the water, the rooster ran away.").

صخونة *ṣxuuna* fever, temperature.

مصخن *mṣaxxan* (p.p. from II صخن *ṣaxxan*) p. *-iin* feverish, hot, running a temperature. الدختر عطاني دوا لاني كنت مريض ومصخن *d-daxtar ᶜaṭaani duwa linni čint mariiḍ w-mṣaxxan.* The doctor gave me medicine because I was ill and running a temperature.

صخي *ṣxy*

صخي *ṣixi* p. *-yyiin* generous, hospitable. البدوي صخي واجد. يكرم كل واحد *li-bdiwi ṣixi waayid. yikrim kill waaḥid.* A Bedouin is very generous. He honors every person.

صخاوة *ṣaxaawa* generosity, hospitability. حصلت صخاوة ما بعدها صخاوة *ḥaṣṣalt ṣaxaawa ma baᶜdaha ṣaxaawa.* I was treated very generously.

ص د ا *ṣdaa*

صدا *ṣida* (coll.) sardines. s. صداة *ṣdaa.* أم القيوين فيها أحسن أنواع الصدا *'umm l-giiween fiiha 'aḥsan 'anwaa^c ṣ-ṣida.* Umm Al-Qaiwain has the best sardines.

ص د ج *ṣdj*

صدق *ṣidj* (v.n.) (less common var. *ṣidg*) truth, truthfulness. ما يقول إلا الصدق *ma yguul 'illa ṣ-ṣidj.* He tells nothing except the truth. صدق إنك شفت الشيخ *ṣidj 'innak čift š-šeex?* Is it true that you have seen the ruler?

صديق *ṣidiij* (less common var. *ṣadiig*) friend. p. أصدقا *'aṣdiga.*

ص د ر *ṣdr*

صدر *ṣidar (يصدر yaṣdur)* 1. to be issued, be handed down. صدر الحكم عليه بالإعدام أمس *ṣidar l-ḥukum ^calee b-l-'i^cdaam 'ams.* The death sentence was issued against him yesterday. 2. to originate, stem, arise. الأمر صدر من الديوان الأميري *l-'amir ṣadar min d-diiwaan l-'amiiri.* The order came from the Emiri court. 3. to be published, to come out. أسامي الناجحين في الامتحان صدرت *'asaami n-naajiḥiin fi li-mtiḥaan ṣidrat.* The names of those who passed the examination were published. 4. to be sent out, go out. خطاب الدعوة صدر اليوم *xiṭaab d-da^cwa ṣidar l-yoom.* The letter of invitation went out today.

صدّر *ṣaddar* II 1. to export. دول الخليج تصدر بترول حق كل العالم *duwal l-xaliij tṣaddir batrool ḥagg kill l-^caalam.* The Gulf States export oil to the whole world. 2. to issue, put out, publish. الحكومة صدرت أوامر بتسفير الأجانب *li-ḥkuuma ṣaddarat 'awaamir b-tasfiir l-'ayaanib.* The government issued orders for the deportation of foreigners.

صادر *ṣaadar* III to confiscate, seize. الحكومة صادرت أملاكه *li-ḥkuuma ṣaadarat 'amlaaka.* The government confiscated his property.

تصدر *tṣaddar* V to be exported. تصدر بترول واجد هذي السنة *tṣaddar batrool waayid haaði s-sana.* A lot of petroleum was exported this year. 2. to take the best seat, have the front seat. الرئيس تصدر المجلس *r-ra'iis tṣaddar l-majlis.* The president sat in the best place in the group.

صدر *ṣadir* 1. (p. صدور *ṣduur*) bosom, chest, breast. واسع الصدر *waasi^c ṣ-ṣadir* open-minded, liberal. انشرح صدره *nširaḥ ṣadra.* He was pleased. 2. (p. صدار *ṣdaar*) poop deck.

صدرية *ṣadriyya* p. صداري *ṣadaari* apron, bib.

مصدر *maṣdar* p. مصادر *maṣaadir* origin, source.

تصدير *taṣdiir* (v.n. from II صدر *ṣaddar*) exporting, exportation. إجازة تصدير واستيراد *'ijaazat taṣdiir w-stiiraad* export-import license.

مصادرة *muṣaadara* (v.n. from III صادر *ṣaadar*) confiscation, seizure.

صادر *ṣaadir* (act. part. from صدر *ṣidar*) 1. (with من *min* or عن *^can*) having been issued or handed down from. 2. outbound, going out (letters, etc.)

صادرة *ṣaadira* out-going mail section. صادرات *ṣaadiraat* exports, export goods.

مصدر *mṣaddir* (act. part. from II صدر *ṣaddar*) 1. exporter. 2. having exported. الجابان مصدرة لنا نص مليون سيارة *l-jaabaan mṣaddra la-na nuṣṣ malyoon sayyaara.* Japan has exported to us half a million cars.

ص د ع *ṣd*ᶜ

صدع *ṣadda*ᶜ II to trouble, bother, harass. صدع راسي *ṣadda*ᶜ *raasi.* He gave me a headache.

صداع *ṣudaa*ᶜ headache.

ص د ف *ṣdf*

صادف *ṣaadaf* III 1. to coincide with, occur with, fall on (a certain date). العيد يصادف يوم ميلادي *l-*ᶜ*iid yṣaadif yoom miilaadi.* The feast will coincide with my birthday. أول رمضان يصادف يوم الجمعة *'awwal rumđaan yṣaadif yoom l-yim*ᶜ*a.* The first of Ramadan will fall on a Friday.

صدف *ṣadaf* (coll.) s. صدفة *ṣdifa* 1. seashells. 2. mother-of-pearl. اشتريت هدايا صدف *štireet hadaaya ṣadaf.* I bought gifts made of mother-of-pearl.

صدفة *ṣudfa* p. صدف *ṣudaf* chance, coincidence. بالصدفة *b-ṣ-ṣudfa* by chance. شفتها بالصدفة *čifitta b-ṣ-ṣudfa.* I saw her by chance.

ص د گ *ṣdg*

صدق *ṣidag (يصدق yaṣdig)* to be truthful, tell the truth. الإنسان لازم يصدق في اللي يقوله *l-'insaan laazim yaṣdig fi lli yguula.* People should tell the truth in what they say.

صدق *ṣaddag* 1. to believe, trust s.o. صدقني، إلى ذالحين ما رحت له *ṣaddigni, 'ila đalḥiin ma riḥt-la.* Believe me, up to now I haven't gone to see him. 2. (with على ᶜ*ala*) to endorse. لازم تصدق على الوثيقة هذي *laazim tṣaddig* ᶜ*ala l-waθiiga haađi.* You have to endorse this document.

صادق *ṣaadag* III to befriend s.o. ما تقدر تصادق بنية هني *ma tigdar tṣaadig bnayya hni.* You cannot make friends with a girl here.

تصدق *tṣaddag* V 1. pass. of II صدق *ṣaddag.* الوثيقة تصدقت اليوم *l-waθiiga tṣaddagat l-yoom.* The document was endorsed today. 2. to give alms. دايماً يتصدق على الفقرا *daayman yitṣaddag* ᶜ*ala l-fugara.* He always gives to the poor.

تصادق *tṣaadag* VI to be or become friends with each other. تصادقنا مدة طويلة *tṣaadagna mudda ṭawiila.* We were mutual friends for a long time. لا تتصادق وايا الأشرار *la tiṣṣaadag wiyya l-'ašraar!* Don't make friends with bad people.

صدق *ṣidg* (more common var. صدج *ṣidj*) see under **ص د ج** *ṣdj.*

صدقة *ṣadaga* alms, charity. الصدقة في الإسلام ربع العشر *ṣ-ṣadaga fi l-'islaam rub*ᶜ *l-*ᶜ*ušur.* Alms tax in Islam is one fourth of a tenth.

صداقة *ṣadaaga* friendship.

صديق *ṣadiig* (more common var. صديج *ṣidiij*) p. أصدقا *'aṣdiga* friend.

أصدق *'aṣdag* (elat.) 1. (with من *min*)

more truthful, honest, sincere than. 2. (with foll. n.) the most truthful, honest, sincere.

تصديق *taṣdiig* (v.n. from II صدق *ṣaddag*) endorsement, verification.

صادق *ṣaadig* (act. part. from صدق *ṣidag*) (more common var. صادج *ṣaadj*) p. *-iin* truthful, sincere.

ص د م *ṣdm*

صدمة *ṣadma* (common var. زكمة *začma* and نشلة *našla*) common cold.

ص د ي *ṣdy*

تصدى *tṣadda* V (with ل *l-*) 1. to oppose, resist. تصدى لي وآنا ما عملت له شي يضره *tṣaddaa-li w-aana ma ᶜimalt-la šayy yđ̣urra.* He opposed me though I have done nothing to harm him. 2. to stand in the path of s.o. تصدوا له في الطريق وقتلوه *tṣaddoo-la fi ṭ-ṭiriij w-gitloo.* They stood in his way and killed him.

ص ر ح *ṣrḥ*

صرح *ṣarraḥ* II to make an announcement, declare. الشيخ صرح بأشيا مهمة *š-šeex ṣarraḥ b-'ašya muhimma.* The ruler made an announcement about important things.

صارح *ṣaaraḥ* III to speak openly or frankly to s.o. ليش ما تصارحنا باللي صار؟ *leeš ma tṣaariḥna b-lli ṣaar?* Why don't you speak frankly to us about what has happened? صارحها بسره *ṣaaraḥha b-sirra.* He disclosed his secret to her.

صريح *ṣariiḥ* 1. frank, candid. كون صريح وياي *kuun ṣariiḥ wiyyaay.* Be frank with me.

صراحة *ṣaraaḥa* (v.n.) 1. openness, frankness. أقول لك بكل صراحة ما لك شغل هني *'agul-lak b-kill ṣaraaḥa ma-lak šuġul hini.* Let me tell you frankly, there's no work for you here. 2. clearness, distinctness.

تصريح *taṣriiḥ* 1. (p. *-aat*) declaration, statement. 2. (p. تصاريح *taṣaariiḥ*) official permit, written permission.

ص ر خ *ṣrx*

صاروخ *ṣaaruux* p. صواريخ *ṣuwaariix* 1. rocket, missile. صاروخ موجه *ṣaaruux mwajjah* guided missile. ضربوا صاروخ *đ̣rabaw ṣaaruux.* They fired a missile. 2. male prostitute.

ص ر ر ١ *ṣrr*

صر *ṣarr* (يصر *yṣirr*) 1. to insist, be persistent. صر على الزواج *ṣarr ᶜala z-zawaaj.* He insisted on getting married. 2. to resolve, make up one's mind. صر على انه يروح القنص *ṣarr ᶜala 'inna yruuḥ l-ganaṣ.* He resolved that he would go hunting.

صرة *ṣurra* p. صرر *ṣurar, -aat* 1. cloth bundle, packet. 2. navel.

ص ر ر ٢ *ṣrr*

صر *ṣirr* (coll.) black-headed gulls. s. *-a.*

ص ر ر ٣ *ṣrr*

صر *ṣirr* extreme cold weather. الدنيا صر اليوم *d-dinya ṣirr l-yoom.* It's freezing today.

ص ر ط ن *ṣrṭn*

صرطان *ṣaraṭaan* 1. cancer (med.). 2.

cancer (astron.). مدار الصرطان *madaar ṣ-ṣaraṭaan* Tropic of Cancer.

صرع *ṣr^c*

صـرع *ṣira^c* (يصـرع *yiṣra^c*) to throw down, fell s.o. صرعه في آخر جولة *ṣra^{c}a fi 'aaxir jawla.* He pinned him in the last round.

صارع *ṣaara^c* III to wrestle. متين وقوي؛ يصارع الثيران *mitiin w-gawi; yṣaari^c θ-θiiraan.* He's well-built and fat; he wrestles bulls.

تصارع *tṣaara^c* VI to wrestle each other. تصارع وايا واحد أطول منه *tṣaara^c wiyya waaḥid 'aṭwal minna.* He wrestled with someone taller than he was.

انصرع *nṣira^c* VII pass. of صرع *ṣira^c*. انصرع واجد *nṣira^c waayid.* He was pinned many times.

مصارعة *muṣaara^{c}a* (v.n. from III صارع *ṣaara^c*) wrestling.

مصارع *musaari^c* (act. part. from III صارع *ṣaara^c*) p. *-iin* wrestler.

صرف *ṣrf*

صرف *ṣiraf* (يصرف *yaṣrif*) 1. to spend, expend. نصرف ألفين درهم في الشهر على الأكل بس *naṣrif 'alfeen dirhim fi š-šahar ^{c}ala l-'akil bass.* We spend two thousand dirhams a month for food only. 2. to cash. صرفت الشيك *ṣiraft š-šeek.* I cashed the check. 3. to dismiss, send away. المدرس صرف الأولاد *l-mudarris ṣiraf l-'awlaad.* The teacher dismissed the kids.

صرف *ṣarraf* II 1. to be suitable to s.o. ما تقدر تقول لي هالحين زين. شوف اللي يصرفك *ma tigdar tgul-li halḥiin zeen. čuuf illi yṣarrifk.* You don't want to tell me now. Fine. Go see what's best for you. 2. to change (money). ممكن تصرف لي الدولار؟ *mumkin tṣarrif-li d-duulaar?* Would you please change this dollar for me?

تصرف *tṣarraf* V 1. to conduct oneself, act, behave. تصرف تصرف زين *tṣarraf taṣarruf zeen.* He conducted himself properly. ما يعرف يتصرف *ma y^{c}arf yitṣarraf.* He doesn't know how to behave. 2. to act independently, freely, at one's own discretion. تصرف حسب الظروف *tṣarraf ḥasab ḍ-ḍuruuf.* Act according to the circumstances. سجنوه لانه تصرف بأموال الشركة *sijnoo linna tṣarraf b-'amwaal š-šarika.* They put him in jail because he misappropriated the company property.

انصرف *nṣiraf* VII to be spent. كل الفلوس انصرفت *kill li-fluus nṣirfat.* All the money was spent.

صراف *ṣarraaf* p. *-iin* money changer.

تصرف *taṣarruf* (v.n. from V تصرف *taṣarraf*) 1. behavior, act of conducting oneself. 2. free disposal, right of disposal. تحت تصرف *taḥt taṣarruf* at the disposal of. السيارة تحت تصرفك *s-sayyaara taḥt taṣarrufak.* The car is at your disposal. بتصرف *b-taṣarruf* freely, unrestrictedly.

مصروف *maṣruuf* (p.p. from صرف *ṣiraf*) 1. having been spent. الفلوس كلها مصروفة *li-fluus killaha maṣruufa.* All the money has been spent. 2. (p. مصاريف *maṣaariif*) expense, expenditure.

ص ر ن خ *ṣrnx*

صرناخ *ṣirnaax* (coll.) beetles. s. *-a.*

ص ط ح *ṣṭḥ*

صطح *ṣaṭiḥ* p. صطوح *ṣṭuuḥ* 1. roof (of a house, etc.). 2. surface. صطح الأرض *ṣaṭh l-'arḍ.* the earth, ground surface. صطح البحر *ṣaṭḥ l-baḥar* sea level.

صطحي *ṣaṭḥi* superficial. معرفة صطحية *maᶜrifa ṣaṭḥiyya* superficial knowledge.

ص ط ر *ṣṭr*

صطر *ṣaṭṭar* II to draw lines (on a sheet of paper) with a ruler. صطرت ها الصفحة *ṣaṭṭart haṣ-ṣafḥa.* I drew lines on this page.

صطر *ṣaṭir* p. صطور *ṣṭuur* line (of writing on a sheet of paper).

مصطر *maṣṭara* p. مصاطر *maṣaaṭir* ruler.

ص ط ل *ṣṭl*

صطل *ṣaṭil* p. *-aat,* صطولة *ṣṭuula* bucket, pail (بلك *balak* is more common).

ص ط و ن *ṣṭwn*

صطوانة *ṣṭuwaana* p. *-aat* 1. phonograph record. 2. cylinder. صطوانة غاز *ṣṭuwaanat ġaaz* gas cylinder.

ص ط ي *ṣṭy*

صطى *ṣiṭa (يصطي yiṣṭi)* (with على *ᶜala*) to break into, burglarize. صطوا على البيت وباقوا الفلوس والصوغة *ṣiṭaw ᶜala l-beet w-baagaw li-fluus w-ṣ-ṣooġa.* They broke into the house and stole the money and the jewelry.

ص ع ب *ṣᶜb*

يصعب *yiṣᶜab* (perf. is not used) to be or become difficult, hard, unpleasant. يصعب المشي إلى السوق *yiṣᶜab l-maši 'ila s-suug.* Walking to the marketplace is difficult. It's difficult to walk to the marketplace. يصعب علي أروح وأخليهم بروحهم *yiṣᶜab ᶜalayya 'aruuḥ w-'axaḷḷiihum bruuḥḥum.* It's difficult for me to go and leave them by themselves.

صعب *ṣaᶜᶜab* II to make difficult, hard. البنك صعب عليه ياخذ قرض *l-bank ṣaᶜᶜab ᶜalee yaaxiδ garḍ.* The bank made it difficult for him to get a loan.

استصعب *staṣᶜab* X to find or consider s.th. difficult, hard. استصعب عليه يسلفني ألف درهم *staṣᶜab ᶜalee ysallifni 'alf dirhim.* He found it difficult to lend me a thousand dirhams.

صعب *ṣaᶜb* difficult, hard, unpleasant. درس صعب *dars ṣaᶜb* difficult lesson. رجال صعب *rayyaal ṣaᶜb* difficult, not easy to please, man. صعب عليك تجي وايانا؟ *ṣaᶜb ᶜaleek tiyi wiyyaana?* Is it difficult for you to come with us? عملة صعبة *ᶜimla ṣaᶜba* hard currency.

صعوبة *ṣuᶜuuba* (v.n.) difficulty, hardship.

أصعب *'aṣᶜab* (elat.) 1. (with من *min*) more difficult, unpleasant than. 2. (with foll. n.) the most difficult, unpleasant.

ص ع د¹ *ṣᶜd*

صعد *ṣiᶜad (يصعد yiṣᶜad)* 1. to ascend, go upward. خلنا نصعد لفوق *xaḷḷna* *nis^cad li-foog.* Let's go upstairs. صعد على السلم *ṣi^cad ^cala s-sillam.* He went up in the elevator. 2. (with على *^cala*) to climb up, mount. صعد على الميز *ṣi^cad ^cala l-meez.* He got up on the table.

مصعد *maṣ^cad* p. مصاعد *maṣaa^cid* elevator (سلم *sillam* or أصانصير *'aṣanṣeer* is more common).

ص ع د [2] *ṣ^cd*

صعود *ṣ^cuud* (common var. صعيد *ṣi^ciid*) ablution (performed by striking the soil or dirt with one's hand). (prov.) لا حصل الماي بطل الصعود *la ḥiṣal l-maay biṭal ṣ-ṣ^cuud.* (lit., "If water is at hand, صعود *ṣ^cuud* is nullified.").

ص ع ل ك *ṣ^clk*

صعلوك *ṣa^cluuk, ṣu^cluuk* p. صعاليك *ṣa^caaliik* 1. pauper, destitute person. 2. bum, vagrant.

ص غ ر *ṣġr*

صغر *ṣaġġar* II 1. to make smaller. صغر الحفيز *ṣaġġar l-ḥafiiz.* He made the office smaller. 2. to reduce, decrease. صغرت عمرها سنتين لاجل تدش المدرسة *ṣaġġart ^cumurha santeen lajil ddišš l-madrasa.* I reduced her age two years in order to enter school.

تصغر *tṣaġġar* V to be made smaller. ها الكندورة ما تتصغر *hal-kandoora ma titṣaġġar.* This dishdash cannot be made smaller.

استصغر *staṣġar* X to find or consider s.th. small, little, insignificant. لا تستصغر من هو أصغر منك *la tistaṣġir man huw 'aṣġar minnak.* Don't underestimate those who are younger than you. راح هناك واستصغر نفسه *raaḥ hnaak w-staṣġar nafsa.* He went there and felt inferior.

صغر *ṣuġur* (v.n.) 1. smallness, littleness. 2. young age. رجال زين. شعلينا من صغره وكبره؟ *rayyaal zeen. š-^caleena min SuGra w-kubra?* He's a good man. What have we got to do with his young or old age?

صغير *ṣaġiir* (common var. زغير *zaġiir*) p. صغار *ṣġaar* small, little. هذا ولد صغير؛ ما عليك منه *haaða walad ṣaġiir; ma ^caleek minna.* This is a little boy; leave him be. صغير على *ṣaġiir ^cala* too young to do s.th. أنت صغير على الزواج *'inta ṣaġiir ^cala z-zawaaj.* You are too young to get married. هي صغيرة عليك *hiya ṣaġiira ^caleek.* She is too young for you.

صغيرون *ṣġayruun* (common var. زغيرون *zġayruun*) dim. of صغير *ṣaġiir.*

أصغر *'aṣġar* (elat.) 1. (with من *min*) smaller, younger than. 2. (with foll. n.) the smallest or youngest.

ص ف ح *ṣfḥ*

صفحة *ṣafḥa* p. *-aat* 1. page, leaf (of a book). اقلب الصفحة! *'iglib ṣ-ṣafḥa!* Turn the page! صفحة خمسين *ṣafḥa xamsiin* page fifty.

ص ف ر [1] *ṣfr*

صفر *ṣufar (*يصفر *yuṣfur)* to whistle. الشرطي صفر له لاجل يوقف *š-širṭi ṣufar-la lajiil yoogaf.* The policeman whistled at him so he might stop.

صفر *ṣaffar* II intens. of صفر *ṣufar.*

صفارة *ṣuffaara, ṣaffaara* 1. whistle. 2. siren. صفارة الإنذار *ṣuffaarat l-'inðaar* warning siren.

ص ف ر ٢ *ṣfr*

اصفر *ṣfarr* IX 1. to turn yellow. اصفرت أوراق الشجرة ووقعت *ṣfarrat 'awraag li-šyara w-wugᶜat.* The leaves of the tree turned yellow and fell. 2. (of the face) to become pale, turn pale. خاف واصفر وجهه *xaaf w-ṣfarr weeya.* He got scared and his face turned pale.

صفر *ṣifir* (coll.) 1. brass. 2. bronze. 3. copper.

صفار *ṣfaar* 1. yellowness. 2. paleness. أبو صفار *'ubu ṣfaar* jaundice. صفار البيض *ṣfaar l-beeḍ* egg yolk.

أصفر *'aṣfar* f. صفرا *ṣafra* p. صفر *ṣufur,* صفرين *ṣufriin.* 1. yellow. 2. pale.

صفري *ṣfiri* autumn, fall. الصفري يكون عقب القيظ *li-ṣfiri ykuun ᶜugb l-geeḍ.* Autumn is after summer.

صفار *ṣaffaar* p. صفافير *ṣifaafiir* coppersmith. سوق الصفافير *suug ṣ-ṣifaafiir* the coppersmiths' market place (in Dubai). (prov.) ضرطة في سوق الصفافير *ḍarṭa fi suug ṣ-ṣifaafiir* A drop in the bucket. (lit. "A fart in the coppersmiths' market.").

ص ف ر ٣ *ṣfr*

صفر *ṣifir* p. اصفار *ṣfaar* zero, naught.

ص ف ر ٤ *ṣfr*

صفر *ṣafar* Safar (name of the second month of the Muslim year).

ص ف ط *ṣfṭ*

صفط *ṣaffaṭ* II to stack up, line up. صفط الكتب على الرف *ṣaffiṭ l-kutub ᶜala r-raff.* Stack the books on the shelf. صفطهم خمسة خمسة *ṣaffiṭhum xamsa xamsa.* Arrange them in rows of five.

صفطة *ṣafṭa* p. *-aat* pile, stack.

مصفط *mṣaffaṭ* (p.p. from II صفط *ṣaffaṭ*) organized, ordered.

ص ف ف *ṣff*

صف *ṣaff* (يصف *yṣuff*) 1. to line up, set in a row or line. صف الطلاب صفين *ṣaff ṭ-ṭullaab ṣaffeen.* He lined the students up in two lines. 2. (v.i.) to stand in a row or line, queue. صف واحد بس. لا تصفوا صفين *ṣaff waaḥid bass. la tṣuffu ṣaffeen.* One line only. Don't stand in two lines.

صفف *ṣaffaf* II to arrange, set s.th. in order. صففت شعرها *ṣaffafat šaᶜarha.* She arranged her hair.

انصف *nṣaff* VII pass. of صف *ṣaff.* انصفوا صفين *nṣaffu ṣaffeen.* They lined up in two lines.

صف *ṣaff* p. صفوف *ṣufuuf* 1. row, line, queue. 2. grade, class (in school). في الصف السادس *fi ṣ-ṣaff s-saadis* in the sixth grade. صف العربي *ṣaff l-ᶜarabi* the Arabic class. 3. classroom.

ص ف گ *ṣfg*

صفق *ṣufag* (يصفق *yuṣfug*) to slam. كان حمقان وصفق الباب *čaan ḥamgaan w-ṣufag l-baab.* He was angry and slammed the door.

صفق *ṣaffag* II to clap, applaud, clap the hands. تبي خبز أكثر؟ صفق للولد *tabi xubiz 'akθar? ṣaffig lil-walad.* Do you want more bread? Clap for the waiter (to come). صفقوا له لين وقف *ṣaffagoo-la leen wugaf.* They applauded him when he stood up.

صفقة *ṣafga* p. *-aat* 1. slap, smack. 2. clap. 3. round of applause, ovation. 4. leaf (of a double door or window).

ص ف ن *ṣfn*

صفن *ṣufan* (يصفن *yuṣfun*) to ponder, meditate, brood. صفنت شوية بس ما تذكرت اسمه *ṣufant šwayya bass ma taðakkart 'asma.* I pondered for a short while, but I didn't remember his name. ديماً يصفن قبل لا يجاوب *daayman yuṣfun gabil-la yjaawib.* He always reflects before he answers.

صفنة *ṣafna* (n. of inst.) p. *-aat* period of daydreaming.

صافن *ṣaafin* (act. part. from صفن *ṣufan*) 1. pondering, meditating, brooding. 2. daydreaming.

ص ف و *ṣfw*

صفى *ṣaffa* II 1. to refine. يصفون البترول هني *yṣaffuun l-batrool hni.* They refine oil here. 2. to settle, clear up, straighten out. صفى حسابه قبل ما سافر *ṣaffa ḥsaaba gabil-ma saafar.* He settled his account before he left town. صفى شغله *ṣaffa šuġla*. He cleared up his work. 3. to purify, make pure. صفى الماي *ṣaffa l-maay.* He purified the water.

تصفى *tṣaffa* V pass. of II صفى *ṣaffa.*

مصفاة *muṣfaa* p. مصافي *maṣaafi* 1. refinery. 2. filter, strainer.

صافي *ṣaafi* clear, pure, unpolluted, unmixed. السما صافي اليوم *s-sama ṣaafi l-yoom.* The sky is clear today. ماي صافي *maay ṣaafi* clear, pure water. ربح صافي *ribḥ ṣaafi* net profit.

ص ف ي *ṣfy*

صفة *ṣifa* see under وص ف *wṣf.*

ص گ ر *ṣgr*

صقر *ṣagir* p. صقور *ṣguur* falcon, hawk. الصقر من نوع الشاهين *ṣ-ṣagir min nooᶜ š-šaahiin.* A falcon is of the same kind as a peregrine. (prov.) اللي ما يعرف الصقر يشويه *'illi ma yᶜarf ṣ-ṣagir yišwii.* Don't kill the goose that lays the golden egg.

صقار *ṣaggaar* p. *-a* a falcon trainer.

ص گ ط *ṣgṭ*

صقط *ṣigaṭ* (يصقط *yuṣguṭ*) 1. to fail, flunk. صقط في الامتحان *ṣigaṭ fi li-mtiḥaan.* He failed the examination. 2. to fall, topple, collapse. صقطت الوزارة مرتين هذي السنة *ṣigṭaṭ l-wazaara marrateen haaði s-sana.* The ministry fell twice this year. صقط في الانتخابات *ṣigaṭ fi li-ntixaabaat.* He didn't win the elections. 3. to drop, sink down, decline. صقط من عيني *ṣigaṭ min ᶜeeni.* He dropped in my estimation.

صقط *ṣaggaṭ* II 1. to fail, flunk. المدرس صقطه لانه غش من اللي يمه *l-mudarris ṣaggaṭa linna ġašš min illi yamma.* The teacher flunked him because he copied from the one next to him. 2. to cause to fall, topple, collapse.

صاقط *ṣaagiṭ* (act. part. from صقط *ṣigaṭ*) 1. having failed, flunked. صاقط في الامتحان *ṣaagiṭ fi li-mtiḥaan.* He has failed the examination. 2. disreputable, notorious. رجال صاقط *rayyaal ṣaagiṭ* disreputable man.

مصكوك *maṣkuuk* (p.p. from صك *ṣakk*) closed, shut. الباب مصكوك *l-baab maṣkuuk.* The door is closed.

صلب[1] *ṣlb*

صلب *ṣilab* (يصلب *yuṣlub)* to crucify. صلبوه على الصليب *ṣilboo ᶜala ṣ-ṣaliib.* They crucified him (on the cross).

صليب *ṣaliib* p. صلبان *ṣilbaan* cross.

صليبي *ṣaliibi* 1. (p. *-yyiin*) crusader. 2. having to do with the cross. الحروب الصليبية *l-ḥuruub ṣ-ṣaliibiyya* the Crusades.

صلب[2] *ṣlb*

صليب *ṣiliib* (invar.) 1. hard, stiff, firm. أرض صليب *'arḍ ṣiliib* hard soil. 2. clear, audible (voice). صوت صليب *ṣoot ṣiliib* full audible voice.

صلبخ *ṣlbx*

صلبخ *ṣalbax* (يصلبخ *yṣalbix)* to calcify, be or become calcareous. البيب صلبخ وما ينزل منه ماي بعد *l-peep ṣalbax w-ma yinzil minna maay baᶜad.* The pipe has calcified and no water comes down from it anymore.

صلبوخ *ṣalbuux* (coll.) pebbles, small rocks. s. *-a.*

صلح *ṣlḥ*

صلح *ṣilaḥ* (يصلح *yiṣlaḥ)* 1. to be proper, good, right. لا تقول ها الكلام. ما يصلح *la tguul hal-kalaam. ma yiṣlaḥ.* Don't say these words. It's not proper. 2. to be suitable, useful, fit. ها السيارة تصلح لك؟ *has-sayyaara tiṣlaḥ-lak?* Would this car suit you? يصلح يكون مطارزي *yiṣlaḥ ykuun maṭaarzi.* He's fit to be a bodyguard.

صگع[1] *ṣgᶜ*

صقع *ṣigaᶜ (يصقع yiṣgaᶜ)* to yell, shriek. لين شاف البايق قام يصقع *leen čaaf l-baayig gaam yiṣgaᶜ.* When he saw the thief, he started to yell. صقع الديك *ṣigaᶜ d-diič.* The rooster crowed.

صگع[2] *ṣgᶜ*

صقع *ṣigaᶜ* (يصقع *yiṣgaᶜ)* to strike (with a heavy object). صقعه بحديدة على راسه *ṣigᶜa b-ḥadiida ᶜala raasa.* He struck him with a piece of iron on his head.

صگل *ṣgl*

صقل *ṣigal* (يصقل *yuṣgul)* to smooth, polish. صقل السيف *ṣigal s-seef.* He polished the sword.

صقلاوي *ṣaglaawi* p. *-yya* one who makes swords.

صگه *ṣgh*

أصقه *'aṣgah* f. صقها *ṣagha* p. صقهين *ṣaghiin* deaf (more common var. أصمخ *'aṣmax.* See under صمخ *ṣmx*)

صقه *ṣagah* deafness.

صكك *ṣkk*

صك *ṣakk (يصك yṣikk)* to close, shut (e.g., the door). صك الباب لين طلع *ṣakk l-baab leen ṭilaᶜ.* He closed the door when he went out. !صك حلقك *ṣikk ḥaljak!* Shut up!

صكة *ṣakka* p. *-aat* 1. tribal feud. 2. calamity.

صاك *ṣaakk* (act. part. from صك *ṣakk*) having closed, shut. آنا صاكه قبل ساعة *'aana ṣaakka gabil saaᶜa.* I closed it an hour ago. الغيم صاك *l-ġeem ṣaakk.* There's a thick cloud cover.

صلح *ṣallaḥ* II 1. to repair, mend. السيارة كانت خربانة وصلحتها *s-sayyaara čaanat xarbaana w-ṣallaḥitta.* The car was broken and I had it repaired. 2. to prepare. صلح القهوة *ṣallaḥ l-gahwa.* He prepared the coffee.

صالح *ṣaalaḥ* III to make peace with s.o., make up with s.o. كنت حمقان وعقبه جا وصالحني *čint ḥamgaan w-ᶜugba ya w-ṣaalaḥni.* I was mad and later on he came and made peace with me.

أصلح *'aṣlaḥ* IV 1. to improve, reform. أصلحوا الأوضاع الاجتماعية *'aṣlaḥaw l-'awđaaᶜ li-jtimaaᶜiyya.* They have improved social conditions. 2. to bring about peace, act as a mediator. تهاوشوا وبعدين أصلحنا بينهم *thaawšaw w-baᶜdeen 'aṣlaḥna beenhum.* They quarreled among themselves and then we made peace between them.

تصالح *tṣaalaḥ* VI to become reconciled, make peace with each other. جهال؛ يتهاوشون وعقبه يتصالحون *yihhaal; yithaawšuun w-ᶜugba yiṣṣaalḥuun.* They are children; they quarrel among themselves and then they make up.

صلح *ṣulḥ* (v.n.) peace, reconciliation. قاضي الصلح *gaađi ṣ-ṣulḥ* justice of the peace. محكمة الصلح *maḥkamat ṣ-ṣulḥ* the lowest criminal court.

صلاحية *ṣalaaḥiyya* 1. usability, usefulness, use. 2. (p. *-aat*) authority, full power.

مصلحة *maṣlaḥa* p. مصالح *maṣaaliḥ* interest, benefit. هذا شي ما لك فيه أي مصلحة *haađa šayy ma-lak fii 'ayya maṣlaḥa.* This is something in which you don't have any interest.

أصلح *'aṣlaḥ* (elat.) 1. (with من *min*) more suitable, fitting than. 2. (with foll. n.) the most suitable, fitting.

إصلاح *'iṣlaaḥ* (v.n. from IV أصلح *'aṣlaḥ*) reform, improvement.

صالح *ṣaaliḥ* (act. part. from صلح *ṣilaḥ*) 1. useable, suitable, fitting. صالح للاستعمال *ṣaaliḥ lil-'istiᶜmaal* serviceable. ماي غير صالح للشرب *maay ġeer ṣaaliḥ liš-šurb* undrinkable water. 2. good, virtuous, godly. أعمال صالحة *'aᶜmaal ṣaalḥa* good deeds.

مصلح *mṣalliḥ* (act. part. from II صلح *ṣallaḥ*) 1. having repaired, fixed s.th. توني مصلحه. اخذه *tawwni mṣallḥa. 'ixđa.* I have just repaired it. Take it. 2. repairman, fixer.

ص ل خ *ṣlx*

صلخ *ṣilax (*يصلخ *yiṣlax)* to skin (an animal). قنصت غزال وصلخته وكليناه *ginaṣt ġazaal w-ṣilaxta w-kaleenaa.* I hunted a deer, skinned it, and we ate it. القصاب صلخ ذبيحتين *l-gaṣṣaab ṣilax đibiiḥteen.* The butcher skinned two (slaughtered) animals.

مصلخ *maṣlax* p. *maṣaalix* slaughterhouse.

ص ل ط *ṣlṭ*

صلط *ṣallaṭ* II (with على *ᶜala*) to give power over. الله يصلط عليك الشياطين *'aḷḷa yṣalliṭ ᶜaleek š-šayaaṭiin.* May God put the devils in control of you. صلط الكلب على البايق *ṣallaṭ č-čalb ᶜala l-baayig.* He set the dog on the thief.

تصلط *tṣallaṭ* V pass. of II صلط *ṣallaṭ.*

صلطة *ṣulṭa* 1. power, authority. 2. (p. *-aat*) authority, official agency.

ص ل ع *ṣlᶜ*

صلع *ṣallaᶜ* II 1. to uncover the head, remove the head gear. أحسن ما تصلع قبل ما تصلي *'aḥsan ma tṣalliᶜ gabil-ma tṣalli.* It's better not to uncover your head before you pray. 2. to be disclosed, revealed. صلعت المسألة *ṣallaᶜat l-mas'ala.* The truth is out.

مصلع *mṣalliᶜ* (act. part. from II صلع *ṣallaᶜ*) bareheaded. يصلي مصلع *yṣalli mṣalliᶜ.* He prays bareheaded.

ص ل گ *ṣlg*

صلقة *ṣalga* p. *-aat* large amount of money.

ص ل و *ṣlw*

صلى *ṣalla* II to pray. المسلم لازم يصلي ويصوم *l-muṣlim laazim yṣalli w-yṣuum.* A Muslim should pray and fast. صليت صلاة الصبح *ṣalleet ṣalaat ṣ-ṣubḥ.* I performed the morning prayer. صليت الظهر *ṣalleet ḍ-ḍuhur.* I prayed the noon prayer. صلوا على النبي! *ṣallu ᶜala n-nabi!* 1. Be quiet! 2. Listen! Change the topic!

صلاة *ṣalaa* p. صلوات *ṣalawaat* prayer, praying. صلاة المغرب *ṣalaat li-mġarb* the sunset prayer. صلينا صلاة العيد *ṣalleena ṣalaat l-ᶜiid.* We prayed the Feast prayer.

مصلي *mṣalli* (act. part. from II صلى *ṣalla*) 1. having prayed. توني مصلي وياهم *tawwni mṣalli wiyyaahum.* I've just prayed with them. 2. (p. *-iin*) one who prays, worshipper.

ص م خ *ṣmx*

صماخ *ṣmaax* (v.n.) 1. deafness, state of being deaf. 2. (ear) wax.

أصمخ *'aṣmax* (less common var. أصقه *'aṣgah*) f. صمخا *ṣamxa* p. صمخ *ṣimx* deaf.

ص م غ *ṣmġ*

صمغ *ṣammaġ* II to put glue on s.th. صمغ الصور ولزقهم في الكتاب *ṣammaġ ṣ-ṣuwar w-lizaghum fi li-ktaab.* He glued the pictures and pasted them in the book.

صمغ *ṣamuġ* (coll.) glue, paste.

ص م م *ṣmm*

صمم *ṣammam* II 1. to design, plan. منو صمم البناية على السيف؟ *minu ṣammam li-bnaaya ᶜala s-siif?* Who designed the building on the seashore? 2. to make up one's mind, be determined. صمم يجي وايانا *ṣammam yiyi wiyyaana.* He decided to come with us.

صميم *ṣamiim* true, genuine. خليجي صميم *xaliiji ṣamiim* a true Gulf Arab. من صميم القلب *min ṣamiim l-galb* whole-heartedly. ضربة بالصميم *ḍarba b-ṣ-ṣamiim* effective hit.

تصميم *taṣmiim* 1. design, designing. 2. determination, resolution.

ص ن د گ *ṣndg*

صندوق *ṣanduug* p. صناديق *ṣanaadiig* 1. box, crate. حط قشاره في صندوق وسار *ḥaṭṭ gšaara fi ṣanduug w-saar.* He put his personal effects in a box and left. صندوق بريد *ṣanduug bariid* post-office box. 2. money box, till, coffer.

صندوق التوفير *ṣanduug t-tawfiir* savings bank, provident fund. أمين الصندوق *'amiin ṣ-ṣanduug* the treasurer.

ص ن گ ل *ṣngḷ*

صنقل *ṣangaḷ* p. صناقل *ṣanaagiḷ* 1. iron chain. 2. band (watch band). صنقل الساعة *ṣangaḷ s-saaᶜa* the watch band.

ص ن ع ١ *ṣnᶜ*

صنع *ṣinaᶜ* (يصنع *yiṣnaᶜ*) to manufacture, make, produce. هني يصنعون جواتي من بلاستيك *hni yiṣnaᶜuun juwaati min plaastiik.* Here they make plastic shoes. في مصانع تصنع تايرات. *fii maṣaaniᶜ tiṣnaᶜ taayraat.* There are factories that manufacture tires.

صنع *ṣannaᶜ* II to industrialize. الحكومة صنعت ها المنطقة *l-ḥukuuma ṣannaᶜat hal-manṭiga.* The government industrialized this area.

صنعة *ṣanᶜa* p. *-aat, ṣanaayiᶜ* trade, craft.

صناعة *ṣinaaᶜa* (v.n. from صنع *ṣinaᶜ*) industry, manufacturing. عندنا صناعة خفيفة هني *ᶜindana ṣinaaᶜa xafiifa hni.* We have light industry here.

صناعي *ṣinaaᶜi* 1. industrial. منطقة صناعية *manṭiga ṣinaaᶜiyya* industrial district. 2. cultured (pearls), artificial. قماش صناعي *gmaaš ṣinaaᶜi* cultured pearls.

مصنع *maṣnaᶜ* p. مصانع *maṣaaniᶜ* factory.

مصنوع *maṣnuuᶜ* (p.p. from صنع *ṣinaᶜ*) 1. having been manufactured. 2. (p. *-aat*) manufactured article.

ص ن ع ٢ *ṣnᶜ*

صنعا *ṣanᶜa* San'a (capital city of the Republic of Yemen).

ص ن ف *ṣnf*

صنف *ṣannaf* II 1. to joke, jest, kid. ما عليك منه؛ بس يصنف *ma ᶜaleek minna; bass yṣannif.* Don't pay attention to him; he's just kidding. 2. to comment (on a subject, etc.) صنف على الموضوع *ṣannaf ᶜala l-mawḍ̱uuᶜ.* He commented on the subject.

صنف *ṣinf* p. أصناف *'aṣnaaf* kind, sort. من ها الصنف *min haṣ-ṣinf* of this kind, similar to this.

تصنيف *taṣniif* (v.n. from II صنف *ṣannaf*) joking, jesting. راعي تصنيفات *raaᶜi taṣniifaat* funny person.

ص ن م *ṣnm*

صنم *ṣanam* p. أصنام *'aṣnaam* idol, image. فيه ناس يعبدون الأصنام *fii naas yᶜabduun l-'aṣnaam.* There are people who worship idols. واقف مثل الصنم؛ ما يتحرك *waagif miθl ṣ-ṣanam; ma yitḥarrak.* He's standing like a statue; he isn't moving.

ص ن و ب ر *ṣnwbr*

صنوبر *ṣnoobar* (coll.) pine nuts. s. حبة صنوبر *ḥabbat ṣnoobar,* صنوبرة *-a.*

ص ه ل *ṣhl*

صهل *ṣihal* (يصهل *yiṣhal*) to neigh, whinny. لين الحصان شاف الفرس قام يصهل *leen li-ḥṣaan čaaf l-faras gaam yiṣhal.* When the horse saw the mare, it started to neigh.

ص ه ي و ن *ṣhywn*

صهيوني *ṣahyuuni* 1. Zionist, Zionistic. 2. a Zionist.

صهيونية *ṣahyuuniyya* Zionism.

ص و ب *ṣwb*

صاب *ṣaab (يصيب yṣiib)* 1. to fall upon s.o., befall, happen to s.o. صابت الشركة خسارة كبيرة *ṣaabat š-šarika xasaara čibiira.* The company suffered a great loss. 2. to afflict, attack. صابه مرض خبيث *ṣaaba marað xabiiθ.* He was afflicted with a malignant disease. 3. to hit (a target). ما تقدر تصيب الهدف. قرب شوية *ma tigdar tṣiib l-hadaf. garrib šwayya.* You cannot hit the target. Get a little closer. صاب الهدف من بعيد *ṣaab l-hadaf min baᶜiid.* He hit the target from a far distance.

تصاوب *tṣaawab* VI to be shot, hit (by a bullet). تصاوب وخذوه المستشفى. *ṣṣaawab w-xaðoo l-mustašfa.* He got shot and they took him to the hospital.

انصاب *nṣaab* VII to be stricken, afflicted, to catch a disease. انصاب بالسل *nṣaab b-s-sill.* He was stricken with tuberculosis.

صوب *ṣoob* (no p.) 1. direction, side. السبيتار من ذاك الصوب *s-sbeetaar min ðaak ṣ-ṣoob.* The hospital is in that direction. 2. place. ذاك الصوب *ðaak ṣ-ṣoob* that place. اقعد ها الصوب *'igᶜid haṣ-ṣoob.* Sit in this place. 3. (prep.) toward, in the direction of. رحنا صوب البحر *riḥna ṣoob l-baḥar.* We went toward the sea. تعال صوبنا نتعشى ونسولف *taᶜaal ṣoobna nitᶜašša w-nsoolif.* Come to our place so as to eat dinner and chat.

إصابة *'iṣaaba* p. *-aat* 1. score, goal. غلبناهم بإصابتين *ġalabnaahum b-'iṣaabteen.* We beat them by two goals. 2. case, attack of illness or sickness. فيه خمس إصابات بالكوليرا هني *fii xams 'iṣaabaat b-l-koleera hni.* There are five cases of cholera here.

مصيبة *muṣiiba* p. مصايب *maṣaayib* 1. calamity, misfortune. جاتني المصايب من كل مكان *yatni l-maṣaayib min kill mukaan.* I was beset by calamities from everywhere.

مصاب *mṣaab* p. *-iin* casualty, injured or wounded person. حصل دعمة وشليت المصاب حق المستشفى *hiṣal daᶜma w-šalleet li-mṣaab ḥagg l-mustašfa.* There was a car accident and I picked up the injured person and took him to the hospital.

ص و ب ن *ṣwbn*

صوبن *ṣooban (يصوبن yṣoobin)* to wash s.th. with soap. يصوبن ايديه عقب الأكل *yṣoobin 'iidee ᶜugb l-'akil.* He washes his hands with soap after eating.

صابون *ṣaabuun* (coll.) soap. s. *-a.*

صابونة *ṣaabuuna* p. *-aat* 1. bar of soap. 2. kneecap. صابونة الرجل *ṣaabuunat r-riil* the kneecap.

ص و ت *ṣwt* See under ص و ط *ṣwṭ.*

ص و ر *ṣwr*

صور *ṣawwar* II to depict, portray, represent. ها الفلم يصور الحياة في ذاك الوقت *hal-filim yṣawwir l-ḥayaa fi ðaak l-wagt.* This movie depicts life at that time.

تصور *tṣawwar* V to imagine, think, conceive. المعيشة موب غالية مثل ما تتصور *l-maᶜiiša muub ġaalya miθil-ma titṣawwar.* The cost of living isn't as expensive as you imagine. حوادث السيايير هني بشكل ما يتصور *ḥawaadiθ s-siyaayiir hini bi-šakil ma yitṣawwar.* Car accidents here are inconceivable. أتصور يوصل اليوم *'atṣawwar yooṣal l-yoom.* I think he'll arrive today.

صورة *ṣuura* p. صور *ṣuwar* 1. image, likeness. 2. copy, duplicate. 3. sura, chapter of the Quran. 4. way, manner. بأي صورة من الصور *b-'ayy ṣuura min ṣ-ṣuwar* in any way possible, by any means, by hook or by crook. بصورة خاصة *b-ṣuura xaaṣṣa* especially. بصورة عامة *b-ṣuura ᶜamma* generally, in general, by and large.

تصوير *taṣwiir* (v.n. from II صور *ṣawwar*) depiction, portrayal.

صوط *ṣwṭ*

صوط *ṣawwaṭ* II 1. to vote, cast a ballot. الحرمة ما تصوط في بلادنا *l-ḥurma ma tṣawwiṭ fi blaadna.* Women don't (have the right to) vote in our country. 2. (with ل *l-*) to call out, shout to s.o. صوط لي *ṣawwaṭ-li.* He shouted to me.

صوط *ṣooṭ* p. اصواط *ṣwaaṭ* 1. voice. سمعت صوط العيال برة *simaᶜt ṣooṭ li-ᶜyaal barra.* I heard children's voices outside. ديما تلغي وصوطها عالي بعد *daayman tilġi w-ṣooṭha ᶜaali baᶜad.* She's always chattering and her voice is loud too. (prov). صوطٍ عالي ويرجع خالي *ṣooṭin ᶜaali w-yirjaᶜ xaali.* Much cry little wool. 2. sound, noise. 3. vote. حصل ألف صوط *ḥaṣṣal 'alf ṣooṭ.* He got 1,000 votes.

صيط *ṣiiṭ* (good or bad) reputation, fame. صيطه كلش زين بين جماعته *ṣiiṭa killiš zeen been jamaaᶜta.* He has good reputation among his kinsfolk. (prov.) الصيط عالي والبطن خالي *ṣ-ṣiiṭ ᶜaali w-l-baṭin xaali.* Much cry little wool.

صوغ *ṣwġ*

صاغ *ṣaaġ (*يصوغ *yṣuuġ)* to fashion, form, mold. الصايغ صاغ لي الحيول *ṣ-ṣaayiġ ṣaaġ-li li-ḥyuul.* The goldsmith fashioned the bracelets for me.

صوغة *ṣooġa* jewelry. المعرس هو اللي يشتري الصوغة *l-miᶜris huwa lli yištiri ṣ-ṣooġa.* It's the bridegroom who buys the jewelry.

صياغة *ṣiyaaġa* (v.n. from صاغ *ṣaaġ*) goldsmithing, jewelry making.

صايغ *ṣaayiġ* (act. part. from صاغ *ṣaaġ*) 1. having fashioned, molded (a piece of jewelry). توه صايغ لك العقد *tawwa ṣaayiġ-lič l-ᶜigd.* He has just fashioned the necklace for you. 2. (p. صياغ *ṣiyyaaġ,* صواغ *ṣuwwaaġ*) goldsmith, jeweler.

صوف *ṣwf*

صوف *ṣuuf* (coll.) wool. s. جزة صوف *jizzat ṣuuf.* صوف خروف *ṣuuf xaruuf* lamb wool. (prov.) اللي ما يرضى بجزة يرضى بجزة وخروف *'illi ma yirḍa b-jizza yirḍa b-jizza w-xaruuf.* Cut your losses and run. Half a loaf is better than none.

صوم *ṣwm*

صام *ṣaam (*يصوم *yṣuum)* to fast, abstain from food, drink, and sexual intercourse. أنت تصوم وتصلي؟ *'inta tṣuum w-tṣalli?* Do you fast and pray? صام كل شهر رمضان *ṣaam kill šahar rumðaan.* He fasted the whole month of Ramadan.

صوم *ṣawwam* II to cause to fast. صومي عيالك؛ لا تفطريهم *ṣawwmi ᶜyaalič; la tfaṭṭriihum.* Make (f.s.) your children fast; don't let them break the fast.

صايم *ṣaayim* (act. part. from صام *ṣaam*) 1. fasting, observing a fast. أنت صايم والا مفطر؟ *'inta ṣaayim walla miftir?* Are you fasting or not? 2. p. *-iin,* صيام *ṣiyyaam* faster, person observing a fast.

صوم *ṣoom* (v.n. from صام *ṣaam*) fasting (less common var. صيام *ṣiyaam*). شهر الصوم *šahr ṣ-ṣoom* the month of fasting, i.e., Ramadan. صوم عاشورا *ṣoom ᶜaašuura* voluntary fasting on the tenth day of محرم *Muharram.*

ص و ن د *ṣwnd*

صوندة *ṣoonda* p. *-aat* hose, rubber tube.

ص ي ب *ṣyb*

صاب *ṣaab (يصيب yṣiib)* see under **ص و ب** *ṣwb.*

ص ي ب ن *ṣybn*

صيبان *ṣiibaan* (coll.) nits. s. *-a.*

ص ي ت *ṣyt*

صيط *ṣiiṭ* see under **ص و ط** *ṣwṭ.*

ص ي ح *ṣyḥ*

صاح *ṣaaḥ (يصيح yṣiiḥ)* 1. to yell, shout. طاح على الأرض وصاح «آخ»! *ṭaah ᶜala l-'arð w-ṣaaḥ, "'aax!"* He fell and yelled, "Ouch!". المدرس صاح علي *l-mudarris ṣaaḥ ᶜalayya.* The teacher shouted at me. لا تدش قبل ما يصيحون اسمك *la ddišš gabil-ma yṣiiḥuun 'ismak.* Don't enter before they call your name. 2. to call out, address, call. صحتك مية مرة. أنت أصمخ؟ *ṣiḥtak miyat marra. 'inta 'aṣmax?* I called you a hundred times. Are you deaf?

صيح *ṣayyaḥ* II to shout, yell repeatedly. يصيح على عياله *yṣayyiḥ ᶜala ᶜyaaḷa.* He's yelling at his children.

صياح *ṣyaaḥ* (v.n. from صاح *ṣaaḥ*) shouting, yelling.

ص ي خ *ṣyx*

صيخ *ṣiix* p. صياخ *ṣyaax* 1. skewer. حطينا اللحم على صيخ وشويناه *ḥaṭṭeena l-laḥam ᶜala ṣiix w-šaweenaa.* We put the meat on a skewer and grilled it. 2. bar, rod.

ص ي د *ṣyd*

صاد *ṣaad (يصيد yṣiid)* 1. to catch, trap. القطو صاد فار *l-gaṭu ṣaad faar.* The cat caught a mouse. 2. to fish. رحنا نصيد سمك *riḥna nṣiid simač.* We went fishing.

انصاد *nṣaad* VII to be caught, trapped. الفار انصاد *l-faar nṣaad.* The mouse was caught.

صيد *ṣeed* (v.n. from صاد *ṣaad*) 1. fishing. صيد السمك *ṣeed s-simač* fishing. 2. game, prey. حصلنا صيد كلش زين *ḥaṣṣalna ṣeed killiš zeen.* We found very good game.

صياد *ṣayyaad* p. *-iin* 1. hunter. 2.

fisherman.

مصيدة *maṣyada* p. *-aat* 1. trap, snare. 2. slingshot.

ص ي د ل *ṣydl*

صيدلة *ṣaydala* pharmacy, pharmacology. أدرس صيدلة *'adris ṣaydala.* I am studying pharmacy.

صيدلي *ṣaydali* p. صيادلة *ṣayaadila* pharmacist, druggist.

صيدلانية *ṣaydalaaniyya* p. *-aat* female pharmacist.

ص ي ر *ṣyr*

صار *ṣaar (يصير yṣiir)* 1. to happen, take place. شصار؟ *š-ṣaar?* What has happened? ما صار شي *ma ṣaar šayy.* Nothing has happened. إذا ما تروح اليوم، شو يصير؟ *'iða ma truuḥ l-yoom, šu yṣiir?* If you don't go today, what happens? متى صارت الحرب؟ *mita ṣaarat l-ḥarb?* When did the war take place? هالسنة ما صار حر واجد *has-sana ma ṣaar ḥarr waayid.* This year there hasn't been much hot weather. صار له شي بحادث السيارة؟ *ṣaar-la šayy b-ḥaadiθ s-sayyaara?* Has anything happened to him in the car accident? 2. to become, turn out to be, change into s.th. ابني صار دختر *'ibni ṣaar daxtar.* My son became a doctor. لحيته صارت بيضا *liḥyita ṣaarat beeḍa.* His beard turned grey. الماي صار ثلج *l-maay ṣaar θalj.* The water became ice. العشا يصير عقب شوي *l-ᶜaša yṣiir ᶜugb šwayy.* Dinner will be ready in a little while. صار وقت الصلاة *ṣaar wagt ṣ-ṣalaa.* It's time for prayer. صار لنا مدة طويلة ما شفناك *ṣaar-lana mudda ṭawila ma čifnaak.* We haven't seen you for a long time. صار له مريض سبوعين *ṣaar-la mariiḍ subuuᶜeen.* He's been ill for two weeks. 3. to be possible, have a chance of occurrence. يصير تجي وما نشوفك؟ *yṣiir tiyi w-ma nčuufak?* Could it be possible that you come and we don't see you? يصير آخذ السيارة؟ *yṣiir 'aaxið s-sayyaara?* Can I take the car? ما يصير تدش بدون إذن *ma yṣiir ddišš b-duun 'iðin.* You cannot get in without permission. ما يصير. آنا أدفع الحساب *ma yṣiir. 'aana 'adfaᶜ li-ḥsaab.* No, you won't. I will pay the bill. خم الأرض يا سالم! – صار *ximm l-'arḍ ya saalim! — ṣaar.* Mop the floor, Salim! — O.K. 4. (with foll. imperf.) to start, begin to do s.th. صار يمشي *ṣaar yamši.* He started to walk. صرت أداوم الساعة ست الصباح *ṣirt 'adaawim s-saaᶜa siit ṣ-ṣabaaḥ.* I started to report for duty at six in the morning.

صير *ṣiir* (no known p.) island. صير بني ياس *ṣiir bani yaas* and صير بني صير *ṣiir bani ṣiir* two U.A.E. islands.

مصير *maṣiir* fate, destiny. الوزارة تقرر مصيره *l-wazaara tġarrir maṣiira.* The ministry will decide his fate. مصيرك بين ايدينه *maṣiirak been iideena.* He is the master of your fate. حق تقرير المصير *ḥaag taġriir l-maṣiir* the right of self-determination.

ص ي ط *ṣyṭ*

صيط *ṣiiṭ* see under **ص و ط** *ṣwṭ.*

ص ي ط ر *ṣyṭr*

صيطر *ṣayṭar (يصيطر yṣayṭir)* (with على *ᶜala)* 1. to control, dominate, command. ما أقدر أسيطر عليهم *ma 'agdar 'aṣayṭir ᶜaleehum.* I can't control them. صيطر على الوضع *ṣayṭar ᶜala l-waḏiᶜ.* He took control of the situation. 2. to master, acquire a command of s.th. قرا زين وصيطر على الموضوع *gira zeen w-ṣayṭar ᶜala l-mawḏuuᶜ.* He read well and mastered the subject.

صيطرة *ṣaytara* (v.n.) 1. control, command. ما لك سيطرة *ma-lak ṣayṭara ᶜaleehum.* You have no command over them. 2. mastery, command. الصيطرة على الإنكليزي صعبة *ṣ-ṣayṭara ᶜala l-'ingiliizi ṣaᶜba.* Mastery of the English language is difficult.

ص ي ف *ṣyf*

صيف *ṣayyaf* II (with عن *ᶜan*) 1. to get late, be late for s.th. صيف عن الاجتماع *ṣayyaf ᶜan li-jtimaaᶜ.* He was late for the meeting. 2. to spend the summer. نحن دايماً نصيف في لندن *niḥin daayman nṣayyif fi landan.* We always spend the summer in London.

صيف *ṣeef* (more common var. قيظ *geeḏ*) summer, summertime. هني الهوا حار ورطب في الصيف *hni l-hawa ḥaarr w-raṭib fi ṣ-ṣeef.* Here the weather is hot and humid in the summer.

مصيف *maṣiif* p. مصايف *maṣaayif* summer resort.

ص ي م *ṣym*

صايم *ṣaayim* see under **ص و م** *ṣwm.*

ص ي ن *ṣyn*

صين (with the article prefix) الصين *ṣ-ṣiin* China.

صيني *ṣiini* 1. Chinese. 2. a Chinese.

صينية *ṣiiniyya* p. صواني *ṣawaani* tray.

ط

ط ا *ṭaa*

طا *ṭaa* name of the letter ط *ṭ*.

ط ا ب و ر *ṭaabwr*

طابور *ṭaabuur* p. طوابير *ṭuwaabiir* line, column (of soldiers). الطابور الخامس *ṭ-ṭaabuur l-xaamis* the fifth column.

ط ا گ ي *ṭaagy*

طاقية *ṭaagiyya* (more common var. كحفية *gaḥfiyya*) p. طواقي *ṭuwaagi* skull cap (usually worn under a غترة *ġitra* headcloth).

ط ا ر *ṭaar*

طار *ṭaar* p. طيران *tiiraan* tambourine.

ط ا و س *ṭaaws*

طاووس *ṭaawuus* p. طواويس *ṭuwaawiis* peacock.

ط ب ب *ṭbb*

طب *ṭabb* (يطب *yṭubb*) 1. to enter, go in. طب الحجرة *ṭabb l-ḥijra.* He entered the room. 2. to reach. طب البلد *ṭabb l-balad.* He reached the city. طبينا الساعة خمس *ṭabbeena s-saaᶜa xams.* We arrived at five o'clock. 3. to hit the ground. طاح من فوق وطب *ṭaaḥ min foog w-ṭabb.* He fell from above and hit the ground.

طب *ṭibb* 1. medicine, medical science. أبغاك تدرس طب *'abġaak tidris ṭibb.* I want you to study medicine. 2. medical treatment.

طبابة *ṭbaaba* also known as الطب الشعبي *ṭ-ṭibb š-šaᶜbi* folk medicine.

طبي *ṭibbi* medical. فحص طبي *faḥṣ ṭibbi* medical examination.

طبيب *ṭabiib* (more common var. دختر *daxtar*) p. أطبا *'aṭibba* medical doctor, physician. طبيب أسنان *ṭabiib 'asnaan* dentist. طبيب بيطري *ṭabiib beeṭari* veterinarian.

ط ب ج *ṭbj*

طابج *ṭaabaj* III (common var. طابق *ṭaabag*) to agree, correlate with s.th. طابجت البضاعة العينة *ṭaabajat l-biðaaᶜa l-ᶜayyna.* The merchandise is like the sample.

تطابج *tṭaabaj* VI to go together, to be congruent with each other. الكنبة والكرسي يتطابجون *l-kanaba w-l-kirsi yiṭṭaabguun.* The sofa and the chair go together (in color and style).

ط ب خ *ṭbx*

طبخ *ṭubax* (يطبخ *yiṭbax*) to cook. حرمتي طبخت عيش ولحم على العشا *ḥurumti ṭbaxat ᶜeeš w-laḥam ᶜala l-ᶜaša.* My wife cooked rice and meat for dinner. لا تطبخين اليوم. رايح أجيب أكل من المطعم *la tiṭbaxiin l-yoom. raayiḥ 'ayiib 'akil min l-maṭᶜam.* Don't cook today. I'm going to get some food from the restaurant.

انطبخ *nṭubax* VII to be cooked. العيش ينطبخ بساع *l-ᶜeeš yinṭubax b-saaᶜ.* Rice can be cooked quickly.

طبخ *ṭabix* (v.n. from طبخ *ṭubax*) cooking, cuisine.

طبخـــة *ṭabxa* (n. of inst.) p. *-aat* meal, dish.

طباخ *ṭabbaax* p. طبابيخ *ṭubaabiix, -iin.* cook.

مطبـــخ *maṭbax* p. مطـــابخ *maṭaabix* kitchen. (prov.) قطـــو مطـــابخ *gaṭu maṭaabix.* He eats like a pig. (lit., "A cat of kitchens."). المطبخ متروس مواعين وصخـــة *l-maṭbax matruus mawaa^c^iin waṣxa.* The kitchen is full of dirty dishes.

ط ب ع *ṭb^c^*

طبـــع *ṭuba^c^ (يطبع yiṭba^c^)* 1. to drown. اللي يطمع يطبـــع *'illi yiṭma^c^ yiṭba^c^.* He who is greedy will drown. 2. to sink. المركب طبـــع *l-markab ṭuba^c^.* The boat sank. 3. to type. أنت تطبع إنكليزي؟ *'inta tiṭba^c^ 'ingiliizi?* Do you type English? طبعت له الخط *ṭuba^c^t-la l-xaṭṭ.* I typed the letter for him. 4. to print. الجامعـــة طبعـــت لـــه كتـــابين *l-yaam^c^a ṭba^c^at-la ktaabeen.* The university printed two books for him.

انطبـــع *nṭiba^c^* VII 1. to be typed. الخط انطبع لو لا؟ *l-xaṭṭ nṭiba^c^ lo la?* Has the letter been typed or not? 2. to be printed. وين انطبع هـــا الكتـــاب؟ *ween nṭiba^c^ hal-kitaab?* Where was this book printed?

طبـــع *ṭabi^c^* (v.n. from طبع *ṭuba^c^*) 1. printing, typing. تحت الطبع *taḥt ṭ-ṭabi^c^* in press, being printed or typed. 2. temper, disposition, nature. طبعه موب زين اليوم *ṭab^c^a muub zeen l-yoom.* He's ill at ease today.

طبعـــاً *ṭab^c^an* of course, certainly. طبعاً خذيته *ṭab^c^an xaðeeta.* Of course I took it.

طبعـــة *ṭab^c^a* 1. (v.n. from طبع *ṭuba^c^*) drowning, sinking. سنة الطبعـــة *sanat ṭ-ṭab^c^a* the year of violent storms and hurricanes in 1872 (lit., "the year of drowning"). 2. (p. *-aat*) edition, issue (of a publication).

طبيعـــة *ṭabii^c^a* 1. nature. جمال الطبيعة *jamaal ṭ-ṭabii^c^a* the beauty of nature. 2. (p. طبايع *ṭabaayi^c^*) peculiarity, trait.

طبيعـــي *ṭabii^c^i* 1. natural. تاريخ طبيعي *taariix ṭabii^c^i* natural history. 2. normal, ordinary. هذا شي طبيعي *haaða šayy ṭabii^c^i.* This is natural. That's natural.

طباع *ṭabbaa^c^* p. *-iin* printer, typesetter.

مطبعـــة *maṭba^c^a* p. مطابع *maṭaabi^c^* 1. printing press. 2. print shop.

طـــابع *ṭaabi^c^* p. طوابع *ṭuwaabi^c^* postage stamp. عطني طابع بو خمس دراهـــم *^c^aṭni ṭaabi^c^ bu xams daraahim.* Give me a five-dirham stamp.

طابعة *ṭaabi^c^a* p. *-aat* typewriter. كاتب طابعة *kaatib ṭaabi^c^a* typist.

مطبوعـــات *maṭbuu^c^aat* (invar. p.) printed matter.

ط ب گ *ṭbg*

طابق *ṭaabag* see under ط ب ج *ṭbj.*

طـــابق *ṭaabig* p. طوابق *ṭuwaabig* floor, story (of a building). المكتب على الطابق الخامس *l-maktab ^c^ala ṭ-ṭaabig l-xaamis.* The office is on the fifth floor. عنده بناية خمـــس طوابـــق *^c^inda bnaaya xams ṭuwaabig.* He has a five-story building.

طبل *ṭbl*

طبّل *ṭabbal* II to beat the drums. في العرس الناس يطبلون ويغنون *fi l-ᶜirs n-naas yṭabbluun w-yġannuun.* In a wedding people beat drums and sing.

طبل *ṭabil* p. طبول *ṭubuul* drum. ليلة العرس الناس يدقون الطبول ويغنون *leelat l-ᶜirs n-naas ydigguun ṭ-ṭubuul w-yġannuun.* On the wedding night, people beat drums and sing.

طبيلة *ṭbeela* p. *-aat* 1. dim. of طبل *ṭabil* small drum. أبو طبيلة *'ubu ṭbeela* one who uses a tambourine to wake people up to eat the early morning meal during the month of Ramadan. 2. car garage.

طحن *ṭḥn*

طحن *ṭiḥan (يطحن yiṭḥan)* to mill, grind. كنا ناخذ البر حق الطاحون ونطحنه *činna naaxið l-birr ḥagg ṭ-ṭaaḥuun w-nṭaḥna.* We used to take the wheat to the mill and have it milled.

انطحن *nṭiḥan* VII pass. of طحن *ṭiḥan.*

طحين *ṭaḥiin* (coll.) flour.

طاحون *ṭaaḥuun* (common var. طاحونة *ṭaaḥuuna*) p. طواحين *ṭuwaaḥiin* flour mill, grinder.

طحنن *ṭḥnn*

طحنون *ṭaḥnuun* Tahnun (male's name). الشيخ طحنون *š-šeex ṭaḥnuun* Shaikh Tahnun.

طرح[1] *ṭrḥ*

طرح *ṭirah (يطرح yiṭrah)* 1. to cause s.o. to lie down flat, to lay flat. الدختر طرح الجاهل على الميز وضربه إبرة *d-daxtar ṭirah l-yaahil ᶜala l-meez w-ðraba 'ibra.* The doctor laid the child on the table and gave him a shot. 2. to dock, anchor. السفينة طرحت قريب من السيف *s-safiina ṭrahat gariib min s-siif.* The ship docked near the seashore. 3. to have a miscarriage. طاحت على الأرض وطرحت *ṭaaḥat ᶜala l-'arð w-ṭraḥat.* She fell down and had a miscarriage.

انطرح *nṭirah* VII to lie down, prostrate oneself. انطرح على يمبه *nṭirah ᶜala yamba.* He stretched out on his side.

طارح *ṭaariḥ* (act. part. from طرح *ṭirah*) at anchor, having anchored. الجلبوت طارح يم السيف *l-jalbuut ṭaariḥ yamm s-siif.* The jolly-boat is anchored near the seashore.

مطروح *maṭruuḥ* (p.p. from طرح *ṭirah*) laid down, spread out. ليش العيش مطروح على الأرض؟ *leeš l-ᶜeeš maṭruuḥ ᶜala l-'arð?* Why is the rice spread out on the ground?

طرح[2] *ṭrḥ*

طرح *ṭirḥ* p. طروح *ṭruuḥ* American cucumber (kind of large cucumber).

طرد *ṭrd*

طرد *ṭirad (يطرد yuṭrud)* to dismiss, expel, drive away. البشكار باق وطردوه *l-biškaar baag w-ṭradoo.* The servant stole and they dismissed him. إذا ما نجحت هذي المرة، يطردونك *'iða ma nijaḥt haaði l-marra, yuṭurduunak.* If you don't pass (the exam) this time, they will expel you. حرمته المسكينة طردها من البيت *ḥurumta l-maskiina ṭiradha min l-beet.* He threw his poor

ʼams ṭarrašt l-biškaar ḥagg s-suug. Yesterday, I sent out the servant to the market. أمس طرشت البشكار حق السوق

طرشة *ṭarša* p. *-aat* 1. time, turn. هذي الطرشة وبس *haaði t-ṭarša w-bass.* This is the last time. 2. trip, journey. طرشتهم الأولى كانت قبل سنة *ṭaršattum l-'awwala čaanat gabil sana.* Their first trip was a year ago.

طارش *ṭaariš* p. طوارش *ṭuwaariš* 1. messenger. جانا طارش من مكتب الشيخ *yaana ṭaariš min maktab š-šeex.* A messenger came to us from the Shaikh's office. 2. (as act. part.) traveling. الأمير والمطارزية موب هني؛ طارشين *l-'amiir w-l-maṭaarziyya muub hni; ṭaaršiin.* The prince and the bodyguards are not here. They are out of town.

مطرش *mṭarriš* (act. part. from II طرش *ṭarraš*) p. مطرشين *mṭarršiin.* 1. having sent, sent out s.o. or s.th. نحن المطرشينه أمس *niḥin li-mṭarršiina 'ams.* We are the ones who sent it yesterday. 2. sending, forwarding s.th. أنا مطرش لك حيول ذهب *'aana mṭarriš-lič ḥyuul ðahab.* I am sending you (f.s.) gold bracelets. 3. sender (of a letter). آنا المطرش *'aana li-mṭarriš.* I'm the sender.

مطرش *mṭarraš* (p.p. from II طرش *ṭarraš*) having been sent or delivered. الخط مطرش حق التنديل *l-xaṭṭ mṭarraš ḥagg t-tindeel.* The letter has been sent to the foreman.

طرف *ṭrf*

طرف *ṭaraf* p. اطراف *ṭraaf* end, edge, side. من طرف *min ṭaraf* 1. concerning, about. حاكيته من طرف ذيك القضية

wife out of the house.

انطرد *nṭirad* VII pass. of طرد *ṭirad.*

طرد *ṭard* (v.n. from طرد *ṭirad*) 1. dismissal, expulsion. 2. (p. طرود *ṭuruud*) package, parcel. طرشت طرد حق صديقي *ṭarrašt ṭard ḥagg ṣadiigi.* I sent a package to my friend. مكتب الطرود *maktab ṭ-ṭuruud* the parcel office.

طراد *ṭarraad* p. *-aat* 1. motorboat. كنا آنا وبخيت في طراد وعبدالله في طراد ثاني *činna 'aana w-bxeet fi ṭarraad w-ᶜabdaḷḷa fi ṭarraad θaani.* Bakheet and I were in a motorboat and Abdalla was in another one. 2. cruiser (warship).

طرر *ṭrr*

طرارة *ṭraara* (v.n.) begging, asking for alms. (prov.) علمناه الطرارة وسبقنا على البيبان *ᶜallamnaa ṭ-ṭraara w-sibagna ᶜala l-biibaan.* Don't do favors for those who do not appreciate them. (lit., "We taught him how to beg and he came ahead of us at doors.").

طرار *ṭarraar* p. طراروة *ṭaraarwa* beggar. ما تحصل طراروة واجدين هني *ma tḥaṣṣil ṭaraarwa waaydiin hni.* You'll not find many beggars here. (prov.) طرار ويتشرط *ṭarraar w-yitšarraṭ.* Give him an inch and he'll take a mile. (lit., "He is a beggar and has conditions.").

طرش *ṭrš*

طرش *ṭarraš* II 1. to send, forward s.th. طرشت خط جوي مسجل *ṭarrašt xaṭṭ jawwi msajjal.* I sent a registered airmail letter. طرشت له طرد *ṭarrašt-la ṭard.* I sent him a package. 2. to send out, dispatch s.o. أمس طرشت البشكار

ḥaačeeta min ṭaraf ðiič l-gaðiyya. I talked to him concerning that matter. 2. in favor of. والله كلمته واجد من طرفك. *wal̩la kallamta waayid min ṭarafk.* I really talked a lot to him in your favor.

طارفة *ṭaarfa* relatives, relations. كيف حال طارفتك؟ *čeef ḥaal ṭaarfatk?* How are your relatives?

ط ر ف ش ن *ṭrfšn*

طرفشانة *ṭirfišaana* p. *-aat* butterfly.

ط ر گ ١ *ṭrg*

تطرق *taṭarrag* V to touch (on a subject), go into s.th. تطرق إلى موضوع يجهله *taṭarrag 'ila mawðuu^c yijhala.* He touched on a subject he didn't know.

ط ر گ ٢ *ṭrg*

طرق *ṭirag (يطرق yuṭrug)* to slap s.o. or s.o.'s face. طرقه طرقتين *ṭraga ṭraagteen.* He slapped him twice.

طراق *ṭraag* (v.n.) slapping, smacking.

طراقة *ṭraaga* (n. of inst.) p. *-aat* slap, smack. شبع طراق وطرقات *šiba^c ṭraag w-ṭraagaat.* He was slapped so many times.

ط ر گ ٣ *ṭrg*

طراقة *ṭraaga* (common var. ملطة *malṭa*) diarrhea.

ط ر م *ṭrm*

أطرم *'aṭram* f. طرما *ṭarma* p. طرم *ṭirm,* طرمين *ṭirmiin* (more common var. أغتم *'aġtam*) dumb. See أغتم *'aġtam* under **غ ت م** *ġtm.*

ط ر م ب *ṭrmb*

طرمبة *ṭrumba* p. *-aat* water pump.

ط ر و *ṭrw*

طري *ṭiri (يطرى yiṭra)* to be or become fresh, moist, tender. رشيت عليه شوية ماي لاجل يطرى *raššeet ^calee šwayyat maay lajil yiṭra.* I sprinkled it with a little water so it will be fresh. ها اللحم ما يطرى بساع *hal-laḥam ma yiṭra b-saa^c.* This meat doesn't become tender quickly.

طري *ṭiri* fresh (fruit, vegetable), lean (meat, etc.)

طراوة *ṭaraawa* freshness, tenderness.

أطرى *'aṭra* (elat.) 1. (with من *min*) more tender, leaner. 2. (with foll. n.) the most tender, the leanest.

ط ر ي *ṭry*

طاري *ṭaari* reputation, good name. بو ظبي بكل دار شاع طاريها *bu ðabi b-kill daar šaa^c ṭaariiha.* The reputation of Abu Dhabi became widespread in every place.

ط ش ش ١ *ṭšš*

طش *ṭašš (يطش yṭišš)* to vanish, disappear. ما تقول إلا جني وطش *ma tguul 'illa jinni w-ṭašš.* You would only say that he was a demon and vanished.

ط ش ش ٢ *ṭšš*

طش *ṭašš (يطش yṭišš)* 1. to spill (water, etc.). طش الماي *ṭašš l-mayy.* He spilled the water. 2. to scatter, strew around. طش شعير حق الدجاج *ṭašš ša^ciir ḥagg d-diyaay.* He sprinkled barley for the chickens. 3. (with ورا *wara*) to make an effort, endeavor, attempt (to do s.th.) طش ورا رزق عايلته *ṭašš wara rizg ^caayilta.* He made an effort to work for his family's livelihood. 4. to sprinkle, drizzle. المطـر طـش *l-muṭar ṭašš.* It sprinkled.

طـش *ṭašš* (v.n.) light drizzle. يـا هـلا بالطش والرش! *ya hala b-ṭ-ṭašš w-r-rašš!* (Phrase used to welcome a very dear person). You are most welcome here! (as if the person were descending from heaven).

ط ع ص *ṭᶜṣ*

طعـص *ṭiᶜṣ* p. طعـوص *ṭᶜuuṣ* sandhill, dune.

ط ع م *ṭᶜm*

طعم *ṭaᶜᶜam* II 1. to inoculate, vaccinate. طعمـوا أولاد المدرسـة ضـد الكولـيرا *ṭaᶜᶜamaw 'awlaad l-madrasa ðidd l-koleera.* They inoculated the school kids against cholera. 2. to feed, give food to. طعمت عيالها قبل ما راحوا المدرسة *ṭaᶜᶜamat ᶜyaalha gabil-ma raaḥaw l-madrasa.* She fed her kids before they went to school.

طعم *ṭaᶜim* taste, flavor. هذا الأكل ما له طعـم *haaða l-'akil ma-la ṭaᶜim.* This food has no taste. طعمه حامض *ṭaᶜma ḥaamið.* It tastes sour.

طعام *ṭaᶜaam* 1. food. 2. (coll.) date pit. s. *-a.*

ط ع ن *ṭᶜn*

طعن *ṭiᶜan (يطعـن yiṭᶜan)* 1. to stab. طعنـه بـالخنجر مرتـين *ṭiᶜna b-l-xanyar marrateen.* He stabbed him twice with the dagger. 2. (with ب *b-*) to find fault with, discredit. ما تقدر تطعن بأخلاقه *ma tigdar tiṭᶜan b-'aaxlaaga.* You cannot find any fault with his character.

طعنة *ṭaᶜna* p. *-aat* stab, thrust.

طـاعون *ṭaaᶜuun* plague, pestilence. تحيد كم واحد مات في سنة الطـاعون؟ *tḥiid čam waaḥid maat fi sanat ṭ-ṭaaᶜuun?* Do you remember how many people died during the year of the plague?

ط غ ص *ṭġṣ*

طقس *ṭaġṣ* (common var. هـوا *hawa*) weather, climate. كيـف الطقـس اليـوم؟ *čeef ṭ-ṭaġṣ l-yoom?* How is the weather today? الطقس اليوم حار وحاف *ṭ-ṭaġṣ l-yoom ḥaarr w-ḥaaff.* The weather today is hot and dry.

ط غ ي *ṭġy*

طغى *ṭiġa (يطغـى yiṭġa)* 1. to be or become tyrannical, cruel, despotic. لـين صـار ملـك، طغى *leen ṣaar malik, ṭiġa.* When he became king, he became a tyrant. 2. (with علـى *ᶜala*) to overshadow, dominate. جمالها طغى على جمـال كـل البنـات *jamaalha ṭiġa ᶜala jamaal kill l-banaat.* Her beauty overshadowed all the girls' beauty.

طاغي *ṭaaġi* (act. part. from طغى *ṭiġa*) p. طغاة *ṭuġaa* tyrant, despot.

ط ف ح *ṭfḥ*

طفح *ṭufaḥ (yitfaḥ)* 1. (with ب *b-*) to become full of, to be overflowing with. الحفـيز طفـح بالمـاي *l-ḥafiiz ṭufaḥ b-l-maay.* The office was flooded with water. 2. to overflow, run over. طفح المـاي مـن التـانكي *ṭufaḥ l-maay min t-taanki.* The water overflowed from the reservoir.

ط ف ر *ṭfr*

طفر *ṭufar (يطفـر yuṭfur)* to jump. طفر

القطـو مـن الـدرام *ṭufar l-gaṭu min d-draam.* The cat jumped out of the waste basket. يقدر يطفر ستة متر *yigdar yuṭfur sitta mitir.* He can (broad) jump six meters.

طفـر *ṭafur* (v.n.) jumping, leaping. الطفـر بالزانـة *ṭ-ṭafur b-z-zaana* pole vaulting. الطفـر العريـض *ṭ-ṭafur l-ᶜariiḏ̣* long jump.

طفـرة *ṭafra* (n. of inst.) p. *-aat* jump, leap.

ط ف ل *ṭfl*

طفـل *ṭifil* p. أطفال *'aṭfaal* infant, baby. مـا يفتهـم؛ تـوه طفـل جـاهل *ma yiftihim; tawwa ṭifil yaahil.* He doesn't know; he's still a small child. دخـتر أطفـال *daxtar 'aṭfaal* pediatrician.

طفولة *ṭufuula* infancy, childhood.

ط ف ي *ṭfy*

طفـى *ṭaffa* II 1. to put out, extinguish. رجال المطافي طفوا الحريـق *rijaal l-maṭaafi ṭaffaw l-ḥariij.* The firemen put out the fire. 2. to turn off, switch off. طفي الليـت. ليـش شـبيته؟ *ṭaffi l-leet. leeš šabbeeta?* Turn off the light. Why did you turn it on?

تطفى *tṭaffa* V pass. of طفى *ṭufa.*

انطفـى *nṭufa* VII to go out, be extinguished. انطفـى الليـت *nṭufa l-leet.* The light went out. الحريق انطفى *l-ḥariij nṭufa.* The fire was extinguished.

مطفـى *maṭfa* p. مطـافي *maṭaafi* fire extinguisher. رجـال المطـافي *rijaal l-maṭaafi* the firemen.

مطفي *maṭfi* (p.p. from طفى *ṭufa*) turned off, switched off. الليت حق الحجرة مطفي *l-leet ḥagg l-ḥijra maṭfi.* The light in the room is turned off.

ط گ گ *ṭgg*

طق *ṭagg* (يطـق *yṭigg*) 1. to beat, flog s.o. طقـوه امية طقة لانـه كـان سـكران *ṭaggoo 'imyat ṭagga linna čaan sakraan.* They flogged him a hundred lashes because he was drunk. هو اللي طقـني *huwa lli ṭaggani.* He's the one who beat me. 2. to knock at (the door). طـق البـاب *ṭagg l-baab.* He knocked at the door. (prov.) من طق الباب سمع الجواب *man ṭagg l-baab simaᶜ l-jawaab.* Where there's a will there's a way. 3. to hammer. طق المسمار في الحـايط *ṭagg l-mismaar fi l-ḥaayiṭ.* He hammered the nail into the wall. 4. to steal. البايق طق كل الفلوس *l-baayig ṭagg kill li-fluus.* The thief stole all the money.

انطق *nṭagg* VII pass. of طق *ṭagg.*

طق *ṭagg* (v.n. from طق *ṭagg*) 1. beating, flogging. صـار فيهـا طـق نعـل *ṣaar fiiha ṭagg niᶜil.* There was fierce fighting (among a group of people). 2. knocking at (the door). 3. hammering. 4. stealing.

طقة *ṭagga* (n. of inst.) 1. smack, blow, knock. 2. lash, stroke.

ط ل ب *ṭlb*

طلـب *ṭilab* (يطلب *yaṭlub*) 1. to ask for, request, apply for. الكولي طلب زيادة من التنديـل *l-kuuli ṭilab ziyaada min t-tindeel.* The coolie asked the foreman for an increase (in his salary). طلـب مـني أسـلفه ميتـين درهـم *ṭilab minni 'asallfa miiteen dirhim.* He asked me

طلبة *ṭalba,* طلابة *ṭlaaba* p. طلايب *ṭilaayib* 1. dilemma, difficulty, problem. صارت القضية طلابة *ṣaarat l-gaḍiyya ṭlaaba.* The case became very complicated. أبو الطلايب *'ubu ṭ-ṭilaayib* troublemaker. 2. bridal money, dowry. يحطون الطلبة في شنطة ويعطونها حق أبوها *yḥuṭṭuun ṭ-ṭalba fi šanṭa w-y^c^aṭuunha ḥagg 'ubuuha.* They put the bridal money in a bag and give it to her father.

طلاب *ṭallaab* p. طلاليب *ṭlaaliib,* طلابة *ṭallaaba* beggar, one who asks for alms. (prov.) طلاب ويتشرط *ṭallaab w-yitšarraṭ.* Give him an inch and he takes a mile. (lit., "He is a beggar and has conditions.").

مطلب *maṭlab* demand, claim.

طالب *ṭaalib* 1. (p. طلاب *ṭullaab*) student, pupil. 2. (act. part. from طلب *ṭilab* p. *-iin*) asking or having asked for s.th., requesting or having requested s.th. آنا طالب زيادة في معاشي *'aana ṭaalib ziyada fi ma^c^aaši.* I am asking (or I have asked) for an increase in my salary. نحن طالبين يدها من أبوها *niḥin ṭaalbiin yaddaha min 'ubuuha.* We have asked her father for her hand in marriage.

مطلوب *maṭluub* (p.p. from طلب *ṭilab*) 1. having been requested, required, wanted. يا هلا فيكم، بس البنت مطلوبة *ya hala fiikum, bass l-bint maṭluuba.* You are welcome, but the girl's hand in marriage has been asked for. مطلوب من سالم انه... *maṭluub min saalim 'inna...* It has been required of Salim that he... 2. due, owed (money). مطلوب منك خمسين دينار *maṭluub*

to loan him two hundred dirhams. طلبت شغل في الديوان الأميري *ṭilabt šuġul fi d-diiwaan l-'amiiri.* I applied for a job in the Emiri court. 2. to send for s.o. الشرطة طلبوه لانه دعم واحد في السوق *š-širṭa ṭlaboo linna di^c^am waaḥid fi s-suug.* The police sent for him because he had run over someone (with his car) in the marketplace. 3. to order. طلبنا ألف سيارة من الجابان *ṭilabna 'alf sayyaara min l-jaabaan.* We ordered a thousand cars from Japan. 4. to be owed money by, be the creditor of. يطلبني ألف دينار *yaṭlubni 'alf diinaar.* I owe him a thousand dinars.

طالب *ṭaalab* III (with على *^c^ala*) to claim s.th., make a demand for s.th. إذا ما تطالب بحقك، ضاع منك *'iḏa ma tṭaalib b-ḥaggak, ḍaa^c^ minnak.* If you don't ask for what you are entitled to, you'll lose it.

تطلب *tṭallab* V 1. to beg, ask for alms. فيه ناس يتطلبون في الأسواق *fii naas yiṭṭallabuun fi l-'aswaag.* There are people who beg in the marketplaces. 2. to require, necessitate. هذا الشغل يتطلب صبر *haaḏa š-šuġul yiṭṭallab ṣabir.* This work requires patience.

انطلب *nṭilab* VII pass. of طلب *ṭilab.*

طلب *ṭalab* p. *-aat* 1. demand, claim. طلبك على الراس والعين *ṭalabak ^c^ala r-raas w-l-^c^een.* Your demand will be gladly accepted. 2. request, application. قدمت طلب حق إجازة *gaddamt ṭalab ḥagg 'ijaaza.* I submitted a request for vacation. 3. demand (comm.). عند الطلب *^c^ind ṭ-ṭalab* on demand. العرض والطلب *l-^c^arḍ w-ṭ-ṭalab* supply and demand.

minnak xamsiin diinaar. You owe fifty dinars. 3. (with ل *l-*) indebted to s.o. آنا مطلوب لك *'aana maṭluub-lak.* I am indebted to you. 4. wanted (in classified ads). مطلوب شقة بحجرتين نوم *maṭluub šigga b-ḥijrateen noom.* A two-bedroom apartment is wanted. 5. wanted (by the police, government, etc.) مطلوب للشرطة لانه باق *maṭluub liš-širṭa linna baag.* He's wanted by the police because he has stolen.

طلع *ṭl*ᶜ

طلع *ṭila*ᶜ (يطلع *yiṭla*ᶜ) 1. to go out, get out. موب هني؛ طلع برة *muub hni; ṭila*ᶜ *barra.* He's not here; he went outside. 2. to appear, come into view. القمر يطلع الليلة الساعة تسع *l-gumar yiṭla*ᶜ *l-leela s-saa*ᶜ*a tisi*ᶜ. The moon will appear at nine tonight. طلع اسمك في الجريدة؟ *ṭila*ᶜ *'ismak fi l-jariida?* Has your name appeared in the newspaper? نتيجة الامتحان طلعت *natiijat li-mtiḥaan ṭla*ᶜ*at.* The result of the examination is out. اتركه! ما يطلع خير من وراه *'uturka! ma yiṭla*ᶜ *xeer min waraa.* Leave him! Nothing good will come from him. طلعت لنا مشكلة ثانية *ṭla*ᶜ*at-lana muškila θaanya.* Another problem has come up for us. 2. to grow forth, sprout. التفاح ما يطلع هني *t-tiffaaḥ ma yiṭla*ᶜ *hni.* Apples don't grow here. 3. to gush out. البترول طلع هني من زمان *l-batrool ṭila*ᶜ *hni min zamaan.* Oil gushed out here a long time ago. 4. to leave, exit, depart. سقط في الامتحان وطلع من المدرسة *ṣigaṭ fi li-mtiḥaan w-ṭila*ᶜ *min l-madrasa.* He failed the examination and left school. 5. to come out, rank, turn out to be, prove to be. طلعت الأولى على بنات صفها *ṭla*ᶜ*at l-'uula* ᶜ*ala banaat ṣaffha.* She ranked first among here classmates. طلع عساس وزخوه *ṭila*ᶜ ᶜ*assaas w-zaxxoo.* He turned out to be a spy and they arrested him. 6. (with على ᶜ*ala*) to take after. طلع على أبوه *ṭila*ᶜ ᶜ*ala 'ubuu.* He takes after his father. (prov.) اللي ما يطلع على أبوه نغل *'illi ma yiṭla*ᶜ ᶜ*ala 'ubuu nağal.* Like father like son. (lit., "He who doesn't take after his father is a bastard.").

طلع *ṭalla*ᶜ II 1. to bring out, show, expose. (prov.) اللي في الجدر يطلعه الملاس *'illi fi l-jidir yṭall*ᶜ*a l-millaas.* Time will tell one's good and bad qualities. 2. to obtain, get, acquire. كم درهم تطلع في اليوم؟ *čam dirhim ṭṭalli*ᶜ *fi l-yoom?* How many dirhams do you make a day? طلع ليسن أمس *ṭalla*ᶜ *leesan 'ams.* He got a driving license yesterday. 3. to dismiss, expel, throw out. طلعوه من شغله *ṭalla*ᶜ*oo min šuğla.* They dismissed him from his job. المؤجر طلعه من الشقة *l-mu'ajjiir ṭalla*ᶜ*a min š-šigga.* The landlord evicted him from the apartment.

طالع *ṭaala*ᶜ III 1. see, look at. إذا أنت تبي تتزوج ما تقدر تطالع البنت *'iδa 'inta tabi tizzawwaj ma tigdar ṭṭaali*ᶜ *l-bint.* If you want to get married, you cannot see the girl. طرش أمه وطالعت البنت *ṭarraš 'umma w-ṭaala*ᶜ*at l-bint.* He sent his mother and she looked at the girl. 2. to study. قعد يطالع دروسه *gi*ᶜ*ad yṭaali*ᶜ *druusa.* He started to study his lessons.

طلعة *ṭal*ᶜ*a* p. *-aat* 1. going out. 2. excursion, short trip. البنات عندهن طلعة حق صديقاتهن *l-banaat* ᶜ*indahin ṭal*ᶜ*a* *ḥagg ṣadiigaattin.* The girls are going to see their friends.

استطلاع *stiṭlaa*ᶜ as in حب الاستطلاع *ḥubb li-stiṭlaa*ᶜ curiosity.

ط ل گ *ṭlg*

طلقت *ṭlagat (تطلق tiṭlag)* to be in labor. خذوها المستشفى لانها كانت تطلق *xaðooha l-mustašfa linha čaanat tiṭlag.* They took her to the hospital because she was in labor.

طلق *ṭallag* II to divorce. طلقها لانها ما جابت جهال *ṭallagha linha ma yaabat yihhaal.* He divorced her because she didn't bear children. (prov.) قال طلقها واخذ أختها. قال الله يلعن الثنتين *gaal ṭalligha w-'ixið 'uxutta. gaal 'aḷḷa yil*ᶜ*an θ-θinteen.* Between the devil and the deep blue sea. Hobson's choice.

تطلق *tṭallag* V pass. of II طلق *ṭallag.*

طلاق *ṭalaag* divorce.

طالق *ṭaalig* p. *-aat* divorcee, divorced woman. إذا قلت حق حرمتك، «أنت طالق» ثلاث مرات، صارت محرمة عليك *'iða gilt ḥagg ḥurumtak, "'inti ṭaalig," θalaaθ marraat ṣaarat muḥarrama* ᶜ*aleek.* If you say to your wife, "You are divorced," three times, she is no longer your wife legally.

ط ل ي *ṭly*

طلي *ṭili* (common var. كبش *čabš*) p. طلاي *ṭlaay* ram, male sheep. الطلي ذكر النعجة *ṭ-ṭili ðakar li-n*ᶜ*aya.* A ram is the male of a ewe.

ط م ا ط *ṭmaaṭ*

طماط *ṭamaaṭ* (coll.) tomatoes. s. طماطة *-aa,* حبة طماط *ḥabbat ṭamaaṭ,* p. حبات طماط *ḥabbaat ṭamaaṭ.* الطماط غالي اليوم *ṭ-ṭamaaṭ ġaali l-yoom.* Tomatoes are expensive today. اشتريت طمام *štireet ṭamaaṭ.* I bought (some) tomatoes.

ط م ط م *ṭmṭm*

طمطم *ṭamṭam (يطمطم yṭamṭim)* to cover up, conceal, hide. طمطموا القضية وخلاص *ṭamṭamaw l-gaḍiyya w-xaḷaaṣ.* They covered up the story and that was the end of it.

ط م ع *ṭm*ᶜ

طمع *ṭuma*ᶜ *(يطمع yiṭma*ᶜ*)* 1. to be or become greedy. لا تطمع! من طمع طبع *la tiṭma*ᶜ*! man ṭuma*ᶜ *ṭuba*ᶜ. Don't be greedy! He who is greedy will drown. 2. (with في *fi*) to covet, envy, be envious of. اللي يطمع في مال غيره يخسر ماله *'illi yiṭma*ᶜ *fi maal ġeera yxasir maala.* He who covets somebody else's wealth will lose his. 3. to be anxious, to aspire, wish, yearn. يطمع يصير حاكم *yiṭma*ᶜ *yṣiir ḥaakim.* He's anxious to become a ruler.

طمع *ṭama*ᶜ (v.n.) greed, greediness, covetousness.

طماع *ṭammaa*ᶜ p. *-iin* greedy, avaricious. خسر المناقصة لانه طماع *xisar l-munaagaṣa linna ṭammaa*ᶜ. He lost the bid because he was greedy. لا تكون طماع! *la tkuun ṭammaa*ᶜ*!* Don't be greedy!

ط م غ *ṭmġ*

طمغ *ṭumaġ (يطمغ yuṭmuġ)* to stamp. اطمغ لي ها الورقة قبل ما آخذها حق المدير *'uṭmuġ-li hal-wurga gabil-ma 'aaxiðha ḥagg l-mudiir.* Stamp this paper for me before I take it to the director.

طمغة *ṭamġa* p. *-aat* 1. impression, imprint. 2. stamp, seal. هذا الخط وهذي طمغة الوزارة *haaða l-xaṭṭ w-haaði ṭamġat l-wazaara.* This is the letter and this is the seal of the ministry.

طمم *ṭmm*

طم *ṭamm* (يطم *yṭumm*) 1. to bury, cover over. طم الخمام في الخندق *ṭamm li-xmaam fi l-xandag.* He buried the garbage in the ditch. 2. (used with ثم *θamm*) to shut up. طم ثمه *ṭamm θamma.* He shut up.

انطم *nṭamm* VII pass. of طم *ṭamm* 1. to be buried, covered up. 2. (imp. only) !انطم *nṭamm!* Shut up! Be quiet!

طم *ṭamm,* طمام *ṭmaam* (v.n.) 1. burying, covering up. 2. roofing.

طنز *ṭnz*

طنز *ṭannaz* II 1. to kid, joke. موب جدي. دايماً يطنز *muub jiddi. daayman yṭanniz.* He's not serious. He's always cracking jokes. 2. (with على *ᶜala*) to ridicule, make fun of. عيب عليك! لا تطنز عليهم *ᶜeeb ᶜaleek! la ṭṭanniz ᶜaleehum.* Shame on you! Don't ridicule them.

تطانز *tṭaanaz* VI to ridicule, make fun of each other.

طنزة *ṭanza,* طناز *ṭnaaz* mockery, scorn, scorning.

مطنزة *maṭnaza* p. مطانز *maṭaaniz* object of ridicule, laughing stock.

طنن *ṭnn*

طن *ṭann* p. اطنان *ṭnaan* ton. حمولة اللوري خمسين طن *ḥumuulat l-loori xamsiin ṭann.* The truck freight tonnage is fifty tons.

طهر *ṭhr*

طهر *ṭahhar* II 1. to purge, clean, purify. الحكومة طهرت الجهاز الفاسد *l-ḥukuuma ṭahharat l-jihaaz l-faasid.* The government purged the system of corruption. 2. to circumcise (more common var. ختن *xitan*). See under خ ت ن *xtn*.

تطهر *tṭahhar* V pass. of II طهر *ṭahhar.*

طهور *ṭuhuur* (common var. ختان *xitaan*) circumcision. الطهور واجب على كل مسلم *ṭ-ṭuhuur waajib ᶜala kill muslim.* Circumcision is required of every Muslim.

طاهر *ṭaahir* religiously clean, pure. إذا أنت مسلم تصلي وتصوم لازم تكون طاهر *'iða 'inta muslim tṣalli w-tṣuum laazim tkuun ṭaahir.* If you are a Muslim, and you pray and fast, you must be clean.

طوب *ṭwb*

طوب *ṭuub* p. طواب *ṭwaab* cannon.

طور *ṭwr*

تطور *tṭawwar* V (common var. تطور *taṭawwar*) to develop, evolve. صناعة البتروكيماويات تطورت في الإمارات *ṣinaaᶜat l-betrookiimaawiyyaat taṭawwarat fi l-'imaaraat.* The industry of petrochemicals has developed in the Emirates.

طوز *ṭwz*

طوز *ṭooz* dust, dust storm.

طوف ṭwf

طاف *ṭaaf (يطوف yṭuuf)* 1. (with حول *ḥool*) to circumambulate, run around, walk around. طفنا حول الكعبة سبع مرات *ṭufna ḥool l-kacba sabac marraat.* We circumambulated the Kaaba seven times. 2. to float. الحطب يطوف في الماي *l-ḥaṭab yṭuuf fi l-maay.* Wood floats in water. 3. to be or become flooded. لين تمطر الشوارع تطوف *leen tumṭur š-šawaaric ṭṭuuf.* When it rains, the streets get flooded. 4. (with على *cala*) to exceed, be greater than. رجال عود عمره طاف على الستين *rayyaal cood cumra ṭaaf cala s-sittiin.* He's an old man who is more than sixty years old. 5. to finish, come to an end. طاف الوقت *ṭaaf l-wagt.* The time is up. طاف وقت وصول الطايرة *ṭaaf wagt wuṣuul ṭ-ṭaayra.* The arrival time of the plane has passed.

طوف *ṭawwaf* II 1. to guide, show around. فيه مطوفين يطوفون الحجاج *fii mṭawwfiin yṭawwfuun l-ḥijjaaj.* There are pilgrims' guides (in Mecca) who guide pilgrims around. 2. to build a wall around, to fence. طوفوا الفندق بطوفة من حديد *ṭawwafaw l-fundug b-ṭoofa min ḥadiid.* They constructed an iron fence around the hotel.

طوفة *ṭoofa* p. إطوف *'iṭwaf* mud wall.

طايف *ṭaayif* (act. part. from طاف *ṭaaf*) 1. having made a circumambulation (of the Kaaba). توني طايف حول الكعبة *tawwni ṭaayif ḥool l-kaaba.* I have just circumambulated the Kaaba. 2. floating. 3. (with على *cala*) having exceeded.

طوس ṭws

طاس *ṭaas* p. *-aat cymbals.*

طاسة *ṭaasa* p. طوس *ṭuus* 1. drinking bowl, cup. 2. special sieve for determining the size of pearls.

طوش ṭwš

طواشة *ṭwaaša* dealing in pearls, buying and selling of pearls.

طواش *ṭawwaaš* p. طواويش *ṭawaawiiš* pearl dealer. الغواوصة يبيعون القماش حق الطواش *l-ġawaawṣa ybiicuun li-gmaaš ḥagg ṭ-ṭawwaaš.* Pearl divers sell pearls to the pearl dealer.

طوع ṭwc

طاع *ṭaac (يطيع yṭiic)* 1. to obey, be obedient. ولد زين. يطيع والدينه *walad zeen. yṭiic waaldeena.* He's a good boy. He obeys his parents. 2. to heed. يطيع كلام الله *yṭiic kalaam 'aḷḷa.* He heeds God's words.

طاوع *ṭaawac* III to comply with, accede to the wishes of. طاوع تعاليم دينه *ṭaawac tacaaliim diina.* He complied with the teachings of his religion.

تطوع *tṭawwac* V (common var. تطوع *taṭawwac*) to volunteer. تطوع في الجيش *taṭawwac fi l-jeeš.* He volunteered for the army. تطوع يشتغل وايانا *taṭawwac yištaġil wiyyaana.* He volunteered to work with us.

استطاع *staṭaac* X (more common var. قدر *gidar*) see under **گ د ر** *gdr*.

طاعة *ṭaaca* (common var. طوع *ṭooc*) obedience, submission to. على المسلم طاعة الله *cala l-muslim ṭaacat 'aḷḷa.* A Muslim should obey God.

طايفة *ṭaayfa* p. طوايف *ṭawaayif* tribe, family. أنـت تخـص أي طايفـة؟ *'inta txiṣṣ 'ayy ṭaayfa?* Which tribe do you belong to?

مطوف *mṭawwif* (act. part. from II طوف *ṭawwaf*) 1. having guided, shown s.o. around. توه مطوف خمـس حجـاج *tawwa mṭawwif xamas ḥijjaaj.* He has just guided five pilgrims around (the Kaaba). 2. p. *-iin* pilgrim's guide to Mecca.

طول *ṭwl*

طال *ṭaal* (يطول *yṭuul*) 1. to reach get to s.th. (prov.) اللي ما يطول العنقود يقـول حـامض *'illi ma yṭuul l-ᶜanguud yguul ḥaamiḍ̄.* Sour grapes. طال الفلـوس مـن الكيـس *ṭaal li-fluus min č-čiis.* He got the money out of the bag. غـاب عـن الديـرة وطـالت غيبتـه *ġaab ᶜan d-diira w-ṭaalat ġeebta.* He went away from his town and didn't come back for a long time. طـال عمـرك! *ṭaal ᶜumrak!* (introductory courteous phrase) May you live long! God prolong your life!

طول *ṭawwal* II 1. to linger long, last long. أقول لك وما أطـول عليـك *'agul-lič w-ma 'aṭawwil ᶜaleeč.* I will tell you (f.s.) and won't take too long. راح وطول. تريتـه *raaḥ w-ṭawwal. trayyeeta.* He went and lingered long. I waited for him. 2. to lengthen, extend, prolong. ممكـن تطـول لي هـا الكنـدورة؟ *mumkin ṭṭawwil-li hal-kandoora?* Will you please lengthen this dishdash for me? طول شعره *ṭawwal šaᶜra.* He let his hair grow long. طول بالك! دقيقة *ṭawwil baalak! digiiga.* Hold your horses! Just a minute. طول الله عمرك، الله يطول عمـرك *ṭawwal aḷḷa ᶜumrak, 'aḷḷa yṭawwil ᶜumrak.* May God prolong your life.

تطول *tṭawwal* V to be lengthened. ها النفنـوف مـا يتطـول *han-nafnuuf ma yiṭṭawwal.* This dress cannot be lengthened.

استطول *staṭwal* X to consider long, too long. استطول المدة *staṭwal l-mudda.* He considered the time to be too long.

طالما *ṭaala-ma* (conj.) as long as, while. طالما هـو المديـر، مـا فيـه زيـادة في المعـاش *ṭaala-ma huwa l-mudiir, ma fii ziyaada fi l-maᶜaaš.* As long as he's the manager, there's no increase in salary.

طول *ṭuul* 1. length. كم طول الميز؟ *čam ṭuul l-meez?* How long is the table? خط الطول *xaṭṭ ṭ-ṭuul* the (geographical) longitude, the meridian. بطـول *b-ṭuul* the same length as. أبغى سـيارة بطـول هـذي *'abġa sayyaara b-ṭuul haaðī.* I want a car the same length as this. على طـول *ᶜala ṭuul* always, all the time. الصبـح آنـا علـى طـول في الـوزارة *ṣ-ṣubḥ 'aana ᶜala ṭuul fi l-wazaara.* In the morning, I am always in the ministry. 2. height, tallness. كـم طولـك؟ *čam ṭuulak?* How tall are you? (prov.) الطول طول نخلة والعقل عقـل صخلـة *ṭ-ṭuul ṭuul nxaḷa w-l-ᶜagil ᶜagil ṣxaḷa.* The mind of a child and the body of a man. طول العمارة *ṭuul li-ᶜmaara* the height of the building. 3. (prep.) throughout, during. طـول الليـل *ṭuul l-leel* all night long. طول الوقت *ṭuul l-wagt* throughout the whole time. طول عمـره جـراخ *ṭuul ᶜumra čarraax.* He's always a liar.

طولما *ṭuul-ma* = طالما *ṭaala-ma.*

طوي *ṭwy*

طوى *ṭuwa (يطـوي yaṭwi)* to fold, fold up, roll up. طويت القراطيس وحطيتهم في بقشة *ṭuweet l-garaaṭiis w-ḥaṭṭettum fi bugša.* I folded the papers and put them in an envelope. طوى الزولية وشالها *ṭuwa z-zuuliyya w-šaalha.* He rolled up the carpet and carried it.

طي ب *ṭyb*

طاب *ṭaab (يطيـب yṭiib)* 1. to be or become pleasant, enjoyable, agreeable. عقب شـهرين الهـوا يطيـب *ᶜugub šahreen l-hawa yṭiib.* In two months the weather will be pleasant. طـابت لـه القعـدة في البيـت *ṭaabat-la l-gaᶜda fi l-beet.* Staying at home was pleasant for him. He liked staying at home. 2. to heal, recover (from an illness). جرحـي بعـده مـا طـاب *jurḥi baᶜda ma ṭaab.* My wound hasn't healed yet. طبـت مـن ذاك المـرض *ṭibt min ðaak l-maraḍ.* I recovered from that illness.

طيـب *ṭayyab* II 1. to cure, heal. اللي يطيب هـو الله سـبحانه وتعـالى *'illi yṭayyib huwa ḷḷaah subḥaanahu wa-taᶜaalaa.* The one who cures is God, be He praised and exalted. 2. to make delicious, tasty. الثـوم يطيـب الأكـل *θ-θoom yṭayyib l-'akil.* Garlic makes the meal delicious.

تطيب *taṭayyab* V to perfume, scent oneself. النـاس هـني يتطيبـون عقـب الأكـل *n-naas hni yiṭṭayyabuun ᶜugb l-'akil.* People here perfume themselves after eating.

طيـب *ṭiib* 1. goodness. بـالطيب والا بالغصب *b-ṭ-ṭiib walla b-l-ġaṣb* by hook or by crook. هذا مـن طيب قلبـه *haaða min ṭiib galba.* This is out of the goodness of his heart. عن طيب خاطر *ᶜan ṭiib xaaṭir* gladly. 2. incense.

طيـب *ṭayyib* 1. delicious, tasty. الدجاج المشـوي طيـب *d-diyaay l-mašwi ṭayyib.* Grilled chicken is delicious. 2. fine, well, in good health. شـلونك؟ طيـب، مشـكور *šloonak? ṭayyib maškuur.* How are you? I am fine, thank you. 3. good, nice. المديـر رجـال طيـب *l-mudiir rayyaal ṭayyib.* The director is a good man.

أطيـب *'aṭyab* (elat.) 1. (with من *min*) more delicious than, etc. 2. (with foll. n.) the most delicious, etc.

طي ح *ṭyḥ*

طاح *ṭaaḥ (يطيح yṭiiḥ)* 1. to fall (down), drop. دعم راعي السيكل وطاح على الأرض *diᶜam raaᶜi s-seekal w-ṭaaḥ ᶜala l-'arḍ.* He hit (in a car accident) the cyclist and he (the cyclist) fell to the ground. (prov.) إذا طـاح البعـير كـثرت سـكاكينه *'iða ṭaaḥ l-biᶜiir kiθrat sičaačiina.* When it rains, it pours. 2. to fall ill, become sick. ضربها وطاحت مريضـة *ḍirabha w-ṭaaḥat mariiḍa.* He hit her and she fell ill. 3. to be in season. الهمبـة طـاحت السـوق بـس غاليـة *l-hamba ṭaaḥat s-suug bass ġaalya.* Mangoes are in season but they are expensive. 4. to lie down. طاح على جنبه اليمـين *ṭaaḥ ᶜala janba l-yimiin.* He lay down on his right side. 5. (with من *min*) to despise, look down upon. طاح من عيني لانـه يسـكر *ṭaaḥ min ᶜeeni linna yiskar.* I despise him because he drinks (alcohol).

طيح *ṭayyaḥ* II to drop, cause to fall.

عقب ما غسل الماعون طيحه *ᶜugub-ma ġisal l-maaᶜuun ṭayyaḥa.* After he had washed the platc, he dropped it. ضربه وطيحه على الأرض *ḍraba w-ṭayyaḥa ᶜala l-'arḍ.* He hit him and caused him to fall down.

طيح *ṭeeḥ* (v.n. from طاح *ṭaaḥ*) falling.

طيحة *ṭeeḥa* (n. of inst.) p. *-aat* a fall. (prov.) يا ماشي درب الزلق لا تيمن طيحتك *ya maaši darb z-zalag la teeman ṭeeḥtak.* Don't stand in harm's way. (lit., "If you are on a slippery road, don't guarantee that you won't fall down.").

طايح *ṭaayiḥ* (act. part. from طاح *ṭaaḥ*) 1. falling down. شفت واحد طايح من فوق وطب *čift waaḥid ṭaayiḥ min foog w-ṭabb.* I saw someone falling down from above and hit the ground. 2. low, inexpensive. أسعار الطماط طايحة في الأسواق *'asᶜaar ṭ-ṭamaaṭ ṭaayha fi l-'aswaag.* The prices of tomatoes are low in the marketplaces. 3. lying down. حصلته طايح على جنبه اليمين *ḥaṣṣalta ṭaayiḥ ᶜala janba l-yimiin.* I found him lying down on his right side.

ط ي ر *ṭyr*

طار *ṭaar (يطير yṭiir)* to fly off, fly away, take off. الطير طار وحط على الشجرة *ṭ-ṭeer ṭaar w-ḥaṭṭ ᶜala li-šyara.* The bird flew off and perched in the tree. الطايرة طارت متأخرة *ṭ-ṭaayra ṭaarat mit'axxra.* The plane took off late. طرت من بو ظبي إلى قطر *ṭirt min bu ḍabi 'ila giṭar.* I took a plane from Abu Dhabi to Qatar. 2. to fly up. القميص طار من الهوا *l-gamiiṣ ṭaar min l-hawa.* The shirt flew up because of the wind.

طير *ṭayyar* II 1. to cause to fly. الهوا طير القميص *l-hawa ṭayyar l-gamiiṣ.* Thc wind blew the shirt away. جمال ها البنية طير عقلي *jamaal hal-ibnayya ṭayyar ᶜagḷi.* This girl's beauty drove me mad. 2. to fly s.th. العيال طيروا طياراتهم لأن كان فيه هوا زين *li-ᶜyaaḷ ṭayyaraw ṭayyaaraattum li'an čaan fii hawa zeen.* The kids flew their kites because there was a good breeze.

طير *ṭeer* p. طيور *ṭuyuur* bird. الشاهين والقطا من طيور الخليج *š-šaahiin w-l-gaṭaa min ṭuyuur l-xaliij.* The peregrine and the sand grouse are among the birds that come from the Gulf. طيور سهيل *ṭuyuur sheel* migratory birds (that come from East Africa to the Gulf in the spring).

طوير *ṭwayyir* dim. of طير *ṭeer* small or young bird.

طيار *ṭayyaar* p. *-iin* pilot, flyer, aviator.

طيارة *ṭayyaara* (common var. طايرة *ṭaayra*) p. *-aat,* طياير *ṭiyaayiir* 1. airplane. 2. kite (toy).

طيران *ṭayaraan* (v.n. from طار *ṭaar*) 1. aviation, air. طيران الخليج *ṭayaraan l-xaliij* Gulf Aviation, Gulf Air. 2. flight, flying.

مطار *maṭaar* p. *-aat* airport, airfield. مطار عسكري *maṭaar ᶜaskari* military airport.

ط ي ش *ṭyš*

طاش *ṭaaš (يطيش yṭiiš)* 1. to boil over. طاش الحليب *ṭaaš l-ḥaliib.* The milk boiled over. 2. to be or become furious, very upset. طاش من الغضب

ṭaaš min l-ġađ̣ab. He became furious. طاش البحر *ṭaaš l-baḥar.* The sea was stormy.

طيع *ṭyᶜ*

طيع *ṭayyaᶜ* II = طوع *ṭawwaᶜ* II. See under **طوع** *ṭwᶜ*.

طين *ṭyn*

طين *ṭiin* (coll.) mud, clay. s. *-a.* طوفة من طين *ṭoofa min ṭiin* mud wall. زاد الطين بلة *zaad ṭ-ṭiin balla.* He made things worse.

ظ

ظ ا د *ḍaad*

ضاد *ḍaad* name of the letter ض *ḍ*.

ظ ب ب *ḍbb*

ضب *ḍabb* p. ضبان *ḍibbaan* large, desert lizard.

ظ ب ا ب *ḍbaab*

ضباب *ḍabaab* (coll.) mist, fog (in Bahraini). طل *ṭall* (in Qatari and U.A.E.). الطايرة ما تقدر تحط من الضباب *ṭ-ṭaayra ma tigdar tḥuṭṭ min ḍ-ḍabaab.* Airplanes cannot land because of the fog.

ظ ب ط *ḍbṭ*

ضبط *ḍibaṭ (*يضبط *yuḍbuṭ)* 1. to control, maintain control over. ها المعلم ما يقدر يضبط الصف *hal-mu^c^allim ma yigdar yuḍbuṭ ṣ-ṣaff.* This teacher cannot control the class. اضبط روحك وصك حلقك! *'uḍbuṭ ruuḥak w-ṣikk ḥaljak!* Control yourself and shut up! 2. to keep records of. يضبط حسابات الشركة *yuḍbuṭ ḥsaabaat š-šarika.* He keeps the books of the company. ما يضبط مصروفه الشهري *ma yuḍbuṭ maṣruufa š-šahri.* He doesn't keep records of his monthly expenses. 3. to set, regulate, adjust. خلنا نضبط ساعاتنا *xaḷḷna nuḍbuṭ saa^c^aatna.* Let's set our watches.

انضبط *nḍibaṭ* VII pass. of ضبط *ḍibaṭ.*

ضبط *ḍabṭ* (v.n. from ضبط *ḍibaṭ*) 1. control, discipline. ضبط الصف *ḍabṭ ṣ-ṣaff* class control. 2. observation, checking. 3. exactness, precision. بالضبط *b-ḍ-ḍabt* exactly, precisely.

مضبطة *maḍbaṭa* p. مضابط *maḍaabiṭ* petition.

انضباط *nḍibaaṭ* 1. discipline. لجنة انضباط *lajnat nḍibaaṭ* disciplinary board. 2. military policeman. جندي انضباط *jindi nḍibaat* military policeman.

ضابط *ḍaabiṭ* p. ضباط *ḍibbaaṭ* 1. officer, military officer. 2. (act. part. from ضبط *ḍibaṭ*) control, device, regulator. ضابط الصوت *ḍaabiṭ ṣ-ṣoot* sound regulator. بدون ضابط *b-duun ḍaabiṭ* out of control.

مضبوط *maḍbuuṭ* 1. accurate, precise. اللي تقوله مضبوط *'illi tguula maḍbuuṭ.* What you say is accurate. 2. (p.p. from ضبط *ḍibaṭ*) controlled, regulated. الضغط مضبوط *ḍ-ḍaġṭ maḍbuuṭ.* The pressure is controlled.

ظ ب ع *ḍb^c^*

ضبع *ḍabi^c^* p. ضباع *ḍbaa^c^* hyena. f. ضبعة *ḍab^c^a* (also known as أم عامر *'umm ^c^aamir).*

ظ ب ي *ḍby*

ظبي *ḍabi* p. ظبيان *ḍibyaan* deer, gazelle. أبو ظبي *'abu ḍabi,* بو ظبي *bu ḍabi* Abu Dhabi.

ظبياني *ḍibyaani* 1. (p. *-yyiin*) an Abu Dhabian. 2. characteristic of Abu Dhabi.

ظ ج ج *ðjj*

ضجة *ðajja* uproar, noise, clamor.

ظ ح چ *ðḥč*

ضحك *ðiḥač (يضحك yiðḥač)* 1. to laugh. قام يضحك لين شاف ذاك المنظر. *gaam yiðḥač leen čaaf ðaak l-manðar.* He started to laugh when he saw that scene. 2. (with على *ᶜala*) to make fun of, to ridicule. ما عليك منه؛ يضحك عليك *ma ᶜaleek minna; yiðḥač ᶜaleek.* Don't pay attention to him; he's just making fun of you. 3. to cheat s.o. ضحك عليه وخذ فلوسه *ðiḥač ᶜalee w-xað fluusa.* He cheated him and took his money.

ضحك *ðaḥḥač* to make s.o. laugh. هذا فلم يضحك *haaða filim yðaḥḥič.* This is a film that makes people laugh. لا تضحكني! *la ððaḥḥični!* Don't make me laugh!

تضحك *tðaḥḥač* V = ضحك *ðiḥač.*

انضحك *nðiḥač* VII (with على *ᶜala*) to be fooled, gotten the best of. ترى شيطان. ما ينضحك عليه *tara šeeṭaan. ma yinðiḥič ᶜalee.* I warn you he's a clever rascal. He cannot be fooled.

ضحك *ðiḥič* (v.n. from ضحك *ðiḥač*) laughter, laughing.

ضحكة *ðiḥča* (n. of inst.) p. *-aat* laugh.

ظ ح ي *ðḥy*

ضحى *ðaḥḥa* II (with ب *b-*) to sacrifice, offer up. ضحى بكل شي لاجل بلاده *ðaḥḥa b-kill šayy lajil blaada.* He sacrificed everything for the sake of his country.

ضحى *ðiḥa* time of day between morning and noon, forenoon. ضحى الاثنين *ðiḥa l-'aθneen* late morning on Monday. كسلان. ما ينش إلا الضحى *kaslaan. ma yništ 'illa ð-ðiḥa.* He's lazy. He wakes up only before noon.

ضحية *ðiḥiyya* p. ضحايا *ðaḥaaya* 1. slaughter animal. الحج هو اللي يدفع فلوس الضحية *l-ḥajj huwa lli yidfaᶜ fluus ð-ðiḥiyya.* The pilgrim is the one who pays for the slaughter animal. 2. victim. راحت ضحية الجهل *raaḥat ðiḥiyyat l-yahil.* She was the victim of ignorance. عيد الضحية *ᶜiid ð-ðiḥiyya,* عيد الأضحى *ᶜiid l-'aðḥa.* Greater Bairam, a sacrificial feast observed on the tenth day of the last month of the Islamic year.

ظ د د *ðdd*

ضد *ðidd* 1. against. هو ضدي *huwa ðiddi.* He's against me. لعبنا ضدهم وخسرنا المباراة *liᶜabna ðiddhum w-xisarna l-mubaaraa.* We played against them and lost the game. نقلوني ضد رغبتي *nigalooni ðidd raġbati.* They transferred me against my will. 2. -proof, anti-. ضد الماي *ðidd l-maay* waterproof. ضد النار *ðidd n-naar* fireproof. ضد الكسر *ðidd l-kasir* shockproof.

ظ ر ب *ðrb*

ضرب *ðirab (يضرب yuðrub)* 1. to strike, hit, beat. ضربني وانحاش *ðirabni w-nḥaaš.* He hit me and ran away. ضربوه بالرصاص وقتلوه *ðraboo b-r-raṣaas w-gitloo.* They shot him with bullets and killed him. الممرضة ضربتني إبرة *l-mumarriða ðrabatni 'ibra.* The nurse gave me a shot. ضربتني

الشمس *ḍrabatni š-šams.* I had a sunstroke. ضرب الرقم القياسي في السباق *ḍirab r-ragam l-giyaasi fi s-sibaag.* He broke the record in the race. ضربه المرض *ḍraba l-maraḍ.* He fell ill. ضرب الجرس *ḍirab l-jaras.* The bell rang. ما تحتاج جوتي جديد. اضربه باليس *ma tiḥtaay juuti yidiid. 'uḍurba baaliis.* You don't need new shoes; shine them. يضرب بالرمل *yuḍrub b-r-ramil.* He practices geomancy. 2. to fire, go off. فطرنا عقب ما ضرب المدفع *fiṭarna ᶜugub-ma ḍirab l-madfaᶜ.* We ended our fast after the cannon went off. 3. to multiply. ما ضربت خمسة في ستة *ma ḍirabt xamsa fi sitta.* You didn't multiply five by six. 4. to mate with, have sexual intercourse with. البعير ضرب الناقة *l-biᶜiir ḍirab n-naaga.* The camel mated with the female camel.

أضرب *'aḍrab* IV to go on strike, refuse to work. المساجين أضربوا عن الأكل *l-masaajiin 'aḍrabaw ᶜan l-'akil.* The inmates went on a hunger strike. الكولية أضربوا *l-kuuliiyya 'aḍrabaw.* The coolies went on strike.

تضارب *tḍaarab* VI 1. to exchange blows, hit each other. عيال؛ يتضاربون وعقبه يتصالحون *ᶜyaaḷ; yiḍḍaarbuun w-ᶜugba yiṣṣaalḥuun.* They are children; they exchange blows and later on they make up. 2. to conflict, be in disagreement. أخبار استقالة الوزارة تضاربت *'axbaar stigaalat l-wazaara ḍḍaarabat.* The reports
tion of the ministry conflicted.

انضرب *nḍirab* VII to be hit, struck. راسه انضرب بحجر *raasa nḍirab b-hiyar.* He got hit on the head by a rock. كرم هالرجال ينضرب فيه المثل *karam har-rayyaal yinḍirib fii l-maθal.* Legends are told about this man's generosity.

ضرب *ḍarb* (v.n. from ضرب *ḍirab*) 1. beating, striking, hitting. زخوه وضربوه ضرب شديد *zaxxoo w-ḍraboo ḍarb šadiid.* They caught him and beat him up. 2. multiplication. جدول الضرب *jadwal ḍ-ḍarb* the multiplication table.

ضربة *ḍarba* (n. of inst.) p. *-aat* 1. a blow. 2. strong wind that causes destruction, esp. to ships. 3. a beating. ضربة شمس *ḍarbat šams* sunstroke.

ضريبة *ḍariiba* p. ضرايب *ḍaraayib* tax, duty. ضريبة المطار *ḍariibat l-maṭaar* airport tax. ضريبة الدخل *ḍariibat d-daxil* income tax.

إضراب *'iḍraab* (v.n. from IV أضرب *'aḍrab*) p. *-aat* strike.

اضطراب *ḍṭiraab* p. *-aat* disturbance, unrest, commotion.

ضارب *ḍaarib* (act. part. from ضرب *ḍirab*) having hit, struck, beaten s.o. هو اللي ضاربني *huwa lli ḍaaribni.* He's the one who hit me.

مضروب *maḍruub* (p.p. from ضرب *ḍirab*) 1. having been hit, struck, beaten. 2. multiplied (math.).

ظ ر ر *ḍrr*

ضر *ḍarr* (يضر *yḍurr*) to be harmful to, to harm. ما تضر إلا نفسك *ma ḍḍurr 'illa nafsak.* You harm only yourself. لا تضر غيرك *la ḍḍurr ġeerak.* Don't cause harm to others.

تضرر *tḍarrar* V to suffer, undergo

harm or damage. ناس واجدين تضرروا من الطوفان *naas waaydiin ḍḍarraraw min ṭ-ṭuufaan.* A lot of people suffered damage in the flood. الشركة تضررت واجد بهاالصفقة *š-šarika ḍḍarrarat waayid b-haṣ-ṣafga.* The company suffered a great loss on this deal.

انضر *nḍarr* VII to be harmed, hurt, injured. ماحد ينضر إلا الفقير هذي الأيام *maḥḥad yinḍarr 'illa l-fagiir haaði l-'ayyaam.* No one will be hurt except the poor these days.

اضطر *ḍṭarr* VIII 1. to force, compel s.o. to do s.th. اضطروني أسويها بروحي *ḍṭarrooni 'asawwiiha b-ruuḥi.* They forced me to do it myself. 2. to be compelled, be hard pressed. رفضت تجي واياي؛ اضطريت أسافر بروحي *rfaḍat tiyi wiyyaay; ḍṭarreet 'asaafir b-ruuḥi.* She refused to come with me; I had to travel alone.

ضرة *ḍarra* p. *-aat* another wife, wife other than the first of a plural marriage. المشاكل ما تجي إلا من تحت راس الضرة *l-mašaakil ma tiyi 'illa min taḥat raas ḍ-ḍarra.* Problems are caused only by a second wife.

ضرر *ḍarar* p. أضرار *'aḍraar* harm, damage, loss.

ضرير *ḍariir* 1. blind. 2. blind man.

ضرورة *ḍaruura* necessity, need. ما فيه ضرورة تروح بالسيارة *ma fii ḍaruura truuḥ b-s-sayyaara.* There's no need for you to go by car.

ضروري *ḍaruuri* 1. necessary, imperative. هذا شي ضروري *haaḍa šayy ḍaruuri.* This is a necessary thing. ضروري تروح هناك *ḍaruuri truuḥ hnaak.* It's necessary that you go there. You must go there. 2. (p. *-yyaat*) necessity, necessary thing.

مضرة *maḍarra* = ضرر *ḍarar.*

أضر *'aḍarr* 1. (with من *min*) more harmful, etc. than. 2. (with foll. n.) the most harmful, etc.

اضطرار *ḍṭiraar* (v.n. from VIII اضطر *ḍṭarr*) compulsion, necessity. عند الاضطرار *ʿind li-ḍṭiraar* in case of emergency.

اضطراري *ḍṭiraari* compulsory, necessary, mandatory. باب خروج اضطراري *baab xuruuj ḍṭiraari* emergency exit.

مضر *muḍirr* harmful, disadvantageous.

ظ ر س *ḍrs*

ضرس *ḍirs* p. ضروس *ḍruus* tooth. ضرسي يعورني *ḍirsi yʿawwirni.* I have a toothache. شلع ضروسه *čilaʿ ḍruusa.* He had his teeth pulled out.

ظ ر ط *ḍrṭ*

ضرط *ḍiraṭ* (يضرط *yaḍruṭ*) to fart, break wind.

ضرط *ḍarraṭ* II to break wind repeatedly.

ضرطة *ḍarṭa* p. *-aat* a fart. (prov.) ضرطة في سوق الصفافير *ḍarṭa fi suug ṣ-ṣafaafiir.* A drop in the bucket.

أضرط *'aḍraṭ* (elat.) 1. (with من *min*) more lowly, contemptible than. 2. (with foll. n.) the most lowly, contemptible.

ضراط *ḍraaṭ* (v.n. from ضرط *ḍiraṭ*)

farting, act of breaking wind. (prov.) ايش على الذيب من ضراط النعجة؟ *eeš ᶜala ð-ðiib min ḍraaṭ li-nᶜaya.* (lit., "What harm can the farting of a ewe do to the wolf?").

ظ ع ف ١ *ðᶜf*

ضعف *ḍiᶜaf (يضعف yiḍᶜaf)* 1. to be or become frail, slim, skinny. ما ياكل زين؛ رايح يضعف *ma yaakil zeen. raayiḥ yiḍᶜaf.* He doesn't eat well. He's going to get weak. كان متين؛ هالحين ضعف *čaan mitiin; halḥiin ḍiᶜaf.* He was fat; now he lost weight. 2. to weaken, become weaker. مركزه في الحكومة ضعف *markiza fi li-ḥkuuma ḍiᶜaf.* His position in the government weakened.

ضعف *ḍaᶜᶜaf* II 1. to make frail, thin. ها الدوا يضعف الآدمي *had-duwa yḍaᶜᶜif l-'aadmi.* This medicine weakens people. 2. to weaken, enfeeble. حرب الخليج ضعفت العراق *ḥarb l-xaliij ḍaᶜᶜafat li-ᶜraag.* The Gulf war weakened Iraq.

ضعيف *ḍaᶜiif* p. *-iin,* ضعفا *ḍuᶜafa* weak, feeble.

أضعف *'aḍᶜaf* 1. (with من *min*) weaker, more feeble than. 2. (with foll. n.) the weakest, the most feeble.

ظ ع ف ٢ *ðᶜf*

ضاعف *ḍaaᶜaf* III to double, redouble. الحكومة ضاعفت عدد المواطنين في البنك *l-ḥukuuma ḍaaᶜafat ᶜadad li-mwaaṭn-iin fi l-bank.* The government doubled the number of citizens in the bank. ضاعف دخله من ها المشروع *ḍaaᶜaf daxla min hal-mašruuᶜ.* He redoubled his income from this project.

تضاعف *tḍaaᶜaf* VI pass. of ضاعف *ḍaaᶜaf.* تضاعف عدد الطلاب *ṭḍaaᶜaf ᶜadad ṭ-ṭullaab.* The number of students has doubled.

ضعف *ḍiᶜf* p. أضعاف *'aḍᶜaaf* 1. double, twice as much. 2. multiple, several times as much. ثلاث أضعاف *θalaaθ 'aḍᶜaaf* three times as much.

ظ غ ط *ðġṭ*

ضغط *ḍiġaṭ (يضغط yiḍġaṭ)* 1. to compress, squeeze, press. ضغط الهوا *ḍiġaṭ l-hawa.* He compressed the air. 2. (with على *ᶜala*) to exert pressure on, press on. ضغط على التنديل لين وافق *ḍiġaṭ ᶜala t-tindeel leen waafag.* He exerted pressure on the foreman until he agreed.

ضغط *ḍaġṭ* pressure, compression. الضغط الجوي *ḍ-ḍaġṭ l-jawwi* atmospheric pressure. ضغط الماي *ḍaġṭ l-maay* water pressure. ضغط الدم *ḍaġṭ d-damm* blood pressure.

مضغوط *maḍġuuṭ* (p.p.) compressed. هوا مضغوط *hawa maḍġuuṭ* compressed air.

ظ ف ر *ðfr*

ظفر *ðufir* p. أظافر *'aðaafir* fingernail, claw.

ظ ل ع *ðlᶜ*

ضلع *ḍilᶜ* p. ضلوع *ḍluuᶜ* 1. hill, elevation. 2. rib (of a person). طاح على الأرض وانكسرت ضلوعه *ṭaaḥ ᶜala l-'arḍ w-nkasrat ḍluuᶜa.* He fell to the ground and his ribs were broken.

ظ ل ف *ðlf*

ظلف *ðilf* p. ظلوف *ðluuf* cloven hoof.

كـل حيـوان بظلـف ينوكـل في الإسـلام *kill ḥayawaan b-ḍilf yinwikil fi l-'islaam.* Every animal with a cloven hoof can be (or is permissible to be) eaten in Islam.

ظ ل ل *ḍll*

ظـل *ḍall (يظـل yḍall)* 1. (with foll. imperf.) to continue to do s.th. ظـل يشـتغل هنـاك *ḍall yištaġil hnaak.* He continued to work there. 2. to stay, remain, last. ظليـت سـاعة أتريـاه *ḍallet saa^ca 'atrayyaa.* I stayed an hour waiting for him. ظـل هنـاك يومـين *ḍall hnaak yoomeen.* He stayed there two days. ما ظـل عنـدي فلـوس *ma ḍall ^cindi fluus.* I don't have any money left. ما ظـل وقـت. خلنـا نسـير *ma ḍall wagt. xaḷḷna nsiir.* There's no time left. Let's go.

ظل *ḍill* shade, shadow.

مظلة *mḍalla* p. *-aat* parachute.

مظلـي *maḍalli* p. *-yyiin* 1. paratrooper. 2. parachutist.

ظ ل م *ḍlm*

ظلـم *ḍilam (يظلم yaḍlim)* 1. to oppress, be tyrannical to, do wrong. هذا طاغية. يظلـم النـاس *haaḍa ṭaaġiya. yaḍlim n-naas.* This is a tyrant. He oppresses people. 2. to treat unjustly, do wrong to s.o. هو رجال ما يظلم أحـد ومـا يفشـل أحـد *huwa rayyaal ma yaḍlim 'aḥad w-ma yfaššil 'aḥad.* He's a man who doesn't treat anyone unjustly and who doesn't let anyone down.

انظلـم *nḍilam* VII to be treated unjustly. مـا سـويت شـي. انظلمـت *ma sawweet šayy. nḍilamt.* I haven't done anything. I was treated unjustly.

ظلـم *ḍulm* (v.n. from ظلم *ḍilam*) injustice, unfairness. (prov.) ظلـم بالسـوية عـدل بالرعيـة *ḍulmin b-s-sawiyya ^cadlin b-r-a^ciyya.* Injustice done to all people equally is preferable to justice to some and injustice to others.

ظـلام *ḍalaam* darkness, gloom. الدنيـا ظلام *d-dinya ḍalaam.* It's dark.

ظـالم *ḍaalim* (act. part. from ظلم *ḍilam*) 1. unjust, unfair. 2. tyrannical, harsh. حـاكم ظـالم *ḥaakim ḍaalim* tyrannical ruler. 3. (p. *-iin*) oppressor, tyrant, despot. كل ظالم اله نهاية *kill ḍaalim 'ila nihaaya.* Every oppressor has an end.

مظلـوم *maḍluum* (p.p. from ظلم *ḍilam*) p. *-iin* unjustly treated, wronged. مظلـوم بشـغله *maḍluum b-šuġla.* He's discriminated against in his job.

مظلم *muḍlim* dark, gloomy.

ظ م م *ḍmm*

ضـم *ḍamm (يضـم yḍumm)* 1. to take s.th. away. ضم الكتب والقراطيس *ḍamm l-kutub w-l-garaaṭiis.* He took away the books and the papers. 2. to save, put away for safekeeping. ضم شوية من معاشـه *ḍamm šwayya min ma^caaša.* He saved a little of his salary. 3. to embrace. ضمهـا إلى صـدره *ḍammha 'ila ṣadra.* He embraced her.

انضـم *nḍamm* VII (with ل *l-*) to join, enter. انضم للحزب *nḍamm lal-ḥizib.* He joined the (political) party.

ظ م ن *ḍmn*

ضمـن *ḍiman (يضمن yiḍman)* to guarantee, make sure, be certain. تقدر تضمن

البضاعـــة توصـــل بـــاكر؟ *tigdar tiḍman l-biḍaaᶜa tooṣal baačir?* Can you guarantee that the merchandise will get here tomorrow?

ضمــن *ḍimin* (prep.) in, within, inside of, among. الضريبة ضمن سعر التذكـــرة *ḍ-ḍariiba ḍimin siᶜr t-taðkara.* The tax is included in the price of the ticket. من ضمن الأشيـــا *min ḍimn l-'ašya.* among the things. *'aana min ḍimn l-yamaaᶜa.* I am one of the group.

أضمن *'aḍman* (elat.) 1. (with من *min*) more guaranteed, safer than. أضمن لك تسير وايانـــا *'aḍman-lak tsiir wiyyaana.* It's safer for you to come with me.

ظ ن ن *ḍnn*

ظــن *ḍann* (يظــن *yḍinn*) 1. to think, believe. أظن انه هذا التنديل *'aḍinn 'inna haaða t-tindeel.* I think that this is the foreman. 2. (with في *fi*) to be suspicious of. أظن فيه *'aḍinn fii.* I am suspicious of him. 3. to expect from s.o., think s.o. capable of. ما ظنيته يخون بلاده *ma ḍanneeta yxuun blaada.* I didn't expect him to betray his country.

ظــن *ḍann* (v.n.) 1. thought, idea. ظنك انه هنـــاك ذالحـــين؟ *ḍannak 'inna hnaak ðalḥiin?* Do you think he is there now? ظنك في محله *ḍannak fi maḥalla.* You are right. 2. opinion. حسن الظـــن *ḥusun ḍ-ḍann* good opinion. خاب ظني فيـــه *xaab ḍanni fii.* I was disappointed in him. 3. (p. ظنـــون *ḍunuun*) doubt, uncertainty. ما عندي أي ظـــن *ma ᶜindi 'ayya ḍann.* I don't have any doubt.

ظنـــة *ḍanna* usually known as جبل ظنة *yibal ḍanna* Mount Dhanna (in the north of Abu Dhabi).

ظ ه ر *ḍhr*

ظهر *ḍihar* (يظهر *yiḍhar*) 1. to appear, come into view, emerge. ظهر القمـــر *ḍihar l-gumar.* The moon appeared. الحق ظهر *l-ḥagg ḍihar.* The truth is out. 2. to leave, go away. الوزير ظهر *l-waziir ḍihar.* The minister has left. 3. to be or become apparent, clear, obvious. يظـــهر انـــك مشغـــول *yiḍhar 'innak mašġuul.* It seems that you are busy. ظهر لي انه جلاخ *ḍihar-li 'inna čallaax.* It was clear to me that he was a liar. على ما يظهر *ᶜala ma yiḍhar* apparently, according to the evidence. على ما يظهر أفلست الشركـــة *ᶜala ma yiḍhar 'aflasat š-šarika.* Evidently, the company went bankrupt.

تظاهر *tḍaahar* VI 1. to pretend, feign. في الحقيقة هو موب مريض. ولكن يتظاهر انه مريض *fi l-hagiiga huwa muub mariiḍ. walaakin yiḍḍaahar 'inna mariiḍ.* Actually, he's not sick, but he pretends to be sick. 2. to demonstrate. الناس تظاهروا قدام الســـفارة *n-naas ḍḍaahraw jiddaam s-safaara.* The people demonstrated in front of the embassy.

ظـــهر *ḍahar* p. ظهور *ḍhuur* 1. back, rear, rear side. ظـــهره يعـــوره *ḍahra yᶜawwra.* He has back pain. ظهر البعير *ḍahar l-biᶜiir* the camel's back. 2. deck. علـــى ظـــهر البـــاخرة *ᶜala ḍahr l-baaxra* on board the ship. 3. backing, support. اللي ما عنده ظهر ما يحصل شـــي *'illi ma ᶜinda ḍahar ma yḥaṣṣil šayy.* He who doesn't have backing can't get anything. 4. tribe. ظهري منصوري *ḍahri manṣuuri.* I am one of the Mansuri tribe. I am a Mansuri tribesman.

ظهر *ḍuhur* noon, midday, noontime. عقب الظهر *ᶜugb ḍ-ḍuhur* in the afternoon. صلاة الظهر *ṣalaat ḍ-ḍuhur* the noon prayer. ثنعش الظهر *θnaᶜaš ḍ-ḍuhur* twelve noon.

ظهور *ḍuhuur* (v.n. from ظهر *ḍihar*) 1. appearance, coming into view, emergence. 2. pomp, splendor, ostentation. حب الظهور *ḥubb ḍ-ḍuhuur* love of pomp and splendor.

مظهر *maḍhar* p. مظاهر *maḍaahir* external appearance, looks.

مظاهرة *muḍaahara* p. *-aat* public demonstration, rally.

ظاهر *ḍaahir* visible, obvious, distinct, clear. الظاهر *ḍ-ḍaahir* apparently. الظاهر عرس *ḍ-ḍaahir ᶜarras.* Apparently, he got married. حسب الظاهر *ḥasab ḍ-ḍaahir* = الظاهر *ḍ-ḍaahir.*

ظاهري *ḍaahiri* p. ظواهر *ḍawaahir* one of the Dhawahir tribe in the U.A.E.

ظاهرة *ḍaahira* p. ظواهر *ḍawaahir* phenomenon.

متظاهر *mitḍaahir* (act. part. from VI تظاهر *tḍaahar*) 1. demonstrating. الناس متظاهرين قدام السفارة *n-naas mitḍaahriin jiddaam s-safaara.* The people are demonstrating in front of the embassy. 2. demonstrator.

ظ و ج *ḍwj*

ظاج *ḍaaj (يظوج yḍuuj)* to get fed up, become restless, bored. هد المدرسة لانه ظاج من الدراسة *hadd l-madrasa linna ḍaaj min d-diraasa.* He dropped out of school because he got fed up with studying.

ظوج *ḍawwaj* II 1. to bore s.o. ها الفلم ظوجني *hal-filim ḍawwajni.* This movie bored me. 2. to annoy, upset, irritate s.o. ظوجني واجد بحكيه *ḍawwajni waayid b-ḥačya.* His talk annoyed me a lot.

ظوج *ḍooj*, **ظوجة** *ḍooja* (v.n. from ظاج *ḍaaj*) 1. boredom. 2. annoyance, irritation.

ظ و گ *ḍwg*

ذاق *ḍaag (يذوق yḍuug)* 1. to taste, sample (food, drink, etc.). ذاق اللحم وقال موب زين *ḍaag l-laḥam w-gaal muub zeen.* He tasted the meat and said it wasn't good. 2. to taste, experience, go through, suffer. ذاق الحلو والمر في حياته *ḍaag l-ḥilu w-l-murr fi ḥayaata.* He tasted the sweet and the bitter in his lifetime.

ذوق *ḍawwag* II to give a taste of, let taste. ذوقني طباخه *ḍawwagni ṭbaaxa.* He gave me a taste of his cooking.

ذوق *ḍoog* (v.n. from ذاق *ḍaag*) 1. tasting. 2. experiencing, going through s.th.

ظ و و *ḍww*

ضوى *ḍawwa* II to light, light up, illuminate. هذا الليت يضوي حجرتين *haaḍa l-leet yḍawwi ḥijirteen.* This bulb lights two rooms.

ضو *ḍaww* 1. fire. شب الضو *šibb ḍ-ḍaww.* Start the fire. نكوي الجرح بالضو *ničwi l-jurḥ b-ḍ-ḍaww.* We treat wounds with cauterization. طفيت الضو *ṭaffeet ḍ-ḍaww.* I extinguished the fire.

2. (p. أضـواء *'aḍwaa'*) light. ضو الشمس *ḍaww š-šams* sunlight. ضو القمر *ḍaww l-gumar* moonlight. أضـــواء المدينـــة *'aḍwaa' l-madiina* the city lights.

ظ ي ع *ḍy*c

ضـاع *ḍaa*c (يضيـع *yḍii*c) to get lost, be lost. ضعت في ذيك الديرة لـين طبيـت فيهـا أول مـرة *ḍi*c*t fi ḍiič d-diira leen ṭabbeet fiiha 'awwal marra.* I got lost in that place when I went there for the first time. ضـاع المفتـاح *ḍaa*c *l-miftaaḥ.* The key was lost. ما قدمـت طلـب وضـاعت علــي الفرصـــة *ma gaddamat ṭalab w-ḍaa*c*at* c*alayya l-furṣa.* I didn't submit an application, and the opportunity had passed me by.

ضيع *ḍayya*c 1. to lose. ضيـع المفتـاح *ḍayya*c *l-miftaaḥ.* He lost the key. ضيعت فلوسي في الســوق *ḍayya*c*t fluusi fi s-suug.* I lost my money in the marketplace. السـوق كـان مـتروس نـاس وضيعـت ولـدي *s-suug čaan matruus naas w-ḍayya*c*t wildi.* The marketplace was full of people and I lost my son. 2. to cause to get lost. كان وايانا واحد ضيعنــا في ذاك الفريـــج *čaan wiyyaana waaḥid ḍayya*c*na fi ḍaak l-firiij.* There was someone with us who got us lost in that neighborhood. 3. to waste, squander. ضيع وقتـه علـى اللعـب *ḍayya*c *wağta* c*ala l-li*c*ib.* He wasted his time playing. (prov.) بين حانا ومانا ضيعنا لحانا *been ḥaana w-maana ḍayya*c*na lḥaana.* Caught in the middle. Between the devil and the deep blue sea.

ظ ي ف *ḍyf*

ضيـف *ḍayyaf* II to take s.o. as a guest, receive hospitably. ضيفونـي في بيتهـــم ســبوع *ḍayyafooni fi beettum subuu*c*.* They took me into their house as a guest for a week.

استضاف *staḍaaf* = II ضيف *ḍayyaf.*

ضيــف *ḍeef* p. ضيـوف *ḍuyuuf* guest. (common var. خـاطر *xaaṭir* p. خطـار *xuṭṭaar.* See under **خ ط ر** *xṭr*).

ضيافـة *ḍiyaafa* 1. hospitality. دار الضيافة *daar ḍ-ḍiyaafa* guest house. 2. hospitable reception.

مضيـف *maḍiif* p. مضـايف *maḍaayif* = دار الضيافـة *daar ḍ-ḍiyaafa* guest house. سـكنت في المضيـف علـى حسـاب الحكومـة *sikant fi l-maḍiif* c*ala ḥisaab l-ḥukuuma.* I lived in the guest house at the expense of the government.

مضيف *muḍayyif* p. *-iin* steward, host.

ظ ي گ *ḍyg*

ضـاق *ḍaag* (يضيـق *yḍiig*) to be or become narrow. ضـاقت الشـوارع *ḍaagat š-šawaari*c*.* The streets became narrower.

ضيق *ḍayyag* II 1. to make s.th. narrow or narrower. ضيقــوا الشـــوارع *ḍayyagaw š-šawaari*c*.* They made the streets narrower. 2. (with على c*ala*) to harass, oppress, restrain. ضيقـوا علينـا بهالمراقبـــــة *ḍayyagaw* c*aleena b-hal-muraagaba.* They harassed us with their surveillance. لا تضيـق علـى روحـك *la ḍḍayyig* c*ala ruuḥak.* Don't set limits on yourself.

تضـايق *tḍaayag* VI to be or become irritated, annoyed. يتضـايق مـن أي شـي *yiḍḍaayag min 'ayya šayy.* He gets irritated at anything.

ضيق *ðiig* (v.n. from ضاق *ðaag*) 1. need, distress, poverty. وقت الضيق *wagt ð-ðiig* the time of need. كنا في ضيق وذالحين الله أنعم علينا *činna fi ðiig w-ðalḥiin 'aḷḷa 'an^c^am ^c^aleena.* We were living in poverty, but now God has given us everything. 2. narrowness.

ضيق *ðayyig* 1. narrow. شارع ضيق *šaari^c^ ðayyig* narrow street. ضيق الخلق *ðayyig l-xulg* impatient. 2. limited, confined. ضيق المجال *ðayyig l-majaal* limited in scope.

أضيق *'aðyag* (elat.) 1. (with من *min*) narrower, more confining than. 2. (with foll. n.) the narrowest, the most confining.

مضيق *maðiig* p. مضايق *maðaayig* straits, narrow passage. مضيق هرمز *maðiif hirmiz* the Straits of Hormuz.

مضايقة *mðaayaga* p. *-aat* annoyance, irritation, harassment.

ع

ع ا ن *ᶜaan*

عانـة *ᶜaana* p. *-aat* old coin equivalent to a nickel.

ع ب د *ᶜbd*

عبـد *ᶜibad (يعبد yᶜabid)* 1. to worship. كلنـا نعبـد الله *killana nᶜabid 'aḷḷa.* We all worship God. 2. to adore. فيه ناس يعبـــدون الفلـــوس *fii naas yᶜabduun li-fluus.* There are people who worship money.

عبـد *ᶜabbad* II to pave. لازم يعبدون ها الطريـــق *laazim yᶜabbduun haṭ-ṭariig.* They have to pave this road.

استعبد *staᶜbad* X to en gate. استعبدوهم عقــب مــا استولوا عليهــم *staᶜbaduuhum ᶜugub-ma stawlaw ᶜaleehum.* They enslaved them after they had conquered them.

عبـد *ᶜabd* p. عبيد *ᶜabiid* 1. slave, serf. تجارة العبيـد *tijaarat l-ᶜabiid* slave trade. 2. Negro. 3. (with foll. epithet of God) servant. عبد الرحيـم *ᶜabd r-raḥiim* Abd Al-Rahim, lit. "servant of the Compassionate." عبـد الرحمـن *ᶜabd r-raḥmaan* Abd Al-Rahman, lit. "servant of the Merciful."

عبودية *ᶜabuudiyya* slavery, serfdom.

عبود *ᶜabbuud* (common var. عبيد *ᶜbeed* dim. of عبدالله *ᶜabdaḷḷa*) Abdalla.

معبـد *maᶜbad* p. معابد *maᶜaabid* temple, place of worship.

ع ب ر *ᶜbr*

عبر *ᶜibar (يعبر yᶜabir)* to cross (a street, a river, etc.) لـين راعـي السـيكل عـبر الشـارع دعمتـه سيارة وطـاح علـى الأرض *leen raaᶜi s-seekal ᶜibar š-šaariᶜ diᶜmata sayyaara w-ṭaaḥ ᶜala l-'arḍ.* When the cyclist crossed the street, a car hit him and he fell to the ground.

عـبر *ᶜabbar* II 1. (with عن *ᶜan*) to express, voice, state clearly. عبر عن رايه *ᶜabbar ᶜan raaya.* He expressed his opinion. 2. to take s.o. across, send across. مسـكته بـاليد وعبرتـه الشـارع *misakta b-l-yadd w-ᶜabbarta š-šaariᶜ.* I held him by his hand and took him across the street.

انعبر *nᶜibar* VII to be crossed. النهر عميـق؛ مـا ينعـبر *n-nahir ᶜamiig; ma yinᶜabur.* The river is deep; it cannot be crossed.

اعتبر *ᶜtibar* VIII 1. to learn a lesson, take warning. هذي عبرة لي ولـك ولكل واحـد يريـد يعتـبر *haaði ᶜibra li wa-lak wa-la kill waaḥid yriid yiᶜtabir.* This is a lesson for me, you, and any other person who wants to take heed. 2. to consider, regard as. أعتبرك مثـل أخـوي *'aᶜtibrak miθil 'uxuuy.* I consider you my brother. 3. to respect, show consideration or regard. لازم تعتبر اللي أكـبر منـك *laazim tiᶜtabir illi 'akbar minnak.* You have to respect those who are older than you.

عبري *ᶜibri* p. *-yya* passenger (paying).

عـبرة *ᶜibra* p. عبر *ᶜibar* lesson, warning, example. هذي عبرة حق كـل واحـد يعبـد الفلـوس *haaði ᶜibra ḥagg kill waaḥid* *ycabid li-fluus.* This is a lesson for everyone who worships money.

عبارة *cibaara* phrase, expr tence. عبارة عن *cibaara can* actually, really, merely. الختان، الله يسلمك، عبارة عن الطهور *li-xtaan, 'alla ysallimk, cibaara can ṭ-ṭuhuur.* Circumcision, God protect you, is actually cleansing.

عبّارة *cabbaara* p. *-aat* ferry boat.

معبر *macbar* p. معابر *macaabir* place for crossing.

اعتبار *ctibaar* (v.n. from VIII اعتبر *ctibar*) 1. respect, regard, esteem. ما يقيم له أي اعتبار *ma ygiim-la 'ayya ctibaar.* He doesn't show him any respect. 2. lesson learned, warning. هذا اعتبار لي ولك ولكل واحد يعبد الفلوس *haaða ctibaar li wa lak w-la kill waaḥid ycabid li-fluus.* This is a lesson for me, you, and any other person who worships money.

اعتباراً من *ctibaaran min* beginning, starting with, effective. اعتباراً من باكر، الدوام من تسعة إلى ثلاثة *ctibaaran min baačir, d-dawaam min tisca 'ila θalaaθa.* Beginning tomorrow, the office hours will be from nine to three.

ع ب ي *cby*

عباة *cabaa* p. عبي *cibi* cloak, loose garment worn over a كندورة *kandoora* or a دشداشة *dišdaaša.*

ع ت ب *ctb*

عاتب *caatab* III to blame, scold, censure. إذا جيت متأخر، ما أعاتبك *'iða yiit mit'axxir, ma 'acaatibk.* If you come late, I won't blame you. عاتبته على اللي سواه *caatabta cala lli sawwaa.* I scolded him for what he had done.

تعاتب *tcaatab* VI to find fault with each other, blame each other. تعاتبنا وعقبه تصالحنا *tcaatabna w-cugba ṣṣaalaḥna.* We blamed each other and then we made up.

عتب *catab* (v.n.) blame, censure, rebuke. عتبي عليك *catabi caleek.* I blame you.

عتبة *ctaba* p. *-aat* window or door sill, step. عتبة مسجد *ctabat msiid* (lit., "a mosque sill") very pious person.

ع ت ت *ctt*

عت *catt* (يعت *ycitt*) to drag s.o. (by the hand). عتيته من يده *catteeta min yadda.* I dragged him by his hand.

ع ت د *ctd*

عتاد *citaad* ammunition, war material.

ع ت گ *ctg*

عتق *citag* (يعتق *ycatig*) to get or grow old. السيارة عتقت؛ لازم أبدلها *s-sayyaara citgat; laazim 'abaddilha.* The car has gotten old; I will have to trade it in.

عتيق *catiig* (common var. عتيج *catiij*) p. *-iin,* عتق *cittag* 1. (with inanimate n.) old, ancient. سيارة عتيقة *sayyaara catiiga* old car. 2. (with animate n.) former, ex-. حرمته العتيقة *ḥurumta l-catiiga* his ex-wife. 3. old-fashioned, obsolete. طابعة عتيقة *ṭaabica catiiga* old-fashioned typewriter.

أعتق *'actag* (elat.) 1. (with من *min*) older than, etc. 2. (with foll. n.) the oldest, etc.

ع ت م ᶜtm

عتم ᶜ*attam* II to darken, black out. عتمـوا المدينـة ᶜ*attamaw l-madiina.* They blacked-out the city.

تعتيم *ta*ᶜ*tiim* (v.n.) blackout.

ع ت و ᶜtw

عتـوي ᶜ*itwi* p. عتاويـة ᶜ*taawya* big tomcat.

ع ث ث ᶜθθ

انعث *n*ᶜ*aθθ* VII to become moth-eaten. البنطلـون الصـوف في ذاك الـدولاب انعـث *l-banṭaloon ṣ-ṣuuf fi ðaak d-duulaab n*ᶜ*aθθ.* The wool pants in that cabinet got moths in them.

عـث ᶜ*iθθ* (coll.) moths. s. *-a* a moth. p. *-aat.*

ع ث ر ᶜθr

عـثر ᶜ*iθar (*يعثر *y*ᶜ*aθir)* 1. to trip, stumble. عثر بالحجر وطـاح على الأرض ᶜ*iθar b-l-ḥiyar w-ṭaaḥ* ᶜ*ala l-'arḍ.* He tripped over the rock and fell to the ground. 2. (with على ᶜ*ala*) to find, run into. عثرت عليه في الدكان ᶜ*iθart* ᶜ*alee fi d-dikkaan.* I found it in the shop.

عثرة ᶜ*aθra* (v.n.) stumbling, tripping.

ع ج ب ᶜjb

عجـب ᶜ*ijab (*يعجـب *y*ᶜ*ajib)* to please, delight. عجبتـني السيارة الجديـدة ᶜ*ijbatni s-sayyaara l-yidiida.* The new car pleased me. I liked the new car. يعجبني الهـوا هـني في الشـتا *yi*ᶜ*jibni l-hawa hini fi š-šita.* I like the weather here in the winter. يعجبـني أدوخ سـبيل *yi*ᶜ*jibni 'aduux sbiil.* I'd like to smoke a pipe.

تعجب *t*ᶜ*ajjab* V to be surprised, astonished, amazed. ليش تتعجـب؟ مـا في اليد ولا حيلـة *leeš tit*ᶜ*ajjab? ma fi l-yadd wala ḥiila.* Why are you surprised? There's nothing we can do. لين قلت له تعجـب *leen git-la t*ᶜ*ajjab.* When I told him, he was astonished. أتعجب كيف حصل فلوس ها القـد *'at*ᶜ*ajjab čeef ḥaṣṣal fluus hal-gadd.* I'm amazed at how he got this much money.

عجـب ᶜ*ajab* 1. oddity, strange occurrence. عجب ما نشوفه إلا يوم الجمعة ᶜ*ajab ma nčuufa 'illa yoom l-yim*ᶜ*a.* It's odd we see him only on Friday. 2. astonishment, amazement.

عجيـب ᶜ*ajiib* strange, odd, remarkable, amazing. شي عجيب *šayy* ᶜ*ajiib* strange thing. عجيب انـه يقـول هـذا ᶜ*ajiib 'inna yguul haaða.* It's strange that he says this. حادثـة عجيبـة *ḥaadθa* ᶜ*ajiiba* extraordinary event.

أعجـب *'a*ᶜ*jab* (elat.) 1. (with من *min*) more astonishing, remarkable than. 2. (with foll. n.) the most astonishing, remarkable.

ع ج ج ᶜjj

عجـاج ᶜ*ajaaj* (common var. عيـاي ᶜ*ayaay*) dust, dust storm. فيه عجاج اليوم *fii* ᶜ*ajaaj l-yoom.* It's dusty today.

ع ج د ᶜjd

عقيـد ᶜ*ijiid* p. عقـدان ᶜ*ijdaan* military rank, approx. colonel.

ع ج ز ᶜjz see under ع ي ز ᶜ*yz.*

ع ج ع ج ᶜjᶜj

عجعـج ᶜ*aj*ᶜ*aj (*يعجعج *y*ᶜ*aj*ᶜ*ij)* to stir up dust. لا تعجعـج! هـذي مـوب رسـتة *la t*ᶜ*aj*ᶜ*ij! haaði muub rasta.* Don't stir up the dust! This isn't a paved road.

ع ج ف *ᶜjf*

عجف *ᶜijaf (yᶜajif)* to call s.o. bad names. هو اللي عجفني *huwa lli ᶜijafni.* He's the one who called me bad names.

ع ج ل *ᶜjl* see under **ع ي ل** *ᶜyl.*

ع ج م *ᶜjm* see also under **ع ي م** *ᶜym.*

عجمان *ᶜajmaan* (common var. عيمان *ᶜaymaan*) Ajman.

ع ج ن *ᶜjn* see under **ع ي ن** *ᶜyn.*

ع چ ف *ᶜčf*

عكف *ᶜičaf (*يعكف *yᶜačif)* to comb (the hair). لين شافتني قامت تعكف شعرها *leen čaafatni gaamat tᶜačif šaᶜarha.* When she saw me, she started to comb her hair.

عكاف *ᶜaččaaf* p. *-iin,* عكاكيف *ᶜičaačiif* hypocrite. ما عليك منه. هذا عكاف ما نصدقه *ma ᶜaleek minna. haaða ᶜaččaaf ma nṣaddga.* Don't pay attention to him. He's a hypocrite who cannot be believed.

ع چ و *ᶜčw*

عكوة *ᶜačwa* p. عكاوي *ᶜačaawi* stick.

ع د د[1] *ᶜdd*

عد *ᶜadd (*يعد *yᶜidd)* 1. to count, number. عد فلوسك *ᶜidd fluusak.* Count your money. يقدر يعد إلى المية *yigdar yᶜidd 'ila l-miya.* He can count to a hundred. 2. to consider, think. ما نقدر نعده من المواطنين *ma nigdar nᶜidda min li-mwaaṭniin.* We cannot consider him one of the citizens.

انعد *nᶜaad* VII to be considered. ما ينعد من المواطنين *ma yinᶜadd min li-mwaṭniin.* He cannot be considered one of the citizens.

استعد *staᶜadd* X to prepare oneself, get ready. استعديت حق الامتحان *staᶜaddeet ḥagg li-mtiḥaan.* I prepared for the exam.

عد *ᶜadd* (v.n. from عد *ᶜadd*) counting, enumeration. خيرات بلادنا ما لها عد *xayraat blaadna ma laha ᶜadd.* The riches of our country are innumerable.

عدة *ᶜidda* 1. waiting period during which a woman may not remarry after being divorced or widowed. 2. (with foll. n. عدة *ᶜiddat*) several, many, a number of. فيه عندنا عدة أشغال يبغى لها خبرة *fii ᶜindana ᶜiddat 'ašġaal yibġaa-lha xibra.* We have many jobs that require experience. كلها عدة أيام وينقضي القيظ *killha ᶜiddat 'ayyaam w-yingaḍi l-geeḍ.* It's a matter of a few days and the summer will be over.

عدد *ᶜadad* p. أعداد *'aᶜdaad* 1. number, numeral. 2. (with من *min*) a number of. 3. number, issue (of a journal, a newspaper, etc.).

عداد *ᶜaddaad* p. *-aat* counter, meter (for electricity, water, etc.) عداد الماي *ᶜaddaad l-maay* the water meter.

إعدادي *'iᶜdaadi* preparatory, junior high (school). مدرسة إعدادية *madrasa 'iᶜdaadiyya* junior high school.

استعداد *stiᶜdaad* (v.n. from X استعد *staᶜadd*) 1. preparation, preparedness. استعداد للسفر *stiᶜdaad l-s-safar* preparation for travel. 2. willingness, readiness. ما عندي استعداد حق هذا الشغل

ma ᶜindi stiᶜdaad ḥagg haaða š-šuġul. I'm not willing to do this kind of work.

معدود *maᶜduud* (p.p. from عد *ᶜadd*) limited in number, a few. مدارس ثانوية معدودة *madaaris θaanawiyya maᶜduuda* a few secondary schools.

مستعد *mistiᶜidd* (act. part. from X استعد *staᶜadd*) ready, prepared. هو مستعد حق كل شي *huwa mistiᶜidd ḥagg kill šayy.* He's prepared for anything. آمر! مستعدين *'aamir! mistiᶜiddiin.* At your service! We are ready.

ع د د ٢ *ᶜdd*

عد *ᶜidd* p. عدود *ᶜduud* artesian well. ماي عد *maay ᶜidd* potable well water.

ع د س *ᶜds*

عدس *ᶜadas* (coll.) lentils. s. حبة عدس *ḥabbat ᶜadas,* عدسة *ᶜdisa.* العدس ما يطلع هني *l-ᶜadas ma yiṭlaᶜ hini.* Lentils do not grow here.

عدسة *ᶜadasa* p. *-aat* lens.

ع د ل *ᶜdl*

عدل *ᶜidal (*يعدل *yᶜadil)* 1. (with بين *been*) to be impartial toward, not to discriminate between. تهاشوا والشيخ عدل بينهم *thaawšaw w-š-šeex ᶜidal beenhum.* They quarreled among themselves and the ruler acted impartially toward them. 2. (with عن *ᶜan*) to drop, give up. عدل عن فكرة الزواج *ᶜidal ᶜan fikrat z-zawaaj.* He dropped the idea of getting married.

عدل *ᶜaddal* II 1. to straighten, make straight. عدل القضيب بالشاكوش *ᶜaddal l-gaḍiib b-č-čaakuuč.* He straightened the iron bar with the hammer. 2. to put in order, straighten out. الإنسان لازم يعدل أموره *l-'insaam laazim yᶜaddil 'umuura.* People should get their affairs in order. 3. to amend, improve, change. وزارة الداخلية عدلت قانون الهجرة *wazaarat d-daaxiliyya ᶜaddalat gaanuun l-hijra.* The ministry of the interior amended the emigration law.

عادل *ᶜaadal* III 1. to find the equivalent of, evaluate. وزارة الخارجية ممكن تعادل لك الشهادة *wazaarat l-xaarijiyya mumkin tᶜaadil-lak š-šahaada.* The foreign ministry might evaluate your degree. 2. to be equal to, equal, be the equal of. هذا يعادل شغل أربع كولية *haaða yᶜaadil šuġul 'arbaᶜ kuuliyya.* This is equal to the work of four coolies.

تعدل *tᶜaddal* V 1. to be straightened. 2. to straighten oneself, straighten up. تعدل! لا تقعد ها الشكل *tᶜaddal! la tugᶜud haš-šikil.* Straighten up! Don't sit like this. 3. to be straightened out, made smooth. لازم تتعدل الأمور، انشاالله *laazim titᶜaddal l-'umuur, nšaaḷḷa.* Matters will be straightened out, hopefully. 4. to be amended, changed. القانون تعدل *l-gaanuun tᶜaddal.* The law has been amended.

تعادل *tᶜaadal* VI to tie, be tied. فريقنا وفريقهم تعادلوا في المباراة *fariigna w-fariiggum tᶜaadlaw fi l-mubaara.* Our team and their team tied in the game.

عدل *ᶜadil* 1. justice. وزارة العدل *wazaarat l-ᶜadil* the ministry of justice. الحاكم لازم يحكم بالعدل *l-ḥaakim* *laazim yḥakim b-l-ᶜadil.* A ruler should rule justly. 2. (adj.) straight, upright, vertical. ها الطوفة موب عدلة *hat-ṭoofa muub ᶜadla.* This wall isn't straight. 3. (adv.) honest(ly), fair(ly), well. يحكي عدل *yiḥči ᶜadil.* He tells the truth. يمشي عدل *yamši ᶜadil.* He's honest. يشتغل عدل *yištaġil ᶜadil.* He works well. 4. (adj.) whole, unbroken, sound. خبزة عدلة *xubza ᶜadla* whole loaf, piece of bread.

عدال *ᶜdaal* (prep.) (common var. عدال *ᶜiddaal*) near, close to. قعد عدالي *giᶜad ᶜdaali.* He sat near me. بيتنا عدال بيتهم *beetna ᶜdaal beettum.* Our house is close to their house.

عدالة *ᶜadaala* justice, fairness.

أعدل *'aᶜdal* (elat.) 1. (with من *min*) straighter than. 2. (with foll. n.) the straightest.

تعديل *taᶜdiil* p. *-aat* (v.n. from II عدل *ᶜaadal*) amendment, change. تعديل الوزارة *taᶜdiil l-wazaara* cabinet reshuffle.

معادلة *muᶜaadala* (v.n. from III عادل *ᶜaadal*) 1. evaluation, evaluating. معادلات الشهادات *muᶜaadalat š-šahaadaat* the evaluation of degrees.

عادل *ᶜaadil* (act. part. from عدل *ᶜidal*) just, fair. حكم عادل *ḥukum ᶜaadil* just decision.

معتدل *miᶜtadil* 1. mild, clement. جو معتدل *jaww miᶜtadil* mild weather. 2. moderate, temperate. معتدل بتصرفاته *miᶜtadil b-taṣarrufaata.* He's moderate in his dealings.

ع د م *ᶜdm*

عدم *ᶜidam* (يعدم *yᶜadim*) to execute, put to death. عدموا القاتل ساعة الصبح *ᶜidmaw l-gaatil saaᶜat ṣ-ṣubḥ.* They executed the killer early in the morning.

إعدام *'iᶜdaam* (v.n.) execution. راح إعدام *raaḥ 'iᶜdaam* They executed him. الحكم بالإعدام *l-ḥukum b-l-'iᶜdaam* the death sentence.

ع د ن *ᶜdn*

عدن *ᶜadan* Aden. جنة عدن *jannat ᶜadan* Eden, Paradise.

عدني *ᶜadani* 1. characteristic of Aden. 2. person from Aden.

معدن *maᶜdan* p. معادن *maᶜaadin* 1. metal. 2. mineral.

ع د و *ᶜdw*

عدى *ᶜida* (يعدي *yᶜadi*) to infect. لا تقعد يمه، ترى يعديك *la tigᶜid yamma, tara yᶜadiik.* Don't sit by him or he'll infect you. ها المرض يعدي *hal-maraḍ yᶜadi.* This disease is infectious.

عادى *ᶜaada* III 1. to treat as an enemy. أعادي كل واحد يخون بلاده *'aᶜaadi kill waaḥid yxuun blaada.* I consider anyone who betrays his country as my enemy. 2. to turn against, oppose s.o. لا تعادي التنديل *la tᶜaadi t-tindeel.* Don't turn against the foreman.

تعدى *tᶜadda* V 1. (with على *ᶜala*) to insult, be insulting to s.o. هو اللي تعدى علي بحكيه *huwa lli tᶜadda ᶜalayya b-ḥačya.* He's the one who insulted me with his words. 2. to exceed. الحرارة ما تتعدى امية في القيظ *l-ḥaraara ma* *titᶜadda 'imya fi l-geeḍ.* The temperature won't exceed a hundred degrees in the summer. الحق عليك. تعديت الحدود *l-ḥagg ᶜaleek. tᶜaddeet li-ḥduud.* You are at fault. You went too far.

اعتدى *ᶜtida* VIII (with على *ᶜala*) to commit aggression against, attack. العراق اعتدى على الكويت *li-ᶜraag ᶜtida ᶜala li-kweet.* Iraq committed aggression against Kuwait. اعتدى علي واشتكيت عليه *ᶜtida ᶜalayya w-štikeet ᶜalee.* He attacked me and I filed a complaint against him.

عدو *ᶜadu* p. عدوين *-wwiin,* أعداء *'aᶜdaa'* enemy.

عداوة *ᶜadaawa* (v.n.) enmity, hostility. فيه عداوة بينهم *fii ᶜadaawa beenhum.* They are enemies.

اعتداء *ᶜtidaa'* (v.n. from VIII اعتدى *ᶜtida*) aggression, attack.

معدي *muᶜdi* (act. part. from عدى *ᶜida*) contagious, infectious. مرض معدي *maraḍ muᶜdi* contagious disease.

ع ذ ب *ᶜðb*

عذب *ᶜaððab* II 1. to torture. عذبوه لين اعترف بالجريمة *ᶜaððaboo leen ᶜtiraf b-l-jariima.* They tortured him until he confessed to the crime. 2. to torment, pain, afflict. تعذب خواتها *tᶜaððib xawaatta.* She torments her sisters. 3. to punish. الله يعذبك إذا ما تصلي وتصوم *'aḷḷa yᶜaððibk 'iða ma tṣalli w-tṣuum.* God will punish you if you don't pray and fast.

تعذب *tᶜaððab* V pass. of II عذب *ᶜaððab.*

عذاب *ᶜaðaab* (v.n.) torture.

ع ذ ر *ᶜðr*

تعذر *tᶜaððar* V to make excuses, apologize. عليه دين، بس يتعذر حق اللي يطلبونه *ᶜalee deen, bass yitᶜaððar ḥagg illi yuṭulbuuna.* He's in debt, but he always makes excuses to those who lent him the money. الحق موب علي. ليش أتعذر؟ *l-ḥagg muub ᶜalayya. leeš 'atᶜaððar?* I'm not at fault. Why should I apologize?

اعتذر *ᶜtiðar* VIII to apologize, excuse oneself. آنا المخطي. لازم أتعذر منه *'aana l-mixṭi. laazim 'aᶜtaðir minna.* I'm at fault. I ought to apologize to him.

عذر *ᶜuður* p. أعذار *'aᶜðaar* excuse. ما لك عذر *ma lak ᶜuður.* You have no excuse.

عذرا *ᶜaðra* p. عذارى *ᶜaðaara* virgin. العذرا مريم *l-ᶜaðra maryam* the Virgin Mary.

ع ذ ر ب *ᶜðrb*

عذروب *ᶜiðruub* p. عذاريب *ᶜiðaariib* defect, fault, flaw. فيه عذروب *fii ᶜiðruub.* It's defective. ويش عذروبه؟ *weeš ᶜiðruuba?* What's his fault?

ع ر ب *ᶜrb*

عرب *ᶜarab* (coll.) Arabs. عرب دار *ᶜarab daar* pure, bona fide Arabs.

عربي *ᶜarabi* p. عرب *ᶜarab* 1. an Arab. 2. Arabic, Arabian. أكل عربي *'akil ᶜarabi* Arabic food. حصان عربي *ḥṣaan ᶜarabi* Arabian horse. 3. Arabic (lang.) تتكلم عربي زين؟ *titkallam ᶜarabi zeen?* Do you speak Arabic well? 4. (with ال *l-*) العربي *l-ᶜarabi* Arabic (generic). العربي صعيب *l-ᶜarabi ṣaᶜiib.* Arabic is difficult.

عروبة *ᶜuruuba* Arabism, Pan-Arabism.

عربانة *ᶜarabaana* p. عربباين *ᶜarabaayin* cart, wagon, buggy, carriage. عربانة أم حصان *ᶜarabaana 'umm ḥṣaan* horse-cart.

ع ر ب د *ᶜrbd*

عربيد *ᶜirbiid* p. عرابيد *ᶜaraabiid* large black snake.

ع ر ب ن *ᶜrbn*

عربون *ᶜirbuun* p. عرابين *ᶜaraabiin* deposit, down payment.

ع ر ج¹ *ᶜrj*

عرج *ᶜiraj (يعرج yᶜarij)* to limp (common var. عرج *ᶜiray (يعرج yᶜariy)).* رجله مكسورة. يعرج *riila maksuura. yᶜarij.* His leg is broken. He limps.

عرج *ᶜaray* p. عرج *ᶜiriy.* 1. lame, limping. 2. lame person. f. عرجا *ᶜarya.*

معراج *miᶜraaj*, as in ليلة المعراج *leelat l-miᶜraaj* the night of Muhammad's ascension to the seven heavens.

ع ر ج² *ᶜrj* see also under **ع ر گ** *ᶜrg.*

ع ر س *ᶜrs*

عرس *ᶜarras* II to get married. عرس على بنت خاله *ᶜarras ᶜala bint xaaḷa.* He married his cousin. عرس وجاب درزن جهال. ماشاالله! *ᶜarras w-yaab darzan yihhaal. maašaaḷḷa!* He got married and had a dozen children. Amazing!

عرس *ᶜirs* marriage, wedding.

عروسة *ᶜaruusa* (common var. عروس *ᶜaruus*) p. عرايس *ᶜaraayis* bride. (prov.) الفلوس تجيب العروس *li-fluus tyiib l-ᶜaruus.* Money talks.

معرس *miᶜris* p. عرسان *ᶜirsaan* bridegroom. المعرس هو اللي يدفع فلوس الصوغة والهدوم وكل شي ثاني *l-miᶜris huwa lli yidfaᶜ fluus ṣ-ṣooġa w-li-hduum w-kill šayy θaani.* The bridegroom is the one who pays the money for the jewelry, the clothes, and everything else.

ع ر ظ *ᶜrđ*

عرض *ᶜirađ (يعرض yᶜariđ)* 1. to dance العرضة *l-ᶜarđa.* (See عرضة *ᶜarđa* below). 2. to submit, turn in, suggest. عرضت الفكرة على الشيخ *ᶜirađt l-fikra ᶜala š-šeex.* I submitted the idea to the ruler. 3. to offer. عرض علينا سعر خاص *ᶜirađ ᶜaleena siᶜir xaaṣṣ.* He made a special offer to us. عرض الأثاث للبيع *ᶜirađ l-'aθaaθ lal-beeᶜ.* He offered his furniture for sale.

عرض *ᶜarrađ* II 1. to widen, broaden. عرضوا الشارع اللي قدام بيتنا *ᶜarrađaw š-šaariᶜ illi jiddaam beetna.* They widened the street in front of our house. 2. to expose. عرض نفسه للخطر *ᶜarrađ nafsa lal-xaṭar.* He exposed himself to danger.

عارض *ᶜaarađ* III to oppose, object to. ماحد يعارض سياسة الحكومة *maḥḥad yᶜaariđ siyaasat l-ḥukuuma.* Nobody opposes government policy.

تعرض *tᶜarrađ* V pass. of II عرض *ᶜarrađ.*

تعارض *tᶜaarađ* VI to be in conflict, be contradictory. ها الإعلام يتعارض وايا سياسة الحكومة *hal-'iᶜlaan yitᶜaarađ* *wiyya siyaasat l-ḥukuuma.* This announcement is in conflict with the government policy. زامي يتعارض وايا زامه *zaami yitᶜaaraḍ wiyya zaama.* My work schedule conflicts with his work schedule.

انعـــــرض *nᶜiraḍ* VII to be submitted, proposed. المشروع انعرض علـــى اللجنـــة *l-mašruuᶜ nᶜiraḍ ᶜala l-lajna.* The project was submitted to the committee.

اعترض *ᶜtiraḍ* VIII (with على *ᶜala*) to object to, oppose, protest. المدير اعترض على القرار *l-mudiir ᶜtiraḍ ᶜala l-ġaraar.* The director objected to the decision.

استعرض *staᶜraḍ* X to review, inspect. الشيخ اســـتعرض حـــرس الشـــرف *š-šeex staᶜraḍ ḥaras š-šaraf.* The ruler reviewed the honor guard.

عـــــرض *ᶜurḍ* width, breadth. كم عرض المـــــيز؟ *čam ᶜurḍ l-meez?* How wide is the table? بالعرض *b-l-ᶜurḍ* crosswise.

عرضـــــة *ᶜarḍa* p. *-aat* (usually with the article prefix ال *l-*, العرضة *l-ᶜarḍa*) male dance, in which men stand in two opposite lines and dance with rifles and swords, swaying their bodies left and right. العرضة النجدية *l-ᶜarḍa n-najdiyya* is performed by Najdis in Saudi Arabia.

عريض *ᶜariiḍ* wide, broad. شارع عريض *šaariᶜ ᶜariiḍ* wide street. عريض الكتف *ᶜariiḍ č-čatf* broad-shouldered.

عريضة *ᶜariiḍa* p. عرايض *ᶜaraayiḍ* petition.

معـــرض *maᶜraḍ* p. معارض *maᶜaariḍ* 1. exhibition, show. 2. showroom. 3. fair, exposition.

معارضة *mᶜaaraḍa* (v.n. from III عارض *ᶜaaraḍ*) opposition.

اعـــتراض *ᶜtiraaḍ* (v.n. from VIII اعترض *ᶜtiraḍ*) objection, protest.

استعراض *stiᶜraaḍ* (v.n. from X استعرض *staᶜraḍ*) parade review. اســـتعراض عســـكري *stiᶜraaḍ ᶜaskari* military parade.

معـــارض *mᶜaariḍ* (act. part. from III عارض *ᶜaaraḍ*) opponent, opposer.

ع ر ع ر *ᶜrᶜr*

عرعور *ᶜarᶜuur* p. عراعير *ᶜaraaᶜiir* (less common var. عرف *ᶜurf*) crest, comb (of a rooster or a hen). عرف الديك *ᶜurf d-diič* the rooster's crest.

ع ر ف *ᶜrf*

عـــرف *ᶜiraf (*يعرف *yᶜarif)* 1. to know. عرفت الجـــواب *ᶜiraft l-jawaab.* I knew the answer. أنت تعرفـــه؟ *'inta tᶜarafa?* Do you know him? 2. (with foll. imperf.) to know how to. يعرف يقرا ويكتب *yᶜarf yigra w-yiktib.* He knows how to read and write. 3. to recognize. عرفته من صوته *ᶜirafta min ṣoota.* I recognized him by his voice. 4. to realize, perceive, see. ذالحين عرفت مبغاه *ðalḥiin ᶜiraft mabġaa.* Now I realized what he wants. تعرف شو اللي صاير هني؟ *tᶜarf šu lli ṣaayir hni?* Are you aware of what's going on here? 5. to figure out, find out, discover. ما أقدر أعرف ليش فنش *ma 'agdar 'aᶜrif leeš fannaš.* I can't figure out why he resigned. عقبه عرفنـــا الســـبب *ᶜugba ᶜirafna s-sabab.* Later, we found out the reason.

عـــرف *ᶜarraf* II to introduce. تبغاني

عمل لي معروف ما أنساه أبد *ᶜimal-li maᶜruuf ma 'ansaa 'abad.* He has done me a favor I'll never forget.

ع ر گ ᶜrg

عرق *ᶜirig (يعرق yᶜarig)* 1. to sweat, perspire. عرق وهو يشتغل *ᶜirig w-huwa yištaġil.* He perspired while he was working. 2. to work hard to get s.th. عرق لاجل يحصل زيادة *ᶜirig lajil yḥaṣṣil ziyaada.* He worked hard to get a raise.

عرق *ᶜirg* p. عروق *ᶜruug* (common var. عرج *ᶜirj* p. عروج *ᶜruuj*). 1. root. 2. stem, branch (of a plant, of a leaf) عرق النسا *ᶜirg n-nisa* sciatica (med.) عرق الهيل *ᶜirg l-heel* cardamom plant (the leaves of which are used in folk medicine or as a spice). 3. vessel, vein. عروق الدم *ᶜruug d-daam* the blood vessels. 4. descent, background, family. العرق دساس *l-ᶜirg dassaas.* Blood will tell.

عرق *ᶜarag* sweat, perspiration.

عرقان *ᶜargaan* sweaty, perspiring.

العراق *li-ᶜraag* Iraq.

عراقي *ᶜraagi* 1. characteristic of Iraq, from Iraq. 2. (p. *-yyiin*) an Iraqi.

ع ر گ ب ᶜrgb

عرقب *ᶜargab (يعرقب yᶜargib)* to trip s.o. عرقبني لين كنت ماشي *ᶜargabni leen čint maaši.* He tripped me while I was walking.

عرقوب *ᶜarguub* (v.n. of عرقب *ᶜargab*) 1. tripping s.o. طقيت له عرقوب *ṭaggeet-la ᶜarguub.* I tripped him. 2. (p. عراقيب *ᶜaraagiib*) hamstring.

أعرفك عليهم؟ *tibġaani 'aᶜarrifk ᶜaleehum?* Do you want me to introduce you to them?

تعرف *tᶜarraf* V (with على *ᶜala*) to get acquainted with, to meet. تعرفت عليهم في الشارجة *tᶜarraft ᶜaleehum fi š-šaarja.* I got acquainted with them in Sharja. تعال! لازم تتعرف على صديقي. *taᶜaal! laazim titᶜarraf ᶜala ṣidiiji.* Come! You have to meet my friend.

انعرف *nᶜiraf* VII pass. of عرف *ᶜiraf.*

اعترف *ᶜtiraf* VIII (with ب *b-*) 1. to confess to, admit. اعترف بالجريمة *ᶜtiraf b-l-jariima.* He confessed to the crime. أعترف ان هذي كانت غلطتي *'aᶜtirif 'inna haaδi čaanat ġalṭati.* I admit that this was my mistake. 2. to recognize, grant recognition to. الحكومة اعترفت بكوريا الشمالية *l-ḥukuuma ᶜtirfat b-kuurya š-šamaaliyya.* The government recognized North Korea.

عريف *ᶜariif* p. عرفا *ᶜurafa* sergeant. نايب عريف *naayib ᶜariif* corporal.

أعرف *'aᶜraf* (elat.) 1. (with من *min*) more knowledgeable than. 2. (with foll. n.) the most knowledgeable.

معرفة *maᶜrifa* (v.n. from عرف *ᶜiraf*) knowledge, learning, knowing.

تعارف *taᶜaaruf* getting acquainted. حفلة تعارف *ḥaflat taᶜaaruf* get-acquainted party.

اعتراف *ᶜtiraaf* (v.n. from VIII اعترف *ᶜtiraf*) 1. confession, admission. 2. recognition, acceptance.

معروف *maᶜruuf* (p.p. from عرف *ᶜiraf*) 1. well-known. حقيقة معروفة *ḥagiiga maᶜruufa* well-known fact. 2. favor.

ع ر گ ل ᶜrgl

عرقل ᶜargal (يعرقل yᶜargil) to complicate, hinder, obstruct. أنت اللي عرقلت القضية *'inta lli ᶜargalt l-gaḏiyya.* You're the one who fouled up the case.

تعرقل tᶜargal (يتعرقل yitᶜargal) pass. from عرقل *ᶜargal.*

ع ر ك¹ ᶜrk

معركة maᶜraka p. معارك maᶜaarik battle, combat.

ع ر ك² ᶜrk

عرك ᶜirak (يعرك yᶜarik) to rub. عرك عيونه *ᶜirak ᶜyuuna.* He rubbed his eyes.

ع ر م ط ᶜrmṭ

عرمط ᶜarmaṭ (يعرمط yᶜarmiṭ) to have a ravenous appetite, to eat ravenously. الي يعرمط نقول عنه قطو مطابخ *'illi yᶜarmiṭ nguul ᶜanna gaṭu maṭaabix.* We say about the one who eats ravenously, "He eats like a pig." (lit., "A cat of kitchens.").

عرموط ᶜarmuuṭ (coll.) pears. s. -*a* p. عراميط *ᶜaraamiit.*

ع ر ن ص ᶜrnṣ

عرنوص ᶜarnuuṣ p. عرانيص ᶜaraaniiṣ corncob.

ع ر و ᶜrw

عروة ᶜirwa p. عراوي ᶜaraawi handle of a cup, pitcher, teapot, etc.

ع ر ي ᶜry

عرى ᶜarra II . See II فصخ *faṣṣax* under **ف ص خ** *fṣx.*

عريان ᶜiryaan = مفصخ *mfaṣṣax* p. -*iin.* (prov.) عريان لافي على مفصخ *ᶜiryaan laafi ᶜala mfaṣṣax.* The blind leading the blind.

ع ز ب ᶜzb

عزب ᶜazzab II 1. to be a guest, stay overnight. رحت الدوحة وعزبت عند رفيقي *riḥt d-dooḥa w-ᶜazzabt ᶜind rifiiji.* I went to Doha and stayed with my friend. 2. to give lodging to s.o., take s.o. in. إذا تروح هناك، ناس واجدين يعزبونك *'iḏa truuḥ hnaak, naas waaydiin yᶜazzbuunak.* If you go there, a lot of people will give you lodging.

عزب ᶜazab p. عزبان ᶜizbaan unmarried man, bachelor. ما نسكن عزبان في هذي الشقة *ma nsakkin ᶜizbaan fi haaḏi š-šigga.* We don't rent this apartment to bachelors.

معزب mᶜazzib p. -*iin* 1. host. معزبي الشيخ *mᶜazzbi š-šeex.* My host is the Shaikh. 2. boss, chief. معزبي التنديل *mᶜazzbi t-tindeel.* My boss is the foreman.

معزبة mᶜazzba p. -*aat* 1. hostess. 2. wife.

ع ز ز ᶜzz

اعتز ᶜtazz VIII to be proud, pride oneself. أعتز بقومي وعشيرتي *'aᶜtazz b-goomi w-ᶜašiirati.* I feel proud of my fellow tribesmen and family.

عز ᶜizz glory, honor. أيام العز *'ayyaam l-ᶜizz* the good old days. مات في عز شبابه *maat fi ᶜizz šabaaba.* He died in the prime of his youth.

عزيز ᶜaziiz p. -*iin* dear, beloved. صديقي العزيز *ṣidiiji l-ᶜaziiz* my dear friend, Dear friend! عزيز على *ᶜaziiz* ᶜala dear to. هو صديق عزيز علينا *huwa ṣidiij ᶜaziiz ᶜaleena.* He is a friend dear to us.

أعز *'aᶜazz* (elat.) 1. (with من *min*) dearer than. 2. (with foll. n.) the dearest.

ع ز ل ᶜzl

عزل *ᶜizal (يعزل yᶜazil)* 1. to separate, sort. عزل العيش عن البر *ᶜizal l-ᶜeeš ᶜan l-burr.* He separated the rice from the wheat. 2. to isolate. لازم نعزل المصابين بالكوليرا عن الباقي *laazim nᶜazil l-muṣaabiin b-l-koleera ᶜan l-baagi.* We have to isolate the cholera patients from the rest. 3. to discharge, dismiss. عزلوا المهندس لانه كان يسكر *ᶜizlaw li-mhandis linna čaan yiskar.* They fired the engineer because he used to get drunk.

انعزل *nᶜizal* VII pass. from عزل *ᶜizal.*

عزل *ᶜazil* (v.n. from عزل *ᶜizal*) isolation.

ع ز م ᶜzm

عزم *ᶜizam (يعزم yᶜazim)* to invite. عزمني على العشا *ᶜizamni ᶜala l-ᶜaša.* He invited me to dinner.

عزم *ᶜazzam* II (with على *ᶜala*) to decide to do s.th. عزمنا على السفر *ᶜazzamna ᶜala s-safar.* We decided to travel.

عازم *ᶜaazim* (act. part. from عزم *ᶜizam*) (*ᶜaazmin-* + suff. pron.) having invited. هو اللي عازمني على العشا *huwa lli ᶜaazminni ᶜala l-ᶜaša.* He's the one who has invited me to dinner.

عزيمة *ᶜaziima* 1. invitation. 2. (p. عزايم *ᶜazaayim*) banquet, dinner party. يقزرون فلوسهم على العزايم *ygazzruun fluushum ᶜala l-ᶜazaayim.* They waste their money on banquets.

ع س س ᶜss

عساس *ᶜassaas* p. *-a* 1. spy. ماميش عساسين هني *maamiiš ᶜassaassiin hni.* There are no spies here. 2. informer, detective.

ع س ك ر ᶜskr

عسكر *ᶜaskar* (coll.) army. s. *-i* soldier p. عساكر *ᶜasaakir* armies.

عسكري *ᶜaskari* 1. soldier. 2. military, army. لباس عسكري *libaas ᶜaskari* military uniform. ضابط عسكري *ðaabiṭ ᶜaskari* military officer.

عسكرية *ᶜaskariyya* military service.

معسكر *muᶜaskar* p. *-aat* army camp, camp.

ع س ل ᶜsl

عسل *ᶜasal* (coll.) honey, molasses. (prov.) ان كان رفيقك عسل لا تلحسه كله *nčaan rifiijak ᶜasal la tilḥasa killa.* Don't use up all of your credit at once. شهر العسل *šahar l-ᶜasal* the honeymoon.

ع س ي ᶜsy

عسى *ᶜasa* 1. (with foll. v.) hopefully, I hope that. عسى ما حصل شي *ᶜasa ma ḥiṣal šayy.* I hope nothing (bad) has happened. 2. (with suff. pron.) I hope that, may. عساهم جاوا *ᶜasaahum yaw.* I hope they came. عساك طيب *ᶜasaak ṭayyib.* I hope you are fine.

ع ش ب ᶜšb

عشب ᶜišib (coll.) grass, pasture. العشب ترعاه الغنم *l-ᶜišib tirᶜaa l-ġanam.* Goats and sheep eat grass.

عشبة ᶜišba herbs (for gastric distress, esp. diarrhea).

ع ش ر ᶜšr

عاشر ᶜaašar III to associate closely with s.o., be on intimate terms with s.o. عاشرته أيام الدراسة وعرفت انه خوش رجال *ᶜaašarta 'ayyaam d-diraasa w-ᶜiraft 'inna xooš rayyaal.* I associated closely with him during my studies and I found out he was a good man.

عشر ᶜušur p. اعشار ᶜšaar one tenth, tenth part. الزكاة في الإسلام ربع العشر *z-zakaa fi l-'islaam rubᶜ l-ᶜušur.* Alms tax in Islam is one quarter of a tenth (2.5%).

عشرة ᶜašara p. *-aat* 1. ten, the numeral ten. عندي عشرة ᶜ*indi* ᶜ*ašara.* I have ten. عشرة دينار ᶜ*ašara diinaar* ten dinars. عشرة كيلو ᶜ*ašara keelu* ten kilograms. 2. (with foll. genit.) عشر ᶜ*ašir,* عشرة ᶜ*ašarat.* كنا عشر أنفار *činna* ᶜ*ašir 'anfaar.* We were ten people.

عشيرة ᶜašiira p. عشاير ᶜašaayir tribe, clan. قانون العشاير *gaanuun l-ᶜašaayir* tribal law.

عاشورة ᶜaašuura the tenth day of Muharram (the first Islamic month). يصوم عاشورة *yṣuum ᶜaašura.* He fasts on the tenth day of Muharram.

عشرين ᶜišriin twenty, the numeral twenty. توه جاهل. يعد إلى العشرين بس. *tawwa yaahil. yᶜidd 'ila l-ᶜišriin bass.* He's only a child. He counts only to twenty. عشرين درهم ᶜ*išriin dirhim* twenty dirhams. خمسة وعشرين *xamsa w-ᶜišriin* twenty-five. امية وعشرين *'imya w-ᶜišriin* 120.

عاشر ᶜaašir tenth. عاشر يوم ᶜ*aašir yoom* the tenth day. عاشرهم ᶜ*aaširhum* the tenth one of them.

ع ش ر ج ᶜšrj

عشرج ᶜišrij chamomile (used as treatment for constipation).

ع ش ش ᶜšš

عشش ᶜaššaš II to build a nest. الطير عشش على شجرتنا *ṭ-ṭeer ᶜaššaš ᶜala šyaratna.* The bird built a nest on our tree.

عش ᶜišš p. عشوش ᶜšuuš nest.

عشة ᶜišša p. عشيش ᶜišiiš hut, shack, shanty.

ع ش گ ᶜšg

عشق ᶜišig (يعشق yᶜašig) to be passionately in love with s.o. عشقها وطلب يدها من أبوها ᶜ*išigha w-ṭilab yaddha min 'ubuuha.* He fell in love with her and asked her father for her hand in marriage.

عشق ᶜišig (v.n.) love, passion. ما ينام الليل من العشق *ma ynaam l-leel min l-ᶜišig.* He doesn't sleep at night because of love. العشق يا خوي يموت. اسأل مجرب *l-ᶜišig ya xuuy ymawwit. 'is'al mjarrib.* Love, my dear brother, is deadly. Ask someone who has experienced it.

عاشق ᶜaašig (act. part.) 1. having fallen in love with s.o. هو عاشق بنت

عمه *huwa ᶜaašig bint ᶜamma* He has fallen in love with his cousin. 2. p. *-iin* lover.

معشوق *maᶜšuug* (p.p.) beloved, sweetheart (f.).

ع ش ي *ᶜšy*

عشى *ᶜašša* II to give s.o. a dinner. عشت عيالها قبل ما نيمتهم *ᶜaššat ᶜyaalḥa gabil-ma nayyamattum.* She gave dinner to her children before she put them to bed.

تعشى *tᶜašša* V to have dinner, dine. تعشيت عيش ولحم *tᶜaššeet ᶜeeš w-laḥam.* I had rice and meat for dinner. أتعشى الساعة تسع *'atᶜašša s-saaᶜa tisiᶜ.* I have dinner at 9 o'clock.

عشا *ᶜaša* p. عشيات *-yaat* 1. dinner, supper. عقب العشا شربنا قهوة *ᶜugb l-ᶜaša šribna gahwa.* After dinner, we had coffee. 2. dinner party. كان عندنا عشا أمس *čaan ᶜindana ᶜaša 'ams.* We gave a dinner party yesterday.

عشا *ᶜiša* (usually with the article prefix العشا *l-ᶜiša*) evening (approx. two hours after sunset). رحنا صوبهم العشا *riḥna ṣoobhum l-ᶜiša.* We went to their place at night. صلاة العشا *ṣalaat l-ᶜiša* the evening prayer.

ع ص ب *ᶜṣb*

عصب *ᶜaṣab* p. أعصاب *'aṣaab* nerve.

عصابة *ᶜiṣaaba* p. *-aat* gang, band.

تعصب *taᶜaṣṣub* 1. prejudice. 2. fanaticism.

ع ص د *ᶜṣd*

عصيدة *ᶜaṣiida* thick porridge made of flour, butter, and sugar.

ع ص ر *ᶜṣr*

عصر *ᶜiṣar* (يعصر *yᶜaṣir*) 1. to squeeze, press. عصر برتقالتين *ᶜiṣar burtugaalateen.* He squeezed two oranges. (prov.) عصر وزارة وجا *ᶜiṣar wzaara w-ya.* He returned empty-handed. 2. to ring out. غسلت الهدوم وعصرهم *ġsalat li-hduum w-ᶜṣarattum.* She washed the clothes and wrung them out.

عصر *ᶜaṣir* 1. (usually with the article prefix ال *l-*) later afternoon. صلاة العصر *ṣalaat l-ᶜaṣir* the afternoon prayer. 2. in the afternoon. رحت هناك العصر *riḥt hnaak l-ᶜaṣir.* I went there in the afternoon.

عصير *ᶜaṣiir* juice.

عصارة *ᶜaṣṣaara* p. *-aat* juicer, squeezer, press.

ع ص ص *ᶜṣṣ*

عص *ᶜiṣṣ* p. عصاعص *ᶜaṣaaᶜiṣ* (common var. عصعص *ᶜiṣᶜiṣ* p. عصاعص *ᶜaṣaaᶜiṣ*) tailbone. (prov.) عصعص الكلب عوج لو عدلته *ᶜiṣᶜiṣ č-čalb ᶜaway lo ᶜaddalta.* A leopard cannot change its spots.

ع ص ع ص *ᶜṣᶜṣ*

عصعص *ᶜiṣᶜiṣ* = عص *ᶜiṣṣ.*

ع ص ف *ᶜṣf*

عاصوف *ᶜaaṣuuf* p. عواصيف *ᶜawaaṣif* storm, violent wind.

ع ص ف ر *ᶜṣfr*

عصفر *ᶜiṣfir* (coll.) safflower. s. عرج عصفر *ᶜirj ᶜiṣfur.*

عصفور ^{c}ṣfwr

عصفور ^{c}aṣfuur p. عصافير ^{c}aṣaafiir 1. sparrow. 2. any small bird. نحن ما ناكل العصافير *niḥin ma naakil l-^{c}aṣaafiir.* We don't eat small birds. ضرب عصفورين بحجر *ðirab ^{c}aṣfuureen b-ḥiyar.* He killed two birds with one stone.

عصم ^{c}ṣm

عاصمة ^{c}aaṣima p. عواصم ^{c}awaaṣim capital city.

معصوم ma^{c}ṣuum p. *-iin* infallible, sinless. ماحد معصوم من الخطا *maḥḥad ma^{c}ṣuum min l-xaṭa.* No one is free of error.

عصمل ^{c}ṣml

عصملية ^{c}uṣmalliyya p. *-aat* old Turkish rifle.

عصي ١ ^{c}ṣy

عصا ^{c}aṣa p. عصي ^{c}iṣi 1. stick. طقيته بالعصا *ṭaggeeta b-l-^{c}aṣa.* I hit him with the stick. 2. cane, walking stick. رجال عود لحيته بيضا والعصا بيده *rayyaal ^{c}ood liḥyita beeða w-l-^{c}aṣa b-yadda.* He's an old man with a grey beard and a cane in his hand.

عصي ٢ ^{c}ṣy

عصى ^{c}iṣa (يعصي y^{c}aṣi) to disobey, resist, oppose. عصا أبوه وسار ^{c}iṣa *'ubuu w-saar.* He disobeyed his father and left. ما تقدر تعصي الحكومة *ma tigdar t^{c}aṣi l-ḥukuuma.* You cannot resist the government.

استعصى sta^{c}ṣa X 1. (with على ^{c}ala) to be difficult, hard. استعصى عليه يصالحهم *sta^{c}ṣa ^{c}alee yṣaaliḥḥum.* He found it difficult to reach a compromise with them. 2. to be incurable, malignant. استعصى المرض *sta^{c}ṣa l-marað.* The disease was incurable.

عصيان ^{c}iṣyaan (v.n. from عصى ^{c}iṣa) revolt, mutiny.

عاصي ^{c}aaṣi (act. part from عصى ^{c}iṣa) p. *-yiin* rebellious, disobedient.

معصية ma^{c}ṣiya p. معاصي ma^{c}aaṣi sin, disobedience to God.

عطر ^{c}ṭr

عطار ^{c}aṭṭaar p. عطاطير ^{c}aṭaaṭiir, *-a* dealer in spices, perfume, herbs, incense, etc. سوق العطاطير *suug l-^{c}aṭaaṭiir* the spice vendors' market.

عطس ^{c}ṭs

عطس ^{c}iṭas (يعطس y^{c}aṭis) to sneeze.

عطش ^{c}ṭš

عطش ^{c}iṭiš (يعطش y^{c}aṭiš) to be or become thirsty. كان يشتغل في الشمس وعطش *čaan yištaġil fi š-šams w-^{c}iṭiš.* He was working in the sun and became thirsty.

عطش ^{c}aṭṭaš II to make s.o. thirsty. ها الأكل المالح عطشني *hal-'akil l-maaliḥ ^{c}aṭṭašni.* This salty food made me thirsty.

عطش ^{c}aṭaš (v.n. from عطش ^{c}iṭiš) thirst.

عطشان ^{c}aṭšaan p. *-iin* thirsty. كنا عطشانين وجوعانين بعد *činna ^{c}aṭšaaniin w-juu^{c}aaniin ba^{c}ad.* We were thirsty and hungry too.

عطل ^{c}ṭl

عطل ^{c}aṭṭal II 1. to delay, hinder,

hamper. آنـا مسـتعجل. لا تعطلـني *'aana mista^cyil. la t^caṭṭilni.* I am in a hurry. Don't delay me. 2. to close up, close down. الدوايـــر تعطـــل يـــوم الجمعـــة *d-dawaayir t^caṭṭil yoom l-yim^ca.* Offices are closed on Fridays.

تعطل *t^caṭṭal* 1. to be stopped, interrupted. ترييته، بس تعطل *trayyeeta, bass t^caṭṭal.* I waited for him but he was late. 2. to be out of order. السيارة تعطلـت *s-sayyaara t^caṭṭalat.* The car was out of order. 3. to be injured. وقع علـى الأرض وتعطـل *wuga^c ^cala l-'arḏ w-t^caṭṭal.* He fell to the ground and was injured.

عطلة *^cuṭla* p. عطل *^cuṭal* 1. holiday. بـاكر الجمعـة، عطلـة. السـوق مبنـد *baačir l-yim^ca, ^cuṭla. s-suug mbannid.* Tomorrow is Friday, a holiday. The marketplace will be closed.

عاطل *^caaṭil* p. *-iin* 1. unemployed, jobless, out-of-work. مـاحد عـاطل عـن العمـل هـني *mahhad ^caaṭil ^can l-^camal hni.* No one is unemployed here. 2. worthless, useless. رجال عاطل *rayyaal ^caaṭil* worthless man.

ع ط و *^cṭw*

عطى *^ciṭa* (يعطي *y^caṭi*) 1. to give s.th., give s.o. s.th. عطاهـا حبـة *^caṭaaha ḥabba.* He gave her a kiss. عطـاني خمسين درهم *^caṭaani xamsiin dirhim.* He gave me fifty dirhams. ما أقدر أتفـاهم وايـاه. مـا يـاخذ ويعطـي *ma 'agdar 'atfaaham wiyyaa. ma yaaxiḏ w-y^caṭi.* I can't come to terms with him. He doesn't give and take. 2. to offer. عطاني ألف درهم حق الساعة بـس مـا بعتهـا *^caṭaani 'alf dirhim ḥagg s-saa^ca bass ma bi^citta.* He offered me a thousand dirhams for the watch, but I didn't sell it. (prov.) عطوهـا رجـل وقـالت عـور *^caṭooha riil w-gaalat ^cawar.* Give him an inch and he'll take a mile. 3. to give up, give away. أبو البنت عطاها حق ابن أخـوه *'ubu l-bint ^caṭaaha ḥagg 'ibin 'uxuu.* The girl's father gave her in marriage to his nephew. (prov.) عطي الخباز خبزك ولـو بـاق نصـه *^caṭi l-xabbaaz xubzak walaw baag nuṣṣ.* Half a loaf is better than none.

انعطى *n^ciṭa* VII pass. of عطى *^ciṭa.*

عطا *^caṭa* 1. gift, present. عطا من الله *^caṭa mi 'aḷḷa* gift from God. 2. (v.n. from عطـى *^ciṭa*) giving. ما فيه أخذ وعطا *ma fii 'axḏ w-^caṭa.* There's no give and take.

ع ظ ظ *^cḏḏ*

عـض *^caḏḏ* (يعـض *y^caḏḏ*) to bite. هـا الكلـب يعـض *hač-čalb y^caḏḏ.* This dog bites. عضه في رقبتـه *^caḏḏa fi rgubta.* He bit him on his neck. (prov.) من عضه الداب ينقـز مـن الحبل *man ^caḏḏa d-daab yangiz min l-ḥabil.* Once bitten twice shy.

عضة *^caḏḏa* (n. of inst.) p. *-aat* bite.

ع ظ م *^cḏm*

عظـم *^caḏḏam* to magnify, enlarge, make greater. عظم الله أجركـم *^caḏḏam aḷḷaahu 'ajrakum.* (said by someone to offer condolences after burial of a deceased person) May God make your reward greater (in heaven).

عظـم *^caḏim* (coll.) bones. s. عظمـة *^caḏma* p. عظام *^cḏaam.*

عظمـة *^caḏama* 1. majesty. عظمة الملك

ᶜaðamat l-malik His Majesty the King. 2. highness. عظمة الحاكم *ᶜaðamat l-ḥaakim* His Highness the Ruler.

عظيم *ᶜaðiim* 1. p. *-iin,* عظما *ᶜuðama* great, magnificent, splendid. ضربة عظيمة في الكول *ðarba ᶜaðiima fi l-gool* great kick in the goal (in soccer). 2. (with the article prefix ال *l-*) the magnificent (one of the epithets of God). أستغفر الله العظيم! *'astaġfiru aḷḷahi l-ᶜaðiim!* I seek God's forgiveness! Please don't say so! Not at all!

أعظم *'aᶜðam* (elat.) 1. (with من *min*) greater than. 2. (with foll. n.) the greatest.

ع ظ و *ᶜðw*

عضو *ᶜuðu* p. أعضا *'aᶜða* 1. member (of an organization). الإمارات عضو في مجلس التعاون الخليجي *l-'imaaraat ᶜuðu fi majlis t-taᶜaawun l-xaliiji.* The U.A.E. is a member of the G.C.C. 2. member, limb, organ (of the body).

عضوة *ᶜuðwa* p. *-aat* female member.

عضوية *ᶜuðwiyya* p. *-aat* membership (of an organization).

ع ف ر *ᶜfr*

عفرا *ᶜafra* p. عفرات *-aat* 1. white female camel. 2. Afra (female's name).

عافور *ᶜaafuur* dust, soil, earth. (prov.) لو حصل الماي بطل العافور *lo ḥiṣal l-maay biṭal l-ᶜaafuur.* (lit., "If water can be found, ablution with clean earth is nullified.").

ع ف ر ت *ᶜfrt*

عفريت *ᶜafriit* p. عفاريت *ᶜafaariit* 1. elf, devil, demon. 2. mischievous. ولد عفريت *walad ᶜafriit* mischievous boy. 3. clever, capable. 4. cunning, sly, crafty.

ع ف س *ᶜfs*

عفس *ᶜifas* (يعفس *yᶜafis)* 1. to scatter. عفس الأوراق *ᶜifas l-'awraag.* He scattered the pieces of paper. 2. to throw into disorder, disarrange. عفس الدنيا *ᶜifas d-dinya.* He turned things upside down. He moved heaven and earth.

عفسة *ᶜafsa* state of disorder, confusion, hustle and bustle. الدنيا عفسة *d-dinya ᶜafsa.* The world is in turmoil.

ع ف و *ᶜfw*

عفى *ᶜifa* (يعفي *yᶜafi)* 1. to forgive (s.o.), pardon (s.o.). الغلطة غلطتي. اعفيني *l-ġalṭa ġalṭati. 'iᶜfiini.* It's my mistake. Forgive me. عقب ما اعترف، عفينا عنه *ᶜugub-ma ᶜtiraf, ᶜafeena ᶜanna.* After he had confessed, we pardoned him. (prov.) عفى الله عما مضى *ᶜafa ḷḷaahu ᶜamma maða.* Let bygones be bygones. 2. to exempt, excuse. عفوه من الرسوم *ᶜafoo min r-rusuum.* They exempted him from the fees. أرجوك اعفيني. ما أقدر أجي اليوم *'arjuuk iᶜfiini. ma 'agdar 'aji l-yoom.* Please excuse me. I can't come today.

عافى *ᶜaafa* III (said of God) to restore to good health, heal, cure. الله يعافيك *'aḷḷa yᶜaafiik.* May God grant you good health.

تعافى *tᶜaafa* VI regain health, recuperate. تعافى، الحمد لله، وترك المستشفى *tᶜaafa, l-ḥamdu li-llaah, w-tirak l-mustašfi.* He regained his health, thank God, and he left the hospital.

عفو *ᶜafu* 1. pardon, forgiveness. 2. amnesty. الحاكم أصدر عفو عام *l-ḥaakim 'aṣdar ᶜafu ᶜaamm.* The ruler declared a general amnesty.

عفية *ᶜafya* bravo! very good! عفية عليك! كيف سويتها؟ *ᶜafya ᶜaleek! čeef sawweetta?* Bravo (for you)! How did you do it?

عافية *ᶜaafya* good health. الله يعطيك الصحة والعافية *'aḷḷa yᶜaṭiik ṣ-ṣiḥḥa w-l-ᶜaafya.* (lit., "May God give you good health and well-being.").

معفي *maᶜfi* (p.p. from عفى *ᶜifa*) exempt. معفي من الجمرك *maᶜfi min l-jimrig* exempt from customs duties. معفي من الخدمة العسكرية *maᶜfi min l-xidma l-ᶜaskariyya* exempt from military service.

ع ف ي *ᶜfy* see under ع ف و *ᶜfw.*

ع گ ب *ᶜgb*

عاقب *ᶜaagab* III to punish. المدرس عاقبني لاني ما كنت عاقل في الصف *l-mudarris ᶜaagabni linni ma čint ᶜaagil fi ṣ-ṣaff.* The teacher punished me because I didn't behave well in class. الشرطة تعاقب المسرع *š-širṭa tᶜaagib l-misriᶜ.* The police punish speeding motorists. عاقب على *ᶜaagab ᶜala* to punish s.o. for s.th. عاقبوه على البوق *ᶜaagabuu ᶜala l-boog.* They punished him for stealing.

تعاقب *tᶜaagab* VI pass. of III عاقب *ᶜaagab.*

عقب *ᶜugub* (prep.) after. عقب الصلاة *ᶜugb ṣ-ṣalaa* after prayer. عقب الظهر *ᶜugb ḍ-ḍuhur* in the afternoon. عقب هذا وذاك *ᶜugub haaða w-ðaak* after all of this. عقب ايش! *ᶜugbeeš!* after hard work. اي نعم حصلتها، لكن عقب ايش *'ii naᶜam ḥaṣṣalitta, lakin ᶜugbeeš.* Yes, indeed, I got it after hard work.

عقب ما *ᶜugub-ma* (conj.) after. تريقت عقب ما سبحت *trayyagt ᶜugub-ma sibaḥt.* I had breakfast after I took a bath. (prov.) عقب ما شاب ختنوه *ᶜugub-ma šaab xatanuu.* You cannot teach an old dog new tricks. Too late! (lit., "After he grew up, they circumcised him.")

عقوبة *ᶜuguuba* (v.n. from III عاقب *ᶜaagab*) punishment, penalty. قانون العقوبات *gaanuun l-ᶜuguubaat* the penal code.

ع گ د *ᶜgd*

عقد *ᶜigad (يعقد yᶜagid)* 1. to hold (a meeting, a session, etc.) عقدوا اجتماع في البلدية *ᶜigdaw jtimaaᶜ fi l-baladiyya.* They held a meeting in the municipal office. 2. to conclude, effect a transaction. الحكومة عقدت اتفاق تجاري ويا انكلترا *l-ḥukuuma ᶜigdat ttifaag tijaari wiyya ngiltara.* The government concluded a trade agreement with England. 3. (with على *ᶜala*) to sign a marriage contract with. عقد عليها قبل سنة *ᶜigad ᶜaleeha gabil sana.* He signed a marriage contract with her a year ago. 4. to knot, tie. عقد الحبل *ᶜigad l-ḥabil.* He knotted the rope.

عقد *ᶜaggad* II to complicate, make

difficult. لا تعقـد الأمـور *la t^{c}aggid l-'umuur.* Don't complicate things.

تعقد *t^{c}aggad* V be or become complicated. المشـكلة تعقـدت *l-muškila t^{c}aggadat.* The problem became complicated.

تعاقد *t^{c}aagad* VI to contract, make a contract. الحكومة تعاقدت وايانا لاجل نبني بيـوت شـعبية *l-ḥukuuma t^{c}aagadat wiyyaana lajil nabni byuut ša^{c}biyya.* The government contracted with us for building low income housing.

انعقد *n^{c}igad* VII pass. of عقد *^{c}igad.*

اعتقد *^{c}tigad* VIII 1. (with ب *b-*) to believe in. كافر. ما يعتقد بالله *kaafir. ma yi^{c}tagid b-'aḷḷa.* He's an atheist. He doesn't believe in God. 2. (with ان *'inn-*) to think (that). أعتقد انه جاي اليوم *'a^{c}tagid 'inna yaay l-yoom.* I think that he's coming today.

عقد *^{c}agd* p. عقود *^{c}guud* contract, lease. وقعت العقـد وايـا شـركة «أدمـا» *wagga^{c}t l-^{c}agd wiyya šarikat 'adma.* I signed the contract with the ADMA company. عقـد زواج *^{c}agd zawaaj* marriage contract.

عقد *^{c}igd* p. عقود *^{c}guud* necklace.

عقدة *^{c}ugda* p. عقـد *^{c}ugad* 1. knot. ما أقـدر أفـك هـا العقـدة *ma 'agdar 'afičč hal-^{c}ugda.* I cannot untie this knot. 2. problem, difficulty. عقدة نفسـية *^{c}ugda nafsiyya* psychological problem, personality problem.

عقيد *^{c}agiid* p. عقـدا *^{c}ugada* colonel (milit.)

تعقيد *ta^{c}giid* (v.n. from II عقد *^{c}aggad*) 1. complication, entanglement. 2. p. only تعقيـدات *-aat* complicated problems.

اعتقاد *^{c}tigaad* (v.n. from VIII اعتقـد *^{c}tigad*) belief, faith.

معقد *m^{c}aggad* (p.p. from II عقـد *^{c}aggad*) complicated, entangled, difficult. قضية معقدة *gaḏiyya m^{c}aggada* complicated problem. شخص معقد *šuxṣ m^{c}aggad* mixed-up person.

ع گ ر ب *^{c}grb*

عقرب *^{c}agrab* p. عقـارب *^{c}agaarib* 1. scorpion. 2. hand (on a clock or a watch). عقارب الساعة *^{c}agaarib s-saa^{c}a* the clock, watch hands.

ع گ ل *^{c}gl*

اعتقل *^{c}tigal* VIII to arrest, apprehend (for political reasons). اعتقلـوه في بيتـه *^{c}tigaloo fi beeta.* They arrested him in his house.

عقل *^{c}agil* p. عقول *^{c}guul* mind, intellect, sense. عقله مخربـط *^{c}agla mxarbaṭ.* He's mixed up. (prov.) الطـول طـول نخلـة والعقـل عقـل صخلـة *ṭ-ṭuul ṭuul nxaḷa w-l-^{c}agil ^{c}agl ṣxaḷa.* The mind of a child and the body of a man.

عقلي *^{c}agli* mental. مستشـفى الأمـراض العقلية *mustašfi l-'amraaḏ l-^{c}agliyya* the sanatorium.

عقال *^{c}gaaḷ* p. عقلة *^{c}ugḷa,* عقـل *^{c}ugiḷ* headband. معظم الناس هني يلبسـون الغـترة والعقال *mu^{c}ḏam n-naas hini yilbisuun l-ġitra w-li-^{c}gaaḷ.* Most people here wear the headcloth and the headband.

أعقل *'a^{c}gaḷ* (elat.) 1. (with من *min*) more sensible than. 2. (with foll. n.) the most sensible.

معقـــول *ma^cguul* reasonable, sensible, rational. طلب معقـــول *ṭalab ma^cguul* reasonable request. معقول انك سويت كذي؟ *ma^cguul 'innak sawweet čiđi?* Is it possible that you behaved in this manner?

معتقـل *mu^ctagal* 1. (p.p. from VIII اعتقل *^ctigal*) arrested, confined. 2. (p. *-aat*) detention center.

ع ك ر *^ckr*

عكـــار *^cakkaar* p. *-iin, -a.* peasant, farmer. ذالحين ما تحصل عكارين واجدين لانهم يشتغلـــون في التجـــارة *đalḥiin ma tḥaṣṣil ^cakkaariin waaydiin linhim yištaġluun fi t-tijaara.* Now you won't find many peasants because they deal in trade.

ع ك س *^cks*

عكس *^cikas* (يعكس *y^cakis)* 1. to reflect. هذي تعكس نـــور الشمـــس *haađi t^cakis nuur š-šams.* This reflects sunlight. 2. to reverse, invert. الوزير عكس قـــرار اللجنة *l-waziir ^cikas garaar l-lajna.* The minister reversed the committee decision.

عـــاكس *^caakas* III to oppose, contradict. عاكســـني في اللـــي اقترحتـــه *^caakasni fi lli gtaraḥta.* He was in opposition to what I had suggested.

انعكس *n^cikas* VII pass. of عكس *^cikas.*

عكس *^caks* 1. (p. عكوس *^ckuus*) photograph. هذا الطلب يبغى له خمس عكـــوس *haađa ṭ-ṭalab yibġaa-la xams ^ckuus.* This application needs five photographs. خذيت عكســـه *xađeet ^caksa.* I took a picture of him. 2. (prep.) opposite (of). طويل عكس قصير *ṭawiil ^caks gaṣiir.* Tall is the opposite of short. بالعكس *b-l-^caks* on the contrary. بالعكس، دبي أبعد *b-l-^caks, dbayy 'ab^cad.* On the contrary, Dubai is farther away. عكس مـــا *^caks-ma* (conj.) contrary to, opposite to. سوى عكس ما قلـــت لـــه *sawwa ^caks-ma git-la.* He did the opposite of what I had told him.

عكـــاس *^cakkaas* p. *-iin, -a* photographer.

عكاسة *^cakkaasa* p. *-aat* camera. النجدة يعرفون المسرع بواسطة العكاسات *n-najda y^carfuun l-misri^c b-waasiṭat l-^cakkaasaat.* The police squad knows speeding motorists by means of cameras.

ع ك ك *^ckk*

عكة *^cikka* p. عكيك *^cikiik* leather bag in which butter is kept.

ع ل ب *^clb*

علـــب *^callab* II to can, tin. فيه معامل تعليب طمام ومشمش *fii ma^caamil ta^cliib ṭamaaṭ w-mišmiš.* There are factories that can tomatoes and apricots.

تعليب *ta^cliib* (v.n. from II علب *^callab*) canning. معمل تعليـــب *ma^cmal ta^cliib* canning factory.

ع ل ج *^clj*

عـــالج *^caalaj* III to treat (a patient, a disease, a subject). عالجوني في المستشفى شهرين *^caalajooni fi l-mustašfi šahreen.* They treated me in the hospital for two months. يعالج الإمساك بـــالعشرج *y^caalij l-'imsaak b-l-^cišrij.* He treats constipation with chamomile. هـــذا موضـــوع لازم يتعـــالج بالصـــبر *haađa mawđuu^c laazim yit^caalaj b-ṣ-ṣabir.*

This is a subject that should be treated patiently.

معالجة *mu^c^aalaja* (v.n. from III عالج *^c^aalaj*) treatment. مركز معالجة السرطان *markaz mu^c^aalajat s-saraṭaan* the cancer treatment center.

علاج *^c^ilaaj* 1. treatment. 2. cure.

ع ل چ *^c^lč*

علك *^c^ilač (يعلك y^c^alič)* to chew (gum). اللي يعلكون هم العيال *'illi y^c^alčuun hum li-^c^yaaḷ.* Those who chew gum are the children.

علك *^c^ilič* chewing gum.

ع ل ف *^c^lf*

علف *^c^alaf* (coll.) cattle feed. s. حفنة علف *ḥafnat ^c^alaf.*

ع ل گ *^c^lg*

علق *^c^ilag (يعلق y^c^alig)* to stick. هذي الطوابع ما تعلق *haaði ṭ-ṭuwaabi^c^ ma t^c^alig.* These stamps do not stick.

علق *^c^allag* II 1. to hang s.th. علق الصورة على الطوفة *^c^allag ṣ-ṣuura ^c^ala ṭ-ṭoofa.* He hung the picture on the wall. 2. to comment, make comments. علق على الأخبار *^c^allag ^c^ala l-'axbaar.* He commented on the news.

تعلق *t^c^allag* V 1. pass. from II علق *^c^allag.* 2. (with ب *b-*) to be attached, devoted to, fond of. بعده جاهل. يتعلق واجد بأمه *ba^c^da yaahil. yit^c^allag waayid b-'umma.* He's still a child. He is very attached to his mother. 3. (with ب *b-*) to concern s.o., have s.th. to with s.o. هذا شي ما يتعلق بك *haaða šayy ma yit^c^allag biik.* This is something that doesn't concern you.

علاقة *^c^alaaga* p. *-aat* connection, relation, relevance. ما فيه علاقة بين الثنتين *ma fii ^c^alaaga been θ-θinteen.* There is no connection between the two. العلاقات العامة *l-^c^alaagaat l-^c^aamma* the public relations. علاقاتنا زينة وايا الدول الأوروبية *^c^alaagaatna zeena wiyya d-duwal l-'uroopiyya.* Our relations are good with the European countries.

تعليق *ta^c^liig* (v.n. from II علق *^c^allag*) comment, commentary.

معلق *mu^c^allig* (act. part. from II علق *^c^allag*) commentator (radio or press).

معلق *m^c^allag* (p.p. from II علق *^c^allag*). 1. suspended, hanging. كبري معلق *kubri m^c^allag* suspension bridge. 2. pending, undecided. المسألة معلقة *l-mas'ala m^c^allaga.* The case is pending.

علاقة *^c^illaaga* p. *-aat* coat hanger.

ع ل گ م *^c^lgm*

علقم *^c^algam* (coll.) colocynth (bot.). طعمه مر مثل العلقم *ṭa^c^ma murr miθl l-^c^algam.* It tastes as bitter as colocynth.

ع ل م *^c^lm*

علم *^c^ilim (يعلم y^c^alim)* 1. to know. الله يعلم كل شي *'aḷḷa y^c^alim kill šayy.* God knows everything. يعلم بالغيب *y^c^alim b-l-ġeeb.* He's clairvoyant. 2. learn, find out, come to know. علمت انك عرست وسافرت لندن *^c^limt 'innak ^c^arrast w-saafart landan.* I found out that you got married and traveled to London.

علم *^c^allam* II 1. to teach, instruct. آنا أعلمك تسوق سيارة *'aana 'a^c^llimk tsuug sayyaara.* I'll teach you to drive a car.

2. to tell, let s.o. know. تعال علمني. باعطيك درهم *ta^c^aal ^c^allimni. b-a^c^ṭiik dirhim.* Come tell me. I'll give you a dirham.

تعلم *t^c^allam* V to learn. تعلم إنكليزي *t^c^allam 'ingiliizi.* He learned English.

علم *^c^ilim* 1. knowledge, information. ما عندي علم بهالشي *ma ^c^indi ^c^ilim b-haš-šayy.* I don't have any knowledge of this thing. العلم عند الله *l-^c^ilim ^c^ind aḷḷa.* God knows (this thing). 2. (p. علوم *^c^luum*) news. ويش علومك؟ *weeš ^c^luumak?* What news do you have? ما عندي أي علوم *ma ^c^indi 'ayy ^c^luum.* I don't have any news.

علم *^c^alam* p. اعلام *^c^laam.* flag, banner.

عالم *^c^aalam* 1. world. 2. people. في عالم واجدين في السوق *fii ^c^aalam waaydiin fi s-suug.* There are many people in the marketplace.

عالمي *^c^aalami* world (adj.). بطل عالمي *baṭal ^c^aalami* world champion.

علام *^c^alaam* (with suff. pron.) why? علامك ما تجي ويانا؟ *^c^alaamak ma tiyi wiyyana?* Why don't you come with us?

علامة *^c^alaama* p. *-aat* 1. mark, sign. علامة مسجلة *^c^alaama msajjala* registered trademark. 2. grade, mark, point. علامة الامتحان *^c^alaamat li-mtiḥaan* the examination grade. حصلت ثمانين علامة *ḥaṣṣalt θamaaniin ^c^alaama.* I got eighty points.

استعلام *sti^c^laam* p. *-aat* information, inquiry. الاستعلامات *l-'isti^c^laamaat* information, inquiry. مكتب الاستعلامات *maktab l-'isti^c^laamaat* the information desk.

عالم *^c^aalim* p. علما *^c^ulama* 1. (act. part. of علم *^c^ilim*) knowing, cognizant. الله هو العالم بكل شي *'aḷḷaa huwa l-^c^aalim b-kill šayy.* God is the Omniscient. 2. scientist, scholar. عالم فيزيا *^c^aalim fiizya* physicist. علما الدين *^c^ulama d-diin* the religious scholars.

أعلم *'a^c^lam* (elat.) 1. (with من *min*) more knowledgeable, learned than. 2. (with foll. n.) the most knowledgeable, learned.

معلوم *ma^c^luum* (p.p. of علم *^c^ilim*) 1. having been known, known. هذا شي معلوم *haaða šayyin ma^c^luum.* This is a known thing. 2. fixed, specific. كمية معلومة *kammiyya ma^c^luuma* fixed quantity.

معلومية *ma^c^luumiyya* p. *-aat* information, data. أبي أزيدك معلومية عني *'abi 'aziidak ma^c^luumiyya ^c^anni.* I would like to give you more information about me.

معلم *mu^c^allim* p. *-iin.* 1. teacher, instructor. 2. (as act. part. from II علم *^c^allam*) having taught. هو معلمني الملاكمة *huwa m^c^allimni l-mulaakama.* He taught me how to box.

ع ل ن *^c^ln*

أعلن *'a^c^lan* IV 1. to announce, declare. ما أعلنوا الأخبار بعد *ma 'a^c^lanaw l-'axbaar ba^c^ad.* They haven't announced the news yet. أعلنوا الحرب على جيرانهم *'a^c^lanaw l-ḥarb ^c^ala yiiraanhum.* They declared war on their neighbors. الشركة أعلنت الإفلاس *š-šarika 'a^c^lanat l-'iflaas.* The

ع ل ن …ده مد رجلك على قد لحـــافك *midd riilak ᶜala gadd l-ḥaafak.* As you make your bed you must lie in it. على كيفـــك *ᶜala keefak* slowly, carefully. امشي علـــى كيفـــك *'imši ᶜala keefak.* Walk (or drive) slowly and carefully. 3. about, on, concerning. حكى على القضية ساعتين *ḥiča ᶜala l-gaðiyya saaᶜteen.* He talked about the case for two hours. آنا شعلي منه؟ *'aana š-ᶜalayya minna?* Why should I care about him? على حساب *ᶜala ḥsaab* on account of, on behalf of. 4. against. يحكى عليك في غيابك *yḥači ᶜaleek fi ġyaabak.* He talks about you in your absence. (prov.) على هامان يا فرعون! *ᶜala haamaan ya farᶜoon!* You can't pull the wool over my eyes. You can't fool me. (prov.) ايش على الذيب من ضراط النعجـــة؟ *'eeš ᶜala ð-ðiib min ðraaṭ li-nᶜaya?!* (lit., "What harm can the fart of a ewe do to the wolf?!"). 5. for, over, about. يموت على فلس *ymuut ᶜala fils.* He will die for a penny. يبكي علـــى أيـــام زمـــان *yibči ᶜala 'ayyaam zamaan.* He cries over the good old days.

أعلـــى *'aᶜla* (elat.) 1. (with من *min*) higher, more elevated than. 2. (with foll. n.) the highest, most elevated.

عـــالي *ᶜaali* 1. high, tall, elevated. طوفة عالية *ṭoofa ᶜaalya* high wall. عمارة عالية *ᶜmaara ᶜaalya* tall building. جبل عالي *yibal ᶜaali* high mountain. 2. high, inflated. سعر عالي *siᶜir ᶜaali* high price. 3. loud, strong (voice). صوت عالي *ṣoot ᶜaali* loud voice. ضغط عالي *ðaġṭ ᶜaali* high pressure. 4. high-ranking, exalted. وظيفة عاليـــة *waðiifa ᶜaalya* high position. درجة عالية *daraja ᶜaalya* high

company declared bankruptcy. 2. to advertise. أعلنوا في الجريدة الهم محتـــاجين قزازيـــن *'aᶜlanaw fi l-jariida 'inhum miḥtaayiin gazzaaziin.* They announced in the newspaper that they were in need of (land) surveyors.

علنـــاً *ᶜalanan* (adv.) openly, publicly. قالهـــا علنـــاً *gaalha ᶜalanan.* He said it openly.

إعلان *'iᶜlaan* (v.n. from IV أعلن *'aᶜlan*) p. *-aat* 1. announcement, declaration. لوحة الإعلانـــات *lawḥat l-'iᶜlaanaat* the bulletin board. 2 advertisement, ad.

ع ل ي *ᶜly*

علـــي *ᶜili* (يعلى *yiᶜla*) to rise, ascend. ذالحين الحرارة تعلى يوم بعـــد يـــوم *ðaḥlin l-ḥaraara tiᶜla yoom baᶜd yoom.* Now, the temperature rises every day. الطايرة تعلى شوية شويـــة *ṭ-ṭaayra tiᶜla šwayya šwayya.* The airplane is climbing slowly.

علـــى *ᶜalla* II to raise. علي صوتك؛ ما أقـــدر أسمعـــك *ᶜalli ṣootak; ma 'agdar 'asmaᶜk.* Raise your voice; I cannot hear you.

تعـــال *taᶜaal*, تعالي *taᶜaali* see under ت ع ل *tᶜl*

علو *ᶜilu* (v.n. from علي *ᶜili*) height. شقد علـــو العمـــارة؟ *š-gadd ᶜilu li-ᶜmaara?* How high is the building?

علـــى *ᶜala* 1. on, on top of. على الطوفة *ᶜala ṭ-ṭoofa* on the wall. على كيسي *ᶜala čiisi* on my bill, at my expense. على هاالخشـــم *ᶜala hal-xašim.* Gladly, with pleasure. 2. in accordance with, according to. على قد الحـــال *ᶜala gadd l-ḥaal* to a limited extent. (prov.) مد

degree.

ع م ب ر ᶜmbr

عمبر ᶜambar var. of عنبر ᶜanbar. See under **ع ن ب ر** ᶜnbr.

ع م ج ᶜmj var. of ᶜmg. See under **ع م گ** ᶜmg.

ع م د ᶜmd

تعمد tᶜammad V 1. to do s.th. intentionally. تعمد يكذب علينا tᶜammad yičðib ᶜaleena. He intentionally lied to us. 2. to intend. تعمد وعيب علينا قدام الناس tᶜammad w-ᶜayyab ᶜaleena jiddaam n-naas He intentionally insulted us in front of the people.

اعتمد ᶜtimad VIII (with على ᶜala) to depend on, rely on. اعتمد على نفسك. لا تعتمد على الغير ᶜtimid ᶜala nafsak. la tiᶜtimid ᶜala l-ġeer. Depend on yourself. Don't depend on others.

عميد ᶜamiid p. عمدا ᶜumada 1. general (mil. rank). ترفع إلى رتبة عميد traffaᶜ 'ila rutbat ᶜamiid. He was promoted to the rank of general. 2. dean. عميد الكلية ᶜamiid l-kulliyya the college dean.

عمداً ᶜamdan (adv.) intentionally, deliberately. سواها عمداً sawwaaha ᶜamdan. He did it on purpose.

اعتماد ᶜtimaad (v.n. from VIII اعتمد ᶜtimad) reliance, dependence. الاعتماد على النفس li-ᶜtimaad ᶜala n-nafs self-reliance. اوراق اعتماد wraag ᶜtimaad credentials (of a diplomat).

ع م ر ᶜmr

استعمر staᶜmar X to colonize. الفرنسيين استعمروا لبنان عقب الحرب l-faransiyyiin staᶜmaraw libnaan ᶜugb l-ḥarb. The French colonized Lebanon after the war.

عمر ᶜumur p. اعمار ᶜmaar 1. age (of a person). كم عمرك؟ čam ᶜumrak? How old are you? عمري ستين سنة ᶜumri sittiin sana. I'm sixty years old. 2. life, lifetime. الاعمار بيد الله li-ᶜmaar b-yadd illaah. (lit., "One's life, lifetime, is in God's hands.") approx.: I'll take my chances. He passed away; it's God's will.

عمارة ᶜmaara p. عماير ᶜamaayir building. جود فلوس وبنى عمارتين على السيف jawwad fluus w-bina ᶜmaarteen ᶜala s-siif. He saved some money and built two buildings on the seashore.

عمار ᶜamaar (no recorded p.) chain or rope to which the anchor of a merchant vessel is tied.

عمران ᶜimraan construction, building, development. فيه حركة عمران هني fii ḥarakat ᶜimraan hni. There is construction activity here.

معماري miᶜmaari architectural, structural. مهندس معماري muhandis miᶜmaari architect.

استعمار stiᶜmaar (v.n. from X استعمر staᶜmar) colonization, colonizing.

استعماري stiᶜmaari 1. imperialistic. 2. imperialist.

مستعمرة mistaᶜmara p. -aat colony, settlement.

ع م گ ᶜmg

عمق ᶜumg (common var. عمج ᶜumj) depth, deepness. كم عمق البير؟ čam ᶜumg l-biir? How deep is the well?

عميــق ^c^amiig (common var. عميــج ^c^amiij) deep. بير عميق *biir ^c^amiig* deep well.

ع م ل ^c^ml

عمل ^c^imal (يعمل y^c^amil) 1. to do s.th. عمل اللازم ^c^imal l-laazim. He did what was required. عمل جهده ^c^imal jihda. He did his best. 2. to make s.th. عمل قهوة ^c^imal gahwa. He made coffee.

عــامل ^c^aamal III to treat, deal with. عاملني باحــترام ^c^aamalni b-ḥtiraam. He treated me with respect. من ذاك اليوم ما عاملتـــه. جــلاخ. *min ðaak l-yoom ma ^c^aamalta. čallaax.* Since that day I haven't dealt with him. He's a liar.

تعــامل t^c^aamal VI to deal, trade. ما نتعامل وايا بعض الشركات *ma nit^c^aamal wiyya ba^c^ð š-šarikaat.* We don't deal with some companies.

اســتعمل sta^c^mal X to use, utilize. لا تستعمل السيارة *la tista^c^mil s-sayyaara.* Don't use the car.

عمل ^c^amal 1. work, employment. هذا مــن عمــل الشيطــان *haaða min ^c^amal š-šayṭaan.* This is the work of the devil. 2. (p. أعمال *'a^c^maal*) operation, deed. أعمال الشركة *'a^c^maal š-šarika* the company operations.

عمليــة ^c^amaliyya p. *-aat* operation (med.). حجــرة العمليــات *ḥijrat l-^c^amaliyyaat* the operating room. عمل عمليــة ^c^imal ^c^amaliyya. He had an operation.

عملــة ^c^umla p. *-aat* currency (in circulation). عملة صعبــة ^c^umla ṣa^c^ba hard currency.

عميل ^c^amiil p. عملا ^c^umala agent. واحد من عملانــا *waaḥid min ^c^umalaana* one of our agents. عميل اســتعمار ^c^amiil sti^c^maar agent of imperialism.

معمــل ma^c^mal p. معامل ma^c^aamil factory, plant.

معاملــة mu^c^aamala (v.n. from III عامل ^c^aamal) 1. treatment. عاملني معاملة زينة ^c^aamalni mu^c^aamala zeena. He treated me well. 2. (p. *-aat*) business dealings.

اســتعمال sti^c^maal (v.n. from X استعمل sta^c^mal) use, usage. ممنوع استعمال الهارن *mamnuu^c^ sti^c^maal l-haaran.* The use of the horn is prohibited.

عامل ^c^aamil p. عمال ^c^ummaal laborer, worker. يشتغل عامل في البلديــة *yištaġil ^c^aamil fi l-baladiyya.* He works as a laborer for the municipality. قانون العمل والعمــال *gaanuun l-^c^amal w-l-^c^umaal* labor law. حزب العمال *ḥizb l-^c^ummaal* the labor party.

ع م ل گ ^c^mlg

عمــلاق ^c^imlaag p. عمالقة ^c^amaalga 1. giant. 2. huge, gigantic.

ع م م ^c^mm

عم ^c^amm (يعم y^c^imm) to be or become prevalent, general, to prevail, spread. عقب ما انتــــهت الحــرب الســلام عــم *^c^ugub-ma ntihat l-ḥarbs-salaam ^c^amm.* After the war had ended, peace prevailed.

عمــم ^c^ammam II to make generally known (and applicable). الوزير عمــم القانون الجديد على كل الدوايـــر *l-waziir ^c^ammam l-gaanuun l-yidiid ^c^ala kill d-dawaayir.* The minister made the new law generally known and applicable to all the departments.

عم ^{c}*amm* p. اعمام ^{c}*maam* 1. paternal uncle. عمي وخالي كانوا في العرس ^{c}*ammi w-xaaḷi čaanaw fi l-*^{c}*irs.* My paternal and maternal uncles were at the wedding. ابن عمي *'ibin* ^{c}*ammi* my cousin (on the father's side). بنت عمي *bint* ^{c}*ammi* my female cousin (on the father's side). 2. master, employer. عمي ^{c}*ammi* my master (said by a domestic servant).

عمة ^{c}*amma* p. *-aat* 1. paternal aunt. 2. lady (of the house), mistress. عمتي ^{c}*ammati* my lady (said by a domestic servant).

عمة ^{c}*imma* p. عمايم ^{c}*amaayim* holy man's turban (symbol of piety). (prov.) بالنهار عمايم وبالليل خمايم *b-n-nahaar* ^{c}*amaayim w-b-l-leel xamaayim.* Fair without and foul within. (lit. "In daylight they are turbans, i.e., holy men with turbans, and at night they are garbage, i.e., rascals, knaves, etc.").

عمومي ^{c}*umuumi* public. تلفون عمومي *talafoon* ^{c}*umuumi* public telephone.

عام ^{c}*aamm* 1. public. وزارة الأشغال العامة *wazaarat l-'ašġaal l-*^{c}*aamma* the ministry of public works. حديقة عامة *ḥadiiga* ^{c}*aamma* public garden, park. المصلحة العامة *l-maṣlaḥa l-*^{c}*aamma* the public welfare. 2. general. مدير عام *mudiir* ^{c}*aamm* director general.

عامي ^{c}*aammi* p. عوام ^{c}*awaamm* 1. common man, ordinary person. 2. illiterate person. f. عامية ^{c}*aamiyya.*

ع م ن[1] ^{c}*mn*

عمان ^{c}*ammaan* Amman (capital of Jordan).

ع م ن[2] ^{c}*mn*

عمان ^{c}*maan* 1. Oman (the Sultanate of Oman). 2. Al-Ain and vicinity, the Al-Ain area. سرنا عمان *sirna* ^{c}*maan.* We went to the Al-Ain area.

عماني ^{c}*maani* 1. characteristic of Oman. لومي عماني *luumi* ^{c}*maani* Omani lemons. 2. (p. *-yya, -yyiin* Omani person, Omani citizen.

ع م ي ^{c}*my*

انعمى *n*^{c}*ima* VII to be or become blind, lose one's eyesight. صار كبير وانعمى *ṣaar čibiir w-n*^{c}*ima.* He became old and went blind.

عمى ^{c}*ima* blindness.

عمي ^{c}*amay* f. عميا ^{c}*amya* p. عميان ^{c}*imyaan* 1. blind. عمي القلب ^{c}*amay l-gaḷb* blind of heart. 2. blind person. (prov.) العور بين العميان باشا *l-*^{c}*awar been l-*^{c}*imyaan baaša.* The one-eyed man in the country of the blind is king.

ع ن ^{c}*n*

عن ^{c}*an* (prep.) 1. about, on. رمسته عن ذيك القضية *rammasta* ^{c}*an ðiič l-gaðiya.* I talked to him about that matter. 2. away from, off. راحوا عن ديرتهم *raaḥaw* ^{c}*an diirattum.* They went away from their country. ابعد عن الشر *'ib*^{c}*id* ^{c}*an š-šarr.* Keep away from evil. 3. out of, due to. سويت هذا عن خطا *sawweet haaða* ^{c}*an xaṭa.* I did that by mistake. عن جهل ^{c}*an jahil* out of ignorance. عن إخلاص ^{c}*an 'ixlaaṣ* faithfully, out of sincere concern. عن رغبـــــة *ᶜan raġba* willingly. 4. as protection from, against. لابس كشمة عن الشمـــس *laabis čašma ᶜan š-šams.* He's wearing glasses as protection from the sun. 5. per, for. خمسة دينار عن كل نفـــر *xamsa diinaar ᶜan kill nafar* five dinars per person. دفعت عشـــرة درهم عن كل يـــوم *difaᶜt ᶜašara dirhim ᶜan kill yoom.* I paid ten dirhams for each day. عن طريق *ᶜan ṭariig* by way of, via. سافرت لندن عن طريق البحريـــن *saafart landan ᶜan ṭariig l-baḥreen.* I traveled to London by way of Bahrain.

ع ن ب *ᶜnb*

عنـــب *ᶜinab* grapes (coll.). العنب غالي *l-ᶜinab ġaali.* Grapes are expensive. فيه عنب في السوق *fii ᶜinab fi s-suug.* There are grapes in the market. اشتريت عنب *štireet ᶜinab.* I bought (some) grapes. حبة عنب *ḥabbat ᶜinab* a grape.

ع ن ب ر ١ *ᶜnbr*

عنبر *ᶜanbar* (coll.) ambergris.

ع ن ب ر ٢ *ᶜnbr*

عنـــبر *ᶜanbar* p. عنابر *ᶜanaabir* storehouse. عنـــابر الشركـــة في دبي *ᶜanaabir š-šarika fi dbayy.* The company storehouses are in Dubai. كاتب العنبر *kaatib l-ᶜanbar* the storekeeper.

ع ن ب ر ٣ *ᶜnbr*

عنـــبر *ᶜanbar* Anbar (name of a slave). (prov.) عنبر أخو بلال *ᶜanbar 'uxu bḷaaḷ.* Two peas in a pod.

ع ن ت ك *ᶜntk*

عنتيكة *ᶜantiika* (invar.) old, antiquated. سيارة عنتيكة *sayyaara ᶜantiika* old car. طفايـــــة عنتيكـــة *ṭaffaaya ᶜantiika* antiquated ashtray.

ع ن ت و ت *ᶜntwt*

عنتـــوت *ᶜantuut* p. عنـــاتيت *ᶜanaatiit* clitoris.

ع ن د *ᶜnd*

عنـــد *ᶜannad* II to be or become stubborn, to insist. عند وما سمع كلام أبـــوه *ᶜannad w-ma simaᶜ kalaam 'ubuu.* He got stubborn and didn't obey his father. عند إلا يروح يشوفها *ᶜannad 'illa yruuḥ yšuuffa.* He insisted on going to see her.

عـــاند *ᶜaanad* III to disobey, oppose, resist. لا تعاند أمـــك وأبـــوك *la tᶜaanid 'ummak w-'ubuuk.* Don't disobey your parents.

عند *ᶜind* 1. (with foll. human n.) with. الســـيارة عنـــد جارنـــا *s-sayyaara ᶜind yaarna.* The car is (parked) at our neighbor's. التنديل عند الوزيـــر *t-tindeel ᶜind l-waziir.* The foreman is with the minister. 2. (with foll. suff. pron.) to have. عنده فلـــوس واجـــد *ᶜinda fluus waayid.* He has a lot of money. عندي لك خبر زين *ᶜindi lak xabar zeen.* I have good news for you. جاوا عندنا وسولفنا *jaw ᶜindana w-soolafna.* They came to our place and we talked. بتنا عندهم ليلة *bitna ᶜindahum leela.* We stayed overnight at their place. 3. (with foll. non-human n.) at, near, by. عند الضيق *ᶜind ḍ-ḍiig* at the time of distress. عند الحاجة *ᶜind l-ḥaaja* at the time of need, in an emergency. السفارة عنـــــد وزارة الخارجيـــــة *s-safaara ᶜind wazaarat l-xaarijiyya.* The embassy is near the foreign ministry.

عنيد ^c^*aniid* 1. stubborn, obstinate. 2. stubborn person.

ع ن د گ ^c^*ndg*

عندق ^c^*andag* (coll.) red mullet. s. *-a* a red mullet.

ع ن ز ^c^*nz*

عنز ^c^*anz* p. عنز ^c^*inaz* nanny goat. التيس هو ذكر العنز *t-tees huwa ðakar l-*^c^*anz.* A billy goat is the male of a nanny goat. (prov.) العنز ما تطالع شقها *l-*^c^*anz ma ṭṭaali*^c^ *šiggha.* approx.: He's one who refuses to see his own faults. (prov.) عنز الجبل تحب التيس الغريب ^c^*anz l-yibal tḥibb t-tees l-ġariib.* approx.: Variety is the spice of life.

ع ن گ د ^c^*ngd*

عنقود ^c^*anguud* p. عناقيد ^c^*anaagiid* cluster (of grapes). (prov.) اللي ما يطول العنقود يقول حامض *'illi ma yṭuul l-*^c^*anguud yguul ḥaamiḍ.* Sour grapes.

ع ن ك ب و ت ^c^*nkwbt*

عنكبوت ^c^*ankabuut* p. عناكب ^c^*anaakib* spider.

ع ن و ن ^c^*nwn*

عنون ^c^*anwan* (يعنون *y*^c^*anwin)* to address. كتب الخط وعنونه باسم الشركة *kitab l-xaṭṭ w-*^c^*anwana b-'asim š-šarika.* He wrote the letter and addressed it with the company's name.

عنوان ^c^*inwaan* 1. address. شو عنوانك؟ *šu* ^c^*inwaanak?* What's your address? 2. title (of a lecture, a book, etc.) بعنوان *bi-*^c^*inwaan* entitled, by the title of. في محاضرة اليوم بعنوان «الزكاة في الإسلام» *fii muḥaaḍara l-yoom bi-*^c^*inwaan z-zakaa fi l-'islaam.* There is a lecture today entitled "Alms (tax) in Islam."

ع ن ي ^c^*ny*

عنى ^c^*ina* (يعني *y*^c^*ani)* to mean, to have in mind. ويش تعني بهالكلام؟ *weeš t*^c^*ani b-hal-kalaam?* What do you mean by these words?

يعني *y*^c^*ani* 1. that is, in other words. يعني بتاخذينه بالطيب والا بالغصب *y*^c^*ani b-taaxðiina b-ṭ-ṭiib walla b-l-ġaṣb.* In other words, you take him (as a husband) by hook or by crook. 2. (parenthetical remark, approx.: then, therefore) أريد أعرس. يعني أبغى فلوس *'ariid 'a*^c^*arris. y*^c^*ani 'abġa fluus.* I would like to get married. Therefore, I want money.

اعتنى ^c^*tina* VIII (with ب *b-*) to take care of. يعتني بصحته واجد *yi*^c^*tini b-ṣiḥḥata waayid.* He takes good care of his health.

عناية ^c^*inaaya* (with ب *b-*) taking care of, caring for. العناية بالجهال *l-*^c^*inaaya b-l-yihhaal* taking care of children. العناية بالوالدين *l-*^c^*inaaya b-l-waaldeen* taking care of parents.

معنى *ma*^c^*na* p. معاني *ma*^c^*aani* meaning, sense. شو معنى ها الكلمة؟ *šu ma*^c^*na hač-čalma?* What's the meaning of this word? بكل معنى الكلمة *b-kill ma*^c^*na č-čalma* in every sense of the word. حكي ما له معنى *ḥači ma la ma*^c^*na* meaningless talk. شمعنى تجي وما تمر علينا؟ *š-ma*^c^*na tiyi w-ma tmurr* ^c^*aleena?* What do you mean by coming and not stopping at our place?

ع ه د ^c^*hd*

تعهد *t*^c^*ahhad* V 1. to promise. تعهد ما

يسويها مرة ثانية tᶜahhad ma ysawwiiha marra θaanya. He promised not to do it again. 2. to undertake, obligate oneself, pledge oneself. القزاز تعهد يقز الأرض باكر l-gazzaaz tᶜahhad ygizz l'arḍ baačir. The surveyor undertook to survey the land tomorrow. 3. to guarantee, take on oneself. تعهد لنا بالمبلغ tᶜahhad lana b-l-mablaġ. He guaranteed us the (sum of) money.

تعاهد *tᶜaahad* VI to vow, make a mutual pledge. تعاهدوا يبقون حبايب *tᶜaahdaw yibguun ḥabaayib.* They vowed to remain dear friends.

عهد *ᶜahd* 1. pledge, promise. 2. (with ب *b-*) knowledge. عهدي بي، ما يكلخ *ᶜahdi bii, ma yčallix.* To my knowledge, he doesn't lie. 3. time, era. في ذاك العهد *fi ðaak l-ᶜahd* during that time. ولي العهد *wali l-ᶜahd* the crown prince.

عهدة *ᶜuhda* (with ب *b-*) in the charge of, under the care of. توكل على الله وخلي كل شي بعهدتي *twakkal ᶜala ḷḷa w-xaḷḷi kill šayy b-ᶜuhdati.* Trust in God, and leave everything in my charge.

معهد *maᶜhad* p. معاهد *maᶜaahid* institute. معهد الإنكليزي *maᶜhad l-'ingiliizi* the English language institute.

معاهدة *muᶜaahada* p. *-aat* treaty.

متعهد *mitᶜahhid* p. *-iin* contractor, supplier.

ع ه ر ᶜhr

عاهرة *ᶜaahira* p. *-aat* prostitute, harlot.

ع و ج ᶜwj see under **ع و ي** *ᶜwy.*

ع و د ᶜwd

عاد *ᶜaad* (يعود *yᶜuud*) to return, come back. ترييناه الين عاد *trayyeenaa 'ileen ᶜaad.* We waited for him until he returned.

عاد *ᶜaad* (*yᶜiid*) 1. to repeat. لا تعيد ها الكلام! *la tᶜiid hal-kalaam!* Don't repeat these words. عيد اللي قلته مرة ثانية *ᶜiid illi gilta marra θaanya.* Repeat what you have said again. عاد النظر *ᶜaad n-naḍar* to reconsider. القاضي عاد النظر في القضية *l-ġaaḍi ᶜaad n-naḍar fi l-gaḍiyya.* The judge reconsidered the case. 2. to return, send back, give back. عادوا الحيول حق الصايغ *ᶜaadaw li-ḥyuul ḥagg ṣ-ṣaayiġ.* They returned the bracelets to the jeweler. عادوه للسجن *ᶜaadoo l-s-sijin.* They sent him back to jail.

عود *ᶜawwad* II 1. to return, go back. اشتغل في الخارج وعود عقب خمس سنين *štiġal fi l-xaarij w-ᶜawwad ᶜugub xams siniin.* He worked abroad and returned after five years. عود من هني *ᶜawwid min hni.* Go back from here. 2. (with على *ᶜala*) to make s.o. get used to s.th., accustom s.o. to s.th. عودوه على النش الفجر *ᶜawwadoo ᶜala n-našš l-fajir.* They made him get used to getting up at daybreak.

تعود *tᶜawwad* V to get accustomed to, to accustom oneself to. تعود يدش الزام متأخر *tᶜawwad ydišš z-zaam mit'axxir.* He got accustomed to going to work late.

انعاد *nᶜaad* VII 1. to be returned, taken back. الحيول انعادوا حق الصايغ *li-ḥyuul nᶜaadaw ḥagg ṣ-ṣaayiġ.* The bracelets were returned to the jeweler. 2. to be repeated.

عــود *ᶜuud* p. اعواد *ᶜwaad* 1. (wood) stick. عطــر العــود *ᶜiṭir l-ᶜuud* kind of incense. (prov.) كل عود فيه دخان *kill ᶜuud fii dxaan.* approx.: Nothing is perfect. Every gem has a flaw. 2. lute.

عود *ᶜood* (no p.) f. عودة *ᶜooda* 1. big, large. المسجد العــود *li-msiid l-ᶜood* the big mosque. 2. old. حرمة عودة *ḥurma ᶜooda* old woman.

عــاد *ᶜaad* (with preced. or foll. imp.) then, therefore. هاك درهم! يالله علمــني عاد! *haak dirhim! yaḷḷa ᶜallimni ᶜaad!* This is a dirham for you! Tell me then!

عــادي *ᶜaadi* 1. regular, ordinary. أبغى بانزين عادي، موب ممتــاز *'abġa baanziin ᶜaadi, muub mumtaaz.* I want regular gasoline, not premium. شي عادي *šayy ᶜaadi* ordinary thing. 2. (p. *-yyiin*) simple, plain, ordinary (person). شخص عادي *šuxṣ ᶜaadi* simple person.

عيــادة *ᶜiyada* p. *-aat* 1. clinic, infirmary. هالحين تحصل عيادة في كل مكــان *halḥiin tḥaṣṣil ᶜiyaada fi kill mukaan.* Nowadays, you'll find a clinic in every place. 2. physician's office. رحــت السبيتار وقال الدختر، «تعــال شوفــني في العيــادة» *riḥt s-sbeetaar w-gaal d-daxtar, "taᶜaal šuufni fi l-ᶜiyaada."* I went to the hospital and the doctor said, "Come see me at my private office." عيــادة خارجيــة *ᶜiyaada xaarijiyya* outpatient clinic.

اعتيــاد *ᶜtiyaad* getting accustomed. الاعتياد على الصــوم مــن الصغــر زيــن *li-ᶜtiyaad ᶜala ṣ-ṣoom min ṣ-ṣiġar zeen.* Getting accustomed to fasting at an early age is good.

عايد *ᶜaayid* (act. part. from عاد *ᶜaad*) p. *-iin* having returned. توني عايد من ناك *tawwni ᶜaayid min naak.* I have just returned from there.

معيــد *muᶜiid* p. *-iin* 1. teaching assistant (in a university or a college). 2. repeater (in a class) هو معيد في هــذا الصــف *huwa muᶜiid fi haaða ṣ-ṣaff.* He's repeating this class.

متعود *mitᶜawwid* (act. part. from V تعود *tᶜawwad*) used to, accustomed. متعود يــدش الشغــل متــأخر *mitᶜawwid ydišš š-šuġul mit'axxir.* He's used to going to work late. متعــود علــى الرذالــة *mitᶜawwid ᶜala r-raðaala* He's used to profanity.

معتاد *miᶜtaad* = متعود *mitᶜawwid.*

عوذ *ᶜwð*

عــاذ *ᶜaað (يعــــود yᶜuuð)*: أعوذ بالله! *'aᶜuuðu b-l-laah!* (used when something evil, shameful, etc., is mentioned) God forbid! God save me from that! Heaven forbid! (lit., "I seek refuge in God.").

عيــاذ *ᶜiyaað:* العيــاذ بــالله! *l-ᶜiyaaðu b-l-laah!* = أعوذ بالله! *'aᶜuuðu b-l-laah!*

عور *ᶜwr*

عور *ᶜawwar* II to injure, hurt. عور يده وفنــش *ᶜawwar yadda w-fannaš.* He injured his hand and resigned. بس! عورتــه *bass! ᶜawwarta.* Enough! You hurt him. راسي يعورني *raasi yᶜawwirni.* I have a headache.

تعــور *tᶜawwar* V to be injured, to get

hurt. تعورت يده وفنش *tᶜawwarat yadda w-fannaš.* His hand was injured and he resigned. طاح على الأرض وتعور *ṭaaḥ ᶜala l-'arḍ w-tᶜawwar.* He fell to the ground and was hurt.

عور *ᶜawar* p. عوران *ᶜiwraan* f. عورة *ᶜoora* 1. one-eyed, blind in one eye. 2. one-eyed man. (prov.) العور بين العميان باشا *l-ᶜawar been l-ᶜimyaan baaša.* In the country of the blind, the one-eyed man is king. (prov.) العورة تعيب على أم زر *l-ᶜoora tᶜayyib ᶜala 'umm zirr.* The pot is calling the kettle black.

عوار *ᶜawaar* 1. pain (esp. stomach pain). 2. injury.

عوز *ᶜwz*

عاز *ᶜaaz* (يعوز *yᶜuuz*) to be needed, to be lacking. الحمد لله! ما يعوزني شي *l-ḥamdu li-llaah! ma yᶜuuzni šayy.* Praise be to God! I don't need anything. ها السيارة يعوزها رنق جديد *has-sayyaara yᶜuuzha rang yidiid.* This car needs new paint.

عوسج *ᶜwsj*

عوسج *ᶜoosaj* (coll.) boxthorn, boxthorn plant.

عوظ *ᶜwḍ*

عوض *ᶜawwaḍ* II to compensate, recompense. الشركة عوضته عن العوار اللي صابه *š-šarika ᶜawwaḍata ᶜan l-ᶜawaar illi ṣaaba.* The company compensated him for the injury he had suffered.

عوض *ᶜawaḍ* compensation, recompense, indemnity. (prov.) العوض ولا القطيعة *l-ᶜawaḍ wala l-gaṭiiᶜa.* Something is better than nothing. Half a loaf is better than none.

تعويض *taᶜwiiḍ* (v.n. from عوض *ᶜawwaḍ*) act of compensating, reparation. تعويض عن الخسارة *taᶜwiiḍ ᶜan l-xasaara* compensation for the loss. طالب بالتعويض *ṭaalab b-t-taᶜwiiḍ.* He demanded compensation.

عوف *ᶜwf*

عاف *ᶜaaf* (يعيف *yᶜiif*) to feel disgust at s.th., detest s.th., have an aversion to s.th. عفت اللي قاله *ᶜift illi gaala.* I felt disgusted at what he had said. عفت ذيك العادة وهديتها *ᶜift ðiič l-ᶜaada w-haddetta.* I detested that habit and gave it up.

عوف *ᶜoof* (v.n.) disgust, aversion.

عوگ *ᶜwg*

عوق *ᶜoog* disease, ailment, malady. شو عوقك؟ *šu ᶜoogak?* What ails you? عوقي بصري *ᶜoogi baṣari.* My eyesight is failing.

عوم *ᶜwm*

عام *ᶜaam* (يعوم *yᶜuum*) 1. to swim. تقدر تعوم هني؟ *tigdar tᶜuum hni?* Can you swim here? 2. to float. الحطب يعوم فوق الماي *l-ḥaṭab yᶜuum foog l-maay.* Wood floats in water.

عوم *ᶜawwam* II to set afloat, to float s.th.

عوم *ᶜoom* (v.n. from عام *ᶜaam*) swimming.

عام *ᶜaam* p. أعوام *'aᶜwaam* year. في ذاك العام *fi ðaak l-ᶜaam* in that year. العام الماضي *l-ᶜaam l-maaḍi* last year.

عايم *ᶜaayim* (act. part. from عام *ᶜaam*) floating. كبري عايم *kubri ᶜaayim* floating bridge.

عون ᶜwn

عان ᶜ*aan (يعين yᶜiin)* to help, assist, aid. الله يعينـــك *'aḷḷa yᶜiinak!* God help you! الله يعينك على هـــا العايلـــة الكبـــيرة *'aḷḷa yᶜiinak ᶜala hal-ᶜaayla č-čibiira.* God help you with this big family.

عـــاون ᶜ*aawan* III to help, assist, aid. تقدر تعاونني أشيل هـــا الصنـــدوق؟ *tigdar tᶜaawinni 'ašiil haṣ-ṣanduug?* Can you help me carry this box?

تعـــاون *tᶜaawan* VI to cooperate, help each other. خوش رجال. يتعاون وايا كل واحـــد *xooš rayyaal. yitᶜaawan wiyya kill waaḥid.* He's a good man. He cooperates with everyone. لازم نتعاون لاجل نخلـــص الشغـــل *laazim nitᶜaawan lajil nxaḷḷis š-šuġul.* We have to help each other in order to finish the work.

اســـتعان *staᶜaan* X to seek help. لحيةٍ غانمة. كل واحـــد يســـتعين فيـــه *liḥyatin ġaanma. kill waaḥid yistaᶜiin fii.* He's a man with an irresistible appeal. Everyone goes to him for help.

عون ᶜ*oon* (v.n. from عان ᶜ*aan*) 1. help, assistance. عنده عايلة كبيرة. الله يكون في عونه! ᶜ*inda ᶜaayla čibiira. 'aḷḷa ykuun fi ᶜoona!* He has a big family. God help him! 2. (p. أعوان *'aᶜwaan*) helper, supporter. هو من أعوان الوزير *huwa min 'aᶜwaan l-waziir.* He's one of the supporters of the minister.

معونة *maᶜuuna* = عون ᶜ*oon.*

عوينـــة ᶜ*weena* = عون ᶜ*oon.* يا عوينة الله عليـــه! *ya ᶜweent aḷḷa ᶜalee!* approx.: He'll want God's assistance for that.

تعـــاون *taᶜaawun* (v.n. from VI تعاون *taᶜaawan*) cooperation. مجلس التعـــاون الخليجي *majlis t-taᶜaawun l-xaliiji* the Gulf Cooperation Council.

معين *muᶜiin* supporter, helper, assistant (said only of God). الله هو المعين *'aḷḷaah huwa l-muᶜiin* (lit., "God is the supporter.") approx: God will provide. يا الله يا معين! *ya 'aḷḷaah ya muᶜiin!* (said in time of distress, or when lifting a heavy weight, pushing an object, etc.).

تعـــاوني *taᶜaawuni* cooperative. جمعية تعاونيـــــــة *jamᶜiyya taᶜaawuniyya* cooperative society.

عوه ᶜwh

عاهـــة ᶜ*aaha* p. *-aat* (bodily) defect, physical handicap.

عوي ١ ᶜwy

عـــوى ᶜ*iwa (يعوي yᶜawi)* to howl (dog, wolf, jackal). الكلب كان يعوي *č-čalb čaan yᶜawi.* The dog was barking. الذيب كان يعوي لانه كان جوعـــان *ð-ðiib čaan yᶜawi linna čaan juuᶜaan.* The wolf was howling because it was hungry.

عوي ٢ ᶜwy

عوى ᶜ*iwa (يعوي yᶜawi)* to bend, twist. عوى القضيب ᶜ*iwa l-gaḍiib.* He bent the rod.

انعـــوى *nᶜiwa* VII to be or become bent, twisted. دعامة السيارة انعويت بسبب الدعمة *daᶜᶜaamaat s-sayyaara nᶜiwyat b-sabab d-daᶜma.* The car bumper got bent because of the collision.

عـــوي ᶜ*away* p. عوي ᶜ*uuy* f. عوية ᶜ*ooya*

1. bent, crooked, twisted, not straight. (prov.) ذنب الكلب عوي *ðanab č-čalb ᶜaway.* A leopard cannot change his spots. 2. winding, twisting. رستة عوية *rasta ᶜooya* (paved) winding road.

ع ي ب ᶜyb

عاب *ᶜaab (يعيب yᶜiib)* (with على *ᶜala*) 1. to call s.o. bad names. هاوشني وعاب عليّ *haawašni w-ᶜaab ᶜalayya.* He quarreled with me and called me bad names.

عيب *ᶜayyab* II 1. (with على *ᶜala*) to make fun of s.o. الجاهل قام يعيب على أخته *l-yaahil gaam yᶜayyib ᶜala 'uxta.* The child started to make fun of his sister. 2. to insult. هو اللي عيب علينا وهاوشنا *huwa lli ᶜayyab ᶜaleena w-haawašna.* He's the one who insulted us and quarreled with us.

عيب *ᶜeeb* p. عيوب *ᶜyuub* 1. defect, blemish. 2. shame, disgrace. عيب عليك! *ᶜeeb ᶜaleek!* Shame on you!

ع ي د ᶜyd

عيد *ᶜayyad* II to celebrate or observe a feast. عيدنا في العين *ᶜayyadna fi l-ᶜeen.* We celebrated the feast in Al-Ain. جا وعيد علينا في عيد الحي *ya w-ᶜayyad ᶜaleena fi ᶜiid l-ḥayy.* He came and celebrated the Pilgrimage Feast with us.

عيد *ᶜiid* p. أعياد *'aᶜyaad* feast, festival, holiday. عيد رمضان *ᶜiid rumðaan* the Ramadan Feast, Lesser Bairam. عيد الضحية *ᶜiid ð-ðiḥiyya* (also known as عيد الحي *ᶜiid l-ḥayy*) the Pilgrimage Feast, Greater Bairam. فيه أعياد دينية ووطنية *fii 'aᶜyaad diiniyya w-waṭaniyya.* There are religious and national holidays. عيد الجلوس *ᶜiid l-yiluus* accession day, coronation day.

ع ي ز ᶜyz

عجز *ᶜiyaz (يعجز yᶜayiz)* 1. to be or become weak, lack strength. ما يقدر يشيل الصندوق لانه عجز *ma yigdar yšiil ṣ-ṣanduug linna ᶜiyaz.* He can't lift the box because he has become weak.

عجز *ᶜayyaz* II to age, grow old. لحيته بيضا والعصا بيده. عجز *liḥyita beeḍa w-l-ᶜaṣa b-yadda. ᶜayyaz.* His beard is grey and the cane is in his hand. He has grown old.

عجز *ᶜayz* deficit, shortage. في عجز في الميزانية *fii ᶜayz fi l-miizaaniyya.* There's a deficit in the budget.

عجوز *ᶜayuuz* p. عجايز *ᶜayaayiz* m. شيبة *šeeba* p. شواب *šuwwaab* 1. old woman, elderly lady. شفت عجوز في سوق السمك *čift ᶜayuuz fi suug s-simač.* I saw an old lady in the fish market. 2. old, elderly. حرمة عجوز *ḥurma ᶜayuuz* old lady.

عاجز *ᶜaayiz* (act. part. from عجز *ᶜiyaz*) 1. weak, feeble. رجال عاجز *rayyaal ᶜaayiz* feeble man. 2. (with عن *ᶜan*) unable to do s.th. عاجز عن الشغل *ᶜaayiz ᶜan š-šuġul* unable to work.

معجزة *miᶜiyza* p. *-aat* miracle (esp. one performed by a prophet).

ع ي س ᶜys

عيس *ᶜiis* (coll.) camels = بعارين *baᶜaariin* s. بعير *biᶜiir.*

ع ي ش ᶜyš

عاش *ᶜaaš (يعيش yᶜiiš)* 1. to live, be

ع ي ف ᶜyf

عـاف ᶜ*aaf* (يعيف *y*ᶜ*iif*). See under **ع و ف** ᶜ*wf.*

ع ي ل ᶜyl

عيـل ᶜ*ayal* (conj.) therefore, for that reason, then. عيل، ما تروح الدختر ᶜ*ayal, ma truuḥ d-daxtar.* Therefore, you won't go to see the doctor. عيـل، مـا تقـدر تشـتغل بـاكر ᶜ*ayal, ma tigdar tištaġil baačir.* Then, you cannot work tomorrow.

عايلة ᶜ*aayla* p. عوايل ᶜ*awaayil* family. عنده عايلة كبيرة ᶜ*inda* ᶜ*aayla čibiira.* He has a large family. هذا مكان حق العوايل *haaða mukaan ḥagg l-*ᶜ*awaayil.* This is a place for families.

عيـل ᶜ*ayyil* p. عيال ᶜ*yaaḷ* child. عيال سالم ᶜ*yaaḷ saalim* Salim's children. عنـده عيـال واجديـن ᶜ*inda* ᶜ*yaaḷ waaydiin.* He has many children.

عيـال ᶜ*ayyaal* p. عيالة *-a* male dancer. f. نعاشـة *na*ᶜᶜ*aaša* p. *-aat.* العيالة يرقصون بالسـيف والخنجـر والبندقيـة *l-*ᶜ*ayyaala yarguṣuun b-s-seef w-l-xanyar w-l-bindigiyya.* Male dancers dance with swords, daggers, and rifles.

ع ي م ᶜym

عجمـي ᶜ*aymi* p. عجـم ᶜ*iyam* (less common var. ᶜ*ajmi* p. ᶜ*ijam*) 1. a Persian. عجمي. مـا يتكلـم عربـي ᶜ*aymi. ma yitkallam* ᶜ*arabi.* He's a Persian. He doesn't speak Arabic. 2. illiterate, unlearned person.

عجمـان ᶜ*aymaan* (common var. ᶜ*ajmaan*) Ajman.

alive (for a period of time), live in a certain manner. عـاش اميـة سـنة ᶜ*aaš 'imyat sana.* He lived a hundred years. عـاش وايـا مـرة أبـوه ᶜ*aaš wiyya murt 'ubuu.* He lived with his step-mother. عـاش ملـك ᶜ*aaš malik.* He lived like a king. 2. to make a living, exist. معاشه علـى قـد الحـال. مـا أدري شـلون يعيـش *ma*ᶜ*aaša* ᶜ*ala gadd l-ḥaal. ma 'adri šloon y*ᶜ*iiš.* His salary doesn't go far. I don't know how he makes a living. 3. to reside, dwell. عشت في بو ظبي عشرين سـنة ᶜ*išt fi bu ḍabi* ᶜ*išriin sana.* I lived in Abu Dhabi for twenty years. ...عاش ᶜ*aaš...* long live... !عاش الشيخ زايد ᶜ*aaš š-šeex zaayid!* Long live Shaikh Zayid! !عاشت ايدك ᶜ*aašat 'iidak!* (said to s.o. who has handed you s.th.) lit., "May your hand live long." f. !عاشت ايدك ᶜ*aašat 'iidič!*

عيـش ᶜ*eeš* (coll.) rice. حبة عيش *ḥabbat* ᶜ*eeš* grain of rice. كليـت عيـش وسمـك *kaleet* ᶜ*eeš w-simač.* I ate rice and fish. العيـش نشـتريه بـالكيس *l-*ᶜ*eeš ništirii b-č-čiis.* We buy rice by the (canvas) sack.

عيش ᶜ*ayyaš* II to support, provide for. الحكومـة تعيـش الفقير *l-ḥukuuma t*ᶜ*ayyiš l-faġiir.* The government helps poor people with living expenses.

عيشة ᶜ*iiša* life, living.

معاش *ma*ᶜ*aaš* salary, pay, stipend.

معيشة *ma*ᶜ*iiša* life, living.

ع ي ظ ᶜyḍ

استعاض *sta*ᶜ*aaḍ* X. See under **ع و ظ** ᶜ*wḍ.*

ع ي ن ᶜyn

عـيـن *ᶜayyan* II 1. to appoint, assign. عينوه مطـارزي حـق الشيـخ *ᶜayyanuu maṭaarzi ḥagg š-šeex.* They appointed him a bodyguard for the Shaikh. 2. to specify, designate. عين لي اللي يبغيـني أجيبه *ᶜayyan-li illi yabġiini 'ayiiba.* He specified what he wanted me to bring.

تعـين *tᶜayyan* V 1. to be appointed, assigned. تعين قزاز في البلديـة *tᶜayyan gazzaaz fi l-baladiyya.* He was appointed a surveyor in the municipality. 2. to be set, fixed, designated. يوم العرس مـا تعـين بعـد *yoom l-ᶜirs ma tᶜayyan baᶜad.* The wedding date hasn't been set yet.

عـين *ᶜeen* p. عيون *ᶜyuun* 1. eye. البنت عيوهـا صاحيـة *l-bint ᶜyuunha ṣaaḥya.* The girl's eyes are sound. The girl has good eyesight. على الراس والعين! *ᶜala r-raas w-l-ᶜeen!* or على راسي وعيـني! *ᶜala raasi w-ᶜeeni!* Gladly! Willingly! (a reply to a request). (prov.) عين ما شـافت مـا لامـت *ᶜeen ma šaafat ma laamat* seeing is believing. 2. water spring. عين عذاري *ᶜeen ᶜaðaari* famous water spring in Bahrain. 3. (stove) burner. كولة أم أربع عيـون *čuula 'umm 'arbaᶜ ᶜyuun* four burner stove. 4. name of the letter ع *ᶜ*.

تعيـين *taᶜyiin* (v.n. from II عين *ᶜayyan*) 1. (p. *-aat*) assignment, appointment. تعيينات المعلمين صدرت في الجريدة أمـس *taᶜyiinaat l-muᶜallimiin ṣadarat fi l-yariida 'ams.* The teachers' (school) assignments were published in the newspaper yesterday. 2. specification, designation. بدون تعيين *b-duun taᶜyiin* at random.

عيان *ᶜayaan* (invar.): شاهد عيان *šaahid ᶜayaan* eyewitness.

معين *mᶜayyan* (p.p. from II عين *ᶜayyan*) 1. appointed, set, fixed. جيت له في وقت معين *yiit-la fi wagt mᶜayyan.* I came to him at an appointed time. 2. having been appointed, assigned. معين معلـم *mᶜayyan muᶜallim.* He has been appointed as a teacher. 3. certain, specific. نحن محتاجين حق أشخاص عندهم مؤهلات معينـة *niḥin miḥtaayiin ḥagg 'ašxaaṣ ᶜindahum mu'ahhalaat mᶜayyana.* We are in need of people who have certain qualifications.

ع ي ي ᶜyy

عـي *ᶜayya* II (with عن *ᶜan*) to refuse. عي عـن العمـل *ᶜayya ᶜan l-ᶜamal.* He refused to work. (with foll. imperf.) to refuse to do s.th. عي يسير وايانا *ᶜayya ysiir wiyyaana.* He refused to come with us.

عياي *ᶜayaay* see under ع ج ج *ᶜjj.*

غ

غ ا د *ġaad*

غاد *ġaad* over there, there. روح غاد *ruuḥ ġaad.* Go there. روح غاد. خلني بروحي! *ruuḥ ġaad. xaḷḷni b-ruuḥi!* Go away! Leave me alone.

غ ا ز *ġaaz*

غاز *ġaaz* (common var. *qaaz*) p. *-aat* gas.

غ ب ش *ġbš*

غبش *ġabbaš* II to go very early in the morning. يغبش لين يدش الشغل *yġabbiš leen ydišš š-šuġul.* He leaves at dawn when he goes to work.

غبشة *ġubša* 1. early morning. 2. in the early morning. يدش الشغل الغبشة *ydišš š-šuġul l-ġubša.* He goes to work at dawn.

غ ب گ *ġbg*

غبقة *ġabga* p. *-aat* light meal, usually taken late at night.

غبوق *ġubuug* late night.

غ ب ن *ġbn*

غبن *ġubun* loss. (prov.) الحي يحييك والميت يزيدك غبن *l-ḥayy yiḥyiik w-l-mayyit yziidak ġubun.* lit., "A living person gives you (new) life and a dead person makes your loss greater." صابه غبن لين اشترى السيارة *ṣaaba ġubun leen štira s-sayyaara.* He got a raw deal when he bought the car.

غ ب ي *ġby*

غبي *ġabi* (more common var. قبي *qabi*) See under **ق ب ي** *qby.*

غ ت ر *ġtr*

غترة *ġitra* p. غتر *ġitar* men's headcloth. غترة وعقال *ġitra w-ᶜgaaḷ* headcloth and head band (known as the head gear; the عقال *ᶜgaaḷ* holds the غترة *ġitra* in place).

غ ت م *ġtm*

غتم *ġatam* f. غتمة *ġatma* p. غتمان *ġitmaan* 1. dumb. 2. mute.

غ ث ث *ġθθ*

غث *ġaθθ (يغث yġiθθ)* to bother, upset, trouble. هذي المشكلة تغث الإنسان *haaði l-muškila tġiθθ l-'insaan.* This problem bothers people. لا تغث روحك! *la tġiθθ ruuḥak!* Don't bother yourself. منو اللي غثك؟ *minu lli ġaθθak?* Who upset you?

انغث *nġaθθ* VII pass. of غث *ġaθθ.*

غثة *ġiθθa* (v.n. from غث *ġaθθ*) bother, trouble.

غ د ر *ġdr*

غدر *ġidar (يغدر yġadir)* to act treacherously toward s.o., doublecross, deceive. هذا موب صديق، ترى يغدرك *haaða muub ṣidiij, tara yġadrak.* This is not a friend; I warn you he will turn on you. غدر بنا *ġidar biina.* He deceived us.

غدير *ġadiir* p. غدران *ġidraan* 1. pool, pond of rain water. 2. stream, brook.

غدار *ġaddaar* p. *-iin* deceitful. اخذ

بـــالك مـــن الغـــدار! *'ixiδ baalak min l-ġaddaar!* Beware of deceitful people.

غ د ي *ġdy*

غدى *ġida (يغدي yġadi)* to become, turn into. البنت غدت كبـــيرة ولازم نزوجـــها. *l-bint ġadat čibiira w-laazim nzawwijha.* The girl has become old, and we will have to marry her off.

غدى *ġadda* II 1. to give lunch to s.o. العيال جاوا من المدرســـة وأمـــهم غدتهـــم *li-cyaaḷ yaw min l-madrasa w-'ummhum ġaddattum.* The kids came from school and their mother gave them lunch. 2. to treat s.o. to lunch, buy lunch for s.o. ساعدته اليوم وغداني *saacadta l-yoom w-ġaddaani.* I helped him today and he treated me to lunch.

تغدى *tġadda* V (common var. V تقدى *tqadda*) to have lunch. تغدينا لحم وعيش. *tġaddeena laḥam w-ceeš.* We had meat and rice for lunch. (prov.) تغدى فيه قبل مـــا يتعشـــى فيـــك *tġadda fii gabil-ma yitcašša fiik.* The early bird gets the worm.

غ ر ا م *ġraam*

غرام *ġraaam* p. *-aat* gram.

غ ر ء ن *ġr'n*

قـــرآن *ġur'aan* (common var. *qur'aan*) Quran.

غ ر ب *ġrb*

غرب *ġurab (يغرب yġarib)* to set (sun, moon). متى تغرب الشمـــس هـــني؟ *mita tġarib š-šams hini?* When does the sun set here?

غـــرب *ġarrab* II to go to a foreign country. غرب لاجل يشتغل ويطرش فلوس حق هلـــه *ġarrab lajil yištaġil w-yṭarriš fluus ḥagg hala.* He left his country in order to work and send money to his family.

تغرب *tġarrab* V = غرب *ġarrab* II.

استغرب *staġrab* X to be surprised. آنا أستغرب من تصرفاته *'aana 'aštaġrib min taṣarrufaata.* I am surprised by his behavior. لا تستغرب. هذي عادة قديمة. *la tistaġrib. haaδi caada gadiima.* Don't be surprised. This is an old custom.

غرب *ġarb* west. الغرب *l-ġarb* the West. الشرق والغرب *š-šarg w-l-ġarb* east and west. شمال غرب *šamaal ġarb* northwest (n.). غرب البلد *ġarb l-balad* west of the city.

غـــربي *ġarbi* 1. (as n.) westerly wind. الغربي يجيب هوا بارد وحاف *l-ġarbi yiyiib hawa baarid w-ḥaaff.* The westerly wind brings cool and dry weather. 2. (as adj.) occidental, Western, European. 3. Westerner, European.

غربة *ġurba* absence from one's homeland.

غـــراب *ġraab* p. غربان *ġirbaan* crow, raven. (prov.) لو في الغراب مرق ما فات الصيـــاد *lo fi li-ġraab marag ma faat ṣ-ṣayyaad.* It's a worthless thing.

غريـــب *ġariib* p. *-iin*, غربا *ġuraba* 1. stranger, foreigner, outsider. هو غريب. ما عنده أحد يســـاعده *huwa ġariib. ma cinda 'aḥad ysaacda.* He's a foreigner. He doesn't have anybody to help him. 2. strange, foreign. لبس غريب *libs ġariib* strange clothing.

أغـــرب *'aġrab* (elat.) 1. (with من *min*)

more unusual than, stranger than. 2. (with foll. n.) the most unusual, the strangest.

المغرب *l-maġrib* 1. (more common var. *li-mġarb*) sunset. المغرب الساعة ستة *li-mġarb s-saaᶜa sitta.* Sunset is at six o'clock. صلاة المغرب *ṣalaat li-mġarb* the sunset prayer. 2. at sunset. سرنا المغرب *sirna li-mġarb.* We left at sunset. 3. المغرب *l-maġrib* 1. Morocco. 2. northwest Africa.

مغربي *maġirbi* p. مغاربة *maġaarba* 1. person from Morocco. 2. Moroccan, from Morocco. 3. North African. 4. person from North Africa.

غ ر ب ل ġrbl

غربل *ġarbal (يغربل yġarbil)* 1. to bother, irritate s.o. البرد غربلني *l-bard ġarbalni.* The cold bothered me. الله يغربلك! *'aḷḷa yġarbilk!* Damn you! God's curse be upon you! 2. to sift, sieve. الحرمة غربلت البر *l-ḥurma ġarbalat l-burr.* The woman sifted the wheat.

تغربل *tġarbal (يتغربل yitġarbal)* pass. of غربل *ġarbal.*

غربلة *ġarbala* (v.n. from غربل *ġarbal*) 1. bother, irritation. 2. sifting.

غ ر ر ġrr

غر *ġarr (يغر yġurr)* to deceive, mislead. لا يغرك مظهره، ترى جلاخ *la yġurrak maðhara, tara čallaax.* Don't let his appearance fool you, because he's a liar.

غتر *ġtarr* VIII to be or become conceited. لا تغتر بروحك! *la tiġtarr b-ruuḥak!* Don't be taken with yourself!

غرة *ġurra:* غرة الشهر *ġurrat š-šahar* the first day of the month.

مغرور *maġruur* p. *-iin* مغرور بنفسه واجد *maġruur b-nafsa waayid.* He is much taken with himself.

غ ر ز ġrz

غرز *ġarraz* II (common var. II قرز *qarraz*) to get stuck or plunged. غرزت السيارة في الرمل *ġarrazat s-sayyaara fi r-ramil.* The car got stuck in the sand.

غ ر س ġrs

غرس *ġiras (يغرس yġaris)* to plant. غرسوا شجر على طول شارع المطار *ġirsaw šiyar ᶜala ṭuul šaariᶜ l-maṭaar.* They planted trees along the airport road.

غ ر ش ġrš

غرشة *ġarša* p. غراش *ġraaš* bottle. عطني غرشة بيبسي *ᶜaṭni ġaršat bebsi.* Give me a bottle of Pepsi-Cola.

غ ر ظ ġrð

غرض *ġarað* p. اغراض *ġraað* thing, possession, belonging. لم اغراضك وفي امان الله! *limm ġraaðak w-fi maan-illaa!* Gather your things and go away!

غ ر غ ر ġrġr

غرغر *ġarġar (يغرغر yġarġir)* to gargle. غرغر بماي وملح *ġarġar b-maay w-milḥ.* He gargled with water and salt.

غرغرة *ġarġara* (v.n.) gargling, gargle.

غ ر گ ġrg

غرق *ġirig (يغرق yġarig)* 1. to be drowned, to go under the water. غرق وماحد قدر ينتشله من الماي *ġirig* *w-maḥḥad gidar yintašla min l-maay.* He drowned and nobody could pull him out of the water. 2. to sink. الطوفان ضرب الباخرة وغرقت *ṭ-ṭuufaan đirab l-baaxra w-ġrigat.* The storm hit the ship and it sank. 3. to be flooded, immersed, submerged. الشوارع غرقت من المطر *š-šawaari^c ġrigat min l-muṭar.* The streets were flooded by the rain.

غرق *ġarrag* II 1. to drown s.o., cause s.o. to drown. الطوفان غرقه *ṭ-ṭuufaan ġarraga.* The storm drowned him. 2. to sink, cause to sink. الغواصة غرقت الباخرة *l-ġawwaaṣa ġarragat l-baaxra.* The submarine sank the ship.

غرقان *ġargaan* 1. drowned. 2. submerged, flooded.

غارق *ġaarig* p. *-iin* swamped, snowed under. غارق في الشغل *ġaarig fi š-šuġul* swamped with work.

غ ر م *ġrm*

غرم *ġarram* II 1. to fine, impose a fine on s.o. القاضي غرمني امية درهم *l-ġaađi ġarramni 'imyat dirhim.* The judge fined me one hundred dirhams. 2. to charge, dock s.o. إذا أبطيت في الدفع يغرمونك *'iđa 'abṭeet fi d-dafi^c yġarrmuunak.* If you don't pay on time, they will charge you.

تغرم *tġarram* V pass. of II غرم *ġarram.*

غرام *ġaraam* love, infatuation, passion.

غرامي *ġaraami* (adj.) love, passionate. قصة غرامية *ġiṣṣa ġaraamiyya* love story.

غرامة *ġaraama* p. *-aat* 1. fine. 2. penalty.

غ ر ي *ġry*

قرية *ġarya* (less common var. *qarya*) p. قري *ġaray* village. هيلي قرية صغيرة أثرية في بو ظبي *hiili ġarya ṣaġiira 'aθariyya fi bu đabi.* Hili is a small archeological village in Abu Dhabi.

غ ز ر *ġzr*

غزر *ġazir* 1. (common var. عمق *^cumg, ^cumj*) depth, deepness. كم غزر الخليج هني؟ *čam ġazir l-xaliij hni?* How deep is the Gulf here? 2. gist, essence. غزر القصيدة *ġazir l-gaṣiida* the gist of the poem.

غ ز ل *ġzl*

غزل *ġizal (يغزل yġazil)* to spin. اشترت صوف خروف وغزلته *štirat ṣuuf xaruuf w-ġizlata.* She bought sheep's wool and spun it.

غازل *ġaazal* III to court, flirt with s.o. إذا تغازل بنت في السوق يزخونك ويودونك السجن *'iđa tġaazil bint fi s-suug yzixxuunak w-ywadduunak s-sijin.* If you flirt with a girl in the marketplace, they will arrest you and put you in jail.

غزل *ġazal* 1. yarn, spun thread. (prov.) زمان أول تحول والغزل انقلب صوف *zamaan 'awwal tḥawwal w-l-ġazal ngalab ṣuuf.* Times change. Things are no longer the same. 2. (v.n. from III غازل *ġaazal*) flirtation. شعر الغزل *ši^cr l-ġazal* love poetry.

غزال *ġazaal* p. غزلان *ġizlaan* gazelle, deer. لحم الغزال طيب *laḥam l-ġazaal ṭayyib.* Venison is delicious. f. غزالة *-a* female gazelle.

غ ز و ġzw

غزى *ġaza (يغزي yġazi)* to raid, attack, carry out a tribal expedition on, invade. ذيك القبيلة غزتهم وخذت كل اغراضهم *ðiič l-gabiila ġazattum w-xaðat kill ġraaḍḍum.* That tribe raided them and took all their possessions. البضايع الجابانية غزت الأسواق في الخليج *l-baḍaayiᶜ l-jaabaaniyya ġazat l-'aswaag fi l-xaliij.* Japanese goods have invaded the markets in the Gulf.

غزو *ġazu* (v.n.) raiding, invading, attacking.

غزوة *ġazwa* (n. of inst.) p. *-aat* a raid, a tribal attack.

غ س ل ġsl

غسل *ġisal (يغسل yġasil)* to wash. يغسلون هدومهم كل سبوع *yġasluun hduumhum kill subuuᶜ.* They wash their clothes every week.

غسل *ġassal* 1. to wash thoroughly. غسل ايدينه وقعد ياكل *ġassal 'iideena w-giᶜad yaakil.* He washed his hands and sat down to eat. (prov.) الزين زين لو قعد من منامه والشين شين لو غسل بصابون *z-zeen zeenin law giᶜad min manaama w-š-šeen šeenin law ġassal b-ṣaabuun.* A leopard cannot change his spots. 2. to wash, bathe s.o. or a corpse. يغسلون المعرس ليلة العرس *yġassluun l-miᶜris leelt l-ᶜirs.* They bathe the bridegroom on the wedding night. غسلوا الميت ودفنوه *ġassalaw l-mayyit w-difnoo.* They washed the corpse and buried it.

اغتسل *ġtisal* VIII to perform major ritual ablution (i.e., to wash the whole body, esp. after intercourse). قوم اغتسل قبل ما تصلي *guum ġtisil gabil-ma tṣalli.* Go cleanse yourself before you pray.

غسالة *ġassaala* p. *-aat* washing machine. هالحين تحصل غسالة في كل بيت *halḥiin tḥaṣṣil ġassaala fi kill beet.* Now, you will find a washing machine in every house.

مغسل *maġsal* p. مغاسل *maġaasil* sink, washbowl.

غ س م ġsm

قسم *ġisam (يقسم yġasim)* (less common var. *qisam*) 1. to divide, split. قسم القرص قسمين *ġisam l-garṣ ġismeen.* He divided the loaf of bread into two pieces. 2. to will, destine, foreordain. الله، سبحانه وتعالى، قسم لنا كذي *'aḷḷaah, subḥaanahu wa taᶜaalaa, ġisam lana čiði.* God, be He praised and exalted, willed it this way for us.

قسم *ġassam* II to divide, distribute. قسم الأرباح علينا *ġassam l-'arbaaḥ ᶜaleena.* He divided the proceeds among us.

تقسم *tġassam* V pass. of II قسم *ġassam.*

قسم *ġisim* (common var. *gisim*) 1. (p. أقسام *'aġsaam*) section, department. 2. part, section. قسمين *ġismeen* two parts. 3. (p. إقسوم *'iġsuum*) shape, figure. (prov.) إقسوم لولا الهدوم خرفان لولا الكلام *'iġsuum loola li-hduum xirfaan loola l-kalaam.* Fair without and foul within.

قسمة *ġisma* (v.n. from قسم *ġisam*) 1. dividing, splitting. 2. destiny, fate (foreordained by God), lot. اللي حصل قسمة ونصيب *'illi ḥiṣal ġisma w-naṣiib.* What has happened is foreordained by God.

غ س ي *ġsy*

قاسي *ġaasi* (less common var. *gaasi*) 1. harsh, severe, cruel. قاضي قاسي *ġaaḍi ġaasi* harsh judge. قاسي على عياله *ġaasi* *ᶜala ᶜyaaḷa.* He's harsh with his kids. 2. hard, solid, stiff. قاسي مثل الحجر *ġaasi miθl l-ḥiyar* hard as rocks.

غ ش ش *ġšš*

غش *ġašš (يغش yġišš)* 1. to cheat, swindle. ما أشتري منه. يغش الزبون *ma 'aštiri minna. yġišš z-zibuun.* I won't buy from him. He cheats customers. نجح في الامتحان لانه غش *nijaḥ fi li-mtiḥaan linna ġašš.* He passed the examination because he cheated. 2. to adulterate, dilute. فيه مطاعم تغش الأكل مالها *fii maṭaaᶜim tġišš l-'akil maalha.* There are restaurants that adulterate their food.

انغش *nġašš* VII pass. of غش *ġašš.*

غش *ġišš* (v.n. from غش *ġašš*) fraud, swindling. الغش والخداع موب من شيمة البدوي *l-ġišš w-l-xidaaᶜ muub min šiimat li-bdiwi.* Fraud and deception are not among the attributes of Bedouins.

غشاش *ġaššaaš* p. غشاشة *ġaššaaša, -iin* cheat, swindler, cheater.

مغشوش *maġšuuš* (p.p. from غش *ġašš*) 1. having been cheated. أنت اشتريت ذولا بألف درهم؟ مغشوش *'inta štireet ðoola b-'alf dirhim? maġšuuš.* Did you buy those for a thousand dirhams? You have been cheated. 2. adulterated. حليب مغشوش *ḥaliib maġšuuš* adulterated milk. زبد مغشوش *zibid maġšuuš* adulterated butter.

غ ش م *ġšm*

غشيم *ġašiim* p. غشم *ġiššam, -iin* 1. inexperienced, untrained. غشيم بالشغل *ġašiim b-š-šuġul* inexperienced at work. 2. greenhorn.

غ ش م ر *ġšmr*

غشمر *ġašmar (يغشمر yġašmir)* 1. to kid s.o. أنت تغشمر، موب كذي؟ *'inta tġašmir, muub čiði?* You are kidding, aren't you? 2. to make fun of s.o. غشمرني قدام الناس *ġašmarni jiddaam n-naas.* He made fun of me in front of the people.

غ ش ي *ġšy*

غشى *ġiša (يغشي yġaši)* to faint, lose consciousness. غشى في السوق *ġiša fi s-suug.* He fainted in the marketplace.

غشيان *ġašyaan* fainted, unconscious. طاح غشيان *ṭaaḥ ġašyaan.* He fainted.

غ ص ب *ġṣb*

غصب *ġiṣab (يغصب yġaṣib)* to force, compel. غصبها تتزوج ابن عمها *ġiṣabha tizzawwaj 'ibin ᶜammaha.* He forced her to marry her cousin.

انغصب *nġiṣab* VII pass. of غصب *ġiṣab.* انغصب يروح باكر *nġiṣab yruuḥ baačir.* He was forced to go tomorrow.

اغتصب *ġtiṣab* VIII to rape, ravish. سجنوه عشر سنين لانه اغتصبها *sijnoo ᶜašar siniin linna ġtiṣabha.* They jailed him for ten years because he had raped her.

غصب *ġaṣb* (v.n. from غصب *ġiṣab*) force, compulsion. غصب عني *ġaṣb ᶜanni* in spite of me, against my will. بالغصب *b-l-ġaṣb* by force. إذا ما جات بالطيب، بتجي بالغصب *'iða ma yat b-ṭ-ṭiib, b-tiyi b-l-ġaṣb.* If she doesn't come willingly, she will have to come by force.

غ ص ص *ġṣṣ*

قاصص *ġaaṣaṣ* III (less common var. *qaaṣaṣ*) to punish. المعلم قاصصني لاني تأخرت عن الدرس *l-muᶜallim ġaaṣaṣni linni ta'axxart ᶜan d-dars.* The teacher punished me because I was late for class.

قصة *ġiṣṣa* (less common var. *giṣṣa*) p. قصص *ġiṣaṣ* story, tale. عندي قصة باعلمك بها *ᶜindi ġiṣṣa b-aᶜallimk biiha.* I have a story to tell you. شو قصة التنديل؟ *šu ġiṣṣat t-tindeel?* What's with the supervisor?

قصاص *ġaṣaaṣ* (less common var. *gaṣaaṣ*) punishment.

غ ط ط *ġṭṭ*

غط *ġaṭṭ (yġiṭṭ)* 1. to dip, immerse. غط يده في الماي *ġaṭṭ yadda fi l-maay.* He dipped his hand in the water. 2. to set (the sun, the moon). غطت الشمس *ġaṭṭat š-šams.* The sun set. غطت عينه *ġaṭṭat ᶜeena.* He fell asleep. ليلة أمس ما غطت عيني النوم *leelat 'ams ma ġaṭṭat ᶜeeni n-noom.* Last night I couldn't sleep.

غ ط ع *ġṭᶜ*

قطع *ġiṭaᶜ* (يقطع *yġaṭiᶜ*) (less common var. *gaṭaᶜ*) 1. to cut, cut off, break off. لا تقطع الورد *la tiġṭaᶜ l-ward.* Don't pick the roses. ماحد يقطع الشجر هني *maḥḥad yġaṭiᶜ š-šiyar hni.* Nobody cuts down trees here. البايق يقطعون يده *l-baayig yġaṭᶜuun yadda.* They cut off the hand of the thief. 2. to buy, get (a ticket). قطع تذكرة حق السينما *ġiṭaᶜ taðkara ḥagg s-siinama.* He bought a ticket for the cinema. اقطع لي تذكرتين *'iġṭaᶜ-li taðkarateen.* Get me two tickets. 3. to break off, sever. ما قطعوا العلاقات ويا دول أوروبا الشرقية *ma ġaṭᶜaw l-ᶜalaagaat wiyya duwal 'oroobba š-šargiyya.* They didn't sever relations with the Eastern European countries. 4. to cut off, stop, interrupt. قطعوا الكهربا والماي عنا *ġiṭᶜaw l-kahraba w-l-maay ᶜanna.* They cut off the electricity and the water to us. مسكين. فنشوه وقطعوا رزقه *maskiin. fannašoo w-ġiṭᶜaw rizga.* Poor man. They laid him off and cut off his livelihood. يقطعون معاشك إذا ما تداوم *yġaṭᶜuun maᶜaašak 'iða ma ddaawim.* They will cut off your salary if you don't report for duty. 5. to block, stop. صار دعمة. الشرطي قطع المرور *ṣaar daᶜma. š-širṭi ġiṭaᶜ l-muruur.* There was an accident. The policeman blocked the traffic. 6. to cover, traverse. قطع المسافة في خمس دقايق *ġiṭaᶜ l-masaafa fi xams digaayig.* He covered the distance in five minutes.

قطع *ġaṭṭaᶜ* II 1. to carve (meat). القصاب قطع اللحم *l-gaṣṣaab ġaṭṭaᶜ l-laḥam.* The butcher carved the meat. 2. to cut into pieces, cut up. قطع الورقة *ġaṭṭaᶜ li-wruga.* He cut the paper into pieces. 3. to wear out, tear up. قطع

غ ط و *ġṭw*

غطى *ġaṭṭa* II to cover. غطي القدر لاجل يستوي اللحـــم *ġaṭṭi l-jidir lajil yistiwi l-laḥam.* Cover the pot so that the meat will get cooked.

تغطى *tġaṭṭa* V 1. to be or become covered. تغطينـا بـالرمل مـن الهبـوب *tġaṭṭeena b-r-ramil min l-habuub.* We were covered with sand from the dust of the storm. 2. to cover oneself, cover up. هاك البرنوص! تغطى فيه *haak l-barnuuṣ! tġaṭṭa fii.* Take the blanket! Cover up with it.

غطا *ġaṭa* p. غطيان *ġiṭyaan* cover, lid. (prov.) قـدر ولقـي غطـاه *jidir w-ligi ġaṭaa.* A man is known by the company he keeps. Birds of a feather flock together. (lit., "A pot and it found its lid.").

مغطى *mġaṭṭa* (p.p. from II غطى *ġaṭṭa*) 1. covered. القدر مغطى *l-jidir mġaṭṭa.* The pot is covered. 2. veiled, obscure. الحرمة وجهـها مغطى *l-ḥurma weehha mġaṭṭa.* The woman's face is veiled.

غ ظ ب *ġḍb*

غضب *ġiḍib (يغضب yġaḍib)* to be or become furious, angry, irritated. أبوه غضب عليه *'ubuu ġiḍib ᶜalee.* His father became furious with him. يغضب على ما ميش *yġaḍib ᶜala ma miiš.* He gets mad for nothing. He gets mad at anything.

غضب *ġaḍab* (v.n. from غضب *ġiḍab*) 1. anger, indignation. ساعة الغضب *saaᶜt l-ġaḍab* time of anger. 2. wrath, rage, fury. !غضب الله عليك *ġaḍab aḷḷa*

الجوتي حقه واشترى واحـد جديـد *ġaṭṭaᶜ l-juuti ḥagga w-štira waaḥid yidiid.* He had worn out his shoes and bought new ones.

تقطع *tġaṭṭaᶜ* V (less common var. *tgaṭṭaᶜ*) pass. of II قطع *ġaṭṭaᶜ.*

انقطع *nġiṭaᶜ* VII (less common var. *ngiṭaᶜ*) 1. to break, tear, snap. انقطع حبل الغسيل *nġiṭaᶜ ḥabl l-ġaṣiil.* The clothesline broke. 2. to stop. انقطع الماي *nġiṭaᶜ l-maay.* The water stopped flowing. 3. to be cut off. انقطع المعاش *nġiṭaᶜ l-maᶜaaš.* The salary was cut off. فنشوني وانقطـع رزقـي *fannašooni w-nġiṭaᶜ rizgi.* They laid me off and my livelihood was cut off.

قطع *ġaṭiᶜ* (v.n. from قطع *ġiṭaᶜ*) 1. cutting off, cutting, breaking off. 2. buying, getting (a ticket). قطع التذاكر عقب الظـهر *ġaṭiᶜ t-taḍaakir ᶜugb ḍ-ḍuhur.* Buying tickets is in the afternoon. 3. selling (of tickets). شغلي قطع تذاكـر *šuġli ġaṭiᶜ taḍaakir.* I sell tickets. 4. breaking off, severing. قطع العلاقـات *ġaṭᶜ l-ᶜalaagaat* breaking off relations.

قطعة *ġiṭᶜa* p. قطع *ġiṭaᶜ* (less common var. *giṭaᶜ*) piece, portion. قطعة خـبز *ġiṭᶜat xubiz* piece of bread.

مقطع *mġaṭṭaᶜ* (p.p. from II قطع *ġaṭṭaᶜ*) (less common var. *mgaṭṭaᶜ*) 1. broken, broken in many places. شريط مقطـع *šariiṭ mġaṭṭaᶜ* broken, much broken (cassette) tape. 2. torn up, worn out. هدوم مقطعـة *hduum mġaṭṭaᶜa* torn up clothes. جوتي مقطع *juuti mġaṭṭaᶜ* worn out shoes, torn up shoes.

ᶜaleek! May the wrath of God be on you!

غضبـــان *ġaðbaan* mad, furious, indignant. غضبان على ولـــده *ġaðbaan ᶜala wilda* mad at his son. غضبان علـــيّ *ġaðbaan ᶜalayya* mad at me.

غ ف ر *ġfr*

غفـــر *ġifar (يغفر yġafir)* to pardon, forgive. الله هو اللي يغفر الذنـــوب *'aḷḷaah huwa lli yġafir ð-ðunuub.* It's God who pardons sins.

اســتغفر *staġfar* X to ask (God's) forgiveness. أستغفر الله *'astaġfiru ḷḷaah.* I ask God's forgiveness.

غفور *ġafuur* forgiving (esp., of God) = غفار *ġaffaar.*

غفار *ġaffaar* = غفور *ġafuur.*

غفـــران *ġufraan* (v.n. from غفر *ġifar*) pardon, forgiveness.

مغفـــور *maġfuur* (p.p. from غفر *ġifar*): المغفور له *l-maġfuur lahu* the deceased, the late...

غ ف ل *ġfl*

غفلة *ġafla* inattention, heedlessness. في غفلة *fi ġafla* suddenly, surprisingly. كنا في غفلـــــة *činna fi ġafla.* We were inattentive. على غفلة *ᶜala ġafla* all of a sudden, unawares.

غفـــلان *ġaflaan* unaware, inattentive, heedless. كنت غفلان عن ذيك القضيـــة *čint ġaflaan ᶜan ðiič l-gaðiyya.* I wasn't aware of that problem.

مغفل *mġaffal* 1. easily duped, gullible. 2. sucker, simpleton.

غ ف و *ġfw*

غفـــى *ġifa (يغفي yġafi)* to doze off, fall asleep. كان تعبان. جلس على الكنبة وغفى *čaan taᶜbaan. yilas ᶜala l-kanaba w-ġifa.* He was tired. He sat on the sofa and dozed off.

غفوة *ġafwa* (n. of inst.) p. *-aat* nap, cat nap, doze. خذت عيني غفوة *xaðat ᶜeeni ġafwa.* I fell asleep.

غ ل ب *ġlb*

غلب *ġilab (يغلب yġalib)* 1. to beat, be victorious over s.o. غلبونا في مباراة كرة القـــــدم *ġalaboona fi mubaaraat kurat l-ġadam.* They beat us at the soccer match. تقدر تغلبـــه في الملاكمـــة؟ *tigdar tġalba fi l-mulaakama?* Can you beat him at boxing? 2. to get the best of, get the better of s.o. القصاب غلبني بسعر اللحم *l-gaṣṣaab ġalabni b-siᶜr l-laḥam.* The butcher got the best of me on the price of the meat.

تغلـــب *tġallab* V (with على *ᶜala*) to overcome, surmount. الحمد لله. تغلبت على كـــل الصعوبـــات *l-ḥamdu li-llaah. tġallabt ᶜala kill ṣ-ṣuᶜuubaat.* Praise be to God. I have overcome all the difficulties.

أغلـــب *'aġlab* (with foll. n. or pron.) most of, the majority of. أغلب الأحيان *'aġlab l-'aḥyaan* most of the time. أغلبـــهم *'aġlabhum* most of them. أغلب الظـــن *'aġlab ḍ-ḍann* most probably, most likely.

أغلبيـــة *'aġlabiyya* 1. (with the article prefix ال *l-*) the majority. الأغلبية جاوا *l-'aġlabiyya yaw.* The majority came. Most of them came. 2. (with foll. n. or pron.) most of, the majority of. أغلبية الناس *'aġlabiyyat n-naas* most of the people. أغلبيتهم *'aġlabiyyattum* most of them.

غالب *ġaalib* (act. part. from غلب *ġilab*) 1. having beaten, having been victorious over s.o. هو اللي غالبني *huwa lli ġaalibni.* He's the one who has beaten me. 2. winner, victor.

مغلوب *maġluub* (p.p. from غلب *ġilab*) having been beaten. فريقهم المغلوب *fariiġġum l-maġluub.* Their team is the one that has been beaten. الفريق المغلوب *l-fariiġ l-maġluub* the losing team.

غ ل ج *ġlj*

غلج *ġalj* difficult, hard, complicated. هالقضية غلجة *hal-ġaðiyya ġalja.* This problem is difficult. الحياة صارت غلجة *l-ḥayaa ṣaarat ġalja.* Life has become complicated. مكان غلج *mukaan ġalj* difficult place to get to.

غ ل ف ا *ġlfa*

غلفا *ġalfa* (common var. قلفا *galfa*) 1. fresh water spring in Ajman. 2. Galfa (water) bottling company.

غ ل ط *ġlṭ*

غلط *ġilaṭ (يغلط yġaliṭ)* (common var. *ġiliṭ*) 1. to make a mistake, commit an error, be mistaken. آنا غلطت في الحساب *'aana ġliṭṭ fi li-ḥsaab.* I made a mistake in computing. 2. (with على *ᶜala*) to be disrespectful, impudent to s.o. لا تغلط عليه؛ أكبر منك *la tġaliṭ ᶜalee; 'akbar minnak.* Don't be disrespectful to him; he's older than you. غلط على أبوه *ġiliṭ ᶜala 'ubuu.* He was impudent to his father.

غلط *ġallaṭ* II to cause s.o. to make a mistake. اسكت! غلطتني بالحساب *'iskit! ġallaṭṭani b-li-ḥsaab.* Shut up! You made me make a mistake in computing.

غلط *ġalaṭ* 1. (adj. invar.) wrong, incorrect. نمرة غلط *numra ġalaṭ* wrong number. جواب غلط *jawaab ġalaṭ* wrong answer. 2. (n.) wrongdoing, s.th. wrong. سوى غلط *sawwa ġalaṭ.* He did something wrong. He made a mistake. فيه شي غلط *fii šayy ġalaṭ.* There's a hitch somewhere.

غلطة *ġalṭa* p. أغلاط *'aġlaaṭ, -aat* mistake, error. غلطة كبيرة *ġalṭa čibiira* big mistake. غلطتي *ġalṭati.* (It's) my mistake.

غلطان *ġalṭaan* mistaken, wrong, in error. آنا غلطان وأطلب منك السماح *'aana ġalṭaan w-'aṭlub minnak s-samaaḥ.* I am mistaken, and I ask for your forgiveness.

غ ل گ *ġlg*

غلق *ġallag* II 1. to close, shut. غلق الباب من فضلك! *ġallig l-baab min faðlak!* Close the door, please! البنك غلق *l-bank ġallag.* The bank is closed. 2. to be or become full (of s.th.) الثلاجة غلقت بالسمك *θ-θallaaja ġallagat b-s-simač.* The refrigerator was full of fish.

غ ل ل *ġll*

استغل *staġall* X 1. to take advantage of, exploit. استغل الموقف *staġall l-mawgif.* He took advantage of the situation. ماحد يشاركه. يستغل كل واحد *maḥḥad yšaarka. yistaġill kill waaḥid.*

No one enters into partnership with him. He takes advantage of everyone. 2. to utilize, make a profit, invest profitably. الحكومة تستغل مصـــادر الـــثروة *l-ḥukuuma tistaġill maṣaadir θ-θarwa.* The government is utilizing the resources of wealth.

استغلال *stiġlaal* (v.n.) 1. exploitation, taking advantage of s.th. 2. utilization, investing profitably.

استغلالي *stiġlaali* 1. exploitative. 2. (p. *-yyiin*) exploiter.

غ ل و *ġlw*

غلى *ġila* (يغلي *yġali)* to be or become expensive, high priced. تكاليف المعيشة غلت *takaaliif l-maᶜiiša ġilat.* The cost of living has become expensive. الأســـعار غلـــت *l-'asᶜaar ġilat.* Prices have risen.

غلـــى *ġalla* II to raise the price of. غلوا أســـعار الســـيارات *ġallaw 'asᶜaar s-sayyaarat.* They have raised the prices of cars.

غـــلا *ġala* high prices of things, high cost. الدنيا في غـــلا *d-dinya fi ġala.* We are in a period of high cost of living. فيه غلا في الأســـعار *fii ġala fi l-'asᶜaar.* Prices have risen.

أغلـــى *'aġla* (elat.) 1. (with من *min*) more expensive than. الذهب أغلى من الفضة *ð-ðahab 'aġla min l-fiðða.* Gold is more expensive than silver. 2. (with foll. n.) the most expensive. الذهب أغلى المعادن؟ *ð-ðahab 'aġla l-maᶜaadin?* Is gold the most expensive metal?

غـــالي *ġaali* 1. expensive, high-priced. الذهب غالي اليوم *ð-ðahab ġaali l-yoom.* Gold is expensive today. 2. dear, beloved. بنتي الغاليـــة *binti l-ġaalya* my dear daughter. بنتي غالية عنـــدي *binti ġaalya ᶜindi.* My daughter is dear to me.

غ ل ي *ġly*

غلـــى *ġila* (يغلي *yġali)* 1. to boil. الماي غلى *l-maay ġila.* The water has boiled. 2. to cause to boil, make s.th. boil. اغلي الماي قبل لا تشربـــه *'iġli l-maay gabil-la tišraba.* Boil the water before you drink it.

غ م ج *ġmj*

غـــامق *ġaamij* dark (color). لون غامق *loon ġaamij* dark color.

غ م ر *ġmr*

غمر *ġumar* (يغمر *yġamir)* to faint, lose consciousness. غمر وطاح على الأرض في الســـوق *ġumar w-ṭaaḥ ᶜala l-'arḍ fi s-suug.* He fainted and fell down in the marketplace.

غمـــران *ġamraan* having fainted, lost consciousness.

غ م ز ي *ġmzy*

غمازي *ġammaazi* p. غماميز *ġimaamiiz* 1. weather vane. 2. wind sock.

غ م م *ġmm*

غمام *ġmaam* (coll.) clouds. s. *-a.*

غ ن چ *ġnč*

غنجة *ġanča* p. *-aat* ship with two sails, oval in shape, and about one hundred feet long.

غ ن د *ġnd*

قنـــد *ġand* (common var. *qand*) p. قنود

ġnuud solid sugar in the shape of a cone.

غ ن د ن *ġndn*

قنـدون *ġanduun* p. قنـادين *ġanaadiin* sugar bowl, sugar bin.

غ ن ص ل *ġnṣl*

قنصـل *ġunṣul* (less common var. *gunṣul*) p. قنـاصل *ġanaaṣil* consul. القنصـل عطـاني ويـزة *l-ġunṣul ᶜaṭaani wiiza.* The consul gave me a visa.

قنصلية *ġunṣuliyya* (less common var. *gunṣuliyya*) consulate. القنصليـة الأمريكانيـة *l-ġunsuliyya l-'amriikaan-iyya* the American Consulate.

غ ن ط ر *ġnṭr*

غنطر *ġanṭar (*يغنطر *yġanṭir)* to contract, bid. غنطر يبـني العمـارة على مليـون درهـم. *ġanṭar yibni li-ᶜmaara ᶜala malyoon dirhim.* He contracted to construct the building for a million dirhams.

مغنطر *mġantir* contractor.

غ ن م *ġnm*

اغتنـم *ġtinam* VIII to seize (the opportunity), take advantage of. اغتنم الفرصـة *ġtinam l-furṣa.* He seized the opportunity. اغتنـم فرصـة وجـود الشـيخ *ġtinam furṣat wujuud š-šeex.* He seized the opportunity of the Shaikh's presence.

غنـم *ġanam* (coll.) sheep, goats. s. غنمة *ġnama.* لحـم غنـم *laḥam ġanam* lamb, mutton.

غنـام *ġannaam* Ghannam (prominent Kuwaiti family).

غـانم *ġaanim* successful. سـالم وغـانم *saalim w-ġaanim* safe and sound. وصل سالم وغانم *wiṣal saalim w-ġaanim.* He arrived safe and sound. لحيةٍ غانمـة *liḥyatin ġaanma* very nice man, man with an irresistible appeal.

غنيمة *ġaniima* p. غنايم *ġanaayim* spoils, plunder, loot.

غ ن ن *ġnn*

قـانون *ġaanuun* (less common var. *gaanuun*) p. قوانـين *ġawaaniin.* كليـة القـانون *kulliyyat l-ġaanuun* the college of law.

غ ن ي *ġny*

غنـى *ġina (*يغني *yġani)* to enrich, make rich. توفـق والله غنـاه *twaffag w-'aḷḷa ġanaa.* He was successful and God enriched him.

غنى *ġanna* II (common var. *qanna*) to sing. منـو يغـني؟ *minu yġanni?* Who's singing?

اغتنـى *ġtina* VIII to become rich. فرشـوا نهـالي في بيوتهـم واغتنـوا *frašaw nhaali fi byuuttum w-ġtinaw.* They carpeted their homes and became rich.

اسـتغنى *staġna* X (common var. *staqna*) 1. to become rich = VIII اغتنـى *ġtina.* جـود فلـوس واجـد واسـتغنى *jawwad fluus waayid w-staġna.* He made a lot of money and became rich. 2. (with عن *ᶜan*) to do without. ما أقدر أسـتغني عـن السـيارة *ma 'agdar 'astaġni ᶜan s-sayyaara.* I cannot do without the car. 3. have no need for, be in no need of. استغنوا عن خدماته *staġnaw ᶜan xadamaata.* They had no need for his services. They laid him off.

غنى *ġina* (common var. *qina*) 1. singing. 2. wealth, richness.

غـــني *ġani* (common var. *qani*) p. أغنيا *'aġniya, -yyiin* rich, prosperous, wealthy.

أغنية *'uġniya* (common var. *'uqniya*) p. أغاني *'aġaani, 'aqaani* song.

مغني *mġanni* (common var. *mqanni*) p. مغنيـين *mqaniyiin* singer. f. مغنية *-ya, maqanniya* singer.

غ و ر *ġwr*

غار *ġaar (يغير yġiir)* (with على *ᶜala*) to invade, attack, raid. القبيلة غارت على ديرتنـــا *l-gabiila ġaarat ᶜala diiratna.* The tribe invaded our (Bedouin) homeland. الدواسـر غـــاروا علينـــا *d-duwaasir ġaaraw ᶜaleena.* The Dosari tribe attacked us.

غـــار *ġaar* (common var. *qaar*) p. غيران *ġiiraan, qiiraan* cave, cavern.

غـــارة *ġaara* (common var. *qaara*) p. *-aat* raid, attack. غـــارة جويـــة *ġaara jawwiyya* air raid.

غ و ر ل *ġwrl*

غوريلا *ġoreella* p. غوريلات *-aat* gorilla.

غ و ر ي *ġwry*

غوري *ġuuri* (common var. قوري *quuri*) p. غواري *ġawaari* tea kettle.

غ و ز ي *ġwzy*

غوزي *ġuuzy* (common var. قوزي *quuzi)* 1. (p. غوازي *ġuwaazi,* قوازي *quwaazi*) little lamb, spring lamb. 2. (coll.) stuffed lamb (known as مفتح *mfattaḥ* among the Bedouins).

غ و ص *ġwṣ*

غـــاص *ġaaṣ (يغوص yġuuṣ)* 1. to dive, plunge, submerge. غاص في الماي *ġaaṣ fi l-maay.* He dived into the water. 2. to become stuck (in the sand, mud). السـيارة غـــاصت في الرمـــل *s-sayyaara ġaaṣat fi r-ramil.* The car became stuck in the sand. 3. to dive for pearls. الغيص يقدر يغوص إلى أرض البحـــر *l-ġeeṣ yigdar yġuuṣ 'ila 'arḍ l-baḥar.* A pearl diver can dive to the bottom of the sea.

غـــواص *ġawwaaṣ* (more common var. غيص *ġeeṣ*) p. غواويص *ġuwaawiiṣ*, غاصة *ġaaṣa* pearl diver, diver.

غيص *ġeeṣ* = غواص *ġawwaaṣ.*

غواصة *ġawwaaṣa* p. *-aat* submarine.

غ و ط ي *ġwṭy*

غوطي *ġuuṭi* (more common var. قوطي *guuṭi*). See under ق و ط ي *gwṭy.*

غ و ي *ġwy*

غـــاوي *ġaawi* p. *-yiin* beautiful, handsome. حرمة غاوية *ḥurma ġaawya* beautiful woman.

غ ي ب *ġyb*

غـــاب *ġaab (يغيب yġiib)* (common var. *qaab*) (with عن *ᶜan*) 1. to be absent, be or stay away from, to disappear. غاب عن الصف *ġaab ᶜan ṣ-ṣaff.* He was absent from class. ما حصلناه. غاب *ma ḥaṣṣalnaa. ġaab.* We didn't find him. He disappeared. 2. to set, go down. غابت الشمـــس *ġaabat š-šams.* The sun went down. غاب عن البـــال *ġaab ᶜan l-baal* to slip one's mind.

غيب *ġeeb*: الغيب *l-ġeeb* the unknown, the supernatural. ما يعلم بالغيب إلا الله

ma yi^{c}lam b-l-ġeeb 'illa 'aḷḷa. Only God is clairvoyant.

غيبة *ġeeba* p. *-aat* absence. لا تطول الغيبة *la ṭṭawwil l-ġeeba.* Don't stay away for a long time.

غياب *ġiyaab* (v.n. from غاب *ġaab*) absence, being away. الحضور والغياب *l-ḥuðuur w-l-ġiyaab* attendance (and absences).

غيابي *ġiyaabi* (adj.) in absentia. حكم غيابي *ḥukum ġiyaabi* sentencing in absentia. محاكمة غيابية *muḥaakama ġiyaabiyya* trial in absentia.

غايب *ġaayib* (act. part. from غاب *ġaab*) 1. absent. غايب عن الصف *ġaayib ^{c}an ṣ-ṣaff* absent from class. 2. person who is absent. (prov.) الغايب عذره وياه *l-ġaayib ^{c}iðra wiyyaa.* The absent party is not so faulty.

غ ي ر *ġyr*

غار *ġaar (يغار yġaar)* (common var. *qaar*) 1. to be jealous. يغار من أخوه الكبير *yġaar min 'uxuu č-čibiir.* He's jealous of his older brother. 2. to be zealous, vie (for). يغار على وطنه *yġaar ^{c}ala waṭana.* He's a zealous patriot.

غير *ġayyar* II (common var. *qayyar*) 1. to change, alter, make different. قوم اسبح وغير هدومك *guum isbaḥ w-ġayyir hduumak.* Go take a bath and change your clothes. ! غير التاير *ġayyir t-taayir!* Change the tire! 2. to exchange. ما يعجبني ها الجوتي. أبغى أغيره *ma y^{c}ajibni hal-juuti. 'abġa 'aġayyra.* I don't like these shoes. I'd like to exchange them.

تغير *tġayyar* V 1. to be changed. الزام تغير. لازم أدش الشغل الساعة ثمان *z-zaam tġayyar. laazim 'adišš š-šuġul s-saa^{c}a θamaan.* The work schedule has changed. I have to go to work at eight. 2. to be replaced. غيروا التنديل بواحد أحسن *ġayyaraw t-tindeel b-waaḥid 'aḥsan.* They replaced the foreman with a better one.

غير *ġeer* (common var. *qeer*) 1. other than, except, else. عطني غير هذا *^{c}aṭni ġeer haaða.* Give me something other than this. غيري *ġeeri* other than me. ما عندنا غير هذا *ma ^{c}indana ġeer haaða.* We don't have anything except this. هذي موب فلوسك. فلوس غيرك *haaði muub fluusak. fluus ġeerak.* This isn't your money. It's someone else's money. 2. another, other, different. غير واحد *ġeer waaḥid* another one, someone else. تعال غير يوم *ta^{c}aal ġeer yoom.* Come another day. 3. (an interrogative used in replying to a question or statement, approx.:) wasn't it, what else but, could it be anything but. غير هو اللي قال لي تعال باكر؟ *ġeer huwa lli gal-li ta^{c}aal baačir?* Wasn't it he who told me to come the following day? غير هو ما بغى يعرس؟ *ġeer huwa ma baġa y^{c}arris?* What else but that he didn't want to get married. 4. not, non-, in-, etc. غير ضروري *ġeer ðaruuri* not necessary, unnecessary. غير معقول *ġeer ma^{c}guul* unreasonable, not reasonable. غير مالي *ġeer maali* nonfinancial. غير كامل *ġeer kaamil* incomplete.

غيرة *ġiira* (v.n. from غار *ġaar*) 1. jealousy. 2. zeal, vigilant care.

غ ي ظ *ġyð*

غاظ *ġaað (يغيظ yġiið)* to anger, make

s.o. angry. غـاظني بتصرفاتـه *ġaađ̣ni b-taṣarrufaata.* He made me angry with his behavior.

اغتـاظ *ġtaađ̣* VIII to be or become angry, to get mad. يغتاظ من كل واحد *yiġtaađ̣ min kill waaḥid.* He gets angry at everybody.

غ ي م *ġym*

غيـم *ġayyam* II to be or become cloudy. الدنيا غيمـت *d-dinya ġayyamat.* It got cloudy. The sky got cloudy.

مغيـم *mġayyim* (act. part.) cloudy, gloomy. الدنيا مغيمـة *d-dinya mġayyma.* It's cloudy.

غيم *ġeem* (coll.) clouds. s. *-a.*

غ ي ن *ġyn*

غين *ġeen* name of the letter غ *ġ.*

غ ي ي *ġyy*

غايـة *ġaaya* p. *-aat* object, objective, intent, purpose. للغايـة *lal-ġaaya* extremely, very. مهـم للغايـة *muhimm lal-ġaaya* extremely important.

ف

ف ا *faa*

فا *faa* name of the letter ف *f.*

ف ا ت و ر *faatwr*

فاتورة *faatuura* p. فواتير *fuwaatiir* invoice, bill.

ف ا ر *faar*

فار *faar* p. فيران *fiiraan* mouse. (prov.) لا غاب القطو العب يا فار *la ġaab l-gaṭu 'ilᶜab ya faar.* While the cat's away, the mice will play.

ف ا ر س *faars*

فارس *faaris,* as in بلاد فارس *blaad faaris* Persia, Iran.

فارسي *faarsi* 1. Persian, the Persian language. 2. Persian, characteristic of Persia. 3. (p. فرس *furs*) a Persian.

ف ا س[1] *faas*

فاس *faas* p. فوس *fuus* ax, hatchet. يشتغل بالفاس *yištaġil b-l-faas.* He works with an ax.

ف ا س[2] *faas*

فاس *faas* Fez (city in Morocco).

ف ا ش س ت *faašst*

فاشستي *faašisti* 1. fascist, fascistic. 2. a fascist.

الفاشستية *l-faašistiyya* fascism.

ف ا ص و ل ي *faaṣwly*

فاصوليا *faaṣuulya* (coll.) beans. s. حبة فاصولية *ḥabbat faaṣuulya.*

ف ا ل[1] *faal*

فال *faal* fortune, sign, omen. فتح الفال *fitaḥ l-faal.* He predicted the future. قطاط الفال *gaṭṭaaṭ l-faal,* فتاح الفال *fattaaḥ l-faal* the fortune-teller. (prov.) فال الله ولا فالك! *faal aḷḷa wala faalak!* (approx.) Contrary to what you have just said, I hope things will turn out to be good.

ف ا ل[2] *faal*

فالة *faala* light meal, snack (usually eaten late at night).

ف ا ن ي ل *faanyl*

فانيلة *faaniila* p. *-aat* tee-shirt, undershirt.

ف ا و ل *faawl*

فاول *faawil* foul, penalty (in games). فاول عليهم *faawil ᶜaleehum* penalty against them. ضربة فاول *ḍarbat faawil* penalty kick (in soccer).

ف ء ف ء *f'f'*

فأفأ *fa'fa'* (يفأفئ *yfa'fi'*) to stammer. يفأفئ في الكلام *yfa'fi' fi l-kalaam.* He stammers.

ف ب ر ي ر *fbryr*

فبراير *fabraayir* February. فبراير هو شباط *fabraayir huwa šbaaṭ.* February is *šbaaṭ.*

ف ت ت *ftt*

فتت *fattat* II to break into small pieces. لا تقط الخبز. فتته وعطيه للطيور *la tgiṭṭ l-xubiz. fattita w-ᶜaṭii liṭ-ṭyuur.*

Don't throw away the bread. Crumble it and give it to the birds.

تفتت *tfattat* V pass. of II فتت *fattat*. الصخر تفتت *ṣ-ṣaxar tfattat*. The rock broke up into fragments.

فتيت *fatiit* (coll.) s. *-a* dish consisting of small pieces of bread, meat, and meat broth. (common var. بثيث *baθiiθ*).

ف ت ح *ftḥ*

فتح *fitaḥ* (يفتح *yfatiḥ*) 1. to open. فتح الدريشة *fitaḥ d-diriiša*. He opened the window. 2. to start, open. فتحنا حساب مشترك في البنك *fitaḥna ḥsaab mištarak fi l-bank*. We opened a joint account in the bank. فتح دكان في مركز حامد *fitaḥ dikkaan fi markaz ḥaamid*. He opened a store in Hamid Center. الشارع كان مسدود؛ البلدية فتحته *š-šaari*ᶜ *čaan masduud. l-baladiyya ftiḥata* The road was closed. The municipality opened it. 3. to turn on. فتح الماي *fitaḥ l-maay*. He turned on the water. فتح الراديو *fitaḥ r-raadyo*. He turned on the radio. هذا يفتح الفال *haaδa yiftaḥ l-faal*. This person tells people's fortune. الفلفل يفتح الشهية *l-filfil yiftaḥ š-šahiyya*. Hot pepper stimulates the appetite. 4. to conquer, capture (a city). الجيش فتح المدينة *l-jeeš fitaḥ l-madiina*. The army conquered the city.

فتح *fattaḥ* II 1. to open. البنك يفتح الساعة عشر ويبند الساعة ثنتين *l-bank yfattiḥ s-saa*ᶜ*a* ᶜ*ašir w-ybannid s-saa*ᶜ*a θinteen*. The bank opens at ten and closes at two. فتح عينك، فتح عيونك! *fattiḥ* ᶜ*eenak, fattiḥ* ᶜ*yuunak!* Open your eyes! Be careful! Be on the lookout! 2. to bloom, open (flowers). الورد يفتح في الربيع *l-ward yfattiḥ fi r-rabii*ᶜ. Flowers bloom in the spring.

فاتح *faataḥ* III to approach, speak to. فاتحته بالموضوع، بس ما وافق *faataḥta b-l-mawδuu*ᶜ*, bass ma waafag*. I brought the subject up with him, but he didn't agree.

انفتح *nfitaḥ* VII pass. of فتح *fitaḥ*.

افتتح *ftitaḥ* VIII to open, inaugurate. الرئيس رحب بالحضور وعقبه افتتح الاحتفال *r-ra'iis raḥḥab b-l-ḥuδuur w-*ᶜ*ugba ftitaḥ li-ḥtifaal*. The president welcomed the attendance and then he opened the ceremony.

فتح *fatiḥ* (v.n. from فتح *fitaḥ*) 1. opening. 2. starting, opening (a bank account). 3. turning on (water, radio, etc.). 4. conquering, capturing (a city). منظمة فتح *munaδδamat fatiḥ* the Palestine Liberation Organization (PLO).

فتاح *fattaaḥ*, as in فتاح الفال *fattaaḥ l-faal* the fortuneteller.

فتاحة *fattaaḥa* p. *-aat* 1. can opener, bottle opener. 2. corkscrew.

مفتاح *miftaaḥ* p. مفاتيح *mafaatiiḥ* 1. key. مفتاح الباب *miftaaḥ l-baab* the door key. 2. switch (el.) مفتاح الكهربا *miftaaḥ l-kahraba* the electric switch.

افتتاح *ftitaaḥ* (v.n. from VIII افتتح *ftitaḥ*) opening, inauguration. افتتاح الاحتفال *ftitaaḥ li-ḥtifaal* the opening of the ceremony.

فاتح *faatiḥ* (act. part. from فتح *fitaḥ*) 1. having opened s.th. من فاتح الدريشة؟ *man faatiḥ d-diriiša?* Who has opened the window? 2. conqueror, victor. 3. (adj.) light (color). خضر فاتح *xaðar faatiḥ* light green. لون فاتح *loon faatiḥ* light color.

فاتحة *faatḥa* p. فواتح *fawaatiḥ* beginning, start. فاتحة خير *faatḥat xeer* beginning of a good time, good start. الفاتحة *l-faatiḥa* name of the first sura of the Quran.

مفتوح *maftuuḥ* (p.p. from فتح *fitaḥ*) 1. open, opened. القوطي مفتوح *l-guuṭi maftuuḥ*. The can is open. دش! الباب مفتوح *dišš! l-baab maftuuḥ*. Enter! The door is open. 2. open, open for business. الأسواق مفتوحة *l-'aswaag maftuuḥa*. The stores are open. 3. on. ليش الماي مفتوح؟ *leeš l-maay maftuuḥ?* Why is the water on?

ف ت خ *ftx*

فتخة *fatxa* p. *-aat* 1. ring, usually worn on a toe. 2. wedding ring.

ف ت ر *ftr*

فتر *fitir* p. افتار *ftaar* the span between the extended thumb and the index finger (used as a unit of measurement).

فترة *fatra* p. *-aat* period, interval of time. بين فترة وفترة *been fatra w-fatra* from time to time.

ف ت ش *ftš*

فتش *fattaš* II 1. to search. زخوه وفتشوه *zaxxoo w-fattašoo*. They arrested and searched him. فتشوا البيت *fattašu l-beet*. They searched the house. 2. (with على *ᶜala*) to look for s.o. or s.th. فتش على المفتاح *fattiš ᶜala l-miftaaḥ*. Look for the key.

تفتيش *taftiiš* (v.n.) search, inspection.

ف ت ل *ftl*

فتل *fital (يفتل yaftil)* 1. to braid, plait. البنت فتلت شعرها *l-bint ftalat šaᶜarha*. The girl braided her hair. فتل الخيوط وسوى منهم حبل *fital li-xyuuṭ w-sawwa minhum ḥabil*. He braided the threads and made a rope out of them. 2. to twist together. فتل الحبلين *fital l-ḥableen*. He twisted the two ropes together.

فتيلة *fitiila* p. فتايل *fitaayil* wick (of a lamp or a candle).

فتال *fattaal* p. فتاتلة *fataatla*, *-iin* one who spins pieces of string to make ropes, cordmaker, ropemaker.

ف ت ن *ftn*

فتن *fitan (يفتن yaftin)* (with على *ᶜala*) to tell on s.o. فتن عليّ *fitan ᶜalayya*. He told on me. فتن عليّ عند المدير *fitan ᶜalayya ᶜind l-mudiir*. He told on me to the director.

فتنة *fitna* p. فتن *fitan* discord, dissension.

فتان *fattaan* 1. (adj.) captivating, charming. جمالها فتان *jamaalha fattaan*. Her beauty is captivating. 2. (n. p. *-iin*) informer, slanderer, talebearer.

ف ت و *ftw*

أفتى *'afta* IV to give a formal legal opinion. المفتي أفتى بهالشي *l-mufti 'afta b-haš-šayy*. The mufti gave a religious opinion on this thing.

فتوى *fatwa* p. فتاوي *fataawi* formal ruling on a religious matter.

مفـــــتي *mufti* official interpreter of Islamic law.

ف ج ر *fjr*

فجـــــر *fajjar* II to explode s.th. فجروا قنبلة *fajjaraw gumbula.* They exploded a bomb.

تفجر *tfajjar* V 1. pass. of II فجر *fajjar.* 2. to burst forth, gush out, erupt. شفت بترول يتفجر من البير *čift batrool yitfajjar min l-biir.* I saw petroleum bursting forth from the well.

انفجر *nfijar* VII to explode, burst, go off. القنبلة انفجـــــرت *l-gumbula nfijrat.* The bomb exploded.

فجر *fajir* daybreak, morning twilight. الفجــــر *l-fajir* at daybreak. يدش الشغل الفجــــر *ydišš š-šuġul l-fajir.* He goes to work at daybreak.

انفجار *nfijaar* p. *-aat* explosion.

ف ج ل *fjl*

فجــــل *fijil* (coll.) radishes. نحن ما نعرف الفجل؛ نقول لـــه الرويـــد *niḥin ma ncarf l-fijil; ngul-la r-rweed.* We don't know *fijil*; we call it *rweed.*

ف چ چ ١ *fčč*

فــك *fačč* (يفــك *yfičč*) 1. to settle (a quarrel, a dispute). ما يفك الهـــواش إلا الشيخ *ma yfičč li-hwaaš 'illa š-šeex.* No one can settle the fight except the Shaikh. 2. to take apart, disassemble. فك الماكينة لاجل ينظفها *fačč l-maakiina lajil ynaððifha.* He took the engine apart in order to clean it. 3. to open. فــك البـــاب ودش الحجـــرة *fačč l-baab w-dašš l-ḥijra.* He opened the door and entered the room. 4. to unscrew, loosen. إذا تفك السكرو الجام يطيح علـــى الأرض *'iða tfičč s-sikruu, l-jaam yṭiiḥ cala l-'arð̣.* If you unscrew the screw, the glass will fall to the ground. 5. (with من *min*) to rid s.o. of s.th., put an end to s.th. فكنا من ها المشكلـــة *fiččna min hal-muškila.* Put an end to this problem.

ف چ چ ٢ *fčč*

فـــك *fačč* p. فكاك *fčaač* jaw, jawbone. فكي يعـــــورني *fačči ycawwirni.* My jaw hurts.

ف ح ص *fḥṣ*

فحص *fiḥaṣ* (يفحص *yafḥaṣ*) to examine s.o. (med.) فحصني الدختر وقال لازم أنام في الســـبيتار *fiḥaṣni d-daxtar w-gaal laazim 'anaam fi s-sbeetaar.* The doctor examined me and said that I had to be hospitalized.

انفحـــص *nfiḥaṣ* VII pass. of فحص *fiḥaṣ.*

فحـــص *faḥṣ* examination, check up (medical or physical).

ف ح م *fḥm*

فحــــم *faḥam* (coll.) charcoal. s. فحمة *fḥama* piece of charcoal. (prov.) موب كل بيضة شحمة ولا كل سودة فحمة *muub kill beeða šḥama wala kill sooda fḥama.* You cannot judge a book by its cover.

ف خ خ *fxx*

فــخ *faxx* p. فخاخ *fxaax* bird trap. نصب الفخ وصاد عصفورين *niṣab l-faxx w-ṣaad caṣfuureen.* He set the trap and caught two birds.

ف خ ف خ fxfx

فخفخة *faxfaxa* arrogance, haughtiness. الفخفخة خصلة شينة *l-faxfaxa xiṣla šeena.* Arrogance is a bad quality. الفخفخة ما تليق لك *l-faxfaxa ma tliig lak.* Arrogance doesn't become you.

ف خ م fxm

فخم *faxim* magnificent, impressive, stately. ها القصر فخم *hal-gaṣir faxim.* This palace is magnificent.

فخامة *faxaama* (title of respect usually given to a prime minister). فخامة رئيس الوزراء *faxaamat ra'iis l-wuzara.* His Excellency the Prime Minister.

ف د ن fdn

فدان *faddaan* p. فدادين *fadaadiin* (land) square measure, approx. 4,200 m^2.

ف د ي fdy

فدى *fida (يفدي yifdi)* to sacrifice for or to. كلنا نفدي وطننا بأرواحنا *killana nifdi waṭanna b-'arwaaḥna.* We all sacrifice our souls for our country.

تفادى *tfaada* VI to avoid. حاول يتفادى الخطر بس ما قدر *ḥaawal yitfaada l-xaṭar bass ma gidar.* He tried to avoid danger but he couldn't.

فدى *fida* (v.n. from فدى *fida*) sacrifice. مات فدى الوطن *maat fida l-waṭan.* He died for his country.

فداوي *fdaawi* p. *-yya* 1. one who sacrifices himself (for his country). 2. commando, guerrilla, member of fedayeen. 3. bodyguard.

ف ر ج ١ frj

فرج *firaj (يفرج yafrij)* to relieve, cause

ف خ ذ fxð

فخذ *faxð* p. افخاذ *fxaað,* فخوذ *fxuuð.* 1. thigh. 2. leg (of meat). اشتريت فخذ خروف *štireet faxð xaruuf.* I bought a leg of lamb. 3. (p. فخايذ *fuxaayið*) subdivision of a tribe. هو من فخذ بني تميم *huwa min faxð bani tamiim.* He belongs to the Tamim tribe.

ف خ ر ١ fxr

تفاخر *tfaaxar* VI (with ب *b-*) to boast about. يتفاخر بأجداده *yitfaaxar b-'aydaada.* He boasts about his ancestors.

افتخر *ftixar* VIII = VI تفاخر *tfaaxar.*

فخر *faxir* (v.n.) 1. glory, pride, honor. 2. boasting. بدون فخر *b-duun faxir,* بليا فخر *b-layya faxir* without boasting. 3. s.o. or s.th. to be proud of. لاعب ها الكرة فخر بلادنا *laa^c^ib hal-kuura faxir blaadna.* This soccer player is the object of our country's pride.

فخري *faxri* honorary. رئيس فخري *ra'iis faxri* honorary chairman.

افتخار *ftixaar* (v.n. from VIII افتخر *ftixar*) 1. boasting, begging. ما يفكر ان هذي إهمال؛ هذي موب افتخار *ma yfakkir 'inna haaði 'ihmaal; haaði muub ftixaar.* He doesn't think this is negligence; it's not boasting.

ف خ ر ٢ fxr

فخار *fuxxaar* (coll.) pottery. فيه مواعين من فخار في متحف العين *fii muwaa^c^iin min fuxxaar fi matḥaf l-^c^een.* There are utensils of pottery in the Al-Ain Museum.

to come to a happy ending. الله فرجها علينا *'aḷḷa firjaha ᶜaleena.* God relieved us. God caused things to come to a happy ending for us.

فرج *farraj* = فرج *firaj.*

فرج *faraj* (v.n. from فرج *firaj*) relief, happy ending. الفرج بيد الله *l-faraj b-yadd 'aḷḷa.* Relief is in God's hands. (prov.) الصبر مفتاح الفرج *ṣ-ṣabir miftaaḥ l-faraj.* Patience is the key to a happy ending.

ف ر ج ٢ *frj*

فريج *firiij* p. فرجان *firjaan* neighborhood, quarter or section of a city. أنت من تركت الفريج حتى مر تمر *'inta min tirakt l-firiij ḥatta marr ma tmurr.* Since you left the neighborhood, you haven't even come by for a visit.

ف ر ح *frḥ*

فرح *firaḥ* (يفرح *yifraḥ*) to be happy, delighted, glad. فرح لين سمع انه نجح في الامتحان *firaḥ leen simaᶜ 'inna nijaḥ fi li-mtiḥaan.* He was happy when he heard that he had passed the examination.

فرح *farraḥ* II to make happy, delight. نجاحه في الامتحان فرحنا *najaaḥa fi li-mtiḥaan farraḥna.* His passing the examination made us happy.

فرح *faraḥ* 1. (v.n. from فرح *firaḥ*) happiness, joy, gladness. ها الخبر طيرني من الفرح *hal-xabar ṭayyarni min l-faraḥ.* This news made me jump for joy. 2. (p. أفراح *'afraaḥ*) wedding celebration. عندهم فرح اليوم *ᶜindahum faraḥ l-yoom.* They have a wedding celebration today.

فرحة *farḥa* (n. of inst.) joy, mirth.

فرحان *farḥaan* happy, joyful, glad. شقد فرحان! *š-gad farḥaan!* How happy he is! ساعةٍ شفته، كان فرحان *saaᶜtin čifta, čaan farḥaan.* When I saw him, he was happy.

ف ر د *frd*

فرد *fard* p. فرود *fruud* pistol.

مفرد *mfarrad* single, lone. بالمفرد *b-li-mfarrad* by retail. نبيع بالجملة؛ ما نبيع بالمفرد *nbiiᶜ b-l-jumla; ma nbiiᶜ b-li-mfarrad.* We sell wholesale; we don't sell retail.

ف ر د و س *frdws*

الفردوس *l-firdoos* Paradise. الفردوس والنعيم *l-firdoos w-n-naᶜiim* Paradise and (God's) blessings.

ف ر ر *frr*

فرر *farrar* II to show around. خذيته بسيارتي وفررته في المدينة *xaðeeta b-sayyaarti w-farrarta fi l-madiina.* I took him in my car and showed him around the city.

افتر *ftarr* VIII 1. to wander around, go around. افتر هني وهناك وما حصل شي *ftarr hni w-hnaak w-ma ḥaṣṣal šayy.* He wandered around here and there and didn't find anything. 2. to spin. هذا التاير ما يفتر. ما ادري شبيه *haaða t-taayir ma yiftarr. ma dri š-bii.* This tire doesn't spin. I don't know what's wrong with it.

فرة *farra* p. *-aat* 1. revolution, turn, spin. كم فرة في الدقيقة؟ *čam farra fi d-dagiiga?* How many revolutions per minute?

مفر *mafarr* escape, flight. ما فيه مفر *ma fii mafarr.* There's no way out. It's unavoidable.

ف رز١ *frz*

فرز *firaz* (يفرز *yafriz)* to stake boundaries (of a lot), to set apart. القزاز فرز لي الأرض *l-gazzaaz firaz-li l-'arḍ.* The surveyor staked the boundaries of my lot.

ف رز٢ *frz*

فرز *farraz* II to turn to ice, freeze. ها الثلاجة باردة كلش. الحليب فرز *haθ-θallaaja baarda killiš. l-ḥaliib farraz.* This refrigerator is very cold. The milk turned into ice.

ف رس١ *frs*

فرس *faras* p. افراس *fraas* mare. فرس البحر *faras l-baḥar* hippopotamus.

فريسة *fariisa* p. فرايس *faraayis* 1. prey (of a wild animal). 2. victim. وقعت فريسة بين ايدينه *wugᶜat fariisa been 'iideena.* She became his victim.

فروسية *furuusiyya* 1. horsemanship. 2. chivalry.

فارس *faaris* p. فرسان *fursaan* knight.

مفترس *miftaris* predatory. حيوان مفترس *ḥayawaan miftaris* beast of prey.

ف رس٢ *frs*

بلاد فارس *blaad faaris* Iran, Persia.

فارسي *faarsi* 1. Persian. خط فارسي *xaṭṭ faarsi* Farsi script. 2. a Persian. 3. the Persian language, Farsi. تتكلم فارسي؟ *titkallam faarsi?* Do you speak Persian?

ف رش *frš*

فرش *firaš* (يفرش *yafriš)* 1. to provide (e.g., a house) with things like rugs, cushions, pieces of furniture, etc. المعرس هو اللي لازم يفرش البيت *l-miᶜris huwa lli laazim yafriš l-beet.* The bridegroom is the one who should furnish the house. 2. to prepare a bed, spread out the bedding. فرشت له لاجل يرقد *frišat-la lajil yargid.* She prepared the bed for him so that he might sleep.

فرش *farš* (v.n.) furnishing. فرش البيت على المعرس *farš l-beet ᶜala l-miᶜris.* Furnishing the house is the bridegroom's responsibility.

فراش *fraaš* 1. mattresses, bedding. 2. bed.

فراشة *faraaša* p. *-aat* butterfly.

فراش *farraaš* p. فراريش *faraariiš, -iin* 1. office custodian. صدق كل موظف يبغى له فراش؟ *ṣidj kill muwaððaf yibġaa-la farraaš?* Is it true that every employee wants an office custodian? 2. doorman.

ف رص *frṣ*

فرصة *furṣa* p. فرص *furaṣ* opportunity, chance. انتهز الفرصة *ntihaz l-furṣa.* He seized the opportunity. طال عمرك هذي فرصة ما لازم تفوتك *ṭaal ᶜumrak haaði furṣa ma laazim tfuutak.* May you live long, this is an opportunity you shouldn't miss.

ف رظ *frð*

فرض *firað* (يفرض *yafrið)* 1. to suppose, assume. افرض نفسك مكاني. شو لازم تسوي؟ *'ifrið nafsak mukaani. šu laazim tsawwi?* Suppose you were in

مفـــرع *mfarri*c (act. part. from II فرع *farra*c) having uncovered one's head.

ف رع و ن *fr*c*wn*

فرعـــون *far*c*oon* p. فراعنـــة *faraa*c*na* Pharaoh. (prov.) على هامان يا فرعـــون c*ala haamaan ya far*c*oon.* You cannot pull the wool over my eyes. You cannot fool me.

ف رغ *frġ*

فـــرغ *firaġ* (يفرغ *yafriġ*) 1. to be or become empty. أصطوانة القاز فرغـــت *'usṭuwaanat l-qaaz friġat.* The gas cylinder became empty. تانكي الماي فرغ *taanki l-maay firaġ.* The water tank became empty. 2. to be or become vacant. فرغت وظيفة قزاز في البلدية. روح قـــدم طلـــب *friġat waðiifat gazzaaz fi l-baladiyya. ruuḥ gaddim ṭalab.* A job for a surveyor was vacated in the municipality. Go submit an application. 3. to be or become free. مشغول هالحين. أفرغ الســـاعة خمـس *mašġuul halḥiin. 'afriġ s-saa*c*a xams.* I'm busy now. I will be free at five o'clock.

فـــرغ *farraġ* II 1. to empty. فرغ تانكي الماي لاجل ينظفـــه *farraġ taanki l-maay lajil ynaððfa.* He emptied the water tank to clean it. فـــرغ مخبـــاك! *farriġ maxbaak!* Empty your pocket. 2. to pour out. فرغ الماي *farriġ l-maay.* Pour out the water. 3. to unload. الكولية هـــالحين يفرغـــون اللوريـــات *l-kuuliyya halḥiin yfarrġuun l-looriyyaat.* The coolies are now unloading the lorries.

تفـــرغ *tfarriġ* V 1. p.p. of II فرغ *farraġ.* 2. to devote oneself, apply oneself. أتفرغ حق أي شي تريده بـــاكر *'atfarraġ ḥagg 'ayya šayy triida*

my place. What should you do? 2. to impose. الحكومة فرضت ضرايب جديـــدة *l-ḥukuuma fraðat ðaraayib yidiida.* The government has imposed new taxes. هذا شي الله فرضه *haaða šayy 'aḷḷa fraða.* This is something God ordained to us.

افترض *ftirað* VIII = فرض *firað.*

فـــرض *farð* p. فروض *furuuð* 1. duty, religious duty. الصلاة فرض على كـــل مســـلم *ṣ-ṣalaa farð* c*ala kill muslim.* Prayer is every Muslim's duty. 2. one of five obligatory prayers. 3. assumption, supposition, hypothesis. على فرض انـــه... c*ala farð 'inna...* on the assumption that...

فرضة *furða* p. فرض *furað* harbor, small seaport. السفينة رست قريب من الفرضـــة *s-safiina risat gariib min l-furða.* The ship laid anchor near the harbor.

فريضة *fariiða* p. فرايض *faraayið* religious duty, religious obligation.

ف رع *fr*c

فرع *farra*c II to uncover (one's head), take off one's غترة *gitra* or hat.

تفرع *tfarra*c V to branch, branch out, spread in all directions. فيه شجر يتفرع وشجـــر مـــا يتفـــرع *fii šiyar yitfarra*c *w-šiyar ma yitfarra*c. There are trees that branch and (other) trees that don't branch.

فـــرع *far*c p. فـــروع *fruu*c 1. branch, branch office. 2. branch, twig.

فرعي *far*c*i* subsidiary, sub-, secondary. شركة فرعيـــة *šarika far*c*iyya* subsidiary company. لجنة فرعية *lajna far*c*iyya* subcommittee.

baačir. I will devote myself to anything you want tomorrow.

فراغ *faraaġ* 1. free time, leisure. 2. empty space, emptiness.

فارغ *faariġ* 1. empty, void. بطالة فارغة *bṭaala faarġa* empty bottles. حكي فارغ *ḥači faariġ* empty talk. 2. vacant, unoccupied. بيت فارغ *beet faariġ* vacant house. وظيفة فارغة *waðiifa faarġa* vacant job. 3. not busy, unoccupied. آنا فارغ هالحين *'aana faariġ halḥiin.* I am free now.

مفروغ *mafruuġ* (p.p. from فرغ *firaġ*): مفروغ منه *mafruuġ mina* having been settled, finished. ها المشكلة مفروغ منها *hal-muškila mafruuġ minha.* This problem has been settled.

ف ر گ *frg*

فرق *firag (يفرق yafrig)* 1. to be different. المكتب يفرق عن الحفيز *l-maktab yafrig* ᶜ*an l-ḥafiiz.* A *maktab* is different from a *ḥafiiz.* يفرق واجد *yafrig waayid.* It differs quite a bit. 2. to make a difference. ما تفرق *ma tafrig.* It doesn't make any difference. شتفرق؟ *š-tafrig?* What difference does it make? 3. to be less (by a certain amount). يفرق خمسة كيلو *yafrig xamsa keelu.* It is less by five kilograms. It's five kilograms short.

فرق *farrag* II 1. to distinguish, differentiate (between). ثنينهم توم؛ ما تقدر تفرق بينهم *θneenhum toom; ma tigdar tfarrig beenhum.* Both of them are twins; you cannot distinguish between them. 2. to divide. فرق علينا الفلوس *farrag* ᶜ*aleena li-fluus.* He divided the money among us. فرق تسد *farrig tasud.* Divide and conquer. 3. to disperse, scatter. فرقوا الجمهور *farragaw l-jumhuur.* They dispersed the crowd. فرقنا الزمان *farragna z-zamaan.* Time has separated us. 4. to distribute. البنك فرق الربح على المساهمين *l-bank farrag r-ribḥ* ᶜ*ala l-musaahmiin.* The bank distributed the interest among the shareholders.

فارق *faarag* III to leave s.o. or s.th., depart, separate from s.o. or s.th. فارق هله وسافر *faarag hala w-saafar.* He left his family and traveled.

تفرق *tfarrag* V to be or become separated. عقب الحرب تفرقوا ناس واجدين ᶜ*ugb l-ḥarb tfarragaw naas waaydiin.* After the war, many people became separated. تفرق شملهم *tfarrag šamlahum.* They were disunited.

افترق *ftirag* VIII = تفرق *tfarrag* V.

فرق *farg* p. فروق *fruug* difference. أنت وانا إخوان؛ ما فيه فرق بيناتنا *'inta w-aana 'ixwaan; ma fii farg beenaatna.* You and I are brothers; there's no difference between us. الفرق بين عشرة وخمسة خمسة *l-farg been* ᶜ*ašara w-xamsa xamsa.* The difference between ten and five is five.

فرقة *firga* p. فرق *firag* 1. band, orchestra. 2. team.

فريق *fariig* p. فرقا *furaga,* فرق *firag.* 1. team (of players). فريق الكورة *fariig l-kuura* the soccer team. 2. lieutenant general. ترفع إلى رتبة فريق أول *traffa*ᶜ *'ila rutbat fariig 'awwal.* He was promoted to the rank of lieutenant general.

فراق *fraag* farewell, departure. (prov.) فراقه عيد *fraaga* ^c^*iid.* Good riddance.

ف ر ك *frk*

فرك *firak* (يفرك *yafruk*) to rub. الجاهل فرك عيونه *l-yaahil firak* ^c^*yuuna.* The child rubbed his eyes.

فرك *farrak* II intens. of فرك *firak.*

ف ر ك و ت *frkwt*

فركوت *farkoot* p. *-aat* overcoat.

ف ر ن *frn*

فرن *firn* p. فران *fraan* 1. oven. الدجاج توه طالع من الفرن *d-diyaay tawwa ṭaali*^c^ *min l-firn.* The chicken has just come out of the oven. 2. bakery. اشتريت خبز حار من الفرن *štireet xubiz ḥaarr min l-firn.* I bought hot bread from the bakery.

ف ر ن س *frns*

فرنسا *faransa* France.

فرنسي *faransi* 1. French, characteristic of France. 2. (p. *-yyiin*) Frenchman. 3. French, the French language. تتكلم فرنسي؟ *titkallam faransi?* Do you speak French?

ف ر و *frw*

فرو *faru* (coll.) fur. كوت فرو *kuut faru* fur coat.

فروة *farwa* p. *-aat* overcoat (made from sheep skin and lined with wool).

ف ز ز *fzz*

فز *fazz* (يفز *yfizz*) 1. to stand up. لين رمسه الشيخ، فز *leen rammasa š-šeex, fazz.* When the Shaikh talked to him, he stood up. 2. to wake up. فز من النوم *fazz min n-noom.* He woke up.

ف ز ع *fz*^c^

فزع *fiza*^c^ (يفزع *yifza*^c^) (with ل *l-*) to go to s.o.'s aid, go to help s.o. كانوا يريدون يضربونه، بس أخوه فزع له *čaanaw yriiduun yađribuuna, bass 'uxuu fiza*^c^*-la.* They wanted to hit him, but his brother came to his aid.

ف س ت ا ن *fstaan*

فستان *fustaan* p. فساتين *fasaatiin* (more common var. نفنوف *nafnuuf*) woman's dress.

ف س د *fsd*

فسد *fisad* (يفسد *yafsid*) 1. to spoil, go bad, become rotten. فسد الحليب *fisad l-ḥaliib.* The milk spoiled. 2. to be or become corrupt, bad. فسد من الجماعة اللي صاحبهم *fisad min l-jamaa*^c^*a lli ṣaaḥbahum.* He became corrupt because of the people he associated with.

فسد *fassad* II 1. to corrupt, spoil s.o. صديقه فسده *ṣadiiga fassada.* His friend corrupted him. 2. to mess up s.th. فسد علينا كل شي *fassad* ^c^*aleena kill šayy.* He messed up everything for us.

فساد *fasaad* corruption, immorality.

فاسد *faasid* (act. part. from فسد *fisad*) 1. immoral, wicked. 2. spoiled, rotten. بيض فاسد *beeđ faasid* rotten eggs.

ف س ر *fsr*

فسر *fassar* II to explain, interpret. المطوع يقدر يفسر لك ها الأشياء *li-mṭawwa*^c^ *yigdar yfassir-lak hal-'ašya.* The religious man can explain these things to you. المعلم فسر لنا الدرس *l-mu*^c^*allim fassar lana d-dars.* The teacher explained the lesson to us. تقدر تفسر هـا الظـاهرة *tigdar tfassir haδ-δaahira?* Can you explain this phenomenon?

تفسر *tfassar* V pass. of II فسر *fassar.*

استفسر *stafsar* X to inquire, ask. رايح أستفسر وأعرف الجـواب *raayiḥ 'astafsir w-'a^c rif l-jawaab.* I am going to inquire and know the answer.

تفسير *tafsiir* (v.n. from II فسر *fassar*) explanation, interpretation. تفسير القرآن *tafsiir l-ġur'aan* interpretation and commentary on the Quran.

مفسر *mfassir* (act. part. from II فسر *fassar*) interpreter, commentator. مفسر الأحلام *mfassir l-'aḥlaam* interpreter of dreams.

ف ش گ *fšg*

فشق *fišag* (coll.) cartridges, bullets. s. فشقة *fišga, fšiga.*

ف ش ل *fšl*

فشل *fišal* (يفشل *yifšal*) to fail, be unsuccessful. بطال. فشل في حياته *baṭṭaal. fišal fi ḥayaata.* He's a bad person. He was a failure in his life.

فشل *faššal* II 1. to let s.o. down, disappoint s.o. خوش رجال. ما يفشل أحد *xooš rayyaal. ma yfaššil 'aḥad.* He's a good man. He doesn't let anyone down. روح شوف الشيخ والشيخ ما يفشلك *ruuḥ čuuf š-šeex w-š-šeex ma yfaššilk.* Go see the Shaikh and he will not disappoint you. 2. to embarrass, ridicule. استح على وجهك! فشلته قدام الناس *'istaḥ ^c ala weehak! faššalta jiddaam n-naas.* Shame on you! You embarrassed him in front of the people.

تفشل *tfaššal* V pass. of II فشل *faššal.*

فشل *fašal* (v.n. from فشل *fišal*) failure, state of being unsuccessful.

فاشل *faašil* (act. part. from *fišal*) 1. having failed, having been unsuccessful. فاشل في الامتحان *faašil fi li-mtiḥaan.* He's failed the examination. 2. unsuccessful, failing. فاشل في حياته *faašil fi ḥayaata.* He's no good. He's a failure in his life.

ف ص خ *fṣx*

فسخ *fuṣax* (يفسخ *yfaṣix*) 1. to dissolve, cancel, void. فسخ العقد *fuṣax l-^c agd.* He broke the contract. 2. to take off (one's clothes). فسخ هدومه وتسبح *fuṣax hduuma w-tsabbaḥ.* He took off his clothes and took a bath. 3. to take apart, disassemble. فسخ الماكينة *fuṣax l-maakiina.* He took the engine apart.

تفسخ *tfaṣṣax* V to take off one's clothes. قوم تفسخ واسبح وتعال ناكل *guum tfaṣṣax w-isbaḥ w-ta^c aal naakil.* Go take off your clothes, take a bath, and come so that we might eat.

مفسخ *mfaṣṣax* (p.p. from II فسخ *faṣṣax*) 1. having been taken apart. الماكينة مفسخة *l-maakiina mfaṣṣaxa.* The engine has been taken apart. 2. (p. *-iin*) naked. (prov.) عريان ولافي على مفسخ *^c iryaan w-laafi ^c ala mfaṣṣax.* Two peas in a pod.

ف ص ص *fṣṣ*

فص *faṣṣ* first, the best. فص كلاس *faṣṣ klaas* first class.

ف ص ل *fṣl*

فصل *fiṣal (يفصل yafṣil)* to separate. في أمريكا ما يفصلون الأولاد عن البنات في المدارس *fi 'amriika ma yfaṣluun l-'awlaad ᶜan l-banaat fi l-madaaris.* In America they do not separate boys from girls in schools.

فصل *faṣṣal* II to interpret, explain. أنت ما تقدر تفصل مثل المطوع *'inta ma tigdar tfaṣṣil miθil li-mṭawwaᶜ.* You cannot interpret things like a religious man does. فصل تفصيلات معقولة *faṣṣal tafṣiilaat maᶜguula.* He gave reasonable interpretations.

انفصل *nfiṣal* VII pass. of فصل *fiṣal.*

فصل *faṣil* 1. (v.n. from فصل *fiṣal*) separation. 2. (p. فصول *fuṣuul*) chapter (in a book, a play, etc.) 3. season. 4. semester, term.

فصلي *faṣli* (adj.) semester, term. رسوم فصلية *rusuum faṣliyya* semester fees.

فصيل *faṣiil* p. فصايل *faṣaayil* platoon (mil.), squadron.

مفصل *mafṣal* p. مفاصل *mafaaṣil* joint.

تفصيل *tafṣiil* 1. (v.n. from II فصل *faṣṣal*) interpretation, explanation. 2. (p. *-aat*) detail.

ف ط ر *fṭr*

فطر *fiṭar (يفطر yafṭir)* to break the fast, eat and drink after a fast. أي ساعة تفطرون هني؟ *'ayya saaᶜa tfaṭruun hni?* What time do you break your fast here? أول شي نفطر على تمر بس *'awwal šayy nafṭir ᶜala tamir bass.* We break our fast with dates only.

فطر *faṭṭar* 1. to cause s.o. to break his fast. شرب الماي يفطر *šurb l-maay yfaṭṭir.* Drinking water breaks the fast. التدخين يفطر بعد *t-tadxiin yfaṭṭir baᶜad.* Smoking breaks the fast also. 2. to allow s.o. to break his fast. الدختر فطرها لانها حامل *d-daxtar faṭṭarha linha ḥaamil.* The doctor excused her from fasting because she was pregnant.

فطر *fiṭir*: عيد الفطر *ᶜiid l-fiṭir* (also known as عيد رمضان *ᶜiid rumðaan*) Lesser Bairam, feast of the end of Ramadan.

فطور *fuṭuur* (v.n. from فطر *fiṭar*) 1. breaking one's fast at sundown during Ramadan. 2. the first meal after the daily fast in Ramadan.

مفطر *mifṭir* not fasting (adj.). أنت صايم والا مفطر اليوم؟ *'inta ṣaayim walla mifṭir l-yoom?* Are you fasting or not fasting today? مفطر لني مريض *mifṭir linni mariiḍ.* I am not fasting because I am sick.

ف ط س *fṭs*

فطيسة *fiṭiisa* p. فطايس *fiṭaayis* dead animal, carrion, animal carcass.

أفطس *'afṭas* 1. (p. فطس *fuṭs,* فطسين *fuṭsiin*) flat-nosed person. 2. flat and wide nose. خشم أفطس *xašim 'afṭas* flat nose.

ف ط م *fṭm*

فطم *fiṭam (يفطم yufṭum)* to wean. فطمت ابنها لين كان عمره سنتين *fṭimat 'ibinha leen čaan ᶜumra sanateen.* She weaned her son when he was two years old.

فطام *fṭaam* (v.n.) weaning.

مفطوم *maftuum* (p.p.) weaned, having been weaned. *maftuum walla ba^c^da?* Is he weaned or not yet?

ف ظ ح *fðḥ*

فضح *fiðaḥ* (يفضح *yifðaḥ*) to expose, disclose or uncover s.o.'s faults or offenses. فضحهم قدام الناس *fiðaḥḥum jiddaam n-naas.* He exposed them in front of the people.

فضيحة *faðiiḥa* p. فضايح *faðaayiḥ* disgrace, scandal.

ف ظ ظ *fðð*

فضة *fiðða* silver (coll.). حيول (من) فضة *ḥyuul (min) fiðða* silver bracelets.

فضي *fiðði* silver, silvery. لون فضي *loon fiðði* silver color.

ف ظ ع *fð^c^*

فظيع *faðii^c^* 1. horrible, disgusting, atrocious, hideous. جريمة فظيعة *jariima faðii^c^a* horrible crime. 2. excellent, splendid. ضربة زاوية فظيعة *ðarbat zaawya faðii^c^a* excellent corner kick (in soccer).

أفظع *'afða^c^* (elat.) 1. (with من *min*) a. more horrible, disgusting, etc. than. b. more excellent than. 2. (with foll. n.) a. the most horrible, disgusting. b. the most splendid.

ف ظ ل *fðl*

فضل *faððal* II to prefer. الوقت متأخر. أفضل أروح *l-wagt mit'axxir. 'afaððil 'aruuḥ.* It's getting late. I prefer to go. أفضل القهوة على الشاي *'afaððil l-gahwa ^c^ala č-čaay.* I prefer coffee to tea.

تفضل *tfaððal* V (only as imp., approx. meaning:) please, go ahead, help yourself, be my guest, come in. تفضل، استريح *tfaððal, stariiḥ.* Please, sit down. تفضل! أنت أول *tfaððal! 'inta 'awwal.* Go ahead! You first. تفضل! اسأل! *tfaððal! 'is'al!* Go ahead! Ask! الأكل بارز. تفضلوا! *l-'akil baariz. tfaððlu!* The food is ready. Help yourselves! تفضلي اشربي شاي! *tfaððli 'išrabi čaay!* Here, have some tea! الباب مفتوح. تفضل *l-baab maftuuḥ. tfaððal.* The door's open. Come on in!

فضل *faðil* 1. favor, grace. اله فضل عليّ *'ila faðil ^c^alayya.* I owe him a favor. من فضلك، كم الساعة؟ *min faðlak, čam s-saa^c^a?* What time is it, please? 2. كل هذا حصلته من فضل الله *kill haaða ḥaṣṣalta min faðl aḷḷa.* I have gotten all of this, thanks to God.

فضيلة *faðiila* p. فضايل *faðaayil* virtue, good quality. قول الصدق فضيلة *gool ṣ-ṣidj faðiila.* Telling the truth is a virtue. هذي فضيلة والا رذيلة؟ *haaði faðiila walla raðiila?* Is this a virtue or a vice? صاحب الفضيلة *ṣaaḥib l-faðiila* His Holiness, His Eminence.

أفضل *'afðal* (elat.) 1. (with من *min*) better than, more desirable than. 2. (with foll. n.) the best, the most desirable.

أفضلية *'afðaliyya* precedence, priority. قضية الأمن لها أفضلية على أي قضية ثانية *gaðiyyat l-'amin laha 'afðaliyya ^c^ala 'ayya gaðiyya θaanya.* The problem of security has priority over any other problem.

فاضل *faaðil* distinguished, eminent, respected. عالم فاضل *^c^aalim faaðil* distinguished scholar.

ف ظ و *fðw*

فضـاء *faðaa'* space, empty space, cosmos. رائد الفضـاء *raa'id l-faðaa'* the astronaut.

ف ع ل *f^c^l*

فعل *fi^c^il* p. فعايل *fi^c^aayil,* أفعال *'af^c^aal* deed, action. شـو هـا الفعـايل؟! *šu hal-fi^c^aayil?!* What deeds are these?! بـالفعل *b-l-fi^c^il* indeed, actually, really. بـالفعل! يبي يعرس *b-l-fi^c^il! yabi y^c^arris.* Yes, indeed! He wants to get married. بـالفعل، جيـت وايـاهم *b-l-fi^c^il, yiit wiyyaahum.* Actually, I came with them.

فعلاً *fi^c^lan* = بالفعل *b-l-fi^c^il.*

فعال *fa^cc^aal* active, effective. عضو فعال *^c^uðu fa^cc^aal* active member.

فـاعل *faa^c^il* (act. part.) 1. having done s.th. منو فـاعل هـا الشـي؟ *minu faa^c^il haš-šayy?* Who has done this thing? 2. (p. *-iin*) doer, perpetrator.

ف گ ا گ *fgaag*

فقاق *fgaag* (coll.) pied weatherer. s. *-a.*

ف گ ر *fgr*

فقـر *faggar* II to make s.o. poor, impoverish s.o. هـا الدكـان فقـره لانـه مـا يعرف كيـف يديـره *had-dikkaan faggara linna ma y^c^arf keef ydiira.* This store made him poor because he didn't know how to manage it.

افتقـر *ftigar* VIII to become poor. من يـوم مـا شـارك أخـوه افتقـر *min yoom-ma šaarač 'uxuu ftigar.* Since the day he entered into a partnership with his brother, he has become poor.

فقـر *fagir* poverty, impoverishment. جا الفقـر لـين تـزوج الثانيـة *yaa l-fagir leen tazawwaj θ-θaanya.* He became poor when he married his second wife. فقر دم *fagir damm* anemia.

فقـير *fagiir* p. *-iin,* فقرا *fagaara* 1. poor. يطـر في الشـوارع لانـه فقـير *yṭirr fi š-šawaari^c^ linna fagiir.* He begs on the streets because he's poor. 2. pauper. 3. simple (person). ما يقول شي. رجال فقـير *ma yguul šayy. rayyaal fagiir.* He doesn't say anything. He is a simple man.

أفقـر *'afgar* (elat.) 1. (with مـن *min*) poorer than. 2. (with foll. n.) the poorest.

ف گ س *fgs*

فقـس *figas* (يفقـس *yufgus*) to hatch. رقدت الدجاجة على البيضة وفقست *rgadat d-diyaaya ^c^ala l-beeða w-figsat.* The hen sat on the egg and it hatched.

فقس *faggas* II = فقس *figas.* البيض فقس *l-beeð faggas.* The eggs hatched.

ف گ ع *fg^c^*

فقـع *fagi^c^* (common var. *fugu^c^*) mushroom (coll.). s. فقعة *fag^c^a.*

ف ك ر *fkr*

فكـر *fakkar* II to think over, meditate, reflect. لين علمته بذاك الشي قام يفكر *leen ^c^allamta b-ðaak š-šayy gaam yfakkir.* When I told him about that matter, he started to think it over. لين يركـب لـه السيارة يفكر انه حـاكم بلـد *leen yirkab-la sayyaara yfakkir 'inna ḥaakim bald.* Whenever he drives a car, he thinks he's a ruler of a country. مـا عـرف الجـواب لانـه مـا فكـر زيـن *ma ^c^iraf l-jawaab linna ma fakkar zeen.* He didn't know the answer because he didn't think hard.

افتكــــر *ftikar* VIII to think, be of the opinion. أفتكر انه جا *'aftakir 'inna ya.* I think he has come. افتكرته أمريكــــي *ftikarta 'amriiki.* I thought he was an American.

فكــــر *fikir* thinking, reflection, meditation. شو فكرك؟ *šu fikrak?* What do you think? فكرها بالدراسة والنجــــاح *fikirha b-d-diraasa w-n-najaaḥ.* Her mind is on studying and passing (the examination).

فكــرة *fikra* p. فكــــر *fikar, -aat* idea, thought, notion.

مفكرة *mufakkara* p. *-aat* 1. datebook. 2. diary.

ف ك ك *fkk* (more common var. *fčč*). See under **ف چ چ** *fčč.*

افتك *ftakk* VIII (with من *min*) to get rid of s.o. or s.th. افتكيــت منــه *ftakkeet minna.* I got rid of it. افتكينا من هـــا الورطـــة *ftakkeena min hal-warṭa.* We got rid of this problem.

فــك *fakka* escape, outlet. ماكو فكة *maaku fakka.* There's no escape.

مفكوك *mafkuuk* (p.p. from فك *fakk*) 1. open. تفضل! البـــاب مفكــوك *tfaððal! l-baab mafkuuk.* Come in. The door is open. 2. loose. سكرو مفكوك *sikruu mafkuuk* loose screw.

ف ك ه *fkh*

فاكهة *faakiha* p. فواكه *fawaakih* fruit.

ف ل ت¹ *flt*

فلــــت *filat (يفلت yaflit)* to come lose, escape, get away. إذا ما تشد الحبل زين، تري يفلـــت *'iða ma tšidd l-ḥabil zeen, tara yaflit.* If you don't tie the rope well, let me tell you, it will come loose. فلت من يدي وطار *filat min yaddi w-ṭaar.* It slipped out of my hand and flew away.

ف ل ت² *flt*

فلت *flit* insecticide, bug spray.

ف ل ج¹ *flj*

فالج *faalij* paralysis.

مفلوج *mafluuj* paralyzed, stricken with paralysis.

ف ل ج² *flj*

فلــــج *falaj* (common var. فلي *falay*) p. أفلاج *'aflaaj,* فلجان *filjaan* brook, little stream.

ف ل چ *flč*

فلكــــة *filka* Filka (more common var. *filča*) (Kuwaiti Island, known as a historical site).

ف ل ح *flḥ*

فــلاح *fallaaḥ* p. *-iin,* فلاليح *filaaliiḥ* farmer, peasant.

ف ل خ *flx*

فلــــخ *filax* to run away. فلخ من الشرطة *filax min š-širṭa.* He ran away from the police.

ف ل س *fls*

فلــــس *fallas* II to be or become bankrupt, go broke. فلست الشركة بســـبب الفلوس اللـــي لهـــا علـــى النـــاس *fallasat š-šarika b-sabab li-fluus illi laha ᶜala n-naas.* The company went broke because of the money people owed it.

فلس *fils* p. فلوس *fluus* 1. one *fils* coin = 1/1000 dinar in Bahrain or 1/100 dirham in the U.A.E. 2. (p. only) money. (prov.) الفلوس تجيب العـــروس *li-fluus tyiib l-ᶜaruus.* Money talks. (lit., "Money brings the bride.").

إفلاس *'iflaas* bankruptcy. الشركة أعلنت إفلاســها وســـارت *š-šarika 'aᶜlanat iflaassa w-saarat.* The company declared bankruptcy and left.

مفلس *miflis* bankrupt, insolvent, broke. شركة مفلســـة *šarika mifilsa* insolvent company. أشوف أنت مفلس اليوم *'ačuuf 'inta miflis l-yoom.* I see that you are broke today.

ف ل س ط ي ن *flsṭyn*

فلسطين *falasṭiin* Palestine.

فلسطيني *falasṭiini* 1. Palestinian, characteristic of Palestine. منظمة التحريـــر الفلســـــطينية *munaððamat t-taḥriir l-falasṭiiniyya* the P.L.O. 2. (p. *-yyiin, -yya*) a Palestinian.

ف ل س ف *flsf*

تفلسف *tfalsaf* (يتفلسف *yitfalsaf*) to pretend to be a philosopher. بـــس اسكت! لا تتفلسف بحكيك! *bass iskit! la titfalsaf b-ḥačyak!* Enough! Be quiet! Don't pretend to be such a philosopher with your talk!

فلسفة *falsafa* philosophy.

فيلســـوف *faylasuuf* p. فلاسفة *falaasfa* philosopher.

ف ل ع *flᶜ*

فلع *fallaᶜ* II 1. to cause to crack open. الثلج فلع الغرشـــة *θ-θalj fallaᶜ l-ġarša.* The ice has caused the bottle to crack open. 2. to split open. الرمان فلـــع *r-rummaan fallaᶜ.* The pomegranates have split open.

انفلع *nfilaᶜ* VII = II فلع *fallaᶜ* to split open.

فلعة *falᶜa* p. *-aat* crack, split.

ف ل ف ل *flfl*

فلفـــل *filfil* (coll.) 1. pepper. فلفل أسود *filfil 'aswad* black pepper. فلفل حــــار *filfil ḥaarr* hot pepper. 2. green peppers. s. فلفلة *filifla,* حبة فلفل *ḥabbat filfil.*

ف ل ك *flk*

فلك *falak* (no known p.) circuit, orbit (of celestial bodies). علم الفلـــك *ᶜilm l-falak* astronomy.

فلكـــة *filka* (more common var. *filča*). See under ف ل چ *flč.*

ف ل ل *fll*

فلـــة *falla* (invar.) wonderful, terrific, splendid. ضربة زاوية فلة *ðarbat zaawya falla* wonderful corner kick (in soccer). بنتي فلة في العلـــوم *binti falla fi l-ᶜuluum.* My daughter is terrific in science. عليها جمال فلة *ᶜaleeha jamaal falla.* She is of terrific beauty.

ف ل م *flm*

فلم *filim* p. أفلام *'aflaam* 1. film, roll of film. 2. movie, film. فيه فلم زين الليلة *fii filim zeen l-leela.* There's a good movie tonight.

ف ل ن *fln*

فـــلان *flaan* f. *-a* so-and-so, such-and-such. لافـــلان ولا عـــلان *la flaan wala ᶜillaan.* nobody, not a single person.

فـــلاني *fulaani* (adj. of فلان *flaan*) فلان الفـــلاني *flaan l-fulaani* John Doe. المكان الفـــلاني *l-mukaan l-fulaani* such and such a place.

ف ن ت ي ر *fntyr*

فنتير *fintiir* p. فناتير *finaatiir* flamingo.

ف ن ج ن *fnjn*

فنجـــان *finjaan* (more common var. *finyaan*). See under **ف ن ي ن** *fnyn.*

ف ن د گ *fndg*

فنـــدق *fundug* p. فنادق *fanaadig* hotel, inn. فنـــدق درجـــة أولى *fundug daraja 'uula* first class hotel. فندق الهلتـــون *fundug l-hilton* the Hilton Hotel.

ف ن د ل *fndl*

فندال *findaal* (coll.) sweet potatoes. s. *-a.*

ف ن ر *fnr*

فنار *fanaar* p. *-aat* lighthouse.

ف ن ش *fnš*

فنـــش *fannaš* II 1. to resign. اشتغل حق الشركة خمس ســنين وفنـــش *štaġal ḥagg š-šarika xams siniin w-fannaš.* He worked five years for the company and resigned. 2. to fire, discharge s.o. (from work). فنشوه لانه ما يشتغل زيـــن *fannašoo linna ma yištaġil zeen.* They fired him because he didn't work well.

تفنيـــــش *tafniiš* (v.n.) dismissal, discharge (from work).

مفنـــش *mfanniš* (act. part.) 1. having resigned. هو مفنش العام المـــاضي *huwa mfanniš l-ᶜaam l-maaḏi.* He resigned last year. 2. having fired, discharged s.o. التنديل هو المفنش الكوليـــة *t-tindeel huwa li-mfanniš l-kuuliyya.* The foreman is the one who fired the coolies.

مفنش *mfannaš* (p.p.) having been fired. خمس كوليـــة مفنشـــين *xamas kuuliyya mfannašiin.* Five coolies have been fired.

ف ن ل ن د *fnlnd*

فنلنـــدا *finlanda* (common var. فللندا *fillanda*) Finland.

ف ن ن *fnn*

تفنـــن *tfannan* V to be versatile, to be inventive. ها القاري يتفنـــن في التجويـــد *hal-gaari yitfannan fi t-tajwiid.* This reader is versatile at Quranic recitation.

فـــن *fann* p. فنون *fnuun* art. يدرس فن *yidriss fann.* He's studying art. فـــن التجميل *fann t-tajmiil* the art of cosmetics. مدرسة الفنـــون الجميلـــة *madrasat li-fnuun l-jamiila* the school of fine arts.

فني *fanni* 1. technical. 2. artistic. لوحة فنيـــة *lawḥa fanniyya* artistic piece of work.

فنان *fannaan* artist.

ف ن ي ل *fnyl*

فنيلة *faniila* p. *-aat* undershirt. اشتريت فنيلتين وخمس هافـــات *štireet faniilteen w-xams haafaat.* I bought two undershirts and five shorts.

ف ن ي ن *fnyn*

فنيـــان *finyaan* (common var. فنيـــال *finyaal*; less common var. فنجـــان *finjaan*) p. فنـــايين *fanaayiin* small porcelain cup. فنيان قهوة *finyaan gahwa* cup of coffee, coffee cup.

ف ه د *fhd*

فهد *fahad* p. فهود *fuhuud* 1. leopard, panther. 2. Fahad (male's name). فهد العسكر *fahad l-ᶜaskar* Fahad Al-Askar (Kuwaiti singer and man of letters).

ف ه ر س *fhrs*

فهرس *fahras* p. فهارس *fahaaris* index, table of contents.

ف ه م *fhm*

فهم *fiham* (يفهم *yifham)* to understand. ليش سويت هذا؟ ما أقدر أفهمك *leeš sawweet haaða? ma 'agdar 'afhamk.* Why have you done this? I can't understand you.

فهم *fahham* II to make s.o. understand or see, to instruct s.o., to explain to s.o. قلت له: «اقعد! آنا أفهمك الدرس» *git-la: "'igᶜid! 'aana 'afahhimk d-dars."* I said to him, "Sit down! I'll make you understand the lesson." ما تقدر تفهمه لاجل هو عنيد *ma tigdar tfahhma lajil huwa ᶜaniid.* You can't make him see things because he's stubborn. فهمني ليش ما جا *fahhimni leeš ma ya.* Explain to me why he hasn't come.

تفاهم *tfaaham* VI 1. to come to an understanding, come to an agreement, reach an understanding. بس خلنا نقعد نتفاهم *bass xaḷḷna nigᶜid nitfaaham.* Let's just sit down and come to an understanding. أنت مخبل! روح تفاهم وياهم *'inta mxabbal! ruuḥ tfaaham wiyyaahum.* You are crazy! Go and reach an understanding with them. 2. to communicate with each other. صحيح هو غتم. تفاهمنا بالإشارة *ṣaḥiih huwa ġatam. tfaahamna b-l-'išaara.* It's true that he's mute. We communicated by gesture.

افتهم *ftiham* VIII 1. to understand, comprehend s.th. ما افتهمت شو اللي يبغيه *ma ftihamt šu lli yabġii.* I didn't understand what he had wanted. 2. to learn, find out. افتهمت من كلامه انه واقع في مشكلة كبيرة *ftihamt min kalaama 'inna waagiᶜ fi muškila čibiira.* I learned from what he said that he was involved in a big problem.

استفهم *stafham* X to inquire, ask. روح استفهم عن ها القضية *ruuḥ stafhim ᶜan hal-gaḍiyya.* Go inquire about this case.

فهم *fahim* (v.n. from فهم *fiham*) understanding. سوء فهم *suu' fahim* misunderstanding.

تفاهم *tafaahum* (v.n. from VI تفاهم *tfaaham*) mutual understanding, mutual agreement.

فهم *faahim* (act. part. from فهم *fiham*) 1. having understood s.th. أنت فاهم الدرس؟ *'inta faahim d-dars?* Have you understood the lesson? 2. knowledgeable, competent. قاضي فاهم *gaaḍi faahim* knowledgeable judge.

مفهوم *mafhuum* (p.p. from فهم *fiham*) 1. understood, having been understood. هذا شي مفهوم *haaða šayy mafhuum.* This is an accepted fact. 2. certainly, sure, of course, fine. مفهوم، بس أنت رجال عود *mafhuum, bass 'inta rayyaal ᶜood.* I know, but you are an old man. المفهوم *l-mafhuum* it is said, it is known that... المفهوم انه جاي باكر

l-mafhuum 'inna yaay baačir. It is said that he's coming tomorrow.

ف ه و *fhw*

فـاهي *faahi* (invar.) 1. light, faint (color). حمر فاهي *ḥamar faahi* light red. 2. weak, flat-tasting. شـاي فـاهي *čaay faahi* weak tea.

ف و ت ١ *fwt*

فـات *faat* (يفـوت *yfuut)* 1. to go, pass. توه فـات مـني *tawwa faat minni.* He just went by here. فات من قدامـي *faat min giddaami.* He passed by me. تفضل فوت *tfaððal fuut.* Please, go ahead. فوت! البـاب مفكـوك *fuut! l-baab mafkuuk.* Come in! The door is unlocked. 2. to pass, go by. فات الوقت *faat l-wagt.* The time has passed. فاتتني الفرصـة *faatatni l-furṣa.* I missed the opportunity. فاتتني الطـايرة *faatatni ṭ-ṭaayra.* I missed the plane. (prov.) اللي فات مـات *'illi faat maat.* Let bygones be bygones. (prov.) اللـي يبغـى الصـلاة مـا تفوتـه *'illi yibġa ṣ-ṣalaa ma tfuuta.* Where there is a will there is way. الشهر اللي فات *š-šahar illi faat* the past month, last month.

فـوت *fawwat* II 1. to cause to go by, cause to pass. لا تفوت الفرصة عليك *la tfawwit l-furṣa ᶜaleek.* Don't miss the opportunity. 2. to allow to pass, allow to go by. فوتـني. أبغـى أشـوف الوزيـر *fawwitni. 'abġa 'ašuuf l-waziir.* Let me in. I want to see the minister. لا تفوت الشغلة مـن يـدك *la tfawwit š-šaġla min yaddak.* Don't let the job slip away from your hand.

فوات *fawaat* (v.n. from فات *faat*) passing, lapse. قبل فوات الأوان *gabil fawaat l-'awaan* before it's too late.

ف و ت ٢ *fwt*

فـوت *fuut* p. أفوات *'afwaat* foot (unit of measure). الميز طولهـا سـتة فـوت *l-meez ṭuulha sitta fuut.* The table is six feet long.

ف و ح *fwḥ*

فـاح *faaḥ* (يفوح *yfuuḥ)* to boil. فاح الماي *faaḥ l-maay.* The water boiled. الماي يفـوح. روح سـوي شـاي *l-maay yfuuḥ. ruuḥ sawwi čaay.* The water is boiling. Go make some tea.

فـوح *fawwaḥ* II to boil s.th. فوح الماي قبـل لا تحـط الشـاي فيـه *fawwiḥ l-maay gabil-la tḥuṭṭ č-čaay fii.* Boil the water before you put the tea in it.

ف و ر م ن *fwrmn*

فورمـن *foorman* p. *-iyya* foreman, supervisor. يشـتغل فورمـن *yištaġil foorman.* He works as a foreman.

ف و ز *fwz*

فـاز *faaz* (يفـوز *yfuuz)* 1. to win, be victorious. من اللي فـاز ذالحـين؟ *man illi faaz ðalḥiin?* Who is the one who won this time? 2. (with على *ᶜala*) to beat s.o., defeat s.o. لعبوا الفريقين وفريقنا فاز عليهـم *liᶜbaw l-fariigeen w-fariigna faaz ᶜaleehum.* The two teams played and our team beat them.

فـوز *fooz* (v.n.) winning, victory, success. الفـوز في الانتخابـات *l-fooz fi li-ntixaabaat* winning the elections.

فـايز *faayiz* (act. part.) 1. having won, having been victorious. 2. winner, victor. فريقنا الفايز *fariigna l-faayiz.* Our team is the winner.

ف و ط *fwṭ*

فوطة *fuuṭa* p. إفـوط *'ifwaṭ* bath towel, towel.

ف و ظ *fwð̣*

فـوض *fawwað̣* II to authorize, empower. منو فوضك توقع هذيل الطلبات *minu fawwað̣k twaggi^c haðeel ṭ-ṭalabaat?* Who authorized you to sign these requests?

فـاوض *faawað̣* III to negotiate with. الشركة فاوضت الحكومة على استيراد مـواد غذائيـة *š-šarika faawað̣at l-ḥukuuma ^cala stiiraad mawaadd ġiðaa'iyya.* The company negotiated with the government about importing foodstuffs.

فوضـى *fawð̣a* disorder, confusion, chaos.

تفويـض *tafwiið̣* (v.n. from II فـوض *fawwað̣*) authorization, empowerment.

مفاوضة *mufaawaḍa* (v.n. from III فاوض *faawað̣*) negotiation.

ف و گ *fwg*

فـاق *faag (يفوق yfuug)* (with على *^cala*) to be superior to s.o., to beat s.o. (in sports, studies, etc.). فـاق على كـل المشـتركين في المسـابقة *faag ^cala kill l-mištarkiin fi l-musaabaga.* He beat all the participants in the contest.

تفـوق *tfawwag* V (with على *^cala*) = فـاق على *faag ^cala.* بنتي تفوقت على بنات صفهـا في الدراسـة *binti tfawwagat ^cala banaat ṣaffha fi d-diraasa.* My daughter beat her classmates in school studies.

فـوق *foog* (prep.) 1. above, over. فوق الأرض *foog l-'arð̣* above the ground. فـوق النخـل *foog n-naxal* doing very well, living very comfortably. 2. on, on top of. فوق الميز *foog l-meez* on top of the table, on the table. فوق السيارة *foog s-sayyaara* on top of the car. 3. beyond, more than. فـوق طـاقتي *foog ṭaagti* beyond my ability. فوق الحد *foog l-ḥadd* boundless, unlimited. جا فـوق الامية نفـر *ya foog l-'imyat nafar.* More than one hundred people came. 4. (adv.) up, upstairs, above, on top. من فـوق *min foog* from up (there). راح فوق *raaḥ foog.* He went upstairs. ابتدا من فـوق *btida min foog.* He started from the top. فـوق حـدر *foog ḥadir* upside down.

فوقـي *foogi* located higher or above, higher, upper. الـدور الفوقـي *d-door l-foogi* the upper floor. مـا أبغـى هـذا؛ أبغـى الفوقـي *ma 'abġa haaða; 'abġa l-foogi.* I don't want this; I want the upper one.

فوقاني *foogaani* = فوقي *foogi.*

متفـوق *mitfawwig* (act. part. from V تفـوق *tfawwag*) excellent, outstanding (person).

ف و ل ١ *fwl*

فـول *fuul* (coll.) fava beans. فول سوداني *fuul suudaani* peanuts.

ف و ل ٢ *fwl*

فـول *fuul* comprehensive, complete, full. عندي فـول بيمـة *^cindi fuul biima.* I have comprehensive car insurance.

ف و ل ٣ *fwl*

فاول *faawil* see under **ف ا و ل** *faawl.*

ف ي *fy*

في *fi* 1. at, in. في البيت *fi l-beet* at home. في المدرسة *fi l-madrasa* at school. في مخباك *fi maxbaak* in your pocket. في الحقيقة *fi l-ḥagiiga* in fact. في أمان الله *fi 'amaan l-laah!* Good-bye! (lit., "in God's protection"). في خير *fi xeer* (adv.) (living) in abundance, (living) comfortably. 2. on. في هذي المناسبة *fi haaði l-munaasaba* on this occasion. في خمسة نيسان *fi xamsa niisaan* on May 5. 3. within, during. لازم تسد المبلغ في خمسة أيام *laazim tsidd l-mablaġ fi xamsat 'ayyaam.* You must pay back the money within five days. 4. times, by, multiplied by. خمسة في ستة ثلاثين *xamsa fi sitta θalaaθiin.* Five times six is thirty. الحجرة خمسة متر في عشرة *l-ḥijra xamsa mitir fi ᶜašara.* The room is five meters by seven (width and length).

فيه *fii* 1. there is. فيه قهوة *fii gahwa.* There's coffee. ما فيه شي *ma fii šayy.* There's nothing. 2. there are. فيه ناس واجد في السوق *fii naas waayid fi s-suug.* There are a lot of people in the marketplace.

كان فيه *kaan fii* 1. there was. كان فيه قهوة *kaan fii gahwa.* There was coffee. ما كان فيه قهوة *ma kaan fii gahwa.* There was no coffee. 2. there were. كان فيه رجاجيل وحريم في السوق *kaan fii rayaayiil w-ḥariim fi s-suug.* There were men and women in the marketplace.

ف ي ت ر *fytr*

فيتر *feetar* p. *-iyya* pipe fitter.

ف ي د *fyd*

فاد *faad* (يفيد *yfiid*) 1. to benefit, help, be of use, be useful, helpful, beneficial. هذا يفيدك واجد *haaða yfiidak waayid.* This will help you a lot. شوما تسوي له ما يفيد *š-ma tsawwii-la ma yfiid.* No matter what you do for him, it doesn't do any good. 2. to inform, let know, notify. خلني أفيدك بشي ما تعرفه *xaḷḷni 'afiidak b-šayy ma tᶜarfa.* Let me inform you of something you have no knowledge of. جا وفادنا بمعلومات جديدة *ya w-faadna b-maᶜluumaat yidiida.* He came and let us in on new bits of information.

استفاد *stafaad* X to benefit, profit. استفاد واجد من التجارة *stafaad waayid min t-tijaara.* He benefited a lot from trade.

أفيد *'afyad* (elat.) 1. (with من *min*) more useful, beneficial than. 2. (with foll. n.) the most useful, beneficial.

فايدة *faayda* p. فوايد *fawaayid* 1. usefulness, benefit, advantage. شو الفايدة؟ *šu l-faayda?* What's the use? ما لك فيها أي فايدة *ma lak fiiha 'ayy faayda.* You don't have any (material) benefit in it. 2. interest (on money) البنك يعطي فايدة خمسة في الامية *l-bank yᶜaṭi faayda xamsa fi l-'imya.* The bank gives a 5% interest.

مفيد *mufiid* useful, beneficial, advantageous.

ف ي ز ي *fyzy*

فيزيا *fiizya* physics.

ف ي ظ *fyð̣*

فـاض *faað̣ (يفيـض yfiið̣)* to overflow, flow over, run over. تانكي الماي فـاض *taanki l-maay faað̣.* The water tank overflowed.

فيضـان *fayað̣aan* (v.n.) 1. overflowing, flowing over. 2. (p. *-aat*) flood.

فـايض *faayið̣* (act. part.) having overflowed. النهر فايض *n-nahir faayið̣.* The river has overflowed. الشـوارع فايضـة بالماي *š-šawaari*[c] *faayð̣a b-l-maay.* The streets are flooded with water.

ف ي ل *fyl*

فيل *fiil* p. افيال *fyaal* elephant.

ف ي ن ر ي *fynry*

فيـنري *feenari* p. فناري *fanaari* refinery, oil refinery. فيـه فيـنري في الأحمـدي *fii feenari fi l-'aḥmadi.* There's an oil refinery at Ahmadi (in Kuwait).

ف ي ه *fyo*

فايهـة *faayha* p. فوايه *fuwaayih* rumor. لا تدير بـال! هـذي فايهـة بـس *la ddiir baal! haaði faayha bass.* Don't worry! It's only a rumor.

فيه *fii* see under ف ي *fy.*

ق

ق ا ف *qaaf*

قـاف *qaaf* (less common var. *ġaaf*) name of the letter ق *q*.

ق ا م و س *qaamws*

قـاموس *qaamuus* (less common var. *ġaammuus*) dictionary. قـاموس عربـي أنكلـيزي *qaamuus ᶜarabi 'ingiliizi* Arabic-English dictionary.

ق ب ر *qbr*

قـبر *qabir* (less common var. *gabir*) grave, tomb. دفنوه في قبر قريب من البيت *difanoo fi qabir gariib min l-beet.* They buried him in a grave near the house. قبر النبي في المدينـة *qabir n-nabi fi l-madiina.* The tomb of the Prophet (Muhammad) is in Medina.

مقـبرة *maqbara* (less common var. *magbara*) p. مقابر *maqaabir* cemetery, graveyard.

ق ب ي *qby*

قبي *qabi* (less common var. غبي *ġabi*) p. *-yyiin* 1. stupid, foolish. قبي ما يفتهم *qabi ma yiftihim.* He's stupid. He doesn't understand. 2. stupid person.

ق ت ل *qtl*

قتل *qital* (more common var. *gital*). See under **گ ت ل** *gtl.*

ق د س *qds.* See under **گ د س** *gds.*

ق د ي *qdy*

تقـدى *tqadda* V (common var. V تغدى *tġadda*). See under **غ د ي** *ġdy.*

قـدا *qada* (common var. غـدا *ġada*) lunch.

ق ر ز *qrz*

قـرز *qarraz* II (common var. غـرز *ġarras*). See under **غ ر ز** *ġrz.*

ق ر ي *qry.* See under **گ ر ي** *gry.*

ق س م *qsm.* See under **غ س م** *ġsm.*

ق ص ي *qṣy.* See under **گ ص ي** *gṣy.*

ق ن د *qnd*

قند *qand* (common var. غند *ġand*). See under **غ ن د** *ġnd.*

ق ن ي *qny* See under **غ ن ي** *ġny.*

ق ه ر *qhr*

قهـر *qihar* (يقهـر *yiqhar*) 1. to annoy, irritate, upset. قهرنـي واجـد *qiharni waayid.* He annoyed me a lot. 2. to sadden, grieve. فشـل في الامتحـان وقهـر والدينـه *fišal fi li-mtiḥaan w-qihar waaldeena.* He failed the examination and made his parents sad.

انقهـر *nqihar* VII 1. to be or become annoyed, irritated, upset. لين علمته بذاك الشي انقهـر *leen ᶜallamta b-ðank š-šayy nqihar.* When I told him about that matter, he got upset. 2. to be or become saddened, grieved. اتقهـروا والدينه لانـه فشـل في الامتحـان *nqahraw waaldeena linna fišal fi li-mtiḥaan.* His parents became sad because he failed the examination.

قهـر *qahar* (v.n. from قهر *qihar*) grief, sadness. مـات مـن القهـر *maat min* *l-qahar.* He died of grief. بقهر *b-qahar* unwillingly. وافقت تاخذه بقهر *waafagat taaxða b-qahar.* She agreed to take him (as husband) unwillingly.

القـاهرة *l-qaahira* (less common var. *l-ġaahira*) Cairo. رحنـا القـاهرة وتونسـنا *riḥna l-qaahira w-twannasna.* We went to Cairo and had a good time.

ق و ر ي *qwry*

قوري *quuri* (common var. غوري *ġuuri*) p. قـواري *qawaari,* غواري *ġawaari* tea kettle, teapot.

ق و ز ي *qwzy*

قـوزي *quuzi* (common var. غـوزي *ġuuzi*). See under **غ و ز** *ġwz.*

ق و ي *qwy.* See under **گ و ي** *gwy.*

ق ي ر *qyr.* See under **غ ي ر** *ġyr.*

ك

ك ا ر *kaar*

كار *kaar* p. *-aat* job, business, vocation. هديت ذاك الكار واشتغلت بالتجـــارة *haddeet ðaak l-kaar w-štaġalt b-t-tijaara.* I quit that job and became a businessman.

ك ا ر و ك *kaaruuk*

كاروك *kaaruuk* p. كواريك *kuwaaariik* baby cradle. اشتريت كاروك حق العيـــل *štireet kaaruuk ḥagg l-ᶜayyil.* I bought a cradle for the baby.

ك ا ش ي *kaašy*

كاشي *kaaši* (coll.) tiles. s. *-yya.* عقب ما انتهينا من البنا اشترينا الكاشي *ᶜugub-ma ntiheena min l-bina štireena l-kaaši.* After we were through with the construction we bought the tiles.

ك ا غ د *kaaġd*

كـــاغد *kaaġid* (coll.) paper. s. *-a* p. كواغد *kawaaġid* sheet, piece of paper. ما عندي كاغد *ma ᶜindi kaaġid.* I don't have paper. كاغد جـــام *kaaġid jaam* sand-paper.

ك ا ف *kaaf*

كاف *kaaf* name of the letter ك *k.*

ك ا م ر ا *kaamraa*

كاميرا *kaamra* p. *-aat* camera.

ك ا ن و ن *kaanwn*

كـــانون *kaanuun*, as in كـــانون أول *kaanuun 'awwal* December. كانون ثاني *kaanuun θaani* January.

ك ا و چ و ك *kaawčwk*

كـــاوشوك *kaawčuuk* (coll.) rubber, caoutchouc.

ك ا و ل ي *kaawly*

كاولي *kaawli* p. *-yya* vagabond, tramp.

ك ب ا ب *kbaab*

كباب *kabaab* (coll.) kabob, meatballs broiled on a skewer. كليت كباب *kaleet kabaab.* I ate kabob. ماعون كبـــاب *maaᶜuun kabaab* kabob dish, dish of kabob.

ك ب ت *kbt*

كبـــت *kabat* p. *-aat* 1. cupboard. فيه مواعـــين في الكبـــت *fii muwaaᶜiin fi l-kabat.* There are pots and pans in the cupboard. 2. wardrobe. حط هدومه في الكبت *ḥaṭṭ hduuma fi l-kabat.* He put his clothes in the wardrobe.

ك ب د *kbd*

كبـــد *kabd* (more common var. *čabd*). See under **چ ب د** *čbd.*

ك ب ر *kbr*

كـــبر *kubar* (يكبر *yikbar)* 1. to grow, become large and big. البنت كبرت وما تروح السوق بروحها *l-bint kubrat w-ma truuḥ s-suug b-ruuḥḥa.* The girl has grown and she won't go to the market-place alone. عايلتنا كبرت ولازم ننتقل إلى بيت أكـــبر *ᶜaaylatna kubrat w-laazim nintagil 'ila beet 'akbar.* Our family became too big and we have to move to a larger house.

كبر *kabbar* II 1. to make big, large, enlarge, amplify, widen. كبرنا البيت واجد *kabbarna l-beet waayid.* We made the house very big. إذا تكبر هذا العكس كم يكلفني؟ *'iða tkabbir haaða l-ᶜaks čam ykallifni?* If you enlarge this photograph, how much will it cost me? 2. to praise, glorify (God). كبروا وصلوا صلاة الصبح *kabbaraw w-ṣallaw ṣalaat ṣ-ṣubḥ.* They praised God and prayed the morning prayer.

تكبر *tkabbar* V 1. to be enlarged. ها العكس ما يتكبر *hal-ᶜaks ma yitkabbar.* This photograph cannot be enlarged. 2. (with على *ᶜala*) to be overbearing toward s.o. لا تتكبر على ربعك *la titkabbar ᶜala rabᶜak.* Don't look down upon your people.

كبر *kubur* (v.n. from كبر *kubar*) 1. size, largeness. 2. old age. تقولين شيبة. شعلينا من كبره وصغره *tguuliin šeeba. š-ᶜaleena min kubra w-zuġra.* You say, "An old man." We have nothing to do with his old age or youthfulness. His old age and youthfulness are not important to us. 3. age. أنت ذالحين شكبرك؟ *'inta ðalḥiin š-kubrak?* How old are you now? رجال عود شكبره! *rayyaal ᶜood š-kubra!* What an old man he is!

كبير *kabiir, čibiir* p. كبار *kbaar* 1. big, large. بيت كبير *beet čibiir* big house. 2. old. رجال كبير *rayyaal čibiir* old man. بنتي الكبيرة *binti č-čibiira* my oldest daughter.

أكبر *'akbar* (elat.) 1. (with من *min*) bigger, larger than. 2. (with foll. n.) the oldest, the biggest.

تكبير *takbiir* (v.n. from II كبر *kabbar*) 1. enlarging, enlargement, amplifying. تكبير العكس يكلف خمسة درهم *takbiir l-ᶜaks ykallif xamsa dirhim.* Enlarging the photograph costs five dirhams. 2. praise, glorification (of God). 3. saying, الله أكبر *"'aḷḷaahu 'akbar."* God is the greatest.

مكبر *mukabbir* (act. part. from II كبر *kabbar*) p. *-aat* amplifier. مكبر الصوت *mukabbir ṣ-ṣoot* loudspeaker.

ك ب ر ي ت *kbryt*

كبريت *kabriit* (more common var. *čabriit*). See under **چ ب ر ي ت** *čbryt.*

ك ب س *kbs*

كبيسة *kabiisa*: سنة كبيسة *sana kabiisa* leap year.

كابوس *kaabuus* nightmare, incubus.

مكبس *makbas* p. مكابس *makaabis* packing house for dates.

مكبوس *makbuus* (common var. *mačbuus*) 1. cooked rice (usually with meat and raisins). 2. (p.p.) having been pressed or squeezed.

ك ب ش *kbš*

كبش *kabš* (more common var. *čabš*). See under **چ ب ش** *čbš.*

ك ب و س *kbws*

كبوس *kabbuus* p. كبابيس *kabaabiis* (Western) hat. نحن ما نلبس الكبوس *niḥin ma nilbis l-kabbuus.* We don't wear Western hats.

ك ت ب *ktb*

كتب *kitab* (يكتب *yiktib*) 1. to write down, write, record. اكتب أساميهم *'iktib* *'asaamiihum.* Write down their names. كتبت اسمي بالعربي *kitabt 'asmi b-l-ᶜarabi.* I wrote my name in Arabic. كتبت له خط *kitabt-la xaṭṭ.* I wrote him a letter. 2. to leave s.th. in one's will, bequeath. كتبت لك البناية اللي على السيف *kitabt-lič li-bnaaya lli ᶜala s-siif.* In my will I left you the building on the beach.

كتب *kattab* II to make write. كتبنا كل الدرس *kattabna kill d-dars.* He made us write the whole lesson.

انكتب *nkitab* VII pass. of كتب *kitab.*

كتاب *ktaab* (common var. *kitaab*) p. كتب *kutub* 1. book. أهل الكتاب *'ahil li-ktaab* people who have sacred scriptures, i.e., Christians and Jews. 2. business letter.

كتابة *ktaaba* (common var. *kitaaba*) (v.n. from كتب *kitab*) writing, handwriting. ما يعرف القراية ولا الكتابة *ma yᶜarf li-graaya wala li-ktaaba.* He can't read or write.

كتيبة *katiiba* p. كتايب *kataayib* battalion, regiment.

مكتب *maktab* p. مكاتب *makaatib* 1. office. يدش المكتب الساعة تسع *ydišš l-maktab s-saaᶜa tisiᶜ.* He enters the office at nine o'clock. مكتب البريد *maktab l-bariid* the post office. 2. bureau.

مكتبة *maktaba* p. *-aat* 1. library. مكتبة الجامعة *maktabat l-yaamᶜa* the university library. تسلفت كتابين من المكتبة الوطنية *tsallaft ktaabeen min l-maktaba l-waṭaniyya.* I borrowed two books from the national library. 2. bookstore.

كاتب *kaatib* 1. (act. part. from كتب *kitab*) having written. هو كاتب الخط *huwa kaatib l-xaṭṭ.* He's the one who has written the letter. 2. (p. كتّاب *kittaab*) a: author, writer. b: clerk, clerical employee.

مكتوب *maktuub* (p.p. from كتب *kitab*) foreordained, predestined. (prov.) المكتوب ما عنه مهروب *l-maktuub ma ᶜanna mahruub.* Whatever will be, will be. (lit., "What's written cannot be avoided.").

ك ت ف *ktf* See under **چ ت ف** *čtf.*

ك ت ل ي *ktly*

كتلي *kitli* p. كتالي *kataali* teakettle.

ك ت م *ktm*

كتم *kitam* (يكتم *yiktim*) to conceal, keep s.th. secret. لا تقل له شي. ما يقدر يكتم السر *la tgul-la šayy. ma yigdar yiktim s-sirr.* Don't tell him anything. He can't keep a secret.

كاتم *kaatim*: كاتم الصوت *kaatim ṣ-ṣoot* the muffler.

مكتوم *maktuum* (p.p.) 1. concealed, kept secret. 2. classified (e.g., letter, correspondence, etc.).

ك ث ر *kθr*

كثر *kiθar* (يكثر *yakθir*) 1. to be plentiful. الخضار تكثر في الشتا *li-xḍaar takθir fi š-šita.* Vegetables become plentiful in the winter. 2. to increase, multiply. كثر عدد سكان أبو ظبي *kiθar ᶜadad sikkaan 'abu ḍabi.* The population of Abu Dhabi has increased a lot. (prov.) إذا طاح البعير كثرت سكاكينه *'iða ṭaaḥ* *l-bicíir kiθrat sičaačiina.* When it rains, it pours. Misfortune comes in groups.

كثر *kaθθar* II 1. to increase, augment, make more of. كثر الشكر في الشاي حقي *kaθθir š-šakar fi č-čaay ḥaggi.* Put a lot of sugar in my tea. الله كثر علينا الخير *'aḷḷa kaθθar caleena l-xeer.* God gave me a lot of wealth. كثر الله من أمثالك *kaθθar aḷḷa min 'amθaalak.* May God allow more of the likes of you. 2. to overdo s.th., to go to extremes. لا تكثر الكلام! *la tkaθθir l-kalaam!* Don't talk so much.

تكاثر *tkaaθar* VI to multiply, grow in number. الدجاج يتكاثر بسرعة في هذي المزرعة *d-diyaay yitkaaθar b-surca fi haaði l-mazraca.* Chickens multiply quickly on this farm.

استكثر *stakθar* X to consider excessive, regard as too much. استكثرت السعر *stakθart s-sicir.* I thought the price was too high. استكثر عليّ السيارة *stakθar calayya s-sayyaara.* He thought I didn't deserve the car.

كثر *kiθir* amount. عطني ها الكثر *caṭni hal-kiθir.* Give me this much. قل لي شكثر تريد *gul-li š-kiθir triid.* Tell me how much you want. (prov.) كثر التكرار يعلم الحمار *kiθir t-takraar ycallim li-ḥmaar.* (lit., "Repetition teaches donkeys.").

كثير *kaθiir* See واجد *waayid* under وجد *wjd.*

كثرة *kaθra* abundance, large quantity, great number. بكثرة *b-kaθra* in abundance. (prov.) الكثرة تغلب الشجاعة *l-kaθra tġalib š-šajaaca.* Numbers beat bravery. Strength in numbers.

أكثر *'akθar* (elat.) 1. (with من *min*) more than. أكثر من هذا *'akθar min haaða* more than this. على الأكثر *cala l-'akθar* most probably, most likely. أكثر من اللازم *'akθar min l-laazim* more than necessary. 2. (with foll. n.) the most, most of the. أكثر الكولية *'akθar l-kuuliyya* most of the coolies.

أكثرية *'akθariyya* majority. الأكثرية موجودين *l-'akθariyya mawjuudiin.* The majority are present. أكثرية الناس *'akθariyyat n-naas* most of the people.

ك ح ح *kḥḥ*

كح *kaḥḥ* (يكح *ykiḥḥ)* to cough. كان مريض ومسخن ويكح *čaan mariiḍ w-mṣaxxan w-ykiḥḥ.* He was sick, running a temperature and coughing.

كحة *kaḥḥa* 1. (v.n.) coughing. عنده كحة قوية *cinda kaḥḥa gawiyya.* He has a bad cough. 2. a cough.

ك ح ل *kḥl*

كحل *kaḥḥal* II to put kohl on one's eyes, beautify (eyes) with kohl. كحلت عيونها وطلعت بره *kaḥḥalat cyuunha w-ṭlacat barra.* She put kohl on her eyes and went out. (prov.) يبغى يكحلها عماها *yibġa ykaḥḥilha camaaha.* He wanted to improve things, but he made them worse.

تكحل *tkaḥḥal* V to beautify the eyes with kohl. تكحلت وطلعت بره *tkaḥḥalat w-ṭlacat barra.* She put on eye make-up and went out.

كحل *kuḥul* (coll.) kohl, eye cosmetic.

كحول *kuḥuul* (coll.) alcohol.

كحيلة *kḥeela* p. *-aat* 1. well-bred she-camel. 2. thoroughbred mare. (prov.) باع الكحيلة بعشا ليلة *baaᶜ li-kḥeela b-ᶜaša leela.* Penny wise and pound foolish.

ك خ خ *kxx*

كخ *kixx* (invar.) (baby talk) Icky! It's dirty. Don't touch it!

ك د د *kdd*

كد *kadd* (يكد *ykidd)* to work hard, labor, toil. لين يشتغل يكد كد *leen yištaġil ykidd kadd.* Whenever he works, he works very hard.

كد *kadd* (v.n.) toil, labor, hard work.

ك د ش *kdš*

كديش *kidiiš* p. كدش *kudš*, كدّش *kiddaš* mule.

ك ذ ا *kðaa*

كذا وكذا *kaða w-kaða.* See under **چ ذ ي** *čðy.*

ك ذ ب *kðb*

كذب *kiðab*, etc. See under **چ ذ ب** *čðb.*

ك ر ا ن ي *kraany*

كراني *karraani* p. *-yya* clerk. يشتغل كراني *yištaġil karraani.* He works as a clerk.

ك ر ب و ن *krbwn*

كربون *karboon* carbon. ورق كربون *warag karboon* carbon paper.

ك ر ت *krt*

كرت *kart* p. *-aat,* كروت *kruut* card. اترس هذا الكرت *'itris haaða l-kart.* Fill in this card.

ك ر ت و ن *krtwn*

كرتون *kartoon* (coll.) heavy paper, thin cardboard. s. *-a* sheet of كرتون *kartoon.*

ك ر د *krd*

كردي *kurdi* 1. Kurdish. 2. (p. أكراد *'akraad*) Kurd, person from Kurdistan.

ك ر ر *krr*

كرر *karrar* II to repeat, do again, do repeatedly. لا تكرر اللي أقوله *la tkarrir illi 'aguula.* Don't repeat what I say.

تكرر *tkarrar* V pass. of II كرر *karrar.*

مكرر *mkarrar* (p.p. from II كرر *karrar*) having been repeated, reiterated.

ك ر س *krs*

كرسي *kirsi* p. كراسي *karaasi* chair. فيه كنبة وكرسيين في المجلس *fii kanaba w-kirsiyyeen fi l-maylis.* There are a sofa and two chairs in the living room.

ك ر ش *krš*

كرش *karš* p. كروش *kruuš* belly, pot belly. كرشه مترس عيش ولحم وسمك وماادري شبعد *karša matruus ᶜeeš w-laḥam w-simač w-ma dri š-baᶜad.* His belly is full of rice, meat, fish, and I don't know what else. أبو كرش *'ubu karš* glutton, heavy eater.

كرشة *karša* p. *-aat* stomach.

ك ر ع *krᶜ*

كراع *kraaᶜ* p. *-iin,* كرعان *kirᶜaan* lower leg and foot of a sheep or cow (esp. as food).

ك ر ف ا ي *krfaay*

كرفاية *kirfaaya* p. *-aat* bed. حجرة النوم فيها كرفايتين *ḥijrat n-noom fiiha kirfaayteen.* There are two beds in the bedroom.

ك ر م *krm*

كرم *kiram (يكرم yikram)* (with على *ᶜala*) to be generous to s.o. سيرنا عليه وكرم علينا *sayyarna ᶜalee w-kiram ᶜaleena.* We went to visit him (in his home) and he was generous to us.

كرم *karram* II to honor, treat with respect (and food). العرب يكرمون الخطار *l-ᶜarab ykarrmuun l-xuṭṭaar.* The Arabs honor guests. كرمتنا؛ كرمك الله *karramtana; karramk aḷḷa.* You were extremely nice to us; may God honor you.

تكرم *tkarram* V (with على *ᶜala*) to show generosity to s.o. تكرم علينا بكل شي؛ بيض الله وجهه *tkarram ᶜaleena b-kill šayy; bayyaḏ aḷḷa weeyha.* He was very generous to us; may God make him happy. طال عمرك! ممكن تتكرم علينا بشورك؟ *ṭaal ᶜumrak! mumkin titkarram ᶜaleena b-šoorak?* May you live long! Will you honor us with your decision?

كرم *karam* generosity, magnanimity. العرب مشهورين بالكرم *l-ᶜarab mašhuuriin b-l-karam.* The Arabs are famous for (their) generosity.

كرامة *karaama* nobility, honor, dignity.

كريم *kariim* p. *-iin*, كرما *kurama* 1. generous, magnanimous. البدوي مشهور بأنه كريم *li-bdiwi mašhuur b-'anna kariim.* A bedouin is known by the fact that he's generous. 2. noble, eminent, distinguished. كريم الأخلاق *kariim l-'axlaag* noble-minded. كريم عين *kariim ᶜeen* (euphemism for) one-eyed.

أكرم *'akram* (elat.) 1. (with من *min*) more generous, etc., than. 2. (with foll. n.) the most generous, etc.

إكرامية *'ikraamiyya* p. *-aat* bonus.

ك ر ن ت ي ن *krntyn*

كرنتينة *karantiina* p. *-aat* quarantine (place in which people under quarantine are kept). ودوه الكرنتينة لانه عنده كوليرا *waddoo l-karantiina linna ᶜinda koleera.* They took him to the quarantine because he had cholera.

ك ر ه *krh*

كره *karah (يكره yikrah)* to hate, detest, loathe. يكره الشغل في الليل *yikrah š-šuġul fi l-leel.* He hates work at night.

كره *karrah* II to make hate, cause to hate. ظل يحكي على صديقي لين كرهني اياه *ḏall yḥači ᶜala ṣidiiji leen karrahni-yyaa.* He kept saying bad things about my friends until he made me hate him.

انكره *nkarah* VII pass. of كره *karah.* انكره يعني كره نفسه *nkirah yaᶜni karrah nafsa.* "nkirah" means he made himself hated.

كره *kurh* (v.n. from كره *karah*) hatred, hate. الكره من شيمته *l-kurh min šiimta.* Hatred is one of his qualities.

مكروه *makruuh* (p.p. from كره *karah*) hated, detested, hateful.

ك ر ه ب *krhb*

كرهب *karhab* (less common var. كهربا *kahraba*) electricity. ها المكان بعيد لكن فيه كرهب وماي *hal-mukaan ba^c^iid laakin fii karhab w-maay.* This place is far, but it has electricity and water.

ك ر و *krw*

كروة *karwa* p. *-aat* wage, fare, charge. كروة العامل موب ها القد *karwat l-^c^aamil muub hal-gadd.* A workman's wage doesn't go far.

ك ر و م *krwm*

كروم *kroom* chrome. فيه معادن في عجمان مثل الكروم وحجر المرمر *fii ma^c^aadin fi ^c^aymaam miθil li-kroom w-ḥiyar l-marmar.* There are metals in Ajman such as chrome and marble.

ك ر ي م *krym*

كريمة *kreema* p. *-aat* pudding (made of milk, eggs, and sugar).

ك ر ي ن *kryn*

كرين *kreen* p. *-aat* crane (machine).

ك س ب *ksb*

كسب *kisab (يكسب yiksab).* See ربح *ribaḥ* under **ر ب ح** *rbḥ.*

ك س ت ب ا ن *kstbaan*

كستبان *kistbaan.* See under **ك ش ت ب ا ن** *kštbaan.*

ك س د *ksd*

كسد *kisad (يكسد yiksad)* to find no market, sell badly. ها البضاعة تكسد إذا ما ترخص السعر *hal-biðaa^c^a tiksad 'iða ma traxxiṣ s-si^c^ir.* There won't be a market for these goods if you don't lower the price.

كساد *kasaad* (v.n.) recession, depression.

ك س ر *ksr*

كسر *kisar (يكسر yaksir)* 1. to break, shatter, fracture. كسر الجام *kisar l-jaam.* He broke the glass. 2. to break (fig.) كسر خاطري *kisar xaaṭri.* He made me sad. كسر الرقم القياسي في سباق الامية متر *kisar r-ragam l-giyaasi fi sibaag l-'imyat mitir.* He broke the record in the 100-meter dash.

كسر *kassar* II 1. to smash, shatter. كسر كلاص الماي *kassar gḷaaṣ l-maay.* He smashed the water glass. 2. to break up. كسر الجوز بس لا تاكله *kassir l-jooz bass la taakla.* Break the walnuts and don't eat them.

تكسر *tkassar* pass. of II كسر *kassar.*

انكسر *nkisar* VII 1. = V تكسر *tkassar.* 2. to be defeated, destroyed. انكسر الجيش العراقي في حرب الخليج *nkisar l-jeeš li-^c^raagi fi ḥarb l-xaliij.* The Iraqi army was defeated in the Gulf War. 3. to go bankrupt, be broken. انكسرت الشركة *nkisrat š-šarika.* The company went bankrupt.

كسر *kasir* p. كسور *kusuur* fracture, break. كسر في العظم *kasir fi l-^c^aðim* fracture of the bone.

تكسير *taksiir* (v.n. from II كسر *kassar*) 1. smashing, shattering. 2. breaking up (of nuts, etc.).

انكسار *nkisaar* (v.n. from VII انكسر *nkisar*) defeat, rout. هذا انكسار للعرب ما عقبه انكسار *haaða nkisaar lal-^c^arab ma ^c^ugba nkisaar.* This is a defeat unparalleled by any other defeat for the Arabs.

كسارة *kassaara* p. *-aat* 1. nutcracker. كسارة جوز *kassaarat jooz* walnut cracker. 2. crusher, wrecker. كسارة صخر *kassaarat ṣaxar* rock crusher.

مكسور *maksuur* (p.p. from كسر *kisar*) 1. broken, smashed. الجام مكسور *l-jaam maksuur.* The glass is broken. 2. out of order. الماكينة ما تشتغل؛ مكسورة *l-maakiina ma tištaġil; maksuura.* The machine doesn't work; it's out of order. 3. bankrupt. الشركة مكسورة *š-šarika maksuura.* The company is bankrupt.

مكسر *mkassar* (p.p. from II كسر *kassar*) 1. smashed, shattered. جام مكسر *jaam mkassar* smashed glass. 2. broken up. جوز مكسر *jooz mkassar* broken walnuts.

مكسرات *mkassaraat* walnuts, almonds, etc.

ك س ف *ksf*

تكسف *tkassaf* V to be humiliated. تكسف قدام الناس في السوق لانه ما كان صايم *tkassaf jiddaam n-naas fi s-suug linna ma čaan ṣaayim.* He was humiliated in front of the people in the marketplace because he wasn't fasting.

انكسف *nkisaf* VII 1. = V تكسف *tkassaf.* 2. to be eclipsed. انكسفت الشمس وصارت الدنيا ظلام *nkisfat š-šams w-ṣaarat d-dinya ðalaam.* The sun was eclipsed and it became dark.

كسيف *kasiif* 1. useless, worthless. أنت واحد كسيف *'inta waaḥid kasiif.* You are a useless person. كلام كسيف *kalaam kasiif* idle talk. 2. bad, horrible. حالة كسيفة *ḥaala kasiifa* bad situation, predicament.

كسافة *kasaafa* = حالة كسيفة *ḥaala kasiifa* misery, predicament. السكن في هالفريج كسافة *s-sakan fi hal-firiij kasaafa.* Living in this neighborhood is misery.

كسوف *kusuuf* solar eclipse. نقول، طال عمرك، «كسوف الشمس وخسوف القمر» *nguul, ṭaal* ᶜ*umrak, "kusuuf š-šams w-xusuuf l-gumar."* We say, may you live long, "solar eclipse and lunar eclipse."

ك س ل *ksl*

كسل *kassal* II to make lazy. هالشغل كسلني *haš-šuġul kassalni.* This kind of work made me lazy.

كسل *kasal* laziness, sluggishness. الحر في القيظ يسبب الكسل *l-ḥarr fi l-geeð ysabbib l-kasal.* Hot weather in the summer causes laziness.

كسلان *kaslaan* 1. lazy, indolent. دايماً قاعد. كسلان *daayman gaa*ᶜ*id. kaslaan.* He's always sitting down. He's lazy. 2. (p. كسلانين *kaslaaniin*, كسالة *kasaala*) lazy person.

أكسل *'aksal* (elat.) 1. (with من *min*) more indolent, lazy, etc. 2. (with foll. n.) the most indolent, lazy, etc.

ك س ي *ksy.* See under چ س ي *čsy.*

ك ش ت *kšt*

كشت *kišat* (يكشت *yakšit*) to go on a picnic, have an outing. كشتنا ليلة قمر وتونسنا *kišatna leelat gumar w-twannasna.* We went on a picnic on a moonlit night and had a good time.

كشت *kaššat* II to take s.o. on a picnic. ليش ما تكشتنا يا يبا؟ *leeš ma tkaššitna ya yuba?* Why don't you take us on a picnic, Dad?

كشتة *kašta* p. *-aat* picnic, outing. علمنا عن كشتتكم يا خوي؟ *ᶜallimna ᶜan kaštatkum ya xuuy.* Tell us about your picnic, brother.

كشات *kaššaat* p. *-a* picnicker. في القيظ تحصل كشاتة واجدين على السيف *fi l-geeđ tḥaṣṣil kaššaata waaydiin ᶜala s-siif.* In the summer, you find many picnickers on the beach.

ك ش ت ب ا ن *kštbaan*

كشتبان *kištbaan* (less common var. كستبان *kistbaan*) p. كشاتبين *kišaatbiin* thimble.

ك ش خ *kšx*

كشخ *kišax* (يكشخ *yikšax*) to show off, be boastful, brag. كشخ بهدومه الجديدة *kišax b-hduuma l-yidiida.* He showed off with his new clothes. لا تكشخ قدامي. أنا عرف أصلك وفصلك *la tikšax jiddaami. 'aana ᶜarf 'aṣlak w-faṣlak.* Don't brag in my presence. I know your origin and ancestry.

كشخة *kašxa* 1. showing off, bragging, boasting. على ويش هـا الكشخة؟ *ᶜala weeš hal-kašxa?* Why this showing off? 2. elegance. تعالي! تعالي! شو ها الكشخة! *taᶜaali! taᶜaali! šuu hal-kašxa!* Come! Come! You look elegant.

كاشخ *kaašix* p. *-iin* wearing elegant clothes. أشوفك اليوم كاشخ *'ašuufak l-yoom kaašix.* I see that you are elegantly dressed today.

ك ش ر *kšr*

كشر *kaššar* (يكشر *ykaššir*) to show one's teeth, bare one's teeth. إذا يكشر يعني حمقان *'iđa ykaššir yaᶜni ḥamgaan.* If he shows his teeth, it means he's angry.

ك ش ش *kšš*

كش *kašš* (يكش *ykišš*) 1. (with عن *ᶜan*) to refrain from. كش عن الأكل *kašš ᶜan l-'akil.* He refrained from eating. 2. to shrink. إذا تغسل ها الثوب يكش *'iđa tġasil haθ-θoob ykišš.* If you wash this dress, it will shrink.

كشة *kašša* p. *-aat* thick lock of hair. شها الكشة! *š-hal-kašša!* What thick lock of hair this is! أبو كشة *'ubu kašša* one who has thick long hair.

ك ش ف *kšf*

كشف *kišaf* (يكشف *yakšif*) 1. to uncover, unveil, remove a covering or a lid. لا تكشفين وجهك لين تطلعين *la tkašfiin weehič leen tiṭlaᶜiin.* Don't uncover your face when you go out. الماعون حار. لا تكشفه بيدك *l-maaᶜuun ḥaarr. la tkašfa b-yaddak.* The pot is hot. Don't uncover it with your hand. 2. (with على *ᶜala*) to inspect, investigate, examine. البلدية رايحة تكشف على البيوت الشعبية *l-baladiyya raayḥa tikšif ᶜala li-byuut š-šaᶜbiyya.* The municipal council is going to inspect the low income housing. 3. (with على *ᶜala*) to examine (medically). كشف عليّ الدختر وقال لازم أنام في المستشفي *kišaf ᶜalayya d-daxtar w-gaal laazim 'anaam fi l-mustašfi.* The doctor examined me, and said that I had to be hospitalized.

تكشف *tkaššaf* V to uncover oneself. كنت حران وتكشفت *čint ḥarraan w-tkaššaft.* I was hot and threw off the covers.

انكشف *nkišaf* VII to be revealed, disclosed. هالحين انكشف كل شي *halḥiin nkišaf kill šayy.* Now everything has been revealed.

اكتشف *ktišaf* VIII to discover, find out, detect. من اكتشف أمريكا؟ *man ktišaf 'amriika?* Who discovered America? اكتشفت انه محتال *ktišaft 'inna muḥtaal.* I found out that he was a swindler.

كشف *kašf* (v.n. from كشف *kišaf*) 1. inspecting, inspection, examining. 2. (p. كشوف *kšuuf, -aat*) report, account. كشف طبي *kašf ṭibbi* medical examination.

كشاف *kaššaaf* p. *-a* boy scout. نور كشاف *nuur kaššaaf* search light.

اكتشاف *ktišaaf* p. *-aat* discovery.

مكشوف *makšuuf* (p.p. from كشف *kišaf*) 1. uncovered, unveiled. 2. open, evident. ورقة مكشوفة *wruga makšuufa* card lying face up. حكي مكشوف *ḥači makšuuf* frank talk. عالمكشوف *ᶜal-makšuuf* openly. خلنا نتكلم عالمكشوف *xaḷḷna nitkallam ᶜal-makšuuf.* Let's talk openly.

مكتشف *muktašif* (act. part. from VIII اكتشف *ktišaf*) explorer, discoverer.

ك ش م *kšm.* See under **چ ش م** *čšm.*

ك ع ب *kᶜb.* See under **چ ع ب** *čᶜb.*

ك ف ح *kfḥ*

كافح *kaafaḥ* III to fight against, struggle against, combat. نكافح المخدرات في كل مكان *nkaafiḥ li-mxaddaraat fi kill mukaan.* We are fighting against drugs everywhere.

كفاح *kifaaḥ* struggle, fight.

مكافحة *mkaafaḥa* = كفاح *kifaaḥ.*

ك ف ر *kfr*

كفر *kifar* (يكفر *yakfur*) not to believe (in God), to be irreligious, be an infidel. يكفر بالله *yakfur b-'aḷḷa.* He doesn't believe in God. ما يخاف من الله؛ يكفر *ma yxaaf min aḷḷa; yakfur.* He doesn't fear God; he's sacrilegious.

كفر *kaffar* II 1. to curse, to blaspheme. يسب ويكفر لين يكون حمقان *ysibb w-ykaffir leen ykuun ḥamgaan.* He curses and blasphemes when he is mad. 2. to infuriate, madden. كفرتني. ما تصك حلقك عاد! *kaffartani. ma ṣṣik ḥaljak ᶜaad!* You're infuriating. Why don't you shut up! 3. to atone, make amends, do penance. إذا تحج وتصلي وتصوم تكفر عن ذنوبك *'iða tḥijj w-tṣalli w-tṣuum tkaffir ᶜan ðnuubak.* If you go on pilgrimage, pray, and fast, you'll atone for your sins.

كافر *kaafir* (act. part. from كفر *kifar*) p. كفار *kiffaar* atheist, infidel, unbeliever. كل واحد ما يامن بالله كافر *kill waaḥid ma yaamin b-aḷḷa kaafir.* Anyone who doesn't believe in God is an atheist.

ك ف ل *kfl*

كفل *kifal* (يكفل *yikfal*) to be responsible, liable, answerable for s.o., post bail for s.o., vouch for s.o. الشركـــة تكفلني *š-šarika tikfalni.* The company will be responsible for me. The company will be my sponsor. إذا مـــاحد يكفلك، ما تقدر تحصل الفلوس من البنـــك *'iða maḥḥad yikfalk, ma tigdar tḥaṣṣil li-fluus min l-bank.* If you don't have anyone to cosign for you, you cannot get the money from the bank. أبوه كفله بألفين درهم *'ubuu kifla b-'alfeen dirhim.* His father posted bail for him in the amount of two thousand dirhams.

تكفـــل *tkaffal* V 1. to be sponsor, be guarantor for, to cosign for. لازم واحد يتكفلك إذا بغيـــت تشتغـــل هـــني *laazim waaḥid yitkaffalk 'iða bağeet tištağil hni.* You have to have a sponsor if you want to get a job here. البنك عطاني مليون درهم سلف والوزير تكفلـــني *l-bank ᶜaṭaani malyoon dirhim salaf w-l-waziir tkaffalni.* The bank lent me one million dirhams and the minister cosigned for me. 2. be responsible, answerable for. دفع ألفين دينار وأبـــوه تكفله بالبـــاقي *difaᶜ 'alfeen diinaar w-'ubuu tkaffala b-l-baagi.* He paid two thousand dinars and his father was responsible for the payment of the rest.

كفالـــة *kafaala* p. *-aat* 1. pledge, deposit, collateral. 2. bail. طلع من السجن بكفالـــة *ṭilaᶜ min s-sijin b-kafaala.* He got out of jail on bail.

كفيـــل *kafiil* p. كفلا *kufala* guarantor, sponsor, co-signer. إذا ما عندك كفيل، ما تقدر تتسلف فلوس *'iða ma ᶜindak kafiil, ma tigdar titsallaf fluus.* If you don't have a guarantor, you cannot borrow any money. كفيلـــي الحكومـــة *kafiili l-ḥukuuma.* My sponsor is the government.

ك ف ن *kfn.* See under **چ ف ن** *čfn.*

ك ف ي *kfy*

كفى *kifa* (يكفي *yikfi)* to be enough, to be sufficient. هذا يكفيني طـــول حيـــاتي *haaða yikfiini ṭuul ḥayaati.* This is enough for me for the rest of my life. يكفي! *yikfi!* That's enough! اللي عطيتني اياه مـــا يكفيـــني *'illi ᶜaṭeetni-yyaa ma yikfiini.* What you have given me won't be enough for me.

كفى *kaffa* II = كفى *kifa.*

اكتفـــى *ktifa* VIII to be satisfied, to content oneself. اكتفى باللي حصله *ktifa b-illi ḥaṣṣala.* He was satisfied with what he had gotten.

كفاية *kifaaya* sufficient amount. عطاني كفايـــة *ᶜaṭaani kifaaya.* He gave me enough. خذوا كفايتهم من الأكل قبل مـــا كشتـــوا *xaðaw kifaayattum min l-'akil gabil-ma kištaw.* They took all the food they needed before they went on a picnic.

كافي *kaafi* enough, sufficient, adequate. بس كافي! لا تـــاخذ أكـــثر *bass kaafi! la taaxið 'akθar.* That's enough (for you)! Don't take more. هذا موب كافي *haaða muub kaafi.* That's not enough.

ك ل *kl*

كـــل *kal* (less common var. أكل *'akal*) *(*ياكل *yaakil)* 1. to eat. عزمناه على العشا وكلينـــا لحـــم *ᶜazamnaa ᶜala l-ᶜaša w-kaleena laḥam.* We invited him to dinner and we ate meat. شو كليت؟ *šu kaleet?* What have you eaten? ما كليت شـــي *ma kaleet šayy.* I haven't eaten anything. (prov.) لا تزق في ماعون كليت

كليت منه *la zzigg fi maa*c*uun kaleet minna.* Don't bite the hand that feeds you. Be good to those who have done you a favor. (lit., "Don't defecate in a plate from which you have eaten."). 2. to eat up, consume. ها السيارة تاكل بانزين واجد *has-sayyaara taakil baanziin waayid.* This car uses a lot of gasoline. This car is a gas guzzler. 3. to eat away, gnaw, corrode. الحلى كل البيب *l-ḥala kal l-peep.* The rust has eaten away the pipe. 4. to take, get s.th. unpleasant. لا تاكل مسبات من أي واحد *la taakil masabbaat min 'ayya waaḥid.* Don't take insults from anyone. كلها غير أكلة *kalha ġeer 'akla.* He was severely penalized. أكلتها؛ ساعدني *'akalitta; saa*c*idni.* I've had it. Help me. 5. to capture, take. الجندي ياكل الحصان *l-jindi yaakil li-ḥṣaan.* The pawn will capture the knight. ياكل حرام *yaakil ḥaraam.* He's very dishonest. ياكل ربا *yaakil riba.* He takes usurious interest. ليش كليت حقي؟ *leeš kaleet ḥaggi?* Why have you cheated me out of what was mine? كل عليّ درهم *kal* c*alayya dirhim.* He cheated me out of a dirham.

أكل *akkal* II to feed s.o., make s.o. eat. أكلت الجهال قبل ما راحوا المدرسة *akkalat l-yihhaal gabil-ma raaḥaw l-madrasa.* She fed the children before they went to school.

انوكل *nwikal* VII pass. of كل *kal.* كل الأكل انوكل *kill l-'akil nwikal.* All the food has been eaten.

أكل *'akil* 1. eating, dining. حجرة الأكل *ḥijrat l-'akil* the dining room. 2. food. فيه أكل واجد *fii 'akil waayid.* There's a lot of food.

أكلة *'akla* (n. of inst.) p. *-aat* meal, morsel, repast.

ماكولات *maakuulaat* (p. only) food-stuffs, food. ماكولات مثلجة *maakuulaat mθallaja* frozen foods. ماكولات معلبة *maakuulaat m*c*allaba* canned foods.

ك ل ب *klb.* See under **چ ل ب** *člb.*

ك ل چ *klč*

كلچ *kalač* p. *-aat* car clutch. خذيت السيارة حق أبو الكلچ *xaðeet s-sayyaara ḥagg 'ubu l-kalač.* I took the car to the one who repairs clutches.

ك ل س *kls*

كلسات *kalsaat* (p. only) pairs of stockings.

ك ل ف *klf*

كلف *kallaf* II 1. to cost. كم يكلف؟ *čam ykallif?* How much will it cost? كلفني امية درهم *kallafni 'imyat dirhim.* It cost me a hundred dirhams. 2. to ask, require, assign. لا تكلف أحد يسويها *la tkallif 'aḥad ysawwiiha.* Don't ask anyone else to do it. كلفته بذيك المهمة *kallafta b-ðiič l-muhimma.* I assigned that important job to him. كلف غيري يسويها *kallif ġeeri ysawwiiha.* Have someone else do it. 3. to bother, inconvenience. لا تكلف روحك *la tkallif ruuḥak.* Don't bother yourself. Don't trouble yourself.

تكلف *tkallaf* V 1. to go to a lot of trouble, burden oneself. تكلف واجد على شان خطري *tkallaf waayid* c*ala šaan xaṭri.* He went to a lot of trouble for my sake. 2. (with ب *b-*) to be affected, unnatural, pretentious. يتكلف واجد بحكيه *yitkallaf waayid b-ḥačya.* He's speaking like someone who has put on airs.

كلفة *kulfa* 1. trouble, inconvenience. 2. cost, expense. 3. assignment, requisition, task.

تكليف *takliif* (v.n. from II كلف *kallaf*) p. تكاليف *takaaliif* 1. cost. تكاليف المعيشة *takaaliif l-maᶜiiša* the cost of living. 2. imposition, bother.

تكلف *takalluf* (v.n. from V تكلف *tkallaf*) affected behavior, mannerisms, airs.

ك ل ف ت *klft*

كلفت *kalfat (يكلفت ykalfit)* to caulk. كلفتنا الحمام لانه كان يسيل *kalfatna l-ḥammaam linna čaan ysiil.* We caulked the bathroom because it was leaking.

كلفات *kilfaat* (v.n.) caulking.

ك ل ك *klk*

كلك *kalak* p. كلاكة *klaaka* water bucket.

ك ل ل ١ *kll*

كل *kall (يكل ykill)* to be or become tired, fatigued, exhausted. ظليت أشتغل لين كليت *ḍalleet 'aštağil leen kalleet.* I kept working until I became tired.

ك ل ل ٢ *kll*

كل *kill* (common var. *kull*) 1. (with foll. indef. n.) each, every. كل واحد *kill waaḥid* each one. كل شي *kill šayy* everything. كل شي صار زين *kill šayy ṣaar zeen.* Everything went well. (prov.) موب كل بيضة شحمة ولا كل سودة فحمة *muub kull beeḍa šḥama wala kull sooda fḥama.* You cannot judge a book by its cover. (lit., "Not every white thing is a piece of suet, neither is every black thing a piece of charcoal."). على كل حال *ᶜala kull ḥaal* at any rate, in any case. 2. (with foll. def. n. or suff. pron.) all of the, the whole of. كل الناس *kill n-naas* all the people. كل الكتاب *kill li-ktaab* the whole book. الكتاب كله *li-ktaab killa* = كل الكتاب *kill li-ktaab.* كلنا *killana* all of us. كل ابوهم *kill ubuuhum* all of them. 3. الكل *l-kull* everyone, everybody. علمت الكل *ᶜallamt l-kull.* I told everyone. الكل جا *l-kull ya.* Everybody came. الكل في الكل *l-kull fi l-kull:* ما أقدر أسوي أي شي. هو الكل في الكل *ma 'agdar asawwi 'ayya šayy. huwa l-kull fi l-kull.* I can't do anything. He is the only person with authority.

كل *killin* 1. everyone, everybody. (prov.) كلٍ حليبة يجيبه *killin ḥaliiba yjiiba.* Like father, like son. (prov.) كلٍ يمد رجله على قد لحافه *killin ymidd riila ᶜala gadd lḥaafa.* As you make your bed, you must lie in it. 2. (with على *ᶜala*): على كل *ᶜala kullin* = على كل حال *ᶜala kull ḥaal.*

كلما *kull-ma* (rel. adv.) 1. whenever. كلما يسافر يجي صوبنا *kull-ma ysaafir yiji ṣoobna.* Whenever he travels, he comes to our place. 2. everything that, whatever, all that. عطيته كلما عندي *ᶜaṭeeta kull-ma ᶜindi.* I gave him everything I had.

كلية *kulliyya* college, school (of a university). كلية الطب *kulliyyat ṭ-ṭibb* the college of medicine. كلية الشرطة

kulliyyat š-širta the police academy. كليـة الدراسـات العليـا *kulliyyat d-diraasaat l-ᶜulya* the college of graduate studies.

ك ل ل ش *kllš*

كلـش *killiš* (adv.) 1. very, extremely, highly. كلش مريض *killiš mariiđ.* He's very sick. كلش زيـن *killiš zeen* very good, very well. 2. very much. عجبني الفلم كلش *ᶜajabni l-filim killiš.* I liked the film very much. 3. (with neg.) not ... any. ما عندي فلوس كلـش *ma ᶜindi fluus killiš,* كلش ما عندي فلـوس *killiš ma ᶜindi fluus.* I don't have any money.

ك ل م *klm*

كلـم *kallam* II to talk to, speak to, speak with. كلمته عـن ذاك الموضـوع *kallamta ᶜan đaak l-mawđuuᶜ.* I talked to him about that subject.

تكلـم *tkallam* V to speak, talk. تتكلم عربي زيـن *titkallam ᶜarabi zeen.* You speak Arabic well. لا تتكلـم! *la titkallam!* Don't talk. تكلم! *tkallam!* Speak up!

كلمة *kalma.* See under **چ ل م** *člm.*

كلام *kalaam* 1. talk, talking, speaking. أنا شايف كلامك ما له معنى *'aana šaayif kalaamak ma la maᶜna.* I see that your talk makes no sense! هذا كلام! *haađa kalaam!* This is just talk. كلام فـارغ *kalaam faariġ* idle talk, nonsense. 2. words, statement, remark. يسمع كلام أبوه *yismaᶜ kalaam 'ubuu.* He heeds his father's words. He listens to what his father says.

مكالمة *mukaalama* p. *-aat* conversation (esp., on the telephone).

ك ل ي چ *klyč*

كليشـة *kleeča* (coll.) cookies made from flour, sugar, cardamom, and ginger. s. كليشاية *-aaya.*

ك م *km*

كم *kam* (more common var. *čam*). See under **چ م** *čm.*

ك م ب ل *kmbl*

كمبـل *kambal* p. كنابل *kanaabil* blanket.

ك م ب ي ا ل *kmbyaal*

كمبيالـة *kumbyaala* p. *-aat* bill of exchange, draft.

ك م ل *kml*

كمـل *kimal* (يكمـل *yikmal)* 1. to be finished, done, completed. ها الشغلـة كملت *haš-šaġla kimlat.* This piece of work was finished. البنا يكمل عقـب شـهرين *l-bina yikmal ᶜugub šahreen.* The construction will be completed in two months. 2. to be concluded, come to a close. كملت الصلاة *kimlat ṣ-ṣalaa.* The prayer was over.

كمـل *kammal* II to complete, finish. كمل دراسته *kammal draasta.* He completed his studies. كمل شغله وطلـع *kammal šuġla w-ṭilaᶜ.* He finished his work and left.

تكمـل *tkammal* V pass. of II كمل *kammal.*

كمال *kamaal* perfection. الكمال لله بس *l-kamaal li-llaah bass.* Only God is perfect.

كـامل *kaamil* (act. part. from كمـل

kimal) 1. complete, full. كل شي كامل *kill šayy kaamil.* Everything is complete. 2. entire, whole. صف كامل من المصلين *ṣaff kaamil min li-mṣalliin* an entire line of worshippers. المدينة بكاملها استقبلت الشيخ *li-madiina b-kaamilha stagbalat š-šeex.* The whole city received the Shaikh.

ك م م[1] *kmm*

كمية *kammiyya* p. *-aat* quantity, amount.

ك م م[2] *kmm*

كمامة *kammaama* p. *-aat* 1. gas mask. 2. muzzle.

ك م ن ج *kmnj*

كمنجة *kamanja* p. *-aat* 1. violin. 2. fiddle.

ك م و ن *kmwn*

كمون *kammuun* (coll.) cumin, cumin seed.

ك ن د ر *kndr*

كندر *kandar* p. كنادر *kanaadir, -aat* yoke (of a water carrier).

كندري *kandari* p. كندرية *kandariyya* water carrier.

ك ن د و ر *kndwr*

كندورة *kandoora* p. كنادر *kanaadir* man's or woman's dress. كندورة اسم قديم. ثوب والا دشداشة الاسم الجديد *kandoora 'asim gadiim. θoob walla dišdaaša l-'asim l-yidiid. kandoora* is an old name. *θoob* or *dišdaaša* are the new names.

ك ن د ي س *kndys*

كنديسة *kandeesa* p. *-aat* condenser.

ك ن د ي ش ن *kndyšn*

كنديشن *kandeešin* air conditioning. هذا الحفيز ما فيه كنديشن *haaða l-ḥafiiz ma fii kandeešin.* This office doesn't have air conditioning.

كنديشة *kandeeša* p. *-aat* air conditioner.

مكندش *mkandaš* (p.p.) air conditioned. كل الحفيزات مكندشة *kill l-ḥafiizaat mkandaša.* All the offices are air conditioned.

ك ن ز *knz*

كنز *kinaz* (يكنز *yakniz*) to pile up, amass (money). ما يروح يتونس؛ بس يكنز فلوس *ma yruuḥ yitwannas; bass yakniz fluus.* He doesn't go to have a good time; he just piles up money.

كنز *kanz* p. كنوز *knuuz* (buried) treasure.

ك ن س *kns*

كنس *kinas.* See under **خ م م** *xmm.*

كنيسة *kaniisa* p. كنايس *kanaayis* church. فيه خمسة كنايس هني عندنا في الكويت *fii xamsat kanaayis hini ᶜindana fi l-kweet.* We have five churches here in Kuwait.

ك ن ع د *knᶜd* See under **چ ن ع د** *čnᶜd.*

ك ن ك ر ي *knkry*

كنكري *kankari* (coll.) gravel. s. *-yya.*

ك ه ر ب *khrb*

كهربا *kahraba* (more common var. كرهب *karhab*). See under **ك ر ه ب**

krhb).

كوافير *kwaafyr*

كوافير *kwaafeer* p. *-iin* coiffeur.

كوب *kwb*

كوب *kuub* p. أكواب *'akwaab* 1. cup. كوب شاي *kuub čaay* tea cup; cup of tea. 2. glass (of s.th.). كوب ماي *kuub maay* glass of water.

كوت *kwt*

كوت *kuut* p. أكوات *'akwaat* 1. coat. كوت صوف *kuut ṣuuf* woolen coat. 2. jacket.

كوخ *kwx*

كوخ *kuux* p. اكواخ *kwaax* hut, shack.

كوخة *kuuxa* p. *-aat* snare, trap (esp., for catching falcons).

كواخ *kawwaax* p. *-a* 1. falcon hunter. 2. falcon trainer.

كود *kwd*

كود *kawwad* II (common var. II كوم *kawwam*) to pile, pile up, stack up. كودوا السامان قدام الحفيز *kawwadaw s-saamaan jiddaam l-ḥafiiz.* They piled the things in front of the office.

تكود *tkawwad* V pass. of II كود *kawwad.*

كود *kood* 1. (more common var. *čood*). See under **چود** *čwd.* 2. (p. اكواد *kwaad*) heap, pile. بالكود *b-l-kood* wholesale. يبيع بالكود *ybiiᶜ b-l-kood.* He sells wholesale.

مكود *mkawwad* (p.p. from II كود *kawwad*) heaped, piled up.

كور *kwr*

كور *kuur* p. اكوار *kwaar,* كيران *kiiraan* bellows.

كورة *kuura* (كرة *kurat* as first term of إضافة) p. *-aat* 1. ball. كرة السلة *kurat s-salla* basketball. كرة الطاولة *kurat t-ṭaawla* table tennis. كرة الطايرة *kurat t-ṭaayra* volleyball. 2. soccer. خلنا نلعب كورة *xal̮l̮na nilᶜab kuura.* Let's play soccer.

مكور *mkawwar* (p.p.) ball-shaped, round.

كوريا *kwryaa*

كوريا *kuurya* Korea. كوريا الجنوبية *kuurya l-januubiyya* South Korea. كوريا الشمالية *kuurya š-šamaaliyya* North Korea.

كوري *kuuri* 1. Korean, characteristic of Korea. 2. (p. *-yyiin*) a Korean.

كوس *kws*

كوس *koos* hot summer wind (usually accompanied by high humidity).

كوسا *kwsaa*

كوسا *kuusa* (coll.) squash, zucchini. s. كوساية *kuusaaya.*

كوع *kwᶜ*

كوع *kuuᶜ* p. اكواع *kwaaᶜ* elbow. كوع البيب *kuuᶜ l-peep* kneepiece or elbow of a pipe. (prov.) ما يعرف كوعه من بوعه *ma yᶜarf kuuᶜa min buuᶜa.* He's a stupid person. (lit., "He doesn't know his knee from his elbow.").

كوف *kwf*

الكوفة *l-kuufa* Kufa (city in Iraq).

ك و ك ب *kwkb*

كوكب *kookab* p. كواكب *kawaakib* star. كواكب السينما *kawaakib s-siinama* the movie stars.

ك و ك ت ي ل *kwktyl*

كوكتيل *kookteel* cocktail. حفلة كوكتيل *ḥaflat kookteel* cocktail party.

ك و ل ي *kwly*

كولي *kuuli* p. *-yya* coolie, workman, laborer. فنشوا الكولية وسفروهم *fannašaw l-kuuliyya w-saffaruuhum.* They laid off the coolies and deported them.

ك و م *kwm*

كوم *kawwam* II. See under **ك و د** *kwd.*

ك و ن *kwn*

كان *kaan* (more common var. *čaan*) See under **چ و ن** *čwn.*

كون *kawwan* II to form, produce, bring into being. فيه جماعة يكونون لهم عصابات *fii jamaaᶜa ykawwnuun-lahum ᶜiṣaabaat.* There are some people who form gangs. الله، سبحانه وتعالى، كون الكون *'aḷḷa, subḥaanah wa taᶜaala, kawwan l-koon.* God, be He praised and exalted, created the world.

تكون *tkawwan* II 1. pass. of II كون *kawwan.* 2. (with من *min*) to be made up of, composed of. المتحف جديد ويتكون من ثلاثة أقسام *l-matḥaf yidiid w-yitkawwan min θalaaθat 'ağsaam.* The museum is new and is made up of three sections.

الكون *l-koon* the world, the universe. الله خلق الكون *'aḷḷa xilag l-koon.* God created the world.

مكان *mukaan* p. أماكن *'amaakin* 1. place, site, location. في كل مكان *fi kill mukaan* everywhere. مكان الولادة *mukaan l-wilaada* place of birth, birthplace. البيت في مكان زين *l-beet fi mukaan zeen.* The house is in a good location. 2. seat, place. قام من مكانه وقعد الشيبة العود *gaam min mukaana w-gaᶜᶜad š-šeeba l-ᶜood.* He got up from his seat and seated the old man. 3. room, space. ما لك مكان هني *ma-lak mukaan hini.* There's no room for you here. ما تقدر تبني هني؛ ما فيه مكان كافي *ma tigdar tibni hni; ma fii mukaan kaafi.* You can't build here; there isn't enough space. 4. position, rank, place. منو رايح يحل مكانه إذا فنش؟ *minu raayiḥ yḥill mukaana 'iða fannaš?* Who's going to fill his position if he resigns? لو كنت مكاني، كان عرفت *loo čint mukaani, čaan ᶜiraft.* If you had been in my place, you would have known.

مكانة *makaana* p. *-aat* standing, position, rank, importance. الشيخ اله مكانة كلش زينة بين المواطنين *š-šeex 'ila makaana killiš zeena been li-mwaaṭniin.* The Shaikh has excellent standing among the citizens. الحاسب الآلي اله مكانته ذالحين *l-ḥaasib l-'aali 'ila makaanta ðalḥiin.* Computers have considerable importance nowadays.

ك و ي ت *kwyt*

الكويت *li-kweet* Kuwait.

كويتي *kweeti* 1. Kuwaiti, characteristic of Kuwait. 2. (p. *-yya, -yyiin*) a Kuwaiti.

ك ي ت *kyt*

كيت *keet:* كيت وكيت *keet w-keet* such and such. روح شوفه. قال عنك كيت وكيت *ruuḥ čuufa. gaal ᶜannak keet w-keet.* Go see him. He said such and such about you.

ك ي س *kys.* See **چ ي س** *čys.*

ك ي ش *kyš*

كيش *keeš* (invar.) cash, ready money. أبيع لك إذا تدفع كيش *'abiiᶜ-lak 'iδa tidfaᶜ keeš.* I'll sell you if you pay cash.

ك ي ف *kyf*

كيف *kayyaf* II 1. to condition, adjust. تقدر تكيف هوا الحجرة *tigdar tkayyif hawa l-hijra.* You can condition the air in the room. 2. to adapt, adjust. تقدر تكيف نفسك هناك *tigdar tkayyif nafsak hnaak.* You can adapt yourself there.

تكيف *tkayyaf* V pass. of II كيف *kayyaf.*

كيف *keef.* See *čeef* under **چ ي ف** *čyf.*

ك ي ك *kyk*

كيك *keek* (coll.) cakes. s. *-a.* كيكة عيد الميلاد *keekat ᶜiid l-miilaad* the birthday cake; the Christmas cake.

ك ي ل *kyl* See **چ ي ل** *čyl.*

ك ي ل و *kylw*

كيلو *keelu* p. كيلوات *-waat* kilogram. كم كيلو تابي؟ *čam keelu tabi?* How many kilograms do you want? كيلو شكر *keelu šakar* kilogram of sugar. كم الكيلو؟ *čam l-keelu?* How much is a kilogram?

ك ي ل و م ت ر *kylwmtr*

كيلومتر *keelumitir* p. *-aat* kilometer. السرعة خمسين كيلومتر في الساعة *s-surᶜa xamsiin keelumitir fi s-saaᶜa.* The speed is fifty kilometers per hour.

ك ي ل و ط *kylwṭ*

كيلوط *keeluwaṭ* kilowatt. خمسة كيلوط *xamsa keeluwaṭ* five kilowatts.

ك ي م ي ا *kymyaa*

كيميا *kiimya* chemistry.

كيماوي *kiimaawi* chemical. هندسة كيماوية *handasa kiimaawiyya* chemical engineering.

كيماويات *kiimaawiyyaat* chemicals.

گ

گ ا ر *gaar*

جار *gaar* (coll.) asphalt, tar.

گ ا ر ي *gaary*

جاري *gaari* p. جواري *guwaari* wagon, cart.

گ ا ز *gaaz*

جـــاز *gaaz* (coll.) kerosene. جاز خانة *gaaz xaana.* 1. place where kerosene is stored or sold. 2. gas station. الجاز خانة مبندة هالحين *l-gaaz xaana mbannda halḥiin.* The gas station is closed now.

گ ا ز ي ن و *gaazynw*

جــــازينو *gaaziino* p. جازينوات *-waat* 1. casino, night club. 2. coffeehouse, cafe. رحنا الجـــــازينو ولعبنـــا ورق *riḥna l-gaaziino w-li*ᶜ*abna warag.* We went to the coffeehouse and played cards.

گ ا ط *gaaṭ*

قاط *gaaṭ* see under **گ و ط** *gwṭ.*

گ ا ف *gaaf*

قاف *gaaf* name of the letter ق *g.*

گ ب ب¹ *gbb*

قبـــــة *gubba* p. *-aat* (common var. تمبة *tamba*) small ball, ball of rags.

گ ب ب² *gbb*

قبـــة *gubba* p. قبب *gubab* dome (of a building), cupola.

گ ب ح *gbḥ*

قبيح *gabiiḥ* 1. ugly, repulsive. وجه قبيح *weeh gabiiḥ* ugly face. 2. shameful, disgraceful, foul. سلوك قبيـــــح *suluuk gabiiḥ* shameful behavior.

أقبح *'agbaḥ* 1. (with من *min*) a. uglier than. b. more infamous than. 2. (with foll. n.) a. the ugliest. b. the most infamous.

گ ب ر *gbr* See under **ق ب ر** *qbr.*

گ ب ر ص *gbrṣ*

قبرص *gubruṣ* Cyprus.

قـــــبرصي *guburṣi* 1. Cyprian, from Cyprus. 2. a Cypriot.

گ ب گ ب *gbgb*

قبقاب *gabgaab* p. قباقيب *gabaagiib* pair of wooden clogs. نحن ما نلبس القــــباقيب *niḥin ma nilbis l-gabaagiib.* We don't wear wooden clogs.

گ ب گ و ب *gbgwb*

قبقـــوب *gabguub* (coll.) 1. lobster. 2. lobster meat. s. *-a.* الناس هني ما ياكلون القبقوب واجد *n-naas hni ma yaakluun l-gabguub waayid.* People here don't often eat lobster.

گ ب ل *gbl*

قبـــل *gibil* (يقبل *yigbal*) 1. to accept. ما قبلت ذيك الهدية من المعرس *ma giblit ðiič l-hadiyya min l-mi*ᶜ*ris.* She didn't accept that gift from the bridegroom. وظيفة زينة. ليش ما قبلتها؟ *waðiifa zeena. leeš ma gbiltaha?* It's a good job. Why didn't you accept it. بناتنا ما يقبلن وظيفة مضيفـــة *banaatna ma yigbalin waðiifat muðiifa.* Our girls don't accept the job of an air hostess. 2. to agree to s.th.

هذي شروط صعبة. ما أقبلها *haaði šruuṭ ṣa^cba. ma 'agbalha.* These are difficult terms. I won't agree to them. قبل يروح وايانا *gibil yruuḥ wiyyaana.* He agreed to go with us. 3. to admit. كلية الطب قبلتني *kulliyyat ṭ-ṭibb giblatni.* The college of medicine admitted me.

قابل *gaabal* III (less common var. *jaabal*) 1. to meet, receive. كنت ماشي في سوق السمك وقابلته *čint maaši fi suug s-simač w-gaabalta.* I was walking in the fish market and I met him. قابلته وجه لوجه *gaabalta weeh l-weeh.* I met him face to face. 2. to have an interview with s.o., to interview s.o. قابلت التنديل *gaabalt t-tindeel.* I had an interview with the foreman. المدير قابلني حق ذيك الوظيفة *l-mudiir gaabalni ḥagg ðiič l-waḏiifa.* The manager interviewed me for that job. 3. to encounter, face. قابل مشاكل كثيرة في حياته *gaabal mašaakil kaθiira fi ḥayaata.* He encountered many problems in his life. 4. to meet with s.o., get together with s.o. لازم أقابل الشيخ على ها القضية *laazim 'agaabil š-šeex ^cala hal-gaḏiyya.* I will have to see the Shaikh about this case.

تقابل *tgaabal* VI to meet each other. رايحين نتقابل باكر الساعة خمس *raayḥiin nitgaabal baačir s-saa^ca xams.* We are going to meet tomorrow at five. تقابلت واياهم؟ *tgaabalt wiyyaahum?* Did you meet with them? Did you get together with them?

انقبل *ngibal* VII to be accepted. انقبلت الهدية *ngiblat l-hadiyya.* The gift was accepted. انقبل في الكلية *ngibal fi l-kulliyya.* He was accepted by the college.

استقبل *stagbal* 1. to meet, go to meet. استقبلته في المطار *stagbalta fi l-maṭaar.* I met him at the airport. 2. to receive. استقبلني في الديوان الأميري *stagbalni fi d-diwaan l-'amiiri.* He received me at the Emiri Court.

قبل *gabil* 1. (prep.) before. قبل أمس *gabl ams* (the day) before yesterday. جا قبل الساعة خمس *ya gabl s-saa^ca xams.* He came before five o'clock. جا قبل ساعة *ya gabil saa^ca.* He came an hour ago. 2. (adv.) before, earlier, previously, formerly. جيت هني قبل؟ *yiit hini gabil?* Have you been here before? أنا جيت قبل *'aana yiit gabil.* I came earlier.

قبل ما *gabil-ma* (conj.) before. لا تسير قبل ما يوصل *la tsiir gabil-ma yooṣal.* Don't leave before he arrives.

قبلة *gibla* kiblah (direction to which Muslims turn to pray toward the Kaaba).

قبول *gubuul* (v.n. from قبل *gibil*) acceptance.

قبيلة *gabiila* p. قبايل *gabaayil* tribe. الناس هني قبايل وعشاير *n-naas hini gabaayil w-^cašaayir.* People here belong to tribes and clans.

مقابلة *mugaabala* (v.n. from III قابل *gaabal*) 1. encounter, meeting. 2. interview.

استقبال *stigbaal* (v.n. from X استقبل *stagbal*) reception. حفلة استقبال *ḥaflat stigbaal* reception party, a reception.

قابل *gaabil* (act. part. from قبل *gibil*) 1. having accepted. هو قابل الوظيفة *huwa* *gaabil l-waðiifa.* He has accepted the job. 2. having agreed to s.th. موب قابل ها الشــروط *muub gaabil haš-šruuṭ.* He hasn't agreed to these terms.

قابل *gaabil* (common var. *jaabil*) next, coming. الليلـــة القابلـــة *l-leela l-jaabla* tomorrow night. الشهر القابل *š-šaahar l-jaabil* next month.

قابليـــة *gaabiliyya* ability, capacity, power.

مقبول *magbuul* (p.p. from قبل *gibil*) 1. having been accepted. ها الشروط هذي كلــها مقبولــة *haš-šruuṭ haaði killaha magbuula.* All of these terms are accepted. 2. having been admitted. أنت مقبولة في كلية التمريض؟ *'inti magbuula fi kulliyyat t-tamriiḍ?* Have you been admitted to the College of Nursing? 3. acceptable, reasonable. سلوك غير مقبول *suluuk ġeer magbuul* improper behavior.

مقـــابل *mgaabil* 1. (act. part.) from III قـــابل *gaabal*) a. having met, received s.th. b. having had an interview with s.o., having interviewed s.o. 2. (prep.) opposite, facing. مقابل شيشة البـــترول *mgaabil šiišat l-batrool* opposite the gas station. 3. in return for, in compensation for. اشتغلت سبوع مقابل لا شي *štiġalt subuuc mugaabil la šayy.* I worked for a week for nothing.

مستقبل *mustagbal* future.

گ ب ن *gbn*

قبن *gabban* II to weigh (with a steelyard). قبن قلات الســح *gabban gaḷḷaat s-siḥḥ.* He weighed the sacks of dates.

قبان *gabbaan* p. *-aat* 1. steelyard, large balance scale. حط كيس العيش علـــى القبـــان *ḥuṭṭ čiis l-ceeš cala l-gabbaan.* Put the sack of rice on the steelyard. 2. weighbridge. كل شاحنة لازم تـــروح القبـــان *kill šaaḥina laazim truuḥ l-gabbaan.* Every truck has to go to the weighbridge.

گ ت ت *gtt*

جـت *gatt* (more common var. *jatt*). See under ج ت ت *jtt.*

گ ت ل *gtl* (less common var. قتل *qtl*).

قتـــل *gital* (يقتل *yagtil*) 1. to kill, murder. قتلوه في بيتـــه *gitloo fi beeta.* They killed him in his house. قتل نفسه *gital nafsa.* He committed suicide. قتل نفسه في الشغـــل *gital nafsa fi š-šuġul.* He worked very hard. 2. to beat up. كان يلعـــب وايـــاهم وقتلـــوه *čaan yilcab wiyyahum w-gitloo.* He was playing with them and they beat him up.

قتـــل *gattal* II to slaughter, massacre, butcher. قتلوهم كل أبوهم *gattaluuhum kill ubuuhum.* They slaughtered all of them without exception.

تقتـــل *tgattal* V pass. of II قتل *gattal.* ناس واجدين تقتلوا في حرب الخليـــج *naas waaydiin tgattalaw fi ḥarb l-xaliij.* Many people were killed in the Gulf War.

انقتل *ngital* VII pass. of قتل *gital.*

قتـــل *gatil* (v.n. from قتل *gital*) killing, murdering. حادثة قتل *ḥaadθat gatil* a murder. مات قتـــل *maat gatil.* He was murdered.

قاتل *gaatil* (act. part. from قتل *gital*) 1. having killed, murdered s.o. 2. (p. *-iin*) killer, murderer.

مقتـــول *magtuul* (p.p. from قتل *gital*) p. *-iin* murdered, killed. (prov.) القـــاتل مقتـــول *l-gaatil magtuul.* He who lives by the sword, dies by the sword.

گ ح ب *gḥb*

قحبة *gaḥba* p. قحاب *gḥaab* prostitute, whore.

گ ح ط *gḥṭ*

قحـــط *gaḥṭ* 1. famine. أيام القحـــط *'ayyaam l-gaḥṭ* the days of famine. 2. drought, state of rainlessness.

گ ح ف *gḥf*

قحافي *gaḥḥaafi* p. *-iyya* shrike, woodchat.

گ ح ف ي *gḥfy*

قحفيـــة *gaḥfiyya* p. قحافي *gaḥaafi*, *-aat* skullcap (worn under the غـــترة *ġitra* men's headcloth).

گ د ح *gdḥ*

قـــدح *gidaḥ* (يقدح *yigdaḥ*) to spark, make sparks. الصوفان يقدح *ṣ-ṣuufaan yigdaḥ.* Touchwood sparks.

قداحـــة *gaddaaḥa* p. *-aat* cigarette lighter.

گ د د ١ *gdd*

قـــد *gadd* equal to. هذا موب قد هذاك *haaða muub gadd haðaak.* This is not equal to that one. عطني قد ما عطيته *ᶜaṭni gadd-ma ᶜaṭeeta.* Give me (something) equal to what you have given him. على قـــد *ᶜala gadd* according to, in proportion to. (prov.) كل يمد رجله على قـــد لحافـــه *killin ymidd riila ᶜala gadd l-ḥaafa.* As you make your bed, you must lie in it. (lit., "One can stretch one's leg according to one's quilt."). اصرف على قد معـــاشك *'iṣrif ᶜala gadd maᶜaašak.* Spend according to your salary. المعاش على قد الحال *l-maᶜaaš ᶜala gadd l-ḥaal.* The salary isn't much. أنا أعرف أقرا وأكتب بس على قد الحال *'aana 'aᶜrif 'agra w-'aktib bass ᶜala gadd l-ḥaal.* I know how to read and write only to the extent of my abilities. هذا الجوتي على قد رجلك *haaða l-juuti ᶜala gadd riilak.* These shoes fit you.

شقد *šgadd.* See under ش *š-*

هالقد *halgadd.* See under ه *h.*

گ د د ٢ *gdd*

قـــدد *gaddad* II to dry, make s.th. dry (e.g., meat, fruit, fish, etc.) من زمـــان الناس كانوا يقددون اللحم والســـمك *min zamaan n-naas čaanaw ygaddiduun l-laḥam w-s-simač.* Some time ago, people used to dry meat and fish.

قد *gadd* (coll.) pieces of dried meat or fish, jerked meat. s. *-a.*

گ د ر *gdr*

قـــدر *gidar* (يقدر *yigdar*) 1. to be able to, be capable of. يقدر يقرا ويكتـــب *yigdar yigra w-yikib.* He can read and write. توه جاهل بعد؛ ما يقدر يمشي *tawwa yaahil baᶜad; ma yigdar yamši.* He's still a child; he cannot walk. 2. (with علـــى *ᶜala*) to have power over s.o., be master of. ماحد يقـــدر عليـــه *maḥḥad yigdar ᶜalee.* Nobody can control him. Nobody can handle him. قدر عليـــهم كلهم *gidar ᶜaleehum killahum.* He was able to beat all of them.

قدر *gaddar* II 1. to estimate, evaluate. تقدر تقدر قيمته؟ *tigdar tgaddir giimta?*

Can you estimate its value? التنديل ما قدر يقدر لي المعاش ذالحين *t-tindeel ma gidar ygaddir-li l-ma*c*aaš ðalḥiin.* The foreman couldn't estimate my salary now. 2. to appreciate, esteem highly, think highly of. ما يقدر أعمالي *ma ygaddir 'a*c*maali.* He doesn't appreciate what I do. كل الناس يقدرونه ويحترمونه. *kill n-naas ygaddruuna w-yiḥtirmuuna.* All the people think highly of him and respect him. 3. (of God) to predetermine, foreordain. لا قدر الله! *la gaddar aḷḷa!* God forbid!

قدر *gadir* 1. = قد *gad.* 2. esteem, regard. اله قدر كبير عند الناس. *'ila gadir čibiir* c*ind n-naas.* He's highly esteemed by the people. ليلة القدر *leelat l-gadir* night of the 26th of Ramadan, celebrating the revelation of the Quran to Muhammad.

قدر *gadar* fate, destiny. القضا والقدر. *l-gaða w-l-gadar* fate and divine decree.

قدرة *gudra* (v.n. from قدر *gidar*) ability, capability, capacity. عندك قدرة تقوم بهالشغل؟ c*indak qudra tguum b-haš-šuġul?* Do you have the ability to do this work? عاش امية سنة بقدرة الله c*aaš 'imyat sana b-gudrat 'aḷḷa.* He lived for a hundred years by the power of God.

أقدر *'agdar* (elat.) 1. (with من *min*) more capable than. 2. (with foll. n.) the most capable.

مقدار *migdaar* p. مقادير *magaadiir* amount.

تقدير *tagdiir* (v.n. from II قدر *gaddar*) estimate, valuation. على أقل تقدير c*ala 'agall tagdiir* at least. على أكثر تقدير. c*ala 'akθar tagdiir* at most.

قادر *gaadir* (act. part. from قدر *gidar*) being able, powerful to do s.th. موب قادر أمشي *muub gaadir 'amši.* I cannot walk. القادر *l-gaadir* (one of the epithets of God). بقدرة القادر *b-gudrat l-gaadir* by the power of God. قادر على الشغل *gaadir* c*ala š-šuġul.* He's able to work. He's capable of working.

مقدر *mgaddar* (p.p. from II قدر *gaddar*) decreed, fore-ordained, predestined.

گ د س *gds*

القدس *l-guds* Jerusalem. صلينا في المسجد الأقصى في القدس *ṣalleena fi l-masyid l-'agṣa fi l-guds.* We prayed in the Al-Aqsa Mosque in Jerusalem.

گ د م *gdm*

قدم *gaddam* II 1. to apply, submit (an application). قدمت طلب حق شغل في البلدية *gaddamt ṭalab ḥagg šuġul fi l-baladiyya.* I submitted an application for a job in the municipality. 2. (with على c*ala*) to give s.o. preferential treatment, to place s.o. or s.th. at the head of. قدمني عليه *gaddamni* c*alee.* He gave me preferential treatment to him. المدرس قدم ابنه على باقي الطلاب *l-mudarris gaddam 'ibna* c*ala baagi ṭ-ṭullaab.* The teacher placed his son ahead of the rest of the students. 3. to set ahead (a watch). في الصيف نقدم ساعاتنا ساعة واحدة *fi ṣ-ṣeef ngaddim saa*c*aatna saa*c*a waḥda.* In the summer we set our watches ahead one hour. 4. to gain, be fast (a watch). ساعتي تقدم دقيقتين في اليوم *saa*c*ti* *tgaddim digiigteen fi l-yoom.* My watch gains two minutes a day.

تقـدم *tgaddam* V 1. to be submitted. طلبات واجدة تقدمـت *ṭalabaat waayda tgaddamat.* Many requests were submitted. 2. to progress, make progress. الصناعة هني تقدمت واجد *ṣ-ṣinaaᶜa hni tgaddamat waayid.* Industry here has progressed a lot. تقدمـت في الرياضيات *tgaddamat fi r-riyaaḍiyyaat.* She made progress in mathematics. 3. (with على *ᶜala*) to precede, go before s.o. تقدمت علينـا لانهـا حرمـة عـودة *tgaddamat ᶜaleena linha ḥurma ᶜooda.* She preceded us because she was an old woman.

اسـتقدم *stagdam* X to bring in, summon, ask to come. نستقدم خبرا من كل العـالم *nistagdim xubara min kill l-ᶜaalam.* We bring in experts from all over the world.

قدم *gadam.* See under **ج د م** *jdm.*

قـديم *gidiim* (less common var. *jidiim*) 1. old, ancient. القصر القـديم *l-gaṣir l-gidiim* the old palace. آثـار قديمـة *'aaθaar gidiima* ancient ruins. 2. former, previous. حرمتي القديمة *ḥurumti l-gidiima* my former wife. من قـديم الزمان *min gidiim z-zamaan* from time immemorial. 3. (being) an old-timer. هو قديم في ها الدايرة؛ يعرف كل شي *huwa gidiim fi had-daayra; yᶜarf kill šayy.* He's an old-timer in this department; he knows everything.

قدام *giddaam.* See *jiddaam* under **ج د م** *jdm.*

أقـدم *'agdam* (elat.) 1. (with من *min*) older than, more ancient. 2. (with foll. n.) the oldest, the most ancient.

أقدمية *'agdamiyya* seniority.

تقـديم *tagdiim* (v.n. from II قـدم *gaddam*). See II قدم *gaddam.*

تقـدم *tagaddum* (v.n. from V تقـدم *tagaddam*). See V تقدم *tagaddam.*

قـادم *gaadim* (act. part.) p. *-iin* 1. having come, having arrived. أنت قادم من ويـن؟ *'inta gaadim min ween?* Where have you come from? 2. arrival, one who has arrived. القـادمين *l-gaadimiin* the arrivals.

مقـدم *mgaddim* (act. part. from II قدم *gaddam*) see II قدم *gaddam.*

متقـدم *mitgaddim* (act. part. from V تقدم *tgaddam*) see V تقدم *tgaddam.*

گ د و *gdw*

قدو *gadu* p. قداو *gdaaw* (less common var. نارجيلة *naariila*) hubble-bubble, water pipe. ما يدوخ جقاير؛ يدوخ قدو *ma yduux jigaayir; yduux gadu.* He doesn't smoke cigarettes; he smokes a hubble-bubble.

گ ر ء *gr'.* See under **ج ر ي** *gry.*

گ ر ا ج *graaj*

كـراج *garaaj* p. *-aat.* وديت السـيارة الكراج *waddeet s-sayyaara l-garaaj.* I took the car to the garage.

گ ر ب *grb*

قرب *garrab* II (with من *min*) 1. to get close, cause to come near s.o. or s.th. فكر في طريقة تقربه منها *fakkar fi ṭariiga tgarrba minha.* He thought of a way that would get him close to her. 2. (with بين *been*) to make peace among (people), reconcile people. قرب بـين القبيلتـين *garrab been l-gabiilteen.* He made peace between the two tribes.

تقرب *tgarrab* V (with من *min*) to curry favor with s.o., seek to gain s.o.'s favor. دايماً يتقرب من التنديـل *daayman yitgarrab min t-tindeel.* He always curries favor with the foreman.

استقرب *stagrab* X 1. to regard as near, find as near. استقربت ها الطريـق لكن ضعـت *stagrabt haṭ-ṭariig laakin ðiᶜt.* I figured this road was nearer, but I got lost. 2. to come by (s.o.'s house), to drop in. استقرب وتقهوى وايانا *stagrib w-tgahwa wiyyaana.* We are close. Come on and have coffee with us.

قرب *gurb* 1. (v.n.) closeness, proximity, nearness. ما دريت ان الحفيز ها القرب *ma dareet 'inna l-ḥafiiz hal-gurb.* I didn't know that the office was this near. جا يطلب القرب مني في يد بنـتي *ya yaṭlub l-gurb minni fi yadd binti.* He came to ask for my daughter's hand in marriage. 2. (prep.) near, close to. الدكان قـرب المدرسـة *d-dikkaan gurb l-madrasa.* The shop is near the school.

قربة *girba* (common var. *jirba*) p. قرب *girab* water bag (made of canvas).

قريب *gariib* 1. (with من *min*) near, close to. قريب من المستشفي *gariib min l-mustašfi* near the hospital. 2. close, nearby. السفارة قريبـة، مـوب بعيـدة *s-safaara gariiba, muub baᶜiida.* The embassy is close, not far. 3. (p. قرايب *garaayib*) relative, relation. هو مـن قرايبي *huwa min garaaybi.* He's one of my relatives. نحن قرايب *niḥin garaayib.* We are relatives.

قرابة *garaaba* relation, relationship, kinship.

أقرب *'agrab* (elat.) 1. (with من *min*) nearer, closer than, etc. 2. (with foll. n.) the nearest, the closest, etc.

تقريباً *tagriiban* (common var. تقريب *tagriib*) approximately, about. تقريبـاً نص ساعة بالطـايرة مـن هـني إلى قطـر *tagriiban nuṣṣ saaᶜa b-ṭ-ṭaayra min hni 'ila giṭar.* It's about half an hour by plane from here to Qatar.

گ ر ح *grḥ*

قرح *garraḥ* II to ebb (water). قرح البحر *garraḥ l-baḥar.* The sea ebbed.

اقترح *gtiraḥ* VIII to suggest, recommend. اقترح عليّ أطلب يدها من أبوهـا *gtiraḥ ᶜalayya 'aṭlub yaddha min 'ubuuha.* He suggested that I ask her father for her hand in marriage.

قرحة *gurḥa* p. *-aat* ulcer.

قراح *graaḥ* ebb (of the sea).

اقتراح *gtiraaḥ* p. *-aat* suggestion, proposal.

گ ر د *grd*

قرد *gird* p. قرود *gruud* monkey, chimpanzee, ape. (prov.) القرد في عين أمـه غـزال *l-gird fi ᶜeen 'umma ġazaal.* Beauty is in the eye of the beholder.

گ ر ر *grr*

قر *garr* (يقر *ygirr*) to confess, admit. إذا مـا تقـر يعذبونـك *'iða ma tgirr yᶜaððbuunak.* If you don't confess, they will torture you. قر بذنبـه *garr b-ðanba.* He confessed to his crime.

قرر *garrar* II 1. to decide. قرر يروح وايـــاي *garrar yruuḥ wiyyaay.* He decided to go with me. 2. to assign, decide on, approve. المدرس قرر الكتاب *l-mudarris garrar li-ktaab.* The teacher assigned the book. وزارة المعارف تقرر المنهـج *wazaarat l-maᶜaarif tgarrir l-manhaj.* The ministry of education decides on the syllabus. 3. to interrogate. ظلوا يقررون فيه لين اعترف *ḍallaw ygarriruun fii leen ᶜtiraf.* They continued to interrogate him until he confessed.

تقـرر *tgarrar* V 1. to be decided. تقرر ترفيعـه *tgarrar tarfiiᶜa.* It was decided he'd be promoted. 2. to be set, determined, decided on. المنهج بعده ما تقـــرر *l-manhaj baᶜda ma tgarrar.* The syllabus hasn't been set yet.

استـقر *stagarr* X 1. to calm down, settle, be stabilized. صعب يستقر الوضع في الشرق الأوســط *ṣaᶜb yistagirr l-waḍiᶜ fi š-šarg l-'awṣaṭ.* It's difficult for the situation to settle in the Middle East. 2. to settle down, take up residence. ما قــدر يســتقر في ذاك المكـــان *ma gidar yistagirr fi ðaak l-mukaan.* He wasn't able to settle in that place. 3. (with علـى *ᶜala*) to make up one's mind to do s.th., determine on s.th. ما يقدر يستقر على راي *ma yigdar yistagirr ᶜala raay.* He can't make up his mind (to do anything).

قـرار *garaar* decision, resolution. قراره كان في مكانه *garaara čaan fi mukaana.* He made the right decision. قرار المحكمة *garaar l-maḥkama* the court decision.

مقـر *magarr* headquarters. مقر الشركة *magarr š-šarika* the company headquarters.

تقرير *tagriir* (v.n. from II قرر *garrar*) p. تقـارير *tagaariir* report, account. كتب تقرير عن اللـي سـواه *kitab tagriir ᶜan illi sawwaa.* He wrote a report about what he had done. تقرير المصير *tagriir l-maṣiir* self-determination.

گ ر ش *grš*

قـرش *girš* p. قروش *gruuš* piaster (1/100 dirham).

گ ر ص *grṣ*

قـرص *giraṣ* (يقـرص *yugruṣ*) 1. to bite. البق يقرص *l-bagg yugruṣ.* Bugs bite. 2. to pinch.

انقرص *ngiraṣ* pass. of قرص *giraṣ*

قـرص *garṣ* 1. (v.n. from قرص *giraṣ*) 1. biting, pinching. 2. (p. قراص *graaṣ*) flat round loaf of bread.

قرصة *garṣa* (n. of inst.) p. *-aat* 1. bite, sting (of an insect). 2. pinch.

قـارص *gaariṣ* 1. (act. part. from قرص *giraṣ*) having bitten. توهـا قـارصتني *tawwha gaarṣatni.* It has just bitten me. 2. (coll.) bugs, mosquitoes. s. *-a.*

گ ر ط *grṭ*

قرط *gurṭ* p. أقراط *'agraaṭ* earring.

گ ر ط ا س *grṭaas*

قرطـاس *girṭaas* (coll.) paper. s. *-a.* ما عنـدي قرطـاس *ma ᶜindi girṭaas.* I don't have paper. عطـني قرطاســتين *ᶜaṭni girṭaasteen.* Give me two sheets of paper. (prov.) لا هـو بـالكيس ولا بالقرطـــاس *la huwa b-č-čiis wala b-l-girṭaas.* He's (or It's) neither here nor there. It's unimportant. (lit.,

"He's neither in the bag nor [wrapped] in the paper."). 2. (p. قراطيس *giraaṭiis*) paper bag. حط السامان بقرطـــــاس *ḥuṭṭ s-saamaan b-girṭaas.* Put the things in a paper bag.

گ رظ *grð̣*

مقراضة *migraað̣a* p. مقاريض *migaariið̣* 1. can opener. فتحت القوطي بالمقراضـــة *fitaḥt l-guuṭi b-l-migraað̣a.* I opened the can with the can opener. 2. nail clipper.

گ رع *gr^c^*

قرع *garra^c^* II to make bald. المحسن قرع راســـي *li-mḥassin garra^c^ raasi.* The barber made me bald-headed.

أقـــرع *'agra^c^* p. قرعان *gir^c^aan* f. قرعا *gar^c^a* bald-headed, bald person. (prov.) يتعلم الحســـانة في روس القرعـــان *yit^c^allam li-ḥsaana fi ruus l-gur^c^aan.* The blind leading the blind. (lit., "He learns barbering on bald people's heads.").

گ رف *grf*

قرفـــة *girfa* (more common var. *jirfa*). See under **ج رف** *jrf.*

گ رگ ر *grg^c^*

قرقع *garga^c^* (يقرقع *ygargi^c^*) to make a loud noise, be noisy. العيال يقرقعون تحت *li-^c^yaaḷ ygargi^c^uun taḥat.* The children are making a loud noise downstairs.

قرقعة *garga^c^a* (v.n.) loud noise, uproar.

گ رگ ور *grgwr*

قرقـــور *garguur* p. قراقير *garaagiir* fish trap (metal cage shaped like a beehive used for trapping fish).

گ رن *grn*

قـــارن *gaaran* III (with بين *been*) to compare. لا تقارن بينه وبـــين أخـــوه *la tgaarin beena w-been 'uxuu.* Don't compare him with his brother.

قرن *garn* p. قرون *gruun* 1. horn (of an animal). (prov.) لو حجت البقر علـــى قرونهـــا *lo ḥajjat l-bagar ^c^ala gruunha.* (This thing is) impossible. (lit., "If cows go on pilgrimage on their horns."). 2. century. القرن العشرين روانا أشيا ما عرفناها من قبـــل *l-garn l-^c^išriin rawwaana 'ašya ma ^c^irafnaaha min gabil.* The Twentieth Century has shown us things we haven't known before.

گ رن ا ص *grnaaṣ*

قرنـــاص *girnaaṣ* p. قرانيص *garaaniiṣ* young falcon. قرناص عـــــامين *girnaaṣ ^c^aameen* two-year old falcon.

گ رن ف ل *grnfl*

قرنفل *grunful* (coll.) carnation. s. *-a.*

گ ر ي١ *gry*

قـــرا *gira* (يقرا *yigra*) 1. to read. يقرا ويكتب إنكليزي *yigra w-yiktib 'ingiliizi.* He reads and writes English. أقـــرا وأكتب بس على قد الحـــال *'agra w-aktib bass ^c^ala gadd l-ḥaal.* I read and write only to the extent of my abilities. 2. to recite, chant. قرا سورة من القـــرآن *gira suura min l-ġur'aan.* He recited a chapter from the Quran. اقرا عليه السلام *'igra ^c^alee s-salaam.* Kiss it good-bye. You won't see it again. 3. to study. اقرا زين. عنـــدك امتحـــان بـــاكر *'igra zeen. ^c^indak mtiḥaan baačir.* Study well. You have an examination tomorrow.

قـرا *garra* II 1. to cause to read. المدرس قراهم امية صفحـة *l-mudarris garraahum 'imyat ṣafha.* The teacher made them read a hundred pages. 2. to teach s.o. قريتـه الـدرس *garreeta d-dars.* I taught him the lesson.

انقرا *ngira* VII pass. of قرا *gira.*

قراية *graaya* 1. (v.n. from قرا *gira*) recitation, reading. القرايـة والكتابـة *li-graaya w-li-ktaaba* reading and writing. 2. (p. *-aat*) readings.

قـرآن *ġur'aan* Quran, the holy book of Muslims. القــرآن الكريــم *l-ġur'aan l-kariim* the Holy Quran. كـان يـروح المسجد ويقـرا مـن القـرآن *čaan yruuḥ li-msiid w-yigra min l-ġur'aan.* He used to go to the mosque and recite from the Quran.

گ ر ي[2] *gry*

قريـة *garya* (more common var. *ġarya*). See under غ ر ي *ġry.*

گ ز ز *gzz*

قـز *gazz (يقـز ygizz)* to survey (land). البلديـة تقـز الأرض *l-baladiyya tgizz l-'arḍ.* The municipality surveys land.

قـزاز *gazzaaz* p. *-iin* surveyor (of land). يشـتغل قـزاز حق البلديـة *yištaġil gazzaaz ḥagg l-baladiyya.* He works as a surveyor for the municipality.

گ ش ر *gšr*

قشـر *gaššar* II to peel, pare, shell. قشر التفاحة قبل لا تاكلها *gaššir t-tiffaaḥa gabil-la taakilha.* Peel the apple before you eat it.

تقشر *tgaššar* II pass. of II قشر *gaššar.*

قشـر *gišir* (coll.) 1. peel, rind, skin. s. *-a.*

قشـرة *gišra* a peeling, piece of rind or skin (e.g., of a fruit), shell (of a nut, an egg, etc.). قشـرة الـراس *gišrat r-raas* dandruff.

گ ش ا ر *gšaar*

قشـار *gšaar* things, objects, odds and ends. شـل قشــاره ومشــى *šall gšaara w-miša.* He picked up his things and left.

گ ش ط *gšṭ*

قشـط *gišaṭ (يقشـط yagšuṭ)* to scratch, nick, chip. قشـط الميز *gišaṭ l-meez.* He scratched the table. الرصاصة قشـطت راسه *r-raṣaaṣa gšaṭat raasa.* The bullet grazed his head.

قشـط *gaššaṭ* 1. to peel off, scratch off. قشــط الرنــق القديــم *gaššaṭ r-rang l-gadiim.* He peeled off the old paint. 2. to rob, strip s.o. of his belongings. هجمـوا عليـه وقشـطوه *hajmaw ʿalee w-gaššaṭoo.* They attacked him and robbed him.

تقشـط *tgaššaṭ* V pass. of II قشـط *gaššaṭ.*

گ ص ب[1] *gṣb*

قصـب *giṣab (يقصـب yagṣib)* to cut meat. القصـاب يقصـب اللحـم *l-gaṣṣaab yagṣib l-laḥam.* A butcher cuts meat.

قصب *gaṣṣab* II intens. of قصب *giṣab.* لا تقصـب هـذا اللحـم *la tgaṣṣib haaða l-laḥam.* Don't cut up this meat.

قصابـة *gṣaaba* (v.n. from قصب *giṣab*) butchering, meat cutting, butcher's trade.

قصاب *gaṣṣaab* p. قصاصيب *gaṣaaṣiib* butcher, meat cutter. ما أشتري اللحم إلا من القصاب *ma 'aštiri l-laḥam 'illa min l-gaṣṣaab.* I buy meat only from a butcher.

مقصبة *magṣaba* p. مقاصب *magaaṣib* 1. butcher's shop. 2. slaughterhouse.

گ ص ب ٢ *gṣb*

قصب *gaṣab* (coll.) 1. stalks, reeds. s. قصبة *gṣuba.* قصب السكر *gaṣab s-sukkar* sugar cane. 2. gold and silver thread or embroidery.

قصبة *gaṣaba* reed, stalk. القصبة الهوائية *l-gaṣaba l-hawaa'iyya* the windpipe.

گ ص د *gṣd*

قصد *giṣad (يقصد yagṣid)* to mean, intend, have in mind. شتقصد؟ *š-tagṣid?* What do you mean? ما قصدت شي *ma giṣatt šayy.* I didn't mean anything. قصد يقول ما عنده فلوس *giṣad yguul ma ᶜinda fluus.* He intended to say he didn't have any money.

اقتصد *gtiṣad* VIII to be economical, frugal, thrifty. إذا ما تقتصد ما تقدر تعيش *'iða ma tigtaṣid ma tigdar tᶜiiš.* If you don't economize, you can't make much of your life.

قصد *gaṣd* intent, intention. عن قصد *ᶜan gaṣd* intentionally. بدون قصد *b-duun gaṣd* unintentionally, inadvertently. شقصدك؟ *š-gaṣdak?* What do you mean? قصدي الكمبيالات *gaṣdi l-kumbyaalaat.* I mean (bank) drafts.

قصيدة *gaṣiida* p. قصايد *gaṣaayid* poem.

اقتصاد *gtiṣaad* (v.n. from VIII اقتصد *gtiṣad*) 1. economy, economization. اقتصاد سياسي *gtiṣaad siyaasi* political economy. 2. economics. يدرس اقتصاد *yidris 'igtiṣaad.* He's studying economics. كلية الاقتصاد *kulliyyat l-igtiṣaad* the college of economics.

اقتصادي *gtiṣaadi* 1. thrifty, frugal. 2. economic. الوضع الاقتصادي *l-waðᶜ l-igtiṣaadi* the economic situation.

گ ص ر *gṣr*

قصر *giṣir (يقصر yigṣar)* to be or become short, shorter. في الصيف الليل يقصر *fi ṣ-ṣeef l-leel yigṣar.* In the summer nights become shorter. قصر عليك الثوب. اشتري واحد ثاني *giṣir ᶜaleek θ-θoob. štiri waaḥid θaani.* The dress is too short for you. Buy another one.

قصر *gaṣṣar* II 1. to shorten, make short or shorter. ها الحبل طويل. قصره *hal-ḥabil ṭawiil. gaṣṣra.* This rope is long. Shorten it. 2. (with في *fi*) to fail (an examination). قصر في الامتحان *gaṣṣar fi li-mtiḥaan.* He failed the examination. 3. to fall behind, lag behind (in s.th.). قصر في شغله *gaṣṣar fi šuġla.* He didn't do a good job. أبوه رجال زين؛ ما يقصر *'ubuu rayyaal zeen; ma ygaṣṣir.* His father is a good man; he doesn't let anyone down. أحسنت! ما قصرت *'aḥsant! ma gaṣṣart.* Bravo! You did your best.

تقصر *tgaṣṣar* V to be shortened. ها الكوت ما يتقصر *hal-kuut ma yitgaṣṣar.* This coat cannot be shortened.

قصر *giṣar* (v.n. from قصر *giṣir*) shortness, smallness. قصر نظر *giṣar naðar* shortsightedness, nearsightedness.

قصـــر *gaṣir* p. قصـــور *gṣuur* castle, palace. قصـــر الشيـــخ *gasr š-šeex* the Shaikh's palace. قصر السيف *gaṣr s-siif* the palace by the seashore.

قصـــير *gaṣiir* p. *-iin,* قصار *gṣaar* short. سالم قصير، مـــوب طويـــل *saalim gaṣiir, muub ṭawiil.* Salim is short, not tall. المسافة قصـــيرة؛ تقـــدر تمشـــي *l-masaafa gaṣiira; tigdar tamši.* The distance is short; you can walk. قصير نظـــر *gaṣiir naðar* shortsighted.

أقصـــر *'agṣar* (elat.) 1. (with من *min*) shorter than. 2. (with foll. n.) the shortest.

قصـــور *gṣuur* (v.n. from قصر *giṣir*) 1. deficiency, shortcoming. 2. negligence, neglectfulness.

قـــاصر *gaaṣir* (v.n. from قصر *giṣir*) 1. (p. *-iin,* قصـــر *giṣṣar*) minor, legal minor. مات وترك وراه قصر *maat w-tirak waraa giṣṣar.* He died and left minor children. 2. unable (to do s.th.), incapable (of doing s.th.). يدي قاصرة *yaddi gaaṣra.* I am powerless. I can't do anything.

گ ص ص *gṣṣ*

قص *gaṣṣ (يقص ygiṣṣ)* 1. to cut, cut off, clip (s.th. with scissors). قص القرطاس *gaṣṣ l-girṭaas.* He cut the paper. قص لي لحمة من الفخذ *giṣṣ-li laḥma min l-faxið.* Cut a piece of meat for me from the leg. 2. to lie, tell lies. دير بالك منه. ترى يقـــص عليـــك *diir baalak minna. tara ygiṣṣ ᶜaleek.* Be careful with him because he will lie to you. 3. to incite to evil, tempt. قص عليه الشيطـــان *gaṣṣ ᶜalee š-šayṭaan.* The devil has talked evil to him. 4. to make s.o. tired, weary, fatigued. الشغل قصـــه *š-šuġul gaṣṣa.* Work made him tired.

قصـــى *giṣa* (v.n. from قص *gaṣṣ*) tiredness, weariness, fatigue. ماحد منـــهم بقصـــاي *maḥḥad minhum b-giṣaaya.* None of them works as hard as I do. None of them is as tired as I am.

مقـــص *mgaṣṣ* p. *-aat* pair of scissors, shears. (prov.) لحية ولحيّة وكل شارب اله مقص *liḥya w-lḥayya w-kill šaarib 'ila mgaṣṣ.* Your fingers are not the same. Different strokes for different folks. (lit., "A beard and a little beard and each mustache has its scissors.").

گ ص گ ص *gṣgṣ*

قصقص *gaṣgaṣ (ygaṣgiṣ)* to cut s.th. up (e.g., paper, cloth, hair, etc.), cut s.th. into pieces. قصقـــص الثـــوب *gaṣgaṣ θ-θoob.* He cut up the dress. قصقص القرطاس *gaṣgaṣ l-girṭaas.* He shredded the paper.

تقصقـــص *tgaṣgaṣ (يتقصقص yitgaṣgaṣ)* pass. of قصقص *gaṣgaṣ.*

گ ط ر *gṭr*

قطـــر *gaṭṭar* II 1. to distill. قطر الماي *gaṭṭar l-maay.* He distilled the water. 2. to drop, drip, fall into drops. عيوني موب صاحية؛ رحـــت لاجـــل أقطرهـــم *ᶜyuuni muub ṣaaḥya; riḥt lajil 'agaṭṭirhum.* My eyes are not good; I went to have eyedrops put in them.

قطـــر *giṭar* Qatar (the State of Qatar). الدوحة عاصمة قطـــر *d-dooḥa ᶜaaṣimat giṭar.* Doha is the capital of Qatar.

قطـــري *gṭari* (common var. *giṭri*) 1. characteristic of Qatar, from Qatar. هذي دشداشـــة قطريـــة *haaði dišdaaša* *gṭariyya.* This is a dishdash from Qatar. 2. (p. *-yyiin*) a Qatari, person from Qatar. أنا قطري من الوكرة *'aana gṭari min l-wakra.* I am a Qatari from Al-Wakra.

قطرة *gaṭra* p. *-aat* 1. drop. قطرة من بحر *gaṭra min baḥar* drop in the ocean. (prov.) قطرة على قطرة وتصبح غدير *gaṭra* *ᶜala gaṭra w-tiṣbiḥ ġadiir.* If you take care of your pennies, the dollars will take care of themselves.

قطار *giṭaar* p. *-aat* (railroad) train. سافر بالقطار *saafar b-l-giṭaar.* He traveled by train.

قطارة *gaṭṭaara* p. *-aat* eyedropper.

تقطير *tagṭiir* (v.n. from II قطر *gaṭṭar*) distilling, distillation.

مقطر *mgaṭṭar* (p.p. from II قطر *gaṭṭar*) distilled. ماي مقطر *maay mgaṭṭar* distilled water.

گ ط ط *gṭṭ*

قط *gaṭṭ* (يقط *ygiṭṭ*) 1. to throw s.th. away, discard. قطه في الدرام *gaṭṭa fi d-draam.* He threw it away in the garbage can. 2. to put, place. قط السامان بالستور *giṭṭ s-saamaan b-s-stoor.* Put the merchandise in the storehouse. 3. to drop s.o. (at some place), to cause to get off, disembark. خذني بالسيارة وقطني عند الدار *xiðni b-s-sayyaara w-giṭṭni ᶜind d-daar.* Take me by car and drop me off at the house.

قط *gaṭṭ* (v.n.) 1. throwing away, discarding. 2. putting, placing, causing to get off.

گ ط ع *gṭᶜ*. See under غ ط ع *ġṭᶜ*.

گ ط ن *gṭn*

قطن *giṭin* (coll.) cotton. القطن ما يطلع هني *l-giṭin ma yiṭlaᶜ hni.* Cotton doesn't grow here.

قطان *gaṭṭaan* p. *-iin* cotton merchant, cotton manufacturer.

گ ط و *gṭw*

قطو *gaṭu* p. قطاوة *gṭaawa* f. قطوة *gaṭwa* cat. (prov.) قطو مطابخ *gaṭu maṭaabix.* He eats like a pig. (lit., "A cat of kitchens.").

گ ط ي *gṭy*

قطا *gaṭa* (coll.) sand grouse. s. قطاة *-a.* القطا من طيور الجزيرة العربية *l-gaṭa min ṭyuur l-jaziira l-ᶜarabiyya.* Sand grouse are among the birds of the Arabian peninsula.

گ ظ ب *gðb*

قظب *giðab* (يقظب *yagðib*) 1. to hold, hold fast. (prov.) اقظب مجنونك لا يجيك أجن منه *'igðab maynuunak la yiik 'ayann minna.* A bird in the hand is worth two in the bush. (lit., "Hold on to your crazy person lest a crazier one comes to you."). 2. to grab, seize. قظب الفلوس *giðab li-fluus.* He grabbed the money. قظب المنبر *giðab l-mimbar.* He mounted the pulpit.

گ ظ ل *gðl*

قظلة *gaðla* hair style. أبو قظلة ممشطة *'ubu gaðla mmaššaṭa* one with a nice hair style.

گ ع د *gᶜd*

قعد *giᶜad* (يقعد *yagᶜid*) 1. to sit down, take a seat. جا وقعد *ya w-giᶜad.* He came and sat down. تفضل اقعد! *tfaððal* ig^c^id! Please sit down. 2. to sit, be sitting. أبغى أقعد قدام *'abġa 'ag^c^id jiddaam.* I would like to sit in front. قعدنا في الحفيز نتطره *gi^c^adna fi l-ḥafiiz nanṭura.* We sat in the office waiting for him. 3. to remain, stay, dwell, live. قعدنا في دبي سنة وبعدين انتقلنا *gi^c^adna fi dbayy sana w-ba^c^deen ntigalna.* We lived in Dubai for a year, and then moved. 4. (with foll. imperf.) to start to do s.th. قعد يدرس *gi^c^ad yidris.* He started to study. قعدنا نسولف من الساعة تسع إلى نص الليل *gi^c^adna nsoolif min s-saa^c^a tisi^c^ 'ila nuṣṣ l-leel.* We started to chat from nine to midnight.

قعد *ga^cc^ad* II to seat s.o., make s.o. sit down. المدرس قعدني قدامه *l-mudarris ga^cc^adni jiddaama.* The teacher seated me in front of him. جاسم قعد ولده في المدرسة ولو انه صغيرون *jaasim ga^cc^ad wlida fi l-madrasa wala inna ṣġayyruun.* Jasim entered his son in school although he was very young.

تقاعد *tgaa^c^ad* VI to retire. رايح أتقاعد السنة الجاية انشالله *raayiḥ 'atgaa^c^ad s-sana l-yaaya nšaaḷḷa.* I am going to retire next year, God willing.

انقعد *ngi^c^ad* VII (with في *fi*) to be lived in, be occupied. ها الفريج وسخ؛ ما ينقعد فيه *hal-firiij waṣx; ma yingi^c^id fii.* This neighborhood is dirty; it can't be lived in.

قعدة *ga^c^da* 1. sitting. قعدة على السيف *ga^c^da ^c^ala s-siif* sitting by the seashore. 2. getting together, session. تعال يمنا. القعدة زينة *ta^c^aal yammna. l-ga^c^da zeena.* Come to our place. Getting together is good.

قعدة *gi^c^da*: ذو القعدة *ðu l-gi^c^da* name of the eleventh month of the Muslim year.

قعود *gu^c^uud* p. قعدان *gi^c^daan,* قواعيد *guwaa^c^iid.* 1. mature young camel. 2. period of mourning or grief.

قعيدة *gi^c^iida* p. *-aat*: قعيدة دار *gi^c^iidat daar* housewife, homemaker.

مقعد *mag^c^ad* p. مقاعد *magaa^c^id* seat, bench.

تقاعد *tagaa^c^ud* (v.n. from VI تقاعد *tgaa^c^ad*) retirement, pension. سن التقاعد *sinn t-tagaa^c^ud* the age of retirement. حالوه على التقاعد *ḥaaluu ^c^ala t-tagaa^c^ud.* They pensioned him off. They forced him to retire.

قاعد *gaa^c^id* (act. part. from قعد *gi^c^ad*) 1. sitting, sitting down. هو هني قاعد ويانا *huwa hni gaa^c^id wiyyaana.* He's here, sitting with us. 2. unemployed, idle. قاعد. ما حصل شغل بعد *gaa^c^id. ma ḥaṣṣal šuġul ba^c^ad.* He's unemployed. He hasn't gotten a job yet. 3. (with foll. imperf.) in the process of doing s.th., engaged in. قاعد يدرس *gaa^c^id yidris.* He's studying. قاعدين يتحاكون *gaa^c^diin yitḥaačuun.* They are engaged in a conversation.

گ ف ش *gfš*

قفشة *gafša* 1. (p. قفاش *gfaaš*) a. spoon. b. ladle. 2. (p. *-aat*) fluke of an anchor.

گ ف ف *gff*

قفة *guffa* p. قفف *gufaf, -aat* large basket made from palm leaves.

گ ف ل gfl

قفل *gaffal* II 1. to lock, lock up. قفل الباب لين طلع *gaffal l-baab leen ṭilaᶜ.* He locked the door when he went out. الحارس قفل كل البيبان *l-ḥaaris gaffal kill l-biibaan.* The guard locked up all the doors. 2. (with على *ᶜala*) to block (one's way). قفل عليّ الطريق *gaffal ᶜalayya ṭ-ṭariig.* He blocked my way.

انقفل *ngifal* VII to be locked, locked up. كل البيبان انقفلت *kill l-biibaan ngiflat.* All the doors were locked up. ها الخزنة ما تنقفل *hal-xazna ma tingifil.* This safe cannot be locked up.

قفل *gufiḷ* p. اقفال *gfaaḷ* 1. lock. 2. padlock.

قفال *gfaaḷ* (common var. قفّال *gaffaaḷ*) end of the pearling season (usually at the end of the summer).

قافلة *gaafla* p. قوافل *gawaafiḷ* 1. caravan. 2. convoy.

گ ل ا ص gḷaaṣ

كلاص *gḷaaṣ* p. *-aat* drinking glass.

گ ل ب gḷb

قلب *giḷab (يقلب yagḷib)* 1. to turn, turn over. اقلب الصفحة *'igḷib ṣ-ṣafḥa.* Turn the page. 2. to turn upside down, turn over. حصل دعمة وسيارة من السياير قلبت *ḥiṣal daᶜma w-sayyaara min s-siyaayiir gḷubat.* There was a car accident and one of the cars turned upside down. لين سمع باللي صار قلب الدنيا *leen simaᶜ b-lli ṣaar giḷab d-dinya.* When he heard about what had happened, he raised heaven and earth. 3. to invert, reverse. تقدر تقلب هذا الكوت وتلبسه *tigdar tagḷib haaða l-kuut w-tilibsa.* You can turn this coat inside out and wear it. 4. to turn somersaults, tumble. فيه بعض حمام يقلب *fii baᶜð ḥamaam yagḷib.* There are some pigeons that turn somersaults. 5. to upset, overturn, topple. القطو قلب الجدر *l-gaṭu giḷab l-jidir.* The cat upset the pot.

قلب *gaḷḷab* II 1. to stir, stir up. قلب الأكل لا يحترق *gaḷḷib l-'akil la yiḥtirig.* Stir up the food so it doesn't burn. 2. to examine, study, scrutinize. قلب الكتاب قبل ما اشتراه *gaḷḷab li-ktaab gabil-ma štiraa.* He examined the book before he bought it.

تقلب *tgaḷḷab* V 1. to toss and turn. تقلب في الكرفاية ساعة قبل ما رقد *tgaḷḷab fi l-kirfaaya saaᶜa gabil-ma rigad.* He tossed and turned in bed for an hour before he fell asleep. 2. to be fickle, changeable, variable. لا تصدقه؛ يتقلب *la tṣaddga; yitgaḷḷab.* Don't believe him; he's fickle. الأسعار تتقلب *l-'asᶜaar titgaḷḷab.* Prices are subject to change. Prices fluctuate.

انقلب *ngiḷab* VII 1. to turn upside down. انقلب اللوري *ngiḷab l-loory.* The truck turned upside down. 2. to change into, turn into, become. (prov.) زمان أول تحول والغزل انقلب صوف *zamaan 'awwal tḥawwal w-l-ġazal ngiḷab ṣuuf.* Times change. Things are no longer the same. (lit., "The olden times have changed and spun thread has changed into wool."). 3. (with على *ᶜala*) to turn on or against s.o. كان زين بس انقلب على صديقه بعدين *čaan zeen bass ngiḷab ᶜala ṣidiija baᶜdeen.* He was very good, but he turned on his friend later on.

قلب *gaḷb* p. قلوب *gḷuub* 1. heart. (prov.) قلبي على ولدي وقلب ولدي على صخر *gaḷbi ᶜala wlidi w-gaḷb wlidi ᶜala ṣaxar.* (lit., "I worry about my son, but my son's heart is rocks."). وافق من كل قلبه *waafag min kill gaḷba.* He agreed wholeheartedly. يهواها من كل قلبه *yihwaaha min kill gaḷba.* He loves her with all his heart. (prov.) القلب قلب ذيب والثوب ثوب نعجة *l-gaḷb gaḷb ðiib w-θ-θoob θoob nᶜaya.* A lion in sheep's clothing. قاسي القلب *gaasi l-gaḷb* cruel, hardhearted. ضعيف القلب *ḍaᶜiif l-gaḷb* cowardly, fainthearted.

قلاب *gaḷḷaab* p. قلاليب *gaḷaaḷiib, -aat* dump truck.

قلابي *gaḷḷaabi*: حمام قلابي *ḥamaam gaḷḷaabi* pigeons that turn somersaults.

انقلاب *ngiḷaab* p. *-aat* coup d'etat, overthrow.

مقلوب *magḷuub* (p.p. from قلب *giḷab*) 1. turned upside down, turned over. بالمقلوب *b-l-magḷuub* upside down. لا تخلي الجوتي حقك بالمقلوب *la txaḷḷi l-juuti ḥaggak b-l-magḷuub.* Don't leave your shoes upside down. 2. wrong side out. لبس قميصه بالمقلوب *libas gamiiṣa b-l-magluub.* He put on his shirt inside out. يظهر انه لابس دلاغه بالمقلوب *yiðhar 'inna laabis dlaaġa b-l-magḷuub.* It seems that he's wearing his socks inside out.

متقلب *mitgaḷḷib* (act. part. from V تقلب *tgaḷḷab*) fickle, changeable, capricious.

گ ل د *gld*

قلد *gallad* II 1. to imitate, copy. القرد يقلد الإنسان *l-gird ygallid l-'insaan.* Monkeys imitate human beings. 2. to forge, counterfeit. لا تقلد إمضا غيرك *la tgallid 'imða ġeerak.* Don't forge other people's signatures.

تقليد *tagliid* (v.n.) 1. imitation. 2. forging, counterfeiting.

تقليدي *tagliidi* traditional, customary, conventional.

گ ل ع *glᶜ*

قلعة *galᶜa* p. قلاع *glaaᶜ* 1. fortress, army fort. تحصل قلعة كبيرة في كل إمارة *tḥaṣṣil galᶜa čibiira fi kill 'imaara.* You will find a big fortress in every emirate. 2. big rock.

گ ل ل *gll*

قل *gall* (يقل *ygill*) to decrease, diminish, to be or become less, little, smaller, fewer. أعمال الخير قلت هالأيام *'aᶜmaal l-xeer gallat hal-ayyaam.* Charitable deeds have decreased these days. معاشه ما يقل عن عشرة ألف درهم في الشهر *maᶜaaša ma ygill ᶜan ᶜašara 'alf dirhim fi š-šahar.* His salary is not less than ten thousand dirhams a month. قلت قيمته عند الناس لانه كذب *gallat giimta ᶜind n-naas linna čiðab.* He lost the respect of the people because he lied.

قلل *gallal* II to reduce, decrease, lessen. القصاب قلل سعر اللحم اليوم *l-gaṣṣaab gallal siᶜr l-laḥam l-yoom.* The butcher has reduced the price of meat today. ليش قللت من زياراتك صوبنا؟ *leeš gallatt min zyaaraatak ṣoobna?* Why have you reduced the frequency of your visits to us? إذا تقلل الميزان

يحطونـك في السـجن *'iδa tgallil l-miizaan yḥuṭṭuunak fi s-sijin.* If you short-weigh the scales, they will put you in jail.

تقلل *tgallal* V pass. of II قلل *gallal.*

اسـتقل *stagall* X to be or become independent. بـو ظـبي، طـال عمـرك، اسـتقلت مـن زمـان *bu đabi, ṭaal ᶜumrak, stagallat min zamaan.* Abu Dhabi, may you live long, became independent a long time ago. الأولاد هـني في أمريكـا يسـتقلون قبـل العشـرين *l-'awlaad hni fi 'amriika yistagilluun gabl l-ᶜišriin.* Youngsters here in America live independently before the age of twenty.

قلـة *gilla* (v.n. from قل *gall*) lack, scarcity, shortage. قلة فهم *gillat fahim* lack of understanding. قلـة شـعور *gillat šuᶜuur* insensitivity. قلة حيا *gillat ḥaya* shamelessness, insolence. قلة حيا منـك تطلعـين بـدون برقـع *gillat ḥaya minnič tiṭlaᶜiin b-duun birgiᶜ.* It's shameful of you to go out without a veil.

قليـل *giliil* (less common var. *jiliil*) 1. not many or much, a few, a little. عنده كتـب قليلـة *ᶜinda kutub giliila.* He has a few books. عطني قهوة قليل *ᶜaṭni gahwa giliil.* Give me a little coffee. 2. insufficient, meager, scanty, small. الفلوس اللي عنـدي قليلـة *li-fluus illi ᶜindi giliila.* The money I have is insufficient. معاشي قليل. ما أقدر أشـتري بيـت *maᶜaaši giliil. ma 'agdar 'aštiri beet.* My wages are meager. I can't buy a house. 3. rare, scarce. اللي يمشون حق الحفيز قليلين *'illi yimšuun ḥagg l-ḥafiiz giliiliin.* Those who walk to the office are rare. 4. (foll. by v.) rarely, scarcely. قليـل أروح دبـي *giliil 'aruuḥ dbayy.* I rarely go to Dubai.

أقـل *'agall* (elat.) 1. (with من *min*) less than. أقل من امية درهم *'agall min 'imyat dirhim* less than a hundred dirhams. دفعـت أقـل *difaᶜt 'agall.* I paid less. 2. (with foll. n.) the least. دفعت أقل شي *difaᶜt 'agall šayy.* I paid the least. على الأقـل *ᶜala l-'agall* at least. إذا مـا تـبي تـاكل علـى الأقـل تقهـوى *'iδa ma tabi taakil ᶜala l-'agall tagahwa.* If you don't want to eat, at least have some coffee. على أقل تقدير *ᶜala 'agall tagdiir* at the lowest estimate.

أقلية *'agalliyya* p. *-aat* minority.

اسـتقلال *stiglaal* (v.n. from X اسـتقل *stagall*) independence.

مسـتقل *mistagill* (act. part. from X اسـتقل *stagall*) 1. independent. 2. separate. حفـيز مسـتقل *ḥafiiz mistagill* separate office.

گ ل ل *gḷḷ*

قلـة *gaḷḷa* p. *-aat* large basket or sack (usually of dates). قلة سـح *gaḷḷat siḥḥ* basket of ripe dates.

گ ل م *glm*

قلـم *gallam* II to prune, trim (trees, bushes, etc.) لازم تقلـم الشـجر ذالحـين *laazim tgallim š-šiyar δalḥiin.* You have to prune trees now.

تقلم *tgallam* V pass. of II قلم *gallam.*

قلـم *gaḷam* p. قلامة *gḷaama*, اقلام *gḷaam* 1. pencil, pen. يكتـب بقلـم حـبر *yikitb b-gaḷam ḥibir.* He writes with a fountain pen. بقلم *b-gaḷam* written by. الروايـة بقلـم سـالم الفقعـان *r-riwaaya* *b-gaḷam saalim l-fagᶜaan.* The play is written by Salim Al-Fag'an. 2. department, section. قلـم الحســابات *gaḷam l-ḥisaabaat* the accounting department. قلم المـرور *gaḷam l-muruur* the traffic bureau.

گ ل ي *gly*

قلـى *giḷa* (يقلـي *yigḷi*) to fry. قلى بيضتين *giḷa beeðteen.* He fried two eggs. قلى السمك *giḷa s-simač.* He fried the fish.

قلـى *gaḷḷa* II = قلى *gila.* قلى لي بيضتين *gaḷḷii-li beeðteen* = اقلـي لي بيضتـين *'igḷii-li beeðteen.* Fry two eggs for me.

تقلى *tgaḷḷa* pass. of II قلى *gaḷḷa.*

مقلـى *magḷa* p. مقـالي *magaaḷi* frying pan.

مقلـي *magli* fried. سمـك مقلـي *simač magḷi* fried fish.

گ م ر ١ *gmr*

قـامر *gaamar* III to gamble. قامر وخسر كـل فلوسه *gaamar w-xisar kill fluusa.* He gambled and lost all his money.

مقـامر *mgaamir* (act. part.) p. *-iin* gambler.

قمـار *gmaar* gambling. القمـار حـرام في الإسـلام *li-gmaar ḥaraam fi l-'islaam.* Gambling is forbidden in Islam.

گ م ر ٢ *gmr*

قمـر *gumar* p. أقمار *'agmaar* moon. قمر عيـني *gumar ᶜeeni* my sweetheart (said to a child). طلع القمر *ṭilaᶜ l-gumar.* The moon rose.

قمـرة *gamra* p. *-aat* 1. moonlit night. كشتنا ليلة أمس وكانت قمـرة زينـة *kišatna leelat 'ams w-čaanat gamra zeena.* We went on a picnic last night and it was a beautiful moonlit night. 2. moonlight.

گ م ش *gmš*

قمـاش *gmaaš* (common var. لولو *luulu*) (coll.) pearls. s. *-a.* تجارة القماش تجـارة قديمـة *tijaarat li-gmaaš tijaara gidiima.* The pearl trade is an old trade. قماش صناعي *gmaaš ṣinaaᶜi* cultured pearls.

گ م ص *gmṣ*

قميص *gamiiṣ* p. قمصـان *gumṣaan* 1. shirt. 2. gown, dress. قميص نوم *gamiiṣ noom* night gown.

گ م ط *gmṭ*

قمطـة *gamṭa* p. *-aat* handful. قمطة عدس *gamṭat ᶜadas* handful of lentils. (prov.) اللي يدري يدري واللـي مـا يـدري يقـول قمطـة عـدس *'illi yidri yidri w-illi ma yidri yguul gamṭat ᶜadas.* Fair without and foul within.

گ م ل *gmḷ*

قمـل *gammaḷ* II to be or become infested with lice. راسـه قمـل مـن الوسـخ *raaṣa gammaḷ min l-waṣax.* His head became lice-infested from the filth.

قمل *gamuḷ* (coll.) lice. s. *-a.*

گ م م *gmm*

قمـة *gimma* p. قمـم *gimam* 1. top, summit. قمة الجبل *gimmat l-yibal* the top of the mountain. 2. summit (conference). مؤتمـر قمـة *mu'tamar gimma* summit conference.

گ ن ب ل *gnbl*

قنبلـــة *gumbula, gunbula* p. قنـــابل *ganaabil* bomb.

گ ن ص gnṣ

قنص ginaṣ (يقنص yagniṣ) to hunt. طلعنا نقنص *ṭilacna nagniṣ.* We went hunting. قنص غزال *ginaṣ ġazaal.* He hunted a deer.

قنص ganaṣ (v.n.) hunting. القنص يستوي زين في الشتا *l-ganaṣ yistawi zeen fi š-šita.* Hunting is good during the winter.

قناص gannaaṣ p. *-a, -iin* hunter. تحصل قناصة زينين بين البدو *tḥaṣṣil gannaaṣa zeeniin been l-badu.* You will find good hunters among the bedouins.

گ ن ص ل gnṣl

قنصل gunṣul (more common var. *ġunṣul*). See under غ ن ص ل *ġnṣl.*

گ ن ط ر gnṭr

قنطر ganṭar. See under غ ن ط ر *ġnṭr.*

گ ن ع gnc

قنع ginac (يقنع yignac) to be or become convinced, persuaded. عنيد؛ ما يقنع أبد *caniid; ma yignac 'abad.* He's obstinate; he won't be convinced. قنع لين علمته بكل شي *ginac leen callamta b-kill šayy.* He became convinced when I told him everything.

قنع gannac II to persuade, convince. قنعني أسافر لندن وياه *gannacni 'asaafir landan wiyyaa.* He persuaded me to travel to London with him.

تقنع tgannac V pass. of II قنع *gannac.*

اقتنع gtinac VIII = قنع *ginac.*

گ ن ن gnn

قانون gaanuun (more common var. *ġaanuun*). See under غ ن ن *ġnn.*

گ ن و gnw

قناة ganaa p. قنوات *ganawaat* canal. قناة السويس *ganaat s-swees* the Suez Canal.

گ ه ر ghr

قهر gihar. See under ق ه ر *qhr.*

گ ه و ghw

قهوى gahwa (يقهوي ygahwi) to give coffee to s.o., welcome s.o. with coffee. قهويت الخطار كلهم *gahweet l-xuṭṭaar killahum.* I gave coffee to all the guests. صديقي قهواني. ما كان واياي فلوس *ṣidiiji gahwaani. ma čaan wiyyaay fluus.* My friend bought me coffee. I didn't have any money with me.

تقهوى tagahwa (يتقهوى yitgahwa) to drink coffee, have coffee (with s.o.). جاوا عندنا وتقهوا ويانا *yaw cindana w-tagahwaw wiyyaana.* They came to our place and had coffee with us. تفضل تقهوى! *tfaððal tagahwa!* Please have some coffee!

قهوة ghawa (common var. *gahwa*) 1. coffee. شربت قهوة *šribt ghawa.* I had some coffee. 2. (p. قهاوي *gahaawi*) coffeehouse, coffee shop, cafe. يسهر في القهاوي *yishar fi l-gahwaawi.* He stays up at night in coffeehouses.

گ و ت ر gwtr

قوترة gootra (adv., invar.) 1. by force. خذيتها منه قوترة *xaðeetta minna gootra.* I took it from him by force. 2. chaos, confusion, disorder. المسألة قوترة عندك؟ *l-mas'ala gootra cindak?* Why are you creating this chaos?

گ و د *gwd*

قـاد *gaad (*يقـود *yguud)* 1. to lead, command. القـايد يقـود الجنـود *l-gaayid yguud li-jnuud.* A commander leads soldiers. 2. to drive, steer (e.g., a car). تعلـم كيـف يقـود السـيارة *tᶜallam keef yguud s-sayyaara.* He learned how to drive a car.

قـود *gawwad* II to procure, pimp. فيه نـاس يقـودون لـك *fii naas ygawwduun-lak.* There are people who will procure for you.

قـوادة *gwaada* (v.n.) 1. procurement, pimping. 2. prostitution.

قـواد *gawwaad* p. قواويد *giwaawiid* 1. pimp, procurer. تحصل قواويد في البـارات في الخارج *tḥaṣṣil giwaawiid fi l-baaraat fi l-xaarij.* You find pimps in bars abroad. 2. قـوادة *gawwaada* p. *-aat* madam, manager of a house of prostitution.

گ و س *gws*

قـوس *goos* p. أقـواس *'agwaas* 1. bow, longbow. قوس ونشـاب *goos w-niššaab* bow and arrow. 2. arch, vault. 3. قوسين (*gooseen*) parentheses. بين قوسين *been gooseen* in parentheses.

گ و ط ي *gwṭi*

قوطي *guuṭi* (less common var. *ġuuṭi*) p. قواطـي *guwaaṭi* 1. tin, can. اشـتريت قوطيين طماط *štireet guuṭiyyeen ṭamaaṭ.* I bought two cans of tomatoes. 2. pack, packet. قوطـي جكـاير *guuṭi jigaayir* pack of cigarettes.

گ و ع *gwᶜ*

قـاع *gaaᶜ* 1. ground, earth. 2. land. عنـدي قـاع في راس الخيمـة *ᶜindi gaaᶜ fi raas l-xeema.* I own a piece of land in Ras Al-Khaima. 3. floor. رقد على القاع *rigad ᶜala l-gaaᶜ.* He slept on the floor. 4. (p. قيعان *giiᶜaan*) bottom. قاع البحـر *gaaᶜ l-baḥar* the bottom of the sea.

گ و ل ١ *gwl*

قـال *gaal (*يقول *yguul)* 1. to say, tell. أنا مـا قلـت هـذا *'aana ma gilt haaða.* I didn't say this. قال إنه موب جاي اليـوم *gaal 'inna muub yaay l-yoom.* He said that he wasn't coming today. قـول الصـدق! *guul ṣ-ṣidj!* Tell the truth! (prov.) نقول ثور، يقول حلبه *nguul θoor, yguul ḥilba.* (lit., "We say, 'Bull,' and he says, 'Milk it.'") describes s.o. who argues for an impossible thing. (prov.) اللي ما يطول العنقود يقـول حـامض *'illi ma yṭuul l-ᶜanguud yguul ḥaamiḍ.* Sour grapes. (prov.) قال طلقها قال الله يلعـن الثنتـين *gaal ṭalligha gaal 'aḷḷa yilᶜan θ-θinteen.* Between the devil and the deep blue sea. Hobson's choice. أقول! *'aguul!* (Used to draw s.o.'s attention) Hey! Listen! 2. (with ل *li-*) to tell. قال لي مـوب رايـح *gal-li muub raayiḥ.* He told me he wasn't going. ويش قال لك؟ *weeš gal-lak?* What did he tell you?

انقـال *ngaal* VII pass. of قال *gaal.* شي مـا ينقـال *šayy ma yingaal* something that shouldn't be said. خله! ما ينقال له شـي *xaḷḷa! ma yingaal-la šayy.* Leave him! He cannot be told anything.

القـال والقيـل *l-gaal w-l-giil,* القيل والقال *l-giil w-l-gaal* idle talk, prattle, gossip.

قـول *gool* (v.n. from قـال *gaal*) 1. saying. القول شي والفعل شي ثاني *l-gool* *šayy w-l-fi^cil šayy θaani.* Saying something and doing something are two different things. على قول المثل *cala gool l-maθal* as the proverb says. 2. (p. أقوال *'agwaal*) saying, proverb.

مقال *magaal* p. *-aat* article, piece of writing. كتب مقال في الجريدة *kitab magaal fi l-jariida.* He wrote an article in the newspaper. مقال افتتاحي *magaal 'iftitaaḥi* editorial, leading article.

مقاولة *mugaawala* p. *-aat* deal, transaction, undertaking.

قايل *gaayil* (act. part. from قال *gaal*) having said s.th. أهو القايل ولد الكلب كلبٍ مثله *'uhu l-gaayil wild č-čalb čalbin miθla.* He's the one who has said, "Like father, like son." أنا قايل له لا تروح هناك *'aana gaayil-la la truuḥ hnaak.* I have told him not to go there.

مقاول *mgaawil* contractor (usually building contractor).

گول ٢ *gwl*

كول *gool* p. كوال *gwaal* goal (in sports).

كوجي *goolči* p. *-yya* goalkeeper.

گوم *gwm*

قام *gaam* (يقوم *yguum*) 1. to get up, stand up, rise. قال له «قوم»! *gaal-la, "guum!"* He said to him, "Get up!" قمت من مكاني وقعدت الشيبة *gumt min mukaani w-ga^{cc}att š-šeeba.* I got up from my place and seated the old man. 2. (with ب *b-*) to carry out, do, perform. لازم تقوم بواجبك *laazim tguum b-waajbak.* You have to carry out your duty. الفرق الشعبية تقوم ببعض الاحتفالات *l-firag š-ša^cbiyya tguum b-ba^cḍ li-ḥtifaalaat.* Popular folk troupes perform some of the celebrations. 3. (with على *cala*) to rise up against, revolt, rebel against. الشعب قام على الحكومة *š-ša^cb gaam cala l-ḥukuuma.* The people rose up against the government. 4. to break out, flare up. قامت الحرب بين القبيلتين على ما ميش *gamaat l-ḥarb been l-gabilteen cala ma miiš.* War broke out between the two tribes for nothing. 5. (with foll. imperf.) to begin, start to do s.th. قام يدرس *gaam yidris.* He began to study. 6. to start, begin. قامت الصلاة *gaamat ṣ-ṣalaa.* The time of prayer has come.

قوم *gawwam* II to make get up, make stand up. صوت الماكينة قومني من النوم *ṣoot l-maakiina gawwamni min n-noom.* The noise of the engine woke me up. قومته من مكانه وقعدت الحرمة العودة *gawwamta min mukaana w-ga^{cc}att l-ḥurma l-^cooda.* I got him out of his seat and seated the old lady.

قاوم *gaawam* III 1. to resist, oppose. الكولي ما يقدر يقاوم التنديل *l-kuuli ma yigdar ygaawim t-tindeel.* A coolie cannot stand up against a foreman. 2. to rise up against, rebel against. قاوموا الاحتلال *gaawmaw li-ḥtilaal.* They rose up against the occupation.

قوم *goom* (v.n. from قام *gaam*) 1. getting up, standing up, rising. 2. (with ب *b-*) carrying out, performing. 3. (p. أقوام *'agwaam,* قوام *gwaam*) kinsfolk, tribesmen.

قامة *gaama* p. *-aat* fathom (measure of length, approx. six feet).

قيامة *gyaama* resurrection. يوم القيامة

yoom li-gyaama the day of resurrection. كنيسة القيامة *kaniisat li-gyaama* the Church of the Holy Sepulcher. قامت القيامة *gaamat li-gyaama.* There was uproar, turmoil, and excitement.

مقام *magaam* p. *-aat* 1. shrine, sacred place, tomb of a saint. 2. occasion. في هذا المقام *fi haaða l-magaam* on this occasion. 3. standing, position, rank. ما له مقام عندي *ma la magaam ᶜindi.* I don't respect him.

تقويم *tagwiim* 1. calendar. التقويم الهجري *t-tagwiim l-hijri* the Hegira calendar, the Muslim calendar. التقويم الغربي *t-tagwiim l-ġarbi* the Gregorian calendar.

مقاومة *mgaawama* (v.n. from III قاوم *gaawam*) resistance. دخل الجيش البلد بدون مقاومة *dixal l-jeeš l-balad b-duun mgaawama.* The army entered the city without resistance. مقاومة ضد الأمراض *mgaawama ḍidd l-'amraaḍ* resistance to disease.

إقامة *'igaama* residence, stay. ما تقدر تشتغل بدون إقامة *ma tigdar tištaġil b-duun 'igaama.* You cannot work without a residence permit.

قايم *gaayim* (act. part. from قام *gaam*) 1. having waked up. توه قايم من النوم *tawwa gaayim min n-noom.* He has just waked up. 2. (with ب *b-*) carrying out, performing, doing. قايم بواجبه *gaayim b-waajba.* He's carrying out his duty. قايم بالأعمال *gaayim b-l-'aᶜmaal* chargé d'affaires (dipl.)

قايمة *gaayma* p. قوايم *gawaayim* 1. list, roster. 2. pillar, support. قوايم المسجد *gawaayim li-msiid* the mosque pillars. 3. menu, bill of fare. قايمة الأكل *gaaymat l-'akil* the menu.

مستقيم *mustagiim* 1. honest, righteous, upright. هذا رجال مستقيم؛ ما يتبرطل *haaða rayyaal mustagiim; ma yitbarṭal.* This is an honest man; he cannot be bribed. 2. straight. خط مستقيم *xaṭṭ mustagiim* straight line.

گ و ن ي *gwny*

قونية *guuniyya* p. قواني *guwaani* 1. large bag or sack (made of canvas or burlap). نشتري العيش بالقونية *ništari l-ᶜeeš b-l-guuniyya.* We buy rice by the sack. 2. weight, approx. fifty kilograms.

گ و ي *gwy*

قوي *giwi* (يقوى *yigwa)* 1. to be or become strong. هالحين ولدي كبر وقوي *halḥiin wildi kubar w-giwi.* Now my son has grown up and become strong. إذا تسقي ها الشجرة تقوى *'iða tisgi hali-šyara tigwa.* If you water this tree, it will be strong. 2. to gain power, increase in power. التنديل بدا يقوى وصار أقوى *t-tindeel bida yigwa w-ṣaar 'agwa.* The foreman began to gain power and became stronger. 3. (with على *ᶜala*) to be superior to. بنتي قويت على بنات صفها *binti giwyat ᶜala banaat ṣaffha.* My daughter was superior to her classmates.

قوى *gawwa* II to strengthen, make strong. قوينا مجلس التعاون (الخليجي) بزيادة ميزانيته *gawweena majlis t-taᶜaawun (l-xaliiji) b-ziyaadat miizaaniita.* We strengthened the Gulf Cooperation Council by increasing its budget. !الله يقويـك *'aḷḷa ygawwiik!* (possible answer to القـوة *l-guwwa?* How are you?).

تقـوى *tgawwa* V pass. of II قـوى *gawwa.*

قــوة *guwwa* 1. strength. القـوة؟ *l-guwwa?* How are you? بـالقوة *b-l-guwwa* by force. 2. power. قـوة الماكينـة *guwwat l-maakiina* the engine power. قـوة خمسـين حصـان *guwwat xamsiin ḥṣaan* fifty horsepower. 3. (p. *-aat*) armed force. قـوة جويـة *guwwa jawwiyya* air force. قـوة بحرية *guwwa baḥriyya* naval force. قـوة الحـدود *guwwat li-ḥduud* the border patrol, the border guard. القوات المسلحة *l-guwwaat l-musallaḥa* the armed forces, the troops.

قـوي *gawi* p. *-yyiin* f. قوية *gawiyya* 1. strong, powerful. رجـال قـوي *rayyaal gawi* strong man. سيارة قوية *sayyaara gawiyya* strong car. 2. serious, intense. دعمة قوية *da^cma gawiyya* serious car accident.

أقـوى *'agwa* (elat.) 1. (with من *min*) stronger than. 2. (with foll. n.) the strongest.

گ ي د *gyd*

قيـد *gayyad* II 1. to list, enter, record, write down. قيد اسمي وايا الجماعة *gayyid asmi wiyya l-jamaa^ca.* List my name with the group. كل شي تـاخذه قيـده في الدفـتر *kill šayy taaxða gayyda fi d-daftar.* Enter everything you take in the notebook. 2. to enlist. قيـدت في الجنديـة *gayyatt fi l-jindiyya.* I enlisted in the army. 3. to tie, fetter, shackle. زخوه وقيـدوه *zaxxoo w-gayyadoo.* They arrested him and hand-cuffed him. 4. to restrict, limit, confine. قيدنـي. مـا قــدرت أروح *gayyadni. ma gidart 'aruuḥ.* He restricted me. I couldn't leave.

تقيد *tgayyad* V pass. of قيد *gayyad.*

قيـد *geed* 1. list, record, tally. 2. restriction, limitation.

تقييـد *tagyiid* (v.n. from II قيد *gayyad*) 1. registering, registration. 2. enlisting. 3. fettering, shackling.

مقيد *mgayyad* (p.p. from II قيد *gayyad*) 1. listed, recorded. 2. enlisted. 3. tied, fettered, shackled. 4. restricted, limited, confined.

گ ي س *gys*

قـاس *gaas* (يقيس *ygiis*) 1. to measure, take the measurements of. قاس القـاع *gaas l-gaa^c.* He measured the land. قاس الحجرة وقال «أربعـة مـتر في سـتة مـتر» *gaas l-ḥijra w-gaal, "'arba^ca mitir fi sitta mitir."* He took the measurements of the room and said, "Four meters by six meters." 2. (with علـى *^cala*) to infer, draw conclusions from. قيس على هــذي المعلوميـة *giis ^cala haaði l-ma^cluumiyya.* Draw conclusions based on this information.

قـايس *gaayas* III to compare. إذا تقايس بينهــم، تحصـل فـرق كـبير *'iða tgaayis beenhum, tḥaṣṣil farg čibiir.* If you compare between (the two of) them, you will find a big difference.

قيـاس *gyaas* (v.n. from قـاس *gaas*) p. *-aat* 1. dimensions, measurement. كم قيـاس الحجـرة؟ *čam gyaas l-ḥijra?* What are the dimensions of the room? 2.

size. قياس كبير *gyaas čibiir* large size. كم قياس الجوتي حقك؟ *čam gyaas l-juuti ḥaggak?* What size are your shoes? بدون قياس *b-duun gyaas* extremely, disproportionately.

قياسي *giyaasi* in keeping with the model or norm. رقم قياسي *ragam giyaasi* (athletic) record. سجل رقم قياسي في المية متر *sajjal ragam giyaasi fi l-miyat mitir.* He set a record in the one hundred meter dash.

گ ي ظ *gyð̣*

قيظ *gayyað̣* II to spend the summer (as a holiday). كل سنة نقيظ في البريمي *kill sana ngayyið̣ fi li-breemi.* Every year we spend the summer in Buraimi.

قيظ *geeð̣* (less common var. صيف *ṣeef*). See under **ص ي ف** *syf.*

گ ي ل *gyl*

قيل *gayyal* II to take a midday nap, take a siesta. عند القايلة قيلوا هم وبعارينهم *ᶜind l-gaayla gayyalaw hum w-baᶜaariinhum.* At midday they and their camels took a siesta. تعال تغدى وقيل عندنا *taᶜaal tġadda w-gayyil ᶜindana.* Come have lunch and take a siesta at our place. هني الناس يتغدون ويقيلون *hni n-naas yitġadduun w-ygayyluun.* Here people have lunch and take a nap.

قايلة *gaayla* 1. midday nap, siesta. هالحين الوقت وقت القايلة *halḥiin l-wagt wagt l-gaayla.* Now it's time for a midday nap. 2. midday heat.

مقيل *mgayyil* (act. part. from II قيل *gayyal*) 1. taking a siesta. هو مقيل هالحين *huwa mgayyil halḥiin.* He's taking a siesta now. 2. having taken a siesta. توني مقيل عندهم *tawwni mgayyil ᶜindahum.* I have just taken a siesta at their place. 3. will take a siesta, going to take a siesta. أقيل عندكم انشاالله *'agayyil ᶜindakum nšaaḷḷa.* I will take a siesta at your place, God willing.

ل

ل ١ *l*

ال *l-* (article prefix) the.

ل ٢ *l*

ل *l-* (with foll. def. n.) ل *'il-/l-* (with suff. pron. and with pron. suffix after v.) *-l-*. 1. for إذا تنزل السعر، أدفع لـك كـاش *'iða tnazzil s-si^c^ir, 'adfa^c^-lak kaaš.* If you lower the price, I'll pay you cash. لك عندي خمسين درهـم *lak ^c^indi xamsiin dirhim.* I owe you fifty dirhams. كم صار لك هني؟ *čam ṣaar-lič hni?* How long have you been here? ما لك أي حـق تطقـه *ma lak 'ayya ḥagg ṭṭigga.* You have no right to hit him. للمرة الثانيـة *lil-marra θ-θanya* for the second time. الها سـنتين تشتغـل *'ilha santeen tištaġil.* She's been working for two years. 2. for, in favor of, to the benefit of. شهدوا لي في المحكمة *šihdoo-li fi l-maḥkama.* They testified for me in court. طرشت لـك اياهـا *ṭarrašt-lič-iyyaaha.* I sent it for you. 3. for, for the purpose of. ماي النل هني موب زيـن للشرب *maay n-nall hni muub zeen lišš-šurb.* Tap water here isn't good for drinking. سـافر لنـدن للونسـة *saafar landan lil-winsa.* He traveled to London for pleasure. 4. to (of the dative). قلت له ما يدير بـال *git-la ma ydiir baal.* I told him not to worry. جبتـها لـك *yibthaa-lič.* I brought it to you. أمري لله *'amri lil-laah.* My destiny is up to God.

لأن *li-'an* (usually transcribed *li'an*) because. أريد أشرب بارد لأني حران *'ariid ašrab baarid li'anni ḥarraan.* I want to have a soft drink because I am hot. أبغى أصلي في المسـجد العـود لأن اليـوم الجمعـة *'abġa 'aṣalli fi li-msiid l-^c^ood li'an l-yoom l-yim^c^a.* I would like to pray in the grand mosque because today is Friday. (See also لن *lin* under **ل ن ن** *lnn*).

ل ا *laa*

لا *la* 1. no. لا، موب هني *la, muub hni.* No, he's not here. 2. there is no, there is not. لا شك *la šakk* there's no doubt. لا إله إلا الله *la 'ilaaha 'illa l-ḷaa.* There is no God but He. لا بد *la bidd* there's no escape from, it's inevitable that. لا بد نسافر بـاكر *la bidd nsaafir baačir.* We are destined to travel tomorrow. لا بـد للـهبوب مـن السـكون *la bidd la li-hbuub min s-sikuun.* It's inevitable that there will be quiet after the storm. لا بـاس *la baas* there's no objection, there's nothing wrong. لا باس تروحـين وايـاهم *la baas truuḥiin wiyyaahum.* There's no objection to your going with them. كيف حالك؟ *čeef ḥaalak?* How are you? لا باس *la baas.* I'm fine. (There's nothing wrong with me.) لا... ولا *la... wala...* neither... nor... لا سـالم ولا بيـات *la saalim wala byaat* neither Salim nor Byat. (prov.) لا ينام ولا يخلي الناس تنام *la ynaam wala yxaḷḷi n-naas tnaam.* A dog in the manger. (lit., "He neither sleeps, nor lets people sleep."). 3. (with foll. v., expressing neg. command) don't. لا تدير بـال *la ddiir baal.* Don't worry. 4. (foll. by perf. v.) if. (prov.) لا حصل الماي بطل العافور *la ḥiṣal l-maay biṭal l-ᶜaafuur.* (lit., "If there is water, ablution with clean dirt is nullified."). 5. (foll. a statement to express a question tail). جيت وياهم، لا؟ *yiit wiyaahum, la?* You came with them, didn't you? تفضل، لا؟ *tfaððal, la?* Come in, won't you? موب هني، لا؟ *muub hni, la?* He's not here, is he?

لاسلكي *laa-silki* wireless.

ل ا ت ر ي *laatry*

لاتري *laatri* lottery. خسر كل فلوسه في اللاتري *xisar kill fluusa fi l-laatri.* He lost all his money on the lottery.

ل ا س ت ي ك *laastyk*

لاستيك *laastyk* 1. (adj.) elastic. 2. (p. *-aat)* rubber band.

ل ا ك ن *laakn*

لكن *laakin* but, however. هو عاقل لكن مرات مخبل *huwa ᶜaagil laakin marraat mxabbaḷ.* He's rational, but sometimes he's crazy. الهوا كان زين أمس لكن اليوم حار ورطب *l-hawa čaan zeen 'ams laakin l-yoom ḥaarr w-raṭib.* The weather was fine yesterday, but today it's hot and humid. لكن إذا جيت مرة ثانية، علمنا يا خوي *laakin 'iða yiit marra θaanya, ᶜallimna ya xuuy.* However, if you come again, let us know, my friend.

ل ء م *l'm.* See ل ي م *lym.*

ل ب ب *lbb*

لب *libb* (coll.) seeds (e.g., watermelon, sunflower seeds). s. لبة *libba.*

ل ب ل ب ي *lblby*

لبلبي *liblibi* (coll.) large chick peas. s. *-yya.*

ل ب س *lbs*

لبس *libas* (يلبس *yilbas)* 1. to get dressed, put on, clothe oneself. لبس هدومه وطلع *libas hduuma w-ṭilaᶜ.* He got dressed and went out. البس هالقحفية *'ilbas hal-gaḥfiyya.* Put on this hat. 2. to wear, be dressed in. في العيد الناس يلبسون هدوم جديدة *fi l-ᶜiid n-naas yilibsuun hduum yidiida.* During the feast (celebration) people wear new clothes.

لبس *labbas* 1. to dress, clothe. لبست عيالها قبل الريوق *labbasat ᶜyaalha gabil r-ryuug.* She dressed her kids before breakfast. لبسوا المعرس قبل الزفة *labbasaw l-miᶜris gabil z-zaffa.* They dressed the bridegroom before the wedding procession. 2. to put on, slip on. المعرس لبس الحلقة بصبع العروسة *l-miᶜris labbas l-ḥilga b-ṣubiᶜ l-ᶜaruusa.* The bridegroom put the ring on the bride's finger.

انلبس *nlibas* VII to be worn. هالكندورة البيضا ما تنلبس في الشتا *hal-kandoora l-beeḍa ma tinlibis fi š-šita.* This white dress isn't worn in the winter.

متلبس *mitlabbis* (with ب *b-*) redhanded, in the act of. الشرطة زخوه متلبس بالجريمة *š-širta zaxxoo mitlabbis b-l-jariima.* The police caught him redhanded.

ل ب ا ن *lbaan*

لبـــان *lbaan* (coll.) gum, chewing gum (usually known as علـك لبـان *ᶜilič lbaan*).

ل ب ن *lbn*

لـبن *laban* 1. (coll.) yoghurt, leban, sour milk. 2. (p. ألبان *'albaan*) dairy product. مصنع ألبـــان *maṣnaᶜ 'albaan* dairy. s. لبنة *lbana.*

لبنان *labnan* Lebanon. رحت لبنان؟ *riḥt labnaan?* Have you been to Lebanon?

لبنـــاني *labnaani* 1. Lebanese, from Lebanon. 2. (p. *-yyiin*) a Lebanese.

ل ب ي *lby*

لـــبى *labba* II to carry out (an order), comply with (a request). لبيت له كـل طلباتـــه *labbeet-la kill ṭalabaata.* I carried out all his orders. I complied with all his requests.

لبيـــك *labbeek!* Here I am! At your request!

ل ت ر *ltr*

لتر *liter* p. *-aat* liter.

ل ث م *lθm*

لثم *laθθam* II to cover the lower part of the face, veil the face. لثم وجهه من الغبار *laθθam weeha min li-ġbaar.* He covered his face because of the dust.

تلثـــم *tlaθθam* V to cover one's face. تلثموا قبل مـا بـاقوا البنـك *tlaθθamaw gabil-ma baagaw l-bank.* They masked themselves before they robbed the bank.

لثام *lθaam* p. *-aat* 1. veil (covering the lower part of the face). 2. mask.

ل ج ل *ljl*

لاجـــل *lajil* (corruption of لأجل *li-'ajl*) (conj.) in order to, for the sake of, so that. رحت لاجل آكل *riḥt lajil 'aakil.* I went in order to eat. يعمل لاجل بلاده *yᶜamil lajil blaada.* He works for the sake of his country. علمته بكل شي لاجل يعرف كيف يتصرف *ᶜallamta b-kill šayy lajil yᶜarf čeef yitṣarraf.* I told him everything so that he might know how to conduct himself.

ل ج م *ljm*

لجـــم *lijam* (يلجم *yaljim)* to bridle, put the bridle on. البغل قام يرفس لانه لجمـــه قبل ما وكلـــه *l-baġal gaam yarfis linna ljama gabil-ma wakkala.* The mule started to kick because he had bridled it before he fed it.

لجم *lajjam* II = لجم *lijam.*

لجام *ljaam* p. *-aat* 1. bridle, rein.

ل ج ن *ljn*

لجنـــة *lajna* p. *-aat,* لجان *lijaan* committee, board, council. لجنة المراقبـــة *lajnat li-mraagaba* the investigating committee. لجنة الامتحان *lajnat li-mtiḥaan* the board of examiners, the examination board.

ل ج ي *ljy*

لجـــي *liji* p. لجاية *lgaaya* four-year old camel. القعود أكبر من اللجـــي *l-guᶜuud 'akbar min l-liji.* A قعـــود *guᶜuud* is older than a لجي *liji.*

ل ح ح *lḥḥ*

لح *laḥḥ* (يلح *yliḥḥ)* 1. to persist. لا تلح. ما أقدر أســـوي لـــك اياهـــا *la tliḥḥ. ma 'agdar 'asawwii-lak-iyyaaha.* Don't be persistent. I can't do it for you. 2. (with على *cala*) to keep after, pester, harass. لحت عليه، وأخيراً اشترى لها عقد *laḥḥat calee, w-'axiiran štiraa-lha cigd.* She kept after him and, finally, he bought her a necklace.

إلحاح *'ilḥaaḥ* (v.n.) insisting, pestering, harassment.

ل ح س *lḥs*

لحس *liḥas (يلحس yilḥas)* to lick. دايماً يلحس المواعين *daayman yilḥas l-muwaaciin.* He always licks pots and pans.

لاحوس *laaḥuus* food poisoning.

ل ح ظ *lḥð̣*

لاحظ *laaḥað̣* III to notice, observe, be aware of. ما لاحظت عليه أي شي جديد *ma laaḥað̣t calee 'ayya šayy yidiid.* I didn't notice anything new about him. بس أبغاك تلاحظ اللي يصير *bass 'abġaak tlaaḥið̣ illi yṣiir.* I just want you to be aware of what's happening.

لحظة *laḥð̣a* p. *-aat* moment, instant. لحظة! *laḥð̣a!* Just a minute! ترياني لحظة بس *trayyaaani laḥð̣a bass.* Wait for me only a moment. بلحظة *b-laḥð̣a* instantly.

ملاحظة *mulaaḥað̣a* (v.n. from III لاحظ *laaḥað̣*) p. *-aat* 1. observation, remark, comment. 2. note, post-script.

ل ح ف *lḥf*

لحاف *lḥaaf* p. لحفان *liḥfaan* quilt. (prov.) مد رجلك على قد لحافك *midd riilak cala gadd lḥaafak.* As you make your bed, lie in it.

ل ح گ *lḥg*

لحق *liḥag (يلحق yilḥag)* 1. to catch up with s.o. لحقني وسبقني *liḥagni w-sibagni.* He caught up with me and passed me. 2. to follow, trail after. أنا أدلك على الطريق. بس الحقني *'aana 'adillak cala ṭ-ṭariig. bass ilḥagni.* I'll show you the way. You just follow me. 3. to chase, pursue. لحقه الشرطي وزخه *lḥaga š-širṭi w-zaxxa.* The policeman chased him and arrested him.

لحق *laḥḥag* II 1. to have time for, have a chance to. ما لحقت أروح وأرجع بنص ساعة *ma laḥḥagt 'aruuḥ w-'arjac b-nuṣṣ saaca.* I didn't have time to go and come back in half an hour. 2. (with على *cala*) to be on time. إذا تمشي، ما تلحق على الدوام. اخذ تكسي *'iða tamši, ma tlaḥḥig cala d-dawaam. 'ixið taksi.* If you walk, you won't report on time for duty. Take a taxi. لحقت على الموعد *laḥḥagt cala l-mawcid.* I was on time for the appointment.

التحق *ltiḥag* VIII (with ب *b-*) to join, enroll in, become a member of. التحق بالجيش *ltiḥag b-l-jeeš.* He joined the army. التحق بالكلية العسكرية *ltiḥag b-l-kulliyya l-caskariyya.* He enrolled in the military academy.

ملاحقة *mulaaḥaga* (v.n.) pursuit, chase. ملاحقة المجرمين *mulaaḥagat l-mijirmiin* the pursuit of criminals.

التحاق *ltiḥaag* (v.n. from VIII التحق *ltiḥag*) (with ب *b-*) joining, entry, affiliation.

لاحق *laaḥig* (act. part. from لحق *liḥag*) 1. following, trailing after. منو لاحقك؟

minu laaḥgak? Who is following you? 2. chasing, pursuing. الشرطي لاحق المجرم *š-širṭi laaḥig l-mijrim.* The policeman is chasing the criminal.

ملحق *mulḥag* 1. (p. *-iin*) attaché. ملحق عسكري *mulḥag ᶜaskari* military attaché. ملحق ثقافي *mulḥag θagaagi* cultural attaché. 2. supplement, extra section. 3. (p. ملاحق *malaaḥig*) appendix. 4. annex. ملحق الدايرة *mulḥag d-daayra* the department annex.

ل ح م *lḥm*

لحم *liḥam* (يلحم *yalḥim)* 1. to weld, solder. البيب انكسر. لازم تلحمه *l-peep nkisar. laazim talḥima.* The pipe broke. You have to weld it. 2. to heal. الجرح لحم *l-jarḥ liḥam.* The wound healed. 3. to patch, mend. المكانيكي لحم التيوب *l-mikaaniiki liḥam t-tyuub.* The mechanic patched the (tire) tube.

انلحم *nliḥam* VII pass. of لحم *liḥam.*

لحم *laḥam* (coll.) meat. s. *-a* piece of meat. اشتريت لحم *štireet laḥam.* I bought some meat. اللحم غالي *l-laḥam ġaali.* Meat is expensive. لحم خروف *laḥam xaruuf* lamb. لحم غنم *laḥam ġanam* mutton. لحم بقر *laḥam bagar* beef.

لحام *lḥaam* (v.n. from لحم *liḥam*) welding, soldering.

لحام *laḥḥaam* p. لحاحيم *laḥaaḥiim* welder, solderer.

ل ح ن *lḥn*

لحن *laḥḥan* II to compose music. اللي لحن ها الأغنية خليجي *'illi laḥḥan hal-'uġniya xaliiji.* The one who wrote the music for this song is a Gulf Arab.

لحن *laḥin* p. ألحان *'alḥaan* tune, melody.

ملحن *mulaḥḥin* p. *-iin* composer (of music).

ل ح ي *lḥy*

لحية *liḥya* p. لحى *liḥa* beard. لحيةٍ غانمة *liḥaytin ġaanma* very good man, man with an irresistible appeal. (prov.) لحية ولحيّة وكل شارب اله مقص *liḥya w-lḥayya w-kill šaarib 'ila mgaṣṣ.* Your fingers are not the same. Different strokes for different folks. لحية التيس *liḥyat t-tees* herb, used for medicinal purposes.

لحية *lḥayya* p. *-aat* dim. of لحية *liḥya.* small beard.

ل خ ب ط *lxbṭ*

لخبط *laxbaṭ* (يلخبط *ylaxbiṭ)* (common var. خربط *xarbaṭ*). For لخبط *laxbaṭ,* تلخبط *tlaxbaṭ,* ملخبط *mlaxbiṭ,* and ملخبط *mlaxbaṭ* see خربط *xarbarṭ,* تخربط *txarbaṭ,* خربطة *xarbaṭa,* مخربط *mxarbiṭ* and مخربط *mxarbaṭ* under **خ ر ب ط** *xrbṭ.*

ل خ خ *lxx*

لخ *laxx* (يلخ *ylixx)* to hit, strike s.o. عقب ما صفعه لخه *ᶜugub-ma ṣfaᶜa laxxa.* After he had slapped him on the face, he hit him.

ل خ م *lxm*

لخمة *luxma* p. *-aat,* لخم *luxam* stingray.

ل ذ ذ *lðð*

لذة *laðða* p. *-aat* delight, joy, pleasure. ما فيه لذة في ها الأكل *ma fii laðða fi hal-'akil.* This food is not delicious.

لذيذ *laðiið* delicious. الكباب لذيذ *l-kabaab laðiið.* Kabob is delicious.

ألذ *'alaðð* (elat.) 1. (with من *min*) more delicious than. لحم الخروف ألذ من الدجاج *laḥam l-xaruuf 'alaðð min d-diyaay.* Lamb is more delicious than chicken. 2. (with foll. n.) the most delicious.

ل ز گ *lzg*

لزق *lizag (يلزق yilzag)* 1. to stick, adhere. هذي الطوابع ما لزقت على البقشة *haaði ṭ-ṭuwaabiᶜ ma lizgat ᶜala l-bugša.* These stamps didn't stick to the envelope. لزق فيني. ما خلاني أروح بروحي *lizag fiini. ma xaḷḷaani 'aruuḥ bruuḥi.* He stuck to me. He didn't let me go alone. 2. to affix, paste, stick. الزق الطابع هني *'ilzag ṭ-ṭaabiᶜ hni.* Affix the stamp here.

لزق *lazzag* II intens. of لزق *lizag.*

تلزق *tlazzag* V pass. of II لزق *lazzag.*

لزقة *lazga* p. *-aat* plaster, stupe, mustard plaster.

ل ز م *lzm*

لزم *lizam (يلزم yilzam)* 1. to get hold of, catch, grab. الزم هذا! *'ilzam haaða!* Get hold of this. الشرطة لزموه وهو متلبس بالجريمة *š-širṭa lizmoo w-huwa mitlabbis b-l-jariima.* The police caught him redhanded. لزم الفلوس وانهزم *lizam li-fluus w-nhizam.* He grabbed the money and ran away. لجنة التحقيق ما لزموا عليه شي *lajnat t-taḥgiig ma lizmaw ᶜalee šayy.* The investigating committee didn't get anything on him. 2. to be required, requisite, necessary. يلزم انكليزي *yilzam ingiliizi.* English is required. يلزم تشوف الوزير *yilzam tšuuf l-waziir.* It's necessary that you see the minister. 3. to befall, set upon, descend upon. لزمتنا زحمة السيارات *lizmatna zaḥmat s-sayyaaraat.* We were caught in the traffic jam. أمس في الليل لزمتني الصخونة *'ams fi l-leel lizmatni ṣ-ṣxuuna.* Last night, I got a fever. 4. to keep in one place, hold, maintain. الزم سيدك! *'ilzam seedak!* Stay in your lane (said to a driver). ها الكيس ما يلزم كل السامان *hač-čiis ma yilzam kill s-saamaan.* This bag won't hold all the things. تقدر تلزم حساب في ها الدكان؟ *tigdar tilzam ḥsaab fi had-dikkaan?* Can you maintain an accounting in this shop?

التزم *ltizam* VIII (with ب *b-*) to take responsibility for. المعرس التزم بكل المصاريف *l-miᶜris ltizam b-kill l-maṣaariif.* The bridegroom took the responsibility for all the expenses.

لزوم *luzuum* need, necessity. ما فيه لزوم تجي وايانا *ma fii luzuum tiyi wiyyaana.* There is no need for you to come with us. عند اللزوم *ᶜind l-luzuum* in case of need, as necessary. أروح أشاوره عند اللزوم *'aruuh ašaawra ᶜind l-luzuum.* I go to consult with him if necessary. عندك لزوم بهالشي؟ *ᶜindak luzuum b-haš-šayy?* Does this matter concern you? لا. أنا ما لي لزوم *la. 'aana ma-li luzuum.* No. It's of no concern to me. It's not important to me.

لازم *laazim* 1. necessary, required, imperative, obligatory. لازم تجي وايانا *laazim tyi wiyyaana.* You have to come with us. موب لازم تجي وايانا *muub laazim tyi wiyyaana.* You don't have to come with us. لازم ما تجي وايانا. *laazim ma tyi wiyyaana.* You shouldn't come with us. كان لازم تجي وايانا *čaan laazim tyi wiyyaana.* You should have come with us. موب لازم. *muub laazim.* It's not important. Never mind. موب لازم. غيرت رايي *muub laazim. ġayyart raayi.* Never mind. I changed my mind. 2. (adj.) required, necessary. هذا شي لازم *haaða šayy laazim.* This is a necessary thing.

لوازم *lawaazim* (p. only) necessities, requisites. لوازم البيت *lawaazim l-beet* the home necessities.

ملزوم *malzuum* (p.p. from لزم *lizam*) 1. obligated, under obligation. أنا موب ملزوم أخم الحفيز كل يوم *'aana muub malzuum 'aximm l-ḥafiiz kill yoom.* I am not obligated to sweep the office every day. 2. (with ب *b-*) responsible for, liable for. أنا موب ملزوم بهالسامان إذا انباق *'aana muub malzuum b-hassaamaan 'iða nbaag.* I am not responsible for these things if they are stolen. كل واحد ملزوم بضريبة المطار *kill waaḥid malzuum b-ḏariibat l-maṭaar.* Everyone is liable for the airport tax.

ملازم *mulaazim* p. *-iin* lieutenant. ملازم أول *mulaazim 'awwal* first lieutenant. ملازم ثاني *mulaazim θaani* second lieutenant.

ل س ن *lsn*

لسان *lsaan* p. *-aat* tongue. على لسانه *ᶜala lsaana* from his mouth. الكلمة نسيتها. على راس لساني *č-čalma naseetta. ᶜala raas lsaani.* I have forgotten the word. It's on the tip of my tongue. طويل السان *ṭawiil l-lsaan* insolent, impertinent.

ل ط ف *ltf*

لطف *laṭṭaf* II to make nice, enjoyable, pleasant. الشجر يلطف الهوا *š-šiyar ylaṭṭif l-hawa.* Trees make the weather nice.

تلطف *tlaṭṭaf* V 1. pass. of لطف *laṭṭaf.* تلطف الهوا عقب المطر *tlaṭṭaf l-hawa ᶜugb l-maṭar.* The weather was nice after the rain. 2. to be so kind as to, have the kindness to do s.th. تلطف عليهم الشيخ وعطاهم فلوس *tlaṭṭaf ᶜaleehum š-šeex w-ᶜaṭaahum fluus.* The Sheikh was very kind to them and gave them money.

تلاطف *tlaaṭaf* VI 1. to be polite, courteous, nice. بس يتلاطفون *bass yitlaatfuun.* They are just being polite to each other. 2. to joke with each other. ما عرفت انه كان يتلاطف واياي *ma ᶜiraft 'inna čaan yitlaaṭaf wiyyaay.* I didn't know that he was just kidding around with me.

لطف *lutf* (v.n.) kindness, politeness, courtesy. مشكور، هذا لطف منك *maškuur, haaða lutf minnak.* Thank you, that is kind of you. بلطف *b-lutf* gently, softly. احكي واياها بلطف *'iḥči wiyyaaha b-lutf.* Speak gently to her.

لطيف *laṭiif* nice, pleasant, enjoyable. الهوا لطيف هني في الشتا *l-hawa laṭiif hni fi š-šita.* The weather is nice here in the winter. ها البنية شقد لطيفة! *ha-li-bnayya š-gadd laṭiifa!* How nice and pleasant this girl is!

ألطف *'alṭaf* (elat.) 1. (with من *min*) more enjoyable, pleasant than. 2.

(with foll. n.) the most enjoyable, pleasant.

ل ط م *lṭm*

لطم *liṭam* (يلطم *yalṭim*) to strike the face with the hands in grief or despair. لين سمعت انه ابنها مات في الدعمة قامت تلطم *leen simcat 'inna 'ibinha maat fi d-dacma gaamat talṭim.* When she heard that her son had died in the car accident, she began to slap herself.

لطمة *laṭma* (n. of inst.) p. *-aat* slap, blow with the hand on the face.

ل ع ب *lcb*

لعب *licab* (يلعب *yilcab*) 1. to play. سبحنا ولعبنا على السيف *sibaḥna w-licabna cala s-siif.* We swam and played on the beach. يلعب كورة *yilcab kuura.* He plays soccer. لعبنا ورق واستانسنا *licabna warag w-staanasna.* We played cards and had a good time. 2. (with ب *b-* or على *cala*) to mess with, toy with, fool around with. دير بالك! لا تلعب بالكهربا *diir baalk! la tilcab b-l-kahraba.* Be careful! Don't mess with the electricity. فيه ناس يلعبون بالفلوس لعب *fii naas yilcabuun b-li-fluus licib.* There are people who have money to burn. لا تلعب براسي. أنا أخبرك *la tilacb b-raasi. 'aana 'axbark.* Don't make a fool of me. I know you well. لعب علينا وشرد *licab caleena w-širad.* He tricked us and took off. يلعب على الحبلين *yilcab cala l-ḥableen.* He plays both sides of the fence. 3. to act, play, perform. يلعب دور مهم *yilcab door muhimm.* He plays an important role. 4. to dance. العيال يلعب *l-cayyaal yilcab.* The male dancer is dancing. النعاشات يلعبن *n-naccaašaat yilcabin.* The female dancers are dancing.

لعّب *laccab* II to make or let play. لعبوني كورة وياهم *laccabuuni kuura wiyyaahum.* They let me play soccer with them.

انلعب *nlicab* VII pass. of لعب *licab.* هذا رجال ما ينلعب عليه *haaδa rayyaal ma yinlicib calee.* This is a man who cannot be fooled. ها الميز ما ينلعب عليه *hal-meez ma yinlicib calee.* This table cannot be played on.

لعب *licib* 1. (v.n. from لعب *licab*) playing. لعبنا لعب زين، بس خسرنا المباراة *licabna licib zeen, bass xisarna l-mubaaraa.* We played well, but we lost the match. لعب القمار *licib li-gmaar* gambling. 2. (p. ألعاب *'alcaab*) play. ألعاب رياضية *'alcaab riyaaḍiyya* athletics, sports. ألعاب سحرية *'alcaab siḥriyya* magic, sleight of hand.

لعبة *licba* (n. of inst.) p. *-aat,* ألعاب *'alcaab* 1. game. 2. catch, trick. لازم فيه لعبة في ها القضية *laazim fii licba fi hal-gaḍiyya.* There must be a catch somewhere in this affair.

ملعب *malcab* p. ملاعب *malaacib* 1. athletic field. ملعب الكورة *malcab l-kuura* the soccer field. 2. playground.

لاعب *laacib* 1. (act. part. from لعب *licab*) having played. تعبان. توني لاعب كورة *tacbaan. tawwni laacib kuura.* I'm tired. I have just played soccer. 2. (p. *-iin*) player, athlete. لاعب كورة *laacib kuura* soccer player. لاعب جنباز *laacib jimbaaz* gymnast, athlete.

ملعوب *malᶜuub* (p.p. from لعب *liᶜab*) 1. being played. الكورة ملعوبة *l-kuura malᶜuuba.* The soccer game is going on. 2. (with في *fi*) having been tampered with. ها الجهاز خربان. ملعوب فيه *hal-jihaaz xarbaan. malᶜuub fii.* This apparatus is out of order. It's been tampered with. 3. (with على *ᶜala*) having been tricked, fooled.

ل ع ن *lᶜn*

لعن *liᶜan (يلعن yilᶜan)* to damn, curse s.o. or s.th. الله يلعنك! *'aḷḷaah yilᶜank!* Damn you! لعن الله إبليس! *liᶜan aḷḷaah 'ibliis!* May God's curse be upon the devil!

لعنة *laᶜna* p.*-aat* curse. لعنة الله عليه! *laᶜnat aḷḷaah ᶜalee!* God's curse upon him!

لعين *laᶜiin,* ملعون *malᶜuun* cursed, damned. ذاك اللعين! عمري ما شفت أخس منه *ðaak l-laᶜiin! ᶜumri ma čift 'axass minna.* That damned (person)! I've never seen a meaner person.

ل ع و ز *lᶜwz*

لعوز *laᶜwaz (يلعوز ylaᶜwiz)* to bother s.o. لعوزنا بروحاته وجياته *laᶜwazna b-rooḥaata w-yayyaata.* He bothered us with going and comings.

تلعوز *tlaᶜwaz* pass. of لعوز *laᶜwaz.* تلعوزت بأسئلته الكثيرة *tlaᶜwazt b-'as'ilta l-kaθiira.* I was bothered by his many questions.

لعوزة *laᶜwaza* (v.n. from لعوز *laᶜwaz*) mess, disorder, confusion.

ملعوز *mlaᶜwiz* (act. part. from لعوز *laᶜwaz*) 1. having bothered s.o. توه ملعوز العيال *tawwa mlaᶜwiz li-ᶜyaaḷ.* He has just bothered the kids. 2. bothering. هو اللي ملعوزنا *huwa lli mlaᶜwizna.* He's the one who is bothering me.

ل غ ز *lġz*

لغز *laġz* p. ألغاز *'alġaaz* riddle, puzzle.

ل غ م *lġm*

لغم *laġam* p. ألغام *'alġaam* (explosive) mine.

ل غ و *lġw*

لغى *liġa (يلغي yalġi)* 1. to talk incessantly, prattle, chatter. ما يعطيك أي فرصة تتكلم. دايما يلغي *ma yᶜaṭiik 'ayya furṣa titkallam. daayman yalġi.* He won't give you any chance to talk. He always talks on and on endlessly.

ألغى *'alġa* IV 1. to cancel (a project, festivities, celebrations, etc.). وزارة الزراعة ألغت المشروع *wazaarat z-ziraaᶜa 'alġat l-mašruuᶜ.* The ministry of agriculture cancelled the project. ألغوا الاحتفالات *'alġaw li-ḥtifaalaat.* They cancelled the celebrations. 2. to abolish, annul, put an end to. الحكومة ألغت قانون الهجرة *l-ḥukuuma 'alġat ġaanuun l-hijra.* The government abolished the emigration law. القاضي ألغى عقد الزواج *l-ġaaḍi 'alġa ᶜagd z-zawaaj.* The cadi annulled the marriage contract. وزارة الإعلام والسياحة ألغت بعض الكتب *wazaarat l-'iᶜlaam w-s-siyaaḥa 'alġat baᶜḍ l-kutub.* The ministry of information and tourism put an end to the use of some of its books.

انلغى *nliġa* VII (pass. of لغى *liġa*) to be cancelled, nullified.

لغة *luġa* p. *-aat* language.

لغوة *laġwa* 1. (v.n. from لغى *liġa*) chattering, talking incessantly. 2. empty talk, aimless chatter, babbling. 3. (p. *-aat*) dialect, vernacular. لغوة أهل عمان *laġwat 'ahil* *ᶜmaan* the dialect of the Al-Ain people

ل ف ت *lft*

لفت *lifat (يلفت yalfit)*: لفت النظر *lifat n-naðar* 1. to catch the eye, attract attention. هـا البناية لفتت نظري *hal-binaaya liftat naðari.* This building caught my eye. ها الشي يلفت النظر *haš-šayy yalfit n-naðar.* This thing attracts one's attention. 2. to caution, give notice to s.o. المدير لفت نظري وقال: «المرة الثانية نفنشك». *l-mudiir lifat naðari w-gaal: "l-marra θ-θanya nfannišk."* The manager warned me and said: "Next time we will lay you off."

تلفت *tlaffat* V to look around, glance around. ليش تتلفت؟ بتدور على أحد؟ *leeš titlaffat? biddawwir ᶜala 'aḥad?* Why are you looking around? Are you looking for someone?

التفت *ltifat* VIII = تلفت *tlaffat* V.

ل ف ح *lfḥ*

لفح *lifaḥ (يلفح yilfaḥ)* to burn, scorch, sear. الهوا الحار يلفح الوجه *l-hawa l-ḥaarr yilfaḥ l-weeh.* Hot weather burns one's face.

ل ف ف *lff*

لف *laff (يلف yliff)* 1. to turn (left, right, etc.) عند الدوار لف يمين *ᶜind d-dawwaar liff yimiin.* At the roundabout turn right. ريوس هني وبعدين لف يسار *reewis hni w-baᶜdeen liff yisaar.* Back up here and then turn left. 2. to go around, make a detour. هذي تحويلة قدامك. لف من هني *haaði taḥwiila jiddaamak. liff min hni.* This is a detour in front of you. Go around from here. 3. to roll, coil. لفيت له جيكارة *laffeet-la jigaara.* I rolled a cigarette for him. لا تلف ها السيم *la tliff has-siim.* Don't coil this wire. 4. to wrap, envelope, cover. لا تلف ها القراطيس *la tliff hal-garaaṭiis.* Don't wrap these sheets of paper. لف الجاهل بالبرنوص *liff l-yaahil b-l-barnuuṣ.* Cover the child with the blanket. 5. to steal, swipe, make off with. لف فلوس الجمعية الخيرية وشرد *laff fluus l-jamᶜiyya l-xayriyya w-širad.* He stole the money of the charitable organization and fled. 6. (with على *ᶜala*) to make a round of calls on, visit. لف على أقاربه وعيد عليهم *laff ᶜala 'agaarba w-ᶜayyad ᶜaleehum.* He made a round of calls on his relatives and wished them a merry feast.

التف *ltaff* VIII 1. (with حول *ḥool*) to rally, gather, assemble around. جا الشيخ والتف حوله مواطنين واجدين *ya š-šeex w-ltaff ḥoola mwaaṭniin waaydiin.* The Shaikh came and many citizens rallied around him. 2. to wrap, cover oneself. التف بالبرنوص *ltaff b-l-barnuuṣ.* He wrapped himself up with the blanket.

لاف *laaff* (act. part. from لف *laff*) having turned. لين شفته كان لاف يمين *leen čifta čaan laaff yimiin.* When I saw him, he had already turned right. 2. having rolled, coiled s.th. 3. having made a round of calls on, having visited.

لـف *laff* : جكاير لف *jigaayir laff* hand-rolled cigarettes.

لفة *laffa* p. *-aat* 1. turn, rotation. 2. coil, twist.

ملـف *malaff* p. *-aat* file, folder, dossier. ملفـات الموظفـين *malaffaat li-mwaḏḏafiin* the employees' files.

متلـف *mitlaff* 1. (with حـول *ḥool*) gathered, assembled around. 2. rolled up, rolled together.

ل ف ل ف *lflf*

لفلف *laflaf* (يلفلف *ylaflif*) 1. to grab up, snatch up. يلفلف أي شي يحصله *ylaflif 'ayya šayy yḥaṣṣla.* He grabs up anything he finds. 2. to wrap up, bundle up. لفلف روحه من البرد *laflaf ruuḥa min l-bard.* He wrapped himself up because of the cold.

تلفلف *tlaflaf* (يتلفلف *yitlaflaf*) to wrap oneself up, cover oneself. موب لازم تتلفلف هني في الشتا *muub laazim titlaflaf hini fi š-šita.* You don't have to wrap yourself up in the winter here.

ل ف ي *lfy*

لفى *lifa* (يلفي *yilfi*) (with على *ᶜala*) to go to see or visit s.o. لفى علينا *lifa ᶜaleena.* He came to see us.

لافي *laafi* (act. part. from لفى *lifa*) p. *-yiin* having come to visit. هو لافي علينا *huwa laafi ᶜaleena.* He has come to visit me.

ل گ ب *lgb*

لقب *lagab* p. ألقاب *'algaab* 1. last name, family name. 2. agnomen or cognomen. 3. title (at the end of one's name).

ل گ ح *lgḥ*

لقحة *lagḥa* p. *-aat* pregnant animal.

ل گ ط *lgṭ*

لقط *ligaṭ* (يلقط *yulguṭ*) to pick up, pick out. الجهال يلقطون الحكي بساع *l-yihhaal ylugṭuun l-ḥači b-saaᶜ.* Children pick words up fast. أمي قاعدة تلقط الحصا من العيش *'ummi gaaᶜda tulguṭ l-ḥaṣa min l-ᶜeeš.* My mother is picking the small pebbles from the rice.

ل گ ف *lgf*

لقف *ligaf* (يلقف *yulguf*) to catch, seize, grab. ارمي الكورة وأنا ألقفها *'irmi l-kuura w-aana 'algufha.* Throw the ball and I will catch it.

انلقف *nligaf* VII pass. of لقف *ligaf.*

ل گ ل گ *lglg*

لقلق *laglag* p. لقالق *lagaalig* stork.

ل گ م *lgm*

لقم *laggam* II: لقم القهوة *laggam l-gahwa.* He stirred the ground coffee into hot water

تلقم *tlaggam* V pass. of II لقم *laggam.*

لقمة *lugma* p. لقم *lugam* bite, mouthful. خلنا نروح ناكل لقمة *xaḷḷna nruuḥ naakil lugma.* Let's go and get a bit to eat.

ل گ ن[1] *lgn*

لقن *laggan* II 1. to teach s.o., instruct s.o. in s.th. العيال اللي يلعب واياهم يلقنوه ها الحكي *li-ᶜyaaḷ illi yilᶜab wiyyaahum ylaggnuu hal-ḥači.* The children he plays with teach him these words. 2. to prompt. لازم يكون فيه واحد يلقنه

laazim ykuun fii waaḥid ylaggna. There must be someone prompting him.

ل گ ن [٢] *lgn*

لقن *ligan* p. لقان *lgaan* 1. large metal wash basin. 2. food tray.

ل گ ي *lgy*

لقى *liga* (يلقى *yilga*), لقي *ligi* (يلقى *yilga*) 1. to find s.o., s.th. لقيته في السوق *ligeeta fi s-suug.* I found him in the marketplace. ما نقدر نلقى أحسن منه *ma nigdar nilga 'aḥsan minna.* We cannot find anything better than this. ما تقدر تلقى لي شقة رخيصة؟ *ma tigdar tilgaa-li šigga raxiiṣa?* Can't you find me an inexpensive apartment? (prov.) جدر ولقي غتاه *jidir w-ligi ġaṭaa.* A man is known by the company he keeps. (lit., "A cooking pot and it has found its lid."). 2. to encounter, meet, run into. لقي مشاكل واجدة في حياته *ligi mašaakil waayda fi ḥayaata.* He encountered many problems in his life.

لاقى *laaga* III = لقى *liga,* لقي *ligi.*

تلاقى *tlaaga* VI to meet each other, get together, come together. تلاقينا وايا هل العروسة واتفقنا على المهر *tlaageena wiyya hal l-ᶜaruusa w-ttafagna ᶜala l-mahar.* We met with the bride's folks and we came to an agreement concerning the dowry. خلنا نتلاقى على العشا *xallna nitlaaga ᶜala l-ᶜaša.* Let's get together for dinner. تلاقيت واياه في سوق السمك *tlaageet wiyyaa fi suug s-simač.* I ran into him in the fish market.

انلقى *nliga* pass. of لقى *liga.* ما ينلقي أوتيل رخيص هني *ma yinligi 'uteel raxiiṣ hni.* An inexpensive hotel cannot be found here. ما ينلقي إلا في المسجد عقب صلاة المغرب *ma yinligi 'illa fi li-msiid ᶜugub ṣalaat li-mġarb.* You can see him only in the mosque after the sunset prayer.

لاقي *laagi* (act. part. from لقى *liga* or لقي *ligi*) p. *-yiin* having found s.o. or s.th. موب لاقيين أحسن منه *muub laagyiin 'aḥsan minna.* We cannot find a better person than he is.

ل ك ك *lkk*

لك *lakk* p. *-aat* very large amount, approx. 100,000. المهر ذالحين لكين والا أكثر *l-mahar ðalḥiin lakkeen walla 'akθar.* A dowry now is 200,000 (dirhams) or more.

ل ك م *lkm*

لكم *likam* (يلكم *yulkum*) to punch, strike with the fist. لكمه على وجهه وطاح على الأرض *lkama ᶜala weeha w-ṭaaḥ ᶜala l-'arḓ.* He punched him on the face and he fell down.

لاكم *laakam* III to box with s.o., engage s.o. in a fist fight. إذا تلاكمه يوقعك *'iða tlaakma ywaggiᶜk.* If you box with him, he will knock you down.

لكمة *lakma* p. *-aat* punch, blow with the fist.

ملاكمة *mulaakama* boxing, fist fighting.

ملاكم *mulaakim* (act. part. from III لاكم *laakam*) p. *-iin* boxer.

ل ك ن *lkn.*

See under **ل ا ك ن** *laakn.*

ل م ب lmbr

لمبر *lambar* p. *-aat* number, numeral.

ل م پ lmp

لمبة *lampa* p. *-aat* light bulb.

ل م ح lmḥ

لمح *limaḥ* (يلمح *yalmaḥ*) to catch a glimpse of, glimpse, catch sight of. لمحته يسوق السيارة *limaḥta ysuug s-sayyaara.* I caught a glimpse of him driving the car.

لمحة *lamḥa* p. *-aat* glance, quick look.

ملامح *malaamiḥ* (p. only) outward appearance, looks, features.

ل م س lms

لمس *limas* (يلمس *yilmas*) 1. to touch, feel. لا تلمس الجام! *la tilmas l-jaam!* Don't touch the glass. الرنك جديد. لا تلمسه *r-rang yidiid. la tilimsa.* The paint is fresh. Don't touch it. 2. to feel, sense, have a hunch. لمست انه عنده تحيز ضد العرب *limast 'inna ᶜinda taḥayyuz ḍidd l-ᶜarab.* I felt that he was prejudiced against the Arabs.

ملموس *malmuus* (p.p. from لمس *limas*) 1. noticeable, tangible. فيه تحسن ملموس في العلاقات الدبلوماسية *fii taḥassun malmuus fi l-ᶜalaagat d-diblomaas-iyya.* There's a noticeable improvement in the diplomatic relations. 2. touched, felt.

ل م ع lmᶜ

لمع *limaᶜ* (يلمع *yilmaᶜ*) to shine, glisten, gleam. الحيول حق هذي الحرمة تلمع *li-ḥyuul ḥagg haaḏi l-ḥurma tilmaᶜ.* This woman's bracelets are shining.

لمع *lammaᶜ* II to shine, make shine. ضرب الجوتي حقه باليص ولمعه *ḏirab l-juuti ḥagga baaliiṣ w-lammaᶜa.* He polished (applied shoe polish to) his shoes and shined them.

لماع *lammaaᶜ* bright, shiny, sparkling.

ل م ل م lmlm

لملم *lamlam* (يلملم *ylamlim*) to gather up, gather s.th. لملم سامانك وفي امان الله *lamlim saamaanak w-fi maan-i-llaa.* Gather up your things and goodbye.

ل م م lmm

لم *lamm* (يلم *ylimm*) to gather, collect, gather together. لم الأوراق وحطهم على الميز *lamm l-'awraag w-ḥaṭṭhum ᶜala l-meez.* He gathered the sheets of paper and put them on the table. لمينا تبرعات حق الجمعية الخيرية *lammeena tabarruᶜaat ḥagg l-jamᶜiyya l-xayriyya.* We collected donations for the charitable organization. صار لي ألم طوابع عشر سنين *ṣaar-li 'alimm ṭuwaabiᶜ ᶜašar siniin.* I have been collecting stamps for ten years. التنديل لم الكولية *t-tindeel lamm l-kuuliyya.* The foreman called all the coolies together.

انلم *nlamm* VII pass. of لم *lamm.*

التم *ltamm* VIII to gather, come together, assemble. الناس التموا عند الدعمة *n-naas ltammaw ᶜind d-daᶜma.* The people gathered near the (scene of the) car accident. ناس واجدين التموا حول الشيخ *naas waaydiin ltammaw ḥool š-šeex.* Many people rallied around the Shaikh.

لم *lamm* (v.n. from لم *lamm*) gathering, collection, gathering together. لم الشمل

lamm š-šamil reunion, reunification

ملموم *malmuum* (p.p. from لم *lamm*) gathered, collected, assembled.

ل م م ا *lmmaa*

لما *lamma* (conj.) 1. when, as, at the time when. لما جيت، كنت أشتغل *lamma yiit, čint 'aštaġil.* When you came, I was working. 2. until, till the time when. تريته لما جا *trayyeeta lamma ya.* I waited for him until he came. خلها وياك لما أرجع *xalḷha wiyyaak lamma 'arja^c^.* Keep it with you until I return.

ل ن چ *lnč*

لنش *lanč* p. *-aat* launch, motorboat. رحنا السعديات باللنش *riḥna s-sa^c^diyyaat b-l-lanč.* We went to Sadiyat Island by launch.

ل ن د ن *lndn*

لندن *landan* London.

ل ن ن *lnn*

لان *linn* (conj., corruption of MSA لأن *li'an*) because. See *li-'an* under ل *l-*.

ل ه ب *lhb*

التهب *ltihab* VIII 1. to catch fire, flare up, burn brightly. الكراج التهب واحترق كله *l-garaaj ltihab w-ḥtiraj killa.* The garage caught fire and burned to the ground. 2. to become inflamed. اللوز حقه التهبت *l-luwaz ḥagga ltihbat.* His tonsils were inflamed.

لهب *lahab* flame, blaze, flare.

التهاب *ltihaab* inflammation. التهاب اللوز *ltihaab l-luwaz* tonsilitis.

ملتهب *miltahib* (act. part. from التهب *ltihab*) 1. aflame, ablaze, burning. 2. inflamed.

ل ه ج *lhj*

لهجة *lahja* p. *-aat* dialect. اللهجة البدوية ما نفتهمها *l-lahja li-bdiwiyya ma niftihimha.* We don't understand the Bedouin dialect. مثل ما نقول بلهجتنا *miθil-ma nguul b-lahjatna* as we say in our dialect.

ل ه ي *lhy*

لهى *lahha* II 1. (with عن *^c^an*) to distract s.o. from s.th., divert s.o.'s attention from. لهاني عن الدراسة *lahhaani ^c^an d-diraasa.* He distracted me from studying. لهي المدير حتى أقرا الجريدة *lahhi l-mudiir ḥatta 'agra l-jariida.* Hold the manger's attention so I can read the newspaper. 2. to entertain, amuse, distract. العيال يحتاجون واحد يلهيهم *li-^c^yaaḷ yiḥtaajuun waaḥid ylahhiihum.* The children need someone to entertain them.

تلهى *tlahha* V pass. of II لهى *lahha.*

التهى *ltiha* VIII = V تلهى *tlahha.*

لهو *lahu* 1. diversion, pastime. 2. amusement, fun.

لهاية *lahhaaya* p. *-aat* pacifier (for babies).

ملهى *malha* p. ملاهي *malaahi* night club, cabaret.

ل و *lw*

لو *loo* (conj.) if. 1. لو تجي وايانا تشوفه *loo tyi wiyyaana ččuufa.* If you come with us, you will see him. لو تروح هناك تستانس *loo truuḥ hnaak tistaanis.* If you go there, you will have a good time. لو سوى كذي كان أحسن *loo* *sawwa čiði čaan 'aḥsan.* If he did like this, it would be better. (prov.) لو يدري عمير كان شق ثوبه *loo yadri ᶜmeer čaan šagg θooba.* Ignorance is bliss. (lit., "If Omeer had known, he would have ripped his clothes."). (prov.) لو فيه خير كان ما هده الطير *loo fii xeer čaan ma hadda ṭ-ṭeer.* It's worthless. (lit., "If it had been of any use, the bird would not have discarded it."). 2. even though, although. (prov.) خشمك منك لو كان عوج *xašmak minnak loo čaan ᶜaway.* Don't be ashamed of your folks. (lit.,"Your nose is a part of you although it is crooked.") لو...لو *loo... loo...* either... or... لو هذا لو ذاك *loo haaða loo ðaak* either this or that. لو تجي لو تروح *loo tyi loo truuḥ.* Either you come or you go. لو بعد *loo baᶜad* or not, yet. جا لو بعد *ya loo baᶜad?* Has he come or not? 3. I wish...! if only...! لو عندي مليون درهم! *loo ᶜindi malyoon dirhim!* I wish I had one million dirhams. لولا *loola* if it weren't (hadn't been) for. لولاهم كان متنا من الجوع *loolaahum čaan mitna min l-yuuᶜ.* If it weren't for them, we would have starved to death.

ل و ب ي *lwby*

لوبيا *luubya* (coll.) beans, string beans. كم اللوبيا اليوم؟ *kam l-luubya l-yoom?* How much are string beans today? اللوبيا غالية *l-luubya ġaalya.* String beans are expensive. عندنا لوبيا *ᶜindana luubya.* We have string beans.

ل و ح *lwḥ*

لوح *looḥ* p. ليحان *liiḥaan* plank (of wood). لوح أسود *looḥ 'aswad* blackboard.

لايحة *laayḥa* p. لوايح *lawaayiḥ* bill. لايحة الأكل *laayḥat l-'akil* the menu or bill of fare.

ل و ر ي *lwry*

لوري *loori* p. *-yyaat,* لواري *lawaari* lorry, truck.

ل و ز *lwz*

لوز *looz* (coll.) almonds. s. *-a* p. *-aat.*

لوزة *looza* p. لوز *luwaz* tonsil. التهاب اللوز *ltihaab l-luwaz* tonsilitis.

ل و ل و *lwlw*

لولو *luulu* (coll.) pearls. s. لولوة *luulwa.* (common var. قماش *gmaaš.* See under **گ م ش** *gmš*).

ل و م *lwm*

لام *laam (*يلوم *yluum)* to blame, rebuke, censure. لا تلومني على ما فعلت *la tluumni ᶜala ma faᶜalt.* Don't blame me for what I have done.

انلام *nlaam* VII (pass. of لام *laam*) to be blamed, rebuked, censured. زين سوى. ما ينلام على اللي سواه *zeen sawwa. ma yinlaam ᶜala lli sawwaa.* He did the right thing. He can't be blamed for what he had done.

لوم *loom* (v.n.) blame, rebuke, censure.

ل و م ي *lwmy*

لومي *luumi* (coll.) s. *-yya* p. *-aat.* 1. lemons. اللومي رخيص اليوم *l-luumi raxiiṣ l-yoom.* Lemons are inexpensive today. اشتريت عشر لوميات *štireet ᶜašar luumiyyaat.* I bought ten lemons. 2. limes.

ل و ي *lwy*

لوى *luwa* (يلوي *yilwi)* 1. to bend. ما أقدر ألوي هـا السيم *ma 'agdar 'alwi has-siim.* I cannot bend this wire. 2. to twist, wrench. لوى يده ووقعه على الأرض *luwa yadda w-wagga*ᶜ*a* ᶜ*ala l-'arḍ.* He twisted his arm and knocked him on the ground.

تلوى *tlawwa* V 1. to writhe. تلويت من المـرض *tlawweet min l-maraḍ.* I writhed in pain. 2. slither, wriggle. شـوف! الـداب يتلـوى في الرمـل *čuuf! d-daab yitlawwa fi r-ramil.* Look! The snake is slithering in the sand. الدودة تتلوى لـين تمشـي *d-duuda titlawwa leen tamši.* A worm wriggles when it moves.

انلوى *nluwa* VII pass. of لوى *luwa.*

التوى *ltuwa* VIII = VII انلوى *nluwa.*

لـوا *liwa* p. ألوية *'alwiya* 1. major general (mil. rank). ترفع إلى رتبة لوا *traffa*ᶜ *'ila rutbat liwa.* He was promoted to the rank of major general. 2. brigade. أمير لوا *'amiir liwa* brigadier general. 3. district, province.

ملوي *malwi* (p.p. from لوى *luwa*) bent, twisted, coiled.

ملتـوي *miltuwi* 1. = ملـوي *malwi* 2. winding, meandering. احكـي عـدل! لا تقـول كـلام ملتـوي *'iḥči* ᶜ*adil! la tguul kalaam miltuwi.* Talk straight! Don't beat around the bush.

ل ي ب ي ا *lybyaa*

ليبيا *liibya* Libya.

ليـبي *liibi* 1. Libyan, characteristic of Libya. 2. (p. *-yyiin*) a Libyan. هو ليبـي مـن طرابلس *huwa liibi min ṭaraablis.*

ل و ن *lwn*

لـون *lawwan* II to color, add color to. لون الرسـم حمـر *lawwan r-rasim ḥamar.* He colored the picture red.

تلـون *tlawwan* V 1. (pass of II لون *lawwan*) to be colored. هـذا مـا يتلـون خضـر *haaða ma yitlawwan xaðar.* This cannot be colored green. 2. to be changeable or fickle, to shift with the wind. يتلـون مثـل مـا تريـد *yitlawwan miθil-ma triid.* He is as fickle as he can be.

لـون *loon* p. الوان *lwaan* 1. color, hue, complexion. لـون خضـر *loon xaðar* green color. لـون حمـر *loon ḥamar* red color. لونـه بلـون بـني *lawwna b-loon bunni.* Color it brown. 2. kind, sort. عطـني مـن هـا اللـون ᶜ*aṭni min hal-loon.* Give me (something) of this kind.

شلون *šloon* (see under **ش ل و ن** *šlwn*).

تلويـن *talwiin* (v.n. from II لون *lawwan*) coloring.

ملـون *mlawwan* (p.p. from II لـون *lawwan*) colored, tinted. فلم ملون *filim mlawwan* color film, color movie. اقـلام ملونـة *gḷaam mlawwana* colored pencils.

متلون *mitlawwin* (act. part. from V تلون *tlawwan*) changeable, fickle, unreliable. ما نقدر نعتمد عليه؛ متلـون *ma nigdar ni*ᶜ*timid* ᶜ*alee; mitlawwin.* We cannot depend on him; he's changeable.

ل و ه *lwh*

لـوه *looh* (elat.) common cormorant. s. *-a* p. *-aat.*

He's a Libyan from Tripoli.

ل ي ت *lyt*

ليت *leet* p. *-aat* 1. lightbulb. هذا الليت محروق. بدله *haaða l-leet maḥruug. baddla.* This lightbulb is burned. Change it. 2. light, electric light. شب الليت *šibb l-leet.* Turn the light on. بند الليت *bannid l-leet.* Turn the light off.

ل ي خ *lyx*

ليخ *liix* p. ليوخ *lyuux* fishing net. الليخ يصيدون فيه السمك *l-liix yṣiiduun fii s-simač.* They catch fish in a fishing net.

ل ي س ت *lyst*

ليستة *liista* p. *-aat* list, roster.

ل ي س ن *lysn*

ليسن *leesan* p. لياسن *liyaasin* driver's license. وين الليسن والملكية؟ *ween l-leesan w-l-milkiyya?* Where are (your) driver's license and title of your car?

ل ي ش *lyš*

ليش *leeš* (less common var. لويش *liweeš,* الويش *'ilweeš*) why, for what reason, what for. ليش رحت؟ *leeš riḥt?* Why did you go? ليش من هني؟ *leeš min hini?* Why from here? ما ادري ليش *ma dri leeš.* I don't know why. ليش ما عطيته اياه؟ *leeš ma ᶜaṭeeta-yyaaha?* Why didn't you give it to him? ليش بس ليش؟ *leeš bass leeš?* Why (on earth)?

ل ي ص ا ن ص *lyṣaanṣ*

ليصانص *leeṣaanṣ* p. *-aat* B.A. degree. من وين حصلت الليصانص؟ *min ween ḥaṣṣalt l-leeṣaanṣ?* Where did you get your B.A. degree.

ل ي ف *lyf*

ليف *layyaf* II to scour, scrub. لازم تليف المقلى زين *laazim tlayyif l-magḷa zeen.* You have to scour the frying pan well. لين كنت جاهل أمي كانت تليفني *leen čint yaahil 'ummi čaanat tlayyifni.* When I was a child, my mother used to scrub me.

ليف *liif* (coll.) plant fibers, bast.

ليفة *liifa* p. *-aat,* لياف *lyaaf* luffa, bath sponge, scouring pad.

ل ي ل *lyl*

ليل *leel* night, nighttime. زامي في الليل *zaami fi l-leel.* My shift is at night. ليل نهار *leel nahaar* day and night. موب لازم تشتغل ليل نهار *muub laazim tištaġil leel nahaar.* You don't have to work day and night. يسهر إلى نص الليل *yishar 'ila nuṣṣ l-leel.* He stays up until midnight. (prov.) بالليل عمايم وبالنهار خمايم *b-l-leel ᶜamaayim w-b-n-nahaar xamaayim.* Fair without and foul within. (lit., "During the day they are turbans, and at night they are garbage.").

ليلة *leela* p. ليالي *layaali* (one) night. ليلة أمس *leelat 'ams* last night. الليلة *l-leela* tonight. ليلة العرس *leelat l-ᶜirs* the wedding night.

ل ي م *lym*

لايم *laayam* III to agree with, suit, be good for. الهوا هني في الصيف يلايم المريضين *l-hawa hni fi ṣ-ṣeef ylaayim l-mariiðiin.* The weather here in the summer agrees with (the health of) sick people. ما يلايمني أشتغل في الليل *ma* *ylaayimni 'aštaġil fi l-leel.* It's not convenient for me to work at night. هالأكل مـا يلايمـني *hal-'akil ma ylaayimni.* This food is not good for me.

ملايـم *mlaayim* (act. part. from III لايم *laayam*) opportune, favorable, suitable. وقت ملايـم *wagt mlaayim* opportune time. مناسبة ملايمـة *munaasaba mlaayuma* favorable occasion.

ل ي ن *lyn*

لـين *leen* (conj.) 1. when لين توصل هناك علمـني *leen tooṣal hnaak ᶜallimni.* When you get there, let me know. تعـال صوبنـا لـين تجـي هـني *taᶜaal ṣoobna leen tyi hni.* Come to our place when you come here. 2. until, till. رمسته لين قـال «زيـن» *rammasta leen gaal, "zeen."* I talked to him until said, "Fine." نطرته لـين جـا *niṭarta leen ya.* I waited for him until he came.

ل ي و *lyw*

ليـوة *leewa* 1. Liwa, oasis in Abu Dhabi. 2. African dance in which men and women sing, dance, and beat the drums.

م

م ا *maa*

مـا *ma* (neg. part.) 1. بعد ما نش من النوم *baaᶜad ma našš min n-noom.* He hasn't woke up yet. ما يخالف! *ma yxaalif!* Never mind! It doesn't matter. مريض. ما يقدر يمشي *mariið. ma yigdar yamši.* He's ill. He cannot walk. ما أقدر أروح ذالحين *ma 'agdar aruuḥ ðalḥiin.* I cannot go now. (prov.) اللي ما يعرف الصقر يشويه *'illi ma yᶜarf ṣ-ṣagir yišwii.* Don't kill the goose that lays the golden egg. باكر ما يدش الزام *baačir ma ydišš z-zaam.* He won't report for duty tomorrow. ها القوطي ما يتبطل *hal-guuṭi ma yitbaṭṭal.* This can cannot be opened. ما قصرت! *ma gaṣṣart!* Bravo! You've done well. ويش بلاك؟ *weeš balaak?* What has happened to you? ما بلاني شي *ma balaani šayy.* Nothing has happened to me. ما فيه قهوة *ma fii ghawa.* There's no coffee. ما عندي فلوس واجد *ma ᶜindi fluus waayid.* I don't have much money. ما كان فيه طمام في الكرينهوز *ma kaan fii ṭamaat fi li-griinhooz.* There weren't any tomatoes in the greenhouse. ما عليه ديون *ma ᶜalee dyuun.* He doesn't owe any money. (prov.) اللي ما له أول ما له تالي *'illi ma la 'awwal ma la taali.* Everything should have a sound beginning. (lit., "He who doesn't have a beginning doesn't have an end."). ماحد *maḥḥad* (corruption of ما أحد *ma 'aḥad*). ماحد في الدار *maḥḥad fi d-daar.* There isn't anyone in the house. ما عليك! *ma ᶜaleek!* Never mind. 2. (rel. pron.) that which, which. ماشاالله! *maašaaḷḷa!* Splendid! (lit., "that which God willed."). Amazing. 3. (with foll. دام *daam*) as long as. ما دمت حي *ma dumt ḥayy* as long as I live. ما دام هني، روح سلم عليه *ma daam hini, ruuḥ sallim ᶜalee.* As long as he's here, go greet him.

ما *-ma* (suff. to prep. inter. part., elat. and certain other forms). قبل ما *gabil-ma ydišš* before he enters. شما يقول *š-ma yguul* whatever he says. شما يبغى *š-ma yibġa* whatever he wants. أحسن ما عندي *'aḥsan-ma ᶜindi* the best I have. كلما تشوفه *kull-ma ččuufa* whenever you see him.

م ا ر س *maars*

مـارس *maaris* (common var. آذار *'aaðaar*) March.

م ا ر ك *maark*

ماركة *maarka* p. *-aat* brand, make. ماركة الوزة *maarkat l-wazza* the goose brand (of tea). ماركة أوميغا *maarkat 'omeega* Omega brand. من ها الماركة *min hal-maarka* of this kind.

م ا ر ي *maary*

مارية *maariyya* p. *-aat* trade-mark. لا تشتري شي ما عليه مارية *la tištiri šayy ma ᶜalee maariyya.* Don't buy anything that doesn't bear a trade-mark.

م ا ع و ن *maaᶜwn*

ماعون *maaᶜuun* p. مواعين *muwaaᶜiin* 1. dish, plate. ماعون عيش ولحم *maaᶜuun* ᶜeeš w-laḥam dish of rice and meat. ماعون زلاطة maaᶜuun zalaaṭa salad plate. 2. (p. only) dishes, pots and pans. اغسل المواعين 'iġsil l-muwaaᶜiin. Do the dishes. اشترينا مواعين أمس štireena muwaaᶜiin 'ams. We bought pots and pans yesterday.

م ا ك و *maakw*

ماكو *maaku* (Kuwaiti) there isn't, there aren't. ماكو شي *maaku šayy.* There's nothing.

م ا ك ي ن *maakyn*

ماكينة *maakiina* p. مكاين *makaayin,* مواكن *mawaakiin* 1. engine. ماكينة السيارة *maakiinat s-sayyaara* the car engine. بند الماكينة *bannid l-maakiina.* Turn the engine off. 2. machine.

م ا م ي ش *maamyš*

ماميش *maamiiš* (Qatari) there isn't, there aren't. قهوة ماميش *ghawa maamiiš*. There's no coffee.

م ا ن ا *maanaa*

مانا *maanaa* Mana (female's name made famous by the proverb بين حانا ومانا ضيعنا لحانا *been ḥaana w-maana ḏayyaᶜna lḥaana.* Caught in the middle. Between the devil and the deep blue sea).

م ا ي *maay*

ماي *maay* (less common var. ميّ *mayy,* مية *mayya*) water. ماي حلو *maay ḥilu* sweet water. ماي مالح *maay maaliḥ* salty, saline water. ماي مطر *maay muṭar* rain water. ماي ورد *maay ward* rose water. (prov.) يوم سخنا الماي شرد الديك *yoom saxxanna l-maay širad d-diič.* Forewarned is forearmed. (lit., "When we heated the water, the rooster ran away.")

م ا ي و *maayw*

مايو *maayo* (common var. أيار *'ayyaar*) May. في شهر مايو الهوا يكون حار *fi šahar maayo l-hawa ykuun ḥaarr.* In May, the weather will be hot.

م ء ن *m'w*

مية *miya*. See under م ي *my.*

م ت ر *mtr*

متر *mitir* p. امتار *mtaar* meter (measure of length or distance). من هني إلى الدكان تقريب ميتين متر *min hini 'ila d-dikkaan tagriib miiteen mitir.* From here to the shop, it's about 200 meters.

م ت ل ي ك *mtlyk*

متليك *matliik* old coin of insignificant value. ما عندي ولا متليك *ma ᶜindi wala matliik.* I don't have any money, not even a plugged nickel.

م ت ن *mtn*

متن *mitin (يمتن yimtan)* 1. to become fat, plump, stout. بس ياكل ويمتن *bass yaakil w-yimtan.* He just eats and gets fat. 2. to gain weight. قطو مطابخ بس ما يمتن *gaṭu maṭaabix bass ma yimtan.* He eats like a pig, but he doesn't gain weight.

متن *mattan* II to fatten, make fat. الخضار والفواكه ما تمتن *li-xḏaar w-l-fawaakih ma tmattin.* Vegetables and fruits are not fattening.

متين *mitiin* 1. (p. -iin) fat, plump, stout. عكس متين ضعيف والا دقيق *ᶜaks mitiin ḏaᶜiif walla dijiij.* The opposite of *mitiin* is *ḍaᶜiif* or *dijiij.* 2. thick. حبل متين *ḥabil mitiin* thick rope.

م ث ل *mθl*

مثل *maθθal* II 1. to act, play (a role). يمثـل دور السـكران *ymaθθil door s-sakraan.* He acts the role of a drunkard. 2. to represent. الحكومـة طرشت مندوب يمثلها *li-ḥkuuma ṭarrašat manduub ymaθθilha.* The government sent a delegate to represent it. 3. to show, demonstrate. سلوكه يمثل تربيتـه *suluuka ymaθθil tarbiyata.* His behavior is an indication of his upbringing.

مثل *miθil* 1. like, similar to, the same as. مثل أجداده *miθil 'aydaada* like his forefathers. هو مثلهم *huwa miθilhum.* He's just like them. يتكلم إنكليزي مثلك *yitkallam 'ingiliizi miθlak.* He speaks English as well as you do. بالمثل *b-l-miθil* in kind, in the same manner, likewise. ها المدير ما يعـامل الموظفـين بالمثـل *hal-mudiir ma yᶜaamil li-mwaḍḍafiin b-l-miθil.* This manager doesn't treat employees the same way. المعاملة بالمثل *l-muᶜaamala b-l-miθil* eye for an eye, the principle of reciprocity. 2. (p. أمثال *'amθaal*) similar person or thing, person or thing of the same kind. أمثال حمد *'amθaal ḥamad* people like Hamad. هـو وأمثالـه *huwa w-'amθaala* He and all of his kind.

مثلمـا *miθil-ma* (conj.) as, just as, the same as. مثلما يقول المثل *miθil-ma yguul l-maθal* as the proverb goes. سويه مثلما قلت لك *sawwii miθil-ma git-lak.* Do it just as I have told you.

مثل *maθal* p. أمثال *'amθaal* 1. proverb, saying, proverbial phrase. على قول المثل *ᶜala gool l-maθal* as the proverb says. 2. example. نزين. عطنا مثل *nzeen. ᶜaṭna maθal.* O.K. Give us an example.

مثلاً *maθalan* for example, for instance.

مثيـل *maθiil* equal, match. ما لك مثيل *ma-lak maθiil.* You have no equal.

تمثال *timθaal* p. تماثيل *tamaaθiil* statue.

تمثيل *tamθiil* (v.n. from II مثل *maθθal*) acting.

تمثيليـة *tamθiiliyya* p. *-aat* play, stage presentation.

ممثـل *mumaθθil* p. *-iin* 1. actor. 2. representative, agent.

م ث ن *mθn*

مثانـة *maθaana* p. *-aat* (urinary) bladder.

م ج ر *mjr*

المجـر *l-majar* (common var. هنغاريـا *hanġaarya*) Hungary.

مجري *majari* 1. Hungarian, characteristic of Hungary. 2. (p. مجر *majar*) a Hungarian.

م ج و س *mjws*

مجـوس *majuus* Magi, adherents of Mazdaism.

مجوسي *majuusi* p. مجوس *majuus* Majian.

مجوسية *majuusiyya* Mazdaism.

م ح ا ح *mḥaaḥ*

محاح *maḥaaḥ* (coll.) egg yolk. s. *-a* p. *-aat* محاح البيض كلش زين حق الأطفـال *maḥaaḥ l-beeḍ killiš zeen ḥagg l-'aṭfaal.* Egg yolk is very good for babies.

م ح ا ر *mḥaar*

محار *maḥaar* (coll.) sea shells, oyster shells, snail shells. s. *-a* p. *-aat.*

م ح د *mḥd*

مـاحد *maḥḥad* (corruption of ما أحد *ma 'aḥad*). See under **م ا** *maa.*

م ح گ *mḥg*

امحـق *'imḥag* (in Bedouin speech) Damn it! Darn it!

محقة *maḥga* chaos, utter confusion.

م ح ن *mḥn*

امتحـن *mtiḥan* VIII 1. to take an examination. امتحنـت وسـقطت في الرياضيـات *mtiḥant w-ṣagaṭṭ fi r-riyaaḍiyyaat.* I took an examination and failed mathematics. 2. to test, examine. المدرس امتحنا في الإنكليزي *l-mudarris mtiḥanna fi l-'ingiliizi.* The teacher tested us in English.

امتحان *mtiḥaan* p. *-aat* examination, test. خذوا عليّ امتحان *xaðu ᶜalayya mtiḥaan.* They gave me an examination. نجحـت في الامتحـان *nijaḥt fi li-mtiḥaan.* I passed the examination.

م ح ي *mḥy*

محى *miḥa (يمحي yamḥi)* 1. to erase, rub out. امحي هذا السطر *'imḥi haaða s-saṭir.* Erase this line (of words). 2. to wipe out, eradicate, exterminate. الجيش محاهم عن بكرة أبيهم *l-jeeš maḥaahum ᶜan bakrat 'abiihim.* The army wiped them out to the last man.

محّى *maḥḥa* II to erase repeatedly. لا تمحّي ها القد *la tmaḥḥi hal-gadd.* Don't erase so much.

انمحى *nmiḥa* VII pass. of محى *miḥa.*

محّاية *maḥḥaaya* p. *-aat* pencil eraser.

ممحي *mamḥi* (p.p. from محى *miḥa*) having been erased, rubbed out. الكلمة ممحية *č-čalma mamḥiyya.* The word has been erased.

م خ ا *mxaa*

المخا *l-maxa* Mocha (city and seaport in SW Yemen).

م خ خ *mxx*

مخ *muxx* p. مخاخ *mxaax* 1. brain. مخ الغنم طيب *muxx l-ġanam ṭayyib.* Sheep brain is delicious. هذا شي ما يدش المخ *haaða šayy ma ydišš l-muxx.* This is an unacceptable thing. (lit., "This is something that cannot enter one's mind.") 2. mind, intelligence. 3. marrow.

م د ا ل ي *mdaaly*

مدالية *madaalya* p. *-aat* medal.

م د ح *mdḥ*

مدح *midaḥ (يمدح yimdaḥ)* to praise, commend. الكل يمدحه *l-kill ymadḥa.* Everyone praises him. مدح الشيخ بقصيدة نبطية *midaḥ š-šeex b-gaṣiida nabaṭiyya.* He praised the Shaikh in a vernacular poem.

انمدح *nmidaḥ* VII pass. of مدح *midaḥ.*

مدح *madḥ* (v.n. from مدح *midaḥ*) praise. مدح النبي *madḥ n-nabi* praising the Prophet. المدح الكثير موب زين *l-madḥ l-kaθiir muub zeen.* Too much praise is not good.

م د د *mdd*

مد *madd (يمد ymidd)* 1. to stretch out

(e.g., one's leg), extend, stretch. مديت رجولي لاجل أستريح *maddeet ryuuli lajil 'astariiḥ.* I stretched out my legs in order to rest. (prov.) مد رجلك على قد لحافك *midd riilak ᶜala gadd lḥaafak.* As you make your bed, you must lie in it. الطرار مد لي يده *t-ṭarraar madd-li yadda.* The beggar extended his hand to me. 2. to lay, lay out, spread out. شركة البترول مدت بيبات جديدة *šarikat l-batrool maddat peepaat yidiida.* The oil company laid new pipes. 3. to sail, set sail. الغواويص مدوا *l-ġuwaawiiṣ maddaw.* The pearl divers sailed.

مدد *maddad* II 1. to extend, lengthen. مددوا عطلة العيد يومين *maddadaw ᶜuṭlat l-ᶜiid yoomeen.* They extended the feast holiday two more days. المدرس مدد وقت الامتحان نص ساعة *l-mudarris maddad wagt li-mtiḥaan nuṣṣ saaᶜa.* The teacher prolonged the examination time half an hour. 2. to expand, extend. ما تعرف انه الحرارة ما تمدد الحطب؟ *ma tᶜarf 'inna l-ḥaraara ma tmaddid l-ḥaṭab?* Don't you know that heat doesn't expand wood? 3. to stretch out, spread out. مددوه على الميز وعملوا له العملية *maddadoo ᶜala l-meez w-ᶜamaloo-la ᶜamaliyya.* They stretched him out on the table and operated on him.

تمدد *tmaddad* V pass. of II مدد *maddad.*

امتد *mtadd* VIII to extend, run, stretch (over a distance). حدود دولة الإمارات تمتد من بو ظبي على طول الساحل العربي *ḥduud dawlat l-'imaaraat timtadd min bu ḍabi ᶜala ṭuul s-saaḥil l-ᶜarabi.* The borders of the U.A.E. extend from Abu Dhabi to the full length of the Arabian coast.

مدة *mudda* p. مدد *mudad, -aat* 1. period of time. مدة سنة *muddat sana* period of one year. 2. while. مدة طويلة *mudda ṭawiila* long time.

تمديد *tamdiid* (v.n. from II مدد *maddad*) extension, lengthening. تمديد الوقت *tamdiid l-wagt* the extension of time.

امتداد *mtidaadd* (v.n. from VIII امتد *mtadd*) extension, stretching. على امتداد *ᶜala mtidaad* along, along the side of.

مادة *maadda* p. مواد *mawaadd* 1. material, matter, substance. مواد بنا *mawaadd bina* building materials. مواد أولية *mawaadd awwaliyya* raw materials. 2. course, subject, field of study. فيه عليّ ثلاث مواد *fii ᶜalayya θalaaθ mawaadd.* I have to take three courses. مادة الفيزيا *maaddat l-fiizya* the physics course. 3. article, paragraph (of a law, contract, etc.) المادة الثانية من القانون *l-maadda θ-θaaniya min l-ġaanuun* article two of the law.

ممتد *mimtadd* extended, outstretched.

م د ن *mdn*

تمدن *tmaddan* V to be or become urbanized, modernized, civilized. ناس واجدين تمدنوا في الخليج *naas waaydiin tmaddanaw fi l-xaliij.* Many people have become urbanized in the Gulf. معظم القري في الإمارات تمدنت *muᶜḍam l-ġaray fi l-'imaaraat tmaddanat.* Most of the villages in the U.A.E. have become quite modern.

مدينة *madiina* p. مدن *mudun* city, town.

؟من أي مدينة *min 'ayya madiina?* From which city? المدينـــة المنـــورة *l-madiina l-munawwara* Medina (city in Saudi Arabia). مدينـــة زايـــد *madiinat zaayid* Zaid City (in Abu Dhabi).

مدني *madani* 1. civil, civic, city. الطيران المـــــــدني *ṭ-ṭaayaraan l-madani* civil aeronautics. قـــانون مـــدني *ġaanuun madani* civil law. مراكز مدنية *maraakiz madaniyya* civic centers. 2. civilian (as opp. to military). ملابـــس مدنيـــة *malaabis madaniyya* civilian clothes.

مدنية *madaniyya* civilization.

م ر ا ك ش *mraakš*

مراكش *maraakiš* 1. Marrakech (city in Morocco). 2. Morocco.

مراكشي *maraakši* 1. characteristic of Marrakech or Morocco. 2. a native of Marrakech or a Moroccan.

م ر ج ح *mrjḥ.* See under م ر ي ح *mryḥ.*

م ر خ *mrx*

المريخ *l-marriix* Mars (planet).

م ر ر ١ *mrr*

مر *marr* (يمر *ymurr*) 1. to pass, drop in (on s.o. or s.th.), drop by, go through. تمر من هني شاحنات كل يـــوم *tmurr min hini šaaḥinaat kill yoom.* Big trucks pass through here every day. مر مـــن هـــني؟ *marr min hini?* Did he pass by here? مر علينا الليلة؛ نسولف ونســـتانس *murr ʿaleena l-leela; nsoolif w-nistaanis.* Drop in on us tonight; we will chat and have a good time. طلب الشغل حقك مر على عـــدة جـــهات *ṭalab š-šuġul ḥaggak marr ʿala ʿiddat jihaat.* Your job application went through many channels. مساكين! أيـــام صعبة مرت عليـــهم *masaakiin! 'ayyaam ṣaʿba marrat ʿaleehum.* Poor people! They have experienced hard times. 2. to pass, elapse, go by. مرت مدة طويلة *marrat mudda ṭawiila.* A long period of time passed.

مرر *marrar* II to let pass. المرور ما يمرر اللوريات من هـــني *l-muruur ma ymarrir l-looriyyaat min hini.* The traffic won't let lorries pass from here.

استمر *stamarr* X 1. to continue, keep on, persist. استمر يشتغـــل الـــين تعـــب *stamarr yištaġil 'ileen tiʿab.* He continued to work until he got tired. سافر لنـــدن واســـتمر في دراســـته *saafar landan w-stamarr fi diraasta.* He traveled to London and went on with his studies. 2. to last, go on. عطلة العيد استمرت أربع أيام *ʿuṭlat l-ʿiid stamarrat 'arbaʿ 'ayyaam.* The feast holiday lasted four days.

مـــر *marr* (v.n. from مر *marr*) passing by, stopping. من زمان ما شفناك. حتى مر ما تمـــر *min zamaan ma šifnaak. ḥatta marr ma tmurr.* We haven't seen you for a long time. You don't even stop by.

مـــرة *marra* p. *-aat* once, time. رحت هناك مرة وحدة بـــس *riḥt hnaak marra waḥda bass.* I went there only once. مرتين *marrateen* twice. مرة ثانية *marra θaanya* once more, once again. كم مرة قلت لك ما تروحين السوق وحـــدك؟ *čam marra git-lič ma truuḥiin s-suug waḥdič?* How many times have I told you not to go to the marketplace alone? أكثر من مـــرة *'akθar min marra* more than once, many times. مرة أدوخ

مرة أدوخ سبيل جكاير ومرة أدوخ *marra 'aduux jigaayir w-marra 'aduux sbiil.* Sometimes I smoke cigarettes and sometimes I smoke a pipe. هذي أول مرة تجي هني؟ *haaðі 'awwal marra tyi hni?* Is this the first time you come here? إي نعم، أول مرة وآخر مرة *'ii naᶜam, 'awwal marra w-'aaxir marra.* Yes indeed, the first time and the last time. بالمرة *b-l-marra* (usually neg.) at all, never. ما شفته بالمرة *ma čifta b-l-marra.* I haven't seen him at all. كم مرة قلت لك؟ ما تفتهم بالمرة؟ *čam marra git-lak? ma tiftihim b-l-marra?* How many times have I told you? Don't you ever know?

مرور *muruur* (v.n. from مر *marr*) 1. passing, passage. 2. (with ال *l-*) المرور *l-muruur* the traffic police.

ممر *mamarr* p. *-aat* passageway, corridor.

م ر ر ٢ *mrr*

مر *murr* 1. bitter. ما أشرب هذي القهوة. مرة *ma 'ašrab haaðі l-gahwa. murra.* I won't drink this coffee. It's bitter. مر مثل العلقم *murr miθl l-ᶜalgam* bitter as colocynth. 2. (with ال *l-*) hardship, hard time. صبر على المر *ṣibar ᶜala l-murr.* He's put up with hardship. ذاق المر *ðaag l-murr.* He's experienced a hard time.

مرارة *maraara* 1. bitterness. ما قدرت أفكر من المرارة اللي كنت فيها *ma gidart 'afakkir min l-maraara lli čint fiiha.* I wasn't able to think because of my bitterness. 2. (p. *-aat*) gall bladder.

أمر *'amarr* (elat.) 1. (with من *min*) more bitter than. أمر من العلقم *'amarr min l-ᶜalgam* more bitter than colocynth. 2. (with foll. n.) the most bitter. الأمرين *l-'amarreen* (originally, the two worst things, probably poverty and old age). ذاق الأمرين *ðaag l-'amarreen.* He experienced many hardships.

م ر ز ب *mrzb*

مرزاب *mirzaab* p. مرازيب *miraaziib* roof gutter. ماي المطر ينزل في المرزاب ويروح البير *maay l-muṭar yanzil fi l-mirzaab w-yruuḥ l-biir.* Rain water flows down the roof gutter and goes to the well.

م ر ظ *mrḍ*

مرض *miriḍ* (يمرض *yimraḍ*) to get sick, become sick. طاح مريض وماحد من هله مرض *ṭaaḥ mariiḍ w-maḥḥad min hala miriḍ.* He fell ill and none of his family became sick.

مرض *marraḍ* II to make sick. ها الأكل يمرض *hal-'akil ymarriḍ.* This food makes people sick.

تمرض *tmarraḍ* V = مرض *miriḍ*. تمرضت من ذاك الشغل. فنشت وهديته *tmarraḍt min ðaak š-šuġul. fannašt w-haddeeta.* I got sick and tired of that work. I resigned and let it go.

تمارض *tmaaraḍ* VI to pretend to be sick, feign illness. تمارض وما دش الشغل اليوم *tmaaraḍ w-ma dašš š-šuġul l-yoom.* He pretended to be sick and didn't go to work today.

مرض *maraḍ* p. أمراض *'amraaḍ* disease, illness.

مريض *mariiḍ* p. *-iin*, مرضى *marḍa.* 1. sick, ill. رحت الدختر لاني كنت مريض

ومسخن riḥt d-daxtar linni čint mariiđ w-mṣaxxan. I went to the doctor because I was sick and running a temperature. 2. sick person, patient.

تمريض tamriiđ nursing, nursing the sick. كلية التمريض kulliyyat t-tamriiđ the college of nursing.

ممرض mumarriđ p. -iin male sick nurse.

ممرضة mumarriđa p. -aat female sick nurse.

م ر گ mrg

مرق marag (coll.) meat juice, broth. (prov.) إذا عطاك الشيخ مرق حطه بشليلك *'iđa cataak š-šeex marag ḥuṭṭa b-šiliilak.* Make hay while the sun shines.

م ر م ر mrmr

مرمر marmar (coll.) 1. marble. عجمان تشتهر بحجر المرمر *caymaan tištihir b-ḥiyar l-marmar.* Ajman is known for its marble. 2. alabaster.

م ر ن mrn

مرن marran II to drill, train s.o. مدرس الرياضة قاعد يمرن الطلاب *mudarris r-riyaađa gaacid ymarrin ṭ-ṭullaab.* The athletics teacher is drilling the students. مرنهم على الحكي بالإنكليزي *marranhum cala l-ḥači b-l-ingiliizi.* He trained them to speak English.

تمرن tmarran V (with على cala) to practice, exercise, rehearse. قبل لا تسافر أمريكا، لازم تتمرن على الحكي بالإنكليزي *gabil-la tsaafir 'amriika, laazim titmarran cala l-ḥači b-l-ingiliizi.* Before you travel to America, you have to practice speaking English. تمرن على دوره في التمثيلية *tmarran cala doora fi t-tamθiiliyya.* He has rehearsed his role in the play.

تمرين tamriin p. تمارين tamaariin, -aat exercise, practice, training. تمارين رياضية *tamaariin riyaađiyya* sports.

م ر ه م mrhm

مرهم marham p. مراهم maraahim ointment, healing or soothing ointment.

م ر ي mry

مراية mraaya (common var. مرية *mrayya*) p. -aat, مري *miri* mirror.

م ر ي ح mryḥ

مريح maryaḥ (يمريح *ymariyḥ*) to rock, swing s.o.

تمريح tmaryaḥ (يتمريح *yitmaryaḥ*) to swing, swing back and forth. الجهال قاعدين يتمريحون *l-yihhaal gaacdiin yitmaryaḥuun.* The children are swinging.

مريحانة maryaḥaana p. -aat swing.

م ر ي م mrym

مريم maryam Miryam (common female's name in the U.A.E.).

مريمو maryamoo, مريوم *maryuum* dim. of مريم *maryam.*

م س ح msḥ

تمساح timsaaḥ p. تماسيح tamaasiiḥ 1. crocodile. دموع التماسيح *dumuuc t-tamaasiiḥ* crocodile tears. 2. alligator.

م س ك msk

مسك misak (يمسك *yamsik*) 1. to catch,

seize. البايق مسكوه في السوق *l-baayig miskoo fi s-suug.* They caught the thief in the marketplace. 2. to hold. مسكت يده *misakt yadda.* I held his hand. 3. to keep (e.g., the accounts, the books) نبغى واحد يمسك الحسابات *nibġa waaḥid yamsik li-ḥsaabaat.* We need someone to keep the accounts.

أمسك *'amsak* IV to stop eating, start fasting (during Ramadan). ذالحين نمسك الساعة أربع الصبح *ðalḥiin nimsik s-saa^c^a 'arba^c^a ṣ-ṣubḥ.* Nowadays, we start fasting at 4:00 a.m.

تمسك *tmassak* V (with ب *b-*) to stick to, adhere to. ما وافق. تمسك برايه *ma waafag. tmassak b-raaya.* He didn't agree. He stuck to this opinion.

مسك *mask* (v.n. from مسك *misak*) keeping (the books, the accounts). مسك الدفاتر *mask d-dafaatir* book-keeping, accounting.

إمساك *'imsaak* (v.n. from IV أمسك *'amsak*) 1. the time of day for beginning the Ramadan fast. 2. (med.) constipation. دوا الإمساك العشرج *duwa l-'imsaak l-^c^išrij.* Camomile is the best medicine for constipation. عندك إمساك؟ *^c^indak 'imsaak?* Are you constipated?

إمساكية *'imsaakiyya* p. *-aat* Ramadan calendar (showing the times of إمساك *'imsaak* and فطور *fuṭuur*).

م س ك ت *mskt*

مسكت *maskat* Muscat (capital of Oman).

مسكتي *maskati* 1. of Muscat, characteristic of Muscat. 2. (p. *-yya*) person from Muscat.

م س ك ن *mskn*

مسكين *maskiin* p. مساكين *masaakiin* poor, miserable, wretched person.

م س و *msw*

مسى *massa* II to bid s.o. good evening, wish s.o. a good evening. مساك الله بالخير! *massaak aḷḷa b-l-xeer!* Good evening!

مسا *masa* (less common var. مساء *masaa'*) evening, night. مسا الخير *masa l-xeer!* Good evening! (less common than مساك الله بالخير! *massaak aḷḷa b-l-xeer!*) مسا البارحة *masa l-baarḥa* last night, yesterday evening. مسا الخميس *masa l-xamiis* Thursday night. *l-masa* in the evening, at night. أشوفك الساعة ستة المسا *'ačuufak s-saa^c^a sitta l-masa.* I'll see you at six in the evening.

مسائي *masaa'i* (adj.) evening. جريدة مسائية *jariida masaa'iyya* evening newspaper.

م ش ش *mšš*

مش *mašš* (يمش *ymišš*) to wipe, wipe off, dust. كل يوم البشكار يمش الكراسي والميوز *kill yoom l-biškaar ymišš l-karaasi w-li-myuuz.* The servant wipes the chairs and the tables every day. (prov.) ياكل ويمش يده بالطوفة *yaakil w-ymišš yadda b-ṭ-ṭoofa.* Don't do favors for those who do not appreciate or deserve them. (lit., "He eats and wipes his hands on the wall.").

مشاشة *maššaaša* p. *-aat* rag or towel used for dusting and cleaning.

Move along! You cannot wait here. 5. to associate, keep company. أنا ما أمشي وايا ناس مثلك! *'aana ma 'amši wiyya naas miθlak!* I don't associate with people like you. 6. to go with, match. ها القميص ما يمشي وايا البنطلون. *hal-gamiiṣ ma yamši wiyya l-banṭaluun.* This shirt doesn't go with the pants. 7. to run, work. سيارتي ما تمشي؛ خربانة *sayyaarti ma timši; xarbaana.* My car doesn't run; it's broken down. مشت عليه الحيلة *mišat ᶜalee l-ḥiila.* The trick worked on him.

مشى *mašša* II 1. to walk s.o., let s.o. walk. مسكته من يده ومشيته *misakta min yadda w-maššeeta.* I held his hand and walked him. 2. to make or let go, send. عطيناه حقوقه ومشيناه *ᶜaṭeenaa ḥguuga w-maššeenaa.* We gave him what was due him and let him go. مشيت عايلتي حق لبنان في الصيف *maššeet ᶜaayilti ḥagg labnaan fi ṣ-ṣeef.* I sent my family to Lebanon in the summer. 3. to advance, promote, further. لا تعطل الشغل؛ مشيه *la tᶜaṭṭil š-šuġul; maššii.* Don't delay the work; get it going. مشيه؛ هو أول واحد *maššii; huwa 'awwal waaḥid.* Hurry up with him; he's the first one. نزلوا سعر البضاعة لاجل يمشونها *nazzlaw siᶜir li-bḍaaᶜa lajil ymaššuunha.* They lowered the price of the merchandise in order to increase sales. هو بس يبغي يمشي مصلحته الشخصية *huwa bass yabġi ymašši maṣlaḥta š-šaxṣiyya.* He just wants to further his own personal interests. 4. to pass, allow s.o. to advance. ما سوى زين في الامتحان، بس المدرس مشاه *ma sawwa zeen fi li-mtiḥaan, bass l-mudarris maššaa.* He

م ش ط *mšṭ*

مشط *maššaṭ* II to comb. قبل ما يطلع يمشط شعره ويتخنن *gabil-ma yiṭlaᶜ ymaššiṭ šᶜara w-yitxannan.* Before he goes out, he combs his hair and puts on perfume.

تمشط *tmaššaṭ* V to comb one's hair. تمشط قبل لا تطلع *tmaššaṭ gabil-la tiṭlaᶜ.* Comb your hair before you go out. الشعر الوسخ ما يتمشط زين *š-šaᶜar l-waṣx ma yitmaššaṭ zeen.* Dirty hair cannot be combed well.

مشط *mišṭ* p. مشاط *mšaaṭ* 1. comb. 2. clip (of bullets).

م ش م ش *mšmš*

مشمش *mišmiš* (coll.) apricots. s. *-a.* المشمش ما يطلع هني *l-mišmiš ma yiṭlaᶜ hini.* Apricots don't grow here. اشتريت مشمش *štireet mišmiš.* I bought (some) apricots.

مشمشة *mišmiša* p. *-aat* 1. apricot tree. 2. apricot.

م ش ي *mšy*

مشى *miša (يمشي yamši)* 1. to walk, go on foot. إذا ما تقدر تمشي، اخذ تكسي *'iða ma tigdar tamši, 'ixið taksi.* If you cannot walk, take a taxi. 2. to leave, depart. أنا باقي هني، بس سالم مشى *'aana baagi hni, bass saalim miša.* I am staying here, but Salim has left. الباص مشى قبل نص ساعة *l-paaṣ miša gabil nuṣṣ saaᶜa.* The bus left half an hour ago. 3. to go. باكر أمشي دبي انشاالله *baačir 'amši dbayy nšaaḷḷa.* Tomorrow I'll go to Dubai, God willing. 4. to move along, proceed. امشي! ما تقدر توقف هني *'imši! ma tigdar toogaf hini.*

didn't do well on the examination, but the teacher passed him.

ماشى *maaša* III 1. to walk with s.o., engage s.o. in walking. ماشيته *maašeeta.* I walked with him. 2. to get along with, go along with. لازم تماشي التنديل إذا بغيت تترفع *laazim tmaaši t-tindeel 'iðaa bağeet titraffa*ᶜ. You'll have to get along with the foreman if you want to be promoted. ماشيه على قد عقله *maašii* ᶜ*ala gad* ᶜ*agla.* Deal with him at his own level.

تمشى *tmašša* V to stroll, take a walk, walk leisurely. أمس عقب العصر تمشينا على السيف *'ams* ᶜ*ugub l-*ᶜ*aṣir tmaššeena* ᶜ*ala l-siif.* Yesterday, late in the afternoon, we strolled on the beach.

مشي *maši* (v.n. from مشى *miša*) 1. walking. 2. (adv.) on foot. رحنا مشي *riḥna maši.* We went there on foot. تقدر تروح مشي *tigdar truuḥ maši.* You can go on foot.

مشية *mašya* (n. of inst.) p. *-aat* manner of walking, gait.

ماشي *maaši* (act. part. from مشى *miša*) 1. having walked. أنا ماشي كيلومتر *'aana maaši keelumitir.* I've walked one kilometer. 2. on foot, walking. رحت البيت ماشي *riḥt l-beet maaši.* I went home on foot. 3. (p. مشاة *mušaa* only) infantry.

ماشية *maašiya* p. مواشي *mawaaši* cattle, livestock.

م ص خ *mṣx*

ماصخ *maaṣix* tasteless, flat, needing salt. ها العيش ماصخ؛ ما ينوكل *hal-*ᶜ*eeš maaṣix; ma yinwikil.* This rice is tasteless; it cannot be eaten.

م ص ر *mṣr*

مصر *maṣir* Egypt. القاهرة عاصمة مصر *l-qaahira* ᶜ*aaṣimat maṣir.* Cairo is the capital of Egypt.

مصري *maṣri* 1. Egyptian. 2. (p. *-yiin,* مصاروة *maṣaarwa*) an Egyptian. في مصريين كثيرين في الخليج *fii maṣriyyiin kaθiiriin fi l-xaliij.* There are many Egyptians in the Gulf. 3. donkey, ass (old word infrequently used).

م ص ر ن *mṣrn*

مصران *muṣraan* p. مصارين *maṣaariin* intestine, gut.

م ص ص *mṣṣ*

مص *maṣṣ* (يمص *ymuṣṣ*) 1. to suck, suck up, suck in, absorb. الجاهل يمص صبعه *l-yaahil ymuṣṣ ṣub*ᶜ*a.* The child is sucking his finger. 2. to sip. ما تقدر تمص القهوة بالمصاصة *ma tigdar tmuṣṣ l-gahwa b-l-maṣṣaaṣa.* You cannot sip coffee with a straw.

انمص *nmaṣṣ* VII to be sucked. حبة الأسبرين تنبلع؛ ما تنمص *ḥabbat l-'asbiriin tinbili*ᶜ*; ma tinmaṣṣ.* An aspirin tablet is to be swallowed; it shouldn't be sucked.

امتص *mtaṣṣ* VIII to absorb, suck up. السيارة البيضا تمتص الحرارة *s-sayyaara l-beeða timtaṣṣ l-ḥaraara.* White cars absorb heat.

مص *maṣṣ* (v.n. from مص *maṣṣ*) 1. sucking, sucking up. 2. sipping.

مصة *maṣṣa* (n. of inst.) p. *-aat* a sip.

مصاصة *maṣṣaaṣa* p. *-aat* 1. (drinking) straw. 2. lollipop, sucker. 3. pacifier.

ماص *maaṣ* p. *-aat* magnet.

م ص ط ر *mṣṭr.* See under **ص ط ر** *ṣṭr.*

م ص ل *mṣl*

مصل *maṣil* p. أمصال *'amṣaal* 1. serum. 2. plasma.

م ص م ص *mṣmṣ*

مصمص *maṣmaṣ (يمصمص ymaṣmiṣ)* 1. to suck on. فيه ناس يحبون يمصمصون العظم *fii naas yḥibbuun ymaṣimṣuun l-ᶜaðim.* There are people who like to suck on bones. 2. to neck, kiss and caress. قاعدين يمصمصون في السيارة *gaaᶜdiin ymaṣimṣuun fi s-sayyaara.* They are necking in the car.

م ط ر *mṭr*

مطر *muṭar (يمطر yimṭir)* مطرت الدنيا *muṭrat d-dinya.* It rained. هني ما تمطر واجد *hini ma timṭir waayid.* Here, it doesn't rain a lot.

مطر *muṭar* rain.

مطارة *maṭṭaara* p. مطاطير *maṭaaṭiir, -aat* canteen, flask. مطارة ربل *maṭṭaarat rabal* hot water bottle.

م ط ر ز ي *mṭrzy*

مطارزي *maṭaarzi* p. *-yya* bodyguard. يشتغل مطارزي عند الأمير *yištaġil maṭaarzi ᶜind l-'amiir.* He works as a bodyguard for the Emir.

م ط ي *mṭy*

مطية *maṭiyya* p. مطايا *maṭaaya* riding animal, such as a donkey or a mule.

م ظ م ظ *mðmð*

مضمض *maðmað (يمضمض ymaðmið)* to rinse out (the mouth). مضمض حلقك بهالدوا *maðmið ḥaljak b-had-duwa.* Rinse out your mouth with this medicine.

تمضمض *tmaðmað (يتمضمض yitmaðmað)* to rinse out one's mouth. لين تتوضا لازم تتمضمض بالماي *leen titwaððа laazim titmaðmað b-l-maay.* When you perform ablution (before prayer), you have to rinse out your mouth with water.

مضمضة *maðmaða* (v.n. from مضمض *maðmað*) rinsing out the mouth

م ظ ي *mðy*

مضى *maða (يمضي yimði)* 1. to pass, go by, elapse. مضت مدة طويلة وما رحت أشوفهم *maðat mudda ṭawiila w-ma riḥt 'ačuuffum.* A long period of time passed and I didn't go to see them. 2. to sign one's name, affix one's signature. امضي هني في آخر الطلب *'imði hni fi 'aaxir ṭ-ṭalab.* Sign your name here at the end of the application.

مضى *maðða* II 1. to spend, pass (time). مضينا وقت طويل في البريمي *maððeena wagt ṭawiil fi li-breemi.* We spent a long time in Buraimi. بس يلعبون ويمضون وقت *bass ylaᶜbuun w-ymaððuun wagt.* They are just playing and killing time. 2. to make, cause s.o. to sign. مضيته قدام شاهدين قبل ما عطيته فلوس *maððeeta jiddaam šaahdeen gabil-ma ᶜaṭeeta fluus.* I made him sign in the presence of two witnesses before I gave him any money.

إمضا *'imða* signature, signing.

ماضي *maaði* (act. part. from مضى

maḍa) 1. having signed. أشوف أنت ماضي هني *'ačuuf 'inta maaḍi hni.* I see that you have signed your name here. 2. past, bygone, last. في الوقت الماضي *fi l-waġt l-maaḍi* during the past time. السبوع الماضي *s-subuu^c l-maaḍi* last week. السنة الماضية *s-sana l-maaḍya* last year. 3. (as n.) past life, history. لا تصادقه. هذا رجال معروف ماضيه *la tṣaadga. haaða rayyaal ma^cruuf maḍii.* Don't befriend him. This is a man whose past is known. الماضي *l-maaḍi* the past. شعلينا من الماضي؟ *š-^caleena min l-maaḍi?* Why should we care about the past?

م ع *m^c*

مع *ma^c* (prep.) 1. with, in the company of. مع السلامة! *ma^c s-salaama!* Good-bye! مع الأسف *ma^c l-'asaf* unfortunately. 2. in spite of, despite. مع هذا *ma^c haaða* in spite of this, nevertheless. 3. (with suff. pron.) to have. معه فلوس واجد *ma^ca fluus waayid.* He has a lot of money. معها ولدين *ma^cha waladeen.* She has two kids. معك حق *ma^cak ḥagg.* You are right.

م ع ا م ي ل *m^caamyl*

معاميل *ma^caamiil* (no singular) coffee pots, cups, etc.

م ع د ١ *m^cd*

معدة *mi^cda* p. *-aat* stomach.

م ع د ٢ *m^cd*

معيدي *m^ceedi* p. *-yya* uncouth person.

م ع ز *m^cz*

معزة *mi^cza* = عنز *^canz.* See عنز *^canz* under ع ن ز *^cnz.*

م ع ن *m^cn*

ماعون *maa^cuun.* See under م ا ع و ن *maa^cwn.*

م ك ر ف و ن *mkrfwn*

ميكروفون *mikrofoon* p. *-aat* 1. microphone. 2. loud speaker

م ك ك *mkk*

مكة *makka* Mecca.

م ك ن *mkn*

أمكن *'amkan* (يمكن *yamkin*) IV to be possible. إذا أمكنك تجي، أهلا وسهلا *'iða 'amkank tyi, 'ahlan wa sahlan.* If it's possible for you to come, you're welcome. يمكن تمطر الدنيا اليوم *yamkin timṭir d-dinya l-yoom.* It might rain today. Maybe it'll rain today.

تمكن *tmakkan* V to be able, be in a position. ما تمكنت أروح وياهم *ma tmakkant 'aruuḥ wiyyaahum.* I wasn't able to go with them.

إمكان *'imkaan* (v.n. from IV أمكن *'amkan*) (usually with suff. pron.) power, capacity, capability. موب إمكاني أحصل لك زيادة *muub 'imkaani 'aḥaṣṣil-lak ziyaada.* It's not in my power to get you an increment. بإمكانك تساعده؟ *b-'imkaanak tsaa^cda?* Can you help him? حسب الإمكان *ḥasb l-'imkaan* as much as possible. رايح أساعده حسب الإمكان *raayiḥ 'asaa^cda ḥasb l-'imkaan.* I am going to help him as much as I can.

'مكانية *'imkaaniyya* (v.n.) possibility. ما فيه إمكانية *ma fii 'imkaaniyya.* It's not possible.

م ل ح mlḥ

ملح *mallaḥ* II to salt. إذا ما تملح العيش يستوي ماصخ *'iða ma tmalliḥ l-ᶜeeš yistiwi maaṣix.* If you don't salt the rice, it will be tasteless.

ملح *milḥ* (coll.) salt. s. حبة ملح *ḥabbat milḥ* pinch of salt.

ملاحة *milaaḥa* navigation, shipping. شركة ملاحة *šarikat milaaḥa* navigation company, shipping company.

مليح *maliiḥ* nice, pleasant, agreeable.

أملح *'amlaḥ* f. ملحا *malḥa* p. ملح *milḥ* grey, salt-colored. حصان أملح *ḥṣaan 'amlaḥ* grey horse. ناقة ملحا *naaga malḥa* grey she-camel.

أملح *'amlaḥ* (elat.) 1. (with من *min*) more salty than. 2. (with foll. n.) the most salty.

مالح *maaliḥ* salt, salty, saline. سمك مالح *simač maaliḥ* salty fish. ماي مالح *maay maaliḥ* salty water. محلول مالح *maḥluul maaliḥ* saline solution.

م ل س mls

أملس *'amlas* f. ملسا *malsa* p. ملسين *malsiin* smooth, sleek.

م ل ا س mlaas

ملاس *millaas* p. ملاليس *milaaliis* ladle, large spoon. (prov.) اللي بالجدر يطلعه الملاس *'illi b-l-jidir yṭallᶜa l-millaas.* Time will tell one's good or bad qualities. (lit., "What's in the pot will be shown in the ladle.").

م ل ط mlṭ

أملط *'amlaṭ* f. ملطا *malṭa* p. ملط *milṭ* 1. hairless, one with no hair on one's

ممكن *mumkin* 1. possible. إي نعم. هذا ممكن *'ii naᶜam. haaða mumkin.* Yes, indeed. That's possible. غير ممكن *ġeer mumkin,* موب ممكن *muub mumkin* impossible. 2. (with foll. v.) maybe, perhaps, it's possible that. ممكن أشوفه اليوم *mumkin 'ačuufa l-yoom.* Maybe I'll see him today. ممكن أسألك سؤال؟ *mumkin 'as'alk su'aal?* May I ask you a question?

متمكن *mitmakkin* (act. part. from V تمكن *tmakkan*) (with من *min*) proficient in, having s.th. under control. هو متمكن من الإنكليزي *huwa mitmakkin min l-'ingiliizi.* He's proficient in English.

م ك ي ا ج mkyaaj

مكياج *mikyaaj* make-up.

م ل چ mlč

ملك *milač (يملك yamlič)* (less common var. *milak*) 1. to own, possess, have. يملك البناية اللي على السيف *yamlič li-bnaaya lli ᶜala s-siif.* He owns the building on the beach. ما فيه واحد هني ما يملك ولا شي *ma fii waaḥid hini ma yamlič wala šayy.* There isn't anyone here who doesn't have anything. 2. to contract a marriage, marry (a woman). إذا اتفقوا يملكون ويسجلون الزواج في المحكمة الشرعية *'iða ttafgaw yimilčuun w-ysajjluun z-zawaaj fi l-maḥkama š-šarᶜiyya.* If they come to an agreement, they contract the marriage and record it in the Islamic court. 3. (with على *ᶜala*) to marry. ولدي ملك على بنت عمه *wildi milač ᶜala bint ᶜamma.* My son married his cousin.

See also under م ل ك *mlk.*

face or body. بـارك الله في الحرمـة الملطا *baarak aḷḷa fi l-ḥurma l-malṭa.* God bless hairless women. 2. hairless person. 3. featherless. شـاهين أملـط *šaahiin 'amlaṭ* featherless peregrine.

ملطة *malṭa* diarrhea.

م ل ك *mlk*

ملـك *milak* (يملـك *yamlik*) (more common var. *milač*). See under **م ل چ** *mlč*.

ملـك *mallak* II to make s.o. the owner of. ملكهـا العمـارة اللـي علـى السـيف *mallakha li-ᶜmaara lli ᶜala s-siif.* He made her the owner of the building on the beach. الحكومة ملكت العمـال بيـوت شـعبية *li-ḥukuuma mallakat l-ᶜummaal byuut šaᶜbiyya.* The government deeded the workers houses for low income people.

تملك *tmallak* V to seize, lay hands on, take possession of. الشـركة فلسـت والحكومـة تملكـت كـل أملاكهـا *š-šarika fallasat w-l-ḥukuuma tmallakat kill 'amlaakha.* The company went bankrupt and the government seized all its possessions.

تمالك *tmaalak* VI 1. to control, restrain oneself. ما قدر يتمـالك نفسـه مـن الغضب اللي هـو فيـه *ma gidar yitmaalak nafsa min l-ġaḏ̣ab illi huwa fii.* He couldn't control himself because of his anger. 2. to control, restrain (a feeling, an emotion). ما قدر يتمـالك أعصابـه *ma gidar yitmaalak 'aᶜṣaaba.* He couldn't control his temper.

استملك *stamlak* X 1. to buy, acquire by purchase. الجامعة استملكت بيـوت وأراضـي *l-yaamᶜa stamlakat byuut w-'araaḏ̣i.* The university bought houses and land. 2. to take possession of, appropriate. تقدر تسـتملك الشـقة إذا تدفـع كيـش *tigdar tistamlik š-šigga 'iða tidfaᶜ keeš.* You can take possession of the apartment if you pay cash.

ملـك *milk* p. أمـلاك *'amlaak* property, possessions. البيـت ملكي *l-beet milki.* The house is mine. I own the house. عنده أملاك واجد، بيوت وأراضـي... *ᶜinda 'amlaak waayid, byuut w-'araaḏ̣i...* He has a lot of possessions, houses, land...

ملـك *malik* p. ملوك *muluuk* king, monarch. الأسد ملـك الوحـوش *l-'asad malik li-wḥuuš.* The lion is the king of beasts.

ملكـة *malika* p. *-aat* queen. ملكة جمال *malikat jamaal* beauty queen.

ملاك *malaak* p. ملايكة *malaayka* angel.

ملكي *malaki* royal, kingly. الحرس الملكي *l-ḥaras l-malaki* the royal guard.

ملكيـة *milkiyya* 1. ownership. ملكيـة الأرض *milkiyyat l-'arḏ̣* land ownership. 2. title (e.g., of a car), deed (of property). عطـني الليسـن حقـك والملكيـة *ᶜaṭni l-leesan ḥaggak w-l-milkiyya.* Give me your driver's license and the title of the car.

مـلاك *mallaak* p. *-iin* landowner, land proprietor.

مملكة *mamlaka* p. ممالك *mamaalik* kingdom.

مـالك *maalik* p. مـلاك *millaak, -iin* owner, proprietor.

مـالكي *maalki* 1. belonging to the Malikite school of Islamic theology.

المذهب المــــالكي *l-maðhab l-maalki* the Malikite school of thought. 2. a Maliki.

مملـوك *mamluuk* p. مماليك *mamaaliik* white slave, mameluke.

م ل ل *mll*

ملا *mulla* p. ملالوة *malaalwa* mulla (a person versed in religious matters). الحكومة تعين ملا والا مطـــوع في كـــل مســجد *li-ḥkuuma tᶜayyin mulla walla mṭawaaᶜ fi kill msiid.* The government appoints a mulla or a *mṭawwaᶜ* in every mosque.

م ل ي *mly.* See **ت ر س** *trs.*

م ن ¹ *mn*

من *man* 1. (inter. pron.) who? which one? من عند البــاب؟ *man ᶜind l-baab?* Who is at the door? من أنت؟ *man inta?* Who are you? منت؟ *mant?* Who are you? منتِ؟ *manti?* Who are you (f.s.)? 2. (rel. pron.) he who. (prov.) من عضه الداب ينقز من الحبــل *man ᶜaðða d-daab yangiz min l-ḥabil.* Once bitten, twice shy. (lit., "He who has been bitten by a snake fears a rope."). (prov.) من حب الشجرة حب أغصانها *man ḥabb li-šyara ḥabb 'aġṣaanha.* He who loves me loves my dog. 3. (inter. suff. pron.) whose, who, whom. سيارة من هـــذي؟ *sayyaarat-man haaði?* Whose car is this? فلــوس مـــن خذيــت؟ *fluus-man xaðeet?* Whose money did you take? المن طرشت الخط؟ *'il-man ṭarrašt l-xaṭṭ?* Who did you send the letter to? المن هذا البيـــت؟ *'il-man haaða l-beet?* Whose house is this? حق من هذا القصر؟ *ḥagg man haaða l-gaṣir?* Whose palace is this?

م ن ² *mn*

من *min* (prep., with foll. vowel *minn-*) 1. from, away from, out of. أنا من راس الخيمــة *'aana min raas l-xeema.* I'm from Ras Al-Khaima. تجينا أشيا كثيرة من الخارج *tyiina 'ašya kaθiira min l-xaarij.* We get many things from abroad. طلع من الحفيز *ṭilaᶜ min l-ḥafiiz.* He came out from the office. (prov.) من بره الله الله ومن داخل يعلم الله *min barra 'aḷḷa 'aḷḷa w-min daaxil yiᶜlam 'aḷḷa.* Fair without and foul within. منــاك *minnaak* = من هناك *min hnaak* from there. مني *minnii* = من هني *min hni* from here. طلع مـــن اللعبـــة مغلــــوب *ṭilaᶜ min l-liᶜba maġluub.* He came out of the game defeated. خذوا امية درهم من ألف درهـــم *xaðaw 'imyat dirhim min 'alf dirhim.* They took one hundred dirhams out of one thousand dirhams. 2. since, for, from. من ذاك اليوم وأنا مريض *min ðaak l-yoom w-aana mariiḍ.* I've been ill since that day. من دش الحجرة العيـــال سكتوا *min dašš l-ḥijra, li-ᶜyaaḷ siktaw.* Since he entered the room, the kids have been quiet. أنا هني من زمـــان *'aana hni min zamaan.* I've been here a long time. من زمـــان ونحـــن نــاطرينك *miz zamaan w-niḥin naaṭriinak.* We've been waiting for you for a long time. مـــن اليوم ورايـــح *min l-yoom w-raayiḥ* from now on. شفتك من قبـــل، مـــوب كـــذي؟ *čiftak min gabil, muub čiði?* I've seen you before, haven't I? جـــا من وهل *yaa min wahal.* He came early. 3. from, against. نلبس غـــترة من الحر في القيـــظ والبرد في الشتـــا *nilbas ġitra min l-ḥarr fi l-geeḍ w-l-bard fi š-šita.* We wear a headcloth to protect us from the heat in the summer and the cold in the winter. غطى وجهه من الغبار *ġaṭṭa weeha min li-ġbaar.* He covered his face to protect it from the dust. 4. through, by. دش من الدريشة *dašš min d-diriiša.* He entered through the window. 5. than (with the elative) هذا أحسن من ذاك *haaða 'aḥsan min ðaak.* This one is better than that one. لازم تسمع كلامه؛ هو أكبر منك *laazim tisma^c kalaama; huwa 'akbar minnak.* You have to heed his words; he's older than you. 6. by. مسك الحنش من ذيله *misak l-ḥanaš min ðeela.* He held the snake by the tail. 7. because of, due to, for. كل هذا منك *kill haaða minnak.* This is all because of you. ما أقدر أمشي من الحر *ma 'agdar 'amši min l-ḥarr.* I can't walk because of the heat. مات من الجوع *maat min l-yuu^c.* He starved to death. تعبت من قد ما مشيت *ti^cabt min gadd-ma mišeet.* I got tired from walking so much. 8. when, whenever. من يحكي الكل يسمع له *min yḥači, l-kill yisma^c-la.* When he talks, everyone listens to him. 9. made of, of (material), consisting of. قميص من حرير *gamiiṣ min ḥariir* shirt of silk, silk shirt. خاتم من ذهب *xaatim min ðahab* gold ring.

م ن ح *mnḥ*

منحة *minḥa* p. منح *minaḥ* grant, donation.

م ن خ ١ *mnx*

مناخ *manaax* climate

م ن خ ٢ *mnx*

مناخ *manaax* (no known p.) pasture land, grazing land. (prov.) بقرة مناخ *bgarat manaax* lazy person who lives as a parasite of others.

م ن د ي ل *mndyl*

منديل *mandiil* p. مناديل *manaadiil* handkerchief. هالحين الرجال ما يحمل منديل *halḥiin r-rayyaal ma yḥamil mandiil.* Nowadays, men don't use handkerchiefs.

م ن ز *mnz*

منز *manaz* p. *-aat* crib, cradle.

م ن ع *mn^c*

منع *mina^c* (يمنع *yimna^c*) 1. to prohibit, forbid. منعوا التدخين في الحفيز *min^caw t-tadxiin fi l-ḥafiiz.* They prohibited smoking in the office. منعوه من السفر إلا بإذن من وزارة الداخلية *min^coo min s-safar 'illa b-'iðin min wazaarat d-daaxiliyya.* They prohibited him from traveling except with permission from the ministry of the interior. 2. to prevent, hinder. ما قطع تذكرة؛ منعوه من الدخول *ma ġiṭa^c taðkara; min^coo min d-duxuul.* He had not bought a ticket; they prevented him from entering. صدق الملح يمنع الحلا؟ *ṣidj l-milḥ yimna^c l-ḥala?* Is it true that salt prevents rust?

مانع *maana^c* III to object, oppose, offer resistance. رجال زين؛ ما يمانع *rayyaal zeen; ma ymaani^c.* He's a good man; he won't object. مانع بزواج بنته *maana^c b-zawaag binta.* He was opposed to his daughter's getting married.

امتنع *mtina^c* VIII (with عن *^can*) to stop, abstain from, refrain from. امتنع عن التدخين *mtina^c ^can t-tadxiin.* He stopped smoking.

مناعـة *manaa^c^a* immunity. مناعـة ضـد المـــرض *manaa^c^a ḍidd l-marað* immunity to disease.

مـانع *maani^c^* (act. part. from منع *mina^c^*) p. موانـع *mawaani^c^* 1. objection. مـا عنـدي مـانع *ma ^c^indi maani^c^.* I have no objection. عنـدك أي مـانع؟ *^c^indak 'ayya maani^c^?* Do you have any objection? 2. preventive, preventative. مانع الحـلا *maani^c^ l-ḥala* rust preventative. مانع الرطوبـة *maani^c^ r-ruṭuuba* moisture protection. 3. contraceptive.

ممنـوع *mamnuu^c^* (p.p. from منع *mina^c^*) forbidden, prohibited, banned. التدخين ممنـوع *t-tadxiin mamnuu^c^.* Smoking is forbidden. No smoking. الدخول ممنوع *d-duxuul mamnuu^c^,* ممنـــوع الدخـــول *mamnuu^c^ d-duxuul.* No admittance!

م ن ن ١ mnn

مـن *mann* (يمـن *yminn*) 1. to bless s.o. الله مـن علينـا بنعمتـه *'aḷḷa mann ^c^aleena b-ni^c^imta.* God blessed us with His grace. 2. to desire the return of s.th. عطانا فلوس وعقبه مـن علينـا فيهـا *^c^aṭaana fluus w-^c^ugba mann ^c^aleena fiiha.* He gave us money and then he wanted it back from us.

منـان *mannaan* p. *-iin* one who gives s.th. and then wants it back or expects an equivalent in return, Indian giver.

ممنون *mamnuun* 1. (as a reply to مشكور *maškuur*) You're welcome! 2. grateful, thankful. إذا تسوي هذا، أكـون ممنـون لـك *'iða tsawwi haaða, 'akuun mamnuun-lak.* If you do this, I'll be grateful to you.

ممنونيـة *mamnuuniyya* 1. gratefulness, obligation. 2. pleasure, gladness. بكل ممنونيـة *b-kill mamnuuniyya* with great pleasure.

م ن ن ٢ mnn

مـن *mann* p. منـان *mnaan* measure of weight, approximately 24 kilograms. مـن زمـان كنـا نشـتري العيـش بـالمن *min zamaan činna ništiri l-^c^eeš b-l-mann.* A long time ago we used to buy rice by the *mann.*

م ن ن ٣ mnn

مـن *mann* (with suff. pron. beginning with a vowel) not. مـني رايـح *manni raayiḥ.* I'm not going. مني عارف *manni ^c^aarifk.* I don't know you. منك جايـة وايانا؟ *mannič yaaya wiyyaana?* Aren't you (f.s.) coming with us?

م ن و mnw

منـو *minu* (interr. pron.) = من هو؟ *man huw?* Who? Who is it? منو يتكلم؟ *minu yitkallam?* Who is speaking? منو طرش لـك الخـط؟ *minu ṭarraš-lič l-xaṭṭ?* Who sent you (f.s.) the letter? منو عند الباب؟ *minu ^c^ind l-baab?* Who's at the door?

م ن و ر mnwr

منـور *manwar* p. مناور *manaawir* man-of-war, battleship.

م ن ي mny

تمنـى *tmanna* V to wish. أتمنى لك كل خير *'atmannaa-lak kill xeer.* I wish you the best. تمنيتها تكـون وايانـا *tmanneetta tkuun wiyyaana.* I wished she had been with us. نتمنى لـك السـعادة *nitmannaa-lak s-sa^c^aada.* We wish you happiness.

منـى *mina* Mina (holy place near

Mecca). الحجاج لازم يروحون منى *l-ḥijjaaj laazim yruuḥuun mina.* Pilgrims must go to Mina.

منية *minya* wish desire. منيتها تصير دختورة *minyatta tṣiir daxtoora.* Her wish is to become a doctor.

منية *maniyya* 1. destiny, fate. منيته يموت قتل *maniyyata ymuut gatil.* He's destined to be killed. 2. death. المنية بيد الله *l-maniyya b-yadd aḷḷa.* Death is in God's hands.

م ه ر *mhr*

مهر *mahar* p. مهور *muhuur* dower, bridal money. الشاب ذالحين ما يدور الزواج لان المهر غالي *š-šaabb ðalḥiin ma ydawwir z-zawaaj linn l-mahar ġaali.* Young men nowadays don't want to get married because the dower is expensive.

مهرة *muhra* p. *-aat* filly.

مهارة *mahaara* (v.n.) skill, skillfulness.

ماهر *maahir* skillful, expert. ماهر في الحسانة *maahir fi li-ḥsaana.* He's skillful at giving haircuts. لاعب كورة ماهر *laa^c^ib kuura maahir* skillful soccer player.

م ه ر ج ا ن *mhrjaan*

مهرجان *mahrajaan* p. *-aat* festival, celebration.

م ه ل *mhl*

مهل *mihal* (يمهل *yimhil)* to grant a delay, give s.o. time. امهلني مدة بسيطة وأنا أسد الفلوس اللي عليّ *'imhilni mudda basiiṭa w-aana 'asidd li-fluus illi ^c^alayya.* Grant me a short period of time and I'll pay back the money I owe.

أمهل *'amhal* IV (more common var. مهل *mihal*). See مهل *mihal.*

تمهل *tmahhal* V to proceed slowly and carefully. تمهل في السير *tmahhal fi s-seer.* Drive slowly and carefully.

مهل *mahal* (v.n. from مهل *mihal* or IV أمهل *'amhal*) slowness, ease. على مهلك *^c^ala mahlak.* Take your time. Take it easy. امشي على مهلك *'imši ^c^ala mahlak.* Walk slowly. Drive slowly.

مهلة *muhla* p. *-aat* delay, grace period. عطني مهلة سبوع لاجل أفكر فيها *^c^aṭni muhlat subuu^c^ lajil 'afakkir fiiha.* Give me a week's time in order for me to think it over.

م ه م ا *mhmaa*

مهما *mahma* (conj.) 1. whatever, whatsoever. موب صحيح، مهما يقول *muub ṣaḥiiḥ, mahma yguul.* It's not true, whatever he says. 2. however much, no matter how much. ما يقتنع، مهما حاولت *ma yigtani^c^, mahma ḥaawalt.* He cannot be convinced, however hard you try. رايح أشتريها، مهما كلفت *raayiḥ 'aštiriiha, mahma kallafat.* I'm going to buy it, no matter what it costs. أنطرك، مهما طال الزمان *'anṭurč, mahma ṭaal z-zamaan.* I'll wait for you, however long it takes.

م ه ن *mhn*

مهنة *mihna* p. مهن *mihan* profession, occupation, vocation. التمريض مهنة شريفة *t-tamriið mihna šariifa.* Nursing is a respectable profession.

مهني *mihani* vocational, industrial. مركز التدريب المهني *markaz t-tadriib* *l-mihani* the vocational training center.

م و ب *mwb*

مـوب *muub* (less common var. مو *muu,* مـب *mub*) (neg. part.) not. الهوا مـوب زيـن اليـوم *l-hawa muub zeen l-yoom.* The weather isn't good today. مـوب واجـد *muub waayid* not very much, not a whole lot. مـوب هـني *muub hini* not here. مـوب صـدق *muub ṣidj* not true. اسكت! موب شغلك *'iskit! muub šuǵlak.* Shut up! It's none of your business. اليـوم، مـوب بـاكر *l-yoom, muub baačir* today, not tomorrow. هـا المعـرس مـوب لاقيـين أحسـن منـه *hal-mi*ᶜ*ris muub laagyiin 'aḥsan minna.* We cannot find a better bridegroom. مـوب... ومـوب *muub... w-muub* neither... nor مـوب هـني ومـوب هنـاك *muub hini w-muub hnaak* neither here nor there. موب بارد وموب حـار *muub baarid w-muub ḥaarr* neither cold nor hot. (prov.) موب كل بيضة شحمة وموب كل سودة فحمـة *muub kill beeđa šḥama w-muub kill sooda fḥama.* You cannot judge a book by its cover. (lit., "Not every white thing is a piece of suet, nor is every black thing a piece of charcoal.").

م و ت *mwt*

مـات *maat (يموت ymuut)* to die, become dead. مـات قبـل خمس سـنين *maat gabil xams siniin.* He died five years ago. مات من الكوليرا *maat min l-koleera.* He died of cholera. يحب بنـت عمـه. يمـوت عليها *yḥibb bint* ᶜ*amma. ymuut* ᶜ*aleeha.* He loves his cousin. He would die for her. مات من الجوع *maat min l-yuu*ᶜ. He starved to death.

مـوت *mawwat* II to kill, put to death. اسـتمروا يعذبونـه لـين موتـوه *stammarraw y*ᶜ*ađđbuuna leen mawwatoo.* They continued to torture him until they killed him. مـوت نفسـه مـن الدراسـة *mawwat nafsa min d-diraasa.* He killed himself studying. يحب بنت عمه. مـوت نفسـه عليهـا *yḥibb bint* ᶜ*amma. mawwat nafsa* ᶜ*aleeha.* He loves his cousin. He almost killed himself for her. موت نفسه لين شاف الـدب *mawwat nafsa leen čaaf d-dubb.* He played dead when he saw the bear. خذوا عليه تـراي يمـوت *xadu* ᶜ*alee traay ymawwit.* They gave him an examination that was awfully tough. (prov.) اللي فات مـات *illi faat maat.* Let bygones be bygones. (prov.) الثور الحمر ما يموت إلا حمـر *θ-θoor l-ḥamar ma ymuut 'illa ḥamar.* A leopard cannot change his spots. (derog.) (lit., "A red bull dies only as a red bull.").

استمات *stamaat* X to defy death, risk one's life. الجنود استماتوا في الدفـاع عـن المدينـة *li-jnuud stamaataw fi d-difaa*ᶜ ᶜ*an l-madiina.* The soldiers risked their lives defending the city.

مـوت *moot* death. الموت بيد الله *l-moot b-yadd aḷḷa.* Death is in God's hands.

موتـة *moota* (n. of inst.) p. *-aat* certain kind of death, demise. كا رجال بطال. مات موتـة الكلـب *čaan rayyaal baṭṭaal. maat mootat č-čalb.* He was a bad man. He died like a dog.

ميـت *mayyit* 1. dead, deceased. أبوك طيـب؟ *'ubuuk ṭayyib?* Is your father alive? لا، والله ميـت *la, waḷḷa mayyit.* No, he's dead. طيب والا ميـت؟ *ṭayyib walla mayyit?* Is he dead or alive? ميت من الخـوف *mayyit min l-xoof.* He's scared to death. 2. (p. اموات *mwaat,* أمـوات *'amwaat*) dead man, deceased person. !الله يرحم امواتنا *'aḷḷaah yirḥam mwaatna!* God bless the souls of our dead!

م و ت ر *mwtr*

موتـر *mootar* p. مواتـر *muwaatir, -aat* vehicle, esp. a pickup truck. الموتر عتيق وما يشتغل زين *l-mootar ᶜatiij w-ma yištaġil zeen.* The car is old and doesn't work very well.

م و د ي ل *mwdyl*

موديـل *muudeel* p. *-aat* model. عندي سيارة موديل ستة وتسعين *ᶜindi sayyaara muuddeel sitta w-tisᶜiin.* I have a 1996-model car.

م و ز *mwz*

مـوز *mooz* (coll.) bananas. s. *-a* p. *-aat.* الموز غالي اليوم *l-mooz ġaali l-yoom.* Bananas are expensive today. اشتريت مـوز *štireet mooz.* I bought (some) bananas. كليت موزتين عقب الغدا *kaleet moozteen ᶜugb l-ġada.* I ate two bananas after lunch.

م و س *mws*

مـوس *muus* p. امـواس *mwaas* 1. pen-knife. 2. straight-edged razor. يحسن بالموس *yḥassin b-l-muus.* He shaves with a razor. 3. razor blade.

م و س ي گ *mwsyg*

موسيقى *muusiiga* music.

موسيقي *muusiigi* musical. حفلة موسيقية *ḥafla muusiigiyya* concert.

موسيقار *muusiigaar* p. *-iyya* musician.

م و ع *mwᶜ*

مـاع *maaᶜ* (يميع *ymiiᶜ*) to melt, dissolve. كـل الثلج مـاع *kill θ-θalj maaᶜ.* All the ice melted. الشكر ماع في الماي *š-šakar maaᶜ fii l-maay.* The sugar dissolved in the water.

مـوع *mawwaᶜ* II to melt, dissolve, liquefy s.th. في ها المصنع يموعون المعادن *fi hal-maṣnaᶜ ymawwᶜuun l-maᶜaadin.* In this factory, they melt metals. موع الملح في الماي *mawwaᶜ l-milḥ fi l-maay.* He dissolved the salt in the water.

مايع *maayiᶜ* (act. part. from ماع *maaᶜ*) melted, dissolved.

م و ل¹ *mwl*

مـول *mawwal* II to finance. الحكومة تمـول مشـاريع كثـيرة *li-ḥkuuma tmawwil mašaariiᶜ kaθiira.* The government finances many projects.

مال *maal* p. امـوال *mwaal* 1. wealth, affluence. 2. property, possessions. مـال الحكومـة *maal l-ḥukuuma* the government property. الحكومة صادرت امواله *l-ḥukuuma ṣaadarat mwaala.* The government confiscated his possessions. راسمال *raasmaal* capital. 3. (particle indicating possession or ownership) هـذي السـيارة مـالي *haaði s-sayyaara maali.* This car is mine. مال من ها الشنطة؟ *maal man haš-šanṭa?* Whose bag is this? Who does this bag belong to? 4. for, for the purpose of. ميز مـال طعـام *meez maal ṭaᶜaam* dining table. أنتـين مـال تلفزيـون *'anteen maal talafizyoon* TV antenna.

مـالي *maali* 1. monetary, financial. طوابـع مالية *ṭuwaabiᶜ maaliyya* revenue stamps. 2. fiscal. سنة ماليـة *sana maaliyya* fiscal year.

ماليـة *maaliyya* finance, monetary affairs. وزارة المالية *wazaarat l-maaliyya* the ministry of finance.

تمويـل *tamwiil* (v.n. from II مـول *mawwal*) financing. مـن مسـؤول عـن تمويـل هـا المشـروع؟ *man mas'uul ʿan tamwiil hal-mašruuʿ?* Who's responsible for financing this project?

م و ل ٢ *mwl*

مـوال *mawwaal* p. مواويـل *mawaawiil* song or poem, often sung to the accompaniment of a reed pipe.

م و ل ٣ *mwl*

مـول *muul* (adv.) 1. never. ما يصدق القـول مـول *ma yṣaddig l-gool muul.* He never believes what's said. فلـوس مـا عنـده مـول *fluus ma ʿinda muul.* He doesn't have any money. بعد ما أشوفك مـول؟ *baʿad ma 'ačuufič muul?* Will I ever see you (f.s.) again. 2. exactly. بيتي على الشارع مـول *beeti ʿala š-šaariʿ muul.* My house lies exactly on the street.

م و م ي ا *mwmyaa*

موميا *muumya* mummy.

م و ن *mwn*

مان *maan (يمون ymuun)* (with على *ʿala*) to be on close terms with s.o., be a good friend to s.o. جابوا مديـر جديـد، يتشـدد على العمـال. فيـه أحـد يمـول عليـه؟ *yaabaw mudiir yidiid, yitšaddad ʿala l-ʿummal. fii 'aḥad ymuul ʿalee?* They brought a new manager who is strict with the workmen. Is there anyone close to him?

مـون *mawwan* II to supply with provisions to s.o. الجيش يمون الجنود بكل شي يحتاجونـه *l-jeeš ymawwin li-jnuud b-kill šayy yiḥtaajuuna.* The army provides soldiers with anything they need.

تمـون *tmawwan* V pass. of II مـون *mawwan.* تمونـا بكـل شـي حـق الكشـتة *tmawwana b-kill šayy ḥagg l-kašta.* We supplied ourselves with everything we need for the picnic.

مونة *muuna* provisions.

تمويـن *tamwiin* (v.n. from II مـون *mawwan*) food supply. مراكـز تمويـن *maraakiz tamwiin* food supply centers.

م و ي *mwy*

مـوج *mooy* (coll.) waves. s. *-a* p. *-aat.* السماميك ما يدشون البحر اليوم بسبب الموج *s-simaamiič ma ydiššuun l-baḥar l-yoom b-sabab l-mooy.* The fishermen won't go to sea today because of the waves.

م ي *my*

ميـة *miya* (common var. امية *'imya*) one hundred.

م ي ب ر *mybr*

ميبرة *meebara* p. *-aat* darning needle.

م ي ت *myt*

ميت *mayyit.* See under **م و ت** *mwt.*

م ي د ا ر *mydaar*

ميـدار *miidaar* p. ميـادير *mayaadiir* fishing line, fishing rod. كنـا نحـدق بالميـادير، يعـني بـالخيوط والدجيـج *činna nḥadig b-l-mayaadiir, yaʿni b-li-xyuuṭ w-d-dijiij.* We were fishing with lines, rods and nets.

م ي د ان *mydaan*

ميـدان *miidaan* p. ميادين *mayaadiin* 1. square, open space. 2. field (of contest), arena. ميـدان السـباق *miidaan s-sibaag* the race track, the race course.

م ي ز ١ *myz*

ميز *mayyaz* II 1. (with بين *been*) to distinguish, differentiate. ما أقـدر أميز بـين الاثنـين *ma 'agdar amayyiz been li-θneen.* I can't distinguish between the two. 2. (with عن *ᶜan*) to consider better than. تقدر تميز بو ظبي عن الدوحة؟ *tigdar tmayyiz bu ḍabi ᶜan d-dooḥa?* Would you consider Abu Dhabi better than Doha?

تميز *tmayyaz* V (with عـن *ᶜan*) to be distinguished, be distinct from. يتميز عـن غيره بأنـه لحيةٍ غانمة *yitmayyaz ᶜan ġeera b-'anna liḥyatin ġaanma.* He's distinguished from other men because he's a very nice guy.

امتاز *mtaaz* VIII (with ب *b-*) 1. to be distinguished, be marked by. بـو ظبي تمتاز بهواها الزين في الشتا *bu ḍabi timtaaz b-hawaaha z-zeen fi š-šita.* Abu Dhabi is distinguished by its good weather in the winter. 2. to distinguish oneself. أم النار تمتاز بآثارها *'umm n-naar timtaaz b-'aaθaarha.* Umm al-Nar distinguished itself by its antiquities. 3. (with على *ᶜala*) to surpass, excel, be better than. امتازت عليهن كلهـن بجمالها *mtaazat ᶜaleehin killahin b-jamaalha.* She surpassed all of them in beauty.

مـيزة *miiza* p. *-aat* distinguishing feature, characteristic.

تمييز *tamyiiz* (v.n. from II ميز *mayyaz*) 1. differentiation. بـدون تمييز *b-duun tamyiiz* unintentionally. 2. discrimination, favoritism. تمييز عنصري *tamyiiz ᶜunṣuri* racial discrimination. 3. appeal (jur.) محكمة تمييز *maḥkamat tamyiiz* highest appeal court, court of cassation.

امتياز *mtiyaaz* (v.n. from VIII امتاز *mtaaz*) 1. distinction, honor. نجح في الامتحان بامتياز *nijaḥ fi li-mtiḥaan bi-mtiyaaz.* He passed the examination with distinction. 2. concession, franchise.

ممتاز *mumtaaz* 1. outstanding, excellent, exceptional. طالب ممتاز *ṭaalib mumtaaz* outstanding student. 2. premium super. تبي بانزين عادي والا ممتاز؟ *tabi baanziin ᶜaadi walla mumtaaz?* Do you want regular or premium gasoline?

م ي ز ٢ *myz*

ميز *meez* p. ميوز *myuuz, -aat* 1. table. ميز مال طعام *meez maal ṭaᶜaam* dining table. 2. desk.

م ي ل ١ *myl*

مال *maal* (يميل *ymiil*) 1. (with ل *l-*) to be more in favor of, incline, tend, have a liking to. تميل للشقرا والا للسمرا؟ *tmiil liš-šagra walla lis-samra?* Are you more in favor of a blonde or a brunette? أنا أميل للرياضيات أكثر من العلوم *'aana 'amiil lir-riyaaḍiyyaat 'akθar min l-ᶜuluum.* I tend to like mathematics more than science. 2. to tend, incline, have a tendency. لون

الطوفة يميل للبياض *loon ṭ-ṭoofa ymiil lil-bayaaḏ̣.* The color of the wall tends toward white. !مالت عليك الدنيا *maalat ᶜaleek d-dinya!* May evil befall you!

ميل *mayyal* II 1. to make s.o. sympathetic, favorably disposed, inclined. صرف عليها فلوس واجد لاجل يميلها اله *ṣiraf ᶜaleeha fluus waayid lajil ymayyilha 'ila.* He spent a lot of money on her to make her like him. 2. to tilt, incline. لا تميل اللوح، ترى يوقع *la tmayyil l-looḥ, tara yoogaᶜ.* Don't tilt the board, or it'll fall down.

تمايل *tmaayal* VI to sway, swing. فيه ناس يتمايلون لين يمشون *fii naas yitmaayluun leen yimšuun.* There are people who sway as they walk.

استمال *stamaal* X to win over, bring to one's side, gain favor with s.o. المدير حاول يستميل بعض الموظفين *l-mudiir ḥaawal yistamiil baᶜḏ̣ li-mwaḏ̣ḏ̣afiin.* The manager tried to win over some of the employees.

ميل *meel* p. ميول *myuul* (v.n. from مال *maal*) leaning, inclination, disposition.

مايل *maayil* (act. part. from مال *maal*) 1. leaning, leaning over, bending down. برج بيزا المايل *burj biiza l-maayil* the leaning tower of Pisa. 2. bent, not straight. ليش مايل؟ عدله *leeš maayil? ᶜaddla.* Why is it bent? Make it straight.

م ي ل ٢ *myl*

ميل *miil* p. اميال *myaal* mile. ستين ميل في الساعة *sittiin miil fi s-saaᶜa* sixty miles per hour. مسافة امية ميل *masaafat i'myat miil* distance of one hundred miles.

م ي م *mym*

ميم *miim* name of the letter م *m.*

م ي ن ا *mynaa*

مينا *miina* p. مواني *mawaani* harbor, port.

م ي و *myw*

ميوه *mayoo* p. ميوهات *-haat* woman's bathing suit.

م ي ي ١ *myy*

ميّ *mayy,* مية *mayya* (more common var. ماي *maay*). See under **م ا ي** *maay.*

م ي ي ٢ *myy*

ميّة *miyya* (more common var. مية *miya,* امية *'imya*). See under **م ي** *my.*

ن

ن ا ر ي ل *naaryl*

ناريل *naariil* (coll.) coconuts. s. *-a*. النـاريل نسـتورده مـن الخـارج *n-naariil nistawrida min l-xaarij.* We import coconuts from abroad.

ناريلة *naariila* p. *-aat* hubble-bubble, Persian waterpipe. عمرك دخت ناريلـة؟ *ᶜumrak duxt naariila?* Have you ever smoked a hubble-bubble?

ن ا س *naas*

ناس *naas.* See under **ء ن س** *'ns.*

ن ا م و س *naamws*

نـاموس *naamuus* 1. (p. نواميـس *nuwaamiss*) prize money (for a camel race or horse race). تستاهل الناموس يـا خلفـان *tistaahal n-naamuus ya xalfaan.* You deserve the prize, Khalfan. 2. honor, integrity. ما عنـده نـاموس؛ يخلـي بنتـه تشـتغل بـين الرجـاجيل *ma ᶜinda naamuus; yxaḷḷi binta tištaġil been r-rayaayiil.* He hasn't got any honor; he lets his daughter work among men.

ن ا ي *naay*

نـاي *naay* p. *-aat* kind of flute without mouthpiece.

ن ا ي ل و ن *naaylwn*

نـايلون *naayloon* nylon. قميـص نـايلون *gamiiṣ naayloon* nylon shirt.

ن ب ت *nbt*

نبـت *nibat* (ينبـت *yanbit)* 1. to grow. الزرع ما ينبت في هـذي الأرض *z-zariᶜ ma yanbit fi haaði l-'arḍ.* Plants do not grow in this soil. 2. to sprout, germinate. البـذر اللي تزرعـه في هـذي الأرض ينبـت عقـب سـبوع *l-biðir illi tizraᶜa fi haaði l-'arḍ yanbit ᶜugub subuuᶜ.* The seeds you plant in this soil will sprout in one week.

نبتة *nabta* p. *-aat* seedling, shoot.

نبات *nabaat* (coll.) plants, vegetation.

ن ب ذ *nbð*

نبيذ *nabiið* wine.

منبـوذ *manbuuð* (p.p.) p. *-iin* outcast, pariah.

ن ب ر *nbr*

منـبر *minbar* p. منـابر *manaabir* pulpit. الشـيخ صعـد المنـبر *š-šeex ṣiᶜad l-minbar.* The Shaikh ascended to the pulpit.

ن ب ش *nbš*

نبـش *nibaš* (ينبش *yanbiš)* 1. to dig up, unearth. نبشوا قبره ودفنـوه في مكـان ثـاني *nbašaw gabra w-difanoo fi mukaan θaani.* They dug up his grave and buried him in another place. 2. to bring out into the open, reveal. هذي قضايـا عتيقـة؛ لا تنبشـها *haaði gaḍaaya ᶜatiija; la tinbišša.* These are very old problems; don't bring them out into the open.

نبـش *nabbaš* II 1. to keep digging up, keep unearthing. ظـل ينبـش ضـدي *ḍall ynabbaš ḍiddi.* He kept digging up things against me. 2. = نبش *nibaš*

ن ب ط *nbṭ*

نبطي *nabaṭi* (adj.) colloquial, not literary. شعر نبطي *šiᶜir nabaṭi* colloquial poetry.

ن ب ظ *nbð̣*

نبض *nabuð̣* pulse, hearbeat. الدختر جس نبضي وقال مصخن *d-daxtar jass nabð̣i w-gaal mṣaxxan.* The doctor felt my pulse and said I had a fever.

ن ب ع *nbᶜ*

نبع *nibaᶜ (ينبع yinbaᶜ)* to spring, originate, flow. ها النهر ينبع من الجبل *han-nahir yinbaᶜ min l-yibal.* This river originates in the mountain.

نبع *nabiᶜ* spring, source. ماي نبع *maay nabiᶜ* spring water.

ن ب غ *nbġ*

نابغة *naabiġa* p. نوابغ *nawaabiġ* genius, distinguished person.

ن ب گ *nbg*

نبق *nabig* (coll.) lotus fruit. s. *-a.* شجر النبق يطلع هني *šiyar n-nabig yiṭlaᶜ hni.* Lotus trees grow here.

ن ب ل *nbl*

نبيل *nabiil* 1. (p. *-iin*) noble. إنسان نبيل *'insaan nabiil* noble person. 2. (p. نبلا *nubala*) aristocratic, highborn.

ن ب ه *nbh*

نبه *nabbah* II 1. to remind. نبهته على طلب الزيادة حقي *nabbahta ᶜala ṭalab z-ziyaada ḥaggi.* I reminded him of my request for an increment. 2. to warn, caution. لا تلومني. نبهته ما ينبش الموضوع *la tluumni. nabbahta ma yinbiš l-mawð̣uuᶜ.* Don't blame me. I warned him not to bring out the subject into the open.

تنبه *tnabbah* V pass. of II نبه *nabbah.*

انتبه *ntibah* VIII to pay attention. !انتبه قدامك شرطة *ntabih! jiddaamak širṭa.* Pay attention! There are policemen in front of you. إذا تنتبه، تفتهم *'iða tintibih, tiftihim.* If you pay attention, you'll understand.

نباهة *nabaaha* (v.n.) 1. intelligence. 2. alertness, awareness.

تنبيه *tanbiih* (v.n. from II نبه *nabbah*) 1. warning, cautioning. 2. notification, notice.

انتباه *ntibaah* (v.n. from VIII انتبه *ntibah*) attention.

منتبه *mintabih* (act. part. from VIII انتبه *ntibah*) 1. paying attention. 2. alert, watchful.

ن ب و *nbw*

نبي *nabi* p. أنبيا *'anbiya* prophet. النبي محمد *n-nabi muḥammad* Prophet Muhammad. فلسطين أرض الأنبيا *falasṭiin 'arð̣ l-'anbiya.* Palestine is the land of the Prophets.

نبوي *nabawi* (adj.) of or pertaining to Prophet Muhammad.

ن ت ج *ntj*

نتج *nitaj* 1. (imperf. ينتج *yantij*) to result, be a result (of s.th.). حكي فارغ. ما نتج شي *ḥači faariġ. ma nitaj šayy.* Empty talk. There were no results. نتج شي من ذاك الاجتماع؟ *nitaj šayy min ðaak li-jtimaaᶜ?* Has anything resulted from that meeting? 2. (imperf. ينتج *yintij*) to produce, make, yield.

الإمارات تنتج بترول واجد *l-imaaraat tintij batrool waayid.* The U.A.E. produces a lot of oil. ها المصنع ينتج جواتي *hal-maṣnaᶜ yintij juwaati.* This factory makes shoes. الأرض في العين تنتج أكثر من الأرض في بو ظبي *l-'arđ fi l-ᶜeen tintij 'akθar min l-'arđ fi bu đabi.* The soil in Al-Ain has a greater yield than the soil in Abu Dhabi.

استنتج *stantaj* X to conclude, deduce, infer. استنتجت من كلامك انك موب موافق *stantajt min kalaamak 'innak muub mwaafig.* I concluded from your talk that you weren't in agreement. تقدر تستنتج كل هذا إذا قريت المخطوطة زين *tigdar tistantij kill haađa 'iđa gareet l-maxṭuuṭa zeen.* You can deduce all of this if you read the manuscript well.

نتيجة *natiija* p. نتايج *nataayij* 1. result, outcome, consequence. انشاالله نتيجتك في الامتحان زينة *nšaaḷḷa natiijatk fi li-mtiḥaan zeena.* I hope your examination result will be good. الحكومة قالت «لازم تنزل الأسعار» *li-ḥkuuma gaalat, "laazim tinzil l-'asᶜaar."* The government said, "Prices have to go down." خلنا نشوف النتيجة *xaḷḷna nčuuf n-natiija.* Let's see what happens. هذي نتيجة اللي يسكر *haađi natiijt illi yiskar.* This is the consequence of those who drink. 2. use, benefit. ما فيه نتيجة إذا حكيت واياه. عنيد *ma fii natiija 'iđa ḥačeet wiyyaa. ᶜaniid.* You won't get anywhere if you talk to him. He's stubborn.

إنتاج *'intaaj* (v.n. from نتج *nataj*) 1. production. 2. producing, making, manufacturing.

استنتاج *stintaaj* (v.n. from X استنتج *stantaj*) inference, conclusion.

منتج *mintij* (act. part. from نتج *nataj*) 1. having produced, manufactured. 2. productive.

ن ت ف *ntf*

نتف *nitaf* (ينتف *yantif*) 1. to pluck, pull out (feathers). نتف ريش الدجاجة *nitaf riiš d-diyaaya.* He plucked the feathers of the chicken.

نتف *nattaf* II = نتف *nitaf.*

تنتف *tnattaf* V pass. of II نتف *nattaf.*

منتوف *mantuuf* (p.p. from نتف *nitaf*) plucked, pulled out (feathers).

ن ث ي *nθy*

نثية *niθya* p. *-aat* female. نثية الكبش النعجة *niθyat č-čabš li-nᶜaya.* The female of the ram is the ewe. النثية تاخذ نص ما ياخذ الذكر في الإرث *n-niθya taaxiđ nuṣṣ ma yaaxiđ đ-đakar fi l-'irθ.* The female gets half of what the male gets in inheritance.

ن ج ب *njb*

نجيب *najiib* p. *-iin,* نجبا *nujaba* 1. noble, high-minded person. 2. (adj.) noble, high-minded.

ن ج ح *njḥ*

نجح *nijaḥ* (ينجح *yinjaḥ*) 1. to pass (an examination). نجحت في الامتحان، الحمد لله *nijaḥt fi li-mtiḥaan, l-ḥamdu lil-laah.* I passed the examination, praise be to God. عقب ما نجح، عطوه جايزة *ᶜugub-ma nijaḥ, ᶜaṭoo jaayza.* After he had passed, they gave him a prize. بـو علي نجح للصـف الخـامس في المدرسـة الليليـة *bu ᶜali nijaḥ laṣ-ṣaff l-xaamis fi l-madrasa l-layliyya.* Abu Ali passed the fifth grade at the night school. 2. to succeed, be successful. نجح في التجارة لانه أمـين *nijaḥ fi t-tijaara linna 'amiin.* He succeeded, did well in business, because he was honest. العملية نجحـت وزال الخطـر عنـه، الحمـد لله *l-ᶜamaliyya njaḥat w-zaal l-xaṭar ᶜanna, l-ḥamdu lil-laah.* The operation was a success and he was no longer in danger, praise be to God.

نجح *najjaḥ* II to pass s.o., let s.o. succeed. ما جاوب زين، بس المدرس نجحه *ma jaawab zeen, bass l-mudarris najjaḥa.* He didn't answer well, but the teacher passed him.

نجاح *najaaḥ* (v.n. from نجح *nijaḥ*) 1. passing (an examination). مـبروك بالنجـــاح في الامتحــــان! *mabruuk b-n-najaaḥ fi li-mtiḥaan!* Congratulations on passing the examination. خذ بس درجة نجاح *xað bass darajat najaaḥ.* He took only a passing grade. 2. success. أمانتـه سـبب نجاحـه في حياتـه *'amaanta sabab najaaḥa fi ḥayaata.* His honesty is the reason for his success in his life.

ن ج د *njd*

استنجد *stanjad* X to appeal for aid, ask for help. بعض دول أفريقيا استنجدت بهيئـة الأمـم بسـبب المجاعـة *baᶜǒ duwal 'afriigya stanjadat b-hay'at l-'umum b-sabab l-majaaᶜa.* Some African nations appealed to the United Nations for aid because of the famine.

نجد *najd* Najd (region in Saudi Arabia), the Arabian Plateau as opposed to حجاز *ḥijaaz* Hijaz, the western region of Saudi Arabia.

نجدي *najdi* 1. characteristic of Najd. 2. (p. *-yyiin*) native of Najd. 3. (n., no known p.) kind of goat or lamb.

نجـدة *najda* 1. (v.n.) aid, help, support. 2. (p. *-aat*) squad, such as a police squad. النجـدة تخـالف المسـرع *n-najda txaalif l-misriᶜ.* The police squad issue violation tickets to speeders.

ن ج ر *njr*

نجر *nijar* (more common var. نير *niyar*). See under **ن ي ر** *nyr.*

نجـار *najjaar* p. نجاجـير *najaajiir* carpenter. وصينا على ميز مـال طعـام عنـد النجـار *waṣṣeena ᶜala meez maal ṭaᶜaam ᶜind n-najjaar.* We ordered a dining table from the carpenter's shop.

نجـارة *njaara* (common var. نيـارة *nyaara*) 1. carpentry. 2. wood shavings.

ن ج ل *njl*

نجيلة *nijiila* p. نجـايل *najaayil* 1. palm seedling, palm shoot. 2. young palm.

ن ج م *njm*

نجـم *najim* p. نجـوم *njuum* male movie star.

نجمـة *najma* 1. p. نجوم *njuum* female movie star. 2. (p. *-aat*) star (more common var. نيمـة *niyma*). See under **ن ي م** *nym.*

ن ج و *njw*

نجا *nija* (ينجـى *yinja)* (with من *min*) to escape (s.th.), be saved, be rescued from s.th. نجا من الموت *nija min l-moot.* He escaped death.

نجى *najja* II to save s.o. (from s.th.), rescue, deliver. الله سبحانه وتعالى نجاني من الموت *'aḷḷa subḥaanahu wa taᶜaalaa najjaani min l-moot.* God, may He be praised and exalted, saved me from death. ما ينجيك من ها المصيبة إلا الله *ma ynajjiik min hal-muṣiiba 'illa ḷḷaah.* Only God will save you from this calamity.

نجاة *najaa* (v.n. from نجا *nija*) escape, deliverance, salvation. النجاة من الموت *n-najaa min l-moot* escape from death.

ن چ ت *nčt*

نكت *ničat (ينكت yančit)* to put food into dishes. حرمتي نكت الأكل وتغدينا *ḥurumti ničtat l-'akil w-tġaddeena.* My wife put the food into dishes and we had lunch.

ن ح ت *nḥt*

نحت *niḥat* (ينحت *yinḥat*) to chisel, sculpture. نحتوا اسمه على الصخرة *nḥitaw 'isma ᶜala li-ṣxara.* They chiseled his name on the rock. نحتوا تمثال حق الجندي المجهول *nḥitaw timθaal ḥagg l-jindi l-majhuul.* They sculptured a stature for the unknown soldier.

نحت *naḥt* (v.n.) 1. sculpturing, sculpture. 2. stonecutting.

نحات *naḥḥaat* p. *-a, -iin* 1. sculptor. 2. stonecutter.

ن ح ر *nḥr*

انتحر *ntiḥar* VIII to commit suicide. انتحر لانها تزوجت غيره *ntiḥar linha tazawwajat ġeera.* He committed suicide because she married someone else.

انتحار *ntiḥaar* (v.n.) suicide, committing suicide.

ن ح ز *nḥz*

منحاز *minḥaaz* p. مناحيز *minaaḥiiz* mortar (vessel).

ن ح س *nḥs*

نحاس *nuḥaas* (coll.) copper. أريزونا تشتهر بالنحاس *'arizoona tištahir b-n-nuḥaas.* Arizona is famous for copper. نحاس أصفر *nuḥaas 'aṣfar* brass.

ن ح ش *nḥš*

انحاش *nḥaaš* VII to escape, run away. زخوه الشرطة، بس انحاش منهم *zaxxoo š-širṭa, bass nḥaaš minhum.* The police arrested him, but he escaped from them.

منحاش *minḥaaš* 1. (adj.) fleeing, runaway. 2. (p. *-iin*) fugitive, runaway.

ن ح ل *nḥl*

نحل *naḥal* (coll.) bees. s. نحلة *nḥala* p. *-aat.*

ن ح ن *nḥn*

نحن *niḥin.* See under ح ن ن[2] *ḥnn.*

ن ح و *nḥw*

تنحى *tnaḥḥa* V to move or go far away. تنحى عن جماعته وتاه في البر *tnaḥḥa ᶜan yamaaᶜta w-taah fi l-barr.* He went far away from his group and got lost in the desert.

تنيحى *tneeḥa* VI 1. to speak literary Arabic. فيه ناس قليلين يتنيحون *fii naas* *galiiliin yitneeḥuun.* There are a few people who speak literary Arabic. 2. to philosophize. !بس عـــاد تتنيحى *bass ᶜaad titneeḥa!* I've had enough of your philosophizing! Don't pretend to be such a philosopher any more!

نحو *naḥu* grammar.

نحـــوي *naḥwi* poetry in literary Arabic. هذا نحوي، موب شعر نبطي *haaða naḥwi, muub šiᶜir nabaṭi.* This is literary poetry, not colloquial poetry.

ناحيـــة *naaḥya* p. نواحـــي *nawaaḥi* 1. region, section of a city, province. في ذيـــك الناحيـــة *fi ðiič n-naaḥya* in that region. من كل ناحيـــة *min kill naaḥya* from everywhere. 2. aspect, viewpoint. مـــن كـــل النواحـــي *min kill n-nawaaḥi* in every respect. من ناحيتي أنا، ما عندي مانع *min naaḥiiti 'aana, ma ᶜindi maaniᶜ.* As for me, I have no objection. من ناحية قانونية *min naaḥya gaanuuniyya* from a legal standpoint, de jure. من ناحيـــة ثانيـــة *min naaḥya θaanya* on the other hand.

ن خ ب nxb

انتخـــب *ntixab* VIII 1. to elect. انتخبوه رئيس *ntixboo ra'iis.* They elected him president. 2. to select, choose, pick. انتخب اللي تبغيه *ntaxib illi tabġii.* Select the one you want. Select whatever you want.

انتخاب *ntixaab* p. *-aat* election.

منتخب *muntaxab* (p.p.) 1. having been elected. الرئيـــس المنتخـــــــب *r-ra'iis l-muntaxab* the president-elect. 2. (p. *-aat*) selected team (in sports). منتخب الإمارات لعب ضد منتخب قطر *muntaxab l-'imaaraat liᶜab ðidd muntaxab giṭar.* The U.A.E. national team played the national team of Qatar.

ن خ ر nxr

نخر *nixar* (ينخر *yanxir*) to gnaw on s.th., eat away at s.th. هو مثل السوسة اللـــي تنخر في الليحـــــان *huwa miθl s-suusa lli tanxir fi l-liiḥaan.* He's like a termite that gnaws on planks of wood.

ن خ ل nxl

نخـــل *naxxaḷ* II to sift. نخلت الطحين *naxxḷat ṭ-ṭaḥiin.* She sifted the flour.

تنخل *tnaxxal* V pass. of II نخل *naxxal.*

نخـــل *naxaḷ* (coll.) date palms, palm trees. s. نخلـــة *nxaḷa* p. *-aat.* (prov.) الطول طول نخلة والعقل عقـــل صخلـــة *ṭ-ṭuul ṭuul nxaḷa w-l-ᶜagiḷ ᶜag-ḷ ṣxaḷa.* The mind of a child and the body of a man. (lit., "The height is that of a date palm and the mind is that of a young goat."). فوق النخل *foog n-naxaḷ* doing very well, prosperous.

منخل *munxuḷ* p. مناخل *manaaxiḷ* sieve.

ن خ و nxw

نخـــى *nixa* (ينخى *yanxa)* to arouse the sense of honor. إذا تنخاه، ما يقصـــر *iða tinxaa, ma ygaṣṣir.* If you arouse his sense of honor, he won't let you down.

نخوة *naxwa* (v.n.) sense of honor, pride, dignity. لحيةٍ غانمـــة. صـــاحب نخـــوة *liḥyatin ġaanma. ṣaaḥib naxwa.* He's a good man. He's an honorable man.

ن خ ي nxy

نخي *naxxi* (coll.) (common var. *naxxiy*) chick-peas. s. *-yya.* النخي نطبخه وايا لحم *n-naxxi niṭbaxa wiyya laḥam.* We cook chick-peas with meat.

ن د ب *ndb*

انتدب *ntidab* VIII to authorize, commission, empower (s.o. to do s.th.). الحكومة انتدبته يمثلها في المؤتمر *l-ḥukuuma ntidbata ymaθθilha fi l-mu'tamar.* The government authorized him to represent it in the conference.

مندب *mandab,* as in باب المندب *baab l-mandab* Bab Al-Mandeb (strait between SW Arabia and Africa).

مندوب *manduub* p. *-iin* delegate, representative. الحكومة طرشت مندوب يمثلها في اجتماعات الشركة *l-ḥukuuma ṭarrašat manduub ymaθθilha fi jtimaa*ᶜ*aat š-šarika.* The government sent a delegate to represent it in the company meetings.

منتدب *muntadab* (p.p. from VIII انتدب *ntidab*) delegated, commissioned.

ن د ر *ndr*

نادر *naadir* 1. rare. حالة نادرة *ḥaala naadra* rare case. معدن نادر *ma*ᶜ*dan naadir* rare metal. 2. (p. *-iin*) excellent person. نادر ما *naadir-ma* rarely, seldom. نادر ما أرقد قبل الساعة ثنعش *naadir-ma 'argid gabil s-saa*ᶜ*a θna*ᶜ*aš.* I rarely go to bed before twelve (midnight).

ن د ف *ndf*

ندف *nidaf (يندف yandif)* to fluff or tease, comb (cotton). ندف القطن حق الشبرية *nidaf l-guṭun ḥagg š-šibriyya.* He fluffed the cotton of the mattress.

نداف *naddaaf* p. *-iin,* ندادیف *nadaadiif* one who fluffs the cotton of mattresses, pillows, etc.

ن د م *ndm*

ندم *nidam (یندم yindam)* (with على ᶜ*ala*) to be sorry for. ندم على اللي سواه *nidam* ᶜ*ala lli sawwaa.* He felt sorry for what he had done.

تندم *tnaddam* V = ندم *nidam.* سواه وتندم *sawwaaha w-tnaddam.* He did it and was sorry.

ن د ي *ndy*

نادى *naada* III 1. to call, summon s.o. ناديته وتكلمنا في الموضوع *naadeeta w-tkallamna fi l-mawḏuu*ᶜ. I called him and we talked about the subject. 2. to call out, shout to s.o. ناديته من بعيد *naadeeta min ba*ᶜ*iid.* I called out to him from a distance 3. (with على ᶜ*ala*) to invite s.o. to s.th. ناديناهم على العشا *naadeenaahum* ᶜ*ala l-*ᶜ*aša.* We invited them to dinner.

ندوة *nadwa* p. *-aat* convention, conference.

نادي *naadi* p. نوادي *nawaadi* club, clubhouse. تعشينا في النادي *t*ᶜ*aššeena fi n-naadi.* We had dinner at the club. النادي السياحي *n-naadi s-siyaaḥi* the Tourists' Club. نادي رياضي *naadi riyaaḏi* athletic club. نادي البيتش *naadi l-biič* the Beach Club.

ن ذ ر *nðr*

نذر *niðar (ينذر yinðir)* to vow, make a vow, pledge (a sacrifice) to God. نذرت تذبح كبش إذا جابت ولد *nðarat tiðbaḥ čabš 'iða yaabat walad.* She vowed to sacrifice a ram if she had a baby boy.

أنـــذر *'anðar* IV 1. to warn. كم مرة أنذرتك مـــا تســوي هـــذا؟ *čam marra 'anðartak ma tsawwi haaða?* How many times have I warned you not to do this? 2. to give notice to s.o., notify s.o. أنذرنا نترك الشقـــة *'anðarna nitrik š-šigga.* He gave us notice to vacate the apartment.

نذر *niðir* (v.n. from نذر *niðar*) 1. vow, solemn pledge. 2. (p. نـــذور *nðuur*) offering (to God).

إنذار *'inðaar* (v.n. from IV أنذر *'anðar*) p. *-aat* warning.

ن ذ ل *nðl*

نذل *naðil* p. انذال *nðaal* rogue, rascal, knave.

ن ز ف *nzf*

نزيف *naziif* bleeding, hemorrhage.

ن ز ل *nzl*

نزل *nizal (*ينزل *yanzil)* 1. to go down, come down, descend. نزل من فوق *nizal min foog.* He came down from upstairs. عقب ما نطرته نص ســـاعة، نـــزل. *ᶜugub-ma niṭarta nuṣṣ saaᶜa, nizal.* After I had waited for him for half an hour, he came down. 2. to get off, disembark, get down. نزلت عند وكالـــة السفر *nizalt ᶜind wakaalat s-safar.* I got off at the travel agency. نزلوا المسافرين مـــن الطيـــارة *nizlaw li-msaafriin min ṭ-ṭayyaara.* The travelers deplaned. 3. to land, come down. الطيارة بعد ما نزلت *ṭ-ṭayyaara baᶜad ma nzalat.* The plane hasn't landed yet. 4. to fall. ما ينزل مطر واجد هني *ma yanzil muṭar waayid hni.* It doesn't rain much here. 5. to go down, fall, drop. الأسعار نزلت شويـــة *l-'asᶜaar nzalat šwayyat.* Prices have gone down a little. 6. to stay, take lodging. وين تنزل لين تروح بو ظبي؟ *ween tinzil leen truuḥ bu ḍhabi?* Where do you stay when you go to Abu Dhabi? نزل عندنا *nizal ᶜindana.* He stayed with us. 7. to come into (the market), come in season, appear. اليح ينزل الشهر الجاي *l-yiḥḥ yanzil š-šahar l-yaay.* Watermelons will come to the market next month.

نزل *nazzal* II 1. to unload. نزلنا الشكر من اللوري *nazzalna š-šakar min l-loori.* We unloaded the sugar from the truck. نزلوا طماط السعديات في السوق *nazzalaw ṭamaaṭ s-saᶜdiyyaat fi s-suug.* They took the Sadiyat tomatoes to market. 2. to lower, decrease, lessen. ينزلـــون أسعار اللحم في رمضان *ynazzluun 'asᶜaar l-laḥam fi rumḍaan.* They lower the prices of meat during Ramadan. نزلوه من مدير إلى كراني *nazzaloo min mudiir 'ila karraani.* They demoted him from manager to clerk. 3. to cause to get off, disembark, dismount. نزلـــني يم السفارة *nazzilni yamm s-safaara.* Drop me near the embassy. نزلوا العبرية في آخر الشـــارع *nazzalaw l-ᶜibriyya fi 'aaxir š-šaariᶜ.* They had the passengers get off at the end of the street. 4. to take down, bring down. نزلت الصندوق تحت *nazzalt ṣ-ṣanduug taḥat.* I took the box downstairs. نزلت الولد عن ظهر الحصـــان *nazzalt l-walad ᶜan ḍahar li-ḥṣaan.* I took the boy down from the back of the horse. نزل البردة مـــن الشمس *nazzal l-parda min š-šams.* He let the curtain down because of the sun. الله يـــنزل عليـــك الغضـــب! *'aḷḷa ynazzil ᶜaleek l-ġaḍab!* May God send his wrath down upon you! 5. to land, put ashore (troops). نزلوا جنود على الجزيرة. *nazzalaw jnuud ᶜala l-yiziira.* They landed soldiers on the island. 6. to put up, lodge, accommodate. نزلونا عندهم مدة سبوع *nazzaloona ᶜindahum muddat subuuᶜ.* They put us up at their place for a week. 7. (with على *ᶜala*) to reveal, send down (a revelation to a prophet). الله نزل القرآن على سيدنا محمد. *'aḷḷa nazzal l-ġur'aan ᶜala sayyidna muḥammad.* God revealed the Quran to our prophet Muhammad.

تنزل *tnazzal* V to lower oneself, condescend. ما يتنزل يحكي وايا أحد *ma yitnazzal yiḥči wiyya 'aḥad.* He won't lower himself to talk to anyone.

تنازل *tnaazaal* VI 1. (with عن *ᶜan*) to give up, relinquish. الملك تنازل عن العرش *l-malik tnaazal ᶜan l-ᶜarš.* The king gave up the throne. 2. to give in, yield. عنيد؛ ما يتنازل *ᶜaniid; ma yitnaazal.* He's stubborn; he doesn't give in.

نزول *nzuul* (common var. *nuzuul*) (v.n. from نزل *nizal*) 1. descend, descent, dismounting, getting down or off. 2. landing.

إنزال *'inzaal* (military) landing, invasion.

ن ز ه *nzh*

نزاهة *nazaaha* (v.n.) honesty, purity, integrity.

نزيه *naziih* above reproach, blameless, honest.

منتزه *muntazah* p. *-aat* park, recreation ground. في العيد الناس يروحون المنتزهات والحدايق العامة *fi l-ᶜiid n-naas yruuḥuun l-muntazahaat w-l-ḥadaayig l-ᶜaamma.* During the feast holiday, people go to parks and public gardens.

ن س ب *nsb*

ناسب *naasab* III 1. to become related to s.o. by marriage. ناسبناه بزواج بنتنا *naasabnaa b-zawaaj bintana.* We became related to him by marrying our daughter to him. ولد الشيخ ناسبنا *wild š-šeex naasabna.* The Shaikh's son married into our family. 2. to suit s.o., be comfortable for s.o. هالوقت يناسبك؟ *hal-wagt ynaasibk?* Does this time suit you? ما يناسبني أنش الساعة خمس *ma ynaasibni 'anišš s-saaᶜa xams.* It's not comfortable for me to get up at five o'clock. 3. to be commensurate, compatible, in keeping with. المعاش على قد الحال؛ ما يناسب شغلي *l-maᶜaaš ᶜala gadd l-ḥaal; ma ynaasib šuġli.* The salary isn't much; it's not commensurate with my job.

تناسب *tnaasb* VI pass. of III ناسب *naasab.*

انتسب *ntisab* VIII (with إلى *'ila*) 1. to be relative to, be related to s.o. حمد ينتسب إلى الرميثات *ḥamad yintasib 'ila r-rmeeθaat.* Hamad is a relative of the Rumaithy family. 2. to join, become affiliated, associated with. انتسبت إلى نادي الموظفين *ntisabt 'ila naadi l-muwaððafiin.* I joined the employee's club.

نسب *nasab* p. أنساب *'ansaab* lineage, descent, ancestry. شعلينا من حسبه ونسبه! *š-ᶜaleena min ḥasaba w-nasaba!* What have we got to do with his lineage and ancestry!

نسبة *nisba* p. نسب *nisab* 1. rate, ratio. نسبة الجهل *nisbat l-jahil* the illiteracy rate. نسبة الموت *nisbat l-moot* the death rate. 2. proportion. نسبة مئوية *nisba mi'awiyya* percentage. نسبة الأولاد إلى البنات في هذا الصف عشرين إلى حدعش *nisbat l-'awlaad 'ila l-banaaat fi haaða ṣ-ṣaff ᶜišriin 'ila ḥdaᶜaš.* The proportion of boys to girls in this class is twenty to eleven. بالنسبة إلى *b-n-nisba 'ila* with regards to, concerning, regarding. بالنسبة إلي، ما عندي مانع *b-n-nisba 'ili, ma ᶜindi maaniᶜ.* As far as I am concerned, I have no objections.

نسيب *nisiib* p. نسايب *nisaayib* in-law, relative by marriage. نسيبي، رجل بنتي، جا عندنا *nisiibi, rajil binti, ya ᶜindana.* My son-in-law (my daughter's husband) came to our place. نسيبي، رجل اختي، رجال زين *nisiibi, rajil ixti, rayyaal zeen.* My brother-in-law (my sister's husband) is a good man.

أنسب *'ansab* (elat.) 1. (with من *min*) more suitable, proper than. 2. (with foll. n.) the most suitable, proper.

مناسبة *munaasaba* 1. suitability, appropriateness. 2. (p. *-aat*) occasion. في هذي المناسبة *fi haaði l-munaasaba* on this occasion. مناسبة سعيدة *munaasaba saᶜiida* happy occasion. بمناسبة *b-munaasabat* on the occasion of. بمناسبة ترفيعه *b-munaasabat tarfiiᶜa* on the occasion of his promotion. بالمناسبة *b-l-munaasaba* incidentally, by the way. بالمناسبة، متى عرست؟ *b-l-munaasaba, mita ᶜarrast?* Incidentally, when did you get married?

مناسب *munaasib* appropriate, suitable, proper. وقت مناسب *wagt munaasib* appropriate time.

ن س خ *nsx*

نسخ *nisax* (ينسخ *yinsax*) to copy (s.th.). المدرس ما نجحه لانه نسخ من صديقه *l-mudarris ma najjaḥa linna nisax min ṣidiija.* The teacher didn't pass him because he had copied from his friend.

نسخ *nasx* (v.n.) copying.

نسخة *nusxa* p. نسخ *nusax* copy. عندك نسخة ثانية من التقرير؟ *ᶜindak nusxa θaanya min t-tagriir?* Do you have another copy of the report? نسخة طبق الأصل *nusxa ṭibg l-'aṣil* an exact copy of the original.

ن س ر *nsr*

نسر *nisir* p. نسور *nsuur* eagle.

نسرة *nisra* p. *-aat* small piece of meat given to an eagle, eagle morsel.

ن س ف *nsf*

نسف *nisaf* (ينسف *yansif*) 1. to blow up, blast s.th. نسفوا الجسر *nisfaw l-jisir.* They blew up the bridge. 2. to swoop down, dive down on. النسر نسف الحبارة *n-nisir nisaf l-ḥabaara.* The eagle swooped down on the sand grouse.

نسف *nasf* (v.n.) blowing up, demolishing.

نساف *nassaaf* p. *-aat* tip-truck, dump truck.

ن س ل *nsl*

تناسل *tnaasal* VI to reproduce, propagate, multiply. الفيران تتناسل بسرعة

l-fiiraan titnaasal b-sur^c^a. Mice reproduce rapidly.

نسل *nasil* offspring, progeny. تحديد النسل *taḥdiid n-nasil* birth control.

منسول *mansuul* hair that has been combed.

ن س م *nsm*

نسمة *nasma* p. *-aat* breath of fresh air.

نسيم *nasiim* wind, breeze. نسيم البحر *nasiim l-baḥar* sea breeze. نسيم البر *nasiim l-barr* land breeze.

ن س ن س *nsns*

نسناس *nisnaas* p. نسانيس *nasaaniis* long-tailed monkey.

ن س ي *nsy*

نسى *nisa, nasa* (ينسى *yinsa, yansa)* 1. to forget. نسيت المفتاح في الحفيز *niseet l-miftaaḥ fi l-ḥafiiz.* I forgot the key in the office. لا تنسى ذيك الحزة *la tinsa ðiič l-ḥazza.* Don't forget that appointment. 2. (with foll. imperf.) to forget to do s.th. نسيت أطرش الخط *niseet 'aṭarriš l-xaṭṭ.* I forgot to mail the letter.

نسى *nassa* II to make or cause s.o. to forget. شو اللي نساك ذيك الحزة؟ *šu lli nassaak ðiič l-ḥazza?* What made you forget that appointment?

تناسى *tnaasa* VI 1. to pretend to have forgotten. ذكرته بالموضوع، بس حاول يتناسى *ðakkarta b-l-mawðuu^c^, bass ḥaawal yitnaasaa.* I reminded him of the subject, but he pretended to have forgotten it. 2. to ignore, be or become oblivious to s.th. حاولت أتناسى الموضوع، بس ما قدرت *ḥaawalt 'atnaasa l-mawðuu^c^, bass ma gidart.* I tried to ignore the matter, but I couldn't.

انتسى *ntisa* VIII to be forgotten. هاللي سويته ما ينتسى *hal-li sawweeta ma yintisa.* What you have done cannot be forgotten.

نسيان *nisyaan* (v.n. from نسى *nisa*) forgetfulness, oblivion.

ن ش ب *nšb*

نشب *nišab* (ينشب *yinšab)* (with في *fi*) to stick, cling, adhere (to). نشبت فيني ذيك المشكلة *nišbat fiini ðiič l-muškila.* That problem stayed with me.

ناشب *naašab* III to cause problems, trouble to s.o. قل لي شو اللي تبغاه. لا تناشبني *gul-li šu lli tibġaa. la tnaašibni.* Tell me what you want. Don't cause me trouble.

تناشب *tnaašab* VI (with وايا *wiyya*) = III ناشب *naašab.*

نشب *nišab* (n. of inst.) trouble, annoyance. (prov.) بغيناها طرب صارت نشب *baġeenaaha ṭarab ṣaarat nišab.* A wolf in sheep's clothing.

نشبة *nišba* p. *-aat* problem, difficulty.

نشاب *niššaab* p. نشاشيب *nišaašiib* arrow. قوس ونشاب *goos w-niššaab* bow and arrow.

ن ش د *nšd*

نشد *nišad* (ينشد *yanšid)* to ask for help. إذا تنشده ما يقصر *iða tinšida ma ygaṣṣir.* If you ask him for help, he won't let you down.

ناشد *naašad* III to appeal to, implore s.o. الرئيس ناشد المواطنين يحافظون على

ن ش ش nšš

نـش našš (ينش ynišš) 1. to get up. أنش الســاعة ســت الصبــاح *'anišš s-saaᶜa sitt ṣ-ṣabaaḥ.* I get up at six in the morning. 2. (with مــن min) to leave. نش مــن الحجــرة *našš min l-ḥijra.* He left the room. 3. to stand up. رمسني الشيخ ونشــيت *rammasni š-šeex w-naššeet.* The Shaikh talked to me and I stood up.

ن ش ط nšṭ

نشـط naššaṭ II to invigorate, energize. المشــي ينشــط الإنســان *l-maši ynaššiṭ l-'insaan.* Walking invigorates people.

تنشـط tnaššaṭ V to be or become energetic and strong. إذا تتمشى تتنشط *'iða titmašša titnaššaṭ.* If you walk around, you'll get some energy.

أنشـط 'anšaṭ (elat.) 1. (with من min) more energetic, active than. 2. (with foll. n.) the most energetic, active.

نشاط našaaṭ energy, vigor.

نشـيط našiiṭ energetic, active. ها الكولي كلــش نشــيط *hal-kuuli killiš našiiṭ.* This coolie is very energetic

ن ش ف nšf

نشـف naššaf II (common var. II يبس yabbas) to dry, make s.th. dry. ينشفون الســمك ويصدرونــه *ynaššfuun s-simač w-yṣaddruuna.* They dry the fish and export it. نشف إيدينك *naššif 'iideenak.* Dry your hands.

تنشـف tnaššaf V to dry oneself. تسبح وتنشــف بهالفوطــة الجديــدة *tsabbaḥ w-tnaššaf b-hal-fuuṭa l-yidiida.* Take a bath and dry yourself with this new

الأمــن *r-ra'iis naašad li-mwaaṭniin yḥaafðuun ᶜala l-'amin.* The president appealed to the citizens to preserve peace.

نشـدة nišda p. *-aat* 1. appeal for help. 2 request for information.

ن ش ر nšr

نشـر nišar (ينشــر yanšar) 1. to broadcast, spread around. الإذاعــة نشــرت الأخبــار *l-'iðaaᶜa nišrat l-'axbaar.* The broadcasting station broadcast the news. 2. to publish. نشر المدرس كتاب جديــد *nišar l-mudarris ktaab yidiid.* The teacher published a new book. الجريدة نشرت أسامي الناجحين في الامتحــان *l-jariida nišrat 'asaami n-naajiḥiin fi li-mtiḥaan.* The newspaper printed the names of those who passed the examination.

انتشر ntišar VIII pass. of نشر *nišar.*

نشــرة našra p. *-aat* publication, periodical. نشــرة رسميــة *našra rasmiyya* official publication. نشرة أخبــار *našrat 'axbaar* newscast.

منشار minšaar p. مناشير *manaašiir* saw.

ناشـر naašir (act. part. from نشر *nišar*) p. *-iin* publisher.

منشـور manšuur (p.p. from نشر *nišar*) 1. published, made public. 2. (p. مناشير *manaašiir*) pamphlet, circular.

منتشـر mintašir (act. part. from VIII انتشــر *ntišar*) widespread, current. المــدارس منتشــرة في الإمــارات *l-madaaris mintašra fi l-'imaaraat.* Schools are all over the U.A.E.

bath towel.

ناشف *naašif* (common var. حاف *ḥaaff*) dry, not wet. الهوا ناشف اليوم *l-ḥawa naašif l-yoom.* The weather is dry today. الهدوم ناشفة *li-hduum naašfa.* The clothes are dry.

ن ش ل *nšl*

نشلة *našla* cold, catarrh. صابته نشلة *ṣaabata našla.* He caught a cold.

نشال *naššaal* p. *-iin* pickpocket.

ن ش م *nšm*

نشمي *našmi* (adj.) 1. helpful, willing to be of service. التنديل خوش رجال، ونشمي بعد *t-tindeel xooš rayyaal, w-našmi bacad.* The foreman is a good person, and he is helpful too. 2. (p. نشامة *našaama*) helpful person.

ن ش ي *nšy*

نشى *našša* II to starch (clothes, linen, etc.). لا تنشي القمصان *la tnašši l-gumṣaan.* Don't starch the shirts.

نشى *niša* (coll.) starch, corn starch.

ن ص ب *nṣb*

نصيب *naṣiib* 1. share, portion. هذا نصيبي من الإرث *haaða naṣiibi min l-'irθ.* This is my share of the inheritance. 2. luck, chance. ما له نصيب *ma la naṣiib.* He's not lucky. الدنيا كلها نصيب *d-dinya killaha naṣiib.* Life is only a chance. قسمة ونصيب *jisma w-naṣiib* fate and destiny. صار قسمة ونصيب وخطبنا البنت من أبوها *ṣaar jisma w-naṣiib w-xaṭabna l-bint min 'ubuuha.* We were lucky and we asked the girl's father for her hand in marriage.

يانصيب *yaanaṣiib* (common var. لاتري *laatri*) lottery.

ن ص ح *nṣḥ*

نصح *niṣaḥ (ينصح yinṣaḥ)* to advise, counsel s.o. نصحته ما يسافر ذالحين *niṣaḥta ma ysaafir ðalḥiin.* I advised him not to travel now. انصحه ما يصاحب هذيل الناس *'inṣaḥa ma yṣaaḥib haðeel n-naas.* Advise him not to befriend these people.

نصيحة *naṣiiḥa* p. نصايح *naṣaayiḥ* advice, sincere advice.

ن ص ر *nṣr*

نصر *niṣar (ينصر yunṣur)* to make victorious, grant victory to. الله ينصر المسلمين! *'aḷḷa yunṣur l-muslimiin!* God make the Muslims victorious.

انتصر *ntiṣar* VIII to triumph, be victorious. انتصرنا في حرب الخليج *ntiṣarna fi ḥarb l-xaliij.* We won the Gulf War. جيشهم انتصر على جيش العدو *jeeššum ntiṣar cala jeeš l-cadu.* Their army triumphed over the enemy's army.

نصر *naṣir* (v.n. from نصر *naṣir*) victory, triumph. النصر من الله *n-naṣir min aḷḷa.* Victory is from God.

نصراني *naṣraani* p. نصارى *naṣaara* 1. Christian. في كنيسة حق النصارى على السيف *fii kaniisa ḥagg n-naṣaara cala s-siif.* There's a Christian church on the beach. 2. an American or a European. بالنصراني *b-n-naṣraani* in English. يقرا ويكتب بالنصراني *yigra w-yiktib b-n-naṣraani.* He reads and writes in English.

نصرانية *naṣraaniyya* Christianity.

انتصار *ntiṣaar* (v.n. from VIII انتصر *ntiṣar*) p. *-aat* victory, triumph.

منصوري *manṣuuri* p. مناصير *manaaṣiir* Mansuri tribesman, one belonging to the Mansuri tribe.

ن ص ص ١ *nṣṣ*

نص *naṣṣ* (ينص *ynuṣṣ*) (with على *ᶜala*) to call for, stipulate, specify. القانون ينص على تعليم الحريم *l-gaanuun ynuṣṣ ᶜala taᶜliim l-ḥariim.* The law calls for the educating of women. القانون ينص على انه كل أجنبي لازم يكون عنده إقامة *l-gaanuun ynuṣṣ ᶜala 'inna kill 'aynabi laazim ykuun ᶜinda 'igaama.* The law stipulates that every foreigner must have a residence permit.

نص *naṣṣ* p. نصوص *nuṣuuṣ* 1. text. اقرا لي نص القانون *'igraa-li naṣṣ l-gaanuun.* Read me the text of the law. 2. wording. بالنص *b-n-naṣṣ* verbatim. قريت له الإعلان بالنص *gareet-la l-'iᶜlaan b-n-naṣṣ.* I read him the advertisement verbatim.

ن ص ص ٢ *nṣṣ*

نص *nuṣṣ* p. نصاص *nṣaaṣ* (less common var. نصيفة *naṣiifa* p. نصايف *naṣaayif*) half. نص درهم *nuṣṣ dirhim* half a dirham. نصهم *nuṣṣum* half of them. نص الليل *nuṣṣ l-leel* midnight. الساعة خمسة ونص *s-saaᶜa xamsa w-nuṣṣ.* It's 5:30. زامي يبند الساعة اثنعش نص الليل *zaami ybannid s-saaᶜa θnaᶜaš nuṣṣ l-leel.* My (work) shift finishes at twelve midnight. (prov.) نص المية خمسين *nuṣṣ l-miya xamsiin.* Take it easy. (lit., "Half a hundred is fifty.").

ن ص ف *nṣf*

نصيفة *naṣiifa* p. نصايف *naṣaayif* half (a thing, a quantity, etc.) (prov.) راعي النصيفة سالم *raaᶜi n-naṣiifa saalim.* Half a loaf is better than none.

نصفية *niṣfiyya* p. *-aat* weight, approx. 25 kilograms = ½ *guuniyya*. See قونية *guuniyya* under **گ و ن ي** *gwny.*

إنصاف *'inṣaaf* (v.n.) justice, fairness.

منصف *munṣif* (act. part.) p. *-iin* 1. fair, just. 2. righteous man.

ن ط ح *nṭḥ*

نطح *niṭaḥ* (ينطح *yinṭaḥ*) to butt. الكبش نطح الخروف *č-čabš niṭaḥ l-xaruuf.* The ram butted the lamb.

تناطح *tnaaṭaḥ* VI to butt each other. الكباش يتناطحون *li-kbaaš yitnaaṭḥuun.* The rams are butting each other.

نطحة *naṭḥa* (n. of inst.) p. *-aat* butt, thrust.

ن ط ر *nṭr*

نطر *niṭar* (ينطر *yanṭir*) to wait for, await s.o. نطرناه وبعده ما جا *niṭarnaa w-baᶜda ma ya.* We waited for him, and he hasn't come yet.

ناطر *naaṭir* (act. part.) waiting for, awaiting s.o. من زمان ونحن ناطرينك *min zamaan w-niḥin naaṭrinnak.* We've been waiting for you for a long time.

ناطور *naaṭuur* p. نواطير *nuwaaṭiir* watchman, guard. يشتغل ناطور في الليل *yištaġil naaṭuur fi l-leel.* He works as a night watchman. 2. scarecrow. تحصل نواطير في كل مزرعة *tḥaṣṣil nuwaaṭir fi kill mazraᶜa.* You will find scarecrows in every farm.

ن ط ط *nṭṭ*

نـط *naṭṭ (ينط yniṭṭ)* to butt in, jump in. لا تنـط. هـا الموضـوع مـا يخصـك *la tniṭṭ. hal-mawḍuuᶜ ma yxuṣṣak.* Don't butt in. This matter doesn't concern you.

ن ط گ *nṭg*

نطق *niṭag (ينطق yanṭig)* 1. to speak, utter. كلش تعبان. ما يقـدر ينطـق أي شـي *killiš taᶜbaan. ma yigdar yanṭig 'ayya šayy.* He's very tired. He can't say anything. انطق! ليش سـاكت؟ *'inṭig! leeš saakit?* Speak up! Why are you quiet? 2. to pronounce. تقدر تنطق ها الكلمة؟ *tigdar tanṭig hač-čalma?* Can you pronounce this word?

نطق *naṭṭag* II to make or cause s.o. to speak. الأم تحاول تنطق طفلها *l-'umm tḥaawil tnaṭṭig ṭiflaha.* The mother is trying to make her baby talk.

استنطق *stanṭag* X to interrogate, question, cross-examine s.o. زخـوه وخـذوه الشـرطة لاجـل يستنطقونه *zaxxoo w-xaḍoo š-širṭa lajil yistanṭguuna.* They arrested him and took him to the police station in order to interrogate him.

منطق *manṭig* logic.

منطقة *manṭiga* p. منـاطق *manaaṭig* district, zone.

ن ظ ر *nḍr*

نظر *niḍar (ينظر yanḍur)* (with في *fi*) to look into, examine. المدير رايح ينظـر في الموضوع ويعلمنـا *l-mudiir raayiḥ yanḍur fi l-mawḍuuᶜ w-yᶜallimna.* The manager is going to look into the matter and he will let us know.

انتظر *ntiḍar* VIII = نطر *niṭar*. See نطر under **ن ط ر** *nṭr*.

نظر *naḍar* 1. consideration, examination, contemplation. الطلب حقك تحـت النظر *ṭ-ṭalab ḥaggak taḥt n-naḍar.* Your request is under consideration. ممكـن تعيـد النظـر في الموضـوع؟ *mumkin tᶜiid n-naḍar fi l-mawḍuuᶜ?* Will you please reconsider the matter? أنـت صـادق. هـا القضيـة فيهـا نظر *'inta ṣaadj. hal-gaḍiyya fiiha naḍar.* You are right. This is an unsolved problem. 2. eyesight, vision. قصـير النظـر *gaṣiir n-naḍar* short-sighted. طويل النظر *ṭawiil n-naḍar* far-sighted. 3. opinion, point of view. في نظـري *fi naḍari* in my opinion. شو وجهة نظرك بهـاالموضوع؟ *šu wujhat naḍark b-hal-mawḍuuᶜ?* What's your opinion about the subject?

نظرة *naḍra* (n. of inst.) p. *-aat* look, glance.

نظريـة *naḍariyya* p. *-aat* 1. theory, hypothesis. 2. theorem.

نظرياً *naḍaariyyan* theoretically. نظرياً، أنـا مـوب مسـؤول *naḍariyyaan, 'aana muub mas'uul.* Theoretically, I'm not responsible.

نظـارة *naḍḍaara.* See كشـمة *čašma* under **چ ش م** *čšm*.

منظر *manḍar* p. منـاظر *manaaḍir* 1. sight, view. فيه مناظر حلـوة في بلادنـا *fii manaaḍir ḥilwa fi blaadna.* There are beautiful sights in our country. 2. scene (of a play).

منظرة *manḍara* p. *-aat,* مناظر *manaaḍir* mirror.

ن ظ ف nḍf

نظـف *niḍaf (ينظـف yinḍaf)* to be or become clean. الهدوم غسلتهم ونظفوا *li-hduum ġasalittum w-niḍfaw.* I washed the clothes and they got clean. ها الثوب ما ينظف إلا إذا غسلته باليد *haθ-θoob ma yinḍaf 'illa 'iḍa ġasalta b-l-yadd.* This dress won't get clean unless you wash it by hand.

نظـف *naḍḍaf* II to clean, make clean, cleanse. تنظف الحجرة كل يوم *tnaḍḍif l-ḥijra kill yoom.* She cleans the room every day. نظف الميز حقك قبل لا تطلع *naḍḍif l-meez ḥaggak gabil-la tiṭlaᶜ.* Clear your desk before you leave.

تنظـف *tnaḍḍaf* V pass. of II نظف *naḍḍaf.*

نظافة *naḍaafa* cleanness, cleanliness, neatness. (prov.) النظافة من الإيمان *n-naḍaafa min l-'iimaan.* Cleanliness is next to godliness.

نظيف *naḍiif* p. *-iin*, نظاف *nḍaaf* 1. clean, neat. الحجرة وصخة، موب نظيفة *l-ḥijra waṣxa, muub naḍiifa.* The room is dirty, not clean. 2. good, well-taken care of. سيارة نظيفة *sayyaara naḍiifa* good car.

أنظف *'anḍaf* (elat.) 1. (with من *min*) cleaner, neater than. 2. better, better taken care of. 3. (with foll. n.) the cleanest, neatest. 4. the best.

منظف *munaḍḍif* (act. part. from II نظف *naḍḍaf*) 1. (p. *-iin*) janitor, sweeper. المنظف جا الساعة خمس ونظف الحفيز *l-munaḍḍif ya s-saaᶜa xams w-naḍḍaf l-ḥafiiz.* The janitor came at five and cleaned the office. 2. (p. *-aat*) cleaning agent, cleanser.

ن ظ م nḍm

نظـم *naḍḍam* II 1. to arrange, organize, put in order. نظم الكراني الطلبات حسب الأسبقية *naḍḍam l-karraani ṭ-ṭalabaat ḥasb l-'asbagiyya.* The clerk arranged the applications according to the date received. بنتي نظمت حجرتها *binti naḍḍamat ḥijratta.* My daughter straightened her room. 2. to regulate, adjust. هذا الولف ينظم مجرى الماي *haaḍa l-wilf ynaḍḍim majra l-maay.* This valve regulates the flow of water.

تنظـم *tnaḍḍam* V pass. of II نظم *naḍḍam.*

انتظـم *ntiḍam* VIII to be or become well organized, well arranged. انتظم الشغل لين عينوا مدير جديد *ntiḍam š-šuġul leen ᶜayyanaw mudiir yidiid.* The work became well-organized when they appointed a new manager. هالحجرة منتظمة زين *hal-ḥijra mintaḍma zeen.* This room is very well-arranged.

نظـام *niḍaam* 1. regular arrangement, order. 2. system. نظام الحكم *niḍaam l-ḥukum* the system of government.

نظامي *niḍaami* 1. systematic, orderly. 2. regular. جيش نظامي *jeeš niḍaami* regular army.

تنظيـم *tanḍiim* (v.n. from II نظم *naḍḍam*) 1. arrangement. 2. control. تنظيم المرور *tanḍiim l-muruur* traffic control. 3. regulation, adjustment.

انتظـام *ntiḍaam* (v.n. from VIII انتظم *ntiḍam*) regularity, orderliness. بانتظام *b-ntiḍaam* (adv.) regularly, in an orderly manner, normally.

منظومة *manðuuma* p. *-aat* poem in literary Arabic.

منظم *mnaðð̣am* (p.p. from II نظم *nað̣ð̣am*) 1. well arranged, ordered, tidy. 2. regular. غير منظم *ġeer mnað̣ð̣am* irregular.

منظمة *munað̣ð̣ma* p. *-aat* organization. منظمة فتح *munað̣ð̣amata fatiḥ* the P.L.O.

ن ع ج n^cj

نعجة *na^{c}ja*. See نعية *n^{c}aya* under **ن ع ي** *n^{c}y*.

ن ع س n^cs

نعس *ni^{c}is (ينعس yin^{c}as)* to be sleepy, drowsy. نعست. أبغى أرقد *ni^{c}ist. 'abġa 'argid.* I've gotten sleepy. I want to go to bed.

نعس *na^{cc}as* II to cause to be sleepy, drowsy. ها الأغنية تنعس *hal-'uġniya tna^{cc}is.* This song makes one drowsy.

نعس *na^{c}as* (v.n.) sleepiness, drowsiness. تغلب عليّ النعس ورقدت *tġallab ^{c}alayya n-na^{c}as w-ragatt.* Drowsiness overcame me and I fell asleep.

نعسان *na^{c}saan* sleepy, drowsy.

ن ع ش ١ $n^cš$

نعش *ni^{c}aš (ينعش yan^{c}iš)* to dance, moving the hair left and right in a rhythmic motion. النعاشات قامن ينعشن *n-na^{cc}aašaat gaaman yan^{c}išin.* The female dancers began to dance.

نعيش *ni^{c}iiš* special kind of female dance (see نعش *ni^{c}aš* above). ها النعاشات ينعشن كلش زين *han-na^{cc}aašaat yan^{c}išin killiš zeen.* These female dancers dance very beautifully.

نعاشة *na^{cc}aaša* p. *-aa* female dancer (girl who dances in the manner described above, under نعش *ni^{c}aš*).

ن ع ش ٢ $n^cš$

نعش *ni^{c}aš (ينعش yin^{c}iš)* to refresh, invigorate. ها البارد ينعش الإنسان *hal-baarid yin^{c}iš l-'insaan.* This soft drink refreshes people.

انتعش *nti^{c}aš* VIII to be refreshed, invigorated. روح اسبح وانتعش *ruuḥ isbaḥ w-nti^{c}iš.* Go take a shower and refresh yourself.

نعش *na^{c}aš* p. نعوش *n^{c}uuš,* نعاش *n^{c}aaš* coffin. نغسل الميت ونحطه في نعش قبل ما ندفنه *nġassil l-mayyit w-nḥuṭṭa fi na^{c}aš gabil-ma nidifna.* We wash the dead person and put him in a coffin before we bury him.

إنعاش *'in^{c}aaš* recovery. حجرة الإنعاش *ḥijrat l-'in^{c}aaš* the recovery room (in a hospital). إنعاش اقتصادي *'in^{c}aaš gtiṣaadi* economic boom.

منعش *mun^{c}iš* (act. part. from نعش *ni^{c}aš*) invigorating, refreshing. الهوا منعش اليوم *l-hawa mun^{c}iš l-yoom.* The weather is invigorating today. البارد منعش *l-baarid mun^{c}iš.* A soft drink is refreshing.

ن ع ل n^cl

نعل *na^{c}al* p. نعول *n^{c}uul* pair of sandals.

ن ع م n^cm

نعم *ni^{c}im (ينعم yin^{c}am)* to be or become fine, powdery. ها الهيل ما ينعم أكثر *hal-heel ma yin^{c}am 'akθar.* This cardamom cannot be made finer.

نعم *na*

نعم *na^{c}^{c}am* II to powder, grind. نعم القهوة أكثر *na^{c}^{c}im li-ghawa 'akθar.* Make the coffee beans finer.

أنعم *'an^{c}am* IV (of God) 1. (with على *^{c}ala*) to be bountiful to s.o., to bestow favors upon s.o. الحمد لله! الله أنعم علينا *l-ḥamdu lil-laah! 'aḷḷa 'an^{c}am ^{c}aleena.* Praise be to God! God was good to us. God made our life comfortable. 2. (with على *^{c}ala* and ب *b-*) to give s.o. s.th. الله أنعم عليهم بالخير *'aḷḷa 'an^{c}am ^{c}aleehum b-l-xeer.* God made them wealthy. الله أنعم عليهم بولد *'aḷḷa 'an^{c}am ^{c}aleehum b-walad.* They were blessed with a baby boy.

تنعم *tna^{c}^{c}am* V 1. to live in luxury, lead a life of comfort and ease. متنعمين في حياتهم *mitna^{c}^{c}miin fi ḥayaattum.* They're living in luxury. 2. (with ب *b-*) to enjoy s.th. روح تونس وتنعم بحياتك قبل لا تموت *ruuḥ twannas w-tna^{c}^{c}am b-ḥayaatak gabil-la tmuut.* Go have a good time and enjoy your life before you pass away.

نعم *na^{c}am* (common var. إي *'ii*) 1. yes! نعم، رحت الدختر *na^{c}am, riḥt d-daxtar.* Yes, I went to the doctor. إي نعم! *'ii na^{c}am!* Yes, indeed! Certainly! 2. (asking the speaker to repeat) yes? I beg your pardon! What did you say? نعم؟ ارفع صوتك *na^{c}am? 'irfa^{c} ṣootak.* Yes? Speak louder.

نعمة *ni^{c}ma* p. نعم *ni^{c}am* 1. blessing, grace, benefaction. الحمد لله! هذي نعمة من الله *l-ḥamdu lil-laah! haaði ni^{c}ma min aḷḷa.* Praise be to God! This is a blessing from God. 2. good food. الحمد لله! شبعت. نعمة *l-ḥamdu lil-laah! šibi^{c}t. ni^{c}ma.* Praise be to God! I'm full. This is good food. ابن نعمة *'ibin ni^{c}ma* man from a wealthy family. f. بنت نعمة *bint ni^{c}ma.*

نعامة *na^{c}aama* p. *-aat* ostrich.

نعيم *na^{c}iim* comfort, ease. عايش في نعيم وغيره في جحيم *^{c}aayiš fi na^{c}iim w-ġeera fi jaḥiim.* He's living very comfortably and others are having a bad time. جنات النعيم *jannaat n-na^{c}iim* paradise.

نعيم *ni^{c}iim* (adj.) 1. fine, powdery. شكر نعيم *šakar ni^{c}iim* fine sugar. 2. soft. ها البز نعيم *hal-bazz ni^{c}iim.* This cloth is soft.

أنعم *'an^{c}am* (elat.) 1. (with من *min*) softer than. 2. (with foll. n.) the softest.

ن ع ن ا ع *n^{c}n^{c}*

نعناع *ni^{c}naa^{c}* (coll.) 1. mint. 2. peppermint, mint candy.

ن ع ي *n^{c}y*

نعجة *n^{c}aya* p. *-aat*, نعاج *n^{c}aay* ewe, female sheep. الكبش ذكر النعجة *č-čabš ðakar li-n^{c}aya.* The ram is the male of the ewe. (prov.) إيش على الذيب من ضراط النعجة؟! *'iiš ^{c}ala ð-ðiib min ḍraaṭ li-n^{c}aya?!* (lit., "What harm can the fart of a ewe do to a wolf?!") A drop in the bucket.

ن ع ي م *n^{c}ym*

نعيم *n^{c}eem*: آل نعيم *'aal n^{c}eem* Al-Neem, the ruling family of Ajman.

نعيمي *n^{c}eemi* Neemi, one of the ruling family of Ajman.

ن غ ل *ngl*

نغل *naġaḷ* p. نغول *nġuuḷ*, نغال *nġaaḷ*

bastard, illegitimate child. ابن النغل! النغل *n-naġal 'ibn n-naġal!* (abusive term) son of a bitch! (prov.) اللي ما يطلع على أبوه نغل *'illi ma yiṭla^c ^cala 'ubuu naġal.* (derog.) Like father like son.

ن ف ث *nfθ*

نفاثة *naffaaθa* : طيارة نفاثة *ṭayyaara naffaaθa* jet airplane.

ن ف خ *nfx*

نفخ *nifax* (ينفخ *yanfix*) 1. to inflate, fill with air. نفخنا التيوبات ونزلنا البحر. *nifaxna t-tyuubaat w-nizalna l-baḥar.* We inflated the tubes and went down to the sea. 2. (with على *^cala*) to blow on. breathe on. نفخت على الأكل لاجل يبرد *nifaxt ^cala l-'akil lajil yabrid.* I blew on the food so it would get cool.

انتفخ *ntifax* VIII pass. of نفخ *nifax.* تاير ها السيكل ما ينتفخ *taayir has-seekal ma yintifix.* This bicycle tire cannot be inflated.

نفاخ *nfaax* (v.n. from نفخ *nifax*) 1. inflating, blowing up, filling with air. 2. swelling (e.g., of the stomach).

نفاخة *naffaaxa* p. *-aat* balloon. العيال يبون نفاخات *li-^cyaaḷ yabuun naffaaxaat.* The children want balloons.

نافوخ *naafuux* top of the head.

منفاخ *minfaax* p. منافخ *manaafix* 1. bellows. منفاخ الحداد *minfaax l-ḥaddaad* the blacksmith's bellows. 2. air pump, tire pump.

منفوخ *manfuux* (p.p. from نفخ *nifax*) 1. inflated, blown up. التاير منفوخ *t-taayir manfuux.* The tire is inflated. 2. puffed up, conceited. ليش منفوخ ها الشكل؟ *leeš manfuux haš-šakil?* Why are you so puffed up?

ن ف ذ *nfð*

نفذ *naffað* II 1. to do, perform, discharge. ينفذ اللي تقوله له اياه *ynaffið illi tgul-la-yyaa.* He does what you tell him to do. 2.to carry out, execute (a sentence). نفذوا حكم الإعدام في القاتل أمس الفجر *naffðaw ḥukm l-'i^cdaam fi l-gaatil 'ams l-fajir.* They carried out the death sentence on the killer yesterday at daybreak.

تنفذ *tnaffað* V pass. of II نفذ *naffað* 1. to be carried out, executed. حكم الإعدام تنفذ فيه *ḥukm l-'i^cdaam tnaffað fii.* The death sentence has been carried out on him. 2. to carry out, do. كل أوامر الشيخ تنفذت *kill 'awaamir š-šeex tnaffaðat.* All the Shaikh's orders have been carried out.

تنفيذ *tanfiið* (v.n. from II نفذ *naffað*) 1. carrying out, execution (of orders, etc.). 2. doing, performing.

نفوذ *nufuuð* authority, influence.

ن ف ر *nfr*

نفر *nafar* p. أنفار *'anfaar, -aat* person, individual. كان في السيارة خمسة أنفار. *čaan fi s-sayyaara xamsat 'anfaar.* There were five people in the car. ها السيارة تشل خمسة أنفار بس *has-sayyaara tšill xamsat 'anfaar bass.* This car carries five people only.

نافورة *naafuura* p. نوافير *nawaafiir* fountain.

ن ف س nfs

نفس *naffas* II to leak, let out air. ها التاير ينفس. لازم تاخذه أبو البنشر *hat-taayir ynaffis. laazim taaxða 'ubu l-banšar.* This tire is leaking. You have to take it to the tire repairman.

نافس *naafas* III to compete, vie, fight with s.o. فريق الكورة حقنا قوي؛ ماحد يقدر ينافسه *fariig l-kuura ḥaggana gawi; maḥḥad yigdar ynaafsa.* Our soccer team is strong; no other team can compete with it.

تنفس *tnaffas* V to breathe, inhale and exhale. ما يتنفس؛ يمكن يموت *ma yitnaffas; yamkin ymuut.* He's not breathing; he might die.

تنافس *tnaafas* VI to compete with each other. فرق الكورة تتنافس على البطولة *firag l-kuura titnaafas ᶜala l-buṭuula.* The soccer teams are competing for the championship.

نفس *nafs* p. أنفس *'anfus,* نفوس *nufuus.* 1. self, personal identity. نفسي أجي واياك *nafsi 'ayi wiyyaak.* I like to come with you. اعتمد على نفسك *ᶜtimid ᶜala nafsak.* Depend on yourself. جاني بنفسه *yaani b-nafsa.* He personally came to me. 2. (with foll. n.) the same. نفس الشي *nafs š-šayy* the same thing. نفس البنية *nafs li-bnayya* the same girl. 3. human being, soul, person. في المدينة مليون نفس *fi l-madiina malyoon nafs.* There are a million people in the city. دايرة النفوس *daayrat n-nufuus* the census bureau.

نفسي *nafsi* psychological, mental. حالة نفسية *ḥaala nafsiyya* psychological condition.

نفس *nafas* p. أنفاس *'anfaas* 1. breath. 2. puff (from a pipe, a cigarette, etc.)

نفسة *nafsa* p. *-aat,* نوافس *nawaafis* woman in childbed.

نفساني *nafsaani*: دختر نفساني *daxtar nafsaani* psychiatrist.

نفاس *nfaas* period of confinement for childbirth.

منافس *mnaafis* p. *-iin* competitor, rival

ن ف ش nfš

نفش *nifaš* (ينفش *yanfiš*) to ruffle its feathers (bird), puff up. الطير نفش ريشه *ṭ-ṭeer nifaš riiša.* The bird ruffled its feathers.

نفش *naffaš* II to fluff, make fluffy. القطان نفش لنا القطن *l-gaṭṭaan naffaš lana l-guṭun.* The cotton dealer fluffed the cotton for us.

تنفش *tnaffaš* V pass. of II نفش *naffaš.*

نفيش *nafiiš* (coll.) popcorn.

منفوش *manfuuš* (p.p. of نفش *nifaš*) 1. puffed up, ruffled. 2. disheveled (hair). أبو شعر منفوش *'ub šaᶜar manfuuš* one with disheveled hair.

ن ف ط nfṭ

نفط *nafṭ* petroleum, oil. شركة نفط *šarikat nafṭ* petroleum company.

ن ف ع nfᶜ

نفع *nifaᶜ* (ينفع *yinfaᶜ*) to be useful, beneficial, of use to. هذا ما ينفعك وهالحين مالك إلا الصبر *haaða ma yinfaᶜk w-hal-hiin ma-lak 'illa ṣ-ṣabir.* This is not useful to you, and now you have nothing to do except to be patient. ها الحكي ما ينفع *hal-ḥači ma* *yinfa*ᶜ. This talk is useless.

انتفـــع *ntifa*ᶜ VIII to benefit, profit, gain. ماحد انتفع من ها المشروع *maḥḥad ntifa*ᶜ *min hal-mašruu*ᶜ. No one benefited from this project.

منفعة *manfa*ᶜ*a* (v.n. from نفع *nifa*ᶜ) p. منافع *manaafi*ᶜ benefit, profit, gain.

أنفـــع *'anfa*ᶜ (elat.) 1. (with من *min*) more useful, beneficial than. 2. (with foll. n.) the most useful, beneficial.

نـــافع *naafi*ᶜ (act. part. from نفع *nifa*ᶜ) beneficial, useful, profitable.

ن ف گ *nfg*

نـــافق *naafag* III to be hypocritical, feign honesty. ما شفت أحد ينافق أكـــثر منـــك *ma čift 'aḥad ynaafig 'akθar minnak.* I haven't seen anyone who is more hypocritical than you are.

نفـــق *nafag* p. أنفاق *'anfaag* tunnel, underground passageway.

نفقـــة *nafaga* p. *-aat* 1. expense. ندرس على نفقتنا *nidris* ᶜ*ala nafgatna.* We are studying at our expense. على نفقـــة الحكومـــة ᶜ*ala nafgat l-ḥukuuma* at the government expense. 2. alimony. طلقتها. لازم تدفع لهـــا نفقـــة *ṭallagitta. laazim tidfa*ᶜ *laha nafaga.* You divorced her. You have to pay alimony to her. 3. child support.

نفاق *nifaag* hypocrisy.

منافق *munaafig* (act. part. from III نافق *naafag*) p. *-iin* hypocrite.

ن ف ن و ف *nfnwf*

نفنــوف *nafnuuf* p. نفـــانيف *nafaaniif* (woman's) ornamented dress (esp. one made from delicate material).

ن ف ي *nfy*

نفى *nifa* (ينفي *yanfi*) 1. to deny. الوزارة نفت الخبر *l-wazaara nifat l-xabar.* The ministry denied the news item. 2. to exile, banish. نفوه إلى جزيرة بعيدة *nafoo 'ila yiziira ba*ᶜ*iida.* They exiled him to a distant island.

نـــافى *naafa* III to contradict, be contrary to. اللي قلته ينافي الحقيقـــة *'illi gilta ynaafi l-ḥagiiga.* What you have said is contradicted by the facts.

تنـــافى *tnaafa* VI (with وايا *wiyya* or مع *ma*ᶜ) = نافى *naafa* III. يتنافى وايا الحقيقة *yitnaafa wiyya l-ḥagiiga.* It contradicts the facts.

منفـــى *manfa* p. منافي *manaafi* place of exile.

منفـــي *manfi* (p.p. from نفى *nifa*) 1. having been denied, rejected. الخبر منفي في كـــل الجرايـــد *l-xabar manfi fi kill l-jaraayid.* The news item has been denied in all the newspapers. 2. (p. *-yyiin*) having been exiled, banished. منفي عشر سنين *manfi* ᶜ*ašar siniin.* He's been living in exile for ten years.

ن ق ب *nqb*

نقابـــة *naqaaba* p. *-aat* union, guild, association. نقابـــة المعلمـــين *naqaabat l-mu*ᶜ*allimiin* the teachers' union. نقابة المحـــامين *naqaabat l-muḥaamiin* the bar association.

ن گ د *ngd*

نقد *naggad* II to pay or give money to s.o. نقدوا النعاشة ألف درهـــم *naggdaw n-na*ᶜᶜ*aaša 'alf dirhim.* They gave one thousand dirhams to the (female) dancer.

'anaagišk b-hal-mawđuu^c. I would like to discuss this topic with you.

تناقش *tnaagaš* VI to discuss, argue s.th. with each other. تناقشنا بالموضوع وذلحين كل شي زين *tnaagašna b-l-mawđuu^c w-đalḥiin kill šayy zeen.* We discussed the topic with each other and now everything is fine.

نقش *nagš* (v.n. from نقش *nigaš*) engraving, inscription. النقش من الفنون الجميلة *n-nagš min li-fnuun l-yimiila.* Engraving is one of the fine arts.

نقاش *naggaaš* p. *-iin* 1. engraver. 2. sculptor.

مناقشة *munaagaša* (v.n. from III ناقش *naagaš*) 1. discussion. 2. argument.

ن گ ص ngṣ

نقص *nigaṣ (ينقص yanguṣ)* 1. to decrease, diminish, become less. مستوى الماي نقص في التانكي *mustawa l-maay nigaṣ fi t-taanki.* The level of water decreased in the reservoir. فلوسه تنقص لانه يقامر *fluusa tanguṣ linna ygaamir.* His money dwindles because he gambles. 2. to be lacking in s.th., to be missing, needing s.th. عندي كل شي. ما ينقصني شي *^cindi kill šayy. ma yanguṣni šayy.* I have everything. I am not lacking anything. 3. to be lacking, insufficient, deficient. الأكل رايح ينقص لانه فيه ناس واجدين *l-'akil raayiḥ yanguṣ linna fii naas waaydiin.* The food isn't going to be enough because there are many people.

نقص *naggaṣ* II 1. to reduce, lower, curtail. إذا تنقص السعر أشتري واجد *'iđa tnaggiṣ s-si^cir 'aštiri waayid.* If you

انتقد *ntigad* VIII to criticize, find fault with. قبل ما تنتقد أحد، انتقد نفسك. *gabil-ma tintagid 'aḥad, ntagid nafsak.* Before you criticize anyone, criticize yourself. ينتقد الواحد على أي شي *yintagid l-waaḥid ^cala 'ayya šayy.* He criticizes people for anything.

نقد *nagd* cash, ready money. مؤسسة النقد الدولي *mu'assasat n-nagd d-dawli* the International Monetary Fund.

ن گ ر ngr

نقر *nigar (ينقر yangur)* 1. to peck, peck up. الطيور تنقر الحبوب *ṭ-ṭuyuur tangur li-ḥbuub.* The birds are pecking the grains. 2. to peck at s.o. إذا تقرب منه ينقرك *'iđa tgarrib minna yangurk.* If you get close to it, it will peck at you.

نقر *naggar* II to peck repeatedly.

منقار *mingaar* p. مناقير *manaagiir* beak, bill (of a bird).

ن گ ز ngz

نقز *nigaz (ينقز yangiz)* to leap, jump unexpectedly. (prov.) من عضه الداب ينقز من الحبل *man ^cađđa d-daab yangiz min l-ḥabil.* Once bitten twice shy.

ن گ ش ngš

نقش *nigaš (ينقش yanguš)* to engrave, carve, chisel. انحتوا اسمه على الحجر *nḥitaw 'asma ^cala l-hiyar.* They engraved his name on the rock.

ناقش *naagaš* III 1. to argue with. لا تناقش التنديل، ترى يفنشك *la tnaagiš t-tindeel, tara yfanništk.* Don't argue with the foreman or else he'll lay you off. 2. (with ب *b-*) to discuss s.th. with s.o. أبغى أناقشك بهالموضوع *'abġa*

reduce the price, I'll buy a lot. 2. to decrease, diminish. نقصوا معاشه ألف درهم *naggaṣaw ma^c^aaša 'alf dirhim.* They decreased his salary by one thousand dirhams.

استنقص *stangaṣ* X to consider s.th. insufficient, deficient. إذا تستنقص الكمية رجعها *'iða tistangiṣ l-kammiyya rajji^c^ha.* If you consider the amount insufficient, return it.

مناقصة *munaagaṣa* p. *-aat* invitation for bids on a contract.

أنقص *'angaṣ* (elat.) 1. (with من *min*) more lacking, deficient, etc. than. 2. (with foll. n.) the most lacking, deficient, etc.

ناقص *naagiṣ* 1. (act. part. from نقص *nigaṣ*) having decreased. مستوى الماي في التانكي ناقص *mustawa l-maay fi t-taanki naagiṣ.* The level of water in the reservoir has decreased. 2. deficient, lacking, insufficient. هالوزن ناقص *hal-wazin naagiṣ.* This weight is less than it should be. حكي ناقص *ḥači naagiṣ* insulting words, insult.

ن گ ط *ngṭ*

نقط *naggaṭ* II to drip, fall in drops. الماي في التانكي ينقط *l-maay fi t-taanki ynaggiṭ.* The water in the reservoir is dripping. التانكي ينقط ماي *t-taanki ynaggiṭ maay.* This reservoir is dripping water.

نقطة *nigṭa* p. نقط *nigaṭ* 1. drop (of a liquid). نقطة من بحر *nigṭa min baḥar* drop in the ocean. 2. point, mark. فريقنا حصل خمسين نقطة *fariigna ḥaṣṣal xamsiin nigṭa.* Our team got fifty points. 3. period, full stop. 4. small amount. عطنا نقطة ماي. عطشانين *^c^aṭna nigṭat maay. ^c^aṭšaaniin.* Give us a little water. We are thirsty.

ن گ ع *ng^c^*

نقع *niga^c^* (ينقع *yinga^c^*) 1. to soak. انقع النخي في ماي قبل ما تغليه *'inga^c^ n-naxxi fi maay gabil-ma tġalii.* Soak the chickpeas in water before you boil them. 2. (v.i.) to become thoroughly soaked. طب في البركة وهدومه نقعت *ṭabb fi l-birča w-hduuma nig^c^at.* He fell in the pool and his clothes became thoroughly soaked.

نقع *nagga^c^* II intens. of نقع *niga^c^*.

تنقع *tnagga^c^* V pass. of II نقع *nagga^c^*.

مستنقع *mistanga^c^* p. *-aat* swamp.

ن گ ل *ngl*

نقل *nigal* (ينقل *yangul*) 1. to move, transport, transmit. نقل كل سامانه *nigal kill saamaana.* He moved all his things. من اللي ينقل الأخبار؟ *man illi yangul l-'axbaar?* Who is transmitting the news items? 2. to transfer, translocate. التنديل نقل الكولي *t-tindeel nigal l-kuuli.* The foreman transferred the coolie. 3. to copy. انقل هذي الصفحة *'ungul haaði ṣ-ṣafḥa.* Copy this page. هو اللي نقل مني في الامتحان *huwa lli nigal minni fi li-mtiḥaan.* He's the one who copied from me during the examination. 4. to broadcast. دايماً ينقلون صلاة الجمعة *daayman yanguluun ṣalaat l-yim^c^a.* They always broadcast the Friday (noon) prayer. 5. to spread, communicate (a disease). البق ينقل

المـــــــرض *l-bagg yangul l-marađ.* Mosquitoes spread diseases.

نقل *naggal* II intens. of نقل *nigal.*

تنقـــل *tnaggal* V to move from one place to another, travel around, roam. ما يقدر يقعد في مكان واحد. دايما يتنقل *ma yigdar yagᶜid fi mukaan waaḥid. daayman yitnaggal.* He can't stay in one place. He always moves from one place to another. يتنقـــل بين بو ظبي ودبي *yitnaggal been bu đabi w-dbayy.* He travels between Abu Dhabi and Dubai. البدوي يتنقل في البر *li-bdiwi yitnaggal fi l-barr.* Bedouins move about the desert.

انتقـــل *ntigal* VIII 1. to move, change residence. انتقلنا إلى الشارجـــة *ntigalna 'ila š-šaarja.* We moved to Sharja. 2. pass. of نقل *nigal.* انتقل إلى المالية *ntigal 'ila l-maaliyya.* He was transferred to the finance department. 3. to be communicated, spread. فيه أمراض تنتقل بـــالهوا *fii 'amraađ tintagil b-l-hawa.* There are diseases that are spread by air.

متنقـــل *mitnaggil* 1. (act. part. from V تنقـــل *tnaggal*) roving, roaming, migrant. 2. mobile. عيادة متنقلة *ᶜiyaada mitnaggla* mobile clinic.

ن گ م *ngm*

انتقم *ntigam* VIII (with من *min*) to get revenge on, avenge oneself. الله ينتقـــم منـــك! *'aḷḷa yintagim minnak!* God get revenge on you!

انتقـــام *ntigaam* (v.n. from VIII انتقم *ntigam*) vengeance, revenge.

ناقم *naagim* (with على *ᶜala*) disgusted, angry, indignant at or about. ما ادري ليش ناقم علـــى هـــا الوضـــع *ma dri leeš naagim ᶜala hal-wađiᶜ.* I don't know why he's disgusted by this situation.

ن گ ي *ngy*

استنقى *stanga* X to pick out, choose. استنقى اللي يبغيـــه *stanga lli yabgii.* He picked what he liked. ما تقدر تستنقي في هـــا الدكـــــان *ma tigdar tistangi fi had-dikkaan.* You can't pick and choose at this store.

ن ك ب *nkb*

نكـــب *nikab* (ينكب *yankub)* to cause great suffering, to make miserable, to afflict. الحرب تنكب الناس *l-ḥarb tankub n-naas.* War causes people great suffering.

انتكب *ntikab* VIII pass. of نكب *nikab.*

نكبة *nakba* p. *-aat* calamity, disaster, catastrophe.

منكـــوب *mankuub* (p.p. from نكـــب *nikab*) p. *-iin* victim (of a disaster). منكوبين الحـــــرب *mankuubiin l-ḥarb* the war victims.

ن ك ت *nkt*

نكـــت *nakkat* II 1. to crack jokes, be witty. دايما ينكت *daayman ynakkit.* He always tells jokes. 2. (with على *ᶜala*) to poke fun at s. o., ridicule s.o. دايما ينكتـــون عليـــه في الحفـــــيز *daayman ynakktuun ᶜalee fi l-ḥafiiz.* They always poke fun at him in the office.

نكتـــة *nukta* p. نكت *nukat* joke, witty remark. صاحب نكتة *ṣaaḥib nukta* s.o. who makes many jokes.

ن ك د *nkd*

نكد *nakkad* II (with على *ᶜala*) to make things difficult or miserable for s.o. نكد عليه عيشته *nakkad ᶜalee ᶜiišta.* He made life miserable for him. ليش تنكد علـى هلـك؟ *leeš tnakkid ᶜala halak?* Why do you make life difficult for your family?

نكد *nakad* (v.n.) trouble, misery. عيشته كلها نكد في نكد *ᶜiišta killaha nakad fi nakad.* His life is a multitude of troubles.

منكـد *mnakkid* (act. part. from II نكد *nakkad*) making things miserable or hard. يسكر ويقامر. منكد علينـا عيشتنـا. *yiskar w-ygaamir. mnakkid ᶜaleena ᶜiišatna.* He drinks and gambles. He's making our life miserable.

ن ك ر *nkr*

نكر *nikar* (ينكر *yinkir*) to deny, renege. جبته يشهد واياي، لكنه نكر كل شي قـدام الحاكم *yibta yišhad wiyyaay, laakinna nikar kill šayy jiddaam l-ḥaakim.* I brought him to testify for me, but he denied everything before the judge.

استنكر *stankar* X to denounce, protest. استنكروا قطـع العلاقـات *stankaraw ġaṭᶜ l-ᶜalaagaat.* They denounced the breaking of relations.

نكـران *nukraan* (v.n. from نكر *nikar*) denial. نكران الجميـل *nukraan l-jamiil* ingratitude.

ناكر *naakir* (act. part. from نكر *nikar*) p. *-iin* denying, disavowing. ناكر الجميل *naakir l-jamiil* ungrateful.

منكـر *munkar* p. *-aat* forbidden or reprehensible action.

ن ك س *nks*

نكـس *nakkas* II to fly at half-mast, lower at half-mast. نكسوا الاعلام حداد على الملك *nakksaw li-ᶜlaam ḥdaad ᶜala l-malik.* They flew the flags at half-mast declaring (a period of) mourning for the king.

انتكـس *ntikas* VIII 1. pass. of نكس *nikas.* 2. to suffer a relapse. صحتـه تحسـنت بـس انتكـس بعديـن *ṣiḥḥta tḥassanat bass ntikas baᶜdeen.* His health improved but he had a relapse later on.

نكسة *naksa* p. *-aat* relapse.

ن ك ه *nkh*

نكهة *nakha* p. *-aat* aroma, scent, smell.

ن ل ل *nll*

نل *nall* p. *-aat* faucet.

ن م ر ١ *nmr*

نمـر *nimir* p. نمورة *nmuura* 1. tiger. 2. leopard.

ن م ر ٢ *nmr*

نمـر *nammar* II to number, assign number to. نمر الطلبات حسب الأسـبقية *nammar ṭ-ṭalabaat ḥasab l-'asbagiyya.* He numbered the applications according to the date received.

نمرة *numra* p. إنمر *'inmar* number.

ن م ل *nml*

نمـل *namil* (coll.) ants s. *-a* p. *-aat.* أم النمـل *'umm n-namil* Kuwaiti island. يحلب النملـة *yḥalib n-namla.* (He's so stingy that) he would milk an ant. He's a scrooge.

ن م و ن *nmwn*

نمونة *namuuna* p. نمايم *namaayin* sample, specimen. ورنا نمونة *warrna namuuna.* Show us a sample. من ها النمونة *min han-namuuna* of this kind.

ن م ي *nmy*

تنمية *tanmiya* 1. development. صندوق التنمية *ṣanduug t-tanmiya* the development fund. 2. raising, boost. تنمية روس الأموال *tanmiyat ruus l-'amwaal* the raising of capital. 3. cultivation, breeding (of plants).

ن ه ب *nhb*

نهب *nihab* (ينهب *yinhab*) 1. to rob. جاوا ونهبوا البنك *yaw w-nhabaw l-bank.* They came and robbed the bank. 2. to steal, plunder. نهبوا كل فلوس البنك *nhabaw kill fluus l-bank.* They stole all the money of the bank.

نهب *nahab* (v.n.) 1. robbing, robbery. 2. stealing. يبيعون درزن البيض بعشرين درهم. هذا نهب *ybiiᶜuun darzan l-beeḏ b-ᶜišriin dirhim. haaða nahab.* They sell a dozen eggs for twenty dirhams. This is stealing.

ن ه ج *nhj*

منهج *manhaj* p. مناهج *manaahij* program of study, curriculum.

ن ه ر *nhr*

نهر *nahar* p. انهار *nhaar* river.

نهار *nahaar* p. *-aat* daytime, the daylight hours. زامي في النهار *zaami fi n-nahaar.* I work a daytime shift. برج النهار *burj n-nahaar* Burj an-Nahar (old military fort in Dubai).

نهاري *nahaari* (adj.) day, daytime. زام نهاري *zaam nahaari* daytime shift. مدرسة نهارية *madrasa nahaariyya* day school. (prov.) بالنهار عمايم وبالليل خمايم *b-n-nahaar ᶜamaayim w-b-l-leel xamaayim.* Fair without and foul within.

ن ه ز *nhz*

انتهز *ntihaz* VIII to seize, take advantage of. انتهز الفرصة وروح سلم عليه *ntahiz l-furṣa w-ruuḥ sallim ᶜalee.* Seize the opportunity and go greet him.

انتهازي *ntihaazi* p. *-yyiin* opportunist.

ن ه گ *nhg*

نهق *nihag* (ينهق *yinhag*) to bray. الحمار ينهق ان كان جوعان *li-ḥmaar yinhag nčaan juuᶜaan.* A donkey brays if it's hungry.

ن ه ل *nhl*

منهل *manhal* p. مناهل *manaahil* watering place, spring. قصر المنهل *gaṣr l-manhal* Al-Manhal Palace (presidential palace in Abu Dhabi).

ن ه م *nhm*

نهمة *nahma* p. *-aat* song sung by a نهام *nahhaam* on a ship.

نهام *nahhaam* p. *-a* singer, entertainer on a ship, esp. during the pearling season. شغلة النهام ماتت *šaġlat n-nahhaam maatat.* The work of a *nahhaam* is gone.

ن ه ي *nhy*

نهى *niha* (ينهي *yanhi*) to tell s.o. not to do s.th. هذي غلطتي. أبوي نهاني عن كل هذي الأشيا *haaði ġalṭati. 'ubuuy nahaani ᶜan kill haaði l-'ašya.* This is my mistake. My father told me not to do any of these things.

أنهى *'anha* IV to finish, terminate. أنهوا خدمته *'anhaw xidimta.* They terminated his service. أنهى خدمته وراح يشتغل في التجارة *'anha xidimta w-raaḥ yištaġil fi t-tijaara.* He resigned and went to work in business.

انتهى *ntiha* VIII 1. to come to an end, to be finished, terminated, concluded. الشغل ينتهي الساعة ثنتين *š-šuġul yintahi s-saa^c^a θinteen.* The work ends at two o'clock. العلاقات انتهت بينا وبينهم *l-^c^alaagaat ntihat beena w-beenhum.* The relations are all over between us and them. 2. (with من *min*) to be or become finished with, be through with s.th. انتهيت من الكتاب *ntiheet min li-ktaab.* I'm finished with the book.

نهاية *nihaaya* p. *-aat* 1. end. نهاية القيظ *nihaayat l-geeḍ* the end of summer. في النهاية *fi n-nihaaya* finally, at last, in the end. في النهاية نجح وحصل الشهادة *fi n-nihaaya nijaḥ w-ḥaṣṣal š-šahaada.* Finally, he passed and obtained the certificate.

ن ه ي ا ن *nhyyaan*

نهيّان *nhayyaan*: آل نهيان *'aal nhayyaan* Al-Nhayan (the ruling family in Abu Dhabi).

ن و ب *nwb*

ناب *naab (ينوب ynuub)* (with عن *^c^an*) to represent, act as representative for, substitute for s.o. ما حضرت الاجتماع أمس. عبدالله ناب عني *ma ḥiḍart li-jtimaa^c^ 'ams. ^c^abdaḷḷa naab ^c^anni.* I didn't attend the meeting yesterday. Abdalla represented me. التنديل موب هني اليوم. من ينوب عنه؟ *t-tindeel muub hni l-yoom. man ynuub ^c^anna?* The foreman isn't here today. Who is going to substitute for him?

نوب *nawwab* II to appoint s.o. as representative, agent, or substitute. الشيخ نوب الوزير عنه *š-šeex nawwab l-waziir ^c^anna.* The Shaikh appointed the minister to represent him.

نيابة *niyaaba* (v.n. from ناب *naab*) representation, substitution. نيابة عن *niyaaba ^c^an,* بالنيابة عن *b-n-niyaaba ^c^an* in place of, instead of. ليش ما تروح بالنيابة عني؟ *leeš ma truuḥ b-n-niyaaba ^c^anni?* Why don't you go in my place?

نايب *naayib* p. نواب *nuwwaab* 1. representative (congressman) in parliament. مجلس النواب *majlis n-nuwwaab* house of representatives. 2. vice-, deputy. نايب الرئيس *naayib r-ra'iis* the vice-president. نايب الوزير *naayib l-waziir* the deputy minister.

نوبي *nuubi* p. نوبان *nuubaan* Nubian (adj. and n.). رقصة النوبان *ragṣat n-nuubaan* the Nubian dance.

ن و ح *nwḥ*

نوح *nuuḥ* Noah. سفينة نوح *safiinat nuuḥ* Noah's Ark.

ن و خ ذ *nwxð*

نوخذة *nooxaða* p. نواخذ *nuwaaxið,* نواخذة *nuwaaxða* captain of a sailing vessel. (prov.) نوخذين يطبقون مركب *nooxaðeen yṭabbguun markab.* Too many cooks spoil the broth.

نور nwr

نـــار *naar* p. نيران *niiraan* 1. fire. شبينا النـــار *šabbeena n-naar.* We started the fire. الأسعار ذالحـــين صـــارت نـــار *l-'as^caar ðalḥiin ṣaarat naar.* Prices nowadays have become unbearable. 2. hell. اللي يسكر مصيره النـــار *'illi yiskar maṣiira n-naar.* He who drinks will go to hell. نـــار جـــهنم *naar jahannam* hellfire. أم النـــار *'umm n-naar* Umm al-Nar (archeological site in Abu Dhabi). 3. gunfire.

نـــاري *naari* fiery, fire-. ألعاب ناريـــة *'al^caab naariyya* fireworks. أسلحة نارية *'asliḥa naariyya* firearms.

نور *nuur* light, illumination. نور الشمس *nuur š-šams* sunlight. نور كشاف *nuur kaššaaf* searchlight.

نورو *nuuroo* dim. of نورة *nuura* Nora.

منارة *manaara* p. *-aat* lighthouse.

منـــاورة *mnaawara* p. *-aat* (mil.) maneuver.

نوط nwṭ

نـــوط *nooṭ* p. *-aat,* إنوط *'inwaṭ* bank note, bill. نوط أبو إمية درهم *nooṭ 'ubu 'imyat dirhim* hundred-dirham bill.

نوع nw^c

نـــوع *nawwa^c* II to make different, diversify. قال لي الدختر أنـــوع بـــالأكل *gal-li d-daxtar 'anawwi^c b-l-'akil.* The doctor told me to eat different kinds of foods.

تنـــوع *tnawwa^c* V pass. of II نـــوع *nawwa^c.*

نـــوع *noo^c* p. انواع *nwaa^c* kind, sort, type. شو نوع الأفلام اللي تحبها؟ *šu noo^c l-'aflaam illi tḥibbha?* What kind of films do you like? من ها النـــوع *min han-noo^c* of this kind, similar to this.

نوعيـــة *naw^ciyya* p. *-aat* quality. نوعية البضاعة زينة *naw^ciyyat l-biðaa^ca zeena.* The quality of the merchandise is good.

نوگ nwg

ناقـــة *naaga* p. نياق *nyaag, -aat* female camel. (prov.) جزا ناقة الحج الذبـــح *jaza naagat l-ḥajj ð-ðabḥ.* He repaid evil with good.

نول nwl

نـــول *nawwal* II to rent, hire. نولنا مركب ودشينا البحـــر *nawwalna markab w-daššeena l-baḥar.* We rented a boat and sailed.

نـــول *nool* rent money. دفعنا نول وخذينا المركـــب *difa^cna nool w-xaðeena l-markab.* We paid the rent and took the boat.

نوم nwm

نـــام *naam.* See رقد *rigad* under **رگد** *rgd.*

منام *manaam* sleep. (prov.) الزين زين لو قعد من منامه والشـــين شـــين لـــو غســـل بصـــابون *z-zeen zeenin lo gi^cad min manaama w-š-šeen šeenin lo ġassal b-ṣaabuun.* A leopard cannot change his spots.

المنامة *l-manaama* 1. Manama (capital of Bahrain). 2. Manama (town in Ajman).

تنـــويم *tanwiim* : تنويم مغناطيسي *tanwiim maġnaaṭiisi* hypnosis, hypnotism.

منـــــوم *mnawwim* 1. (adj.) sleep-inducing. دوا منـــوم *duwa mnawwin* soporific, somnifacient. 2. (p. *-iin*): منـوم مغناطيسـي *mnawwim mağnaaṭiisi* hypnotist.

ن و ن *nwn*

نون *nuun* name of the letter ن *n.*

ن و ي *nwy*

نـوى *nuwa (ينوي yanwi)* to intend to do s.th., have s.th. in mind. أنوي أصوم كل شـهر رمضـــان *'anwi 'aṣuum kill šahar rumđaan.* I intend to fast the whole month of Ramadan. الحكومة تنوي تبـني بيـوت شـعبية جديـدة *l-ḥukuuma tanwi tabni byuut šacbiyya yidiida.* The government plans to build new low income houses.

نـوى *nuwa* (coll.) 1. date pits. 2. fruit kernels, stones. s. نواة *-aa.*

نـووي *nawawi* nuclear. أسـلحة نوويـة *'asliḥa nawawiyya* nuclear weapons.

نيـة *niyya* p. نوايـا *nawaaya* intention, intent, purpose. نيـتي أصـوم كـل شـــهر رمضــــــان *niyyati 'aṣuum kill šahar rumđaan.* I intend to fast the whole month of Ramadan. ما لك نية تجي وايانا؟ *ma-lak niyya tyi wiyyaana?* Don't you intend to come with us? حسن النية *ḥusn n-niyya* good intention, good will. قالها بحسـن النيـة *gaal-ha b-ḥusun niyya.* He said it with good intentions.

ن ي ب *nyb*

نـاب *naab* p. نياب *nyaab*, نيوب *nyuub* 1. eyetooth. 2. fang.

ن ي ر ١ *nyr*

نجر *niyar (ينجر yanyir)* 1. to chop, hew (wood). نجر بـالقدوم *niyar b-l-jadduum.* He chopped the piece of wood with a hatchet. 2. to plane (wood).

ن ي ر ٢ *nyr*

نيرة *neera* p. *-aat* gold coin.

ن ي س ا ن *nysaan*

نيسان *niisaan* April.

ن ي ش ن *nyšn*

نيشـن *neešan (ينيشن yneešin)* 1. to aim, point. نيشـن واضـــرب *neešin w-iđrib.* Aim and shoot. 2. (with على *cala*) to aim, take aim at s.o. or s.th. لازم تنيشن على الشـــي قبـل لا تضرب *laazim tneešin cala š-šayy gabil-la tađrib.* You have to aim at the thing before you fire.

نيشـان *niišaan* 1. (p. نياشين *niyaašiin*) medal. حصلـت هـا النيشـان مـن المدرسـة الحربيـــة *ḥaṣṣalt han-niišaan min l-madrasa l-ḥarbiyya.* I got this medal from the military school. 2. aim. خذيــت نيشـــان وضربــت طلقــة *xađeet niišaan w-đirabt ṭalga.* I took aim and fired one shot.

ن ي ل ١ *nyl*

النيـل *n-niil,* نهـر النيـل *nahr n-niil* the Nile.

ن ي ل ٢ *nyl*

نيلة *niila* bluing.

نيلي *niiili: loon niili* light blue color.

ن ي م ١ *nym*

نيـم *nayyam* II = نوم *nawwam* II. See II نوم *nawwam* under **ن و م** *nwm.*

ن ي م ٢ *nym*

نجمة *niyma, niima* p. نجوم *nyuum* star. نجمة الغبشــة *niymat l-ġubša* the morning star.

ن ي ي *nyy*

نية *niyya*. See under **ن و ي** *nwy*.

ه

ه *h-*

هـ *ha-* (with foll. article prefix ال *l-* and noun) this, هـــاالقد *hal-gadd* this much. هاالشكل *haš-šikil* (adv.) in this manner, this way. قلت له يقعد هاالشكل. *git-la yagᶜid haš-šikil.* I told him to sit down like this. هاالأيـــام *hal-ayyaam* nowadays, these days. ما فيه في بلادنـــا فقـــير هاالأيـــام *ma fii fi blaadna fagiir hal-ayyaam.* There are no poor people in our country these days.

ها[١] *haa*

هـــا *haa* (inter.) 1. well! well then! ها! شتـــبي بعـــد؟ *haa! š-tabi baᶜad?* Well! What else do you want? ها يبه! شـــو تقـــول؟ *haa yuba! šu tguul?* Well, father! What do you think? 2. yes. ها أنا هني *haa 'aana hni.* Yes, I'm here. 3. (expresses surprise or amazement) oh? really? ها! جابت ولد وما درينـــا؟ *haa! yaabat walad w-ma dareena?* Oh? She had a baby boy and we didn't know?

ها[٢] *haa*

ها *haa-*: هاك *haak,* fem. *haač,* p. هاكم *haakum* here, here you are. هاك الفلوس *haak li-fluus.* Here's the money. هاك، اخذه *haak, ixða.* Here, take it.

ها[٣] *haa*

ها *haa* name of the letter هـــ *h.*

هاذ *haað*

هـــذا *haaða* f. هــــذي *haaði* p. هذيل *haðeel,* هــــذول *haðool,* ذول *ðool,* ذولا *ðoola,* ذيـــلا *ðeela* this, this one. هذا الكتاب زيـــن *haaða li-ktaab zeen.* This book is good. هذا كتاب زيـــن *haaða ktaab zeen.* This is a good book. هذيل عيـــالي *haðeel ᶜyaaḷi.* These are my children. هذي مالي *haaði maali.* This is mine. هذي ليـــك *haaði lič.* This is for you.

هارن *haarn*

هارن *haaran* p. هوارن *hawaarin, -aat* car horn. لا تـــدق الهـــارن! *la ddigg l-haaran!* Don't sound the horn of your car!

هاس *haas*

هاس *haas* p. *-aat* heart (playing card).

هاف *haaf*

هـــاف *haaf* p. *-aat* under short. اشتريت خمـــس هافـــات *štireet xams haafaat.* I bought five pairs of shorts.

هامان *haamaan*

هامان *haamaan* man's name known in the proverb على هامان يا فرعـــون *ᶜala haamaan ya farᶜoon.* You cannot fool me. You cannot pull the wool over my eyes.

هامور *haamwr*

هامور *haamuur* (coll.) groupers. s. *-a* p. *-aat,* هوامير *hawaamiir.* (prov.) مثل الهامور جالس في البابـــة *miθl l-haamuur jaalis fi l-baaba.* A dog in the manger. (lit. "Like groupers sitting in the entrance to the fishing trap.").

هبب *hbb*

هب *habb (يهب yhibb)* to blow. هب الريح *habb r-riiḥ.* The wind blew. (prov.) إذا هبت هبوبك أذر عنها *'iδa habbat hbuubak 'aδir ᶜanha.* Get out of harm's way. هب ريح *habb riiḥ.* p. هبوب ريح *hbuub riiḥ* daring and courageous man. غيص هب ريح *ġeeṣ habb riiḥ* daring and courageous pearl diver.

هبد *hbd*

هبد *hibad (يهبد yhabid)* to knock out, throw s.o. to the ground. هبده والضربة طيحته الأرض *hbada w-ḍ-ḍarba ṭayyaḥata l-'arḍ.* He hit him and the blow caused him to fall down.

هبر *hbr*

هبر *habur* (coll.) boneless meat (usually with no fat in it). s. *-a* p. *-aat.*

هبش *hbš*

هبش *hibaš (يهبش yhabiš)* to eat ravenously. قطو مطابخ. بس يهبش *gaṭu maṭaabix. bass yhabiš.* He has a bottomless belly. (lit., "He's a cat of kitchens."). He just eats ravenously.

هبل *hbl*

هبل *habal* p. هبلان *hiblaan* dim-witted, weak-minded. موب هبل؛ ما تقدر تضحك عليه *muub habal; ma tigdar tiḍḥač ᶜalee.* He's not dim-witted. You can't fool him.

هتر *htr*

استهتر *stahtar* X (with ب *b-*) to have little respect for, make light of s.th. لا تستهتر بالقانون *la tistahtir b-l-ġaanuun.* Don't have little respect for the law.

استهتار *stihtaar* (v.n.) recklessness, thoughtlessness.

مستهتر *mistahtir* (act. part.) heedless, reckless.

هجج *hjj*

هج *hajj (يهج yihijj)* to run away, escape. لين شاف الشرطي هج *leen čaaf š-širṭi hajj.* When he saw the policeman, he ran away. هج من بلاده *hajj min blaada.* He escaped from his country.

هجج *hajjaj* II to drive away, cause s.o. to flee. الحر هني في القيظ يهجج بعض الناس *l-ḥarr hni fi l-geeḍ yhajjij baᶜḍ n-naas.* Hot weather here in the summer drives some people away.

هجر ١ *hjr*

هجر *hijar (يهجر yhajir)* to abandon, leave behind. حرام عليه. هجر حرمته وعياله *ḥaraam ᶜalee. hijar ḥurumta w-ᶜyaaḷa.* Shame on him. He abandoned his wife and kids.

هاجر *haajar* III to emigrate. ناس واجدين يهاجرون حق أمريكا *naas waaydiin yhaajruun ḥagg 'amriika.* Many people emigrate to America.

هجرة *hijra* (v.n. from III هاجر *haajar*) emigration, exodus. الهجرة *l-hijra* the Hegira (Prophet Muhammad's emigration from Mecca to Medina). يوم الهجرة *yoom l-hijra* on the day of emigration, esp. from Palestine. هجرة الطيور *hijrat ṭ-ṭuyuur* the migration of birds.

هجري *hijri* (adj.) pertaining to Muhammad's emigration. سنة هجرية *sana hijriyya* year of the Muslim era, dating from Muhammad's emigration.

مهجر *mahjar* 1. place of emigration. 2. refuge.

مهاجر *muhaajir* p. *-iin* 1. emigrant. 2. immigrant. 3. refugee. المهاجرين الفلسطينيين *li-mhaajriin l-falaṣṭiiniyyiin* the Palestinian refugees.

مهجور *mahjuur* (p.p. from هجر *hijar*) abandoned. عماير مهجورة *ᶜamaayir mahjuura* abandoned buildings, condemned buildings.

ه ج ر ٢ *hjr*

هاجري *haajri* p. هجر *hajar* one belonging to the tribe of الهواجر *l-hawaajir* or بني هاجر *bani haajir.*

الهاجري *l-haajri* Gulf Arabic family name.

ه ج س *hjs*

هاجوس *haajuus* p. هواجس *hawaajis,* هواجيس *hawaajiis* anxiety, apprehension.

ه ج م *hjm*

هجم *hijam* (يهجم *yhajim)* (with على *ᶜala*) 1. (v.t.) to attack, assault. الجيش هجم على القرية *l-jeeš hijam ᶜala l-ġarya.* The army attacked the village. هجموا علينا بس غلبناهم *hjamaw ᶜaleena bass ġalabnaahum.* They attacked us but we defeated them. 2. (v.i.) to be destroyed, ruined. هجم بيته *hijam beeta.* His house was destroyed.

هاجم *haajam* III 1. to attack, assault. هاجمونا ساعة الصبح *haajmoona saaᶜt ṣ-ṣubḥ.* They attacked us early in the morning. 2. to move in on, pounce upon. هاجمه وخذ الكورة منه وسجل هدف *haajma w-xað l-kuura minna w-sajjal hadaf.* He moved in on him, took the ball away from him and scored a goal.

هجوم *hujuum* (v.n. from هجم *hijam*) 1. attack, charge, assault. كان فيه هجوم على المدينة *čaan fii hujuum ᶜala l-madiina.* There was an attack on the city. 2. forward line, forward positions (in soccer, etc.) يلعب هجوم يمين *yilᶜab hujuum yimiin.* He plays (forward) right-in. هجوم يسار *hujuum yisaar* left-in.

مهاجم *mhaajim* (act. part. from III هاجم *haajam*) 1. attacker, assailant. 2. forward (in soccer, etc.)

ه ج ن *hjn*

هجان *hajjaan* p. *-a* (mounted) camel rider who patrols the desert.

ه د ب *hdb*

هدب *hidb* p. اهداب *hdaab,* هدوب *hduub* eyelash. هدوب عيونها طويلة وجميلة *hduub ᶜyuunha ṭawiila w-yimiila.* Her eyelashes are long and beautiful.

ه د د ١ *hdd*

هد *hadd* (يهد *yhidd)* 1. to throw away, discard s.th. هذا شي ما ينفعك. هده *haaða šayy ma yinfaᶜk. hidda.* This is something that is worthless to you. Throw it away. (prov.) لو فيه خير ما هده الطير *loo fii xeer ma hadda ṭ-ṭeer.* It's a worthless thing. (lit., "If it had been of any value, the bird wouldn't have discarded it."). 2. to leave, quit s.th. هد شغله هني وراح دايرة ثانية *hadd šuġla hni w-raaḥ daayra θaanya.* He left his work here and went to another department. هد المدرسة وراح يشتغل

hadd l-madrasa w-raaḥ yištaġil. He dropped out of school and went to work. 3. to release, set free, turn loose. هدوه عقب ما استجوبوه *haddoo* *ᶜugub-ma stajwaboo.* They released him after they had interrogated him. هديت الطير *haddeet ṭ-ṭeer.* I set the bird free. هدت البنية جديلتها *haddat li-bnayya jadiilatta.* The girl let her braid down.

هدد *haddad* II to threaten. هدد حرمته بالطلاق *haddad ḥurumta b-ṭ-ṭalaag.* He threatened his wife with a divorce. هددني بالقتل *haddadni b-l-gatil.* He threatened me with death.

انهد *nhadd* VII pass. of هد *hadd.*

ه د د ٢ *hdd*

هداد *hdaad:* أيام الهداد *'ayyaam li-hdaad* the days when camels are in heat.

ه د ر *hdr*

هدير *hidiir* grunt, sound of a camel.

ه د ف *hdf*

هدف *hadaf* p. أهداف *'ahdaaf* 1. purpose, aim, goal. عايش بس كذي بدون هدف *ᶜaayiš bass čiđi b-duun hadaf.* He's living just like that, without purpose. 2. goal (in sports) سجل هدفين *sajjal hadafeen.* He scored two goals. 3. target. صاب الهدف من بعيد *ṣaab l-hadaf min baᶜiid.* He hit the target from a far distance.

هداف *haddaaf* p. *-iin* sharpshooter, good shot (esp. in soccer and other sports).

ه د م *hdm*

هدم *hidam (يهدم yhadim)* to tear down, demolish, destroy. البلدية هدمت العماير القديمة *l-baladiyya hidmat l-ᶜamaayir l-gadiima.* The municipality tore down the old buildings.

هدم *haddam* II intens. of هدم *hidam.*

تهدم *thaddam* V pass. of V هدم *haddam.*

انهدم *nhidam* VII to collapse, fall down. العمارة انهدمت لأن أساسها موب زين *li-ᶜmaara nhidmat li'an 'asaassa muub zeen.* The building collapsed because its foundation wasn't good.

هدم *hidim* garment, item of clothing. p. هدوم *hudum* clothes.

هدام *haddaam* destructive. شعارات هدامة *šiᶜaaraat haddaama* destructive slogans. مبادي هدامة *mabaadi haddaama* destructive ideology.

هدمان *hadmaan* p. *-iin* 1. dizzy. 2. seasick. الداو كان يروح كذي وكذي وأنا صرت هدمان *d-daaw čaan yruuḥ čiđi w-čiđi w-aana ṣirt hadmaan.* The boat was moving this way and that way, and I became seasick.

ه د ن *hdn*

هدنة *hudna* p. *-aat,* هدن *hudan* truce, armistice.

ه د ه د *hdhd*

هدهد *hidhid* p. هداهد *hadaahid* hoopoe.

ه د ا و ي *hdaawy*

هداوي *hidaawi* p. *-yya* bodyguard, esp. one for the Shaikh or the Emir.

ه د ي ١ *hdy*

هدى *hida (يهدي yhadi)* 1. to lead s.o.

on the right path. دايماً سكران. الله يهديه ويترك السكر *daayman sakraan. 'aḷḷa yhadii w-yitrik s-sikir.* He's always drunk. Hopefully God will guide him and he will give up drinking. 2. to give as a gift. الشيخ هداني سيارة *š-šeex hadaani sayyaara.* The Shaikh gave me a car as a gift.

هدية *hadiyya* p. هدايا *hadaaya* gift, present. عندي لك هدية تفرحين بها *ᶜindii-lič hadiyya tifraḥiin biiha.* I have a gift for you that will make you happy. هدية العيد *hadiyyat l-ᶜiid* the feast present. هدية عيد الميلاد *hadiyyat ᶜiid l-miilaad* the Christmas present, the birthday present.

هدي² *hdy*

هدي *hidi (*يهدا *yihda)* to calm down, become calm. ليش أنت عصبي؟ بس اهدا شوية *leeš inta ᶜaṣabi? bass ihda šwayya.* Why are you nervous? You just calm down a little.

هود *huud* (v.n.) quietness, calmness. بهود *b-huud* quietly.

هدي *hadi* (adj.) p. *-yyiin* quiet (person). رجال هدي. يرمس بشويش *rayyaal hadi. yarmis b-šweeš.* He's a quiet man. He speaks quietly and slowly.

هادي *haadi*: المحيط الهادي *l-muḥiiṭ l-haadi* the Pacific Ocean.

هذول *hðwl*

هذول *haðool.* See under **هاذ** *haað.*

هرب *hrb*

هرب *harrab* II to smuggle. عدموه لانه كان يهرب مخدرات *ᶜidmoo linna čaan yharrib muxaddiraat.* They executed him because he was smuggling drugs.

تهرب *tharrab* V 1. (with من *min*) to dodge, evade. ما أبغى ولا واحد يتهرب من المسؤولية *ma 'abġa wala waaḥid yitharrab min l-mas'uuliyya.* I don't want anyone to dodge responsibility. سألناه بس هو تهرب من الجواب *si'alnaa bass huwa tharrab min l-jawaab.* We asked him, but he evaded the answer. 2. pass. of II هرب *harrab.*

هارب *haarib* 1. (p. *-iin*) fugitive, runaway. 2. (adj.) fleeing, on the run.

مهرب *mharrib* (act. part. from II هرب *harrab*) smuggler.

هرس *hrs*

هريسة *hariisa* 1. dish of meat and wheat. 2. sweet pastry made of semolina and sugar.

هرول *hrwl*

هرول *harwal (*يهرول *yharwil)* to jog, trot. فيه ناس يهرولون كل يوم على السيف *fii naas yhariwluun kill yoom ᶜala s-siif.* There are people who jog every day on the beach.

هزب¹ *hzb*

هزب *hizab (*يهزب *yhazib)* to call s.o. bad names. هزبني قدام الناس *hizabni jiddaam n-naas.* He called me bad names in front of the people.

هزب² *hzb*

هزب *hazzab.* II ولم *wallam* II and برز *barraz* II are more common. See under **ولم** *wlm* and **برز** *brz,* respectively.

هزز *hzz*

هز *hazz* (يهز *yhizz*) 1. to rock, jolt (to and fro). الأم هزت الكاروكة لاجل يرقد طفلها *l-'umm hazzat l-kaaruuka lajil yargid ṭiflaha.* The mother rocked the cradle so that her baby might fall asleep. 2. to shake, jiggle. لا تهز الشجرة *la thizz li-šyara.* Don't shake the tree. 3. to shake, jiggle. هز راسه *hazz raasa.* He shook his head. الطيارة هزت العمارة *ṭ-ṭayyaara hazzat li-ᶜmaara.* The plane shook the building.

انهز *nhazz* VII pass. of هز *hazz.*

اهتز *htazz* VIII (v.i.) to shake, tremble. اهتزت العمارة *htazzat li-ᶜmaara.* The building shook. اهتز من الخوف *htazz min l-xoof.* He trembled with fear.

هزة *hazza* (n. of inst.) p. *-aat* tremor, shake. هزة أرضية *hazza 'arðiyya* = زلزال *zilzaal* earthquake.

هزل *hzl*

هزلي *hazali* comical, funny. رواية هزلية *riwaaya hazaliyya* comedy. ممثل هزلي *mumaθθil hazali* comedian.

هزم *hzm*

هزم *hizam* (يهزم *yhazim*) to defeat, vanquish. هزمناهم في الكورة *hizamnaahum fi l-kuura.* We defeated them in soccer.

انهزم *nhizam* VII 1. to be vanquished, defeated. انهزم جيشهم في ذيك المعركة *nhizam jeeššum fi ðiič l-maᶜraka.* Their army was defeated in that battle. 2. to run away, flee. لين شاف الشرطي انهزم *leen čaaf š-širṭi nhizam.* When he saw the policeman, he ran away.

هست *hst*

هست *hast* (invar.) there is, there are. neg. ما ميش *ma miiš* there isn't, there aren't. قهوة هست *gahwa hast,* هست قهوة *hast gahwa.* There's coffee.

هظم *hðm*

هضم *hiðam* (يهضم *yhaðim*) to digest. ها الأكل ما يهضمه البطن زين *hal-'akil ma yhaðma l-baṭin zeen.* The stomach cannot digest this food very well.

انهضم *nhiðam* VII pass. of هضم *hiðam.*

هفف *hff*

هف *haff* (يهف *yhiff*) to blow or move air with a fan. ها المهفة ما تهف الهوا زين *hal-mhaffa ma thiff l-hawa zeen.* This fan doesn't blow air well.

مهفة *mhaffa* p. *-aat* hand fan made from tree leaves. مهفة النبي *mhaffat n-nabi* butterfly.

هل ١ *hl*

هل *hal* inter. part. introducing a yes-or-no question. هل المدير هني؟ *hal l-mudiir hni?* Is the manager here?

هل ٢ *hl*

هال (*ha-* plus article prefix). See هـ *ha* under ه *h-*.

هلا *hlaa*

هلا *hala!* Welcome! هلا بيك! *hala biik!* Welcome to you! هلا ومرحبا! *hala w-marḥaba!* You are welcome (to our place, here, etc.)

هلك *hlk*

هلك *hilak* (يهلك *yhalik*) 1. (v.i.) to

die, perish. رايحين نهلك من الحر *raayḥiin nhalik min l-harr.* We're going to die from the heat. هلكت من الشغل *hilakt min š-šuġul.* I'm dead tired from work. 2. (v.t.) to ruin, annihilate. هلكني المشي *hilakni l-maši.* Walking ruined me.

استهلك *stahlak* X to consume, use up, exhaust. ها السيارة تستهلك بانزين واجد *has-sayyaara tistahlik baanziin waayid.* This car consumes a lot of gasoline. استهلكنا كل الطحين *stahlakna kill ṭ-ṭaḥiin.* We used up all the flour.

استهلاك *stihlaak* (v.n. from X استهلك *stahlak*) 1. consumption, usage. استهلاك المواد الغذائية *stihlaak l-mawadd l-ġiðaa'iyya* the consumption of foodstuffs. 2. exhaustion.

ه ل ل *hll*

هل *hall* (يهل *yhill*) 1. to appear, come up. هل الهلال *hall l-hilaal.* The new moon appeared. هل المطر *hall l-muṭar.* Rain fell. 2. to begin. هل شهر رمضان. لازم نصوم *hal šahar rumðaan. laazim nṣuum.* The month of Ramadan began. We have to fast.

هلل *hallal* II 1. to chant لا إله إلا الله *la 'ilaaha 'illa ḷḷaah.* There is no God but He. 2. to rejoice, shout with joy. جاهم ولد وهللوا وطبلوا *yaahum walad w-hallalaw w-ṭabblaw.* They had a baby boy and they rejoiced and beat the drums.

هلال *hilaal* 1. new moon. إذا بغيت تعرف أول الشهر الهجري لازم تشوف الهلال *'iða baġeet tᶜarf 'awwal š-šahar l-hijri laazim ččuuf l-hilaal.* If you want to know the beginning of the Hegira month, you have to see the new moon. 2. crescent, half-moon. الهلال الأحمر *l-hilaal l-'aḥmar* the Red Crescent.

ه ل و *hlw*

هلو *haluw* hello, hi. هلو حمد. كيف حالك؟ *haluw ḥamad. čeef ḥaalak?* Hello, Hamad. How are you? هلو بك! *haluw biik!* You are welcome (here). Nice meeting you.

ه م *hm*

هم *hum* p. of هو *huwa* 1. they (m.) (less common var. همّ *humma,* أهم *'uhum*). 2. (suff. to n.) their. عيالهم *ᶜyaalhum* their kids. 3. (suff. to v. or part.) them. عطاهم *ᶜaṭaahum.* He gave them. واياهم *wiyyaahum* with them.

ه م ب *hmb*

همبة *hamba* (coll.) mangoes. s. همبا *hambaa.* الهمبة كلش طيبة *l-hamba killiš ṭayba.* Mangoes are very delicious.

ه م ج *hmj*

همجي *hamaji* 1. (adj.) savage, barbaric. 2. (p. *-yyiin,* همج *hamaj*) barbarian.

ه م ز *hmz*

همزة *hamza* p. *-aat* name of the letter ء ', the glottal stop.

ه م س *hms*

همس *himas* (يهمس *yhamis*) to whisper. همس بأذني *himas b-iðni.* He whispered in my ear.

همسة *hamsa* p. *-aat* whisper.

ه م ل *hml*

همل *himal* (يهمل *yihmil*) to neglect. فنشوه لانه همل بواجبه *fannašoo linna* *himal b-waajba.* They laid him off because he neglected his duties.

إهمال *'ihmaal* (v.n.) negligence. هذي غلطتي. إهمال مني *haaði ġalṭati. 'ihmaal minni.* This is my mistake. I was negligent.

هم م ۱ *hmm*

هم *hamm* (يهم *yhimm*) 1. to be important, of consequence, to matter. ما يهم. أنا باروح له *ma yhimm. 'aana ba-ruuḥla.* It doesn't matter. I'll go to see him. 2. to concern, affect. هذا شي ما يهمك *haaða šayy ma yhimmak.* This is something that doesn't concern you. مصلحته الشخصية تهمه وايد *maṣlaḥta š-šaxṣiyya thimma waayid.* His personal interest concerns him a lot.

انهم *nhamm* VII to be very unhappy, become distressed, concerned. انهم لين حرمته جابت بنت ثانية *nhamm leen ḥurumta yaabat bint θaanya.* He was very unhappy when his wife gave birth to another baby girl.

اهتم *htamm* VIII 1. to worry, be concerned. لا تهتم. أنا وياك *la tihtamm. 'aana wiyyaak.* Don't worry. I'm with you. لا تدير بال. لا تهتم بقضايا مثل هذي *la ddiir baal. la tihtamm b-gaðaaya miθil haaði.* Don't worry. Don't be concerned about cases like these. 2. (with ل *l-*) to pay attention to, take notice of s.o. or s.th. لا تهتم لحكيه. يلغي وايد *la tihtamm la-ḥačya. yilġi waayid.* Don't pay attention to his words. He talks on and on endlessly. 3. (with ب *b-*) to go to great lengths on behalf of s.o. لين كنا في بو ظبي اهتم بنا وايد *leen činna fi bu ðabi htamm biina waayid.* When we were in Abu Dhabi, he went to great lengths on our behalf.

هم *hamm* p. هموم *hmuum* 1. concern, worry, anxiety. همي أخلص دراستي *hammi 'axaḷḷiṣ diraasti.* My concern is to complete my studies. مسكين. شايل هم كبير *maskiin. šaayil hamm čibiir.* Poor man. He's burdened with worry. 2. grief, sadness. بحر من الهم *baḥar min l-hamm* sea of grief. مات من الهم *maat min l-hamm.* He died from grief.

همة *himma* 1. zeal, eagerness. 2. effort.

أهم *'ahamm* (elat.) 1. (with من *min*) more important than. 2. (with foll. n.) the most important.

أهمية *'ahammiyya* importance, significance. ما له أهمية *ma la 'ahammiyya.* It's not important.

مهم *muhimm* (less common var. *mhimm*) important, significant. المهم في الزواج المحبة *l-muhimm fi z-zawaaj l-maḥabba.* The most important thing in marriage is love.

مهمة *muhimma* p. *-aat* mission, important task. مهمة دبلوماسية *muhimma diblomaasiyya* political mission.

هم م ۲ *hmm*

هم *hamm* also, too, in addition. يدرس هني وهم يشتغل في الليل *yidris hni w-hamm yištaġil fi l-leel.* He studies here, and he works at night also.

هن *hn*

هن *hin* p. of هي *hiya* 1. they (f.). 2. (suff. to n.) their عيالهن *ᶜyaalhin* their kids. 3. (suff. to v. or part.) them. عطاهن *ᶜaṭaahin.* He gave them. وایاهن *wiyyaahin* with them.

ه ن ا ك *hnaak*

هنـاك *hunaak* (common var. *hnaak*) there, over there, in that place. رحت هناك *riḥt hunaak.* I went there. موب هني وموب هنـاك *muub hni w-muub hnaak* neither here nor there. تحصله هنـاك *tḥaṣṣla hnaak.* You'll find him over there.

ه ن د *hnd*

الهند *l-hind* India.

هنـدي *hindi* 1. (adj.) Indian, characteristic of India. عيش هندي *ᶜeeš hindi* Indian rice. السفارة الهنديـة *s-safaara l-hindiyya* the Indian Embassy. 2. (p. هنود *hnuud*) an Indian.

ه ن د س *hnds*

هنـدس *handas* (يـهندس *yhandis)* to design, engineer. منو هندس ذيك العمارة؟ *minu handas ðiič li-ᶜmaara?* Who designed that building?

هندسة *handasa* (v.n.) 1. engineering. يـدرس هندسـة *yidris handasa.* He's studying engineering. 2. geometry. الهندسـة والحسـاب والجـبر *l-handasa w-li-ḥsaab w-l-jabir* geometry, arithmetic and algebra.

مـهندس *muhandis* (common var. *mhandis*) engineer. مـهندس مـدني *muhandis madani* civil engineer.

ه ن د و س *hndws*

هنـدوس *hindoos* (coll.) Hindus. s. هندوسي *-i* Hindu.

ه ن ي ¹ *hny*

هنـا *hanna* II 1. to congratulate, express good wishes to. هنيته بنجاحـه *hanneeta b-najaaḥa.* I congratulated him on his success. راح هناهم بالعيـد *raaḥ hannaahum b-l-ᶜiid.* He went and gave them his best wishes on the occasion of the holiday. 2. to make happy, delight. الله يهنيك بحيـاتك *aḷḷa yhanniik b-ḥayaatak.* God make you happy in your life. هناك الله! *hannaak aḷḷa!* (response to هنياً *haniyyan*) May God make you happy.

هنياً *haniyyan* (said to s.o. who has just eaten or drunk water) I hope you enjoyed it. I hope it would bring you good health.

تهنيـة *tahniya* p. تهـاني *tahaani* congratulation. تهانينا بالنجـاح *tahaaniina b-n-najaaḥ* (Please accept) our congratulations on your success.

مـهني *mhanni* p. *-yiin* congratulator, well-wisher.

ه ن ي ² *hny*

هني *hni* (common var. *hini, 'ihni*) here, in this place. هني الناس مستانسـين *hini n-naas mistaansiin.* Here the people are happy. ترجيته هني *trayyeeta hni.* I waited for him here.

ه و *hw*

هو *huwa* (less common var. *huw, 'uhu, huwwa*) p. هم *hum* he.

ه و ب *hwb*

هوب *hoob!* stop! (said to a driver).

ه و د *hwd*

هود *hawwad* II to slow down. قدامك

هـود. ليـت. *jiddaamak leet. hawwid.* There's a traffic light in front of you. Slow down.

هودج *hwdj*

هودج *hoodaj* p. هوادج *hawaadij* camel litter, howdah.

هور *hwr*

هـور *hoor* p. هـوران *hooraan* shallow marsh. هـور العنز *hoor l-ᶜanz* region in Dubai.

هوري *hwry*

هـوري *huuri* p. هـواري *hawaari* small boat.

هوز *hwz*

هوز *hooz* p. *-aat* water hose.

هوس *hws*

هـوس *hawas* desire, liking. مـا عنـدي هوس بالشـغل *ma ᶜindi hawas b-š-šuġul.* I don't like to work.

هوش¹ *hwš*

هـاوش *haawaš* III 1. to quarrel with s.o. رحت لاجل أتكلم وايـاه بـس هاوشـني *riḥt lajil 'atkallam wiyyaa bass haawašni.* I went to talk to him, but he quarreled with me. 2. to fight, argue, quarrel with s.o. خـلاص. لا تهاوشني مـن فضلـك *xalaaṣ. la thaawišni min faðlak.* It's all over. Please don't fight with me.

هوشة *hooša* fight, quarrel.

مهـاوش *mhaawiš* (act. part.) having quarreled with s.o. أنا ما سويت شي. هو اللي مهاوشـني *'aana ma sawweet šayy. huwa lli mhawišni.* I haven't done anything. He's the one who quarreled with me.

هوش² *hwš*

هـوش *hooš* (coll.) goats, sheep. s. هايشة *haayša* p. هوايش *hawaayiš* goat, sheep.

هول *hwl*

هـول *hawwal* II to exaggerate, overemphasize, magnify. دايماً يهـول الأشـيا *daayman yhawwil l-'ašya.* He always exaggerates things. ليـش هولـت المسـألة إلى ذاك الحد؟ *leeš hawwalt l-mas'ala 'ila ðaak l-ḥadd?* Why did you magnify the matter to that degree?

هــايل *haayil* amazing, astonishing, extraordinary. ضربة كـورة هايلـة *ðarbat kuura haayla* amazing soccer kick. خـبر هــايل *xabar haayil* astonishing news. حـادث هــايل *ḥaadiθ haayil* extraordinary event.

هون *hwn*

هان *haan (*يهـون *yhuun)* 1. to be or become easy, simple. كل شي يهون إلا هـذا *kill šayy yhuun illa haaða.* Everything will become easy except this. 2. (with على *ᶜala*) to be or become easy for s.o. لو تساعدني يهون علـيّ الشـغل *lo tsaaᶜidni yhuun ᶜalayya š-šuġul.* If you help me, the work will be easy for me. 3. (imperf. يهين *yhiin*) to humiliate, treat s.o. with contempt or disdain. لا تـروح لـه. يهينـك *la truuḥ-la. yhiinak.* Don't go to (see) him. He'll humiliate you. المعلـم هانـه قـدام اولاد صفـه *l-muᶜallim haana jiddaam wlaad ṣaffa.* The teacher humiliated him in front of his classmates.

هـون *hawwan* II (with على *ᶜala*) to

make s.th. easy or simple for s.o. هون علينا الشغل لانه ساعدنا *hawwan ᶜaleena š-šuġul linna saaᶜadna.* He made the work easy for us because he had helped us.

تهاون *thaawan* VI to be lax, careless, negligent. فنشوه لانــــه تهــاون بشغلــه *fannašoo linna thaawan b-šuġla.* They fired him because he was lax in his work.

انهــان *nhaan* VII to be humiliated, insulted. انهان قدام الناس *nhaan jiddaam n-naas.* He was humiliated in front of the people.

هين *hayyin* easy, simple. شغل هين *šuġul hayyin* easy work.

إهانة *'ihaana* p. *-aat* insult.

ه و ي ١ *hwy*

هــوا *hawa* 1. weather. كيف الهوا اليوم؟ *čeef l-hawa l-yoom?* How is the weather today? الهوا حار وحاف *l-hawa ḥaarr w-ḥaaff.* The weather is hot and dry. 2. air. فيه هوا واجد اليوم *fii hawa waayid l-yoom.* It's very windy today.

ه و ي ٢ *hwy*

هــوى *hawa (*يهوى *yihwa)* to love s.o. يــهواها *yihwaaha.* He loves her. قلبي يهواها *galbi yihwaaha.* I love her very much. My heart bleeds for her.

هــوى *hawa* (v.n.) love, infatuation. الهوى مــا لــه دوا *l-hawa ma-la duwa.* Love is incurable. واقع في هواها *waagiᶜ fi hawaaha.* He's in love with her.

ه ي *hy*

هي *hiya* (less common var. *hiy*) p. هن *hin* she.

ه ي ء *hy'*

هيئــة *hay'a* p. هيئات *-aat* organization, association, group. هيئة الأمم المتحـــدة *hay'at l-'umam l-mittaḥda* The United Nations Organization. هيئة دبلوماســية *hay'a diblomaasiyya* diplomatic corps.

ه ي ب *hyb*

هاب *haab (*يهاب *yhaab)* 1. to be afraid of s.o. or s.th. قلت له: «لا تهاب» *git-la: "la thaab."* I said to him: "Don't be afraid." لا تبوق ولا تهاب *la tbuug w-la thaab.* If you don't steal, you won't have to be afraid of anyone or anything. 2. to respect. عندهم مدرس كلش زين. يهابونـــه *ᶜindahum mudarris killiš zeen. yhaabuuna.* They have a very good teacher; they respect him.

ه ي ج *hyj*

هــاج *haaj (*يهيج *yhiij)* 1. to become furious, angry. لين علمته باللي صار هاج *leen ᶜallamta b-lli ṣaar haaj.* When I told him about what had happened, he became furious. 2. to be or become stormy, rough, to run high. كان فيه هوا واجد والبحر هاج *čaan fii hawa waayid w-l-baḥar haaj.* It was very windy and the sea became stormy.

هيــج *hayyaj* II 1. to arouse, excite. خنتها هيجتـــني *xinnatta hayyajatni.* Her perfume aroused me. 2. to stir up, provoke, agitate. خطاب عبد الناصر كان يهيج النـــاس *xiṭaab ᶜabd n-naaṣir čaan yhayyij n-naas.* Nasir's speech used to stir up people.

تهيــج *thayyaj* V 1. to get excited, stirred up. اقعــد. لا تتــهيج *'igᶜid. la tithayyaj.* Sit down. Don't get excited.

2. to become aroused, excited. تهيج لين شافها عريانة *thayyaj leen šaaffa* *ᶜiryaana.* He became aroused when he saw her naked.

هيش *hyš*

هايشة *haayša*. See under **هوش**٢ *hwš.*

هيكل *hykl*

هيكل *haykal* p. هياكل *hayaakil* 1. temple, place of worship. هيكل سليمان *haykal sulaymaan* Solomon's Temple. 2. skeleton. 3. framework.

هيل *hyl*

هيل *heel* (coll.) cardamom. قهوة بدون هيل ما تصير *gahwa b-duun heel ma tṣiir.* Coffee without cardamom cannot be coffee.

هيلي *hyly*

هيلي *hiili* Hili (town in Abu Dhabi famous for its historical ruins, esp. tombs of kings and sovereigns). هيلي قرية أثرية في بو ظبي *hiili ġarya 'aθariyya fi bu đabi.* Hili is an archaeological village in Abu Dhabi.

هين *hyn*

هان *haan,* هين *hayyin*, etc. See under **هون** *hwn.*

و

و w

و *w* 1. and, plus. سالم وخميس *saalim w-xmayyis* Salim and Khmayis. وتالي؟ *w-taali?* And then what? What happened next? أنا قلت لك وما يحتاج بعد *'aana git-lak w-ma yiḥtaaj baᶜad.* I have told you and that's it. خمسة وخمسة عشرة *xamsa w-xamsa ᶜašara.* Five plus five is ten. 2. while, as, when. شفته وهو يبكي *čifta w-huwa yabči.* I saw him while he was crying. دعمت سيارة وأنا كنت مريوس *diᶜamt sayyaara w-aana čint mreewis.* I hit a car while I was backing up. 3. (in an oath or exclamation) by. والله! *w-aḷḷa!*, وحق الله! *w-ḥagg aḷḷa!* by God! in the name of God! والله ما ادري *w-aḷḷa ma dri.* By God, I don't know. Honestly, I don't know.

واح waaḥ

واحة *waaḥa* p. *-aat* oasis. واحة البريمي *waaḥat li-breemi* the Buraimi Oasis. فندق الواحة *fundug l-waaḥa* the Oasis Hotel.

وار waar

وار *waar* p. *-aat* yard (measure). اشتريت وارين بز *štireet waareen bazz.* I bought two yards of cloth.

واركوت waarkwt

واركوت *waarkoot* p. *-aat* overcoat.

واشر waašr

واشر *waašir* p. *-aat* washer (of a screw).

وانيت waanyt

وانيت *waaneet* p. *-aat* pickup, small truck. وانيتي كان خربان *waaneeti čaan xarbaan.* My pickup was out of order.

واو waaw

واو *waaw* name of the letter و *w.*

واوي waawy

واوي *waawi* p. *-yya* jackal.

واير waayr

واير *waayir* p. *-aat* wire.

وبر wbr

وبر *wabar* (coll.) camel hair.

وتد wtd

وتد *watad* p. أوتاد *'awtaad* (common var. وتاد *wtaad*) pole, stake. (from the Quran) ﴿وجعلنا الجبال أوتاداً أوتادا﴾ *wa-jaᶜalna l-jibaala 'awtaadan 'awtaada.* We (God) made mountains to be poles. We made mountains to serve as poles.

وتر wtr

وتر *watar* p. أوتار *'awtaar* (common var. وتار *wtaar*) 1. string (of a musical instrument). 2. hypotenuse (geom.).

وثگ wθg

وثق *wiθag (*يوثق *yuuθig)* (with ب *b-*) to trust, have confidence in s.o. عطيته اللي يبغاه؛ أوثق به *ᶜaṭeeta lli yibġaa; 'uuθig bii.* I gave him what he wanted; I trust him. يوثق به *yuuθag bii.* He's trust-worthy, reliable.

وثق *waθθag* II to authenticate, certify (a document). لازم توثق شهاداتك من السفارة *laazim twaθθig šahaadaatak min s-safaara.* You have to have your certificates authenticated at the embassy.

توثق *twaθθag* V pass. of II وثق *waθθag.*

ثقة *θiga* trust, confidence. لك ثقة فيه؟ *lak θiga fii?* Do you trust him? Do you have confidence in him? ثقة بالنفس *θiga b-n-nafs* self-confidence, self-reliance. عرفت هذا من مصدر ثقة *ᶜiraft haaða min maṣdar θiga.* I knew this from a reliable source.

وثيقة *waθiiga* p. وثايق *waθaayig* document, record. مركز الوثايق *markaz l-waθaayig* the document center. وثيقة بالدرجات *waθiiga b-d-darajaat* transcript (of school grades). عطوني وثيقة اني اشتغلت وياهم *ᶜaṭooni waθiiga 'inni štaġalt wiyyaahum.* They gave me a document certifying that I had worked for them.

ميثاق *miiθaag* p. مواثيق *mawaaθiig* charter, pact, covenant. ميثاق هيئة الأمم *miiθaag hay'at l-'umam* the Charter of the United Nations.

توثيق *tawθiig* (v.n. from II وثق *waθθag*) 1. authentication, attestation. توثيق الشهادة *tawθiig š-šahaada* authentication of the certificate. 2. strengthening, consolidation. توثيق العلاقات *tawθiig l-ᶜalaagaat* the strengthening of relations.

و ث ن *wθn*

وثن *waθan* p. أوثان *'awθaan* idol.

وثني *waθani* p. *-yyiin* heathen, pagan.

وثنية *waθaniyya* paganism.

و ج ب *wjb*

وجب *wijab* (يوجب *yuujib*) (with على *ᶜala*) to be one's duty to do s.th., to become obligatory to s.o. موب حامل؛ وجب عليها الصوم *muub ḥaamil; wijab ᶜaleeha ṣ-ṣoom.* She's not pregnant; it's her duty to fast.

وجب *wajjab* II to be courteous or hospitable toward s.o. هلي جاوا عندنا. وجبناهم واجد *hali yaw ᶜindana. wajjabnaahum waayid.* My relatives came to our place. We were very courteous and hospitable toward them.

استوجب *stawjab* X 1. to merit, deserve, be worthy of. المسألة ما تستوجب اهتمام أكثر *l-mas'ala ma tistawjib htimaam 'akθar.* The problem doesn't merit more consideration. 2. to require, necessitate. هذا ما يستوجب حضورك *haaða ma yistawjib ḥuḍuurak.* This doesn't require your presence.

وجبة *wajba* p. *-aat*: وجبة طعام *wajbat ṭaᶜaam* meal, repast. قطو مطابخ. ياكل خمس وجبات في اليوم *gaṭu maṭaabix. yaakil xamas wajbaat fi l-yoom.* He eats like a pig. He eats five meals a day.

واجب *waajib* 1. (with على *ᶜala*) (it's) incumbent upon s.o., necessary for s.o. to do s.th. واجب عليّ أروح أسلم على الشيخ *waajib ᶜalayya 'aruuḥ asallim ᶜala š-šeex.* It's incumbent upon me to go to welcome the Shaikh. 2. (p. *-aat*) duty. هذا واجب عليك *haaða* *waajib* *ᶜaleek.* It's your duty. لنا حقوق وواجبات *lana ḥguug w-waajibaat.* We have rights and duties.

و ج د *wjd*

وجدان *wijdaan* conscience.

واجد *waajid* (more common var. *waayid*). See under **و ي د** *wyd.*

موجود *mawjuud* 1. present, in attendance, around. التنديل موجود في الحفيز *t-tindeel mawjuud fi l-ḥafiiz.* The foreman is in the office. موب موجود في البيت *muub mawjuud fi l-beet.* He's not at home. 2. located, situated. وين خور فكان موجودة؟ *ween xoor fakkaan mawjuuda?* Where's Khor Fakkan located? 3. (p. *-aat*) stock, asset, supply.

و ج ع *wjᶜ*

وجع *wujaᶜ (يوجع yoojaᶜ)* to hurt, pain. بطنه يوجعه من الدوا *baṭna yoojaᶜa min d-duwa.* His stomach is hurting from the medicine. راسي يوجعني *raasi yoojaᶜni.* I have a headache.

وجع *wajjaᶜ* II (more common var. II عور *ᶜawwar*). See under **ع و ر** *ᶜwr.*

توجع *twajjaᶜ* V (more common var. V تعور *tᶜawwar*). See under **ع و ر** *ᶜwr.*

وجع *wujaᶜ* pain, ache.

و ج ه *wjh*

جهة *jiha* p. *-aat* 1. direction. في أي جهة السفارة؟ *fi 'ayy jiha s-safaara?* Which direction is the embassy? 2. side. راح من ذيك الجهة *raaḥ min ðiič l-jiha.* He went from that side. من جهة الشمال *min jihat š-šamaal* from the north. 3. point of view, aspect. من جميع الجهات *min jimiiᶜ l-jihaat* from all points of view. من جهتي أنا *min jihati 'aana* as for me, as far as I am concerned.

وجه *wajih* see *weeh* under **و ي ه** *wyh.*

وجهة *wijha*: وجهة نظر *wijhat naḍar* point of view, viewpoint.

و ح د *wḥd*

وحد *waḥḥad* II 1. to unite, unify, make one. الشيوخ وحدوا الإمارات *š-šyuux waḥḥdaw l-'imaaraat.* The Shaikhs united the Emirates. 2. to standardize. وزارة التربية وحدت المناهج *wazaarat t-tarbiya waḥḥdat l-manaahij.* The ministry of education standardized the programs of study. 3. to declare God to be one. لين المسلم يوحد الله يقول: «لا إله إلا الله» *leen l-muslim ywaḥḥid aḷḷa yguul: "la 'ilaaha 'illa aḷḷa."* When Muslims declare God as a single entity, they say: "There is no god but He."

توحد *twaḥḥad* V pass. of II وحد *waḥḥad.* توحدت الإمارات وصار اسمها الإمارات العربية المتحدة *twaḥḥadat l-'imaaraat w-ṣaar 'asimha l-'imaaraat l-ᶜarabiyya l-mittaḥda.* The emirates were united and their name became the United Arab Emirates.

اتحد *ttiḥad* VIII (v.i.) to unite, be united, form a union. اتحدت الإمارات *ttiḥdat l-'imaaraat.* The emirates united.

وحدة *wiḥda* 1. unity, oneness. وحدة العرب *wiḥdat l-ᶜarab* the unity of the Arabs. 2. loneliness, solitude. يحب الوحدة. دايماً بروحه *yḥibb l-wiḥda.*

daayman bruuḥa. He likes loneliness. He's always by himself. 3. (p. *-aat*) unity, group. وحدات من الجيش *wiḥdaat min l-jeeš* army units, military units.

وحيد *waḥiid* (adj.) only, sole. ابني الوحيد *'ibni l-waḥiid* my only son. بنتي الوحيدة *binti l-waḥiida* my only daughter. السبب الوحيد *s-sabab l-waḥiid* the only reason. همي الوحيد أكمل دراستي يا يبا *hammi l-waḥiid 'akammil diraasti ya yuba.* My only concern is to complete my studies, father. وريثه الوحيد *wariiθa l-waḥiid* his sole inheritor.

اتحاد *'ittiḥaad* (v.n. from VIII اتحد *ttiḥad*) unity, union. اتحاد الدول العربية *'ittiḥaad d-duwal l-ᶜarabiyya* the unity of the Arab States. اتحاد الطلاب *'ittiḥaad ṭ-ṭullaab* the students' union.

واحد *waaḥid* fem. واحدة *waḥda* 1. one (numeral) 2. someone, somebody. واحد عطاني اياه *waaḥid ᶜaṭaani-yyaa.* Someone gave it to me. جاني واحد من الكولية *yaani waaḥid min l-kuuliyya.* One of the coolies came to (see) me. واحد منهم *waaḥid minhum* one of them. كل واحد *kill waaḥid.* everyone, everybody. الواحد ما يقدر يمشي من الحر *l-waaḥid ma yigdar yamši min l-ḥarr.* One cannot walk because of the heat. 3. (in inter. and neg. sentences) أحد *'aḥad* anyone. فيه أحد هني؟ *fii 'aḥad hni?* Is there anyone here? ما فيه أحد *ma fii 'aḥad.* There isn't anyone.

متحد *mittaḥid* united, combined. الإمارات العربية المتحدة *l-'imaaraat l-ᶜarabiyya l-mittaḥda.* The United Arab Emirates. الولايات المتحدة *l-wilaayaat l-mittaḥda.* The United States.

وحش *wḥš*

استوحش *stawḥaš* X 1. to feel lonely. استوحشت في ذيك الديرة. كنت بروحي *stawḥašt fi ðiič d-diira. čint b-ruuḥi.* I felt lonely in that town. I was by myself. 2. (with ل *l-*) to miss s.o. استوحشنا لك لين كنت في أمريكا *stawḥašnaa-lak leen čint fi 'amriika.* We missed you when you were in America.

وحش *waḥš* p. وحوش *wḥuuš* wild animal, wild beast. الظبيان من الوحوش البرية في الخليج *ð̣-ð̣ibyaan min li-wḥuuš l-barriyya fi l-xaliij.* Deer are among wild animals in the Gulf.

وحشي *waḥši* wild, savage. حيوانات وحشية *ḥayawaanaat waḥšiyya* wild animals.

وحشية *waḥšiyya* brutality, savagery.

أوحش *'awḥaš* (elat.) 1. (with من *min*) more untamed than, etc. 2. (with foll. n.) the most untamed, etc.

متوحش *mitwaḥḥiš* 1. wild, barbaric, savage. 2. (p. *-iin*) barbarian, savage.

وحل *wḥl*

وحل *waḥal* (coll.) mud.

وخر *wxr*

وخر *waxxar* II 1. to get out of the way, move aside. وخرت لاجل يفوت من قدامي *waxxart laji yfuut min giddaami.* I got out of the way so he could pass by me. 2. (v.t.) to get s.th. out of the way, move s.th. back. وخر سيارتك *waxxir sayyaaratk.* Move your car out of the way.

توخــر *twaxxar* V pass. of II وخــر *waxxar.*

و د د *wdd*

ود *widd* desire, wish. ودك تروحين وايانا؟ *widdič truuḥiin wiyyaana?* Would you like to go with us? ودي أشوفك *widdi 'ašuufič.* I would like to see you.

ودي *widdi* (adj.) friendly, amicable. علاقــات وديــة *ᶜalaagaat widdiyya* friendly relations.

وداد *wdaad* love, friendship.

و د ع *wdᶜ*

ودع *waddaᶜ* II to say goodbye to s.o., bid s.o. farewell. رحنــا نودعــه في المطــار أمـس *riḥna nwaddᶜa fi l-maṭaar 'ams.* We went to the airport to see him off yesterday. جاني وودعني لانه مسافر *yaani w-waddaᶜni linna msaafir.* He came and said goodbye to me because he was going away.

وداع *wdaaᶜ* (common var. *wadaaᶜ*) farewell, leave-taking.

مـودع *mwaddiᶜ* 1. (act. part. from II ودع *waddaᶜ*) having said goodbye to s.o. أنا مودعه قبل شـوية *'aana mwaddᶜa gabl šwayya.* I said goodbye to him a short while ago. 2. (p. *-iin*) people saying goodbye.

مســتودع *mistawdaᶜ* p. *-aat* warehouse, depot (mil.). مستودع أسلحة *mistawdaᶜ 'asliḥa* arms depot.

و د ي¹ *wdy*

ودى *wadda* II 1. to send. صادوا سمك واجــد وودوه الكــبرة *ṣaadaw simač waayid w-waddoo č-čabra.* They caught a lot of fish and took it to the market. ولـدي ودى لنـا هديـة مـن أمريكـا *wlidi waddaa-lna hadiyya min 'amriika.* My son sent us a gift from America. 2. to take s.o. or s.th. to some place, convey. وديت العيال المدرسة *waddeet li-ᶜyaaḷ l-madrasa.* I took the children to school. وديته سوق الســمك *waddeeta suug s-simač.* I took him to the fish market. ليش ما تودين عليه؟ *leeš ma twaddiini ᶜalee?* Why don't you take me to it? وديت عليه *waddeet ᶜalee.* I sent for him.

وادي *waadi* p. وديـان *widyaan* valley, river valley.

و د ي² *wdy*

دية *diyya* blood money.

و ذ ن¹ *wðn*

وذن *waððan* II (common var. II أذن *'aððan*). See under ء ذ ن *'ðn.*

مؤذن *m'aððin* p. -iin muezzin, one who calls to prayer.

و ذ ن² *wðn*

وذن *wiðin* p. وذون *wðuun.* See under ء ذ ن *'ðn.*

و ر ا *wraa*

See under **و ر ي** *wry.*

و ر ت ي م *wrtym*

ورتيـم *warteem* overtime. في هذي الدايرة مـا فيـه ورتيـم. روح شـوف دايـرة ثانيــة *fi haaði d-daayra ma fii warteem. ruuḥ čuuf daayra θaanya.* In this department there is no overtime (work). Go look for another department.

و ر ث *wrθ*

ورث *wiriθ (*يـورث *yuuraθ)* to inherit.

ورث عمـارتين علـى السـيف *wiriθ ᶜmaarteen ᶜala s-siif.* He inherited two buildings on the seashore.

ورث *warraθ* II to leave, bequeath, will. أبوه ورثه كل أملاكه *'ubuu warraθa kill 'amlaaka.* His father left him all his property. أبـوك ورثـك شـي؟ *'ubuuk warraθk šayy?* Did your father leave you anything?

ورث *wirθ* inheritance, legacy.

ورثة *wirθa* p. ورث *wiraθ* inheritance.

وراثـة *wiraaθa* heredity, hereditary, transmission.

وراثـي *wiraaθi* hereditary. مرض وراثي *maraḍ wiraaθi* hereditary disease.

وريـث *wariiθ* p. ورثـا *wuraθa* heir, inheritor. الورثـا عيالـه وأمهـم وكيلتهـم *l-wuraθa ᶜyaaḷa w-'ummhum wakiilattum.* The heirs are his children and their mother is their guardian.

تـراث *turaaθ* heritage, legacy. الـتراث العربي *t-turaaθ l-ᶜarabi* Arab heritage.

ورچ *wrč*

ورك *wirč* p. وروك *wruuč* 1. thigh. 2. hip.

ورد١ *wrd*

اسـتورد *stawrad* X to import. نستورد أشيا واجدة ونصدر بترول واجـد *nistawrid 'ašya waayda w-nṣaddir batrool waayid.* We import many things and export a lot of oil.

مـورد *mawrid* p. مـوارد *mawaarid* income, revenue.

اسـتيراد *stiiraad* (v.n. from X استورد *stawrad*) import, importation. استيراد وتصديـر *stiiraad w-taṣdiir* import-export.

وارد *waarid* p. *-aat* import. واردات وصـادرات *waaridaat w-ṣaadiraat* imports and exports.

مستورد *mistawrid* 1. (act. part. from X استورد *stawrad*) having imported. تونا مسـتوردين عشـرة طـن عيـش *tawwna mistawirdiin ᶜašara ṭann ᶜeeš.* We have just imported ten tons of rice. 2. (p. *-iin*) importer.

ورد٢ *wrd*

ورد *ward* (coll.) s. وردة *warda* p. *-aat* 1. roses. فيه ورد في البستان اللي ورا البيت. *fii ward fi l-bistaan illi wara l-beet.* There are roses in the backyard. 2. flowers.

وردي *wardi* (adj.) pink, rosy. كـانت لابسـة فسـتان وردي *čaanat laabsa fustaan wardi.* She was wearing a pink dress.

ورس *wrs*

ورس *warras* II to dye (clothes, etc.) المورس هـو اللـي يـورس الهـدوم *li-mwarris huwa lli ywarris li-hduum.* A dyer is the one who dyes clothes.

ورس *wars* (coll.) dye, coloring.

مورس *mwarris* dyer.

ورش *wrš*

ورشة *warša* p. *-aat* workshop.

ورگ *wrg*

ورق *warag* (coll.) p. أوراق *'awraag,* وراق *wraag.* 1. leaves, foliage. ورق الشجر *warag š-šiyar* the tree leaves. 2. paper. ورق حـق الكتابـة *warag ḥagg* *li-ktaaba* writing paper. 3. (playing) cards. لعبنا ورق واستانسنا *li^cabna warag w-staanasna.* We played cards and had a good time.

ورقة *wruga* p. *-aat* 1. leaf. 2. piece of paper, sheet of paper.

ورنيش *wrnyš*

ورنيش *warniiš* (coll.) varnish.

ورور *wrwr*

ورور *warwar* p. وراور *waraawir* revolver, pistol.

وري *wry*

ورا *wara* 1. (prep.) behind, in the rear of, at the back of. فيه موقف سيارات ورا البناية *fii mawgif sayyaaraat wara li-bnaaya.* There's a parking lot behind the building. ليش واقف وراي؟ *leeš waagif waraaya?* Why are you standing behind me? كانت ماشية وراهم *čaanat maašya waraahum.* She was walking behind them. من ورا *min wara* (a) from behind, from the back of. طلع من ورا العمارة *ṭila^c min wara li-^cmaara.* He came out from behind the building. طلع من ورا الباب *ṭila^c min wara l-baab.* He came out from behind the door. (b) from, resultant from, caused by. كل المشاكل من وراك *kill l-mašaakil min waraak.* You are the cause of all the problems. ها المشاكل تجي من ورا الحريم *hal-mašaakil tyi min wara l-ḥariim.* These problems are caused by women. 2. (adv.) behind, at the back, in the rear. سار ورا *saar wara.* He walked behind. لا تقعد ورا. تعال اقعد قدام *la tag^cid wara. ta^caal w-ig^cid giddaam.* Don't sit at the back. Come and sit in front. لورا *l-wara* backward, to the rear. رجع لورا *rija^c li-wara.* He went backward. He backed up.

وراني *warraani* (adj.) rear, back, hind. الباب الوراني *l-baab l-warraani* the rear door. الرجول الورانية حق العنز *r-ryuul l-warraaniyya ḥagg l-^canz* the hind legs of the nanny goat.

وزر ^١ *wzr*

وزرة *wizra,* وزار *wzaar* p. وزر *wizar, -aat* loincloth (usually worn under the كندورة *kandoora* man's dress).

وزر ^٢ *wzr*

وزير *waziir* p. وزرا *wuzara* (cabinet) minister. وزير الخارجية *waziir l-xaarijiyya* the minister of foreign affairs, the secretary of state. رئيس الوزرا *ra'iis l-wuzara* the prime minister. مجلس الوزرا *maylis l-wuzara* the council of ministers.

وزارة *wazaara, wizaara* p. *-aat* ministry. وزارة الأشغال *wazaarat l-'ašġaal* the ministry of (public) works. وزارة البترول *wazaarat l-batrool* the ministry of petroleum. وزارة الخارجية *wazaarat l-xaarijiyya* the foreign ministry, the department of State. وزارة الداخلية *wazaarat d-daaxiliyya* the ministry of the interior. وزارة التربية *wazaarat t-tarbiya* the ministry of education. وزارة الزراعة *wazaarat z-ziraa^ca* the ministry of agriculture. وزارة المواصلات *wazaarat l-muwaaṣalaat* the ministry of communications. وزارة الشؤون *wazaarat š-šu'uun* the ministry of (social) affairs. وزارة الأوقاف *wazaarat l-'awgaaf* the ministry of endowment.

وزارة التخطيط *wazaarat t-taxṭiiṭ* the ministry of planning. وزارة العدل *wizaarat l-ᶜadil* the ministry of justice.

وزاري *wazaari* ministerial. تعديل وزاري *taᶜdiil wazaari* cabinet reshuffle.

وزز *wzz*

وز *wazz* (coll.) geese. s. وزة *-a* p. *-aat.*

وزع *wzᶜ*

وزع *wazzaᶜ* (يوزع *ywazziᶜ*) 1. to deliver. بعد ما وزعوا البريد *baᶜad ma wazzᶜaw l-bariid.* They haven't delivered the mail yet. 2. to distribute, deal out, pass out. الشركة وزعت الأرباح على المساهمين *š-šarika wazzaᶜat l-'arbaaḥ ᶜala l-musaahmiin.* The company distributed the proceeds among the shareholders. المدير وزع الجوايز على الطلاب المتفوقين *l-mudiir wazzaᶜ l-jawaayiz ᶜala ṭ-ṭullaab l-mitfawwgiin.* The principal distributed the awards to the outstanding students.

توزع *twazzaᶜ* V pass. of II وزع *wazzaᶜ.*

توزيع *tawziiᶜ* (v.n. from II وزع *wazzaᶜ*) 1. distribution. 2. delivery.

موزع *mwazziᶜ* (act. part. from II وزع *wazzaᶜ*) 1. having distributed s.th. موزع ثروته بين عياله *mwazziᶜ θariwta been ᶜyaaḷa.* He has distributed his wealth among his children. 2. distributor. موزع البريد *mwazziᶜ l-bariid* the mailman.

موزع *mwazzaᶜ* (p.p. from II وزع *wazzaᶜ*) 1. having been distributed. الأرباح موزعة *l-'arbaaḥ mwazzaᶜa.* The dividends have been distributed. 2. having been delivered. البريد موزع *l-bariid mwazzaᶜ.* The mail has been delivered.

وزن *wzn*

وزن *wuzan* (يوزن *yuuzin*) to weigh, weigh out. آزن لي خمسة كيلو عيش *'aazin-li xamsa keelu ᶜeeš.* Weigh out for me five kilograms of rice.

انوزن *nwuzan* VII pass. of وزن *wuzan.*

وزن *wazin* p. وزان *wzaan* 1. weight. كم وزن ها الكيس؟ *čam wazin hač-čiis?* How much does this bag weigh? وزن ثقيل *wazin θagiil* heavy weight. ما عليك منه. ما له وزن هني *ma ᶜaleek minna. ma la wazin hini.* Don't pay any attention to him. He doesn't carry any weight here. 2. weight (in boxing) وزن الريشة *wazn r-riiša* featherweight. وزن الديك *wazn d-diič* bantamweight.

وزنة *wazna* (n. of inst.) p. *-aat* 1. unit of weight. 2. weight.

ميزان *miizaan* p. موازين *mawaaziin* 1. scale, balance. حط الشنطة على الميزان *ḥuṭṭ š-šanṭa ᶜala l-miizaan.* Put the suitcase on the scale. ميزان حرارة *miizaan ḥaraara* thermometer.

ميزانية *miizaaniyya* p. *-aat* 1. budget. ميزانية السنة الجاية *miizaaniyyat s-sana l-yaaya* next year's budget. 2. control, regulation. نصرف بدون ميزانية *niṣrif b-duun miizaaniyya.* We spend without control.

موزون *mawzuun* (p.p. of وزن *wuzan*) having been weighed, weighed out.

وزي *wzy*

توازى *twaaza* VI to get into trouble.

توازيت وما دريت شوأسوي *twaazzeet w-ma dareet š-asawwi.* I got into trouble and didn't know what to do.

وسخ *wsx*

See وصخ *wṣx.*

وسط *wsṭ*

See وصط *wṣṭ.*

وسع *ws^c^*

وسع *wisa^c^ (*يوسع *yoosa^c^)* to hold, have room for, be large enough for. هالحجرة توسع خمسين نفر *hal-ḥijra toosa^c^ xamsiin nafar.* This room holds fifty people. ذاك المكان وسعنا كلنا *ðaak l-mukaan wisa^c^na killana.* That place held us all.

وسع *wassa^c^* II 1. to make wider, more spacious. هالشارع كان ضيق. البلدية وسعته *haš-šaari^c^ čaan ḍayyig. l-baladiyya wassa^c^ata.* This street was narrow. The municipality widened it. 2. (with ل *l-*) to make room for s.o. وسع لي. أريد أقعد *wassi^c^-li. 'ariid ag^c^id.* Make room for me. I want to sit down. 3. (with على *^c^ala*) to be generous toward s.o., to make s.o. wealthy. الله وسعها علينا *'aḷḷa wassa^c^ha ^c^aleena.* God was generous to us.

توسع *twassa^c^* V 1. to become wider, to expand. الشوارع توسعت بفضل البلدية *š-šawaari^c^ twasssa^c^at b-faðl l-baladiyya.* The streets became wider, thanks to the municipality. الحفريات توسعت في الإمارات *l-ḥafriyyaat twassa^c^at fi l-'imaaraat.* Excavations have expanded in the U.A.E. 2. to have enough room. توسعنا في الدار الجديدة *twassa^c^na fi d-daar l-ydiida.* We had enough room in the new house.

أوسع *'awsa^c^* (elat.) 1. (with من *min*) wider, more spacious than. 2. (with foll. n.) the widest, most spacious.

واسع *waasi^c^* wide, spacious, extensive. الشارع واسع *š-šaari^c^ waasi^c^.* The street is wide. حجرة واسعة *ḥijra waas^c^a* spacious room. الله واسع الرحمة *'aḷḷa waasi^c^ r-raḥma.* God is abounding in mercy. واسع الصدر *waasi^c^ ṣ-ṣadir* patient.

موسوعة *mawsuu^c^a* p. *-aat* encyclopedia.

وسم *wsm*

وسم *wasim* 1. (= وسمي *wasmi*) rainy season that lasts fifty days in autumn. 2. tribal mark, tribal brand. 3. cauterization.

وسام *wisaam* p. أوسمة *'awsima* 1. medal. 2. badge of honor. وسام الاستحقاق *wisaam li-stiḥgaag* order of merit. وسام الشرف *wisaam š-šaraf* Legion of Honor.

موسم *moosam* p. مواسم *mawaasim* season, time of the year. موسم الحج *moosam l-ḥajj* the pilgrimage season.

وسوس *wsws*

وسوس *waswas (*يوسوس *ywaswis)* 1. to whisper. ما بغيت أحد يسمع الحكي. وسوست له بإذنه *ma bağeet 'aḥad yisma^c^ l-ḥači. waswasit-la b-'iðna.* I didn't want anyone to hear my words. I whispered (to him) in his ear. 2. to tempt s.o. with wicked suggestions. وسوس لي الشيطان وذقت الخمر *waswas-li š-šayṭaan w-ðugt l-xamir.* The devil tempted me with wicked thoughts and I tasted wine.

وس ي *wsy*

واسى *waasa* III to comfort, console. رحنا نواسيه لان ولده في السجن *riḥna nwaasii linna wilda fi s-sijin.* We went to comfort him because his son was in jail. مات ابنهم في حادث سيارة. رحنا نواسيهم *maat 'ibinhum fi ḥaadiθ sayyaara. riḥna nwaasiihum.* Their son died in a car crash. We went to offer condolences to them.

مواساة *mwaasaa* (v.n.) consolation.

وش ك *wšk*

وشك *wašak*: على وشك *ᶜala wašak* on the verge of, about to. على وشك الموت *ᶜala wašak l-moot* on the verge of death, about to die.

وش م *wšm*

وشم *wašim* tattoo, tattoo mark.

وص خ *wṣx*

وسخ *waṣṣax* II to make s.th. dirty, filthy. وسخ هدومه *waṣṣax hduuma.* He made his clothes dirty. لا توسخ ايدينك *la twaṣṣix 'iideenak.* Don't get your hands dirty.

توسخ *twaṣṣax* V pass. of II وسخ *waṣṣax.* الهدوم تتوسخ كل يوم من الغبار. *li-hduum titwaṣṣax kill yom min li-ġbaar.* Clothes get dirty every day from the dust.

وسخ *wuṣax* p. وسوخات *wuṣuuxaat* dirt, filth. فيه وسخ على الأرض. خمها *fii wuṣax ᶜala l-'arḍ. ximmha.* There's dirt on the floor. Mop it.

وسخ *waṣix* dirty, filthy, foul. خميت الأرض لانها وسخة *xammeet l-'arḍ linnha waṣxa.* I mopped the floor because it was dirty. المواعين وسخين *l-muwaaᶜiin waṣxiin.* The dishes are dirty. ثم وسخ *θamm waṣix* foul mouth.

وص ط *wṣṭ*

توسط *twaṣṣaṭ* V (with عند *ᶜind*) to cause to intercede with s.o. روح شوف لك واحد يتوسط لك عند الوزير *ruuḥ čuuf-lak waaḥid yitwaṣṣaṭ-lak ᶜind l-waziir.* Go find someone to intercede for you with the minister.

وسط *waṣaṭ* (adj.) 1. middle (course), intermediate. لو هذا لو ذاك. ما فيه حل وسط. *loo haaða loo ðaak. ma fii ḥall waṣaṭ.* Either this or that. There isn't a compromise solution. 2. medium, average. *gyaas waṣaṭ* medium size.

وسط *wiṣṭ* 1. (prep.) in the middle of, in the center of, among. المركز التجاري وسط المدينة *l-markaz t-tijaari wiṣṭ l-madiina.* The commercial center is downtown. وسط الصفري *wiṣṭ li-ṣfiri* in the middle of autumn. 2. center, middle. أنت في الوسط *'inta fi l-wiṣṭ.* You're in the center.

وسطاني *waṣṭaani* (common var. وسطي *waṣṭi*) 1. middle, central. الصندوق الوسطاني *ṣ-ṣanduug l-waṣṭaani* the middle box. 2. medium, medium-sized. أبغى جوتي وسطاني *'abġa juuti waṣṭaani.* I want medium-sized shoes. سكرو وسطاني *sikruu waṣṭaani* medium-sized screw.

أوسط *'awṣaṭ* f. وسطى *wuṣṭa* middle, central. الشرق الأوسط *š-šarg l-'awṣaṭ* the Middle East. أمريكا الوسطى *'amriika l-wuṣṭa* Central America.

واسطة *waasṭa* p. وسايط *waṣaayiṭ* 1. intermediary, interceder, sponsor. 2. means, medium. وسايط النقل *waṣaayiṭ n-nagil* means of transportation. بدون واسطة *b-duun waasṭa* without any means. بواسطة *b-waasṭat* by means of. بواسطة التجارة *b-waasṭat t-tijaara* by means of trade.

متوسط *mitwaṣṣiṭ* 1. (act. part. from V توسط *twaṣṣaṭ*) having interceded. هو متوسط لي عند الوزير *huwa mitwaṣṣiṭ-li ᶜind l-waziir.* He has interceded for me with the minister. 2. centrally located, central. الشارجة متوسطة بين الإمارات الثانية *š-šaarja mitwaṣṣṭa been l-'imaaraat θ-θaanya.* Sharja is centrally located among the other emirates. 3. intermediate, medial. تدرس في المدرسة المتوسطة *tidris fi l-madrasa l-mitwaṣṣṭa.* She is studying in the intermediate (junior high) school. 4. average, mean. درجة متوسطة *daraja mitwaṣṣṭa* average grade.

و ص ف *wṣf*

وصف *wuṣaf* (يوصف *yuuṣif*) 1. to describe, depict. تقدر توصف لي البيت؟ *tigdar tuuṣif-li l-beet?* Can you describe the house to me? وصفته وصف زين *wuṣafta waṣif zeen.* I described it well. 2. to praise, credit. وصف الشيخ بالكرم في قصيدة نبطية *wuṣaf š-šeex b-l-karam fi gaṣiida nabaṭiyya.* He praised the Shaikh for generosity in a colloquial poem.

انوصف *nwuṣaf* VII pass. of وصف *wuṣaf.*

صفة *ṣifa* p. *-aat* quality, characteristic, trait. هذي من صفات كريم الأخلاق *haaði min ṣifaat kariim l-'axlaag.* This is one of the qualities of noble-minded people.

وصفة *waṣfa* p. *-aat*: وصفة طبية *waṣfa ṭibbiyya* medical prescription.

مواصفة *muwaaṣafa* p. *-aat* 1. specification. 2. detailed description. عطنا مواصفة النمونة *ᶜaṭna muwaaṣafat n-namuuna.* Give us a detailed description of the specimen.

مستوصف *mistawṣaf* p. *-aat* clinic.

و ص ل *wṣl*

وصل *wuṣal* (يوصل *yooṣal*) 1. to arrive. أي حزة وصلت؟ *'ayy ḥazza wuṣalt?* At what time did you arrive? متى وصلت دبي؟ *mita wiṣalt dbayy?* When did you arrive in Dubai? 2. to reach s.o. وصلني خط أمس *wuṣalni xaṭṭ 'ams.* I received a letter yesterday. وصلني الخبر *wuṣalni l-xabar.* I received the news.

وصل *waṣṣal* II 1. to give s.o. a ride. تقدر توصلني المطار بسيارتك؟ *tigdar twaṣṣilni l-maṭaar b-sayyaartak?* Can you give me a ride in your car to the airport? 2. to convey, take, bring (s.th. to s.o.). هو اللي وصل لي الخبر *huwa lli waṣṣal-li l-xabar.* He's the one who conveyed the news to me. كل شي نقوله يوصله حق المدير *kill šayy nguula ywaṣṣla ḥagg l-mudiir.* He takes everything we say to the manager. ظلوا يرفعون سعر البانزين إلين وصلوه إلى ثلاثة دولار الليتر *ðallaw yirfaᶜuun siᶜr l-baanziin 'ileen waṣṣaloo 'ila θalaaθa duulaar l-liter.* They kept raising the price of gasoline until they brought it up to three dollars per liter. 3. to connect, hook up, join. البيت جديد وفيه

ماي واجد، بس بعد ما وصلوا الكهربا *l-beet yidiid w-fii maay waayid, bass ba^c^ad ma waṣṣlaw l-kahraba.* The house is new and there is a lot of water, but they haven't connected the electricity yet. إذا تبغى تستأجر الشقة، لازم تسألهم يوصلوا لك الكهربا *'iða tibġa tista'jir š-šigga, laazim tis'alhum ywaṣṣluu-lak l-kahraba.* If you to rent the apartment, you'll have to ask them to hook up the electricity for you.

واصل *waaṣal* III to continue, go on with. واصل دراسته في أمريكا *waaṣal diraasta fi 'amriika.* He continued his studies in America.

توصل *twaṣṣal* V (with إلى *'ila*) to reach, attain, arrive at s.th. توصلنا إلى حل وسط *twaṣṣalna 'ila ḥall waṣaṭ.* We reached a compromise.

اتصل *ttiṣal* VIII (with في *fi*) to contact s.o., get in touch with s.o. صار لي أحاول أتصل فيك من مدة ساعتين *ṣaar-li 'aḥaawil 'attaṣil fiik min muddat saa^c^teen.* I have been trying to contact you for two hours. اتصل فيني بالتلفون *ttiṣal fiini b-t-talafoon.* He contacted me by telephone.

صلة *ṣila* p. *-aat* 1. connection, link. 2. relationship.

وصل *waṣil* (more common var. إيصال *'iiṣaal*). See إيصال *'iiṣaal* below.

وصول *wuṣuul* (v.n. from وصل *wuṣal*) arrival. ساعة الوصول *saa^c^t l-wuṣuul* the time of arrival.

توصيلة *tawṣiila* connection, contact (el.).

وصال *wiṣaal* being together, reunion (of lovers). أبغى وصالك *'abġa wiṣaalič.* I would like to be reunited with you.

مواصلة *muwaaṣala* 1. (p. *-aat*) communication, line of communication. وزارة المواصلات *wazaarat l-muwaaṣalaat* the ministry of communication. سباق المواصلات *sibaag l-muwaaṣalaat* the relay race. 2. continuation.

إيصال *'iiṣaal* p. *-aat* receipt, voucher.

واصل *waaṣil* (act. part. from وصل *wuṣal*) having arrived. توه واصل *tawwa waaṣil.* He has just arrived. أنت أي حزة واصل؟ *'inta 'ayya ḥazza waaṣil?* What time did you arrive?

وص ي *wṣy*

وصى *waṣṣa* II 1. (with foll. v.) to ask, request, order. وصيته يشتري لنا خمسة كيلو سمك *waṣṣeeta yištiri lana xamsa keelu simač.* I asked him to buy us five kilograms of fish. 2. (with على *^c^ala*) to order, place an order for. وصى على كبتات جديدة *waṣṣa ^c^ala kabataat yidiida.* He ordered new cupboards. وصيت لي على شاي؟ *waṣṣeet-li ^c^ala čaay?* Have you ordered me a cup of tea? 3. to advise, recommend. المدرس وصاني ما أهد المدرسة *l-mudarris waṣṣaani ma 'ahidd l-madrasa.* The teacher advised me not to drop out of school. 4. to make a will. وصى قبل ما مات *waṣṣa gabil-ma maat.* He made a will before he passed away.

وصي *waṣi* p. أوصيا *'awṣiya* 1. guardian. هو وصي عليهم *huwa waṣi ^c^aleehum.* He's their guardian. 2. regent. وصي على العرش *waṣi ^c^ala l-^c^arš* (prince) regent.

وصية *waṣiyya* p. وصايا *waṣaaya, -aat* will, testament. ما ترك وصية *ma tirak waṣiyya.* He didn't leave a will.

وظء *wḍ'*

See **وظي** *wḍy.*

وطر *wṭr*

وطر *waṭir* p. اوطار *wṭaar* time, era. وطرنا غير وطر أبهاتنا *waṭirna ġeer waṭir 'abbahaatna.* Our time is different from our ancestors' time. ذاك الوطر ولى *ðaak l-waṭir walla.* Those days are gone forever.

وطن *wṭn*

استوطن *stawṭan* X to settle, take up residence. بعض القبايل استوطنت في البريمي *bacaḍ l-gabaayil stawṭanat fi li-breemi.* Some tribes settled in the Buraimi Oasis.

وطن *waṭan* p. أوطان *'awṭaan* homeland, native country. كل واحد يحن إلى وطنه *kill waaḥid yḥinn 'ila waṭana.* Everyone yearns for their homeland. الفلسطينيين لازم يرجعون إلى وطنهم *l-falasṭiiniyyiin laazim yirjacuun 'ila waṭanhum.* Palestinians must go back to their homeland. حب الوطن *ḥubb l-waṭan* patriotism.

وطني *waṭani* 1. (p. *-yyiin*) nationalist, patriot. 2. national. فيه أعياد دينية وأعياد وطنية *fii 'acyaad diiniyya w-'acyaad waṭaniyya.* There are religious and national holidays. متحف قطر الوطني *matḥaf giṭar l-waṭani* the National Museum of Qatar. بنك أبو ظبي الوطني *bank 'abu ḍabi l-waṭani* the National Bank of Abu Dhabi. 3. native, indigenous. لباس وطني *libaas waṭani* native dress.

وطنية *waṭaniyya* 1. nationalism. 2. patriotism.

مواطن *mwaaṭin* p. *-iin* citizen, national. مواطن إماراتي *mwaaṭin 'imaaraati* U.A.E. citizen.

وظح *wḍḥ*

واضح *waaḍiḥ* 1. clear, plain. واضح مثل نور الشمس *waaḍiḥ miθil nuur š-šams* clear as daylight. 2. evident, obvious. واضح انه التنديل موافق على الزيادة *waaḍiḥ 'inna t-tindeel mwaafig cala z-ziyaada.* It's obvious that the foreman has approved the (salary) increase.

وضيحي *wḍeehi* p. *-yya* oryx. الوضيحي، طال عمرك، مثل الظبي *li-wḍeeḥi, ṭaal cumrak, miθl ḍ-ḍabi.* An oryx, may you live long, looks like a gazelle.

وعد *wcd*

وعد *wucad* (يوعد *yuucid*) to promise. وعدني يحصل لي زيادة *wucadni yḥaṣṣil-li ziyaada.* He promised me to get me an increment. لا توعد بشي ما تقدر تنفذه *la tuucid b-šayy ma tigdar tnaffða.* Don't promise anything you cannot do. وعدها بعقد ذهب *wucadha b-cigd ðahab.* He promised her a gold necklace.

واعد *waacad* III = وعد *wucad.*

تواعد *twaacad* VI to make an appointment. تواعدنا نتقابل ونتشاور ونخطب البنت من أبوها *twaacadna nitgaabal w-niššaawaar w-nxaṭib l-bint min 'ubuuha.* We agreed to meet, deliberate and ask the girl's father for her hand in marriage.

وعد *wa^c^d* p. وعود *w^c^uud* promise. الوعد مثل الدين عليك *l-wa^c^d miθl d-deen ^c^aleek.* A promise is like something you owe.

موعد *maw^c^id* p. مواعيد *mawaa^c^iid* appointment, appointed time. عندي موعد وايا الدختر الساعة تسع *^c^indi maw^c^id wiyya d-daxtar s-saa^c^a tisi^c^.* I have an appointment with the doctor at nine.

وعظ *w^c^ð̣*

وعظ *wu^c^að̣ (*يوعظ *yuu^c^ið̣)* to preach. يوم الجمعة، قبل الصلاة، الإمام يوعظ في الناس *yoom l-yim^c^a, gabl ṣ-ṣalaa, l-'imaam yuu^c^ið̣ fi n-naas.* On Friday, before the prayer, the Imam preaches to the people.

موعظة *maw^c^ið̣a* p. مواعظ *mawaa^c^ið̣* sermon.

وعي *w^c^y*

وعى *wu^c^a (*يوعى *yuu^c^a)* to wake up, awaken. توه وعى من النوم *tawwa wu^c^a min n-noom.* He has just woken up.

وعى *wa^cc^a* II to wake s.o. up. من فضلك وعيني الساعة خمس *min fað̣lak wa^cc^iini s-saa^c^a xams.* Please wake me up at five o'clock.

واعي *waa^c^i* p. *-yiin* awake, conscious. أنا واعي من الفجر *'aana waa^c^i min l-fajir.* I have been awake since daybreak.

وفد *wfd*

وفد *wafd* p. وفود *wfuud* delegation.

وفر *wfr*

وفر *waffar* II 1. to save, be economical. يصرف كل فلوسه. ما يوفر شي *yiṣrif kill fluusa. ma ywaffir šayy.* He spends all his money. He doesn't save anything. 2. (with على *^c^ala*) to save s.o. s.th. سافر بالطيارة. توفر عليك وقت واجد *saafir b-ṭ-ṭayyaara. twaffir ^c^aleek wagt waayid.* Go by plane. It will save you a lot of time. الأكل في البيت يوفر عليك مصاريف كثيرة *l-'akil fi l-beet ywaffir ^c^aleek maṣaariif kaθiira.* Eating at home saves you a lot of expenses.

توفر *twaffar* V 1. to be plentiful, abundant, to abound. اليح يتوفر في الربيع والقيظ *l-yiḥḥ yitwaffar fi r-rabii^c^ w-l-geeð̣.* Watermelons are plentiful in the spring and the summer. 2. to be saved. كم يتوفر من راتبك في الشهر؟ *čam yitwaffar min raatbak fi š-šahar?* How much is saved out of your salary in a month? ما يتوفر ولا متليك *ma yitwaffar wala matliik.* Not a plugged nickel can be saved. 3. to be met, fulfilled. كل الشروط لازم تتوفر فيك *kill š-šruuṭ laazim titwaffir fiik.* You will have to meet all the conditions. إذا ما تتوفر فيك كل الشروط ما يقبلونك *'iða ma titwaffar fiik kill š-šruuṭ ma yigbaluunak.* If you don't fulfill all the requirements, they will not accept you.

توفير *tawfiir* (v.n. from II وفر *waffar*) saving. صندوق التوفير *ṣanduug t-tawfiir* savings bank, provident fund.

متوفر *mitwaffir* (act. part. from V توفر *twaffar*) plentiful, abundant.

وفگ *wfg*

وفق *waffag* II (common var. II *waffaj*) 1. to grant prosperity or success to s.o. الله وفقني وصـــرت المديـــر *'aḷḷa waffagni w-ṣirt l-mudiir.* God granted me success and I became the manager. الله يرضى عليك ويوفقـــك *'aḷḷa yirđa ᶜaleek w-ywaffijk.* May God be pleased with you and make you successful. 2. (with بـــين *been*) to reconcile, make peace between. كانوا زعلانين وايا بعض ووفقنـــا بينـــهم *čaanaw zaᶜlaaniin wiyya baᶜađ w-waffagna beenhum.* They were angry at each other and we made peace between them. صعب توفق بين الشغـــل والدراســـة *ṣaᶜb twaffig been š-šuġul w-d-diraasa.* It's difficult for you to reconcile working with studying.

وافـــق *waafag* III (common var. III *waafaj*) 1. (with على *ᶜala*) to approve, authorize, sanction s.th. التنديل وافق على الزيادة *t-tindeel waafag ᶜala z-ziyaada.* The foreman approved the increase (in salary). 2. (with foll. imperf.) to agree to do s.th. وافق يجي وايانا *waafag yaji wiyyaana.* He agreed to come with us. 3. to suit, be agreeable to s.o. ها الشغل ما يوافقني *haš-šuġul ma ywaafigni.* This work doesn't suit me. 4. to agree, concur with s.o. أنت صادق. أوافقك على كل شي *'inta ṣaadj. 'awaafgak ᶜala kill šayy.* You're truthful. I agree with you on everything. 5. to agree with, be beneficial for s.o. ها الدوا ما يوافقـــني *had-duwa ma ywaafigni.* This medicine doesn't agree with me. 6. to coincide with. تاريخ ميلاده يوافـــق أول رمضـــــان *taariix miilaada ywaafig 'awwal rumđaan.* His birth date coincides with the first of Ramadan. 7. to correspond to, be equivalent to. أول رمضان السنة الجاية يوافق واحد وثلاثين ثنعش *'awwal rumđaan s-sana l-yaaya ywaafig waaḥid w-θalaaθiin θnaᶜaš.* The first of Ramadan next year corresponds to December 31.

توافـــق *twaafag* VI (common var. VI *twaafaj*) 1. to match each other. ها الألـــوان مـــا تتوافـــق *hal-'alwaan ma titwaafag.* These colors don't match. 2. to get along together, agree with each other. إذا تتوافقون كل شي يســـتوي زيـــن *'iđa tiwaafguun kill šayy yistawi zeen.* If you get along together, everything will be good.

اتفـــق *ttifag* VIII to agree, reach an agreement. تشاورنا واتفقنا علـــى المـــهر *ššaawarna w-ttifagna ᶜala l-mahar.* We deliberated and agreed on the dower. زين اتفقنا، بس ما عنـــدك فلـــوس واجـــد *zeen ttafagna, bass ma ᶜindak fluus waayid.* Fine, we agree, but you don't have a lot of money.

توفيق *tawfiig* (v.n. from II وفق *waffag*) success, prosperity. على الله التوفيق *ᶜala ḷḷa t-tawfiig.* Success is given by God. توفيقي في شغلي مـــن الله *tawfiigi fi šuġli min 'aḷḷa.* My success in my work is given by God.

موافقـــة *mwaafaga* (v.n. from III وافق *waafag*) 1. agreement. 2. approval, consent. قدمت طلب حق إجازة وجـــاتني الموافقـــة *gaddamt ṭalab ḥagg 'ijaaza w-yatni li-mwaafaga.* I submitted an application for leave and it was approved.

اتفاق *ttifaag* (v.n. from VIII اتفق *ttifag*) agreement. بالاتفاق *b-li-ttifaag* by (mutual) agreement.

اتفاقية *ttifaagiyya* p. *-aat* agreement, treaty, pact.

موافق *mwaafig* (act. part. from III وافق *waafag*) (common var. *mwaafij*) 1. having approved, authorized s.th. التنديل موافق على الزيادة *t-tindeel mwaafig* ^{c}*ala z-ziyaada.* The foreman has approved the increase (in salary). 2. (adj.) in agreement. أنا موافق *'aana mwaafig.* I agree.

و ف ي *wfy*

توفى *twaffa* V to die, pass away. أبوي، الله يرحمه، توفى يوم العيد *'ubuuy, 'aḷḷa yirḥama, twaffa yoom l-*^{c}*iid.* My father, God bless his soul, passed away on the day of the holiday.

استوفى *stawfa* X to receive in full. استوفيت المبلغ منه بالقوة *stawfeet l-mablaġ minna b-l-guwwa.* I received the full amount from him by force.

وفا *wafa, wufa* loyalty, faithfulness.

وفاة *wafaa* (v.n. from V توفى *twaffa*) p. وفيات *wafayaat* death, passing away.

وفي *wafi* p. أوفيا *'awfiya* true, loyal, faithful. صديق وفي *ṣidiij wafi* true friend.

أوفى *'awfa* (elat.) 1. (with من *min*) more loyal, faithful than. 2. (with foll. n.) the most loyal, faithful.

وافي *waafi* full, complete. مبلغ وافي *mablaġ waafi* full amount.

و گ ت *wgt*

وقت *wagt* p. أوقات *'awgaat* time. في أي وقت؟ *fi 'ayya wagt?* At what time? ما عنده وقت. دايما مشغول *ma* ^{c}*inda wagt. daayman mašġuul.* He has no time. He's always busy. ما أقدر أجي. الوقت متأخر *ma 'agdar 'ayi. l-wagt mit'axxir.* I can't come. It's getting late. على الوقت ^{c}*ala l-wagt* on time. في نفس الوقت *fi nafs l-wagt* at the same time. وقتما *wagt-ma* when, at the time when. وقتما رحت كانت الدنيا ليل *wagt-ma riḥt čaanat d-dinya leel.* When I went, it was nighttime.

توقيت *tawgiit* time, reckoning of time. توقيت صيفي *tawgiit ṣeefi* daylight-saving time. حسب التوقيت المحلي *ḥasab t-tawgiit l-maḥalli* according to local time.

موقت *mwaggat* temporary, provisional. جدول موقت *jadwal mwaggat* temporary schedule.

و گ ع *wg*^{c}

وقع *wuga*^{c} (يوقع *yuuga*^{c}) 1. to fall down, drop. وقع على الأرض وتعور راسه *wuga*^{c} ^{c}*ala l-*^{c}*arḍ w-t*^{c}*awwar raasa.* He fell down and his head was injured. الماعون وقع من يدي وانكسر *l-maa*^{c}*uun wuga*^{c} *min yaddi w-nkisar.* The dish fell down from my hand and broke. 2. to fall. ما يوقع مطر واجد هني *ma yuuga*^{c} *muṭar waayid hni.* Not much rain falls here.

وقع *wagga*^{c} II 1. to cause to fall. دعمت راعي السيكل ووقعته على الأرض *di*^{c}*amt raa*^{c}*i s-seekal w-wagga*^{c}*ta* ^{c}*ala l-'arḍ.* I hit the cyclist and knocked him down on the ground. وقعوا تسع طيارات في الحرب *wagg*^{c}*aw tisi*^{c} *ṭayyaaraat fi l-ḥarb.* They downed nine planes in the war. 2. to drop. وقعت الماعون وانكسر *waggaᶜt l-maaᶜuun w-nkisar.* I dropped the dish and it broke. 3. to sign. وقع الطلب *waggaᶜ ṭ-ṭalab.* He signed the application. ما يوقع. يبصم *ma ywaggiᶜ. yabṣum.* He can't sign. He makes a fingerprint. 4. to cause to sign. المحاسب وقع كل الموظفين *li-mḥaasib waggaᶜ kill l-muwaðᶞafiin.* The accountant had all the employees sign.

توقع *twaggaᶜ* V to be signed. الأوراق كلها توقعت *l-'awraag killaha twaggaᶜat.* All the papers were signed.

تواقع *twaagaᶜ* VI to quarrel, fight, dispute (with each other). تواقعنا على ما ميش *twaagaᶜna ᶜala ma miiš.* We quarreled about nothing. ما يندرى ليش القبايل تتواقع *ma yindara leeš l-gabaayil titwaagaᶜ.* It's not known why the tribes are fighting each other.

وقعة *wagaᶜ* p. *-aat* 1. a fall. 2. battle, combat.

موقع *mawgiᶜ* p. مواقع *mawaagiᶜ* place, location, site.

توقيع *tawgiiᶜ* 1. (v.n. from II وقع *waggaᶜ*) signing. توقيع الأوراق *tawgiiᶜ l-'awraag* signing of the papers. 2. endorsing, endorsement. توقيع الشيكات *tawgiiᶜ š-šeekaat* endorsing the checks. 3. (p. تواقيع *tawaagiiᶜ*) signature.

واقع *waagiᶜ* 1. (act. part. from وقع *wugaᶜ*) having fallen. واقع على الأرض *waagiᶜ ᶜala l-'arð.* He has fallen down. 2. fact, matter of fact. الواقع *l-waagiᶜ* the facts, the truth. في الواقع *fi l-waagiᶜ* in fact, as a matter of fact.

وگف *wgf*

وقف *wugaf* (يوقف *yoogaf*) 1. to stop, come to a standstill. وقف في نص الطريق *wugaf fi nuṣṣ ṭ-ṭariig.* He stopped in the middle of the road. ساعتي وقفت *saaᶜti wugfat.* My watch has stopped. الباص حق المطار وين يوقف؟ *l-paaṣ ḥagg l-maṭaar ween yoogaf?* Where does the airport bus stop? أوقف، قبل لا تروح. العشا الليلة على كيسي *'oogf, gabil-la truuḥ. l-ᶜaša l-leela ᶜala čiisi.* Stop, before you go. Dinner is at my expense tonight. 2. to stand up, rise. لين تسأل سؤال، أوقف *leen tis'al su'aal, 'oogaf.* When you ask a question, stand up. أوقف لين يرمسك الشيخ *'oogaf leen yrammisk š-šeex.* Stand up when the Shaikh talks to you. 3. to place oneself, take one's stand. أوقفوا في سيد واحد *'oogfu fi seed waaḥid.* Stand in one line. 4. (with وايا *wiyya*) to stand up for, support, back. التنديل رجال زين؛ دايماً يوقف وايا العمال *t-tindeel rayyaal zeen; daayman yoogaf wiyya l-ᶜummaal.* The foreman is a good man; he always stands up for the workmen.

وقف *waggaf* II 1. to stop, bring s.o. or s.th. to a stand still. لا توقف السيارة هني *la twaggif s-sayyaara hni.* Don't stop the car here. 2. to park (a car). وقفت سيارتي ورا البنك *waggaft sayyaarti wara l-bank.* I parked my car behind the bank. 3. to cause to stand, to place in an upright position. تقدر توقف على راسك؟ *tigdar twaggif ᶜala raasak?* Can you stand on your head? وقفت الجاهل وخليته يمشي *waggaft l-yaahil w-xalḷeeta yamši.* I stood the child up and let him walk. 4. (with عن *ᶜan*) to suspend, prevent s.o. from. وقفوه عن العمل *waggafoo ᶜan l-ᶜamal.* They suspended him from work. 5. to position, station, place. وقفوا شرطي على باب مكتب الوزير *waggafaw širṭi ᶜala baab maktab l-waziir.* They put a policeman at the door of the minister's office.

توقف *twaggaf* V pass. of II وقف *waggaf.*

وقف *wagf* p. أوقاف *'awgaaf* religious endowment, wakf. وزارة الأوقاف *wazaarat l-'awgaaf* the ministry of religious endowments.

وقفة *wagfa* p. *-aat* 1. stop, halt. 2. position, stance. 3. eve of a religious festival. وقفة عيد رمضان *wagfat ᶜiid rumḏaan* the day preceding the feast of breaking the Ramadan Fast.

وقوف *wuguuf* (v.n. from وقف *wugaf*) 1. stopping, stop. 2. standing up, rising.

موقف *mawgif* p. مواقف *mawaagif* 1. stopping place, (bus) stop. 2. parking lot, parking place. 3. position, stand, opinion.

واقف *waagif* (act. part. from وقف *wugaf*) 1. standing, upright. 2. standing still, motionless. 3. (p. *-iin*) bystanders, onlookers. كان فيه واقفين على طول الشارع *čaan fii waagfiin ᶜala ṭuul š-šaariᶜ.* There were bystanders along the street.

موقوف *mawguuf* (p.p. from وقف *wugaf*) 1. detained, held in custody. 2. (p. *-iin*) person under arrest.

وگي *wgy*

اوقية *wgiya* p. *-aat* unit of weight, approx. ½ kilogram.

وكح *wkḥ*

وكيح *wakiiḥ* p. وكح *wikkaḥ* impudent, insolent. ولد وكيح *walad wakiiḥ* impudent boy.

وكاحة *wkaaḥa* impudence, insolence.

وكر *wkr*

وكر *wakir* p. اوكار *wkaar* bird's nest.

وكري *wakri* p. وكارة *wkaara* young peregrine.

وكل¹ *wkl*

وكل *wakkal* II 1. to authorize, appoint as agent. وكلني أبيع السيارة حقه *wakkalni 'abiiᶜ s-sayyaara ḥagga.* He authorized me to sell his car. 2. to engage s.o. as legal counsel. وكلت محامي يدافع عني *wakkalt mḥaami ydaafiᶜ ᶜanni.* I engaged an attorney to defend me.

توكل *twakkal* V 1. (with ب *b-*) to act as counsel for (a case). المحامي وافق يتوكل بذيك القضية *li-mḥaami waafag yitwakkal b-ðiič l-gaḏiyya.* The attorney agreed to take that case. 2. (with عن *ᶜan*) to act as counsel for s.o. وافق يتوكل عني *waafag yitwakkal ᶜanni.* He agreed to defend me. 3. (with على *ᶜala*) to trust in, put one's confidence in. توكل على الله *twakkal ᶜala 'aḷḷa.* Trust in God.

وكيل *wakiil* p. وكلا *wukala* 1. deputy, vice-. وكيل وزير *wakiil waziir* deputy minister. وكيل وزارة *wakiil wazaara* undersecretary of State. وكيل رئيس

الشركـــــة *wakiil ra'iis š-šarika* the company vice-president. 2. representative, agent. وكيل الشركـــة *wakiil š-šarika* the company representative.

وكالة *wakaala* p. *-aat* 1. agency. وكالة الأخبـــــار *wakaalat l-'axbaar* the news agency. 2. power of attorney. 3. deputyship, proxy. وزير بالوكالـــة *waziir b-l-wakaala* acting minister.

و ك ل ٢ *wkl*

وكـــل *wakkal* II = II أكل *'akkal*. See under **ء ك ل** *'kl.*

و ل ا *wlaa*

ولا *wala* (contraction of *w-la*) 1. nor, and not. لا هذا ولا ذاك *la haaða wala ðaak* neither this nor that. ما يبـــي هذا ولا ذاك *ma yabi haaða wala ðaak.* He doesn't want this or that. 2. not even, not as much as. ما عندي ولا متليك *ma* *ᶜindi wala matliik.* I don't have even a plugged nickel. رحنا نحدق وما صدنا ولا سمكـــة *riḥna nḥadig w-ma ṣidna wala smiča.* We went fishing and didn't catch a single fish. ما قال لي ولا كلمة *ma gal-li wala čalma.* He didn't say to me even one word.

و ل د *wld*

ولد *wilad* (يالد *yaalad)* to give birth to a child, bear a child. حرمتي ولـــــدت وجابت ولـــد، الحمـــد لله *ḥurumti wlidat w-yaabat walad, l-ḥamdu li-llaah.* My wife gave birth to a baby boy, thanks to God.

ولد *wallad* II 1. to assist in childbirth. في الزمان الأولي كانت الداية اللـــــي تولـــد الحرمـــة *fi z-zamaan l-'awwali čaanat d-daaya illi twallid l-ḥurma.* A long time ago, a midwife was the one who helped women in their delivery. 2. to generate. كان صعب من قبل يولدون كهربا حق كـــــل المدينـــة *čaan ṣaᶜb min gabil ywallduun kahraba ḥagg kill l-madiina.* It was difficult some time ago to generate electricity for the whole city. 3. to cause, breed, engender. الصداقة وايا جماعة مثـــــل ذولا تولـــد مشاكل *ṣ-ṣadaaga wiyya yamaaᶜa miθil ðoola twallid mašaakil.* Making friends with people like these causes problems.

تولـــــد *twallad* V to be caused, engendered. ها المشاكل تتولد من الجـــهل *hal-mašaakil titwallad min l-yahil.* These problems are caused by ignorance.

توالـــــــد *twaalad* VI to multiply, reproduce, propagate.

انولـــد *nwilad* VII to be born. وين انولـــدت؟ *ween nwilatt?* Where were you born? انولدت في دبـــــي *nwilatt fi dbayy.* I was born in Dubai.

ولد *walad* (less common var. *wild*) p. اولاد *wlaad* 1. son, child. ولدي *wlidi* my son. ولـــد عبـــدالله *wild ᶜabdaḷḷa* Abdallah's son. 2. boy. طال عمـــرك، هذيل اولاد يتهاوشون ويتصالحون بســـرعة *ṭaal ᶜumrak, haðeel wlaad yithaawšuun w-yiṣṣaalḥuun b-surᶜa.* May you live long, these are boys who fight each other and make up fast. (prov.) ولد الكلب كلب مثله *wild č-čalb čalbin miθla.* Like father like son (derog.). 3. jack (in cards).

ولادة *wilaada* birth, childbirth. مكان الـــولادة *makaan l-wilaada* birth place.

تاريخ الولادة *taariix l-wilaada* date of birth.

مولد *mawlid* p. موالد *mawaalid* birthday (of a prophet). مولد النبي *mawlid n-nabi* the Prophet's (Muhammad's) birthday.

ميلاد *miilaad* 1. birth. 2. time of birth. عيد ميلاد *ciid miilaad* birthday celebration. عيد الميلاد *ciid l-miilaad* Christmas. قبل الميلاد *gabl l-miilaad* before Christ, B.C. بعد الميلاد *bacd l-miilaad* after Christ, A.D.

ميلادي *miilaadi* 1. relating to the birth of Christ. 2. after Christ, A.D. سنة ألفين ميلادي *sanat 'alfeen miilaadi* the year 2000 A.D. سنة ميلادية *sana miilaadiyya* year of the Christian era. سنة هجرية *sana hijriyya* year of the Muslim era, Hegira Year.

توليد *tawliid* (v.n. from ولد *wallad*) 1. delivery, assistance at childbirth. 2. act of generating (electricity). 3. causing, breeding, engendering.

والد *waalid* father. الوالدين *l-waaldeen* one's parents.

والدة *waalida* p. *-aat* mother.

مولود *mawluud* (p.p. of ولد *wilad*) 1. having been born. هو مولود يوم الجمعة *huwa mawluud yoom l-yimca.* He was born on Friday. 2. (p. مواليد *mawaaliid*) age group, age classes, members of an age group. هو من مواليد ألف وتسعمية وخمسين *huwa min mawaaliid 'alf w-tisic imya w-xamsiin.* He's one of the 1950 age group.

ولع *wlc*

تولع *twallac* V (with في *fi*) to be madly or passionately in love with. تولع في هواها *twallac fi hawaaha.* He fell madly in love with her.

ولع *walac* = هوى *hawa.* See under **هوي** *hwy.*

ولف *wlf*

ولف *wilf* p. ولاف *wlaaf, -aat* valve.

ولل *wll*

ول *wall* (interj. expressing surprise or astonishment) how strange! how odd! ول! كيف صار هذا؟ *wall! čeef ṣaar haaða?* How strange! How did this happen?

ولا *wllaa*

ولا *willa* see under **ءلل** *'ll.*

ولله *wllh*

والله *wal̥la* see under **ءلله** *'llh.*

ولم *wlm*

ولم *wallam* II (more common var. II برز *barraz*). See under **برز** *brz.*

والم *waalam* III 1. to suit, fit. ها الشغل ما يوالمني *haš-šuġul ma ywaalimni.* This work doesn't suit me. 2. to be similar to. رايه يوالم رايي *raaya ywaalim raayi.* His opinion is similar to mine.

وليمة *waliima* p. ولايم *walaayim* banquet.

ولو *wlw*

ولو *walaw* (conj.) even though, although. ما آخذه ولو كنت محتاج له *ma 'aaxða walaw čint miḥtaaj-la.* I won't take it even though I am in need of it. (prov.) عطي الخباز خبزك ولو باق نصه *cați l-xabbaaz xubzak walaw baag nuṣṣa.*

approx.: You get what you pay for. (lit., "Give your bread to the baker although he may steal half of it.").

و ل ي *wly*

ولى *walla* II 1. to flee, escape. لين شاف الشرطي، ولى *leen čaaf š-širṭi, walla.* When he saw the policeman, he fled. ما نبغاه. خله يولي! *ma nibġaa. xaḷḷa ywalli!* We don't want him. The hell with him! 2. ليش ما تولي؟ استحي على وجهك! *leeš ma twalli? stiḥi ᶜala weehak!* Why don't you get lost? Shame on you! 3. to appoint as governor, ruler, etc. ولاه حاكم على البلد *wallaa ḥaakim ᶜala l-balad.* He appointed him governor of the city.

تولى *twalla* V 1. to be in charge of, be entrusted with. فيه ناس يتولون المراقبة *fii naas yitwalluun li-mraagaba.* There are people who are in charge of surveillance. 2. to come into power, take over the government. الشيخ طال عمره تولى الحكم قبل عشر سنين *š-šeex ṭaal ᶜumra twalla l-ḥukum gubil ᶜašar siniin.* The Shaikh, may he live long, came into power ten years ago.

استولى *stawla* X (with على *ᶜala*) to capture, seize control of, take possession of. الجيش استولى على المدينة *l-jeeš stawla ᶜala l-madiina.* The army captured the city. استولى على الحكم *stawla ᶜala l-ḥukum.* He came into power. فنشوه واستولوا على أملاكه *fannašoo w-stawlaw ᶜala 'amlaaka.* They fired him and confiscated his property.

ولي *wali* p. أوليا *'awliya* 1. legal guardian. منو ولي أمرك؟ *minu wali 'amrak?* Who is your legal guardian? ولي العهد *wali l-ᶜahd* successor to the throne, crown prince. 2. saint, man close to God (in Islam). الأنبيا والأوليا *l-'anbiya w-l-'awliya* prophets and saints.

ولاية *wilaaya* p. *-aat* 1. state. الولايات المتحدة *l-wilaayaat l-mittaḥda* the United States. ولاية أريزونا *wilaayat 'arizoona* the State of Arizona. 2. sovereignty.

أولى *'awla* (elat.) 1. (with من *min*) more worthy, deserving than. 2. (with foll. n.) the most worthy, deserving.

مولى *mawla* p. موالي *mawaali* master, my lord. مولاي هو الله *mawlaaya huwa ḷḷaah.* My master is God.

متولي *mitwalli* (act. part. from V تولى *twalla*) entrusted, in charge.

و ن س *wns*

ونس *wannas* II to entertain, amuse, show a good time. ها الممثل يونس واجد *hal-mumaθθil ywannis waayid.* This actor is very entertaining. خذيت العيال المنتزه وونستهم *xaðeet li-ᶜyaal l-muntazah w-wannasittum.* I took the kids to the park and showed them a good time.

تونس *twannas* V to have a good time, enjoy oneself. رحنا البحرين وتونسنا *riḥna l-baḥreen w-twannasna.* We went to Bahrain and had a good time. تونسنا في النادي *twannasna fi n-naadi.* We enjoyed ourselves at the clubhouse.

مستانس *mistaanis* (act. part. from X استانس *staanas*). See under **ء ن س** *'ns.*

ونش *wnš*

ونش *winš* p. *-aat* winch.

ونن *wnn*

ون *wann* (يـون *ywinn)* to moan, groan. يون من الوجـع *ywinn min l-wuja^c^*. He's moaning in pain.

ونين *waniin* (v.n.) moaning, groaning.

ونون *wnwn*

ونـون *wanwan* (يونـون *ywanwin)* to moan repeatedly. طاحت مريضة وكانت تونـون *ṭaaḥat mariiða w-čaanat twanwin.* She fell ill and was moaning repeatedly.

وهب *whb*

وهـب *wihab* (يوهب *yoohib)* to donate, give, grant. وهب مليون درهم حق الأيتام *wihab malyoon dirhim ḥagg l-'aytaam.* He donated a million dirhams to the orphans.

هبة *hiba* p. *-aat* present, gift, donation. هذي هبـة مـني لـك *haaði hiba minni lič.* This is a present from me to you.

وهـابي *wahhaabi* p. *-yyiin* Wahabi, Wahabite.

موهبة *mawhiba* p. مواهـب *mawaahib* talent, gift. عنده موهبة في الموسيقى *^c^inda mawhiba fi l-muusiiga.* He has a talent for music. هـذي موهبـة مـن الله *haaði mawhiba min aḷḷa.* This is a gift from God.

موهـوب *mawhuub* (p.p. from وهـب *wihab*) talented, gifted. رسـام موهـوب *rassaam mawhuub* talented draftsman.

وهگ *whg*

وهق *wahhag* II to confuse, mix s.o. up. اللي قلت لي اياه يوهق *'illi gilt-li-yyaa ywahhig.* What you have told me is confusing.

توهق *twahhag* V pass. of II *wahhag.*

وهم *whm*

وهـم *wahham* II 1. to give s.o. a false impression. مـا دريـت. هـو اللـي وهمـني بهاالأشـــيا *ma dareet. huwa lli wahhamnni b-hal-'ašya.* I didn't know. He's the one who gave me a false impression of these things. 2. (with ان *inna*) to make s.o. believe that. وهمني ان الوضـع زيـن *wahhamni 'inna l-waði^c^ zeen.* He made me believe that the situation was good.

اتهـم *ttiham* VIII to accuse, suspect s.o. ما عـرف مـن هـو، بـس اتهمهـم كلهـم *ma ^c^iraf man huw, bass ttihamhum killahum.* He didn't know who it was, but he accused all of them. اتهموه بالقتل *ttihmoo b-l-gatil.* They accused him of murder.

تهمـة *tuhma* p. تهـم *tuham* accusation, charge. أنـت مـا سـويت شـي. هـذي بـس تهمة *'inta ma sawweet šayy. haaði bass tuhma.* You haven't done anything. This is only an accusation.

وهـم *waham* p. أوهـام *'awhaam* 1. wrong impression, delusion, fancy. 2. hallucination.

وهمـي *wahmi* 1. imaginary. 2. fictitious. شـخصية وهميـــة *šaxṣiyya wahmiyya* fictitious character.

اتهـام *ttihaam* (v.n. from VIII اتهـم *ttiham*) p. *-aat* 1. accusation, charge. 2. indictment.

متهـم *mittahim* (act. part. from VIII اتهم

ttiham) 1. (with ب *b-*) accusing or having accused s.o. of s.th. أنا متهمه بالبوق *'aana mittihma b-l-boog.* I'm accusing him of stealing. زخوه لانهم متهمينه بالبوق *zaxxoo linhum mittahmiina b-l-boog.* They arrested him because they accused him of stealing. 2. (p. *-iin*) accuser.

متهم *mittaham* (p.p. from VIII اتهم *ttaham*) (with ب *b-*) having been accused of s.th. متهم بالقتل *mittaham b-l-gatil.* He has been accused of murder.

متوهم *mitwahhim* mistaken, wrong. هو بس متوهم. لا تدير له بال *huwa bass mitwahhim. la ddiir-la baal.* He's just mistaken. Don't pay attention to him.

و ي د *wyd*

واجد *waayid* (less common var. *waajid*) 1. (adj.) فيه ناس واجدين في السوق *fii naas waaydiin fi s-suug.* There are many people in the market-place. 2. (adv.) very. واجد زين *waayid zeen* very good.

و ي ز *wyz*

ويزة *wiiza* p. ويز *wiyaz* visa.

و ي ش *wyš*

ويش *weeš* see أيش *'eeš* under **ء ي ش** *'yš.*

و ي ل *wyl*

ويل *weel* (usually with suff. pron.) distress, woe. ويلي عليهم! *weeli ᶜaleehum!* Poor fellows! I'm so sorry for them. يا ويلاه! *ya weelaah!* Poor me! يا ويلاه! ما أقدر أنام الليل! *ya weelaah! ma 'agdar anaam l-leel.* Poor me! I can't sleep nights.

و ي ن *wyn*

وين *ween* where, what place. وين رحت البارحة؟ *ween riḥt l-baarḥa?* Where did you go yesterday? ما ادري وين هم *ma dri ween hum.* I don't know where they are. وين وقفت السيارة؟ *ween waggaft s-sayyaara?* Where did you park the car? صار لنا مدة ما شفناك. وين كنت؟ *ṣaar-lana mudda ma čifnaak. ween čint?* We haven't see you for some time. Where were you? من وين *min ween* = منين *mneen* from where? منين أنت؟ *mneen inta?* Where are you from? منين جاي؟ *mneen yaay?* Where are you coming from? منين لك ها السيارة؟ *mneen-lak has-sayyaara?* Where did you get this car? أنت وين وهو وين! *'inta ween w-huwa ween!* What a difference between you and him!

وينما *ween-ma* (conj.) wherever. وينما يروح، تروح وياه *ween-ma yruuḥ, truuḥ wiyyaa.* Wherever he goes, she goes with him.

و ي ه *wyh*

وجه *weeh* p. وجوه *wyuuh* face. استحي على وجهك! *stiḥi ᶜala weehak!* Shame on you!

و ي ي *wyy*

وايا *wiyya* with. أبغى أحكي وايا عبدالله *'abġa 'ahči wiyya ᶜabdaḷḷah.* I would like to speak with Abdalla. رحت وياهم؟ *riḥt wiyyaahum?* Did you go with them? شما تقول، أنا وياك *š-ma tguul, 'aana wiyyaak.* Whatever you say, I'm with you.

ي

ي ا[1] *yaa*

يـا *ya* (vocative and exclamatory part. used in addressing s.o. or expressing admiration or surprise) !يـا محمـد *ya mḥammad!* Muhammad! !يا ولد الكلب *ya wild č-čalb!* You son of a bitch! !يا ابـن الحـرام *ya 'ibn l-ḥaraam!* You bastard! !يـا أمـي *ya 'ummi!* (respectful form of address to an old woman) (cf. !يمه *yumma!* Mother!). !يا يبه *ya yuba!* Father! !يـا هـلا ومرحبـا! يـا حي الله *ya hala w-marḥabaa! ya ḥayy aḷḷa!* Welcome! !يا حسرتي *ya ḥasrati!* What a pity! يا حيـف *ya ḥeef* (expression of surprise or sorrow). !يا حيف تعمل هذا *ya ḥeef tᶜamil haaða!* I'm sorry you've done that! How could you have done that? !يا ربـي *ya rabbi!* my God! !يا خوي *ya xuuy!* Brother! My brother! يالله *yaḷḷa* see under **ءلله** *'ḷlh.*

ي ا[2] *yaa*

يا *yaa* name of the letter ي *y.*

ي ا ب ا ن *yaabaan*

اليابـان *l-yaabaan* (less common var. الجابان *l-jaabaan*) Japan.

يابـاني *yaabaani* (less common var. جابـاني *jaabaani*) 1. (adj.) Japanese. سـيارة يابانيـة *sayyaara yaabaaniyya* Japanese car. 2. (p. *-yyiin*) a Japanese.

ي ا ث و م *yaaθwm*

يـاثوم *yaaθuum* (less common var. جاثوم *jaaθuun*) nightmare.

ي ا خ و ر *yaaxwr*

يـاخور *yaaxuur* p. يواخـير *yuwaaxiir* (more common var. جـاخور *jaaxuur*). See under **ج ا خ و ر** *jaaxwr.*

ي ا س *yaas*

يـاس *yaas* : بني ياس *bani yaas* Bani Yas (name of a prominent tribe in the U.A.E.). صـير بـني يـاس *ṣiir bani yaas* island in Abu Dhabi.

ي ا س م ي ن *yaasmyn*

يـاسمين *yaasamiin* (coll.) 1. jasmine (bot.). s. *-a.* 2. jasmine (perfume). واجـد مـن الحريـم يتخننـن بعطـور اليـاسمين *waayid min l-ḥariim yitxannanin b-ᶜuṭuur l-yaasamiin.* Many women wear jasmine perfume.

ي ا ف و خ *yaafwx*

يـافوخ *yaafuux* (less common var. جـافوخ *jaafuux*) p. يوافيخ *yawaafiix* top of the head.

ي ا گ و ت *yaagwt*

ياقوت *yaaguut* (coll.) sapphire. s. *-a.*

ي ا م ل و *yaamlw*

ياملو *yaamlo* p. ياملوات *-waat* rail at the poop of a ship.

ي ا ن س و ن *yaanswn*

يانسون *yaansuun* (coll.) anise, aniseed.

ي ا ن ص ي ب *yaanṣyb*

يانصيب *yaanaṣiib* lottery.

ي ا ه yaah

ياه *yaah* (common var. جاه *jaah*) see under ج ا ه *jaah.*

ي ب ب ybb

يبب *yabbab* II to utter long drawn and trilling sounds by Arab women as a manifestation of joy.

ي ب س ybs

يبس *yibas* (ييبس *yeebas)* to be or become dry. يحطون العنب في الشمس لين ييبس ويصير زبيب *yḥuṭṭuun l-ᶜinab fi š-šams leen yeebas w-yṣiir zibiib.* They put grapes in the sun until they dry up and become raisins.

يبس *yabbas* II to dry, make s.th. dry. في أم القيوين كانوا ييبسون السمك ويصدرونه للخارج *fi 'umm l-giiween čaanaw yyabbsuun s-simač w-yṣaddruuna lal-xaarij.* In Umm Al-Qaiwain they used to dry fish and export it overseas. الهوا اليوم يبس الهدوم *l-hawa l-yoom yabbas li-hduum.* The air today dried the clothes.

تيبس *tyabbas* V pass. of II يبس *yabbas.*

أيبس *'aybas* (elat.) 1. (with من *min*) drier than. 2. (with foll. n.) the driest.

يابس *yaabis* 1. dry, dried out, arid. الهوا يابس اليوم *l-hawa yaabis l-yoom.* The weather is dry today. خبز يابس *xubiz yaabis* dry bread. الهدوم يابسة *li-hduum yaabsa.* The clothes are dry. أرض يابسة *'arḍ yaabsa* arid land. راسه يابس *raasa yaabis.* He's stubborn.

ي ب ل ybl

جبل *yibal* p. جبال *ybaal* mountain. جبل حفيت *yibal ḥafiit* Mount Hafit (near the city of Al-Ain).

جبلي *yibali* mountainous, hilly.

ي ب ه ybh

جبهة *yabha* p. *-aat* forehead. عرفته من جبهته *ᶜirafta min yabihta.* I recognized him from his forehead.

ي ت م ytm

يتم *yattam* II to orphan, deprive of parents. الحرب يتمت جهال واجدين *l-ḥarb yattamat yihhaal waaydiin.* The war left many children fatherless and motherless.

تيتم *tyattam* V to become an orphan, to be deprived of one's parents. تيتم لين كان طفل *tyattam leen čaan ṭifil.* He became an orphan when he was a baby.

يتيم *yatiim* p. يتما *yutama,* أيتام *'aytaam* orphan. دار الأيتام *daar l-'aytaam* orphanage. تبرع بمليون درهم حق دار الأيتام *tbarraᶜ b-malyoon dirhim ḥagg daar l-'aytaam.* He donated one million dirhams to the orphanage.

ي ح ح yḥḥ

يح *yiḥḥ* (coll.) watermelons. s. *-a* p. *-aat.* اشتريت يح *štireet yiḥḥ.* I bought some watermelons. اليح رخيص هالحين *l-yiḥḥ raxiiṣ halḥiin.* Watermelons are cheap now. اشتريت ثلاث يحات *štireet θalaaθ yiḥḥaat.* I bought three watermelons.

ي ح ش yḥš

جحش *yaḥš* see under ج ح ش *jḥš.*

ي ح ي م *yḥym*

جحيم *yaḥiim* (more common var. *jaḥiim*). See under **ج ح م** *jḥm.*

ي د د¹ *ydd*

يد *yadd.* See ايد *'iid* under **ء ي د** *'yd.*

ي د د² *ydd*

جد *yadd* p. أجداد *'aydaad* grandfather. جدي هو أبو أبوي *yaddi huwa 'ubu 'ubuuy.* My grandfather is my father's father. جد جدي *yadd yaddi* my great-grandfather. (prov.) جد البقر ثور *yadd l-bagar θoor.* Do not boast of your ancestors. أجدادنا *'aydaadna* our forefathers.

جدة *yadda* p. *-aat* grandmother.

ي د د³ *ydd*

جدد *yaddad* II 1. to renew. جددنا البيمة حق السيارة *yaddadna l-biima ḥagg s-sayyaara.* We renewed the car insurance. جددت جواز سفري *yaddatt jawaaz safari.* I renewed my passport. 2. to renovate, remodel, modernize. البيت عتيق؛ جددناه *l-beet ᶜatiij; yaddadnaa.* The house is old; we renovated it.

تجدد *tyaddad* V pass. of II جدد *yaddad.*

جديد *yidiid* new, recent. اشترى له بيت جديد *štiraa-la beet yidiid.* He bought himself a new house. من جديد *min yidiid* (adv.) anew, from the start.

ي د ع *ydᶜ*

جدع *yidiᶜ* p. جدوع *yduuᶜ* branch of a tree. جدع الشجرة هذا مكسور *jidiᶜ li-šyara haaða maksuur.* This branch of the tree is broken. هذا الجدع خالي *haaða l-yidiᶜ xaaḷi.* This branch is empty of fruit.

ي ر ب *yrb*

جرب *yarab* (coll.) scabies. الجرب يصيب البعارين مرات *l-yarab yṣiib l-baᶜaariin marraat.* Camels are infested with scabies sometimes.

جربان *yarbaan* infested with scabies. البعارين جربانين *l-baᶜaariin yarbaaniin.* The camels are infested with scabies.

أجرب *'ayrab* = جربان *yarbaan.*

ي ر ب و ع *yrbwᶜ*

يربوع *yarbuuᶜ* p. يرابيع *yaraabiiᶜ* jerboa, desert rat.

ي ر د *yrd*

جراد *yaraad* (coll.) = *jaraad* (coll.) locusts. s. *-a.*

ي ر ر *yrr* See also **ج ر ج ر** *jrjr.*

جر *yarr (يجر yyurr)* to tow, drag along. سيارتي تعطلت. جروها حق الكراج *sayyaarti tᶜaṭṭalat. yarrooha ḥagg l-garaaj.* My car broke down. They towed it to the garage. لا تجر الصندوق. شيله *la tyurr ṣ-ṣanduug. šiila.* Don't drag the box. Carry it. جر البردة *yarr l-parda.* He drew the curtain.

انجر *nyarr* VII pass. of جر *yarr.*

اجتر *ytarr* VIII to ruminate. شوف! البعير يجتر *čuuf! l-biᶜiir yiytaar.* Look! The camel is chewing its cud.

جر *yarr* (v.n. from جر *yarr*) towing, dragging along.

جرة *yarra* p. *-aat* (earthenware) jar.

جرار *yarraar* p. *-aat* drawer (of a desk,

etc.)

ي ر ي ت *yryt*

يـــاريت *yareet* = ياليت *yaleet* if only. يـــاريت أقـــدر أحاكيـــها! *yareet 'agdar 'aḥaačiiha!* I wish I could talk to her.

ي ر ي و ر *yrywr*

يريور *yaryuur* p. يرايير *yaraayiir* shark. زيت السمك ما ياخذونه من كبد الـــيريور *zeet s-simač ma yaaxðuuna min čabd l-yaryuur.* They don't take cod liver oil from the liver of a shark.

ي ع د *y^c^d*

ياعدة *yaa^c^da* p. يواعد *yuwaa^c^id* goat.

ي غ م *yġm*

يغــم *yiġam (*ييغم *yiiġam)* to gulp. يغم كـــلاص البـــيرة *yiġam glaaṣ l-biira.* He drank the glass of beer in one gulp.

يغمـــة *yiġma* (n. of inst.) p. يغم *yiġam* gulp. شرب بطل البـــيرة في يغمتـــين *širib boṭil l-biira fi yiġmateen.* He drank the bottle of beer in two gulps.

ي ف ن *yfn*

جفن *yifin* p. جفون *yfuun* eyelid. جفوني ما عرفت النوم *yfuuni ma ^c^rafat n-noom.* I couldn't sleep.

ي ل د *yld*

جلد *yild* (coll.) leather. جوتي جلد *juuti yild* leather shoes. جاكيت جلد *jaakeet yild* leather jacket. صلخوا جلد الخروف *ṣlaxaw yild l-xaruuf.* They skinned the lamb.

ي ل س *yls* See also **ج ل س** *jls.*

جلس *yilas (*يجلس *yiilis)* 1. = قعد *gi^c^ad.* See also قعد *gi^c^ad* under **گ ع د** *g^c^d.* 2. (with على *^c^ala)* to sit on, e.g., a chair, at a table. تفضل اجلس على الكرســـي *tfaððal iilis ^c^ala l-kirsi.* Please sit down on the chair. جلس على العـــرش *yilas ^c^ala l-^c^arš* to sit on the throne, accede the throne. الملك جلس على العرش *l-malik yilas ^c^ala l-^c^arš.* The king sat on the throne. The king acceded to the throne.

جلس *yallas* II 1. = II قعد *ga^cc^ad.* See II قعد *ga^cc^ad* under **گ ع د** *g^c^d.* 2. (with علـــى *^c^ala)* to seat s.o., e.g., on a chair, at a table, etc. جلس على العرش *yallas ^c^ala l-^c^arš* to crown s.o. جلسوه علـــى العـــــرش *yallasoo ^c^ala l-^c^arš.* They crowned him king.

جلوس *yiluus* (v.n. from جلس *yilas)* 1. sitting. 2. sitting down. جلوس علـــى العـــــرش *yiluus ^c^ala l-^c^arš* accession to the throne. عيد الجلـــــوس *^c^iid l-yiluus* accession day, coronation day.

مجلـــس *maylis* p. مجالس *mayaalis* 1. living room. الشقة فيها مجلس وحجرة نوم *š-šigga fiiha maylis w-ḥijrat noom.* There are a living room and a bedroom in the apartment. 2. council. مجلـــس الشـــورى *maylis š-šuura* the council of state. مجلـــس الأمـــن *maylis l-'amin* the security council. مجلس الدفـــاع *maylis d-difaa^c^* the defense council. مجلـــس البلدية *maylis l-baladiyya* the municipal council. مجلس الشيـــوخ *maylis š-šyuux* the senate. مجلس الوزرا *maylis l-wuzara* the council of ministers. 3. board, commission. مجلـــــس الإدارة *maylis l-'idaara* the board of directors.

جـــالس *yaalis* (act. part. from جلـــس *yilas)* sitting, sitting down.

ي م م[1] *ymm*

تيمم *tyammam* V to substitute dirt or sand for water in ablution. إذا ما فيه ماي، لازم تتيمم قبل ما تصلي *'iđa ma fii maay, laazim tityammam gabil-ma tṣalli.* If there is no water, you have to use sand (or dirt) before you pray.

ي م م[2] *ymm*

يم *yamm* (prep.) next to, beside, near. تعال يمي وعلمني باللي صار *taᶜaal yammi w-ᶜallimni b-lli ṣaar.* Come sit next to me and tell me what has happened. القصر يم الديوان الأميري *l-gaṣir yamm d-diiwaan l-'amiiri.* The palace is near the Emiri Court. رحت يم الشيخ *riḥt yamm š-šeex.* I went to see the Shaikh. من يم *min yamm* on the part of, from the point of view of. من يمي، أنا موافق *min yammi, 'aana mwaafig.* For my part, I agree.

ي م ن *ymn*

اليمن *l-yaman* Yemen.

يمني *yamani* 1. of Yemen, characteristic of Yemen. خنجر يمني *xanyar yamani* Yemeni dagger. 2. (p. *-yyiin,* يمنية *yamaniyya*) a Yemeni, a Yemenite.

يمين *yimiin* right, right side. خذ يمينك! *xiđ ymiinak!* Bear to your right! لفيت على اليمين *laffeet ᶜala l-yimiin.* I turned right. مكتب البريد على اليمين *maktab l-bariid ᶜala l-yimiin.* The post office is on the right. جلس على يميني *yilas ᶜala yimiini.* He sat on my right.

ي ن ا ي ر *ynaayr*

يناير *yanaayir* January.

ي م ر *ymr*

جمر *yamir* (coll.) embers, burning coal or charcoal. s. جمرة *yamra,* p. *-aat.*

ي م ع *ymᶜ* See also ج م ع *jmᶜ.*

جمع *yimaᶜ* (يجمع *yiimaᶜ*) 1. to assemble, call together. المدير جمع كل الموظفين *l-mudiir yimaᶜ kill li-mwađđafiin.* The manager called all the employees together. 2. to collect. جمعوا فلوس حق الشهدا *yimᶜaw fluus ḥagg š-šuhada.* They collected money for the martyrs. يجمعون تبرعات *yiimaᶜuun tabarruᶜaat.* They are collecting donations. 3. to add, add up. جمعت كل الأعداد *yimaᶜt kill l-'aᶜdaad.* I added up all the figures.

جمع *yammaᶜ* II 1. intens. of جمع *yimaᶜ.* 2. to save (money), amass, pile up. جمع فلوس واجد واشترى بيت *yammaᶜ fluus waayid w-štiraᶜ beet.* He saved a lot of money and bought a house.

جمعة *yimaᶜ* 1. male's name. 2. الجمعة *l-yimaᶜ,* يوم الجمعة *yoom l-yimaᶜ* Friday, on Friday. اليوم الجمعة *l-yoom l-yimaᶜ.* Today is Friday. كل جمعة *kill yimᶜa,* كل يوم جمعة *kill yoom yimᶜa* every Friday. صلاة الجمعة *ṣalaaṭ l-yimᶜa* the Friday (noon) prayer.

جامع *yaamiᶜ* p. جوامع *yawaamiᶜ* mosque, esp. one in which the Friday (noon) prayer is performed. الجامع العود *l-yaamiᶜ l-ᶜood* the grand mosque, the big mosque.

جامعة *yaamᶜa* p. *-aat* university

ي م ل *yml*

جميل *yimiil* beautiful, pretty, handsome.

ي ن ز ب ي ل *ynzbyl*

جنزبيل *yanzabiil* (coll.) ginger.

ي ن ن *ynn*

جن *yann* (يجن *yiyinn*) to be or become insane. جنت لين سمعت انه ابنها مات في حادث سيارة *yannat leen sma^cat 'inna 'ibinha maat fi haadiθ sayyaara.* She went insane when she heard that her son had died in a car accident. لين شافها في السوق بدون دفتها، جن *leen čaaffa fi s-suug b-duun daffatta, yann.* When he saw her in the marketplace without her *aba*, he went out of his mind.

جنن *yannan* II to make insane or crazy, madden. الجهال يلعبون في البيت اليوم. جننوني *l-yihhaal yla^cbuun fi l-beet l-yoom. yannanuuni.* The children are playing in the house today. They drove me nuts. جمالها يجنن *jamaalha yyannin.* Her beauty drives people crazy.

انجن *nyann* VII = I جن *yann.*

جن *yinn* (v.n. from جن *yann*) 1. insanity, madness. 2. delusion. 3. (coll.) demons, devils. الانس والجن *l-'ins w-l-jinn* humans and demons.

جني *yinni* p. جنون *ynuun* genie, jinni.

جنة *yanna* p. *-aat*, جنان *ynaan* 1. beautiful garden. ورا البيت جنة *wara l-beet yanna.* There's a beautiful garden behind the house. 2. paradise, heaven. الجنة والنعيم *l-yanna w-n-na^ciim* paradise and the blessings of God.

جنون *ynuun* (v.n. from جن *yann*) = جن *yinn.*

مجنون *maynuun* 1. (adj.) crazy, insane. ما عليك منه. مجنون *ma ^caleek minna. maynuun.* Don't pay attention to him. He's crazy. 2. (p. مجانين *mayaaniin*) mad man, lunatic. مجنون. خذوه العصفورية *maynuun. xaðoo l-^caṣfuuriyya.* He's a mad man. They took him to the lunatic asylum. (prov.) اقضب مجنونك لا يجيك أجن منه *'igḍab maynuunak la yiik 'ayann minna.* A bird in the hand is worth two in the bush. (lit., "Hold on to your crazy person lest a crazier one comes to you.").

أجن *'ayann* (elat.) 1. (with من *min*) more insane, crazier than. 2. (with foll. n.) the most insane, the craziest.

ي ه ل *yhl*

جاهل *yaahil* 1. (p. جهال *yihhaal*) child, baby, youngster. الجهال يلعبون بره *l-yihhaal yla^cbuun barra.* The children are playing outside. 2. (p. *-iin*) ignorant, uneducated person. جاهل. ما يفتهم *yaahil. ma yiftihim.* He's ignorant. He doesn't understand. جاهل. لا يقرا ولا يكتب *yaahil. la yigra wala yiktib.* He's illiterate. He neither reads nor writes.

ي ه و د *yhwd*

يهود *yahuud* (coll.) Jews. s. يهودي *-i.* f. يهودية *-iyya.* اليهود والنصارى أهل الكتاب *l-yahuud w-n-naṣaara 'ahl l-kitaab.* Jews and Christians are the people of the Book (i.e. people who have sacred scriptures).

ي و ع *yw^c*

جوع *yuu^c* (v.n. from جاع *jaa^c*) hunger, starvation. مات من الجوع *maat min l-yooᶜ.* He starved to death.

جوعان *yuuᶜaan* p. *-iin* hungry, starved. كنت جوعان وكليت واجد *čint yuuᶜaan w-kaleet waayid.* I was hungry and ate a lot.

ي و ر *ywr*

جار *yaar* p. جيران *yiiraan* neighbor. جارنا رجال زين *yaarna rayyaal zeen.* Our neighbor is a good man. (prov.) جارك ثم دارك *yaarak θumma daarak.* Your neighbor is more important than your home.

ي و ل *ywl*

جوال *yawwaal* p. جوالة *-a* male dancer.

ي و ل ي *ywly*

جولية *yuulya* July.

ي و م *ywm*

يوم *yoom* p. أيام *'ayyaam* 1. day. جلست هناك يومين *yilast hnaak yoomeen.* I stayed there for two days. عقب ستة أيام *ᶜugub sittat ayyaam* in six days. يوم الخميس *yoom l-xamiis* on Thursday. اليوم *l-yoom* today. (prov.) يوم لك ويوم عليك *yoom lak w-yoom ᶜaleek.* Laugh one day, cry the next. 2. (conj.) when, the day when = يوم ما *yoom-ma.* (prov.) يوم ما سخنا الماي شرد الديك *yoom-ma ṣaxxanna l-maay širad d-diič.* Forewarned is forearmed.

يومي *yawmi* daily. جريدة يومية *jariida yawmiyya* daily newspaper.

يومية *yoomiyya* (adv.) 1. daily, every day. يتصل فيها يومية *yittaṣil fiiha yoomiyya.* He contacts her daily. 2. (p. يوميات *-yyaat*) daily wage, day's pay. يومية الكولي على قد الحال *yoomiit l-kuuli ᶜala gadd l-ḥaal.* A coolie's daily wage is not much. أبوه قال له ما يعطيه يوميته إذا ما يدرس زين *'ubuu gal-la ma yᶜaṭii yoomiita 'iða ma yidris zeen.* His father told him that he wouldn't give him his daily allowance if he didn't study hard.

ي و ن ي *ywny*

يونية *yuunya* June.

ي ي *yy*

جا *ya* (less common var. *ja*) (يجي *yiyi, yaji*) 1. to come, come to. جا قبل أمس *ya gabl ams.* He came before yesterday. متى جيت هني؟ *mita yiit hini?* When did you come here? جات الشارجة *yat š-šaarja.* She came to Sharja. جايني واشتكى *yaayni w-štika.* He came to me and complained. 2. (with foll. imperf.) to come in order to do s.th. جا يدرس *ya yidris.* He came to study. جاك يطلب فلوس *yaak yaṭlub fluus.* He came to you to ask for money. 3. to befall, descend upon. بغيت الفايدة، بس جاتني المصايب واجدة *bağeet l-faayda, bass yatni l-maṣaayib waayda.* I was out to make a profit, but (instead) my disasters struck me. كنت تعبان بس ما جاني الرقاد *čint taᶜbaan bass ma yaani r-rgaad.* I was tired, but I wasn't sleepy. جاتها العادة أمس *yatha l-ᶜaada 'ams.* She had her period yesterday. 4. to come to, come one's way. جاني خبر زين من ولدي في أمريكا *yaani xabar zeen min wildi fi 'amriika.* I received good news from my son in America. شو يجيك من ها المشروع؟ *šu yiik min hal-mašruuᶜ?* What do you get from this project? ما جاتني زيادة إلى ذالحين *ma yatni zyaada 'ila ðalḥiin.* I haven't gotten a raise up to now. 5. (with على *ᶜala*) to fit, be big enough. هالجوتي ما يجـي عليـك *hal-juut ma yaji ᶜaleek.* These shoes are too small for you.

جيية *yayya* (n. of inst.) p. *-aat* 1. coming, arrival. من وين جييتـها؟ *min ween yayyatta?* Where did she come from? يا هلا ومسهلة! جييتك في مكانها *ya hala w-mashala! yayyatk fi mukaanha.* You are welcome! Your arrival is timely. 2. visit. جييتكم عزيزة علينـا *yayyatkum ᶜaziiza ᶜaleena.* Your visit is precious to us. ويش ها الجيية! يومين بـس! *weeš hal-yayya! yoomeen bass!* What a (short) visit this was! That's no visit! Two days only!

ي ي ا *yyaa*

ايا *-yyaa-* (with suff. pron.): عطيته اياهم *ᶜaṭeeta-yyaahum.* I gave them to him.

ي ي ب *yyb*

جـاب *yaab* (يجيب *yiyiib)* 1. to bring, fetch. جبت العيـال مـن المدرسـة *yibt li-ᶜyaaḷ min l-madrasa.* I brought the kids from school. جاب لها حيول ذهـب *yaab laha ḥyuul ðahab.* He brought her gold bracelets. 2. to give birth to, have (a child). حرمتي جابت ولد *ḥurumti yaabat walad.* My wife gave birth to a baby boy. 3. to come up with. إذا ما تجيب الفلوس باكر أشتكي عليـك *'iða ma tyiib li-fluus baačir 'aštiki ᶜaleek.* If you don't come up with the money tomorrow, I will sue you.